KV-637-697

HANDBOOK OF THE ECONOMICS OF EDUCATION
VOLUME 1

HANDBOOKS IN ECONOMICS

26

Series Editors

KENNETH J. ARROW
MICHAEL D. INTRILIGATOR

ELSEVIER

AMSTERDAM • BOSTON • HEIDELBERG • LONDON
NEW YORK • OXFORD • PARIS • SAN DIEGO
SAN FRANCISCO • SINGAPORE • SYDNEY • TOKYO
North-Holland is an imprint of Elsevier

N·H

HANDBOOK OF THE ECONOMICS OF EDUCATION

VOLUME 1

Edited by

ERIC A. HANUSHEK
Stanford University, Stanford, CA

and

FINIS WELCH
Welch Consulting, Bryan, TX

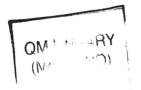

QM LIBRARY
(M... ...D)

ELSEVIER

AMSTERDAM • BOSTON • HEIDELBERG • LONDON
NEW YORK • OXFORD • PARIS • SAN DIEGO
SAN FRANCISCO • SINGAPORE • SYDNEY • TOKYO
North-Holland is an imprint of Elsevier

N·H

North-Holland is an imprint of Elsevier
Radarweg 29, PO Box 211, 1000 AE Amsterdam, The Netherlands
The Boulevard, Langford Lane, Kidlington, Oxford OX5 1GB, UK

First edition 2006

Copyright © 2006 Elsevier B.V. All rights reserved

No part of this publication may be reproduced, stored in a retrieval system or transmitted in any form or by any means electronic, mechanical, photocopying, recording or otherwise without the prior written permission of the publisher

Permissions may be sought directly from Elsevier's Science & Technology Rights Department in Oxford, UK: phone (+44) (0) 1865 843830; fax (+44) (0) 1865 853333; email: permissions@elsevier.com. Alternatively you can submit your request online by visiting the Elsevier web site at http://elsevier.com/locate/permissions, and selecting *Obtaining permission to use Elsevier material*

Notice
No responsibility is assumed by the publisher for any injury and/or damage to persons or property as a matter of products liability, negligence or otherwise, or from any use or operation of any methods, products, instructions or ideas contained in the material herein. Because of rapid advances in the medical sciences, in particular, independent verification of diagnoses and drug dosages should be made

Library of Congress Cataloging-in-Publication Data
A catalog record for this book is available from the Library of Congress

British Library Cataloguing in Publication Data
A catalogue record for this book is available from the British Library

ISBN-13: 978-0-444-51399-1
ISBN-10: 0-444-51399-X

ISSN: 0169-7218 (Handbooks in Economics series)
ISSN: 1574-0692 (Handbook of the Economics of Education series)

For information on all North-Holland publications
visit our website at books.elsevier.com

Printed and bound in The Netherlands

06 07 08 09 10   10 9 8 7 6 5 4 3 2 1

INTRODUCTION TO THE SERIES

The aim of the *Handbooks in Economics* series is to produce Handbooks for various branches of economics, each of which is a definitive source, reference, and teaching supplement for use by professional researchers and advanced graduate students. Each Handbook provides self-contained surveys of the current state of a branch of economics in the form of chapters prepared by leading specialists on various aspects of this branch of economics. These surveys summarize not only received results but also newer developments, from recent journal articles and discussion papers. Some original material is also included, but the main goal is to provide comprehensive and accessible surveys. The Handbooks are intended to provide not only useful reference volumes for professional collections but also possible supplementary readings for advanced courses for graduate students in economics.

KENNETH J. ARROW and MICHAEL D. INTRILIGATOR

CONTENTS OF THE HANDBOOK

VOLUME 1

CONTENTS OF VOLUME 1

PREFACE

There are many ways to date the development of the economics of education. In the 17th Century, Sir William Petty began writing about the valuation of lives in terms of the productive skills of individuals – a precursor of human capital considerations. Adam Smith followed a century later with direct consideration of the organization and finance of education. Yet, the more natural dating is much more recent with the development and legitimization of the study of human capital lead by Gary Becker, Jacob Mincer, and T.W. Schultz. These initial forays have, however, been followed by a torrent of recent work.

The initial human capital contributions focused largely on differential wages of individuals as they related to skills. And, the most natural way to identify differential skills was the amount of schooling by individuals. The continuing power of this early work is seen easily by the myriad of analyses that simply note that they ran a "Mincer earnings function" – with no need to explain or to cite the original source.

The field has developed and expanded in a number of directions for the past half century. The work on the impacts of schooling on observable outcomes – labor market returns, health, and more – has grown. Increasingly detailed and sophisticated analyses have pushed the questions asked and the interpretations of existing work. For example, how does the social return to education relate to the private return? Does the growth of nations relate to schooling?

The economics of education has also reached back in the direction of understanding what goes on in schools. What factors influence the quality and outcomes of schools? How does institutional structure influence outcomes? How does finance interact with the level and distribution of outcomes?

While each of these questions entered the discussion early in the modern history of the economics of education, the recent explosion of work has introduced new developments and new approaches in each of these areas. Indeed, the standards of analysis have changed dramatically as the various subfields have developed.

Part of the explosion is undoubtedly related to the new availability of relevant data. Many countries have developed regularly available large surveys of households along with a variety of "outcome" measures. Extensive panel data sets on labor market outcomes have grown in the U.S. and increasingly in other countries. Administrative data on school operations are increasingly accessible to researchers. These sources of data are being cleverly exploited to build new knowledge about the economics of education.

The heavy influence of governments in educational policy has also contributed. Governments at all levels enter into many supply decisions – and they frequently look for analyses and evaluations that will guide their decisions.

These conditions have induced a complementary growth in the number of researchers working in the economics of education. The upsurge in Ph.D. theses related to education issues is remarkable. Similarly, while the field was once very skewed to work in the U.S. – again related to the availability of U.S. data, this is no longer the case.

One implication of this growth is that the field is rapidly developing and changing. The chapters in these volumes were designed to cover the broad range of existing research and to suggest productive lines of development. They do that. But even the relatively short production lags in these volumes imply that a number of new and exciting works are only hinted at in the chapters. In short, there is much more work to be done as this field unfolds.

A variety of factors went into the selection of authors of these chapters. Quite clearly, a fundamental requirement was that the authors had to be leaders in the intellectual development of the various topics. But, beyond that, authors were selected because they had a point of view, one designed to provoke thought and new work.

The ideas put forward here are likely to be challenged in further work. And, some may not survive such challenges. The idea is not to write the final word on any of these topics, because each is the source of lively current debate. The idea instead is to provide an intermediate assessment of dynamic research areas in order to push the research further. Perhaps the success will be judged by the intensity of future challenges to thinking in each of the areas.

The development of *Handbook* chapters is not an easy task. Blending existing work into a picture that at once categorizes the current position and simultaneously pushes research forward takes skill, insight, and simply a lot of hard work. We wish to thank each of the authors for conscientiously confronting the enormity of their assigned tasks.

The effort was also aided by the editorial and production team that has developed in the *Handbook* series, not the least of which includes the general editors of Kenneth Arrow and Michael Intriligator. It also includes Valerie Teng and the others at Elsevier. We also wish to thank the Bush School of Government and Public Service at Texas A&M. They generously hosted a conference where early versions of these papers were presented.

Eric A. Hanushek
Finis Welch
July 2006

Chapter 1

POST SCHOOLING WAGE GROWTH: INVESTMENT, SEARCH AND LEARNING

YONA RUBINSTEIN

Brown University and Eitan Berglas School of Economics, Tel-Aviv University
e-mail: yona_rubinstein@brown.edu, yonar@post.tau.ac.il

YORAM WEISS

Eitan Berglas School of Economics, Tel-Aviv University
e-mail: weiss@post.tau.ac.il

Contents

Handbook of the Economics of Education, Volume 1
Edited by Eric A. Hanushek and Finis Welch
© 2006 Elsevier B.V. All rights reserved
DOI: 10.1016/S1574-0692(06)01001-4

Abstract

The survey presents basic facts on wage growth and summarizes the main ideas on the possible sources of this growth. We document that wage growth happens mainly early in the life cycle and is then associated with increasing labor force participation and high job mobility. Wage growth during the first decade in the labor market, is about 50% for high school graduates and about 80% for those with college or more. This growth is comparable in size to the accumulated contribution of schooling for these two groups. We describe in detail models of wage growth that can explain these results, including investment in human capital, search and learning. We also discuss the roles of contracts in sharing the risks associated with learning about ability and varying market conditions. Evidence supporting investment is the U shaped life cycle profile for the variance of wages. However, heterogeneity matters and individuals with relatively high life time earnings have both a higher mean and a higher growth. Evidence supporting search is the high wage gains obtained from changing employers early in the career. Evidence for learning are the initially rising hazard of quitting and the rising rewards for AFQT scores that are not observed by the market.

1. Introduction

Perhaps the most widely estimated regression equation in economics is Mincer's log-earnings function that relates the log of individual earnings or wages to observed measures of schooling and potential work experience; with a specification that is linear in years of schooling and quadratic in experience. This simple regression has been estimated in numerous studies, employing various data sets from almost every historical period and country for which micro data are available, with remarkably robust regularities. First, workers' wage profiles are well ranked by education level; at any experience level, workers earn more, on average, as their schooling increases. Second, average wages grow at a decreasing rate until late in one's working lifetime. Most importantly, the estimated coefficients for schooling and experience in all these regressions fall into a sufficiently narrow range to admit a common economic interpretation in terms of rates of return for investment in human capital. The estimated coefficients of the log-earnings function have been applied to a wide variety of issues, including *ceteris paribus* effect of schooling on earnings, wage differentials by gender and race, and the evolution of earnings inequality. Mincer's (1974) earning function was used as the statistical platform in all these studies.[1]

The human capital approach to wage growth over the life cycle, as developed by Becker (1975), Mincer (1958, 1974) and Ben-Porath (1967), emphasizes the role of human capital acquired in school and on the job. Workers face a given trade off between current and future earnings, represented by a human capital "production function", and decide how much to invest. The wage offered to individuals is determined as a product of the worker's stock of human capital and the market-determined "rental rate". Markets operate competitively and workers are compensated for their investments. If individuals are heterogeneous, then compensation applies only at the margin, while non-marginal workers receive rents for their scarce attributes. When market conditions change, due to technological change for instance, the rental rate changes, as does perhaps the production function that describes the investment opportunities. Together, these lead to adjustments in the individual investment decisions that affect wage growth.

Becker (1975), Griliches (1977) and Rosen (1977) have questioned the interpretation that should be given to the regression coefficients of schooling and experience in the Mincer earning equation, and hence the validity of drawing policy conclusions from these coefficients. The main concerns are, first, the role of individual heterogeneity in ability and access to the capital markets and, second, the role of market frictions and specific investments in human capital. These concerns affect the statistical estimation procedures because the unobserved individual attributes that influence investment decisions can bias the schooling and experience coefficients in Mincer's equation. Equally important is the recognition that if markets are non-competitive because of credit constraints or the firm specific investments that create relational rents, then wages and

[1] Heckman, Lochner and Todd provide an insightful perspective on the Mincer earning regression, fifty years later.

productivity need not coincide as well as social and private rates of return for investment in human capital may diverge.

Parallel to the human capital approach, search models have been offered to deal with limited information and market frictions. At the individual level, these models explain wage growth and turnover as outcomes of the (random and intermittent) arrival of job offers that can be rejected or accepted [see Burdett (1978)]. These models also allow for investment in search effort, with the objective of generating job offers rather than enhancing productivity. When combined with learning, search models can provide a framework for explaining the separate roles of tenure and general market experience [see Mincer and Jovanovic (1981), Jovanovic (1984), Mortensen (1988)]. At the market level, search models can explain the aggregate level of unemployment in addition to the distribution of wages in the economy. The policy implications of these models for schooling and training may be quite different than those of the human capital model because of the important role of externalities, relational rents and bargaining [see Mortensen and Pissarides (1999), Wolpin (2003)].

A third important consideration that may explain wage growth is learning [see Jovanovic (1979a, 1979b), Harris and Holmstrom (1982), Gibbons and Waldman (1999a, 1999b)]. Workers are heterogeneous and it takes time to identify their productive capacity with sufficient precision. Therefore, employers must base their payments on predictions of expected output that are repeatedly modified by the worker performance. The arrival of new information which allows the market to sort workers can be individually costly, because it makes wages uncertain. This risk creates incentives for risk sharing between workers and firms. A possible outcome of this process is that all workers obtain partial insurance, to protect them against wage reductions upon failures to perform well. Yet, successful workers will be promoted because information is public and other firms compete for workers based on this information. We thus have wage growth that is triggered by new information rather than by the worker's actions or arrival of job offers.

Although investment, search and learning have similar implications with respect to the behavior of mean wages, implying rising and concave wage profiles, they can be distinguished by their different implications for higher moments, such as the wage variance. For instance, Mincer (1974) pointed out that compensation for past investment in human capital creates a negative correlation between early and late earnings during the life cycle, implying that the interpersonal variance of earnings over the life-cycle has a U-shape pattern. This is not true in the search and learning models, where workers that are initially homogeneous become increasingly heterogeneous as time passes due to their longer exposure to random job offers. In these models, the variance may first increase and then decrease as workers are gradually sorted into their "proper" place.

The purpose of this survey is to provide a synthesis of the alternative explanations for wage growth and relate them to the patterns observed in the data. The first part of the survey provides an initial glance at the data on life cycle wage levels and rates of wage growth, based on cross sectional, synthetic cohorts and panel data. We use all these sources to illustrate the important distinction between life-cycle and time effects and to show that most wage growth occurs early in the work career. These results are associated with high turnover, in and out of the labor force, between employers, occupations and industries. We show that post-schooling wage growth is quantitatively important and is as large as the wage growth attributed to schooling. Moreover, schooling and experience are strongly linked, with more-educated workers generally having higher wage growth and more-stable employment. The second part of the survey presents models of wage growth based on investment, search and learning in a unified framework. This allows us to compare alternative channels for wage growth and identify the connections amongst them. The third part of the survey provides a second glance, based on the empirical literature in the area and our own examination of the data, for the purpose of identifying empirical tests that take into account unobserved heterogeneity and might distinguish alternative models of wage growth.

2. Wages and employment over the life cycle – A first glance

In this section, we take a first glance at the available data on life cycle earnings. Our goal is to summarize the patterns of post schooling wages for workers of different educational attainments, without restricting ourselves to a particular functional form, such as the famous Mincer's wage equation that restricts mean (log) wages to be linear in schooling and quadratic in experience. We take advantage of large bodies of data collected over several decades, a privilege that early research did not have, for reproducing the basic facts on wages over the life cycle.

The data sources are the March Supplements from the Current Population Surveys (CPS) for the years 1964–2002, the Panel Study of Income Dynamics (PSID) for the years 1968–1997 the National Longitudinal Survey of Youth (NLSY) for the years 1979–2000, and the CPS outgoing rotation groups (ORG) for the years 1998–2002.

The March CPS data is a sequence of annual cross sections. The ORG CPS data follows households over 16 months and enables us to create short panels for individuals. The PSID began with a cross-sectional national sample in 1968, with participants interviewed every year until 1993 and then biannually until 1997. In contrast, the NLSY sample includes only individuals aged 14–21 when first interviewed in 1979 and observed until 2000. (A more detailed description of these data sets is available in the Appendix.)

From each source, we selected white males with potential work experience (age – school years – 6) of no more than 40 years. Observations were divided by school completion into five levels: (i) high school dropouts, (ii) high school graduates with twelve years of schooling, (iii) some college, (iv) college graduates with a BA degree and (v) college graduates with advanced/professional education (MBA, PhD). We then examine the hourly or annual wages, whichever is applicable, of workers employed full time and full year.

By restricting ourselves to white US males, we can examine wage patterns for a relatively homogeneous group over a long period of time. This allows us to control for institutional and social differences and to focus on the potential role of the economic forces that affect wage growth, such as investment, search and prices of skills.

2.1. The pooled data

Under stationary conditions, the chronological time of observation would be irrelevant; we can then pool data from different years and cohorts while paying attention only to the stage in the worker's life cycle, as indicated by his potential work experience. Figure 1 shows the mean weekly wage–experience profiles, by schooling, averaged over the 38 years 1964 to 2002 of the March CPS data, using a subsample of fully employed (full time and full year) workers. These (log) wage profiles have the general shape found in previous studies based on single cross sections [see Mincer (1974), Murphy and Welch (1992), Heckman, Lochner and Todd (2001)]. Average wages are well ranked by educational attainments. Mean wages increase rapidly (by approximately 80 percent) over the first 10 to 15 years of a career. As careers progress, we find little change in mean wages.

The sharp growth in wages is associated with a sharp increase in labor supply and regularity of employment, as indicated by the life-cycle profiles of the proportion of workers who work full time, full year (among those who worked some time during the year) and average weekly hours (for those with positive hours). Workers with higher levels of schooling work more and reach a steady level much earlier than do less educated workers (see Figures 2a and 2b). Thus, hours and wages move together over the life cycle, and earnings grow faster than wages.

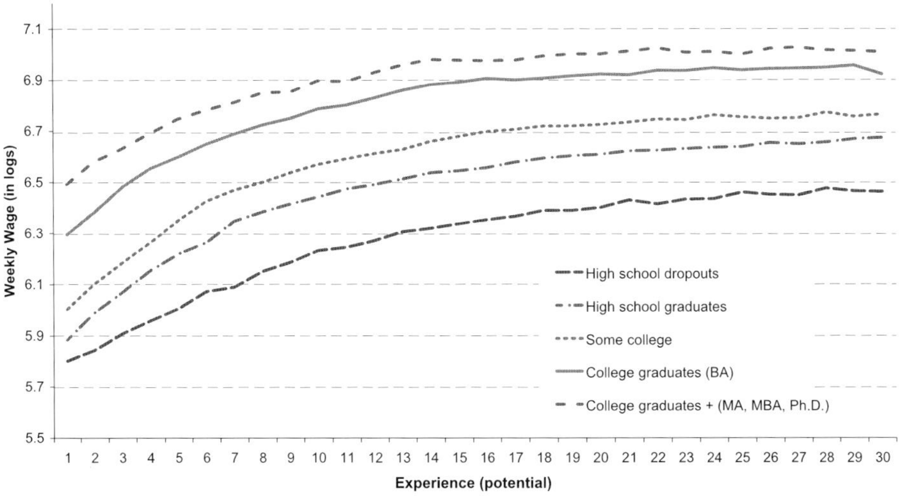

Figure 1. Mean weekly wages (in logs) by education and (potential) experience, white males, full-time full-year workers (52 weeks), CPS, March supplements, 1964–2002.

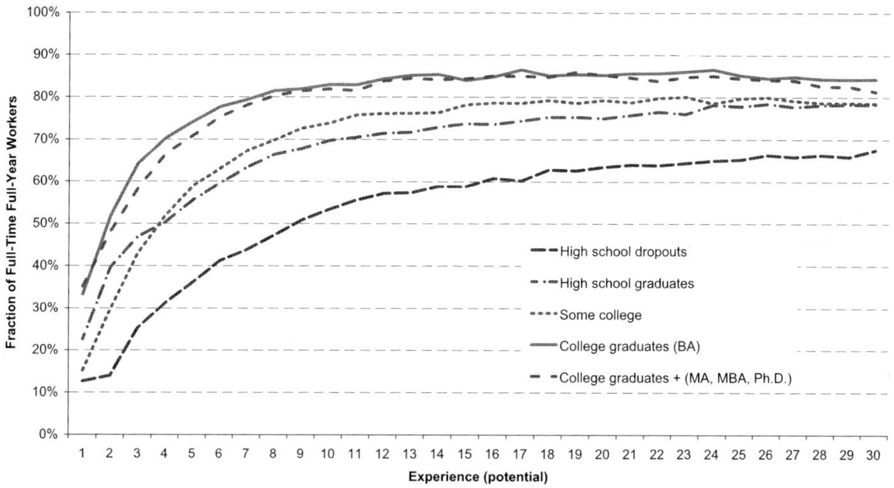

Figure 2a. Fraction of full-time full-year workers and average weekly hours of employed workers by education and experience, CPS, March supplements, 1964–2002.
Fraction of full-time full-year workers.

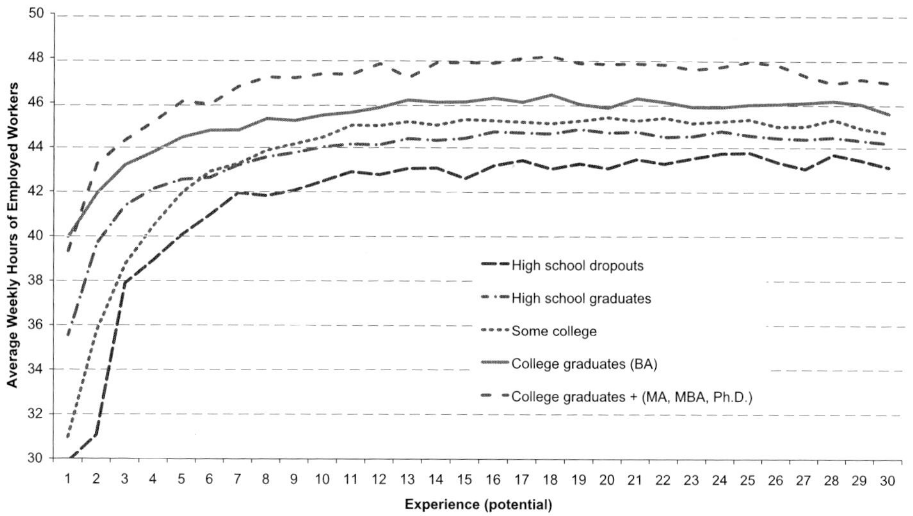

Figure 2b. Fraction of full-time full-year workers and average weekly hours of employed workers by education and experience, CPS, March supplements, 1964–2002.
Average weekly hours of employed workers.

2.2. *Cohorts and cross-sections*

In fact, the economy is not stationary. The wage structure has undergone major changes beginning in the late 1970's, when workers with high level of schooling started to gain relative to those with low levels of schooling, mainly as a result of the decline in the wages of low-skill workers [see Katz and Autor (1999)]. Such changes in returns to skill imply different wage profiles for different cohorts, where workers born in the same year are followed over time, and for cross sections, where workers with different experience (and time of entry into the labor force) are observed at a given year.

Figures 3a and 3b show the wage–experience profiles for the cohort of high school graduates born in 1951–1955 and the cohort of college graduates born in 1946–1950, respectively. These two groups entered the labor market at roughly the same time, 1971–1975. Added to the graphs is the evolution of the cross section wage–experience profiles from 1971 to 2000 in five year intervals, where each such cross section profile shows the mean wages of workers with the indicated schooling and experience in a given time interval. These figures make it very clear that cohort-based wage profiles are affected by changes in market conditions that shift the cross section profiles over time. These shifts differ by level of schooling. High school graduates of *all* experience levels earned lower wages during the period 1970–2000, which is the reason why the mean wage profile of the cohort of high school graduates born between 1951 to 1955 exhibits almost no wage growth after ten years in the labor market (see Figure 3a). In contrast, workers with a college degree or more maintained their earning capacity over time. Consequently, as seen in Figure 3b, the cross section and cohort wage profiles of college graduates are quite similar and rise throughout most of the worker's career.

Although the cross section profile is, by construction, free of time effects, its shape is not necessarily a reflection of life cycle forces because cohorts "quality" can change over time. An important reason for this is that schooling is embodied in the worker early in life and the quality of that schooling may depend on the size of the cohorts with each level of schooling and the state of knowledge at the time of entry. It is impossible to separately identify time cohort and life cycle effects unless one uses some a priori identifying assumptions.[2]

2.3. *Panel data*

Panel data follows the *same* group of individuals over a period of time, in contrast to cohort data, where different individuals are sampled in every period. Having repeated observations for the same individual allows one to calculate individual rates of wage growth and examine their variance. The panel also allows examination of individual transitions among different employers and occupations.

[2] For instance, Borjas (1985) assumed that time effects are common to immigrants and natives to identify cohort effects for immigrants. Weiss and Lillard (1978) assumed that time effects are constant and common to all experience groups in order to identify cohort effects for scientists.

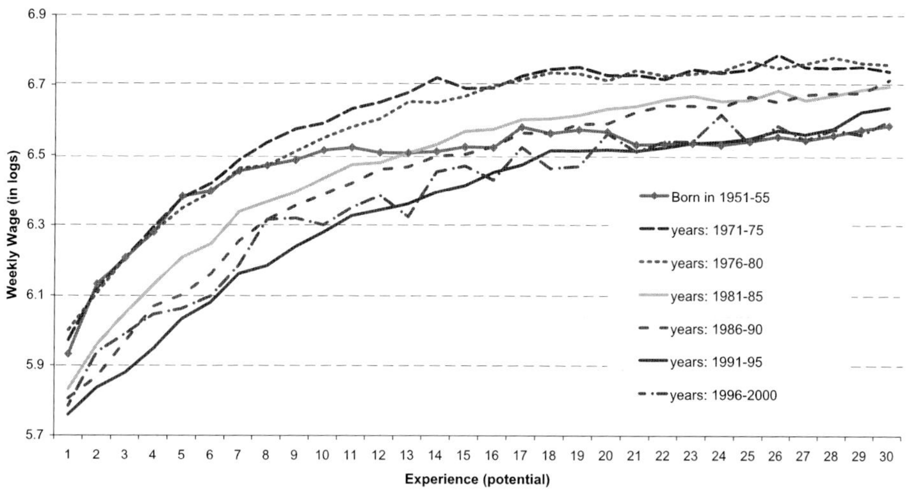

Figure 3a. Cohort and cross-section wage profiles for high school graduates and college graduates, white males, CPS, March supplements, 1964–2002.
High school graduates.

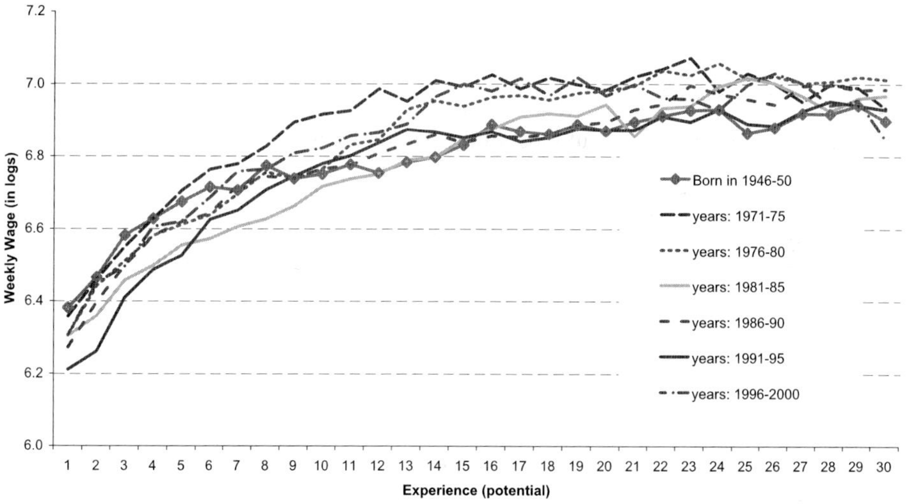

Figure 3b. Cohort and cross-section wage profiles for high school graduates and college graduates, white males, CPS, March supplements, 1964–2002.
College graduates.

Figures 4a and 4b show the average wage profiles constructed from PSID and NLSY data. Basically, the patterns resemble the synthetic cohorts displayed in Figures 3a and 3b, except that the panel profiles are less likely to taper off and decline late in the life cycle for workers with less than a college degree. Note that the NLSY sample

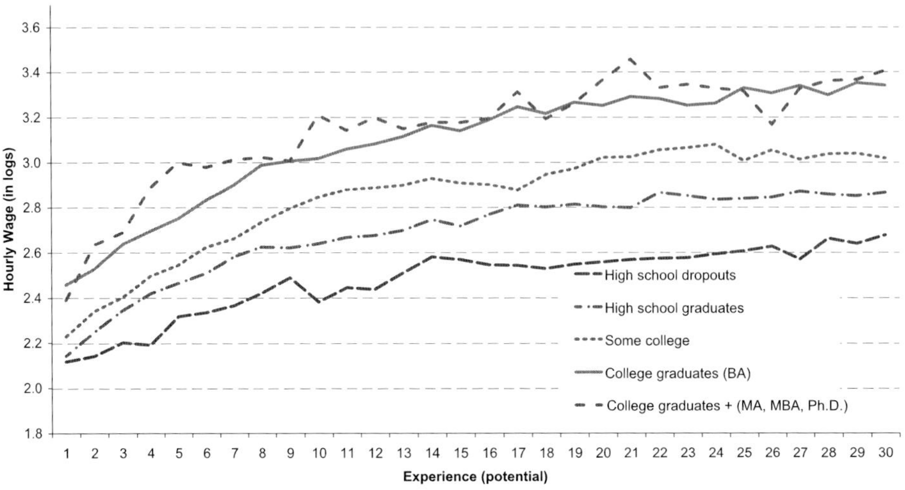

Figure 4a. Mean hourly wages (in logs) by education and experience, PSID, 1968–1997 and NLSY, 1979–2000.
PSID, 1968–1997.

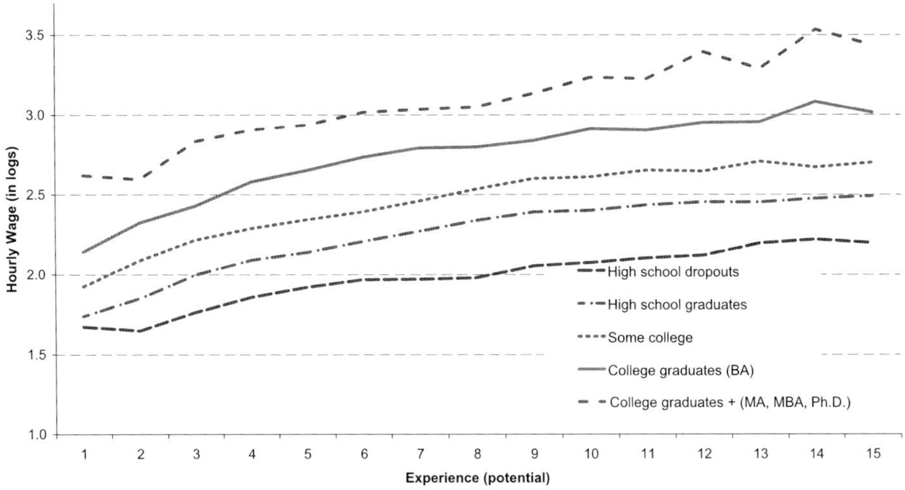

Figure 4b. Mean hourly wages (in logs) by education and experience, PSID, 1968–1997 and NLSY, 1979–2000.
NLSY, 1979–2000.

follows few birth cohorts that are close to each other, at the early stage of the life-cycle, while the PSID covers many cohorts at all stages of the life cycle. Therefore, the NLSY profiles are less concave than the corresponding PSID profiles, which show a pattern that is more similar to the CPS cross section profiles.

Figures 5a and 5b display the life cycle patterns of the monthly proportions of CPS workers that changed occupation and industry, while Figure 5c shows the annual proportions of NLSY workers who changed employers. We see that for all these dimensions of mobility, transitions decline quickly with potential experience and are generally more frequent among the less educated, especially at the early part of their careers. The impact of schooling on movement across employers is weaker than on transitions across occupations or industries. Similar findings are reported by Topel and Ward (1992), Hall (1982), Blau and Kahn (1981), Mincer and Jovanovic (1981), Abraham and Farber (1987), Wolpin (1992) and Farber (1999).

An interesting feature of the transitions among employers is that the proportion of movers initially rises, suggesting a period of experimentation on the job, and continues at a relatively high rate of about 15 percent per year until the end of the worker's career.

2.4. *Individual growth rates*

Table 1 summarizes the main results on wage growth. For each individual, we calculate annual wage growth and then present the averages and standard deviations of these rates, by experience and schooling. For comparison, we also present the predicted average growth rates that would be implied for the same individuals by using Mincer's quadratic specification for wage levels. We report these figures for the CPS short panel as well as the PSID and the NLSY samples. We include only observations in which workers were fully employed in the two consecutive years for which wage growth is calculated (see Appendix).

The average worker's career is characterized by three very different phases. The first, decade-long phase is characterized by a sharp growth of wages. The second, five-year long phase is characterized by moderate wage growth; the late phase of a career has zero or negative growth. The growth rates are substantially higher for workers with higher levels of schooling. This general pattern is revealed in *all* the data sets that we use. However, the CPS short panel shows somewhat lower rates of wage growth because of the absence of time effects.

The average annual growth rates of wages in the initial ten years for the most-educated group are 7.7 in the CPS short panel, and 11.0 and 9.6 in the PSID and NLSY panels, respectively. These rates are quite close to the wage growth associated with schooling. However, the contribution of experience declines with the level of schooling; for high school graduates, average growth rates during the first decade of post schooling experience are 5.6, 5.7 and 7.1 in the CPS, PSID and NLSY, respectively.

There is a sharp decrease in wage growth with labor market experience. As one moves across experience groups for the highly educated, the wage growth in the CPS short panel declines from 7.7 to 5.3 and then to 1.5. In the PSID sample, wage growth declines from 11.0 to 1.3 and then rises stightly to 1.9. The NLSY sample shows no such reduction mainly because it represents few cohorts, all of which gain from the continuous rise in skill prices. For some college and below, we see a decline of wage growth with experience in all samples because these groups gained less from the increase in skill prices.

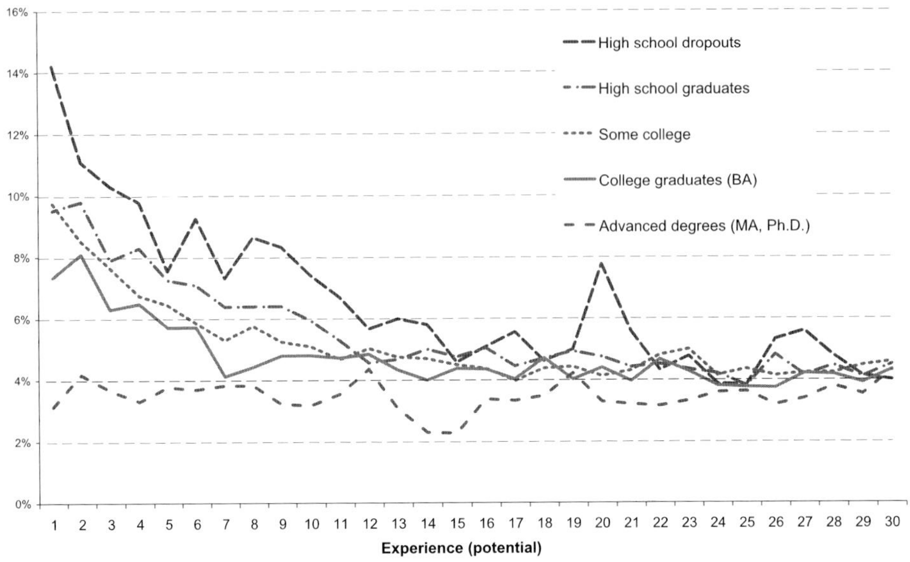

Figure 5a. Proportion of workers who changed occupation, industry or employers by education and experience, full-time workers, CPS-ORG, 1998–2002, and NLSY, 1979–2000.
Proportion of workers who changed occupation (within one month), CPS-ORG, 1998–2002.

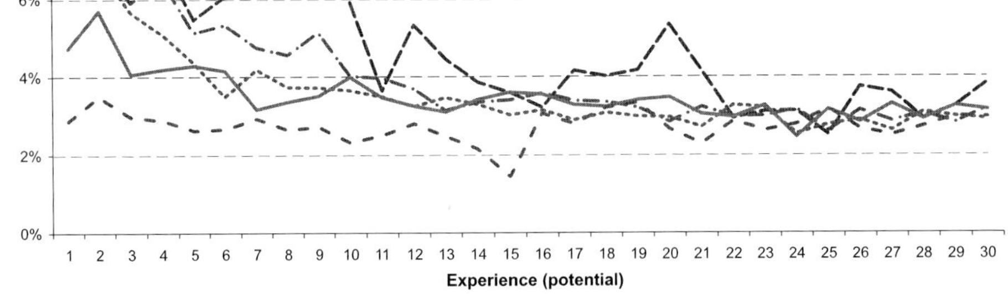

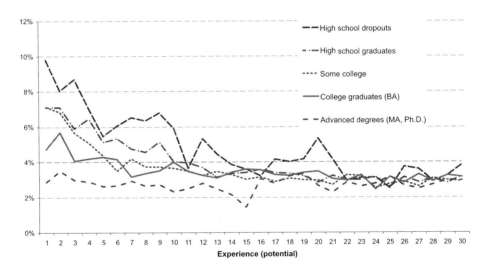

Figure 5b. Proportion of workers who changed occupation, industry or employers by education and experience, full-time workers, CPS-ORG, 1998–2002, and NLSY, 1979–2000.
Proportion of workers who changed industry (within one month), CPS-ORG, 1998–2002.

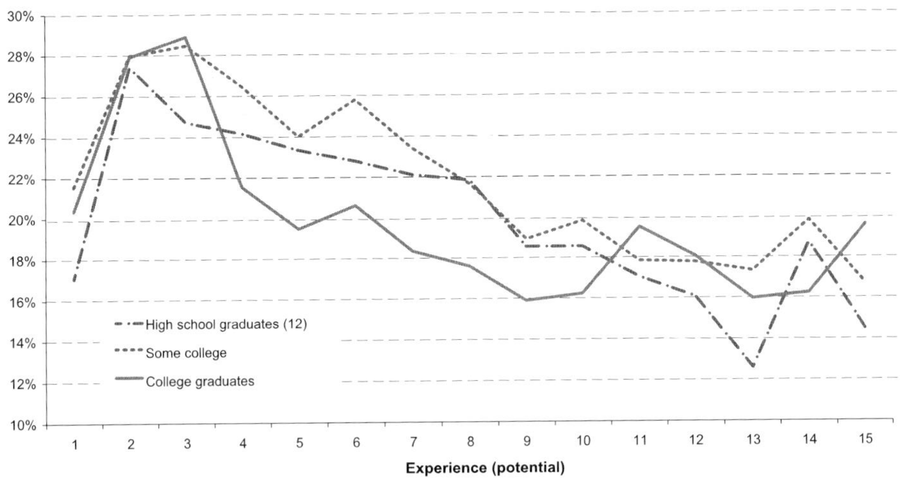

Figure 5c. Proportion of workers who changed occupation, industry or employers by education and experience, full-time workers, CPS-ORG, 1998–2002, and NLSY, 1979–2000.
Proportion of workers who changed employers (within one year), NLSY, 1979–2000.

Differences in average growth rates by schooling levels are substantial. For instance, in the CPS and PSID samples, workers with advanced degrees enjoy a wage growth that is twice as high as that of workers with less than high school degree (.077 vs. .039 and .110 vs. .043, respectively) during the first decade of their career. This important interaction is not captured by the standard Mincer specification; we allow for it here because we estimate the experience coefficients separately for each education group. As seen in Table 1, the averaged individual growth rates are generally higher than the wage growth obtained from Mincer's quadratic specification, especially at the early part of a career. As noted by Murphy and Welch (1990), the quadratic specification overestimates early wages and underestimates late wages. As a consequence of this misspecification, early growth rates are substantially biased downwards.

The variability in the rates of wage growth follows a U-shape pattern with respect to schooling. That is, the standard deviations are lower for workers with high school degree than for workers with more schooling or less, suggesting that, in this regard, the middle levels of schooling are less risky. However, there is no systematic pattern for the standard deviations of wage growth by level of experience.

In Table 2a we show, for each experience and education group, the proportion of observations with a rise, a decline and no change in *reported nominal* wage;[3] for each such subsample, we calculate the average change in *real* hourly wage. Using the CPS short panel, we see that, given a nominal increase, the average real hourly wage grows at a

[3] The wage used for this classification is total annual salary reported in the NLSY and PSID. For the CPS short panel, we use the monthly wage. These are raw data and no correction for hours was made.

Table 1
The average wage growth by education, experience, specification and data source

Experience	Data source	Education categories									
		Less than HSG		HSG (12)		Some college		College graduates		MA, Ph.D.	
		Level	Dif	Level	Dif	Level	Dif	Level	Dif	Level	Dif
0–10											
	CPS-ORG	0.024	0.039	0.032	0.056	0.033	0.063	0.036	0.063	0.029	0.077
		(0.003)	(0.029)	(0.001)	(0.010)	(0.001)	(0.010)	(0.002)	(0.011)	(0.003)	(0.017)
	PSID	0.028	0.043	0.030	0.057	0.038	0.065	0.039	0.076	0.032	0.110
		(0.003)	(0.007)	(0.002)	(0.003)	(0.003)	(0.005)	(0.003)	(0.004)	(0.006)	(0.021)
	NLSY	0.024	0.065	0.034	0.071	0.046	0.081	0.052	0.082	0.055	0.096
		(0.006)	(0.010)	(0.003)	(0.004)	(0.004)	(0.005)	(0.005)	(0.005)	(0.009)	(0.012)
11–15											
	CPS-ORG	0.016	0.007	0.022	0.033	0.022	0.055	0.022	0.045	0.018	0.053
		(0.002)	(0.034)	(0.001)	(0.011)	(0.001)	(0.012)	(0.001)	(0.012)	(0.001)	(0.020)
	PSID	0.019	0.030	0.020	0.021	0.026	0.021	0.027	0.029	0.022	0.013
		(0.002)	(0.007)	(0.001)	(0.004)	(0.002)	(0.005)	(0.002)	(0.005)	(0.004)	(0.016)
	NLSY	0.013	0.024	0.023	0.019	0.026	0.024	0.035	0.067	0.039	0.123
		(0.002)	(0.008)	(0.001)	(0.004)	(0.002)	(0.007)	(0.004)	(0.009)	(0.009)	(0.018)
16–25											
	CPS-ORG	0.010	0.052	0.013	0.022	0.012	0.026	0.009	0.026	0.009	0.015
		(0.001)	(0.021)	(0.000)	(0.007)	(0.000)	(0.008)	(0.001)	(0.009)	(0.001)	(0.012)
	PSID	0.011	0.010	0.012	0.010	0.015	0.014	0.017	0.026	0.014	0.019
		(0.001)	(0.004)	(0.001)	(0.003)	(0.001)	(0.004)	(0.001)	(0.004)	(0.003)	(0.009)
	NLSY	0.003	0.035	0.014	0.038	0.009	0.065	0.021	0.111	0.025	0.044
		(0.004)	(0.009)	(0.003)	(0.005)	(0.005)	(0.013)	(0.009)	(0.015)	(0.022)	(0.035)
25+											
	CPS-ORG	−0.002	0.025	−0.004	0.011	−0.005	0.002	−0.014	−0.002	−0.009	0.012
		(0.003)	(0.017)	(0.001)	(0.007)	(0.001)	(0.008)	(0.002)	(0.011)	(0.003)	(0.013)
	PSID	−0.003	0.004	−0.005	0.006	−0.005	0.010	−0.003	0.000	−0.001	0.011
		(0.001)	(0.003)	(0.002)	(0.003)	(0.003)	(0.005)	(0.004)	(0.005)	(0.005)	(0.006)
	NLSY	−0.015	0.034	−0.003	0.034						
		(0.012)	(0.042)	(0.007)	(0.041)						

Notes: The numbers in the "dif" columns are cell means and standard deviations. The numbers in the "level" columns are growth rates as implied by the estimated coefficients of the experience and experience squared terms in Mincer's wage equation.

hefty rate of 25 percent per year. The corresponding figure for wage reduction is even larger, −33 percent per year. As experience increases, the proportion of gainers (workers with a wage rise) declines and the proportion of losers (workers with a wage decline) rises. However, the conditional means of their respective wage changes remain remarkably similar across experience groups. Similarly, as we compare education groups, the main reason for the higher growth rate among the educated is the larger proportion of

Table 2a
Annual wage growth rates and proportions of gainers and losers, by education and experience; CPS-ORG, 1998–2002

		High school graduates		Some college		College graduates		Advanced degrees	
	Experience	Fraction	Wage growth	Fraction	Wage growth	Fraction	Wage growth	Fraction	Wage growth
All	0–10	1.000	0.056	1.000	0.063	1.000	0.063	1.000	0.077
	11–15	1.000	0.033	1.000	0.055	1.000	0.045	1.000	0.053
	16–25	1.000	0.022	1.000	0.026	1.000	0.026	1.000	0.015
	26–40	1.000	0.011	1.000	0.002	1.000	−0.002	1.000	0.012
Gainers (wage up)	0–10	0.602	0.259	0.621	0.255	0.643	0.263	0.667	0.253
	11–15	0.588	0.254	0.589	0.254	0.602	0.259	0.590	0.274
	16–25	0.562	0.264	0.582	0.257	0.567	0.268	0.567	0.250
	26–40	0.546	0.264	0.555	0.261	0.536	0.287	0.545	0.265
No wage change	0–10	0.048	−0.022	0.043	−0.035	0.055	−0.025	0.080	−0.003
	11–15	0.048	−0.017	0.056	0.001	0.081	−0.026	0.090	−0.038
	16–25	0.049	−0.018	0.053	−0.036	0.090	−0.031	0.083	−0.007
	26–40	0.053	−0.028	0.055	−0.037	0.085	−0.026	0.099	−0.020
Losers (wage down)	0–10	0.349	−0.289	0.336	−0.279	0.301	−0.350	0.253	−0.361
	11–15	0.363	−0.306	0.355	−0.267	0.317	−0.343	0.320	−0.329
	16–25	0.389	−0.325	0.364	−0.334	0.342	−0.359	0.349	−0.363
	26–40	0.401	−0.314	0.391	−0.361	0.378	−0.405	0.356	−0.366

Notes: Gainers (losers) had a nominal wage increase (decrease) between subsequent wage observations.
Fraction is the share within experience groups.

Table 2b
Annual wage growth and proportions of gainers and losers by experience groups and data source

	Experience	CPS-ORG Fraction	CPS-ORG Wage growth	NLSY Fraction	NLSY Wage growth	PSID Fraction	PSID Wage growth
All							
	0–10	1.000	0.062	1.000	0.077	1.000	0.063
	11–15	1.000	0.044	1.000	0.033	1.000	0.024
	16–25	1.000	0.024	1.000	0.049	1.000	0.015
	26–40	1.000	0.007	–	–	–	–
Gainers (wage up)	0–10	0.627	0.259	0.718	0.176	0.726	0.163
	11–15	0.593	0.254	0.644	0.144	0.689	0.122
	16–25	0.568	0.264	0.662	0.168	0.667	0.118
	26–40	0.547	0.264	–	–	–	–
No wage change	0–10	0.053	−0.023	0.071	−0.044	0.040	−0.040
	11–15	0.065	−0.020	0.097	−0.040	0.048	−0.030
	16–25	0.065	−0.023	0.082	−0.041	0.056	−0.046
	26–40	0.066	−0.029	–	–	–	–
Losers (wage down)	0–10	0.319	−0.312	0.211	−0.221	0.234	−0.228
	11–15	0.342	−0.309	0.259	−0.217	0.263	−0.224
	16–25	0.367	−0.339	0.255	−0.232	0.277	−0.220
	26–40	0.388	−0.351	–	–	–	–

Notes: Gainers (losers) had a nominal wage increase (decrease) between subsequent wage observations. Fraction is the share within experience groups.

workers with a nominal wage rise; but given such a change, the average increase is *independent* of the level of schooling.

The same patterns are seen in Table 2b for the NLSY and PSID samples, where due to the smaller size of these samples we classify the data only by experience. Again, the main reason for the reduction of wage growth with experience is the decline in the proportion of gainers, while the conditional means remain the same (except for gainers in the PSID who show some decline).

Finally, Table 2c shows the interaction between gainers, losers, movers and stayers. It is seen that, compared to stayers, workers who change employers are more likely to be losers and suffer a larger reduction in wages if they lose. However, movers obtain higher wage increases if they gain. In this respect, the current job provides workers with some insurance. Taken together, the patterns displayed in Figure 3 strongly suggest that the average wage growth is influenced by the arrival of positive or negative shocks. It is the nature of such shocks (positive or negative) rather than their size that changes over the life cycle.

Table 2c
Annual wage growth and proportions of gainers, losers, movers and stayers in the NLSY, by experience groups

	Experience	All		Stayers		Movers	
		Fraction	Wage growth	Fraction	Wage growth	Fraction	Wage growth
All	0–10	1.000	0.077	0.800	0.082	0.200	0.052
	11–15	1.000	0.033	0.833	0.039	0.167	0.001
	16–25	1.000	0.049	0.833	0.055	0.167	0.014
Gainers (wage up)	0–10	0.718	0.176	0.739	0.170	0.625	0.208
	11–15	0.644	0.144	0.662	0.140	0.549	0.174
	16–25	0.662	0.168	0.680	0.162	0.568	0.207
No wage change	0–10	0.071	−0.044	0.070	−0.046	0.074	−0.034
	11–15	0.097	−0.040	0.100	−0.038	0.080	−0.049
	16–25	0.082	−0.041	0.083	−0.040	0.079	−0.045
Losers (wage down)	0–10	0.211	−0.221	0.191	−0.210	0.301	−0.250
	11–15	0.259	−0.217	0.238	−0.209	0.370	−0.244
	16–25	0.255	−0.232	0.237	−0.218	0.353	−0.283

Notes: Gainers (losers) had a nominal wage increase (decrease) between subsequent wage observations.
Movers (stayers) changed (did not change) employer between subsequent wage observations.
Fraction is the share within experience groups.

2.5. *The questions*

Based on this preliminary glance at the data, the following questions arise:

- What causes the large wage growth at the initial phase of a career?
- Why does wage growth decline?
- What are the interrelationships between wage growth, job change and labor supply?
- What causes the large variance in individual wage growth and who are the gainers and losers?

In the next section, we examine some theoretical models that address these issues. In the subsequent (and last) section, we present further evidence and discuss the support for these explanations that is provided by the data.

3. Models of wage growth

A basic tenet of modern labor economics is that the observed life cycle wage patterns are, to a large extent, a matter of choice. Thus, each worker can influence his future wage by going to school, by choosing an occupation and by searching for a better job. Of course, wage levels and wage growth are also influenced by factors beyond the worker's control, such as aggregate demand and supply, technology, degree of competition and the institutional framework. Nevertheless, individual choice in a given market situation is an important part of the equilibrium analysis of wage outcomes.

In this survey, we present some of the basic approaches that economists have used in the analysis of post-schooling wage growth. The main ideas that we cover are investment, search, and learning. Our purpose is to illustrate how these ideas are used in sufficient detail to enable the reader to use them as tools. We try to use as much a unified framework, as possible, so as to make the conceptual connections and distinctions between these ideas transparent. To achieve this purpose within our space constraints we have omitted important ideas that require separate discussion. In particular, we focus on general training and do not discuss firm-specific investments, mainly because of the difficulties in pinning down the wages. We also do not cover incentive contracts and the relations between wages and effort. The interested reader should consult other surveys for these important and complex issues [Malcomson (1997, 1999), Gibbons and Waldman (1999a, 1999b), Prendergast (1999)]. Finally, we do not discuss the important relationships between wages and hours worked [see Weiss (1986), Blundell and MaCurdy (1999)].

3.1. Investment

Workers have a finite life, T, and time is discrete. Let Y_t denote the earning capacity of the worker with the *current* employer, $t, t = 1, 2, \ldots, T$. We assume that

$$Y_t = R_t K_t, \tag{1}$$

where K_t is the worker's human capital and R_t is the rental rate. In a competitive world, without friction, all firms pay the *same* rental rate.

Workers can accumulate human capital by investment on the job. Let l_t be the proportion of earnings capacity that is forgone when the worker learns on the job. Hence, current earnings are

$$y_t = R_t K_t (1 - l_t). \tag{2}$$

Following the Ben-Porath (1967) model, suppose that human capital evolves according to

$$K_{t+1} = K_t + g(l_t K_t), \tag{3}$$

where $g(\cdot)$ is increasing and concave with $g(0) = 0$. Thus, a worker who directs a larger share of his existing capital to investment has lower current earnings but a higher future earning capacity.

Here we consider only the behavior of workers for a given "production function" $g(\cdot)$. In a more general analysis, this function would be influenced by market forces [see Rosen (1972), Heckman, Lochner and Taber (1998)], but we do not attempt to close the model by deriving the equilibrium trade-off between current and future earnings.

To determine a worker's investment, we form the Bellman equation

$$V_t(K_t) = \underset{l_t}{\mathrm{Max}}\big[R_t K_t(1 - l_t) + \beta V_{t+1}\big(K_t + g(l_t K_t)\big)\big], \tag{4}$$

where β represents the discount factor and $\beta < 1$. This equation states that the value of being employed in period t consists of the current earnings with this employer and the *option* to augment human capital through learning on the job. Each of these terms depends on the level of investment of the worker, and one considers only the optimal choices of the worker in calculating the value of the optimal program.

The first-order condition for l_t in an interior solution is

$$\frac{R_t}{g'(l_t K_t)} = \beta V'_{t+1}(K_{t+1}). \tag{5}$$

The left-hand side of (5) describes the marginal costs of investment in terms of forgone current earnings, while the right-hand side is the marginal value of additional future earnings. In the last period, T, investment is zero because there are no future periods left in which to reap the benefits.

Differentiating both sides of (4) w.r.t. K_t and using (5) we obtain the rule of motion for the marginal value of human capital

$$V'_t(K_t) = R_t + \beta V'_{t+1}(K_{t+1}). \tag{6}$$

Using the end condition that $V_{T+1}(K_{T+1}) = 0$ for *all* K_{T+1}, meaning that human capital has no value beyond the end of the working period, we obtain

$$V'_T(K_T) = R_T. \tag{7}$$

The standard investment model assumes stationary conditions; hence, R_t is a constant that can be normalized to 1. Then, using (7) and solving (6) recursively, the value of an additional unit of human capital at time t is

$$V'_t(K_t) = \frac{1 - \beta^{T+1-t}}{1 - \beta}, \tag{8}$$

which is *independent* of K_t. It follows that the value of being employed at a given current wage *declines* with time, that is, $V'_t(K_t) \geqslant V'_{t+1}(K_{t+1})$ for all periods $t = 1, 2, \ldots, T$. The shorter the remaining work horizon, the less valuable is the current stock of human capital and the lower the incentive to augment that stock. The lack of dependence on history, implicit in the Ben-Porath (1967) specification, is sufficient but not necessary for the result of declining investment, which holds under more general conditions [see Weiss (1986)].

The model can be easily generalized to the case in which R_t is variable over time. In this case, equation (8) becomes

$$V'_t(K_t) = \sum_{\tau=t}^{T} \beta^{\tau-t} R_\tau. \tag{8'}$$

Comparing these expressions, it is seen that if R_t rises with time, then the investment in human capital is higher at each period. The reason is that investment occurs when a worker receives a relatively lower price for his human capital, so that the forgone earnings are relatively low. If the rental rate rises with time at a decreasing rate, this relative price effect weakens with time and investment declines.[4]

The observable implications of this model are clear:

- For a constant R, investment declines as the worker ages and approaches the end of his working life.
- Earnings rise along an optimal investment path. This is caused by two effects that reinforce each other; positive investment increases earning capacity and declining investment induces a rise in its utilization rate.
- If R varies with time, workers that expect exogenous growth in their earning capacity invest at a higher rate and their wage rises at a higher pace. Investment declines if the rate of growth in the rental rate decreases.

3.2. *Investment in school and on the job*

Investment in school and on the job can be viewed as two alternative modes of accumulation of human capital that complement and substitute each other. Complementarity arises because human capital is self-productive, so that human capital accumulated in school is useful for learning on the job. Substitution arises because life is finite and if more time is spent in school, there is less time left for investment on the job. Although the focus of this survey is on post-schooling investments, the fact that these two modes are to some extent jointly determined leads us to expect interactions, whereby individuals completing different levels of schooling will invest differentially on the job and therefore display different patterns of wage growth.

Investment on the job is usually done *jointly* with work, while schooling is done separately. As a consequence, one foregoes less earning when training on the job than in school. However, in school, one typically specializes in the acquisition of knowledge and human capital is consequently accumulated at a faster rate. One can capture these differences by assuming different production (and cost) functions for the two alternative investment channels.

Let p_t be a labor force participation indicator such that $p_t = 1$ if the individual works in period t and $p_t = 0$, otherwise. Suppose that when the individual does not work he

[4] Using (8′) and (5) investment is determined by

$$\frac{1}{g'(l_t K_t)} = \sum_{\tau=t}^{T} \beta^{\tau-t} \frac{R_\tau}{R_t}.$$

If the rental rate R rises with time $\frac{R_\tau}{R_t} > 1$, which raises the incentives to invest at any period. If, in addition, $\frac{R_\tau}{R_t}$ declines in t for all $\tau > t$ then changing prices creates an added incentive to invest early rather than late, which together with the effect of the shortening horizon implies that investment, $l_t K_t$, declines in t.

goes to school and then accumulates human capital according to $K_{t+1} = K_t(1+\gamma)$ where γ is a fixed parameter such that $\gamma K_t > g(l_t K_t)$. We also assume that $(1+\gamma) > \frac{1}{\beta}$, which means that the rate of return from investment in human capital γ exceeds the interest rate. Otherwise, such investment would never be optimal. Assume stationary conditions and let $R_t = 1$. We can now rewrite the Bellman equation in the form

$$V_t(K_t) = \operatorname*{Max}_{p_t, l_t}\left[p_t K_t(1-l_t) + \beta V_{t+1}\left(K_t + p_t g(l_t K_t) + (1-p_t)\gamma K_t\right)\right]. \tag{9}$$

School is the preferred choice in period t if

$$\beta V_{t+1}\left(K_t(1+\gamma)\right) > K_t(1-l_t^*) + \beta V_{t+1}\left(K_t + g(l_t^* K_t)\right), \tag{10}$$

where the optimal level of training on the job, l_t^*, is determined from (5). Finally, the law of motion for the marginal value of human capital is modified to

$$V_t'(K_t) = p_t + \beta V_{t+1}'(K_{t+1})\left(1 + (1-p_t)\gamma\right). \tag{11}$$

This extension has several implications:

- Specialization in schooling occurs, if at all, in the first phase of life. It is followed by a period of investment on the job. In the last phase of the life cycle, there is no investment at all.
- During the schooling period, there are no earnings, yet human capital is accumulated at the maximal rate $(1+\gamma)$. During the period of investment on the job, earnings are positive and growing. In the last phase (if it exists), earnings are constant.
- A worker leaves school at the first period in which (10) is reversed. At this point it must be the case that $l_t^* < 1$, which means that at the time of leaving school, earnings must *jump* to a positive level. This realistic feature is present only because we assume different production (and cost) functions in school and on the job, whereby accumulation in school is faster but requires a larger sacrifice of current earnings.
- A person with a larger initial stock of human capital, K_0, will stay in school for a shorter period and spend more time investing on the job. He will have higher earnings and the same earnings growth throughout life.
- A person with a larger scholastic learning ability, γ, will stay in school for a longer period and spend less time investing on the job. He will also have higher earnings and the same earning growth throughout life.

Although these results depend heavily on the particular form of the production function (3), they illustrate that unobserved characteristics of economic agents can create a negative correlation between the amounts of time spent investing in school and on the job, while there need be no correlation between completed schooling and post schooling wage growth.[5] It should be noted, however, that wage growth is often higher for the more educated, which casts some doubt on the neutrality implied by (3). Uncertainty and unexpected shocks can also affect the correlation between schooling and investment. For instance, the introduction of computers may raise the incentive to invest on the job among educated workers to a larger extent than among uneducated workers because the investment's payoff may be lower for the second group.[6]

3.3. Search

In a world with limited information and frictions, firms may pay a different rental rate, R, because workers cannot immediately find the highest paying firm and must spend time and money to locate employers. If a worker meets a new employer, he obtains a random draw $\tilde{R}$ from the given distribution of potential wage offers $F(R)$. The worker decides whether to accept or reject this offer. To simplify, we assume here that workers are relatively passive in their search for jobs. They receive offers at some fixed exogenous rate λ, but do not initiate offers through active job search.

We discuss here the case with homogenous workers and firms, assuming that workers are equally productive in all firms and their productivity is constant over time. However, firms may pay different wages for identical workers. Specifically, if K is the worker's human capital, then the profits of a firm that pays the worker R are $K - RK$. Firms that post a high R draw more workers and can coexist with a firm that posts a low R and draws few workers. In equilibrium, all firms must have the same profits [see Mortensen and Pissarides (1999)]. Here we consider only the behavior of workers for a given wage distribution, $F(R)$, and do not attempt to close the model by deriving either the equilibrium wage offer distribution or the equilibrium trade-off between current and future earnings. In a more general analysis, the wage distribution is determined by market forces [see Wolpin (2003)].

Lets us momentarily ignore investment and look solely at the implications of search. Consider a worker who receives a rental rate R_t for his human capital from his current employer in period t, so that $Y_t = KR_t$. Now imagine that during period t, the worker is matched with a new employer offering another rental rate, R. Because the worker can follow the same search strategy wherever he is employed, it is clear that the offer will be accepted if $R > R_t$ and rejected if $R < R_t$. If the worker rejects the offer and stays with the current employer, his earning capacity remains the same and $Y_{t+1} = Y_t$. If the

[5] The crucial feature here is that investment depends only the time left to the end of the horizon and is independent of the level of the stock of human capital. An additional simplification is that there is no depreciation, so that earning growth depends only on investment and is thus also independent of history. The results stated in the text can be easily shown using the continuous time version of the problem described in the text and applying phase diagram techniques [see Weiss (1986)].

[6] Weinberg (2003) shows that computer adoption is also related to experience. In industries with the greatest increase in computer use, the returns to experience have increased among high school graduates, but declined among college graduates.

worker accepts the outside offer and moves to the new employer, his new wage, $Y_{t+1} = RK$, must exceed Y_t. The probability that the worker will switch jobs is $\lambda(1 - F(R_t))$ and is *decreasing* in R_t.

The observable implications of this model are:

- A job has an *option value* to the worker. In particular, he can maintain his current wage and move away when he gets a better offer. Consequently, earnings rise whenever the worker switches jobs and remain constant otherwise.
- The higher the worker's current wage, the more valuable is the current job; hence, the offers that the workers accepts must exceed a higher reservation value. Therefore, the quit rate and the expected wage growth decline as the worker accumulates work experience and climbs up the occupational ladder.
- A straight-forward extension is to add involuntary separations. Such separations are usually associated with wage reduction and are more likely to occur at the end of the worker's career, which may explain the reduction in average wages towards the end of the life cycle.

This model can be generalized by allowing the worker to control the arrival of new job offers by spending time on the job in active search [see Mortensen (1986)]. Search effort declines as the worker obtains better jobs, so that the arrival rate of job offers and wage growth decline, too. Towards the end of the career, a worker may reduce his search effort to a level that generates no job offers. Consequently, voluntary quits and wage growth cease.

The same search model can be motivated slightly differently by assuming that workers and firms are heterogeneous. Let workers be ranked by their skill, K. Let firms be ranked by their *minimal* skill requirement R [see Weiss, Sauer and Gotlibovski (2003)]. Assume that worker K employed by firm R produces R if $K \geqslant R$ and 0 otherwise. Because workers with $K \geqslant R$ on job R produce the same amount, irrespective of their K, we can set their wages to R (assuming zero profits). A worker K who is now employed at firm R_t and meets (with probability λ) a random draw from the population of employers, R, is willing to switch if and only if $R > R_t$. However the employer is willing to accept him only if $K \geqslant R$. Transition into a better job thus occurs with probability $\lambda(F(K) - F(R_t))$.

3.4. Comparison of investment and search

The investment and search models have similar empirical implications for *average* growth in earnings, i.e., positive and declining wage growth. In the investment model, the reason for wage growth is that the worker chooses to spend some of his time learning. However, investment declines as a result of the shortened remaining work period, which causes wage growth to taper off. In the search model, wage growth is an outcome of the option that workers have to accept or reject job offers. Acceptance depends on the level of earnings that the worker attained by time t, so that history matters. Two workers of the same age may behave differently because of their different success records in meeting employers. But the general trend is for wage growth to decline because workers who attained a higher wage have a lower incentive to search and are less likely to switch jobs.

Although investment and search have similar implications for wage growth, they can be distinguished by their different patterns in the *variance* of wages and the correlation between wages at different points of the life cycle. As shown by Mincer (1974), the variance in wages first declines and then rises, as we move across age groups in a cross section or follow a cohort. The reason is that a current low wage is compensated for by a future high wage, so that workers who invest more intensely will *overtake* those with a lower investment rate. The minimal variance occurs in the middle range of experience, where individual earning profiles cross. Under search, the cause for variability is not differential investment but different success record in locating suitable job matches and the variability in accepted wage offers. Homogeneous workers become increasingly heterogeneous due to their longer exposure to random job offers. However, selection modifies the impact of such shocks on wages, because wages do not go down when the worker keeps the job and those who have high wages are less likely to get a better offer. Thus, the variance first increases and then declines as workers are gradually climbing up the income distribution. If workers are initially heterogeneous, the variance may also first increase and then decline as workers are gradually sorted into their "right" place. The investment model suggests a negative correlation between wage level and wage growth at the beginning of the worker's career and a positive correlation between wage growth and wage level late in the worker's career, whereas the search model implies a negative correlation between current wage and wage growth at *any* point of the life cycle.

Search and investment also have similar implications for quits, especially if investment has a firm-specific component. To the extent that specific investment can be described by a stochastic learning process on the job, as in Jovanovic (1984) and Mortensen (1988), then both wage growth and mobility can be outcomes of either internal shocks in the form of changes in the quality of a match, or external shocks in the form of outside offers. The average patterns of wage growth and separations will be the same under specific investment or search. However, higher moments, such as the wage variances among stayers and movers, can indicate the importance of specific capital and search, respectively.

3.5. Putting the two together

We now consider the possible interaction between search and investment behavior. To simplify, we continue to assume that workers can reject or accept offers as they arrive at an exogenous rate λ, but cannot initiate offers by investing in search. However, the option of passive search changes the incentives to invest in human capital.

The Bellman equation becomes

$$V_t(R_t, K_t) = \operatorname*{Max}_{l_t}\big\{R_t K_t(1-l_t) + \beta\big[\lambda E\big\{\max\big[V_{t+1}(R_t, K_{t+1}), V_{t+1}(R, K_{t+1})\big]\big\} + (1-\lambda)V_{t+1}(R_t, K_{t+1})\big]\big\}. \tag{12}$$

Because a worker with a given K can follow the same search and investment strategy on any job, it is clear that he will switch jobs if $R > R_t$. Given this reservation value strategy, we can write

$$E\{\max[V_{t+1}(R_t, K_{t+1}), V_{t+1}(\widetilde{R}_{t+1}, K_{t+1})]\}$$
$$= F(R_t)V_{t+1}(R_t, K_{t+1}) + \int_{R_t}^{\infty} V_{t+1}(R, K_{t+1})f(R)\,\mathrm{d}R, \tag{13}$$

where $f(R)$ is the density of wage offers. The first-order condition for l_t is now

$$\frac{R_t}{g'(l_t K_t)} = \beta V_{k,t+1}(R_t, K_{t+1}) + \lambda\beta \int_{R_t}^{\infty} \big(V_{k,t+1}(R, K_{t+1})$$
$$- V_{k,t+1}(R_t, K_{t+1})\big) f(R)\,\mathrm{d}R, \tag{14}$$

where $V_{k,t}$ denotes the partial derivative of $V_t(\cdot,\cdot)$ with respect to K_t. The interaction between investment and search decisions is captured by the second term in Equation (14) which shows that the incentives to invest now include the *capital gains* that the worker obtains if he changes employers. The higher K_t, the more one gains from a favorable draw of R; therefore, the incentive to accumulate human capital is stronger.[7]

This extended model has the following features:

- As long as the worker stays with the same firm, investment in human capital declines because of the shortened work period.
- On any such interval, the worker invests more than he would without search and a fixed R. This result reflects the upward drift in the R which is inherent in the search model and qualitatively similar to the result in the regular investment model when R rises exogenously.
- Investment drops when the worker switches to a new job with a higher R, because the option of switching to a new job becomes less valuable.

3.6. Human capital and skills

Human capital K is an aggregate that summarizes individual skills in terms of production capacity. Different skills are rewarded differentially in different occupations. We

[7] We can simplify these expressions by showing that the value function is *linear* in K_t and can be written in the form

$$V_t(R_t, K_t) = K_t A_t(R_t) + B_t.$$

Hence, investment in period t is determined by

$$\frac{R_t}{g'(l_t K_t)} = \beta A_{t+1}(R_t) + \lambda\beta \int_{R_t}^{\infty} (A_{t+1}(R) - A_{t+1}(R_t)) f(R)\,\mathrm{d}R,$$

where $A_t(x)$ is a sequence of functions that are increasing in x and decreasing in t, with $A_T(x) = 1$ for all x.

assume that this aggregate may be represented as

$$\ln K_j = \sum_s \theta_{sj} S_s, \tag{15}$$

where S_s is the quantity of skill s possessed by the individual and θ_{sj} is a non-negative parameter that represent the contribution of skill s to occupation j. Firms reward individual skills indirectly by renting human capital at the market-determined rental rate, R. Thus, the parameter θ_{sj} is the proportional increase in earning capacity associated with a unit increase in skill x_s if the individual works in occupation j. Having assumed that θ_{sj} is independent of the quantity of skill s possessed by the individual, these coefficients may be viewed as the implicit "prices" (or "rates of return") of skill s in occupation j.[8]

Because we are interested here in the timing of occupational changes, it will be convenient to set the problem in continuous time. We denote by T the duration of the worker's lifetime and by t a point in time in the interval $[0, T]$. We define $h_j(t)$ as the portion of available time spent working in occupation j at time t, so that $0 \leqslant h_j(t) \leqslant 1$ and $\sum_j h_j(t) = 1$. The worker will typically work at one particular occupation in each point in time but is free to switch occupations at any time. The worker's earning capacity is

$$Y(t) = R \sum_j h_j(t) K_j(t). \tag{16}$$

Skills are initially endowed and can then be augmented by acquiring experience. We consider here a "learning by doing" technology whereby work at a rate $h_j(t)$ in a particular occupation j augments skill s by $\gamma_{sj} h_j(t)$. Thus, the change in skill s at time t is

$$\dot{S}_s = \sum_j \gamma_{sj} h_j(t). \tag{17}$$

Note the joint production feature of this technology. Working in any one occupation j can influence many skills that are useful in other occupations. Yet, such experience may be more relevant to some particular skills. In this way, we obtain that work experience is transferable but not necessarily general.

In the static version of this model (the Roy model), individual skills are constant ($\gamma_{sj} = 0$ for all s and j) and the main issue is the mapping between skills and earnings that results from the different occupational choices of workers with different skills. The basic principle that applies there is that each individual will spend *all* his work time in the occupation in which his bundle of skills commands the highest reward [see Willis (1986) and Heckman and Honore (1990)]. Unexpected changes in the prices of skills, θ_{sj}, can cause the worker to switch occupations; however, under static conditions

[8] Each worker can be viewed as a bundle of skills. Because these skills cannot be unbundled from the worker, the law of one price does not apply and different skills have different implicit prices in different uses, depending upon the technology of production. It is only human capital that can be moved freely across uses and, therefore, commands a single price.

there is no occupational mobility. In the dynamic set up that we outline here, skills vary with time, and this variation is influenced by the worker's career choices. In such a context, *planned* occupational switches can arise, even in the absence of shocks, if experience is sufficiently transferable across occupations.

To simplify the exposition, we consider the case of two occupations and two skills[9] and examine the conditions for a single switch. Given our simplifying assumptions, the earnings capacity of a worker in different occupations, K_j grows at constant rates that depend on the occupation in which the worker specializes. Suppose that the worker switches from occupation 1 to occupation 2 at time x and then stays there for the rest of his life. Then, in the early phase, prior to time x, $h_1(t) = 1$ and

$$\begin{aligned} \frac{\dot{K}_1}{K_1} &= \theta_{11}\gamma_{11} + \theta_{21}\gamma_{21} \equiv g_{1,1}, \\ \frac{\dot{K}_2}{K_2} &= \theta_{12}\gamma_{11} + \theta_{22}\gamma_{21} \equiv g_{2,1}. \end{aligned} \tag{18}$$

In the later phase, after x, $h_2(t) = 1$ and

$$\begin{aligned} \frac{\dot{K}_1}{K_1} &= \theta_{11}\gamma_{12} + \theta_{21}\gamma_{22} \equiv g_{1,2}, \\ \frac{\dot{K}_2}{K_2} &= \theta_{12}\gamma_{12} + \theta_{22}\gamma_{22} \equiv g_{2,2}. \end{aligned} \tag{19}$$

The expected lifetime earnings of the worker is

$$V(x) = R\left\{K_1(0)\int_0^x \mathrm{e}^{-rt+g_{1,1}t}\,\mathrm{d}t + K_2(0)\int_x^T \mathrm{e}^{-rt+g_{2,1}x+g_{2,2}(t-x)}\,\mathrm{d}t\right\}. \tag{20}$$

For a switch at time x to be optimal, it is necessary that $V'(x) = 0$ and for $V''(x) < 0$. It can be shown that if work experience in each occupation raises the worker's earnings in that same occupation by more than in the alternative occupation (that is, $g_{1,1} > g_{2,1}$ and $g_{2,2} > g_{2,1}$) then $V'(x) = 0$ implies that $V''(x) > 0$, so that the worker will *never* switch occupations.[10] Instead, the worker will specialize in one occupation throughout his working life and concentrate all his investments in that occupation [see Weiss

[9] More generally, we are interested in the case where there are more occupations than skills. Otherwise some skills will be redundant [see Welch (1969)].

[10] The first derivative can be written in the form

$$\begin{aligned} V'(x) &= R\Big\{K_1(0)\,\mathrm{e}^{-rx+g_{1,1}x} - K_2(0)\,\mathrm{e}^{-rx+g_{2,1}x} \\ &\quad + (g_{2,1} - g_{2,2})K_2(0)\int_x^T \mathrm{e}^{-rt+g_{2,1}x+g_{2,2}(t-x)}\,\mathrm{d}t\Big\} \\ &= R\,\mathrm{e}^{-rx+g_{2,1}x}K_2(0)\Big\{\mathrm{e}^{D+(g_{1,1}-g_{2,1})x} - 1 + (g_{2,1} - g_{2,2})\int_0^{T-x} \mathrm{e}^{-r\tau+g_{2,2}\tau}\,\mathrm{d}\tau\Big\} \end{aligned}$$

(1971)]. However, some occupations require a preparation period in other occupations, that serve as stepping stones [see Jovanovic and Nyarko (1997)]. For instance, it is not uncommon that successful managers start as engineers or physicians rather than junior managers.

Specifically, suppose that

$$\gamma_{11} > \gamma_{12}, \quad \gamma_{21} > \gamma_{22}, \quad \theta_{11} < \theta_{12}, \quad \theta_{21} < \theta_{22}. \tag{21}$$

Then it is easy to verify that, depending on initial conditions, the worker may start in occupation 1 and then switch to occupation 2 because skill 1 is more important in occupation 2, i.e., $\theta_{12} > \theta_{11}$, but occupation 1 is the better place to acquire skill 1, i.e., $\gamma_{11} > \gamma_{12}$. It does not pay to specialize in occupation 1 because the worker will not exploit his acquired skills that are more useful in occupation 2. Nor is it usually optimal to specialize in occupation 2, because then the worker will not acquire sufficient skills. However, a worker with a large endowment of skill 1 or skill 2 may specialize in occupation 2 immediately.

This model illustrates quite clearly the main features of occupations that serve as stepping stones. Basically, these occupations enable the worker to acquire skills that can be used later in other occupations in a cheaper or more effective way.[11] Although these jobs pay less for *all* workers with *given* skills, some workers may still enter them as an investment in training.[12]

The pattern of earnings growth that is implied by this sequence of occupational choices is easy to summarize. At the point of switch, x, earnings *rise* instantaneously, where the proportional jump is $S_1(0)(\theta_{11}-\theta_{12})+S_2(0)(\theta_{21}-\theta_{22})+(g_{1,1}-g_{2,1})x$. The growth rate of earnings may either rise or decline following this change, because the restrictions in (21) are consistent with either $g_{1,1} > g_{2,2}$ or $g_{1,1} < g_{2,2}$. If we assume, however, that the differences between the two occupations in the learning coefficients (the γ's) are more pronounced than the differences in the prices of skills (the θ's) then $g_{1,1} > g_{2,2}$ and the growth rate in earnings will decline, which is the more realistic case.

using $\frac{K_1(0)}{K_2(0)} = e^{S_1(0)(\theta_{11}-\theta_{12})+S_2(0)(\theta_{21}-\theta_{22})} \equiv e^D$ and a change of variable, $t - x = \tau$. The second derivative evaluated at this point is given by

$$V''(x) = R\,e^{-rx+g_{2,1}x} K_2(0)\{(g_{1,1} - g_{2,1})\,e^{D+(g_{1,1}-g_{2,1})x} - (g_{2,1} - g_{2,2})\,e^{(-r+g_{2,2})(T-x)}\}.$$

[11] Because this model assumes learning by doing, the opportunity costs of investment are the forgone earnings that one could receive by switching earlier to the higher-paying occupation. This stands in some contrast to the cases discussed above, where the costs were the loss of effective work time, in the occupation that one has.

[12] Booth, Francesconi and Frank (2002), show that fixed term temporary jobs serve as stepping stones to permanent jobs. Female workers who held 3 consecutive one year fixed-term contracts are initially paid lower wages than comparable workers on permanent jobs but appear to overtake them after about 10 years. Among men, wages are higher for workers who follow the same pattern but overtaking is not observed.

3.7. Wages, productivity and contracts

The presumption, so far, was that a worker's wage is closely tied to his productivity. However, the relation between these two variables may be quite complex, especially when workers and firms develop durable relationships. In such a case, wages and productivity are still tied in terms of long-term averages but, in the short run, systematic differences between wages and productivity may appear that represent credit and risk sharing arrangements, or incentives to exert effort. We shall not attempt to describe the complex issues associated with incentives for effort, about which several excellent recent surveys exist. However, the issues associated with credit and risk sharing are easy to explain.

Trade between workers and employers that extends over time is motivated by some basic asymmetry between the parties. Specifically, firms may have better access to the capital market and may be able to pool some risks. If a worker's output varies over time, and if he has no access to the capital market, the firm may smooth his consumption by offering a flat wage profile which effectively means that the worker borrows from the firm. Similarly, if a worker's output is subject to shocks, the firm may accept these risks and provide the worker with insurance that stabilizes his income. As we shall now show, the ability of firms to provide such credit or insurance arrangements is limited by the commitments that workers (and firms) can make.

Consider a worker with a fixed bundle of skills and suppose that because of random variations in the prices of skills, his/her human capital is subject to capital gains or losses. Specifically,

$$K_{t+1} = \begin{cases} K_t(1+g) & \text{with probability } p, \\ K_t(1-\delta) & \text{with probability } 1-p, \end{cases} \tag{22}$$

where g and δ are fixed parameters that govern the size of capital gains and losses, respectively. We denote by $Q_t(K_{t-1})$ the expected present value of the worker's output over the remainder of his work life, $T - t$. Let h_t be a sequence of zeros and ones, where 1 for the τ element, $\tau = 1, 2, \ldots, t$, indicates the occurrence of a positive shock and a 0 indicates the occurrence of a negative shock in period τ. We refer to such a sequence as the history or sample path. Let $y_t(h_{t-1})$ be the wage that a firm promises to pay a worker with history h_{t-1} in period t and let $Y_t(h_{t-1})$ be the present value of the expected payments over the remainder of the working life, from t to T.[13] We can think of $Y_t(h_{t-1})$ as the worker's *contractual* assets.

[13] For simplicity, assume that the interest rate is zero. Then, $Q_t(K_{t-1})$ satisfies the difference equation

$$Q_t(K_{t-1}) = RK_{t-1} + pQ_{t+1}(K_{t-1}(1+g)) + (1-p)Q_{t+1}(K_{t-1}(1-\delta)),$$

and can be solved recursively, using the end condition that $Q_{T+1}(K_T) = 0$ for all K_T. Similarly,

$$Y_t(h_{t-1}) = y_t(h_{t-1}) + pY_{t+1}(h_{t-1}, 1) + (1-p)Y_{t+1}(h_{t-1}, 0)),$$

can be solved recursively, using the end condition that $Y_{T+1}(h_T) = 0$ for all h_T.

A risk-neutral firm is indifferent between all contingent contracts that yield the same expected value. However, a risk-averse worker with no access to the capital or insurance markets would prefer that the payment stream will be as stable as possible. If the worker can commit to stay with the firm, the competition among firms will force them to offer wage contracts that smooth the wage payments over time and across states of nature. In practice, workers cannot legally bind themselves to a firm; their option to leave the firm limits the insurance and consumption smoothing that firms can provide [see Harris and Holmstrom (1982), Weiss (1984)].

A competitive payment scheme must maximize the expected utility of the worker given the firm's expected profits and the worker's outside options. Therefore, the contract that survives must solve the following program

$$V_t(K_{t-1}, Y_{t-1}) = \operatorname*{Max}_{y, x_1, x_0} \bigl\{(u(y) + pV_{t+1}\bigl(K_{t-1}(1+g), Y_{t-1} + x_1\bigr) \\ + (1-p)V_{t+1}\bigl(K_{t-1}(1-\delta), Y_{t-1} + x_0\bigr)\bigr\}, \tag{23}$$

subject to

$$y + px_1 + (1-p)x_0 = 0, \tag{24a}$$

$$Y_{t-1} + x_1 \geqslant Q_{t-1}\bigl(K_{t-1}(1+g)\bigr) - a, \tag{24b}$$

$$Y_{t-1} + x_0 \geqslant Q_{t-1}\bigl(K_{t-1}(1-\delta)\bigr) - a, \tag{24c}$$

where a is a parameter that represents the costs of mobility across firms, such as loss of firm-specific capital.[14] The state variables at period t are the worker's human capital and the expected payments from the firm under the existing contract (including current obligations $y_t(h_{t-1})$). The control variables, y, x_1, x_0 represent possible revisions of that contract that can make the worker better off, keeping the firm's expected profits constant and keeping the worker with the firm.[15] Constraint (24a) requires that the revisions maintain the cost of the contract to the firm (because Q_{t-1} is fully determined by K_{t-1}, this implies that expected profits are unchanged). Constraints (24b) and (24c) imply that other firms cannot bid workers away. If the firm changes the contract in such a

[14] For simplicity, we treat the mobility cost as a fixed cost. In general, these costs depend on the time spent in a job, firm or industry and on the worker's particular skills.

[15] By definition,

$$Y_t(h_{t-1}) = y_t(h_{t-1}) + pY_{t+1}(h_{t-1}, 1) + (1-p)Y_{t+1}(h_{t-1}, 0) \\ = y + p(Y_t(h_{t-1}) + x_1) + (1-p)(Y_t(h_{t-1}) + x_0),$$

implying

$$y + px_1 + (1-p)x_0 = 0.$$

manner that its obligation falls short of the worker's expected output, it cannot retain the worker because another firm can offer a superior contract and still make non-negative profits.

The first-order conditions are

$$u'(y) - \lambda = 0, \tag{25a}$$

$$\frac{\partial V_{t+1}(K_{t-1}(1+g), Y_{t-1}+x_1)}{\partial Y_t} - \lambda + \frac{\mu_1}{p} = 0, \tag{25b}$$

$$\frac{\partial V_{t+1}(K_{t-1}(1-\delta), Y_{t-1}+x_0)}{\partial Y_t} - \lambda + \frac{\mu_2}{1-p} = 0, \tag{25c}$$

where λ, μ_1, μ_2 are the time-variable non-negative Lagrange multipliers that are associated with the constraints (24a), (24b) and (24c), respectively.

Differentiating (23) with respect to Y_{t-1} and using conditions (25a)–(25c), we have

$$\frac{\partial V_t(K_{t-1}, Y_{t-1})}{\partial Y_{t-1}} = \lambda, \tag{26}$$

which implies that in each period and at any possible state, the marginal utility of consumption, $u'(y)$, is equated to the marginal value of the worker's contractual assets, $\frac{\partial V_t(K_{t-1}, Y_{t-1})}{\partial Y_{t-1}}$. Because the Lagrange multipliers μ_1 and μ_2 are non-negative, it follows from conditions (25b) and (25c) that the payment stream is arranged in such a way that the marginal value of contractual assets never rises. This also means that wage payments never decline as successive realizations of human capital unfold.

These results have a simple economic interpretation. Workers who may suffer either capital gains or capital losses, when skill prices change, would like the firm to transfer wages from "good" states when income is high and marginal utility of income is low to "bad" states when income is low and marginal utility of income is high. The firm is willing to do so only if the expected present value of wage payments does not rise in consequence. Thus, paying a higher current wage in a bad state implies a wage reduction in some future good state. However, the firm can commit to such a transfer policy only if it is able to retain the worker and collect the payment for the insurance that it provides the worker now.

If the cost of mobility across firms, a, is sufficiently high to prevent mobility, then constraints (24b)–(24c) are not binding and $\mu_1 = \mu_2 = 0$. Then, the optimal contract implies that y is a constant, which means that the firm provides *perfect* insurance and consumption smoothing. However, if the cost of mobility across firms, a, is sufficiently low, the constraint (24c) which corresponds to a positive shock is binding, because such a shock makes the worker more attractive to other firms. The wage profile that emerges in this case is one in which the wage rises when workers receive a positive shock but remains unchanged when they receive a negative shock. In this way, the workers receive *partial* insurance from the firm. When a positive shock occurs, wages are raised to the minimal level required to retain the worker. When a negative shock occurs, wages are set above the worker's productivity. This policy requires that workers pay for the insurance by accepting initial wages that fall short of their productivity upon joining the firm.

If the costs of mobility across firms are low, and workers must be induced to stay with the firm, then their *average* wages rise *faster* than their average productivity. This result is reversed if there are substantial costs of mobility across firms and the workers are locked to the firm, a condition that allows the firm to provide perfect insurance. In this case, of course, average wages rise at a *lower* rate than does productivity.

In equilibrium, there is no mobility across firms. However the workers' *option* to leave the firm affects wage growth. Paradoxically, workers are better off when the costs of mobility are high. This holds for two related reasons. First, with high mobility costs, workers are effectively locked in with the firm so that the firm can provide perfect rather than partial insurance. Second, because information is public and workers are equally productive in all firms, mobility serves no productive role. Thus the most efficient arrangement is for workers to stay with their employers. A more complex situation arises if workers can influence skill acquisition and use via occupational switches. Then, workers will receive less insurance from the firm but obtain higher wage growth resulting from investment in skills acquisition. In addition, workers may try to create a more balanced portfolio of skills, a factor supporting mobility and, possibly, multiple job holding.

An important feature of the optimal wage contract is that wages in period t generally depend on the entire history of shocks and not simply on the accumulated human capital at time t. Specifically, $y_t(h_{t-2}, 1, 0)$ may exceed $y_t(h_{t-2}, 0, 1)$. While workers have the same productive capacity in period t in both cases, there are wage gains from having *early* success. This is because early success provides opportunities for sharing risk with potentially more productive realizations in the future, an option not available to workers who experienced early failure. More generally, conditions at the time at which the commitments are taken, e.g., when workers entered the firm, can cause wage differences between workers who are equally productive.[16]

3.8. Unobserved productivity and learning

A particular worker's productivity may be unknown to the worker and potential employers. Over time, the worker's performance is observed; one may use this information to make inferences about the worker's "true" skills. This learning process can create negative and positive shocks to the worker's perceived productivity, similar to those discussed above. However, the learning model has further implications concerning mobility. That is, workers can experiment in an occupation where learning about ability is

[16] Two basic features of this model have been demonstrated empirically. First, nominal wages are indeed rigid downward [see Baker, Gibbs and Holmstrom (1994a, 1994b), McLaughlin (1994)]. However, the prevalence of real wage reduction is problematic for the contracting model. Second, history-dependence is in fact present [see Baker, Gibbs and Holmstrom (1994a), Beaudry and Di Nardo (1991)]. There is also evidence that risk aversion reduces wage growth [Shaw (1996)].

possible and then, as their abilities are gradually revealed, sort themselves into different occupations, based on their realized performance.

Let there be two occupations, one low skill, one high skill, and let there be two types of workers, those of high ability and those of low ability. All workers perform equally well in the low-skill occupation and produce one unit of output per period, irrespective of ability. Workers differ in their ability to perform the required jobs in the high-skill occupation; we denote the expected output, per period of time, as q_l and q_h for the low and high ability workers, respectively. However, neither the workers nor their employers know whether a particular worker is of high or low ability. The common prior probability that a specific worker is of low ability is denoted by π_0. With time, as a worker's performance is observed by all agents (including the worker himself), all agents modify this common prior.[17] Although a worker's productivity remains constant over time, the new information can affect his wages and employment.

We may model the realized output as a simple Bernoulli trials so that q_i is the fixed probability that type i, $i = l, h$, will produce one unit of output in period t and $1 - q_i$ is the probability that type i will produce nothing in period t. Let $n(t)$ be the (random) number of successes that a worker has accumulated up to period t. Based on this information, one can update the probability that he is of the low ability type. Specifically, the posterior probability is

$$\begin{aligned} \pi(t,r) &\equiv \Pr\{q = q_l / n(t) = r\} \\ &= \frac{\pi_0 q_l^r (1-q_l)^{t-r}}{\pi_0 q_l^r (1-q_l)^{t-r} + (1-\pi_0) q_h^r (1-q_h)^{t-r}}, \end{aligned} \tag{27}$$

and the updated expected output per period is

$$q(t,r) = q_l \pi(t,r) + q_h \big[1 - \pi(t,r)\big]. \tag{28}$$

From (27) it follows that $\pi(t,r)$ rises in t for a given r and declines with r for a given t. That is, if a worker did not perform well, a low $n(t)$ up to a given time t, the posterior probability that he is of low ability increases. In contrast, if the worker has a favorable record, the posterior probability that he is of high ability increases. The perceived (expected) output of the worker is correspondingly modified downwards or upwards. (In this respect, the model is similar to the one discussed in the previous section, except that the informational value of the shocks (success or failure) decays over time.) With sufficient time, the process reveals the true identity of the worker.[18]

[17] We examine here only learning that is general for all firms in a particular industry. As already noted, firm-specific learning, involves some complex issues about the nature of the competition among firms that we cannot cover here. See, however, Jovanovic (1979a, 1979b, 1984), Mortensen (1988), Felli and Harris (1996, 2003) and Munasinghe (2003).

[18] Rewrite

$$\pi(t,r) = \frac{1}{1 + \frac{1-\pi_0}{\pi_0}\left(\frac{q_h}{q_l}\right)^r \left(\frac{1-q_h}{1-q_l}\right)^{t-r}}.$$

Consider first the case in which workers are risk-neutral and assume that workers are paid their current perceived output at each point of time. Because all workers are ex ante identical, they will all start at the risky high skill occupation, while attempting to learn their true ability. As the public information about each worker accumulates, workers are separated in terms of wages and employment. Those with inferior performance will receive lower wages and some of them will choose to leave. Those with superior records will receive higher wages and will choose to stay. Because of the finite time horizon and costs of mobility, workers will not move at the end of their career even though their perceived output and wages continue to fluctuate. This mobility pattern continues to hold if workers are risk-averse and if firms provide partial insurance so that wages are rigid downwards. However, an important difference is that such insurance can induce the workers to stay in the skilled sector even if their output in that occupation is low. With efficient contracts, such workers must be forced out, i.e., denied tenure [see Harris and Weiss (1984)].

The "pure" learning model has some strong implications for wage growth that hold for any distribution of shocks provided that we continue to assume that the shocks are independent across time. Suppose that worker i's performance in period t is given by

$$y_{it} = \eta_i + \varepsilon_{it}, \tag{29}$$

where η_i is a fixed parameter that is unknown to the firm, and ε_{it} is a random i.i.d. shock with zero mean. Now if firms pay wages based on workers perceived output at time t, $w_{it} = E(y_{it}/I_t) = E(\eta_i/I_t)$, where I_t is any information available at t. Then, because expectations are linear operators, it follows that $E(\eta_i/I_t) = E(E(\eta_i/I_{t+1})/I_t)$ and

$$w_{it} = E(w_{i,t+1}/w_{it}). \tag{30}$$

This martingale property implies that innovations in the wage process $w_{i,t+1} - E(w_{i,t+1}/I_t) = w_{i,t+1} - w_{it}$ are serially uncorrelated. Intuitively, any particular piece of the agents' information that the researcher observes has already been used by the agents and cannot change the predicted outcome [see Farber and Gibbons (1996)]. However, if one adds contracting and downward rigidity due to risk aversion, then, conditioned on the current wage, history matters. In particular, early success implies higher wages throughout the worker's career. Nevertheless, if a person with an early success is compared to a person with a late success, but both receive the *same current wage* then the late beginner will have the higher future expected wage [see Chiappori, Salenei and Valentin (1999)]. That is, the fact that the early beginner has the same wage as a late beginner speaks against him. In this respect, "what have you done for us lately" matters more.

Farber and Gibbons (1996) and Altonji and Pierret (2001) discuss further empirical implications of such models of public learning. Importantly, they distinguish between

Then, holding r fixed, $\pi(t, r)$ approaches 1 and $q(t, r)$ approaches q_l as t rises. Similarly, holding $t - r$ constant, $\pi(t, r)$ approaches 0 and $q(t, r)$ approaches q_h as t and r rise together.

information available to an outside observer (econometrician) and the information available to the economic agents. If the econometrician can observe a variable that is correlated with ability, even if not observed by the agents, then this variable will have an affect on wages which rises with time, reflecting the accumulation of information by the agents. In contrast, the effects of outcomes that employers observe, other than the worker's output, and that are correlated with ability (such as schooling) will decline over time as their marginal informational content diminishes.

4. Basic findings and their interpretation

In this section we provide a second look at the data, while stressing findings that have some bearing on the alternative models of wage growth.

4.1. Mincer's earnings function

Jacob Mincer discovered an important empirical regularity in the wage (earnings) structure. Average earnings of workers (in a given schooling-experience group) are tied to schooling and work experience in a relatively precise manner as summarized by the now familiar Mincer equation

$$\ln Y_{it} = \alpha + \beta s_i + \gamma(t - s_i) - \delta(t - s_i)^2 + \cdots, \tag{31}$$

where Y_{it} are annual earnings (or weekly or hourly wage) of person i in year t, s_i are the years of schooling completed by person i and $(t - s_i)$ are the accumulated years of (potential) work experience of person i by year t.

In his 1974 book, Mincer estimated this specification for a sample of about 30.000 employed males taken from the US 1960 census; he reported a coefficient of .107 for schooling and .081 and −.0012 for the two experience coefficients. Including weeks worked as an explanatory variable, the effects of experience declined to .068 and −.0009, implying that wages grow less than earnings. The same equation has since been estimated in many countries for different periods and sectors, with similar results.[19]

Mincer's important insight was that this stability is no accident but rather a reflection of powerful and persisting economic forces. In an early (1958, pp. 284–5) paper, he wrote that:

> The starting point of an economic analysis of personal income distribution must be an exploration of the implications of the theory of rational choice. An implication of rational choice is the formation of income differences that are required

[19] Mincer has estimated several variants of this equation. Apart from alternative time shapes for the experience profiles, he was also concerned about whether schooling has a diminishing impact, the interaction between schooling and experience and the role of labor supply. These are empirically important issues yet the version in the text has become most popular in subsequent applications.

to compensate for various advantages and disadvantages attached to the receipts of incomes.... This principle, so eloquently stated by Adam Smith has become a common place in economics. What follows is an attempt to cast one important aspect of this compensation principle into an operational model that provides insights into some features of the aggregative income distribution and into a number of decompositions of it which recent empirical research has made possible. The aspect chosen concerns differences in training among members of the labor force.

To apply the compensation principle to the data, Mincer considered long-lived individuals who operate in a stationary economy with access to a capital market and maximize the present value of their lifetime incomes. Suppose that the different occupations (jobs) pay wages that depend on the worker's schooling and experience and can be described by some earnings (wage) function of the form $Y_j(s, t-s)$. Given that workers can choose schooling and then occupations (jobs) that require different levels of training, what form should these functions have in equilibrium? One basic condition is that the present value of different lifetime earnings streams must be equal. Otherwise, all workers will be attracted to the highest paying j, s option, and no one will choose any other option. This condition alone puts strong restrictions on the equilibrium wage structure and, in particular, it implies that the marginal contribution of schooling is the *same* for all occupations, irrespective of the time shape of the experience profile, which is a form of separability. A simple functional form that satisfies these requirements for a large T is $Y_j(s, t-s) = \mathrm{e}^{rs} y_j(t-s)$, where $\int_0^\infty \mathrm{e}^{-r\tau} y_j(\tau)\,\mathrm{d}\tau$ is a constant that is independent of j.[20] Taking logs, one gets that

$$\log Y_j(s, t-s) = y_0 + rs + \log y^e(t-s) + \varepsilon_{tj}, \tag{32}$$

where $y^e(t-s_j)$ is the mean effect of experience and $\varepsilon_{tj} = \log y_j^e(t-s) - \log y^e(t-s)$ are deviations caused by differences in on the job training across occupations.

This simple model highlights several general points:

- The effect of schooling on the log of wages is determined by the prevailing interest rate, reflecting the delay in receiving income that is implied by investment in schooling. Under this interpretation, it is important that schooling be measured in

[20] Letting $T = \infty$ and writing

$$V_j(s) = \int_s^\infty \mathrm{e}^{-rt} Y_j(s, t-s)\,\mathrm{d}t = \mathrm{e}^{-rs} \int_0^\infty \mathrm{e}^{-r\tau} Y_j(s, \tau)\,\mathrm{d}\tau,$$

we see that

$$V_j'(s) = -rV_j(s) + \mathrm{e}^{-rs} \int_0^\infty \mathrm{e}^{-r\tau} \frac{\partial}{\partial s} Y_j(s, \tau)\,\mathrm{d}\tau.$$

Thus, the conditions that $V_j(s)$ is a constant for all s and j and that $V_j'(s) = 0$ together imply that $\mathrm{e}^{-rs} \int_0^\infty \mathrm{e}^{-r\tau} \frac{\partial}{\partial s} Y_j(s, \tau)\,\mathrm{d}\tau$ is a constant for all s and j. Proceeding in this fashion, we obtain similar conditions for all higher-order derivatives. The specification in the text satisfies all these requirements, provided that $\int_0^\infty \mathrm{e}^{-r\tau} y_j(\tau)\,\mathrm{d}t$ is independent of j.

k, Mincer used these considerations to provide a direct economic ie coefficients of his estimated "human capital earnings function". ficient on schooling in equation (30) reflects "the rate of return for coefficients on experience reflect the shape of the average person's ...stment profile. The reduction in investment is thereby tied to the observed slope and concavity of log earnings-experience profiles.[22]

As pointed out by Rosen (1977), under the model's strict assumptions, in particular the assumption that all earnings profiles yield the same present value, the life cycle pattern of earnings is undetermined. Thus, to use the human capital model, one must specify a particular trade-off between current and future earnings, usually called the "production function" of human capital. Thus, let $\dot{K} = g(I)$, where $I = lK$ and $g(I)$ is rising and concave. The assumptions that $g(I)$ rises and Y declines in I maintain the idea of compensation because one must sacrifice current earnings in order to increase earning capacity (and future earnings). The added assumption of concavity can be justified by the fact that a person must use his own resources to augment his earning capacity. But this would force identical individuals to choose the same investment path on the job. Differences in individual earnings profiles cannot, then, be simply attributed to differences in investments; individual attributes such as ability or access to the capital market, which affect individual "propensity to invest", must be introduced. In this case, it is no longer true that, in equilibrium, all income profiles are equivalent and that the observed wage ratios are independent of demand.

Mincer has often relied on Becker's (1975) analysis (first presented in his 1967 Woytinsky lectures) of the roles of ability and access to the capital market as factors affecting individual differences in investment. He is quite explicit in stating that: "Once ability and opportunity are introduced as determinants of investment, earning differentials can no longer be considered as wholly compensatory. Rents or "profits" from investment in human capital arise..." (1993, vol. 1, p. 59). These rents depend on the individual's attributes and on how much he chooses to invest. Mincer thus often refers to the estimated returns for schooling and experience as average returns.

Nevertheless, the role of individual heterogeneity initiated a major debate about the economic interpretation of the coefficients in the Mincer earnings functions. Given that these rates are based on comparison of different individuals who choose different levels of schooling, the casual effect of schooling is not identified, because it may simply reflect the impact of omitted (unobserved) ability and the positive correlation between ability and schooling [Griliches (1977)]. This debate was further stimulated by theoretical criticisms, based on asymmetric information and signaling, showing that schooling may have a positive effect even if it has no impact on a worker's output. More generally, to the extent that schooling is mainly a sorting device, social rates of return may be far lower than the private returns captured in the cross section.

[22] It is, of course, not necessary to assume investment in human capital to obtain such results. Rising and concave earning profiles can be also motivated by various forms of selection, such as the dismissal of unsatisfactory workers [see Flinn (1997)].

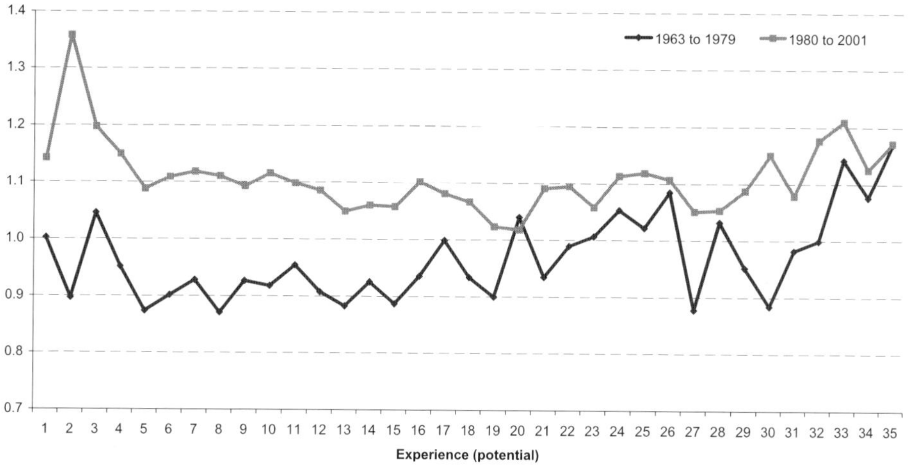

Figure 6e. The gap between workers belonging to the 90'th and 10'th percentiles of the residual log wage distribution for the periods 1963–1979 and 1980–2001, by education and experience, March CPS supplements, 1964 to 2002.
Advanced degrees.

We see that within each experience group, there is a *negative* correlation between the current wage level and subsequent wage growth. This pattern is consistent with search behavior, because high-wage individuals are less likely to obtain superior offers. The investment model would suggest that the correlation is initially negative because low wages imply high investment, but later becomes positive as the high investment results in overtaking. In contrast, we observe negative correlations in all years. Yet, the fact that the correlations weaken as we move to higher experience groups suggests a presence of investment considerations.

To further examine the role of investment, we take a closer look at the covariance between earning levels at different points of time. The correlation matrices in Table 3 display the correlations between wages (and residuals obtained from the estimated Mincer wage equation, with and without individual fixed effects) at different stages of the life cycle. We use a balanced panel from the NLSY, where we again take three year averages. The correlation between income levels at different stages of the life cycle decays with the time distance, but is always positive. This result holds true also when we take residuals, eliminating the effects of schooling and experience. It is only when we eliminate the fixed effect of each person and consider the residual variation around the individual means (over all time periods) and the group average wage growth that we find negative correlations between early and late residuals. Moreover, these correlations become more negative as the time distance increases, providing clear evidence for compensation, whereby an early wage that is below the individual mean is associated with a late wage that is above the individual mean.

Thus, to identify compensation one must eliminate heterogeneity among individuals. Obviously, if individuals differ permanently in their earning capacity a positive corre-

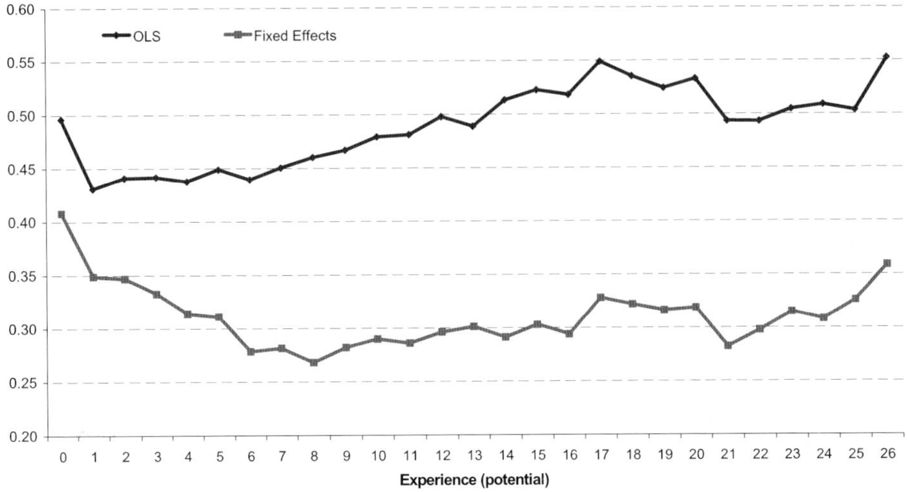

Figure 7a. Standard deviation of residuals in Mincer's wage equation by experience, with and without fixed effects, PSID, 1968–1997 and NLSY, 1979–2000.
PSID, 1968–1997.

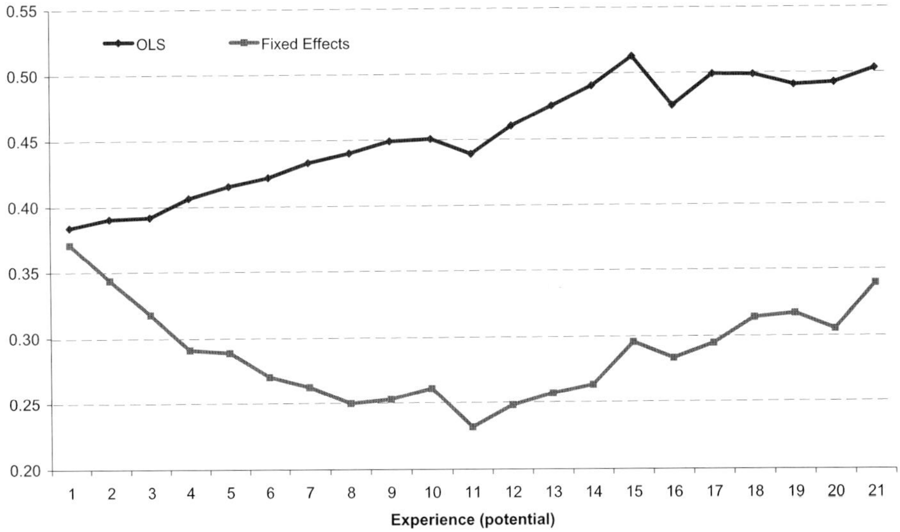

Figure 7b. Standard deviation of residuals in Mincer's wage equation by experience, with and without fixed effects, PSID, 1968–1997 and NLSY, 1979–2000.
NLSY, 1979–2000.

lation will exist between early and late wages within each cohort because individuals who are above the mean are likely to remain above the mean, irrespective of investment. However, there may be more complex forms of heterogeneity that interact with experi-

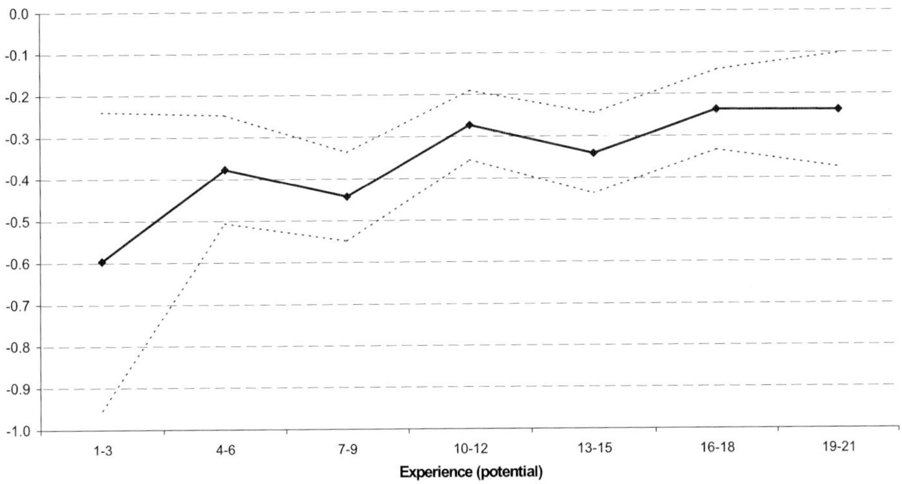

Figure 8a. Regression coefficients and confidence intervals of annual hourly wage growth rates on log hourly wage levels in prior period (3 year averages), by experience and schooling, NLSY, 1979–2000. High school dropouts.

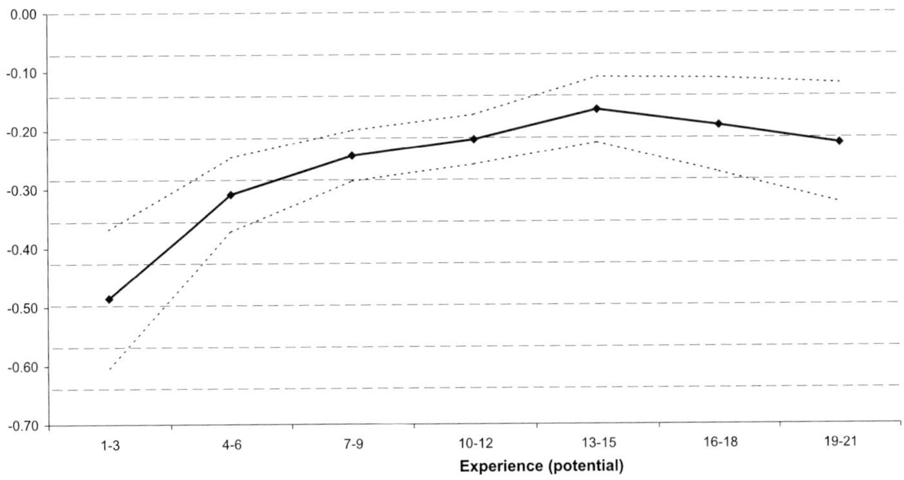

Figure 8b. Regression coefficients and confidence intervals of annual hourly wage growth rates on log hourly wage levels in prior period (3 year averages), by experience and schooling, NLSY, 1979–2000. High school graduates.

ence. In particular, there may be "systematic heterogeneity", whereby individuals with higher initial earning capacity also tend to invest more.[25] As explained in Mincer (1974,

[25] Note that initial earnings understate the individual's initial earning capacity and the bias depends on the propensity to invest. Mincer proposed to estimate initial earning capacity by the level of earnings at the "break even point", which he estimated to be about 10 years of work experience.

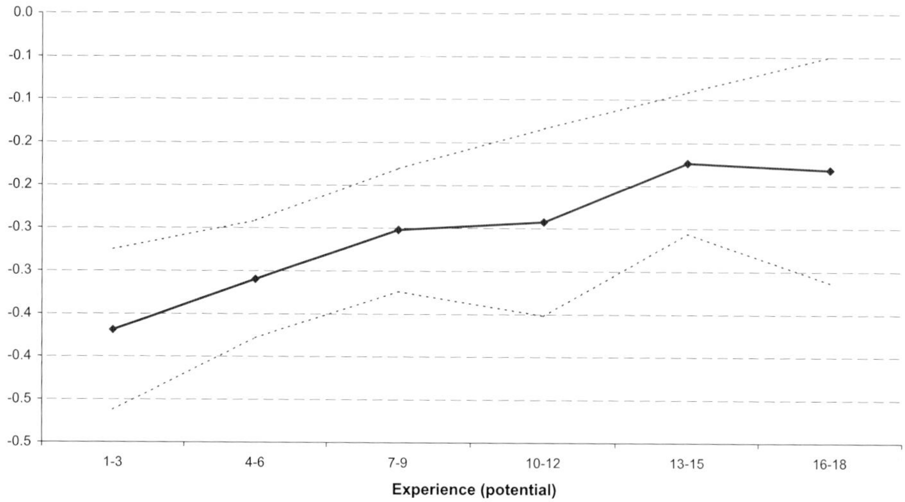

Figure 8c. Regression coefficients and confidence intervals of annual hourly wage growth rates on log hourly wage levels in prior period (3 year averages), by experience and schooling, NLSY, 1979–2000. Some college.

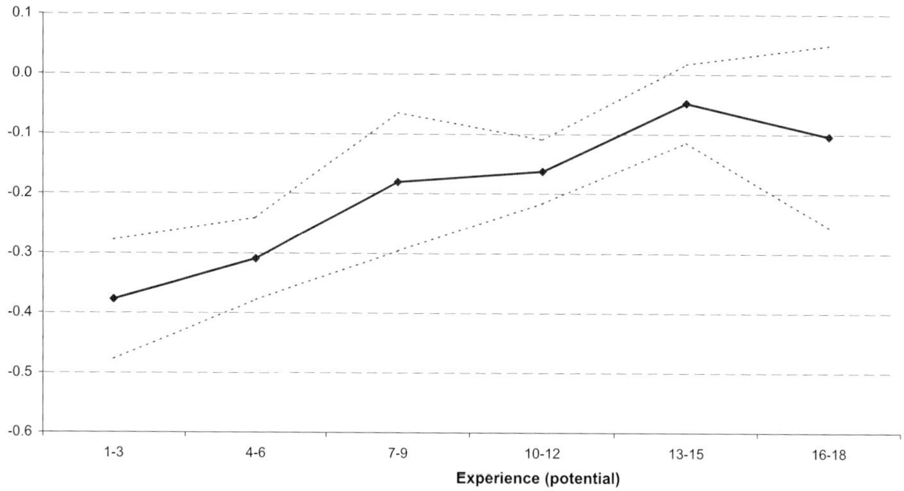

Figure 8d. Regression coefficients and confidence intervals of annual hourly wage growth rates on log hourly wage levels in prior period (3 year averages), by experience and schooling, NLSY, 1979–2000. College graduates.

Ch. 2) such heterogeneity tends to raise the within-cohort variance in earnings with the passage of time and may offset the effects of compensation.

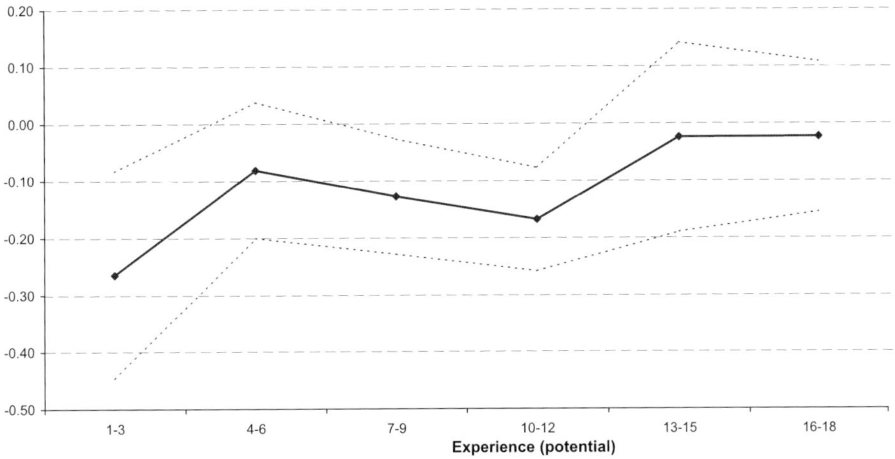

Figure 8e. Regression coefficients and confidence intervals of annual hourly wage growth rates on log hourly wage levels in prior period (3 year averages), by experience and schooling, NLSY, 1979–2000. Advanced degree.

Figure 9a displays estimated coefficients from regressions of individual fixed growth effects on individual fixed level effects, where the level effects are evaluated at two different points in the life cycle. When the level effect is the usual individual fixed effect, i.e., the mean wage residual during an individual career, the relationships between level and growth are significantly positive in all schooling groups but stronger among the highly educated. In such a case, we can interpret the level as a proxy for the individual's initial earning *capacity* and can conclude that individuals with higher "ability to learn" also have higher "ability to earn". However, if one evaluates the fixed effect as the intercept of the individual residual profile at the beginning of the worker's career, the relation becomes negative. In this case, the level effect also reflects investment, and the negative correlation reflects the fact that individuals with a higher propensity to invest forego a larger proportion of their initial earning capacity.[26]

In Figure 9b we present the regression coefficients of the individual slope and level (evaluated at the mean) on AFQT, which is an observable measure of individual ability. We see that *both* the level and growth effects are positively correlated with AFQT, which supports our interpretation of the previous results whereby individuals with higher "ability to learn" also have higher "ability to earn".[27] However, we do not find strong

[26] Baker (1997) and Haider (2001) report a *negative* correlation between the individual slopes and intercepts that evaluate an individual's deviation from the mean at *zero* experience. In contrast, Lillard and Weiss (1979) report a *positive* correlation between individual slopes and the mean residual (averaged over all experience levels). These findings are not inconsistent and indicate the presence of both heterogeneity and compensation.

[27] Although the impact of AFQT on the slope is significant only among the highly educated, it becomes significantly positive when we control for the initial level of the individual intercept. This suggests that the

Table 3
Correlations of log wages and residuals at different stages of the life cycle (three-year averages), full-time workers, NLSY, 1979–2000

(i): Log wage levels

Experience	1–3	4–6	7–9	10–12	13–15	16–18	19–21
1–3	0.195						
4–6	0.606	0.173					
	(0.000)						
7–9	0.476	0.738	0.193				
	(0.000)	(0.000)					
10–12	0.424	0.646	0.817	0.211			
	(0.000)	(0.000)	(0.000)				
13–15	0.374	0.588	0.701	0.789	0.238		
	(0.000)	(0.000)	(0.000)	(0.000)			
16–18	0.314	0.533	0.643	0.691	0.789	0.271	
	(0.000)	(0.000)	(0.000)	(0.000)	(0.000)		
19–21	0.321	0.531	0.629	0.673	0.740	0.783	0.300
	(0.000)	(0.000)	(0.000)	(0.000)	(0.000)	(0.000)	

(ii): Residuals of Mincer's wage function

Experience	1–3	4–6	7–9	10–12	13–15	16–18	19–21
1–3	0.181						
4–6	0.563	0.151					
	(0.000)						
7–9	0.415	0.698	0.166				
	(0.000)	(0.000)					
10–12	0.358	0.592	0.788	0.183			
	(0.000)	(0.000)	(0.000)				
13–15	0.297	0.522	0.653	0.755	0.206		
	(0.000)	(0.000)	(0.000)	(0.000)			
16–18	0.230	0.459	0.586	0.644	0.757	0.236	
	(0.000)	(0.000)	(0.000)	(0.000)	(0.000)		
19–21	0.232	0.453	0.567	0.619	0.699	0.750	0.259
	(0.000)	(0.000)	(0.000)	(0.000)	(0.000)	(0.000)	

(*Continued on next page*)

evidence that the differences in investment magnify the differences in initial human capital endowments, expressed as present value of lifetime wages. This is indicated by the fact that the *initial* residual levels associated with higher wage growth are sufficiently

propensity to invest is related not only to ability but also to taste parameters, such as discounting and risk aversion.

Table 3
(*Continued*)

(iii): Residuals of Mincer's wage function with fixed effects

Experience	1–3	4–6	7–9	10–12	13–15	16–18	19–21
1–3	0.141						
4–6	0.317	0.066					
	(0.000)						
7–9	−0.094	0.157	0.047				
	(0.027)	(0.000)					
10–12	−0.280	−0.209	0.218	0.047			
	(0.000)	(0.000)	(0.000)				
13–15	−0.429	−0.419	−0.267	0.072	0.056		
	(0.000)	(0.000)	(0.000)	(0.089)			
16–18	−0.481	−0.465	−0.351	−0.198	0.203	0.080	
	(0.000)	(0.000)	(0.000)	(0.000)	(0.000)		
19–21	−0.448	−0.437	−0.351	−0.220	0.059	0.291	0.095
	(0.000)	(0.000)	(0.000)	(0.000)	(0.165)	(0.000)	

Note: Significance level in parentheses.

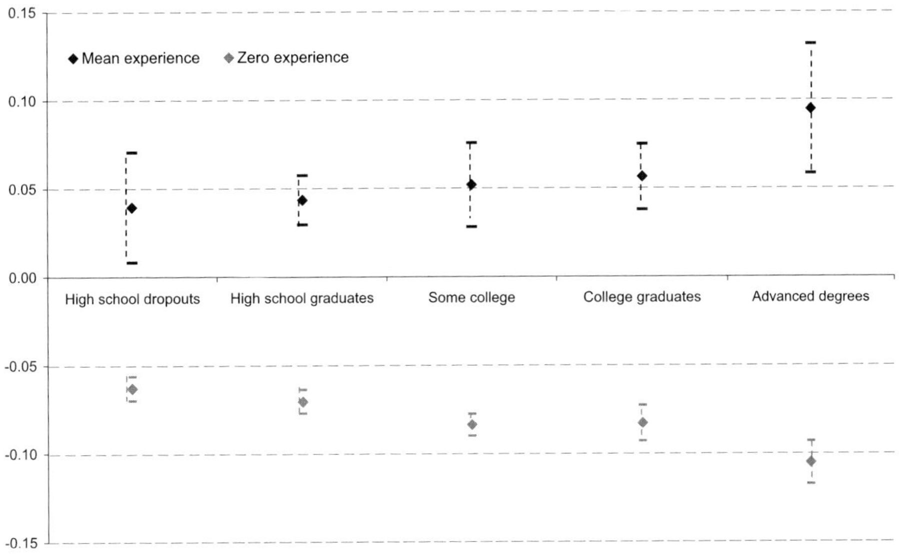

Figure 9a. Regression coefficients of individual growth rates on individual level effects, evaluated at zero experience and the individual's mean experience by education.

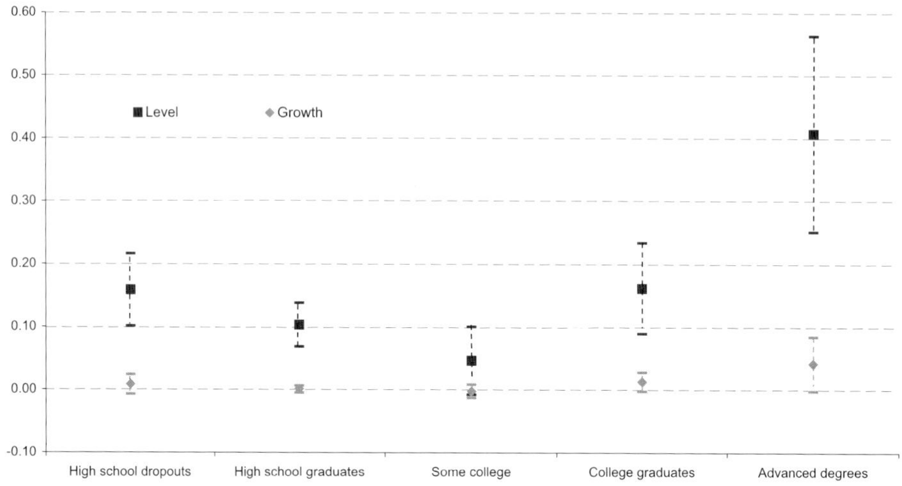

Figure 9b. Regression coefficients of individual growth effects and level effects (evaluated at the mean) on AFQT scores by education.

negative to render the total impact on the present value of lifetime earnings to be rather small.[28]

Although the investment interpretation is consistent with important features of the data on wage *levels*, it cannot explain some important feature of wage *changes*. In particular, it was noted by MaCurdy (1982) and Abowd and Card (1989) that, after accounting for the common wage growth, the growth rates of individual wages are not correlated for periods that are more than few years apart. This finding, confirmed by subsequent studies [Lillard and Reville (1999), Meghir and Pistaferri (2001), Alvarez, Browning and Ejrnaes (2001)], is also shown in Table 4a. Moreover, the correlations between short subsequent periods (one or two years) are negative. This correlation pattern is consistent with search where shocks are random, with those experiencing positive shocks less likely to exhibit high wage growth in subsequent periods. Clearly, measurement errors is another source for a negative short run correlation in individual wage growth rates. However, for sufficiently long periods (4 years) that are distant from each other one obtains a positive and significant correlation (see Table 4b) that is consistent with fixed individual growth rates, indicating that those who have above-average wage growth early in life also have above-average wage growth late in life.[29] Generally, in-

[28] Rubinstein and Tsiddon (2004), who use parents' education as a proxy for ability show that, within education groups, workers with more educated parents have higher wage levels and higher wage growth. Huggett, Ventura and Yaron (2002) show how a positive correlation between learning ability and earning ability can explain the rising variance and skewness of the earnings distribution within cohorts.

[29] The individual growth rates are estimated within cell using the regression:

$$\Delta w_{it} = b_0 + b_1 u_t + b_2 \Delta u_t + \sum d_j E_j + \theta_i + \varepsilon_{it},$$

Table 4
Variances and correlations of the residuals of the first differences of log hourly wages of full-time workers at different stages of the life cycle. NLSY, 1979–2002

a: Three-year averages

Experience (potential)	1–3	4–6	7–9	10–12	13–15	16–18
1–3	**0.092**					
4–6	−0.236	**0.077**				
	(0.000)					
7–9	−0.054	−0.228	**0.077**			
	(0.148)	(0.000)				
10–12	0.024	0.030	0.049	**0.077**		
	(0.534)	(0.266)	(0.067)			
13–15	−0.038	0.037	0.031	−0.230	**0.059**	
	(0.364)	(0.213)	(0.291)	(0.000)		
16–18	−0.058	0.073	0.038	−0.054	−0.243	**0.037**
	(0.227)	(0.032)	(0.250)	(0.067)	(0.000)	

b: Four-year averages (excluding overlapping periods)

Experience (potential)	1 to 4	6 to 9	11 to 14	16 to 19
1 to 4	**0.085**			
6 to 9	−0.076	**0.077**		
	(0.011)			
11 to 14	0.025	0.073	**0.059**	
	(0.439)	(0.004)		
16 to 19	0.067	0.016	−0.226	**0.036**
	(0.055)	(0.572)	(0.000)	

Notes: We calculate individuals' mean residuals for each cell from within cell regressions of the change in log hourly wages on experience and national unemployment rates.
Significance level in parentheses.

vestment is indicated by a positive correlation between early and late earnings, whereas search and learning imply short-term persistence with positive drift and negative correlation in wage growth. The reduction in the variance with experience is consistent with the theoretical prediction that all individuals reduce their investment to zero towards the end of life [see Lillard and Reville (1999)]. However, the NLSY sample up to 2002 maybe too young to recover end of life effects.[30]

where $\Delta w_{it} = \log(w_{it}) - \log(w_{it-1})$ or $((\log(w_{it}) - \log(w_{it-1}))/2$ is wages are reported biannually) and u_t is the national civilian unemployment rate in year t. E_j are dummies for year of potential experience. Tables 4a and 4b report the correlations between the within cells estimates of θ_i.

[30] Indeed Abowd and Card (1989), and Baker (1997), who use a wider age range, find that the variance in earnings rises at old age suggesting that individual wage shocks dominate at this stage of the life cycle.

4.3. Labor mobility and wage growth

Search theory not only competes with the theory of human capital, it also complements that theory. The challenge is to understand the interactions between these two processes. Mincer and Jovanovic (1981) provide the first attempt to integrate these processes. They describe the potential impact of search as follows "Perhaps the best way to summarize the life cycle relation between wages and mobility is to recognize that initial (first decade ?) job search has two major purposes: to gain experience, wages, and skills by moving across firms; and to find sooner or later a suitable job in which one can settle and grow for a long time. The life cycle decline in mobility is, in part, evidence of successful initial mobility, an interpretation which is corroborated by corresponding life cycle growth in wages" [Mincer and Jovanovic (1981, p. 42)].

To identify the actual impacts of search and investment, they consider two different aspects of work experience, tenure in a given firm, T, and general work experience, X. They then examine two jointly determined outcomes; the wage, $w(T, X)$, and the separation rate, $s(T, x)$. The latent variables in this system are investments in general and firm-specific training and search. They use the NLS panel data and run regressions of wages and separations on tenure in the current job and potential work experience. To partially correct for the endogeneity of tenure, they add the number of past moves across firms as an indicator of individual "propensity to move".

Their main results are:

- Tenure has a separate positive and declining effect on wages, which is as important as the effect of total work experience. Tenure effects are much more important for young workers.
- Experience and tenure have negative impacts on separation, but the negative effect of tenure is much larger.
- Past moves have positive effects on separation, suggesting heterogeneity, but have only weak negative effects on wages.
- Controlling for both experience and tenure, education has a negative effect on mobility.
- The positive impact of schooling on wages is unaffected by the inclusion of mobility variables such as tenure and past moves, but the experience effects among young men are reduced substantially. This suggests that search mainly affects the size and interpretation of the experience effect but has little bearing on returns from schooling.

Subsequent work in this area tried to address the potential biases that arise when estimating the tenure effect and the impact of occupational moves. Potential biases arise from a variety of selection issues (i.e., in what ways are stayers different from movers) and in part from the assumed imperfect information and specific investments that create relational rents and give scope to bargaining and other noncompetitive behavior. A rather broad range of estimates for the size of the tenure effects have been obtained, ranging from approximately 7 to 35 percent per ten years of seniority [see Topel (1991), Altonji and Williams (1998, 2004), Dustmann and Meghir (2005)]. Data on wage loss following plan closure also indicate that the loss of wages is higher for workers with more tenure, yielding a tenure effect of about 14 percent [see Farber (1999)]. A positive tenure effect is often attributed to firm-specific human capital that is shared if the worker stays with the firm and lost if he changes employers, although it is not entirely clear why and how wage growth should respond to the accumulation of such specific capital.

A simple indication of the complexity of the relationship between wage growth and mobility is that, on the average, wage growth is associated with mobility, yet when we look at individual data, movers exhibit lower wage growth than stayers (see Figure 10). There are several possible explanations for this discrepancy: (1) If moving is a personal attribute, then firms are less likely to invest in prospective movers. (2) If jobs differ by the quality of match, successful and more productive matches are less likely to come apart. (3) If the firm is subject to exogenous shocks, the better workers are selected to stay with the firm. (4) If the continuation of the match is jointly profitable, the sharing of the gains will depend on outside options. Therefore, the *threat* of mobility rather than realized mobility can cause wage growth; much of the benefit of this threat is captured by the stayers. This threat is reflected by the *average* trends in mobility within a cohort.

Topel and Ward (1992), who examined the mobility and wage growth of young workers, find that

- Wage growth within firms is quite high (7 percent on average) and declines with both tenure and experience.
- Jobs that are going to last longer currently offer higher wage growth.
- Wage growth across jobs is substantial (20 percent on the average) and declines with tenure (at previous job) and experience.

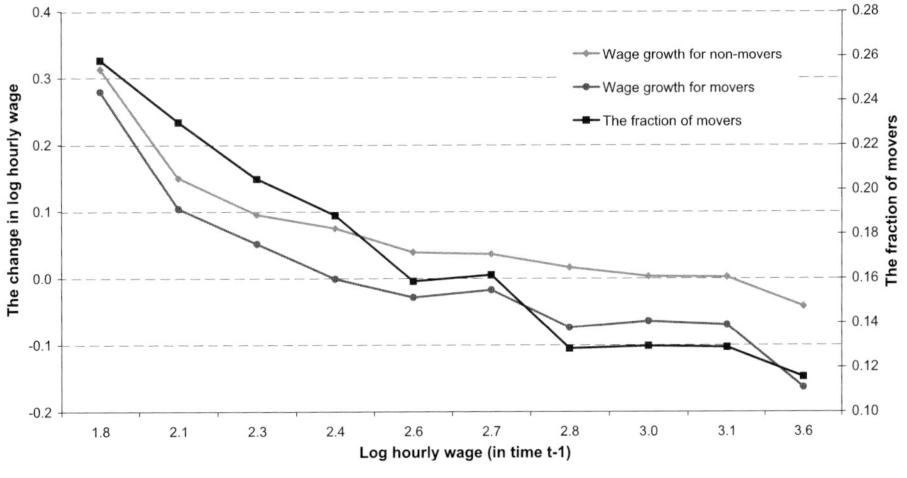

Figure 10. Fraction of movers and annual growth rates in hourly wages of movers and stayers by hourly wage in the previous year, NLSY, 1979–2000.

- Higher wage growth upon transition is obtained when one moves to a job with longer prospective tenure.
- The exit rate from a given job declines with experience and the wage level. However, conditional on the wage, the effect of experience on the job exit rate is positive.

Together these findings provide strong support for the importance of search at early stages of the worker's career.

Changes in occupation and industry are also channels for wage growth. If one ranks occupations or industries by their average wage level at the "prime" ages, 36–45, then we can identify the direction of moves on this scale. We find that the occupation and industry changes of less-educated workers involve transitions to higher paying occupations, while highly educated workers move across similar occupations and industries in terms of their mean wage.[31] In this respect, there is substitution between learning in school and on the job (see Figures 11a and 11b). In contrast, highly educated workers obtain higher wage growth when they change employers, suggesting that education and search are complements.[32] These results are consistent with the findings of Sicherman

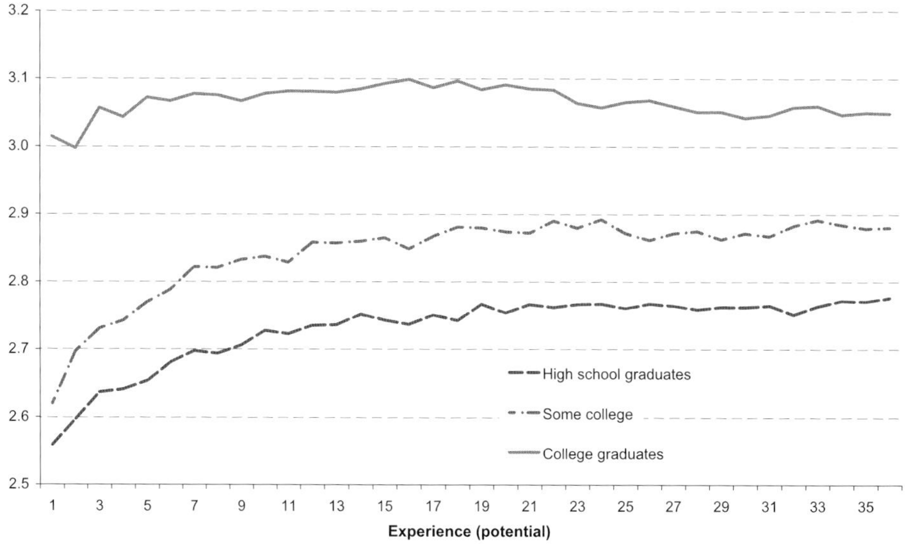

Figure 11a. Mean hourly wages (in logs) of prime aged workers (36–45) in the currently held industry and occupation, by education and experience, CPS-ORG, 1998–2002.
Occupation.

[31] To examine moves across industry and occupation, we use the CPS monthly files from January 1998 to December 2002. Overall, we have in our data 473 occupation categories and 236 industries.

[32] Holding constant experience and previous wage, movers in the NLSY with higher than college degree have the same wage growth as comparable stayers. Movers, with lower levels of schooling have a substantially lower wage growth than comparable stayers.

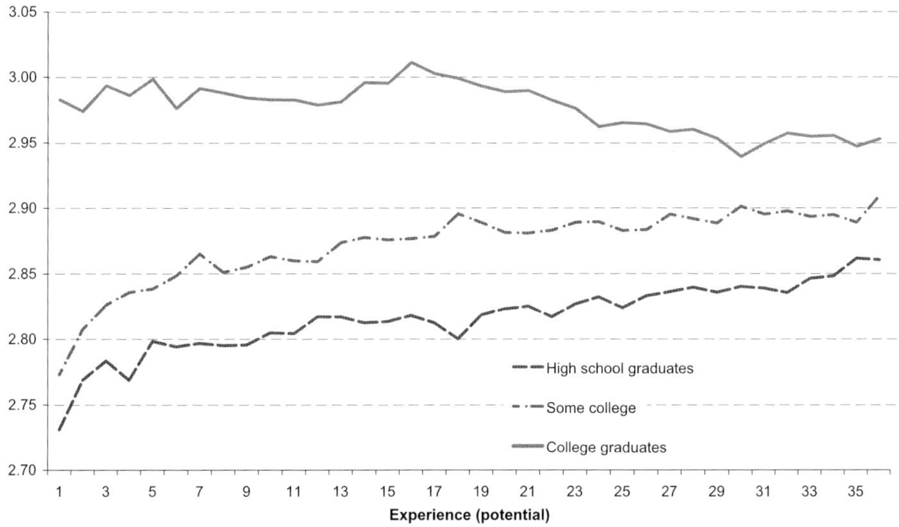

Figure 11b. Mean hourly wages (in logs) of prime aged workers (36–45) in the currently held industry and occupation, by education and experience, CPS-ORG, 1998–2002.
Industry.

(1991) and Neal (1995, 1999) that educated workers are less likely to make a career change and that they also experiment with fewer employers prior to making such a change. A partial explanation is that educated workers learn about their ability in school, which facilitates their career choice. However, educated workers may take more time to find an employer that matches their skills. In fact, workers that report that their education exceeds the requirements of the job they hold are, on average, more educated and less experienced.

One must bear in mind that wage gains or losses that one observes upon job change are partial and possibly misleading indicators of the total value of such moves because workers may anticipate consequences that occur later in their career. Studies of mobility patterns over the business cycle show that movers who obtained wage gains during booms often leave their new jobs and suffer a wage loss during recession [see Keane, Moffitt and Runkle (1988), Barlevy (2001)]. There is, however, no evidence that young movers accept jobs in low-wage industries in exchange for future prospects in those industries [see Bils and McLaughlin (2001)].[33]

[33] Rubinstein and Tsiddon (2003) show that the effect of recessions on labor market outcomes varies by education and parents' education. While educated workers who were born to better-educated parents do not lose wages or jobs during recessions, less educated workers lose both.

4.4. Learning

When employers and workers are uncertain about each other's attributes, it takes time to reduce this uncertainty through experimentation. Such learning can occur within a firm or in the market at large.

As noted by Jovanovic (1979b), learning at the firm level can be inferred from the shape of the hazard function of leaving the firm. That is, if workers and firms learn about the quality of the match after they have spent an initial period together, then the weak matches terminate and the good ones survive. As time passes, learning has been accomplished and the proportion of good matches rises, so that the hazard function first rises and then declines. This is a rather sharp test because a sorting model based on the survival of the fittest usually implies a declining hazard. The hazard function in Figure 12 displays such a pattern, showing that the probability of separation conditional on length of employment peaks at about 15 months. A similar finding is reported by Booth, Francesconi and Garcia-Serrano (1999). In contrast, the data on young men used by Topel and Ward (1992) show a decline in the hazard by tenure (and experience) right from the beginning of the employment relationship. This, of course, does not exclude experimentation but shows that sorting is more important.[34]

As noted by Farber and Gibbons (1996) and Altonji and Pierret (2001), public learning can be inferred from the impact on wages of individual attributes that are not

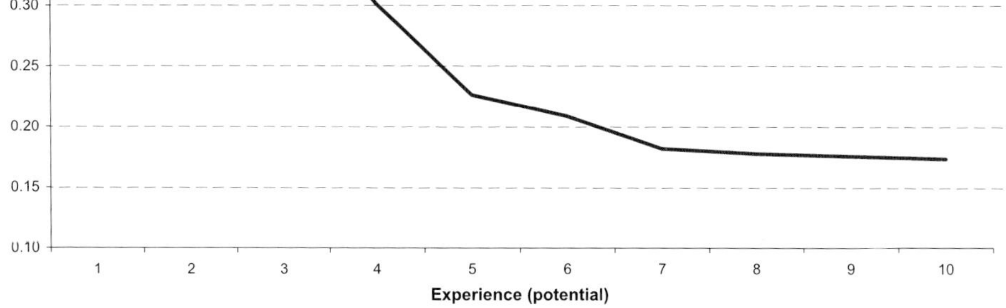

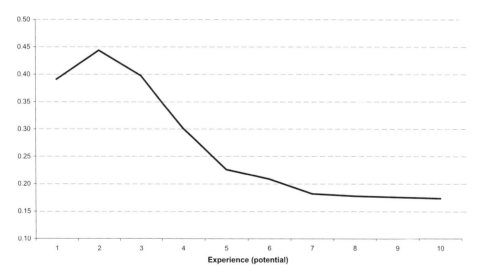

Figure 12. Hazard function of separation from current employer (in annual terms), NLSY, 1979–2000.

[34] It is interesting to note that a rising hazard function that peaks after 3 years was found in the context of divorce [see Weiss and Willis (1997)], suggesting perhaps that it is somewhat more difficult (or useful) to learn about the quality of marriage than about the quality of the job.

directly observed by employers. As time passes and employers observe the worker's performance, they learn about the worker's true productivity and the impact on wages of variables that are observed by the researcher but not by the firm (such as AFQT) increases, while the impact on wages of early signals of ability (such as schooling) declines. In Figures 13a to 13d, we show the marginal impact of AFQT on earning by experience within education groups.[35] The graphs show an increase in the impact of AFQT at early years of experience, especially for high school graduates, suggesting that learning about ability is more relevant for this group.[36] A further indicator of interest is race or ethnicity, which employers may use as a predictor of ability. In Table 5 we show that the increase in the impact of AFQT and the decline in the effect of schooling over the life cycle are substantially higher for blacks and Hispanics. This suggests initial racial statistical discrimination which gradually dissipates, as employers learn about individual ability.

Generally speaking, it is relatively difficult to tease the impact of learning from the data based on the impact of AFQT scores on wage growth.[37] Apart from problems of

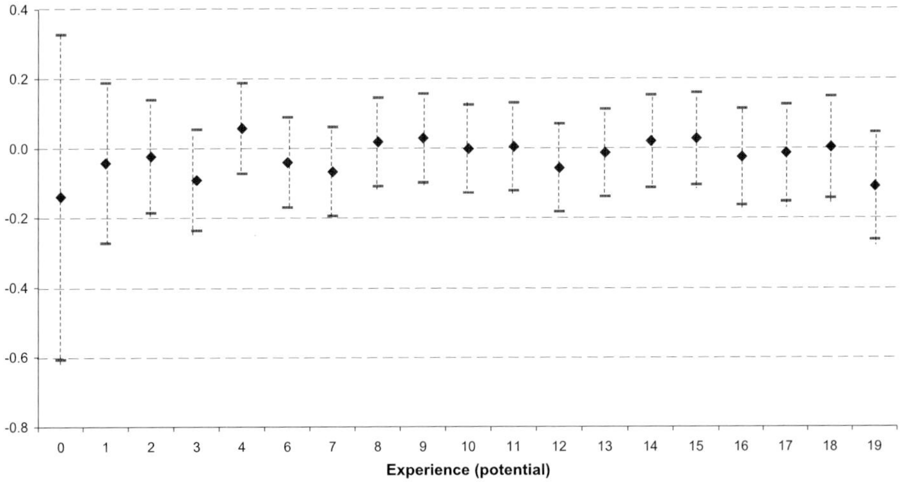

Figure 13a. The effect of AFQT on log hourly wage, by experience and education, point estimates and confidence intervals (relative to the AFQT effect at 5 years of experience), NLSY, 1979–2000. High school dropouts.

[35] Workers are classified by their completed schooling as of age 30. In each education group, and for each year of experience, we run regression with AFQT scores and year effects as explanatory variables. The figures record the estimated coefficient on the AFQT score.

[36] Lange (2003) also finds that employers' learning is concentrated at the early part of the worker's life cycle.

[37] Farber and Gibbons (1996) and Altonji and Pierret (2001) get sharper results by using more heterogeneous samples that include women and blacks, restricting the coefficients of AFQT* experience and schooling* experience to be common across groups.

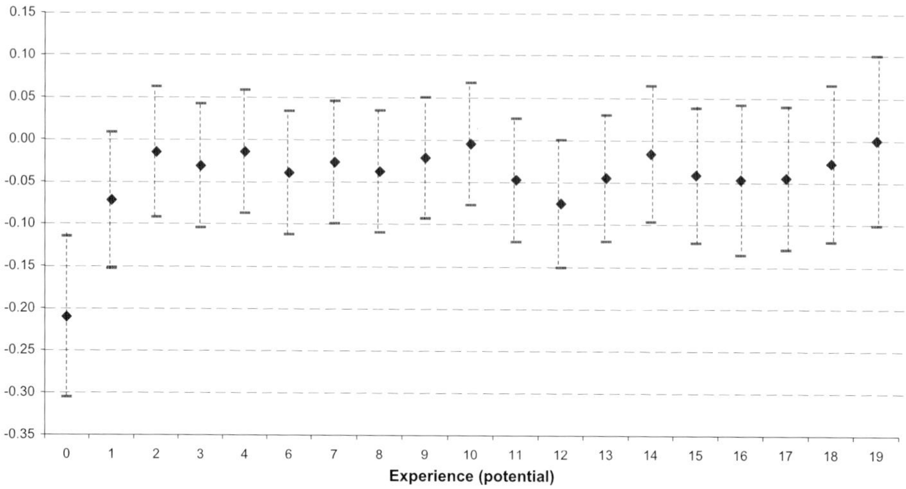

Figure 13b. The effect of AFQT on log hourly wage, by experience and education, point estimates and confidence intervals (relative to the AFQT effect at 5 years of experience), NLSY, 1979–2000. High school graduates.

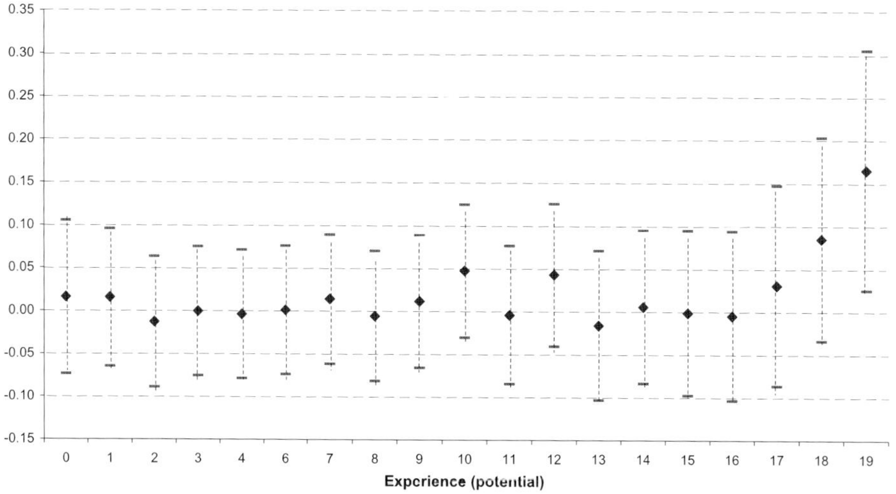

Figure 13c. The effect of AFQT on log hourly wage, by experience and education, point estimates and confidence intervals (relative to the AFQT effect at 5 years of experience), NLSY, 1979–2000. Some college.

separating learning from investment, where AFQT as an indicator of ability can affect both level and growth of wages, there are some deeper problems related to the connections between indicators of ability, such as AFQT, and wages. Willis and Rosen

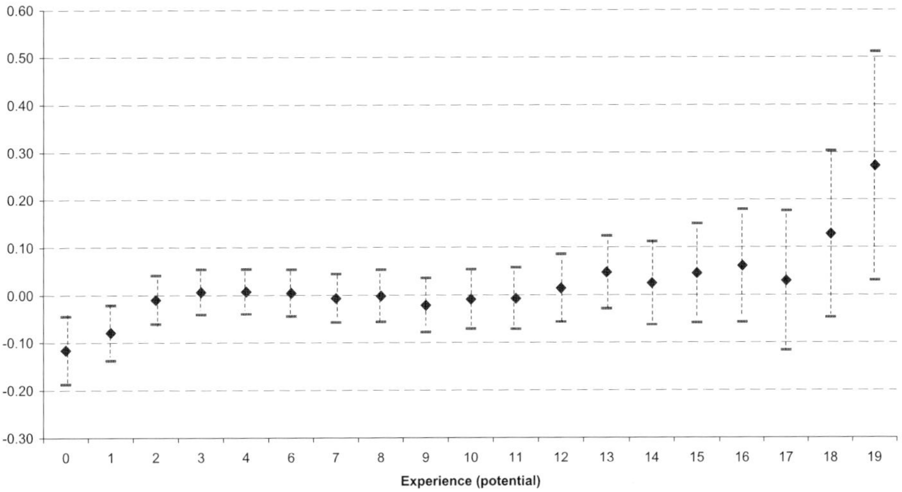

Figure 13d. The effect of AFQT on log hourly wage, by experience and education, point estimates and confidence intervals (relative to the AFQT effect at 5 years of experience), NLSY, 1979–2000. College graduates and advanced degrees.

(1979), Heckman and Rubinstein (2001) and Heckman, Hsee and Rubinstein (2003) have shown that a two factor model that recognizes the role of comparative advantage is more suitable for explaining schooling choices and wage outcomes. Figures 9a and 9b show the strong positive interaction between schooling and AFQT, which suggests that ability is more important among workers who are more educated and thus placed at more "responsible" jobs. Alternatively, the interaction indicates that high-ability individuals who do not acquire high levels of schooling may be lacking valuable non-cognitive traits. Similar issues arise in the context of the impact of AFQT on wage growth. It is quite possible that, conditional on a low level of schooling, high AFQT indicates that the worker is lacking in some other important dimension, such as motivation; as time passes this is confirmed by performance. This substitution may explain the low impact of AFQT among workers with some college and the initially negative interaction between AFQT and experience for this group.

Learning can also influence the variance of wages within a cohort of workers, as workers are gradually sorted out. It is generally difficult to separate this force for increasing variability from other considerations, such as investment, discussed above. In special cases, however, such a separation is possible. An interesting example is when workers move to a new labor market and can be followed based on their time spent in the new country. Eckstein and Weiss (2004) provide such an analysis for the wave of immigration from the former USSR to Israel during 1990–2000. The issue in this case was that employers were uncertain about the quality of schooling received in the former USSR, a factor that affects all immigrants, as well as the quality of particular immigrants. The results show that initially, all immigrants are treated alike and receive the

Table 5
Mincer's wage equation with AFQT, race and ethnicity males NLSY, 1979–2000

Variables	OLS			Fixed effects		
	All	Whites	Blacks and Hispanics	All	Whites	Blacks and Hispanics
	(i)	(ii)	(iii)	(iv)	(v)	(vi)
Black	**−0.093**	–	**−0.103**	–	–	–
	(0.020)		(0.028)			
Hispanic	**0.005**	–	–	–	–	–
	(0.023)					
AFQT	**0.043**	**0.083**	**0.043**	–	–	–
	(0.014)	(0.019)	(0.024)			
School years completed	**0.096**	**0.082**	**0.109**	–	–	–
	(0.008)	(0.010)	(0.012)			
Experience	**0.106**	**0.089**	**0.122**	**0.098**	**0.078**	**0.119**
	(0.011)	(0.014)	(0.017)	(0.006)	(0.007)	(0.010)
Experience square[1]	**−0.024**	**−0.023**	**−0.025**	**−0.027**	**−0.027**	**−0.027**
	(0.002)	(0.003)	(0.003)	(0.001)	(0.002)	(0.002)
Interactions						
Schooling∗experience[1]	**−0.015**	**0.001**	**−0.033**	**−0.001**	**0.015**	**−0.019**
	(0.006)	(0.008)	(0.009)	(0.003)	(0.004)	(0.005)
AFQT∗experience[1]	**0.058**	**0.018**	**0.061**	**0.053**	**0.009**	**0.074**
	(0.011)	(0.016)	(0.020)	(0.006)	(0.008)	(0.010)
Observations	24801	15430	9371	24801	15430	9371
R-squared	0.319	0.318	0.272	0.265	0.306	0.201

Notes: Robust standard errors in parentheses.
[1]Coefficients and standard errors multiplied by 10.

same wage, irrespective of the experience and schooling brought from abroad. As time passes and the market learns about the immigrant's quality, the returns for imported skills rise and immigrants are gradually sorted by their observed attributes. At the same time, the residual variance reflecting unobserved attributes rises, too. The outcome is that both the mean and variance of immigrant wages rise with time spent in the new country.

One issue of interest in learning models is whether individuals move from high risk to low risk occupations or vice versa. It has been shown by Johnson (1978) and Miller (1984) that if workers are unsure about their ability to perform a job, or about the quality of the worker–job match, young workers will willingly try out jobs where success is rare, which the more-experienced have already quit after finding out that they are unsuitable. However, Jovanovic and Nyarko (1997) have shown that if what one learns from experience is how to perform the job – rather than about one's own ability or the job's quality – then the direction of mobility is reversed. Thus, the young first try the safe jobs, as long as experience is sufficiently transferable, because it is better to learn in jobs where mistakes are less costly. In Figures 14a and 14b, we show the stan-

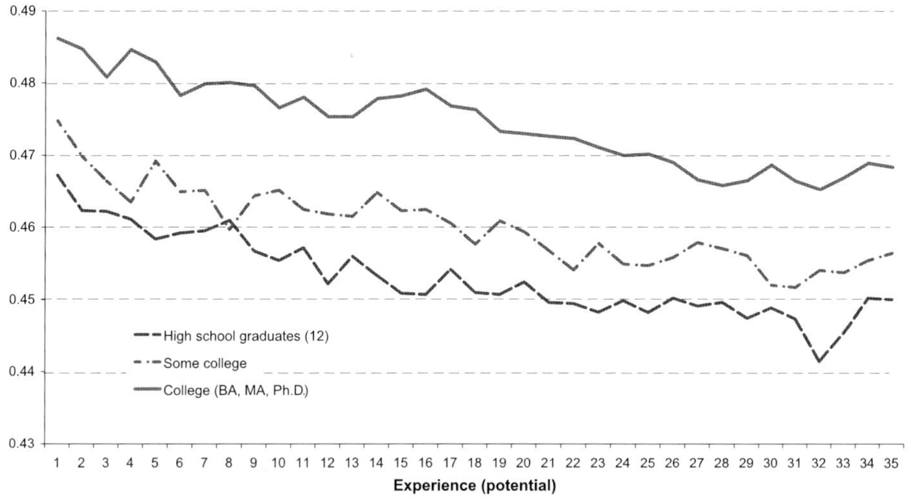

Figure 14a. Standard deviations of the log hourly wages of prime aged workers (36–45) at the industry and at the occupation in which the worker is currently employed, by education and experience, CPS-ORG, 1998–2002.
Industry.

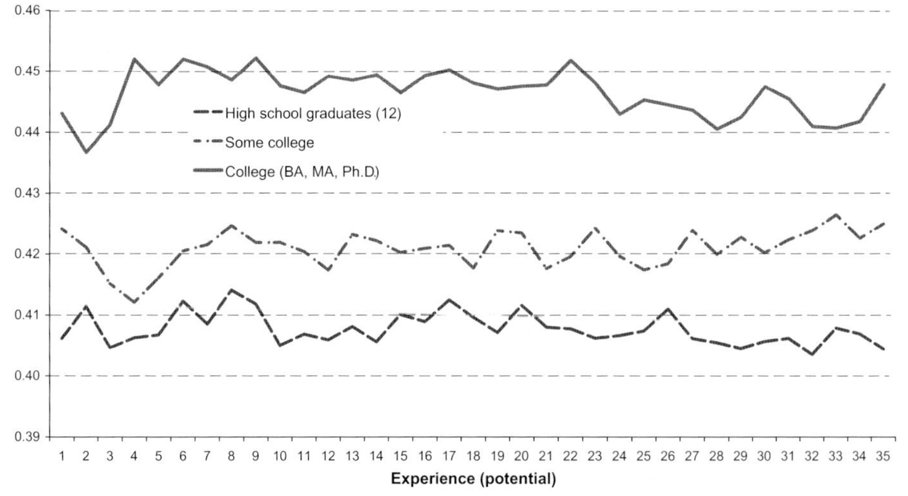

Figure 14b. Standard deviations of the log hourly wages of prime aged workers (36–45) at the industry and at the occupation in which the worker is currently employed, by education and experience, CPS-ORG, 1998–2002.
Occupation.

dard deviations for the occupations and industries in which individuals are employed at different stages of their life cycle. We see that these measures of risk are stable under occupational moves but *decline* as workers change industries. The results suggest experimentation with match quality across industries.

5. Data appendix: Data and sample-inclusion criteria

5.1. The CPS individual-level repeated cross-section data set

These data come from a series of 39 consecutive March *Current Population Surveys* (hereafter: March CPS) for the years 1964 to 2002. These data provide information on employment and wages in the preceding calendar year. Thus, the annual data – taken from the CPS demographic supplement – cover the period of 1963 to 2001. The individual-level repeated cross-section data set is restricted to men aged 18 to 65 with zero (0) to forty (40) years of potential experience, where potential experience is defined as age-6-school years completed.

The main advantage of the March CPS is that micro data samples are available from the mid-1960s onward. On the minus side, the March CPS has no "point-in-time" measure of the wage rate. Wage rates, in many of studies using the March CPS data, are often constructed by dividing total annual earnings in the previous year by an estimate of weeks or hours of work. The task is made more difficult by the absence of information on usual hours of work per week prior to 1976. For these reasons we further restrict this sample to include – Full-Time-Full-Year workers (hereafter: FTFY) – full-time workers (35+ hours per week) who reported working at least 51 weeks of the previous year.

The wage measure in the March CPS data set that we use throughout this paper is the average weekly wage computed as total annual earnings divided by total weeks worked. Top coding has been changed over the years. Until the 1995 survey, the imputed wages/earnings of top-coded workers were set to equal the cutoff point. Since 1996, the imputed wages for the top-coded group are based on the conditional mean earnings of these workers conditional on characteristics such as race, gender and region of residence. In order to deal with the top-coding issue, we employ a unified rule for all years. We calculate for each worker his rank/position on the wage distribution for the year observed and exclude those belonging to either the lower 2 percent or the top 2 percent each year.

Observations are divided by completed schooling, when interviewed, into five categories: (i) high school dropouts – less than twelve grades, (ii) high school graduates (iii) some college completed, (iv) college graduates with 16 years of schooling (BA) and (v) college graduates with advanced/professional education (MBA, PhD).

5.2. The CPS monthly longitudinally matched data

The vast majority of empirical analyses of the Current Population Surveys use either a single cross-section data point or a series of consecutive CPS surveys, treating the latter as a series of repeated cross-sections. The CPS data have, in fact, a longitudinal component. In this paper we take advantage of the CPS basic monthly files – a probability sample of housing units in the US – to construct a panel data set.

The CPS divides housing units into 8 representative sub-samples called "rotation groups". Each unit is interviewed for 4 consecutive months, followed by a break lasting two quarters, and again for another four monthly interviews. Overall, each unit is interviewed for 8 times over 16 months. The CPS monthly files we employ – from the years 1998 to 2002 – include a set of identifier variables that enables us to follow the same housing unit over 16 months. If there is no change in the composition of individuals residing in a particular unit, we have a panel of individuals. Yet, since people do switch locations, it might be the case that the same id number was shared by 2 (or more) individuals over time. Therefore, we follow the Madrian and Lefgren (1999) procedure, whereby individuals are identified in our panel data not only by their id number but also by matching a set of time-invariant characteristics. This procedure make us quite confident that we do not combine different persons into one artificial observation.

Data on schooling, employment, occupation and industry, are available for all interviews. However weekly wage data is collected only during the fourth and the eighth interview – among what is known as the "outgoing rotation groups" hereafter (ORG). We construct two samples. The main sample includes only workers participating in all interviews. This sample is used for the analysis of transitions between industries and occupations. Our second sample is taken from the ORG sample restricted to full-time workers, not enrolled in school and with two wage data points. We exclude observations with a reported hourly wage lower than \$4 or higher than \$2000 (adjusted for 2000 CPI). This sample is used to study wage growth of individuals.

5.3. The panel study of income dynamics

The Panel Study of Income Dynamics (PSID) is a longitudinal, nationwide survey of a representative sample of individuals and the families in which they reside. The PSID began in 1968 with approximately 4,800 white and black households and approximately 18,000 individuals. The sample had expanded as original members formed additional families over the years. We restrict our sample to US born white males aged 21 to 65 during the work year, with non missing demographics. When we discuss wage data, we exclude workers with a reported hourly wage lower than \$4 or higher than \$2000 (adjusted for 2000 CPI) and individuals who worked less than 35 weeks or less than 1000 annual hours. When using wage differences, we restrict the sample according to these cretiria in both consecutive years. Observations are divided by completed schooling into five categories – similar to our definitions using the CPS data.

6. National Longitudinal Survey of Youth (NLSY)

The micro data we use are from the 1979–2000 waves of the National Longitudinal Survey of Youth (NLSY).[38] The NLSY includes a randomly chosen sample of US youths and a supplemental sample that includes Black, Hispanic, and non-Black, non-Hispanic economically disadvantaged young people. Interviewees have been surveyed annually since the initial wave of the survey in 1979, when sample members all ranged between age 14 and 21 in 1979. The military sub-sample and the non-black, non-Hispanic disadvantaged samples are excluded. We further exclude observations with missing data regarding own or parents' education, Armed Forces Qualification Test score (hereafter AFQT), or labor market outcomes. In order to guarantee that AFQT test scores were not influenced by school attendance, AFQT scores are gender-age-school-adjusted (standardized within birth year cohort to mean 0, variance 1). When studying labor market outcomes we exclude individuals enrolled in schooling in the given year. We group respondents into five education categories: high school dropouts, high school graduates (including GED graduates), some college (SC), college graduates and individuals with advanced degrees.

When we discuss wage data, we further exclude workers with a reported hourly wage lower than $4 or higher than $2000 (adjusted for 2000 CPI) and individuals who worked less than 35 weeks or less than 1000 annual hours. When using wage differences, we restrict the sample according to these criteria in both consecutive years.

References

Abowd, J., Card, D. (1989). "On the covariance structure of earnings and hours changes". Econometrica 57, 411–445.

Abraham, K., Farber, H. (1987). "Job duration, seniority and earnings". American Economic Review 77, 278–279.

Altonji, J., Pierret, C. (2001). "Employer learning and statistical discrimination". The Quarterly Journal of Economics 116, 313–350.

Altonji, J., Williams, N. (1998). "The effect of labor market experience, job seniority and wage growth". Polachek, S. (Ed.), Research in Labor Economics 17, 233–276.

Altonji, J., Williams, N. (2004). "Do wages rise with job seniority? A reassessment". Industrial and Labor Relations Review. In press.

Alvarez, J., Browning, M., Ejrnaes, M. (2001). "Modeling income processes with lots of heterogeneity". Unpublished Manuscript, Institute of Economics, Copenhagen University.

Baker, G., Gibbs, M., Holmstrom, B. (1994a). "The internal economics of the firm: Evidence from personnel data". Quarterly Journal of Economics 109, 881–919.

Baker, G., Gibbs, M., Holmstrom, B. (1994b). "The wage policy of a firm". Quarterly Journal of Economics 109, 921–956.

Baker, M. (1997). "Growth rate heterogeneity and the covariance structure of life time earnings". Journal of Labor Economics 15, 837–878.

[38] Exceptions are Tables 3 and 4 where, in order to increase the number of observations at later ages, we also use the survey year 2002.

Barlevy, G. (2001). "Why are the wages of job changers so procyclical?". Journal of Labor Economics 19, 94–135.
Beaudry, P., Di Nardo, J. (1991). "The effect of implicit contracts on the movement of wages over the business cycle: Evidence from micro data". Journal of Political Economy 99, 665–688.
Becker, G. (1975). Human Capital. Columbia University Press.
Ben-Porath, Y. (1967). "The production of human capital and the life cycle earnings". Journal of Political Economy 75, 352–365.
Bils, M., McLaughlin, K. (2001). "Interindustry mobility and the cyclical upgrading of labor". Journal of Labor Economics 19, 94–135.
Blau, F., Kahn, L. (1981). "Causes and consequences of layoffs". Economic Inquiry 19, 270–296.
Blundell, B., MaCurdy, T. (1999). "Labor supply: A review of alternative approaches". In: Ashenfelter, O., Card, D. (Eds.), Handbook of Labor Economics, vol. 3b. North-Holland, Amsterdam.
Booth, A., Francesconi, M., Garcia-Serrano, C. (1999). "Job tenure and job mobility in Britain". Industrial and Labor Relations Review 53, 43–70.
Booth, A., Francesconi, M., Frank, J. (2002). "Temporary jobs: Stepping stones or dead ends?". Economic Journal 112, F585–F606.
Borjas, G. (1985). "Assimilation, changes in cohort quality, and the earning of immigrants". Journal of Labor Economics 3, 463–489.
Burdett, K. (1978). "Job search and quit rates". American Economic Review 68, 212–220.
Card, D. (1999). "The causal effect of education on earnings". In: Ashenfelter, O., Card, D. (Eds.), Handbook of Labor Economics, vol. 3a. North-Holland, Amsterdam.
Card, D. (2001). "Estimating the return to schooling: Progress on some persistent econometric problems". Econometrica 69, 1127–1161.
Chiappori, P., Salenei, B., Valentin, J. (1999). "Early starters versus late beginners". Journal of Political Economy 102, 731–760.
Dustmann, C., Meghir, C. (2005). "Wages, experience and seniority". Review of Economic Studies 72, 77–108.
Eckstein, Z., Weiss, Y. (2004). "On the wage growth of immigrants: Israel 1990–2000". Journal of the European Economic Association 2, 665–695.
Farber, H. (1999). "Mobility and stability: The dynamics of job changes in labor markets". In: Ashenfelter, O., Card, D. (Eds.), Handbook of Labor Economics, vol. 3b. North-Holland, Amsterdam.
Farber, H., Gibbons, R. (1996). "Learning and wage dynamics". Quarterly Journal of Economics 111, 1007–1048.
Felli, L., Harris, C. (1996). "Learning wage dynamics and firm-specific human capital". Journal of Political Economy 104, 838–868.
Felli, L., Harris, C. (2003). "Firm specific training". Unpublished Manuscript, London School of Economics.
Flinn, C. (1997). "Equilibrium wage and dismissal processes". Journal of Business and Economic Statistics 15, 221–236.
Gibbons, R., Waldman, M. (1999a). "A theory of wage and promotion dynamics inside firms". Quarterly Journal of Economics 114, 1321–1358.
Gibbons, R., Waldman, M. (1999b). "Careers in organizations: Theory and evidence". In: Ashenfelter, O., Card, D. (Eds.), Handbook of Labor Economics, vol. 3b. North-Holland, Amsterdam.
Griliches, Z. (1977). "Estimating the returns to schooling: Some econometric problems". Econometrica 45, 1–22.
Haider, S. (2001). "Earning instability and earning inequality of males in the United States: 1967–1991". Journal of Labor Economics 19, 774–798.
Hall, R. (1982). "The minimum wage and job turnover in markets for young workers". In: Freeman, R., Wise, D. (Eds.), The Youth Labor Market. University of Chicago Press, Chicago.
Harris, M., Holmstrom, B. (1982). "A theory of wage dynamics". Review of Economic Studies 49, 315–333.
Harris, M., Weiss, Y. (1984). "Job matching with finite horizon and risk aversion". Journal of Political Economy 92, 758–779.

Heckman, J., Honore, B. (1990). "The empirical content of the Roy model". Econometrica 58, 1121–1149.
Heckman, J., Hsee, J., Rubinstein, Y. (2003). "The GED is a mixed signal: The effect of cognitive skills and personality skills on human capital and labor market outcomes". Unpublished Manuscript, Department of Economics, University of Chicago.
Heckman, J., Lochner, L., Taber, C. (1998). "Explaining rising wage inequality: Explanations with a dynamic equilibrium model of labor earnings with heterogenous agents". Review of Economic Dynamics 1, 1–58.
Heckman, J., Lochner, L., Todd, P. (2001). "Fifty years of Mincer earnings regressions". Unpublished Manuscript, Department of Economics, University of Chicago.
Heckman, J., Rubinstein, Y. (2001). "The importance of noncognitive skills: Lessons from the GED testing program". American Economic Review 91, 145–149.
Huggett, M., Ventura, G., Yaron, A. (2002). "Human capital and earning distribution dynamics". Unpublished Manuscript, Department of Economics, Georgetown University.
Johnson, W. (1978). "A theory of job shopping". Quarterly Journal of Economics 93, 261–277.
Jovanovic, B. (1979a). "Job matching and the theory of turnover". Journal of Political Economy 87, 972–990.
Jovanovic, B. (1979b). "Firm specific capital and turnover". Journal of Political Economy 87, 1246–1260.
Jovanovic, B. (1984). "Matching, turnover and unemployment". Journal of Political Economy 92, 108–122.
Jovanovic, B., Nyarko, Y. (1997). "Stepping Stone mobility". Carnegie-Rochester Conference on Public Economics 46, 289–325.
Katz, L., Autor, D. (1999). "Changes in the wage structure and wage inequality". In: Ashenfelter, O., Card, D. (Eds.), Handbook of Labor Economics, vol. 3a. North-Holland, Amsterdam.
Keane, M., Moffitt, R., Runkle, D. (1988). "Real wages over the business cycle: Estimating the impact of heterogeneity with micro data". Journal of Political Economy 96, 1232–1266.
Lange, F. (2003). "The returns to schooling and ability during the early career: Evidence on job market signaling, employer learning and post-schooling investments". Unpublished Manuscript, Department of Economics, University of Chicago.
Lillard, L., Reville, R. (1999). "Life cycle human capital investment: New evidence on an old issue". Unpublished Manuscript, Rand Corporation.
Lillard, L., Weiss, Y. (1979). "Components of variation in panel earnings data: American scientists 1960–1970". Econometrica 47, 437–454.
MaCurdy, T. (1982). "The use of time series processes to model the error structure of earnings in longitudinal data analysis". Journal of Econometrics 18, 83–114.
Madrian, B.C., Lefgren, L. (1999). "A note on longitudinally matching current population survey (CPS) respondents". NBER Technical Working Paper 247.
Malcomson, J. (1997). "Contracts, hold-up and labor markets". Journal of Economic Literature 35, 1916–1957.
Malcomson, J. (1999). "Individual employment contracts". In: Ashenfelter, O., Card, D. (Eds.), Handbook of Labor Economics, vol. 3b. North-Holland, Amsterdam.
McLaughlin, J. (1994). "Rigid wages?". Journal of Monetary Economics 34, 383–414.
Meghir, C., Pistaferri, L. (2001). "Income variance dynamics and heterogeneity". Institute for Fiscal Studies Discussion Paper 01/07.
Miller, R. (1984). "Job matching and occupational choice". Journal of Political Economy 92, 1086–1120.
Mincer, J. (1958). "Investment in human capital and the personal income distribution". Journal of Political Economy 66, 281–302.
Mincer, J. (1974). Schooling, Experience and Earnings. Columbia University Press, New York.
Mincer, J. (1993). Studies in Human Capital: Collected Essays of Jacob Mincer, vol. 1. Edward Elgar.
Mincer, J., Jovanovic, B. (1981). "Labor mobility and wages". In: Rosen, S. (Ed.), Studies in Labor Markets. University of Chicago Press, Chicago.
Mortensen, D. (1986). "Job search and labor market analysis". In: Ashenfelter, O., Layard, R. (Eds.), Handbook of Labor Economics. North-Holland, Amsterdam.
Mortensen, D. (1988). "Wages separations and job tenure". Journal of Labor Economics 4, 572–586.
Mortensen, D., Pissarides, C. (1999). "New developments in models of search in the labor market". In: Ashenfelter, O., Card, D. (Eds.), Handbook of Labor Economics, vol. 3b. North-Holland, Amsterdam.

Munasinghe, L. (2003). "A theory of wage and turnover dynamics". Unpublished Manuscript, Department of Economics, Barnard College.
Murphy, K., Welch, F. (1990). "Empirical age earnings wage profiles". Journal of Labor Economics 8, 202–229.
Murphy, K., Welch, F. (1992). "The structure of wages". Quarterly Journal of Economics 107, 285–326.
Neal, D. (1995). "Industry specific human capital: Evidence from displaced workers". Journal of Labor Economics 13, 653–677.
Neal, D. (1999). "The complexity of job mobility among young men". Journal of Labor Economics 17, 237–261.
Polachek, S. (2003). "Mincer's overtaking point and the lifecycle earning distribution". Unpublished Manuscript, Department of Economics, SUNY at Binghamton.
Prendergast, C. (1999). "The provision of incentives in firms". Journal of Economic Literature 37, 7–63.
Rosen, S. (1972). "Learning and experience in the labor market". Journal of Human Resources 7, 326–342.
Rosen, S. (1977). "Human capital: A survey of empirical research". In: Ehrenberg, R. (Ed.), Research in Labor Economics, vol. 1. JAI Press, Greenwich.
Rubinstein, Y., Tsiddon, D. (2003). "Born to be unemployed: Unemployment and wages over the business cycle". Unpublished Manuscript, School of Economics, Tel-Aviv University.
Rubinstein, Y., Tsiddon, D. (2004). "Coping with technological progress: The role of ability in making inequality so persistent". Journal of Economic Growth. In press.
Shaw, K. (1996). "An empirical analysis of risk aversion and income growth". Journal of Labor Economics 14, 626–653.
Sicherman, N. (1991). "Over education in the labor market". Journal of Labor Economics 9, 101–122.
Topel, R. (1991). "Specific capital, mobility, and wages: Wages rise with job seniority". Journal of Political Economy 99, 145–176.
Topel, R., Ward, M. (1992). "Job mobility and careers of young men". Quarterly Journal of Economics 107, 339–479.
Weinberg, B. (2003). "Experience and technology adoption". Unpublished Manuscript, Department of Economics, Ohio State University.
Weiss, Y. (1971). "Learning by doing and occupational specialization". Journal of Economic Theory 3, 189–199.
Weiss, Y. (1984). "Wage contracts when output grows stochastically: The role of mobility costs and capital market imperfections". Journal of Labor Economics 2, 155–174.
Weiss, Y. (1986). "The determination of life-time earnings: A survey". In: Ashenfelter, O., Layard, R. (Eds.), Handbook of Labor Economics. North-Holland, Amsterdam.
Weiss, Y., Lillard, L. (1978). "Experience, vintage, and time effects in the growth of earnings: American scientists 1960–1970". Journal of Political Economy 86, 427–448.
Weiss, Y., Sauer, R., Gotlibovski, M. (2003). "Immigration, search and loss of skill". Journal of Labor Economics 21, 557–592.
Weiss, Y., Willis, R. (1997). "Match quality, new information, and marital dissolution". Journal of Labor Economics 15, S293–S329.
Welch, F. (1969). "Linear synthesis of skill distribution". Journal of Human Resources 4, 311–327.
Willis, R. (1986). "Wage determination". In: Ashenfelter, O., Layard, R. (Eds.), Handbook of Labor Economics, vol. 1. North-Holland, Amsterdam.
Willis, R., Rosen, S. (1979). "Education and self selection". Journal of Political Economy 87 (2), S7–S36.
Wolpin, K. (1992). "The determinants of black–white differences in early employment careers: Search, layoffs, quits and endogenous wage growth". Journal of Political Economy 100, 535–560.
Wolpin, K. (2003). "Wage equation and education policy". In: Dewaterpoint, M., Hansen, L., Turnovsky, S. (Eds.), Advances in Economics and Econometrics. Cambridge University Press, Cambridge, UK.

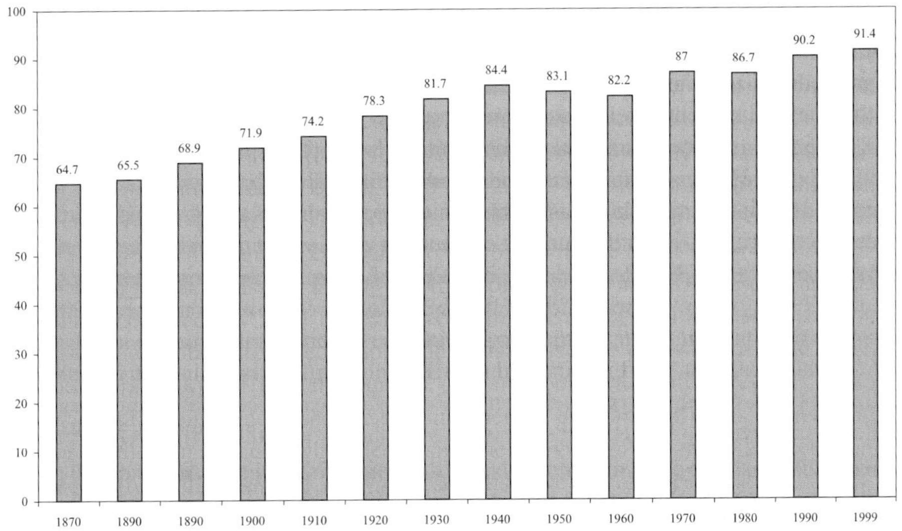

Figure 1. Enrollment as a percent of 5- to 17-year-olds. Source: NCES (2001).

of economic performance well into the nineteenth century, but lagged badly in offering broad access to primary education.

Historians of education typically highlight the fact that the common school movement was one of a number of campaigns for democratization in various social and economic policies that coincided with, or followed shortly after, widespread extension of the suffrage.[9] Despite the sentiments popularly attributed to the Founding Fathers, voting in the United States was largely a privilege reserved for white men with significant amounts of property until early in the nineteenth century. By 1815, only four of the original thirteen states (and seven overall) had adopted universal white male suffrage, but as the movement to do away with political inequality gained strength, they were joined by the rest of the country as virtually all new entrants to the Union extended voting privileges to all white men, as part of a general campaign to attract and retain settlers, and older states revised their laws. The shift to full white manhood suffrage was largely complete by the late 1840s.[10] Overall, the timing of the movements for extending the suffrage as well as for common schools, is consistent with the view that increasing equality in political influence helped realize the increased investments in public schooling, along with the corresponding extension of access to a primary education. That the southern

[9] Cubberley (1920, 1947).

[10] For discussions of the series of reforms involving both the extension of the franchise and the conduct of voting more generally, see Porter (1918), Albright (1942), Keyssar (2000), and Engerman and Sokoloff (2005). For a discussion of how the extension of the franchise in Europe may have contributed to the expansion of public schooling, see Acemoglu and Robinson (2000).

states were generally the laggards in both broadening the electorate and starting common schools, while New England and the western states were leaders in both, likewise provides support for this view.[11] Since doing away with property restrictions on the franchise enhanced the political voice of the groups that would benefit relatively more from the establishment of tax-supported free schools (as they were less able to pay the cost of educating their children), and the most important single source of tax revenue for local and state governments were taxes on property (so the poor would bear relatively less of the additional tax burden), it should not be surprising if the achievement of greater equality in political influence led to the institutional changes that contributed to greater equality in the distribution of human capital.

A related idea is that the greater support for public education institutions in the United States was due not to differences in capacity to pay (as gauged by per capita income), nor to the crude politics of redistribution, but rather to differences across communities in their willingness or ability to mobilize tax revenue for public or quasi-public goods such as public schools. This way of framing the problem highlights issues of social capital, government or administrative structure, as well as of political economy. Although many societies initially gave local or provincial governments responsibility for operating public schools, and granted them authority to levy taxes, the United States was one of very few countries where rather early in its process of development this capability was acted on in a widespread and substantial way. Elsewhere it was generally not until national governments got involved and provided resources that major investments in a broad system of primary schooling were undertaken.[12] Some scholars have suggested the possibility that such differences across communities, or across countries, in the willingness of populations to pay taxes to support public schools may have had something to do with differences in the extent of inequality or social heterogeneity amongst the respective populations.[13] The logic is based on the observation that the well-to-do can always obtain schooling for their children through the private market, but that public investment in schooling systems, or broad access to schooling, generally involves some transfers between those who bear a disproportionate share of the costs and those who realize a disproportionate share of the benefits.[14] Major support for public schooling is therefore more likely where there is relative equality or population homogeneity (where

[11] Later, the southern states were also laggards in establishing public high schools. See Goldin and Katz (1999b).

[12] The role of the national government was more prominent in Europe than in the U.S., and especially so in Latin America.

[13] The idea that social homogeneity is associated with greater social capital, and leads to higher levels of investment in public or quasi-public goods has been receiving increasing attention. For discussion and evidence of this linkage see Goldin and Katz (2000) and Alesina, Baqir and Easterly (1999).

[14] In the nineteenth-century U.S., for example, it was typical for local governments – that provided most of the funds for public schools – to raise the overwhelming share of their revenue through property taxes. Property taxes generally accounted for 90 percent or more of local government tax revenue through the middle of the 20th century. See Copeland (1961).

one expects there to be less severe collective action problems because of greater similarity across households in the balance of costs and benefits, as well as in values and perspective), or where the wealthier segments of the population are more receptive to indirectly supporting their neighbors or countrymen (either because of the social capital of the community or because such investments yield social benefits that the taxpayers will share in, such as the increase in property values that come from attracting a desirable class of migrants). In this view, the United States during the early 19th century enjoyed conditions that were very favorable to substantial investments in public schooling. Not only would the relative political and economic equality (as compared to other parts of the world) and social homogeneity of the population make it easier to overcome collective action problems and take advantage of the returns to investment in primary schooling, but also the general circumstance of scarce labor meant that local communities (and especially property holders) could benefit from investments in public goods that would lure new residents and spur growth.[15] Support for this notion of the significance of social or political equality comes from the coincidence in time between the common school movement of the 1820s and 1830s in the United States and the broadening of the franchise during that same era, from similar associations between suffrage reform and the passage of measures to support public schools in both Canada, England, and elsewhere in Europe, as well as from geographic patterns in the spread of secondary schools discussed below.[16]

The U.S. schools were distinctive not only for the early move to public funding, extensive reach, and decentralized structure, but also for their relatively practical and egalitarian content. The curricula tended to stress basic skills and tools, and were organized around the idea of providing all students, boys and girls, with a "common" academic education. To a remarkable degree, the guiding vision seemed to be that children were quite similar in capacities, and while some might be able to remain longer

[15] For more discussion of the distinctiveness of the U.S. as regards relative equality, and of the significance of labor scarcity for encouraging investments in public goods, see Engerman and Sokoloff (2002, 2005). For evidence that the U.S. was rather different from other countries of the period in having higher literacy outside of cities than in urban centers, see Engerman, Mariscal and Sokoloff (2002). For fascinating evidence of how much early settlers had to gain from attracting migrants and spurring local population growth, see Galenson and Pope (2002).

[16] Also consistent with this view is the cross-sectional correspondence across states between leadership in broadening the franchise and leadership in the establishment of universal common schools. For discussions of the connection between extensions of suffrage and public schooling in many countries and contexts, see the discussions in many chapters of Cubberley (1920). Although the idea that the earlier move to broad provision of public schooling in the United States reflected a more general orientation toward democratic institutions is something of a consensus interpretation, other explanations have been offered. For example, some have suggested that the introduction of widespread public schooling was associated with a desire among certain segments of the elite to socialize, or otherwise prepare, immigrants or other potential workers for employment in large-scale industrial establishments. See Bowles and Gintis (1976). Even if this argument held for an early industrializing state such as Massachusetts, which seems highly debatable, it is surely poorly suited to the overwhelmingly agricultural Midwestern states that established public schools with great enthusiasm.

Table 3
Median years of schooling, by race and gender, 1865–1960

	Total	Male	Female	White	Black
1865	8.0	7.7	8.1	8.2	1.3
1870	8.1	8.0	8.2	8.2	2.9
1875	8.2	8.1	8.2	8.3	3.8
1880	8.3	8.2	8.3	8.4	4.4
1885	8.3	8.2	8.4	8.4	4.8
1890	8.4	8.3	8.4	8.5	5.0
1895	8.5	8.4	8.5	8.6	5.5
1900	8.6	8.6	8.7	8.8	5.8
1905	8.8	8.7	8.9	9.0	6.1
1910	9.5	9.2	9.9	10.0	7.3
1915	10.3	10.1	10.5	10.7	8.3
1920	11.6	11.4	11.8	11.9	9.1
1925	12.1	12.0	12.1	12.3	10.4
1930	12.2	12.1	12.2	12.3	10.7
1935	12.3	12.3	12.3	12.4	12.0
1940	12.5	12.6	12.5	12.6	12.3
1945	12.6	12.7	12.5	12.6	12.4
1950	12.9	13.0	12.8	12.9	12.6
1955	12.9	12.9	12.8	12.9	12.6
1960	12.7	12.7	12.8	12.8	12.6

Note: From 1865 to 1900, the Black group represents Black and Others.
Sources: Current Population Reports: Educational Attainment in the United States: March 1981 and 1980, and Historical Statistics of the United States, Colonial Times to 1970, Part I.

in formal schools than others, and thus move further up the formal educational ladder, all should be provided with the same basic knowledge or training. Not only was it right for each individual, if not quite an individual right, to be equipped with the same basic skills or knowledge, but also, in ensuring this would be so, society would promote civic virtue and a better functioning democracy. The relative absence of parallel schooling tracks for different classes of students was yet another fundamental way in which the schooling system in the U.S. stood in sharp contrast with those in Europe and elsewhere.[17]

Of course, not all segments of the population were equally well served. As seen in Table 3, there has been striking, especially from an international perspective, gender equality in the United States from early in its history (as regards enrollment rates and

[17] European countries were generally much slower to provide broad access to schools, and even when they ultimately did so, they tended to favor systems whereby different groups of students received different programs of instruction training (often geared toward careers in particular occupations or industries) at earlier ages.

literacy, if not in programs of study or quality of instruction). The experience of Black Americans, however, provides an extreme and tragic example of how access to schooling has often been all too closely linked with social or political standing; their education levels have always lagged far behind those of whites. With many states having prohibitions on instructing slaves to read, blacks received very little in the way of schooling before the Civil War. Even after the War, although emancipation, constitutional amendments, and other policies yielded a dramatic expansion in their access to public services, blacks generally had to make do with schools that were *de jure* segregated, and vastly inferior in nearly all dimensions, until well into the 20th century. Plessy v. Ferguson (1896) notwithstanding, the separate schooling was anything but equal – especially after black voting rights were effectively eroded by poll taxes, literacy tests, and a host of other qualifications for suffrage adopted by many states late in the 19th century.[18] Brown v. Board of Education (1954) brought an end to *de jure* segregation, but the *de facto* segregation that endured, and continues to the present day, has highlighted some of the problems that can arise from decentralized structures of public school financing and administration. Students in districts that provide less support to public schools, for whatever reason, have very different experiences in the classroom than do their peers in more fortunate circumstances. Of course, there is no easy solution, especially in a context where there is substantial inequality or heterogeneity. Centralized structures that involve redistribution tend to inspire greater resistance to taxes, as well as encourage households who demand higher quality schooling services to shift to private providers.

3. Public universities

The United States also has a strong history in publicly provided university education. Although the first universities were private, as both the private and social usefulness of institutions of higher learning became apparent, it did not take long for the public sector to expand its role, to innovate a quite new type of education institution, and in so doing broaden access to universities. The earliest colleges – such as Harvard, William and Mary, and Yale – were established through charters from colonial state governments, and each was (with the precursor of the University of Pennsylvania standing out as an exception) associated with a particular religious denomination. They were private, relying primarily on tuition for funding, though they sometimes received support from state authorities. By the early 19th century, however, there was growing expression of public dissatisfaction with how they operated. Institutions of higher learning were already coming to be recognized as of great public significance, not only as avenues for

[18] For superb treatments of how black voting rights were undermined by southern whites after the period of Reconstruction, and how enormous gaps in public provision for white and black schools quickly followed and persisted well into the 20th century, see Du Bois and Dill (1911), Kousser (1974), Welch (1973), and Margo (1990).

personal advancement, but also for their contributions to the intellectual and technological development of society.[19] A democracy required an educated citizenry; in this intensely democratic age, many observers feared that religious denominations might exercise too much control, and were suspicions of aristocratic tendencies. Efforts by state governments to exert more authority over the colleges were generally resisted, as was the attempt by New Hampshire to transform Dartmouth College into a state institution. The Supreme Court ruling that the charter of a college was a contract that could not be altered by legislative fiat was just one of many reasons why state governments turned to creating new universities of their own.

This belief in the importance of higher education, and of broad access to it, together with the demographic, economic, and geographic expansion, fueled a sharp acceleration in the formation of colleges and universities after the Revolution. Only ten were founded before 1780, fourteen more came over the next twenty years, and by the close of 1860 students were attending classes in more than two hundred and forty-five such institutions. Although the overwhelming majority of these institutions were private, state universities accounted for nearly 10 percent of the total and a somewhat larger proportion of students. Whereas the early denominational colleges had relied on very narrow curricula, largely confined to theology, mathematics, philosophy, and ancient languages, those established after the Revolution began to introduce new programs (i.e. medicine, law, and ultimately engineering) that were more practical and often focused on the applications of science or scientific method to current problems or circumstances. Part of the inspiration for these changes may have come from Europe, and especially from the example of the Ecole Polytechnique founded by the revolutionary French government in 1794, but the actual designing and creation of such new programs were carried out by visionary or entrepreneurial academics and patrons whose senses of possibilities had likely been influenced by the concerns of students, state governments, and businessmen. One illustration of this is the significance of the Erie Canal in encouraging the spread of engineering instruction in the U.S. during the first half of the 19th century.[20] The Rensselaer School (founded in 1824, and later renamed the Rensselaer Polytechnic Institute) was the pioneer in focusing its programs on engineering and agricultural science, but as the progress of early industrialization made clear the growing relevance and value of familiarity with technology, many colleges began to expand their offerings in this direction.[21] Harvard and Yale both acted in 1847 to organize the Lawrence Scientific School and the Sheffield Scientific School respectively, and separate departments or schools in science and related areas were becoming commonplace by the 1850s.

[19] One reflection of this sentiment was George Washington's desire for a National University to be established in the nation's capital.

[20] See Edelstein (2002). As Edelstein discusses, it was no coincidence that these early programs were highly concentrated in New York.

[21] Rensselaer is another example of how many Americans conceived of institutions of higher learning in utilitarian terms. The school was founded on the basis of a gift from Stephen Van Rensselaer, who wanted an institution that would promote study and instruction of the application of science to agriculture and manufactures.

The success of private institutions such as Rensselaer in producing graduates who became renowned for their accomplishments and impact on the economy encouraged public authorities to seek to emulate the model. During the late 1840s and early 1850s, state legislatures in New York, Michigan, Illinois, Virginia, and Pennsylvania moved to establish state colleges of agriculture (and often of "mechanic arts" as well), and the federal government soon joined in. Despite some fears that it would adversely affect already existing private schools, in 1862 President Lincoln signed the so-called First Morrill Act, which gave over more than 11 million acres of public land to the states to endow institutions focused on agriculture, mechanic arts, or military science and tactics.[22] Different states exploited these federal land grants in different ways, but the unambiguous effect was an enormous expansion of public college and universities, both by stimulating the organization of new universities such as Ohio State, Purdue, and MIT, as well as by dramatically boosting the resources available to schools that had been struggling with limited funds. The Morrill Act is a vivid demonstration of how government support for broad access to education extended beyond primary schooling, even during the 19th century.

The land grant universities also reflect, however, the deeply utilitarian approach that policy makers, and Americans more generally, took toward educational institutions of higher learning. Public support was grounded on the presumption that they would contribute to the advance of technology and the economy, whether at the national, regional, or local level. They were much more likely to establish programs in agriculture, engineering, the natural sciences, mining, forestry, as well as in other fields of study that would be helpful to local industries than were private institutions of higher learning. In 1890, for example, about 22 percent of all students attending college or university were enrolled in public schools, while roughly 50 percent of engineering degrees were awarded by such institutions (which were the home of nearly 60 percent of engineering programs).[23]

It is interesting to observe that this major expansion of public universities, and their move into more technical fields, coincided in time with the beginning of a major shift in the educational backgrounds of individuals who were making the most important contributions to technological knowledge. Figure 2 displays the level of formal schooling attained for the 409 individuals (408 men and 1 woman) recognized as important inventors in the *Dictionary of American Biography* who were born before 1886 and active in the U.S.[24] Arraying them by birth cohort, and weighting them by the number of patents they received, reveals that their levels of formal schooling were quite modest through the birth cohort of 1820 to 1845; roughly 75 to 80 percent of patents went to those 'great inventors' with only primary or secondary schooling (meaning that their formal schooling had ended no later than age 17). These data indicate that people with rather limited formal technical educations were capable of making important contribu-

[22] A similar bill had been passed by Congress a few years before, but was vetoed by President Buchanan.

[23] Goldin and Katz (2003) and Edelstein, p. 10.

[24] See Khan and Sokoloff (2004) for a discussion of the sample, and further analysis.

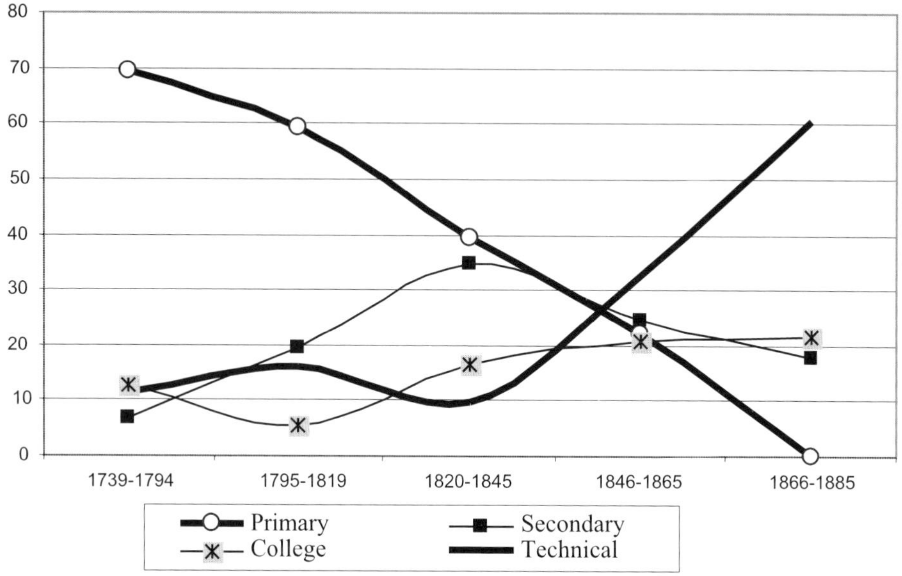

Figure 2. Educational level of great inventors by birth cohort, % distribution of patents. Source: Khan and Sokoloff (2004).

tions to technological knowledge, at least until the very end of the 19th century. The technologically creative seem to have been able to accumulate the skills and knowledge necessary to operate at the frontier largely on their own, or through their work experience as apprentices or younger employees, up until the Second Industrial Revolution. The growing importance of a technical education begins to be evident among the great inventors in the birth cohort of 1846–65, as the proportion of them who had studied at an institution of higher learning, and earned degrees engineering and/or the natural sciences rose sharply. By the next birth cohort, a college education was virtually a necessity, especially one in a technical field (in Figure 2, includes physical or biological sciences, medicine, and engineering).

The coincidence of the expansion of public universities with the major and rather discontinuous increase in the prevalence of college education and degrees in technical fields among great inventors raises a number of intriguing interpretations. One is that the episode is indicative of how responsive U.S. public education institutions, and the government authorities that establish and maintain them, have been to changes in the relative returns to different types of human capital. Moreover, an economic logic might suggest that since the fraction of the population that stood to take direct advantage of the expanded opportunity to obtain a college degree was small, the steps the federal and state governments took were likely based on a presumption that public universities generated significant positive externalities. Another possibility is that the land-grant universities, and their greater orientation toward science and engineering, constituted an innovation in educational institutions, in that whatever else they accomplished, they also introduced a more effective means by which technologically creative individuals could become familiar with the frontiers of technical knowledge. That the shift in the composition of great inventors from those who had accumulated their technical skills and knowledge through work experience to those who had been trained at universities occurred so swiftly, if not discontinuously, does suggest that this avenue was superior for the production of technological leaders.[25] Although part of this apparently remarkable success may have stemmed from the public subsidy to university education, it is worth noting that the late-19th century was also marked by private universities, new as well as old, starting or expanding programs in the engineering, the natural sciences, medicine, and other technical fields.[26]

Over time, public schools came to account for a larger and larger share of institutions of higher education. From less than a quarter in 1890, the fraction of college students enrolled in public schools increased to roughly one half by 1940, and is now over three quarters.[27] This shift in the relative importance of public and private colleges occurred over a period during which the demand for college and university education rose dramatically. Private institution enrollments registered extremely impressive growth, but public sector enrollments truly exploded. The chief reason for this seemingly greater responsiveness or flexibility was likely the greater ease of mobilizing resources. Faced with a burgeoning demand for the education provided by such institutions, and encouraged by the belief that both the presence of the institutions and the stock of individuals so educated generated positive local externalities, public authorities were simply more able and willing to provide the resources needed to expand supply. Of course, there was, and continues to be, substantial and systematic variation across states in their levels of support for public universities. It has, for example, been widely noted that the states that were formed the earliest, and where private colleges were more likely to have been founded during the early history of the country, tend to have markedly lower levels of public support for state universities. Overall, one of the most striking, if not surprising, patterns is a pronounced persistence over time in state and local government spending per capita on higher education.

[25] Another observation that tends to support this sort of interpretation is that the shift toward more highly educated great inventors occurred at roughly the same time in all of the sectors of the economy. Inventors concerned with electric light and power were a bit more likely to have had university degrees in science or engineering than those in other areas, but such differences across sectors were minor compared to the dramatic changes between birth cohorts. See Khan and Sokoloff (2004) for more discussion.

[26] Cornell and the Massachusetts Institute of Technology are of course famous examples of distinguished universities that began as so-called land grant institutions, but Case and Carnegie are among the many distinguished private schools of technology that were established during this era.

[27] U.S. Census Bureau (2002), Table 198.

4. The high school movement

Of course a major factor helping to account for the growth of enrollments in colleges and universities was the expansion of public high schools – a development that did not take place in earnest until the early 20th century. As we have discussed, prior to the 'common school' movement of the first half of the 19th century, most schooling was provided on a private basis – that is, the grammar schools, academies, or colleges were funded primarily by the fees or tuition collected from students and their families. As public provision of primary schooling spread, it was the so-called academies (beginning with institutions such as the Dummer Academy and the Phillips Academy founded in Massachusetts in 1761 and 1778 respectively) that focused on secondary education. These institutions varied in emphasis, but generally provided courses of study that either prepared students for college, or gave them an advanced education (following on common schools) in modern languages, mathematics, the sciences, and history, with the goal of equipping them for success in the professions or the "ordinary business of life". These academies grew in popularity, with the most intense phase of their development coinciding roughly with the common school movement. Some scholars have estimated that by 1850, there were more than 6000 of these academies, staffed by more than 12,000 teachers, and with more than 260,000 students enrolled.[28] That the numbers of these essentially private secondary schools grew so rapidly, and that they were evidently stimulated by the spread of broad-based primary school systems, suggests that this period was characterized by a powerful demand for education among the middle and upper classes of the population. These institutions schooled many boys and girls, some bound for college, but some for other occupations (including teaching in lower schools).

The establishment of free public high schools got under way during the 1820s, with Boston and Portland, Maine opening schools in 1821, and the passage of seminal (if selectively enforced) legislation by Massachusetts in 1827 requiring all towns with 500 or more families to have one. Many towns and especially big cities (Philadelphia in 1838 and New York in 1848, for example) followed, but even in New England where public high schools were for decades highly concentrated, the spread of such institutions was a very slow process. Among the obstacles were the question of cost relative to benefit (given that many adolescents were able to earn significant wage income in the labor market or be productive on the farm), the difficulty of realizing an efficient scale given the relatively dispersed population of the mid-19th century (the private academies were often boarding schools), and the opposition of taxpayers and the advocates for common schools and/or private academies (who might well have had reason to think that public high schools would sap them of scarce resources). Outside of New England and New York, there was considerable resistance to legislation providing for public high schools, including challenges to constitutionality where such laws were actually passed.[29]

[28] Cubberley (1947, p. 247). Goldin and Katz (2003) have suggested that these numbers give an exaggerated sense of how high enrollment rates were among adolescents.

[29] See Cubberley (1947, pp. 262–264) for discussion. Also see Vinovskis (1985).

Table 4
Availability and use of public high schools

	# Free public high schools	% Pupils in public high schools	Approx. % of pupils in HS relative to HS age population
1869–70	c. 500	–	2.0
1878–80	c. 800	–	3.0
1889–90	2,536	68.1	5.0
1894–95	4,712	74.7	7.5
1899–00	6,005	82.4	9.0
1904–05	7,576	86.4	10.0
1909–10	10,213	88.6	12.5
1914–15	11,674	89.6	20.0
1919–20	14,326	91.0	29.0
1924–25	c. 20,000	91.6	47.0
1929–30	c. 22,000	–	52.0

Source: Cubberley (1947, p. 627).

It was not really until the last decades of the 19th century that public high schools began to develop rapidly. As Table 4 shows, between 1880 and 1900 the number of free public high schools increased seven fold, to a point where they accounted for more than 80 percent of secondary school enrollments. Even then, however, only about 10 percent of those of high school age were enrolled in either public or private institutions.[30] Although the early rise of public high schools may seem modest, that they were having major democratizing effects was soon evident. The rather elite backgrounds of those able to afford private secondary education is suggested by estimates that between 50 and 60 percent of high school graduates during the 1880s and early 1890s would go on to graduate from college. With the rapid increase in the numbers of public schools during the late 1890s and beyond, however, this figure dropped to just over 30 percent by 1900, and to nearly 20 percent by 1920.[31] Most of the growth in public high schools before 1900 was in the northern states, and especially New England, where urbanization and the shift to non-agricultural occupations were most advanced. But this regional pattern changed dramatically as the expansion of public high schools accelerated during the first decades of the 20th century.

From less than 10 percent as late as 1910, high school graduation rates rose to over 50 percent by 1940, with the increase accounted for almost exclusively by the rapid expansion of public provision of free secondary school education (see Table 5). As Goldin and Katz highlight in their careful studies, this crucial phase of the 'high school movement'

[30] See the figures in Cubberley (1947, p. 627).

[31] These estimates are based on the ratio of bachelor's degrees granted relative to the number of high school graduates four years earlier. See Snyder (1993, Figure 19).

Table 5
High school graduation rates summary statistics by state

	Unweighted		Weighted	
	Mean	Standard deviation	Mean	Standard deviation
48 States				
1910	0.088	0.049	0.086	0.043
1920	0.180	0.085	0.162	0.069
1928	0.300	0.117	0.270	0.100
1938	0.504	0.145	0.482	0.130
32 Non-Southern States				
1910	0.112	0.043	0.111	0.297
1920	0.223	0.069	0.199	0.281
1928	0.361	0.093	0.321	0.268
1938	0.581	0.097	0.559	0.134

Source: Goldin and Katz (1997) "Why the United States Led in Education", Table 1. Weighted data use the number of the 17-year olds in the state.

proceeded most swiftly in states located in the Great Plains (such as Iowa, Nebraska, Kansas, and South Dakota) and on the pacific coast (such as California or Washington).[32] These regions had lagged New England in the spread of high school education at 1910, but were the first to broadly assume the major new financial commitments required to expand the level of public education offered all children from common or grammar school through high school. An enormous change was effected in but a few decades, with graduation rates in these leading regions jumping from just over 10 percent to the 60 to 75 percent range over this key 1910 to 1940 interval. It was not until the 1960s that the rest of the country caught up, with the national rate leveling off in the 70 to 75 percent range for the remainder of the century.

Fundamental to this movement was the rather high return to having a high school degree. Based on their analysis of the rather unique set of data information provided by the 1915 Iowa State Census, Goldin and Katz estimate that the private return to a high school education was over 10 percent, for either blue- or white-collar occupations. Although neither they, nor other scholars, have a fix on how recently the return to secondary schooling had risen to that level, there is certainly reason to think that the changes in technology associated with the Second Industrial Revolution, the growth in urban centers, the continued sectoral shift out of agriculture, and the surge of immigration from abroad might have boosted the returns to schooling about the turn of the century.

[32] Goldin and Katz (1999a, 1999b, 2000).

Why was it that the populations that took the lead in taxing themselves to provide high school educations to all of their children were in 'America's heartland', far away from the urban centers often associated with progressive attitudes toward education? Goldin and Katz identify a number of factors that help account for the regional pattern, including the high per capita incomes in these areas. The key feature of their explanation, however, is the emphasis on how these states had greater social equality or homogeneity than other regions such as the Northeast (and especially the South), and that these qualities were associated with higher levels of social capital and greater willingness to invest in public or quasi-public goods such as schooling. As they note, the cost of providing universal high school education was substantial – with the cost of the four years of high school roughly equivalent to the cost of the preceding eight years of schooling.[33] Moreover, it is striking that the public decisions about levels of support for schooling were generally made at local levels, such as school districts or counties, even if guided or coordinated from above (state governments). Amongst the evidence they offer for their view is that even within Iowa, a state where social heterogeneity is relatively subtle, counties with greater social homogeneity (such as the proportion of the population with native-born parents) and economic equality (as proxied for by motor vehicle registration per household) made significantly earlier and larger commitments to funding high school education, and had higher rates of attendance. Analyses of variation across states yield similar implications. The Goldin and Katz perspective on the regional diffusion of high schools is, therefore, quite similar to ideas about the common school movement: communities with greater equality or homogeneity were more likely to support public provision of schooling because of greater uniformity across households in the sharing of costs and benefits as well perhaps as greater identification or concern with what was good for others in the community.

5. Challenges and responses in the late 20th century

While social equality and homogeneity among the population seems to have greatly facilitated the growth and expansion of the public school system during the 19th and early 20th centuries, the increasing heterogeneity evident in late 20th century America might be viewed as posing new challenges to the system. Some observers believe that increases in income inequality, major change in the ethnic and age composition of households, changes in the legal environment, as well as the increasing cost of schools in a world in which women (long disproportionately represented among the ranks of teachers) have a broader range of professional career paths available to them may undercut support for maintaining high quality public schools. Certainly there is much concern among the body politic. The state of public schools has returned to center stage in many political campaigns, with calls for overhauling the system, introducing national standardized testing, school vouchers, and expanded choice for parents. Surveys of public opinion indicate that adults give national schools a report card grade of slightly below a "C".

[33] Goldin and Katz (1999a, 1999b, 2000, 2003) and Goldin (2001).

Table 6
Percentage of population attaining upper secondary education or more, by country: 1999

OECD countries	Ages 25–64	Ages 25–34	Ages 35–44	Ages 45–54	Ages 55–64
Australia	57	65	59	55	44
Austria	74	83	78	69	59
Belgium	57	73	61	50	36
Canada	79	87	83	78	62
Czech Republic	86	93	89	85	75
Denmark	80	87	80	79	70
Finland	72	86	82	67	46
France	62	76	65	57	42
Germany	81	85	85	81	73
Greece	50	71	58	42	24
Hungary	67	80	76	70	36
Iceland	56	64	59	53	40
Ireland	51	67	56	41	31
Italy	42	55	50	37	21
Japan	81	93	92	79	60
Korea	66	93	72	47	28
Luxembourg	56	61	57	52	41
Mexico	20	25	22	16	9
New Zealand	74	79	77	71	60
Norway	85	94	89	79	68
Poland	54	62	59	53	37
Portugal	21	30	21	15	11
Spain	35	55	41	25	13
Sweden	77	87	81	74	61
Switzerland	82	89	84	79	72
Turkey	22	26	23	18	12
UK	62	66	63	60	53
US	87	88	88	88	81
OECD mean	62	72	66	58	45

Source: Hanushek (2002, Table 1).

Despite what seems to be growing sentiment among laymen that public schools are in trouble, scholars have been cautious about drawing strong conclusions as regards trends in performance. As Hanushek (1998) has noted, although U.S. students overall do not perform particularly well compared with students from other countries, they never have – especially on math and science exams. In the past, the U.S. stood out not for the average performance of our students, but for the fraction of our population that was schooled. It should not necessarily be alarming that other countries are catching up to us in this latter dimension (see Table 6). Moreover, it may be naïve to think that the performance of our students, or schools, is merely a function of resources. There is, indeed, at best weak evidence of much of a return in terms of student performance to

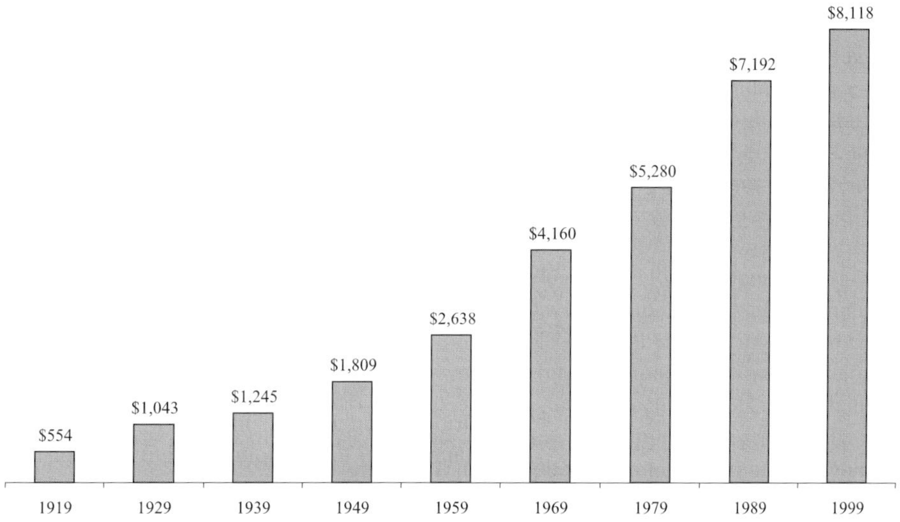

Figure 3. Expenditures per pupil in average daily attendance constant $1998. Source: U.S. Department of Education, NCES (2001).

the steady and large increases in the amount we have invested in primary and secondary schooling. Real per student expenditure on primary and secondary education in the United States has risen from $554 in 1919, to $1,245 in 1939, and to $8,118 in 1990 (see Figure 3). Most of this growth was due to the rising cost of instructional staff (accounting for approximately 40 percent of the expenditure increase), an increase in the intensity of education (with declining pupil-staff ratios), and an increase in the length of the school year. [34]

Although many are reassured by these arguments and numbers, and use them to highlight the possibility that disappointing performance by students may reflect changes in the society rather than a deterioration in the schools, pessimists find grounds for concern about the overall health of the system. They begin with the well-documented absence of a clear link between measured inputs into schools and school performance. In their view, this pattern suggests that there may be gross inefficiency in how resources are being utilized; surely, they contend, we can do better. A second problem is the apparent negative correlation between teacher salaries and teacher quality, coupled with the evidence that the relative wages of high-quality women rose dramatically as their access to more lucrative alternative career paths has widened since the 1960s (see Figure 4). The implication is that the figures indicating increased expenditures on a per pupil basis, because of the increase over time in salaries paid to teachers, may be misleading. The quality of teachers could well have declined, even if their average salary increased,

[34] Hanushek and Rivkin (1997).

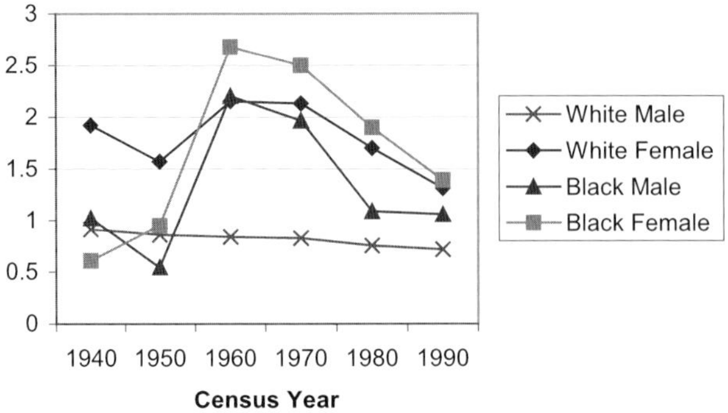

Mean relative earnings over all teacher i's relative to non-teacher college-graduate j's are calculated as $\frac{1}{N_i} \sum_i \frac{y_i}{Y_j}$, where $Y_j \equiv \frac{1}{N_j} \sum_j y_j \mid X_i = X_j$ and X include state of residence, SMSA status, gender, race, education group, and age group. For more details, see discussion in text.

Figure 4. Decline in teacher earnings relative to non-teachers. Source: Bacolod (2003).

as the latter development may have resulted more from technological change in other sectors and the improved labor market opportunities of women, than from the rising productivity or ability of teachers. These changes, along with an increasing presence of unions in the market for teachers, may have had adverse effects on the quality of education in the U.S.

This possibility has been receiving increasing attention from scholars. Flyer and Rosen (1997) discuss the rising costs of elementary and secondary education in the context of the rising value of women's time. They attribute much of the three-fold increase in the direct costs of education to the rising opportunities of women and changing family structure. In a direct examination of changes in teacher quality, Bacolod (2002) focuses on the impact of changing professional opportunities for women on teacher supply and quality. In 1940, 23 percent of women aged 21–30 with at least 2 years of college went into teaching. By 1980, this fraction had dropped to 15 percent, and by 1990 was down to 6 percent. At the same time, the quality of teachers was declining. Among the cohort of women born in 1941–45 who ultimately went into teaching, 41 percent scored about the 80th percentile in IQ and only 8 percent were below the 20th percentile. In sharp contrast, by the cohort born in 1963–64, the fraction above the 80th percentile was only 19 percent and the fraction below the 20th percentile had increased to 19 percent. Bacolod attributes these changes to the sensitivity of educated women to pay differentials; as the pay of teachers increases relative to the pay of other professionals, the profession would be able to attract better teachers. In a similar vein, Corcoran, Evans and Schwab (2002) find evidence that the likelihood that a female from the top of her high school class will eventually enter teaching has fallen significantly from 1964 to 1992, from almost 20 percent to under 4 percent.

If it is a pure supply and demand phenomenon, why doesn't the market adjust to maintain the same quality of teachers or attract higher quality individuals into the profession?

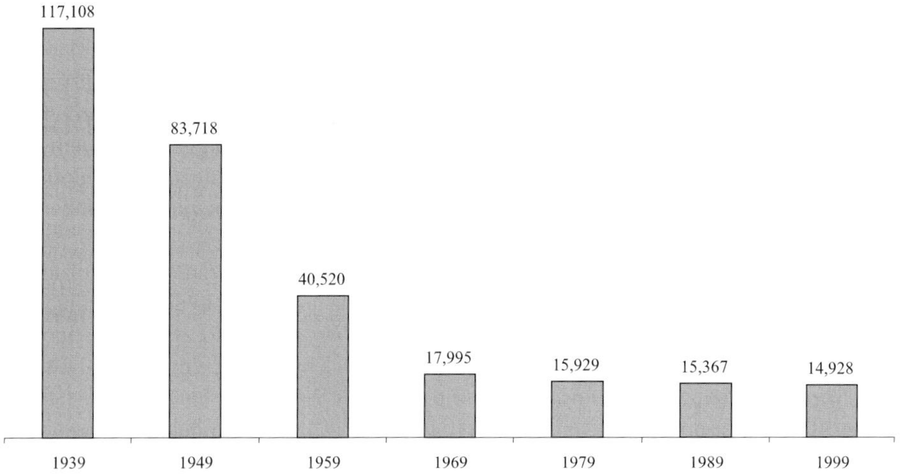

Figure 5. Number of regular public school districts. Source: NCES (1995).

One possibility is that perhaps because of collective action problems, governments are notoriously bad about adjusting the wages of public workers to adjust for inflation and other developments that affect labor markets. Another explanation for the lack of adjustment is the presence of strong anti-competitive pressures such as teachers' unions in the profession.

5.1. The growth of teachers' unions

According to Murphy (1990), it was the growth of cities and the centralization of public school systems that provided the foundation for teacher unionization. The number of public school districts declined dramatically, from approximately 118,000 different regular public school districts in 1939 to fewer than 20,000 by 1969 (see Figure 5). Even with this consistent and long-run trend toward the centralization of public education, however, there were a number of obstacles for teachers unions to overcome. The first obstacle was the requisite notion that women working as teachers be considered "professionals" in order to be unionized. A second problem had to do with the political ideology of the late 1940s and 1950s; anti-communist sentiment – red-baiting – contributed to an atmosphere of fear that inhibited efforts to unionize workers in such a key sector. And finally, Murphy notes the recurring fiscal crises in education as a last major obstacle to teacher unionization. As a result, it was only in the 1960s that teachers' unions really became much of a presence.

The first teachers' unions actually developed out of teachers' professional associations in a few large central city districts beginning to employ union tactics (such as strikes) in order to be recognized. Indeed, it was just such a circumstance that led to the organization of the American Federation of Teachers (AFT). The AFT then induced

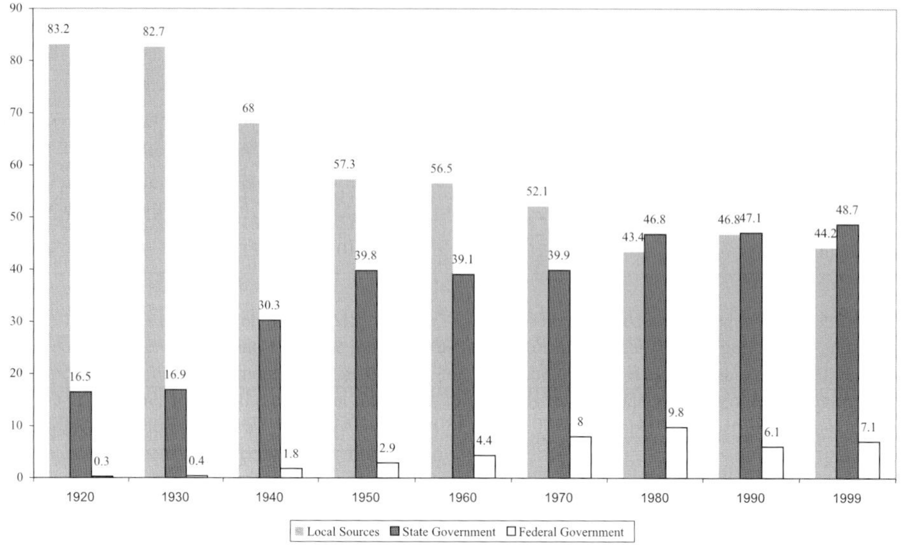

Figure 6. Percentage distribution of revenue receipts for education. Source: NCES (2001).

the National Education Association (NEA) to begin collective bargaining on behalf of teachers. Although the practice spread quickly, with 93 percent of school districts reporting teachers represented by a union as early as 1963, the strength of these organizations varied, and varies, considerably across districts. Hoxby notes that, in 1966, only 8 percent of school districts reported the existence of a collective bargaining agreement between their administration and the teachers' organization, and at least 50 percent of teachers as union members. By 1992, the relative importance of unions had grown, with an increase in the share of school districts having a majority of their teachers in a union to 36 percent (serving approximately 43 percent of the nation's students).

Given the rise of unionization, what has the impact been on teachers and school quality? Although the unions focus on redirecting resources to teachers, their redistributive goals may not be associated with a positive impact on the productivity of teachers or on the performance of students. Hoxby (1996) examines the effect of the growth in unionization by using differences in the introduction of collective bargaining, particularly that when it stems from the passage of state laws facilitating teachers' unionization. She concludes that teachers' unions increase the resources allocated to the school but actually reduce productivity, and this productivity reduction is sufficiently large to have an overall negative effect on student performance.

5.2. School finance reform: Success or failure?

About the same time that teachers' unions were growing in strength, there was a drastic change in the way education was financed. Resources for public schools had traditionally been raised locally, with the dominant share coming from property taxes that went directly to local public schools and other government services. However, in the 1960s, many states reformed their methods of school finance in an effort to equalize per pupil expenditures across districts; funding for schools was no longer so closely tied to local taxes, and what taxpayers contributed were no longer so much directed at local schools and other projects. Figure 6 shows the decline in the percentage of revenues for education raised at the local level. These changes were at least partially driven by changes in thinking encouraged by progressive scholars and lawyer activists, who had become increasingly discontent with the longstanding systems of school finance. Despite the Coleman Report (1966) finding a weak link between expenditures and student outcomes, many found the system of resources for schools coming from local sources to be "unfair." Reformers argued that in allowing children from richer communities to attend better funded schools than their counterparts in poor neighbors, the existing system violated the Fourteenth Amendment to the United States Constitution and denied individuals "equal protection of the law."

However, when the first efforts to persuade the federal government, including the Supreme Court, to attack this problem met with resistance (and the reluctance of the Supreme Court to get involved in questions of state and local finance), the attention of reformers turned to state governments, and state courts in particular. The reformers have been remarkably successful, and since the 1970s, with 19 state funding systems being declared unconstitutional, enormous changes in the way in which schools are financed have been implemented.[35]

In an interesting study of this reform movement, Hoxby (1998) examines whether the school finance reforms to equalize spending across districts that occurred in many states were a response to a genuine failure of the traditional system to provide an equitable allocation of resources for schooling, or whether they are better understood as motivated by changing views about the importance of school finance systems in creating an equitable allocation of resources. Using data from three states, Massachusetts, Illinois, and California, all of which started with local finance through property taxes, and later moved to state government control, Hoxby explores whether the school finance equalization was a response to changes in per-pupil spending inequality, per-pupil valuation inequality, and per-capita income inequality across districts. Large changes prior to the reform might suggest that the traditional system of financing schools was failing, while little to no change would point to the pursuit of new goals or expectations. Her finding of very little change in the extent of inequality in per-pupil spending across districts, and that much of the change in inequality that does occur can be explained by changes in income inequality, suggests that it was not a failing of the existing education finance system that motivated the reform; rather, in her view, the impetus for reform came more

[35] Although many of these decisions were based on interpretation of the "equal protection" clause in state constitutions, others came through the education clauses in state constitutions that require the state to provide a "thorough and efficient" (or similar wording) system of public schools. See Minorini and Sugarman (1999) for more discussion.

from demographic changes, as well as from changes in expectations about the goals of public education.

California was the first state to have its supreme court declare its education finance system unconstitutional. Serrano v. Priest, originally filed by a class of Los Angeles County public school children and their parents, contended that the finance system was unconstitutional because of its reliance on local property taxes for funding. Because of this dependence of funds for schools on local sources, large variations in property wealth led to large variations in school expenditures across districts. The decision has resulted in a substantial equalization across districts in expenditures per pupil, but many observers believe it has also contributed to declining support for public schools in the state. The relative performance of California schools and students has sharply declined in the years since.

The evidence does suggest that school finance equalization efforts did lead to an equalization of spending across districts. In a systematic study comparing school finance reform programs across states, Card and Payne (2002) find that where the school finance system was declared unconstitutional in the 1980s, state governments did respond by allocating relatively more funds to low-income districts; the resulting increase in the relative spending on schools in these districts does seem to have fostered some convergence in spending across richer and poorer districts as well as a narrowing of test score outcomes. The reforms are far from an unmitigated success however. While the school finance equalization schemes do appear to have reduced differences in spending across districts, it is unclear whether they are really raising the bottom districts or pulling down the top. As Hoxby (1998) argues, these policies might reasonably be considered a tax on district's spending on public schools, and could well encourage parents to turn to private schools to provide education for their children. Moreover, while spending may have been equalized, there appears to have been no commensurate improvement in the performance of students from poorer districts.[36]

5.3. *Population heterogeneity and support for public schools*

As we have discussed, the history of schooling in the United States is largely one of a well-supported and innovative public sector. Such a positive outcome was neither natural nor due to serendipity. Rather, the outcome was primarily due to a population that was unusually (from a world perspective) favorably disposed toward bearing the tax burdens required to support strong education institutions. Americans were likely amenable to these arrangements for schooling their children because they enjoyed comfortable living standards, expected further material progress through economic growth,

[36] This pattern, which seems to hold for California and elsewhere, may perhaps not be surprising. Some would argue that spending equality across groups is insufficient for dealing with the problems that afflict certain disadvantaged segments of the population. Duncombe and Yinger (1997) cite inequality of costs as an explanation as to why, despite aid formulas implemented to improve educational outcomes of those in greatest need, central city school districts are unable to improve their educational outcomes.

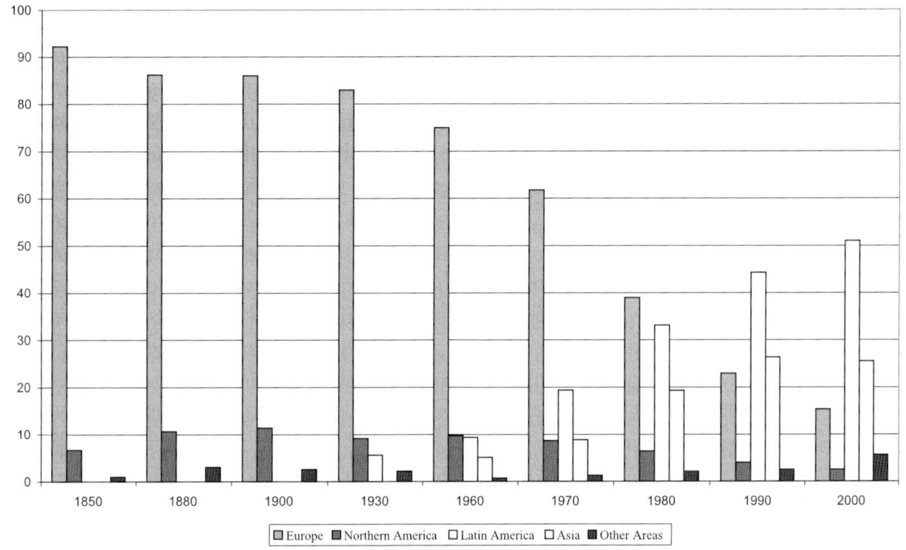

Figure 7. Foreign-born population by region of birth. Source: Census Bureau (2000).

and because a relatively high degree of homogeneity amongst them (and commitment to community) led to reasonably equal sharing of the costs and benefits of such policies. Moreover, local funding and administering of thousands of school districts meant that taxes for schools would be spent close to home, and that there would competition as well as ample scope for adapting school programs to fit local conditions.

Many observers fear that the exceptionally favorable environment for public schooling that has long characterized the United States is under threat. The key concern is, of course, not with whether the level of prosperity in the society is sufficient to sustain the traditional system of offering broad access to a high quality, if somewhat standardized, education. Rather, the chief issue seems to be whether the erosion of social equality and homogeneity, which has long served as the foundation for the public school system, will undercut political and economic support. The challenge seems especially formidable in light of the changes in markets and institutions noted above that have adversely affected the production of high quality education and diminished the degree of local control.

The logic and empirical basis for the concern with the potential consequences of greater population heterogeneity is straightforward. Over the last half-century, there have been dramatic increases in income inequality, in the fraction of households without children, and in the proportion of school-age children (and the population) from ethic and/or racial backgrounds quite different from the historic norm – whites of European descent (see Figures 7, 8 and 9). All of these changes might be expected to exacerbate the collective action problems associated with organizing and funding investments in public and quasi-public goods such as public schools. In addition, the schools are facing increased challenges through recent changes in the percentage of students with difficulty

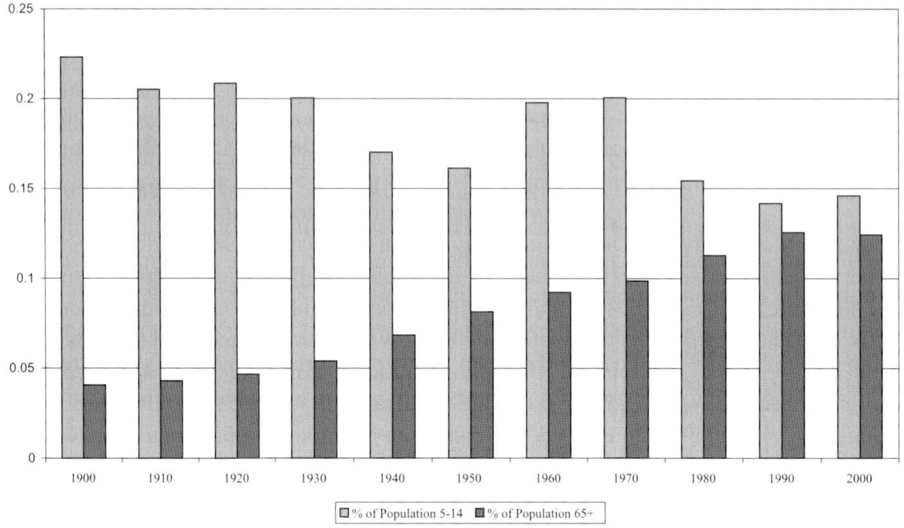

Figure 8. An aging population. Source: Census 2000 Special Reports, Series CNSR-4; Demographic Trends in the 20th Century, 2002.

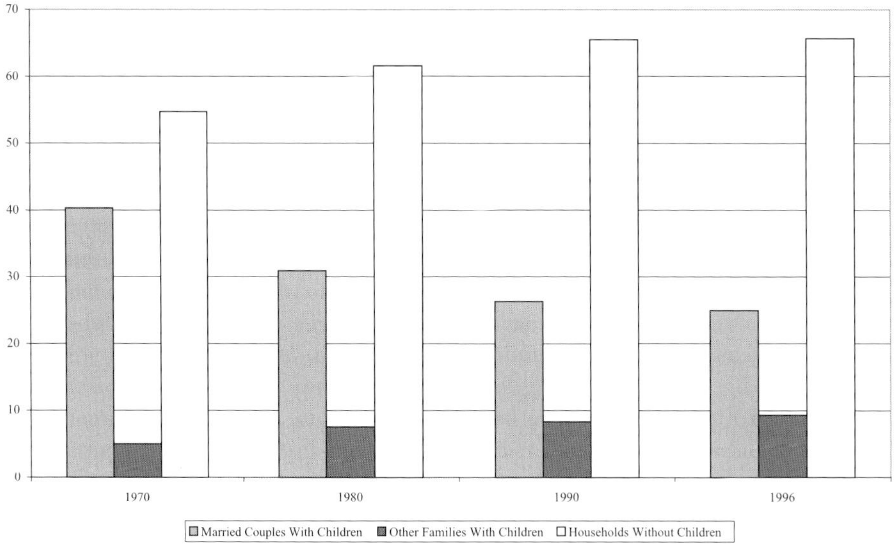

Figure 9. Household composition: 1978–1996. Source: Census Bureau (2002).

speaking English (see Figure 10). As a larger fraction of the nation's income and wealth comes to be concentrated in the hands of high-income and childless households, it may

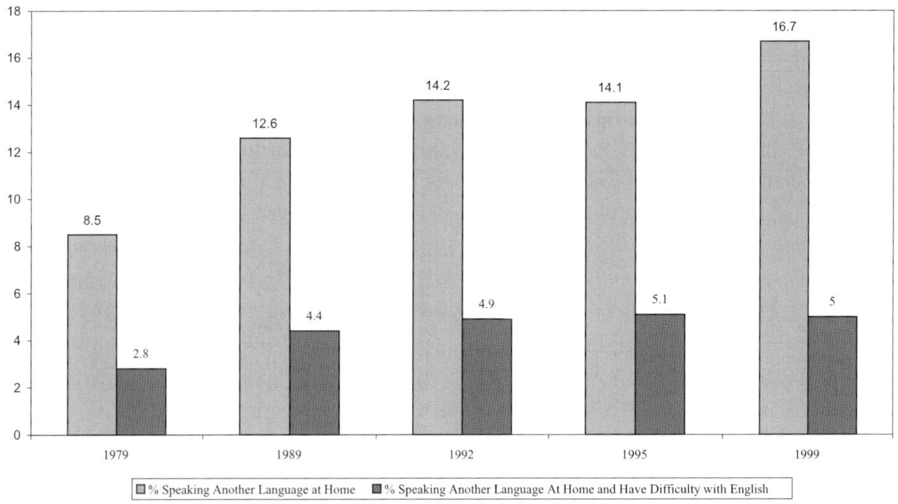

Figure 10. Children who speak a language other than English at home as a percentage of children 5 to 17 years old. Source: Statistical Abstract of the U.S. 2003, Table 217.

not be unreasonable to expect heightened resistance on their part to paying taxes to fund public schools that increasingly serve the children of parents that are poor and/or from very different backgrounds.[37] Thus, some pessimists forecast a decline in the quality of public schools, and a shift toward private schools by parents who value and can afford a better education for their children.

The aggregate data do not provide an obvious case for alarm. As shown in Figure 11, there is no evidence of a major shift toward private schooling. The share of elementary school students enrolled in private schools has been roughly stable, fluctuating between 7 and 11 percent, since the late-19th century. Few attended secondary schools before the advent of the public high school movement, so it is not surprising that more than 30 percent of students so enrolled were at private institutions until late in the 19th century. With the enormous wave of expansion of public high schools during the early 20th century, the share of private schools was reduced to about 7 percent by 1939.

Examinations beyond the aggregate trend do, however, suggest that changes in the composition of the population have effects on private school attendance. Fairlie and Resch (2002) use the National Educational Longitudinal Survey to test for the presence of "white flight" from public schools into private schools in response to minority

[37] Educating the children of immigrants is of course not new to U.S. society. However, it is perhaps worth noting that well-to-do Americans may not only differ from today's immigrants in their ethnic and cultural backgrounds, but also in the type of primary or secondary schooling they want, or is appropriate, for their children. Human capital is more important factor of production, and means for personal advancement, than it was in the past, and thus the appeal and feasibility of common curricula may be less today than they were.

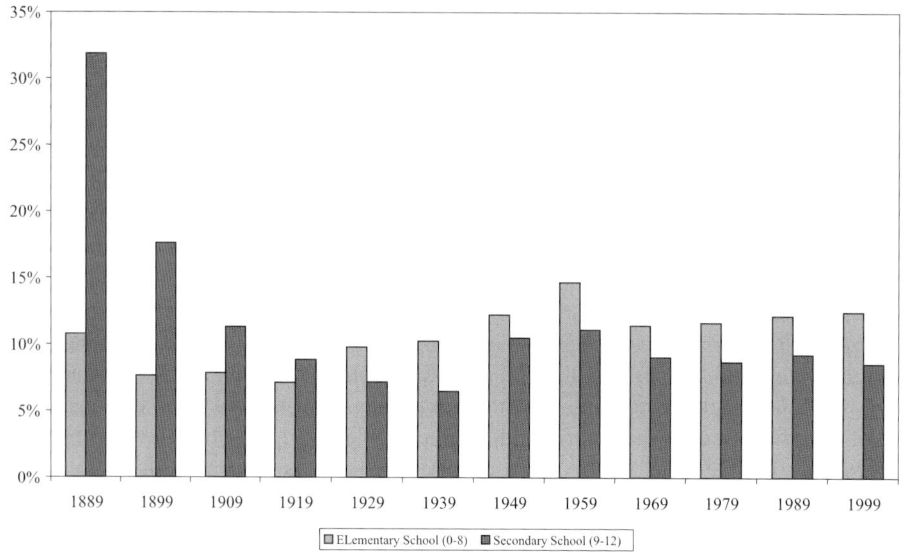

Figure 11. Fraction of enrollment in private schools. Source: NCES (1995).

children; they conclude that families leave schools with higher concentrations of poor minorities. Moreover, in an analysis using 1980 and 1990 census data, Betts and Fairlie (2003) find that immigrants induce native flight among high school students; they estimate that one native student switches to a private school for every four immigrants who arrive in public high schools. Students who leave are predominantly white students, and they seem especially sensitive to non-English speaking immigrants.[38]

Similar implications come from the many studies of the impacts of various desegregation initiatives in the years since Brown v. Board of Education. For example, Clotfelter (1976) explored the doubling of non-Catholic private school enrollment between 1961 and 1971, to get at whether active policies of desegregation affected the demand for private school enrollment by whites.[39] Using data from a sample of U.S. metropolitan areas in 1960 and 1970, along with a sample of counties in Mississippi, he found that

[38] Of course, there is a long history to white Americans of European descent resisting integration of schools, and of discriminating systematically in the funding of schools that serve other groups. See, for example, Margo (1990). For a quite different historical case, see Downes (1996), who looks at variation in the private school share in the early years of California statehood, and concludes that measures of the heterogeneity of school districts, the resultant ability of districts to provide publicly the optimal amount of education for the majority of their residents, and the extent of intergovernmental competition can explain a significant portion of the variation in public and private shares in California counties.

[39] Interestingly, this increase in non-Catholic private school enrollment was accompanied by a significant decline in Catholic private school enrollment (from 5.3 million to 4.0 million) due to a worsening financial crisis among parochial schools.

school desegregation, through its effect on racial composition of students eligible to attend school with whites, increased private school enrollment among whites. However, this effect was only large when the proportion of nonwhites in the school population was large, suggesting the presence of a "tipping" phenomenon.

Evidence that is of perhaps more relevance to the current concerns comes from a study by Betts and Fairlie (2001), who find evidence that in recent years it may be the best students who are leaving the public school system in favor of private schools. Using 1990 census microdata, they document high rates of private school attendance among white natives, white immigrants, and Asian natives, and low rates among black and Hispanic natives and immigrants. Their analysis of the sources of these differentials is handicapped by the omission of religious affiliation, but they report that parental education and family income per capita can explain over 70 percent of the variation in mean private school attendance rates between white natives and all other groups. Those who attend private schools have higher income per capita and parental education.

One of the concerns about the recent changes in the way public schools are financed is that they may stimulate flight from public to private schools by those who especially value education. Attempts to equalize spending and hence public school opportunity could backfire as wealthier individuals, no longer in direct control of financing their local schools, will no longer support the public school system as they shift their children to private schools. In this case, private schools would attract the best students and public school quality would fall, both in terms of spending and average student quality.[40] Although much more work needs to be done, some scholars claim that the evidence does suggest that the move to centralized school finance has led to an increase in the use of private education. Husted and Kenny (2002) examine 159 metropolitan areas in 1970, 1980, and 1990 and find that private school enrollments increase as public spending becomes more equalized. Downes and Schoeman (1998) study what has happened in California, and show that changes in the public provision of schooling that may result from school finance reform can explain a large portion of the growth in the share of students enrolled in private schools.

6. Conclusion

Throughout its history, the United States has been a leader and innovator in schooling institutions. The country was a pioneer in embracing the goal of universal access to primary education, and by the middle of the 19th century, if not before, was recognized as having the most literate population in the world. After centuries of universities functioning primarily as centers reserved for the elite, the state governments of this new republic began to establish public universities, whose programs would not only serve

[40] For further discussion of the general equilibrium theory, see papers by Nechyba (1996) and Epple and Romano (1996).

students from many walks of life, but would also promote the advance and diffusion of technological knowledge and otherwise contribute to the local economy. Later, the U.S. proved just as revolutionary in secondary education. What is perhaps most salient about the overall record is the longstanding commitment to provide broad access to education, but the remarkable creativity and flexibility in developing new approaches to pursuing the goal of how to support and facilitate better use of the progress of knowledge is also extremely impressive. These innovations spread, or are in the process of spreading, across the world. Until rather recently, it has been for other countries to learn from what was being done here, as they sought to improve their own educational institutions.

Given that the United States is so renowned for championing rugged individualism and the efficiency of markets, it may at first seem surprising to note that this country's major innovations in this critical social and economic sphere involve public sector initiatives. Certainly the success of public schooling must be at least partially attributed to the social utility of the state intervening to deal with the difficulty of enforcing debt contracts backed by human capital, and to the positive externalities associated with a better educated and potentially more mobile populace. Among the other important explanatory factors, however, are the decentralized structures employed to finance and administer the public schools, as well as the democratic ethos that has been sustained over time by fundamental political institutions and relative population homogeneity. These features worked together, both in enhancing the flexibility of the education institutions and in ensuring that the political will and resources necessary for their continued vitality would be there. That schools were financed and administered by local or state authorities subject to the judgments of democratic elections did lead to more experimentation overall, as school boards and university regents sought to adapt programs or innovate new ones to better serve their communities. Moreover, that populations understood that their taxes went to support public schools under local (or state) control, and provide benefits they shared with their neighbors, increased their willingness to bear the cost of public provision of education – especially when those neighbors were very much like them in what they wanted from, and would contribute to, the school system.

As the country moves into the 21st century, there are certainly major challenges facing public schools. Changes in the legal environment and in tax structures have weakened the link between taxes paid and the resources available to local schools, and together with the growing social and economic heterogeneity of the population, have sapped the commitment of taxpayers to foot the bill for broad provision of high quality education. A variety of developments, including the expansion of unions and the increased cost of attracting talented teachers, have made management issues all the more daunting. Moreover, the heightened importance of human capital in a global economy poses fundamental questions about the design of curricula, the structures of post-secondary education, and the viability of public provision where the type of schooling demanded is becoming more differentiated. Although the litany of problems is sobering, it must be remembered that similar issues (such as increased population heterogeneity, centralization of finance and administration, and changes in the returns to different types of education) have arisen before, and stimulated very constructive responses by public schools. Will it happen again? Optimists can take heart from the fact that the United States remains a country with vast resources and democratic, flexible institutions. One way or another, it will be fascinating, especially for scholars of long-run economic growth and development, to observe how the society adapts its education institutions yet again to the new conditions of an ever-changing world.

References

Acemoglu, D., Robinson, J.A. (2000). "Why did western Europe extend the franchise?: Democracy, inequality, and growth in historical perspective". Quarterly Journal of Economics 115 (4), 1167–1200.

Albright, S.D. (1942). The American Ballot. American Council on Public Affairs, Washington, DC.

Alesina, A., Baqir, R., Easterly, W. (1999). "Public goods and ethnic divisions". Quarterly Journal of Economics 114 (4), 1243–1284.

Bacolod, M.P. (2002). "A study of teacher supply and quality and school quality: Evidence from the United States and the Philippines". Unpublished Ph.D. dissertation, University of California, Los Angeles.

Bacolod, M.P. (2003). "Do alternative opportunities matter? The role of female labor markets in the decline of teacher supply and teacher quality, 1940–1990". Working Paper 02-03-02, UC Irvine.

Betts, J.R., Fairlie, R.W. (2001). "Explaining ethnic, racial, and immigrant differences in private school attendance". Journal of Urban Economics 50 (1), 26–51.

Betts, J.R., Fairlie, R.W. (2003). "Does immigration induce 'native flight' from public schools into private schools?" Journal of Public Economics 87 (5–6), 987–1012.

Bowles, S., Gintis, H. (1976). Schooling in Capitalist America: Education Reform and the Contradictions of Economic Life. Basic Books, New York.

Card, D., Payne, A.A. (2002). School finance reform, the distribution of school spending, and the distribution of SAT scores. Journal of Public Economic 83 (1), 49–82.

Chadbourne, A.H. (1936). A History of Education in Maine. Science Press, Lancaster, PA.

Clotfelter, C.T. (1976). "School desegregation, 'tipping', and private school enrollment". Journal of Human Resources 11 (1), 28–50.

Copeland, M.A. (1961). Trends in Government Financing. Princeton University Press, Princeton.

Corcoran, S.P., Evans, W.N., Schwab, R.S. (2002). "Changing labor market opportunities for women and the quality of teachers 1957–1992". NBER Working Paper No. 9180.

Cubberley, E.P. (1920). The History of Education. Houghton Mifflin, Boston.

Cubberley, E.P. (1947). Public Education in the United States. Houghton Mifflin, Boston.

Downes, T.A. (1996). "Do differences in heterogeneity and intergovernmental competition help explain variation in the private school share? Evidence from early California statehood". Public Finance Quarterly 24 (3), 291–318.

Downes, T.A., Schoeman, D. (1998). "School finance reform and private school enrollment: Evidence from California". Journal of Urban Economics 43, 418–443.

Du Bois, W.E.B., Dill, A. (1911). The Common School and the Negro American. Atlanta University Press, Atlanta, GA.

Duncombe, W., Yinger, J. (1997). "Why is it so hard to help central city schools?". Journal of Policy Analysis and Management 16 (1), 85–113.

Edelstein, M. (2002). "The production of engineers in New York colleges and universities, 1880–1950: Some new data". Mimeo, Queens College and CUNY.

Engerman, S.L., Haber, S., Sokoloff, K.L. (2000). "Institutions, inequality, and differential paths of growth among new world economies". In: Ménard, C. (Ed.), Institutions, Contracts, and Organizations. Edward Elgar, Cheltenham.

Engerman, S.L., Mariscal, E.V., Sokoloff, K.L. (2002). "The evolution of schooling institutions in the Americas, 1800–1925". Mimeo, University of California, Los Angeles.

Engerman, S.L., Sokoloff, K.L. (2002). "Factor endowments, inequality, and paths of development among new world economies". Economia 3 (2), 41–102.
Engerman, S.L., Sokoloff, K.L. (2005). "The evolution of suffrage institutions in the Americas". Journal of Economic History 65 (4), 891–921.
Epple, D., Romano, R. (1996). "Competition between private and public schools, vouchers, and peer group effects". American Economic Review 88 (1), 33–62.
Fairlie, R.W., Resch, A.M. (2002). "Is there 'white flight' into private schools? Evidence from the national educational longitudinal survey". Review of Economics and Statistics 84 (1), 21–33.
Fishlow, A. (1966). "The common school revival: Fact or fancy". In: Rosovsky, H. (Ed.), Industrialization in Two Systems: Essays in Honor of Alexander Gerschenkron. Wiley, New York.
Flyer, F., Rosen, S. (1997). "The new economics of teachers and education". Journal of Labor Economics 15 (1), S104–S139.
Galenson, D., Pope, C. (2002). "Precedence and wealth: Evidence from nineteenth century Utah". In: Goldin, C., Rockoff, H. (Eds.), Strategic Factors in Nineteenth Century American Economic History: A Volume To Honor Robert W. Fogel. University of Chicago Press, Chicago.
Goldin, C. (2001). "The human capital century and American leadership: Virtues of the past". Journal of Economic History 61 (2), 263–292.
Goldin, C., Katz, L.F. (1999a). "The shaping of higher education: The formative years in the United States, 1890 to 1940". Journal of Economic Perspectives 13 (1), 37–62.
Goldin, C., Katz, L.F. (1999b). "Human capital and social capital: The rise of secondary schooling in America, 1910 to 1940". Journal of Interdisciplinary History 29 (2), 683–723.
Goldin, C., Katz, L.F. (2000). "Education and income in the early twentieth century: Evidence from the prairies". Journal of Economic History 60 (3), 782–818.
Goldin, C., Katz, L.F. (2003). "The 'virtues' of the past: Education in the first hundred years of the new republic". NBER Working Paper 9958.
Hanushek, E.A., Rivkin, S.G. (1997). "Understanding the twentieth-century growth in U.S. school spending". Journal of Human Resources 32 (1), 35–68.
Hanushek, E.A. (1998). "Conclusions and controversies about the effectiveness of school resources". Federal Reserve Bank of New York Economic Policy Review 4 (1), 11–28.
Hanushek, E.A. (2002). "Publicly provided education". In: Auerbach, A.J., Feldstein, M. (Eds.), Handbook of Public Economics, vol. 4. Elsevier Science.
Hoxby, C.M. (1996). "How teachers' unions affect education production". Quarterly Journal of Economics 111 (3), 671–718.
Hoxby, C.M. (1998). "How much does school spending depend on family income? The historical origins of the current school finance dilemma". American Economic Review 88 (2), 309–314.
Husted, T.A., Kenny, L.W. (2002). "The legacy of Serrano: The impact of mandated equal spending on private school enrollment". Southern Economic Journal 68 (3), 566–583.
Kaestle, C.F., Vinovskis, M.A. (1980). Education and Social Change in Nineteenth-Century Massachusetts. Cambridge University Press, New York.
Keyssar, A. (2000). The Right to Vote: The Contested History of Democracy in the United States. New York.
Khan, B.Z., Sokoloff, K.L. (2004). "Institutions and democratic invention in 19th century America". American Economic Review 94 (2), 395–401.
Kousser, J.M. (1974). The Shaping of Southern Politics: Suffrage Restrictions and the Establishment of the One-Party South, 1880–1910. Yale University Press, Basic Books, New Haven.
Margo, R.A. (1990). Race and Schooling in the South, 1880–1950: An Economic History. University of Chicago Press, Chicago.
Minorini, P.A., Sugarman, S.D. (1999). "School finance litigation in the name of educational equity: Its evolution, impact, and future". In: Ladd, H., Chalk, R., Hansen, J. (Eds.), Equity and Adequacy in Education Finance. National Academy Press, Washington, DC.
Mitchell, B.R. (1992). International Historical Statistics: Europe 1750–1988. Stockton Press, New York.
Mitchell, B.R. (1993). International Historical Statistics: The Americas 1750–1988. Stockton Press, New York.

Murphy, M. (1990). Blackboard Unions: The AFT and the NEA, 1900–1980. Cornell University Press, Ithaca and London.
Nechyba, T.J. (1996). "Public school finance in a general equilibrium Tiebout world: Equalization programs, peer effects, and private school vouchers". NBER Working Paper 5642.
Porter, K.H. (1918). A History of Suffrage in the United States. University of Chicago Press, Chicago.
Snyder, T.D. (1993). "120 years of American education: A statistical portrait". U.S. Department of Education, National Center for Education Statistics, Washington, DC.
Soltow, L., Stevens, E. (1981). The Rise of Literacy and the Common School in the United States. University of Chicago Press, Chicago.
Vinovskis, M.A. (1985). The Origins of Public High Schools: A Reexamination of the Beverley High School Controversy. University of Wisconsin Press, Madison.
Vinovskis, M.A. (1995). Education, Society, and Economic Opportunity: A Historical Perspective on Persistent Issues. Yale University Press, New Haven.
Welch, F. (1973). "Education and racial discrimination". In: Ashenfelter, O., Rees, A. (Eds.), Discrimination in Labor Markets. Princeton University Press, Princeton.

Chapter 3

HISTORICAL PERSPECTIVES ON RACIAL DIFFERENCES IN SCHOOLING IN THE UNITED STATES

WILLIAM J. COLLINS

Department of Economics, Vanderbilt University, Nashville, TN 37235
e-mail: william.collins@vanderbilt.edu

ROBERT A. MARGO

Department of Economics, Boston University, Boston, MA 02215
e-mail: margora@bu.edu

Contents

Handbook of the Economics of Education, Volume 1
Edited by Eric A. Hanushek and Finis Welch
© *2006 Elsevier B.V. All rights reserved*
DOI: 10.1016/S1574-0692(06)01003-8

Abstract

In this chapter we present an overview of the history of racial differences in schooling in the United States. We present basic data on literacy, school attendance, educational attainment, various measures of school quality, and the returns to schooling. Then, in the context of a simple model of schooling attainment, we interpret the fundamental trends in an "analytic narrative" that illuminates change over time. Although some of the data presented in the tables carry the story to the late twentieth century, the evidence and narrative we develop focus on the period before 1954, the year of the U.S. Supreme Court's decision in *Brown v. Board of Education of Topeka*.

A theme of convergence is central to the narrative. Slaves were typically forbidden to learn how to read and write, and others were typically forbidden to teach them. Just after the Civil War, more than 80 percent of African Americans over the age of nine were illiterate (compared to 12 percent of whites). After Emancipation, black children continued to face many obstacles in acquiring education. In addition to their relative poverty and their parents' relatively low levels of literacy (on average), society and its educational institutions were overtly racist. The negative implications for black children's schooling were significant and lasted well into the twentieth century. Nonetheless, successive generations of black children did manage to narrow the racial gap in schooling and educational attainment. By 1930, only 12 percent of African Americans were illiterate – finally attaining the level that whites had registered 60 years earlier. The pace of change was not constant, however, and there were some periods of short-run divergence between blacks and whites in educational attainment. The long-term process of convergence, moreover, has yet to fully run its course, and the remaining racial gaps in schooling have proven quite stubborn to eliminate.

Keywords

slavery, literacy, education, Brown v. Board, discrimination

JEL classification: R0, N92, J15

1. Introduction

In this chapter we present an overview of the history of racial differences in schooling in the United States. We present basic data on literacy, school attendance, educational attainment, various measures of school quality, and the labor market returns to schooling. Then, in the context of a simple model of schooling attainment, we develop an "analytic narrative" that discusses the history of racial disparities in schooling. Although some of the data presented in the tables carry the story to the late twentieth century, the evidence and the narrative focus on the period before 1954, the year of the U.S. Supreme Court's landmark decision in *Brown v. Board of Education of Topeka*.[1]

Our focus on racial disparities in educational outcomes can be motivated by the standard human capital earnings function.[2] Written in semi-log form, this function is

$$\mathrm{Ln}\, Y = a + bS + e, \tag{1}$$

where Y represents earnings, S represents years of schooling, a and b are coefficients, and e is a random error term with a zero mean. Let W stand for whites and AA for African Americans. It is well known [see Oaxaca (1973)] that at the sample means,

$$\mathrm{Ln}\, Y_{\mathrm{W}} - \mathrm{Ln}\, Y_{\mathrm{AA}} = b_{\mathrm{W}}(S_{\mathrm{W}} - S_{\mathrm{AA}}) + S_{\mathrm{AA}}(b_{\mathrm{W}} - b_{\mathrm{AA}}). \tag{2}$$

The first term on the right-hand side of Equation (2), $b_{\mathrm{W}}(S_{\mathrm{W}} - S_{\mathrm{AA}})$, is the portion of the racial difference in log earnings that is accounted for by racial differences in schooling. The second term, $S_{\mathrm{AA}}(b_{\mathrm{W}} - b_{\mathrm{AA}})$, is the portion of racial difference in log earnings that is accounted for by racial differences in the b's, the schooling coefficients. Differences in the schooling coefficients may exist because of racial differences in the quality of schooling, racial discrimination in the labor market, or several other plausible factors. This "decomposition" of the mean racial difference in log earnings is not unique (in the sense that the average gap can be partitioned differently), and the phrase "accounted for" in the previous sentences cannot be interpreted in strictly causal or "counterfactual" terms without additional assumptions. Nonetheless, Equation (2) helps motivate economists' study of racial differences in educational attainment because such differences, quantitatively speaking, have accounted for significant portions of mean racial differences in earnings and other economic outcomes in the United States, past and present.

A theme of convergence is central to our narrative of the historical evolution of racial differences in schooling. After the Civil War and emancipation, conditions inherited

[1] The *Brown* decision concluded that "Separate educational facilities are inherently unequal. Therefore, we hold that the plaintiffs ... are, by reason of the segregation complained of, deprived of the equal protection of the laws guaranteed by the Fourteenth Amendment" [quoted in Kluger (1976, p. 782)]. Nonetheless, strict racial segregation in southern schools persisted well into the 1960s.

[2] For reasons of space and cohesion, this chapter focuses on the history of black and white trends in schooling outcomes, but nearly all of the methods and many of the data sources we cite could be used to document other groups' schooling outcomes, including those for Asians, Native Americans, and Hispanics.

from slavery were such that black children faced many obstacles in acquiring education. In addition to their relative poverty and their parents' relatively low levels of literacy (on average), society and its educational institutions were overtly racist. The negative implications for black children's schooling were significant and lasted well into the twentieth century. Nonetheless, successive generations of black children did manage to narrow the racial gap in schooling and educational attainment. The pace of convergence was not constant, however, and it appears that there were periods of divergence and stagnation. The long-term process of convergence, moreover, has yet to fully run its course, and the remaining racial gap in schooling has proven quite stubborn to eliminate [see Neal (2006) in this volume].

Although our focus is on the United States, many of the same issues arise in other "New World" economies where the "Peculiar Institution" of African slavery once thrived. More generally, economic differences between ethnic or racial groups may be partly inherited from the distant past, in the sense that past institutions shaped "initial conditions" adversely (from the perspective of one group relative to another). Given those initial conditions, convergence may be protracted for a variety of reasons. In all such cases, economists may clarify historical and current social issues by delineating the relevant institutions; measuring, when possible, the determinants of levels and disparities in outcomes; and developing models to explain the pace (or lack) of inter-group convergence.

2. Basic statistics

The decennial federal censuses are a basic source of information on the schooling of Americans. Since 1850, every census has included at least one question pertaining to school attendance and at least one question pertaining to educational attainment. Before the Civil War, however, these questions were asked only of the free population.

Until 1940, the sole question on educational attainment pertained to self-reported literacy (see discussion below). The 1940 census was the first to measure educational attainment by "highest grade completed", and this information has been collected ever since, but with a substantial revision in coding starting in the 1990 census. It is commonplace to equate highest grade completed with "years of schooling", although the two concepts are distinct. "Highest grade completed" refers to the completion of a given body of work – a grade – whereas a "year of schooling" means a period of time spent in school – a school year. Today, elementary and secondary schooling is structured such that a student making acceptable progress can complete a grade in a single school year, and a single school year is (generally) 180 days in length. Thus, if a student completes one grade for each year of age, she will complete elementary school eight years (eight grades) after entering the first grade. Four years later, she will have graduated from high school (the twelfth grade).

Historically, there was a much looser association between age and grade, particularly in the South. Indeed, prior to World War One, many Southern schools, particularly schools attended by blacks, were not "graded" *per se*. See Margo (1986a, 1986b) for an analysis of the implications of this phenomenon for interpreting historical trends in years of schooling.

2.1. Literacy

From 1850 to 1930 the census inquired about "literacy" – specifically, whether an individual could read and write. These questions could be answered in the affirmative if they were true in any language, not just English. In view of the high rates of immigration, however, several of the pre-1940 censuses also asked about English language skills if the person was foreign born. It is important to note that the literacy questions were never asked of everyone, but only of individuals who had reached a certain minimum age: 20 years of age before the Civil War, and 10 years of age afterwards.

Census data on literacy are difficult to interpret for several reasons. First, the data were self-reported. Census enumerators did not routinely give objective tests to determine if a respondent was telling the truth, or to determine precisely the level of a person's reading and writing skills. Thus, it is entirely possible that a census respondent in one household might consider a particular individual to be "literate" whereas an individual with exactly the same level of literacy in a second household might be deemed "illiterate" by that household's respondent. Second, even if literacy were defined in the same way by every respondent, a "0–1" indicator, by its very nature, cannot capture the complexity of reading and writing skills.[3] The census might have deemed someone "literate" when that person was able write her name but little else, and so the threshold of competence was quite low.

Two data sources can shed some light on the relationship between literacy and time spent in school. The first is from a survey of white women and children working in North Carolina manufacturing in the early twentieth century.[4] Individuals in the survey reported the total number of months they had spent in school and whether they could read or write. A cross-tab of literacy by months attended suggests a structural break around eighteen months of schooling. Given the average length of the school year over the period of time that persons in the survey would have attended school (roughly six months), this suggests that three "years of schooling" were sufficient to achieve basic literacy skills.

A second survey of adults, conducted by the census just after World War Two, asked about highest grade completed and literacy status [U.S. Bureau of the Census (1948)].

[3] The 1870 census enumerator instructions for the literacy question are interesting in this regard: "It will not do to assume that, because a person can read, he can, therefore, write. The inquiries contained in columns 16 and 17 must be made separately. Very many persons who will claim to be able to read, though they really do so in the most defective manner, will frankly admit that they can not write" (from documentation on IPUMS website: www.ipums.umn.edu).

[4] See Goldin (1990). The discussion in the text derives from Goldin's unpublished work with the North Carolina survey (personal communication).

According to this survey, illiteracy was close to universal (88 percent) among persons with no schooling whatsoever. Among persons who had completed only the first grade, 82 percent were deemed illiterate. Illiteracy fell sharply, however, with completion of the second and third grades.

Judging from this evidence, an "illiterate" person was highly likely to be someone who had attended school for a very short time or who had never attended school.[5] Consequently, while illiteracy is a (fairly) accurate indicator of the absence of formal schooling, literacy *per se* provides no information other than that years of formal schooling probably exceeded the minimal threshold of exposure necessary to be deemed "literate".[6] Many white sub-populations in the United States achieved this minimal level of exposure to formal schooling by the middle of the nineteenth century. For these sub-populations, levels and trends in census literacy yield minimal insights about trends in educational attainment. However, for African Americans, changes over time in illiteracy provide very useful evidence because their illiteracy rates were very high in the immediate aftermath of the Civil War.

Table 1 shows illiteracy rates for African Americans for various census years over the interval 1870 to 1930, arranged by birth year. For most census years the rates are

Table 1
Illiteracy among African-Americans, by birth cohort, 1870–1930

	1870	1880	1890	1900	1910	1920	1930
Panel A: Everyone, age 10–69							
1800–09	0.850						
1810–19	0.864	0.794					
1820–29	0.845	0.806	–				
1830–39	0.833	0.781	–	0.847			
1840–49	0.812	0.729	–	0.747	0.754		
1850–59	0.764	0.656	–	0.617	0.590	0.613	
1860–69		0.627	–	0.454	0.417	0.422	–
1870–79			–	0.373	0.291	0.294	–
1880–89				0.434	0.247	0.212	–
1890–99					0.289	0.186	–
1900–09						0.182	–
1910–19							–
All cohorts	0.808	0.689	0.557	0.482	0.336	0.242	0.146
Observations	66,240	43,711	full count	30,978	28,337	77,770	full count

(*Continued on next page*)

[5] A child might become literate without having gone to school if there were literate individuals (for example, the parents) in the household willing and capable to teach the child to read and write. Further, some children become literate prior to attending school on a formal basis. In such cases, an association between literacy and school attendance would not be causal. However, for the post-bellum period and, for much of this century, we believe that the association is causal for African-Americans.

[6] We say "probably" because some individuals learned to read and write at home, never having attended a regular school.

Table 1
(*Continued*)

	1870	1880	1890	1900	1910	1920	1930
Panel B: Southern born							
1800–09	0.873						
1810–19	0.884	0.812					
1820–29	0.868	0.827	–				
1830–39	0.864	0.806	–	0.866			
1840–49	0.842	0.758	–	0.776	0.773		
1850–59	0.795	0.684	–	0.640	0.609	0.638	
1860–69		0.658	–	0.480	0.442	0.447	–
1870–79			–	0.393	0.307	0.315	–
1880–89				0.460	0.264	0.229	–
1890–99					0.308	0.199	–
1900–09						0.194	–
1910–19							–
All cohorts	0.837	0.717	–	0.507	0.355	0.258	–
Observations	61,769	40,620	–	28,782	26,117	71,121	–
Panel C: Non-southern born							
1800–09	0.408						
1810–19	0.409	0.458					
1820–29	0.479	0.440	–				
1830–39	0.420	0.409	–	0.521			
1840–49	0.416	0.367	–	0.316	0.481		
1850–59	0.374	0.319	–	0.316	0.360	0.292	
1860–69		0.234	–	0.160	0.130	0.135	–
1870–79			–	0.100	0.104	0.082	–
1880–89				0.078	0.057	0.051	–
1890–99					0.035	0.050	–
1900–09						0.026	–
1910–19							–
All cohorts	0.408	0.317	–	0.157	0.109	0.064	–
Observations	4,452	3,085	–	2,178	2,137	6,344	–

Notes: Samples include persons from age 10 to 69. Those who cannot write are counted as illiterate, regardless of ability to read [following census convention according to U.S. Department of Commerce (1975, p. 365)]. Those with birthplace code "U.S., not specified" are not included in the "Southern Born" versus "Non-Southern Born" tabulations. The census inquires about age, but generally not about year of birth; therefore, the birth cohorts listed above are not precise. For example, those aged 60 to 69 at the time of the 1870 census are assigned to the 1800–1809 birth cohort, but some 60 year-olds would have been born in 1810. Given the age categories available in the published census volumes, the 1890 and 1930 figures are calculated for persons from age 10 to 64 (rather than age 10 to 69).

Sources: 1870, 1880, 1900, 1910, and 1920 figures are calculated using the IPUMS census data [Ruggles et al. (1997)]. The figures for 1890 and 1930 are calculated using the published census volumes.

based on samples drawn from the Integrated Public Use Microdata Series [IPUMS, Ruggles et al. (1997)]. Unfortunately, IPUMS samples do not exist for 1890 or (at the time of our writing) for 1930. For the entire United States, reported in panel A, we have included figures from the 1890 and 1930 published census volumes. Birth cohorts are grouped into ten-year intervals (for example, 1840–49). Reading down a column gives the illiteracy rates by birth cohort in a given census year. Reading across a row shows how the rate in a particular birth cohort evolved over time. The figures in panel A are nationally representative samples, whereas those in panels B and C pertain to southern-born and non-southern-born blacks respectively. Table 2 reports similar computations for all whites, and Table 3 shows racial differences (black – white) in illiteracy rates. The foreign born are included in these tables, and their inclusion tends to raise slightly the illiteracy figures for whites. Readers are referred to Table A1 for more detail.

The pre-Civil War censuses only ascertained the literacy of free blacks. Therefore, the 1870 census is the first to provide nationally representative evidence on the literacy

Table 2
Illiteracy among whites, by birth cohort, 1870–1930

	1870	1880	1890	1900	1910	1920	1930
Panel A: Everyone, age 10–69							
1800–09	0.148						
1810–19	0.144	0.136					
1820–29	0.130	0.124	–				
1830–39	0.114	0.107	–	0.114			
1840–49	0.100	0.092	–	0.090	0.087		
1850–59	0.141	0.083	–	0.077	0.072	0.070	–
1860–69		0.104	–	0.058	0.061	0.059	–
1870–79			–	0.047	0.057	0.054	–
1880–89				0.052	0.052	0.051	–
1890–99					0.033	0.033	–
1900–09						0.017	–
All cohorts	0.125	0.100	0.076	0.063	0.053	0.041	0.024
Observations	248,734	312,690	full count	245,281	245,330	710,213	full count
Panel B: Southern born							
1800–09	0.250						
1810–19	0.253	0.226					
1820–29	0.227	0.204	–				
1830–39	0.203	0.188	–	0.183			
1840–49	0.204	0.177	–	0.158	0.144		
1850–59	0.325	0.177	–	0.148	0.124	0.121	
1860–69		0.267	–	0.107	0.095	0.095	–
1870–79			–	0.088	0.073	0.063	–
1880–89				0.140	0.065	0.050	–
1890–99					0.076	0.038	–
1900–09						0.041	–
All cohorts	0.255	0.211	–	0.126	0.083	0.054	–
Observations	64,598	73,993	–	54,973	55,076	161,753	–

(Continued on next page)

Table 2
(*Continued*)

	1870	1880	1890	1900	1910	1920	1930
Panel C: Non-southern born							
1800–09	0.113						
1810–19	0.109	0.109					
1820–29	0.102	0.101	–				
1830–39	0.089	0.085	–	0.098			
1840–49	0.067	0.068	–	0.073	0.071		
1850–59	0.073	0.051	–	0.058	0.058	0.057	
1860–69		0.049	–	0.047	0.053	0.051	–
1870–79			–	0.034	0.052	0.052	–
1880–89				0.020	0.048	0.051	–
1890–99					0.017	0.032	–
1900–09						0.008	–
All cohorts	0.083	0.066	–	0.044	0.044	0.037	–
Observations	184,071	238,614	–	190,170	189,828	546,536	–

Notes: Samples include persons from age 10 to 69. Those who cannot write are counted as illiterate, regardless of ability to read [following census convention according to U.S. Department of Commerce (1975, p. 365)]. Those with birthplace code "U.S., not specified" are not included in the "Southern Born" versus "Non-Southern Born" tabulations. The census inquires about age, but generally not about year of birth; therefore, the birth cohorts listed above are not precise. For example, those aged 60 to 69 at the time of the 1870 census are assigned to the 1800–1809 birth cohort, but some 60 year-olds would have been born in 1810. Given the age categories available in the published census volumes, the 1890 and 1930 figures are calculated for persons from age 10 to 64 (rather than age 10 to 69).

Sources: 1870, 1880, 1900, 1910, and 1920 figures are calculated using the IPUMS census data [Ruggles et al. (1997)]. The figures for 1890 and 1930 are calculated using the published census volumes.

status of African-Americans. According to the 1870 census, fully 81 percent of African-Americans ages 10 and older were illiterate. Illiteracy rates were far higher among those born in the South than those born elsewhere. The national rate, therefore, was so high in 1870 for two proximate reasons: most southern-born blacks were illiterate, and most blacks in 1870 were southern born.

The illiteracy rate of white Americans in 1870 was only 12.5 percent (for native-born whites, the rate was 11.9 percent; see Table A1). Again, illiteracy among whites was higher in the South, but the regional gap was far smaller, and in addition, the geographic distribution of the white population across regions was far more uniform than that of the black population.

There are three reasons why illiteracy rates might decline as a cohort ages. To the extent that the acquisition of literacy occurs primarily because of school attendance, illiteracy rates will decline as the cohort moves from the first age group (10–19) to the second age group (20–29). Some adults may become literate beyond this age, possibly by attending school at night (or Sunday school) or perhaps with assistance from literate children or other relatives. Other reasons for declining illiteracy rates beyond age 30

Table 3
Racial gap in illiteracy (black – white), by birth cohort, 1870–1930

	1870	1880	1890	1900	1910	1920	1930
Panel A: Everyone, age 10–69							
1800–09	0.702						
1810–19	0.720	0.658					
1820–29	0.715	0.682	–				
1830–39	0.719	0.674	–	0.733			
1840–49	0.712	0.637	–	0.657	0.667		
1850–59	0.623	0.573	–	0.540	0.518	0.543	
1860–69		0.523	–	0.396	0.356	0.363	–
1870–79			–	0.326	0.234	0.240	–
1880–89				0.382	0.195	0.161	–
1890–99					0.256	0.153	–
1900–09						0.165	–
All cohorts	0.683	0.589	0.481	0.419	0.283	0.201	0.122
Panel B: Southern born							
1800–09	0.623						
1810–19	0.631	0.586					
1820–29	0.641	0.623	–				
1830–39	0.661	0.618	–	0.683			
1840–49	0.638	0.581	–	0.618	0.629		
1850–59	0.470	0.507	–	0.492	0.485	0.517	
1860–69		0.391	–	0.373	0.347	0.352	–
1870–79			–	0.305	0.234	0.252	–
1880–89				0.320	0.199	0.179	–
1890–99					0.232	0.161	–
1900–09						0.153	–
All cohorts	0.582	0.506	–	0.381	0.272	0.204	–
Panel C: Non-southern born							
1800–09	0.295						
1810–19	0.300	0.349					
1820–29	0.377	0.339	–				
1830–39	0.331	0.324	–	0.423			
1840–49	0.349	0.299	–	0.243	0.410		
1850–59	0.301	0.268	–	0.258	0.302	0.235	
1860–69		0.185	–	0.113	0.077	0.084	–
1870–79			–	0.066	0.052	0.030	–
1880–89				0.058	0.009	0.000	–
1890–99					0.018	0.018	–
1900–09						0.018	–
All cohorts	0.325	0.251	–	0.113	0.065	0.027	–

Notes and Sources: See notes and sources for Table 1 or 2.

are "educational creep" and mortality bias. Educational creep occurs if illiterate adults claim to be literate, and if they are more prone to do so as they age. Mortality bias occurs if literacy and longevity are positively correlated, in which case illiterate adults are more likely to drop out of the sample as age rises (due to early deaths).

Inspection of Tables 1 and 2 reveals evidence of increasing literacy for relatively young people. For both races, illiteracy rates consistently declined within birth cohorts between the first (10–19 years old) and second (20–29 years old) age groups. However, in most cases, illiteracy rates did not decline much after age 30 as cohorts aged, suggesting that the second and third factors (creep and mortality bias) were of relatively minor importance.

Table 1 reveals that African–American illiteracy rates declined sharply after 1870, and that this decline was driven primarily by the replacement of high-illiteracy older cohorts by low-illiteracy young cohorts. It is clear, moreover, that this replacement effect was not in progress prior to 1870. In that year, there was only a nine percentage point spread between the illiteracy rates of the oldest cohort (85 percent) and the youngest cohort (76 percent). By 1900, the spread between the oldest and youngest cohorts had increased to more than 40 percentage points (85 to 43 percent). Thus, the flow of better-educated African-Americans into the adult population was having a large impact on the overall illiteracy rate.

Both southern-born and non-southern-born blacks achieved lower illiteracy rates after 1870. In absolute terms, the reductions in illiteracy were larger in magnitude for southern-born blacks than for non-southern born blacks, and therefore the gap in illiteracy between the two groups declined. But the process of decline was similar for both groups. High illiteracy, older cohorts were replaced by low illiteracy, younger cohorts.

The conventional interpretation of the downward trend in black illiteracy after 1870 is that it represented a structural break from the past. Prior to the Civil War, the vast majority of blacks were southern born, and, as just noted, the vast majority of southern-born blacks were slaves. Historians have used a variety of evidence to gauge the extent of slave literacy, including the "ex-slave narratives" conducted by the Works Progress Administration in the middle of the 1930s, slave autobiographies from the era, and advertisements for runaway slaves. The best current estimate is that, in the late antebellum period, perhaps 10 percent of slaves were literate, a figure that is consistent with evidence from the post-bellum censuses and from our own discussion of emancipation's "treatment effect" on the trend in literacy among blacks [Cornelius (1991, p. 9), see below].

Wage data for clerks suggest that literate free workers earned a premium before the Civil War [Margo (2000)]. If this were the case, why did so few slaves become literate, particularly if their owners could extract all or part of the return? Although some owners were clearly aware of the economic incentives, most slave owners were extremely wary of literate slaves.[7] Literate slaves could forge passes, and passes were used by

[7] While denial of literacy to slaves has not always been the case in slave societies, it does seem to have been the norm in "New World" slave economies; see Fogel (1989) and Engerman, Haber and Sokoloff (2000).

free blacks to travel throughout the South. Slave owners believed that literate slaves were more likely to be dissatisfied with their lot, and more likely to foment rebellion [Genovese (1976)]. Laws making it a crime to teach a slave to read and write date from the seventeenth century and, according to Genovese (1976), became more restrictive over time.

Nevertheless, as suggested by the estimate mentioned above, some slaves did manage to become literate. Some learned from their masters, particularly children of house servants; others learned (as children) from their white playmates on the plantation. Literate slaves taught others, sometimes with the approval of their masters, but often surreptitiously. The motivation was sometimes economic, particularly among urban slaves whose services were rented out. But for many slaves, the economic returns may have been secondary to the religious returns associated with the ability to read the Bible. Although the fraction of slaves who did attain literacy remained small, sufficient numbers existed to aid in the post-Civil War educational effort [Cornelius (1991, p. 10)].

Unfortunately, none of the post-bellum censuses ascertained the ex-slave status of African Americans. However, pre-war southern birth is likely to be a very good indicator of ex-slave status simply because the vast majority of blacks in the South before 1860 were slaves [see Fogel and Engerman (1974)].[8] The illiteracy rate of southern-born blacks among older age cohorts was very high in 1870. For example, 88 percent of those born between 1810 and 1819 and observed in 1870 were illiterate. For those born a generation later, in the 1840s, the illiteracy rate was 84 percent, a difference of only four percentage points. However, for persons born in the South a generation later still, in the 1870s, the illiteracy rate was 39 percent in 1900 (the first date shown for this cohort in the table). If one treats the difference between the 1810s southern birth cohort and the 1840s southern birth cohort as a measure of the ante-bellum inter-generational trend, and if that trend had simply continued after the Civil War, then the predicted illiteracy rate for the 1870s birth cohorts would be 80 percent. This, of course, is far higher than the actual illiteracy rate we observe.

This simple calculation reinforces the point made above. The post-bellum decline in black illiteracy occurred because low illiteracy younger cohorts replaced high illiteracy older cohorts, and this process was not in place before the Civil War. We can refine the estimate of the "treatment effect" of the War and emancipation on black illiteracy in a two-step procedure that is detailed in Table 4. At the same time, we can generate counterfactual trends for slave and free black literacy rates (separately) based on pre-War trends. First, we estimate aggregate black illiteracy rates in 1850 and 1860 (recall

[8] Sacerdote (2005) provides an extended analysis of the post-bellum convergence in literacy rates between southern and non-southern born blacks. Although southern and non-southern born are not synonymous with "slave" and "free", the difference in practice is likely to be slight. In particular, Sacerdote shows that there was initially (in 1880) a gap in literacy and school attendance between the children of southern and non-southern born blacks, but that this gap declined sufficiently over time that substantial convergence was achieved in essentially two generations. Differencing between southern and non-southern born blacks in this manner is tantamount to factoring out the effects of race, thereby identifying the effects of slavery per se.

Table 4
Emancipation and the trend in black illiteracy in 20–29 age cohort

	1: Estimated free black illiteracy	2: Estimated slave black illiteracy	3: Counterfactual aggregate black illiteracy	4: Aggregate black illiteracy	Col. 4 – Col. 3
1850	0.362[a]	0.910	–	0.845	–
1860	0.291[a]	0.899	–	0.833	–
1870	0.220	0.888	0.821	0.812[a]	−0.009
1880	0.149	0.877	0.809	0.656[a]	−0.153
1890	–	–	–	–	–
1900	0.007	0.855	0.785	0.373[a]	−0.412

Notes: Figures are based on actual observations from census data.
Sources: For 1870, 1880, and 1900, we made calculations using IPUMS [Ruggles et al. (1997)]. We calculated the slave and free proportions of the black population in 1850 and 1860 using U.S. Department of Commerce (1975, p. 18).
[a]Those without asterisks are based on assumptions regarding trends in illiteracy rates. "Free black illiteracy" for 1850 and 1860 is calculated using the IPUMS for those years. The 1850 and 1860 aggregate black illiteracy estimates (for 20-29 year olds) are based on observations for 30–39 or 40–49 year olds in 1870 (column 4). The counterfactual aggregate black illiteracy rate (column 3) is a linear extrapolation of the 1850–1860 trend in aggregate black illiteracy (from column 4). The estimated slave black illiteracy rate for 1850 and 1860 (column 2) is calculated by using the aggregate black rate, the free black rate, and the proportion of blacks who were slaves in each year. The 1870–1900 figures are linear extrapolations of the 1850–1860 trend. There was a slight upward trend in the proportion of blacks who were slaves between 1850 and 1860 (approximately one percentage point), and this trend is implicit in the counterfactual aggregate series. Using fixed weights to average columns 1 and 2, based on the average share of blacks who were slaves in 1850 and 1860, gives similar results.

that the 1850 and 1860 censuses only ascertained literacy of free blacks). Our estimate of aggregate black illiteracy in 1850 (1860) assumes that the rate for 20–29 year olds in 1850 equals the rate for the corresponding cohort of 40–49 year olds (30–39 year olds) in 1870.[9] Although the implied levels of slave illiteracy are close to the figure cited above (of 10 percent), the figures may be biased downward if illiteracy declines within a cohort as the cohort ages (e.g., due to mortality bias or late learning). It turns out that plausible adjustments for "cohort drift" have relatively small effects on our substantive conclusions.[10]

Because we know (from the census) the illiteracy rates of free blacks in 1850 and 1860, as well as the proportion of the overall black population that was enslaved, we

[9] All estimates are made for the age group 20–29 although, in principle, they could be made for any age group.

[10] We can adjust for "cohort drift" in illiteracy by resetting the illiteracy rates for 20–29 year-old slaves in 1850 and 1860 to levels that are higher than those observed in 1870 for 30–39 and 40–49 year olds. We did so by setting a plausible upper bound illiteracy rate at 95 percent for slaves in 1850 and 1860. This makes the estimated "treatment effect" somewhat larger – measuring −0.48 in 1900 rather than −0.40.

can use estimates of the aggregate illiteracy rate in 1850 and 1860 to back out estimates of the slave illiteracy rate in each year. Then, we can use the 1850 to 1860 trends to estimate counterfactual black illiteracy rates for 1870, 1880, and 1900. The counterfactual rates reflect trends for free blacks and slaves "as if" the Civil War and emancipation had not yet occurred and "as if" literacy rates for each group had continued to evolve as between 1850 and 1860. The counterfactual illiteracy rate of free blacks was distinctly downward. In 1850, 36.2 percent of free blacks aged 20–29 were illiterate; the corresponding rate in 1860 was 29.1 percent (computed from the IPUMS samples, see Table 4, column 1). Our estimate of slave illiteracy rates in 1850 and 1860 (in panel A) suggests a very slight pre-war downward trend from a relatively high level (column 2). For extrapolation into the post-1860 period, we assume that the share of blacks who were slaves (again, ages 20–29) was the average share observed in 1850 and 1860 (0.886). The "counterfactual aggregate black illiteracy rate" (column 3) is then a weighted average of the counterfactual rates for free blacks and slaves.

Our estimate of the structural break is the difference between the counterfactual illiteracy rate and the actual illiteracy rate (column 5). As is clear from Table 4, had the Civil War, emancipation, and the subsequent expansion of educational opportunity been delayed, black illiteracy in 1880 and 1900 would have been much higher than it actually was. That is, even though the trend in illiteracy among free blacks before the Civil War was downward, a continuation of that downward trend, by itself, cannot account for the observed time series pattern of aggregate black illiteracy rates because such a small portion of blacks was free. There must have been a structural break in black illiteracy associated with the War, and this break must have been due to a significant, indeed an enormous, decline in illiteracy among former slaves and their offspring.[11] The actual illiteracy rate for black, 20–29 year olds in 1900 is 0.37; the counterfactual rate is 0.78, implying a differential trend of more than 40 percentage points.

Illiteracy rates among African-Americans continued to decline in the late nineteenth and early twentieth centuries, both absolutely and relative to whites. In terms of percentage points, these decreases were steeper among southern-born blacks than non-southern-born blacks. At the time of our writing there was no IPUMS sample for 1930, and the published volumes for that year do not distinguish southern-born from non-southern-born blacks. However, given that aggregate illiteracy fell between 1920 and 1930 by more percentage points (10.9 points) than between 1910 and 1920 (9.3 points), that southern-born blacks constituted the overwhelming share of all blacks in 1920, and that illiteracy among non-southern-born blacks ages 10–19 was already very low in 1920, there is no question that illiteracy among southern-born blacks must have continued to decline in the 1920s. Furthermore, it is clear from the age pattern of educational attainment of southern-born blacks in 1940 that further declines occurred in the 1930s. Even so, the illiteracy rate of southern-born blacks in 1940 exceeded that of

[11] As is apparent from Table 4, the adjustment for cohort drift raises the counterfactual black illiteracy rate after the War, and thus increases the size of the estimated treatment effect.

non-southern-born blacks, as well as that of whites. Remaining gaps aside, it is clear that blacks had made enormous progress by the eve of World War Two in eliminating what was surely one of slavery's worst legacies – an extremely high rate of illiteracy.

Improvements in literacy appear to have had tangible benefits for the freedmen. In particular, after the Civil War, literate blacks achieved higher levels of occupational status and, almost surely, higher rates of wealth accumulation than illiterate counterparts [see below and Smith (1984), Collins and Margo (2001)]. Moreover, because higher living standards encouraged parents to send their children to school, subsequent generations of African Americans benefited directly from the economic gains associated with rising literacy among black parents [Margo (1990)].

2.2. *School attendance*

The federal census has included a question on school attendance since 1850.[12] Prior to 1940, the question on school attendance could be answered in the affirmative if the person had attended at least one day of school during the previous (census) year, obviously a minimal level of compliance. In 1900, additional information was collected on the number of months attended. In 1940, the question was modified to refer to attendance during the month prior to the census week (the last week of March).

Panel A of Table 5 shows school attendance rates by race and region of residence (South and non-South) for ages 5 to 19 from 1870 to 1940.[13] In 1870, approximately half of the white children in this age group had attended school during the census year, but only 9.1 percent of the black children had attended school. Regional breakdowns reveal that black and white attendance rates were considerably lower in the South (7.4 percent for blacks, 31.0 percent for whites) than outside the South (34.4 percent for blacks, 60.1 percent for whites). In both regions, however, the black rate was considerably lower than the white rate.

The history of black school attendance from the end of the Civil War to World War Two is a history of convergence between blacks and whites, and between the South and the rest of the country. The aggregate rate (ages 5 to 19) for blacks more than doubled between 1870 and 1880, and it doubled again between 1880 and 1910. The white attendance rate was also increasing, but not nearly as much as the black attendance rate. Consequently, the racial gap in school attendance that existed just after the Civil War (43

[12] In computing rates of attendance from the census data, the usual practice is to convert non-responses to zeroes (non-attendance), and this is the practice that we follow in Table 5. Margo (1990, Chapter 2) shows that the common practice produces a downward bias in school attendance rates in the case of the 1900 census, although the bias appears to be small.

[13] We do not include a 20–24 category (as we do in Table 6) because the 1910 and 1920 censuses did not inquire about school attendance for those over 21, and the 1900 census inquired about those "of school age" without defining an upper limit. We believe that age 19 is a reasonable cutoff for most of the period covered by Table 5.

Table 5
School attendance rate, by race and region (ages 5 to 19), 1870–1940

	1870	1880	1890	1900	1910	1920	1930	1940
Panel A: By region, ages 5–19								
Black	9.7	22.2	32.9	35.5	46.1	56.7	63.6	67.1
South	7.4	20.5	–	34.4	45.0	55.9	–	64.6
Non-South	34.4	41.6	–	49.0	60.7	64.5	–	78.0
White	52.7	55.6	57.8	57.0	65.5	69.6	74.9	75.0
South	31.0	41.4	–	52.0	61.8	66.1	–	68.4
Non-South	60.1	60.6	–	58.9	67.1	71.1	–	77.9
Panel B: By age cohort								
Black								
5–9	6.5	15.7	24.2	26.3	40.4	54.2	–	66.9
10–14	15.3	36.2	51.7	56.7	68.5	79.1	–	89.0
15–19	7.0	14.4	21.5	23.4	29.2	34.3	–	44.3
White								
5–9	49.8	54.0	53.4	51.7	65.3	71.2	–	74.4
10–14	71.3	77.9	84.6	84.5	91.6	94.0	–	94.1
15–19	33.9	32.3	34.6	34.1	40.1	40.1	–	57.3

Notes and Sources: 1870, 1880, 1900, 1910, 1920, and 1940 figures are calculated using the IPUMS census data, based on the "school" variable [Ruggles et al. (1997)]. Figures for 1890 are calculated using Tables 11 (white) and 17 (black) from Volume 1 of the published Census of Population, in combination with the age categories reported by U.S. Department of Commerce (1975, series A 119–134). 1930 figures are calculated using Table 8, Chapter 12, Volume II of the Census of Population.

percentage points in 1870) declined to 19 percentage points by 1910. Convergence continued for the next thirty years, and by the eve of World War Two, the black attendance rate for 5 to 19 year olds was only eight percentage points behind that of whites.

Panel B of Table 5 provides more detail by age. In any given year, attendance rates followed an inverted-U, peaking between the ages of 10 and 14. Proportionately, the largest increases in black school attendance prior to World War Two occurred in the 5 to 9 age group, with the rate increasing by a factor of ten over the seventy-year period. For the age groups 10 to 14 and 15 to 19, the proportional increase was smaller but still very impressive (a factor of 6). It is also noteworthy that the racial gaps, conditional on age, were decreasing between successive census dates with one notable exception – ages 15–19, between 1920 and 1940 (see below).

By 1940, the racial gap in attendance for 10–14 years olds, the age range at which attendance peaked for both groups, had declined to just 5 percentage points, compared with a 56-point gap in 1870. At younger and older ages, the racial gaps were somewhat larger and, despite the progress since 1870, considerable scope remained for racial convergence in attendance rates at all ages on the eve of World War Two. Further, while the rate of college attendance was still relatively low in 1940, it had begun a secular increase that would accelerate in pace after World War Two.

Table 6
School attendance rates, by race and region (ages 5 to 24), 1940–1990

	1940	1950	1960	1970	1980	1990
Panel A: By region, ages 5–24						
Black	52.4	58.9	69.1	72.5	72.3	73.7
South	50.7	58.7	68.4	71.5	71.1	74.1
Non-South	59.8	59.4	70.3	73.8	73.5	73.3
White	57.9	62.4	72.0	74.1	70.6 [70.7]	74.1 [74.7]
South	53.9	58.7	67.6	69.9	69.1 [69.1]	72.9 [73.1]
Non-South	59.6	64.0	73.8	75.8	71.2 [71.4]	74.7 [75.5]
Panel B: By age cohort						
Black						
5–9	66.9	71.9	80.3	84.7	93.9	89.3
10–14	89.0	93.2	95.0	95.6	97.8	95.6
15–19	44.3	52.9	63.7	73.5	75.6	78.6
20–24	3.4	10.0	10.2	13.4	21.2	27.8
White						
5–9	74.4	76.3	83.8	87.8	94.2 [94.4]	89.1 [89.1]
10–14	94.1	95.7	97.4	97.4	99.0 [99.1]	96.4 [96.5]
15–19	57.3	61.8	70.0	78.7	75.2 [75.9]	80.6 [81.7]
20–24	6.9	14.5	15.1	22.2	23.3 [23.8]	33.5 [34.7]

Notes: The figures in brackets exclude Hispanic whites.
Sources: IPUMS [Ruggles et al. (1997)].

Table 6 shows racial differences in school attendance for ages 5–9, 10–14, 15–19, and 20–24, for the census years 1940 to 1990, based on the IPUMS samples. Detailed analysis of the 1950 data (not shown) reveals that the racial gap in the 5–9 age group was especially pronounced at age 5 and (to a lesser extent) age 6. Black children, on average, started school at a later age than white children, with obvious consequences for "age-in-grade" distributions (discussed below). The attendance gaps at age 5 and 6 began to close after World War Two, but substantial progress was not made until the late 1960s and early 1970s with the widespread expansion of kindergarten programs in the South [Cascio (2003)].

The widening of the racial gap in attendance among 15–19 year olds between 1920 and 1940 (Table 5) primarily reflects increased high school attendance among whites, a trend that had begun earlier in the century [Goldin (1998)]. However, the racial gap at ages 15–19 began to close soon after 1940, and by 1980, this gap was very small. Reflecting growth in college attendance, the gap at ages 20–24 widened between 1950 and 1970, but this gap, like the others, eventually narrowed (after 1970).[14] Racial gaps

[14] See Turner and Bound (2003) on the GI Bill's effect on college attendance for black and white veterans.

in school attendance continue to exist today, but they are vastly smaller at all ages than was true a century ago, or even a half-century ago.

2.3. *Years of schooling*

The census first collected data on educational attainment (the highest grade of schooling completed) at the national level in 1940. These data are reasonably comparable between 1940 and 1980. The 1990 and 2000 census data, however, are not directly comparable to earlier years.

To use the census data to construct a time series, one must choose an age by which schooling was typically completed. Customarily, this age is set at 24, though one could argue that 30 is a more reasonable upper bound. Then, using each decade's census data, one can construct short "contemporaneous" time series for those within a fixed age window. For example, we can use the 1950 census to describe educational attainment for those age 30 to 34, and we can use the 1960 census to describe the same age category, but of course, for a later birth cohort.

Data on educational attainment are not available at the national level prior to 1940. Earlier information does exists for North Dakota and Iowa, but very few blacks resided in these states, and therefore the data are not helpful for the study of racial disparities. Nonetheless, the 1940 federal census can be used to "back-cast" educational attainment by race. The idea is to assume that older persons in 1940 are representative of their respective birth cohorts. This back-cast series can then be combined with the contemporaneous series just described.

Table 7 shows race-specific estimates of educational attainment following this procedure, arranged by five-year birth cohorts, and distinguishing between southern-born and non-southern-born individuals.[15] We begin with the 1880–84 birth cohort and end with the 1950–54 birth cohort (the youngest relevant cohort in 1980). As in the previous tables, the basic long-run pattern in Table 7 is one of racial and (for blacks) regional convergence. However, unlike the previous tables, convergence in educational attainment was not continuous. Indeed, there is evidence of racial divergence at the national level for cohorts born between 1880–84 and 1905–09.

The apparent widening in the racial gap in mean educational attainment for cohorts born between 1880–84 and 1905–09 would be even more striking if we presented estimates for the pre-1880 birth cohorts. It is certainly possible to use the 1940 census to back-cast even further than we have [see Smith (1984)] but, on a priori grounds, it seems less likely that persons older than age 60 in 1940 were representative of their respective birth cohorts than were younger persons because of mortality (or creep) bias. Nonetheless, it is almost certainly true that the trend in racial differences in years of schooling for the pre-1880 birth cohorts was one of convergence. Pre-1880 cohorts in-

[15] An interesting aspect of group disparities in educational attainment that is not reflected in Table 7 is that black women in early twentieth century birth cohorts tend have substantially higher educational attainment than black men (by about 0.5 to 0.75 years). Gender gaps among whites are smaller. However, for cohorts born prior to the Civil War, black female illiteracy rates are much higher than for men [Margo (1990, p. 7)].

Table 7
Mean educational attainment, by race, birth cohort, and region of birth

	White	Black	Difference
Panel A: All states			
1880–84 [1940]	7.79	4.66	3.13
1885–89 [1940]	7.99	4.95	3.04
1890–94 [1940]	8.35	5.37	2.98
1895–99 [1940]	8.83	5.58	3.25
1900–04 [1940]	9.27	5.92	3.35
1905–09 [1940]	9.81	6.36	3.45
1910–14 [1950]	10.23	7.23	3.00
1915–19 [1950]	10.62	7.83	2.79
1920–24 [1960]	11.09 (11.12)	8.73 (8.74)	2.36
1925–29 [1960]	11.25 (11.27)	9.22 (9.23)	2.03
1930–34 [1970]	11.70 (11.74)	10.15 (10.17)	1.55
1935–39 [1970]	11.93 (11.97)	10.54 (10.54)	1.39
1940–44 [1980]	12.67 (12.82)	11.67 (11.74)	1.00
1945–49 [1980]	13.04 (13.19)	12.11 (12.17)	0.93
1950–54 [1980]	12.99 (13.08)	12.21 (12.25)	0.78
Panel B: Southern born			
1880–84	7.48	4.41	3.07
1885–89	7.73	4.68	3.05
1890–94	8.04	5.10	2.94
1895–99	8.29	5.32	2.97
1900–04	8.59	5.65	2.94
1905–09	9.03	6.07	2.96
1910–14	9.30	6.90	2.40
1915–19	9.66	7.52	2.14
1920–24	10.17 (10.19)	8.32 (8.33)	1.85
1925–29	10.43 (10.44)	8.79 (8.80)	1.64
1930–34	10.99 (11.02)	9.89 (9.91)	1.10
1935–39	11.34 (11.36)	10.37 (10.37)	0.97
1940–44	12.19 (12.30)	11.49 (11.55)	0.70
1945–49	12.62 (12.73)	11.95 (12.00)	0.67
1950–54	12.68 (12.75)	12.02 (12.04)	0.66
Panel C: Non-southern born			
1880–84	7.87	6.58	1.29
1885–89	8.06	7.21	0.85
1890–94	8.44	7.48	0.96
1895–99	8.99	7.68	1.31
1900–04	9.49	8.19	1.30
1905–09	10.08	8.79	1.29
1910–14	10.57	9.59	0.98
1915–19	10.96	9.75	1.21
1920–24	11.41 (11.44)	10.16 (10.18)	1.25
1925–29	11.55 (11.58)	10.50 (10.51)	1.05

(*Continued on next page*)

Table 7
(*Continued*)

	White	Black	Difference
1930–34	11.96 (12.00)	10.69 (10.70)	1.27
1935–39	12.15 (12.19)	10.87 (10.88)	1.28
1940–44	12.85 (13.01)	12.12 (12.21)	0.73
1945–49	13.19 (13.35)	12.43 (12.51)	0.76
1950–54	13.10 (13.20)	12.53 (12.58)	0.57

Notes: The figures are based on the IPUMS "higrade" variable. The topcoded level of educational attainment changed over time. In 1940 and 1950, the topcode was for five (or more) years of college; in 1960 and 1970, the topcode was for six (or more) years of college; for 1980, the topcode was for eight (or more) years of college. The figures in parentheses do not make any adjustments for the change in topcode. The figures that are not in parentheses apply a topcode of five years of college for all samples. Southern and non-southern regional designations follow census convention.

Sources: The census years in square brackets (panel A, column 1) denote the IPUMS sample from which the data are drawn for that cohort. Figures for the 1880–84 to 1905–09 cohorts are calculated using the 1940 IPUMS; figures for 1910–14 to 1915–19 are calculated using the 1950 IPUMS; figures for 1920–24 to 1925–29 are calculated using the 1960 IPUMS; 1930–34 to 1935–39 are calculated using the 1970 IPUMS; 1940–44 to 1950–54 are calculated using the 1980 IPUMS.

clude African-Americans who were born under slavery, who (as we saw in preceding tables) had extremely high illiteracy rates. Illiteracy rates began to decline precisely when post-bellum cohorts of African-Americans began to attend school in increasing numbers. As they did, we would expect mean educational attainment for blacks to rise relative to that for whites in the pre-1880 cohorts. In line with this expectation, our back-cast estimate (from the 1940 census) of the racial gap in educational attainment for the 1860–64 birth cohort is 4.24 years (not shown in table), considerably larger than the gap observed for the 1880–84 birth cohort.

When the data are arranged by region of birth (panels B and C) it is apparent that *within* regions, blacks did not lose ground relative to whites as they did in the national aggregates (between 1880–84 and 1905–09 cohorts). The national racial divergence appears to be driven by a relatively large increase in educational attainment among whites in the non-South (by 2.2 grades), a period that encompasses the onset of the "high school movement" in the North [Smith (1986), Goldin and Katz (1998)]. Blacks born outside the South experienced similar gains in years of schooling between these cohorts, so the racial gap in the non-South remain unchanged. In the South, blacks gained 1.66 years of education and whites gained 1.55 years of education for the same cohorts, indicating a slight amount of convergence. But because blacks were overwhelmingly concentrated in the South, while whites were more evenly distributed across regions, the national gap widened.[16]

[16] According to Margo (1986a, 1986b), the back-casting procedure used in Table 7 may understate the extent of racial convergence in years of schooling among southern born men between the 1880–84 and 1905–09

In any case, the data in Table 7 reveal a substantial degree of racial convergence in educational attainment for cohorts born after 1910. For cohorts born before World War Two, racial convergence was driven primarily by improvements among southern-born blacks. Not only did they manage to close the gap in years of schooling between themselves and southern-born whites, they also closed the gap between themselves and non-southern-born blacks and whites. Because the majority of blacks at the time were still southern born, and because their gains were so pronounced, racial convergence occurred at the national level despite some racial divergence among non-southern-born persons over the same period.

For cohorts born after 1940, the racial gap in mean educational attainment narrowed for both the southern-born and the non-southern-born. By 1980, the mean difference was less than a grade of school for persons aged 25–34. Thus, taking the data at face value, the racial gap in educational attainment declined by 75 percent between the 1880–84 and 1950–54 birth cohorts.

Table 8 reports the 10th, 50th, and 90th percentiles of educational attainment by race and birth cohort. Table 7's story of convergence at the means is complemented by the median figures in Table 8. For the earlier cohorts (1880–84 to 1910–14), the median black male attained three or four fewer years of education than the median white male, but by the 1940–44 birth cohort, median education levels were essentially equal (at 12 years). As suggested above, the racial gap at the upper end of the educational distribution proved more stubborn: the gap was four years among the earlier cohorts, and narrowed to about two years for cohorts born in 1940 or later.

It was not until the twentieth-century birth cohorts that southern-born black men at the 10th percentile of the distribution had even a single year of education; and it was not until the 1920–24 birth cohort that southern-born black men at the 10th percentile attained the level of education that southern-born white men at the 10th percentile had attained for the 1880–84 cohort (three years of schooling). In other words, among the

cohorts. During the post-bellum period and, indeed, continuing into the early twentieth century many schools in the South were "ungraded"; that is, there was no sorting of students into grades. Ungraded schools had been common in the North and Midwest in the nineteenth century, as well, but had been all but replaced by graded schools by the end of the century [indeed, much earlier in the Northeast; see Perlmann and Margo (2001)]. Ungraded schools persisted for far longer in the South and were common among schools attended by black children. Census officials in 1940 were aware of this problem, and they instructed enumerators to make their best guess as to the appropriate grade completed if an individual had attended an ungraded school. Under various assumptions, it is possible to use contemporary data on school attendance rates to simulate the time path of a series that measures "years of schooling" in a literal sense. When this series is compared with the back-casted series on educational attainment, it suggests that, when faced with an individual in 1940 who had attended an ungraded school, enumerators simply assumed that educational attainment in terms of grades equaled the literal number of years attended [Margo (1986b)]. The effect is to overstate the educational attainment of southern born blacks, but in a way that was non-neutral with respect to year of birth. Specifically, for blacks born in the South after 1880, the likelihood of attending a graded school was increasing over time, and for such persons the reported census data are more accurate. This non-neutrality makes average years of schooling among southern-born blacks appear to increase more slowly after 1880 than would be the case if a constant definition of a "year of schooling" were used to construct the estimates.

Table 8
Distribution of educational attainment, by race, birth cohort, and region of birth (men)

	White			Black		
	10 percentile	50 percentile	90 percentile	10 percentile	50 percentile	90 percentile
Panel A: All states						
1880–84 [1940]	3	8	12	0	4	8
1885–89 [1940]	3	8	12	0	4	8
1890–94 [1940]	4	8	13	0	5	9
1895–99 [1940]	5	8	13	1	5	9
1900–04 [1940]	5	8	14	1	5	10
1905–09 [1940]	6	9	14	2	6	11
1910–14 [1950]	6	10	15	2	7	12
1915–19 [1950]	7	11	15	3	8	12
1920–24 [1960]	7	12	16	3	8	12
1925–29 [1960]	7	12	16	4	9	13
1930–34 [1970]	8	12	17	5	10	14
1935–39 [1970]	8	12	16	6	11	14
1940–44 [1980]	9	12	18	8	12	16
1945–49 [1980]	10	13	18	9	12	16
1950–54 [1980]	10	12	17	9	12	16
Panel B: Southern born						
1880–84	3	7	12	0	4	8
1885–89	3	7	12	0	4	8
1890–94	3	8	12	0	4	8
1895–99	4	8	12	0	5	9
1900–04	4	8	13	1	5	9
1905–09	4	8	13	2	5	10
1910–14	4	9	14	2	6	12
1915–19	5	9	14	2	7	12
1920–24	5	11	16	3	8	12
1925–29	6	11	16	3	8	12
1930–34	6	12	16	5	10	14
1935–39	7	12	16	6	11	13
1940–44	8	12	17	8	12	15
1945–49	9	12	17	8	12	16
1950–54	9	12	16	9	12	15
Panel C: Non-southern born						
1880–84	3	8	12	2	7	12
1885–89	3	8	12	3	7	12
1890–94	4	8	13	3	8	12
1895–99	5	8	14	4	8	12
1900–04	6	8	14	4	8	12
1905–09	7	10	15	4	8	13
1910–14	7	11	16	5	9	13
1915–19	8	12	16	5	10	14
1920–24	8	12	16	6	10	14

(*Continued on next page*)

Table 8
(*Continued*)

	White			Black		
	10 percentile	50 percentile	90 percentile	10 percentile	50 percentile	90 percentile
1925–29	8	12	16	7	11	14
1930–34	8	12	17	6	11	14
1935–39	9	12	17	8	12	14
1940–44	10	12	18	9	12	16
1945–49	11	13	18	10	12	16
1950–54	11	13	17	10	12	16

Notes: The sample includes men only. The figures are based on the IPUMS "higrade" variable.
The number in square brackets refer to the census year from which the data are taken. Southern and non-southern regions follow census convention.
Source: IPUMS samples [Ruggles et al. (1997)].

southern-born, there was a forty-year racial lag in educational attainment at the bottom end of the educational distribution. Subsequent convergence (post-1920 birth cohort) at the 10th percentile was remarkably fast, even though the level of attainment for whites at that percentile increased markedly (from 5 to 9 years). By the 1950–54 birth cohort, black and white southern-born men at the 10th percentile had the same level of educational attainment. The racial gap in the educational distributions was smaller in the non-South than in the South among the early birth cohorts, but there is some evidence of widening at each percentile between the 1885–69 and 1910–14 cohorts, followed by convergence.

2.4. *Age-in-grade distributions*

An "age-in-grade" distribution shows the age distribution of persons attending school, conditional on their having completed no more than a specified grade. Today, children enrolled in elementary school generally take a single school year to complete a grade. If all children enrolled in the first grade at, say, exactly age 6, and advanced accordingly, then the age-in-grade distribution for those who had completed only first grade would be a spike at age 7. However, some children may enter school at a younger age, and others may enter at an older age. Some children may skip a grade, and others might be held back. In the presence of such deviations, the age-in-grade distribution will not be a spike. Even so, if the probability of a deviation from the norm is low, the variance of age, conditional on grade, should be low as well, and relatively few students should be "over age" for their grade level.

Tables 9 to 11 show age-in-grade distributions for students who have finished (only) grades one, four, or eight in 1940, 1960, and 1980. If children enroll in the first grade by age six or seven, an "over-age" child, conditional on having completed just the first

Table 9
Age distributions for children attending school, by highest grade completed, 1940

Age	Completed 1st grade white	Completed 1st grade black	Completed 4th grade white	Completed 4th grade black	Completed 8th grade white	Completed 8th grade black
Panel A: 1940, All states						
Under 6	3.9	2.1				
6	23.9	18.1				
7	42.7	28.0	0.3	0.4		
8	20.6	21.9	1.7	2.0		
9	5.1	12.2	16.1	8.2		
10	1.8	7.8	38.8	17.1		
11	0.7	3.8	23.5	17.4	0.5	1.2
12	0.4	2.4	10.4	17.3	3.1	3.3
13		1.3	4.6	12.7	16.5	10.3
14		1.1	2.2	10.8	36.6	24.2
15		0.4	0.9	5.6	24.2	20.3
16		0.2	0.4	4.0	10.1	19.6
Over 16				4.5	8.7	19.9
Panel B: 1940, Southern states						
Under 6	1.3	1.6				
6	19.7	16.5				
7	38.8	26.1	0.3	0.4		
8	24.9	22.7	1.5	1.7		
9	8.1	13.1	12.4	5.9		
10	3.8	8.8	30.7	14.1		
11	1.5	4.3	23.8	16.0	0.5	0.9
12	1.0	2.8	14.6	18.4	2.4	3.0
13	0.3	1.4	7.9	14.5	14.9	9.1
14	0.3	1.3	4.7	12.6	31.5	20.8
15		0.5	2.0	6.5	25.9	18.7
16		0.2	1.0	4.7	13.5	21.7
Over 16			1.1	5.2	10.9	24.7
Panel C: 1940, Non-southern states						
Under 6	5.1	5.4				
6	25.8	27.5				
7	44.5	39.4	0.2	0.2		
8	18.6	17.2	1.8	3.7		
9	3.7	6.7	17.8	18.6		
10	0.9	1.7	42.5	30.6		0.2
11	0.3	0.9	23.4	24.1	0.5	1.8
12		0.1	8.5	12.1	3.2	3.8
13		0.5	3.1	4.5	16.9	12.1
14			1.1	2.6	37.9	29.4
15			0.4	1.4	23.8	22.7
16				0.5	9.3	16.6
Over 16					8.2	12.7

Notes: Very small figures (less than 0.2 percent) are not shown, and so the figures do not necessarily sum to exactly 100 within columns. The figures represent the age distribution of students (that is, those who have attended school during the census year) who have completed (only) a particular grade level.
Sources: IPUMS [Ruggles et al. (1997)].

Table 10
Age distributions for children attending school, by highest grade completed, 1960

Age	Completed 1st grade white	Completed 1st grade black	Completed 4th grade white	Completed 4th grade black	Completed 8th grade white	Completed 8th grade black
Panel A: 1960, All states						
Under 6	0.5	1.2				
6	4.7	9.3				
7	55.6	45.0				
8	32.5	29.8	0.3	0.7		
9	4.3	9.5	3.0	5.8		
10	0.9	2.6	53.0	39.2		
11	0.2	0.9	33.7	30.7		0.4
12		0.4	6.7	12.5	0.7	1.7
13			1.9	5.7	4.9	8.1
14			0.5	1.9	50.6	32.3
15			0.3	1.1	31.2	30.6
16			0.2	0.4	7.6	14.5
Over 16			0.5	1.8	4.9	12.4
Panel B: 1960, Southern states						
Under 6	0.5	1.1				
6	4.1	7.9				
7	48.6	40.1				
8	36.3	32.9	0.3	0.6		
9	6.7	11.2	2.3	4.5		
10	1.9	3.5	44.9	35.3		
11	0.6	1.2	36.8	30.6		0.4
12	0.2	0.6	9.5	14.5	0.6	1.3
13			3.6	7.1	4.2	7.2
14			1.1	2.7	42.5	29.6
15			0.5	1.6	34.7	31.2
16			0.2	0.6	10.6	16.0
Over 16			0.7	2.3	7.3	14.4
Panel C: 1960, Non-southern states						
Under 6	0.4	1.3				
6	5.0	11.8				
7	58.4	53.9		0.4		
8	31.1	24.2	0.3	1.0		
9	3.4	6.3	3.3	7.9		
10	0.5	1.0	56.2	45.9		
11		0.2	32.5	30.8		0.5
12			5.5	9.1	0.8	2.4
13			1.1	3.2	5.2	9.8
14			0.2	0.5	53.6	37.2
15				0.3	29.8	29.5
16					6.5	11.6
Over 16					4.0	9.0

Notes: Very small figures (less than 0.2 percent) are not shown, and so the figures do not necessarily sum to exactly 100 within columns. Figures represent the age distribution of students (that is, those who have attended school during the census year) who have completed (only) a particular grade level.

Sources: IPUMS [Ruggles et al. (1997)].

Table 11
Age distributions for children attending school, by highest grade completed, 1980

Age	Completed 1st grade white	Completed 1st grade black	Completed 4th grade white	Completed 4th grade black	Completed 8th grade white	Completed 8th grade black
Panel A: 1980, All states						
Under 6	0.2	0.5				
6	1.9	5.4				
7	47.7	47.6				
8	43.5	38.0	0.2	0.6		
9	5.7	7.2	1.7	4.7		
10	0.5	0.9	49.5	47.7		
11			42.1	36.7		
12			5.6	8.2	0.2	0.3
13			0.6	1.4	1.6	2.9
14				0.3	46.6	39.5
15					41.9	38.4
16					6.8	11.8
Over 16					2.9	7.0
Panel B: 1980, Southern states						
Under 6	0.2	0.5				
6	1.9	4.0				
7	46.5	44.9				
8	43.4	40.3	0.2	0.4		
9	6.9	9.1	1.7	3.9		
10	0.8	0.9	48.2	45.0		
11			41.9	38.4		
12			6.6	9.7	0.2	0.3
13			1.0	1.8	1.4	2.5
14			0.3	0.3	44.2	36.8
15				0.3	41.5	39.2
16					8.9	12.9
Over 16					3.8	8.3
Panel C: 1980, Non-southern states						
Under 6	0.2	0.6				
6	1.9	6.9				
7	48.3	50.6				
8	43.6	35.4		0.7		
9	5.2	5.0	1.6	5.5		
10	0.4	0.8	50.0	50.6		
11			42.3	35.0		
12			5.2	6.5	0.2	0.4
13			0.5	1.1	1.7	3.3
14				0.3	47.6	42.4
15					42.1	37.6
16					5.9	10.7
Over 16					2.5	5.6

Notes: Very small figures (less than 0.2 percent) are not shown, and so the figures do not necessarily sum to exactly 100 within columns. Figures represent the age distribution of students (that is, those who have attended school during the census year) who have completed (only) a particular grade level.
Sources: IPUMS [Ruggles et al. (1997)].

grade, will be age nine or older. At the national level in 1940 (Table 9, panel A), approximately 70 percent of black children in 1940 who were enrolled in school and had completed the first grade were age eight or younger. This percentage was considerably below the corresponding figure for white children (91 percent), indicating that a relatively high proportion of black children (30 percent) were "over-age". In part, this reflects the relatively high proportion of "over-age" children in the South for both whites and blacks (see panel B), combined with the regional concentration of blacks in the South. But even within the South, black children were more likely than whites to be "over-age" in 1940.

The racial gaps in the age-in-grade distributions can be traced to two proximate causes: racial differences in starting age and racial differences in progress through grades. Data on school attendance rates (reviewed above) suggest that the first proximate cause was important: black children at age 5 or 6 were less likely to be enrolled in school than white children. At mid-century, this appears to be due to the concentration of blacks in the South, where 5 and 6 year olds (both white and black) were much less likely to be in school than children elsewhere in the country. The second factor (the rate of progress through grades) cannot be documented directly in the census data. However, if black children simply delayed entry into the first grade until no later than age eight or nine, but otherwise completed the first grade in a single school year, all would have completed the first grade by age ten, but this clearly was not the case in 1940.

Delay in entering in the first grade coupled with slow progress through subsequent grades compounded the extent to which black children were "over age" for their grade at higher levels of educational attainment. Consider the columns for students who had finished fourth grade in Table 9. A child entering the first grade by age seven and progressing normally through the fourth grade would be age 11. Yet, in 1940, approximately 55 percent of black students who had completed at most the fourth grade were age 12 or older, compared to 19 percent of whites. Fully 25 percent of black students were age 14 or older, compared to 5 percent of white children.

Because the 1940 census was the first to collect information on educational attainment, national level evidence cannot be provided prior to 1940. However, data on school enrollments by grade collected by Welch (1973) suggests that the same phenomenon (a relatively high proportion of "over age" southern black students) existed prior to 1940.[17]

By 1960 (documented in Table 10), this phenomenon had been significantly mitigated at every grade level, though not completely eroded. Only about 15 percent of black children who had only finished the first grade were above age eight (compared with 30 percent in 1940), and just 23 percent of those who had only finished fourth grade were above age eleven (compared with 55 percent in 1940).

[17] Welch (1973) points out that, assuming a constant rate of entry in the first grade and all students complete at least the second grade, the ratio of first to second grade enrollment should be one. However, in the South, this ratio typically was well in excess of unity for black children.

Comparing Tables 10 and 11, it appears that racial differences in grade completion continued to narrow between 1960 and 1980, although the gaps were still quantitatively non-trivial and tended to widen with age. Nationally, in 1980, about 8.5 percent of black students who had completed only the first grade were older than eight, compared with 6.7 percent of whites; 10.2 percent of blacks who had completed only fourth grade were older than 11, compared with 6.6 percent of whites.[18] The age distribution's right tail was noticeably fatter among black eighth grade finishers than among whites in both the South and the non-South. Nationally, 18.8 percent of black students who had finished only the eighth grade were 16 or older compared with only 9.7 percent of whites. By 1980, it seems highly likely that racial differences in grade repetition drove the relatively wide racial difference in "over age" eighth-grade completers, as compared with first or fourth grade finishers.

2.5. *The quality of schooling*

By "quality of schooling" we refer to conventionally measured educational inputs like the expenditures per pupil, the teacher–pupil ratio, the length of the school year, and similar indicators. We recognize that contemporary research lacks consensus on whether such measures constitute true indicators of school quality, and that studies of "educational production functions" are fraught with methodological problems. As severe as these problems are with contemporary data, they are worse with historical data. Nevertheless, we believe that examining data on school inputs is useful because the racial gaps are strikingly large – so large that, on *a priori* grounds, it seems that they must have influenced school performance and may have influenced long-run labor market outcomes [see Ashenfelter, Collins and Yoon (2006)].

Modern studies of racial differences in school characteristics are based on samples that identify the race of the student and school-level characteristics. Although archival evidence of this type exists, it has yet to be systematically examined by economic historians. Most studies have been based on the published reports of state superintendents of education, which pertain to public schools. Such reports provide no direct evidence on racial differences unless the data in them are so reported. Typically, the only states that reported information separately by race were states that operated legally segregated schools; that is, states in the South.

Table 12, taken from Margo (1990), provides a representative sample of this evidence [for additional data see Welch (1973), Card and Krueger (1992), and Donohue, Heckman and Todd (2002)]. In 1890, the first year shown, black children in some southern states, such as Alabama, received school resources on a per pupil basis that were in rough equivalence to those received by whites. In other states, such as Florida or Maryland, spending per black pupil was considerably lower than spending per white pupil.

[18] The text figures do not correspond exactly to those in the table because the table omits entries that are very small to conserve space.

Table 12
Racial differences in school quality in the south 1890–1950

	Ca. 1890	Ca. 1910	Ca. 1935	Ca. 1950
Panel A: Black/white ratio of per pupil spending on instruction				
Alabama	0.99	0.31	0.33	0.76
Arkansas	–	0.42	0.45	0.62
Delaware	–	0.75	1.00	0.87
Florida	0.49	0.28	0.41	0.8
Georgia	–	0.29	0.27	0.68
Louisiana	0.50	0.17	0.27	0.62
Maryland	0.65	0.59	0.78	0.95
Mississippi	0.50	0.28	0.23	0.31
North Carolina	1.01	0.54	0.64	0.93
South Carolina	–	0.19	0.28	0.64
Tennessee	–	0.67	0.57	0.69
Texas	–	0.63	0.50	0.83
Virginia	0.69	0.42	0.52	0.88
Panel B: Black/white ratio of average class size				
Alabama	1.27	1.45	1.41	1.14
Arkansas	1.08	1.31	1.29	1.20
Florida	1.55	2.00	1.15	1.09
Louisiana	1.74	1.66	1.62	1.24
Mississippi	1.49	2.11	1.39	1.29
North Carolina	0.92	1.22	0.94	1.10
South Carolina	1.92	1.87	1.34	1.10
Tennessee	0.93	1.11	1.20	1.10
Virginia	1.45	1.30	1.03	1.11
Panel C: White – black difference in days of school in academic year				
Alabama	−5	34	17	−1
Florida	0	21	6	0
Louisiana	−3	78	47	2
Mississippi	−6	10	26	22
North Carolina	−2	11	0	0
South Carolina	–	42	46	6
Virginia	−9	15	5	0

Notes: Per pupil expenditures reflect teachers' salaries per student in average daily attendance in public schools. Class size data are based on average daily attendance relative to the number of teachers. "Days of school" data are based on elementary and secondary public schools. See Margo (1990) for more detailed descriptions of the sources and methods of compilation.
Source: Margo (1990).

Most whites, however, did not live in the South, unlike most blacks, and the South was an educational laggard. A proper national average for 1890 would unquestionably show that, relative to schools attended by the typical white child, the school attended by the typical black child was woefully under-financed.

In an absolute sense, per pupil spending in the black schools was low circa 1890 in part because teacher salaries (black or white) were low in the South. Low teacher salaries in the South partly reflected the poor educational qualifications of Southern teachers [Margo (1984a, 1984b)] and partly reflected the relatively low wages southerners earned in most occupations [Margo (2004)].

Teacher's pay was not the only problem, however. Class sizes were generally larger in the black schools (see panel B), and by 1910, the length of the school year for southern black students was shorter than for southern whites (see panel C).

Between 1890 and 1910, the level of real per pupil spending in southern black schools appears to have been flat on average, with some states declining and others, such as Alabama, rising slightly. Relative to the white schools, however, the trend in expenditures was unmistakably downward. Over the same period, relative class sizes for black students increased, and wide gaps opened in the number of days of school per term. The failure of southern schools to live up to the "equal" part of "separate but equal" was glaring by 1910.

From 1910 to 1935, black children in most southern states experienced increases in the absolute level of real spending per pupil, reflecting rising school terms and teacher salaries, and falling class sizes. In some states these increases were sufficient to raise the black-to-white spending ratio, but in other states, such as Tennessee and Texas, the ratio of spending declined. There is evidence of some racial convergence in these measures of school quality in some states between 1910 and 1935, but the record is mixed and the convergence is not strong.

After 1935, however, racial convergence in rough measures of school quality was strong. Moreover, in general, southern schools were improving relative to non-southern schools over the same period, resulting in a decline in regional disparities in school spending [Goldin and Margo (1992)]. In absolute terms, there was more racial equality in the distribution of school resources within the South, and between the South and the rest of the nation, on the eve of the Supreme Court's historic decision in *Brown v. Board of Education*, than in the previous half-century. Although the convergence of school resources began at least 20 years before the *Brown* decision, the NAACP's legal campaign certainly helped raise teachers' salaries in this period and may have induced southern districts to raise the quality of black schools in an effort to head off a direct legal challenge to school segregation. That is, the rapid improvements in relative quality predate *Brown*, but may have been driven by the threat of a *Brown*-like decision.

2.6. *Desegregation*

The NAACP began a legal campaign against inequities in pubic schooling in the early 1930s [Kluger (1976), Tushnet (1987)], starting with teacher salary and graduate school admissions cases, culminating in the *Brown v. Board* case, and continuing thereafter. In 1956, southern congressmen signed the "Southern Manifesto", denouncing the *Brown* decision as an "unwarranted exercise of power by the Court". They pledged to resist school desegregation by all legal means. A landmark event in the Civil Rights Movement occurred when members of the Army's 101st Airborne Division escorted nine black students into Little Rock's Central High School. A full five years after Little Rock, however, less than one percent of southern black students attended school with whites [Southern Education Reporting Service (1965)]. In a notorious manifestation of "massive resistance", Prince Edward County in Virginia closed its public schools from 1959 to 1964 to forestall racial integration [Murrell (1998)].

Ten years after *Brown*, the Civil Rights Act of 1964, the Elementary and Secondary Education Act of 1965, and a series of federal court orders pushed large-scale desegregation forward in the South [Orfield (1969)]. Desegregation plans were ordered and implemented in cities outside the South as well. Boozer, Krueger and Wolkon (1992) and Ashenfelter, Collins and Yoon (2006) use the National Survey of Black Americans, first taken in 1979–80, to document changes in the prevalence of racially segregated schooling. The portrait of change is very clear. Up to around the 1948 birth cohort, it was rare for southern blacks, particularly those in the Deep South, to have attended school with whites. By the 1953 birth cohort, however, the vast majority of southern blacks had not attended all black high schools. Over the same period, a relatively consistent and low proportion of non-southern black respondents reported attending all black high schools.

Orfield (1983), Welch and Light (1987), Reber (2003) and Clotfelter (2004) describe and analyze trends in the degree of school segregation since the 1960s. A key finding, highlighted by Reber (2003) and Clotfelter (2004), is that, although desegregation plans substantially increased black students' "exposure" to white students, this effect was partially undermined by white migration to areas outside the range of desegregation plans and by white enrollment in private schools.

3. Race and the returns to schooling: Historical evidence

Our model of schooling (presented in Section 4) presumes that the returns to schooling were an important determinant of schooling decisions, and therefore racial differences in the returns would influence racial differences in educational attainment. Our focus here is primarily on the period before World War Two. Racial differences in the returns to schooling since 1940 have been the subject of intensive study by labor economists [see, for example, Smith and Welch (1989), Donohue and Heckman (1991), and Card and Krueger (1992)]. These studies, which are based primarily on earnings data from the census and Current Population Survey, generally find that the returns to schooling were initially lower for blacks than for whites, but that racial differences in the returns converged over time. Some of the timing in the convergence in returns suggests that improvements in the relative quality of schools attended by blacks may have been an important causal factor, but other factors, notably increases in the demand for educated black labor resulting from anti-discrimination legislation, were also important [Card and Krueger (1992), Donohue and Heckman (1991)].

Documenting racial differences in the returns to schooling prior to 1940 is difficult because no large samples containing information on race, earnings, and schooling exist prior to the 1940 census. The pre-1940 censuses do contain race-specific information on occupations, and "occupational status" can be indexed in these data by assigning a numerical score to each occupation. Typically these numerical scores are based on mean or median income in the occupation in a particular year. Smith (1984) is the first paper to examine long-term racial trends in occupational status in this manner. Smith's numerical scores were based on race-specific and occupation-specific average income in the 1970 census. Using these scores and the occupational tables in the published census volumes, he produced estimates of the black–white ratio of occupational status by birth cohort for the census years 1890 to 1980.

Smith's work produced two basic findings. First, in the aggregate, the black–white status ratio for men increased only slightly from 1890 to 1940 but then rose sharply from 1940 to 1980. Second, the ratio was generally constant within cohorts as cohorts aged. It follows that the replacement of low status, older, black cohorts by higher status, younger, black cohorts was an important mechanism behind the long term rise in the aggregate status ratio. Because the same process was at work in narrowing the racial gap in schooling, it is natural to hypothesize that the two convergence trends – schooling and status – are related. Moreover, the slow pace of convergence in occupational status prior to World War Two, according to this conjecture, may be related to the continued wide racial gap in years of schooling for cohorts born in the late nineteenth and early twentieth century, and to the apparent decline in the relative quality of black schools in the South at roughly the same time. A regression of the black–white status ratio on the racial difference (white – black) educational attainment does produce a negative and statistically significant coefficient, implying that convergence in years of schooling and in occupational status were positively correlated. However, the regression is not very robust to minor modifications in the specification, which suggests that an aggregate time-series approach may not be the best way to investigate these issues [Margo (1990)].

Another approach is to use the IPUMS samples to estimate regressions of occupational status. For the pre-1940 censuses these regressions cannot reveal the returns to an additional year of schooling, because data on years of schooling were not reported. But the regressions can gauge the returns to literacy. The IPUMS samples come with a ready-made measure of occupational status based on occupation-specific median income in the 1950 census. The IPUMS measure has been used by other scholars, but for our purposes it suffers from several deficiencies. In particular, it does not use race-specific or sex-specific values, nor does it reflect regional differences in income. In its place, we constructed our own measure of occupational status based on median total income for males reported in the 1960 IPUMS sample, partitioned by occupation, region, and race.[19]

[19] We assign scores based on median total incomes for men in three-digit occupational codes, in four regions (Northeast, Midwest, South, and West), and by two race categories (white and non-white).

Table 13
The returns to literacy, by race and region of residence, 1870–1920

	1870	1880	1900	1910	1920
National					
White	0.160	0.133	0.169	0.171	0.188
	(0.004)	(0.004)	(0.005)	(0.005)	(0.004)
	[8.074]	[8.086]	[8.176]	[8.212]	[8.313]
Black	0.109	0.067	0.119	0.138	0.118
	(0.008)	(0.009)	(0.010)	(0.010)	(0.008)
	[7.007]	[7.089]	[7.135]	[7.138]	[7.318]
South					
White	0.175	0.150	0.202	0.243	0.286
	(0.008)	(0.007)	(0.010)	(0.011)	(0.008)
	[7.655]	[7.656]	[7.736]	[7.789]	[7.972]
Black	0.117	0.066	0.120	0.133	0.113
	(0.008)	(0.009)	(0.011)	(0.011)	(0.008)
	[6.915]	[6.997]	[7.019]	[7.008]	[7.111]
Non-South					
White	0.112	0.085	0.119	0.111	0.118
	(0.005)	(0.005)	(0.006)	(0.006)	(0.004)
	[8.196]	[8.218]	[8.309]	[8.345]	[8.413]
Black	0.057	0.031	0.024	0.039	0.004
	(0.020)	(0.024)	(0.027)	(0.032)	(0.014)
	[7.840]	[7.875]	[8.055]	[8.020]	[8.165]

Notes: Each coefficient in the table is from a separate regression of log occupational status on a quartic in age, region dummies (when multiple regions are included), central city and suburban residence dummies, and dummies for inter-regional and international migrants using samples of male workers. Unpaid family farm workers are excluded. The occupational status index is based on the median total income in 1960 for men by race, region (Northeast, Midwest, South, West), and three-digit occupation cells. Standard errors are in parentheses. Mean values of dependent variable (log occupational status) are in square brackets.
Source: Computed from IPUMS samples [Ruggles et al. (1997)].

We estimate regressions in which the dependent variable is the log of occupational status, and the independent variables are a fourth-order polynomial in age, and dummies for literacy, inter-regional migrants, foreign birth, metropolitan residence (central city and suburb dummies), and region of residence (Midwest, South, and West dummies). We used the 1870, 1880, 1900, 1910, and 1920 IPUMS to estimate separate regressions for blacks and whites, first with national samples, and then separately for the South and non-South.

Table 13 reports the coefficients on the literacy variable. Several features of the results are noteworthy. First, the returns to literacy were positive in the South for both whites and blacks, but the black coefficients are roughly half the size of the white coefficients. The lower returns to literacy among blacks may reflect discrimination in the labor market, although other explanations are possible.[20] Second, among whites, the returns to literacy were considerably higher in the South than outside the region. The regional difference in the returns to literacy is consistent with other evidence showing that the skill premium was higher in the South than in the non-South. Among blacks, the returns to literacy outside the South appear to be relatively small.

Third, the mean values (in square brackets) indicate that there was a large gap in occupational status between the South and non-South, in all years, for both races. This gap reflects differences in the occupational structure, to be sure, but it also reflects the fact that, in the immediate aftermath of the Civil War, wages in the South declined sharply relative to the non-South, and a substantial wage gap remained in place well into the 20th century. The existence of a regional wage gap suggests there were potentially substantial economic gains to migrating from the South in the early twentieth century.[21] Margo (1990) shows that better educated southern blacks (and whites) were more likely to leave the South [also see Vigdor (2002)]. Margo (1990) also specifies and estimates a migration model using 1940 data that allows for unobservable factors to influence both the migration decision and the returns to migration from the South.

4. A model of educational attainment

In this section we sketch a simple model of schooling choice that we use to interpret the historical facts presented in the preceding tables. A household in our model consists of a parent and a child. Parental utility is defined over the household's current consumption (C) and the child's future consumption, which depends on the child's earnings, E, and any transfers from the parent to child, X:[22]

$$U = V(C) + \delta(E + X).$$

The budget constraint is:

$$C + \gamma X = Y + w(T - S).$$

Here, Y is the income of the adult, w is the marginal product of the child, and $\gamma = 1/(1 + r)$. The parent decides how much of the child's time endowment T is to be allocated towards production of the consumption good versus schooling.

[20] For example, the average gap in years of schooling between literate and illiterate whites was larger than the analogous gap between literate and illiterate blacks. This alone could result in a higher measured returns to literacy among whites.

[21] Collins (1997) finds that the prevalence of European migrants in non-southern industrial centers tended to dampen the flow of black migrants out of the South, especially before the arrival of immigration restrictions in the 1920s.

[22] These transfers can be thought of as "savings" in the current period, which are transferred to the child in the future and which the child can then use towards consumption.

We assume that $E = E(S, q, Y)$, where q measures the "quality" of schooling. The first derivatives of the earnings function are positive, second derivatives are negative, and the cross-partials are positive. This specification of the earnings function can be rationalized as follows. Let H represent the child's "human capital", and let $E = E(H)$. Also let $H = H(s, q, Y)$. H, in other words, is an educational production function. The parameter δ is the marginal utility (to the parent) of the child's future consumption. The presumption is that $\delta < 1$; that is, the parent subjectively discounts these earnings relative to current consumption.

The parent maximizes the utility function with respect to S and X. The first-order conditions are:

$$wV' = \delta E_s,$$

$$V' = \delta/\gamma.$$

These two conditions can be combined

$$w = \gamma E_s$$

According to this condition the parent allocates the child's time to equate the marginal cost of schooling (w) to the marginal benefits (γE_s).

Several features of this first-order condition are important to our narrative. First, there will be an interior solution if $\gamma E_s(0) > w$. We think of $E_s(0)$ as the marginal returns to going to school for a minimal amount of time, which is the amount of schooling necessary to just become literate. The idea is that $E_s(0)$ in the past was very high. Unless γ was very close to or equal to zero, a parent would generally desire that the child go to school long enough to become literate. The data at hand do not really us to estimate the marginal returns, but we can estimate the average returns (see below).

Second, the likelihood of an interior solution, and the value of s if s is positive, is decreasing in w, holding other exogenous variables in the model constant. In particular, changes over time that reduced the value of child labor relative to the value of adult labor lead to increases in schooling.

Third, increases in factors complementary to s in the production of E – that is, Y and q in the model – will also increase s under the assumptions of the model. Although Y is defined to be the parent's income in the model, in general Y can be thought of as any "family background" variable that is complementary to s in the production of E. Increases in school quality are also associated with increases in S. Further, it is intuitively clear that we could introduce another argument Z in the E function such that, as long as $E_{sz} > 0$, then $\mathrm{d}S/\mathrm{d}Z > 0$. Positive shifts in Z can be thought of as factors that increase the relative demand for educated labor in general, or educated black labor in particular.

The model treats q as exogenous. We could, however, specify a political process in which black (and other) parents participate and through which q is determined. Changes in the price of q would influence the optimal level of school quality, as would changes in the political process that make it easier or more difficult for a particular population group to influence the outcome (see our discussion of disenfranchisement in the next section).[23]

5. Applying the model: An analytic narrative

Since emancipation, African Americans have significantly increased their schooling levels relative to whites. The data from the 1870 census indicate that school attendance rates of black children were very low and rates of adult illiteracy were very high in the immediate aftermath of the Civil War. However, over the next two decades, black school attendance rates increased substantially, as did literacy, and the process of convergence was underway.

Black children emerged from slavery with essentially no exposure to formal schooling. According to our model, as long as the marginal returns to schooling at the initial level (zero) exceeded the marginal cost, black parents would desire to send their children to school. Several pieces of evidence lead us to contend that the marginal returns to schooling were positive for black children during the early post-bellum period. Wage data indicate a substantial premium for educated, white-collar labor circa 1860 [Margo (2000)]. More on point, a previous section documented that, in 1870 and 1880, literate adult blacks held jobs that, on average, had higher earnings than jobs held by illiterate adult blacks, and that these returns were higher in the South than elsewhere in the country. Further, for blacks born in the South, literacy facilitated migration to the North, where wages were higher than in the South [Margo (1990, 2004), Vigdor (2002)].

The adjustment from the initial disequilibrium could not have taken place immediately, however. Adult blacks emerged from slavery with little in the way of physical wealth and few marketable skills, and they worked in a regional economy where wages were low and capital markets were thin. Factors complementary to the production of human capital – Y and q – were low, if not non-existent, for most black children in the immediate aftermath of the War, and this is reflected in the low rates of black school attendance in 1870.

In fact, the large upward adjustment in schooling would have not have taken place – or rather, would only have taken place with substantial out-migration – had educational expansion not occurred in the South in the 1870s. Some schools for black children were established, often by ex-slaves themselves, in occupied areas of the

[23] The model can also accommodate government intervention that specifies a minimum level of S. At the minimum level of S, the demand for S (the E_S) function becomes horizontal. If this occurs above w, there is no effect on S. If this occurs below the current value of w, parents will increase the level of S. Relevant historical examples of such interventions are child labor and compulsory schooling laws. Margo (1990, Chapter 2) presents some evidence that the passage of compulsory laws raised black attendance rates in the South, but the magnitude of the effect was small.

Confederacy during the War. The effort expanded after the Emancipation Proclamation and the establishment of the Freedmen's Bureau in 1865 [Butchart (1980), Morris (1981)]. White teachers from the North, many of them women, were involved in the initial effort to expand educational opportunities in the South [Jones (1980)]. To an extent that surprised contemporaries, former slaves, many whom were barely literate themselves, also contributed to the effort [Anderson (1988)]. Black teachers from the North also went South to assist. According to one recent estimate, slightly more than 10 percent of the Freedmen's Bureau teachers were black [Butchart (1988)]. However, Reconstruction (1866–1877) was the true the catalyst for the establishment of black schools by state governments in the South. During the Reconstruction period, blacks enjoyed some measure of political clout, and this clout helped secure fundamental civil rights legislation and provisions in state constitutions that guaranteed black access to public schools [see, in particular, Anderson (1987)]. As we described earlier, rates of black school attendance jumped markedly between 1870 and 1880, and it is doubtful this would have happened without the Reconstruction period's institutional changes.

Despite the provision of public schools in the South beginning in the 1870s, the constraints on black educational advance were severe. Although black wealth and incomes had begun to converge slowly on white wealth and incomes [Higgs (1982), Margo (1984a, 1984b), Smith (1984)], black parents were still poor and poorly educated, and their children's schooling suffered for it. The South's emphasis on cotton agriculture was another important factor. The productivity of child labor was relatively high in cotton. As a result, schools in cotton counties (black and white) were open fewer days per year than elsewhere to accommodate seasonal demands for child labor.

Reconstruction ended in 1877. Although blacks continued to vote in some states, their political clout was on the wane. Beginning in the 1880s, the states of the former Confederacy passed legislation and amended state constitutions for the purpose of disenfranchising black voters [Kousser (1974)]. These "legal" measures were supplemented by extra-legal ones, including violence, intimidation, and outright electoral fraud. The disenfranchisement movement was highly effective. In Louisiana, for example, slightly more than fifty percent of the electorate was black in 1890, but by 1910, less than 0.1 percent was black [Margo (1982)].

Disenfranchisement was accompanied by changes in school finance. In the late nineteenth century, prior to disenfranchisement, public schools in the South were often financed solely at the state level, deriving revenue from state-levied property, poll, and other taxes. School funds were typically allocated to counties on the basis of the school-age population. Whites living in heavily black counties resisted efforts to levy local property taxes because they feared that the bulk of these taxes would go to the black schools. After disenfranchisement, white-dominated school boards began using state school funds that had been allocated on the basis of the size of the black population for use in the white schools. As one school superintendent remarked at the time "we use their money ... colored people are mighty profitable to us." Opposition to local taxes abated, and whites in predominantly white counties began levying local property taxes to improve their own schools. The upshot of all these changes was deterioration in the relative (black/white) quality of schools attended by black children in the period between 1890 and 1910 [Bond (1934, 1939), Harlan (1958), Smith (1973), Kousser (1980a), Margo (1982), Pritchett (1985, 1989), Walters, James and McCammon (1997)].

At the federal level, *de jure* segregation received constitutional protection with the Supreme Court's decision in *Plessy v. Ferguson* [Lofgren (1987)]. *Plessy*, however, required that accommodations (including schools) be "equal" if they were legally "separate". Another decision, *Cummins v. Georgia* in 1898, demonstrated just how limited in law this protection really was [Kousser (1980b)]. In *Cummins*, the Supreme Court ruled that, in effect, a Georgia school board was not required under the separate-but-equal doctrine to open up a public high school for black children who wished to attend. If a black child wished to attend high school and happened to grow up in a county without one, then either the child or his family would have to bear the costs of migrating to a place that did have a black high school.

Economic historians have investigated whether violations of the equal part of the separate-but-equal doctrine hampered the educational progress of southern black children. Using child-level data from the 1900 census, Margo (1987) regresses months of school attendance on family attributes and county-level school and labor market characteristics. According to his regressions, equalizing black and white school characteristics at the sample means would have reduced the racial gap in months of school attendance by nearly half. This effect, as large as it is, was dwarfed by the impact of racial differences in family background factors, as measured by occupational status and adult literacy. Moehling (2004) reports similar findings with regard to school characteristics [see also Walters, James and McCammon (1990), Walters and James (1992), and Walters and Briggs (1993), for additional studies of racial differences in school enrollment in the early twentieth century South]. Moehling also shows that the schooling of southern black children in the early twentieth century was hampered by a family background factor not considered by Margo – a higher rate of single parenthood.

Other studies have examined the effects of separate-but-equal on racial differences in literacy rates and test scores. Margo (1986a) studies county-level literacy rates in Alabama from 1920 to 1940. He regresses the literacy rate (for 7 to 20 year olds) on the average daily attendance rate in grades one through six, the length of the school year in days, expenditure per pupil per day, the value of school capital per pupil, and the percentage of one-teacher schools. He also includes two family background variables: per capita income and the percentage of families owning their homes. Random effects estimates suggest that expenditures per pupil per day were significant determinants of literacy rates for both races, but the coefficients from fixed effects specifications are small and statistically insignificant. However, both the random and fixed effects estimates indicate that the length of the school year mattered, both economically and statistically. Margo (1986a) argues that equalizing school-term lengths would have narrowed the racial gap in literacy, especially in 1920 and 1930. For example, the black fixed effects coefficient implies that equalizing school terms would cut the literacy gap by about 4 percentage points (out of a total gap of 20 points) in 1920. By 1940, however, the average length of the black school year was similar to that of the white school year, and county-level variation had narrowed considerably.

Fishback and Baskin (1991) examine child literacy in Georgia in 1910. They model child literacy as a function of current school inputs in the county of residence, measured by the value of school capital per child, expenditures on teacher salaries per pupil per day, and the length of term. Additional explanatory variables include the child's age, gender, race, and labor force status, the household head's literacy, age, and occupational status, and (if the head's spouse is present) spouse's age and literacy. The basic results are similar to Margo's. School inputs have positive coefficients, but only length of term is statistically significant.

Like Margo, Fishback and Baskin include a decomposition analysis of literacy rates. Equalizing all school inputs would narrow the gap in literacy by about 40 percent, about half of which can be attributed to the impact of the length of the school year. Variations in the value of the school capital stock per pupil were unimportant, perhaps because they really were (the interpretation favored by Fishback and Baskin), or perhaps because of measurement error. Also as in Margo (1987), Fishback and Baskin find that family background variables, particularly adult literacy, were critical determinants of children's educational outcomes. Equalizing adult literacy rates of both head and spouse, all else equal, would have cut the literacy gap among children nearly in half. Like Moehling (2004), Fishback and Baskin also find that an absent spouse was associated with lower child literacy.

Orazem (1987) is a unique study of racial differences in test scores in primary schools in Maryland in the 1920s and 1930s.[24] The dependent variable is the "proportion of students taking a nationally standardized test of reading skills who meet or exceed the national norm for the test". The state department of education published the results of the test, by race, at the county level for selected years between 1924 and 1938. Orazem finds that the length of the school year influenced black test scores, controlling for a variety of other school quality characteristics (e.g., teacher certification, students per teacher, value of school buildings per student, and so on) and county fixed effects. Based on the black coefficient estimates, racial disparities in school characteristics could account for about one-third of the racial gap in the dependent variable.

Orazem also studies racial differences in average daily school attendance rates (as a proportion of enrollment). In addition to school characteristics, he controls for local economic characteristics (e.g., salaries in manufacturing and the value of crop production per acre). The results suggest that for blacks, school attendance rates were negatively influenced by class size and the proportion of one-teacher schools, and positively associated with the proportion of state certified teachers. Based on the black coefficient

[24] Data for Baltimore were unavailable.

estimates, Orazem argues that eliminating school quality differentials would have eliminated the racial gap in average daily attendance rates (raising the black rate from 76 to 84 percent of enrollment).

These studies should be viewed cautiously as they are based on relatively crude cross-section data. It is easy to imagine, for example, that unobservable factors, rather than a genuine causal link between school characteristics and school outcomes, are driving the results. Nonetheless, the findings are broadly consistent across the studies, and they suggest that if the equal part of "separate but equal" had been enforced, schooling outcomes for southern black children would have been better than they actually were. Earlier we noted that racial convergence in years of schooling appears to have slowed considerably for cohorts born around the turn of the century. The results of the various studies just reviewed suggest that some portion of the slowdown in convergence may be attributable to the violations of *Plessy*.

While southern school boards appear to have violated the equal part of *Plessy*, for the most part, they did not do so completely; that is, separate-but-equal did not usually mean separate-and-non-existent. To be sure, at higher levels of education, especially those supplied by state governments, the sheer absence of any facilities for blacks was a serious problem. But at the elementary level, most southern black children, it seems, had some access to some sort of public school.

The continued funding of black schools even after disenfranchisement has been called "Myrdal's paradox", after Gunnar Myrdal (1944). Myrdal answered his own question by asserting that southern whites, despite their racism, believed it would be a violation of the "American Creed" if blacks were denied basic access to schooling. The fact that any such violations at the elementary level would have been so obviously unconstitutional surely played a role as well. Another resolution to Myrdal's paradox emphasizes economic motives. Freeman (1973) [see also Harris (1985)] suggested that whites were willing to allocate school funds to blacks if schooling made blacks more productive in the labor market in specific ways – better field hands, better cooks, better seamstresses and servants. So-called "industrial education" was a hallmark of the program for black economic advance advocated by Booker T. Washington. However, at the elementary level, the curriculum in the black schools seems to have emphasized more basic skills – literacy, mathematics, and so on – than purely "industrial" skills.

Margo (1991) presents a game-theoretic model of a local government in which the dominant group (whites) supplies a local public good to a minority group (blacks). The local public good is funded by the imposition of a lump sum tax on the minority group. The majority group derives income from capital that it combines with the labor of the minority group. The minority group, however, is partially mobile across jurisdictions. In equilibrium, the local government may have some monopoly power and therefore will tax the minority in excess of the value of any local public service provided to the minority. However, unless the minority group is completely immobile, some amount of the public good will be provided to the minority group. Margo (1991) provides some qualitative and econometric evidence that whites were, indeed, aware of the constraints that black geographic mobility placed on their ability to discrimination in the supply of local public goods, such as schools.

An important corollary of Margo's argument is that increased black demand for better schools could not be totally ignored by local school boards. Even if blacks were unable to vote at the ballot box, they could, and did, vote with their feet. Nonetheless, it seems doubtful that the Tiebout-like incentives emphasized by Margo were the sole factor explaining increases in black school quality that took place prior to *Brown* and voting rights legislation in the 1960s. Private philanthropy played an important role in improving the quality of black schools in the South. Numerous private organizations were involved in providing philanthropic monies; examples include the Peabody Fund, the Jeanes Fund, and, especially, the Rosenwald Foundation. Philanthropic dollars were especially important in the initial establishment of institutions of higher learning for blacks; see Martin (1981) and Peeps (1981).

One might hypothesize that funds provided by philanthropists might have simply substituted, in part, for money that might have been spent anyway, and therefore, some benefits might have flowed indirectly to whites. In an important paper, Donohue, Heckman and Todd (2002) demonstrate that philanthropic dollars do not appear to have been especially fungible in this sense, and thus black children benefited from the efforts of the philanthropists [see also Strong et al. (2000)]. In terms of our model, improvements in black school quality financed by philanthropic efforts increased the economic benefits of black school attendance.

In sum, several factors influenced the pace of convergence in black and white schooling levels. In the initial aftermath of the Civil War, the returns to attending school for even a short time appear to have been substantial. At the same time, school attendance was facilitated by political changes during Reconstruction that forced southern state governments to provide education to black children. This combination of demand for and supply of educational services resulted in an initial period of racial convergence in schooling. By the late nineteenth century, convergence slowed as political factors again intervened, this time in the form of disenfranchisement. Disenfranchisement did not lead to a complete abrogation of black access to elementary schools in the South, but in general, black schools' quality lagged far behind that of southern white schools.

Despite the political turn of events, black educational attainment continued to rise, and the racial gap in attainment started to narrow for cohorts born after 1910. Each generation of black parents was becoming better educated, and parental education had a strong, positive influence on children's education. Moreover, as more blacks left the South, the costs of migrating from the region declined, and the economic returns to migration, which was facilitated by schooling, loomed even larger. Ultimately, an education was a ticket out of the rural South, a ticket that many black children and parents sought eagerly.

The 50-year anniversary of the *Brown* decision has recently passed, accompanied by much journalistic reflection. Surprisingly, the academic literature contains comparatively few econometric efforts to measure the effects of school desegregation on the students who were directly affected by the events.[25] Early contributions to this literature include Braddock, Crain and McPartland (1984) and Crain and Strauss (1985). Braddock, Crain and McPartland (1984) review a group of studies that suggest that desegregation had a positive influence on students' attitudes and eventual matches with colleges, neighborhoods, and employers. Crain and Strauss (1985), who explore data from a randomized desegregation program in Hartford, find that black men and women who attended desegregated schools were more likely to work in white-collar jobs than other blacks in their same cohort, and that the men in particular attained more education.

Boozer, Krueger and Wolkon (1992), who examine the National Survey of Black Americans, find evidence of a negative link between school segregation and outcomes in terms of education and earnings. Guryan (2004) studies black high school dropout rates in the 1970s using census data, and he argues that desegregation caused a two to three percentage point decline in dropouts. Reber (2004) studies high school enrollment and graduation rates for black students in Louisiana. It appears that black students' outcomes were responsive to changes in school funding that were linked to desegregation (more so than to changes in exposure to white students). Using census data from 1990, Ashenfelter, Collins and Yoon (2006) find that southern-born black men who went to school after large-scale desegregation earned higher incomes than southern-born black men who went to school before desegregation (relative to northern-born blacks in the same age cohorts).

These studies cannot clearly identify the channels through which desegregation affected black students' educational and labor market outcomes, but they are highly suggestive of a positive influence. Identifying such channels, and assessing the broader economic implications of school desegregation (for example, for the sorting of families across school districts and long-run trends in school quality) are active areas of research.

6. Conclusions and suggestions for further research

In the contemporary United States racial differences in schooling receive a great deal of public and scholarly attention. Without wishing to minimize the on-going importance of these contemporary differences, our goal has been to place them in historical perspective. From an historical perspective the most important "stylized fact" is that since the Civil War, black schooling levels have converged on white schooling levels. This convergence took place despite formidable barriers to black educational progress and despite pervasive labor market discrimination that might have reduced incentives to invest in higher education for much of the period we surveyed here.

[25] The rest of this section draws heavily on Ashenfelter, Collins and Yoon (2006). There is a larger literature on the racial composition of schools and black students' educational and labor market outcomes in fairly recent cohorts. See Grogger (1996), Rivkin (2000), or Hanushek, Kain and Rivkin (2002).

Our approach in this chapter has been deliberately "broad-brushed" and we have relied very heavily on one source of data, namely the IPUMS. Many features of our "analytical narrative" could be fleshed out with additional effort. For example, archival evidence from school records could shed additional light on the impact of the violations of the equal part of the "separate but equal" doctrine on black school outcomes. Our analysis has concentrated heavily on the South because this was where most black children were born and educated, but also because southern states kept separate records for white and black schools, facilitating the study of racial disparities in resources. The scope for improving our understanding of black education outside the South is considerable.

We have relied on the IPUMS samples to provide evidence on the economic returns to schooling, but by their very nature, these data provide only crude evidence prior to 1940. Although we are very doubtful of finding large bodies of relevant data, it is possible that firm-level records may provide some additional evidence.

Perhaps the most promising extension of the work we have discussed here is to other times and places. Slavery was hardly unique to the United States, and many other countries have equally brutal histories of racial, ethnic, or religious persecution of minorities. Sometimes these histories are abruptly interrupted through revolution, invasion, or spontaneous political change, but invariably, the different groups start the new era with very different initial levels of human capital and wealth. How quickly do the groups converge, if at all? Does convergence take place for every one or does it take place only through a succession of cohorts? Is government policy a force for convergence or a force for maintaining or exacerbating differences? What are the implications of disparities in schooling for disparities in other outcomes, such as health, income, and employment? These questions have motivated the study of the history of racial disparities in schooling in the United States, and many of the same questions, we believe, should motivate the documentation and analysis of group disparities in other contexts.[26]

Acknowledgements

This is a heavily revised version of a paper presented at the George Bush School of Government and Public Service, Texas A&M University, in March 2003. Comments from Derek Neal, William Rodgers, and workshop participants at the Bush School are gratefully acknowledged.

[26] The limited evidence currently available suggests that convergence may have been more rapid in the U.S. than in other New World slave societies. For example, the literacy rate in Brazil in 1920 (ages 10 and over), some three decades, after slavery was abolished was only 30 percent (this figure pertains to the entire population); see Engerman, Haber and Sokoloff (2000, p. 126) for these and other literacy figures pertaining to New World slave societies.

Appendix

Table A1
Illiteracy among whites, by nativity, 1870–1930

	1870	1880	1890	1900	1910	1920	1930
Panel A: Everyone, age 10–69							
Native-Born	0.119	0.095	–	0.050	0.033	0.021	–
Observations	197,571	250,882		198,567	196,498	583,615	
Foreign-Born	0.149	0.121	–	0.116	0.133	0.133	–
Observations	51,163	61,808		46,714	48,832	126,598	
All Cohorts	0.125	0.100	0.076	0.063	0.053	0.041	0.024
Observations	248,734	312,690	full count	245,281	245,330	710,213	full count
Panel B: Southern born							
All Cohorts	0.255	0.211	–	0.126	0.083	0.054	–
Observations	64,598	73,993	–	54,973	55,076	161,753	–
Panel C: Non-southern born							
Native-Born	0.058	0.046	–	0.021	0.014	0.008	–
Observations	132,908	176,806		143,456	140,996	419,938	
Foreign-Born	0.149	0.121	–	0.116	0.133	0.133	–
Observations	51,163	61,808		46,714	48,832	126,598	
All Cohorts	0.083	0.066	–	0.044	0.044	0.037	–
Observations	184,071	238,614	–	190,170	189,828	546,536	–

Notes: See notes to Table 2.
Sources: See sources for Table 2.

References

Anderson, J. (1987). The Education of Black People in the South, 1860–1935. University of North Carolina Press, Chapel Hill.

Anderson, J.D. (1988). The Education of Blacks in the South, 1860–1935. University of North Carolina Press, Chapel Hill.

Ashenfelter, O., Collins, W.J., Yoon, A. (2006). "Evaluating the role of Brown v. Board of Education in school equalization, desegregation, and the income of African Americans". American Law and Economics Review, in press.

Bond, H.M. (1934). The Education of the Negro in the American Social Order. Prentice-Hall, New York.

Bond, H.M. (1939). Negro Education in Alabama: A Study in Cotton and Steel. Associate Publishers, New York.

Boozer, M.A., Krueger, A.B., Wolkon, S. (1992). "Race and school quality since Brown v. Board of Education". Brookings Papers on Economic Activity, Microeconomics: 269–338.

Braddock, J.H., Crain, R.L., McPartland, J.M. (1984). "A long-term view of school desegregation: Some recent students of graduates as adults". Phi Delta Kappan 66, 259–264.
Butchart, R.E. (1980). Northern Schools, Southern Blacks, and Reconstruction: Freedmen's Education, 1862–1975. Greenwood Press, Westport, CT.
Butchart, R.E. (1988). "'We can best instruct our own people': New York African-Americans in the freedmen's schools, 1861–1875". Afro-Americans in New York Life and History 12, 27–49.
Card, D., Krueger, A. (1992). "School quality and black/white relative earnings: A direct assessment". Quarterly Journal of Economics 107, 151–200.
Cascio, E.U. (2003). "Schooling attainment and the introduction of kindergartens in the south". Working Paper, University of California at Berkeley.
Clotfelter, C.T. (2004). After Brown: The Rise and Retreat of School Desegregation. Princeton University Press, Princeton.
Collins, W.J. (1997). "When the tide turned: Immigration and the delay of the great black migration". Journal of Economic History 57, 607–632.
Collins, W.J., Margo, R.A. (2001). "Race and homeownership: A century long view". Explorations in Economic History 38, 68–92.
Cornelius, J.D. (1991). 'When I can Read My Title Clear' Literacy, Slavery, and Religion in the Ante-bellum South. University of South Carolina Press, Columbia.
Crain, R.L., Strauss, J. (1985). School Desegregation and Black Occupational Attainments: Results from a Long-term Experiment. Center for Social Organization of Schools, Johns Hopkins University, Baltimore.
Donohue, J.J., Heckman, J.J. (1991). "Continuous versus episodic change: The impact of affirmative action and civil rights policy on the economic status of blacks". Journal of Economic Literature 29, 1603–1644.
Donohue, J.J., Heckman, J.J., Todd, P. (2002). "The schooling of southern blacks: The roles of legal activism and private philanthropy, 1910–1960". Quarterly Journal of Economics 117, 225–268.
Engerman, S.L., Haber, S.H., Sokoloff, K.L. (2000). "Inequality, institutions, and differential paths of growth among new world economies". In: Menard, C. (Ed.), Institutions, Contracts, and Organizations: Perspectives from New Institutional Economics. Edward Elgar, Cheltenham, UK.
Fishback, P.V., Baskin, J.H. (1991). "Narrowing the black–white gap in child literacy in 1910: The roles of school inputs and family inputs". Review of Economics and Statistics 73, 725–728.
Fogel, R.W. (1989). Without Consent or Contract: The Rise and Fall of American Slavery. W.W. Norton, New York.
Fogel, R., Engerman, S. (1974). Time on the Cross: The Economics of American Negro Slavery. Little and Brown, Boston.
Freeman, R. (1973). "Black–White economic differences: Why did they last so long". Working Paper, Department of Economics, University of Chicago.
Genovese, E. (1976). Roll, Jordan, Roll: The World the Slaves Made. Random House, New York.
Goldin, C. (1990). Understanding the Gender Gap: An Economic History of American Women. Oxford University Press, New York.
Goldin, C. (1998). "America's graduation from high school: The evolution and spread of secondary schooling in the twentieth century". Journal of Economic History 58, 345–374.
Goldin, C., Katz, L. (1998). "America's graduation from high school: The evolution and spread of secondary schooling in the twentieth century". Journal of Economic History 58, 345–374.
Goldin, C., Margo, R.A. (1992). "The great compression: The U.S. wage structure at mid-century". Quarterly Journal of Economics 107, 1–34.
Grogger, J. (1996). "Does school quality explain the recent black/white wage trend?". Journal of Labor Economics 14, 231–253.
Guryan, J. (2004). "Desegregation and black dropout rates". American Economic Review 94, 919–943.
Hanushek, E.A., Kain, J.F., Rivkin, S.G. (2002). "New evidence about Brown v. Board of Education: The complex effects of school racial composition". National Bureau of Economic Research Working Paper 8741.
Harlan, L. (1958). Separate and Unequal: School Campaigns and Racism in the Southern Seaboard States, 1901–1915. University of North Carolina Press, Chapel Hill.

Harris, C.V. (1985). "Stability and change in discrimination against black public schools: Birmingham, Alabama, 1871–1931". Journal of Southern History 51, 375–416.
Higgs, R. (1982). "Accumulation of property by southern blacks before World War One". American Economic Review 72, 725–737.
Jones, J. (1980). Soldiers of Light and Love: Northern Teachers and Georgia Blacks, 1865–1973. University of North Carolina Press, Chapel Hill.
Kluger, R. (1976). Simple Justice: The History of Brown v. Board of Education and Black America's Struggle for Equality. Alfred A. Knopf, New York.
Kousser, J.M. (1974). The Shaping of Southern Politics: Suffrage Restriction and the Establishment of the One Party South, 1880–1910. Yale University Press, New Haven.
Kousser, J.M. (1980a). "Progressivism – for middle class whites only". Journal of Southern History 46, 169–194.
Kousser, J.M. (1980b). "Separate but not equal: The supreme Court's first decision on racial discrimination". Journal of Southern History 46, 17–44.
Lofgren, C. (1987). The Plessy Case: A Legal-Historical Interpretation. Oxford University Press, New York.
Margo, R.A. (1982). "Race differences in public school expenditures: Disfranchisement and school finance in Louisiana, 1890–1910". Social Science History 6, 9–33.
Margo, R.A. (1984a). "Accumulation of property by southern blacks before World War One: Comment and further evidence". American Economic Review 74, 768–776.
Margo, R.A. (1984b). "Teacher salaries in black and white: The South in 1910". Explorations in Economic History 21, 306–326.
Margo, R.A. (1986a). "Educational achievement in segregated school systems: The effects of 'separate-but-equal'". American Economic Review 76, 794–801.
Margo, R.A. (1986b). "Race and human capital: Comment". American Economic Review 76, 1221–1224.
Margo, R.A. (1987). "Accounting for racial differences in school attendance in the American South, 1900: The role of separate-but-equal". Review of Economics and Statistics 6, 661–666.
Margo, R.A. (1990). Race and Schooling in the South, 1880–1950: An Economic History. University of Chicago Press, Chicago.
Margo, R.A. (1991). "Segregated schools and the mobility hypothesis: A model of local government discrimination". Quarterly Journal of Economics 106, 301–310.
Margo, R.A. (2000). Wages and Labor Markets in the United States, 1820–1860. University of Chicago Press, Chicago.
Margo, R.A. (2004). "The North–South wage gap, before and after the Civil War". In: Eltis, D., Lewis, F., Sokoloff, K. (Eds.), Slavery in the Development of the Americas. Cambridge University Press, New York.
Martin, S.D. (1981). "The American Baptist Home Mission Society and black higher education in the South, 1865–1920". Foundations 24, 310–327.
Moehling, C. (2004). "Family structure, school attendance, and child labor in the American South in 1910". Explorations in Economic History 41, 73–100.
Morris, R.C. (1981). Reading, Riting, and Reconstruction: The Education of Freedmen in the South, 1861–1870. University of Chicago Press, Chicago.
Murrell, A.E. (1998). "The 'impossible' Prince Edward case: The endurance of resistance in a Southside county, 1959–65". In: Lassiter, M.D., Lewis, A.B. (Eds.), The Moderates' Dilemma: Massive Resistance to School Desegregation in Virginia. University of Virginia Press, Charlottesville.
Myrdal, G. (1944). An American Dilemma: The Negro Problem and Modern Democracy. Harper & Brothers, New York.
Neal, D. (2006). "Why has black–white skill convergence stopped?". In: Hanushek, E., Welch, F. (Eds.), Handbook of the Economics of Education. North-Holland, Amsterdam, in this issue.
Oaxaca, R. (1973). "Male–female wage differentials in urban labor markets". International Economic Review 14, 693–709.
Orazem, P. (1987). "Black–white differences in school investment and human capital production in segregated school systems". American Economic Review 77, 714–723.

Orfield, G. (1969). The Reconstruction of Southern Education: The Schools and the 1964 Civil Rights Act. Wiley-Interscience, New York.
Orfield, G. (1983). Public School Desegregation in the United States, 1968–1980. Joint Center for Political Studies, Washington, DC.
Peeps, J.M.S. (1981). "Northern philanthropy and the emergence of black higher education – do-gooders, compromisers, or co-conspirators?". Journal of Negro Education 50, 251–269.
Perlmann, J., Margo, R.A. (2001). Women's Work? American Schoolteachers, 1670–1920. University of Chicago Press, Chicago.
Pritchett, J.B. (1985). "North Carolina's public schools: Growth and local taxation". Social Science History 9, 277–291.
Pritchett, J.B. (1989). "The burden of negro schooling: Tax incidence and racial redistribution in post-bellum North Carolina". Journal of Economic History 49, 966–973.
Reber, S.J. (2003). "Court ordered desegregation: Successes and failures integrating American schools since brown". Working Paper, UCLA School of Public Affairs.
Reber, S.J. (2004). "Desegregation and educational attainment for blacks: Evidence from Louisiana". Working Paper, UCLA School of Public Affairs.
Rivkin, S.G. (2000). "School desegregation, academic attainment, and earnings". Journal of Human Resources 35, 333–346.
Ruggles, S., Sobek, M., et al. (1997). Integrated Public Use Microdata Series. Historical Census Projects, University of Minnesota, Minneapolis.
Sacerdote, B. (2005). "Slavery and the intergeneration transmission of human capital". Review of Economics and Statistics. In press.
Smith, J. (1984). "Race and human capital". American Economic Review 74, 685–698.
Smith, J. (1986). "Race and human capital: Reply". American Economic Review 76, 1225–1229.
Smith, J., Welch, F. (1989). "Black economic progress after Myrdal". Journal of Economic Literature 27, 519–564.
Smith, R. (1973). "The economics of educational discrimination in the United States South, 1870–1910". Ph.D. dissertation, Department of Economics, University of Wisconsin, Madison.
Southern Education Reporting Service (1965). Statistical Summary, State by State, of School Segregation–Desegregation in the Southern and Border Area from 1954 to the Present (Nashville).
Strong, D., Walters, P.B., Driscoll, B., Rosenberg, S. (2000). "Leveraging the state: Private money and the development of public education for blacks". American Sociological Review 65, 658–681.
Turner, S., Bound, J. (2003). "Closing the gap or widening the divide: The effects of the G.I. Bill and World War II on the educational outcomes of black Americans". Journal of Economic History 63, 145–177.
Tushnet, M.V. (1987). The NAACP's Legal Strategy Against Segregated Education, 1925–1950. University of North Carolina Press, Chapel Hill.
United States Bureau of the Census (1948). Special Reports of the United States Census: Current Population Reports, series P-20, No. 20. Government Printing Office, Washington, DC.
United States Department of Commerce, Bureau of the Census (1975). Historical Statistics of the United States, Colonial Times to 1970. Government Printing Office, Washington, DC.
Vigdor, J.L. (2002). "The pursuit of opportunity: Explaining selective black migration". Journal of Urban Economics 51, 391–417.
Walters, P.B., Briggs, C.M. (1993). "The family economy, child labor, and schooling: Evidence for the early twentieth century South". American Sociological Review 58, 163–181.
Walters, P.B., James, D.R. (1992). "Schooling for some: Child labor and school enrollment of blacks and white children in the early twentieth century South". American Sociological Review 57, 625–650.
Walters, P.B., James, D.R., McCammon, H.J. (1990). "Schooling or working? Public education, racial politics, and the organization of production in 1910". Sociology of Education 63, 1–26.
Walters, P.B., James, D.R., McCammon, H.J. (1997). "Citizenship and public schools: Accounting for racial inequality in education in the pre- and post-disfranchisement South". American Sociological Review 62, 34–52.

Welch, F. (1973). "Education and racial discrimination". In: Ashenfelter, O., Rees, A. (Eds.), Discrimination in Labor Markets. Princeton University Press, Princeton, pp. 43–81.

Welch, F., Light, A. (1987). New Evidence on School Desegregation. Clearinghouse Publication, vol. 92. U.S. Commission on Civil Rights, Washington, DC.

Chapter 4

IMMIGRANTS AND THEIR SCHOOLING

JAMES P. SMITH

Senior Economist-RAND, 1776 Main Street, P.O. Box 2138, Santa Monica, CA 90407-2138
e-mail: James_Smith@rand.org

Contents

Handbook of the Economics of Education, Volume 1
Edited by Eric A. Hanushek and Finis Welch
© 2006 Elsevier B.V. All rights reserved
DOI: 10.1016/S1574-0692(06)01004-X

Abstract

This chapter deals with several salient issues about immigrants to the US and their education. These issues include a comparison of the schooling accomplishments of immigrants compared to the native-born both contemporaneously as well as over time. These comparisons emphasize the considerable diversity in the schooling accomplishments among different immigrant sub-groups and between legal and undocumented migrants. Finally, the recent literature suggests than any concern that educational generational progress among Latino immigrants has lagged behind other immigrant groups is largely unfounded.

Keywords

immigration, education

JEL classification: I20, I23, I28, J10, J15, J61

Introduction

Since schooling is the most basic index of their skill, how much education immigrants had before they arrived, how much they were able to add while in the United States, and how that schooling helped their performances in the American labor market are critical questions in determining their eventual economic success or failure. In part because of this, education may also be crucial in influencing who decides to migrate to the United States.

This influence may be even more direct if migrants come to attend American schools, especially if some of them then stay on as permanent residents. Finally, immigrants are not only members of today's workforce – they are also parents and grandparents of a major part of the American labor market in the future. Thus, the issue of the size of inter-generational transmission of schooling across immigrant generations is a basic determinant in shaping what the country will look like in the decades ahead.

Immigrants are believed to have much less schooling than do native-born Americans; a disparity thought to be growing over time. Some also see a crisis in American colleges with foreign students first displacing American students and subsequently displacing American workers when they stay on as permanent residents. There is also a common belief that the successful economic assimilation across generations that is part of our folklore for European immigrants in particular may be broken for some of our contemporaneously large migrant ethnic groups. In this essay, I will provide evidence that at a minimum these claims are exaggerated.

This chapter is divided into five sections. Section 1 documents the most salient comparative patterns in the schooling of the foreign-born population in the United States, while the second section examines how nativity differences in education have changed over time. Section 3 highlights the considerable education diversity that exists in schooling accomplishments within the immigrant population. This diversity spans time of arrival, ethnic background, legal status, and the reasons for admission to the United States. Section 4 addresses the issue of the impact of foreign students on American schools. The final section focuses on the inter-generational transmission of schooling.

1. Schooling of migrants and the native-born

Using data obtained from the 2002 Current Population Survey, Table 1 highlights differences in education distributions among three groups – the foreign-born, the native-born, and the recent foreign-born (those who reported arriving within the last five years). Table 2 presents the same three-way division for the principal ethnic origin classifications of people currently living in the US – Asians, Europeans, and Hispanics.[1] Combined,

[1] These ethnic classifications are based on country of birth (first generation) and country of parents' birth (second generation). For the third plus generations (neither they or their parents were foreign born), Asians are those who claimed Asian race, Hispanics were defined by Hispanic ethnicity, and Europeans were those who were neither one or those and who also were not Black or Native-American using the race variable.

Table 1
Schooling distribution of native born and foreign populations – 2002 CPS

All			
Schooling	Foreign-born	Native-born	Recent foreign-born
Less than 5 years	6.4	0.7	7.4
5–8 years	14.1	3.5	12.8
9–11 years	7.9	7.4	6.9
12 years	26.9	34.4	23.9
13–16 years	34.9	45.2	34.9
17–18 years	6.4	6.3	10.0
19+ years	3.6	2.6	4.3
Mean years	12.00	13.31	12.31

Calculations by author using the 2002 March CPS for all persons 25 and over. The recent foreign-born are those who migrated within the last five years.

these two tables reveal the principal salient facts about the comparative education attributes of migrants. On average, migrants to the United States have less schooling than the native-born population does – in 2002, for example, the mean difference was 1.3 years of schooling. Far more dramatic, however, are the differences within the lower part of the education distribution. About one-fifth of the foreign-born had only an elementary school education or less, five times the comparable proportion among the native-born. Among recent immigrants in particular, however, the relative ranking actually shifts in the top part of the education distribution where recent migrants are 47% more likely than those born in the US to have completed more than a college degree.

These differences between the native and foreign-born pale next to the heterogeneity within the migrant population. That diversity already revealed itself in the comparatively fat tails of the foreign-born education distribution in Table 1. But the heterogeneity is even starker in Table 2, which offers a comparison among the three principal types of immigrants (Asians, Europeans, and Hispanics) classified by their place of birth.

The differences amongst these three ethnic groups are large. On one end are recent Europeans migrants who are actually more educated than native-born Americans. Very few of them are low skilled and 29% claim some post-baccalaureate schooling (compared to 9% among all native-born Americans). The skill of European migrants is not only high, but it appears to be rising as reflected in the much higher education levels of recent European migrants compared to all the foreign-born from Europe. I shall return to this issue of secular trends below.

Using schooling as the skill index, Asian migrants score even better. On average, they too are relatively high skilled (with recent immigrants the most skilled), albeit with considerable within-group diversity. While 25% of recent Asian migrants have schooling beyond a college degree, 5% have an eighth grade education or less. Both proportions are more than those for native-born Americans. On the other end of the skill index lie

Table 2
Schooling distributions of native-born and foreign populations – 2002 CPS

Schooling	Asian			European		
	Foreign-born	Native-born	Recent foreign-born	Foreign-born	Native-born	Recent foreign-born
Less than 5 years	2.8	0.2	2.4	1.9	0.4	1.9
5–8 years	5.0	2.1	3.2	6.9	2.9	5.1
9–11 years	4.0	2.6	3.4	4.2	6.2	1.7
12 years	22.4	23.2	16.1	29.5	33.8	22.0
13–16 years	48.4	59.4	50.3	41.7	46.8	41.1
17–18 years	11.7	6.8	18.0	10.4	7.0	19.6
19+ years	5.7	5.6	6.5	5.5	2.9	8.9
Mean years	13.96	14.36	14.73	13.58	13.52	14.61

Schooling	Hispanics		
	Foreign-born	Native-born	Recent foreign-born
Less than 5 years	11.6	3.8	13.3
5–8 years	24.9	8.9	23.3
9–11 years	12.7	12.8	11.6
12 years	27.5	34.5	25.4
13–16 years	21.4	36.1	22.7
17–18 years	1.3	3.0	2.4
19+ years	1.1	0.9	1.4
Mean years	9.81	11.93	9.84

Calculations by author using the 2002 March CPS for all persons 25 and over. The recent foreign-born are those who migrated within the last five years.

Hispanic migrants. On average, Latino migrants are much less skilled than the native-born or than either European or Asian migrants are. To provide a dramatic illustration, among recent migrants Europeans and Asian have almost five years of schooling more than Latino migrants do. The reason is simple – about a third of recent Latino migrants have only eight years of schooling or less.

This simple summary highlights the salient differences in schooling achievements of the native and foreign born. On average, migrants are about a year or so less educated than the typical native-born American is. However, the real differences emerge in the tails. Migrants are simultaneously much more likely to be considerably more educated (have post-baccalaureate schooling) and less educated (without a high school diploma) than are Native-born Americans. A good deal of those differences are differentiated in the three major ethnic groups – compared to native-born Americans, Europeans and Asians migrants are far more likely to have training beyond college while Latino migrants are far more likely not to have gone beyond elementary school.

Before examining whether these schooling differences between the native and foreign born can be explained by a few crucial theoretical and/or institutional factors, I next examine a closely related question – what has happened to these educational disparities by nativity over time?

2. The changing education gap of immigrants

A primary concern in the economics literature is the changing labor market quality of foreign immigrants to the United States [see Borjas (1994, 1995) and Jasso, Rosensweig and Smith (2000)]. Education is the most basic index of skill so it should come as no surprise that this topic has focused both on wages and education gaps of migrants compared to the native born. In this chapter, I will only deal with the education dimension of that debate.[2] On both wages and education, the discussion often begins with the rapidly changing ethnic composition of migrants to the US.

Before the Immigration and Nationality Act amendments of 1965 repealed the national-origin quotas, Europe and Canada were the dominant sources of immigrants to the US. Even as late as 1950, 90% of the foreign-born population was of either European or Canadian heritage. But with the passage of the 1965 amendments, the racial and ethnic composition has changed dramatically and rapidly as the number of migrants was rising during the last half-century.

The two principal changes clearly involved the increasing flows of migrants from Asia and Latin America. During the last two decades, more than 75% of new immigrants were either Latinos or Asians. Since 1970, more than eight million legal Hispanic immigrants arrived in the United States while almost seven million Asians were also admitted. Especially for Latinos, these numbers were augmented by considerable influx of unauthorized migrants. By 1970, the fraction of the foreign-born population from Europe and Canada had been reduced to around two-thirds; this proportion was only a quarter in 1990. In contrast, foreigners from the Caribbean and Latin America were one-in-five of the foreign born in 1970 and 43% by 1990. Finally, Asians went from only 3% of the foreign-born in 1950 to a quarter by 1990.[3]

While the 1965 amendments certainly represented the most substantial change in immigration policy in the last 50 years, other subsequent legislation also had significant impacts on the attributes of migrant flows. While there are many changes, the two most important were the 1986 Immigration Reform and Control Act (IRCA) and a series of laws that encouraged the entry of more skilled immigrants. [For a brief summary of the major legislative changes see Chapter 2 in Smith and Edmonston (1997).]

Besides attempting to limit future illegal immigration by adding more resources for border control and by establishing employer sanctions, IRCA created a program for

[2] This section summarizes and extends Smith (2006).

[3] See Smith and Edmonston (1997, p. 37), for details.

legalizing illegal aliens already residing in the US. Almost three million unauthorized migrants were legalized through this program [see Smith and Edmonston (1997)]. The most important of the recent changes in legal admission policy was the Immigration Act of 1990, which among other things simultaneously reduced the number of visas for unskilled migrants while increasing them for skilled immigrants.

Table 3 attempts to document trends by listing for each of the decennial Censuses between 1940 and 1990 and for the 1996 and 2002 CPS mean education levels of the native and foreign-born populations over age 24. To more closely capture changing flows, means are also presented for the foreign-born population who arrived during the last five years. Separate data are presented for the four principal ethnic groups – Asians, Europeans, Hispanics, and Mexicans.

Table 3
Years of schooling completed, by nativity

	2002	1996	1990	1980	1970	1960	1950	1940
All								
U.S. born	13.31	12.99	12.61	11.78	10.84	10.01	9.43	8.77
Foreign born	12.00	11.51	11.31	10.59	8.97	7.74	7.46	6.68
1–5 years in U.S.	12.32	11.73	11.65	11.25	10.36	9.95	n.a.	8.90
Asian								
U.S. born	14.36	14.00	13.60	13.01	11.84	10.66	10.43	9.66
Foreign born	13.96	13.28	12.94	13.17	11.32	8.37	7.24	7.76
1–5 years in U.S.	14.73	13.13	12.90	12.50	13.46	12.08	n.a.	10.44
"Europeans"								
U.S. born	13.52	13.18	12.82	12.02	11.11	10.34	9.79	9.18
Foreign born	13.58	12.89	11.94	10.29	8.99	7.83	7.39	6.74
1–5 years in U.S.	14.61	14.65	13.63	12.11	10.35	10.32	n.a.	8.95
Hispanics								
U.S. born	11.93	11.52	11.58	9.80	9.47	7.39	7.22	5.79
Foreign born	9.81	9.27	9.23	8.91	7.91	5.99	5.79	4.71
1–5 years in U.S.	9.84	8.41	9.14	8.26	8.40	7.23	n.a.	7.25
Mexican								
U.S. born	n.a.	n.a.	11.15	9.50	8.33	6.80	5.81	4.28
Foreign born	8.66	7.93	7.71	6.74	5.59	4.39	4.53	3.97
1–5 years in U.S.	8.53	7.52	7.83	6.33	5.93	4.58	n.a.	6.06

Calculations by author from 1940–1990 decennial Censuses, 1996 and 2002 CPS. Sample those 25 and above.

Not surprisingly, education levels have moved sharply higher over time for all groups represented in Table 3. Each decade witnessed another increase in schooling accomplishments for our reference group – the US native born. The cumulative change was eventually large – essentially moving the typical adult native-born American from an elementary school graduate in 1940 (8.8 years) to going beyond high school in 2002 (13.3 years). While starting at a lower base (a deficiency of two years in 1940), the foreign-born population has not only moved lockstep with the native-born, but their cumulative change was greater, reducing the education deficit with the native-born to one and a third years by 2002. No doubt reflecting secular improvements in education in the sending countries, recent immigrants tend to have more schooling than the complete resident foreign-born population. However, the gap between them has narrowed so that time series gains in education among the recent foreign-born are smaller than that of all migrants.

Ethnic differences in education are large. Among immigrants in particular, Latino migrants have always lagged behind the others by a substantial margin. Given the better educational opportunities available in the United States compared to many of the sending countries, it is not a surprise that within each of these ethnic groups the native-born tend to have more schooling than their foreign-born counterparts. In fact, the differences among the ethnic groups are far smaller in the native-born population than the foreign-born, an issue to which I return later.

To make trends in disparities with the native-born population more transparent, Figure 1 plots the extent to which the schooling of the native-born population exceeds that of the total and recent foreign-born population. Similarly, using the same reference group, Figure 2 displays the disparity in mean schooling of the different native-born ethnic populations; Figure 3 plots the differentials for the ethnic specific foreign-born populations, and Figure 4 presents education gaps for recent immigrants.

Putting aside for a moment within ethnic trends, two things are particularly striking concerning schooling deficits of the foreign born. First, up to 1980 the schooling disadvantage of the total foreign-born population was declining while it was simultaneously rising for new recent immigrants. These opposing trends are not a contradiction. The stock of migrants is weighted heavily by history toward trends for past European migrants. Moreover, the higher education level of recent younger immigrants increases mean schooling of the total foreign born. But also the steep negative age gradient to mean schooling with a much older immigrant population due to the long stall in migration to the US implies that as some of the older immigrants (with very little schooling) die between the Censuses, the mean education of those who remain will rise. Second, and perhaps more to the point, no matter whether one uses the total or the recent foreign-born population, all this seems much ado about nothing. Over a 60-year period, the full range of change in the foreign born schooling gap was about .7 of a year of schooling and was little over a year when using all recent immigrants.

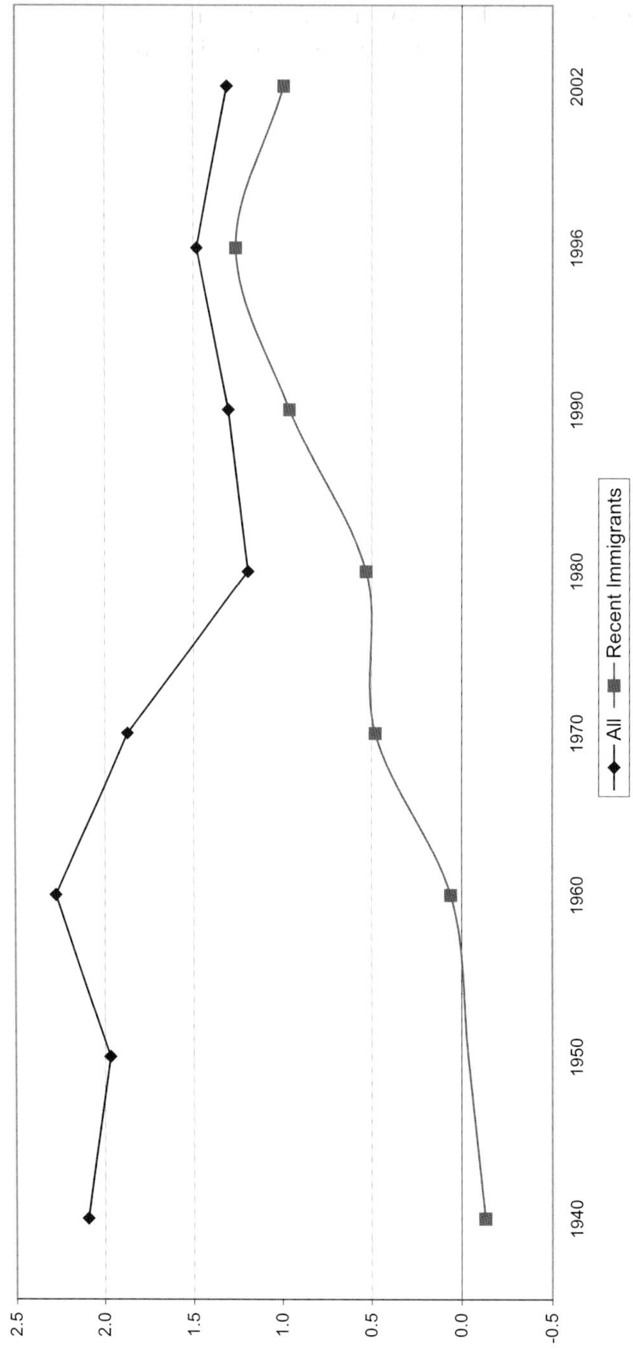

Figure 1. Schooling disparity of all foreign born (comparison group: all native born).

Figure 2 summarizes trends for various native-born populations. Compared to the overall average, the native-born of European descent have slightly less than a half-year[4] advantage, while those of Asian background hover around with a year of schooling advantage. What is remarkable about both Europeans and Asians is how little trend exists in this ethnic gap of the native-born. For example, for the last 60 years, native-born Asians have had about one year more schooling than the average in the US. There is a more detectable, and perhaps surprising to some, steady decline in the schooling gap of native-born Latinos until it is about half as large now as it was in 1940. I return to that issue below.

Figure 3 plots education gaps for ethnic foreign-born populations. In 1940 and 1950, all groups start out with a schooling disadvantage – about two years for Europeans and Asians and twice that much for Hispanics. Subsequently, first for Asians and then for Europeans, these schooling deficits narrowed until currently the total adult foreign-born populations over both groups hold a narrow advantage of the US native-born. In comparison, there is very little change between Hispanics and Mexicans where the education gap among the foreign-born at best drifts slightly downward. The overall downward trend in the foreign-born education gap thus results from a narrowing gap between Asians and Europeans, a basically constant gap among Latinos which combined offset any impact of a shift in relative representation toward Hispanics.

Figure 4 presents the same type of data for recent immigrants. Typically, new Asian and European migrants have had more education than the native-born, an advantage that has become slightly bigger for Europeans and smaller for Asians. Between 1970 and 1996, the education gap for new Latino migrants has risen. All groups appear to have experienced a slight closing of the education gap in the late 1990s.

One question that arises is whether these overall trends are the same for male and female immigrants. To examine this issue, Figure 5 presents data for trends in the sex-specific schooling gap for all migrants while Figure 6 plots similar data on education deficits of recent migrants. While the overall levels are different with a larger sex specific schooling disadvantage among female immigrants, the trends depicted in Figure 5 for all migrants are remarkably similar for men and women. The larger schooling deficit for female migrants primarily reflects the lower schooling accomplishments of female migrants. For example, in 1970 the average male migrant had 9.2 years of schooling compared to 7.6 years of schooling for the average female migrant.

Figure 6 depicts trends in schooling deficits by sex among recent migrants. The slowly expanding education deficit with the native born characterizes both men and women, but the education gap increases at a slower rate among women than among men. This is largely because the typical advantage new male immigrants have had over new female immigrants has been gradually eroding. To illustrate, among recent immigrants in the 1970 Census, men had a year and one third education advantage over

[4] The small differences for Europeans are not surprising since they comprise such a large fraction of the total.

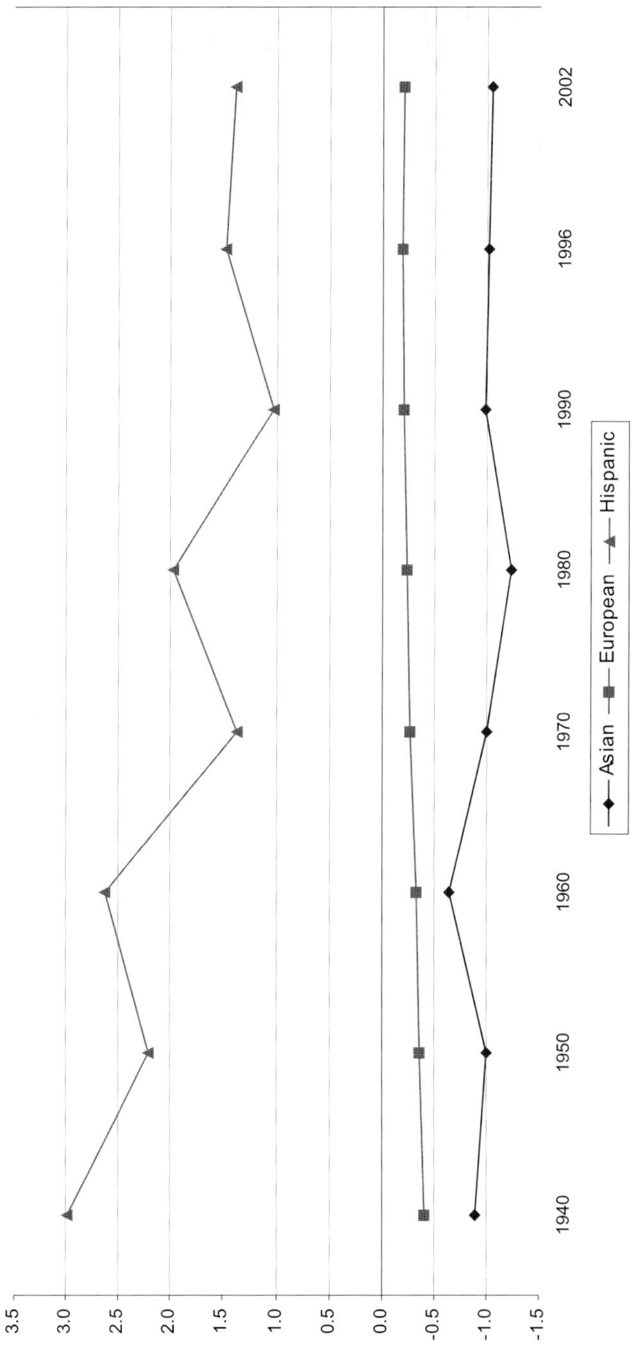

Figure 2. Schooling differences of the native born (comparison group: all native born).

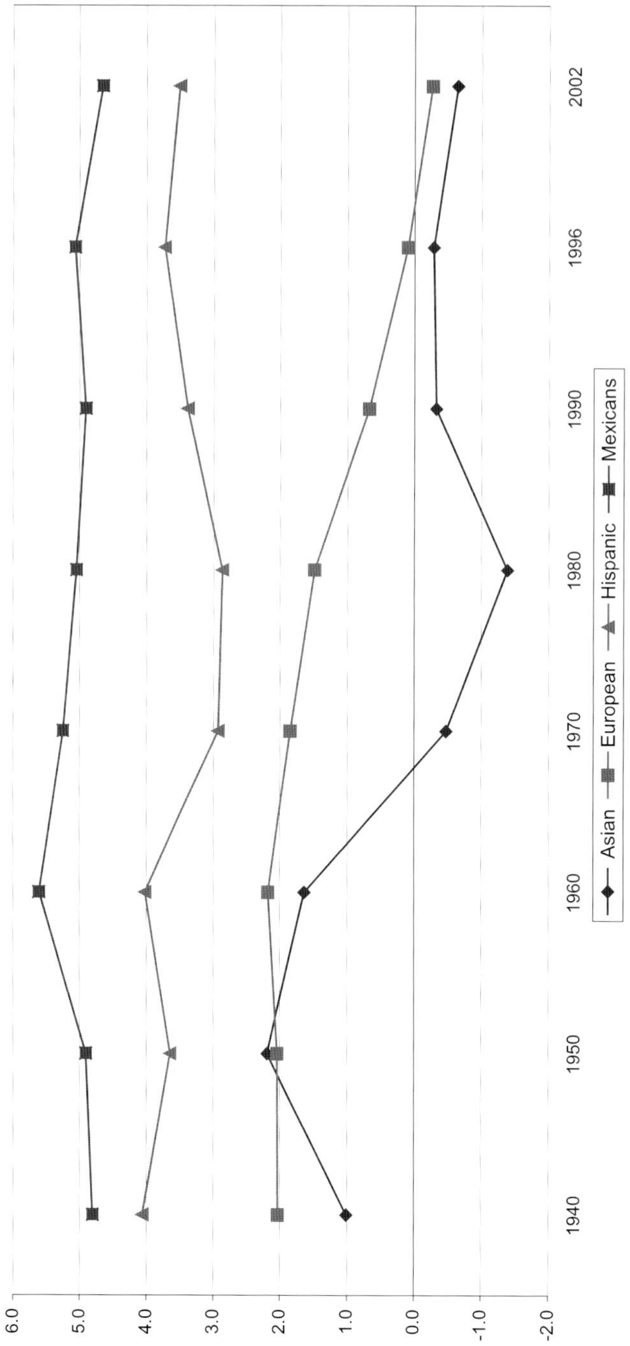

Figure 3. Schooling disparity of all foreign born (comparison group: all native born).

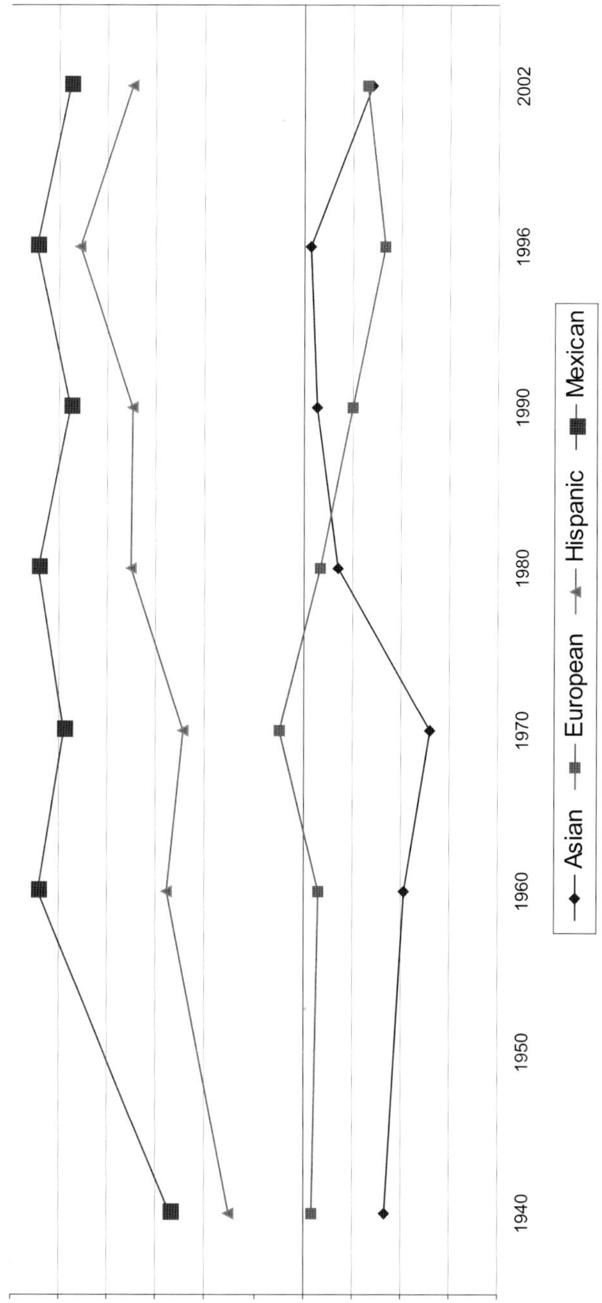

Figure 4. Schooling disparities of recent foreign born (comparison group: all native born).

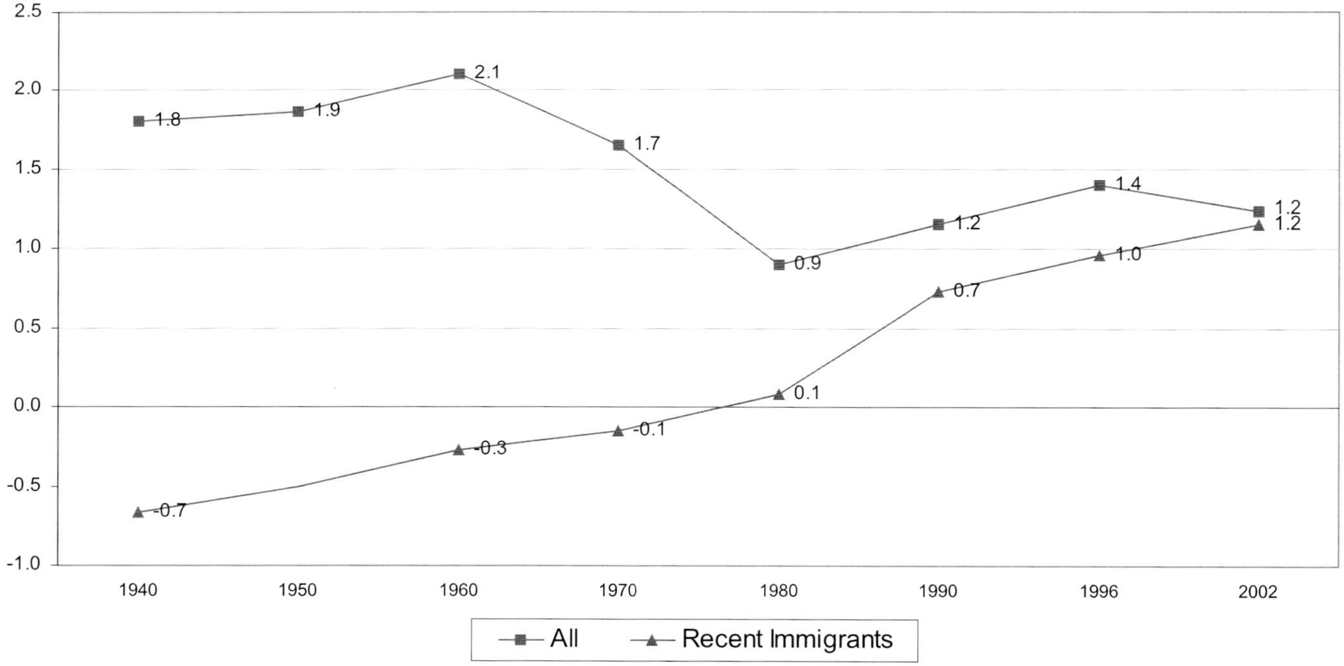

Figure 5. Schooling disparity of males ages 25+ (comparison group: all male native born).

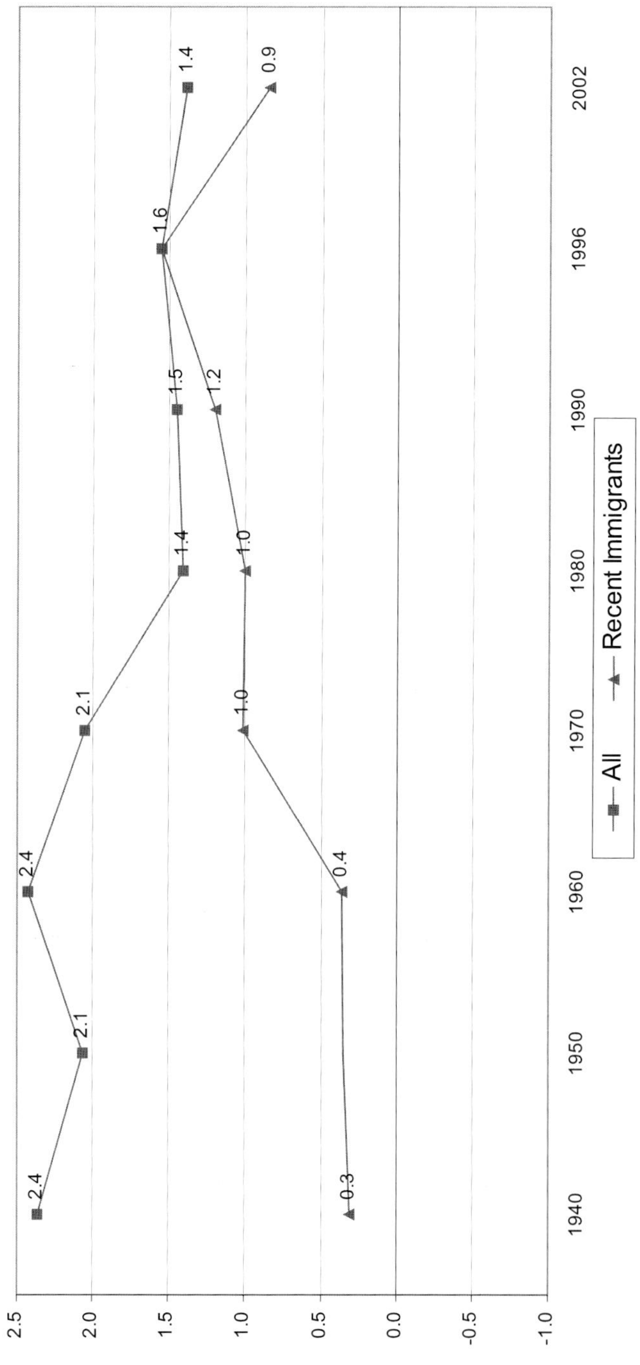

Figure 6. Schooling disparity of females ages 25+ (comparison group: all female native born).

women (11.1 years for men compared to 9.8 years among women). In contrast, by 2002 recent female migrants actually had slightly more schooling than did recent male migrants to the United States – 12.4 years of schooling for women compared to 12.2 for men.

Since they more directly capture flows, data on recent immigrants in Figures 1, 4, 5, and 6 are more sensitive to period changes in legislative and economic incentives in the propensity to migrate. A comparison of the more stable within-ethnic group trends in Figure 4 compared to the slightly widening gap of recent migrants in Figure 1 suggests that the principal impact of the 1965 legislative change was on the composition of migrants – in particular increasingly the representation of less-schooled Latino migrants. Two largely offsetting forces dominated the recent period. On one hand were the legalization of mainly Hispanic migrants through IRCA and the increased flows of unauthorized (again mainly Hispanic) migrants who have less schooling than the average native-born American; on the other, the increased numbers of European and Asian migrants who have education above that of the typical native-born American. A comparison of the 1996 and 2002 CPS may indicate that the second force is now stronger than the first as the education gap of new migrants and native-born Americans is now declining.

An attempt to highlight trends during the 1990s is provided in Table 4, which lists mean schooling of migrants by year of entry into the United States using the 1996 and 2002 CPS. Among all migrants, there is a u-shaped pattern with higher schooling levels among pre-1980 migrants compared to those who came during the 1980s, and then a rapid rise after the mid-1990s. Within ethnic groups, the Asian patterns reflect the same overall picture just described, while there is evidence of a more continuous rise among Europeans. There is little evidence of much of a trend at all among Mexican migrants.

Table 4
Recent trends in immigrant schooling

Time since immigration	All	Asians	Europeans	Hispanics	Mexicans
2002 CPS					
2000–2002	12.51	14.70	14.77	9.87	8.37
1996–2000	12.18	14.51	14.47	9.70	8.75
1990–1996	11.71	13.63	14.41	9.55	8.74
1980–1990	11.79	13.60	14.11	9.88	8.73
< 1980	12.15	14.07	13.01	9.95	8.56
1996 CPS					
1990–1996	11.56	12.80	14.21	8.69	7.89
1980–1990	11.33	13.27	13.68	9.26	7.99
< 1980	11.61	13.63	12.49	9.47	7.90

Source: Calculations by author. Sample those 25 and above.

Since data are provided in both CPSs for the 1990–1996, 1980–1990, and pre-1980 year of entry cohorts, Table 4 allows one in principle to examine the same entry cohort of immigrants six years apart. In every case, mean schooling is higher in the more recent 2002 CPS, and the differences between the two CPS samples are often not small. For example, consider Asian migrants who arrived between 1990 and 1996. In the 1996 CPS, they report having 12.8 years of schooling; by 2002 this had risen to 13.6, an increment of .8 of a year. While the increases for the other ethnic groups are smaller than this example, they often run about half a year of schooling.

There are several possible reasons for this upward drift in mean schooling within entry cohorts. First, it may simply reflect 'grade' inflation, a well-documented trend in census data even for the native-born. Second, it may be produced by the aging of young, more educated immigrants who were 19–24 years old in 1996 but who now qualify for the 25-year-old age restriction by 2002, and the exit of older immigrants with low schooling levels who died between 1996 and 2002. Third, it could reflect a migration selection effect if less educated migrants are more likely to return even temporarily to the sending countries. Circulatory migration of the less educated would produce this pattern since the less educated would be less likely to remain within any specific time since migration interval in successive CPS surveys. Finally, some part of this upward drift may be the consequence of additional post-migration school attendance, an issue to which I return below.

To obtain some notion of the importance of the second and at least a component of the fourth reason, schooling differences with the native-born were calculated for a sample restricted to those aged 31–55 in 1996 and 37–61 in 2002. The younger age threshold of older migrants mitigates against any significant mortality effect while the older age cutoff among the young should reduce the impact of school completion among younger migrants. Finally, the upward adjustment in the age cutoff of the young eliminates the impact of the new entry by 2002 of younger migrants who failed to meet the age threshold in 1996. However, the schooling increments within time since immigration intervals were only marginally different in this sample suggesting that these demographic factors of mortality and 'aging in' are not the major part of the story.

The exclusion of those factors leaves grade inflation, post-migration education selectivity, and post-migration education accumulation as the major options. Some insights into the latter are provided by Table 5, which lists the fraction of new legal immigrants who received some type of education during the year after the receipt of their green cards. The second column lists the fraction of respondents who received some form of training during this period, while the next five columns describe the type of training that took place.

The extent of post-green card training and schooling is impressive. Forty-one percent of all new legal immigrants engaged in some type of training during this year, and even one quarter of those between ages 61 and 80 participated in training. Classes in English as a second language were the most popular form of classes, especially among older immigrants, while some younger immigrants signed up for computer classes.

Table 5
New legal immigrants who attended school in the United States during the year of their receiving their green cards

Age	% Attended	Type of schooling				
		Regular	Language	GED	Computer	Other
21–30	.52	.421	.276	.026	.069	.207
31–40	.41	.268	.314	.027	.104	.287
41–60	.37	.194	.513	.000	.015	.279
61–80	.24	.231	.692	.000	.000	.077
All	.41	.304	.371	.019	.063	.244

Source: 1996 New Immigrant Pilot Survey. Attending is defined as any attendance at or between the baseline and the 12 month follow-up. Type of schooling defined by most recent type of schooling.

But regular school was also an important chosen option. One in eight new legal immigrants between the ages of 21 and 80 attended an American school in the year after the receipt of their green card. That rate rose to one in five among those new immigrants in their twenties.

Among those 25 and over, about half of new immigrants reported that they wanted to attain a high degree in the Unites States. A fifth of these hoped-for degrees were college diplomas, while almost 38% were some type of masters, doctorate, or professional degree. Thus, it seems quite likely that some significant part of this rise in schooling between successive surveys is real – new immigrants do add to their schooling after the receipt of their green card.

But this also seems unlikely to offer a complete explanation. The data in Table 4 show that this increase in mean education takes place even among immigrants who arrived before 1980. By this time, one would have thought that the incremental schooling behavior would have run its course.

This suggests mostly by default that differential out-migration (either temporary or permanent) of the less educated may be an important empirical and under appreciated phenomenon. Greater circular migration alone of less-educated migrants (which seems likely to have taken place) would by itself produce across-year increases of schooling of migrants arrayed by their year of migration. If so, this also implies that the use of the analytical procedure of comparing immigrants stratified by reported time since arrival across surveys taken in different calendar years may be a perilous exercise indeed in spite of how widespread this practice is in the literature.

Several things are clear from this analysis. First, cross-sectional patterns associated with time since immigration may be a quite poor way of assembling evidence for either assimilation or immigrant quality. It is well recognized to be inappropriate when assessing the amount of assimilation since they are obviously members of different cohorts. It may also be problematic for assessing cohort quality as there may be significant post-immigration changes in the composition of entry cohorts as well as their schooling.

Second, when examining outcomes for immigrants, laws do matter. Periodic changes in immigration legislation have had important effects on the skill composition of subsequent immigrant cohorts. The most well documented example concerns the impact of the 1965 National Origin Quota Act, which resulted in a large shift in the ethnic composition of immigrants with fewer Europeans and relatively more Asians and Latinos coming to the United States. During the 1970s and 1980s, this shift toward increasing numbers of Latino immigrants in particular led to an increasing gap between the average education of new immigrants compared to that of the native born.

But the 1965 act was not the end of the story by any means. Subsequent legislative changes, especially a set of revisions during the late 1980s and early 1990s that increased the quotas on skilled employment visas, had the opposite effect of increasing the average skill of new immigrants. The most important of these was 1990 act, which simultaneously increased the total numbers of employment visas (which tend to be more skilled on average) while decreasing the numbers in the unskilled occupations. Consequently, while less well known, these legislative changes resulted in a narrowing of the education gap of migrants and the native-born during the 1990s. These tables and figures indicate that the changing composition of recent immigration alongside the increasing fraction of immigrants within the Hispanic population are two dominant underlying trends.[5]

But laws are not the only thing that matters. First even within the system that admits legal immigrants to the United States there are numerically unlimited categories such as spouses of US citizens that can in some years comprise more than one-third of non-refugee adult admissions. Jasso, Rosensweig and Smith (2000) provide a detailed analysis of the factors determining the skill selectivity of such migrants. For example, they show that a higher cost of migration, say through distance, would imply that the average skill of migrants should rise in order to justify the mobility costs. Thus, migrants from Asia should be more highly selected on their skill (including their education) than migrants who reside in nearby countries such as Mexico and Canada. The empirical estimates in the Jasso et al. study provide strong support for this hypothesis.

Second, many immigrants come to the United States without documents or overstay their visas and therefore reside here illegally. These undocumented migrants tend to be largely but not exclusively Latino and they also have less skill and schooling than those immigrants who come through the legal system. Especially as their relative numbers change, the flows of illegal migrants into the United States can have profound impacts on the overall portrait of the education levels of the native born compared to the foreign born. In the next section, I will discuss this impact in more detail.

[5] See Jasso, Rosensweig and Smith (2000) for a detailed analysis of these changes and the effect of this set of legislation.

3. The educational diversity of migrants – legal and unauthorized immigrants

Most of what we know about immigrants is typically based on comparisons using the foreign-born population in household surveys [Smith and Edmonston (1997)]. The foreign-born population in surveys represents a combination of some very different types of people – legal immigrants, legal nonimmigrants (those with visas that authorize stays for some period of time), and unauthorized or illegal immigrants. These populations are distinct in many ways, including their education. For example, many nonimmigrants come to the United States attracted by its reputation for superior schools, e.g., students on temporary visas attending American colleges and universities. In contrast, illegal immigrants are thought to predominately work in jobs within the bottom tail of the skill distribution, especially in the service and agricultural sectors. Not surprisingly, their schooling is often far below those of most American workers. Finally while legal immigrants come to America for many diverse reasons, especially in recent years some qualify for permanent residence only because they are highly skilled and highly educated. Data on average education of the foreign-born population may be quite sensitive to the relative proportions of these three groups, and consequently aggregate data may poorly describe each of them.

According to the 2000 census, there were 281 million people living in the United States. Of these, 31 million or one in nine were born in another country. While making distinctions is difficult and measurement is far from perfect, the best current Census estimates indicate that roughly 22 million of the foreign born (or about 69%) were prior legal immigrants to the US.

Who are the rest? In the 2000 decennial Census about a million and one half were legal nonimmigrants [INS (2003)] and another 600,000 were people awaiting their formal transition to legal status. The remainder of the foreign born are obviously the most difficult to count, but recent INS estimates indicate that there are 7 million unauthorized residents. Other quite credible estimates produce even higher numbers. For example, Passel, Capps and Fix (2004) estimate that there were 9.3 million undocumented immigrants in the United States in 2002. Given this uncertainty, these estimates may be better thought of as a range – say anywhere between 8 and 12 million undocumented residents. Moreover, the relative proportions of these groups vary significantly across ethnic groups. For example, recent INS estimates claim that among all foreign-born in the 2000 Census, 23% were unauthorized [INS (2003)]. The corresponding fraction authorized for the Asian, European, Hispanic, and Mexico-born population was 6%, 4%, 44%, and 52% respectively.

Unfortunately, hard data documenting the distinct education attributes of these different subgroups of the foreign-born are almost nonexistent, especially if we strive for nationally representative statistics. The reason is simple – there has been no attempt to identify in surveys to which of the three groups a foreign-born respondent belongs. Fortunately, some indirect estimates are now possible since at least one of the three main sub-populations can be separately identified. The New Immigrant Pilot Survey (NIS-P) was a stratified random sample of new immigrants admitted to legal permanent residence in the United States, i.e., granted green cards during the months of July and August 1996 [see Jasso et al. (2000) for details]. Since the NIS samples legal immigrants only, any discrepancy between the CPS and NIS schooling distributions among recent immigrants would reflect the presence of illegal migrants and legal nonimmigrants in the CPS.

The top panel of Table 6 depicts the distribution of schooling of the entire adult NIS-P cohort, along with corresponding data based on the 1996 CPS for the foreign-born who entered the U.S. between 1992 and 1996 ('recent immigrants'). The 1996 CPS is used because it is the same calendar year as the NIS-P. These data are also presented for three subgroups – Hispanics, Asian, and Europeans.

Compared to the CPS recent foreign-born population, there are far more legal immigrants at the top of the educational hierarchy and far fewer at the bottom. The CPS-based proportion for foreign-born recent entrants with less than five years of schooling is 1.6 times as large as the legal immigrant based proportion (10.4% versus 6.6%) while the CPS-based fraction with 17 or more years of schooling among the recent-entrant foreign-born is eight percentage points smaller than in the legal immigrant population (13.3% versus 21%). The CPS and Census foreign-born population apparently does not reflect the legal immigrant population and its use to assess policy on legal immigration is problematic.

Differences between these populations emerge more clearly in Table 7 which lists mean education by place of birth of legal immigrants (in 1996) and for the March 1996 CPS 'recent' foreign-born population. Because roughly half of legal immigrants are adjustees and have been living in the US for several years, the CPS foreign-born population is presented both for those who had arrived in the last three years and for those who had arrived during the last five years. Using recent INS (2003) estimates on legal status of the foreign born population, these differences between the legal immigrant population and the full foreign born population can be used to calculate the implied education level of the nonimmigrant and unauthorized populations combined. These numbers are placed in a parenthesis besides the mean education of the legal population.[6] Finally, Table 7 also provides estimates of mean education for the entire native-born and foreign-born populations.

On average, legal immigrants have more education than the contemporaneously sampled recent CPS foreign-born population, and by implication much more schooling than other types of foreign-born people living in the US. I estimate that in 1996 mean schooling of the foreign-born who are legal immigrants was almost two years larger than the mean schooling of all 'recent' undocumented immigrants and nonimmigrants combined. For all recent migrants, mean schooling of legal immigrants is only slightly below that of the native-born population (a third of a year), but more than a year higher than that of the foreign-born population.

[6] Due to the uncertainty about which is the appropriate comparison group for legal immigrants, the average of the 3 year and 5 year CPS education was used. The percent of the CPS population who were legal immigrants was obtained from the INS (2003) cited earlier in the text.

Table 6
Schooling distributions of legal immigrants and the recent foreign born

Schooling	All	
	New legal foreign-born	Recent foreign-born
Less than 5 years	6.6	10.4
5–8 years	13.6	14.5
9–11 years	13.9	8.1
12 years	12.5	22.4
13–16 years	32.5	31.4
17–18 years	11.9	8.2
19+ years	9.1	5.1
Mean years	12.6	11.7

Schooling	Asian		European	
	New legal foreign-born	Recent foreign-born	New legal foreign-born	Recent foreign-born
Less than 5 years	3.2	7.8	1.3	1.5
5–8 years	8.4	5.2	6.7	3.5
9–11 years	12.7	5.0	11.9	5.6
12 years	15.2	23.2	7.1	18.9
13–16 years	36.7	42.9	42.1	43.8
17–18 years	12.7	10.9	22.2	15.5
19+ years	11.3	5.0	8.7	11.3
Mean years	13.7	13.1	14.4	14.7

Schooling	Hispanics	
	New legal foreign-born	Recent foreign-born
Less than 5 years	14.0	21.3
5–8 years	24.9	29.9
9–11 years	16.5	13.0
12 years	11.9	11.0
13–16 years	23.0	15.5
17–18 years	5.5	4.7
19+ years	4.3	4.6
Mean years	10.1	8.8

Note: Recent immigrants are from the 1996 NIS and the recent foreign-born are from the 1996 CPS. The recent foreign-born entered between 1992–96.

This comparison varies a good deal across ethnic groups. Among Asians and Europeans the relatively small subset of the foreign-born who are not legal immigrants are actually more educated, presumably reflecting the significant numbers of graduate and professional degree attendees in this group. Much different are Latino immigrants,

Table 7
Education levels of recent male immigrants – legal and all recent foreign-born

Place of birth	Foreign born					Native born
	Legal	Not Legal	CPS < 3 years	CPS < 5 years	All FB	
Average education (years)						
All	12.64	(10.79)	12.33	11.73	11.51	12.99
Asia	13.66	(14.14)	14.22	13.13	13.28	14.00
Europe	14.49	(16.86)	14.51	14.65	12.89	13.18
All Hispanics	10.12	(6.90)	8.99	8.41	9.27	11.52

Note: Recent Legal Immigrants obtained from NIS-P. Recent Foreign Born are obtained from the 1996 CPS. These immigrants came either less than 3 years ago (4th column) or less than 5 years ago (5th column).

where undocumented migrants are a large part of the total. The implied mean schooling of non-legal immigrant Hispanics is less than seven years, more than three years less than that of legal Hispanic immigrants.

The diversity amongst the foreign-born population is not limited to differences across these sub-populations. Even within the most numerous group – legal immigrants – there exists great heterogeneity in their prior schooling experiences. Table 8 illustrates this diversity by presenting average education by the type of visa that qualified one for legal immigrant status. Variation by type of visa is enormous with a range of nine years of schooling. The least educated are parents who typically did not complete elementary school, while the best educated are those new immigrants who came on employment visas who on average were college graduates. The influence of positive assortative mating in the marriage market is also evident in the ranking of schooling of those admitted through spousal visas; at the top employment (15.4), followed by spouses of US citizens (13.6), and finally spouses of permanent residents (10.0). This variation by visa type is important because over time legislation has loosened or tightened the numerical limits on different types of visas. The most important of these changes in the last two decades is the increase in numerical limits on employment visas which resulted not only in increased entry of those with employment visas but also in an increase in the average skill of education of legal immigrants [see Jasso, Rosensweig and Smith (2000)].

Table 8 also indicates at the time of the receipt of a green card that most of the prior schooling of legal immigrants was obtained abroad. Only one in five legal immigrants had previously completed at least one year in an American school. Not surprisingly, this fraction is higher (25%) among those who adjusted their immigrant status while in the US (adjustees), twice the rate among new arrivals (12%). Once again, the highest fraction that had completed some prior American schooling were those who had obtained employment visas (one third) while the lowest occurred among those with parent visas (only 3%). However, if we confine our attention to those who had attended some American schooling, their total years of their attendance is not trivial – about three and a quarter years for the full sample.

Table 8
Years of schooling completed among immigrants aged 25 years and over at admission, by visa class

Visa class	Mean	Years in US	Fraction with some US schooling
Spouse of U.S. citizen	13.6	0.9	.249
Spouse of Permanent Resident	10.0	0.3	.125
Parent of (adult) U.S. citizen	7.4	0.1	.029
Sibling, principal and spouse	13.5	0.1	.073
Employment, principal	16.5	1.3	.345
Employment spouse and child	15.4	0.8	.298
Refugee/asylee, principal and spouse	12.7	0.7	.221
Diversity, principal and spouse	14.7	0.1	.048
Adjustees	13.4	0.9	.285
New arrivals	11.8	0.2	.053

Note: Figures are for all immigrants in the NIS-P based on weighted data.

4. Foreign students at American schools

Education plays several roles in influencing who comes to the United States. Education affects earnings opportunities in the host and sending countries and therefore the incentives to want to migrate to the US. In addition, higher education in particular is a product in which it is widely believed the US has a distinct comparative advantage. The worldwide desire to attend American universities represent a strong draw to foreign nationals to live in the US for at least some period of time. Attendance at US colleges and universities is also thought to be a way station to subsequently obtaining legal permanent residence in the US. Foreign students attending schools in the US must obtain temporary visas for their duration of their status as students and are legally classified as nonimmigrants. Other nonimmigrants include temporary visitors for pleasure (tourists) or business, foreign diplomats and officials and their families, as well as a number of other smaller categories.

Figure 7 plots time series trends in the total number of nonimmigrants admitted to the US along with the total numbers on temporary tourist or business visas and those on student visas. Clearly, globalization has a human dimension, as mirrored in the accelerating numbers of nonimmigrants admitted to the US in recent decades. Since 1960, the numbers of nonimmigrants have grown from about 1.1 million in 1960 to almost 33 million by 2001 – a growth of 8.2% per year! Figure 7 also indicates that most of this overall surge is accounted for by a single group, those on temporary visas for tourism or business – which even in 2001 comprised 90% of all nonimmigrants.[7] There

[7] Tourist visas made up 84% of all temporary visas for business or pleasure in 2001.

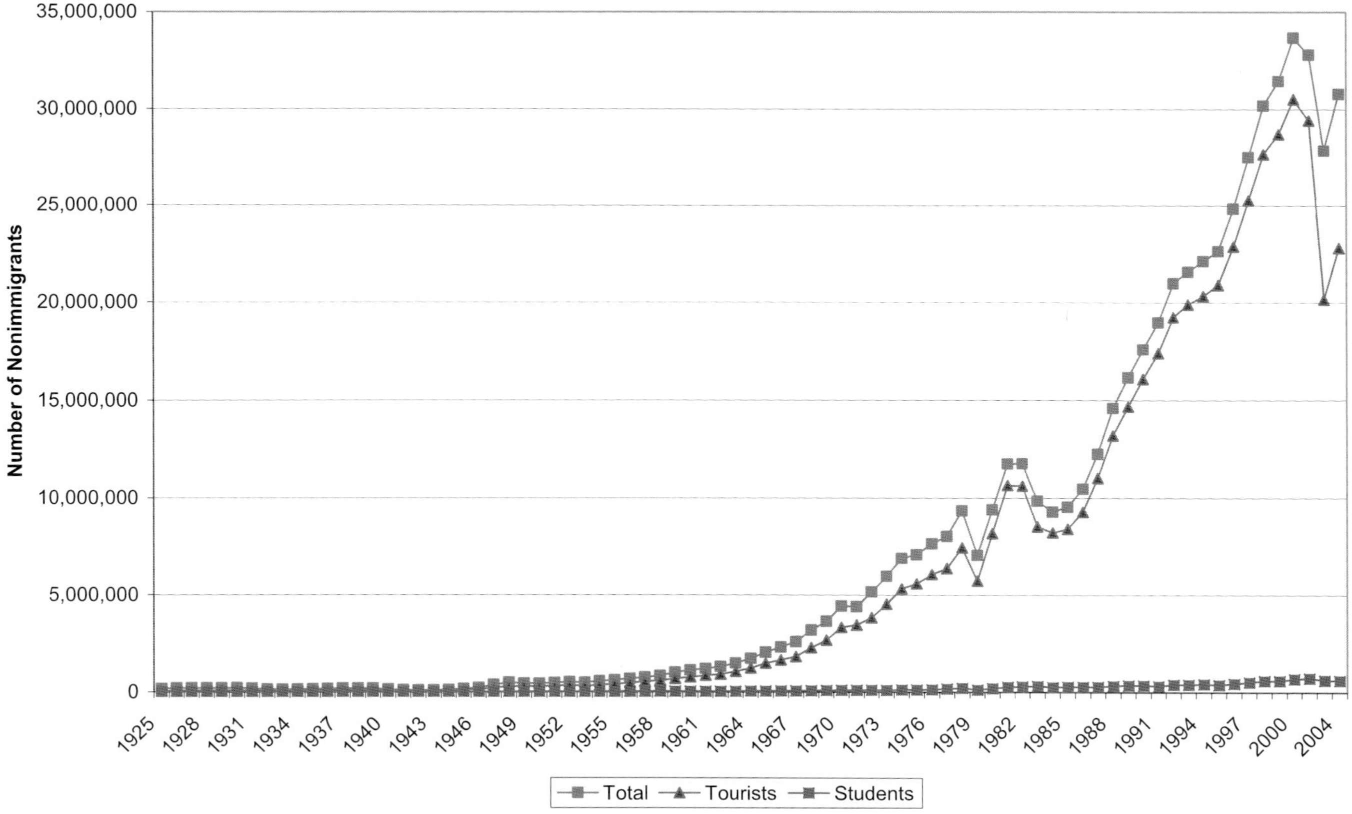

Figure 7. Nonimmigrants admitted, 1925–2004. Source: Historical Statistics of the United States, Millennial Edition, R. Bache, S. Carter, and R. Sutch (Eds.); and 2001 Statistical Yearbook of the Immigration and Naturalization Service.

was not much of a recent slowdown as the number of nonimmigrants basically doubled during the 1990s – that is until September 11. In the calendar year after that event, the total number of nonimmigrant visas fell by almost 5 million. In the three years subsequent to 9-11, the numbers of non-immigrant flows have recovered somewhat but they have not yet reached their pre-9-11 levels. Obviously, given the unusual nature of this event and its aftermath, it remains difficult to project at this point what the permanent impact of the 9/11 terrorist attacks will be.

When placed on the same scale as all nonimmigrants in Figure 7, secular trends for foreign students are barely detectable as they only comprise about 2% of the total. However, when plotted in Figure 8 on a scale more appropriate to their numbers, we see that the same secular expansion took place among foreign student visas. The number of student visas reached three quarters of a million in 2001, more than double the number in 1990 and more than seven times that in 1970.[8] Once again the events of 9/11 had a noticeable impact on these trends, but projecting into the future what the permanent impact will be would be simply guessing.

Another way of gauging the importance of foreign students is to compare them to the size of the total student population. Table 9 does just that by listing the percent of all enrolled students who are foreign nationals for fall semester of 2001. In spite of the rapid growth in student visas, the overall numbers and impact remain modest – about 4% of students at American colleges and universities are foreign nationals. This evaluation could be quite different ten years from now if the growth in foreign students continues unabated. Moreover, foreign student representation varies a great deal by level of schooling and field of study. As Table 9 demonstrates, less than 3% of undergraduates are foreign students, while one in seven of those attending American graduate schools are foreign students.

While the overall impact of foreign students may be modest, their influence on doctoral programs in general and particularly in some sub-fields in the hard sciences is anything but. Table 9B lists the fraction of doctorates that were awarded to foreign students in 2002. Foreign students earned 30% of all doctorates, and more than half of all Ph.D.s in math and engineering went to foreign students in that year.

There is a tremendous amount of variance across fields, with much lower foreign representation in the nonscience and engineering fields (15.6%). Mathematical ability and language issues appear to play some role in the choice of degree. Foreign students receive almost half of all US doctorates in physics but much less in the biological sciences (28.7%). Even in the social sciences, a third of all Ph.D.s in 2001 were earned by foreign students. Psychology, a very large degree-awarding program in the US and a

[8] Student visas in Figure 8 include visas for academic students (F1), vocational students (M1), and the corresponding F2 and M2 visas for their spouses and children. However, in 2001 for example, spouses and children make up only 6% of the total.

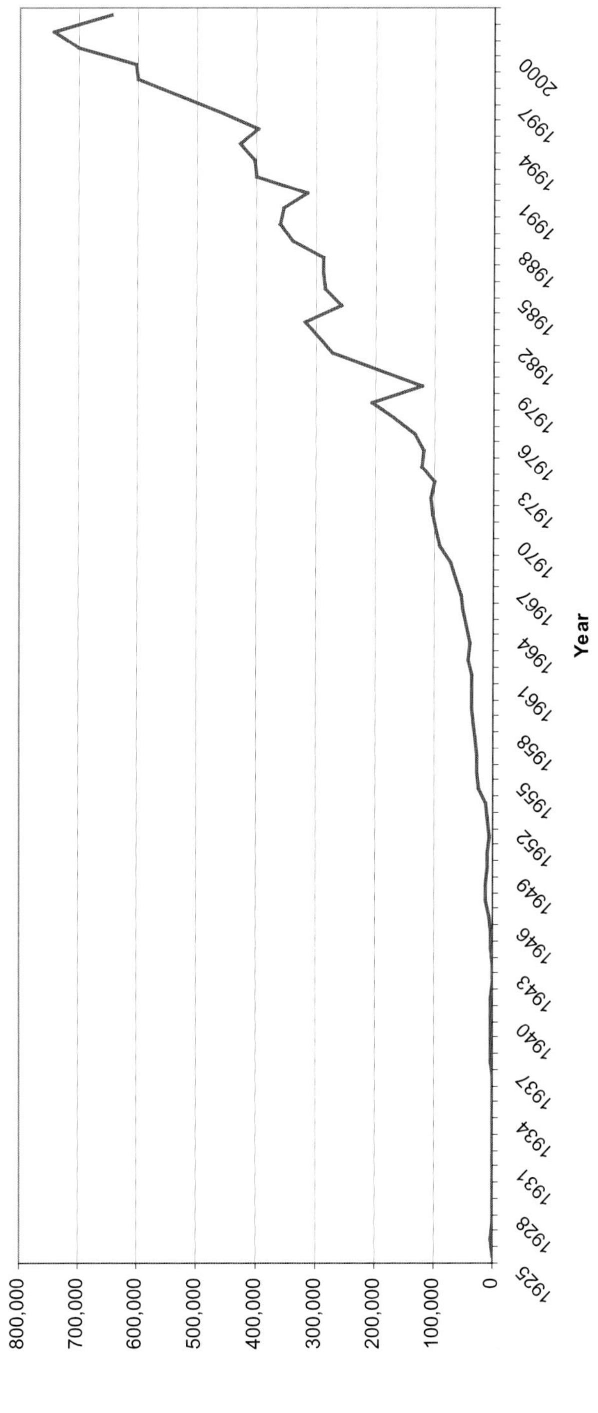

Figure 8. Nonimmigrant students, 1925–2001. Source: Historical Statistics of the United States, Millennial Edition, R. Bache, S. Carter, and R. Sutch (Eds.); and 2001 Statistical Yearbook of the Immigration and Naturalization Service.

Table 9
Enrollment of foreign students

A. By level of degree

Academic level	International students	% of U.S. enrollment
Associate	67,667	1.4
Bachelor's*	193,412	2.8
Graduate**	264,749	13.7
Total	525,828	3.9

B. Percent of doctorates awarded to foreign students holding temporary or permanent visas, by Field: 2001

All science and engineering	.380
Engineering	.583
Sciences	.322
Mathematics	.510
Physics	.428
Biological sciences	.287
Psychology	.072
Other social sciences	.322
Non-science and engineering	.156
All	.301

*College Board Annual Survey of Colleges for Fall 2001 enrollment.
**Includes first professional degrees.

science with both natural and social science arms, awarded only 7.2% of its degrees to foreign students.[9]

Table 10 provides another perspective by listing the percent of American foreign students by their region and country of birth for the academic years 1980–81 and 1999–2000. The most dramatic trend involved Asian students who increased by almost 200,000 during that time frame, increasing their proportionate representation from 30% to more than half. Two countries in particular stand out above all others – China and India. In 1980, there were fewer than 3,000 Chinese students studying in the US – by 1999 there were more than 50,000. Similarly, the numbers of Indian students increased from 9,000 to 42,000. In the rest of the world, the total numbers of European students trebled pretty much uniformly throughout Western Europe. The main area of decline was the Middle East and in particular Iran where the number of students fell from 47,000 in 1980 to less than 2,000 in 1999.

The growing numbers of foreign students receiving doctoral degrees from American universities should be viewed in the larger context of a world-wide surge in the demand

[9] An important issue that has received little rigorous analytical attention is the extent to which these foreign students have displaced American students. Such a question is not answered by just the raw numbers alone. For a thoughtful recent attempt to address this question, see Borjas (2004).

Table 10
Foreign students enrolled in institutions of higher education in the United States by region, and selected countries of origin

	1980–1981		1999–2000	
	Number	Percent	Number	Percent
Asia	94,640	30.3	280,146	54.4
China	2,770	0.9	54,466	10.6
Taiwan	19,460	6.2	29,234	5.7
India	9,250	3.0	42,337	8.2
Europe	25,330	8.1	78,485	15.2
Africa	38,180	12.2	30,292	5.9
Latin America	49,810	16.0	62,098	12.1
Middle East	84,710	27.2	34,897	6.8
North America	14,790	4.7	24,128	4.7

Source: International Comparisons of Education.

for degrees beyond the baccalaureate and increasing competition among relatively few but a growing set of countries (the UK, US, France, Germany, Japan, Australia) for these students. The surge in demand for science and engineering degrees reflects the strong economic growth in Asia and Europe, and only a relatively small part of this demand has been filled by American institutions. In large part, internal supply in Asia and Europe has responded to meet this demand. For example, in 1999 there were 190,000 doctoral degrees awarded world wide in science and engineering and only 45,000 of them were earned in the United States. Nor is the US unique in the presence of foreign students in its advance degree programs. To cite just one example, 44% of doctoral engineering degrees in the UK were earned by foreign students – the comparable numbers in the US and France were 49% and 30% respectively.

In most science fields, American top universities continue to rank among the world's elite, especially in their basic research function. These elite American universities also produce a disproportionate number of some of the best of the next generation of scientists. Many of these trained scientists are now not Americans and this may prove to be the principal legacy of the penetration of foreign students into American universities. The exact contours of that legacy are not yet clear, but the era of dominance of American-born scholars in research in many fields is most likely coming to an end. It is far less certain what will happen to the dominance of American universities in research. In certain fields at least, the best of the foreign students remain to teach and to do research at American universities in part because universities in their home countries still do not offer the same opportunities for merit based advancement and research.

These flow numbers for nonimmigrants contained in Figures 7 and 8 may understate the role of foreign students for two reasons. The first stems from a basic but fundamental stock-flow distinction. Many nonimmigrants on tourist visas have relatively short stays of a few weeks or less, while most students remain for most of the year. If the average tourist stayed in the US for eight and a half days, there would be an equal number of tourists and students living in the US on any given day.

Second, attending school in the US may be a viable route to obtaining a green card and permanent residence in the US. But here too reality may pale next to popular perceptions. Most foreign students return home to stay and most legal immigrants have never attended an American school. At the time they received their green cards, 81% of new legal immigrants in 1996 had not completed a single year in an American school. Going to an American school is a route to legal immigration, but it is by no means among the more important avenues. This route is more important among those with more advanced degrees. In recent decades, about half of the foreign trained doctoral students planned to stay in the United States after graduation, a fraction that has grown to as high as 72% by 2002.[10]

5. Immigrant education and generational assimilation

Economic mobility for yourself and your children is deeply tied to our immigration history. However, the actual documentation of the speed at which different immigrant ethnic groups can secure a better economic lot for their heirs is very sparse. The conventional view is that in terms of generational assimilation the waves of European immigrants who arrived at the end of the 19th century and the beginning of the 20th century were an enormous success. The success of more recent waves is viewed as far more problematic. This concern is particularly strong with Latino immigrants where the existing demographic and economic literature adapts a quite pessimistic tone about the extent of generational progress within the Hispanic population.[11]

It is the alleged inability of successive Hispanic generations to close their schooling gap that led to pessimism about generational assimilation.[12] The first panel in Table 11 lists education levels for three generations of Hispanic men. All data are stratified by age and are obtained from the 1996 CPS. Any other CPS or Census would show similar patterns by generation.

If one considers first these cross-sectional schooling levels by generation for Latino men, it is easy to understand the reasons for pessimism about the alleged inability of successive Hispanic generations to close their schooling gap. Latino male education levels do rise by about three years between the 1st and 2nd generation, but in every age group listed the mean education of the third generation is actually less than that of the second. Across three generations, Latino schooling gains among men were only about two and

[10] See Science and Engineering Indicators (2002) – National Science Foundation.

[11] This section is based on Smith (2003).

[12] One problem in studying assimilation is ambiguity in defining generations across Census and CPS files. Here, generations are defined as follows: 1st generation – born outside the US; 2nd generation – at least one parent born outside the US; 3rd generation or more – both parents born in the US. Thus, while reference is made for convenience to the 3rd generation, it really includes all generations beyond the second.

Table 11
Education by generation

	Age 25–30	31–40	41–50	51–60	All
Hispanic male education					
First	9.99	9.49	9.59	7.78	9.27
Second	12.98	12.60	12.97	11.99	12.14
Third	12.56	12.26	11.98	11.16	11.63

Source: 1996 March *Current Population Survey*.

Table 12
Hispanic and Mexican men's education

Year of birth	Hisp. 1st	Hisp. 2nd	Hisp. 3rd	Mex. 1st	Mex. 2nd	Mex. 3rd
1830–1834			3.17			2.80
1835–1839			4.34			4.61
1840–1844			3.69			3.49
1845–1849			5.30			5.47
1850–1854			5.27			5.43
1855–1859		6.34	5.97		5.50	5.68
1860–1864		5.19	6.62		3.75	6.32
1865–1869		4.46	7.33		3.72	6.96
1870–1874		5.26	7.97		3.70	7.75
1875–1879		4.77	8.40		4.77	8.20
1880–1884	3.12	5.65	9.55	2.67	5.08	9.17
1885–1889	3.62	6.22	10.05	2.79	5.66	9.75
1890–1894	4.98	7.55	10.89	4.56	7.04	10.47
1895–1899	4.68	8.13	11.74	3.80	7.47	11.61
1900–1904	4.55	7.75	12.08	3.81	7.37	12.40
1905–1909	5.06	9.59	12.24	4.27	9.27	12.17
1910–1914	6.10	10.56	12.13	5.02	10.30	12.13
1915–1919	7.41	11.17	12.47	6.20	10.93	12.45
1920–1924	7.91	11.80	12.40	6.22	11.61	12.29
1925–1929	8.28	12.28		5.96	12.04	
1930–1934	8.76	12.10		6.23	11.64	
1935–1939	8.40	12.50		6.15	12.26	
1940–1944	9.09	12.88		6.86	12.51	
1945–1949	9.56	12.42		7.79	12.08	
1950–1954	9.13			7.72		
1955–1959	9.47			8.23		
1960–1964	9.79			8.71		
1965–1969	9.90			9.30		

one half years. Since these generations span at least 50 years, at this pace generation progress could rightly be labeled slow, especially given beliefs about the considerable progress made by the children and grandchildren of the European immigrants.

Cross-sectional data such as that contained in Table 11 have been repeatedly used to evaluate generational assimilation among Hispanics. The evaluation is consistently negative, often with an implicit comparison to the allegedly great generational gains made by the earlier European immigrants or to the educational accomplishments of Asian immigrants. Of course, as we will see momentarily, that data arrayed as in Table 11 are methodologically inappropriate and have little to do with generational assimilation.

These data do not speak to inter-generation assimilation since we should not be comparing 2nd and 3rd generation workers of the same age in the same year. For example, the 1970 40-year-old, 3rd generation Latinos in Table 11 are not sons of 40-year-old, 2nd generation Latino men in the same year, and certainly not the grandsons of the 1970 1st generation immigrants who were 40 years old. To correctly evaluate generational assimilation, the data must be realigned to match up the sons and grandsons of each set of ethnic immigrants.

To obtain a single estimate for each five-year birth cohort cell, means across all Census years since 1940 and groups of CPS years were averaged. To track generation progress, the data in Table 12 are indexed by immigrant generation birth cohorts. With a 25-year lag between generations, education of the 2nd generation refers to 2nd generation born 25 years after the birth-years indexed for immigrants in the first column. A similar 25-year offset is assumed for the 3rd and 2nd generations.

To the extent that schooling is an adequate proxy for labor market quality, reading down the column for the first generation informs us about secular changes in the 'quality' of immigrants.

Conclusions

This chapter deals with a number of issues about immigrants to the United States and their education. In part reflecting the reasons why they come to America, immigrants are more highly represented in both the lowest and highest rungs of the education ladder. On average immigrants have less schooling than the native born, a schooling deficit that reached 1.3 years in 2002. Perhaps as important as the average difference between immigrants and the native-born population, there is considerable diversity in the schooling accomplishments among different immigrant sub-groups. The education of new European and Asian immigrants is higher than that of native-born Americans, while the typical Latino immigrant continues to trail the native-born by about four years of schooling on average.

The education gap of new recent immigrants did rise but only modestly over the last 60 years. This increase was higher among men than among women and appears to be entirely accounted for by the increasing fraction of immigrants who are illegal. Legal immigrants appear to have about the same amount of schooling as native-born

Americans do, and in the top of the schooling hierarchy have a good deal more. Finally, the concern that educational generational progress among Latino immigrants has lagged behind other immigrant groups is largely unfounded.

Acknowledgement

This chapter was presented at a conference on the *Handbook of the Economics of Education* at the Bush Center, Texas A&M University. The research was supported by grants from NIH. The expert programming assistance of David Rumpel and Iva Maclennan is gratefully appreciated.

References

Borjas, G. (1994). "The economics of immigration". Journal of Economic Literature 32, 1667–2717.
Borjas, G. (1995). "Assimilation and changes in cohort quality revisited: What happened to immigrant earnings in the 1980s?". Journal of Labor Economics 13 (2), 201–245.
Borjas, G. (2004). "The impact of foreign students on native enrollment in graduate programs". NBER Working Paper 10349, National Bureau of Economic Research.
Immigration and Naturalization Service (2003). "Estimates of unauthorized immigration population residing in the United States: 1990 to 2000". Office of Policy and Planning, INS.
Jasso, G., Rosensweig, M., Smith, J.P. (2000). "The changing skill of new immigrants to the United States: Recent trends and their determinants". In: Borjas, G. (Ed.), Issues in the Economics of Immigration. University of Chicago Press, Chicago.
Jasso, G., Massey, D., Rosensweig, M., Smith, J.P. (2000). "The New Immigrant Pilot Survey (NIS): Overview and findings about U.S. immigrants at admission". Demography 37 (1), 127–138.
Passel, J.S., Capps, R., Fix, M. (2004). "Undocumented immigrants: Facts and figures". Urban Institute.
Science and Engineering Indicators (2002). Volume 1. National Science Board, National Science Foundation.
Smith, J.P. (2003). "Assimilation across the generations". American Economic Review 93 (2), 315–319.
Smith, J.P. (2006). "Immigrants and the labor market". Journal of Labor Economics 24 (2), 203–233.
Smith, J.P., Edmonston, B. (1997). The New Americans: Economic, Demographic, and Fiscal Effects of Immigration. National Academy Press, Washington, DC.

Chapter 5

EDUCATIONAL WAGE PREMIA AND THE DISTRIBUTION OF EARNINGS: AN INTERNATIONAL PERSPECTIVE

FRANCO PERACCHI

Faculty of Economics, Tor Vergata University, via Columbia, 2, I-00133 Roma, Italy
e-mail: franco.peracchi@uniroma2.it

Contents

Handbook of the Economics of Education, Volume 1
Edited by Eric A. Hanushek and Finis Welch
© 2006 Elsevier B.V. All rights reserved
DOI: 10.1016/S1574-0692(06)01005-1

Abstract

This chapter analyzes the international evidence on the relationship between educational wage premia and the distribution of personal labor earnings. The aim is to review what is known about the contribution of differences in relative wages across schooling levels to the degree of variability, between countries and over time, in the pecuniary returns to work. Definition and measurement problems are of paramount importance in analyses of this kind, and so a large part of the chapter is devoted to some of these issues.

Keywords

educational wage premia, earnings functions, educational attainments, distribution of labor earnings

JEL classification: I20, J24, J31

1. Introduction and summary

This chapter analyzes the international evidence on the relationship between educational wage premia and the distribution of personal labor earnings. The aim is to review what is known about the contribution of differences in relative wages across schooling levels to the degree of variability, between countries and over time, in the pecuniary returns to work. Definition and measurement issues are of paramount importance when trying to address the seemingly simple question of how much schooling pays off. Hence, a large part of the chapter is devoted to these issues.

Educational wage premia are typically defined as the percentage difference between the mean labor earnings of people with different schooling levels. For example, the college wage premium (or college premium for short) is defined as the percentage difference between the mean earnings of people with a college degree and the mean earnings of people with only secondary education completed. Often wage premia are approximated by logarithmic differences. To ensure robustness to outliers or censoring, mean earnings are sometimes replaced by median earnings.

The size of educational premia depends on how schooling levels are defined. It also depends, in a more subtle way, on the time reference for the earnings flow and the way in which the returns to work are defined. Earnings may be defined on an hourly, weekly, monthly or annual basis. If weekly, monthly or annual earnings are considered, educational premia may depend on differences across educational levels in the distribution of hours worked per unit of time. Educational premia are usually computed excluding non-wage benefits, such as employer provided health insurance and pension coverage. They also exclude the effects of education on productivity in self-employment and non-pecuniary returns such as better health status, efficiency in home production, child care, etc. We know little about how the inclusion of all these elements may change the structure of the private returns to schooling.

The distribution of labor earnings is not the same as the distribution of income, and changes in the distribution of labor earnings do not necessarily and immediately translate into equivalent changes in the distribution of income. Analyses of the income distribution typically focus on the distribution of total household income or equalized total household income (that is, total household income divided by some equivalence scale). These income concepts differ from personal earnings for two reasons. One is the role of income earned by other household members. The other is the role of unearned income. Unearned income is especially important at the bottom and the top of the income distribution. The sources of unearned income also differ in the two tails. At the bottom, where unemployment or nonemployment are prevalent, a crucial role is played by transfer income (unemployment benefits, pension income, etc.). At the top, a crucial role is instead played by property income (mainly income from past savings).

In this chapter I follow the approach of the theory of human capital developed by Schultz (1961), Becker (1964, 1967), Ben-Porath (1967) and Mincer (1974). This approach postulates that schooling increases wages by directly increasing a worker's productivity. I shall not consider the ability signaling approach introduced by Spence

(1974), which postulates that education is associated with higher wages because by acquiring higher education a worker signals to firms that she has higher innate ability than a worker with lower education.[1] A central difference between the two approaches is the fact that, in the human capital theory, the schooling choice causes at least part of the productivity differences among workers, whereas in signaling models, schooling is correlated with differences among workers that exist prior to the schooling choice [Weiss (1995)].

I also distinguish between educational wage premia and returns to schooling. The latter are a measure of the causal effect of an extra year of schooling on a worker's earnings.[2] The former represent a convenient statistical summary of the observed differences in the distribution of earnings across schooling levels, but need not have a causal interpretation.

I shall focus on three sets of questions:

1. How are workers distributed by schooling level across countries? How did this distribution change over time?
2. How do educational premia look like across countries, possibly controlling for sex and age or labor market experience? How did they change over time?
3. What is the role of the differences in educational premia and in the population distribution by schooling level in explaining the observed differences in the distribution of personal earnings both across countries and over time?

The remainder of this chapter is organized as follow. Section 2 deals with the crucial issue of comparability of educational attainments and earnings data across countries and over time, and with the problem of how to specify and interpret the statistical relationship between earnings and schooling. Section 3 summarizes the available evidence on differences and trends across countries in the educational composition of the population and the workforce. To help interpret these results, and to guide the discussion of the available empirical evidence, it also presents a simple model of endogenous schooling choice that somewhat resembles the earlier models of Becker (1964, 1967) and Ben-Porath (1967). Section 4 looks instead at the evidence on movements in wage premia over the last 2–3 decades, focusing on differences in time trends across countries. Finally, Section 5 considers how the differences in the evolution of the educational composition of the workforce and the wage premia help explain the differences in the distribution of labor earnings across countries and over time.

2. Measurement and statistical issues

Before addressing the three questions raised in the Introduction, a number of measurement and statistical issues need to be discussed. Measurement issues arise from the fact

[1] See Chapter 8 by Lange and Topel in this Handbook.

[2] See Chapter 7 by Heckman, Lochner and Todd in this Handbook.

that educational attainments and earnings need not be defined or measured in ways that are fully consistent across countries and over time, which complicates the task of drawing inferences from the available data. The main statistical issues have to do with the specification of the statistical model for the relationship between earnings and schooling, and the conditions under which this model may be taken to represent the causal effect of schooling on earnings.

2.1. *Comparability of educational attainments*

How are educational attainments measured? Can they be compared across countries and over time? These questions routinely arise when using micro-economic survey data, where one faces the problem of comparing educational attainments across countries, or over time for the same country. After the seminal paper of Benhabib and Spiegel (1994), they have also received considerable attention in the literature on macroeconomic growth, where a key empirical issue is whether the initial differences in the level of schooling help explain the cross-country differences in GDP growth.

Perhaps the simplest measure of educational attainments is the number of years of full-time schooling completed. This measure has been criticized on several grounds. First, by not counting years of part-time study, it underestimates educational attainments. Second, it ignores differences in the curricular content of schooling within a given country. Third, it takes no account of cross-country differences in educational systems. Thus, for example, Freeman and Schettkat (2000a) argue that "years of education do not provide a particularly good measure of differences in schooling. ... If one compares formal schooling, it is necessary to go beyond years of schooling and establish some form of equivalence between ... educational attainments".

Comparative work on educational attainments and educational wage premia is largely based on the International Standard Classification of Education (ISCED), which was designed by the UNESCO in the early 1970's to serve "as an instrument suitable for assembling, compiling and presenting statistics of education both within individual countries and internationally" [UNESCO (1997)].

The present version of the classification, known as ISCED 1997, was approved by the UNESCO in 1997. Educational programs are cross-classified along two dimensions: level and field of education. The concept of educational level is based on the assumption that educational programs can be grouped into an ordered set of categories, broadly corresponding to the degree of complexity of their content. ISCED 1997 classifies educational programs into the following seven levels:

- Level 0: Pre-primary education (initial stage of organized instruction). Not compulsory in most countries. It is "designed primarily to introduce very young children to a school-type environment".
- Level 1: Primary education or first stage of basic education. It is "designed to give students a sound basic education in reading, writing and mathematics, along with an elementary understanding of other subjects, such as history, geography, natural

science, social science, art and music". It covers in principle 5 to 6 years of full-time schooling, and the customary or legal age of entry is between 4 and 7 years.

- Level 2: Lower secondary or second stage of basic education. It is typically designed to complete the provision of basic education. The programs at this level are usually more subject-focused, and require more specialized teachers. The end of this level, after some 9 years from the beginning of primary education, often coincides with the end of full-time compulsory schooling.
- Level 3: Upper secondary education. Typically starts at 15 or 16 years of age, at the end of full-time compulsory education. Instruction is even more subject-oriented and often teachers need to be more qualified than at ISCED level 2. Education can be general or pre-cocational (two types of education often aggregated) or vocational. Many programs enable access to ISCED level 5.
- Level 4: Post-secondary non-tertiary education. It consists of programs that are at the boundary between upper-secondary and post-secondary (tertiary) education, but cannot be considered as tertiary programs because they are not significantly more advanced than ISCED level 3 programs. Examples include pre-degree foundation courses or short vocational programs.
- Level 5: First stage of tertiary education. It consists of programs that last at least two years, have a more advanced educational content than ISCED levels 3 and 4, but do not lead directly to an advanced research qualification.
- Level 6: Second stage of tertiary education. It consists of programs that lead to the award of an advanced research qualification (Ph.D. or Doctorate). They are devoted to advanced study and original research (and not based on course-work only), and typically require the submission of a thesis or dissertation of publishable quality.

There is considerable variation, both across countries at a given point in time and over time for the same country, in the length, structure and objectives of each of these levels. Just as an example, Table 1 presents the theoretical starting ages at ISCED levels 3 and 5 in the school year 2000–01 for the 15 countries of the European Union (EU). The theoretical length of ISCED level 3 ranges between 2 years in Netherlands, Spain and the UK, and 5 years in Austria and Italy.

An additional difficulty is the fact that the same level of education (either years of schooling or schooling level) may reflect very different levels of literacy in different countries. This is indicated quite clearly by the results of reading and mathematical and scientific literacy tests, such as those carried out through the OECD Programme for International Student Assessment (PISA).[3] These studies also indicate considerable differences in performance within each education system. Such differences are often related to differences in "school quality", a rather vague concept that is meant to capture differences in school and student backgrounds, the human and financial resources available to schools, curricular differences, selection policies and practices, or the way in which teaching is organized and delivered.

[3] See OECD (2002).

Table 1
Theoretical starting age at ISCED levels 3 (level 3A) and 5 (level 5A/5B) in the school year 2000–01 for the countries of the European Union

Country	Level 3	Level 5
Austria	14	18–19
Belgium	14	18
Denmark	16–17	20–21
Finland	16	19
France	15	18
Germany	16	19
Greece	15	18
Ireland	15	18
Italy	14	19
Luxembourg	15	18
Netherlands	16	18
Portugal	15	18
Spain	16	18
Sweden	16	19
UK	16	18

Source: Dunne (2003).

The problem of differences in school quality may be particularly serious for developing countries.[4] Typical proxies for school-quality include the pupil-teacher ratios, the spending per pupil as a fraction of per-capita GDP, the ratio of average salaries of teachers to per-capita GDP, the length of the school year, and the fraction of students that are repeaters and drop out in primary and secondary school. In fact, most of these indicators are simply crude measures of inputs into the schooling production function.

Barro and Lee (1996, 1997) show big differences in these indicators, both across countries and over time. However, without knowledge of the schooling production function, it is not clear how these differences translate into differences in school quality. Hanushek and Kimko (2000) try to circumvent the problem by constructing direct measures of school quality for 39 countries by combining the information on international mathematics and science tests available through 1991.

2.2. Aggregate data on schooling

The main direct sources of aggregate data on schooling are population censuses and educational and labor force surveys. Various international organizations (OECD, UN, UNESCO, etc.) collect and try to harmonize these data to ensure comparability across countries and over time.

[4] See Chapter 16 by Glewwe and Kremer in Volume 2 of this Handbook.

Data availability varies widely across countries. When direct census or survey information is unavailable, school enrollment rates (the ratio of the number of students enrolled in a given educational level to the size of the population in the relevant age group) are often used to construct measures of average educational attainments.

For example, Kyriacou (1991) provides estimates of the average years of schooling of the workforce for a sample of 111 countries at five-year intervals over the period 1965–1985. He first estimates a relationship linking average years of schooling to lagged enrollment rates for an initial cross-section of countries, and then uses this relationship to predict schooling attainments for other countries and years.

Barro and Lee (1993, 1996) compute instead average years of completed education of the population aged 15+ and 25+, broken down by gender, by combining direct survey and census information for some countries with indirect information for other countries obtained from school enrollment data through the perpetual inventory method.[5]

Nehru, Swanson and Dubey (1995) completely ignore census or survey information and use UNESCO school enrollment data to construct time series of educational attainments via the perpetual inventory method adjusted for mortality and, whenever possible, grade repetition and dropouts. Accounting for grade repetition is particularly important in developing countries where enrollment rates may otherwise be grossly overestimated. Unfortunately, their database contains some implausible results.

The practice of using enrollment flows has been criticized by many. For example, Krueger and Lindahl (2001) argue that "despite their aggregate nature, available data on average schooling levels across countries are poorly measured, in large part because they are often derived from enrollment flows".

De la Fuente and Doménech (2000, 2001) focus on 21 high-income OECD countries and produce estimates of the fraction of the population aged 25+ that attended (but not necessarily completed) the various educational levels. They exploit a variety of direct sources of information on educational attainments and remove several anomalies that seem to reflect changes in classification criteria and other inconsistencies of the underlying primary statistics. They explicitly avoid the use of flow estimates based on enrollment data because "they seem to produce implausible time profiles". Compared to the alternative series, their data indicate a larger role for human capital variables in empirical growth equations.[6]

The data set produced by Cohen and Soto (2002) is currently the most complete and comes closest to the data presented in national censuses and OECD or UNESCO databases. It covers 95 countries at ten-year intervals from 1960 to 2010. The data for 2010 are based on the estimates of educational attainments for the year 2000 and the population projections by age taken from the US Census Bureau Web page. The main

[5] The most recent version of their data [Barro and Lee (2000)] comprises at least one observation for 142 countries, of which 107 have complete observations at five-year intervals from 1960 to 2000.

[6] Similar conclusions are obtained by Bassanini and Scarpetta (2002), who show that the long-run elasticity of output per working-age person to the average years of education (about 6% per an additional year of education) is in line with the microeconomic literature on private returns to schooling.

differences with respect to de la Fuente and Domenech (2000, 2001) are due to differences in classification and the methods used to distinguish between primary education and the first stage of secondary education.

It is worth noticing that the importance of measurement errors not only varies significantly across data sets, but also depends on which data transformation is used. De la Fuente and Ciccone (2003) argue that "two of the data sets most widely used in cross-country empirical work, those by Kyriacou (1991) and Barro and Lee (various years), perform relatively well when the data are used in levels, but contain very little signal when the data are differenced. Recent efforts to increase the signal to noise ratio by de la Fuente and Doménech (2001) and Cohen and Soto (2002) seem to have been at least partially successfull, but even in these cases the potential estimation bias remains large".

2.3. *Comparability of earnings data*

Comparability of earnings data is another important issue. Differences across countries and over time may arise from differences in the data sources, the time reference for the earnings flow, the comprehensiveness of the definition of earnings, their tax treatment, etc. They may also arise from differences in data quality.

Household surveys (either cross-sectional or longitudinal) are the main source of information on earnings. Sometimes, administrative data are used, such as income tax records and administrative data from social security. Firm-level data are less frequently used. Relative to survey data, administrative data have the advantage that the earnings information is in principle more accurate. This advantage is often offset by the fact that background information may be limited or of poor quality.

Typically, the self-employed are excluded or their earnings are imputed using the earnings model for the employees. The reason is the difficulty of separating self-employment income from risk premia and the returns to physical capital and entrepreneurial ability.

The time reference for the earnings flows varies, as earnings may be computed on an hourly, daily, weekly, monthly or annual basis. If defined on a daily, weekly, monthly or annual basis, educational premia may depend on differences in the number of hours worked per unit of time by each educational level. On the other hand, the practice of obtaining hourly, daily, weekly or monthly earnings by dividing reported annual earnings by reported hours, days, weeks or months worked per year may add substantial noise to the data. This is especially true when, for example, annual hours of work are obtained as the product of the reported number of weeks worked times the reported usual number of weekly hours of work.

If one is interested in analyzing the allocative role of wages, then earnings should be measured after taxes and transfers, and should include the non-pecuniary advantages of jobs. This is not always done. Educational wage premia are often computed before taxes and transfers, and are typically computed excluding non-wage benefits, such as employer provided health insurance, pension coverage and nursery services. They also exclude the effects of education on productivity in self-employment and non-pecuniary returns such as better health status, efficiency in home production, child care, etc. To what extent the inclusion of these elements may change the structure of private returns to schooling remains an open research issue.

A variety of measurement error problems in earnings data may potentially affect estimates of educational premia and earnings inequality.

First, earnings may be top-coded. In surveys, this typically occurs for confidentiality reasons. Administrative data may also be topcoded because, for some programs, only earnings up to a threshold are relevant. Top-coding biases estimated means and variances downwards but does not necessarily affect estimated percentiles.

Second, reported earnings may be subject to recall and rounding errors. For some categories of workers and some countries, reported earnings may actually be systematically misreported.

Third, a small fraction of individuals reports earnings that appear implausibly low or implausibly high. The log transformation may exacerbate the problem for low earnings. To limit the influence of these cases, it is common practice to drop wage observations below a threshold, and sometimes also above. This practice does not have a formal justification and may actually introduce biases in the estimation of mean, variances and regression relationships.

Fourth, earnings data subject to nonresponse or other forms of missingness may be "completed" by some imputation procedure before being released. Imputation methods vary considerably, but they are almost invariably based on the "missing at random" assumption. Empirical work is divided between two alternative practices. One ignores the fact that a fraction of the data has been imputed and treats them as genuinely occurring values, the other drops observations with imputed values. In both cases, the fact that earnings may not be missing at random creates problems, although of a different nature.

Finally, cross-country comparisons are complicated by differential movements in price levels and exchange rates. Results may be sensitive to the choice of the price indices and the way in which national currencies are converted into a common scale (for example, through exchange rates or purchasing power parities).

2.4. *Statistical earnings functions*

In broad terms, a statistical earnings function is a specification of the conditional distribution of log earnings Y given $S = s$ years of (full-time) schooling and $X = x$ years of potential work experience (years since leaving full-time study).[7] Instead of considering the whole conditional distribution, one typically focuses on the conditional mean $\mu(s, x) = \mathrm{E}(Y \mid S = s, X = x)$ and the conditional variance $\sigma^2(s, x) = \mathrm{Var}(Y \mid S = s, X = x)$ of log earnings, or on selected conditional percentiles, such as the median, the upper and lower quartiles, or the upper and lower deciles.

[7] Potential work experience is often conventionally defined as age minus years of schooling minus 6.

Depending on the data and the model assumptions, a statistical earnings fun provide a cross-sectional or a longitudinal description. In the first case, the $\mu(s, \cdot)$ describes the variability of average earnings, at a given point in tim people with s years of schooling but different experience levels. In the second case, $\mu(s, \cdot)$ describes the expected path of earnings across the working life of people with s years of schooling.

A typical assumption on statistical earnings functions is additive separability in s and x. For example, the specification

$$\mu(s, x) = \alpha + f(s) + g(x),$$

where f and g are smooth functions, implies that $\partial\mu/\partial s$ does not depend on x and $\partial\mu/\partial x$ does not depend on s. When $f(s)$ is linear and $g(x)$ is quadratic, one obtains the earnings function popularized by Mincer (1974)

$$\mu(s, x) = \mathrm{E}(Y \mid S = s, X = x) = \alpha + \beta s + \gamma_1 x + \gamma_2 x^2. \tag{1}$$

I shall refer to (1) as the Mincer model or standard human capital earnings function. Because years of schooling enter (1) linearly, it follows that $\mathrm{E}(Y \mid S = s+1, X = x) - \mathrm{E}(Y \mid S = s, X = x) = \beta$. I shall refer to the parameter β as the (Mincerian) return to education because, under certain conditions,[8] it may be interpreted as the internal rate of return from the investment on one additional year of (full-time) schooling.

Model (1) is easily generalized by replacing the linear term in schooling and the quadratic term in potential experience by more flexible parametric specifications.[9] A semi-parametric alternative is the partially linear model

$$\mu(s, x) = \alpha + \beta s + g(x),$$

where the function g is left unspecified.

A closely related family of models is obtained when additive separability is retained, but years of schooling are replaced by a set of indicators for educational attainments. One interpretation of this model is that the unknown function $f(s)$ is approximated by a piecewise constant function. For example, with three mutually exclusive and totally exhaustive schooling levels (say, "compulsory", "upper secondary" or "high school", and "tertiary" or "college"), a possible specification of the conditional mean of log earnings is

$$\mu(d_2, d_3, x) = \mathrm{E}(Y \mid D_2 = d_2, D_3 = d_3, X = x) = \eta + \sum_{j=2}^{3} \delta_j d_j + g(x),$$

where D_2 and D_3 are 0–1 indicators for completed high school and college, $\eta + g(x)$ is the mean of log earnings for a worker with only compulsory education and x years

[8] See, for example, Willis (1986) and Polachek and Siebert (1993).

[9] See, for example, Heckman and Polachek (1994) and Murphy and Welch (1990).

of potential experience, and δ_2 and δ_3 are the educational premia[10] for workers with exactly the same number of years of potential experience.

When schooling is discretized into categories, the Mincer model (1) implies

$$\mu(d_2, d_3, x) = \eta + \sum_{j=2}^{3} \delta_j d_j + \gamma_1 x + \gamma_2 x^2, \tag{2}$$

where

$$\eta = \alpha + \beta \bar{S}_1, \qquad \delta_2 = \beta(\bar{S}_2 - \bar{S}_1), \qquad \delta_3 = \beta(\bar{S}_3 - \bar{S}_1),$$

and $\bar{S}_j$ is the mean number of years of schooling of workers with the jth schooling level. Notice that the ratio δ_3/δ_2 of the coefficients on the schooling indicators is equal to the ratio $(\bar{S}_3 - \bar{S}_1)/(\bar{S}_2 - \bar{S}_1)$ of the mean number of years that each level requires beyond compulsory schooling.

Sometimes, potential experience is not available because only a coarse classification by educational level is available and the career starting date cannot easily be determined [see Light (1998)]. In these cases, versions of models (1) and (2) are often estimated with potential experience replaced by age. This practice usually ignores the implications of the two models for the conditional mean of log earnings given schooling and age. For example, if (1) holds and potential experience is defined as $X = \text{age} - S - 6$, then

$$\mathrm{E}(Y \mid S = s, \text{age} = a) = \theta_1 + \theta_2 s + \theta_3 s^2 + \theta_4 a + \theta_5 a^2 + \theta_6 as,$$

where $\theta_1 = \alpha - 6\gamma_1 + 36\gamma_2$, $\theta_2 = \beta - \gamma_1 + 12\gamma_2$, $\theta_3 = \theta_5 = -\theta_6/2 = \gamma_2$, and $\theta_4 = \gamma_1 - 12\gamma_2$. Thus, the conditional mean of log earnings now depends on the level and the square of both schooling and age, and on their cross-product.

Because schooling and potential experience are usually recorded as integer valued, a statistical earnings function may in principle be estimated fully nonparametrically at all (s, x) combinations for which the sample size is large enough. Depending on the model specification, estimation methods for additive models or partially linear models may also be considered. Most frequently, however, the parametric models (1) and (2) are estimated from cross-sectional data using ordinary least squares (OLS). Ease of estimation and increasing data availability have resulted in hundreds of estimates of Mincerian returns to schooling from model (1) or educational premia from model (2) for a large number of countries and different periods.

The econometric problems arising when OLS are used to uncover the returns to schooling, that is, the causal effect of one additional year of schooling on the distribution of earnings, have been discussed at length in the literature.[11] These problems include endogeneity of schooling, measurement errors in schooling and potential experience, omitted unobserved individual effects ("ability"), heterogeneity of returns, and

[10] The difference in the mean of log earnings relative to compulsory education.

[11] See, for example, the classical paper of Griliches (1977) and the more recent papers by Card (2001) and Harmon, Oosterbeek and Walker (2003).

sample selection due to either self-selection or the sample inclusion criteria adopted by the analyst.[12]

To tackle the resulting biases, various estimation methods have been proposed. In recent years, two approaches have received considerable attention. The first exploits the differences between siblings or twins in the levels of schooling and earnings. The second employs instrumental variables (IV) techniques using a wide range of instruments typically provided by "natural experiments". The estimates of returns to education obtained from these approaches usually exceed OLS estimates, although this is not true in general.[13] They also tend to be less precise than OLS, possibly because of a weak instrument problem.[14]

Ashenfelter, Harmon and Oosterbeek (1999) argue that, in fact, differences due to the estimation method are much smaller than is sometimes reported. The reason is that estimated returns that are significantly different from zero are more likely to be published and, since the twin studies and IV studies tend to have larger sampling errors in general, a less representative sample of these studies is typically reported.

Recently, the specifications (1) and (2) (and their generalizations) have also been used to model the behavior of the quantiles of the conditional distribution of log earnings given schooling and labor market experience (or age). If $\xi_u(s, x)$ denotes the uth conditional quantile of log earnings ($0 < u < 1$),[15] then the counterpart of model (1) is the linear quantile regression model

$$\xi_u(s, x) = \alpha + \beta s + \gamma_1 x + \gamma_2 x^2,$$

where now the parameters α, β, γ_1 and γ_2 all vary with u, unless the conditional distribution of log earnings is homoskedastic, in which case only the intercept α varies with u. The linear quantile regression model is typically estimated by minimizing an asymmetric least absolute deviations criterion using some version of the simplex method.

2.5. *Measurement errors in micro-level data on schooling*

When individual's education appears as a regressor in a model for some labor market outcome, the validity of inference depends crucially on how accurately educational attainments are measured. The presence of measurement errors in micro-level data on schooling has been recognized for long time.[16] Assessments of their effects on inference about population earnings functions and attempts to correct for their presence typically

[12] For example, focusing only on full-time full-year workers or private-sector non-agricultural employees.

[13] See, for example, the results of Vieira (1999) for Portugal.

[14] See, for example, Bound, Jaeger and Baker (1995).

[15] By definition, $\xi_u(s, x) = \inf\{y\colon F(y \mid s, x) \leqslant u\}$, where $F(\cdot \mid s, x)$ is the conditional distribution function of log earnings given schooling and labor market experience. If $u = .5$, then $\xi_u(s, x)$ is simply the conditional median of log earnings. By the properties of quantiles, $\exp \xi_u(s, x)$ is the conditional quantile of earnings.

[16] See, for example, Griliches (1977).

rest on the assumption that they obey the classical measurement errors model, which essentially treats them as random. How good is this model?

Black, Sanders and Taylor (2003) document the nature of measurement errors in the reporting of higher education in the US Census and Current Population Survey (CPS) data. They find that these errors violate models of classical measurement error in three important ways. First, the level of education is consistently reported as higher than it is. Second, errors in the reporting of education are correlated with covariates that enter the earnings regressions. Third, errors in the reporting of education appear to be correlated with the error term in a model of earnings determination. These findings are unlikely to be unique to the USA.

They conclude that "because measurement error in education is systematically related to both observed earnings-related characteristics and the error term in earnings regressions, it is likely that measurement error is positively correlated across multiple reports on education. If so, instrumental variable (IV) estimates, that rely on multiple reports of education are inconsistent, as are other recently proposed estimators designed to deal with these biases".

3. Educational attainments

Section 3.1 presents international evidence on educational attainments of the population and the workforce over the last 40 years. Although the available data can only provide a broad-brush picture of the differences and trends across countries, they show clear evidence of substantial increases of educational attainments in both developing and developed countries. To help interpret these results, and to guide the discussion of the empirical evidence on educational wage premia, Section 3.2 presents a simple model of endogenous schooling choice that resembles the earlier models of Becker (1964, 1967) and Ben-Porath (1967). The model suggests an important link between schooling attainments and life expectancy, on which Section 3.3 provides some empirical evidence. Finally, Sections 3.4 and 3.5 discuss two crucial aspects which are neglected by the basic model, namely the interaction between supply and demand and the role of expectations about future wage premia.

3.1. Educational composition of the population and the workforce

How is the population distributed by educational level across countries? How is the workforce distributed by educational level across countries? How did these distributions change over time?

Figure 1 plots changes in the educational attainments of the adult population (aged 25+) between 1960 and 2000 against their initial level in 1960. The data are from Cohen and Soto (2002), and cover 95 countries. I present four indicators: the percentage of the adult population with primary, secondary and higher education, and the average number of years of schooling.

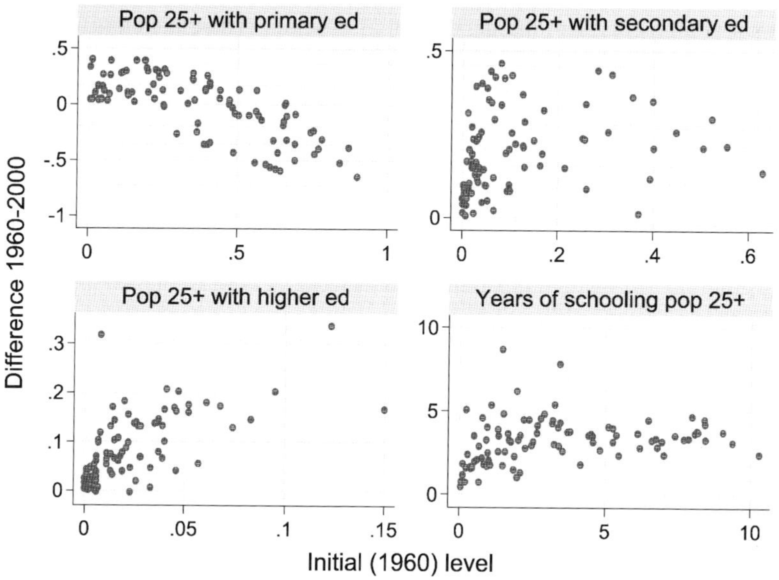

Figure 1. Educational attainments of the population aged 25+ in 1960 and differences between 1960 and 2000.

Between 1960 and 2000, educational attainments increased in both developing and developed countries. On average across countries, the percentage of the adult population with only primary education hardly changed as a result of an increase in developing countries[17] and a decline in developed countries. On the other hand, the percentage of the adult population with secondary education increased by 19 percentage points, the percentage of the adult population with tertiary education increased by about 8 percentage points, whereas the mean number of years of schooling increased by 3.2 years.

The available data show clear evidence of convergence in the percentage of the adult population with only primary education (Figure 1). In fact, the relationship between initial levels and subsequent variation has a negative slope, and one may also observe a decline in the cross-country variation of this indicator. On the other hand, the data show no evidence of convergence for the percentage of the adult population with secondary or higher education, and for the mean number of years of schooling. For these indicators, the available evidence actually shows a substantial increase in cross-country variation.

Much less is known about the educational composition and the educational attainments of the workforce, and their changes over time. Because better educated people tend to have higher labor force participation, the worksforce tends to exhibit higher

[17] An important, but largely unresolved issue, is the role played by prohibition on child labor, increases in mandatory schooling, and various education policies (literacy campaigns, educational radio, etc.) in raising educational attainments in developing countries [see, for example, Glewwe (2002)].

educational attainments than the population as a whole. Thus, the educational attainments of the population provide a lower bound on the educational attainments of the workforce. In general, increases in the educational attainments of the population and the workforce are highly correlated. The precise effect, however, depends on the labor force participation rate of each educational group relative to the aggregate.

3.2. A model of endogenous schooling

To understand the forces behind the massive increase of educational attainments documented in Section 3.1, I now present a partial equilibrium model of schooling choice that may be viewed as the finite-horizon, discrete-time counterpart of the infinite-horizon, continuous-time model used by Card and Lemieux (2000) and Card (2001). It may also be viewed as a simplified version of the microeconomic choice model of Heckman, Lochner and Taber (1998), as I do not consider the equilibrium effects of human capital accumulation decisions and treat earnings by schooling level as exogenous.

At the minimum school-leaving age ($t = 0$), a person with a planning horizon of M years (her known residual life length) decides a consumption path $\{c_t\} = (c_0, c_1, \ldots, c_M)$ and a level S of post-compulsory schooling in order to maximize her lifetime utility. I assume that there are $J + 1$ schooling levels, indexed by the number of extra years $0 = S_0 < S_1 < \cdots < S_J$ that they require, S_0 being the level associated with compulsory schooling. Leaving school is an irreversible decision.

Under these assumptions, lifetime utility may be written

$$V\big(S, \{c_t\}\big) = \sum_{t=0}^{S} \beta^t u(c_t - \phi_t) + \sum_{t=S+1}^{M} \beta^t u(c_t), \tag{3}$$

where β is the rate of time preference, $u(\cdot)$ is a smooth function, and ϕ_t is the relative disutility of school versus work for the tth year of extra schooling. It is useful to write (3) more compactly as

$$V\big(S, \{c_t\}\big) = \sum_{t=0}^{M} \beta^t u(c_t - \phi_{S,t}),$$

where $\phi_{S,t}$ is equal to ϕ_t if $t \leqslant S$ and is equal to zero otherwise. The lifetime budget constraint is

$$\sum_{t=0}^{M} \gamma^t c_t = \sum_{t=0}^{S} \gamma^t (p_t - T_t) + \sum_{t=S+1}^{M} \gamma^t y_{S,t}, \tag{4}$$

where $\gamma = 1/(1 + R)$, R is the real interest rate (assumed fixed), p_t are part-time earnings while at school, T_t are tuition costs, and $y_{S,t}$ are post-schooling earnings of a person with schooling level S. Notice that earnings are defined in broad terms and include unemployment benefits and work-related pensions received after retirement.

This simple model suggests that differences in educational attainments across countries and over time may arise because of differences in the rate of time preference (β), the length of a person's planning horizon (M), the taste for school versus work (ϕ_t), the real interest rate (R), the expected age profile of earnings by schooling level ($\{y_{S,t}\}$), part-time earnings while at school (p_t), and tuition costs (T_t). For simplicity, M, ϕ_t, p_t and T_t are all assumed not to depend on the level of schooling.

The choice problem may be solved in two stages. First, an optimal lifetime consumption path is chosen for each schooling level, resulting in a specific value of lifetime utility. Then the person selects the schooling level that gives the highest value of lifetime utility.

For a given schooling level S, a consumption path $\{c_t\}$ is optimal if it satisfies

$$\beta \frac{u'(c_t - \phi_{S,t})}{u'(c_{t-1} - \phi_{S,t-1})} = \gamma. \tag{5}$$

Given a consumption path $\{c_t\}$ which is optimal for S, the lifetime utility associated with schooling level S is simply $V_S = V(S, \{c_t\})$. An optimal schooling level S^* is one for which the associated lifetime utility is highest. Letting $V^* = V_{S^*}$ and $V_j = V_{S_j}$, the optimal schooling level S^* is characterized by the set of $J + 1$ inequalities $V^* \geqslant V_j$ for all $j = 0, 1, \ldots, J$. Equivalently, letting $\Delta V^* = V^* - V_0$ and $\Delta V_j = V_j - V_0$, S^* is characterized by the set of J inequalities $\Delta V^* \geqslant \Delta V_j$ for all $j = 1, \ldots, J$. If the ΔV_j are all negative, then the optimal choice is to take only compulsory schooling.

In order to obtain analytical results, I follow the common practice of assuming $u(c) = \ln c$. Condition (5) then becomes

$$c_t - \phi_{S,t} = \alpha(c_{t-1} - \phi_{S,t-1}),$$

where $\alpha = \beta/\gamma$. Thus

$$c_t - \phi_{S,t} = \alpha^t(c_0 - \phi_0),$$

and therefore

$$\sum_{t=0}^{M} \gamma^t c_t = \sum_{t=0}^{M} \gamma^t (c_t - \phi_{S,t}) + \sum_{t=0}^{M} \gamma^t \phi_{S,t} = (c_0 - \phi_0)G + \sum_{t=0}^{S} \gamma^t \phi_t,$$

where $G = \sum_{t=0}^{M} \beta^t > 0$. Hence, from the budget constraint (4),

$$(c_0 - \phi_0)G = \sum_{t=0}^{S} \gamma^t (p_t - T_t - \phi_t) + \sum_{t=S+1}^{M} \gamma^t y_{S,t},$$

so $c_0 - \phi_0 = Y_S/G$, where

$$Y_S = \sum_{t=0}^{S} \gamma^t (p_t - T_t - \phi_t) + \sum_{t=S+1}^{M} \gamma^t y_{S,t}.$$

If $\phi_t = 0$ for all t, then Y_S is just the person's net wealth. Under logarithmic utility, the lifetime utility function (3) is therefore

$$V(S, \{c_t\}) = \sum_{t=0}^{M} \beta^t \ln(c_t - \phi_{S,t}),$$

where $c_t - \phi_{S,t} = \alpha^t Y_S / G$. Hence, the lifetime utility associated with schooling level S is

$$V_S = \sum_{t=0}^{M} \beta^t (t \ln \alpha + \ln Y_S - \ln G),$$

and the difference in lifetime utility relative to the case of only compulsory schooling is

$$V_S - V_0 = (\ln Y_S - \ln Y_0) \sum_{t=0}^{M} \beta^t = G \ln \frac{Y_S}{Y_0},$$

where $Y_0 = p_0 - T_0 - \phi_0 + \sum_{t=1}^{M} \gamma^t y_{S_0,t}$.

Given any two schooling levels $S_1 < S_2$, level S_2 is preferred to S_1 whenever $V_2 - V_1 = G \ln(Y_2/Y_1) > 0$, with $Y_j = Y_{S_j}$, $j = 1, 2$. Since $G > 0$, S_2 is preferred to S_1 whenever $Y_2 > Y_1$, that is, whenever

$$\sum_{t=0}^{S_2} \gamma^t (p_t - T_t - \phi_t) + \sum_{t=S_2+1}^{M} \gamma^t y_{2,t} > \sum_{t=0}^{S_1} \gamma^t (p_t - T_t - \phi_t) + \sum_{t=S_1+1}^{M} \gamma^t y_{1,t},$$

where $y_{j,t} = y_{S_j,t}$. Because p_t, T_t and ϕ_t are assumed not to depend on the level of schooling, it follows that S_2 is preferred to S_1 whenever

$$\sum_{t=S_2+1}^{M} \gamma^t (y_{2,t} - y_{1,t}) > \sum_{t=S_1+1}^{S_2} \gamma^t y_{1,t} + \sum_{t=S_1+1}^{S_2} \gamma^t (T_t - p_t + \phi_t),$$

that is, the present value of the earnings differential associated with the higher level of schooling is greater than the sum of two components: the present value of forgone earnings and the present value of the net costs (monetary costs plus relative disutility) of extra schooling. An interesting feature of this result is that the choice between S_1 and S_2 depends on the real interest rate R and the length M of the planning horizon, but not on the rate of time preference β.

Now assume that the earnings function is of the form

$$y_{S,t} = f_S h(t - S), \quad t > S,$$

that is, log earnings are additively separable in schooling and potential work experience $t - S$. Then

$$\sum_{t=S_1+1}^{S_2} \gamma^t y_{1,t} = f_1 \sum_{t=S_1+1}^{S_2} \gamma^t h(t - S_1)$$

and

$$\sum_{t=S_2+1}^{M} \gamma^t (y_{1,t} - y_{2,t}) = \sum_{t=S_2+1}^{M} \gamma^t \big[f_2 h(t - S_2) - f_1 h(t - S_1) \big],$$

where $f_j = f_{S_j}$, $j = 1, 2$. In the special case when earnings do not depend on potential work experience, that is, $h(t) = 1$ for all $t > S$, one has

$$\sum_{t=S_1+1}^{S_2} \gamma^t y_{1,t} = f_1 \sum_{t=S_1+1}^{S_2} \gamma^t$$

and

$$\sum_{t=S_2+1}^{M} \gamma^t (y_{1,t} - y_{2,t}) = (f_2 - f_1) \sum_{t=S_2+1}^{M} \gamma^t.$$

Under the further assumption that $p_t = T_t$ and $\phi_t = 0$ for all t, S_2 is preferred to S_1 whenever

$$(f_2 - f_1) \sum_{t=S_2+1}^{M} \gamma^t > f_1 \sum_{t=S_1+1}^{S_2} \gamma^t,$$

that is, whenever

$$\frac{f_2 - f_1}{f_1} > \frac{\sum_{t=S_1+1}^{S_2} \gamma^t}{\sum_{t=S_2+1}^{M} \gamma^t},$$

where $(f_2 - f_1)/f_1$ is the educational wage premium. Because

$$\sum_{t=a+1}^{b} \gamma^t = \gamma^{a+1} \left(\frac{1 - \gamma^{b-a}}{1 - \gamma} \right),$$

it follows that S_2 is preferred to S_1 whenever $(f_2 - f_1)/f_1 > \kappa$, where

$$\kappa = \frac{\sum_{t=S_1+1}^{S_2} \gamma^t}{\sum_{t=S_2+1}^{M} \gamma^t} = \frac{\gamma^{S_1}}{\gamma^{S_2}} \left(\frac{1 - \gamma^{S_2 - S_1}}{1 - \gamma^{M - S_2}} \right) = \frac{\gamma^{S_1 - S_2} - 1}{1 - \gamma^{M - S_2}}. \tag{6}$$

Notice that the threshold value κ of the educational wage premium depends negatively on the length M of the planning horizon (residual life expectancy), and positively on the real interest rate R and the difference $S_2 - S_1$ in the years of schooling required to reach the higher level. When M is short, a large educational premium is needed to induce a person to acquire more schooling. On the other hand, when M gets longer, smaller educational premia are required. Because expected life length and level of economic development are strongly positively correlated, this prediction of the model is consistent with the observed evidence of falling returns to education by level of economic development.[18]

In the special case when $S_2 = S_1 + 1$, the condition for choosing S_2 over S_1 becomes

$$\frac{f_2 - f_1}{f_1} > \frac{\gamma^{-1} - 1}{1 - \gamma^{M-S_2}} = \frac{R}{1 - \gamma^{M-S_2}}.$$

If $M \to \infty$, that is, the person has an infinite planning horizon, then $(f_2 - f_1)/f_1 > R$, which is the discrete-time analog of the classical condition that equates the marginal return on an extra unit of schooling to the instantaneous real interest rate.[19]

Suppose that S_1 and S_2 are the only possible educational levels. If the educational premium $(f_2 - f_1)/f_1$ varies across individuals and its variability is well described by some distribution function G, then the fraction of the population taking the higher educational level is equal to

$$\pi = \Pr\left\{\frac{f_2 - f_1}{f_1} > \kappa\right\} = 1 - G(\kappa).$$

In particular, if G is the Gaussian distribution function with mean μ and variance σ^2, then

$$\pi = 1 - \Phi\left(\frac{\kappa - \mu}{\sigma}\right) = \Phi\left(\frac{\mu - \kappa}{\sigma}\right),$$

where $\Phi(\cdot)$ denotes the distribution function of the standardized Gaussian distribution.

The model just described has several implications for the behavior of π. First, other things being equal, a shift to the right of the distribution of educational premia (for example, an increase in its mean leaving its shape unchanged) increases π. On the other hand, a mean preserving spread increases π if $\pi < 1/2$ and lowers π if $\pi > 1/2$.

Second, if the planning horizon M increases, then the threshold value κ of the educational premium decreases and π increases. Notice that M changes with life expectancy and the number of years of compulsory schooling. Other things being equal, if life expectancy increases then π increases. On the other hand, if the number of years of compulsory education increases, then M decreases and so π decreases. Nothing instead happens if the number of years of compulsory education and life expectancy increase by the same amount.

Third, other things being equal, a decline of the real interest rate R, due to either improvements in the credit markets or to reduced risk, lowers the threshold value κ and therefore increases π. If R is re-interpreted as the difference between the real interest rate and the macroeconomic growth rate of wages [as in Bils and Klenow (2000)], then higher macroeconomic growth also induces more schooling.

[18] See Psacharopoulos (1994) and Psacharopoulos and Patrinos (2002).

[19] See, for example, Willis (1986).

All three forces may have contributed to the worldwide increase of college education after the Second World War and other historical episodes, such as the great expansion of secondary education in the USA from 1910 to 1940, documented by Goldin (1999), and the sharp increase of household investment in schooling in rural India after the green revolution, documented by Foster and Rosenzweig (1996).

Goldin (1999) explains the "secondary school movement" in the USA as the result of an income effect and changes in labor demand driven by both the technological revolution in the industrial sector and shifts towards the services. These two explanations are not entirely convincing. If it was changes in labor demand, why did the "secondary school movement" start and develop in rural America? If education is mainly an investment, why should changes in income matter so much? Of course, several explanations are possible for a positive income effect on the demand for schooling. For example, Schultz (1963) argues that attending classes may be less onerous than working, especially in developing countries, and that higher education may increase one's ability to enjoy consumption throughout life. Other explanations are that higher income may reduce the importance of borrowing constraints, and that increases in average income may lead to the availability of more schools and therefore to more schooling.

My finite-horizon model suggests a different explanation that requires neither a shift in labor demand nor a positive income effect on the demand for schooling. More simply, increases in productivity and income in rural areas lead to more favorable survival prospects. Assuming that credit markets are not dramatically imperfect, and barring general equilibrium effects, this makes schooling investments more profitable and lead people to acquire more education. These effects are clearly reinforced if more schooling implies better health, and therefore higher survival probabilities and longer life expectancy [see, e.g., Lleras-Muney (2002)].

3.3. Life expectancy and schooling decisions

I now present some empirical evidence on the relationship between schooling attainments and life expectancy. Somewhat surprisingly, this relationship has received little attention in the literature, maybe because of data limitations. Ideally, one would need information on residual life expectancy at the age when compulsory education ends. This age varies considerably across countries, ranging between 9 and 18 years. Further, data on residual life expectancy at various ages for a sufficiently large number of countries can only be found for recent years.

Figure 2 shows the relationship between life expectancy at birth and residual life expectancy at age 10 in year 2000.[20] In countries where life expectancy at birth is high, residual life expectancy at age 10 is about 10 years shorter than at birth. In countries where life expectancy at birth is low, however, residual life expectancy at age 10 is often higher than at birth (Figure 3). As a result, cross-country variability in residual

[20] The data are from the database maintained by the World Health Organization.

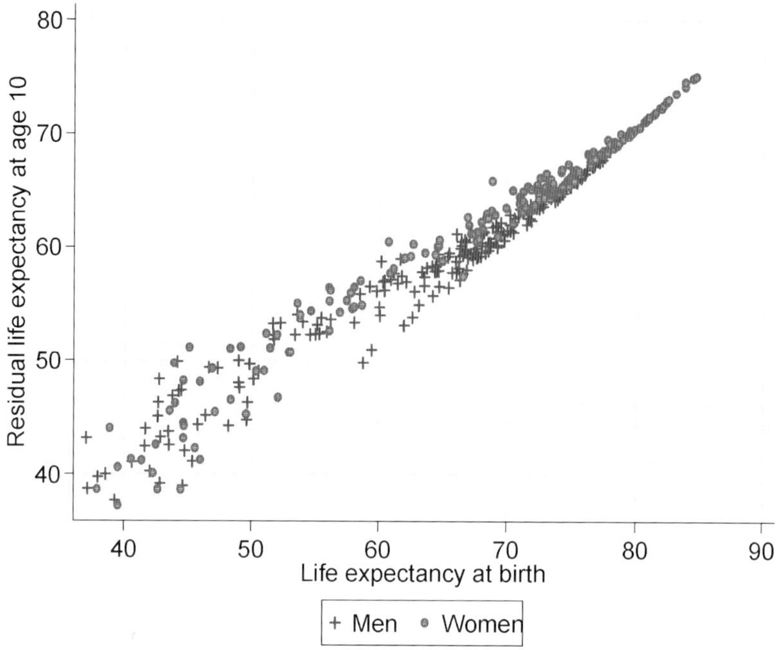

Figure 2. Life expectancy at birth and residual life expectancy at 10 years of age. Year 2000.

life expectancy declines with age, and is much higher at birth than at later ages. Despite this "convergence" process, the ranking of countries in terms of residual life expctancy does not change much with age. Table 2 shows the Spearman rank correlation coefficient between life expectancy at birth and life expectancy at various ages, separately for men and women. The correlation between the various measures is remarkably high up to age 60, which justifies focusing on the relationship between life expectancy at birth and schooling attainments.

Figure 4 plots the increase in life expectancy at birth between 1960 and 2000 against its initial level in 1960.[21] The figure shows an increase in life expectancy for most countries considered and a remarkable reduction of the differences across countries. As pointed out by Bourguignon and Morrisson (2002), this convergence in life expectancy contrasts sharply with the pattern of divergence in per-capita GDP. The convergence process has two notable features, however. First, life-expectancy actually fell in some countries of the former Soviet Union (Belarus, Russia and Ukraine) and in many sub-Saharan countries. Second, the pattern of convergence for the sub-Saharan countries is

[21] The data are from the Population Division of the Department of Economic and Social Affairs of the UN Secretariat.

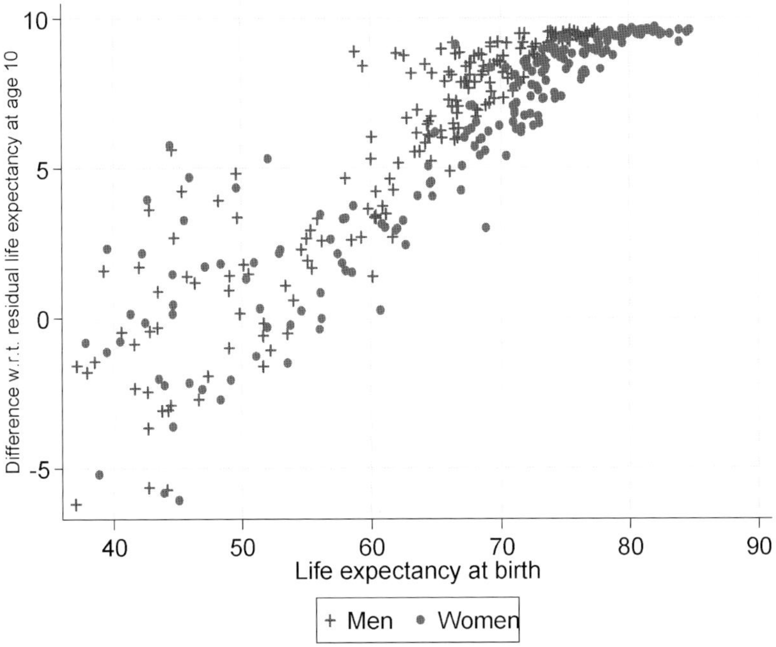

Figure 3. Life expectancy at birth and difference with respect to residual life expectancy at 10 years of ag. Year 2000.

quite different from the other countries considered, as increases in life expectancy are much lower for each initial level.

Figures 5–7 show the relationship between changes in life expectancy and changes in various measures of schooling attainments over the period 1960–2000 for the 95 countries in the Cohen and Soto (2002) data set. The relationship is positive but not particularly strong. In fact, Cohen and Soto (2002) observe that "the reduction of worldwide inequalities regarding life expectancy has not been channeled into a convergence of education patterns across the world". They argue that, over the past 30 years, nearly half of the increase of life expectancy in rich countries has been translated into higher education, but only one fourth in poor countries.

As an answer to this puzzle,[22] Cohen and Soto (2002) produce a model that exhibits a nonlinear relationship between education and life expectancy. Below a critical value T^* of life expectancy, increases in life expectancy are entirely channeled into worklife. Above T^*, the level of education rises with life expectancy and, for large values of life expectancy, the lengthening of life is entirely channeled into education. They also estimate a simple nonlinear cross-sectional relationship between average years of schooling

[22] Which they coin a "Becker paradox".

Table 2
Spearman rank correlation coefficient between life expectancy at birth and life expectancy at various ages. Year 2000

Age	Men	Women
1	.992	.995
5	.985	.989
10	.983	.988
15	.981	.987
20	.978	.985
25	.975	.983
30	.967	.981
35	.962	.979
40	.955	.976
45	.947	.972
50	.937	.965
55	.922	.954
60	.909	.944
65	.890	.930
70	.867	.911
75	.825	.877
80	.751	.832
85	.670	.772
90	.610	.720
95	.586	.675
100	.553	.652

in the population aged 25–29 and life expectancy at age 5, and show that education starts rising significantly only when life expectancy at 5 is above 55. Their estimates imply that the poorest countries are only in the early stage of their education pattern.

3.4. Supply and demand

The model in Section 3.2 is a partial equilibrium model where individuals make their educational choices taking educational premia and institutional settings as given. In fact, as documented in Section 4 below, educational premia show remarkable variation both over time and across countries. Understanding the sources of this variation requires moving to a more general model where wage premia are determined by the interaction of market forces, namely supply and demand of the various kinds of labor, and labor market institutions (wage setting norms, unionization, minimum wages, unemployment benefits and income maintenance programs) that may ease or limit the operation of market forces.

Welch (1970) was among the first to ask the question of what explains the relative stability of educational premia during historical episodes characterized by a sustained

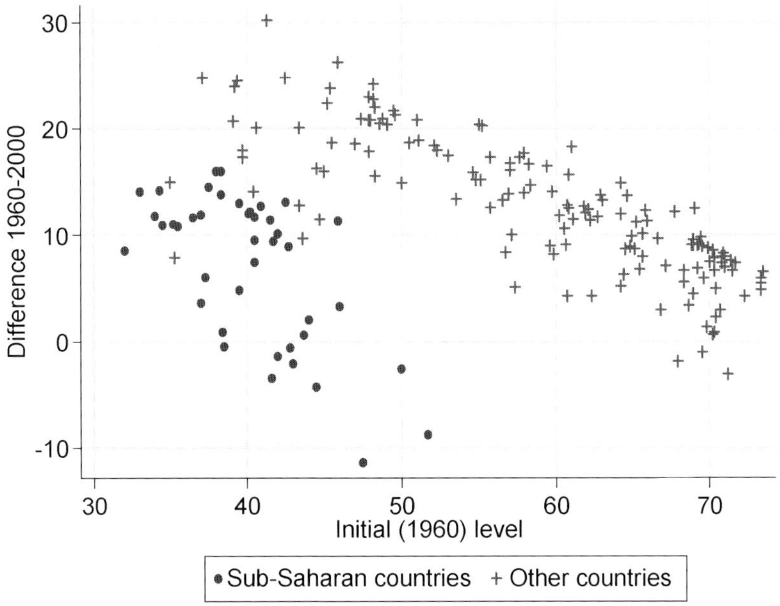

Figure 4. Life expectancy at birth in 1960 and differences between 1960 and 2000.

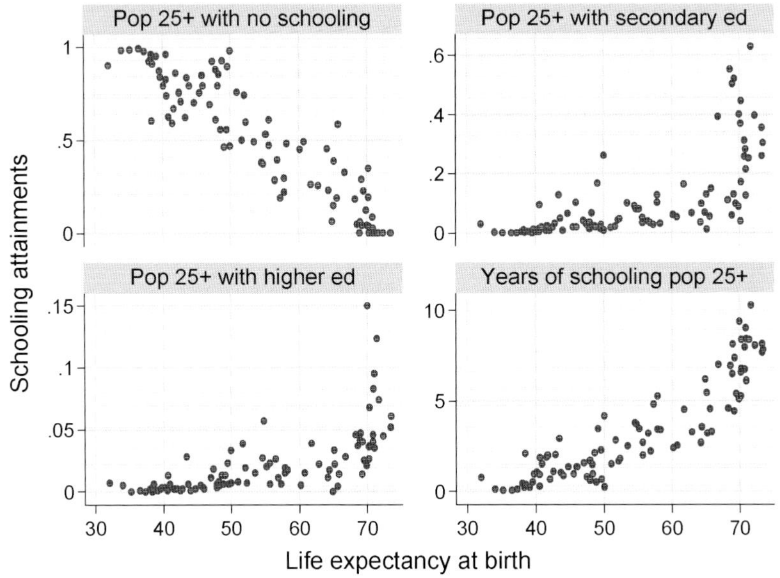

Figure 5. Schooling attainments and life expectancy at birth by country, 1960.

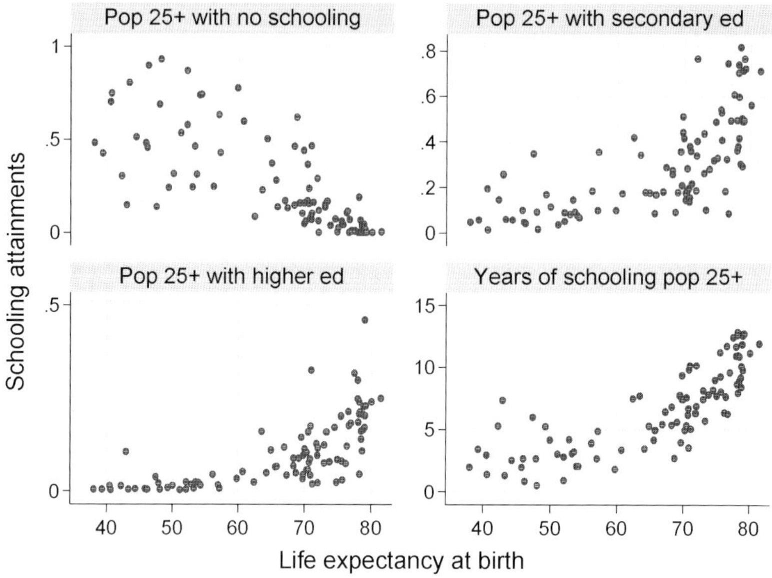

Figure 6. Schooling attainments and life expectancy at birth by country, 2000.

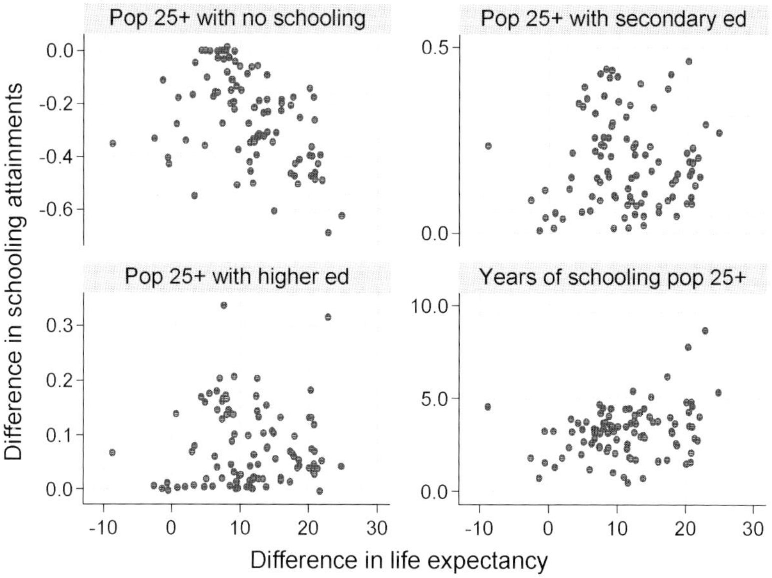

Figure 7. Differences in schooling attainments and differences in life expectancy at birth by country, 1960–2000.

increase in educational attainments. He argues that "changes have occurred to prevent the decline in returns to acquiring education that would normally accompany a rise in average educational levels. Presumably, these changes have resulted in growth in demand for the investment good, education, sufficient to absorb the increased supply with constant or rising returns". Among the possible explanations, he singles out the "changing composition of industrial activity" and the fact that "technical change may not be neutral between skill-classes" defined by years of education and age or labor market experience.

In the very short-run, the supply of skills and labor market institutions may be treated as given. With exogenous variation in the demand of skills, standard theory predicts that the wage premium should vary inversely with the relative supply of skills. If labor market institutions prevent the wage premium from increasing, the consequence of an increased demand for skills is relative unemployment of the unskilled.

A simple generalization of this partial equilibrium story allows both supply and demand for skills to grow exogenously. In the absence of institutional constraints, now the wage premium goes up or down depending on whether demand grows faster than supply, or vice versa. To keep the wage premium constant, supply and demand must grow at the same rate. In this case, two alternative explanations may be offered for an increase in both the skill premium and the relative employment of the skilled. According to the first, the supply of skills grows at a constant rate but demand accelerates. According to the second, the demand for skills grows at a constant rate but supply decelerates. In either case, the model may be further enriched by allowing labor market institutions to affect the way in which wage premia respond to market forces.

Changes in the growth rate of the supply of skills may depend on changes in cohort size, immigration, educational policies, etc. On the other hand, the three main hypotheses for an acceleration in the growth of the demand for skills are: (i) changes in the organization of production (de-industrialization, that is, the shift from manufacturing to services), (ii) globalization (increased trade, especially with less-skilled countries), and (iii) skill-biased technical change.

The skill-biased technical change (SBTC) hypothesis posits that increases in the relative demand of skills are mainly caused by bursts of new technology, such as the "computer revolution" of the 1980s and 1990s.[23] As pointed out by Acemoglu (2002a), one problem with the SBTC hypothesis is that it does not provide an explanation of why technical change seems to be skill-biased in certain periods but not in others. For example, during the nineteenth and early twentieth centuries, "the technical change was 'deskilling' – a major purpose of technical change was to expand the division of labor and simplify tasks previously performed by artisans by breaking them into smaller, less skill-requiring pieces" [Acemoglu (2002a, p. 9)]. Card and DiNardo (2002) raise

[23] A rather subtle distinction is between technological and organizational changes. For example, Mitchell (2001) argues that changes in the skill premium are connected to the organization of production, as summarized by plant size. When production is organized in large plants, jobs become routinized, favoring less skilled workers.

another problem, namely the fact that, in the absence of prior information on how different skill groups are affected by changes in technology, "one can always define SBTC to be present whenever changes in relative wages are not inversely related to changes in relative supply".

In the long-run, two things may happen. First, the growth of supply and demand and the changes in the skill premium are jointly determined. If younger cohorts respond to a permanent upward shift in the relative demand for skills by sharply increasing their college enrollment, then SBTC may actually lower the skill premia in the long run. This suggests the possibility of cycles [Freeman (1975a, 1975b, 1986)]: An excess supply of skills due to high levels of investment in the acquisition of skills may depress the skill premia, leading to reduced college enrollment, subsequent excess demand for skills and rising skill premia. This is one of the explanations put forward for the slowdown in the educational attainments of the cohorts born after 1950 in the USA and most European countries and, at the same time, the rise of college premia in the 1980s and 1990s.[24]

Models of this kind have formally been studied only recently. For example, Heckman, Lochner and Taber (1998) develop a heterogenous-agent dynamic general equilibrium model of labor earnings, estimate it using micro data, and use the estimated model to explore the empirical plausibility of alternative explanations for the rise in wage inequality. Azuma and Grossman (2003) develop a model where innovations that increase the relative demand for more educated labor are concomitant with innovations that increase ability premia. The former cause short-run increases in educational premia but long-run offsetting increases in the relative supply of more educated workers. The latter cause a smaller fraction of workers to choose to become more educated and, as a result, cause educational premia to be larger than otherwise.

Second, in the long run, labor market institutions may change in response to shifts in supply and demand. For example, Freeman and Katz (1995) argue in their Introduction that "economic forces that raise relative wages are likely to lead to less centralized collective bargaining or a reduction in union influence on wage setting". At the moment, the study of how labor market institutions respond to pressures brought about by market forces appears to be an open research area.

3.5. *Expectations formations*

In the simple model of Section 3.2, wage premia are assumed to be perfectly known to economic agents when they make their schooling choices. This is a strong assumption, given the variability of wage premia over time. Relaxing this assumption requires answering a number of crucial questions: How do people form their expectations about future wage premia? Are these expectations rational or adaptive? How big is the variability of forecasts? With few exceptions [Siow (1984), Zarkin (1985)], these questions have received little attention in the literature.

[24] See, for example, the Introduction to Freeman and Katz (1995) and Card and Lemieux (2001).

Recently, several authors have tried to shed some light on the way youth perceive the returns to schooling. Betts (1996) uses a survey of 1,269 undergraduates at the University of California, San Diego, to study students' beliefs about salaries by type of education. He finds strong support for the human capital hypothesis that individuals acquire information about earnings by level of education in order to choose their optimal level of education. Information is not perfect, however, and there is evidence of both overestimation of college premia and learning over time.

Dominitz and Manski (1996) report the evidence from a small-scale computer-assisted self-administered survey eliciting from high school students and college undergraduates their expected earnings under alternative schooling scenarios, and their beliefs about current earnings distributions. They find substantial within-group variation in earnings expectations and in beliefs about current earnings distribution. Despite this variation, and the fact that respondents appear rather uncertain about their future earnings, there is a common belief that the returns to a college education are positive, that earnings rise between ages 30 and 40. They also find that most respondents overestimate the degree of earnings variability.

Brunello, Lucifora and Winter-Ebmer (2001) report the results of a survey of wage expectations and expected employment probabilities of European college students. The survey, the first of this type in Europe, collected data on over 6,829 college undergraduates from 50 university faculties belonging to 32 universities in 10 European countries. Students were asked about their expected monthly earnings in the following contingencies: (i) starting earnings after college graduation, (ii) starting earnings with only a high-school degree, (iii) college earnings 10 years after graduation, and (iv) high-school earnings 10 years after high-school degree. For students enrolled in business and economics, these subjective expectations were then compared to estimated earnings from a standard human capital earnings function. Consistent with the results in Betts (1996) for the USA, the paper finds that expected college premia are higher than average actual premia.

This result, which apparently lends support to the view that students tend to be too optimistic, is not so clearly interpretable. First, the study compares the expectations of business and economics students, that may have better job prospects, with the actual college premia of all students. Further, since expected monthly wage gains are compared with actual hourly wage gains, the result may simply reflect the fact that college graduates work longer hours than high school graduates.

4. Wage premia: Empirical evidence

In this section, I look at the available evidence on movements in wage premia over the last 2–3 decades, focusing on differences in time trends across countries. If country-specific idiosyncrasies, such as differences in educational systems, income measures, data collection procedures, etc., remain relatively constant through time, then cross-country comparisons of time trends in educational premia are likely to be easier than point in time comparisons. On the other hand, as noted by Gottschalk and Smeeding (1997), "if data quality changes over time, if income components that are less (or more) well reported increase in significance over time, or if factors such as top coding have different impacts over time, then trends as well as levels will be affected".

Most of the available information is for developed countries and covers, at best, the last 2 or 3 decades. The USA is the country for which more is known. The evidence for the USA, mainly based on the micro data from the March Annual Demographic File or the Outgoing Rotation Groups of the CPS, has been summarized by several authors.[25] It shows large increases in earnings differentials both between workers with different schooling levels (and also with different ages or years of potential labor market experience) and within workers with the same observable characteristics. More precisely, the college wage premium for full-time full-year workers declined substantially during the 1970s, increased sharply during the 1980s, and continued to rise, albeit much more modestly, through most of the 1990s. The returns to experience also increased, especially among the less educated. The results of these trends has been a substantial decline in the relative position of young workers with no college education.

Although institutional changes, namely the weakening of labor unions and the decline of the minimum wage in real terms, may have played a role, "the fact that the skill intensity increased at the same time as the skill premium increased presents a prima facie case for the importance of demand shifts" [Gottschalk and Smeeding (1997, p. 647)]. The prominent demand side explanations are skill-biased technical change, the effects of trade liberalization, and shifts in derived demand for skilled labor resulting from shifts in the composition of final demand. The effects of demand shifts may have been amplified by a relative shortage of skilled labor due to the cohort-size effects and the slowdown of college enrollment, especially among men. Overall, the available evidence appears insufficient to discriminate between these different hypotheses (also because they are not mutually exclusive), thus providing an important motivation for the interest in other countries' experience.

4.1. Single-country studies

Single-country studies (including pairwise comparisons with the USA) typically provide important details on the countries being studied. Contrasting their results can be difficult, however, because of the differences in the educational systems, the time periods considered, the nature and quality of the data, etc.

Developed economies

Developed economies represent the ideal comparison group for analyzing the US experience because of the similarity of economic, social and political fundamentals, the

[25] See, for example, Bound and Johnson (1992), Levy and Murnane (1992), Juhn, Murphy and Pierce (1993), Gottschalk (1997), Gottschalk and Smeeding (1997), Katz and Autor (1999), Welch (1999), Card and DiNardo (2002), and Chapter 6 by Don Deere and Jelena Vesovic in this Handbook.

availability of micro-data of comparable content and quality, and the large institutional differences in the way educational systems are organized and administered.

Most studies summarized in Table 3 report increases in the educational premia, especially after the mid 1980s, despite the rising educational attainments of the population. The standard interpretation is demand rising faster than supply. In a few countries, large increases in the supply of workers with secondary and tertiary education may have contributed to keep the educational premia stable (Ireland, Norway) or may have led to a decline (Austria, Canada, Spain). Institutional settings (wage bargaining rules, employment protection legislation, etc.) may in some cases (Germany, Italy) have partly or even fully offset the influence of market forces.

Some authors place a special emphasis on the role of labor market institutions. For example, Freeman and Katz (1995) argue in their Introduction that "since developed economies operate in the same world markets with similar technologies, ..., changes in demand move in broadly similar ways across countries. Supply changes will diverge more because different countries expanded their higher education systems at different times, but, even so, the proportion of the workforce that is highly educated has risen in all advanced countries. Differences in the pattern of change in supply and demand are thus unlikely be themselves to explain cross-country variation in changes in wage inequality fully". Because of this, they identify "country differences in wage-setting and other labor market institutions ... as an additional determinant of differing patterns of change in inequality".

Transition economies

The transition process from planned to market economies in Eastern and Central Europe involved dramatic changes in political and economic structures, including labor market institutions. Theoretically, this transition could lead to either increases or decreases in skill premia. For example, if communist ideology overvalued low-skilled blue-collar workers relative to well-educated intellectuals (as is sometimes argued), then returns to education would be lower than in market economies and should therefore increase during the transition. On the other hand, if skills learned under communism are not useful in a market economy, then returns to experience or to pre-transition schooling might actually fall.

In fact, Krueger and Pischke (1995) find that in the late 1980s, just before German reunification, the return to a year of schooling was about the same in East and West Germany. Because higher education took longer in West Germany than in the East, "the higher returns to these degrees in the West are just due to longer schooling, not to higher returns per year of schooling".

Katz (1999) points out that "there are striking similarities in how the productivity of labor and its determinants have been conceptualized in the Soviet wage theory and Western 'human capital' theory". Using a random sample of 1,200 households interviewed in 1989 in Taganrog, a medium-size city located in the South of Russia and dominated by heavy industry, she finds that educational premia are "at the lower end

Table 3
Educational wage premia. Single country studies: Developed economies

Country	Reference	Data set	Years	Main findings
Australia	Gregory and Vella (1995)	Labor Force Survey	1976–90	Although the rate of return to education does not appear to be increasing, the same change in earnings dispersion as in the USA is observed.
Austria	Fersterer and Winter-Ebmer (2003)	Microcensus	1981–97	Falling returns to an additional year of schooling.
Canada	Bar-Or et al. (1995)	Survey of Consumer Finances (SCF)	1971–1991	While there appears to have been some decline in the return to university education during the 1970s, the return did not rebound much during the 1980s except for the youngest experience group.
	Beaudry and Green (2000)	SCF	1971–93	The college wage premium remained constant or fell, but the dispersion of wage earnings widened.
	Murphy, Riddell and Romer (1998)	SCF	1981–94	The stability of the college wage premium is a consequence of the substantial growth in post-secondary education.
	Burbidge, Magee and Robb (2001)	SCF, Survey of Labour Income Dynamics	1981–99	The college wage premium has remained stable for men and has trended downwards for women.
Germany	Abraham and Houseman (1995)	Survey of Compensation, GSOEP	1964–89	Relative constancy of differentials across education groups, stable or narrowing differentials by age group.
	Freeman and Schettkat (2000a, 2000b)			
	Beaudry and Green (2003)	GSOEP	1979–95	"Stable education-wage differences with rises in real wages for most workers".
Ireland	Barrett, Fitzgerald and Nolan (2002)	1987 ESRI survey, 1994 and 1997 ECHP	1987, 1994, 1997	Increase in returns to university education for the middle or older age groups between 1987 and 1994, but not between 1994 and 1997.

(*Continued on next page*)

Table 3
(*Continued*)

Country	Reference	Data set	Years	Main findings
Israel	Weisberg (1995)	1974 Labor Mobility Survey, 20% sample of the 1983 Census	1974, 1983	Increase of the educational premia for all age groups.
Italy	Erickson and Ichino (1995)	SHIW	1978–87	Weak trend towards lower returns to secondary education (relative to primary) and higher returns to college.
	Casavola, Gavosto and Sestito (1996)	Administrative data from Social Security	1986–90	Weak evidence of increasing wage premia for white-collar jobs.
Netherlands	Hartog, Oosterbeek and Teulings (1993)	Structure of Earnings Survey	1962–89	Returns to education dropped continuously between 1962 and 1985, while the level of education of the labor force increased steadily. After 1985, returns to education stabilized with no indication of a slowdown in the rise of educational attainments.
Norway	Kahn (1998)	Level of Living Survey	1980–91	Stable returns to education, largely because of the centralized wage bargaining process.
	Hoegeland, Klette and Salvanes (1999)	1980 Census, 1990 Survey of Population and Housing	1980, 1990	Stable returns to education, because of the increasing supply of highly educated workers.
Portugal	Machado and Mata (2001)	Census of firms and their workers (*Quadros de Pessoal*)	1982, 1994	Increase in college wages relative to wages of workers with only compulsory education.
	Hartog, Pereira and Vieira (2001)	*Quadros de Pessoal*	1982, 1986, 1992	Returns to education were stable between 1982 and 1986, but increased substantially between 1986 and 1992.
Spain	Abadie (1997)	Family Budget Survey	1980/81, 1990/91	Substantial decline in the educational premium, mainly for young and elderly workers.
	Vila and Mora (1998)	Family Budget Survey	1980/81, 1990/91	Falling returns to primary and lower secondary education, stable or increasing returns to higher education.

(*Continued on next page*)

Table 3
(*Continued*)

Country	Reference	Data set	Years	Main findings
Sweden	Edin and Holmlund (1995)	Level of Living Survey, HUS	1968–91	Wage differentials shrank from the mid-1960s up to the early 1980s, and then widened from the mid-1980s. Returns to schooling and experience fell during the first period, and increased during the second. Argue that "a simple demand and supply framework can account for movements in educational wage differentials".
UK	Harmon and Walker (1995)	Family Expenditure Survey (FES)	1978–86	No evidence of time trends in the returns to education.
	Schmitt (1995)	General Household Survey (GHS)	1974–88	U-shaped pattern of educational premia for high- and mid-level qualifications, with the gains over the 1980s offsetting the decline during the late 1970s.

of an international spectrum, but not extreme". She argues that in order to explain these relatively lower (but not extremely low) returns, no assumption of ideologically motivated bias is necessary. "One thing that the USSR did achieve was wide access to education, for women as well as for men. With a large supply of educated and skilled labor, market forces were exerting a downward pressure on returns to schooling."

Svejnar (1988) summarizes the studies that investigate the changes in the returns to education during the earlier stages of the transition to a market economy. In general, these studies find increases in the returns to schooling and greater incentives to human capital investments, especially among men.

Rutkowski (2001) updates the results of several earlier papers on the structure of earnings in Central Europe (CE), including the Baltic states but excluding the countries of the former Soviet Union. He argues that "returns to education have considerably increased in all transition economies of CE (for which the relevant data are available) and now by and large they are comparable to those observed in advanced market economies. [...] Especially strong was the increase in the university earnings premium, while the premium to secondary education increased much more modestly". Table 4 summarizes a few other recent studies.

Table 4
Educational wage premia. Single country studies: Transition economies

Country	Reference	Data set	Years	Main findings
Czech Republic	Flanagan (1998)	1988 Microcensus, 1996 Survey of Economic Expectations and Attitudes	1988, 1996	Rapidly rising returns to schooling rose during the transition to a market economy. By the mid-1990s, they approximated those found in many market economies. It is argued that the driving force behind this process initially was the reallocation of economic activity between sectors but, after 1992, it was the rapid growth of the private sector.
	Filer, Jurajda and Plánovský (1999)			Confirm the results in Flanagan (1998), but with much larger increases in the return to education.
Poland	Keane and Prasad (2002)	Household Budget Survey	1985–96	Educational premia rose rapidly during the transition, whereas the premium for labor market experience declined in the early years of transition and the position of older workers deteriorated relative to younger workers.

Developing economies

During the last 30 years, developing economies have been characterized by substantial increases in the educational attainments of the population and the workforce. At the same time, changes in the industrial structure in response to economy-wide reforms (privatizations, liberalizations, tax reforms, labor market reforms, etc.) have altered the demand for labor. Hence, these economies represent ideal cases for studying the relative importance of supply and demand factors on the structure of earnings. Unfortunately, this task is not easy, mainly because of problems of data availability and quality.

An important difference between developed and developing economies is the fact that employees outnumber the self-employed in the former, while the opposite is often true in the latter. The importance of self-employment in developing economies (and in some developed economies as well) raises both problems of self-selection (why do people choose to be self-employment?) and unresolved issues of how income and work effort should be measured. Further, whenever the employees are a relatively small fraction of the workforce, they also tend to be disproportionately concentrated in the public sector where, because of the way wages are set, the link between educational premia and worker productivity tends to be weaker.

Table 5 summarizes some recent studies. While coverage of Latin American countries is good, much less is known for African and Asian countries. Notice that the experience of workers in most African countries has been different from those in developed economies and other developing countries, as real wages fell substantially between the early 1970s and the 1990s. Latin American countries have instead been characterized by a process of trade liberalization and economy-wide reforms.

Several studies focus on the impact of the Mexican trade liberalization of 1985–1987 on the wage structure. All these studies find an increase in the skill premium, but offer different (not necessarily mutually exclusive) explanations. Hanson and Harrison (1995) argue that the rising skill premium is associated to changes internal to industries, or even internal to plants. Revenga (1995) instead argues that it reflects the fact that production (low-skilled) workers are more concentrated in industries that experienced a larger decline in tariffs protection. Cragg and Epelbaum (1996) relate the increase in the skill premium to a rise in the demand of more educated workers resulting from capital-skill complementarity. López-Acevedo (2001) takes a broader look at the effects of Mexico's structural changes on earnings inequality. She argues that "there was a shift in demand towards high-skilled labor that was not met by an increase in supply. This probably occurred as a result of the rapid rate of skill-biased technological change, whose transmission to Mexico was facilitated by the economy's increased openness".

4.2. *Multi-country studies*

Starting from the mid 1990s, increasing attention has been devoted to multi-country studies. As emphasized by Davis (1992), the importance of multi-country study is threefold: (i) "they represent a powerful tool for discriminating among competing explanations and for identifying the causal component of institutional changes and government interventions", (ii) "they serve as useful inputs into detailed studies on individual countries by suggesting when to pursue explanations that stress factors common to many countries and when to pursue explanations that stress country-specific factors", (iii) "they are likely to highlight certain hypotheses or suggest additional explanations that fail to surface in studies on particular countries".

One hypothesis that has received considerable attention is a description of US and European labor markets during the 1970s and 1980s that goes roughly as follows. There has been a substantial increase in the relative demand for skills, possibly driven by pervasive SBTC.[26] In countries where wages are flexible (UK, USA), this generated substantial increases in skill premia (decline in the relative wages of the unskilled). In countries where wages are rigid (continental Europe), the consequence was instead a large rise of unemployment among the unskilled (young or low educated workers).

[26] Berman, Bound and Machin (1998) find that SBTC during the 1970s and 1980s was "pervasive throughout the developed world".

Table 5
Educational wage premia. Single country studies: Developing economies

Country	Reference	Data set	Years	Main findings
Africa				
Ghana	Teal (2000)	Panel of firms	1991–95	As average earnings fell, their dispersion widened, with the lowest paid experiencing the largest fall in real wages.
Zambia	Skyt Nielsen and Rosholm (2001)	Household Survey	1991, 1993, 1996	Average real wages declined steadily during the period considered.
Asia				
India	Duraisamy (2002)	National Sample Survey	1983, 1993/94	While returns to upper secondary and college education changed little, returns to primary and lower secondary education declined and those to technical diploma/certificate increased substantially.
Korea	Kim and Topel (1995)	Occupational Wage Survey	1971–89	Huge drop in the college premium due to an exceptionally fast growth in the share of the workforce with a college degree.
Latin America				
Brazil	Blom, Holm-Nielsen and Verner (2001)	Monthly Labor Force Survey	1982–98	Substantial increases in the educational attainments of the Brazilian workforce, the largest expansion being for the intermediate education levels. Tertiary education increased significantly during the 1980s, but slowed down during the 1990s. During the same period, returns to tertiary education increased sharply, while returns to primary and secondary education dropped substantially.
	Ferreira (2002)	Nationwide Household Sample	1976–98	Sustantial increases in the college wage premium despite a significant increase in the relative supply of male workers with a college degree.

(Continued on next page)

Table 5
(*Continued*)

Country	Reference	Data set	Years	Main findings
Chile	Montenegro (2001)	National Socioeconomic Survey (CASEN)	1990–98	Stability of returns to education during the period considered. Returns to education increase moving from the lower to the upper part of the wage distribution. Women have higher returns to education than men in the lower part of the wage distribution, and similar returns in the upper part.
Colombia	Cárdenas and Bernal (1999)	quarterly Household Survey and annual Manufacturing Survey	1974–96	Decrease of the college wage premium between 1976 and 1981 attributed to the increase in the relative supply of more educated workers. The post-1991 increase is attributed to the rapid increase in their relative demand fostered by structural economic reforms.
Costarica	Funkhouser (1998)	National Survey of Households, Employment and Unemployment	1976–92	Returns to education fell by about one fourth between 1977 and 1983, followed by a slight rebound after 1983. This behavior appears to be negatively correlated with measures of supply of education and positively correlated with measures of demand.
Mexico	Hanson and Harrison (1995)	plant level data (Annual Manufacturing Survey)		Increases in the skill premium, but little changes in relative employment. They argue that the rising skill premium is associated to changes internal to industries, or even internal to plants.
	Revenga (1995)	Annual Manufacturing Survey		Increases in the skill premium, attributed to the fact that production (low-skilled) workers are more concentrated in industries that experienced a larger decline in tariffs protection.

(*Continued on next page*)

Table 5
(*Continued*)

Country	Reference	Data set	Years	Main findings
	Cragg and Epelbaum (1996)	Urban Employment Survey	1987–93	Increases in the skill premium, attributed to a rise in the demand of more educated workers resulting from capital-skill complementarity.
	López-Acevedo (2001)	Urban Employment Survey, Household Income and Expenditure Survey	1987–98	She argues that "there was a shift in demand towards high-skilled labor that was not met by an increase in supply. This probably occurred as a result of the rapid rate of skill-biased technological change, whose transmission to Mexico was facilitated by the economy's increased openness".
Uruguay	Gonzáles and Miles (2001)	Household Survey	1986–97	Returns to college education increased significantly while returns to primary education diminished at basically every quantile. During the same period, wage bargaining moved from a completely centralized process towards a more decentralized system.

Davis (1992) summarizes a variety of heterogeneous information on 9 developed countries[27] and 4 developing countries[28] for the 1970s and the 1980s. He finds that education differentials fell sharply for developed countries during the 1970s, and became flat or rising during the 1980s. The USA is the only developed country to show a net increase in the college wage premium over the two decades as a whole.

Nickell and Bell (1996) compare Germany, UK and the USA during the 1970s and 1980s. They observe that "in most European countries there has been a significant increase in skilled unemployment as well as in unskilled unemployment". Further, "the relative wages of the unskilled have not fallen in Germany but have fallen substantially in Britain and the United States". As an explanation, they suggest the fact that "education and training levels in the bottom half of the ability range are far higher in Germany than in Britain or the United States".

[27] Australia, Canada, France, Germany, Japan, Netherlands, Sweden, UK and USA.

[28] Brazil, Colombia, South Korea, and Venezuela.

Card and Lemieux (2001) compare Canada, the UK and the USA. The US data cover the period 1959–1996 and are drawn from the 1960 census and the March CPS from 1970 to 1997. The UK data cover the period 1974–1996 and are drawn from the General Household Survey. The data for Canada cover the period 1981–1996 and are drawn from the 1981, 1986, 1991 and 1996 Censuses. Their earnings measure is log weekly wages of full-time male workers aged 26 to 60. They show that, in all three countries, the college/high school wage gap has increased for younger men, but has remained nearly constant for older men. They explain the shift in the age structure of the wage premium with intercohort shifts in the relative supply of highly educated workers driven by the slowdown in the growth of educational attainments that began with the cohorts born in the early 1950s.

Some recent multi-country studies focus in more detail on the countries of Western Europe. Brunello, Comi and Lucifora (2000) compare the differences in the male college wage gap (both the college–high school wage gap and the college–less than college wage gap) in 10 European countries[29] for two cohorts (people born in 1940–49 and 1950–59). The original data were drawn from individual micro surveys and collapsed into cohort data. Their earnings measure is average hourly wages before taxes (after taxes in Austria and Italy) of full-time employees. They find evidence of significant differences, both across countries and across cohorts, in the level and growth of the college wage gap. In some countries the college wage gap increased over the period (Denmark, Finland, Italy, Portugal, Switzerland, UK), while in other countries it did not change (France, Germany, Netherlands) or even declined (Austria). Estimated growth appears to be negatively correlated to changes in relative supply and positively correlated both to an index of between-industries demand shocks and to the long-run rate of labor productivity growth. Institutional changes also appear to matter, as countries that have experienced a decline in union density, centralization of the wage bargain, and employment protection have also had a faster growth in the college wage gap.

The volume edited by Harmon, Walker and Westergaard-Nielsen (2001) collects the results of a research project entitled Public Funding and Private Returns to Education (PURE), whose main objective was to estimate the returns to education for 15 European countries.[30] Early versions of each country report were published in Asplund and Pereira (1999). Each country team estimated Mincerian returns to education, separately for men and women, using the available cross-sectional data for the period from the mid-1975 to the mid-1995. A variety of checks were carried out to study the robustness of the results to model specification.[31]

[29] Austria, Denmark, Finland, France, West Germany, Italy, Netherlands, Portugal, Switzerland and the UK.

[30] Austria, Denmark, Finland, France, Germany, Greece, Ireland, Italy, Netherlands, Portugal, Spain, Sweden, Switzerland and UK.

[31] Potential experience versus age, ordinary least squares versus instrumental variables and quantile regressions, returns to different subgroups of the population, sensitivity to the choice of the other right-hand side variables, sensitivity to the inclusion of corrections for sample selection, etc.

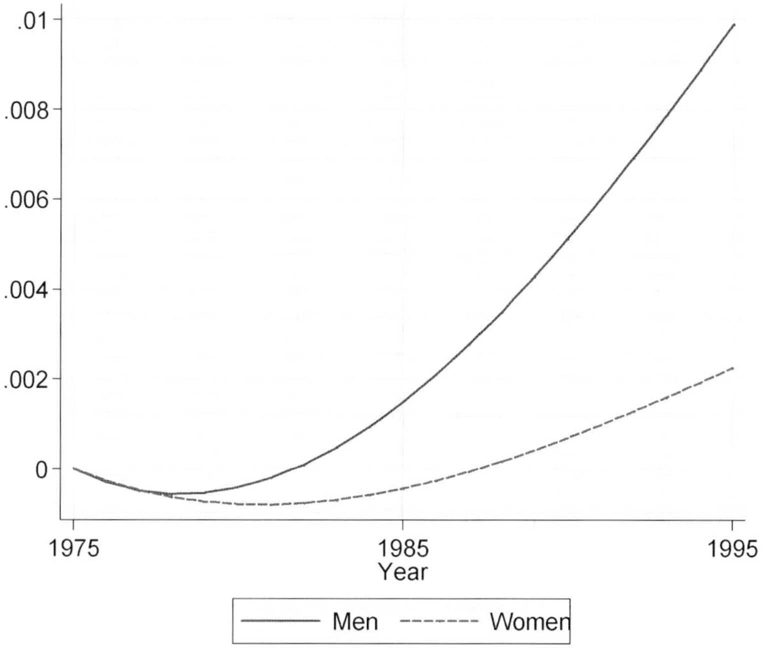

Figure 8. Average time-profile of the returns to schooling by sex in the 15 countries of the PURE project.

Figure 8 summarizes the results of the project. It presents the average time profiles of Mincerian returns to an extra year of schooling, taking 1975 as the baseline, separately for men and women. The two profiles have been obtained by using a regression model with a cubic time trend and a set of country dummies to fit the returns estimated by the various country team for each available year between 1975 and 1995. Qualitatively, the two profiles are very similar. They fall until the late 1970s or early 1980s, and rise afterwards. For men, the decline stops earlier and the subsequent rise is faster than for women, with an average gain of about 1 percentage point between 1980 and 1995.

Behavior across European countries differs widely. Table 6, corresponding to Table 1.1 in Harmon, Walker and Westergaard-Nielsen (2001), summarizes the relative size of Mincerian returns in the 1980s and the trends between 1975 and 1995, separately for men and women. Returns to schooling decreased in Austria and Sweden, but increased in Denmark, Italy and Portugal. Other countries showed no trend at all (France, Germany, Greece, Ireland, Norway and Switzerland), or different behavior of male and female returns (Finland, Netherlands, Spain and UK).

To my knowledge, only few studies cover developing countries. Davis (1992) looks at the experience of Brazil, Colombia, South Korea and Venezuela during the 1970s and 1980s, and finds sharply declining education differentials during the 1980s. Behrman, Birdsall and Székely (2000) analyze the impact of economy-wide reforms on wage differentials using data for 18 Latin American countries for the period 1980–

Table 6
Relative size of returns in the 1980s and trends in returns for the countries in the PURE project: + indicates relatively high returns,: indicates relatively low returns, 0 indicates returns close to the average, and – indicates no obvious trend

Country	Returns in 1980s		Trend	
	Men	Women	Men	Women
Austria	+	+	Down	Down
Denmark	:	:	Up	Up
Finland	+	+	–	Up
France	0	0	–	–
Germany	+	+	–	–
Greece	:	0	–	–
Ireland	+	+	– (Up)	–
Italy	:	:	Up	Up
Netherlands	:	:	Up	Down
Norway	:	:	–	–
Portugal	+	+	Up	Up
Spain	:	+	–	Up
Sweden	:	:	Down	Down
Switzerland	+	+	–	–
UK	:	+	Up	–

Source: Table 1.1 in Harmon, Walker and Westergaard-Nielsen (2001).

1998. They find that educational premia have increased considerably, especially in the 1990s. Domestic financial market reforms, capital account liberalizations, tax reforms and labor market reforms appear to have had a strong positive effect on wage differentials, but this effect tends to fade away rapidly. Privatizations have a negative effect, whereas trade openness has no overall effect, "perhaps because it triggers many countervailing forces that cancel each other out". Duryea, Jaramillo and Pagés (2002) present estimates of the returns to an extra year of schooling for primary, secondary and tertiary education during the 1990s, obtained from samples of urban males aged 30–50 for several Latin American countries. They show that returns to secondary education fell slightly during the period considered, whereas returns to tertiary education rose.

4.3. Studies based on harmonized cross-national data

The patterns emerging from multi-country studies, or from a comparison of single-country studies, may be regarded with some skepticism due to the difficulty of making direct comparisons. Recently, greater richness in cross-country studies is possible thanks to the increasing availability of harmonized micro data.

There are two main types of harmonized micro data. The first type consists of data originally collected by national statistical agencies that have been subsequently processed in order to produce greater uniformity in cross-national comparisons. Leading examples are the Luxembourg Income Study (LIS) and the Cross-National Equivalent File BHPS-GSOEP-PSID-SLID produced by the Department of Policy Analysis and Management at Cornell University and the German Institute for Economic Research (DIW) in Berlin. As argued by Gottschalk and Joyce (1998), "attempts to make these data sets has costs as well as benefits. The major cost is that we are forced to use the lowest common denominator in defining variables and samples".

The second type consists of data collected for a number of countries using a similar questionnaire and a harmonized survey design. Leading examples are the International Social Survey Programme (ISSP) and the European Community Household Panel (ECHP). These data sets usually come much closer to the ideal of a single survey instrument applied to all countries.

For either type of data, an important question that would deserve more careful consideration is to what extent the efforts to ensure comparability across countries and over time have been successfull.[32]

The LIS

The LIS is a collection of micro data sets obtained from annual income surveys in several (mainly developed) countries.[33] The LIS contains a historical database for 5 countries (Canada, Germany, Sweden, UK and USA), covering the period from the late 1960s to the mid 1970s, and 5 waves of data covering the subsequent period at roughly 5-year intervals. Wave IV, currently the most complete, is centered around 1995 and collects data on 26 countries, of which 20 are European.

Prior to inclusion into the LIS database, each survey goes though a "lissyfication" process that, in principle, should enhance comparability across countries and over time. In fact, comparability remains a problem because, except for a few variables (such as age, marital status and relationship to the household head), definitions and codings are not standardized. Key variables such as earnings, labor force status and education are defined and coded differently in the various countries or over time, with LIS making little attempts at harmonizing them. Further, not all variables listed in the LIS database are available for each country/year. In particular, the early LIS waves contain very limited information on education, usual hours per week, and weeks worked per year. Thus, for example, education is not available for Norway and the UK until 1986, and for Sweden until 1992.

Gottschalk and Joyce (1998) use LIS data from the late 1970s to the early 1990s for 8 countries[34] to estimate changes in returns to age and education over time and across countries. Their statistical model is a version of model (2), with occupational dummies

[32] See Atkinson and Brandolini (2001) for a discussion.

[33] See Smeeding, O'Higgins and Rainwater (1990).

[34] Australia, Canada, Finland, Israel, Netherlands, Sweden, UK and USA.

replacing educational dummies in Sweden and the UK. They focus attention on the subsample of male employees aged 25–54 who are heads of household and work full-time. They find that the increase in the educational premium in the USA between 1979 and 1986 was the largest across all countries. The increase between 1986 and 1991 was also large, but not much larger that what was experienced during the same period by several other countries. Further, for most countries considered, changes in the returns to skill are strongly negatively related to changes in the relative supplies of skills, although the evidence is weaker for the educational premium. They conclude that "market forces can be used to explain much of the cross-national differences that have been attributed in the literature to differences in labor market institutions".

Peracchi (2001) compares the US trends from the March CPS with the evidence for 12 countries in the LIS[35] over a longer period from the mid 1970s to the mid 1990s, focusing attention on the subsample of full-time (male and female) employees aged 25–59. He finds that most of the stylized facts observed for the USA also hold for a large majority of the countries included in the LIS database. Therefore, far from being unique, the US experience appears to be part of a phenomenon that is common to most developed countries. The intensity of the trends does differ across countries, but not their nature.

He finds that educational premia vary considerably across countries, partly reflecting problems of comparability of educational attainments. For the same country, however, they are remarkably similar at different quantiles, indicating that higher education implies a uniform shift to the right in the distribution of earnings. Israel and the USA are among the countries where educational premia are initially highest.

His evidence suggests classifying countries into three groups. The first group (Australia, Finland, Germany, and Norway) contains countries where no increase in the educational premia is observed, neither for men nor for women. The second group (Canada, Poland, and the USA) contains instead countries where all educational premia have increased, both for men and for women. Finally, the third group (Israel, Italy, Netherlands, Taiwan and the UK) contains countries were the patterns are mixed. According to his estimates, the average annual increase in the high-school premium for US males has been the highest among all countries considered, whereas the increase in the college premium in the USA remains below that observed for other countries such as Italy and Poland.

One explanation for some of the differences with respect to the previous literature is the fact that Peracchi (2001) includes the early and mid 1990s, thus capturing an increase in earnings inequality that was not yet present in the data for the 1980s. This raises the interesting, and largely unexplored, question of why the USA has been leading the other developed countries. The issue of timing may further help discriminate between alternative explanations for the observed trends.

Acemoglu (2002b) also compares the US trends from the CPS with the LIS evidence to see whether the relative supply-and-demand framework with a common technology

[35] Australia, Canada, Finland, Germany, Israel, Italy, Netherlands, Norway, Poland, Sweden, Taiwan and UK.

trend for all countries provides a satisfactory explanation for the differential behavior of skill premia in the USA and Europe. He argues that it does not, and develops a model where labor market institutions creating wage compression also encourage more investment in technologies that increase the productivity of less-skilled workers and are therefore less skill-biased.

The ISSP

The ISSP is a voluntary grouping of national study teams, each of which collects repeated cross-sectional information using a common questionnaire. In addition to an annual theme question concerning social attitudes on topics such as political views or issues of work and family, the ISSP each year collects basic demographic and income information from respondents. The ISSP has grown from 4 countries in 1984 (Australia, Germany, UK and USA) to the current 38 countries.

Unfortunately, the size of the ISSP samples tends to be quite small. Further, most countries provide earnings only in bracketed amounts that differ across countries and over time. As a result, the ISSP data may not replicate the patterns from other data sets that provide nonbracketed amounts from larger samples. In particular, "the ISSP data for the United States does not show the upward trend in inequality found in the CPS and other data sets" [Gottschalk and Joyce (1998)].

Trostel, Walker and Wooley (2002) use the ISSP data for the period 1985–1995 to estimate the Mincerian return to education separately for 28 countries, both developed and developing. With log hourly wages of employees aged 21–59 as the outcome variable, they obtain pooled estimates of the rate of return to schooling just under 5% for men and a little under 6% for women, but find the cross-country variation in the estimates "quite striking" and "difficult to explain". Returns are generally higher outside Continental Europe, "but this seems to be the only clear pattern". There is "tenous evidence that the rate of return declines with average educational attainment [...], per capita income and [...] relative spending on education". Consistently with progressivity of labor income taxation, there is "somewhat stronger evidence that the estimated rate of return is higher when wages are measured before taxes than after taxes". Looking at time trends over the 1985–1995 period, they find no evidence for a worldwide rising rate of return to education. For women, they actually find some evidence of a declining rate.

The ECHP

The ECHP is a standardized multi-purpose annual longitudinal survey carried out at the level of the European Union (EU) between 1994 and 2001 (in 12 countries from 1994 and all 15 countries from 1996). The survey was centrally designed and coordinated by the Statistical Office of the European Communities (Eurostat), and covered demographics, labor force behavior, income, health, education and training, housing, migration, etc. It was aimed at being both cross-sectionally and longitudinally representative, with changes in the population over time reflected by the continuous evolution of the sample

– through births to sample households and the formation of new households from the split off of existing ones.[36]

In this section, I present estimates of model (2) from the first seven waves of the ECHP[37] and from the US March CPS for the period 1994–2000. I consider average weekly earnings of full-time employees, defined as the ratio between the sum of wage and salary earnings in the calendar year prior to the survey divided by the number of weeks worked. For both the CPS and the ECHP, wages and salaries consist of all forms of cash wage and salary income (including employer bonuses, 13th month bonus, etc.) and, with the exception of Finland, France and the USA, are post-tax. Weeks worked are directly reported in the CPS, whereas for the ECHP they are obtained multiplying the number of months worked by 4. Unfortunately, the monthly calendar of main activity is not available for the Netherlands and Sweden, which are therefore excluded from the sample.

For both the CPS and the ECHP, educational attainments are measured by the highest level of education completed. The classification adopted by the ECHP is very coarse, however, for it only distinguishes three levels: the first level ("less than second stage of secondary education") corresponds to ISCED levels 1 and 2, the second level ("second stage of secondary education") corresponds to ISCED levels 3 and 4, and the last one ("recognized third level education") corresponds to ISCED levels 5 and 6. The fact that the ECHP does not separate primary and lower secondary education is a serious problem for Southern European countries (Greece, Italy, Portugal and Spain), where a large fraction of people of older age at most have completed primary education.

I estimate model (2) by OLS for each country, separately for men and women, with potential experience replaced by age. To capture trends in the structure of wages, the educational dummies and the quadratic age term are fully interacted with a linear time trend. The parameters presented in Table 7 correspond to the level of the educational premia in 1993 and their average annual variation between 1993 and 1999. Cross-country differences in the initial level of the educational premia are not easy to interpret because they reflect differences in the average annual return to education as well as differences in the number of years that each educational level requires beyond the first (less than second stage of secondary education) and the earnings concept used (pre- or post-tax). There is clear evidence of an increase of educational premia for the USA, whereas the evidence for the European countries is mixed. For example, the college premium is increasing for both men and women in Greece, only for men in Germany and Luxembourg, and only for women in Belgium and Denmark, but is decreasing for men in Ireland and Italy.

[36] See Peracchi (2002) for more details.

[37] For Germany, Luxembourg and the UK, the public-use version of the ECHP contains two data sets for the first three waves, one from the original ECHP and the other from pre-existing national panels, namely the German Socioeconomic Panel (SOEP), the Luxembourg's Social Economic Panel, and the British Household Panel Survey (BHPS), whereas for the later waves it only contains the comparable data derived from the national panels. For these three countries, I disregard the original ECHP data and only work with the data from the national panels.

Table 7
Educational wage premia in the countries of the European Union and the USA. Initial level in 1993 and trend in 1993–1999

	College premium		High-school premium	
	Level	Trend	Level	Trend
Men				
Austria	.437**	.008	.197**	−.017
Belgium	.280**	.010	.032	.008
Denmark	.251**	.002	.108**	−.004
Finland	.481**	−.020	.177*	−.038
France	.618*	.009	.116**	.014
Germany	.234**	.022**	.032	−.003
Greece	.370**	.020**	.200**	.011
Ireland	.502**	−.020*	.249**	−.015*
Italy	.457**	−.023**	179**	−.000
Luxembourg	.616**	.021*	.277**	.004
Portugal	.995**	−.003	.381**	.029**
Spain	.507**	.004	.267**	.007
UK	.273**	.002	.109**	.016
USA	.787**	.012**	.400**	.003
Women				
Austria	.577**	−.036	.265**	−.010
Belgium	.271**	.022*	.106**	.014
Denmark	.193**	.015*	.110**	.007
Finland	.372**	−.005	.143	−.019
France	.521**	−.008	.143**	−.002
Germany	.207**	.018	.022	.011
Greece	.399**	.037**	.279**	.003
Ireland	.644**	.003	.282**	−.002
Italy	.424**	.004	.322**	−.001
Luxembourg	.714**	−.007	.353**	.005
Portugal	1.015**	.010	.540**	.005
Spain	.649**	−.006	.357**	−.008
UK	.355**	−.003	.195**	.004
USA	.859**	.010*	.391**	.012**

**denotes an observed significance level below 1%,
*denotes an observed significance level between 1 and 5%.

5. Education and the distribution of personal earnings

I now turn to the implication of the differences in the educational composition of the workforce and the evolution of educational wage premia for the differences in the distribution of labor earnings across countries and over time. How much of the variability of earnings can be accounted for by the differences in wage premia? How much do changes in wage premia across countries and over time help explain changes in the distribution of earnings?[38]

5.1. Methodological aspects

The literature offers various ways of formally looking at the relationship between educational premia, relative supply of workers by schooling levels, and the distribution of personal earnings. One exploits the decomposition of the total variance of log earnings into three components, reflecting respectively the variation between schooling levels, the variation between other characteristics within each schooling level, and the residual variation within schooling levels and other characteristics. Another tries instead to decompose changes in the conditional quantiles of log earnings. More recently, some attention has also been devoted to the decomposition of earnings inequality into permanent and transitory components.[39]

Variance decomposition

Let μ and σ^2 respectively denote the unconditional mean and variance of log earnings Y, let $\mu(s)$ and $\sigma^2(s)$ respectively denote the conditional mean and the conditional variance of log earnings among workers with schooling level $S = s$, and let $\mu(s, x)$ and $\sigma^2(s, x)$ respectively denote the conditional mean and the conditional variance of log earnings among workers with schooling level $S = s$ and other observable characteristics $X = x$ (age, potential labor market experience, etc.).

The unconditional mean of log earnings may be written

$$\mu = \sum_s \mu(s)p(s) = \sum_s \left[\sum_x \mu(s, x)p(x \mid s)\right]p(s) = \sum_{s,x} \mu(s, x)p(s, x), \tag{7}$$

where $p(s)$ denotes the relative frequency of workers with schooling level s, $p(x \mid s)$ denotes the relative frequency of workers with characteristics x among those with schooling level s, and $p(s, x) = p(x \mid s)p(s)$ denotes the relative frequency of workers with schooling level s and other observable characteristics x. This relationship can be used to formally decompose the difference $\mu_{jt} - \mu_{kt}$ between country j and country k at a given time t, or the difference $\mu_{jt} - \mu_{jr}$ between time r and time t for the same country j. For example,

$$\begin{aligned}\mu_{jt} - \mu_{jr} &= \sum_{s,x} \left[\mu_{jt}(s, x) - \mu_{jr}(s, x)\right]p_{jt}(s, x) \\ &\quad + \sum_{s,x} \mu_{jr}(s, x)\left[p_{jt}(s, x) - p_{jr}(s, x)\right].\end{aligned}$$

[38] A much more complicated problem, not addressed here, is how changes in the distribution of earnings contribute to changes in the distribution of total household income.

[39] In what follows, I ignore the complications arising from the fact that the relevant population concepts are typically unknown and must be estimated using sample counterparts.

Clearly, $\mu_{jt} - \mu_{jr} = \sum_{s,x} [\mu_{jt}(s,x) - \mu_{jr}(s,x)] p_{jt}(s,x)$ if the distribution of workers by schooling level and other observable characteristics does not change over time, and $\mu_{jt} - \mu_{jr} = \sum_{s,x} \mu_{jr}(s,x)[p_{jt}(s,x) - p_{jr}(s,x)]$ if instead the conditional mean of log earnings does not change over time.

Similarly, the unconditional variance of log earnings may be decomposed as follows

$$\begin{aligned}\sigma^2 &= \sum_s [\mu(s) - \mu]^2 p(s) + \sum_s \sigma^2(s) p(s) \\ &= \sum_s [\mu(s) - \mu]^2 p(s) + \sum_{s,x} [\mu(s,x) - \mu(s)]^2 p(s,x) \\ &\quad + \sum_{s,x} \sigma^2(s,x) p(s,x).\end{aligned} \tag{8}$$

This may be written

$$\sigma^2 = \sum_s [A(s) + B(s) + W(s)] p(s),$$

where the first term

$$\sum_s A(s) p(s) = \sum_s [\mu(s) - \mu]^2 p(s)$$

measures the contribution of the variation of mean log earnings across schooling levels, the second term

$$\sum_s B(s) p(s) = \sum_{s,x} [\mu(s,x) - \mu(s)]^2 p(x \mid s) p(s)$$

measures the contribution of the variation of mean log earnings across workers with the same schooling level but different values of the other observable characteristics, and the third term

$$\sum_s W(s) p(s) = \sum_{s,x} \sigma^2(s,x) p(x \mid s) p(s)$$

measures the contribution of the residual variation of log earnings within groups of workers with the same observable characteristics (within-group inequality). If $\mu(s,x) = \alpha_s + g(x)$ and $\sigma^2(s,x) = \omega^2$ (homoskedastic partially linear model), then

$$\begin{aligned}\sum_s A(s) p(s) &= \sum_s (\alpha_s - \bar{\alpha} + \bar{g}_s - \bar{g})^2 p(s), \\ \sum_s B(s) p(s) &= \sum_{s,x} [g(x) - \bar{g}_s]^2 p(x \mid s) p(s), \\ \sum_s W(s) p(s) &= \omega^2,\end{aligned}$$

where $\bar{\alpha} = \sum_s \alpha_s p(s)$, $\bar{g}_s = \sum_x g(x) p(x \mid s)$, and $\bar{g} = \sum_s \bar{g}_s p(s)$.

The ratio

$$\frac{\sum_s W(s)p(s)}{\sigma^2} = 1 - \frac{\sum_s [A(s) + B(s)]p(s)}{\sum_s [A(s) + B(s) + W(s)]p(s)}$$

measures the relative contribution of the within-group variation to the total variance of log earnings. This ratio is equal to one minus the population R^2 in a regression of log earnings on schooling and other observable characteristics. Hence, the importance of the within-group inequality depends crucially on what worker characteristics are considered beside schooling, and may be reduced by controlling for more worker characteristics or by specifying a more flexible model for the conditional mean $\mu(s, x)$.

More compactly, (8) may be written

$$\sigma^2 = \sum_s C(s)p(s),$$

where $C(s) = A(s) + B(s) + W(s)$. This gives a straightforward way of formally decomposing the difference $\sigma_{jt}^2 - \sigma_{kt}^2$ between country j and country k at a given time t, or the difference $\sigma_{jt}^2 - \sigma_{jr}^2$ between time r and time t for the same country j.[40] For example

$$\sigma_{jt}^2 - \sigma_{jr}^2 = \sum_s \bigl[C_{jt}(s) - C_{jr}(s)\bigr]p_{jt}(s) + \sum_s C_{jr}(s)\bigl[p_{jt}(s) - p_{jr}(s)\bigr].$$

Clearly $\sigma_{jt}^2 - \sigma_{jr}^2 = \sum_s [C_{jt}(s) - C_{jr}(s)]p_{jt}(s)$ if the marginal distribution of workers by schooling level does not change over time, and $\sigma_{jt}^2 - \sigma_{jr}^2 = \sum_s C_{jr}(s)[p_{jt}(s) - p_{jr}(s)]$ if only the marginal distribution of workers by schooling level changes over time.

Other approaches

In practice, the variance decomposition (8) has three main drawbacks. First, it focuses only on the first two moments of the conditional distribution of earnings. Second, the variance of log earnings is mathematically convenient but need not be a good measure of dispersion, unless earnings are approximately log normal. Third, standard estimates of $\mu_{jt}(s, x)$ and $\sigma_{jt}^2(s, x)$ are very sensitive to the presence of outliers.

To avoid reliance on the variance as a measure of earnings dispersion, and to increase the robustness of the decomposition into between and within (residual) variation, Juhn, Murphy and Pierce (1993) assume the following linear model for log earnings Y_{ijt} of individual i in country j at time t

$$Y_{ijt} = \gamma_{jt} Z_{ijt} + U_{ijt},$$

[40] See, for example, Katz and Autor (1999) and Welch (1999).

where Z_{ijt} is a vector of observable worker characteristics (including education), γ_{jt} is a (row) vector of prices of the observable skills, and U_{ijt} is an unobservable determinant of log earnings (or "residual") whose conditional distribution given Z_{ijt} is represented by a continuous and invertible distribution function F_{jt}. Dropping for simplicity the subscript j and letting $\theta_{it} = F_t(U_{it})$ denote the conditional percentile position of individual i given Z_{it}, one can write

$$Y_{it} = \gamma_t Z_{it} + F_t^{-1}(\theta_{it}),$$

where F_t^{-1} denotes the conditional quantile function of the residual. Notice that both the percentile position θ_{it} and the quantile function F_t^{-1} may change over time.

If γ_r and F_r^{-1} denote skill prices and the quantile function of the residual for some base period r,[41] then

$$Y_{it} = \gamma_r Z_{it} + (\gamma_t - \gamma_r) Z_{it} + F_r^{-1}(\theta_{it}) + \left[F_t^{-1}(\theta_{it}) - F_r^{-1}(\theta_{it})\right]. \tag{9}$$

If skill prices and the distribution function of the regression error did not change between time r and time t, then individual earnings would be given by

$$Y_{it}^{(1)} = \gamma_r Z_{it} + F_r^{-1}(\theta_{it}).$$

Thus, Juhn, Murphy and Pierce (1993) attribute changes through time in the distribution of $Y_{it}^{(1)}$ to changes in observable skills. On the other hand, if only the distribution function of the unobservable component did not change over time, then individual earnings would be given by

$$Y_{it}^{(2)} = Y_{it}^{(1)} + (\gamma_t - \gamma_r) Z_{it}.$$

Thus, they attribute the additional changes through time in the distribution of $Y_{it}^{(2)}$ to changes in skill prices. Finally, because

$$Y_{it} = Y_{it}^{(2)} + \left[F_t^{-1}(\theta_{it}) - F_r^{-1}(\theta_{it})\right],$$

they attribute the residual changes through time in the distribution of Y_{it} to changes in the distribution of the unobservables.

Both (8) and (9) only require repeated cross-sectional data to be estimated. This largely explains their popularity. With the increasing availability of long panel data, however, it becomes possible to decompose changes in annual earnings inequality into a persistent component (lifetime earnings becoming more or less equal) associated with the returns to education and other permanent worker characteristics, and a transitory component (lifetime earnings becoming more or less unstable). Unfortunately, the results of this kind of decomposition appear to be very sensitive to the choice of model for earnings dynamics.[42] Further, unless sample attrition is ignorable, using long panel data raises delicate problems of self-selection into the sample.

[41] The choice of the base period matters. For example, Goldin and Margo (1992) find that "the choice of base year greatly affects the importance of changes in the distribution of residuals relative to changes in both prices and quantities".

[42] See Haider (2001).

5.2. Empirical evidence

Unlike the evidence on educational premia, that on the distribution of earnings is much more scattered and unsystematic. The vast majority of the available evidence is for the USA. The stylized facts for the USA, on which there is a broad consensus, may be summarized as follows. First, inequality has increased both between groups, and within group. Second, the increase in between-group inequality is entirely due to the increase in age and schooling differentials, whereas gender and race differentials have instead declined. Third, the increase in between-group inequality accounts for a smaller share of the growth in inequality relative to residual inequality, that is, increased dispersion within groups. Fourth, lifetime earnings inequality has also increased [Haider (2001)].

As pointed out by Katz and Autor (1999), however, "trends in overall and residual inequality ... are less consistent across data sources and are more sensitive to the choice of the lower cut-off (i.e., handling of outliers), top-coding, and choice of sample (full-time, all), earnings concept (weekly, hourly) and weights (bodies, weeks, labor hours supplied)". They conclude that "although all data sources point to a growth of residual inequality starting in the 1970s, the relative magnitude, precise timing, and sample-specificity of this trend are elusive. These vagaries are unfortunate because shifts in the residual earnings distribution are less well understood than 'between group' inequality and, moreover, account for the preponderance of recent inequality growth by most estimates. To make further progress in understanding these trends, researchers should carefully explore the robustness of their conclusions to choice of data source, sub-sample and methodology".

In the remainder of this section I briefly review some of the available evidence for other countries, mainly developed economies. Most of the studies considered adopt decompositions similar to (8) or (9). In fact, no country except the USA and Canada seem to have the long panel data needed in order to estimate the decomposition of the variance of log earnings into a permanent and a transitory component.

Single-country studies

Table 8 reviews some recent single-country studies, focusing on developed countries because of the very limited evidence available for transition economies and developing countries. This review is only meant to provide an illustration of the heterogeneity in the data and the findings of these studies.

Multi-country studies

Katz, Loveman and Blanchflower (1995) analyze the trends in the wage structure and the overall wage inequality in France, Germany, UK and the USA during the 1970s and the 1980s. Although their data and earnings measures are only roughly comparable, they find that "all four countries share a pattern of rising wage inequality among both men and women in the 1980s, but the magnitude of the increases differ substantially".

Table 8
Earnings inequality. Single country studies

Country	Reference	Data set	Years	Main findings
Canada	Burbidge, Magee and Robb (1997)	SCF	1971–93	There was an increase in overall wage dispersion between 1975 and 1985, more pronounced for female workers, and a leveling off after 1985. Wage dispersion appears to have risen for all educational and experience groups, except older male and female university graduates. For all educational groups, the most significant increase in wage dispersion occurred for younger workers.
	Baker and Solon (2003)	Random sample of income tax forms issued by employers (T-4 Supplementary Tax File)	1976–92	They decompose the growth of earnings inequality in Canada during the period into a persistent (long-run) and a transitory component. They find that "the increase in the persistent component may have played a somewhat larger role".
Germany	Fitzenberger et al. (2001)	Random sample of Social Security accounts	1976–84	They find that the German wage structure was fairly stable during the period considered, although wage inequality within age-education groups increased slightly above the median. They interpret this evidence as the outcome of the institutional aspects of wage setting in Germany and the baby boom effect on cohort size.
Netherlands	ter Weel (2003)	OSA survey	1986–98	Using decomposition (9), he finds that wage inequality did not increase much during the period considered, that most of the changes in wage inequality are accounted for by changes in the educational level and experience composition of the labor force, and that residual wage inequality does not play an important role.

(*Continued on next page*)

Table 8
(*Continued*)

Country	Reference	Data set	Years	Main findings
Portugal	Cardoso (1998)	*Quadros de Pessoal*	1983–1992	Rising earnings inequality, especially after 1986, due to a substantial widening of the wage gap across schooling levels, with the returns to college education sharply increasing relative to the other schooling levels. "Forces operating within industries have contributed to switch the relative demand in favor of very qualified workers". At the same time, "the minimum wage legislation and collective bargaining . . . contributed to compress the bottom part of the wage distribution in the early eighties, whereas wage drift led to rising dispersion at the top of the distribution".
UK	Gosling, Machin and Meghir (2000)	FES, GHS	1966–95	Using decomposition (9), they find that about a third of the increase in wage dispersion during the period is due to increases in educational premia, a third is due to a continuous decline in the growth rate of wages of successive cohorts entering the labor market, and the remaining third is within group, as successive cohorts enter the labor market with increased dispersion of wages. This increased dispersion may partly have to do with the increased heterogeneity of educational qualifications of people with the years of schooling.

The UK and the USA both display a sharp increase, while the increase in Japan is much more moderate. France experience declining inequality until 1984 and a moderate increase from 1984 to 1990. Changes in education/occupation differentials appear to be the driving force. A unique feature of the UK and the USA, however, is the fact that wage inequality increased for both men and women with similar education and experience levels. They argue that "simple supply and demand measures go a reasonable distance towards explaining the differences and similarities between these countries in patterns of relative wage movements. ... Institutional differences across the countries translated the relative demand shifts against less educated workers into similar outcomes of sharply rising inequality in the United States and Britain in the 1980s but a very different outcome in France through the mid-1980s. ... Finally, the strength of the Japanese manufacturing sector may partially account for the much smaller magnitude of changes in skill differentials in Japan than in Britain and the United States".

Blau and Kahn (1996) compare the level of male earnings inequality in the USA and 9 other industrialized countries[43] around the mid-1980s using the decomposition (9). In addition to ISSP data for Austria, Germany, Hungary, Norway, Switzerland, UK and USA, they employ a variety of other sources.[44] After examining indices of relative supplies and demands of skills across countries, they observe that "low-skill workers should fare worse relative to middle-skill workers in other countries than they do in the United States". They conclude that "market forces [...] do not appear to be a viable explanation for international differences, further increasing our confidence that [labor market] institutions are important".

Gottschalk and Smeeding (1997) review the evidence from various studies that contrast the US experience during the 1980s with that of other developed countries.[45] They summarize the available evidence on the levels of earnings inequality as follows:

1. "At any given time there are wide differences across modern countries in the level of earnings inequality for both men and women".
2. "Nations with centralized wage bargaining (e.g., Sweden, Germany) have greater equality than nations with less centralized bargaining (e.g., the United States and Canada)".

They summarize the trends in earnings inequality as follows:[46]

1. "Almost all industrial economies experienced some increase in wage inequality among prime aged males during the 1980s (Germany and Italy are the exceptions)".
2. "But large differences in trends also exist across countries, with earnings inequality increasing most in the United States and the United Kingdom and least in Nordic countries".

[43] Australia, Austria, Germany, Hungary, Italy, Norway, Sweden, Switzerland, and the UK.

[44] The other sources are the 1986 Income Distribution Survey for Australia, the 1987 Survey of Household Income and Wealth (SHIW) for Italy, the Class Structure and Class Consciousness (CSCC) data base for Norway (1982) and Sweden (1980), the 1984 Household Market and Nonmarket Activities Survey (HUS) for Sweden, and the 1984 Panel Study of Income Dynamics (PSID) for the USA.

[45] Australia, Canada, Finland, France, Germany, Israel, Italy, Japan, Netherlands, Sweden, and the UK.

[46] They also claim that "as a result of allowing market forces to influence wages, Russia, Hungary, and the former East Germany experienced considerably larger percentage changes in earnings inequality than the United States or the United Kingdom".

3. "The increasing demand for more skilled workers, coupled with differences across countries in the growth in supply of skilled workers, explains a large part of differences in trends in returns to education and experience".
4. "Institutional constraints on wages also seem to matter. The rise in the relative unemployment rates of the least skilled in some, but not all, countries with centralized wage setting institutions suggests that constraints were at least partially responsible for limiting the rise in inequality".

Gottschalk (1997) classifies developed countries into four groups. One extreme is occupied by the UK and the USA, with very large increases in inequality, the other by Germany, "the only country that seems to have avoided any increase in inequality during the 1970s, 1980s or 1990s". A unique feature of the UK and the USA is the fact that they experienced large increases in the returns to both education and experience, as well as increases in inequality within groups. In between, he puts two groups of countries: those which experienced large but not extreme increases in inequality (Canada, Australia, Israel and New Zealand), and those which experienced small but positive changes in inequality (Finland, France, Italy, Japan, Netherlands and Sweden).

Gottschalk and Joyce (1998) use the LIS database to examine the contribution of changes in inequality between group and within group to changes in overall inequality of full-time male earnings. They find that the small overall increase in earnings inequality in many countries (and the small overall decline in some of them) actually reflects large but offsetting changes in returns to skill and changes in inequality within age-education cells, and conclude that "there is no clear relationship between the ranking of countries in changes in overall inequality and changes in within-group inequality".

Katz and Autor (1999) summarize the evidence provided by OECD (1996) on trends in wage inequality for men in 14 OECD countries[47] between 1979 to 1994. They find that "the United States and the United Kingdom experienced sharp increases in overall wage inequality, residual wage inequality and educational and occupational wage differentials of similar magnitude. ... The pattern of declining wage inequality apparent throughout the OECD (except the United States) in the 1970s ceased in the 1980s and 1990s in almost all nations (with Germany and Norway as possible exceptions). Canada, Australia, Japan, and Sweden had modest increases in wage inequality and educational/occupational differentials starting in the early 1980s. Wage differentials and inequality narrowed through the mid-1980s in Italy and France with some hint of expanding in France in the late 1980s and with a large increase in inequality in Italy in the 1990s". They argue that "these patterns are suggestive of an important role of differences and changes in labor market institutions and regulations. ... But differences in supply and demand factors may also play a role".

Devroye and Freeman (2001) look at the differences between Germany, Netherlands, Sweden and the USA in the sensitivity of the variance decomposition (8) to two alternative measures of skills, namely years of schooling and adult literacy scores in the OECD

[47] Australia, Austria, Canada, Finland, France, Germany, Italy, Japan, Netherlands, New Zealand, Norway, Sweden, UK and USA.

International Adult Literacy Survey. They reject the hypothesis that cross-country differences in the distribution of skills are the main determinants of cross-country differences in earnings inequality and instead conclude that "the explanation for cross-country differences in inequality lies, not in the distribution of skills, but in the mechanism by which different pay systems produce dispersion among otherwise similar people in similar situation".

Europe versus the USA

In this final section I compare the experience of the countries of the European Union (except Netherlands and Sweden) to that of the USA during the 1990s employing the variance decomposition (8). As before, I use the ECHP for the European Union and the March CPS for the USA. Since the earnings measure is average weekly earnings of full-time employees in the calendar year prior to the survey, the period considered goes from 1993 to 1999.

I begin by presenting some cross-sectional evidence obtained by pooling all the available waves of the data. Figure 9 shows the age-profile of the variance of log earnings for men and women. For all countries, except the UK, this variance tends to increase with age. Figure 10 shows the age-profile of the relative importance of the within-group

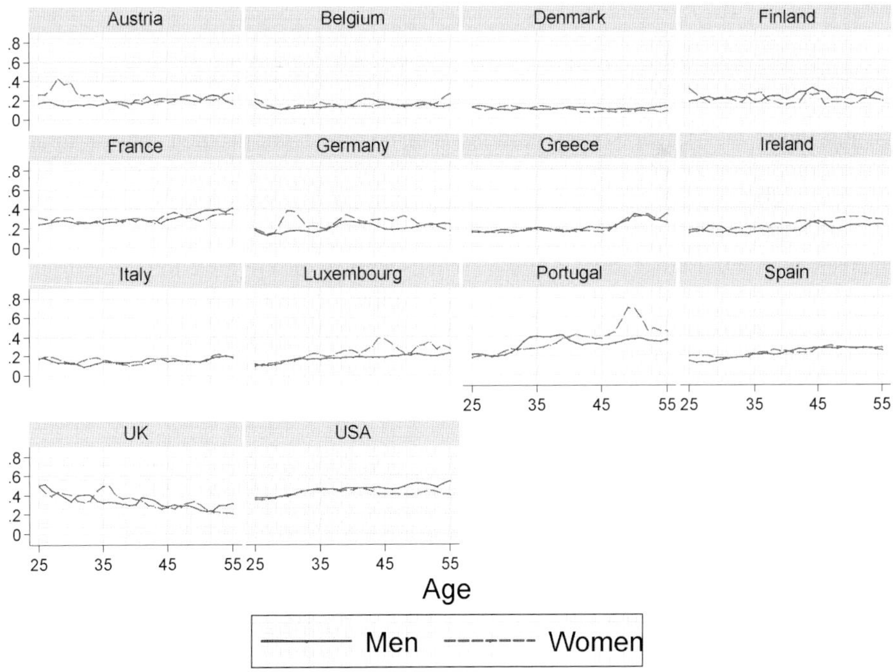

Figure 9. Variance of log earnings by age.

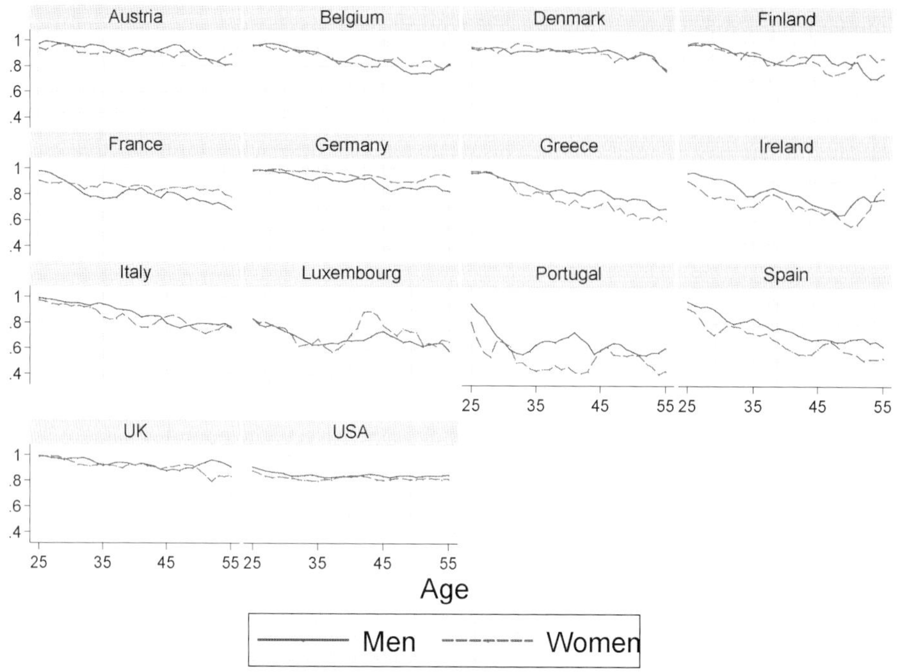

Figure 10. Contribution of the within-group component to the variance of log earnings by age.

component of the variance of log earnings. For both men and women and for all ages, more than half of the contribution to the variance of log earnings comes from the variation within educational levels. The importance of this component is generally higher for men than for women in Greece, Ireland, Portugal, Spain and the USA, whereas the opposite is true in France and Germany. What seems to differentiate the USA from the other countries is the fact that the contribution of the variation within educational levels is relatively stable at about 85 percent, irrespective of age. For most European countries, on the contrary, the importance of this component is very high at younger ages, but then declines with age. This decline appears to be quite rapid for Greece, Ireland, Portugal and Spain.

Figure 11 shows instead the time-profile of the total variance of log earnings separately for men and women. There is some evidence of an upward trend for Finland, Luxembourg and Portugal, but not for the other countries. Figures 12–14 show the time-profile of the relative contribution of the three components that enter the decomposition (8). Figure 12 shows the importance of the variance between schooling levels. The importance of this first component appears to be relatively stable in the UK and the USA, but rising in several European countries. Figure 13 shows the importance of the variance between ages within schooling levels. The importance of this second component appears to be stable in the UK and declining in the USA, but rising in most

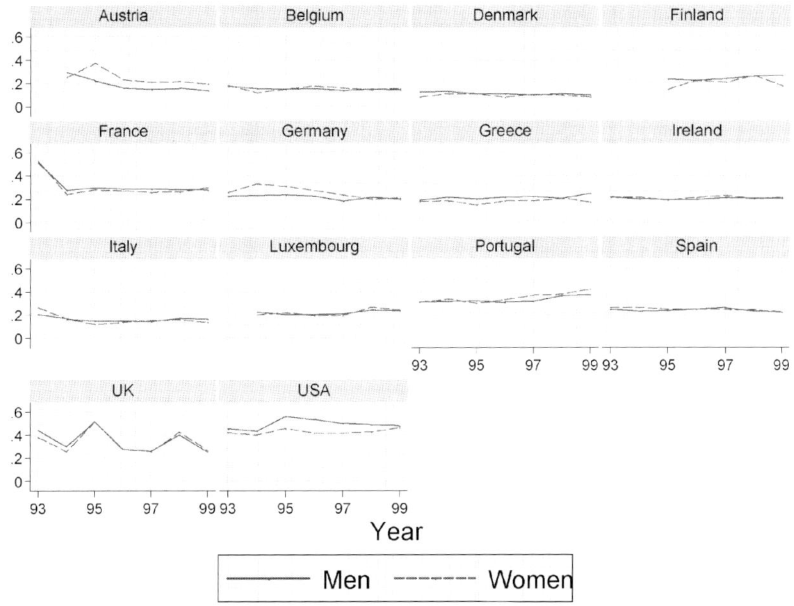

Figure 11. Total variance of log earnings.

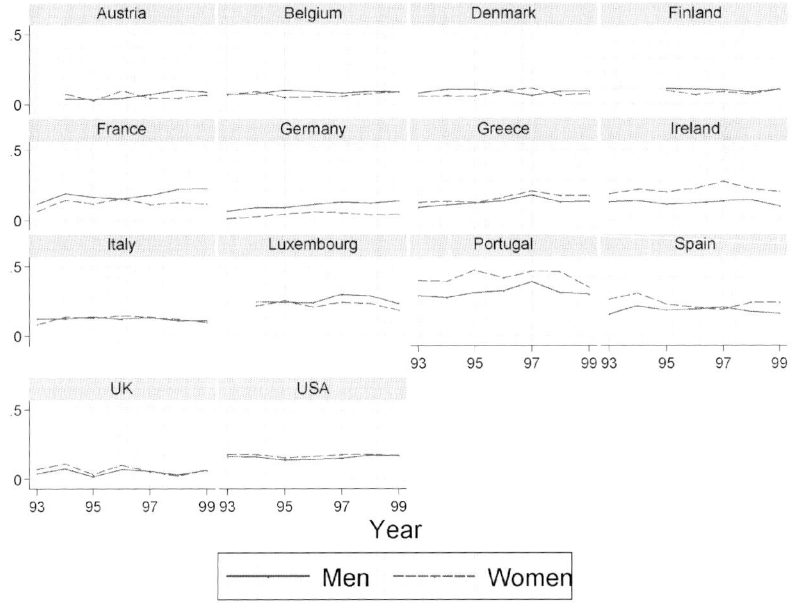

Figure 12. Relative contribution of the variance between schooling levels to the total variance of log earnings.

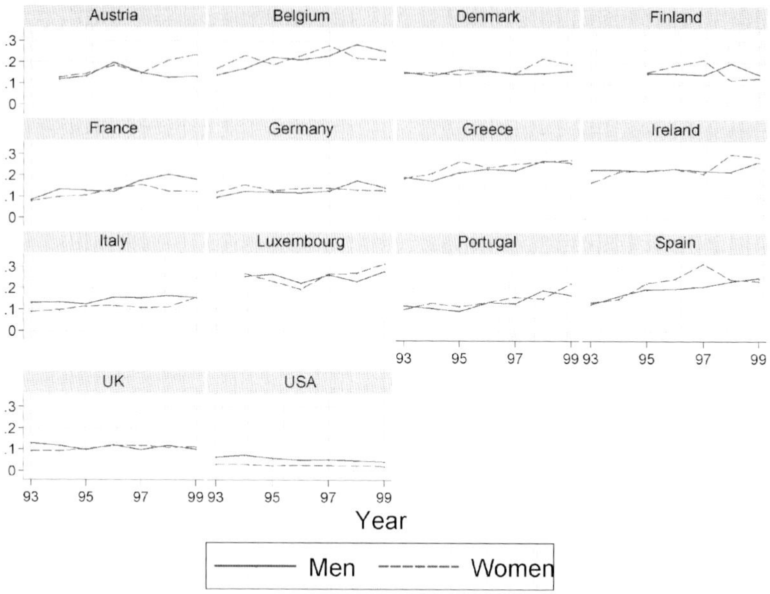

Figure 13. Relative contribution of the variance between ages within schooling levels to the total variance of log earnings.

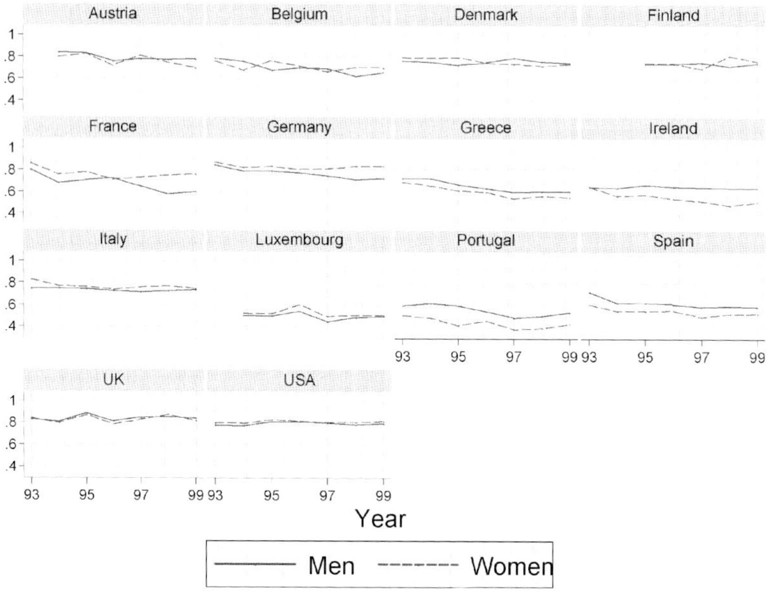

Figure 14. Relative contribution of the residual variance within age and schooling to the total variance of log earnings.

other European countries. Finally, Figure 14 shows the importance of the residual variation within age and schooling. The importance of this third component appears to be increasing in the UK and the USA, but appears to be stable or even declining in most other European countries.

Acknowledgements

I would like to thank Antonio Ciccone, Don Deere, Ric Hanushek and especially Finis Welch for helpful comments.

References

Abadie, A. (1997). "Changes in Spanish labor income structure during the 1980s: A quantile regression approach". Investigaciones Economicas 21, 253–272.

Abraham, K.G., Houseman, S.N. (1995). "Earnings inequality in Germany". In: Freeman, R.B., Katz, L.F. (Eds.), Differences and Changes in Wage Structures. University of Chicago Press, Chicago.

Acemoglu, D. (2002a). "Technical change, inequality, and the labor market". Journal of Economic Literature 40, 7–72.

Acemoglu, D. (2002b). "Cross-country inequality trends". NBER Working Paper No. 8832.

Ashenfelter, O., Harmon, C., Oosterbeek, H. (1999). "A review of estimates of the schooling/earnings relationship, with tests for publication bias". Labour Economics 6, 453–470.

Asplund, R., Pereira, P.T. (1999). Returns to Human Capital in Europe. ETLA, The Research Institute of the Finnish Economy, Helsinki.

Atkinson, A.B., Brandolini, A. (2001). "Promise and pitfalls in the use of 'secondary' data sets: Income inequality in OECD countries as a case study". Journal of Economic Literature 39, 771–799.

Azuma, Y., Grossman, H.I. (2003). "Educational inequality". Labour 17, 317–335.

Baker, M., Solon, G. (2003). "Earnings dynamics and inequality among Canadian men, 1976–1992: Evidence from longitudinal income tax records". Journal of Labor Economics 21, 289–321.

Bar-Or, Y., Burbidge, J., Magee, L., Robb, A.L. (1995). "The wage premium to a university education in Canada". Journal of Labor Economics 13, 762–794.

Barrett, A., FitzGerald, J., Nolan, B. (2002). "Earnings inequality, returns to education and immigration in Ireland". Labour Economics 9, 665–680.

Barro, R., Lee, J.W. (1993). "International comparisons of educational attainment". Journal of Monetary Economics 32, 363–394.

Barro, R., Lee, J.W. (1996). "International measures of schooling years and schooling quality". American Economic Review Papers and Proceedings 86, 218–223.

Barro, R., Lee, J.W. (1997). "Schooling quality in a cross-section of countries". NBER Working Paper No. 6198.

Barro, R., Lee, J.W. (2000). "International data on educational attainment, updates and implications". NBER Working Paper No. 7911.

Bassanini, A., Scarpetta, S. (2002). "Does human capital matter for growth in OECD countries? A pooled mean-group analysis". Economics Letters 74, 399–405.

Beaudry, P., Green, D. (2000). "Cohort patterns in Canadian earnings: Assessing the role of skill premia in inequality trends". Canadian Journal of Economics 3, 907–936.

Beaudry, P., Green, D. (2003). "Wages and employment in the United States and Germany: What explains the difference?" American Economic Review 93, 573–602.

Becker, G.S. (1964). Human Capital. Columbia University Press, New York.

Becker, G.S. (1967). Human Capital and the Personal Distribution of Income. University of Michigan Press, Ann Arbor.
Behrman, J.R., Birdsall, N., Székely, M. (2000). "Economic reform and wage differentials in Latin America". Inter-American Development Bank, Research Department Working Paper No. 435.
Benhabib, J., Spiegel, M.M. (1994). "The role of human capital in economic development: Evidence from aggregate cross-country data". Journal of Monetary Economics 34, 143–174.
Ben-Porath, Y. (1967). "The production of human capital and the life cycle of earnings". Journal of Political Economy 75, 352–365.
Berman, E., Bound, J., Machin, S. (1998). "Implications of skill-biased technological change: International evidence". Quarterly Journal of Economics 113, 1245–1279.
Betts, J.R. (1996). "What do students know about wages? Evidence from a survey of undergraduates". Journal of Human Resources 31, 27–56.
Bils, M., Klenow, P.J. (2000). "Does schooling cause growth?". American Economic Review 90, 1160–1183.
Black, D., Sanders, S., Taylor, L. (2003). "Measurement of higher education in the Census and Current Population Survey". Journal of the American Statistical Association 98, 545–554.
Blau, F.D., Kahn, L.M. (1996). "International differences in male wage inequality: Institutions versus market forces". Journal of Political Economy 104, 791–836.
Blom, A., Holm-Nielsen, L., Verner, D. (2001). "Education, earnings and inequality in Brasil, 1982–98". World Bank Policy Research Working Paper No. 2686.
Bound, J., Jaeger, D., Baker, R. (1995). "Problems with instrumental variables estimation when the correlation between the instruments and exogenous explanatory variables is weak". Journal of the American Statistical Association 90, 443–450.
Bound, J., Johnson, G. (1992). "Changes in the structure of wages in the 1980's: An evaluation of alternative explanations". American Economic Review 82, 371–392.
Bourguignon, F., Morrisson, C. (2002). "Inequality among world citizens: 1820–1992". American Economic Review 92, 727–744.
Brunello, G., Comi, S., Lucifora, C. (2000). "The college wage gap in 10 European countries: Evidence from two cohorts". IZA Discussion Paper No. 228.
Brunello, G., Lucifora, C., Winter-Ebmer, R. (2001). "The wage expectations of European college students". Mimeo.
Burbidge, J.B., Magee, L., Robb, A.L. (1997). "Canadian wage inequality over the last two decades". Empirical Economics 22, 181–203.
Burbidge, J.B., Magee, L., Robb, A.L. (2001). "The education premium in Canada and the USA". QSEP Research Paper No. 364, McMaster University, Hamilton, Ontario.
Card, D. (2001). "Estimating the returns to schooling: Progress on some persistent econometric problems". Econometrica 69, 1127–1160.
Card, D., Lemieux, T. (2000). "Dropout and enrollment trends in the post-war period: What went wrong in the 1970s?". NBER Working Paper No. 7658.
Card, D., Lemieux, T. (2001). "Can falling supply explain the rising return to college for younger men? A cohort-based analysis". Quarterly Journal of Economics 116, 705–746.
Card, D., DiNardo, J.E. (2002). "Skill-biased technological change and rising wage inequality: Some problems and puzzles". Journal of Labor Economics 20, 733–783.
Cárdenas, M., Bernal, R. (1999). "Wage inequality and structural reforms: Evidence from Colombia". Mimeo.
Cardoso, A. (1998). "Earnings inequality in Portugal: High and rising?". The Review of Income and Wealth 3, 325–343.
Casavola, P., Gavosto, A., Sestito, P. (1996). "Technical progress and wage dispersion in Italy: Evidence from firms' data". Annales d'Économie et de Statistique 41–42, 387–412.
Cohen, D., Soto, M. (2002). "Why are some countries poor? Another look at the evidence and a message of hope". OECD Development Centre, Technical Paper No. 197.
Cragg, M.I., Epelbaum, M. (1996). "Why has wage dispersion grown in Mexico? Is the incidence of reforms or the growing demand for skills?". Journal of Development Economics 51, 99–116.

Davis, S.J. (1992). "Cross-country patterns of change in relative wages". NBER Working Paper No. 4085.
de la Fuente, A., Doménech, R. (2000). "Human capital in growth regression: How much difference does quality data make". CEPR Discussion Paper No. 2466.
de la Fuente, A., Doménech, R. (2001). "Educational attainment in the OECD, 1960–1995".
de la Fuente, A., Ciccone, A. (2003). Human Capital in a Global and Knowledge-Based Economy. Final Report. Office for Official Publications of the European Communities, Luxembourg.
Devroye, D., Freeman, R. (2001). "Does inequality in skills explain inequality of earnings across advanced countries". NBER Working Paper No. 8140.
Dominitz, J., Manski, C.F. (1996). "Eliciting student expectations of the returns to schooling". Journal of Human Resources 31, 1–26.
Dunne, M. (2003). "Education in Europe. Key statistics 2000/01". Statistics in Focus. Theme 3 (Population and Social Conditions). 13/2003. Eurostat, Luxembourg.
Duraisamy, P. (2002). "Changes in returns to education in India, 1983–94: By gender, age-cohort and location". Economics of Education Review 21, 609–622.
Duryea, S., Jaramillo, O., Pagés, C. (2002). "Latin American labor markets in the 1990s: Deciphering the decade". Mimeo, Research Department, Inter-American Development Bank.
Edin, P., Holmlund, B. (1995). "The Swedish wage structure: The rise and fall of solidarity wage policy?". In: Freeman, R.B., Katz, L.F. (Eds.), Differences and Changes in Wage Structures. University of Chicago Press, Chicago.
Erickson, C.L., Ichino, A. (1995). "Wage differentials in Italy: Market forces, institutions and inflation". In: Freeman, R.B., Katz, L.F. (Eds.), Differences and Changes in Wage Structures. University of Chicago Press, Chicago.
Ferreira, S.G. (2002). "The evolution of the college-high school wage differential for males in Brasil: Does an increasing supply of college-educated labor explain it". Department of Economics, University of Wisconsin-Madison.
Fersterer, J., Winter-Ebmer, R. (2003). "Are Austrian returns falling over time?" Labour Economics 10, 73–89.
Filer, R.K., Jurajda, S., Plánovský, J. (1999). "Education and wages in the Czech and Slovak Republics during transition". Labour Economics 6, 581–593.
Fitzenberger, B., Hujer, R., MaCurdy, T.E., Schnabel, R. (2001). "Testing for uniform wage trends in West-Germany: A cohort analysis using quantile regression for censored data". In: Fitzenberger, B., Koenker, R., Machado, J.A.F. (Eds.), Economic Applications of Quantile Regression. Physica Verlag, Heidelberg.
Flanagan, R.J. (1998). "Were communists good human capitalists? The case of the Czech Republic". Labour Economics 5, 295–312.
Foster, A.D., Rosenzweig, M.R. (1996). "Technical change and human-capital returns and investment: Evidence from the green revolution". American Economic Review 86, 931–953.
Freeman, R.B. (1975a). "Supply and salary adjustments to the changing science manpower market: Physics, 1948–1973". American Economic Review 65, 27–39.
Freeman, R.B. (1975b). "Legal cobwebs: A recursive model of the market for new lawyers". Review of Economics and Statistics 57, 171–179.
Freeman, R.B. (1986). "Demand for education". In: Ashenfelter, O., Layard, R. (Eds.), Handbook of Labor Economics, vol. 1. North-Holland, Amsterdam.
Freeman, R.B., Katz, L.F. (1995). Differences and Changes in Wage Structures. Chicago University Press, Chicago.
Freeman, R.B., Schettkat, R. (2000a). "The role of wage and skill differences in US-German employment differences". NBER Working Paper No. 7474.
Freeman, R.B., Schettkat, R. (2000b). "Skill compression, wage differentials and employment: Germany versus the US". NBER Working Paper No. 7610.
Funkhouser, E. (1998). "Changes in the returns to education in Costa Rica". Journal of Development Economics 57, 289–317.
Glewwe, P. (2002). "Schools and skills in developing countries: Education policies and socio-economic outcomes". Journal of Economic Literature 40, 436–482.

Goldin, C. (1999). "Egalitarianism and the returns to education during the great transformation of American education". Journal of Political Economy 107, S65–S94.
Goldin, C., Margo, R.A. (1992). "The great compression: The wage structure in the United States at mid-century". Quarterly Journal of Economics 107, 1–34.
González, X., Miles, D. (2001). "Wage inequality in a developing country: Decrease in minimum wage or increase in education returns". In: Fitzenberger, B., Koenker, R., Machado, J.A.F. (Eds.), Economic Applications of Quantile Regression. Physica Verlag, Heidelberg.
Gosling, A., Machin, S., Meghir, C. (2000). "The changing distribution of male wages in the UK". Review of Economic Studies 67, 635–666.
Gottschalk, P. (1997). "Inequality, income growth, and mobility: The basic facts". Journal of Economic Perspectives 11, 21–40.
Gottschalk, P., Joyce, M. (1998). "Cross-national differences in the rise of earnings inequality: Market and institutional factors". Review of Economics and Statistics 80, 489–502.
Gottschalk, P., Smeeding, T.M. (1997). "Cross-national comparisons of earnings and income inequality". Journal of Economic Literature 35, 633–681.
Gregory, R.G., Vella, F. (1995). "Real wages, employment, and wage dispersion in US and Australian labor markets". In: Freeman, R.B., Katz, L.F. (Eds.), Differences and Changes in Wage Structures. University of Chicago Press, Chicago.
Griliches, Z. (1977). "Estimating the returns to schooling: Some econometric problems". Econometrica 45, 1–22.
Haider, S.J. (2001). "Earnings instability and earnings inequality of males in the United States: 1967–1991". Journal of Labor Economics 19, 799–836.
Hanson, H.G., Harrison, A. (1995). "Trade, technology and wage inequality". NBER Working Paper No. 5110.
Hanushek, E.A., Kimko, D.D. (2000). "Schooling, labor-force quality, and the growth of nations". American Economic Review 90, 1184–1208.
Harmon, C., Oosterbeek, H., Walker, I. (2003). "The returns to education: Microeconomics". Journal of Economic Surveys 17, 115–155.
Harmon, C., Walker, I. (1995). "Estimates of the economic returns to schooling for the UK". American Economic Review 85, 1279–1286.
Harmon, C., Walker, I., Westergaard-Nielsen, N. (2001). Education and Earnings in Europe. A Cross Country Analysis of the Returns to Education. Elgar, Cheltenham, UK.
Hartog, J., Oosterbeek, H., Teulings, C. (1993). "Age, wages and education in the Netherlands". In: Johnson, P., Zimmermann, K. (Eds.), Labour Markets in an Aging Europe. Cambridge University Press, Cambridge, UK.
Hartog, J., Pereira, P., Vieira, J. (2001). "Changing returns to education in Portugal during the 1980s and early 1990s: OLS and quantile regression estimators". Applied Economics 33, 1021–1037.
Heckman, J.J., Lochner, L., Taber, C. (1998). "Explaining rising wage inequality: Explorations with a dynamic general equilibrium model of labor earnings with heterogeneous agents". NBER Working Paper No. 6384.
Heckman, J.J., Polachek, S.W. (1994). "Empirical evidence on the functional form of the earnings-schooling relationship". Journal of the American Statistical Association 69, 350–354.
Hoegeland, T., Klette, T.J., Salvanes, K.G. (1999). "Declining returns to education in Norway? Comparing estimates across cohorts, sectors and over time". Scandinavian Journal of Economics 101, 555–576.
Juhn, C., Murphy, K.M., Pierce, B. (1993). "Wage inequality and the rise in returns to skill". Journal of Political Economy 101, 410–442.
Kahn, L.M. (1998). "Against the wind: Bargaining, recentralization and wage inequality in Norway 1987–1991". Economic Journal 108, 603–645.
Katz, K. (1999). "Where there no returns to education in the USSR? Estimates from Soviet-period household data". Labour Economics 6, 417–434.
Katz, L.F., Autor, D.H. (1999). "Changes in the wage structure and earnings inequality". In: Ashenfelter, O., Card, D. (Eds.), Handbook of Labor Economics, vol. 3A. North-Holland, Amsterdam.

Katz, L.F., Loveman, G.W., Blanchflower, D.G. (1995). "A comparison of changes in the structure of wages in four OECD countries". In: Freeman, R.B., Katz, L.F. (Eds.), Differences and Changes in Wage Structures. University of Chicago Press, Chicago.

Keane, M.P., Prasad, E.S. (2002). "Changes in the structure of earnings during the Polish transition". IMF Working Paper WP/02/135.

Kim, D., Topel, R.H. (1995). "Labor markets and economic growth: Lessons from Korea's industrialization, 1970–1990". In: Freeman, R.B., Katz, L.F. (Eds.), Differences and Changes in Wage Structures. University of Chicago Press, Chicago.

Krueger, A.B., Lindahl, M. (2001). "Education for growth: Why and for whom?". Journal of Economic Literature 39, 1101–1136.

Krueger, A.B., Pischke, J. (1995). "A comparative analysis of East and West German labor markets: Before and after unification". In: Freeman, R.B., Katz, L.F. (Eds.), Differences and Changes in Wage Structures. University of Chicago Press, Chicago.

Kyriacou, G. (1991). "Level and growth effects of human capital". C.V. Starr Center Working Paper No. 91-26.

Levy, F., Murnane, R. (1992). "U.S. earnings levels and earnings inequality: A review of recent trends and proposed explanations". Journal of Economic Literature 30, 1331–1381.

Light, A. (1998). "Estimating the returns to schooling: When does the career begin". Economics of Education Review 17, 31–45.

Lleras-Muney, A. (2002). "The relationship between education and adult mortality in the United States". NBER Working Paper No. 8986.

López-Acevedo, G. (2001). "Evolution of earnings and rates of return to education in Mexico". World Bank Policy Research Working Paper No. 2691.

Machado, J.A.F., Mata, J. (2001). "Earnings functions in Portugal 1982–1994: Evidence from quantile regression". In: Fitzenberger, B., Koenker, R., Machado, J.A.F. (Eds.), Economic Applications of Quantile Regression. Physica Verlag, Heidelberg.

Mincer, J. (1974). Schooling, Experience and Earnings. Columbia University Press, New York.

Mitchell, M.F. (2001). "Specialization and the skill premium in the 20th century". Federal Reserve Bank of Minneapolis, Research Department Staff Report 290.

Montenegro, C.E. (2001). "Wage distribution in Chile: Does gender matter? A quantile regression approach". World Bank Policy Research Report on Gender and Development Working Paper Series No. 20.

Murphy, K.M., Riddell, W.C., Romer, P.M. (1998). "Wages, skills and technology in the United States and Canada". NBER Working Paper No. 6638.

Murphy, K.M., Welch, F. (1990). "Empirical age-earnings profiles". Journal of Labor Economics 8, 202–229.

Nehru, V., Swanson, E., Dubey, A. (1995). "A new database on human capital stocks in developing and industrial countries: Sources, methodology and results". Journal of Development Economics 46, 379–401.

Nickell, S., Bell, B. (1996). "Changes in the distribution of wages and unemployment in OECD countries". American Economic Review Papers and Proceedings 86, 302–308.

OECD. (1996). Employment Outlook. OECD, Paris.

OECD. (2002). Education at a Glance. OECD Indicators 2002. OECD, Paris.

Peracchi, F. (2001). "Earnings inequality in international perspective". In: Welch, F. (Ed.), The Causes and Consequences of Increasing Inequality. University of Chicago Press, Chicago.

Peracchi, F. (2002). "The European Community Household Panel: A review". Empirical Economics 27, 63–90.

Polachek, S.W., Siebert, S.W. (1993). The Economics of Earnings. Cambridge University Press, Cambridge, UK.

Psacharopoulos, G. (1994). "Returns to investment in education: A global update". World Development 22, 1325–1343.

Psacharopoulos, G., Patrinos, H.A. (2002). "Returns to investment in education: A further update". World Bank Policy Research Working Paper 2881.

Revenga, A. (1995). "Employment and wage effects of trade liberalization: The case of Mexican manufacturing". World Bank Policy Research Working Paper No. 1524.
Rutkowski, J.J. (2001). "Earnings inequality in transition economies of Central Europe: Trends and patterns during the 1990s". World Bank Social Protection Discussion Paper No. 0117.
Schultz, T.W. (1961). "Investment in human capital". American Economic Review 51, 1–17.
Schultz, T.W. (1963). The Economic Value of Education. Columbia University Press, New York.
Schmitt, J. (1995). "The changing structure of male earnings in Britain, 1974–1988". In: Freeman, R.B., Katz, L.F. (Eds.), Differences and Changes in Wage Structures. University of Chicago Press, Chicago.
Siow, A. (1984). "Occupational choice under uncertainty". Econometrica 52, 631–645.
Smeeding, T., O'Higgins, M., Rainwater, L. (1990). Poverty, Inequality and Income Distribution in Comparative Perspective. Luxembourg Income Study (LIS). Urban Institute Press, London.
Svejnar, J. (1988). "Labor markets in the transitional central and east European countries". In: Ashenfelter, O., Card, D. (Eds.), Handbook of Labor Economics, vol. 3B. North-Holland, Amsterdam.
Skyt Nielsen, H.S., Rosholm, M. (2001). "The public-private sectore wage gap in Zambia in the 1990s: A quantile regression approach". In: Fitzenberger, B., Koenker, R., Machado, J.A.F. (Eds.), Economic Applications of Quantile Regression. Physica Verlag, Heidelberg.
Spence, A.M. (1974). "Job market signaling". Quarterly Journal of Economics 87, 355–374.
Teal, F. (2000). "Real wages and the demand for skilled and unskilled male labour in Ghana's manufacturing sector: 1991–1995". Journal of Development Economics 61, 447–461.
ter Weel, B. (2003). "The structure of wages in the Netherlands, 1986–1998". Labour 17, 361–382.
Trostel, P., Walker, I., Wooley, P. (2002). "Estimates of the economic return to schooling for 28 countries". Labour Economics 9, 1–16.
UNESCO. (1997). International Standard Classification of Education. ISCED 1997.
Vieira, J.A.C. (1999). "Returns to education in Portugal". Labour Economics 6, 535–541.
Vila, L., Mora, J. (1998). "Changing returns to education in Spain during the 1980s". Economics of Education Review 12, 173–178.
Weisberg, J. (1995). "Returns to education in Israel: 1974 and 1983". Journal of Education Review 14, 145–154.
Weiss, A. (1995). "Human capital vs. signalling explanations of wages". Journal of Economic Perspectives 9, 133–154.
Welch, F. (1970). "Education in production". Journal of Political Economy 78, 312–327.
Welch, F. (1999). "In defence of inequality". American Economic Review Papers and Proceedings 89, 2–17.
Willis, R.J. (1986). "Wage determinants: A survey and reinterpretation of human capital earnings functions". In: Ashenfelter, O., Layard, R. (Eds.), Handbook of Labor Economics. North-Holland, Amsterdam.
Zarkin, G.A. (1985). "Occupational choice: An application to the market for public school teachers". Quarterly Journal of Economics 100, 409–446.

Chapter 6

EDUCATIONAL WAGE PREMIUMS AND THE U.S. INCOME DISTRIBUTION: A SURVEY

DONALD R. DEERE

Texas A&M University and Unicon Research Corporation
e-mail: deere@tamu.edu

JELENA VESOVIC

Texas A&M University
e-mail: jvesovic@econmail.tamu.edu

Contents

Handbook of the Economics of Education, Volume 1
Edited by Eric A. Hanushek and Finis Welch
© 2006 Elsevier B.V. All rights reserved
DOI: 10.1016/S1574-0692(06)01006-3

Abstract

This chapter discusses the large literature and numerous issues regarding education-related differences in income in the U.S. Early analyses of skill-related differences compared the earnings of workers across occupations. The general consensus of these investigations was that skill premiums narrowed substantially between 1900 and 1950. The large increase in the supply of high-school graduates relative to the increased demand for skilled workers is the likely explanation. Following the 1940 Decennial Census, which collected information on educational attainment and on earned income and time worked, empirical analyses concentrated directly on education-related differences in earnings. The human capital revolution of the late 1950s/early 1960s greatly expanded the research on education and income and shifted the focus to wages. The human capital approach modeled income as endogenous and sought to understand the variation in earnings by providing a framework for estimating the returns to education and experience. Recent analyses of education and wages have built on this foundation and have been embedded in a large literature that seeks to document and understand the substantial increase in wage inequality over the last 40 years. The consensus is that increases in the demand for skill are the main culprit, though the reasons for such increases are still an open question. We use census data to document the overall increase in education-related income differences over the past 60 years for several income measures. We also document concomitant changes in enrollment and provide a preliminary analysis suggesting that enrollment has responded to the increase in education–wage premiums. We use NLSY data to document the variation in enrollment patterns for those who attend college and to show how these differences are related to pre-schooling characteristics and to post-schooling earnings. We conclude with a brief discussion of the main issues for future research raised throughout the chapter.

Keywords

education, wages, human capital, enrollment, income

JEL classification: J24, J31, I20

1. Introduction

This chapter tries to provide some guidance to the vast literature and numerous issues concerning education-related differences in income in the U.S. The next section reviews the early literature that largely involved examining differences in incomes across skill-groups identified by occupation. With the advent of the 1940 Decennial Census that, for the first time, included data on educational attainment as well as on earned income and time worked, the analysis could focus on education differences directly. The third section discusses the development of the human capital model and the human capital earnings function and their implications. The theory of human capital has provided a powerful and compact approach for examining the relationship between education and earnings, as well as providing a foundation for a broad ranging analysis of individual self-investment choices. Section four provides a selective review of the literature of the past 20 years or so that has focused on the relationship between education and earnings. Much of this has been in the context of examining the substantial changes in education–wage premiums, and the general increases in wage inequality, that occurred since the 1960s. These three sections set the stage for the data analysis contained in the subsequent two sections of the chapter.

The first data section, section five, uses census data to describe the changes in education–income premiums over the past 60 years. Several measures of income are used from hourly wages to household incomes. Census data also are used to document the large changes in educational attainment and in enrollment rates during this period. The section ends with a preliminary analysis and discussion of the relationship between changes in education–wage premiums and college enrollment and speculates about the relationship between widening college premiums and the increased emphasis on public school quality. Section six is the other data section, which presents preliminary analysis of the National Longitudinal Survey of Youth 1979. These data show the extensive variety of college enrollment patterns that are observed and how differences in enrollment choices relate to observable differences in individual and family characteristics on the one hand and to post-college earnings on the other. A final section seven concludes with a brief recap of the issues raised for future research.

2. Educational wage premiums and the income distribution – early approaches

Historically, interest in the distribution of income often focused on the extent of Morgan (1962), changes in Lampman (1954), or sources of Copeland (1947) inequality, or the distribution of income by source [Schuller (1953)]. There also was interest in the log-normal shape of the income distribution and why this differed from the perceived normal distribution of abilities [Staehle (1943), Roy (1950)]. The focus on differences in earned income, and wages in particular, began with comparisons of wages across occupations and occupation groups.

2.1. Occupation and wages

Early analyses of wage differentials concentrated on occupation differentials partly due to data availability and also because this was a handy categorization of skill. Prime interest was in the skilled/unskilled differential as wage differentials among occupations of different skill levels were important for attracting labor to the skilled trades that require years of training. Occupational wage differentials were analyzed either within one or several industries or a composite sample of many occupations in many industries was used. Examples are Lebergott (1947), Ober (1948), Bell (1951), Woytinsky (1953), Blank and Stigler (1957), and Keat (1960).

Lebergott (1947) compared the 1900 and 1940s occupational wage structure of selected manufacturing industries. Data for 1900 comes from a special 1900 Census of Population survey and from the Monthly Labor Review for the 1940s. The hierarchy of occupational wages remained much the same but the wage premiums between the top and bottom rates narrowed. Empirically, he finds that this narrowing resulted from small increases in earnings in occupations that had the highest earnings in 1900 and relatively large increases in earnings in lower-paid occupations.

Ober (1948) and Bell (1951) examined the trend, and cyclical variation, in occupational wage differentials in the first half of the 20th century. Ober grouped occupational titles into skilled, semiskilled and unskilled in order to calculate percentage differentials. The data cover 1907–1947 and are assembled from Bureau of Labor Statistics (BLS) publications. The analysis indicates that the skilled-occupation wage premium narrows by about half over these 40 years. The rates of reduction in the premium were not uniform across sub-periods. The largest declines occurred during the two World Wars and the respective immediate postwar years. There was a period of relative stability between WWI and the 1930s followed by some widening of the wage differential during the Depression.

Bell (1951) uses data from a relatively large number of sources, including BLS industry studies, BLS union wage scale publications and National Industrial Conference Board surveys of 25 industries, to examine wage differentials for several hundred occupations. Bell (1951) discusses a similar cyclical pattern to that reported by Ober (1948), but with less evidence of a widening differential during the Depression. With regard to the overall trend Bell (1951) claims that Lebergott (1947) and Ober (1948) "present an unwarranted generalization about the trend in the occupational wage structure," [Bell (1951, p. 335)] prior to WWII. It appears, however, that his reported results are more consistent with a general narrowing of wage differentials over time, particularly in the most expansionary sub-periods.

Woytinsky (1953) also found a broad decline in the skilled/unskilled wage premium during 1907–1947. There was some regional variation in the magnitude of the narrowing of wage differentials, but the narrowing occurred in all regions. Woytinsky (1953) expressly considers supply and demand considerations as an explanation for the changes in wage premiums. Comparing the 1910 and 1940 censuses, he finds an increase in the proportion of the labor force in semi-skilled occupations, especially at the higher grades.

Assuming greater overlap in the skill requirements of skilled and higher semi-skilled occupations, he concludes that shifts in relative supplies were a chief factor affecting wage differentials. Blank and Stigler (1957) reach a similar supply-based explanation from examining the relative earnings of scientific professionals compared to the rapid expansion in the number of trained professionals.

Keat (1960) also makes a broad comparison of occupational wage structures in two widely separated years, 1903 and 1956, using data from BLS publications and other sources. As did Lebergott (1947) and others, he finds that differentials narrowed, while rank order changed little. Keat (1960) also makes a systematic assessment of potential explanations for the narrowing, including demographic shifts in sex, race, and age, changes in union influence, reductions in immigration and the costs of training and education. He concludes that, "changes in the cost and time of education and training can conceivably explain a large part of the change in the skilled-unskilled wage differential" [Keat (1960, 600-01)]. Though there is some disagreement about timing, the broad consensus of this literature is that occupational wage differentials narrowed rather substantially during the first half of the 20th century.

2.2. Education and income – early analyses

In the first half of the 20th century there was relatively little analysis of education and income. Part of the reason for this, undoubtedly, was the paucity of data, but the view of education as advancing citizenship generally and having a consumption aspect also likely played a role.

An early example is Ellis (1917), which begins with the acknowledgment that all admit the value of school education for general culture and esthetic appreciation and as a preparation for citizenship, but only a few see the relationship between education and the production of wealth. The author adds that even fewer understand how wealth-producing power depends on the quantity and quality of education, pointing out how natural resources are worthless without education [see also Welch (1970), on this point] and how the necessity for education had increased and would continue to rise with the advance in the complexity of the process of civilization. The paper cites a positive relationship between a states' expenditures on an educational system and a states' productivity, measured by the ratio of the products of farms, factories, mines and quarries to the population of the state from the 1910 census.

At the individual level, Ellis (1917) presents numerous comparisons of wages and incomes showing the premium received by those with more education. Interestingly, Ellis (1917) notes the sharply disproportionate membership of the more educated among successful men, as measured by a listing in "Who's Who in America" for 1899–1900. He then highlights the selection issue, "let it be understood that the remarkable superiority of the educated must not be attributed entirely to their education" [Ellis (1917, p. 15)]. Ellis notes that the educated were a select few both in terms of ability and wealth, but concludes, "after due allowance for all these factors is made there remains still a large margin of superior efficiency on the part of the educated that one must credit to education or do violence to common sense" [Ellis (1917, p. 16)].

Fisher (1932) emphasizes the role of education in determining the distribution of wealth in addition to the role it plays in wealth production. He provides an early analysis of the effect of supply changes from increases in education on the skill–wage premium. Fisher credits the steady extension of education with reducing "the relative number of people who are unable to offer the world anything but unskilled labour" [Fisher (1932, p. 747)]. He also notes that, "It has long been common to deplore the narrowing of the margin between skilled and unskilled wages, and to suggest that it means a weakening of the incentive to acquire skill" [Fisher (1932, p. 750)]. Some 50 years later, the incentive issue seems to have been lost, as the lament came over widening wage gaps and "the rich getting richer."

In the aptly named article, "Capital Concept Applied to Man," Walsh (1935), using multiple data sources, compares the estimated lifetime earnings across education groups with estimated costs of the education. Besides comparing group averages, the paper also notes substantial dispersion within groups and points to ability differences as a primary cause. As with Ellis (1917) above, Walsh (1935) also notes the selection issue by commenting that the differences in average earnings across education groups are not all due to the differences in education, especially for the college–high school comparison. He concludes that, "the investments made in professional abilities and material capital act in the same way. Within this range the capital theory fittingly applies to men" [Walsh (1935, p. 285)].

2.3. *Improved measurement and analysis – education and wages after the 1940 census*

Two developments prior to the 1940 census were to result in nothing short of a gold mine for data analysts. The first was the large economic upheavals of the 1930s and the Great Depression, while the second, and much more obscure, was the use of sampling in the census.[1] The former placed greater urgency on the collection of a broader set of economic data, particularly related to employment and income, and the latter made this feasible by collecting data on certain items from only a (representative) subset of the population. The 1940 census collected, for the first time, information on educational attainment, income, and time worked. The sampling also made it feasible for detailed cross-tabulations to be made of such variables as education and income. Time worked, of course, allowed the calculation of wage rates. Economists, especially labor economists, have been crunching data ever since.

A number of studies examine education and the distribution of income using Census and Census-type (e.g., the Current Population Survey) data following release of

[1] Jenkins (1985) and Anderson (2000) provide discussions of the changes to the 1940 census and note in particular the role of the Committee on Government Statistics and Information Services (COGSIS).

the 1940 census. Most of these studies also highlight the difficulty in interpreting differences in average income across education groups as a "return" due to the biases associated with correlation between income and ability and/or family income/wealth.

Miller (1960) provides a comprehensive description and analysis of differences in income across education levels using the 1940 and 1950 censuses and Current Population Surveys from the mid-1940s and mid- and late-1950s. The successive cross-section approach presages later analyses, such as the results presented later in this chapter. Miller (1960) presents wage premiums by education and age and presents evidence of alternate narrowing and then widening of wage premiums between 1940 and 1960. He also notes the substantial overlap in the income distributions for high school and college graduates. Miller (1960) examines the relationship between changing premiums and educational attainment, noting that the college premium has remained roughly constant overall as college graduates have become relatively more plentiful and concludes, "the demand for more highly educated workers has kept pace with the increased supply of such workers" [Miller (1960, p. 985)].

Other papers of interest from this period include Glick and Miller (1956), who find that education–income premiums are larger for white men than for black men. They also suggest that more widespread information about the magnitude of the college premium would result in even greater increases in educational attainment. Glick and Miller (1956) also identify a higher "return" to graduation and suggest this may result in part from the relationship between persistence in school and capability. Renshaw (1960) addresses specifically many of the issues surrounding interpreting average income differences as returns, including ability bias, differences within compared to between occupations, and the longer work hours of the more educated. The latter point hints that labor supply curves are positively sloped. Houthakker (1959) shows how the shape of estimated age–earnings profiles varies by education level and notes that because of selection (on ability and family income) the real return to education could be zero. Finally, Bristol (1958) examines longitudinal data and documents regression to the mean in general, but also notes that dispersion across education groups does not regress, and may increase, over time.

While these early analyses are clearly aware of the investment aspects of education and often note the difficulties of interpreting education premiums as returns, they essentially pre-date the formal development of the human capital model and the resulting human capital earnings function. The human capital earnings function, discussed in the next section, provides a compact, powerful, and quite tractable tool for the analysis of education wage premiums and the income distribution. Before turning to this discussion, we first highlight papers by Claudia Goldin and coauthors that provide modern analyses of the relationship between education and wages during the earlier parts of the 20th century.

Goldin and Katz (2001) demonstrate, using multiple data sources, that the first half-century was a period of narrowing wage inequality, in contrast to the widening inequality of the last 50 years, and that overall wage inequality was lower at the end of the century than at the beginning. Focusing on education, the authors combine Iowa state census data with U.S. census data to find education–wage premiums, both high school relative to elementary and college/high school, fell between 1914 and 1949. Goldin and Katz (2001) discuss supply and demand factors, technological change, and institutional factors, such as unionism, as potential causes of these changes.

Goldin (1999) documents the substantial expansion in high school graduation between 1910 and 1940 and suggests this was an important factor in explaining the decline in the premium to white collar workers. Goldin and Katz (1995) examine the wages of office workers relative to production workers as a proxy for the high school wage premium. This ratio showed little change from 1890 to 1910, declined substantially from 1910 to 1920 and changed slightly from 1920 to 1930. The authors attribute this change primarily to the increased demand for blue-collar workers during World War I, the increased relative supply of educated workers, and a reduction in the immigration flows. Goldin and Margo (1992) analyzed education–wage premiums using 1940, 1950 and 1960 census data. They document a significant reduction of education premiums during the 1940s. The authors discuss the increased relative demand for less-educated workers, the increase in the supply of educated labor, and institutional changes related to stronger unions and a rising minimum wage as causal factors.

3. The human capital revolution

While the concept of human capital had existed for some time [e.g., Walsh (1935)], the phrase "Human Capital Revolution" in labor economics generally applies to the literature that began around the early 1960s, including in particular, Mincer (1958, 1962) and Becker (1962, 1975) and the other papers in a special issue of the *Journal of Political Economy* (1962) entitled, "Investments in Human Beings." In introducing this volume, Schultz notes that investments in people are substantial and that such investments are key to understanding growth, the structure of relative earnings, and the distribution of personal income.

The human capital literature, which Becker notes in the introduction to the second edition of *Human Capital* (1975) grew at a tremendous rate, is primarily distinguished by treating earnings as an endogenous variable and seeking to explain the sources of variation in earnings. Education has received the most attention as a type of human capital investment, partly because of data availability (see the papers in the special issue of the *Journal of Political Economy*, 1979). Training is, however, a close second, especially when equated with labor market experience as measured by the passage of time since leaving school. The concept of investment in human capital also has been applied to migration [Bowles (1970), Topel (1986)], including immigration [Borjas (1987)], health [Mushkin (1962), Grossman (1972)], and search [Stigler (1962)]. The point of this section is to provide a brief introduction to the human capital earnings function as a basis for the empirical examination of education wage premiums.

3.1. The human capital earnings function

Mincer (1970) provides an excellent exposition of the human capital earnings function, its use in analyzing earnings differences, and its relationship to earlier approaches to the study of the income distribution, while Mincer (1974) provides a more detailed development and analysis. Becker (1962, 1975) provides an expansive theoretical foundation for analyzing several aspects of human capital investment, including the distinction between general and specific training. Mincer (1970) emphasizes that the human capital approach focuses on the determinants of labor incomes with resulting implications for the distribution of income. In particular, the role of individual economic decisions is central to the human capital model. He contrasts this with the earlier analyses of the income distribution that concentrate on the functional or factor-share approach and then notes that the primary source of income variation is differences in labor earnings – leading to the importance of the determinants of labor earnings. The human capital approach shifted the explanation of income inequality from differences in ability, with the concomitant puzzle over the (perceived) normal distribution of abilities yet the log-normal distribution of incomes, to differences in investments. A shift other social sciences might describe as from ascribed to achieved characteristics. The fundamental notion is that greater investments would be undertaken only if greater earnings resulted, thus providing a link to the Smithian principle of equalizing differences.

Consider a simple model of education investment in which all schooling is undertaken prior to entering the labor force, education is measured by time in school, the only cost of schooling is foregone earnings, the flow of earnings is constant after leaving school, and worklife does not vary with schooling. Equalization of the present value of lifetime earnings for years of schooling, s, and for no schooling implies:

$$\log E_s = A + Bs, \tag{1}$$

where $\log E_s$ is the natural logarithm of annual earnings with s years of schooling, A is the logarithm of annual earnings with no schooling and B is the rate of return on the investment in schooling. Thus, this basic model implies that log earnings are linear in years of schooling, providing the basic specification for examining earnings differences across education groups.

Mincer (1970, 1974) emphasizes that the "schooling model" given by (1) does not hold if there is additional investment in human capital after entering the labor force. If work experience, notably on-the-job training that sacrifices some current output for greater future output, leads to increased earnings, then post-school investments in human capital must be included in the analysis. Let $C_t = k_t E_{st}$ be the cost of post-schooling investment in period t since leaving school. This is measured as the fraction, k_t, of gross earnings (i.e., earnings capacity) in period t with years of schooling s, denoted E_{st}, that is devoted to training. Earnings capacity in post-schooling period t is given by:

$$E_{st} = E_{s0} \prod (1 + r_t k_t), \tag{2}$$

with r_t the return on investment in post-schooling period t. Taking logs and assuming $k_t \leqslant 1$ and r_t small gives:

$$\log E_{st} = \log E_{s0} + \sum r_t k_t. \tag{3}$$

Noting that observed earnings in period t for schooling s, denoted Y_{st}, is net of investment in period t, $Y_{st} = E_{st}(1 - k_t)$, and substituting from (1) gives:

$$\log Y_{st} = A + Bs + \sum r_t k_t + \log(1 - k_t). \tag{4}$$

Given that time in (4) is measured post-schooling implies that the shape of the experience–earnings profile depends on the time path of investments, k_t, and their returns, r_t. The incentives for these investments to be undertaken nearer the beginning of the working life, because of the greater return from the remaining working life and the lower cost due to lower earnings, coupled with depreciation or obsolescence of human capital later in the working life, suggests a concave shape. Thus the basic empirical specification for the human capital earnings function is:

$$\log Y_{st} = A + Bs + Ct - Dt^2, \tag{5}$$

with s measuring years of schooling and t measuring post-schooling years of experience, often proxied by (estimated) years since leaving school. Note that most applications of (5) use the logarithm of wages rather than of earnings, or include the log of weeks worked as a regressor, in order to control labor supply responses.

3.2. *Issues, interpretation and extension*

Ben-Porath (1967) provides a detailed theoretical analysis of life cycle earnings and human capital investments and the possible time-paths of each and their relationship. Murphy and Welch (1990) show that a fourth-order polynomial better tracks the rapid increase in earnings over the first few years of experience compared to the quadratic specification in (5). Card (1999) notes that though less restrictive functional forms are often used for schooling, the linear specification in (5) provides a good fit.

Beyond specification topics, several issues regarding measurement as well as the interpretation and estimation of (5) have arisen. Foremost among these are ability bias, signaling, heterogeneity in education returns and the measurement of experience and of education. Mincer (1970) mentions each of these except signaling, while Becker (1975) provides a response to the signaling hypothesis [see Taubman and Wales (1973), Spence (1973, 1974), and Chapter 8 by Lange and Topel in this Handbook].

The plausible notion that more able individuals invest in more schooling, which results in biased estimates of B in (5) thereby overstating the return to education, is compelling. Card (1999), and earlier Griliches (1977), however, conclude that the overall evidence on this suggests that OLS estimation of (5) provides estimates of B that are relatively uncontaminated by ability bias. One reason may be that measurement error in education, which would tend to attenuate the estimate of B, works to offset the ability bias. Another reason may be that good instruments or techniques for obtaining unbiased estimates are rather elusive (see also Chapter 7 by Heckman, Lochner and Todd in this Handbook).

Willis (1986) provides an extended discussion of the human capital earnings function and gives an interpretation consistent with a structural model including heterogeneous returns [see also Willis (1979)]. Willis (1986) provides a link between the equalizing differences model of Smith, which provides a foundation for the original development of the human capital earnings function, and the Mills/Cairn models of income differences based on non-competing groups. Card (1999) provides a detailed discussion of the heterogeneous returns issue and the various resulting estimation approaches. He concludes that OLS appears to provide a good estimate of the average marginal return to education.

Mincer (1974) notes that for those with weaker/non-continuous attachment to the labor force, such as women, actual experience is a much better measure than potential experience in explaining earnings. Mincer and Polachek (1974), Mincer and Ofek (1982) and Light and Ureta (1995) provide analyses of the implications of this difference for measuring gender wage differentials. Mincer (1970) notes that years in school may be a poor reflection of the education received. Welch (1966), Betts (1996) and Strayer (2002) examine aspects of the returns to school quality and Ureta and Welch (1998) probe the empirical content of the 1990 change in the Census Bureau's measurement of education.

The human capital earnings function/model is one of the most successful, and almost certainly the most estimated, relationships in economics. The model and its empirical content suggest that differences in the quantity of human capital investments, both education and post-school training, explain a large portion of earnings inequality, longitudinally as well as in a cross-section. This explanatory power increases noticeably if/when the quality of these investments also is taken into account. In addition, the model reconciles the early puzzle of the skewed shape of the income distribution with the symmetric shape of the ability distribution. Also of importance, the focus on individual choice in the human capital model suggests that investment decisions are affected by shifts in the returns to human capital, thereby raising issues about how enrollment and labor supply (given time worked affects training) respond to wage differences.

In the next section, we discuss some aspects of the research on education–wage differentials as part of the large literature on changes in the wage structure. In a subsequent section we return to the issue of responses to changes in these education–wage premiums.

4. Increases in the return to human capital and the wage structure

Much of the literature from the past two decades that rests on the foundation of the human capital earnings function has focused on documenting and explaining the large changes in the wage structure that occurred since the 1960s. The primary issue addressed in this literature is increasing wage inequality. Changes in education–wage differentials are only one, though an important, part of this body of research. Other aspects of the wage structure examined alongside the changing education premiums are the premium for experience, dispersion in wages within education and experience groups, and, to a lesser extent, changes in gender and race differentials.

The general consensus on the primary source of increased wage inequality is an increase in the relative demand for skill, with education being one of the two (experience is the other) common, observable indicators of skill. There is less consensus on the source of the shifts in relative demand. There also is some discussion of shifts in supply and of institutional changes as sources of the movements in wage premiums. This section attempts to provide some highlights of this literature, with particular focus on changes in education premiums.

4.1. Documenting facts about the changing wage structure

Murphy and Welch (1989) document the pattern of changes in the education premiums from the early 1960s to the mid-1980s, showing the reduction during the 1970s and the sharp increase in the 1980s. Levy and Murnane (1992) provide a comprehensive look at wage inequality facts and issues that goes beyond education premiums. They also note, among many other facts, the decline in education premiums during the 1970s followed by a sharp increase in wage differentials between education groups in the 1980s. They suggest that changes in the relative supply of and demand for skill groups is necessary to explain observed trends in relative wages, and they also raise the issue of the role of institutional changes. Juhn, Murphy and Pierce (1993) provide a more explicit link between changes in relative wages, including education premiums, and changes in the relative demand for skilled workers. They note that the increase in wage dispersion between education and experience groups has a different time pattern than the increase in wage dispersion within these groups. They suggest that changes in the composition or quality of the work force across cohorts explains little of the increased wage premiums as within- and between-cohort wage inequality has increased similarly. Gottschalk (1997) provides a more recent survey that also includes some discussion of mobility. Katz and Autor (1999) provide a comprehensive discussion of the issues and literature on changes in the wage structure, including some international comparisons. They include a framework for emphasizing the roles of supply and demand in understanding wage inequality and for examining the interaction of market forces with labor market institutions. Deere (2001) provides a compilation of facts about trends in wage inequality, including the college/high school premium, and notes the relationship between increased men's participation and changes in wages.

Juhn (1999) uses Decennial Census data, rather than Current Population Survey data, to examine wage inequality and relative demand shifts and finds that the supply and demand framework explains the movement in education premiums rather well. Haider (2001) uses Panel Study of Income Dynamics data to examine changes in lifetime income inequality and instability. He finds that lifetime income instability increased a similar amount to lifetime income inequality and that a large part of the increase in lifetime inequality is due to permanent changes in wage across education groups.

Murphy and Welch (1992) document the alternating pattern of education premiums, increasing in the 1960s, narrowing in the 1970s, and rising sharply in the 1980s. They also attribute the cause of increased premiums to relative demand shifts, but highlight the role of relative supply from the entry of the well-educated baby boom cohort in the 1970s narrowing of education premiums. Freeman (1976) and Welch (1979) are earlier papers that examine the reduced college/high school wage premium during the 1970s, with the former concluding that both demand and supply shifts were the cause, and the latter focusing on supply shifts. Freeman (1976) also points out the decline in college enrollment resulting from the reduced college wage premium.

Katz and Murphy (1992) demonstrate the positive relationship between changes in relative wages for skilled workers and changes in employment shares during 1963–1987 and suggest this is strong evidence of an increased relative demand for skill. Similarly, Murphy and Welch (1993) highlight the substantial increase in education attainment during 1940–1990 alongside the overall, though not monotonic, increase in education–wage premiums during this period as indicative of an increase in the relative demand for education.

4.2. Causes of changes in the wage structure

Davis and Haltiwanger (1991), Bound and Johnson (1992, 1995), Berman, Bound and Griliches (1994) and Johnson (1997) focus on the reason for the increased relative demand for skill and conclude that skill-biased technical change is the primary source. The basic reasoning is that the education intensity of each sector has increased as opposed to there being a large shift of employment toward education-intensive sectors. Krueger (1993) and Autor, Katz and Krueger (1998) examine the role of computerization in changing wage premiums and suggest this as a source of the skill-biased technological change. Levy and Murnane (1996) and DiNardo and Pischke (1997) cast some doubt on the causal relationship between computerization and wage premiums.

Bartel and Sicherman (1999) use NLSY 1979 panel data in a fixed effects model to examine the relationship between technological change and education premiums and find that a substantial portion is due to sorting on unobserved heterogeneity. Bartel and Lichtenberg (1987) is an early paper that examines technical change and wages and concludes that while more educated workers have an advantage in implementing new technology, the relative demand for more educated workers declines as the equipment ages. Doms, Dunne and Troske (1997) note that there is a positive cross-sectional relationship between the presence of educated workers and use of new technology, but find little evidence of a longitudinal relationship between skill-upgrading and the adoption of new technologies.

Katz and Goldin (1998) offer an interesting potential counterpoint to the technical change source of the increase in the demand for skill. They provide evidence of substantial skill-biased technical change in the early 1900s – change that was accompanied by a narrowing of education– and skill–wage premiums. They suggest that this different response (compared to recent times) of wage premiums to technical change may have resulted from an even larger expansion in the supply of (high school-) educated workers.

Murphy and Welch (2001a) raise questions about the nature of the technical change favoring skilled workers because the growth in education levels is so pervasive across sectors to suggest that it is unrelated to industry-specific production techniques. Gould (2002) develops and analyzes a multi-sector model of occupation selection and provides evidence that sectors are becoming more similar in their pricing of skills, consistent with an increasing emphasis on general skills. Card and Lemieux (2001) and Card and DiNardo (2002) question the role of relative demand shifts driven by technical change in explaining changes in wage premiums, especially related to education, and highlight the role of supply shifts.

In addition to the role of skill-biased technical change, the increasing openness of the U.S. economy has been noted as a source of the relative demand shift for skilled workers. Indirectly through international trade or directly from immigration, there has been a relative increase in the supply of less skilled workers. Johnson (1997) examines both the international trade and technical change hypotheses. Some of the other papers that examine the trade issue are Lawrence and Slaughter (1993), Feenstra and Hanson (1996), Sachs and Shatz (1996), and Borjas and Ramey (1994, 1995) focusing on trade and Borjas, Freeman and Katz (1996, 1997) that include immigration.

Other papers that address additional issues about the source of increasing wage inequality include Blackburn and Neumark (1993), which concludes that changes in the ability bias of the education coefficient cannot explain the observed increase in the OLS-measured return to schooling. Juhn, Murphy and Pierce (1993) conclude that changes in the quality of college compared to high school graduates can not explain the college/high school wage premium given that the premium changes have been similar for older as well as younger cohorts.

Grogger and Eide (1995) use data from the National Center for Education Statistics (National Longitudinal Study of the High School Class of 1972 and the High School and Beyond survey) to compare the impact of changes in pre-college skills and skills acquired in college on the college/high school wage premium. They conclude that changes in the skills of men attending college had no effect on wage premiums, but that returns to math ability rose for women, so that the increase in the college premium for women is overstated to some degree.

DiNardo, Fortin and Lemieux (1996) and Fortin and Lemieux (1997) examine the impact of institutional changes, principally declining minimum wages, de-unionionization and increased deregulation, on increased wage inequality. They find that these factors were an important source of increased inequality, with declining unionization more important for men and a drop in the real minimum wage more important for women.

Pierce (2001) examines a broader measure of compensation than wages and finds an increase in inequality that is somewhat larger than the increase measured for wages.

Pension and health insurance costs fell for low-wage workers and increased for higher-paid workers.

One of the issues in the early literature on skill-based wage differentials is the issue of incentives. Recall that Fisher (1932) was concerned about the reduced incentive to acquire skill as the skill premiums narrowed. With the large increase in skill premiums, particularly those associated with a college degree, there has been some recognition that investments in education will increase in response and thereby mitigate wage inequality. This reasoning lies behind the explanation of Goldin and Katz (1998) for the opposite reaction of the wage premium to the technology changes in the early 1900s. While most of the recent literature has been concerned with increases in inequality and its causes (and also the measured stagnation of real wages), Topel (1997), Mincer (1998), Welch (1999), Murphy and Welch (2001b) and Deere and Welch (2002) raise the issue of the incentives provided by skill-based wage premiums, particularly the college/high school wage difference. They note the increases in education attainment and/or enrollment that have occurred since 1980, when the college premium began its sharp rise. This supply response of increased investment in human capital should result ultimately in a reduction in wage inequality.

5. Trends in education–wage premiums and the relationship to enrollment

The previous sections have attempted to provide some guidance to the vast literature about the relationship between education and earnings. In this section we first document the changes in the relationship between education and income over the past 60 years. Several measures of income are used – from hourly wages to household income. We also document changes in enrollment over this period. The section ends with a preliminary examination of the relationship between changes in education–wage premiums and changes in enrollment rates. We also include a brief discussion of research on public school quality and relate this to the changes in education premiums.

5.1. Education and income

While education may not necessarily be a ticket on a ride to riches, over the past 50 years it appears increasingly to have at least greased the wheels. Figure 1 presents an "Education Lorenz" curve using data from the 1950 and 2000 Decennial Censuses. For each of four sex/race groups, educational attainment is measured in groups along the horizontal axis. Because of very large changes in the distribution of educational attainment over this period, the vertical axis measures the ratio of the cumulated income share of an education group to its cumulated population share. Thus, if every educational group had an income share equal to its share of the population, this "Lorenz" curve would be horizontal and equal to 1.0. By construction, the curve must equal 1 for the highest education group. An upward slope to the curve implies that groups with less education have a disproportionately (compared to their population share) small share of

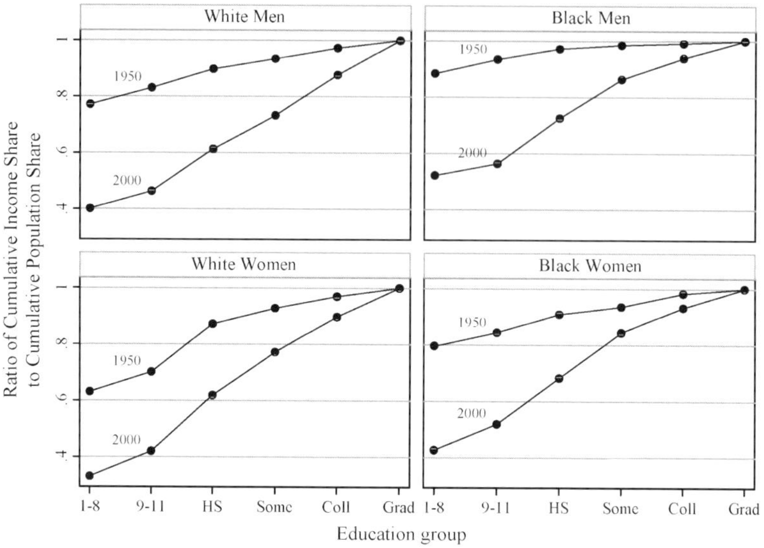

Figure 1. "Education Lorenz curves": Changes in the distribution of income across education groups 1950 to 2000, by sex and race. Source: Authors' calculations using Decennial Censuses from 1950 and 2000.

income. The greater the slope, the greater the disparity in income relative to population shares.

Inspection of the figure for 1950 shows that, with two exceptions, the relative income shares are essentially at or above .8 for all education groups for all sex/race groups. The exceptions are white women with less than a high school degree, who have relative income shares of .63 and .70. For 2000, the only groups with relative income shares above .8 are those with at least some college, and, for whites, a college degree is necessary to have a relative income share this high. The curves are more steeply sloped in 2000, with relative income shares for those with no more than a high school degree substantially lower than in 1950. The relative income shares for high school graduates are just above .6 for white men and women and about .7 for black men and women. For those with less than a high school degree, relative income shares are below .5 for whites and below .6 for blacks.

Alongside this growth in income disparity across education groups, there has been a sharp increase in educational attainment. Table 1 presents the distribution of educational attainment by sex and race from each of the Decennial Censuses from 1940–2000. The six education groups, which match those displayed in Figure 1, are 0–8 years, 9–11 years, high school graduates, some college, college graduates (bachelor's only), and those with some post-graduate work (whether with an additional degree or not).

The table shows a substantial increase in reported educational attainment. In 1940, well over one-half the working-age population did not have a high school degree, with this figure about 90% for blacks. By 2000, these low education groups had diminished

Table 1
Distribution of education al attainment for those not enrolled in school, 1940–2000, by sex and race

	Educational attainment					
	0–8 years	9–11 years	High school graduates	Some college	College graduates	Post graduates
A. White men						
1940	51.0	19.6	17.9	5.6	4.0	1.8
1950	37.5	21.5	24.7	8.0	5.2	3.2
1960	26.6	21.7	29.7	10.2	6.6	5.2
1970	15.6	18.9	37.1	12.5	8.4	7.5
1980	9.3	13.5	38.4	17.0	11.3	10.6
1990	5.6	11.9	30.9	26.0	16.0	9.6
2000	3.6	9.8	29.2	28.1	18.5	10.8
B. Black men						
1940	83.3	9.5	4.3	1.6	1.0	0.4
1950	71.0	16.0	8.5	2.8	1.1	0.6
1960	53.3	23.0	16.2	4.5	1.8	1.3
1970	31.1	29.0	29.0	6.8	2.3	1.9
1980	15.6	24.1	37.9	14.1	4.6	3.8
1990	6.3	24.1	34.5	24.2	7.5	3.5
2000	3.5	19.8	35.9	27.5	9.1	4.2
C. White women						
1940	45.4	20.7	23.1	6.8	3.2	0.8
1950	31.6	21.7	32.0	9.1	4.0	1.6
1960	21.6	22.4	38.5	10.7	4.9	1.9
1970	12.3	19.9	45.7	12.8	6.4	2.8
1980	7.8	14.5	46.8	16.8	8.8	5.3
1990	4.6	11.6	35.4	27.8	14.2	6.4
2000	2.8	8.2	29.5	31.5	18.5	9.4
D. Black women						
1940	77.2	12.9	6.5	2.2	1.0	0.2
1950	63.3	19.6	11.5	3.2	1.8	0.6
1960	44.3	27.1	20.4	4.8	2.5	1.0
1970	24.7	31.9	32.0	6.6	3.2	1.6
1980	12.1	25.1	40.0	14.6	4.9	3.4
1990	4.8	22.9	33.5	26.6	8.4	3.9
2000	2.8	18.0	32.3	31.4	10.4	5.0

Source: Authors' calculations from Decennial Censuses from 1940–2000.

by a factor of about 4, while those with at least some college comprised at least 40% (and for whites, over half) of the population. There are surely many reasons for this large increase in human capital investment over the past 60 years, but the relationship between higher income and more education is worthy of further scrutiny.

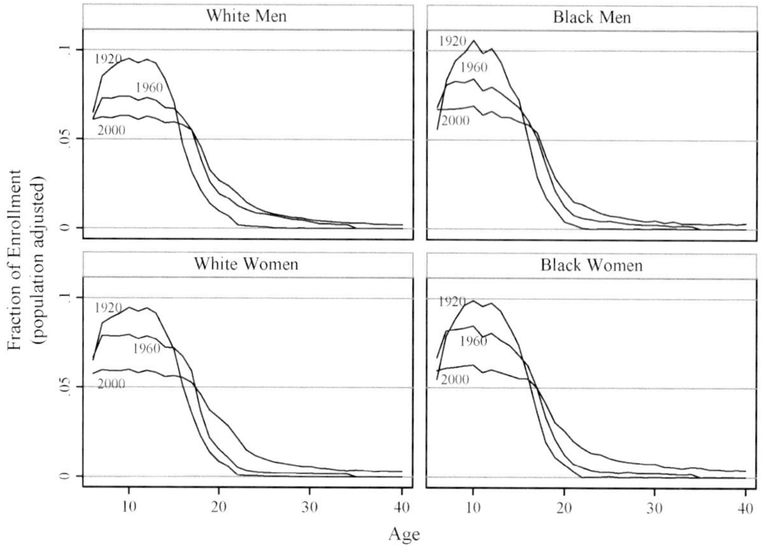

Figure 2. Changes in the age distribution of individuals enrolled in school from 1920 to 1960 to 2000, by sex and race. Source: Authors' calculations using Decennial Censuses from 1920, 1960 and 2000.

Before looking in a bit more detail at the relationship between income and education, it is useful first to examine changes in school enrollment patterns. Figure 2 graphs the age distribution of enrollment from the 1920, 1960, and 2000 Decennial Censuses. The horizontal axis measures the age, from 6 to 40, of the enrolled population, while the vertical axis measures the fraction of all enrolled individuals who are of a given age (adjusted for population shifts). The resulting graphs are discrete probability density functions (connected by a smooth line) conditional on age 40 or younger.

Between 1920 and 1960, there is an increase in the share of enrollment in the typical late high school and college ages (the 1920 and 1960 densities cross around 15 years). The differences for men extend to later ages. Between 1960 and 2000, there is another shift of enrollment to ages in the 20s and beyond. This increase in enrollment shares beyond the typical college years is more pronounced for women.

By 2000, individuals over 30 accounted for between 5% and 9% of enrollment across sex/race groups. The shares for women and blacks are higher than for men and whites. These compare to over-30 enrollment shares of less than 1% in 1920 and even in 1960. Further, enrollment shares for ages beyond 40, which are not shown on the graph, are between 2% and 2.5% for men in 2000 and between 3 and 3.5% for women. These compare to over-40 enrollment shares of essentially zero for all sex/race groups in 1920 and 1960. As educational attainment increased it is, of course, not surprising that enrollment shifted to older ages. The substantial increase in enrollment shares for ages well beyond the typical college years, however, raises interesting questions to which we return below.

5.2. *Education and wages*

In this section we examine differences in hourly wages across education groups by sex and race from 1940–2000. The hourly wage rate represents the price of labor and it is useful to begin by comparing the prices of different "types" of labor distinguished by education. Education is one of the two (potential experience being the other) common observable measures of human capital used by economists to measure, or at least reflect, differences in productivity.

The data used here come from the 1940–2000 Decennial Censuses. The data appendix provides a more detailed description of the "wage sample" used in this section, but here are the highlights. The data are restricted to individuals who are black or white, not enrolled in school, are wage and salary employees (including the incorporated self-employed from 1970 on), worked at least 27 weeks and 35 hours per week in the prior year, and have potential experience of 1–40 years.

Figures 3a and 3b present trends in wage differences across education groups by sex/race. In each year, within sex/race groups, the average wage is calculated for each education group, and this average is then expressed as a percentage of the average wage for high school graduates in that year to provide a measure of the education–wage premiums by year for each sex/race group. Thus the vertical axis of Figures 3a and 3b measures wages as a percentage of the average high school graduate wage, while the horizontal axis denotes year. For clarity, the education groups are divided, with Figure 3a showing relative wages for groups with at least a high school degree and Figure 3b including groups with at most a high school degree. The horizontal line at 100 in both figures for high school graduates identifies this group as the "numeraire." While the relative wages are not always ordered monotonically by education level, that is the norm.

As relative wages draw nearer to 100, for example as from 1940 to 1950, dispersion decreases and the education–wage premiums shrink. As relative wages move away from 100, for example as from 1980 to 1990, the education–wage premiums increase. The overall pattern, familiar to most students of labor economics, is one of reduced premiums from 1940 to 1950 and increasing premiums after that, except for the reversal in 1980. Note that the premiums above high school seem to move more than those below, and in particular that the premiums above high school increase between 1990 and 2000, while the premiums below high school tend to decrease in this period.

There also appear to be some differences for women compared to men, with white women having larger premiums in 1940 with a sharper drop to 1950, and black women experiencing smaller changes in premiums above high school and generally diminishing premiums (i.e., reduced wage dispersion) below high school. Part of the reason for the differences for women lies in the greater changes in women's labor market experiences over time, so that the average high school female is a rather volatile base group. This affects not only measures of wages, but especially measures that include participation as will be evident below.

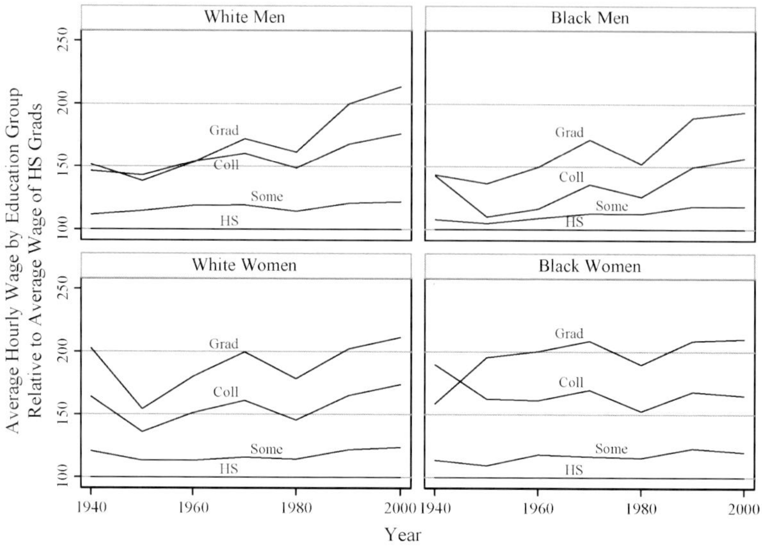

(a)

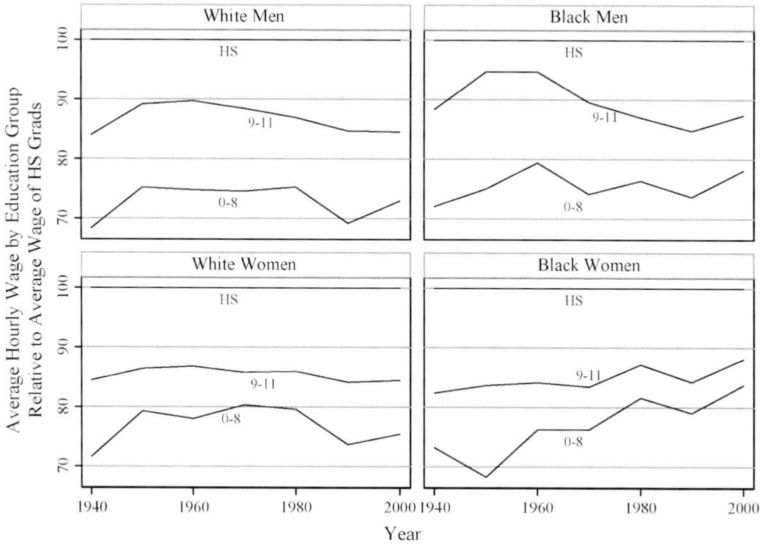

(b)

Figure 3. Trends in hourly wages by education for groups with at least (a) and at most (b) a HS degree relative to wages of HS graduates 1940–2000, by sex and race. Source: Authors' calculations using Decennial Censuses from 1940–2000.

Table 2 provides companion information to the figures by reporting the relative wages in 1950, when the premiums are generally the smallest, and the differences in premiums compared to 1950 for the other years. For example, the number −5.2 for white men with 9–11 years of education in 1940 implies that the premium for white men finishing high school was 5.2 percentage points larger in 1940 than in 1950. Note that a negative difference in the education premium compared to 1950 for education levels below high school means that wages became more dispersed for these groups. Likewise, the number 6.6 for black men college graduates in 1960 implies that the college/high school premium for black men was 6.6 percentage points larger in 1960 than in 1950. Most of the changes in premiums subsequent to 1950 occur above high school, as noted above.

The college/high school premium increases after 1950 for men and for white women in every year but 1980. Cumulating the year-to-year changes from 1950 to 2000, the college/high school premium is 33 points higher for white men, 47 points higher for black men, and 38 points higher for white women. Black women stand out as having a relatively stable college/high school premium over the period, though the college/high school wage ratio in 1950 was noticeably higher at 162.5% than for the other groups. The pattern in the premium for post-graduate work relative to high school is similar, rising by 75 percentage points for white men between 1950 and 2000.

As a prelude to examining differences in incomes across education groups, we first take a look at how hours of work have changed. Figure 4 presents "labor supply" curves by sex and race groups at the beginning and end of the period. The vertical axis uses educational attainment to measure wages, thereby capturing the wage premiums reflected in the previous figure. The horizontal axis measures quantity as the average annual hours of work for each education group relative to average hours for high school graduates.

The figure shows that each sex/race group had a backward-bending "labor supply" curve in 1940 and that by 2000 these curves were virtually uniformly positively sloped. The picture is very similar if the data for 1970 are used instead of for 1940. The obvious implication is that, at least among those in this wage sample, differences in hours worked across education groups now reinforce wage differences resulting in larger education–earnings premiums.

5.3. Wage dispersion within education groups

Before turning our attention to investigate education–income differences for a broader group of the population that also includes those who work only part-time or not at all, we digress to take a brief look at differences in wages within education groups. Figures 3a and 3b traced increases in the dispersion of average wages across education groups from 1950 to 2000. While education (and experience) are the most easily observed indicators of human capital, there are many other, unobserved factors that affect productivity and therefore wages.

Alongside the increased dispersion in wages across education (and experience) levels since 1950, there has been an increase in wage dispersion within education and experience, presumably related to shifts in the premiums for these unobservable factors. In

Table 2
Changes in relative wages for 1940–2000 compared to 1950, by sex and race

	Educational attainment					
	0–8 years	9–11 years	High school graduates	Some college	College graduates	Post graduates
A. White men						
1940	−6.8	−5.2	0.0	−3.0	3.3	13.2
1950	75.2	89.2	100.0	114.7	143.0	138.3
1960	−0.4	0.6	0.0	4.2	11.0	14.7
1970	−0.6	−0.7	0.0	4.7	17.4	33.5
1980	0.1	−2.2	0.0	−0.2	5.6	23.0
1990	−6.0	−4.5	0.0	6.1	24.9	61.8
2000	−2.2	−4.7	0.0	7.3	33.2	75.2
B. Black men						
1940	−2.9	−6.4	0.0	3.0	32.3	7.1
1950	75.0	94.8	100.0	104.8	110.1	136.4
1960	4.4	−0.1	0.0	4.4	6.6	13.3
1970	−0.9	−5.3	0.0	8.0	25.5	35.2
1980	1.4	−7.8	0.0	7.6	15.9	15.7
1990	−1.3	−10.0	0.0	13.8	39.7	52.7
2000	3.2	−7.4	0.0	13.5	46.5	57.0
C. White women						
1940	−7.7	−2.0	0.0	7.4	28.1	48.0
1950	79.3	86.5	100.0	113.3	136.1	154.4
1960	−1.3	0.4	0.0	−0.1	15.4	25.4
1970	1.1	−0.6	0.0	2.5	25.1	45.0
1980	0.3	−0.5	0.0	1.0	9.7	24.2
1990	−5.6	−2.3	0.0	8.6	29.2	47.9
2000	−3.9	−2.0	0.0	10.6	37.9	57.0
D. Black women						
1940	4.9	−1.3	0.0	4.2	27.1	−36.5
1950	68.3	83.7	100.0	109.6	162.5	195.2
1960	8.0	0.5	0.0	8.6	−0.9	4.9
1970	8.0	−0.3	0.0	7.1	7.3	13.2
1980	13.3	3.5	0.0	6.0	−9.7	−5.4
1990	10.8	0.5	0.0	13.6	5.8	13.5
2000	15.5	4.4	0.0	10.4	3.0	15.0

Source: Authors' calculations using Decennial Censuses from 1940–2000.
Note: Numbers for 1950 are average wage of the education group relative to average wage of high school graduates; numbers for the other years are difference from the 1950 value.

fact, the increase in within group dispersion has almost exactly matched the increase in across group dispersion so that the share in the variance in log wages explained by education and experience (and sex and race) has remained virtually constant. In 1950,

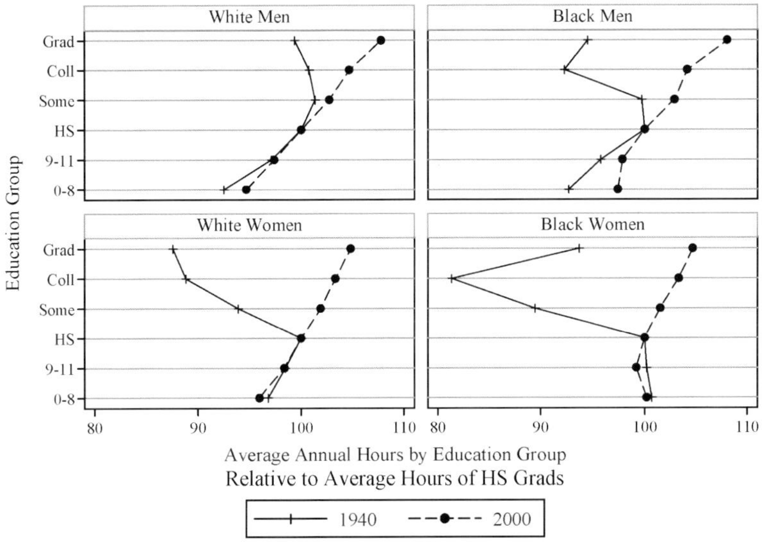

Figure 4. Changes in "labor supply" across education groups relative to HS graduates 1950 to 2000, by sex and race. Source: Authors' calculations using Decennial Censuses from 1940 and 2000.

the R^2 from a regression of log hourly wage on a fully interacted set of indicator variables for race, sex, education group and experience, is .297, and the R^2 from the same regression in 2000 is .306.

An implication of this essentially constant relative dispersion in wages is that the overlap of the wage distribution for high school graduates with the wage distribution for college graduates has also remained about the same. One way of measuring this overlap is with the average percentile location of college graduates in the high school wage distribution. This measure, a type of Mann–Whitney statistic, also indicates the probability that a randomly chosen college graduate will have a higher wage than a randomly chosen high school graduate. Table 3 gives these average percentiles by sex and race groups for each of the census years 1940 through 2000.

In contrast to the overall pattern of increased dispersion in average wages across education groups shown in Figures 3a and 3b, the overlap shows no general trend. There is evidence of some compression in wages in 1950, especially for black men, and also in 1980, and of dispersion in 1990, but there is little overall trend. In particular, the overlap in 1970 is virtually identical to the overlap in 2000, even though dispersion in average wages increased substantially during these thirty years. The relatively constant overlap in wages alongside the increase in wage dispersion (both across and within education groups) and the increase in college enrollment suggest that the education choice/productivity relationship goes beyond a simple single factor model. Instead, these facts point toward a more complex selection model driven by comparative advantage considerations [see Dahl (2002)].

Table 3
Average percentile location of college graduates in the high school wage distribution 1940–2000, by sex and race

	Men		Women	
	White	Black	White	Black
1940	74.1	72.6	79.4	82.2
1950	72.2	60.1	74.9	76.0
1960	74.6	66.1	80.5	81.0
1970	76.5	72.5	81.4	82.5
1980	70.7	68.6	75.4	77.1
1990	75.5	75.4	79.4	80.7
2000	76.3	75.2	79.9	80.6

Source: Authors' calculations using Decennial Censuses from 1940–2000.

5.4. *Education and earnings*

The patterns seen above for wages across education groups translate rather directly to the relationship between income and education. For the "education–income" premiums we consider a broader population group. The data again come from the 1940–2000 Decennial Censuses and include all individuals who are black or white, not enrolled in school, and with potential experience of 1–40 years. The data appendix provides a more detailed description of this "income sample."

As was evident from the "labor supply" curves in Figure 4, hours of work have become positively related to wages for those working full-time and at least half-year. The increase in the slope of the education–hours relationship is even greater when non-participants are included. Figure 5a traces the average annual work hours of each education group by race for men. There has been a significant increase in the dispersion of hours, with education groups above high school showing a small increase in hours while the average hours for groups with high school degrees and below have dropped sharply. Figure 5b shows the education–hours trends by race for women. There has been an increase in hours dispersion that is positively related to education, but the dominant trend is that women's hours have increased across the education spectrum.

Those with more education are increasingly more likely to work and to work more hours relative to those with less education. This increasingly positive relationship between education levels and work reinforces the increasing education–wage premiums, resulting in increasing education–earnings premiums. Figure 6a shows the earnings by education level relative to high school graduates' earnings by race for men. There has generally been an increase in education–earning differences, with 1980, and to a lesser extent 1950, showing some earnings compression. Compared to 1950, the earnings of college graduates relative to high school graduates increased by 47 percentage points for white men and by 83 percentage points for black men. The earnings of those with 9–11 years of education relative to high school graduates fell by 10 and 20 percentage points, respectively, for white and black men. Labor supply responses for men have resulted in increases in education–earnings premiums that are greater than the increases in education–wage premiums alone.

Because of the large increases in work hours, the picture is somewhat different for women. Figure 6b reports the trends in education–earnings premiums by race for women. Overall, these premiums, again measured relative to high school graduate earnings, generally shrink between 1940 and 1980. The substantial increases in hours worked by all women, including high school graduates, means that the metric in Figure 6a is changing sharply, which masks to some degree the trend in earnings dispersion. After 1980, there are notable increases in education–earnings premiums, especially for white women with more than a high school education. Between 1980 and 2000, the college–high school earnings premium increased by 50 percentage points for white women and by 23 percentage points for black women.

On average during the working years, earned income provides a substantial percentage of an individual's total income. For men, earned income as a percentage of total income averaged about 95% during 1950–1970 and about 90% during 1980–2000, and for women this percentage has remained virtually constant at 85% during 1950–2000.[2] Despite these high, and rather constant, percentages, there are a couple of interesting points to be gleaned from comparing education–earnings and education–income premiums.

Figure 7a plots these premiums by race for men. The premiums track almost identically until 2000, then there is a substantial increase in the total income premium relative to the earnings premium for white men with at least a college degree. This divergence in the total income premium does not extend to the lower education levels, where there is a slight decrease in the education–income premium relative to the education–earnings premium. One suspects that capital income is the story for the differences at the higher education levels, while transfer income may affect the picture at the lower education levels.

Figure 7b compares the income and earnings premiums by race for women. Here the story is not diverging trends but rather persistent differences in levels. For white women, the education–income premiums are larger than the education–earnings premiums above high school, but are smaller below high school. For black women, the education–income premiums are uniformly smaller than the education–earnings premiums. At the lower education levels, transfer payments undoubtedly play role. For the higher education levels, the role of capital income raises both labor supply and household composition issues. Capital incomes are certainly higher on average for white women, and the affect this has on labor supply may explain the reversal of the relative

[2] The 1940 census does not include total income as a variable.

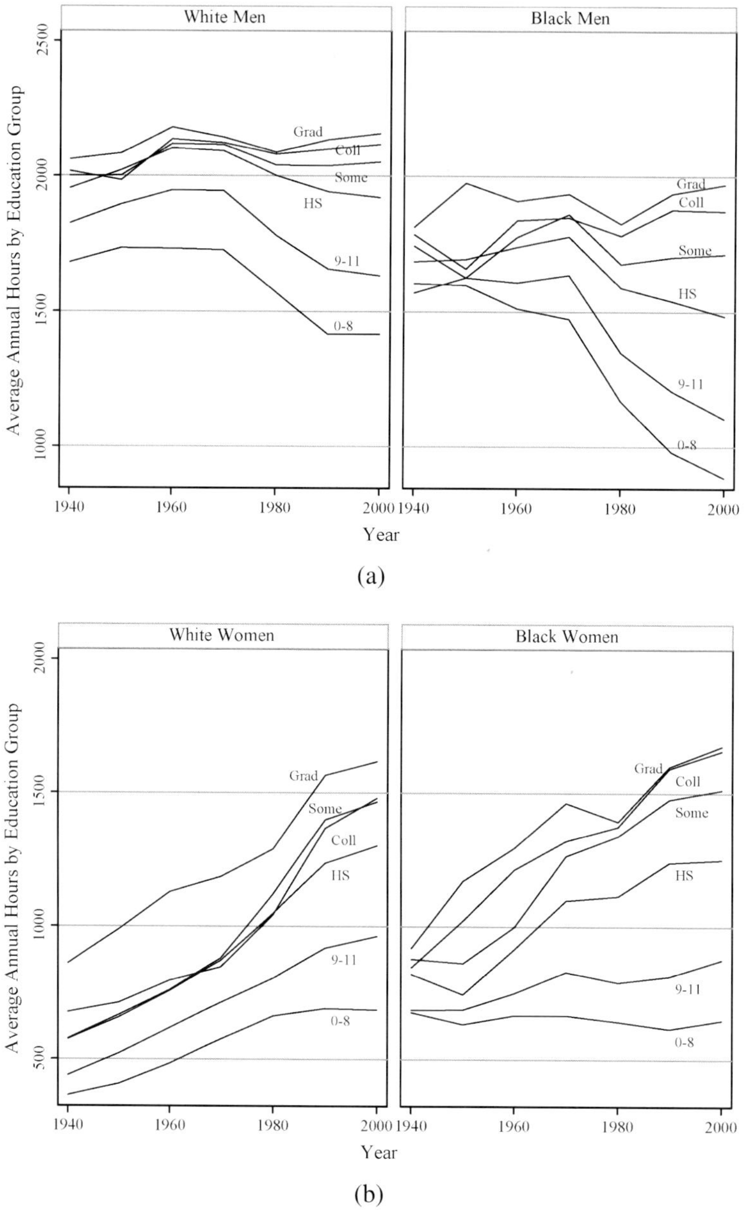

Figure 5. Trends for men (a) and women (b) in average annual hours worked by education group 1940–2000, by race. Source: Authors' calculations using Decennial Censuses from 1940–2000.

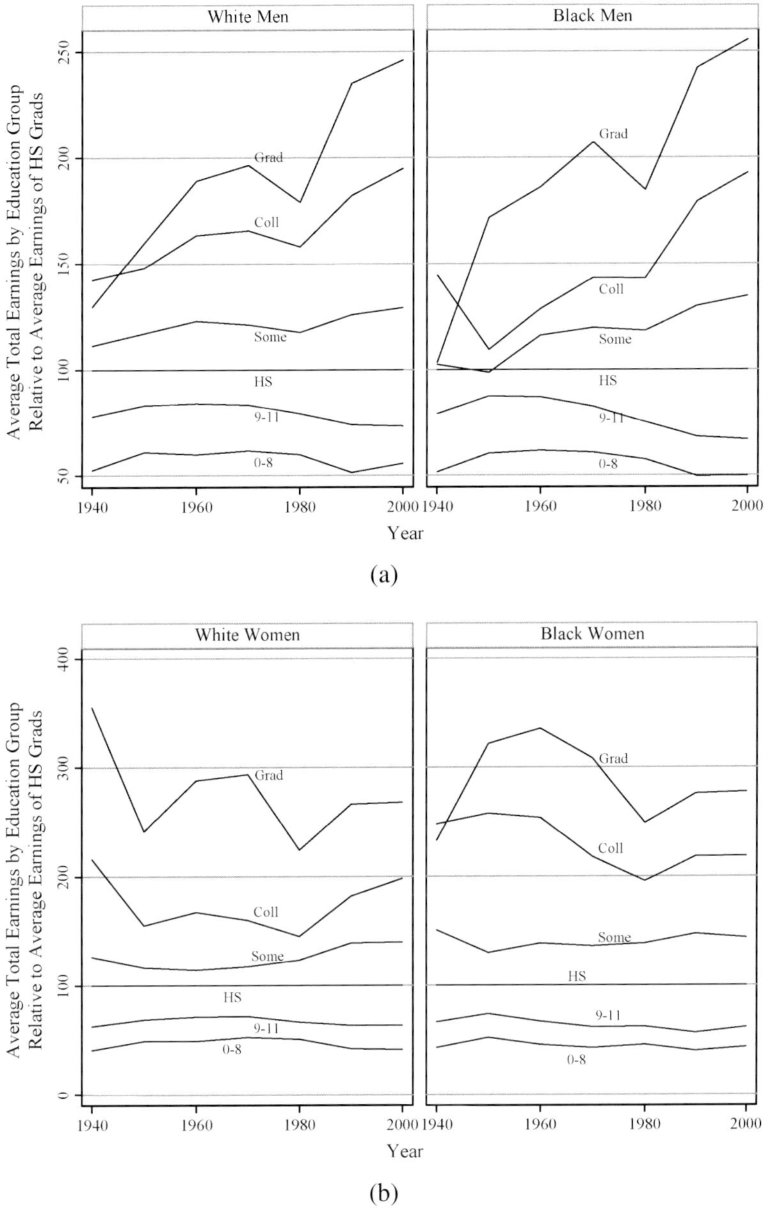

Figure 6. Trends for men (a) and women (b) in total earnings by education group relative to earnings of HS graduates 1940–2000, by race. Source: Authors' calculations using Decennial Censuses from 1940–2000.

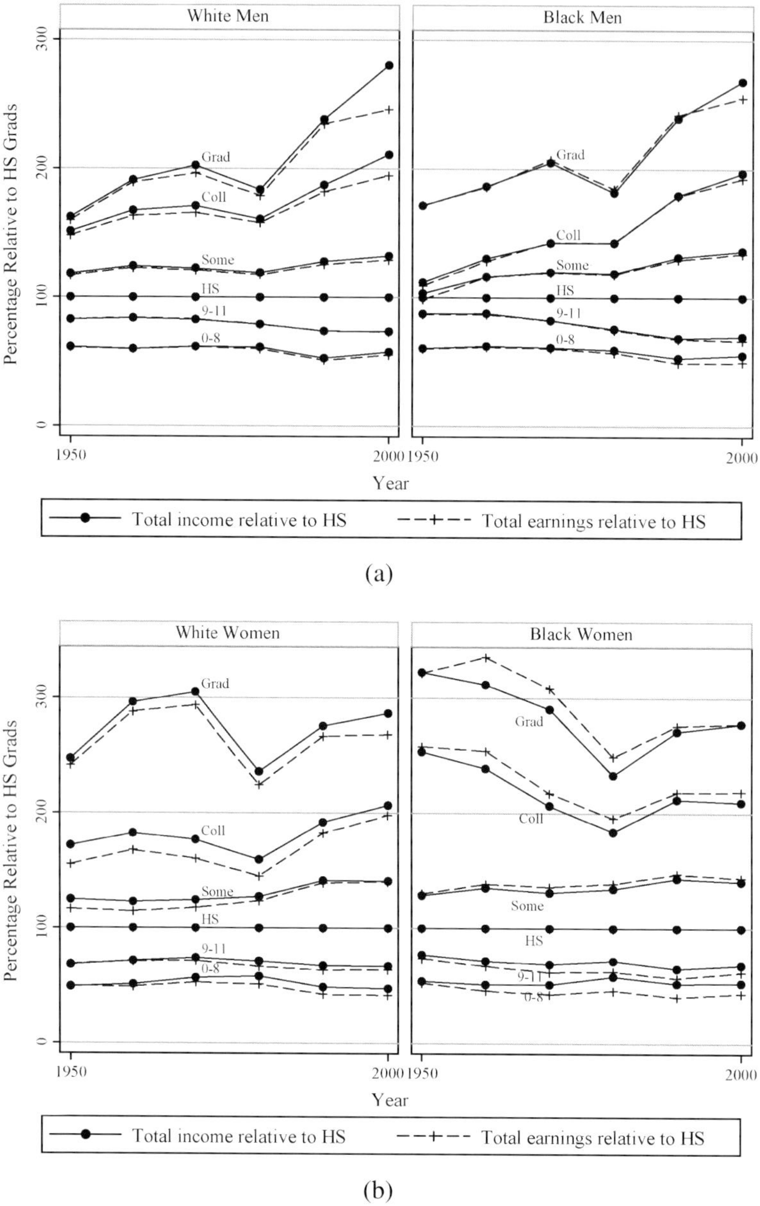

Figure 7. Comparing trends for men (a) and women (b) in relative earnings and relative total income by education group 1950–2000, by race. Source: Authors' calculations using Decennial Censuses from 1950–2000.

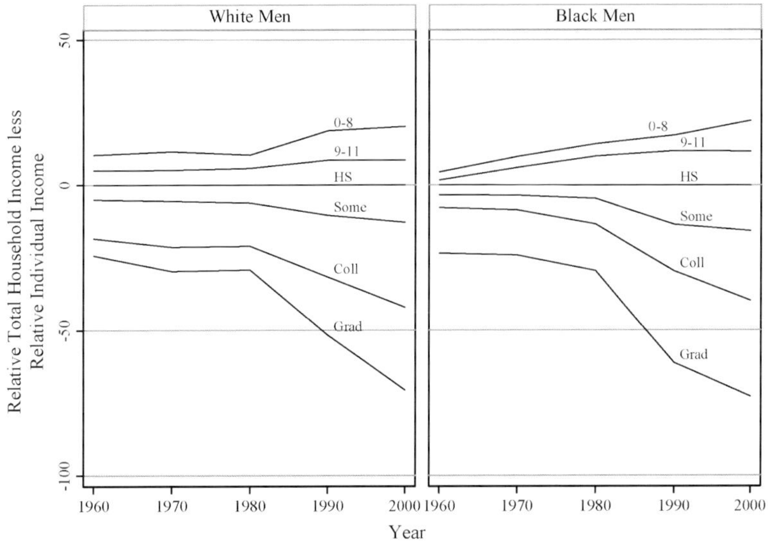

Figure 8. Trends in the difference of relative total household income and relative individual income by education group for men 1960–2000, by race. Source: Authors' calculations using Decennial Censuses from 1960–2000.

size of the income and earnings premiums for white and black women. Further, differences in capital income raise the issue of household composition and how household incomes vary by education level.

5.5. Education and household income

Differences in household incomes by education level would be expected to show a similar pattern to those for individual income – those with more education reside in households with higher incomes on average. This is, of course, true. With regard to education-related premiums, the more interesting issue is the size of these differences in household income across education levels and how these premiums change over time relative to the premiums for individual income.

Figure 8 traces the difference in the household income premiums and the individual income premiums by race for men from 1960 to 2000.[3] Note that the lines in this graph are in reverse order than all the previous graphs – the education levels are higher for the lower lines. This pattern reflects that the education premiums for household income

[3] The 1940 and 1950 censuses do not include information on household income. Household income is measured for all men in the income sample and then averaged by education group for each year and then divided by the average for high school graduates in that year. The plotted trends are for this relative household income less relative individual income.

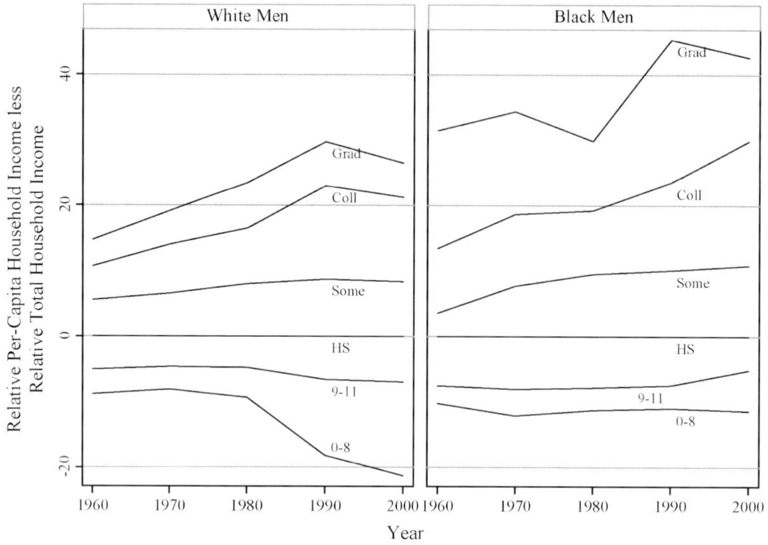

Figure 9. Trends in the difference of relative per-capita household income and relative total household income by education group for men 1960–2000, by race. Source: Authors' calculations using Decennial Censuses from 1960–2000.

are uniformly smaller than the education premiums for individual income. The smaller differences in household income premiums also appear if household incomes are averaged for women's education levels, though there is little overall trend. The widening of these lines for men, particularly noticeable after 1980, means that the household income premiums are not increasing as rapidly during this period as are the individual income premiums.

Education–household income differences have the same overall pattern as do individual income premiums, but the household income premiums, and the trend toward increased premiums, are more muted. Household income premiums are more muted compared to individual income premiums because of the imperfect correlation between the incomes of individuals residing in the same household. Before we take a closer look at one aspect of the intra–household income relationship by focusing on married couples, we first look at how per capita household income relates to education levels.

Figure 9 graphs the differences in the per capita and total household income premiums by education groups for white and black men. In contrast to Figure 8, the ordering of the lines has the higher education levels nearer the top. This order reflects that education–per capita household income differences are uniformly larger than education–total household income differences. In addition, the trends suggest that per capita household income premiums have generally, though not always, increased relative to total household income premiums. This relative increase in per capita income premiums reflects underlying changes in household composition. While average house-

Figure 10. Trends in marriage rates by education group less the marriage rate of HS graduates for men 1960–2000, by race. Source: Authors' calculations using Decennial Censuses from 1960–2000.

hold size for the income sample decreased by about .8 persons between 1960 and 2000, this decrease was not uniform across education levels. As a result, by 2000, the differences in average household size between education levels were about 50% greater than in 1960.

Marriage rates have decreased between 1960 and 2000 as age at first marriage has risen and divorce rates have increased. For the income sample the percentage of men who are married with a spouse present decreased from about 77% to 59% between 1960 and 2000 adjusting for differences in the age distribution. This decrease has not been uniform across education levels. The positive relationship between education and marriage that existed in 1960 has become stronger, and this in turn, has implications for household income.

Figure 10 shows the marriage rates for men by education level compared to the marriage rates for high school graduates for 1960–2000 by race. Similar to the figures above, the vertical axis measures the percentage of men who are married by education group less this percentage for high school graduates. Thus, the high school graduate group has a constant marriage rate difference of 0 in all years. The figure shows the increased dispersion of marriage rates across education groups, especially for black men. By 2000, college graduates were at least 10 percentage points more likely to be married compared to high school graduates. The marriage differences between college graduates and high school dropouts (9–11 years) were 15 and 22 points, respectively, for white and black men. The relative increase in marriage for more educated men affects household in-

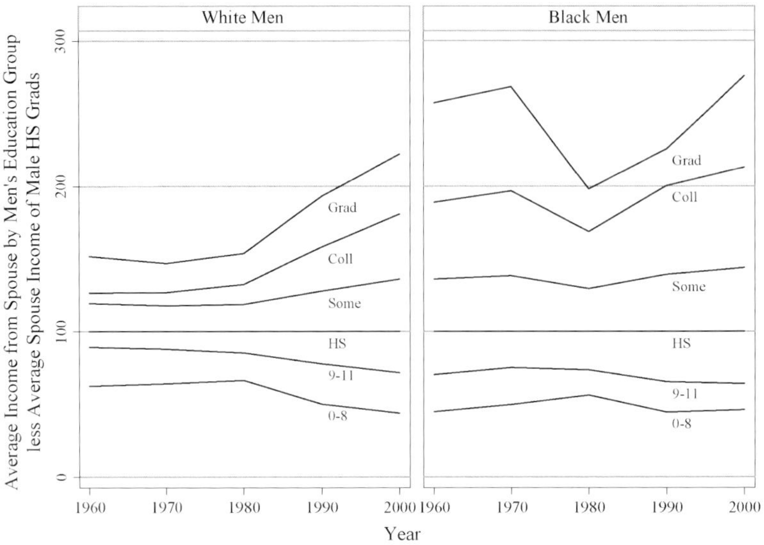

Figure 11. Trends in average spouse's income by education group less the average spouse income for HS graduates for men 1960–2000, by race. Source: Authors' calculations using Decennial Censuses from 1960–2000.

come in an obvious way, but the pattern of marriages across education levels also has an impact.

Not only are more educated men increasingly more likely to be married than less educated men, but, given marriage, the relative odds of being married to a spouse with the same education have increased. In 1960 for the income sample, the empirical odds of being married to someone with the same education were 1.33, compared to the theoretical odds of .54 if marriage occurred at random across education groups. Thus assortative mating in 1960 can be measured by the relative odds of $2.46 = (1.33/.54)$. By 2000 there was a greater variance in educational attainment, implying that the odds of being married to a spouse with the same education if marriage occurred at random were lower, at .39. The empirical odds of the same education among spouses were 1.08, yielding an assortative mating measure of $2.77 = (1.08/.39)$.

Figure 11 shows the effect on spouse incomes from the changes in marriage rates and assortative mating. The figure traces, for white and black men, the average income of wives by the education level of their husbands relative to the average income for the wives of high school graduates. The calculation of average spouse income includes a zero for individuals who are not married. Relative spouse income is fairly stable for whites and becomes more compressed for blacks between 1960 and 1980. From 1980 to 2000 these "spouse income premiums" increase, most noticeably at the higher education levels. The effect of marriage and spouse income is to increase the differences

Table 4
School enrollment rates by age group 1940–2000, by sex

	Age group					
	6–18	19–23	24–29	30–39	40–49	50+
A. Men						
1940	82.2	12.2	2.1	0.7	0.5	0.4
1950	86.1	22.5	12.5	–	–	–
1960	91.0	24.3	9.7	2.0	0.0	0.0
1970	93.4	33.3	11.5	4.0	1.0	0.6
1980	93.6	29.6	11.8	5.7	2.6	0.9
1990	92.8	40.3	14.1	7.7	4.4	1.7
2000	96.1	40.5	14.3	6.4	3.8	1.4
B. Women						
1940	82.3	8.6	1.0	0.6	0.5	0.3
1950	86.0	11.9	3.2	–	–	–
1960	90.5	14.9	3.2	1.1	0.0	0.0
1970	92.6	23.3	4.6	2.6	1.2	0.7
1980	93.5	28.4	9.7	6.3	3.6	1.1
1990	93.1	41.8	14.2	9.7	6.9	1.9
2000	96.5	46.6	15.6	7.8	5.4	1.6

Source: Authors' calculations using Decennial Censuses from 1940–2000.

in household income across education groups above what they would be had marriage rates and patterns remained unchanged.[4]

5.6. *Enrollment and education–wage premiums*

We turn now to the implications of increases in education–wage premiums. Recall that Figure 2 showed the shift in the age distribution of enrollment toward older ages, particularly those above the traditional college ages. Table 4 reports enrollment rates by age group separately for men and women over the period 1940 to 2000.[5] For men, there are two sharp increases driven by policy change – in 1950 for 18–23 and 24–29 year-olds due to the GI bill, and in 1970 for 18–23 year-olds due to Vietnam draft deferments. Besides the two spikes for men, which result in a decline in enrollment rates in the subsequent census, there is a steady rise in enrollment rates for men and women from 1940 through 1990 across all ages, and through the year 2000 for ages below 30.

[4] This does not imply, as would be contrary to Figure 8, that household income premiums exceed individual income premiums. Let Mc and Mh be the average incomes of men with college and high school degrees, respectively, and let Sc and Sh be the average incomes for everyone else in the household of these men. $Sc > Sh$ does not necessarily imply that $(Mc + Sc)/(Mh + Sh) > Mc/Mh$.

[5] The 1950 census does not have enrollment for individuals ages 30 and greater.

Table 5
School enrollment rates as a percentage of high school graduates by age group 1940–2000, by sex

	Age group				
	19–23	24–29	30–39	40–49	50+
A. Men					
1940	21.4	4.5	1.3	0.8	0.6
1950	36.0	18.2	–	–	–
1960	30.1	12.1	2.4	0.0	0.0
1970	38.3	14.6	5.2	1.3	0.5
1980	34.4	13.5	6.6	3.3	1.4
1990	44.6	15.4	8.2	4.7	2.0
2000	44.9	15.6	6.8	4.0	1.6
B. Women					
1940	14.1	1.8	1.0	0.9	0.5
1950	16.8	4.0	–	–	–
1960	16.9	2.4	0.9	0.0	0.0
1970	26.4	5.6	3.1	1.4	0.6
1980	32.3	10.8	7.2	4.6	1.6
1990	45.5	15.1	10.1	7.5	2.3
2000	50.4	16.6	8.2	5.7	1.8

Source: Authors' calculations using Decennial Censuses from 1940–2000.

Table 5 reports estimates of college enrollment rates calculated by including only those individuals who report having at least a high school degree. The pattern is very similar to that for overall enrollment rates with the 1950 and 1970 spikes for men and almost uniform increases everywhere else through 1990 and through 2000 for those younger than 30. Note that the enrollment rate for women in their 30s in 1990 is above 10%. Though this rate drops to 8.2% in 2000, it remains quite high by historical standards.

The general pattern of rising enrollment rates coincides with the general pattern of rising education–wage premiums. Of course, enrollment has generally been rising for a much longer period, hence cross-section analysis may provide more compelling evidence of a link between wage premiums and enrollment. Table 6 presents results of simple regressions of college enrollment rates on the college/high school wage premium. There are two measures of college enrollment. The first is the number of individuals ages 19 to 29 with a high school degree who are enrolled, divided by the number of individuals in this age range with a high school degree. The second includes in the numerator those with a college degree. The first measure is a true enrollment rate, while the second rate includes those with a degree as well as those pursuing one. The regression includes year and sex-by-race indicators and is estimated at the division-by-year level using weighted least squares on first-differences in averages of the enrollment rate and the college/high school wage premium. The results show a positive and statistically

Table 6
Enrollment responses to changing education premiums

	Percentage of high school graduates	
	Enrolled	Enrolled or with a college degree
Impact*100	3.94 (1.59)	5.57 (1.92)
Number of observations	208	208
R-squared:	0.52	0.43

Source: Authors' calculations using Decennial Censuses from 1940–2000. Standard errors are in parenthesis.
Note: Controls for year, race and sex are included. Average college/high school premium in the sample is 57.15% and average enrollment rate is 21.04%, while the average of the enrollment plus college graduate rate is 33.96%. Regressions are estimated at the region-by-year level using first differences.

significant relationship between the wage premium and college enrollment. The magnitudes imply an elasticity of 0.1 for the response of enrollment to the college/high school wage premium.

5.7. Public school quality

The poor quality of public schools was highlighted in "A Nation at Risk" [NCEE (1983)]. While this worked to spur reform, it might be argued that an important push for better schools was the value of a college education. The increase in the college/high school earnings premium that had become apparent by the late 1980s, certainly did not go unnoticed outside of academia. As noted above, much of the reaction to this increase in inequality has been one of dismay, though there also has been recognition of the increased payoff to college. In addition to college testing preparation and resume enhancement via extracurricular activities, parents and legislators understand that the quality of pre-college schooling plays a significant role not only in college admission, but also in the efficacy of college investment.

Economists have contributed to the growing debate about how to improve school quality by, among other things, trying to assess the factors that affect school quality. The traditional production function approach generally concluded that there was no simple relationship between school output and school inputs [Hanushek (1986)]. An interesting, and relatively, recent aspect of this literature is a shift in the focus to the incentives schools face, how schools respond to competition, and the resulting implications for learning. For example, Hoxby (2000) estimates how the choice among multiple public school districts, "Tiebout choice," affects schools, Rouse (1998) examines the impact of having vouchers, Sander (1999) assesses the effect of private school competition, and Deere and Strayer (2003) examine the implications of a state-mandated accountability system.

While economists can argue about the value of the true return to education and how to estimate it, the outside world, and parents in particular, are convinced that college is very much a good, and increasingly valuable, investment. Whether this is due to human capital acquisition or to signaling does not matter, as Becker (1975) notes, because in either case there is a private return. There seems little doubt then that the increased (perceived) value of a college education will only enhance interest in and, as a result, research on improvements in school quality and the implications for human capital acquisition.

6. Differences in enrollment, characteristics and earnings

Labor income differentials are viewed according to the human capital approach as differences in the human capital stock across individuals and over time. As noted above, human capital theory provides a link between the life cycle of earnings and the time profile of human capital investments. A pioneer model of the lifetime accumulation of human capital was developed by Ben-Porath (1967). The optimal path of human capital investments over the individual's life cycle was derived from the maximization of the expected present value of lifetime earnings net of investment costs. Investment costs include both opportunity costs and direct expenditures. The life cycle changes in investment costs and the returns to investment predict that individuals become less likely to take on additional schooling investments as they age. By undertaking schooling investments early in life, individuals minimize opportunity costs and ensure that the return to the investment will be received for as many years as possible.

Rising school enrollment rates among older individuals (by schooling standards) suggest that increasing numbers of individuals delay a portion of regular schooling. The schooling histories for the cohort in the National Longitudinal Survey of Youth (NLSY) 1979 diverge from these paths predicted by the simple human capital model. In this section, we provide some preliminary evidence on differences in enrollment patterns and how these relate to differences in individual and family characteristics and to earnings.

6.1. Patterns of college enrollment

To begin, high school graduates, including GED recipients, represent 89.4% of all men and 92.7% of all women from the cohort represented by the NLSY 1979. Out of the high school graduates, 62.7% of men and 67.8% of women enrolled in college, with 42.2% of men and 38.0% of women earning a bachelor's degree. Among bachelor's degree recipients, 51.2% of men and 54.6% of women ever attended graduate school.

Figure 12 presents summary information on the patterns of college enrollment for the NLSY 1979 cohort. The figure gives the respective percentages of high school graduates who enroll in college either right after high school or with some delay and of those who never enroll in college. These groups are further divided into those who go straight through college and those who interrupt their college enrollment. The figure shows that 40.5% of men and 42.9% of women high school graduates enrolled in college straight out of high school, while 22.2% of men and 24.9% of women delayed their first enrollment in college for at least six months. Roughly one-fifth of all high school graduates, and one-third of all students who eventually attended college, delayed their college enrollment. Individuals who are more likely to have delays between high school graduation and college enrollment are also more likely to make interruptions of at least six months during their undergraduate studies than are those who go straight to college. 28.9% of men and 35.5% of women who went straight to college interrupted their undergraduate studies for six months or longer, while the analogous percentages for those who delayed enrollment in college are 39.7% for men and 41.1% for women.

Along these different paths of delays and interruptions in college enrollment, there are big differences in the fraction who earn a bachelor's degree. Approximately two-thirds of all individuals who had no delay or interruptions since high school graduation acquired a bachelor's degree, while only 10.0% of men and 17.4% of women who delayed enrollment in college and made interruptions during undergraduate studies received a degree. Less than one-third of students who went straight to college, but took at least six months off during their studies, graduated from college. Out of those who went through college with no interruptions but delayed enrollment in college, only 14.7% of men and 12.4% of women obtained a bachelor's degree. The delay of college enrollment after high school graduation and the interruption of college enrollment are prevalent occurrences that are strongly related to the observed likelihood of college completion.

Students who delay or prolong their stay in college affect measured enrollment rates at older ages. The numbers in the parentheses below the percentages in Figure 12 for the straight-to-college sub-groups correspond to the average time, period measured in years, between the beginning of the first college enrollment spell and the ending of the last college enrollment spell as an undergraduate student. It took a bit over four years on average for students who did not interrupt their schooling to earn a bachelor's degree. In contrast, more than ten years passed (including all interruptions) for students who interrupted their undergraduate studies to finish a bachelor's degree. Students who enrolled in college straight out of high school but did not earn a bachelor's degree spent on average 1.9 years in school if they did not make any interruptions. Those with interruptions spent 9.4 and 10.6 years, respectively for men and women, in and out of college without receiving a bachelor's degree.

For the sub-groups with delayed college enrollment, the numbers in parentheses immediately below the percentages refer to the average delay, in years, prior to first enrollment. The numbers in the second row of parentheses measure average time between first enrollment and the end of the last enrollment spell. Among students who eventually obtained a bachelor's degree, the average delay is between 2.3 and 3.4 years,

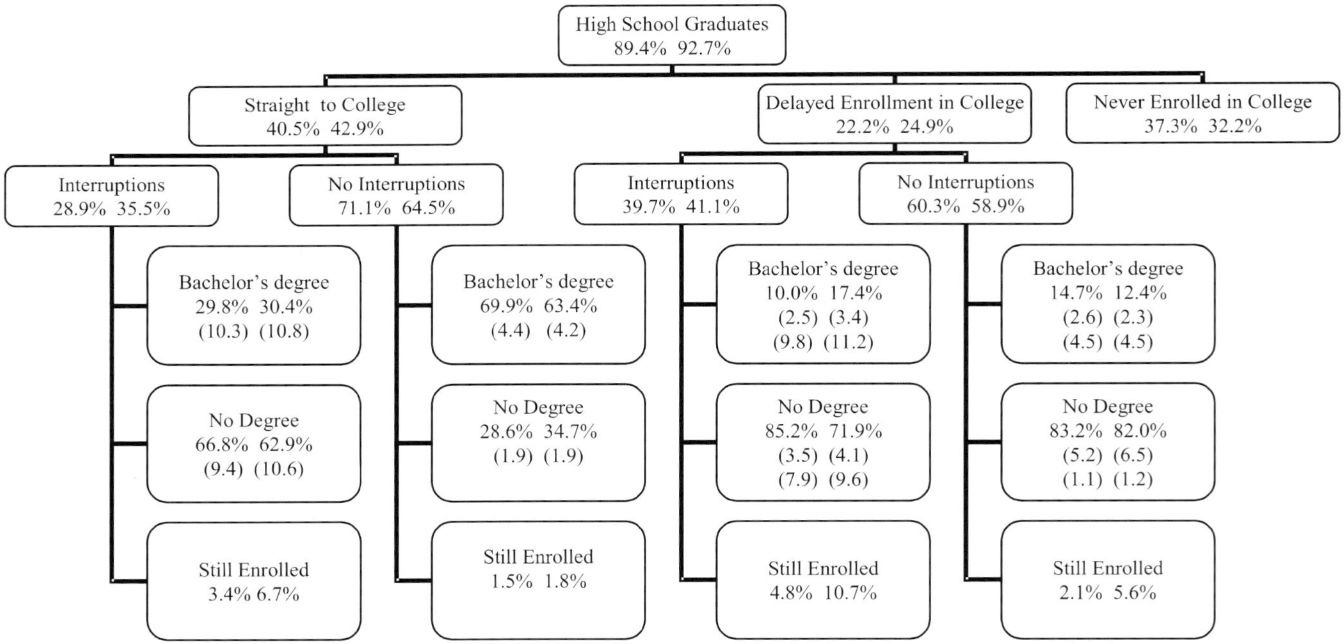

Figure 12. College enrollment patterns by sex from the National Longitudinal Survey of Youth 1979. Source: Authors' calculations using NLSY 1979. Note: In each of the categories, the numbers to the left refer to men and numbers to the right to women. The numbers in the parentheses for the people who went straight to college measure time from the beginning of the first enrollment spell in college until the end of the last enrollment spell. For those who delayed entry to college, average delay as well as time between the beginning of the first enrollment spell and the end of the last enrollment spell is reported.

while for students who did not receive a degree, the average delay ranges from 3.5 to 6.5 years. In contrast to the differences in degree completion associated with enrollment delays and interruptions noted above, the time spent in (and out of) college does appear to differ across the enrollment delay sub-groups. Those without interruptions take just over four years to finish their degree whether there was an initial delay or not. Likewise, those who do interrupt enrollment take about the same amount to complete degree requirements.

The obvious first question arising from inspection of Figure12 concerns the possible explanations for the observed patterns. Theoretical models that might help to understand these choices include those with borrowing constraints [Wallace and Ihnen (1975)], limited transferability of education and experience across occupations [Weiss (1971)], intertemporal variation in the schooling/leisure trade-off over the early career [Ryder, Stafford and Stephan (1976)] and unexpected changes in the environment or uncertainty [Williams (1979), Dorthan and Williams (1981), Kodde (1986)]. Whether there are differences in observable characteristics, such as ability measures or family background, that can explain these differences and what the individuals who delay or interrupt their schooling are doing during the non-enrollment spells are worthy of further examination.

6.2. *Differences in ability and family background*

Table 7, which provides information on ability measures (i.e., AFQT scores) and family background characteristics across college graduates with different schooling paths, reveals several differences related to enrollment patterns. The average AFQT score for all bachelor's degree recipients (last column) is 70.7 for men and 65.5 for women. The highest average AFQT scores are for those who went straight to and through college, 73.2 for men and 68.9. The lowest scores are for those who delayed entry to college and interrupted their undergraduate studies, 56.4 for both men and women.

Bachelor's degree holders who had no delay or any interruptions in their schooling from high school to college graduation appear to have more advantaged family background measures. Their family income in 1979 averaged $29,279 and $27,262 for men and women, respectively. The family income in 1979 for those who delayed and interrupted their schooling averaged $17,462 and $21,159, respectively for men and women. College graduates whose schooling was continuous come from families with more educated parents as compared to their discontinuously schooled peers. The highest grade completed by mothers and fathers of continuously schooled college graduates averaged 13.2 and 12.9 for mothers of men and women, respectively, and 13.9 and 13.6 for fathers of men and women. Parental education is lowest for the college graduates who delayed entry to college and interrupted their undergraduate studies. For these men, father's highest grade completed was 11.8 and mother's was 11.0, and for women, the education levels are 11.7 and 11.8 for fathers and mothers, respectively.

Table 8 provides analogous information on ability and family background comparing college graduates and college non-finishers. The first two columns for all college degree recipients are copied from the last two columns of Table 7. For both men and women,

Table 7
Characteristics of bachelor's degree holders by enrollment history, NLSY 1979

	Straight to college and interruptions		Straight to college and no interruptions		Delayed college and interruptions		Delayed college and no interruptions		All bachelor's degree holders	
	Men	Women	Men	Women	Men	Women	Men	Women	Men	Women
Mother's highest grade	12.7	12.4	13.2	12.9	11.0	11.8	12.5	12.7	13.0	12.7
Father's highest grade	13.5	13.5	13.9	13.6	11.8	11.7	13.4	12.9	13.7	13.4
AFQT score	64.7	59.2	73.2	68.9	56.4	56.4	65.7	58.7	70.7	65.5
Family income in 1979	21,782	24,348	29,279	27,262	17,462	21,159	26,450	26,972	27,543	26,340
Number of observations	128	180	641	623	34	67	67	61	870	931
Enrolled in graduate school	47%	50%	54%	57%	37%	53%	42%	47%	51%	55%

Source: Authors' calculations using NLSY 1979.
Note: The number of observations in the table correspond to the actual number of individuals who earned a bachelor's degree. The summary of the family background characteristics as well as AFQT scores is based on the subset of people with a valid code for the same characteristics.

Table 8
Comparison of the characteristics of bachelor's degree holders and those who enrolled in college but earned no degree

	All bachelor's degree holders		No degree	
	Men	Women	Men	Women
Mother's highest grade	13.0	12.7	11.2	10.9
Father's highest grade	13.7	13.4	11.4	10.9
AFQT score	70.7	65.5	44.2	40.2
Family income in 1979	27,543	26,340	18,758	16,851
Number of observations	870	931	1490	1807

Source: Authors' calculations using NLSY 1979.

those who do not finish college have substantially lower AFQT scores and relatively disadvantaged family backgrounds than those who finish college. A breakdown (not shown) of the non-finishers across the delay and interruption categories does not show much variation, in contrast to Table 7. The characteristics are weaker across the board – all average AFQT scores are below 50, all average parental education levels are below 12 years, and all average family incomes are below $20,000.

6.3. Differences in earnings

The rising income inequality across education and experience groups has coincided with rising within-group (defined by education and experience) inequality. Within a group of bachelor's degree recipients and within a given calendar year, depending on the year when the bachelor's degree was earned, there are substantial differences in wage and salary income as shown in Table 9. The table presents average full-time wage and salary income for college graduates in the 1994–2000 surveys by time of degree and by sex.

Given the varied enrollment patterns for degree recipients highlighted in Figure 12 above, all college graduates within a given calendar year do not have the same amount of potential post-degree experience. For example, in 1994, individuals who earned a bachelor's degree before or in 1980, have at least 14 years of potential post-degree work experience, while those who graduated from college in the 1990s have only a few years of potential post-degree work experience. In 1994, men who graduated from college in the late 1970s had an annual income from wages and salaries exceeding $57,000, compared to those who graduated during 1981–1983 and earned $53,725 on average. Moving down the column, average earnings decline monotonically as the potential experience window narrows. In all four survey years, men who graduated from college in earlier years, earn more on average then men who earned bachelor's degree in later years.

If age differences are negligible, men who graduated from college in later calendar years are the ones who either delay entry in college or stayed longer in college. Though

Table 9
Earnings differences in the same year among those with bachelor's degree, the impact of year of degree, 1994–2000, by sex

	Calendar year							
	1994		1996		1998		2000	
	Men	Women	Men	Women	Men	Women	Men	Women
Year of degree								
Before or in 1980	57,493	40,285	65,208	42,914	77,991	42,909	79,039	46,871
	42	27	43	25	40	28	31	30
	36.2	36.1	37.9	38.0	39.8	39.2	42.1	41.9
1981–83	53,725	39,757	59,105	42,922	63,767	47,968	79,459	52,493
	140	85	137	95	125	80	123	84
	34.4	34.3	36.3	35.9	38.3	38.0	40.4	40.1
1984–86	46,409	33,967	49,814	40,254	56,140	39,910	64,672	46,201
	147	128	157	94	158	98	146	93
	31.8	31.7	33.7	33.7	35.6	35.6	37.8	37.9
1987–89	39,030	31,755	47,096	36,399	54,758	39,420	64,631	43,125
	63	36	60	33	68	27	61	23
	31.2	31.8	33.1	34.0	34.8	35.9	37.1	38.2
After or in 1990	29,673	30,444	40,975	30,402	40,511	31,746	47,209	39,912
	18	24	25	31	26	38	37	40
	31.4	32.4	33.4	34.6	35.3	36.3	37.9	38.4

Source: Authors' calculations using NLSY 1979.
Note: The sample consists of bachelor's degree recipients with no advance degree who have a valid code for wage and salary income in the previous calendar year, were not enrolled in school and worked full-time, full-year during the previous calendar year. Income values are deflated using the Personal Consumption Expenditure price index from the GDP accounts, with 1996 as the base year. Number of observations and average age also are reported.

ages are somewhat higher for the graduates in the first two rows, average age is virtually constant across the last three rows, suggesting that the reduced experience from delayed and interrupted college is related to earnings. The same pattern holds for women but the variation in income within a given calendar year is much smaller for women than for men. The table suggests that late finishers pay a price compared to their early finishing counterparts who have more post-degree potential experience.

Table 10 presents the income earnings comparisons controlling for actual post-degree potential experience. The table contrasts those with continuous schooling from those with delayed or interrupted enrollment for men and women. At the same level of potential post-degree experience, discontinuously schooled men have somewhat higher earnings up to five years of experience, $33,767 as compared to $31,515. Discontinuously schooled women have higher earnings up to ten years of experience, $28,384 compared to $25,660 for 0–5 years of experience and $34,160 compared to $33,040 for 5–10 years. At the higher levels of potential post-degree experience men and women with continuous schooling have higher earnings. One explanation may be that in the early

Table 10
Earnings profile differences for continuously and discontinuously schooled bachelor's degree holders

	Actual years of potential post degree experience			
	Less than or equal to 5	5–10	10–15	More than 15
A: Men				
Continuously	31,515	43,722	57,156	72,990
	1101	1407	913	339
	26.0	30.1	34.9	39.5
Discontinuously	33,766	42,675	51,880	66,563
	347	333	169	32
	29.7	32.5	37.0	41.0
B: Women				
Continuously	25,660	33,040	41,310	48,270
	916	1076	548	227
	25.6	29.9	34.8	39.4
Discontinuously	28,384	34,160	37,499	44,284
	333	297	113	34
	29.8	33.1	36.7	39.9

Source: Authors' calculations using NLSY 1979.
Note: The sample consists of bachelor's degree recipients with no advance degree who have a valid code for wage and salary income in the previous calendar year, were not enrolled in school and worked full-time, full-year during the previous calendar year. Income values are deflated using the Personal Consumption Expenditure price index from the GDP accounts, with 1996 as the base year. Number of observations and average age also are reported.

career pre-degree experience does matter and discontinuously schooled peers are older and potentially have more pre-degree experience. The table suggests this advantage is short-lived as discontinuously schooled college graduates have flatter experience–earnings profiles and that holds for both men and women.

6.4. Summary

There are several issues raised by the preliminary results presented in this section. First, there are substantial differences in patterns of college enrollment among those who attend college and even among those who complete college. Why do such differences exist? Part of the explanation likely lies in the fact that the enrollment differences are rather strongly related to differences in individual and family characteristics. A second issue involves the earnings implications of the different patterns of schooling investment. The results here suggest that estimated potential experience (i.e., age-education-6, which is a poor measure of experience for women because of interruptions in labor force participation for family reasons, also may be a poor measure of experience for men because of interruptions in education. There also is the issue of what individuals who have yet to complete their schooling are doing during these interruptions and whether and what the returns are to pre-degree experience.

7. Concluding remarks

At various points in this chapter questions have been raised yet little offered in the way of answers. The two data sections suggest two broad areas that would seem ripe for detailed and careful study.

It is indisputable that education–income premiums have widened overall during the past 60 years, especially since 1980. While the extent to which this represents an increase in the true return to education (and whether social or only private) and why these premiums have increased remain of interest, there would appear to be much gained by focusing some future research on the implications of these changes. We have hinted at adjustments in college enrollment and in labor supply, noted the complicated interrelationship with household formation, and raised the issue of an increased focus on public school quality. The extent to which individuals have adjusted their human capital investment behavior in response to these changes and the resulting implications for productivity and income or earnings inequality are interesting, and important, questions.

A greater understanding of the nature of the human capital investment process also would be quite useful. We have presented preliminary evidence to suggest that the school-to-work transition is far from simple or uniform and that it is systematically related both to pre-schooling individual characteristics and post-schooling earnings. This likely has been compounded by the changes in education premiums as well. The reasons individuals delay or interrupt school, or, alternatively, the reasons they return to school, and the implications of this extended enrollment are important not only to improving our measurement and assessment of human capital, but, even more, to our understanding of human capital formation and economic growth.

Appendix

Census data

Data from the Decennial U.S. Census were used for all calculations in the fourth section of the chapter. The source was the 1% PUMS samples for 1940–2000 available from IPUMS [Ruggles et al. (2003)]. There were two primary samples created from these data – the wage sample and the income sample. The former, used to calculate hourly wage premiums, is a proper subset of the latter, which was used to calculated earnings and total income premiums. All of the calculations using Census data are restricted to blacks and whites only, with calculations typically made separately by sex and race.

The wage sample includes those not living in group quarters, not enrolled in school, not self-employed, who worked at least 27 weeks and 35 (usual) hours per week in the previous year, and with between 1 and 40 years of potential labor market experience. Usual weekly hours were imputed for years prior to 1970 using the relationship in 1980 by race and sex between usual hours per week in the previous year and weeks worked in the previous year and hours worked in the previous week. Potential experience is the difference between age and years of education plus six, with a minimum labor force entry age of 14 for years prior to 1980 and 16 for 1980 and after. Weeks worked in the previous year were imputed for 1960 and 1970 from the relationship by race, sex, potential experience and education between detailed and interval measures of weeks worked in the previous year during 1950 and 1980. Hourly wages were calculated as the ratio of wage and salary income in the previous year to the product of weeks worked in the previous year and usual hours per week in the previous year. Observations with calculated hourly rates less than one-half of the prevailing federal minimum wage were omitted.

The income sample is more inclusive. It includes those living in households, not enrolled in school and with between 1 and 40 years of potential labor market experience. Potential experience is the difference between age and years of education plus six, with a minimum labor force entry age of 14 for years prior to 1980 and 16 for 1980 and after. In order to calculate annual hours worked for these individuals, usual weekly hours were imputed for years prior to 1970 and weeks worked in the previous year were imputed for 1960 and 1970 as described above for the wage sample. The household income calculations are made for all of the men in the income sample.

Income values were adjusted for the impact of top-coding. Top-coded values were replaced by the ratio of the median of all values above the top-code to the top-code value. These ratios were calculated separately by state using the 1990 values, which are included in the 1990 PUMS, and then applied to the other years. This enhances comparability, but probably results in some understatement in the increase in wage premiums from 1980 through 2000.

The wage sample across the seven Censuses includes 3.2 million individuals, while the income sample includes 5.9 million persons. Given that some of the samples are not equi-probability samples, the individual population weights were used in the analysis. The sum of the population weights for the wage and income samples are 342 million and 645 million, respectively. The 1950 sample is about one-third the size of the 1940 and 1960 censuses because many supplementary questions, including the education, work, and income questions were asked of only sample-line individuals. This also explains why there is no information on spouses or households in 1950. In 1940, the only information collected on unearned income was whether income totaled $50 or more, hence total individual income and also household income cannot be determined in 1940.

NLSY data

The National Longitudinal Survey of Youth (NLSY) 1979 [U.S. Department of Labor, Bureau of Labor Statistics (2001)] was designed to represent the youth population born during the period 1957–1964 and living in the United States on January 1, 1979. It consists of three independent sub-samples. The first is a nationally representative or "cross-sectional" sample of youth aged 14 to 21 as of December 31, 1978. The second is designed to over-sample civilian black, Hispanic and economically disadvantage white youths of the same age. And the third represents youth of the same age serving in the military as of September 30, 1978. The total number of respondents in 1979 was 12,686 and they were interviewed annually from 1979 to 1994 and biennially thereafter. The last available wave of the survey is from 2000.

In our analysis, we used the nationally representative sample as well as the supplemental samples of blacks and Hispanics. The cross-sectional sample consists of 6,111 individuals and the supplemental samples include 2,172 blacks and 1,480 Hispanics. Total number of respondents in our preliminary sample is 9,763. Due to the over-sampling in the supplemental samples, the 1979 sampling weights are used for tabulating population characteristics.

There is a very detailed section in the NLSY questionnaire devoted to regular school, i.e., schooling that leads to a high school diploma or a bachelor's or graduate degree. Respondents were asked if they had attended regular school at any point since the date of the previous interview. If they were attending school at the time of the interview they were asked the grade in which they were enrolled. If not attending school, they were asked the month and year they were last enrolled in regular school, the reason for leaving school and the highest grade attended as well as highest grade completed. If the respondent didn't have a high school diploma or equivalent at the date of the previous interview, then the questions regarding whether the respondent received a degree and when it was earned were asked.

In most of the years, there were questionnaire items regarding academic or college degrees. In 1979–1984, the question regarding type of college degree earned was included while the question referring to the date of the degree was asked in 1979–1981. The next time information regarding college degrees was collected is 1988. In that year, from all individuals, data regarding highest degree ever received (including high school diploma or GED) and date of the degree was gathered from all respondents holding a high school diploma or its equivalent. Beginning with the 1989 interview, respondents were asked if they received a college degree since the previous interview and the type and date of the highest degree obtained.

Information on college enrollment also was collected in most years. If the respondent had been enrolled in college or university since the previous interview, information regarding that institution was compiled as well as the dates of the first and last enrollment, college major, full- or part-time status, the number of credit hours earned, whether a loan covered any of the college expenses and total dollar value of all the loans received during enrollment. Questions regarding name and location of the college and whether the institution is a 2- or 4-year school were part of the interview. For the 1979–1983 survey years, data regarding only the college most recently attended were collected. From 1984 on, the questionnaires allowed for up to three colleges attended since the previous interview. None of the questions regarding college attendance or college characteristics were queried in 1987 and 1991 due to funding cuts.

Even with this rich schooling information, there remain 64 individuals whose schooling attainment and enrollment were indeterminate and they are dropped from the sample: 37 from the cross-sectional sample, 16 from the supplemental black sample and 11 from the supplemental Hispanic sample. We are left with a final sample of 9,699 individuals – 4,810 men and 4,889 women. As of the 2000 survey, the overall attrition rate for our sample is 19.2%; 7,838 individuals are interviewed in the 2000 wave – 4,927 in the cross-sectional sample, 1,755 in the supplemental sample of blacks and 1,155 in the supplemental sample of Hispanics. The respective attrition rates are 18.9%, 18.6% and 21.4%, for the cross-sectional and black and Hispanic supplemental samples.

For the 9,699 individuals in our final sample, educational attainment and school enrollment could be reported with error and we had to address inconsistencies within an interview year as well as across years. We have used all of the available information, starting with high school, to arrange school enrollment and non-enrollment spells and assign dates when various degrees were earned. According to the survey design, there is only one year in which a person can report having a high school diploma or equivalent and the date it was earned. The date of the first enrollment in college corresponds to the first entry to college after high school graduation or passing a GED test. A person is classified as delaying college enrollment if the time between high school graduation/GED and college enrollment is greater than six months. School enrollment spells can be of any length, while non-enrollment spells must be greater than six months, which corresponds to a person not being enrolled for at least one semester. We classify a person as still enrolled in regular school if he/she was enrolled within six months of the last interview date.

If a person never reported being enrolled in college but reported having a degree, we assumed there was no college degree. For the degrees reported in 1981 though 1984, the dates are not provided. No information regarding degrees received is available in the 1985–1987 surveys. For these years, degrees and dates are imputed from the degrees reported in surveys prior to 1985 and the highest degree earned that is reported in 1988. We compared the 1988 reporting of highest degree ever earned with the reported earned degrees in previous years. If the reported degrees in different survey years match, we used the date from 1988. If the degree reported in 1988 is higher, we imputed dates for the degrees earned in those preceding years.

References

Anderson, M.J. (2000). Encyclopedia of the U.S. Census. Congressional Quarterly Press, Washington, DC.

Autor, D.H., Katz, L.F., Krueger, A.B. (1998). "Computing inequality: Have computers changed the labor market?". Quarterly Journal of Economics 113, 1169–1213.

Bartel, A.P., Lichtenberg, F.R. (1987). "The comparative advantage of educated workers in implementing new technology". Review of Economics and Statistics 69, 1–11.

Bartel, A.P., Sicherman, N. (1999). "Technological change and wages: An interindustry analysis". Journal of Political Economy 107, 285–325.

Becker, G.S. (1962). "Investment in human capital: A theoretical analysis". Journal of Political Economy 70, 9–49.

Becker, G.S. (1975). Human Capital: A Theoretical and Empirical Analysis, with Special Reference to Education. NBER, New York. Distributed by Columbia University Press.

Bell, P.W. (1951). "Cyclical variations and trend in occupational wage differentials in American industry since". The Review of Economics and Statistics 33, 329–337.

Ben-Porath, Y. (1967). "The production of human capital and the life cycle of earnings". Journal of Political Economy 75, 352–365.

Berman, E., Bound, J., Griliches, Z. (1994). "Changes in the demand for skilled labor within U.S. manufacturing: Evidence from the annual survey of manufacturers". Quarterly Journal of Economics 109, 367–397.

Betts, J.R. (1996). "Do school resources matter only for older workers?". Review of Economics and Statistics 78, 638–652.

Blackburn, M.L., Neumark, D. (1993). "Omitted-ability bias and the increase in the return to schooling". Journal of Labor Economics 11, 521–544.

Blank, D.M., Stigler, G.J. (1957). The Demand and Supply of Scientific Personnel. NBER, New York.

Borjas, G.J. (1987). "Self-selection and the earnings of immigrants". American Economic Review 77, 531–553.

Borjas, G.J., Freeman, R., Katz, L.F. (1996). "Searching for the effect of immigration on the labor market". American Economic Review 86, 246–251.

Borjas, G.J., Freeman, R., Katz, L.F. (1997). "How much do immigration and trade affect labor market outcomes?" Brookings Papers on Economic Activity, 1–67.

Borjas, G.J., Ramey, V.A. (1994). "Time-series evidence on the sources of trends in wage inequality". American Economic Review 84, 10–16.

Borjas, G.J., Ramey, V.A. (1995). "Foreign competition, market power and wage inequality". Quarterly Journal of Economics 110, 1075–1110.

Bound, J., Johnson, G. (1992). "Changes in the structure of wages in the 1980's: An evaluation of alternative explanations". American Economic Review 82, 371–392.

Bound, J., Johnson, G. (1995). "What are the causes of rising wage inequality in the United States". Economic Policy Review (Federal Reserve Bank of New York) 1, 9–17.

Bowles, S. (1970). "Migration as investment: Empirical tests of the human investment approach to geographic mobility". Review of Economics and Statistics 52, 356–362.

Bristol, R.B. Jr. (1958). "Factors associated with income variability". American Economic Review 48, 279–290.

Card, D. (1999). "The causal effect of education on earnings". In: Ashenfelter, O., Card, D. (Eds.), Handbook of Labor Economics, vol. 3a. North-Holland, Amsterdam, pp. 1801–1863.

Card, D., DiNardo, J.E. (2002). "Skill-biased technological change and rising wage inequality: Some problems and puzzles". Journal of Labor Economics 20, 733–783.

Card, D., Lemieux, T. (2001). "Can falling supply explain the rising return to college for younger men? A cohort-based analysis". Quarterly Journal of Economics 116, 705–746.

Copeland, M.A. (1947). "The social and economic determinants of the distribution of income in the United States". American Economic Review 37, 56–75.

Dahl, G.B. (2002). "Mobility and the return to education: Testing a Roy model with multiple markets". Econometrica 70, 2367–2420.

Davis, S.J., Haltiwanger, J. (1991). "Wage dispersion between and within U.S. manufacturing plants, 1963–86". Brookings Papers on Economic Activity. Microeconomics, 115–180.

Deere, D.R. (2001). "Trends in wage inequality in the United States". In: Welch, F. (Ed.), The Causes and Consequences of Increasing Inequality. The University of Chicago Press, Chicago, pp. 9–35.

Deere, D.R., Strayer, W. (2003). "Competitive incentives: School accountability and student outcomes in Texas". Mimeo, Texas A&M University.
Deere, D.R., Welch, F. (2002). "Inequality, incentives and opportunity". Social Philosophy and Policy 19, 84–109.
DiNardo, J.E., Fortin, N.M., Lemieux, T. (1996). "Labor market institutions and the distribution of wages, 1973–1992: A semiparametric approach". Econometrica 64, 1001–1044.
DiNardo, J.E., Pischke, J.-S. (1997). "The return to computer use revisited: Have pencils changed the wage structure too?". Quarterly Journal of Economics 112, 291–303.
Dorthan, U., Williams, J. (1981). "Education as an option". Journal of Business 54, 117–139.
Dums, M., Dunne, T., Troske, K.R. (1997). "Workers, wages and technology". Quarterly Journal of Economics, 253–290.
Ellis, C.A. (1917). The Money Value of Education. Department of the Interior, Bureau of the Education, Bulletin No. 22, Washington.
Feenstra, R.C., Hanson, G.H. (1996). "Globalization, outsourcing and wage inequality". American Economic Review 86, 240–245.
Fisher, A.G.B. (1932). "Education and relative wage rates". International Labour Review 25, 742–764.
Fortin, N.M., Lemieux, T. (1997). "Institutional changes and rising wage inequality: Is there a linkage?". Journal of Economic Perspectives 11, 75–96.
Freeman, R. (1976). "Overinvestment in college training". Journal of Human Resources 10, 287–311.
Glick, P.C., Miller, H.P. (1956). "Educational level and potential income". American Sociological Review 21, 307–312.
Goldin, C. (1999). "Egalitarianism and the returns to education during the great transformation of American education". Journal of Political Economy 107, S65–S94.
Goldin, C., Katz, L.F. (1995). "The decline of non-competing groups: Changes in the premium to education, 1890–1940". NBER Working Paper #5202.
Goldin, C., Katz, L.F. (1998). "The origins of technology-skill complementarity". Quarterly Journal of Economics, 693–732.
Goldin, C., Katz, L.F. (2001). "Decreasing and then increasing inequality in America: A tale of two half-centuries". In: Welch, F. (Ed.), The Causes and Consequences of Increasing Inequality. The University of Chicago Press, Chicago, pp. 37–82.
Goldin, C., Margo, R.A. (1992). "The great compression: The wage structure in the United States at mid-century". Quarterly Journal of Economics 107, 1–34.
Gottschalk, P. (1997). "Inequality, income growth and mobility: The basic facts". Journal of Economic Perspectives 11, 21–40.
Gould, E.D. (2002). "Rising wage inequality, comparative advantage and the growing importance of general skills in the United States". Journal of Labor Economics 20, 105–147.
Griliches, Z. (1977). "Estimating the returns to schooling: Some econometric problems". Econometrica 45, 1–22.
Grogger, J., Eide, E. (1995). "Changes in college skills and the rise in the college wage premium". Journal of Human Resources 30, 280–310.
Grossman, M. (1972). "On the concept of health capital and the demand for health". Journal of Political Economy 80, 223–255.
Haider, S. (2001). "Earnings instability and earnings inequality of males in the United States: 1967–1991". Journal of Labor Economics 19, 799–836.
Hanushek, E.A. (1986). "The economics of schooling: Production and efficiency in public schools". Journal of Economic Literature 24, 1141–1177.
Houthakker, H.S. (1959). "Education and income". The Review of Economics and Statistics 41, 24–28.
Hoxby, C.M. (2000). "Does competition among public schools benefit students and taxpayers?". American Economic Review 90, 1209–1238.
Jenkins, R.M. (1985). Procedural History of the 1940 Census of Population and Housing. The University of Wisconsin Press, Wisconsin.

Johnson, G.E. (1997). "Changes in earnings inequality: The role of demand shifts". Journal of Economic Perspectives 11, 41–54.
Juhn, C. (1999). "Wage inequality and demand for skill: Evidence from five decades". Industrial and Labor Relations Review 52, 424–443.
Juhn, C., Murphy, K.M., Pierce, B. (1993). "Wage inequality and the rise in returns to skill". Journal of Political Economy 101, 410–442.
Katz, L.F., Autor, D.H. (1999). "Changes in the wage structure and earnings inequality". In: Ashenfelter, O., Card, D. (Eds.), Handbook of Labor Economics, vol. 3a. North-Holland, Amsterdam, pp. 1463–1555.
Katz, L.F., Murphy, K.M. (1992). "Changes in relative wages, 1963–1987: Supply and demand factors". Quarterly Journal of Economics 107, 35–78.
Keat, P. (1960). "Long-run changes in occupational wage structure, 1900–1956". Journal of Political Economy 68, 584–600.
Kodde, D.A. (1986). "Uncertainty and the demand for education". Review of Economics and Statistics 68, 460–467.
Krueger, A.B. (1993). "How computers have changed the wage structure: Evidence from microdata, 1984–1989". Quarterly Journal of Economics 108, 33–60.
Lampman, R.J. (1954). "Recent changes in income inequality reconsidered". American Economic Review 44, 251–268.
Lawrence, R.Z., Slaughter, M.J. (1993). "International trade and American wages in the 1980s: Giant sucking sound or small hiccup?". Brookings Papers on Economic Activity. Microeconomics, 161–210.
Lebergott, S. (1947). "Wage structures". The Review of Economic Statistics 29, 274–285.
Levy, F., Murnane, R.J. (1992). "U.S. earnings levels and earnings inequality: A review of recent trends and proposed explanations". Journal of Economic Literature 30, 1333–1381.
Levy, F., Murnane, R.J. (1996). "With what skills are computers a complement?" American Economic Review 86, 258–262.
Light, A., Ureta, M. (1995). "Early-career work experience and gender wage differentials". Journal of Labor Economics 13, 121–154.
Miller, H.P. (1960). "Annual and lifetime income in relation to education: 1939–1959". American Economic Review 50, 962–986.
Mincer, J. (1958). "Investment in human capital and personal income distribution". Journal of Political Economy 66, 281–302.
Mincer, J. (1962). "On-the-job training: Costs, returns and some implications". Journal of Political Economy 70, 50–79.
Mincer, J. (1970). "The distribution of labor incomes: A survey with special reference to the human capital approach". Journal of Economic Literature 8, 1–26.
Mincer, J. (1974). Schooling, Experience and Earnings. National Bureau of Economic Research, New York.
Mincer, J. (1998). "Investments in U.S. education and trainings as a supply responses". Research in Labor Economics 17, 277–304.
Mincer, J., Ofek, H. (1982). "Interrupted work careers: Depreciation and restoration of human capital". Journal of Human Resources 17, 3–24.
Mincer, J., Polachek, S. (1974). "Family investment in human capital: Earnings of women". Journal of Political Economy 82, 76–108.
Morgan, J. (1962). "The anatomy of income distribution". Review of Economics and Statistics 44, 270–283.
Murphy, K., Welch, F. (1989). "Wage premiums for college graduates: Recent growth and possible explanations". Educational Researcher, 17–26.
Murphy, K.M., Welch, F. (1990). "Empirical age–earnings profiles". Journal of Labor Economics 8, 202–229.
Murphy, K.M., Welch, F. (1992). "The structure of wages". Quarterly Journal of Economics 107, 285–325.
Murphy, K.M., Welch, F. (1993). "Occupational change and the demand for skill, 1940–1990". American Economic Review 83, 122–126.
Murphy, K.M., Welch, F. (2001a). "Industrial change and the demand for skill". In: Welch, F. (Ed.), The Causes and Consequences of Increasing Inequality. The University of Chicago Press, Chicago, pp. 263–284.

Murphy, K.M., Welch, F. (2001b). "Wage differentials in the 1990s: Is the glass half-full or half-empty?". In: Welch, F. (Ed.), The Causes and Consequences of Increasing Inequality. The University of Chicago Press, Chicago, pp. 341–364.

Muskin, S.J. (1962). "Health as an investment". Journal of Political Economy 70, 129–157.

National Commission on Excellence in Education. (1983). A Nation at Risk: The Imperative of Educational Reform.

Ober, H. (1948). "Occupational wage differentials, 1907–1947". Monthly Labor Review LXVII, 127–134.

Pierce, B. (2001). "Compensation inequality". Quarterly Journal of Economics 116, 1493–1525.

Renshaw, E.F. (1960). "Estimating the returns to education". The Review of Economics and Statistics 42, 318–324.

Rouse, C.E. (1998). "Private school vouchers and student achievement: An evaluation of the Milwaukee parental choice program". Quarterly Journal of Economics 113, 553–602.

Roy, A.D. (1950). "The distribution of earnings and of individual output". The Economic Journal 60, 489–505.

Ruggles, S., Sobek, M., et al. (2003). Integrated Public Use Microdata Series: Version 3.0. Historical Census Projects, University of Minnesota, Minneapolis. http://www.ipums.org.

Ryder, H.E., Stafford, F.P., Stephan, P.E. (1976). "Labor, leisure and training over the life cycle". International Economic Review 17, 651–674.

Sachs, J.D., Shatz, H.J. (1996). "U.S. trade with developing countries and wage inequality". American Economic Review 86, 234–239.

Sander, W. (1999). "Private schools and public school achievement". Journal of Human Resources 34, 697–709.

Schuller, G.J. (1953). "The secular trend in income distribution by type, 1869–1948: A preliminary estimate". Review of Economics and Statistics 35, 302–324.

Spence, A.M. (1973). "Job market signaling". Quarterly Journal of Economics 87, 355–374.

Spence, A.M. (1974). Market Signaling: Informational Transfer in Hiring and Related Screening Processes. Harvard University Press, Cambridge.

Staehle, H. (1943). "Ability, wages and income". Review of Economics and Statistics 25, 77–87.

Stigler, G.J. (1962). "Information in the labor market". Journal of Political Economy 70, 94–105.

Strayer, W. (2002). "The returns to school quality: College choice and earnings". Journal of Labor Economics 20, 475–503.

Taubman, P.J., Wales, T.J. (1973). "Higher education, mental ability and screening". Journal of Political Economy 81, 28–55.

Topel, R.H. (1986). "Local labor markets". Journal of Political Economy 94, 111–143.

Topel, R.H. (1997). "Factor proportions and relative wages: The supply-side determinants of wage inequality". Journal of Economic Perspectives 11, 55–74.

U.S. Department of Labor, Bureau of Labor Statistics. (2001). National Longitudinal Survey of Youth 1979 cohort: 1979–2000. Center for Human Resource Research, Ohio State University, Columbus, OH.

Ureta, M., Welch, F. (1998). "Measuring education attainment: The new and old census and BLS taxonomies". Economics of Education Review 17, 15–30.

Wallace, T.D., Ihnen, L.A. (1975). "Full-time schooling in life-cycle models of human capital accumulation". Journal of Political Economy 83, 137–156.

Walsh, J.R. (1935). "Capital concept applied to man". Quarterly Journal of Economics 49, 255–285.

Weiss, Y. (1971). "Learning by doing and occupational specialization". Journal of Economic Theory 3, 189–198.

Welch, F. (1966). "Measurement of the quality of schooling". American Economic Review 56, 379–392.

Welch, F. (1970). "Education in production". Journal of Political Economy 78, 35–59.

Welch, F. (1979). "Effects of cohort size on earnings: The baby boom babies' financial bust". Journal of Political Economy 87, S65–S97.

Welch, F. (1999). "In defense of inequality". American Economic Review 89, 1–17.

Williams, J.T. (1979). "Uncertainty and the accumulation of human capital over the life cycle". Journal of Business 52, 521–548.

Willis, R.J. (1986). "Wage determinants: A survey and reinterpretation of human capital earnings functions". In: Ashenfelter, O., Layard, R. (Eds.), Handbook of Labor Economics, vol. 1. North-Holland, Amsterdam, pp. 525–602.

Willis, R.J., Rosen, S. (1979). "Education and self-selection". Journal of Political Economy 87, 7–36.

Woytinsky, W.S. and associates. (1953). Employment and Wages in the United States. Twentieth Century Fund, New York.

Chapter 7

EARNINGS FUNCTIONS, RATES OF RETURN AND TREATMENT EFFECTS: THE MINCER EQUATION AND BEYOND[1]

JAMES J. HECKMAN

Department of Economics, University of Chicago, 1126 East 59th Street, Chicago, IL 60637, USA
e-mail: jjh@uchicago.edu

LANCE J. LOCHNER

Department of Economics, University of Western Ontario, 1151 Richmond Street N, London, ON, N6A 5C2, Canada
e-mail: llochner@uwo.ca

PETRA E. TODD

Department of Economics, University of Pennsylvania, 20 McNeil, 3718 Locust Walk, Philadelphia, PA 19104, USA
e-mail: petra@athena.sas.upenn.edu

Contents

[1] Heckman is Henry Schultz Distinguished Service Professor of Economics at the University of Chicago and Distinguished Professor of Science and Society, University College Dublin. Lochner is Associate Professor of Economics at the University of Western Ontario. Todd is Professor of Economics at the University of Pennsylvania. The first part of this chapter was prepared in June 1998. It previously circulated under the title "Fifty Years of Mincer Earnings Regressions". Heckman's research was supported by NIH R01-HD043411, NSF 97-09-873, NSF SES-0099195 and NSF SES-0241858. We thank Christian Belzil, George Borjas, Pedro Carneiro, Flavio Cunha, Jim Davies, Reuben Gronau, Eric Hanushek, Lawrence Katz, John Knowles, Mario Macis, Derek Neal, Aderonke Osikominu, Dan Schmierer, Jora Stixrud, Ben Williams, Kenneth Wolpin, and participants at the 2001 AEA Annual Meeting, the Labor Studies Group at the 2001 NBER Summer Institute, and participants at Stanford University and Yale University seminars for helpful comments. Our great regret is that Sherwin Rosen, our departed friend and colleague, who thought long and hard about the issues discussed in this chapter could not give us the benefit of his wisdom.

Handbook of the Economics of Education, Volume 1
Edited by Eric A. Hanushek and Finis Welch
© 2006 Elsevier B.V. All rights reserved
DOI: 10.1016/S1574-0692(06)01007-5

Abstract

Numerous studies regress log earnings on schooling and report estimated coefficients as "Mincer rates of return". A more recent literature uses instrumental variables. This chapter considers the economic interpretation of these analyses and how the availability of repeated cross section and panel data improves the ability of analysts to estimate the rate of return. We consider under what conditions the Mincer model estimates an *ex post* rate of return. We test and reject the model on six cross sections of U.S. Census data. We present a general nonparametric approach for estimating marginal internal rates of return that takes into account tuition, income taxes and forms of uncertainty. We also contrast estimates based on a single cross-section of data, using the synthetic cohort approach, with estimates based on repeated cross-sections following actual cohorts. Cohort-based models fitted on repeated cross section data provide more reliable estimates of *ex post* returns.

Accounting for uncertainty affects estimates of rates of return. Accounting for sequential revelation of information calls into question the validity of the internal rate of return as a tool for policy analysis. An alternative approach to computing economic rates of return that accounts for sequential revelation of information is proposed and the evidence is summarized. We distinguish *ex ante* from *ex post* returns. New panel data methods for estimating the uncertainty and psychic costs facing agents are reviewed. We report recent evidence that demonstrates that there are large psychic costs of schooling. This helps to explain why persons do not attend school even though the financial rewards for doing so are high. We present methods for computing distributions of returns *ex ante* and *ex post*.

We review the literature on instrumental variable estimation. The link of the estimates to the economics is not strong. The traditional instruments are weak, and this literature has not produced decisive empirical estimates. We exposit new methods that interpret the economic content of different instruments within a unified framework.

Keywords

rate of return to schooling, internal rate of return, uncertainty, psychic costs, panel data, distribution

JEL classification: C31

1. Introduction

Earnings functions are the most widely used empirical equations in labor economics and the economics of education. Almost daily, new estimates of "rates of return" to schooling are reported, based on numerous instrumental variable and ordinary least squares estimates. For many reasons, few of these estimates are true rates of return.

The internal rate of return to schooling was introduced as a central concept of human capital theory by Becker (1964). It is widely sought after and rarely obtained. Under certain conditions which we discuss in this chapter, high internal rates of return to education relative to those of other investment alternatives signal the relative profitability of investment in education. Given the centrality of this parameter to economic policy making and the recent interest in wage inequality and the structure of wages, there have been surprisingly few estimates of the internal rate of return to education reported in the literature and surprisingly few justifications of the numbers that are reported as rates of return. The reported rates of return largely focus on the college–high school wage differential and ignore the full ingredients required to obtain a rate of return. The recent instrumental variable literature estimates various treatment effects which are only loosely related to rates of return.

In common usage, the coefficient on schooling in a regression of log earnings on years of schooling is often called a rate of return. In fact, it is a price of schooling from a hedonic market wage equation. It is a growth rate of market earnings with years of schooling and not an internal rate of return measure, except under stringent conditions which we specify, test and reject in this chapter. The justification for interpreting the coefficient on schooling as a rate of return derives from a model by Becker and Chiswick (1966). It was popularized and estimated by Mincer (1974) and is now called the Mincer model.[1]

This model is widely used as a vehicle for estimating "returns" to schooling quality,[2] for measuring the impact of work experience on male–female wage gaps,[3] and as a basis for economic studies of returns to education in developing countries.[4] It has been estimated using data from a variety of countries and time periods. Recent studies in growth economics use the Mincer model to analyze the relationship between growth and average schooling levels across countries.[5]

Using the same type of data and the same empirical conventions employed by Mincer and many other scholars, we test the assumptions that justify interpreting the coefficient on years of schooling as a rate of return. We exposit the Mincer model, showing conditions under which the coefficient in a pricing equation (the "Mincer" coefficient) is

[1] See, e.g., Psacharopoulos (1981), Psacharopoulos and Patrinos (2004) and Willis (1986) for extensive surveys of Mincer returns.

[2] See Behrman and Birdsall (1983) and Card and Krueger (1992).

[3] See Mincer and Polachek (1974).

[4] See Glewwe (2002).

[5] See Bils and Klenow (2000).

also a rate of return. These conditions are not supported in the data from the recent U.S. labor market. We then go on to summarize other methods that use repeated cross section and panel data to recover *ex ante* and *ex post* returns to schooling.

This chapter makes the following points:

(1) We test important predictions underlying the Mincer model using six waves of U.S. Census data, 1940–1990.[6] We find, as does other recent literature, that Mincer's original model fails to capture central features of empirical earnings functions in recent decades. The empirical analysis in this chapter is more comprehensive than previous analyses and tests more features of the model, including its predictions about the linearity of log earnings equations in schooling, parallelism in log earnings–experience profiles, and U-shaped patterns for the variance of log earnings over the life cycle.

(2) In response to the evidence against the Mincer specification of the earnings function, we estimate more general earnings models, where the coefficient on schooling in a log earnings equation is not interpretable as a rate of return. From the estimated earnings functions, we compute marginal internal rates of return to education for black and white men across different schooling levels and for different decades. Our estimates account for nonlinearities and nonseparabilities in earnings functions, taxes and tuition. A comparison of these estimated returns with estimated Mincer coefficients shows that both levels and trends in rates of return generated from the Mincer model are misleading. Caution must be used in applying the Mincer equation to modern economies to estimate rates of return.

The estimated marginal rates of return are often implausible, calling into question the empirical conventions followed by Mincer and the recent U.S. Census-based/Current Population Survey-based literature reviewed by Katz and Autor (1999) that ignore endogeneity of schooling, censoring and missing wages, uncertainty, sequential revelation of information and psychic costs of schooling.

(3) We explore the importance of Mincer's implicit stationarity assumptions, which allowed him to use cross-section experience–earnings profiles as guides to the life cycle earnings of persons. In recent time periods, life cycle earnings–education–experience profiles differ across cohorts. Thus cross-sections are no longer useful guides to the life cycle earnings or schooling returns of any particular individual. Accounting for the nonstationarity of earnings over time has empirically important effects on estimated rates of return to schooling. Since many economies have nonstationary earnings functions, these lessons apply generally.

(4) Mincer implicitly assumes a world of perfect certainty about future earnings streams. We first consider a model of uncertainty in a static economic environment without updating of information, which can be fit on cross sections or repeated cross sections. Accounting for uncertainty substantially reduces high estimated internal rates of return to more plausible levels. These adjustments introduce *ex ante* and *ex post* distinctions into the analysis of the earnings functions, something missing in the Mincer model, but essential to modern dynamic economics.

[6] Mincer's analysis focused on 1960 U.S. census data (earnings for 1959).

(5) We next consider a dynamic model of schooling decisions with the sequential resolution of uncertainty. Following developments in the recent literature, we allow for the possibility that, with each additional year of schooling, information about the value of different schooling choices and opportunities becomes available. This generates an option value of schooling.[7] Completing high school generates the option to attend college and attending college generates the option to complete college. Our findings suggest that part of the economic return to finishing high school or attending college includes the potential for completing college and securing the high rewards associated with a college degree. Both sequential resolution of uncertainty and non-linearity in returns to schooling can contribute to sizeable option values.[8]

Accounting for option values challenges the validity of the internal rate of return as a guide to the optimality of schooling choices. The internal rate of return has been a widely sought-after parameter in the economics of education since the analysis of Becker (1964). When schooling decisions are made at the beginning of life, there is no uncertainty and age-earnings streams across schooling levels cross only once. In this case, the internal rate of return (IRR) can be compared with the interest rate to produce a valid rule for making education decisions [Hirshleifer (1970)]. If the IRR exceeds the interest rate, further investment in education is warranted. However, when schooling decisions are made sequentially as information is revealed, a number of problems arise that invalidate this rule. We examine the consequences of option values in determining rates of return to schooling. Our analysis points to a need for more empirical studies that incorporate the sequential nature of individual schooling decisions and uncertainty about education costs and future earnings to help determine their importance. We report evidence on estimated option values from the recent empirical literature using rich panel data sources that enable analysts to answer questions that could not be answered with the cross section data available to Mincer in the 1960s.

(6) We then consider models that control for unobserved heterogeneity and endogeneity of schooling in computing "the rate of return to schooling" starting with the Card (1995, 1999) model and moving into the more recent analyses of Carneiro, Heckman and Vytlacil (2005). These models focus on identifying the growth of earnings with respect to schooling (the causal effect of schooling) and not internal rates of return. In many papers, an instrument, rather than some well-posed question, defines the parameter of interest. The models ignore the sequential resolution of uncertainty but account for heterogeneity in responses to schooling where "returns" are potentially correlated with schooling levels. This correlation is ignored in the Census/CPS-based literature on "returns" to schooling. We review some new analytical results from the instrumental

[7] Weisbrod (1962) developed the concept of the option value of schooling. For one formalization of his analysis, see Comay, Melnik and Pollatschek (1973).

[8] Schooling choices are made sequentially. Thus if the function relating the value of completing schooling at each year of schooling is nonconcave, the return to one stage may be low but the return to the next stage may be high, hence creating an option value at the stage with low terminal payoff. The earlier stage must be completed to obtain the higher return arising at the later stage.

variables literature that aid in interpreting reported "Mincer coefficients" (growth rates of earnings in terms of years of schooling) within a willingness to pay framework. We link the rate of return literature to the recent literature on treatment effects.

(7) The literature on the returns to schooling focuses on certain mean parameters. Yet the original Mincer (1974) model entertained the possibility that returns varied in the population. Chiswick (1974) and Chiswick and Mincer (1972) estimate variation in rates of return as a contributing factor to overall income inequality. We survey recent developments in the literature that use rich panel data to estimate distributions of the response of earnings to schooling using the modern theory of econometric counterfactuals. They reveal substantial variability in *ex post* returns to schooling.

(8) Finally, we review research from a very recent literature that decomposes variability in returns to schooling into components that are not forecastable by agents at the time they make their schooling decisions (uncertainty) and components that are predictable (heterogeneity). Both predictable and unpredictable components of *ex post* returns are found to be sizeable in most recent studies. This analysis highlights the distinction between *ex ante* and *ex post* returns to schooling and the importance of accounting for uncertainty in the analysis of schooling decisions. This literature also identifies psychic costs of schooling, which are estimated to be substantial. Conventional rate of return calculations assume that they are negligible. These components help to explain why many people who might benefit financially from additional schooling do not take it up.

In this chapter, we use the Mincer model as a point of departure because it is so influential. Mincer's model was developed to explain cross sections of earnings. While the model is no longer a valid guide for accurately estimating rates of return to schooling, the Mincer vision of using economics to explain earnings data remains valid.

This chapter proceeds in the following way. Section 2 reviews two distinct theoretical arguments for using the Mincer regression model to estimate rates of return. They are algebraically similar but their economic content is very different. Section 3 presents empirical evidence on the validity of the widely used Mincer specification. Using nonparametric estimation techniques, we formally test and reject key predictions of Mincer's model, while others survive. The predictions that are rejected call into question the practice of interpreting the Mincer coefficient as a rate of return. Section 4 extracts internal rates of return from nonparametric estimates of earnings functions fit on cross sections. We show the effects on estimated rates of return of accounting for income taxes, college tuition and psychic costs, and length of working life that depends on the amount of schooling. We also consider how accounting for uncertainty affects estimated marginal internal rates of return.

Section 5 introduces a dynamic framework for educational choices with sequential resolution of uncertainty, which produces an option value for schooling. We discuss why in such an economic environment the internal rate of return is no longer a valid guide for evaluating schooling investments. A more general measure of the rate of return used in modern capital theory is more appropriate. Section 6 considers the interpretation of Mincer regression estimates based on cross-section data in a changing economy. We contrast cross-sectional estimates with those based on repeated cross-sections drawn from the CPS that follow cohorts over time. Mincer's assumption that cross sections of earnings are accurate guides to the life cycles of different cohorts is not valid in recent years when U.S. labor markets have been changing.

Section 7 discusses the recent literature on the consequences of endogeneity of schooling for estimating growth rates of earnings with schooling. We describe Card's (1999) version of Becker's Woytinsky Lecture (1967) and some simple instrumental variables (*IV*) estimators of the mean growth rate of earnings with schooling. Section 8 discusses the modern theory of instrumental variable estimation and interprets what *IV* estimates in the general case where growth rates of schooling are heterogeneous and potentially correlated with schooling levels. We consider what economic questions *IV* answers. The modern *IV* literature defines the parameter of interest by an instrument, rather than an economic question, and produces estimates of "rates of return" that have little to do with true rates of return.

Section 9 surveys a recent literature that estimates distributions of *ex post* returns. Section 10 decomposes the distributions of returns and growth rates of earnings with schooling into *ex ante* and *ex post* components and presents option values for schooling as well as estimates of the psychic costs of schooling. Our analysis links the classical literature on rates of return to the modern literature on counterfactual analysis. Section 11 concludes.

2. The theoretical foundations of Mincer's earnings regression

The most widely used specification of empirical earnings equations and the point of departure for our analysis is the Mincer equation:

$$\ln\left[Y(s,x)\right] = \alpha + \rho_s s + \beta_0 x + \beta_1 x^2 + \varepsilon, \tag{1}$$

where $Y(s,x)$ is the wage or earnings at schooling level s and work experience x, ρ_s is the "rate of return to schooling" (assumed to be the same for all schooling levels) and ε is a mean zero residual with $E(\varepsilon|s,x) = 0$.[9] This regression model is motivated by two conceptually different frameworks used by Mincer (1958, 1974). While algebraically similar, their economic content is very different. In Section 3, we formally test and reject predictions of these models on the type of Census data originally used by Mincer. In Section 4, we implement a more general nonparametric approach to estimating internal rates of return that does not require an explicit model specification.

2.1. The compensating differences model

The original Mincer model (1958) uses the principle of compensating differences to explain why persons with different levels of schooling receive different earnings over

[9] Psacharopoulos (1981) and Psacharopoulos and Patrinos (2004) provide surveys of an enormous Mincer-based earnings literature.

their lifetimes. Individuals have identical abilities and opportunities, credit markets are perfect, the environment is perfectly certain, but occupations differ in the amount of schooling required. Individuals forego earnings while in school, but incur no direct costs. Because individuals are *ex ante* identical, they require a compensating wage differential to work in occupations that require a longer schooling period. The compensating differential is determined by equating the present value of earnings streams net of costs associated with different levels of investment. This framework implicitly ignores uncertainty about future earnings as well as nonpecuniary costs and benefits of school and work, which Section 10 shows are important determinants of the return to schooling and its distribution.

Let $Y(s)$ represent the annual earnings of an individual with s years of education, assumed to be constant over his lifetime. Let r be an externally determined interest rate and T the length of working life, assumed not to depend on s. The present value of earnings associated with schooling level s is

$$V(s) = Y(s) \int_s^T \mathrm{e}^{-rt}\,\mathrm{d}t = \frac{Y(s)}{r}\left(\mathrm{e}^{-rs} - \mathrm{e}^{-rT}\right).$$

Equilibrium across heterogeneous schooling levels requires that individuals be indifferent between schooling choices, with allocations being driven by demand conditions. Equating earnings streams across schooling levels and taking logs yields

$$\ln Y(s) = \ln Y(0) + rs + \ln\left(\left(1 - \mathrm{e}^{-rT}\right)/\left(1 - \mathrm{e}^{-r(T-s)}\right)\right).$$

The final term on the right-hand side is an adjustment for finite life, which vanishes as T gets large.[10]

This model implies that people with more education receive higher earnings. When T is large, the percentage increase in lifetime earnings associated with an additional year of school, ρ_s, must equal the interest rate, r. Because the internal rate of return to schooling represents the discount rate that equates lifetime earnings streams for different education choices, it will also equal the interest rate in this model. Therefore, ρ_s in Equation (1) yields an estimate of the internal rate of return, and when $\rho_s = r$, the education market is in equilibrium. If $\rho_s > r$, there is underinvestment in education.

2.2. *The accounting-identity model*

The model used by Mincer (1974), and now widely applied, is motivated differently from the compensating differences model, but yields an algebraically similar empirical specification of the earnings equation. It is much less clearly tied to an underlying optimizing model, although some of the assumptions are motivated by the dynamic human capital investment model of Ben-Porath (1967). Mincer's accounting identity model

[10] This term also disappears if the retirement age, T, is allowed to increase one-for-one with s (i.e., $\frac{\partial T(s)}{\partial s} = 1$), so post-school working life is the same for persons of all schooling levels.

emphasizes life cycle dynamics of earnings and the relationship between observed earnings, potential earnings, and human capital investment, for both formal schooling and on-the-job investment. Persons are *ex ante* heterogeneous, so the compensating differences motivation of the first model is absent. ρ_s varies in the population to reflect heterogeneity in returns.[11]

Let P_t be potential earnings at age t, and express costs of investments in training C_t as a fraction k_t of potential earnings, $C_t = k_t P_t$. Let ρ_t be the *average* return to training investments made at age t. Potential earnings at t are

$$P_t \equiv P_{t-1}(1 + k_{t-1}\rho_{t-1}) \equiv \prod_{j=0}^{t-1}(1 + \rho_j k_j)P_0.$$

Formal schooling is defined as years spent in full-time investment ($k_t = 1$), which is assumed to take place at the beginning of life and to yield a rate of return ρ_s that is constant across all years of schooling. Assuming that the rate of return to post-school investment is constant over ages and equals ρ_0, we can write

$$\begin{aligned}\ln P_t &\equiv \ln P_0 + s\ln(1+\rho_s) + \sum_{j=s}^{t-1}\ln(1+\rho_0 k_j)\\ &\approx \ln P_0 + s\rho_s + \rho_0\sum_{j=s}^{t-1}k_j,\end{aligned}$$

where the last approximation is obtained for "small" ρ_s and ρ_0.

Mincer approximates the Ben-Porath (1967) model by assuming a linearly declining rate of post-school investment: $k_{s+x} = \kappa(1 - \frac{x}{T})$ where $x = t - s \geqslant 0$ is the amount of work experience as of age t. The length of working life, T, is assumed to be independent of years of schooling. Under these assumptions, the relationship between potential earnings, schooling and experience is given by

$$\ln P_{x+s} \approx \ln P_0 + s\rho_s + \left(\rho_0\kappa + \frac{\rho_0\kappa}{2T}\right)x - \frac{\rho_0\kappa}{2T}x^2.$$

Observed earnings are potential earnings less investment costs, producing the relationship for observed earnings known as the Mincer equation,

$$\begin{aligned}\ln Y(s,x) &\approx \ln P_{x+s} - \kappa\left(1 - \frac{x}{T}\right)\\ &= [\ln P_0 - \kappa] + \rho_s s + \left(\rho_0\kappa + \frac{\rho_0\kappa}{2T} + \frac{\kappa}{T}\right)x - \frac{\rho_0\kappa}{2T}x^2.\end{aligned}$$

[11] Chiswick and Mincer (1972) explicitly analyze income inequality with this model. We discuss earnings distributions and distributions of rates of return in Section 10.

This expression is Equation (1) without an error term. Log earnings are linear in years of schooling, and linear and quadratic in years of labor market experience. Parameter ρ_s is an *average rate of return across* all schooling investments and not, in general, an internal rate of return or a marginal return that is appropriate for evaluating the optimality of educational investments. In many studies [see, e.g., Psacharopoulos (1981), Psacharopoulos and Patrinos (2004)], estimates of ρ_s are simply referred to as "rates of return" without any justification for doing so. In this formulation, ρ_s is the *ex post average* growth rate of earnings with schooling. It communicates how much average earnings increase with schooling, but it is not informative on the optimality of educational investments which requires knowledge of the *ex ante* marginal rate of return.

In most applications of the Mincer model, it is assumed that the intercept and slope coefficients in Equation (1) are identical across persons. This implicitly assumes that P_0, κ, ρ_0 and ρ_s are the same across persons and do not depend on the schooling level. However, Mincer formulates a more general model that allows for the possibility that κ and ρ_s differ across persons, which produces a random coefficient model,

$$\ln Y(s_i, x_i) = \alpha_i + \rho_{si} s_i + \beta_{0i} x_i + \beta_{1i} x_i^2.$$

Letting $\bar{\alpha} = E(\alpha_i)$, $\bar{\rho}_s = E(\rho_{si})$, $\bar{\beta}_0 = E(\beta_{0i})$, $\bar{\beta}_1 = E(\beta_{1i})$, we may write this expression, dropping individual subscript "i" as

$$\begin{aligned}\ln Y(s, x) &= \bar{\alpha} + \bar{\rho}_s s + \bar{\beta}_0 x + \bar{\beta}_1 x^2 \\ &\quad + \left[(\alpha - \bar{\alpha}) + (\rho_s - \bar{\rho}_s)s + (\beta_0 - \bar{\beta}_0)x + (\beta_1 - \bar{\beta}_1)x^2\right],\end{aligned}$$

where the terms in brackets are part of the error.[12] Mincer originally assumed that $(\alpha - \bar{\alpha})$, $(\rho_s - \bar{\rho}_s)$, $(\beta_0 - \bar{\beta}_0)$, $(\beta_1 - \bar{\beta}_1)$ are independent of (s, x); although he relaxes this assumption in later work [Mincer (1997)]. Allowing for correlation between ρ_s and s motivates an entire instrumental variables literature which we survey in Sections 7 and 8.

Implications for log earnings–age and log earnings–experience profiles and for the interpersonal distribution of life-cycle earnings

Both Mincer models predict that log earnings are linear in years of schooling although the two models have very different economic content. We test and reject this prediction on widely used Census and CPS data. Assuming that post-school investment patterns are identical across persons and do not depend on the schooling level, the accounting identity model also predicts that

(i) *log-earnings experience profiles are parallel across schooling levels* ($\frac{\partial \ln Y(s,x)}{\partial s \partial x} = 0$),

and

[12] In the random coefficients model, the error term of the derived regression equation is heteroskedastic.

(ii) *log-earnings age profiles diverge with age across schooling levels* ($\frac{\partial \ln Y(s,x)}{\partial s \partial t} = \frac{\rho_0 \kappa}{T} > 0$).

In Section 3, we extend Mincer's original empirical analysis of white males from the 1960 Census to white and black males from the 1940–1990 Censuses. The data from the 1940–1950 Censuses provide some empirical support for predictions (i) and (ii). The 1960 and 1970 data are roughly consistent with the model; prediction (i) does not pass conventional statistical tests for whites, although they pass an "eyeball" test.[13] Data from the more recent Census years (1980–1990) are much less supportive of these predictions of the model, due in large part to the nonstationarity of recent labor markets.

Another implication of Mincer's model is that for each schooling class, there is an age in the life cycle at which the interpersonal variance in earnings is minimized. Consider the accounting identity for observed earnings in levels at experience x and schooling s, which we can write as

$$Y(s, x) \equiv P_s + \rho_s \sum_{j=s}^{s+x-1} C_j - C_{s+x}.$$

This says that earnings at schooling level s equals initial endowment from schooling plus the return on past investments less the cost of current investment at age $s + x$ or experience class x.

In logs,

$$\ln Y(s, x) \approx \ln P_s + \rho_s \sum_{j=0}^{x-1} k_{s+j} - k_{s+x}.$$

Interpersonal differences in observed log earnings of individuals with the same P_0 and ρ_s arise because of differences in $\ln P_s$ and in post-school investment patterns as determined by k_j. When $\ln P_s$ and κ or the k_{s+j} are uncorrelated, the variance of log earnings reaches a minimum when experience is approximately equal to $1/\rho_0$. (See the derivation in Appendix A.) At this experience level, variance in earnings is solely a consequence of differences in schooling levels or ability and is unrelated to differences in post-school investment behavior. Prior to and after this time period (often referred to as the 'overtaking age'), there is an additional source of variance due to differences in post-school investment. Thus, the model predicts

(iii) *the variance of earnings over the life cycle has a U-shaped pattern.*

We show that this prediction of the model is supported in Census data from both early and recent decades.[14]

[13] Mincer (1974) provided informal empirical support for the implications using 1960 Census data.

[14] In addition to Mincer (1974), studies by Schultz (1975), Smith and Welch (1979), Hause (1980), and Dooley and Gottschalk (1984) also provide evidence of this pattern for wages and earnings.

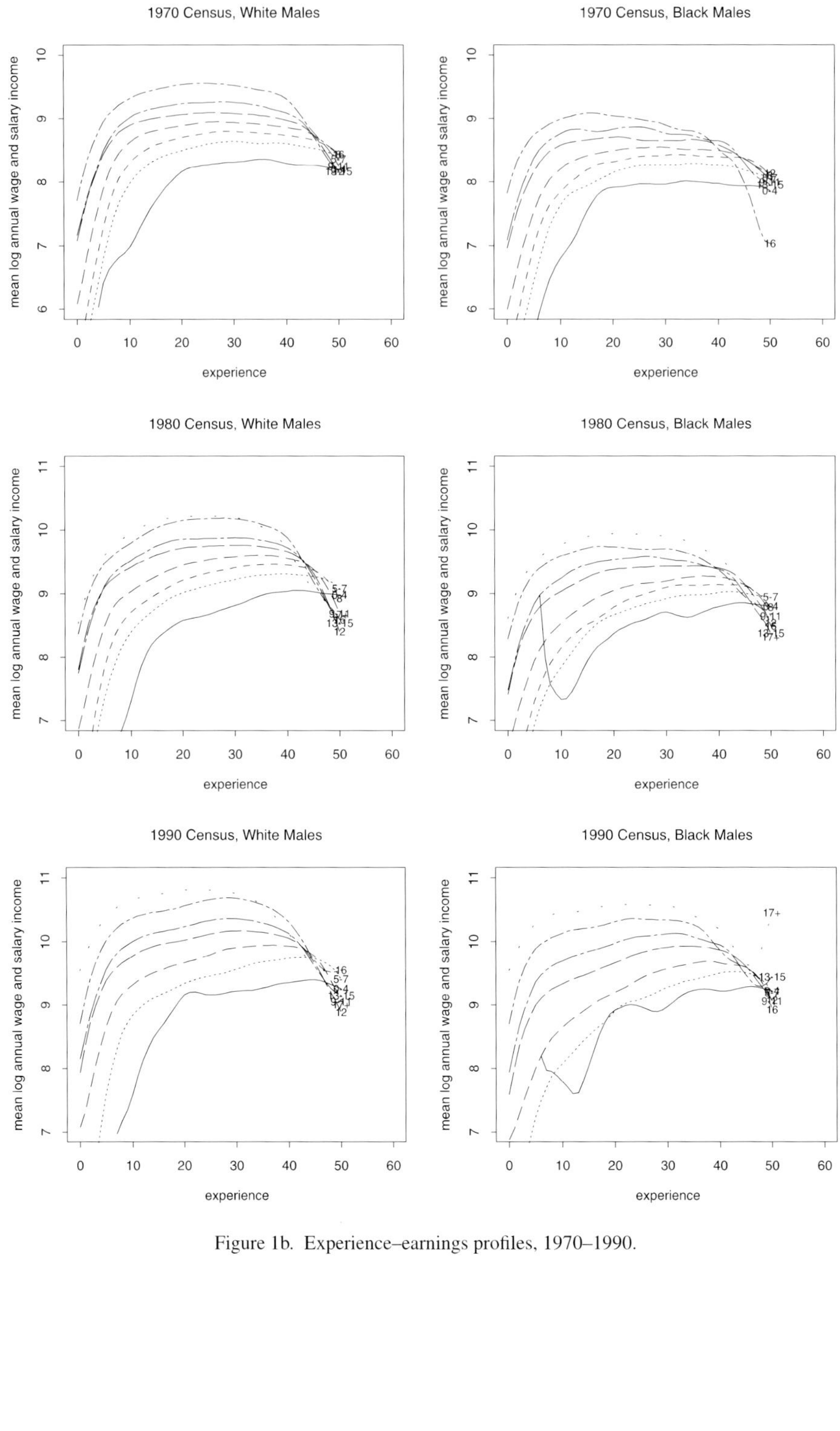

Figure 1b. Experience–earnings profiles, 1970–1990.

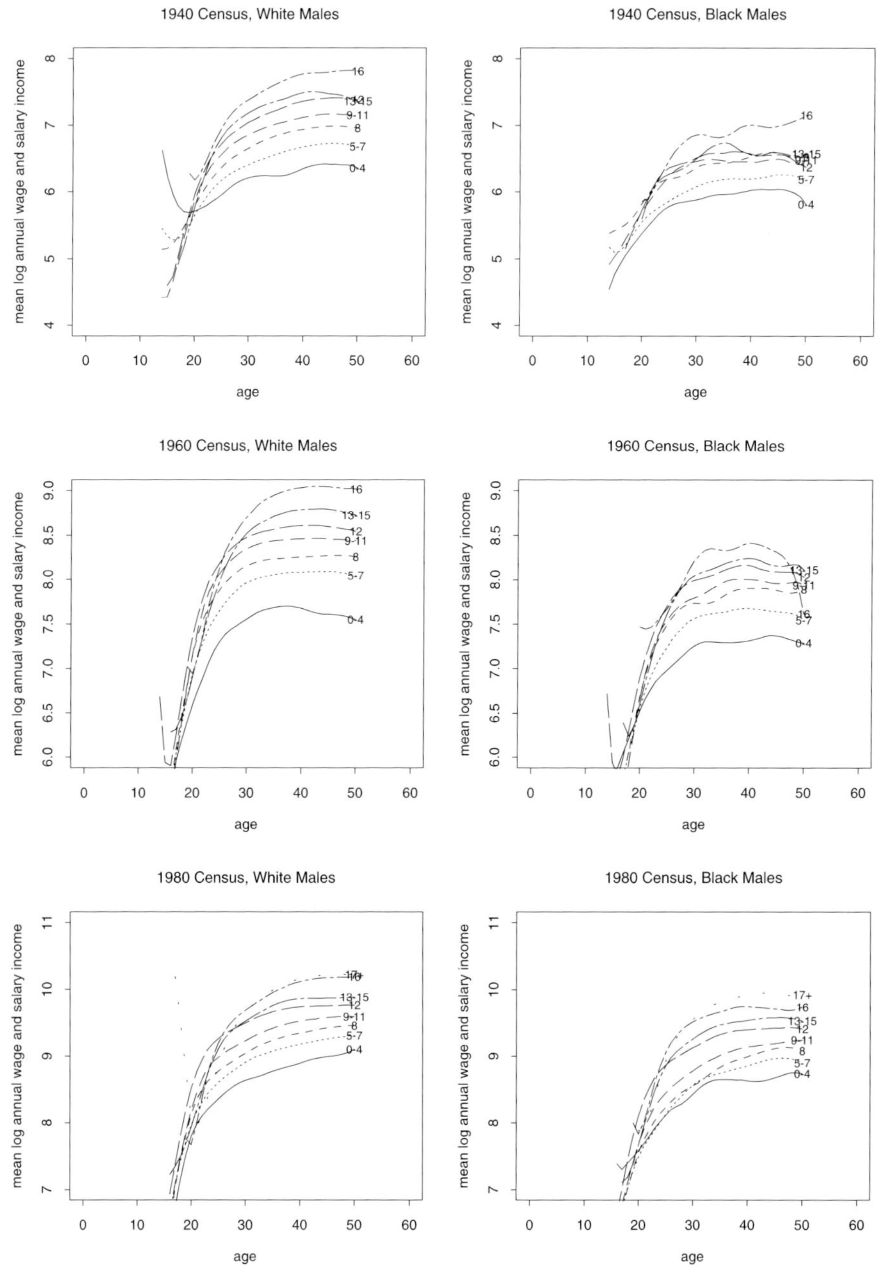

Figure 2. Age–earnings profiles, 1940, 1960, 1980.

Table 1
Tests of parallelism in log earnings experience profiles for men

Sample	Experience level	Estimated difference between college and high school log earnings at different experience levels					
		1940	1950	1960	1970	1980	1990
Whites	10	0.54	0.30	0.46	0.41	0.37	0.59
	20	0.40	0.40	0.43	0.49	0.45	0.54
	30	0.54	0.27	0.46	0.48	0.43	0.52
	40	0.58	0.21	0.50	0.45	0.27	0.30
	p-value	0.32	0.70	<0.001	<0.001	<0.001	<0.001
Blacks	10	0.20	0.58	0.48	0.38	0.70	0.77
	20	0.38	0.05	0.25	0.22	0.48	0.69
	30	−0.11	0.24	0.08	0.33	0.36	0.53
	40	−0.20	0.00	0.73	0.26	0.22	−0.04
	p-value	0.46	0.55	0.58	0.91	<0.001	<0.001

Notes: Data taken from 1940–90 Decennial Censuses without adjustment for inflation. Because there are very few blacks in the 1940 and 1950 samples with college degrees, especially at higher experience levels, the test results for blacks in those years refer to a test of the difference between earnings for high school graduates and persons with 8 years of education. See Appendix B for data description. See Appendix C for the formulae used for the test statistics.

Figure 3 examines the support for implication (iii) – a U-shaped variance in earnings – for three different schooling completion levels: eighth grade, twelfth grade, and college (16 years of school). For the 1940 Census year, the variance of log-earnings over the life cycle is relatively flat for whites. It is similarly flat in 1950, with the exception of increasing variance at the tails. However, data for black and white men from the 1960–1990 Censuses clearly exhibit the U-shaped pattern predicted by Mincer's accounting-identity model. The evidence in support of predictions (ii) and (iii) gives analysts greater confidence in using the Mincer model to study earnings functions and rates of return to schooling, while failure of prediction (i) in recent decades raises a note of caution.[20] A major limitation of cross sectional analyses of variances is that they are silent about which components are predictable by the agent and which components represent true uncertainty, which is important in assessing the determinants of schooling decisions. We discuss this issue in Section 10.

Table 2 reports standard cross-section regression estimates of the Mincer return to schooling for all Census years derived from earnings specification (1). The estimates indicate an *ex post* average rate of return to schooling of around 10–13% for white men and 9–15% for black men over the 1940–1990 period. While estimated coefficients on schooling tend to be lower for blacks than whites in the early decades, they are higher

[20] The U-shaped profile of the variance of earnings argues against the Rutherford (1955) model of earnings as revived by Atkeson and Lucas (1992).

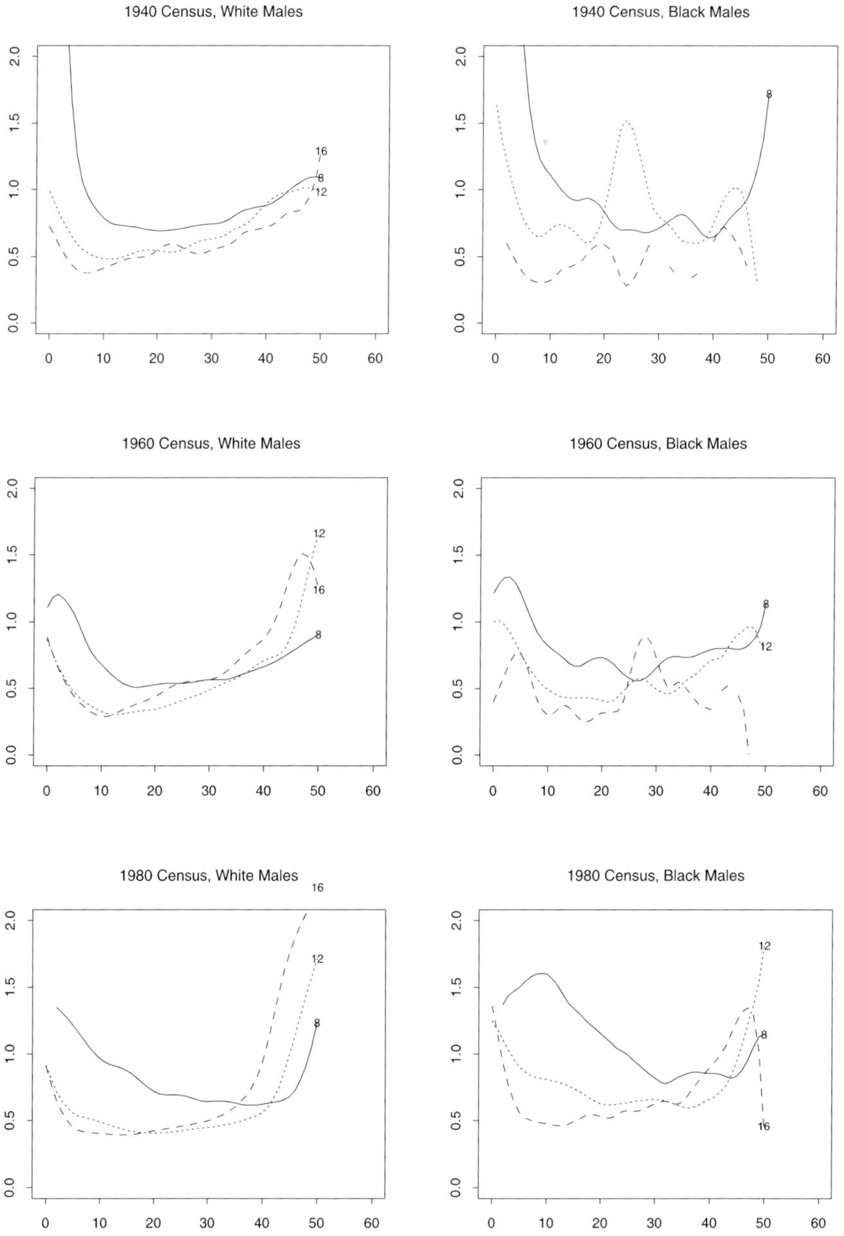

Figure 3. Experience–variance log earnings.

Table 2
Estimated coefficients from Mincer log earnings regression for men

		Whites		Blacks	
		Coefficient	Std. Error	Coefficient	Std. Error
1940	Intercept	4.4771	0.0096	4.6711	0.0298
	Education	0.1250	0.0007	0.0871	0.0022
	Experience	0.0904	0.0005	0.0646	0.0018
	Experience-squared	−0.0013	0.0000	−0.0009	0.0000
1950	Intercept	5.3120	0.0132	5.0716	0.0409
	Education	0.1058	0.0009	0.0998	0.0030
	Experience	0.1074	0.0006	0.0933	0.0023
	Experience-squared	−0.0017	0.0000	−0.0014	0.0000
1960	Intercept	5.6478	0.0066	5.4107	0.0220
	Education	0.1152	0.0005	0.1034	0.0016
	Experience	0.1156	0.0003	0.1035	0.0011
	Experience-squared	−0.0018	0.0000	−0.0016	0.0000
1970	Intercept	5.9113	0.0045	5.8938	0.0155
	Education	0.1179	0.0003	0.1100	0.0012
	Experience	0.1323	0.0002	0.1074	0.0007
	Experience-squared	−0.0022	0.0000	−0.0016	0.0000
1980	Intercept	6.8913	0.0030	6.4448	0.0120
	Education	0.1023	0.0002	0.1176	0.0009
	Experience	0.1255	0.0001	0.1075	0.0005
	Experience-squared	−0.0022	0.0000	−0.0016	0.0000
1990	Intercept	6.8912	0.0034	6.3474	0.0144
	Education	0.1292	0.0002	0.1524	0.0011
	Experience	0.1301	0.0001	0.1109	0.0006
	Experience-squared	−0.0023	0.0000	−0.0017	0.0000

Notes: Data taken from 1940–90 Decennial Censuses. See Appendix B for data description.

in 1980 and 1990. The estimates suggest that the rate of return to schooling for blacks increased substantially over the 50 year period, while it first declined and then rose for whites. The coefficient on experience rose for both whites and blacks over the five decades.

The economic content of these numbers is far from clear. What does a high "rate of return" – really a high growth rate of earnings with schooling – mean? The clearest interpretation is as a marginal price of schooling in the labor market and not as an internal rate of return. We next show how to use empirical earnings functions to estimate marginal internal rates of return.

4. Estimating internal rates of return

Given the evidence against the validity of the Mincer earnings specification presented in Section 3 and in recent studies of the changing wage structure [e.g., Murphy and Welch (1990), Katz and Murphy (1992), Katz and Autor (1999)], it is fruitful to develop an alternative approach to estimating marginal internal rates of return without imposing the Mincer specification on the data. Using a simple income maximizing framework under perfect certainty of the sort developed in Rosen (1977) and Willis (1986), this section first presents estimates of the internal rate of return based on progressively more general formulations of the earnings function. We then relax the assumption of perfect certainty in Section 4.2 below, as well as in Section 5 and Section 10.

We initially assume that individuals choose education levels to maximize the present value of their lifetime earnings. They take as given a post-school earnings profile, which may be determined through on-the-job investment as in the previous accounting-identity model. The model estimated in this section relaxes many of the conditions of the models in Section 2, such as the restriction that log earnings increase linearly with schooling and the restriction that log earnings–experience profiles are parallel across schooling classes.

To estimate marginal internal rates of return, which we refer to as internal rates of return in this section, analysts must account for direct costs, including both monetary and psychic costs as well as indirect costs. They must also account for income taxes and length of working life that may depend on the schooling level. With these additional considerations, the coefficient on schooling in a log earnings equation need no longer equal the real interest rate (the rate of return on capital), and it loses its interpretation as the internal rate of return to schooling. However, the internal rate of return can still be estimated using an alternative direct solution method, as we discuss below.[21]

Let $Y(s,x)$ be wage income at experience level x for schooling level s; $T(s)$, the last age of earnings, which may depend on the schooling level; v, private tuition and nonpecuniary costs of schooling; τ, a proportional income tax rate; and r, the before-tax interest rate.[22] Individuals are assumed to choose s to maximize the present discounted value of lifetime earnings,[23]

$$V(s) = \int_0^{T(s)-s} (1-\tau)\,\mathrm{e}^{-(1-\tau)r(x+s)}\,Y(s,x)\,\mathrm{d}x - \int_0^s v\,\mathrm{e}^{-(1-\tau)rz}\,\mathrm{d}z. \tag{2}$$

[21] To estimate social rates of return, we need to account for the social opportunity costs of funds and full social returns including crime reduction. On the last point, see Lochner and Moretti (2004).

[22] The standard framework implicitly assumes that individuals know these functional relationships, credit markets are perfect, education does not enter preferences, and there is no uncertainty.

[23] This expression embodies an institutional feature of the U.S. economy where income from all sources is taxed but one cannot write off tuition and nonpecuniary costs of education. However, we assume that agents can write off interest on their loans. This assumption is consistent with the institutional feature that persons can deduct mortgage interest, that 70% of American families own their own homes, and that mortgage loans can be used to finance college education. The expressions based on (2) can easily be modified to account for other tax treatments of tuition.

The first-order condition for a maximum yields

$$\begin{aligned}&\left[T'(s)-1\right]\mathrm{e}^{-(1-\tau)r(T(s)-s)}Y\left(s,T(s)-s\right)\\&\quad-(1-\tau)r\int_0^{T(s)-s}\mathrm{e}^{-(1-\tau)rx}Y(s,x)\,\mathrm{d}x\\&\quad+\int_0^{T(s)-s}\mathrm{e}^{-(1-\tau)rx}\frac{\partial Y(s,x)}{\partial s}\,\mathrm{d}x-v/(1-\tau)=0.\end{aligned}\tag{3}$$

Defining $\tilde{r}=(1-\tau)r$ (the after-tax interest rate) and re-arranging terms yields

$$\begin{aligned}\tilde{r}&=\underbrace{\frac{[T'(s)-1]\,\mathrm{e}^{-\tilde{r}(T(s)-s)}Y(s,T(s)-s)}{\int_0^{T(s)-s}\mathrm{e}^{-\tilde{r}x}Y(s,x)\,\mathrm{d}x}}_{\text{(Term 1)}}\\&\quad+\underbrace{\frac{\int_0^{T(s)-s}\mathrm{e}^{-\tilde{r}x}\left[\frac{\partial\log Y(s,x)}{\partial s}\right]Y(s,x)\,\mathrm{d}x}{\int_0^{T(s)-s}\mathrm{e}^{-\tilde{r}x}Y(s,x)\,\mathrm{d}x}}_{\text{(Term 2)}}-\underbrace{\frac{v/(1-\tau)}{\int_0^{T(s)-s}\mathrm{e}^{-\tilde{r}x}Y(s,x)\,\mathrm{d}x}}_{\text{(Term 3)}}.\end{aligned}\tag{4}$$

Term 1 represents a life-earnings effect – the change in the present value of earnings due to a change in working-life associated with additional schooling (expressed as a fraction of the present value of earnings measured at age s). Term 2 is the weighted average effect of schooling on log earnings by experience, and Term 3 is the cost of tuition and psychic costs expressed as a fraction of lifetime income measured at age s.

The special case assumed by Mincer and many other economists writes $v=0$ (i.e., no tuition or psychic costs). The traditional assumption is that tuition costs are a small (and negligible) component of total earnings or that earnings in college offset tuition. In light of the substantial estimates of psychic costs presented in Carneiro, Hansen and Heckman (2003), Cunha, Heckman and Navarro (2005, 2006) and Cunha and Heckman (2006a, 2006b), the assumption that $v=0$ is very strong even if tuition costs are a small component of the present value of income. We discuss this evidence in Section 10. Accounting for psychic costs lowers the internal rate of return.

Consider the additional commonly invoked assumption that $T'(s)=1$ (i.e., no loss of work life from schooling). These assumptions simplify the first-order condition to

$$\tilde{r}\int_0^{T(s)-s}\mathrm{e}^{-\tilde{r}x}Y(s,x)\,\mathrm{d}x=\int_0^{T(s)-s}\mathrm{e}^{-\tilde{r}x}\frac{\partial Y(s,x)}{\partial s}\,\mathrm{d}x.$$

As noted in Section 2, Mincer's model implies multiplicative separability between the schooling and experience components of earnings, so $Y(s,x)=\mu(s)\varphi(x)$ (i.e., log earnings profiles are parallel in experience across schooling levels). In this special case, $\tilde{r}=\mu'(s)/\mu(s)$. If this holds for all s, then wage growth must be log linear in schooling and $\mu(s)=\mu(0)\,\mathrm{e}^{\rho_s s}$, where $\rho_s=\tilde{r}$. If all of these assumptions hold, then the coefficient on schooling in a Mincer equation (ρ_s) estimates the internal rate of return to schooling, which should equal the after-tax interest rate.

From Equation (4) we observe, more generally, that the difference between after-tax interest rates (and the marginal internal rate of return) and the Mincer coefficient can be decomposed into three parts: a life-earnings part (Term 1), a second part which depends on the structure of the schooling return over the life cycle, and a tuition and psychic cost part (Term 3). Term 2 is averaged over all experience levels. Under multiplicative separability, it is the Mincer rate of return estimated from Equation (1). In general nonseparable models, it is not the Mincer coefficient.

The evidence for 1980 and 1990 presented in Section 3 and in the recent literature argues strongly against the assumption of multiplicative separability of log earnings in schooling and experience. In recent decades, cross section log earnings–experience profiles are not parallel across schooling groups. In addition, college tuition costs are nontrivial and are not offset by work in school for most college students. These factors account for some of the observed disparities between the after-tax interest rate and the steady-state Mincer coefficient.

One can view $\tilde{r}$ as a marginal internal rate of return to schooling after incorporating tuition costs, earnings increases, and changes in the retirement age. That is, $\tilde{r}$ is the discount rate that equates the net lifetime earnings for marginally different schooling levels at an optimum. As in the model of Mincer (1958), this internal rate of return should equal the interest rate in a world with perfect credit markets, once all costs and benefits from schooling are considered.

After allowing for taxes, tuition, variable length of working life, and a flexible relationship between earnings, schooling and experience, the coefficient on years of schooling in a log earnings regression need no longer equal the internal rate of return. However, it is still possible to calculate the internal rate of return using the observation that it is the discount rate that equates lifetime earnings streams for two different schooling levels.[24] Typically, internal rates of return are based on nonmarginal differences in schooling. Incorporating tuition (and psychic costs) and taxes, the internal rate of return for schooling level s_1 versus s_2, $r_I(s_1, s_2)$, solves (suppressing the argument of $r_I(s_1, s_2)$)

$$\int_0^{T(s_1)-s_1} (1-\tau)\,\mathrm{e}^{-r_I} Y(s_1, x)\,\mathrm{d}x - \int_0^{s_1} v\,\mathrm{e}^{-r_I z}\,\mathrm{d}z$$
$$= \int_0^{T(s_2)-s_2} (1-\tau)\,\mathrm{e}^{-r_I} Y(s_2, x)\,\mathrm{d}x - \int_0^{s_2} v\,\mathrm{e}^{-r_I z}\,\mathrm{d}z. \tag{5}$$

As with $\tilde{r}$ above, r_I will equal the Mincer coefficient on schooling under the assumptions of parallelism in experience across schooling categories (i.e., $Y(s, x) = \mu(s)\varphi(x)$), linearity of log earnings in schooling ($\mu(s) = \mu(0)\,\mathrm{e}^{\rho_s s}$), no tuition and psychic costs ($v = 0$), no taxes ($\tau = 0$), and equal work-lives irrespective of years of schooling ($T'(s) = 1$).[25] In the next section, we compare rate of return estimates based on specification (1) to those obtained by directly solving for r_I in Equation (5).

[24] Becker (1964) states this logic and Hanoch (1967) applies it.

[25] When tuition and psychic costs are negligible, proportional taxes on earnings will have no effect on estimated internal rates of return, because they reduce earnings at the same rate regardless of educational choices.

4.1. How alternative specifications of the Mincer equation and accounting for taxes and tuition affect estimates of the internal rate of return (IRR)

Using data for white and black men from 1940–1990 decennial Censuses, we examine how estimates of the internal rate of return change when different assumptions about the model are relaxed. Tables 3a and 3b report internal rates of return to schooling for each Census year and for a variety of pairwise schooling level comparisons for white and black men, respectively.[26] These estimates assume that workers spend 47 years working irrespective of their educational choice (i.e., a high school graduate works until age 65 and a college graduate until 69). To calculate each of the IRR estimates, we first estimate a log wage equation under the assumptions indicated in the tables. Then, we predict earnings under this specification for the first 47 years of experience, and the IRR is taken to be the root of Equation (5).[27] As a benchmark, the first row for each year reports the IRR estimate obtained from the Mincer specification for log wages (Equation (1)). The IRR could equivalently be obtained from a Mincer regression coefficient.[28]

Relative to the Mincer specification, row 2 relaxes the assumption of linearity in schooling by including indicator variables for each year of schooling. This modification alone leads to substantial differences in the estimated rate of return to schooling, especially for schooling levels associated with degree completion years (12 and 16) which have much larger returns than other schooling years. For example, the IRR to finishing high school is 30% for white men in 1970, while the rate of return to finishing 10 rather than 8 years of school is only 3%. In general, imposing linearity in schooling leads to upward biased estimates of the rate of return to grades that do not produce a degree, while it leads to downward biased estimates of the degree completion years (high school or college). Sheepskin effects are an important feature of the data.[29] There is a considerable body of evidence against linearity of log earnings in schooling. [See, e.g., Heckman, Layne-Farrar and Todd (1996), Jaeger and Page (1996), Hungerford and Solon (1987).] Row 3 relaxes both linearity in schooling and the quadratic specification for experience, which produces similar estimates. The assumption that earnings are quadratic in experience is empirically innocuous for estimating returns to schooling once linearity in years of schooling is relaxed.

Finally, row 4 relaxes all three Mincer functional form assumptions. Earnings functions are nonparametrically estimated as a function of experience, separately within

[26] As lower schooling levels are reported only in broader intervals in the 1990 Census, we can only compare 6 years against 10 years and cannot compare 6 years against 8 years or 8 against 10 years as we do for the earlier Census years. We assume the private cost to elementary and high school is zero in all the calculations.

[27] Strictly speaking, we solve for the root of the discrete time analog of Equation (5).

[28] They would be identical if our internal rate of return calculations were computed in continuous time. Because we use discrete time to calculate internal rates of return, $r_I = e^{\rho_s} - 1$, which is approximately equal to ρ_s when it is small.

[29] We use the term "sheepskin effects" to refer to exceptionally large rates of return at degree granting years of schooling. We cannot, however, distinguish in some years of the Census data which individuals receive a diploma among individuals reporting 12 or 16 years of completed schooling.

Table 3a
Internal rates of return for white men: earnings function assumptions (specifications assume work lives of 47 years)

	Schooling comparisons					
	6–8	8–10	10–12	12–14	12–16	14–16
1940						
Mincer specification	13	13	13	13	13	13
Relax linearity in S	16	14	15	10	15	21
Relax linearity in S & quad. in exp.	16	14	17	10	15	20
Relax lin. in S & parallelism	12	14	24	11	18	26
1950						
Mincer specification	11	11	11	11	11	11
Relax linearity in S	13	13	18	0	8	16
Relax linearity in S & quad. in exp.	14	12	16	3	8	14
Relax linearity in S & parallelism	26	28	28	3	8	19
1960						
Mincer specification	12	12	12	12	12	12
Relax linearity in S	9	7	22	6	13	21
Relax linearity in S & quad. in exp.	10	9	17	8	12	17
Relax linearity in S & parallelism	23	29	33	7	13	25
1970						
Mincer specification	13	13	13	13	13	13
Relax linearity in S	2	3	30	6	13	20
Relax linearity in S & quad. in exp.	5	7	20	10	13	17
Relax linearity in S & parallelism	17	29	33	7	13	24
1980						
Mincer specification	11	11	11	11	11	11
Relax linearity in S	3	−11	36	5	11	18
Relax linearity in S & quad. in exp.	4	−4	28	6	11	16
Relax linearity in S & parallelism	16	66	45	5	11	21
1990						
Mincer specification	14	14	14	14	14	14
Relax linearity in S	−7	−7	39	7	15	24
Relax linearity in S & quad. in exp.	−3	−3	30	10	15	20
Relax linearity in S & parallelism	20	20	50	10	16	26

Notes: Data taken from 1940–90 Decennial Censuses. In 1990, comparisons of 6 vs. 8 and 8 vs. 10 cannot be made given data restrictions. Therefore, those columns report calculations based on a comparison of 6 and 10 years of schooling. See Appendix B for data description.

each schooling class as shown in Figure 1. This procedure does not impose any assumption other than continuity on the earnings–experience relationship. Comparing these results with those of row three provides a measure of the bias induced by assuming separability of earnings in schooling and experience. In many cases, especially in recent

Table 3b
Internal rates of return for black men: earnings function assumptions (specifications assume work lives of 47 years)

	Schooling comparisons					
	6–8	8–10	10–12	12–14	12–16	14–16
1940						
Mincer specification	9	9	9	9	9	9
Relax linearity in S	18	7	5	3	11	18
Relax linearity in S & quad. in exp.	18	8	6	2	10	19
Relax linearity in S & parallelism	11	0	10	5	12	20
1950						
Mincer specification	10	10	10	10	10	10
Relax linearity in S	16	14	18	−2	4	9
Relax linearity in S & quad. in exp.	16	14	18	0	3	6
Relax linearity in S & parallelism	35	15	48	−3	6	34
1960						
Mincer specification	11	11	11	11	11	11
Relax linearity in S	13	12	18	5	8	11
Relax linearity in S & quad. in exp.	13	11	18	5	7	10
Relax linearity in S & parallelism	22	15	38	5	11	25
1970						
Mincer specification	12	12	12	12	12	12
Relax linearity in S	5	11	30	7	10	14
Relax linearity in S & quad. in exp.	6	11	24	10	11	12
Relax linearity in S & parallelism	15	27	44	9	14	23
1980						
Mincer specification	12	12	12	12	12	12
Relax linearity in S	−4	1	35	10	15	19
Relax linearity in S & quad. in exp.	−4	6	29	11	14	17
Relax linearity in S & parallelism	10	44	48	8	16	31
1990						
Mincer specification	16	16	16	16	16	16
Relax linearity in S	−5	−5	41	15	20	25
Relax linearity in S & quad. in exp.	−3	−3	35	17	19	22
Relax linearity in S & parallelism	16	16	58	18	25	35

Notes: Data taken from 1940–90 Decennial Censuses. In 1990, comparisons of 6 vs. 8 and 8 vs. 10 cannot be made given data restrictions. Therefore, those columns report calculations based on a comparison of 6 and 10 years of schooling. See Appendix B for data description.

decades, there are large differences. This finding is consistent with the results reported in Section 3, which show that earnings profiles in recent decades are no longer parallel in experience across schooling categories.

The general estimates in Tables 3a and b show a large increase in the return to completing high school for whites (Table 3a), which goes from 24% in 1940 to 50% in 1990, and even more dramatic increases for blacks (Table 3b). The estimates for 1990 seem implausible but are the rates of return that are implicit in recent Census- and CPS-based estimates. It is possible that these increases in rates of return over time partially reflect a selection effect, stemming from a decrease in the average quality of workers over time who drop out of high school. Given the limitations of Census and CPS data, we do not correct for censoring or selection bias in our analysis of these data.[30] Sections 7 and 8 consider estimation when schooling choices are endogenous.

Since 1950, there has been a sizeable increase over time in the marginal internal rate of return to attending and completing college, consistent with changes in demand favoring highly skilled workers. For most grade comparisons and years, the Mincer coefficient implies a lower return to schooling than do the nonparametric estimates, with an especially large disparity for the return to high school completion. For whites, the return to a 4-year college degree is similar under the Mincer and nonparametric models, but for blacks the Mincer coefficient substantially understates the return in recent decades. While the recent literature has focused on rising returns to college relative to high school, the increase in returns to completing high school appears to have been substantially greater.

A comparison of the IRR estimates based on the most flexible model for black males and white males shows that for all years except 1940, the return to high school completion is higher for black males, reaching a peak of 58% in 1990 (compared with 50% for whites in 1990). The internal rate of return to completing 16 years is also higher for blacks in most years (by about 10% in 1990).

Estimated internal rates of return differ depending on the set of assumptions imposed by the earnings model. Murphy and Welch (1990) note that allowing for quartic terms in experience is empirically important for fitting the earnings equation (the hedonic pricing equation), but do not report any effects of relaxing the quadratic-in-experience assumption on estimated marginal rates of return to schooling. We find that imposing the quadratic-in-experience assumption is fairly innocuous for computing rates of return. The assumptions of linearity in schooling and separability in schooling and experience are not. Comparing the unrestricted estimates in row 4 with the Mincer-based estimates in row 1 reveals substantial differences for nearly all grade progressions and all years. If imposing linearity and separability is innocuous, relaxing these conditions should not have such a dramatic effect on estimates of rates of return.

[30] Though, it is worth noting that the fraction of white men completing high school as measured by the Census is relatively stable after 1970. Among black men, high school graduation rates continued to increase until the early 1980s. Heckman, Lyons and Todd (2000), Chandra (2003) and Neal (2004) show the importance of selection adjustments in estimating wage functions, but there have been few adjustments of rates of return for selection. This important topic is neglected in the recent literature.

Table 4
Internal rates of return for white & black men: accounting for taxes and tuition (general nonparametric specification assuming work lives of 47 years)

		Schooling comparisons					
		Whites			Blacks		
		12–14	12–16	14–16	12–14	12–16	14–16
1940	No taxes or tuition	11	18	26	5	12	20
	Including tuition costs	9	15	21	4	10	16
	Including tuition & flat taxes	8	15	21	4	9	16
	Including tuition & prog. taxes	8	15	21	4	10	16
1950	No taxes or tuition	3	8	19	−3	6	34
	Including tuition costs	3	8	16	−3	5	25
	Including tuition & flat taxes	3	8	16	−3	5	24
	Including tuition & prog. taxes	3	7	15	−3	5	21
1960	No taxes or tuition	7	13	25	5	11	25
	Including tuition costs	6	11	21	5	9	18
	Including tuition & flat taxes	6	11	20	4	8	17
	Including tuition & prog. taxes	6	10	19	4	8	15
1970	No taxes or tuition	7	13	24	9	14	23
	Including tuition costs	6	12	20	7	12	18
	Including tuition & flat taxes	6	11	20	7	11	17
	Including tuition & prog. taxes	5	10	18	7	10	16
1980	No taxes or tuition	5	11	21	8	16	31
	Including tuition costs	4	10	18	7	13	24
	Including tuition & flat taxes	4	9	17	6	12	21
	Including tuition & prog. taxes	4	8	15	6	11	20
1990	No taxes or tuition	10	16	26	18	25	35
	Including tuition costs	9	14	20	14	18	25
	Including tuition & flat taxes	8	13	19	13	17	22
	Including tuition & prog. taxes	8	12	18	13	17	22

Notes: Data taken from 1940–90 Decennial Censuses. See discussion in text and Appendix B for a description of tuition and tax amounts.

Table 4 examines how the IRR estimates for post-secondary education change when we account for income taxes (both flat and progressive) and college tuition.[31] Below, in

[31] Because we assume that schooling is free (direct schooling costs are zero) through high school and because internal rates of return are independent of flat taxes when direct costs of schooling are zero, internal rates of return to primary and secondary school are identical across the first three specifications in the table. Empirically, taking into account progressive tax rates has little impact on the estimates for these school completion levels. (Tables are available upon request.) For these reasons, we only report in Table 4 the IRR estimates for comparisons of school completion levels 12 and 14, 12 and 16, and 14 and 16.

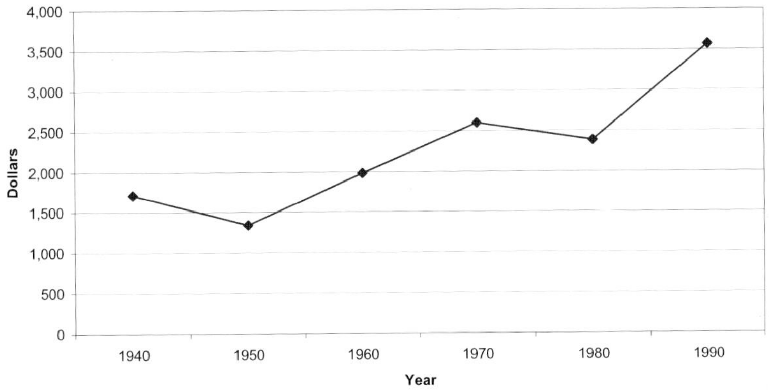

Figure 4a. Average college tuition paid (in 2000 dollars).

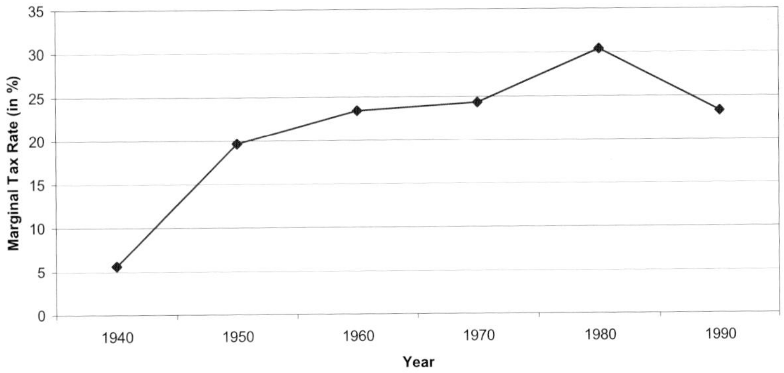

Figure 4b. Marginal tax rates [from Barro and Sahasakul (1983), Mulligan and Marion (2000)].

Section 10, we discuss the relevance of psychic costs. For ease of comparison, the first row for each year reports estimates of the IRR for the most flexible earnings specification, not accounting for tuition and taxes. (These estimates are identical to the fourth row in Tables 3a and 3b.) All other rows account for private tuition costs for college (v) assumed equal to the average college tuition paid in the U.S. that year. The average college tuition paid by students increased steadily since 1950 as shown in Figure 4a. In 1990, it stood at roughly \$3,500 (in 2000 dollars).[32] Row three of Table 4 accounts

[32] Average college tuition was computed by dividing the total tuition and fees revenue in the U.S. by total college enrollment that year. Federal and state support are not included in these figures. See Appendix B for further details on the time series we used for both tuition and taxes. We lack data on psychic costs, although the estimates from structural models suggests that they may be sizeable. See Carneiro, Hansen and Heckman (2003) and Cunha, Heckman and Navarro (2005).

for flat wage taxes using estimates of average marginal tax rates (τ) from Barro and Sahasakul (1983) and Mulligan and Marion (2000), which are plotted for each of the years in Figure 4b. Average marginal tax rates increased from a low of 5.6% in 1940 to a high of 30.4% in 1980 before falling to 23.3% in 1990. The final row of Table 4 accounts for the progressive nature of our tax system using federal income tax schedules (Form 1040) for single adults with no dependents and no unearned income. (See Appendix B for details.)

When costs of schooling alone are taken into account (comparing row 2 with row 1), the return to college generally falls by a few percentage points. Because the earnings of blacks are typically lower than for whites but tuition payments are assumed here to be the same, accounting for tuition costs has a bigger effect on the estimates for the black samples. For example, internal rates of return to the final two years of college decline by about one-fourth for whites and one-third for blacks. Further accounting for taxes on earnings (rows 3 and 4) has little additional impact on the estimates. Interestingly, the progressive nature of the tax system typically reduces rates of return by less than a percentage point. Overall, failure to account for tuition and taxes leads to an overstatement of the return to college, but the time trends in the return are fairly similar whether or not one adjusts for taxes and tuition. As discussed in Section 10, however, accounting for psychic costs has a substantial effect on estimated rates of return.

Figure 5 graphs the time trend in the IRR to high school completion for white and black males, comparing estimates based on (i) the Mincer model and (ii) the flexible nonparametric earnings model accounting for progressive taxes and tuition. Estimates based on the Mincer specification tend to understate returns to high school completion and also fail to capture the substantial rise in returns to schooling that has taken place

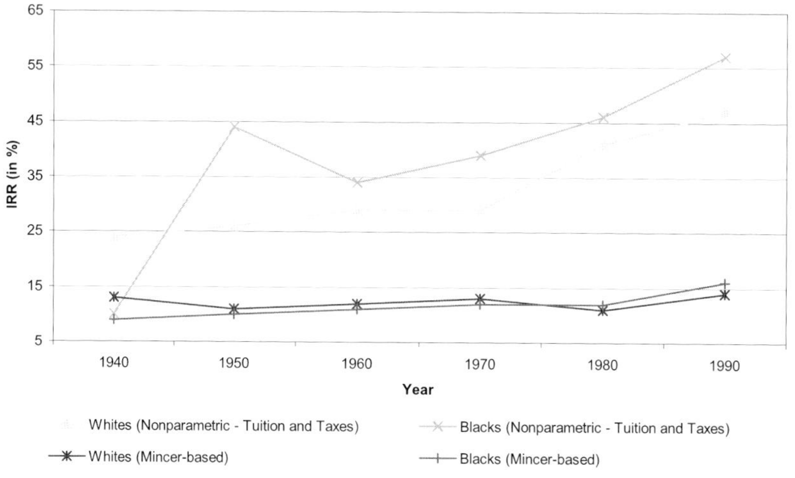

Figure 5. IRR for high school completion (white and black men).

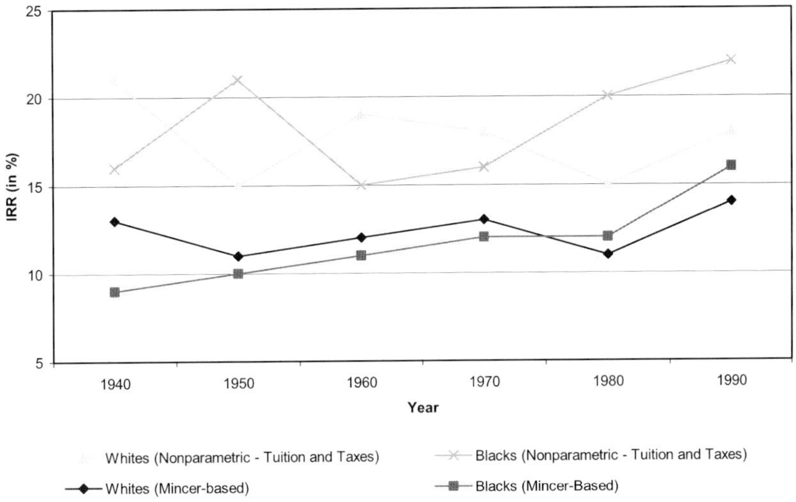

Figure 6. IRR for college completion (white and black men).

since 1970. Furthermore, the sizeable disparity in returns by race is not captured by the estimates based on the Mincer equation.

Figure 6 presents similar estimates for college completion (14 vs. 16 years of school). Again, the Mincer model yields much lower estimates of the IRR in comparison with the more flexible model that also takes into account taxes and tuition. Nonparametric estimates of the return to college completion are generally 5–10% higher than the corresponding Mincer-based estimates even after accounting for taxes and tuition. Additionally, the more general specification reveals a substantial decline in the IRR to college between 1950 and 1960 for blacks that is not reflected in the Mincer-based estimates.

Using our flexible earnings specification, we also examine how estimates depend on assumptions about the length of working life, comparing two extreme cases. The estimates just reported assume that individuals work for 47 years regardless of their schooling (i.e., $T'(s) = 1$). An alternative assumption posits that workers retire at age 65 regardless of their education (i.e., $T'(s) = 0$). We find virtually identical results for all years and schooling comparisons for both assumptions about the schooling – worklife relationship.[33] Because earnings at the end of the life cycle are heavily discounted, they have little impact on the total value of lifetime earnings and, therefore, have little effect on internal rate of return estimates.

[33] Results available from authors upon request.

4.2. Accounting for uncertainty in a static version of the model

To this point, we have computed internal rates of return using fitted values from estimated earnings equations. Mincer's approach and more general nonparametric approaches pursued in the literature make implicit assumptions about how individuals forecast their future earnings. The original formulations ignore uncertainty, making no distinction between *ex post* and *ex ante* returns. It is essential to know *ex ante* returns in order to understand schooling choices, because they are the returns on which individuals act.

In this subsection, we explore alternative approaches for estimating the IRR used by agents in making their schooling choices that are based on alternative assumptions about expectation formation mechanisms. These analyses are based on cross section data. We present a more general dynamic analysis in the next section.

As previously discussed, it is common in the literature to use log specifications for earnings. Thus, using a general notation, it is common to assume $\ln Y = Z\gamma + \varepsilon$, so $Y = \mathrm{e}^{Z\gamma}\mathrm{e}^{\varepsilon}$ and that expected earnings given Z are

$$E(Y|Z) = \mathrm{e}^{Z\gamma} E(\mathrm{e}^{\varepsilon}).$$

Assume for the sake of argument (but contrary to the evidence in Section 3) that Equation (1) describes the true earnings process and that $E(\varepsilon|x, s) = 0$. To this point, when we have fit Mincer equations, we have estimated internal rates of return using fitted values for Y in place of the true values. That is, we use the following estimate for earnings: $\widehat{Y}(s, x) = \exp(\hat{\alpha}_0 + \hat{\rho}_s s + \hat{\beta}_0 x + \hat{\beta}_1 x^2)$, where $\hat{\alpha}_0$, $\hat{\rho}_s$, $\hat{\beta}_0$, and $\hat{\beta}_1$ are the regression estimates. This procedure implicitly assumes that individuals place themselves at the mean of the log earnings distribution when forecasting their earnings and making their schooling choices.[34] Individuals take fitted log earnings profiles as predictions for their own future earnings, ignoring any potential person-specific deviations from that profile. Ignoring taxes, for this case, the IRR estimator $\hat{r}_I$ solves

$$\sum_{x=0}^{T} \frac{\widehat{Y}(s+j, x)}{(1+\hat{r}_I)^{s+j+x}} - \sum_{x=0}^{T} \frac{\widehat{Y}(s, x)}{(1+\hat{r}_I)^{s+x}} - v \sum_{x=1}^{j} \frac{1}{(1+\hat{r}_I)^{s+x}} = 0,$$

which is the discrete time analogue to the model of Equation (2) for two schooling levels s and $s + j$.[35] If tuition and psychic costs are negligible ($v = 0$),

$$\operatorname{plim} \hat{r}_I = \mathrm{e}^{\rho_s} - 1 \approx \rho_s.$$

Given our assumptions on expectations, this is an *ex ante* rate of return. *Ex ante* returns are the theoretically appropriate ones for studying schooling behavior, because they are the returns on which schooling decisions are based.

[34] Assuming a symmetric distribution for ε, this is equivalent to placing themselves at the median of the earnings distribution.

[35] We assume here that $T(s) - s = T$ for all s, or that $T'(s) = 1$.

Suppose instead that agents base their expectations of future earnings at different schooling levels on the mean earnings profiles for each schooling level, or on $E(Y|s, x)$. In this case, the estimator of the *ex ante* rate of return is given by the root of

$$\sum_{x=0}^{T} \frac{E(Y(s+j,x)|s,x)}{(1+\hat{r}_I)^{s+j+x}} - \sum_{x=0}^{T} \frac{E(Y(s,x)|s,x)}{(1+\hat{r}_I)^{s+x}} - \sum_{x=1}^{j} \frac{v}{(1+\hat{r}_I)^{s+x}} = 0. \tag{6}$$

If $v = 0$ and Mincer's assumptions hold, this formula specializes to

$$\frac{e^{\rho_s j}}{(1+\hat{r}_I)^j} \sum_{x=0}^{T} \frac{e^{\beta_0 x+\beta_1 x^2} E(e^{\varepsilon(s+j,x)}|s,x)}{(1+\hat{r}_I)^x} = \sum_{x=0}^{T} \frac{e^{\beta_0 x+\beta_1 x^2} E(e^{\varepsilon(s,x)}|s,x)}{(1+\hat{r}_I)^x}.$$

If $E[e^{\varepsilon(s,x)}|s,x] = E[e^{\varepsilon(s+j,x)}|s,x]$ for all x, then the two sums are equal and $\text{plim}\ \hat{r}_I = e^{\rho_s} - 1$ as before. In this special case, using $\widehat{Y}(s,x) = \exp(\hat{\alpha}_0 + \hat{\rho}_s s + \hat{\beta}_0 x + \hat{\beta}_1 x^2)$ or $E(Y(s,x)|s,x)$ will yield estimates of the internal rate of return that are asymptotically equivalent. However, if $E(e^{\varepsilon(s+j,x)}|s,x)$ is a more general function of s and x, then the estimators of the *ex ante* return will differ.

In the more general case, using estimates of $E(Y(s,x)|s,x)$ under a Mincer specification yields an estimated rate of return with a probability limit

$$\text{plim}\ \hat{r}_I = e^{\rho_s}\big[M(s,j)\big]^{1/j} - 1 \approx \rho_s + \frac{1}{j}\big(\ln M(s,j)\big),$$

where

$$M(s,j) = \frac{\sum_{x=0}^{T} e^{\beta_0 x+\beta_1 x^2} E(e^{\varepsilon(s+j,x)}|s,x)(1+r_I)^{-x}}{\sum_{x=0}^{T} e^{\beta_0 x+\beta_1 x^2} E(e^{\varepsilon(s,x)}|s,x)(1+r_I)^{-x}}. \tag{7}$$

This estimator of the *ex ante* internal rate of return will be larger than ρ_s if the variability in earnings is greater for more educated workers (i.e., $M(s,j) > 1$) and smaller if the variability is greater for less educated workers (i.e., $M(s,j) < 1$). If individuals use mean earnings at given schooling levels in forming expectations, then this estimator is more appropriate. However, this approach equates all variability across people with uncertainty, even though some aspects of variability across persons are predictable. We discuss how to decompose variability into predictable and unpredictable components in Section 10. Inspection of Figure 3 reveals that, at young ages, the variability in earnings for low education groups is the highest among all groups. If discounting dominates wage growth with experience, we would expect that $M(s,j) < 1$.[36]

These calculations assume that agents are forecasting the unknown $\varepsilon(s,x)$ using (s,x). If they also use another set of variables q, then the rate of return should be defined conditional on q ($\hat{r}_I = \hat{r}_I(q)$) and we would have to average over q to obtain

[36] More generally if $v \neq 0$, then $\hat{r}_I$ converges to the root of Equation (6). Neglecting this term leads to an upward bias, as previously discussed.

the average *ex ante* rate of return. If agents know $\varepsilon(s, x)$ at the time they make their schooling decisions, then the *ex ante* return and the *ex post* return are the same, and $\hat{r}_I$ now depends on the full vector of "shocks" confronting agents. Returns would then be averaged over the distribution of all "shocks" to calculate an expected return. Due to the nonlinearity of the equation used to calculate the internal rate of return, the rate of return based on an average earnings profile is not the same as the mean rate of return. Thus, mean *ex ante* and mean *ex post* internal rates of return are not the same.

When ρ_s varies in the population, these results must be further modified. Assume that ρ_s varies across individuals, that $E(\rho_s) = \bar{\rho}_s$, and that ρ_s is independent of x and $\varepsilon(s + j, x)$ for all x, j. Also, assume $v = 0$ for expositional purposes (no tuition or psychic costs). Using fitted earnings, $\hat{w}(s, x)$, to calculate internal rates of return yields an estimator, $\hat{r}_I$, that satisfies

$$\operatorname{plim} \hat{r}_I = e^{\bar{\rho}_s} - 1 \approx \bar{\rho}_s.$$

This estimator calculates the *ex ante* internal rate of return for someone with the mean increase in annual log earnings $\rho_s = \bar{\rho}_s$ and with the mean deviation from the overall average $\varepsilon(s, x) = \varepsilon(s + j, x) = 0$ for all x.

On the other hand, assuming agents cannot forecast ρ_s, using estimates of mean earnings $E(Y(s, x)|s, x)$ will yield an estimator for r with

$$\operatorname{plim} \hat{r}_I = e^{\bar{\rho}_s}\big[kM(s, j)\big]^{1/j} - 1 \approx \bar{\rho}_s + \frac{1}{j}\big[\ln k + \ln M(s, j)\big],$$

where $k = \frac{E(e^{(s+j)(\rho_s - \bar{\rho}_s)}|s,x)}{E(e^{s(\rho_s - \bar{\rho}_s)}|s,x)}$ and $M(s, j)$ is defined in Equation (7).

For $\bar{\rho}_s > 0$, it is straightforward to show that $k > 1$, which implies that everything else the same, the estimator, $\hat{r}_I$, based on mean earnings will be larger when there is variation in the return to schooling than when there is not. Furthermore, the internal rate of return is larger for someone with the mean earnings profile than it is for an individual with the mean value of ρ_s. Again, if agents know ρ_s, we should compute $\hat{r}_I$ conditioning on ρ_s and construct the mean rate of return from the average of those $\hat{r}_I$. Again, the mean *ex post* and *ex ante* rates of return are certain to differ unless agents have perfect foresight.

Table 5 reports estimates of the *ex ante* IRR based on our general nonparametric specification. We compute the IRR under two alternative assumptions: (i) that agents forecast future earnings using the earnings function that sets $\varepsilon = 0$ ("unadjusted earnings") and (ii) that agents forecast using mean earnings within each education and experience category rather than using predicted earnings placing themselves at $\varepsilon = 0$ ("adjusted earnings"). Procedure (ii) is described in Equation (6). Procedure (i) sets $E(e^{\varepsilon(s,x)}|s, x) = 1$ for all s, x. Both the adjusted and unadjusted estimates account for tuition and progressive taxes. The adjusted estimates generate much lower (and more reasonable) IRR estimates than the unadjusted ones.[37]

[37] We lack the required panel data on individuals to compute *ex post* rates of return. See the discussion in Section 10.

Table 5
Internal rates of return for white & black men: residual adjustment (general nonparametric specification accounting for tuition and progressive taxes)

			Schooling comparisons					
			6–8	8–10	10–12	12–14	12–16	14–16
a. Whites								
	1940	Unadjusted	12	14	24	8	15	21
		Adjusted	2	2	8	9	13	16
	1950	Unadjusted	25	26	26	3	7	15
		Adjusted	17	19	14	5	8	14
	1960	Unadjusted	21	27	29	6	10	19
		Adjusted	13	19	16	7	11	16
	1970	Unadjusted	16	27	29	5	10	18
		Adjusted	11	18	16	6	10	16
	1980	Unadjusted	14	64	41	4	8	15
		Adjusted	9	28	24	5	8	13
	1990	Unadjusted	19	19	47	8	12	18
		Adjusted	11	11	31	8	12	17
b. Blacks								
	1940	Unadjusted	11	0	10	4	10	16
		Adjusted	3	0	−8	4	6	7
	1950	Unadjusted	33	14	44	−3	5	21
		Adjusted	53	8	21	1	9	15
	1960	Unadjusted	20	14	34	4	8	15
		Adjusted	14	12	16	6	6	8
	1970	Unadjusted	14	25	39	7	10	16
		Adjusted	12	16	22	7	10	12
	1980	Unadjusted	9	43	46	6	11	20
		Adjusted	7	21	29	6	9	15
	1990	Unadjusted	16	16	57	13	17	22
		Adjusted	8	8	42	11	15	20

Notes: Data taken from 1940–90 Decennial Censuses. In 1990, comparisons of 6 vs. 8 and 8 vs. 10 cannot be made given data restrictions. Therefore, those columns report calculations based on a comparison of 6 and 10 years of schooling. See discussion in text and Appendix B for a description of tuition and tax amounts. Unadjusted sets the residual from the earnings equation to be the same for everyone (= 0). Adjusted uses mean earnings within each age-schooling cell.

Using mean earnings rather than earnings for someone with the mean residual generally leads to lower estimated *ex ante* internal rates of return for most schooling comparisons. Even if the Mincer specification for log earnings is correct, the internal rate of return guiding individual decisions is lower than the Mincer estimated rate of return when individuals base their schooling decisions on average earnings levels within schooling and experience categories. In other words, predicted earnings obtained using the coefficients from a log earnings regression evaluated where $\varepsilon = 0$ is an inaccurate measure of the average earnings within each schooling and experience category.

The adjustment for uncertainty reported in this section based on mean earnings makes the strong assumption that all variation is unforecastable at the time schooling decisions are made. A better approach is to extract components of variation that are forecastable at the time schooling decisions are being made (heterogeneity) from components that are unforecastable (true uncertainty). Only the latter components should be used to compute $M(s, j)$. Methods for separating forecastable heterogeneity from uncertainty are available [Carneiro, Hansen and Heckman (2003), Cunha, Heckman and Navarro (2005), Heckman and Navarro (2006)] but require panel data and cannot be applied to Census cross-sections. We review the evidence from the panel literature in Section 10.

Another major issue about the entire enterprise of calculating rates of return is whether the marginal rate of return is an economically interesting concept when agents are sequentially revising their information about returns to schooling. As shown in the next section, in general it is not. This casts doubt on the policy relevance of the entire rate of return literature, that was initially motivated by Becker (1964), and suggests that the literature should be refocused to account for intrinsic uncertainty.

5. The internal rate of return and the sequential resolution of uncertainty

Human capital theory was developed in an era before the tools of dynamic decision making under uncertainty were fully developed. Concepts central to human capital theory like the internal rate of return are not generally appropriate to the evaluation of investment programs under sequential resolution of uncertainty. The recent literature has made progress towards empirical analysis of schooling decisions in dynamic settings.[38] Our analysis of this issue in this section is mainly theoretical and aimed at clarifying a number of important features of dynamic schooling decisions under uncertainty. We discuss other dynamic models with option values developed in the recent dynamic literature in Section 10.[39]

This section makes three main points. First, ignoring the sequential revelation of information, Mincer's assumption of the linearity of log earnings in years of schooling rules out option values that can arise even in an environment where the agent perfectly anticipates future earnings. We show how nonlinearity is a source of option values, and accounting for option values affects estimated returns to schooling. Second, sequential revelation of information is an additional source of option values. Accounting for information updating is a force toward generating a *downward* bias in least squares estimates of returns to schooling. Intuitively, people drop out of school when they have good draws, leaving only the unlucky to continue on in their schooling. This result runs counter to the intuition often expressed in the conventional ability bias literature that

[38] See Keane and Wolpin (1997), Belzil and Hansen (2002), Cunha, Heckman and Navarro (2005) and Heckman and Navarro (2006) for such models.

[39] See Heckman and Navarro (2006).

the most able continue on to school. [For a survey of the conventional literature see, e.g., Griliches (1977).] Third, we show that the internal rate of return is not a correct investment criterion when earnings are uncertain and there are option values.

For two reasons, the dynamic nature of schooling suggests that the returns to education may include an option value. First, the return to one year of school may include the potential for larger returns associated with higher levels of education when the returns to school are not constant across all schooling levels. For example, finishing high school provides access to college, and attending college is a necessary first step for obtaining a college degree. Given the large increase in earnings associated with college completion, the total return to high school or college attendance includes the potential for even greater returns associated with finishing college. The return in excess of the direct return (the lifetime income received at a given schooling level) is the option value. Mincer's assumption that earnings are log linear in schooling implicitly rules out this type of option value if the growth rate in earnings is the same as the interest rate. The traditional approach to schooling computes the rate of return using the lifetime income arising from stopping at schooling level s with the lifetime income from stopping at $s + 1$ using the direct return, i.e., the return of stopping at s versus the return from stopping at $s + 1$, and does not consider the continuation value.

Second, when there is uncertainty about college costs or future earnings and when each additional year of schooling reveals new information about those costs or earnings, the full returns to schooling will include the expected value of newly revealed information that can be acted on. Finishing high school opens the possibility of attending college, which will be realized if tuition costs and opportunity costs turn out to be low. Therefore, the returns to high school completion include both the increase in earnings associated with completing high school and the *ex ante* expected value of continuing beyond high school, including the expected value of all future information, including information about wage shocks, costs of additional schooling, ability in various tasks and the like. The value of this information depends on the probability that the individual decides to continue on to college and the expected return if he does so. Failing to finish high school precludes an individual from learning the information that arises from high school completion as well as the value of exercising the option to go to college. Dropping out eliminates the college option. Earnings each period may also be uncertain. The decision to continue on in school will depend on both current and expected future labor market conditions. By ignoring uncertainty, the literature based on the Mincer earnings equation neglects this source of option values. Sequential arrival of information implies that education decisions are made sequentially and should not be treated as a static discrete choice problem made once in a lifetime by individuals – the traditional approach used in human capital theory [see, e.g., Mincer (1958), Willis and Rosen (1979), Willis (1986), Card (2001)].

The empirical evidence presented in Section 3 [see also Bound, Jaeger and Baker (1995), Heckman, Layne-Farrar and Todd (1996), Hungerford and Solon (1987)] strongly rejects Mincer's (1958) implicit assumption that marginal internal rates of return to each year of schooling are identical and equal to a common interest rate, i.e., the assumption that log earnings are linear in years of schooling. This observation alone undermines the interpretation of the coefficient on schooling in a log earnings regression as a rate of return. But this nonlinearity, combined with the sequential resolution of uncertainty, creates additional problems for estimating rates of returns using Mincer regressions. Because the returns to college completion are high, it may be worthwhile to finish high school to keep open the option of attending college. The total return to high school and earlier schooling choices includes a nontrivial option value.

To analyze this option value, we present two simple dynamic models with uncertainty about the value of future schooling choices. Following most of the literature, we assume that individuals maximize the expected value of lifetime earnings given their current education level and the available information. We briefly discuss more general dynamic models with option values in Section 10.

To gain some understanding about the separate roles of nonlinearity and uncertainty in generating option values, we first consider the option value framework of Comay, Melnik and Pollatschek (1973), which assumes that there is no uncertainty about earnings conditional on final schooling attainment but that individuals face an exogenously specified probability ($\pi_{s+1,s}$) of being accepted into grade $s+1$ if they choose to apply after finishing grade s.[40] Thus they face a lottery where the chance of being admitted to the next round of schooling does not depend on earnings. For someone attending exactly s years of school, define the discounted present value of lifetime earnings as of the schooling completion date as:

$$Y_s = \sum_{x=0}^{T} (1+r)^{-x} Y(s, x),$$

where the interest rate, r, is assumed to be exogenously specified and common across persons. This expression is assumed to be known with certainty. If an individual who chooses to apply for grade $s + 1$ is rejected, he or she begins working immediately, earning Y_s. This is the direct value of schooling as conventionally measured. In this environment, the total expected value of attaining $s \in \{1, 2, \ldots, \bar{S}\}$ years of school, given the information available at the end of stage $s - 1$, is

$$E_{s-1}(V_s) = (1 - \pi_{s+1,s})Y_s + \pi_{s+1,s} E_{s-1} \max\left\{Y_s, \frac{E_s(V_{s+1})}{1+r}\right\}$$

for $s < \bar{S}$ and $E_{\bar{S}-1}(V_{\bar{S}}) = Y_{\bar{S}}$. This expression assumes that each grade of school takes one period and that direct costs of schooling are negligible.

The *ex ante* option value of grade s as perceived at the end of $s - 1$ is defined as the difference between the total expected value of that opportunity, $E_{s-1}(V_s)$, and the direct value or the present discounted value of earnings if the person does not continue

[40] They also analyze models with positive probability of failing conditional on attending the next grade. The results from such an analysis are quite similar to those discussed here.

in school, Y_s:

$$\begin{aligned} O_{s,s-1} &= E_{s-1}[V_s - Y_s] \\ &= E_{s-1}\max\left\{0, \pi_{s+1,s}\left(\frac{E_s(V_{s+1})}{1+r} - Y_s\right)\right\} \\ &= \max\left\{0, \pi_{s+1,s}\left(\frac{E_{s-1}(V_{s+1})}{1+r} - Y_s\right)\right\}, \end{aligned}$$

where the final equality follows from the assumption that there is no uncertainty about earnings conditional on the final schooling outcome. Notice that if the growth rate of earnings is the same as the interest rate, as is assumed by Mincer (1958), or if the growth in earnings with schooling is at the same rate as the individual-specific interest rate in the accounting identity model, then $Y_s = \frac{Y_{s+1}}{1+r}$ for each individual and all s. Under this assumption, Mincer's assumption of linearity of log earnings in schooling implicitly rules out any option value of schooling.[41] Intuitively, if the earnings profiles associated with all schooling choices provide the same present value when discounted back to the same date, then there is no value attached to the possibility of continuation of schooling. Thus, linearity of log wages in years of schooling with a growth rate equal to the interest rate implies no option value of education in the Comay, Melnik and Pollatschek (1973) framework.

This model generates option values when future wage growth is greater than $1+r$ for an additional year of schooling. For example, if college graduation offers large returns, finishing high school will carry an option value since there is some probability that an individual will be accepted into college. In this case, the total value of a high school degree includes the value of a lottery ticket that pays the rewards of a college degree to 'winners'. The option value of high school represents the value of this lottery ticket scaled by the probability that the option will arise. Notice that even if the probability of being accepted to college is one ($\pi_{s+1,s} = 1$), if s corresponds to the state of high

[41] PROOF. $V_{\bar{S}} = Y_{\bar{S}}$ at $\bar{S}$, so

$$E_{\bar{S}-2}(V_{\bar{S}-1}) = (1 - \pi_{\bar{S},\bar{S}-1})Y_{\bar{S}-1} + \pi_{\bar{S},\bar{S}-1}\max\left\{Y_{\bar{S}-1}, \frac{Y_{\bar{S}}}{1+r}\right\},$$

since there is no uncertainty about earnings conditional on each schooling level. For proportional earnings growth at rate r, both versions of the Mincer model imply that $Y_s = \frac{1}{1+r}Y_{s+1}$ for all s. Thus, people may differ in their earnings levels and face different individual specific interest rates as in the accounting identity model. They may also face different $\pi_{s+1,s}$. For any sequence of $\pi_{s+1,s}$ and r, we obtain

$$E_{\bar{S}-2}(V_{\bar{S}-1}) = Y_{\bar{S}-1} = \frac{Y_{\bar{S}}}{1+r}.$$

Backward induction produces $E_{s-2}(V_{s-1}) = Y_{s-1} = \frac{Y_s}{1+r}$ for all s, which implies no option value for any schooling level.

school graduation, there is an option value. Thus even in a certain environment, because of the staged nature of the schooling process, option values may arise.[42]

The Comay, Melnik and Pollatschek (1973) model assumes that the probability of transiting to higher grades is exogenously determined by a lottery. Because there is no uncertainty about future earnings paths conditional on schooling or about the future costs, their model isolates the role played by a nonlinear log earnings–schooling relationship in determining option values.

We now consider an economically more interesting model of the schooling choice problem that incorporates uncertainty in future earnings (or school costs) and sheds light on the impact of that uncertainty on the option value of education. This model motivates recent work in the economics of education by Keane and Wolpin (1997), Belzil and Hansen (2002) and Heckman and Navarro (2006). Suppose that there is uncertainty about net earnings conditional on s, so that actual lifetime earnings for someone with s years of school are

$$Y_s = \left[\sum_{x=0}^{T}(1+r)^{-x}Y(s,x)\right]\varepsilon_s.$$

This form of uncertainty is a one time, schooling-specific shock. The literature discussed in Section 10 considers more general models with age or period-specific shocks, but we start with this simple set up to motivate ideas. We assume that $E_{s-1}(\varepsilon_s) = 1$ and define expected earnings associated with schooling s conditional on current schooling $s-1$,

$$\bar{Y}_s = E_{s-1}(Y_s).$$

The disturbance, ε_s, may represent a shock to additional schooling costs or to current earnings that is revealed after the decision to attend grade s is made at the end of $s-1$ but prior to any future schooling decisions. Individuals with s years of schooling must decide whether to quit school and receive lifetime earnings of Y_s, or continue on in school for an additional year and receive an expected lifetime earnings of $E_s(V_{s+1})$.

The decision problem for a person with s years of schooling given the sequential revelation of information is to complete another year of schooling if

$$Y_s \leqslant \frac{E_s(V_{s+1})}{1+r},$$

so the value of schooling level s, V_s, is

$$V_s = \max\left\{Y_s, \frac{E_s(V_{s+1})}{1+r}\right\}$$

[42] An influential book by Dixit and Pindyck (1994) defines option values as arising only in an environment of uncertainty. This definition is too restrictive. Options include any extra choices created by completing one stage of schooling beyond stopping and earning at that stage.

for $s < \bar{S}$. At the maximum schooling level, $\bar{S}$, after all information is revealed, we obtain $V_{\bar{S}} = Y_{\bar{S}} = \bar{Y}_{\bar{S}}\varepsilon_{\bar{S}}$.

The endogenously determined probability of going on from school level s to $s+1$ is

$$p_{s+1,s} = \Pr\left(\varepsilon_s \leqslant \frac{E_s(V_{s+1})}{(1+r)\bar{Y}_s}\right),$$

where $E_s(V_{s+1})$ may depend on ε_s because it enters the agent's information set. The average earnings of a person who stops at schooling level s are

$$\bar{Y}_s E_{s-1}\left(\varepsilon_s \,|\, \varepsilon_s > \frac{E_s(V_{s+1})}{(1+r)\bar{Y}_s}\right). \tag{8}$$

Thus, the expected value of schooling level s as perceived at current schooling $s-1$ is:

$$E_{s-1}(V_s) = (1 - p_{s+1,s})\bar{Y}_s E_{s-1}\left(\varepsilon_s \,|\, \varepsilon_s > \frac{E_s(V_{s+1})}{(1+r)\bar{Y}_s}\right) + p_{s+1,s}\left(\frac{E_{s-1}(V_{s+1})}{1+r}\right).$$

The first component is the direct return. The second component arises from the option to go on to higher levels of schooling.

Assuming that schooling choices are irreversible, the *option value* of schooling s, as perceived after completing $s-1$ levels of schooling given that the agent has the information about all of the shocks ε_{s-j}, $j \geqslant 1$, is the difference between the expected value of the earnings associated with termination at schooling level s and the corresponding value function:

$$O_{s,s-1} = E_{s-1}[V_s - Y_s].$$

These option values can be defined for all s. Option values are non-negative for all schooling levels, since $V_s \geqslant Y_s$ for all s. The option value for the highest schooling level is zero, since there is no tomorrow and $V_{\bar{S}} = Y_{\bar{S}}$ although in reality even final schooling opens up other choices beyond schooling.

The *ex ante* rate of return to schooling s as perceived at the end of stage $s-1$, before the information is revealed, is

$$R_{s,s-1} = \frac{E_{s-1}(V_s) - Y_{s-1}}{Y_{s-1}}. \tag{9}$$

This expression assumes no direct costs of schooling. If there are up-front direct costs of schooling, C_{s-1}, to advance beyond level $s-1$, the *ex ante* return is

$$\widetilde{R}_{s,s-1} = \frac{E_{s-1}(V_s) - (Y_{s-1} + C_{s-1})}{Y_{s-1} + C_{s-1}}.$$

This expression assumes that tuition or direct costs are incurred up front and that returns are revealed one period later.

$\widetilde{R}_{s,s-1}$ is an appropriate *ex ante* rate of return concept because if

$$Y_{s-1} + C_{s-1} \leqslant \frac{E_{s-1}(V_s)}{1+r}, \tag{10}$$

i.e.,

$$r \leqslant \frac{E_{s-1}(V_s) - (Y_{s-1} + C_{s-1})}{Y_{s-1} + C_{s-1}} = \widetilde{R}_{s,s-1},$$

then it would be optimal to advance one more year of schooling (from $s - 1$ to s) given the assumed certain return on physical capital r. The *ex post* return as of period s is

$$\frac{V_s - (Y_{s-1} + C_{s-1})}{Y_{s-1} + C_{s-1}}.$$

The distinction between *ex ante* and *ex post* returns to schooling is an important one that is not made in the conventional literature on "returns to schooling" surveyed in Willis (1986) or Katz and Autor (1999). In Section 10, we survey a literature that demonstrates that uncertainty is an empirically important feature of lifetime earnings. Hence, option values play an important role in computing the theoretically motivated *ex ante* return.[43]

This analysis highlights the sequential nature of the schooling choice problem under uncertainty. The schooling allocations that arise out of this framework differ from those implied by the standard Mincer approach, which uses a static decision rule based on expected earnings profiles as of some initial period. The sequential approach recognizes that individuals face uncertainty at the time they make their schooling decisions and that some of that uncertainty is resolved after each schooling decision is made. After completing a schooling level, individuals observe the shock associated with that level and can base their decision to continue in school on its realization. This, along with any nonlinearity in the reward function, can create an option value of attending school. If the shock at stage s is bad, one can always continue to the next higher schooling level, $s + 1$.

It is interesting to note that even when $\overline{Y}_s = \frac{\overline{Y}_{s+1}}{1+r}$ as assumed by Mincer's models, there is still an option value in this framework. This is so because after completing s, new information about the actual returns associated with that choice offers the option of continuing on to level $s + 1$ with fresh draws of the ε. This is in contrast to the role of uncertainty in the simple Comay, Melnik and Pollatschek (1973) model. More generally, when future earnings choices (Y_{s+1} vs. Y_s in this example) offer very large expected returns, the option value might be quite substantial – both sources of option values are at work.

Conventional rate of return calculations for comparing the "returns" to schooling levels s and $s + 1$ base the calculation only on the direct or terminal earnings streams associated with s and $s + 1$. Taking into account the option value also requires consideration of the earnings stream associated with higher schooling levels. That is, the value of graduating from high school instead of dropping out is affected by the expected earnings associated with graduating from college.

[43] Our definition of the *ex post* return is a bit ambiguous because at different stages after $s - 1$, information about V_s (which is defined over streams of future earnings at different stages of schooling) is revealed. We use V_s as the full information, end of life version when all information is in.

Keane and Wolpin (1997) develop sequential models of schooling. Although not the focus of their analysis, option values can be derived from the estimated value functions associated with different schooling levels.[44] Heckman and Navarro (2006) present a more general approach to information revelation by allowing for serially correlated unobservables. They also establish semiparametric identification of their model. We briefly discuss their work in Section 10.

To illustrate the role of uncertainty and nonlinearity of log earnings in terms of schooling, we simulate a five schooling-level version of our model with uncertainty. Results are reported in Tables 6a and 6b. In both tables, we assume an interest rate of $r = 0.1$ and further assume that ε_s is independent and identically distributed log-normal: $\log(\varepsilon_s) \sim N(0, \sigma)$ for all s.[45] We assume that $\sigma = 0.1$ in the results presented in the tables. Table 6a reports various outcomes related to the returns to schooling when we assume log earnings are linear in years of schooling (i.e., $\overline{Y}_{s-1} = \overline{Y}_s/(1+r)$). Schooling continuation probabilities ($p_{s,s-1}$) and the proportional increase in $\overline{Y}$ associated with an increase in schooling from $s - 1$ to s are shown. By assumption, the latter is equal to $r = 0.1$ for all education levels. Column 4 displays the proportional increases in observed earnings (where observed earnings are measured by Equation (8)) from period $s - 1$ to s, which are always less than r. In the presence of uncertainty, self-selection leads to a substantial *downward* bias in the observed returns to schooling, especially for the schooling transitions associated with higher grades. The traditional ability bias model discussed below in Section 8 predicts an *upward* bias in *OLS* estimates of the return to schooling. In a sequential model with serially independent shocks, people with a good draw at lower schooling levels drop out, thus producing a downward bias.[46]

Option values as a fraction of the total expected value of a schooling level ($O_{s,s-1}/E_{s-1}(V_s)$) are reported in column 5. They show a pattern of decline with schooling levels attained. The final three columns report average measures of the return to schooling for different sets of individuals. Column 6 reports the average return for

[44] In the ordered choice models in Cameron and Heckman (1998) and Cunha, Heckman and Navarro (2007), there is no option value arising from sequential resolution of uncertainty, because of the assumed one sided nature of the information revelation process.

[45] We also considered models with an AR(1) process for the shocks: $\log(\varepsilon_s) = \rho \log(\varepsilon_{s-1}) + v_s$ where $v_s \sim N(0, \sigma)$ but for the sake of brevity we do not report them. The case where $\rho = 0$ corresponds to Tables 6a and 6b. For $\rho = 1$, $E(\varepsilon_{s+1}|\varepsilon_s) = \varepsilon_s$ and a good or bad shock affects expected future outcomes in the same proportion as current outcomes. In this model, the outcome of ε_s has no effect on schooling decisions. In the linear case corresponding to Table 6a, expected rates of return as measured by $E_{s-1}(R_{s,s-1})$ range between those reported in the table (when ρ is zero) and the linear increase in earnings, $r = 0.10$ (when ρ is near one). Expected returns for the more general nonlinear case differ little from those shown in Table 6b, since nearly everyone chooses to attend the highest level of schooling regardless of the value for ρ. This implies that returns always reflect the expected increase in earnings between the current schooling level and the highest possible schooling level, which is, on average, independent of ρ.

[46] Note that our model is highly simplified. A more general model would analyze the lifecycle evolution of wages age by age.

the entire population ($E_{s-1}[R_{s,s-1}]$), while column 7 reports estimates of the return for those who choose to continue on to grade s ("treatment on the treated") and column 8 reports the expected return that would be received by those who choose not to continue in school ("treatment on the untreated"). Here the treatment is schooling at the stated level. Comparing average returns with the proportional increase in $\bar{Y}$ with schooling or in observed earnings with schooling, observe that total rates of return to schooling are substantially higher for all but the final schooling transition due to the additional effect of the option value of school and the self-selection that takes place. When log earnings are linear in schooling, true returns are actually declining in accumulated schooling since option values are decreasing in s.[47] Returns for those who choose to continue in school are noticeably larger than average returns, while returns for those who choose not to continue are all less than r. The least squares estimate of the rate of return to school (i.e., the coefficient on schooling in a log earnings regression or the "Mincer coefficient") is only 0.063, far below the estimates of the true average growth rate (*ATE*) or treatment on the treated (*TT*), the growth rate among the treated. It also under-estimates the rate of increase in expected earnings, $\bar{Y}_s$, and does not accurately reflect the pricing relationship for wages and schooling. Even under linearity of mean log earnings in schooling, Mincer-based estimates of the return are substantially downward biased in the presence of sequential resolution of uncertainty. Not surprisingly, this bias (along with option values) disappears as the variance of ε_s goes to zero. However, we find a bias as large as -0.01, roughly 10% of the true return, when σ is as low as 0.01.[48]

Table 6b adds nonlinearity in the wage equation in terms of schooling to the base model to demonstrate its added effect on rates of return and option values. The simulation reported in this table assumes that increases in population mean log earnings from the first to the second and third to fourth levels of school are both 0.1, but the increase associated with going from level two to three is 0.3 and from four to five is 0.2. This roughly mimics the patterns observed in the later Census years with schooling levels three and five representing high school and college graduation, respectively. These simulations show substantially larger returns to the lower school transitions as a result of the sizeable sheepskin effects in later years. Option values are particularly large in early schooling years. In general, the greater the nonlinearity, the greater the option value. Estimates from a Mincer regression suggest a rate of return of only 0.060, substantially less than the true average growth rate or the treatment on the treated growth rate estimates, which range from 0.21 to 0.46. While true returns increase relative to those reported in Table 6a, the Mincer estimate actually declines slightly. Because most individuals are choosing to continue to higher schooling levels in this simulation, there

[47] We have assumed that individuals cannot choose to recall the wage streams associated with earlier schooling choices (i.e., someone with s years of school cannot choose to work at a lower schooling level and obtain Y_{s-1} or $Y_{s-2}, \ldots$) if they receive a low realization for Y_s. Allowing people to have access to all of the earnings opportunities created at all earlier schooling levels provides a force offsetting the tendency for option values to decline with schooling. These opportunities provide the agent with a form of insurance.

[48] Results available from the authors upon request.

is little difference between "average returns" and estimated treatment on the treated parameters.

The simulations presented in Tables 6a and 6b point to the potentially important role of both sources of option values in determining total returns to schooling. Turning to real data, we use the nonparametrically estimated earnings profiles for white males in the 1990 Census to compute the option value of high school completion and college attendance for a range of reasonable schooling transition probabilities, p, and interest rates, r. These estimates are unbiased measures of the option value within the framework of Comay, Melnik and Pollatschek (1973) where $p_{s+1,s} = \pi_{s+1,s}$ are the empirical transition probabilities for the schooling levels we examine because selection is random with respect to individual earnings levels. For a model of sequential resolution of uncertainty, where $p_{s+1,s}$ is $\Pr(\varepsilon_s \leqslant \frac{E_s(V_{s+1})}{(1+r)\overline{Y}_s})$ and ε_s is in the information set used to define E_s, they under-estimate the option value and return to schooling, since observed earnings are $\overline{Y}_s E_{s-1}(\varepsilon_s | \varepsilon_s > \frac{E_s(V_{s+1})}{(1+r)\overline{Y}_s})$ rather than $\overline{Y}_s$ (i.e., observed earnings are based on a sample selecting not to continue). Table 7 reports the average discounted lifetime earnings for individuals making different schooling choices, denoted by $\widehat{Y}_s$. It also reports the total expected value of a schooling choice, $E_{s-1}(V_s)$, the implied option value, $\widehat{O}_{s,s-1}$, and return to schooling, $R_{s,s-1}$. The table reports estimates based on interest rates of 7% and 10% and transition probabilities ranging from 0.1 to 0.5 (empirically, about half of all 1990 high school graduates attended college and about half of those went on to graduate). As expected, both the present value of earnings for each schooling choice and the option value of continuing are declining in the interest rate. Option values rise with increases in the transition probability. The option value for high school completion ranges from a low of only \$370 when the interest rate is 10% and $p = 0.1$ to a high of \$22,000 when interest rates are 7% and $p = 0.5$. The major component of this option value comes from the return to completing college rather than the return to attending college, because the difference in earnings between high school graduates and those with some college is quite small. Accordingly, option values are noticeably higher for college attendance, reaching a high of \$35,000 when the interest rate is 7% and $p = 0.5$. Simply comparing the earnings streams for two schooling levels fails to recognize a potentially important component of the returns to education. Rates of return, shown in the final two columns, increase by about 50% for college attendance when the transition probability is raised from 0.1 to 0.5. Returns to high school completion are less sensitive to assumptions about p and the option values. Failing to consider option values leads to biased estimates of the true return to schooling.

We conclude this section by considering whether the internal rate of return has any relevance in a model with sequential updating of information or in a model with a lottery structure, like the framework of Comay, Melnik and Pollatschek (1973). Investment criterion (10) based on (9) is the appropriate criterion for *ex ante* calculations. *Ex post*

Table 7
Present value of earnings, option values, and return to schooling (white men, 1990 Census)

Interest rate	Transition probability	PV lifetime earnings (in \$1000's)			Option value (in \$1000's)		Total value (in \$1000's)		Return to schooling	
r	p	$\widehat{Y}_{12}$	$\widehat{Y}_{14}$	$\widehat{Y}_{16}$	$\widehat{O}_{12,10}$	$\widehat{O}_{14,12}$	$E(V_{12})$	$E(V_{14})$	$\widehat{R}_{12,10}$	$\widehat{R}_{14,12}$
0.07	0.1	226.46	274.15	394.97	1.92	7.08	228.38	281.23	0.24	0.11
0.07	0.3	226.46	274.15	394.97	9.47	21.25	235.92	295.40	0.26	0.14
0.07	0.5	226.46	274.15	394.97	21.96	35.41	248.42	309.56	0.30	0.17
0.1	0.1	149.26	181.17	266.12	0.37	3.88	149.63	185.05	0.27	0.11
0.1	0.3	149.26	181.17	266.12	3.02	11.63	152.29	192.80	0.28	0.14
0.1	0.5	149.26	181.17	266.12	8.24	19.38	157.51	200.56	0.31	0.16

Notes: Transition probability, p, represents the probability of continuing in school conditional on current education. "PV of lifetime earnings" is $\widehat{Y}_s = \sum_{x=0}^{65}(1+r)^{-x}\widehat{Y}(s,x)$ where $\widehat{Y}(s,x)$ is the nonparametrically estimated earnings for a white man with s years of school and x years of experience (based on the 1990 Census). "Total value", $E(V_s) = (1-p)\widehat{Y}_s + p(1+r)^{-1}E(V_{s+1})$, is recursively solved backward from $E(V_{16}) = \widehat{Y}_{16}$. "Option value" is $\widehat{O}_{s,s-1} = E(V_s) - \widehat{Y}_s$. "Return to school" $\widehat{R}_{s,s-1} = \frac{E(V_s)-\widehat{Y}_{s-1}}{\widehat{Y}_{s-1}}$ is annualized. See Appendix B for data description.

returns, of the sort traditionally reported in the labor economics literature, are obtained by using realized values of earnings.[49]

The natural generalization of the IRR to an environment with sequential revelation of information would be as that rate that equates value functions across different schooling levels defined relative to some information set at the date schooling choices are being made. However, even for a particular information set, single crossings of realized age–earnings profiles, a near universal feature of schooling–earnings data, do not guarantee unique internal rates of return applied to the valuation function when option values are taken into account. Hirshleifer (1970) shows that there is always a unique positive internal rate of return when comparing two deterministic earnings streams which cross at only one age. This is the typical case when comparing the earnings profiles for any two schooling levels. Accounting for options to continue in school, it is possible for multiple roots to arise in the computation of more sophisticated internal rates of return that account for the option value of schooling even if earnings are monotonically increasing in schooling for workers conditional on age, and there are single crossings of any two earnings streams. Intuitively, the value function is a weighted average of future earnings streams so a single crossing property for earnings streams is not enough to guarantee unique internal rates of return for value functions.

To explore this intuition formally, consider a model of exogenous schooling transition probabilities like that of Comay, Melnik and Pollatschek (1973) for the case where earnings are zero until the end of school, age s, at which time they jump up to $\alpha_s + \beta s$ and linearly increase thereafter at rate $\beta > 0$.[50] Assume that there are no direct or psychic costs of schooling. As long as $\alpha_s > \alpha_{s'}$ for all $s > s'$, any two earnings streams will only cross once at the age where the higher schooling level ends. Letting $Y(s, a)$ denote the earnings for someone with s years of school at age a, we have

$$Y(s, a) = \begin{cases} 0 & \text{if } a < s, \\ \alpha_s + \beta a & \text{if } a \geqslant s. \end{cases}$$

Consider three schooling choices, $s \in \{0, s_1, s_2\}$. Suppose p is the exogenously specified probability that someone with $s_1 < s_2$ years of school continues on to s_2 years. The expected earnings stream at age a of someone choosing to attend s_1 years of school with the option of continuing will be $\overline{Y}(a) = (1 - p)Y(s_1, a) + pY(s_2, a)$. An option value arises because the agent has a chance of getting into schooling level s_2 after completing schooling level s_1.

For $\alpha_0 < \alpha_{s_1} < \alpha_{s_2}$, $\overline{Y}(a)$ will cross $Y(0, a)$ three times whenever

$$\frac{\alpha_0 + \beta s_1}{\alpha_{s_1} + \beta s_1} < 1 - p < \frac{\alpha_0 + \beta s}{\alpha_{s_1} + \beta s}$$

49 As information unfolds after s, one could define a sequence of *ex post* value functions depending on what is revealed after stage s.

50 The example can easily be extended to account for tuition costs and more general lifecycle earnings profiles.

for any s, where $s_1 < s < s_2$.[51] This possibility is illustrated in Figure 7. Because $\bar{Y}(a)$ crosses $Y(0, a)$ three times, the internal rate of return equations for the value functions produced from this model can generate multiple roots.[52,53] Even if pairwise earnings streams cross only once, there may be multiple internal rates of return when we use the

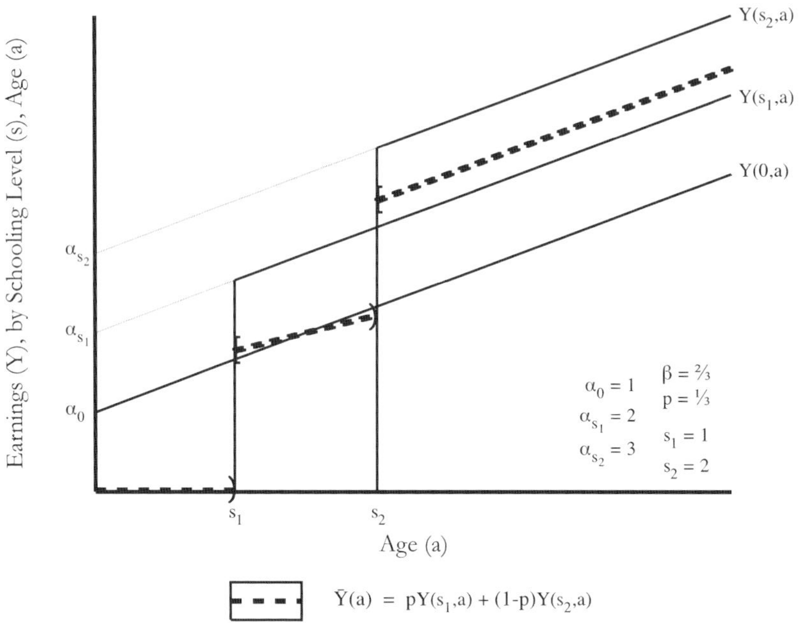

Figure 7. Three crossings of prospective earnings profiles in a model with option values.

[51] The left-hand side of this condition ensures that $\bar{Y}(a)$ jumps from zero to some point above $Y(0, a)$ at age s_1. Over the interval $[s_1, s_2)$, $\bar{Y}(a)$ increases with age at a slower rate ($[1-p]\beta$) than does $Y(0, a)$ (β). The right-hand condition guarantees that at some later age s, in the interval $[s_1, s_2)$, $\bar{Y}(a)$ will be below $Y(0, a)$. Finally, we know at age s_2, $\bar{Y}(a)$ will jump above $Y(0, a)$, since both α_{s_1} and α_{s_2} are both greater than α_0.

[52] See Hirshleifer (1970) for a discussion of multiple roots and the internal rate of return.

[53] For the case with schooling options of 0 years, $s_1 = 1$ years, and $s_2 = 2$ years, when individuals live forever, the value associated with choosing exactly $s = 0$ is $Y_0 = \int_0^\infty \mathrm{e}^{-ra}(\alpha_0 + \beta a)\,\mathrm{d}a = \frac{\alpha_0 r + \beta}{r^2}$. Consider the value of one year of school discounted to date 0, which contains the option value of continuing on to two years. p is the probability of continuing on to the second year of schooling.

$$V_1 = (1-p)\int_1^\infty \mathrm{e}^{-ra}(\alpha_1 + \beta a)\,\mathrm{d}a + p\int_2^\infty \mathrm{e}^{-ra}(\alpha_2 + \beta a)\,\mathrm{d}a$$
$$= (1-p)\mathrm{e}^{-r}\left[\alpha_1 \frac{1}{r} + \beta\left(\frac{1}{r} + \frac{1}{r^2}\right)\right] + p\,\mathrm{e}^{-2r}\left[\alpha_2 \frac{1}{r} + \beta\left(\frac{2}{r} + \frac{1}{r^2}\right)\right].$$

IRR equates $Y_0 = V_1$, so assuming $r \neq 0$, $\alpha_0 r + \beta = (1-p)\,\mathrm{e}^{-r}[(\alpha_1 + \beta)r + \beta] + p\,\mathrm{e}^{-2r}[(\alpha_2 + \beta)r + 2\beta]$, which is a transcendental equation and may have multiple roots.

appropriate value function, invalidating their use as a guide to selecting human capital investment projects.

In the more general case of sequential resolution of uncertainty, the schooling transition probability is not exogenous. Multiple roots are even more likely in this case, since the transition probability depends on the discount rate. Writing equations out explicitly in terms of interest rate r, we obtain

$$E_{s-1}\big(V_s(r)\big) = \Pr_{s-1}\left(\varepsilon_s \geqslant \frac{E_s[V_{s+1}(r)]}{(1+r)\overline{Y}_s(r)}\right)\overline{Y}_s(r)E_{s-1}\left(\varepsilon_s \mid \varepsilon_s \geqslant \frac{E_s[V_{s+1}(r)]}{(1+r)\overline{Y}_s(r)}\right) + \Pr_{s-1}\left(\varepsilon_s < \frac{E_s[V_{s+1}(r)]}{(1+r)\overline{Y}_s(r)}\right)\frac{E_{s-1}[V_{s+1}(r)]}{(1+r)}.$$

In this setting, the natural generalization of the IRR is the value (or values) of r_I that solves

$$Y_s(r_I) = \frac{E_{s-1}(V_{s+1}(r_I))}{1+r_I}.$$

Take a three period example. In this case, the IRR for the second level of schooling solves

$$\overline{Y}_1(r_I) = \Pr_1\left(\varepsilon_2 \geqslant \frac{\overline{Y}_3(r_I)}{(1+r_I)\overline{Y}_2(r_I)}\right)\frac{\overline{Y}_2(r_I)}{1+r_I}E_1\left(\varepsilon_2 \mid \varepsilon_2 \geqslant \frac{\overline{Y}_3(r_I)}{(1+r_I)\overline{Y}_2(r_I)}\right) + \Pr_1\left(\varepsilon_2 < \frac{\overline{Y}_3(r_I)}{(1+r)\overline{Y}_2(r_I)}\right)\frac{\overline{Y}_3(r_I)}{(1+r_I)^2}.$$

The fact that the continuation probabilities also depend on r_I makes multiple roots more likely. To gain some intuition in this case, take a limiting case where the variance of ε_2 goes to zero. This implies that the probability of continuing to level three will be either zero or one, depending on whether or not $\overline{Y}_2$ is greater or less than $\frac{\overline{Y}_3}{(1+r_I)}$. We may, therefore, get two valid solutions to the above IRR equation:

Case 1 (individual always continues): r_I^1 satisfies

$$\overline{Y}_1\big(r_I^1\big) = \frac{\overline{Y}_3(r_I^1)}{(1+r_I^1)^2} > \frac{\overline{Y}_2(r_I^1)}{1+r_I^1}.$$

The latter inequality guarantees that the person always wants to continue to schooling level three upon reaching level two.

Case 2 (individual never continues): r_I^2 satisfies

$$\overline{Y}_1\big(r_I^2\big) = \frac{\overline{Y}_2(r_I^2)}{(1+r_I^2)} > \frac{\overline{Y}_3(r_I^2)}{(1+r_I^2)^2}.$$

The latter inequality guarantees that the person always stops his schooling at level two.

Both of these cases can arise for the same person depending on the realization of ε_2 as long as $\mathrm{Var}(\varepsilon_2) > 0$, if log earnings are not parallel in experience. Consider the case where wage gaps are small initially and large later in the life cycle. In this case, r_I^1

would be less than r_I^2. In Case 1, the high wage differential later on is not discounted very much, so the individual always wants to attend schooling level three. A low IRR must, therefore, equate level one earnings with discounted level three earnings. On the other hand, the high late wage differential may be discounted so much with a high discount rate that the individual never chooses to go on to college at that rate. In this case, a high IRR, r_I^2, must equate level one earnings with discounted level two earnings. These examples are extreme, but multiple roots can arise more generally as long as the variance of ε_s is not too large. This type of multiplicity of roots could also come more directly out of the Comay, Melnik and Pollatschek (1973) type of model, where the probability of continuing to level three would be either zero (if individuals do not want to continue) or p (if individuals wish to continue), depending on the discount rate. Given the lack of parallelism in cross section log earnings profiles, multiplicity of roots is likely to be empirically important.

These issues call into serious question the usefulness of internal rates of return as a measure of the return to education in an environment where the schooling decision is dynamic and sequential. A central tool of policy evaluation from classical human capital theory loses its validity in the presence of option values. Criterion (9) does not suffer from this criticism and is the appropriate measure of the *ex ante* rate of return to use but it is rarely reported. For an exception, see Cunha, Heckman and Navarro (2005) and Cunha and Heckman (2006b) who estimate this rate of return. In the absence of sequential resolution of uncertainty and option values, $R_{s,s-1}$ is the same as the classical internal rate of return applied to pairwise earnings streams, so it is the natural generalization of that concept.

Empirical work on the option value of schooling is in its infancy. If option values are empirically relatively unimportant in models with the sequential resolution of uncertainty, conventional investment evaluation methods based on the IRR may well be informative on the optimality of schooling investments. Even if option values are negligible, the analysis presented throughout this paper suggests that the Mincer model will not estimate theoretically appropriate rates of return to schooling. In the absence of option values, other key assumptions required to equate Mincer coefficients with internal rates of return are violated. Even in an environment without the sequential resolution of uncertainty, more general methods of the type presented in Section 4 are required to obtain internal rates of return.

We next turn to an analysis of cross section bias. In doing so, we ignore option values, following conventions in the labor economics literature, and focus on "rates of return" as conventionally measured to concentrate on the issue of whether cross section estimates of "rates of return" are valid for life cycle "rates of return."

6. How do cross-sectional IRR estimates compare with cohort-based estimates?

Thus far we have considered estimation of rates of return to schooling using cross-section data which applies the standard synthetic cohort approach followed by most of the literature. For an *ex ante* analysis it assumes that younger workers base their earnings expectations on the current experiences of older workers. For an *ex post* analysis, it assumes that the experiences of older workers at a point in time will be those of younger workers when they reach those ages. If skill prices are changing over time and workers at least partially anticipate these changes, the estimates of the *ex ante* return to different schooling levels based on cross-sectional data may not represent the *ex ante* rates of return governing human capital investment decisions. Similarly, if the environment is nonstationary, the *ex post* returns of the younger cohort are not accurately estimated. While estimates based on cross-section data reflect current price differentials and opportunity costs, they do not capture future skill price differentials that forward-looking individuals would take into account. The U.S. labor market in recent years is highly nonstationary as are the labor markets of many economies around the world.

If cohorts anticipate future changes in the skill premium, they will base their schooling decisions on their true cohort-specific rate of return and not the rate of return estimated from a cross-section of current workers. However, if individuals do not anticipate the future price changes, cross-section estimates may better represent their expectations about the returns to school. Expectations play a crucial role in determining whether cross-section or cohort-based estimates of the rate of return influence schooling decisions.

Another possible source of discrepancy between cross-section and cohort-based rate of return estimates is change in cohort quality, as might arise from changes in the quality of schools over time. If relative skills for some schooling classes increase permanently, then cohort rates of return jump up with the first 'new' cohort and remain higher for all succeeding cohorts. Cross-section estimates only reflect the changes slowly as more high quality cohorts enter the sample each year. As a result, they under-estimate true rates of return for cohorts entering the labor market after the change in school quality, with the bias disappearing as time progresses. While future price changes are difficult to predict, changes in cohort or school quality are more identifiable.

Mincer (1974) addressed cross section bias in his pioneering work. He found that patterns for wage growth in a 1956 cross-section of male workers were quite similar to the 1956 to 1966 growth in wages for individual cohorts. The empirical discrepancy between cross-section and cohort-based estimates was relatively small. Recent analyses reveal that wage patterns have changed dramatically across cohorts and that cross-sections no longer approximate cohort or life cycle change [MaCurdy and Mroz (1995), Card and Lemieux (2001)]. While these studies do not agree on whether or not these changes are due to changes in relative skill prices or cohort quality, there is little question in the U.S. data that life cycle earnings profiles based on a cross-section of workers no longer accurately reflect the true earnings patterns for any given cohort. As a result, the rates of return to schooling estimated from cross-sections of workers reported in the previous section are likely to differ from the rates of return faced by cohorts making their schooling decisions.

Next, we present a cohort analysis focusing on the actual returns earned by each cohort without taking a position on whether changes in those returns over time are due to changes in cohort quality or skill prices. Arias and McMahon (2001) present a similar analysis in estimating *ex post* dynamic rates of return. We study how the actual *ex post* returns earned by individual cohorts compare with returns estimated from a cross-section of individuals at the time those cohorts made their schooling decisions. We use repeated cross-section data from the 1964–2000 Current Population Survey (CPS) March Supplements, comparing cross-section estimates of the return to schooling with estimates that combine all years of the CPS to follow cohorts over their life cycles. Given the sensitivity noted in the previous sections of this chapter to specifications of the functional forms of earnings equations, we adopt a flexible earnings specification and compute internal rates of return to high school completion (12 vs. 10 years of schooling) and college completion (16 vs. 12 years of schooling) that relax the assumptions that log earnings are parallel in experience and linear in schooling. Our estimates also take into account average marginal tax rates and tuition costs using the time series generated from CPS data.[54] Because earnings are not observed at every experience level for any cohort in the sample (an obvious practical problem in estimating cohort rates of return), a fully nonparametric approach is infeasible. To extrapolate the earnings function to work experience levels not observed in the data, we assume that log earnings profiles are quadratic in experience in a specification that allows the intercept and coefficients on experience and experience-squared to vary by schooling class and year or cohort of data. We estimate log earnings for each year or for each cohort using regressions of the form

$$\log\bigl(Y(s,x)\bigr) = \alpha_s + \beta_{0s}x + \beta_{1s}x^2 + \varepsilon_s,$$

where the regression coefficients are allowed to vary by schooling group.[55] Two sets of estimates are generated: (i) regressions are estimated separately for each year of CPS data (to produce a set of cross-section estimates), and (ii) all CPS cross-sections are combined and separate regressions are estimated for each cohort by following them over their life cycles (to produce a set of cohort-based estimates). Both sets of estimates are used to generate predicted life cycle earnings profiles for each cohort or cross-section of individuals, which are then used to compute internal rates of return to high school and college by the method described in Section 4 setting the residual of the wage equation to its mean.[56]

[54] An average marginal tax rate of 25% is assumed for all years after 1994, the final year of tax rates reported in Mulligan and Marion (2000). This corresponds to the average of all rates since 1950, after which rates changed very little from year to year.

[55] In estimating earnings profiles for those with 10 years of education, we combine individuals with 9–11 years, with separate intercept terms for each of the education levels. This is done to increase precision in estimation. See Appendix B for additional details on the coding of the education variables.

[56] In addition to the quadratic specification, we also tried using a cubic and quartic in experience to extrapolate for the missing experience levels. For cohorts with 25 or fewer years of data, extrapolations based on higher-order polynomial specifications were unreliable, so we adopted the more parsimonious quadratic specification.

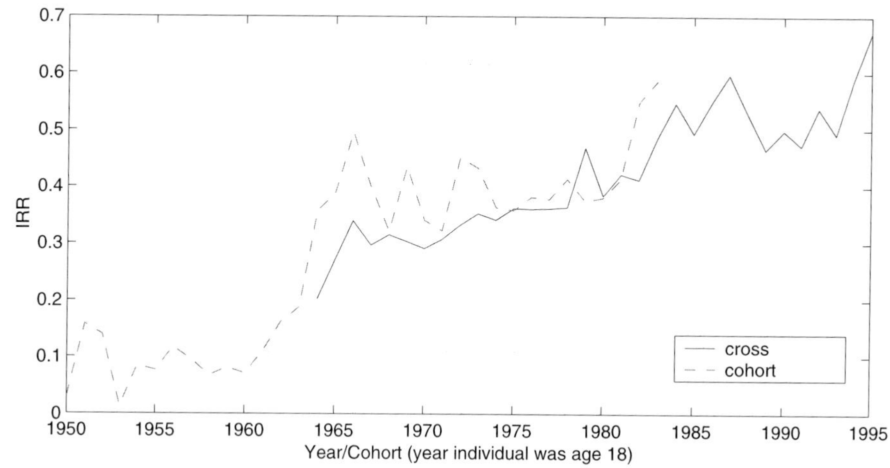

Figure 8a. IRR for 10 vs. 12 years of education for white men (1964–2000 CPS).

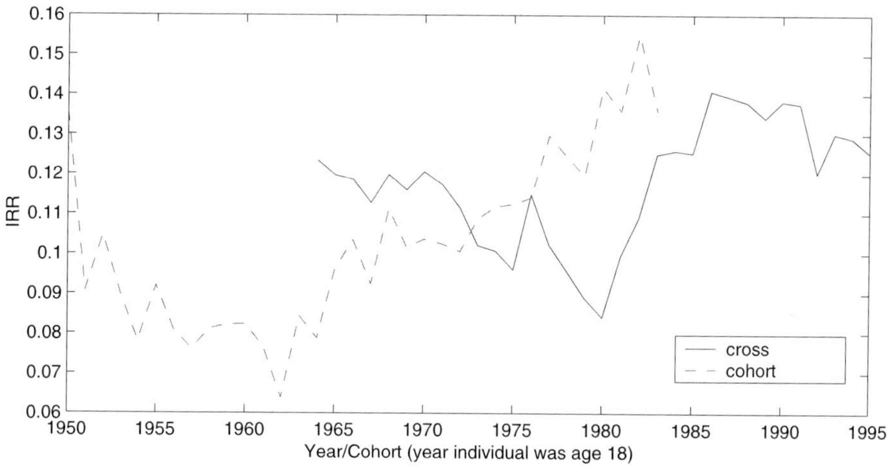

Figure 8b. IRR for 12 vs. 16 years of education for white men (1964–2000 CPS).

Figures 8a and 8b show cohort and cross-section high school and college completion IRR estimates for white men, which are based on the CPS estimates reported in Table 8a. Cross-section estimates are shown for each year of the sample from 1964–1995, and cohort-based estimates are shown for cohorts turning age 18 in 1950 through 1983.[57]

[57] We do not estimate returns for cohorts beyond 1983, since there are too few years of earnings observations for those cohorts to produce stable and reliable estimates.

Table 8a
Internal rates of return for white men: best Census and CPS estimates

Schooling comparison	Year	Mincer	Census data: General spec. (no residual adjustment)	Census data: General spec. (residual adjustment)	CPS data: Cross section	CPS data: Cohort
10 vs. 12	1940	13	24	8	–	–
	1950	11	26	14	–	3
	1960	12	29	16	–	7
	1970	13	29	16	29	34
	1980	11	41	24	38	38
	1990	14	47	31	50	–
12 vs. 16	1940	13	15	13	–	–
	1950	11	7	8	–	14
	1960	12	10	11	–	8
	1970	13	10	10	12	10
	1980	11	8	8	8	14
	1990	14	12	12	14	–

Notes: Mincer estimates make no adjustment for taxes or tuition. Census General Specification estimates account for tuition and progressive taxes with a fully nonparametric wage specification. CPS cross section estimates use cross sectional data and a general wage specification accounting for tuition and flat taxes. CPS Cohort estimates follow a cohort turning age 18 in the reported year, using a general wage specification accounting for tuition and flat taxes. See Appendix B for data description.

The cohort-based estimates reported in Figure 8a reveal relative stability in the return to high school for cohorts making their high school completion decisions prior to 1960, followed by a large increase in the IRR for cohorts making their decisions over the first half of the 1960s, followed by another period of relative stability. Returns increased from around 10% among 1950–60 cohorts to around 40% for post-1965 cohorts. Cross-section based estimates increase slowly but consistently over most of the 1964–1995 period. In general, cross-section estimated rates of return under-estimate the true rates of return earned by cohorts of white men making their schooling decisions in the late 1960s and 1970s. However, basic time patterns are consistent across the two sets of estimates. More dramatic differences are observed for the college-going decision of white men as shown in Figure 8b. While cross-section estimates show declining "returns" to college over the 1970s (from 12% down to 8%), cohort-based estimates show continually increasing returns from the early 1960s to the early 1980s. The rate of return estimated from cross-sections does not begin to increase until 1980. Cross-section estimates overestimate the rate of return faced by cohorts making their college attendance decisions around 1965 by as much as 4 percentage points, while estimates in the early 1980s under-estimate the return by nearly the same amount. Table 8b reports comparable numbers for black men.

Table 8b
Internal rates of return for black men: best Census and CPS estimates

Schooling comparison	Year	Mincer	Census data		CPS data	
			General spec. (no residual adjustment)	General spec. (residual adjustment)	Cross section	Cohort
10 vs. 12	1940	9	10	−8	–	–
	1950	10	44	21	–	4
	1960	11	34	16	–	18
	1970	12	39	22	32	49
	1980	12	46	29	55	70
	1990	16	57	42	64	–
12 vs. 16	1940	9	10	6	–	–
	1950	10	5	9	–	15
	1960	11	8	6	–	6
	1970	12	10	10	12	14
	1980	12	11	9	14	17
	1990	16	17	15	16	–

Notes: Mincer estimates make no adjustment for taxes or tuition. Census General Specification estimates account for tuition and progressive taxes with a fully nonparametric wage specification. CPS cross section estimates use cross sectional data and a general wage specification accounting for tuition and flat taxes. CPS Cohort estimates follow a cohort turning age 18 in the reported year, using a general wage specification accounting for tuition and flat taxes. Each CPS estimate is based on three adjoining years/cohorts worth of data. See Appendix B for data description.

If the observed discrepancies between cross-section and cohort-based estimated "rates of return" are due to price changes over time that could be at least partly anticipated or are due to changing cohort quality, then cross-section estimates would not reflect the *ex ante* "rates of return" that governed schooling decisions. On the other hand, if changes in skill prices were entirely unanticipated, then cross-section estimates may provide a better indication of the *ex ante* returns governing schooling decisions than would the actual *ex post* returns experienced by each cohort. A better understanding of the underlying causes for such dramatic changes in wages and of individual expectations is needed. Buchinsky and Leslie (2000), Carneiro, Hansen and Heckman (2003) and Cunha, Heckman and Navarro (2005) present empirical explorations of alternative expectation–formation models. We review methods for estimating agent information sets in Section 10.

In summary, cross-section estimates of the "rate of return" to schooling should be cautiously interpreted, particularly when skill prices are changing over time or when cohort quality is changing. If one is interested in empirically estimating historical rates of return, a cohort analysis is clearly preferable. Data from the 1964–2000 March CPS suggest that "returns" estimated from a cross-section of workers are not only biased in levels, but they also suggest patterns that sometimes differ from those obtained using a cohort-based estimation strategy. If one is interested in estimating the conventional rates of return governing school investment decisions, then whether to use cross-section or cohort-based estimates depends on the extent to which individuals are able to forecast future changes in wages and skill prices. We next turn to a review of the recent instrument-based "rate of return" literature.

7. Accounting for the endogeneity of schooling

Much of the CPS-Census literature on the returns to schooling ignores the choice of schooling and its consequences for estimating "the rate of return". It ignores uncertainty. It is static and ignores the dynamics of schooling choices and the sequential revelation of uncertainty. It also ignores ability bias.[58] Economists since C. Reinhold Noyes (1945) in his comment on Friedman and Kuznets (1945) have raised the specter of ability bias, noting that the estimated return to schooling may largely be a return to ability that would arise independently of schooling. Griliches (1977) and Willis (1986) summarize estimates from the conventional literature on ability bias. For the past 30 years, labor economists have been in pursuit of good instruments to estimate "the rate of return" to schooling, usually interpreted as a Mincer coefficient. However, the previous sections show that, for many reasons, the Mincer coefficient is not informative on the true rate of return to schooling, and therefore is not the appropriate theoretical construct to gauge educational policy. Card (1999) is a useful reference for empirical estimates from instrumental variable models.

Even abstracting from the issues raised by the sequential updating of information, and the distinction between *ex ante* and *ex post* returns to schooling, which we discuss further below, there is the additional issue that returns, however defined, vary among persons. A random coefficients model of the economic return to schooling has been an integral part of the human capital literature since the papers by Becker and Chiswick (1966), Chiswick (1974), Chiswick and Mincer (1972) and Mincer (1974).[59] In its most stripped-down form and ignoring work experience terms, the Mincer model writes log earnings for person i with schooling level S_i as

$$\ln y_i = \alpha_i + \rho_i S_i, \tag{11}$$

where the "rate of return" ρ_i varies among persons as does the intercept, α_i. For the purposes of this discussion think of y_i as an annualized flow of lifetime earnings. Unless the only costs of schooling are earnings foregone, and markets are perfect, ρ_i is a percentage growth rate in earnings with schooling and not a rate of return to schooling. Let $\alpha_i = \bar{\alpha} + \varepsilon_{\alpha_i}$ and $\rho_i = \bar{\rho} + \varepsilon_{\rho_i}$ where $\bar{\alpha}$ and $\bar{\rho}$ are the means of α_i and ρ_i. Thus the

[58] See Katz and Autor (1999) for a survey. An exception is Angrist and Krueger (1991). For an analysis of the quality of their instruments see Staiger and Stock (1997).

[59] Recall our discussion of the random coefficients model in Section 2.2.

means of ε_{α_i} and ε_{ρ_i} are zero. Earnings equation (11) can be written as

$$\ln y_i = \bar{\alpha} + \bar{\rho} S_i + \{\varepsilon_{\alpha_i} + \varepsilon_{\rho_i} S_i\}. \tag{12}$$

Equations (11) and (12) are the basis for a human capital analysis of wage inequality in which the variance of log earnings is decomposed into components due to the variance in S_i and components due to the variation in the growth rate of earnings with schooling (the variance in $\bar{\rho}$), the mean growth rate across regions or time ($\bar{\rho}$), and mean schooling levels ($\bar{S}$). [See, e.g., Mincer (1974), Willis (1986).]

Given that the growth rate ρ_i is a random variable, it has a distribution that can be studied using the methods surveyed in Sections 9 and 10. Following the representative agent tradition in economics, it has become conventional to summarize the distribution of growth rates by the mean, although many other summary measures of the distribution are possible. For the prototypical distribution of ρ_i, the conventional measure is the "average growth rate" $E(\rho_i)$ or $E(\rho_i | X)$, where the latter conditions on X, the observed characteristics of individuals. Other means are possible such as the mean growth rates for persons who attain a given level of schooling.

The original Mincer model assumed that the growth rate of earnings with schooling, ρ_i, is uncorrelated with or is independent of S_i. This assumption is convenient but is not implied by economic theory. It is plausible that the growth rate of earnings with schooling declines with the level of schooling. It is also plausible that there are unmeasured ability or motivational factors that affect the growth rate of earnings with schooling and are also correlated with the level of schooling. Rosen (1977) discusses this problem in some detail within the context of hedonic models of schooling and earnings. A similar problem arises in analyses of the impact of unionism on relative wages and is discussed in Lewis (1963).

Allowing for correlated random coefficients (so S_i is correlated with ε_{ρ_i}) raises substantial problems that are just beginning to be addressed in a systematic fashion in the recent literature. Here, we discuss recent developments starting with Card's (1999) random coefficient model of the growth rate of earnings with schooling, a model that is derived from economic theory and is based on the analysis of Becker's model by Rosen (1977).[60] We consider conditions under which it is possible to estimate the mean effect of schooling and the distribution of returns in his model. The next section considers the more general and recent analysis of Carneiro, Heckman and Vytlacil (2005).

In Card's (1999, 2001) model, the preferences of a person over income (y) and schooling (S) are

$$U(y, S) = \ln y(S) - \varphi(S), \quad \varphi'(S) > 0, \quad \text{and} \quad \varphi''(S) > 0.$$

The schooling–earnings relationship is $y = g(S)$. This is a hedonic model of schooling, where $g(S)$ reveals how schooling is priced out in the labor market. This specification

[60] Random coefficient models with coefficients correlated with the regressors are systematically analyzed in Heckman and Robb (1985, 1986). They originate in labor economics with the work of Lewis (1963). Heckman and Robb analyze training programs but their analysis clearly applies to estimating the returns to schooling.

is written in terms of annualized earnings and abstracts from work experience.[61] It assumes perfect certainty and abstracts from the sequential resolution of uncertainty that is central to the modern literature. In this formulation, discounting of future earnings is kept implicit. The first order condition for optimal determination of schooling is

$$\frac{g'(S)}{g(S)} = \varphi'(S). \tag{13}$$

The term $\frac{g'(s)}{g(s)}$ is the percentage change of earnings with schooling or the "growth rate" at level s. Card's model reproduces Rosen's (1977) model if r is the common interest rate at which agents can freely lend or borrow and if the only costs are S years of foregone earnings. In Rosen's setup, an agent with an infinite lifetime maximizes $\frac{1}{r}\,\mathrm{e}^{-rS}g(S)$ so $\varphi(S) = rS + \ln r$, and $\frac{g'(S)}{g(S)} = r$.

Linearizing the model, we obtain

$$\frac{g'(S_i)}{g(S_i)} = \beta_i(S_i) = \rho_i - k_1 S_i, \quad k_1 \geqslant 0,$$

$$\varphi'(S_i) = \delta_i(S_i) = r_i + k_2 S_i, \quad k_2 \geqslant 0.$$

Substituting these expressions into the first-order condition (13), we obtain that the optimal level of schooling is $S_i = \frac{(\rho_i - r_i)}{k}$, where $k = k_1 + k_2$. Observe that if both the growth rate and the returns are independent of S_i ($k_1 = 0, k_2 = 0$), then $k = 0$ and if $\rho_i = r_i$, there is no determinate level of schooling at the individual level. This is the original Mincer (1958) model.[62]

One source of heterogeneity among persons in the model is ρ_i, the way S_i is transformed into earnings. [School quality may operate through the ρ_i for example, as in Behrman and Birdsall (1983), and ρ_i may also differ due to inherent ability differences.] A second source of heterogeneity is r_i, the "opportunity cost" (cost of schooling) or "cost of funds." Higher ability leads to higher levels of schooling. Higher costs of schooling results in lower levels of schooling.

We integrate the first-order condition (13) to obtain the following hedonic model of earnings,

$$\ln y_i = \alpha_i + \rho_i S_i - \frac{1}{2} k_1 S_i^2. \tag{14}$$

To achieve the familiar looking Mincer equation, assume $k_1 = 0$.[63] This assumption rules out diminishing "returns" to schooling in terms of years of schooling. Even under

[61] Adding work experience in a multiplicatively separable way produces one Mincer model.

[62] In that model, aggregate allocations of persons to schooling are determined by an arbitrage condition that returns must be equalized across choices.

[63] The Card model (1999) produces a Mincer-like model where ρ_i is the Mincer return for individual i. The mean return in the population is $E(\rho_i)$. It is an *ex post* return derived under the assumption that log earnings are linear in schooling, contrary to the literature, previously discussed, that shows pronounced nonlinearities and sheepskin effects. (See the discussion in Sections 3 and 4.)

this assumption, ρ_i is the percentage growth rate in earnings with schooling, but is not in general an internal rate of return to schooling. It would be a rate of return if there were no direct costs of schooling and everyone faces a constant borrowing rate. This is a version of the Mincer (1958) model, where $k_2 = 0$, and r_i is constant for everyone but not necessarily the same constant. If $\rho_i > r_i$, person i takes the maximum amount of schooling. If $\rho_i < r_i$, person i takes no schooling and if $\rho_i = r_i$, schooling is indeterminate. In the Card model, ρ_i is the person-specific growth rate of earnings and overstates the true rate of return if there are direct and psychic costs of schooling.[64]

This simple model is useful in showing the sources of endogeneity in the schooling earnings model. Since schooling depends on ρ_i and r_i, any covariance between $\rho_i - r_i$ (in the schooling equation) and ρ_i (in the earnings function) produces a random coefficient model. Least squares will not estimate the mean growth rate of earnings with schooling unless, $COV(\rho_i, \rho_i - r_i) = 0$.

Dropping the i subscripts, the conditional expectation of log earnings given s is

$$E(\ln y|S = s) = E(\alpha|S = s) + E(\rho|S = s)s.$$

The first term produces the conventional ability bias if there is any dependence between s and raw ability α. Raw ability is the contribution to earnings independent of the schooling level attained. The second term arises from sorting on returns to schooling that occurs when people make schooling decisions on the basis of growth rates of earnings with schooling. It is an effect that depends on the level of schooling attained.

In his Woytinsky Lecture, Becker (1967), points out the possibility that many able people may not attend school if ability (ρ_i) is positively correlated with the cost of funds (r_i). A meritocratic society would eliminate this positive correlation and might aim to make it negative. Schooling is positively correlated with the growth rate (ρ_i) if $COV(\rho_i, \rho_i - r_i) > 0$. If the costs of schooling are sufficiently positively correlated with the growth rate, then schooling is negatively correlated with the growth rate.

Observe that S_i does not directly depend on the random intercept α_i. Of course, α_i may be statistically dependent on (ρ_i, r_i). In the context of Card's model, we consider conditions under which one can identify $\bar{\rho}$, the mean growth rate of earnings in the population as well as the full distribution of ρ. First we consider the case where the marginal cost of funds, r_i, is observed and consider other cases in the following subsections.[65]

7.1. *Estimating the mean growth rate of earnings when r_i is observed*

A huge industry surveyed in Card (1999) seeks to estimate the mean growth rate in earnings, $E(\rho_i)$, calling it the "causal effect" of schooling. For reasons discussed earlier

[64] Recall the discussion of Section 4. From Equation (4) if term 1 is zero, and we assume multiplicative separability (or no experience) then ρ_i (= term 2) $= \tilde{r} +$ term 3 which arises from tuition and psychic costs where $\tilde{r}$ is the opportunity cost of funds.

[65] Our discussion is based in part on Heckman and Vytlacil (1998).

in this chapter, in general, it is not an internal rate of return. However, it is one of the ingredients used in calculating the rate of return as we develop further in Section 8.2. The "causal effect" may also be of interest in its own right if the goal is to estimate pricing equations for labor market characteristics. We discuss some simple approaches for identifying causal effects before turning to a more systematic analysis in Section 8.

Suppose that the cost of schooling, r_i, is measured by the economist. Use the notation "$\perp\!\!\!\perp$" to denote statistical independence. Assume

$$r_i \perp\!\!\!\perp (\rho_i, \alpha_i).$$

This assumption rules out any relationship between the cost of funds (r_i) and raw ability (α_i) with the growth rate of earnings with schooling. For example, it rules out fellowships based on ability. We make this assumption to illustrate some ideas and not because of its realism. Observing r_i implies that we observe ρ_i up to an additive constant. Recall that $S_i = \frac{(\rho_i - r_i)}{k}$, so that $\rho_i = r_i + kS_i$ and $\bar{\rho} = E(\rho_i) = \bar{r} + kE(S_i)$.

r_i is a valid instrument for S_i under the assumption that $k_1 = 0$. It is independent of α_i, ρ_i (and hence $\varepsilon_{\alpha i}, \varepsilon_{\rho i}$) and is correlated with S_i because S_i depends on r_i. Form

$$\begin{aligned}\frac{COV(\ln y_i, r_i)}{COV(S_i, r_i)} &= \frac{E\{(r_i - \bar{r})[(\alpha_i - \bar{\alpha}) + (\rho_i - \bar{\rho})(S_i - \bar{S}) + \bar{\rho} S_i + \rho_i \bar{S} - \bar{\rho}\bar{S})]\}}{E\{[\frac{\rho_i - r_i}{k}][r_i - \bar{r}]\}} \\ &= \frac{\frac{1}{k}E[(\Delta r)(\Delta \rho)(\Delta \rho - \Delta r)] - \frac{\bar{\rho}}{k}\sigma_r^2}{-\frac{\sigma_r^2}{k}},\end{aligned}$$

where $\Delta X = X - E(X)$. As a consequence of the assumed independence between r_i and (α_i, ρ_i), $E[(\Delta r)(\Delta \rho)^2] = 0$ and $E[(\Delta r)^2 \Delta \rho] = 0$, so

$$\left[\frac{COV(\ln y_i, r_i)}{COV(S_i, r_i)}\right] = \bar{\rho}.$$

Observe that $\bar{\rho}$ is not identified by this argument if $\rho_i \not\perp\!\!\!\perp r_i$ (so the mean growth rate of earnings depends on the cost of schooling).[66] In that case, $E[(\Delta r)(\Delta \rho)^2] \neq 0$ and $E[(\Delta r)^2(\Delta \rho)] \neq 0$. If r_i is known and $r_i = L_i \gamma + M_i$, where the L_i are observed variables that explain r_i and $E(M_i | L_i) = 0$, then γ is identified, provided a rank condition for instrumental variables is satisfied.[67] We require that L_i be at least mean independent of (M_i, ρ_i, α_i). From the schooling equation we can write $S_i = (\rho_i - L_i \gamma - M_i)/k$ and k is identified since we know γ.

Observe that we can estimate the distribution of ρ_i since $\rho_i = r_i + kS_i$, k is identified and (r_i, S_i) are known. This is true even if there are no instruments L ($\gamma = 0$), provided that $r_i \perp\!\!\!\perp (\rho_i, \alpha_i)$. With the instruments that satisfy at least the mean independence condition, we can allow $r_i \not\perp\!\!\!\perp \rho_i$ and all parameters and distributions are still identified. The

[66] The symbol $\not\perp\!\!\!\perp$ means "not independent of."

[67] See, e.g., Greene (2003).

model is fully identified provided r_i is observed and $L_i \perp\!\!\!\perp (M_i, \rho_i, \alpha_i)$.[68] Thus, we can identify the mean return to schooling.

7.2. *Estimating the mean growth rate when r_i is not observed*

If r_i is not observed and so cannot be used as an instrument, but we know that r_i depends on observed factors L_i and M_i, $r_i = L_i\gamma + M_i$ and $L_i \perp\!\!\!\perp (M_i, \alpha_i, \rho_i)$, then the analysis of Section 7.1 carries over and the mean growth rate $\bar{\rho}$ is identified. Recall that $\ln y_i = \alpha_i + \bar{\rho} S_i + (\rho_i - \bar{\rho}) S_i$. Substitute for S_i to get an expression of y_i in terms of L_i, $\ln y_i = \alpha_i + \rho_i(\rho_i - L_i\gamma - M_i)/k$. We obtain the vector moment equations:

$$COV(\ln y_i, L_i) = \bar{\rho}\, COV(S_i, L_i),$$

so $\bar{\rho}$ is identified from the population moments because the covariances on both sides are available.[69] Partition $\gamma = (\gamma_0, \gamma_1)$, where γ_0 is the intercept and γ_1 is the vector of slope coefficients. From the schooling equation, we obtain

$$\begin{aligned} S_i &= \frac{\rho_i - L_i\gamma_1 - M_i}{k} - \frac{\gamma_0}{k} \\ &= -L_i\frac{\gamma_1}{k} + \frac{\rho_i - M_i}{k} - \frac{\gamma_0}{k}. \end{aligned}$$

We can identify γ_1/k from the schooling equation, as well as the mean growth rate $\bar{\rho}$. However, we cannot identify the distribution of ρ_i or r_i unless further assumptions are invoked. We also cannot separately identify γ_0, γ_1 or k. Heckman and Vytlacil (1998) show how to define and identify a version of "treatment on the treated" for growth rates in the Becker–Card–Rosen model.

7.3. *Adding selection bias*

Selection bias can arise in two distinct ways in the Becker–Card–Rosen model: through dependence between α_i and ρ_i and through dependence between α_i and r_i. Allowing for selection bias,

$$E(\ln y_i|S_i) = E(\alpha_i|S_i) + E(\rho_i S_i|S_i) = E(\alpha_i|S_i) + E(\rho_i|S_i)S_i.$$

If there is an L_i that affects r_i but not ρ_i and is independent of (α_i, M_i), i.e., $L_i \perp\!\!\!\perp (\alpha_i, \rho_i, M_i)$, and $E(r_i|L_i)$ is a nontrivial function of L_i, in the special case of a linear schooling model as in Section 7.2,

$$E(\ln y_i|L_i) = E(\alpha_i|L_i) + E(\rho_i S_i|L_i) = \eta + \bar{\rho} E(S_i|L_i).^{70}$$

[68] As we have stressed, the independence conditions are overly strong, but can be weakened to a mean independence assumption provided that we only seek to recover conditional means.

[69] One can use the GMM formula presented in Hansen (1982) to construct an efficient estimator if there is more than one nonconstant element in L_i.

[70] $\eta = \bar{\alpha} + \left(\frac{\sigma_\rho^2}{k}\right) - \frac{E(\rho_i M_i)}{k}$, where $\sigma_\rho^2 = VAR(\rho_i)$.

Since we can identify $E(S_i|L_i)$ we can identify $\bar{\rho}$. Thus, under the stated conditions, the instrumental variable (IV) method identifies $\bar{\rho}$ when there is selection bias. In a more general nonparametric case for the schooling equation, which we develop in the next section of this chapter, this argument breaks down and $\bar{\rho}$ is not identified when ρ_i determines S_i in a general way. The sensitivity of the IV method to assumptions about special features of Card's model is a simple demonstration of the fragility of the method. We return to this model in Section 10 and use it to motivate recent developments in the literature on identifying information available to agents when they make their schooling decisions.

7.4. *Summary*

Card's version of the Becker (1967)–Rosen (1977) model is a useful introduction to the modern literature on heterogeneous "returns to schooling." ρ_i is, in general, a person-specific growth rate of log earnings with schooling and not a rate of return. There is a distribution of ρ_i and no scalar measure is an adequate summary of this distribution. Recent developments in this literature, to which we now turn, demonstrate that standard instrumental variable methods are blunt tools for recovering economically interpretable parameters.

8. Accounting systematically for heterogeneity in returns to schooling: What does *IV* estimate?

To understand what IV estimates in a more general setting, this section analyzes a simple version of (11) in which there are only two levels of schooling. Our discussion can be generalized [see Heckman and Vytlacil (2005), Heckman, Urzua and Vytlacil (2006)], but for purposes of exposition it is fruitful to focus on a two outcome model. It links IV to the analysis of Willis and Rosen (1979) and Willis (1986), who focus on a two outcome model of schooling in which the ρ_i of Equation (14) varies in the population. Recent research on instrumental variables in the correlated coefficient model establishes a close link between IV and the selection model [Heckman (1976)] that Willis and Rosen apply to obtain their estimates. As shown in Heckman, Urzua and Vytlacil (2006), the contrast between IV and selection methods emphasized by Angrist and Krueger (1999) and echoed throughout the literature is not valid once the IV method for the correlated random coefficient model is correctly understood.

Because schooling is usually received in integer amounts, and most well posed models of schooling choice are based on nonlinear discrete choice frameworks, the simple Card model abstracts from key features of the schooling choice – earnings outcome model which can be captured in a simple way by a discrete outcome model.[71] Heckman

[71] Card's model becomes nonlinear if one constrains it to rule out negative schooling and schooling above observed magnitudes.

(1997) and Heckman and Vytlacil (1998) show how models of schooling that capture key features of economic theory are intrinsically nonlinear.

In the model of Section 7, the mean growth rate of earnings with schooling, $\bar{\rho}$, was assumed to be the parameter of interest without any good justification. While statisticians sometimes call such averages the "average causal effect" (ACE), there is no reason to focus on this parameter to the exclusion of other parameters that can be derived from the distribution of ρ_i.

Moreover, as we shall show in this section, the instrumental variable estimators set forth in the recent literature do not in general estimate ACE or any of the other standard treatment effects of schooling on earnings when schooling choices are discrete. They do not estimate rates of return to schooling, nor are they designed to. Instead, they estimate certain weighted averages of individual growth rates where the weights can sometimes be negative.

Following Heckman and Vytlacil (2000, 2005, 2007b), Heckman, Urzua and Vytlacil (2006), and Carneiro, Heckman and Vytlacil (2005), consider the following generalized Roy model of schooling and its "return." A version of it is applied by Willis and Rosen to the problem of choice of college using tools developed in the econometrics of selection bias. Our analysis of this model links the modern *IV* literature to the classical selection literature.[72]

Let Y_1 denote the present value of earnings from college. Y_0 is the present value of earnings from high school. There is a distribution of $G = Y_1 - Y_0$ and another distribution of $G - C$ in the population where C denotes the cost of schooling and G denotes earnings gains from college. No single number summarizes either distribution, although much of the literature focuses on one conditional mean or some other single number as the object of economic and econometric interest. Attention has focused in recent years on *IV* estimates of the coefficient of schooling in a regression of log earnings on schooling. In the special cases analyzed in Section 7, *IV* can sometimes identify the mean growth rate in earnings ($E(\rho_i)$) which is usually not the same as the rate of return. But more generally, *IV* does not even identify this parameter. This section considers what *IV* estimates in general cases.

If G varies in the population but everyone faces the same C, individuals decide to enroll in school ($S = 1$) if $G - C > 0$. Figure 9 plots the hypothetical density of G in this example, $f(G)$, and also presents the cost that everyone faces, C. Individuals who have values of G to the right of C choose to enroll in school, while those to the left choose not to enroll. The gross gain for the individuals who choose to go to school, $E(G|G \geqslant C)$, is computed with respect to the normalized density of $f(G)$ that is to the right of C. The marginal return (the return for individuals at the margin) is exactly equal to C. Figure 9 presents both the average and the marginal return for this example.

Suppose that we want to estimate the effect on earnings of compulsory college attendance. Those individuals who are induced to enroll in school by this policy have G

[72] Heckman, Urzua and Vytlacil (2006) systematically compare these literatures. See also Heckman and Vytlacil (2005, 2007b).

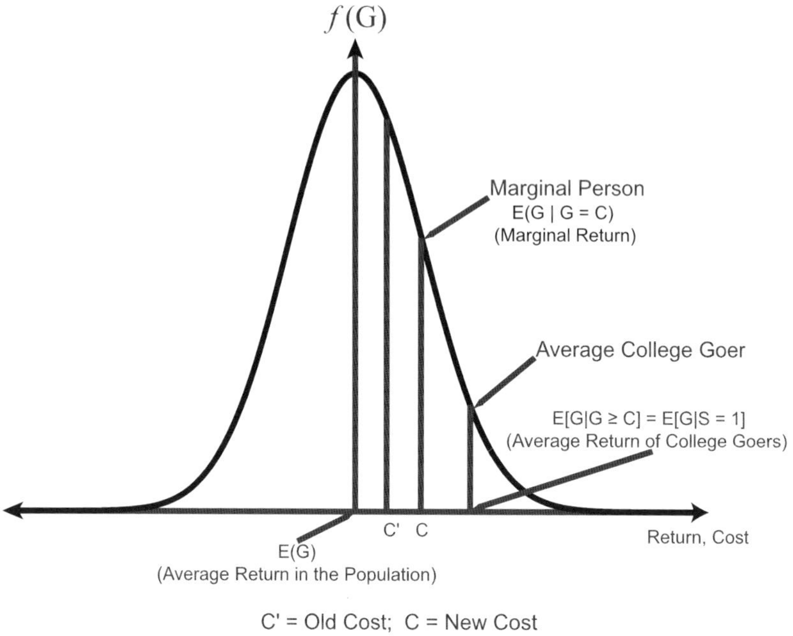

Figure 9. Density of absolute returns.

below C (they were not enrolled in school before the policy), and the average "return" for these individuals is $E(G|G \leqslant C)$. Alternatively, one might be interested in analyzing the effect of a tuition subsidy that changes the cost of attending school from C to C' for everyone in the economy. Those individuals who are induced to enroll in school by this policy have G below C (they were not enrolled in school before the policy) and G above C' (they decide to enroll after the policy), and the average "return" for these individuals is $E(G|C' < G \leqslant C)$. One needs different parameters to evaluate each of these two different policies ($E(G|G \leqslant C)$ vs. $E(G|C' < G \leqslant C)$). Neither is estimated by the average growth rate, and hence by the *IV* method discussed in Section 7. In this example, the marginal entrant into college has a lower return than the average entrant, and the return for the average student is not the relevant return to evaluate either policy.[73]

Standard estimates of the returns to schooling, such as the ones obtained using the method of least squares, as in the vast literature surveyed by Katz and Autor (1999), or using the method of instrumental variables, as surveyed by Card (1999), are not designed to produce either of the policy parameters just described. It is unusual in

[73] There is an additional assumption behind this example which we will maintain throughout this chapter: that the policy does not have important general equilibrium effects.

the recent literature on the "returns to schooling" for researchers estimating "the effect" of schooling to specify a policy or economic question of interest and address it directly. Following Card (1999) and Angrist and Krueger (1999), many define the probability limits of instrumental variable estimators (*LATE*, defined below) as "the" return to schooling without stating what economic questions these statistical objects address. Different instruments define different parameters. These parameters answer different, implicitly defined, economic questions. Moreover the commonly accepted interpretation of LATE – that it estimates the returns for those induced to change their schooling status by the change in the instrument – assumes that everyone responds to the instrument in the same direction (i.e., all increase their schooling or all decrease it). This is a strong assumption that rules out heterogeneity in the response of schooling choices to instruments.[74]

In this section we distinguish between policy parameters of interest, conventional evaluation parameters and standard estimates of the "returns to schooling." We show how these parameters answer different questions, and how we can recover each of them from the data. We illustrate the empirical importance of accounting for heterogeneity and the fragility of instruments even in an ideal data set with far richer instruments than are available in the widely used CPS or Census data analyzed in earlier sections of this survey. This section draws from Heckman and Vytlacil (2005, 2007b), Heckman, Urzua and Vytlacil (2006) and Carneiro, Heckman and Vytlacil (2005). They estimate the growth rate of earnings in schooling relevant for evaluating a particular education policy such as a tuition subsidy (in a partial equilibrium framework) and find that it is very different from the conventional program evaluation parameters usually defined in the literature, such as the "return to schooling" for the average person, or the "return to schooling" for the average student in college. It also differs from the estimates obtained by applying least squares or instrumental variables methods, the two methods most often used to estimate "returns" to schooling.

We clarify the interpretation of what is usually labeled "ability bias" and "selection bias" in this literature. Standard intuitions break down in a model of heterogeneous returns. They can be very misleading when comparing *OLS* and *IV* estimates of the growth rates of earnings with respect to schooling [see Heckman and Vytlacil (2005)].

Instrumental variables estimates of the "return to schooling" (really growth rates of earnings with schooling) are usually interpreted as estimating an average "return" to schooling for individuals induced to go to school by changes in the values of the instrument, following the *LATE* (local average treatment effect) interpretation of Imbens and Angrist (1994). Angrist and Krueger (1999) are ardent and influential proponents of this approach. We discuss the relationship of *LATE* to treatment effects and rates of return below.

[74] Heckman and Vytlacil (2005) and Heckman, Urzua and Vytlacil (2006) present an extensive discussion of this issue.

Intuitions about ability bias break down in a particularly serious way if individuals have multiple skills and sort across schooling levels in such a way that the best individuals in one schooling level are the worst in the other, and vice versa.[75] Heckman and Robb (1985, 1986) make the point that *IV* does not identify interpretable parameters in a selection model or a generalized Roy model.

8.1. The generalized Roy model of schooling

To focus the discussion, and motivate the empirical literature, we consider a two outcome model. Heckman and Vytlacil (2005, 2007b) and Heckman, Urzua and Vytlacil (2006) extend this discussion to ordered choice and general unordered choice models with multiple outcomes.

As noted in Section 7, from its inception, the modern literature on the "returns to schooling" has recognized that returns may vary across schooling levels and across persons of the same schooling level.[76] The early literature was not clear about the sources of variation in returns. The Roy model (1951) and its extensions [see Heckman (1976, 1979)], as applied by Willis and Rosen (1979), gives a more precise notion of why returns vary and how they depend on S. In the generalized Roy framework, the potential outcomes associated with two different schooling levels are generated by two random variables (U_0, U_1):

$$\ln Y_0 = \alpha + U_0, \tag{15a}$$

$$\ln Y_1 = \alpha + \bar{\beta} + U_1, \tag{15b}$$

where $E(U_0) = 0$ and $E(U_1) = 0$ so α $(= E(\ln Y_0))$ and $\alpha + \bar{\beta}$ $(= E(\ln Y_1))$ are the mean potential outcomes for $\ln Y_0$ and $\ln Y_1$ respectively. The common coefficient model assumes $U_0 = U_1$. We implicitly condition on X, the regressors determining potential outcomes. Let $C(Z)$ denote costs of schooling measured in proportional terms. The Z are the variables determining costs. The individual level "causal effect" of educational choice $S = 1$ is

$$\beta = \ln Y_1 - \ln Y_0 = \bar{\beta} + U_1 - U_0.$$

In general, this is not a rate of return but a growth rate of earnings with schooling. There is a distribution of β in the population.

Observed earnings are written in a "switching regression" form,

$$\begin{aligned}\ln Y &= S \ln Y_1 + (1 - S) \ln Y_0 = \alpha + \beta S + U_0 \\ &= \alpha + \bar{\beta} S + \{U_0 + S(U_1 - U_0)\}.\end{aligned} \tag{16}$$

[75] As opposed to what we would expect from a single skill model where the best individuals in one sector would also be the best individuals in the sector they did not choose if they were placed there instead.

[76] See Becker and Chiswick (1966), Chiswick (1974) and Mincer (1974).

Persons live once and we only observe them in one or the other education state (recall $S = 0$ or 1). This equation captures the literature on counterfactual states that was developed by Roy (1951). It is also a version of Quandt's (1958, 1972) switching regression model. It is equivalent to the familiar semilog specification of the earnings–schooling equation popularized by Mincer (1974), given in Equation (11), which in the current notation writes log earnings $\ln Y$ as a function of S,

$$\ln Y = \alpha + \bar{\beta} S + U, \tag{17}$$

where $U = U_0 + S(U_1 - U_0)$.[77] In terms of the notation of Section 7, $U_0 = \varepsilon_\alpha$, $U_1 - U_0 = \varepsilon_\rho$.

In the generalized Roy framework, the choice of schooling is explicitly modeled. In its simplest form

$$S = \begin{cases} 1 & \text{if } \ln Y_1 - \ln Y_0 \geqslant C \Longleftrightarrow \beta \geqslant C, \\ 0 & \text{otherwise.} \end{cases} \tag{18}$$

If agents know or can partially predict β at the time they make their schooling decisions, there is dependence between β and S in Equation (16). This produces the "correlated random coefficient model" that is often applied to general versions of (16). Decision rules similar to (18) characterize many other economic choices.

The conventional approach to estimating selection models postulates normality of (U_0, U_1) in Equations (15a) and (15b), writes $\bar{\beta}$ and α as linear functions of X and postulates independence between X and (U_0, U_1). Parallel normality and independence assumptions are made for the unobservables and observables in selection equation (18). From estimates of the structural model, it is possible to answer a variety of economic questions and to construct the various treatment parameters and distributions of treatment parameters.[78] However in recent years these assumptions have often been viewed as unacceptably strong by empirical labor economists [see, e.g., Angrist and Krueger (1999)].[79]

A major advance in the recent literature in econometrics is the development of frameworks that relax conventional linearity, normality and separability assumptions to estimate various economic parameters. Heckman and Vytlacil (2000, 2005, 2007b) develop

[77] For simplicity, throughout this section we suppress explicit notation for dependence of the parameters on the covariates X unless it is clarifying to make this dependence explicit.

[78] Willis and Rosen (1979) is an example of the application of the generalized Roy model. Textbook treatments of the normal selection model are available in Amemiya (1985) and Ruud (2000). Aakvik, Heckman and Vytlacil (2005), Heckman, Tobias and Vytlacil (2001, 2003) and Heckman and Vytlacil (2007a) derive all of the treatment parameters and distributions of treatment parameters for several parametric models including the normal. The Heckman, Tobias and Vytlacil papers present one elementary discussion of the normal selection model applied to the generalized Roy framework. Carneiro, Hansen and Heckman (2003) and Cunha, Heckman and Navarro (2005) estimate the distribution of treatment effects under semiparametric assumptions. We review this work in the last two sections of this chapter.

[79] A large literature, starting with Heckman and Sedlacek (1985) and exemplified most recently by Blundell, Reed and Stoker (2003) shows that correcting for selection and sectoral choices, a log normality assumption for sectoral earnings fits the data well.

a framework for estimating rates of return to schooling (mean growth rates of earnings with schooling) that do not depend on normality, independence of the conditioning variables with the regressors, separability or linearity of the estimating equations. Their work unites *IV* and selection models and presents a new local *IV* approach as a way to estimate selection models. Heckman, Urzua and Vytlacil (2006) and Heckman and Vytlacil (2005) present extensive discussions of the relationship between the two approaches.

Heckman and Vytlacil work with general nonseparable models,

$$\ln Y_1 = \mu_1(X, U_1) \quad \text{and} \quad \ln Y_0 = \mu_0(X, U_0). \tag{19}$$

The growth rate of earnings due to schooling is $\ln Y_1 - \ln Y_0 = \beta = \mu_1(X, U_1) - \mu_0(X, U_0)$, which is a general nonseparable function of (U_1, U_0). It is not assumed that $X \perp\!\!\!\perp (U_0, U_1)$, so X may be correlated with the unobservables in potential outcomes. As demonstrated by Heckman and Vytlacil (2000, 2005, 2007a), one needs exogeneity of X only if one is seeking to make out of sample projections. Like virtually the entire microeconomic literature, they ignore any general equilibrium effects of policies on Y_1, Y_0 or β.[80]

A latent variable model that captures decision rule (18) in a general way is:

$$\begin{aligned} S^* &= \mu_S(Z) - U_S, \\ S &= 1 \quad \text{if } S^* \geqslant 0. \end{aligned} \tag{20}$$

In this notation the Z can include all of the variables in the outcome equations plus the variables in the cost function which are a source of exclusion restrictions. $\mu_S(Z)$ is a general function of the observables where U_S is an unobservable arising from Y_1, Y_0 and C. A person goes to school ($S = 1$) if $S^* \geqslant 0$. Otherwise $S = 0$. In this notation, (Z, X) are observed and (U_1, U_0, U_S) are unobserved. U_S may depend on U_1 and U_0 and the unobservables in C in a general way. The Z vector may include some or all of the components of X.

The separability between Z and U_S in (20) plays a crucial role in the entire modern instrumental variables literature based on *LATE* and its extensions. It produces the "monotonicity" or "uniformity" condition of Imbens and Angrist (1994). Without the separability, changes in the instruments in Z can induce two-way flows into and out of treatment and cause *IV* to break down as a method for estimating treatment effects. See Heckman and Vytlacil (2005, 2007b) and Heckman, Urzua and Vytlacil (2006). Those authors explore the consequences of a simple random coefficient choice model $\mu_S(Z) = Z\gamma$, where γ is a random coefficient that is statistically independent of Z and U_S. If γ can assume both positive and negative values, then monotonicity can be

[80] Heckman, Lochner and Taber (1998) analyze generalized Roy models of schooling in a general equilibrium framework.

violated. But it can also be violated if γ is a nonnegative random vector since different components of γ would differ across persons experiencing the same change in Z.

The separability that is required to justify (20) and that underlies the entire *LATE*-based literature cannot be justified in many choice-theoretic models of schooling including dynamic discrete choice models. The Bellman equation producing the value function in multiperiod settings generates nonseparability between observables and unobservables in the choice equation in early stage decisions even if final stage choices are separable in those variables [see Cunha, Heckman and Urzua (2006)]. The method of *IV* applied to a heterogeneous outcome model is fundamentally asymmetric. It allows for heterogeneity in responses to schooling (i.e., it imposes no restrictions on β which may be general random variables). At the same time, it restricts the heterogeneity in responses of schooling choices to changes in Z. Consider the special case $\mu_s(Z) = Z\gamma$. The "monotonicity conditions" invoked in the recent literature to justify *IV* as estimating the return to schooling for people induced into schooling by a change in instrument rules out a random coefficient model for γ except for very special cases. Thus it does not allow for heterogeneity in choices, but it allows for heterogeneity in outcomes. See the discussion in Heckman and Vytlacil (2005, 2007b) and Heckman, Urzua and Vytlacil (2006).

Heckman and Vytlacil (2001a, 2007b) assume that (a) Z has some variables that shift $\mu_S(Z)$ given X (the other variables) – an exclusion condition that is standard in the *IV* literature; (b) The unobservables (U_0, U_1, U_S) are independent of Z given X (a standard instrumental variables condition) and (c) $0 < \Pr(S = 1|X) < 1$, so in large samples there are some people who have $S = 1$ and some who have $S = 0$, so comparisons between treated and untreated persons can be made for those values of X. They make additional mild regularity assumptions. Under these conditions it is possible to interpret *IV* as a weighted average of willingness to pay measures called the marginal treatment effect (*MTE*). A version of this treatment effect was introduced into the econometrics literature by Björklund and Moffitt (1987) for a linear-in-parameters model.[81]

Let $P(z)$ be the probability of receiving schooling level 1, $S = 1$ conditional on $Z = z$, $P(z) \equiv \Pr(S = 1|Z = z) = F_{U_S}(\mu_S(z))$ where F_{U_S} is the distribution of U_S. Without loss of generality, one may write $U_S \sim \text{Unif}[0, 1]$ so $\mu_S(z) = P(z)$.[82] (If $S^* = \nu(Z) - V_S$, and V_S is a continuous random variable, one can always reparameterize the model using simple transformation of variable rules so $\mu_S(Z) = F_{V_S}(\nu(Z))$, where F_{V_S} is the distribution of V and $U_S = F_{V_S}(V_S)$.) The propensity score $P(z)$ is a monotonic transformation of the mean utility of attending school and we will refer to it as the mean utility.

[81] Vytlacil (2002) shows that under the conditions stated in this paragraph, separability (20) implies and is implied by the monotonicity and independence conditions of Imbens and Angrist (1994) and Angrist and Imbens (1995). Heckman and Vytlacil (2005, 2007b) present three alternative definitions of the *MTE* for a general nonlinear model which are equivalent in a linear model.

[82] We say a random variable is uniformly distributed over [0, 1] if its density is identically equal to 1 over this interval.

When β varies in the population, the growth rate of earnings with schooling is a random variable and there is a distribution of "causal effects." There are various ways to summarize this distribution and, in general, no single statistic will capture all aspects of the distribution.

Many summary measures of the distribution of β are used in the recent literature. Among them are

$$\begin{aligned} E(\beta|X=x) &= E(\ln Y_1 - \ln Y_0|X=x) \\ &= \bar{\beta}(x) \end{aligned}$$

the return to the population average person given characteristics $X = x$. This quantity is sometimes called "the" causal effect of S.[83] Others report the "return" for those who attend school:

$$\begin{aligned} E(\beta|S=1, X=x) &= E(\ln Y_1 - \ln Y_0|S=1, X=x) \\ &= \bar{\beta}(x) + E(U_1 - U_0|S=1, X=x).^{84} \end{aligned}$$

This is the parameter emphasized by Willis and Rosen (1979) where $E(U_1 - U_0|S = 1, X = x)$ is the sorting gain – how people who take $S = 1$ differ from randomly sampled persons.

Another parameter is "the return" for those who are currently not going to school:

$$\begin{aligned} E(\beta|S=0, X=x) &= E(\ln Y_1 - \ln Y_0|S=0, X=x) \\ &= \bar{\beta}(x) + E(U_1 - U_0|S=0, X=x). \end{aligned}$$

Angrist and Krueger (1991) and Meghir and Palme (2001) estimate this parameter and we discuss it further below. In addition to these "effects" is the effect for persons indifferent between the two levels of schooling, which in the simple Roy model without costs ($C = 0$) is $E(\ln Y_1 - \ln Y_0| \ln Y_1 - \ln Y_0 = 0) = 0$.

Depending on the conditioning sets and the summary statistics desired, a variety of "causal effects" can be defined. Different causal effects answer different economic questions. As noted by Heckman and Robb (1986), Heckman (1997) and Heckman and Vytlacil (2005, 2007b), under one of two conditions,

I: $U_1 = U_0$ (common effect model),

or more generally,

II. $\Pr(S = 1|X = x, \beta) = \Pr(S = 1|X)$ (conditional on X, β does not affect choices),

[83] It is the Average Treatment Effect (*ATE*) parameter. Card (1999, 2001) defines it as the "true causal effect" of education. See also Angrist and Krueger (1999, 2001). Our chapter demonstrates that there is no unique "true causal effect."

[84] It is the Treatment on the Treated parameter as discussed by Heckman and Robb (1985).

all of the mean treatment effects conditional on X collapse to the same parameter. The second condition is the one implicitly used by Mincer (1974). It assumes that schooling decisions are not made on the basis of any component of the growth rate β. If neither condition is satisfied, there are many candidates for the title of causal effect. This ambiguity has produced considerable confusion in the empirical literature as different analysts use different definitions in reporting empirical results and many of the estimates are not strictly comparable.[85]

Which, if any, of these effects should be designated as "the" causal effect? We have already noted that conventional "causal effects" are not estimates of a marginal internal rate of return, but instead are estimates of some average growth rate of earnings with schooling. Instead of hoping that a treatment effect or estimator answers an interesting economic question, a better approach is to state an economic question and find the answer to it. This obvious and traditional approach is not pursued in the recent literature. Heckman and Vytlacil (2001c, 2005, 2007b) develop this approach using a standard welfare framework. They introduce the notion of a policy relevant treatment effect. Aggregate per capita outcomes under one policy are compared with aggregate per capita outcomes under another. One of the policies may be no policy at all. For utility criterion $V(Y)$, a standard welfare analysis compares an alternative policy with a baseline policy. The Policy Relevant Treatment Effect (*PRTE*) is

$$E\big(V(Y)|\text{Alternative Policy}\big) - E\big(V(Y)|\text{Baseline Policy}\big). \tag{21}$$

Adopting the common coefficient model, so $\beta = \bar{\beta}$, a log utility specification ($V(Y) = \ln Y$) and ignoring general equilibrium effects, where β is a constant, $\bar{\beta}$, the mean change in welfare is

$$E(\ln Y|\text{Alternative Policy}) - E(\ln Y|\text{Baseline Policy}) = \bar{\beta}(\Delta P),$$

where (ΔP) is the change in the proportion of people induced to attend school by the policy. This can be defined conditional on $X = x$ or overall for the population. In terms of gains per capita to recipients, the effect is $\bar{\beta}$. This is also the mean change in log income if β is a random variable but independent of S if conditions I or II apply. In the general case, when agents partially anticipate β, and comparative advantage dictates schooling choices, none of the traditional treatment parameters plays the role of $\bar{\beta}$ in (21) or answers the stated economic question. Heckman and Vytlacil (2001c, 2005, 2007b) show how the policy relevant treatment effect can be represented as a weighted average of the *MTE*. The weights are given in Table 9b. See Heckman, Urzua and Vytlacil (2006) for further examples.

In the empirical literature on the returns to schooling the aim is often to estimate $E(\beta|X = x)$, although this is unlikely to be the answer to many relevant policy

[85] For example, Heckman and Robb (1985) note that in his survey of the union effects on wages, Lewis (1986) confuses these different "effects." This is especially important in his comparison of cross section and longitudinal estimates where he inappropriately compares conceptually different parameters.

questions. The standard estimation method is instrumental variables. However, in the presence of heterogeneity and self-selection, we cannot identify $E(\beta|X = x)$ by using standard instrumental variables methods. Instead, we identify *LATE* [Imbens and Angrist (1994)], or a weighted average of *LATE* parameters, which is an instrument dependent parameter. It is usually broadly defined as the "average 'return' to schooling for individuals induced to change their schooling by the observed change in the instrument". The economic interpretation of this parameter is unclear. In general, *LATE* does not correspond to a policy relevant parameter or a rate of return. The *LATE* parameter of Imbens and Angrist (1994) is often invoked by empirical analysts to justify an instrumental variable estimate, without providing any precise definition of the economic question it addresses.

One way to make this general point is to explore what is estimated by using compulsory schooling as an instrument. Compulsory schooling is sometimes viewed as an ideal instrument [see Angrist and Krueger (1991)]. But when "returns" are heterogeneous, and agents act on that heterogeneity in making schooling decisions, compulsory schooling used as an instrument identifies only one of many possible treatment parameters and in general does not estimate a rate of return to schooling.

Compulsory schooling selects at random persons who ordinarily would not be schooled ($S = 0$) and forces them to be schooled. It is straightforward to establish that it identifies treatment on the untreated:

$$E(\ln Y_1 - \ln Y_0|X = x, S = 0) = E(\beta|X = x, S = 0)$$

but not $ATE = E(\ln Y_1 - \ln Y_0) = \bar{\beta}$, treatment on the treated $TT = E(\ln Y_1 - \ln Y_0|X = x, S = 1) = E(\beta|X = x, S = 1)$, or the marginal internal rate of return.[86]

Treatment on the untreated answers an interesting policy question. It is informative about the earnings gains for a policy directed toward those who ordinarily would not attend school and who are selected into school at random from this pool. If the policy the analyst seeks to evaluate is compulsory schooling then the instrumental variable estimand[87] and the policy relevant treatment effect coincide. More generally, if the instrumental variable we use is exactly the policy we want to evaluate, then the *IV* estimand and the policy relevant parameter are the same. But whenever that is not the case, the *IV* estimand does not identify the effect of the policy when returns vary among people and they make choices of treatment based on those returns.[88] For example, if the policy we want to consider is a tuition subsidy directed toward the very poorest within the pool of nonattenders, then an instrumental variable estimate based on compulsory schooling will not be the relevant return to evaluate the policy.[89]

[86] See Carneiro, Heckman and Vytlacil (2005).

[87] An estimand is the probability limit of an estimator.

[88] See Heckman, Urzua and Vytlacil (2006) for an analysis of this case.

[89] Heckman and Vytlacil (2005) show that for every policy it is possible in principle to define an instrumental variable that generates the correct policy relevant treatment effect. However, such an instrument may not be feasible in any given data set because of support problems. (Support is the range of a random variable where it has positive density.) Different policies define different policy relevant instrumental variables.

8.2. Defining treatment effects in the generalized Roy model and relating them to true rates of return

The index model (18) and (20) can be used to define the marginal treatment effect (*MTE*),

$$\Delta^{MTE}(x, u_S) \equiv E(\beta | X = x, U_S = u_S).$$

This is the mean gain to schooling for individuals with characteristics $X = x$ and with unobservable $U_S = u_S$.[90] It is a willingness to pay measure for an additional year of

Table 9a
Treatment effects and estimands as weighted averages of the marginal treatment effect

$ATE(x) = \int_0^1 MTE(x, u_S)\,du_S$	(Average Treatment Effect)
$TT(x) = \int_0^1 MTE(x, u_S)h_{TT}(x, u_S)\,du_S$	(Treatment on the Treated)
$TUT(x) = \int_0^1 MTE(x, u_S)h_{TUT}(x, u_S)\,du_S$	(Treatment on the Untreated)
$PRTE(x) = \int_0^1 MTE(x, u_S)h_{PRT}(x, u_S)\,du_S$	(Policy Relevant Treatment Effect)
$IV(x) = \int_0^1 MTE(x, u_S)h_{IV}(x, u_S)\,du_S$	
$OLS(x) = \int_0^1 MTE(x, u_S)h_{OLS}(x, u_S)\,du_S$	

Source: Heckman and Vytlacil (2001a, 2001b, 2005, 2007b).

Table 9b
Weights*

$$h_{TT}(x, u_S) = \left[\int_{u_S}^1 f(p|X = x)\,dp\right]\frac{1}{E(P|X=x)}$$

$$h_{TUT}(x, u_S) = \left[\int_0^{u_S} f(p|X = x)\,dp\right]\cdot\frac{1}{E((1-P)|X=x)}$$

$$h_{PRT}(x, u_S) = \left[\frac{F_{P*,X}(u_S) - F_{P,X}(u_S)}{\Delta P}\right]$$

$$h_{IV}(x, u_S) = \left[\int_{u_S}^1 (p - E(P|X = x)) f(p|X = x)\,dp\right]\frac{1}{\mathrm{Var}(P|X=x)}$$

$$h_{OLS} = \frac{E(U_1|X=x, U_S=u_S)h_1(x, u_D) - E(U_0|X=x, U_S=u_S)h_0(x, u_S)}{MTE(x, u_S)}$$

$$h_1(x, u_S) = \left[\int_{u_S}^1 f(p|X = x)\,dp\right]\frac{1}{E(P|X=x)}$$

$$h_0(x, u_S) = \left[\int_0^{u_S} f(p|X = x)\,dp\right]\frac{1}{E((1-P)|X=x)}$$

Source: Heckman and Vytlacil (2001a, 2001b, 2005, 2007b).
* $f(p|X = x)$ is the density of $P(Z)$ given $X = x$.

90 Björklund and Moffitt (1987) introduced this parameter in the context of the parametric normal Roy model. See Heckman and Vytlacil (2005, 2007a, 2007b) for a discussion of this literature.

schooling for persons indifferent between attending or not attending college at a mean utility $P(Z) = u_S$.

Under their assumptions, Heckman and Vytlacil (1999, 2001b, 2005, 2007b) establish that all of the conventional treatment parameters used in the program evaluation literature are different weighted averages of the *MTE* where the weights integrate to one. The conventional treatment parameters are the average treatment effect or *ATE*, $E(Y_1 - Y_0|S = 1, x)$, and treatment on the untreated or *TUT*, $E(Y_1 - Y_0|S = 0, x)$. See Table 9a [from Heckman and Vytlacil (2000, 2005, 2007b)] for the treatment parameters expressed in terms of *MTE* and Table 9b for the weights. The analysis of Heckman and Vytlacil (2001b, 2005, 2007b) unites the selection literature and the modern *IV* literature using a common analytical framework. Heckman, Urzua and Vytlacil (2006) discuss how to construct the weights.[91]

These tables also show how one can write the *IV* and *OLS* estimates and the Policy Relevant Treatment Effect as weighted averages of the *MTE*. The crucial observation to extract from this table is that the weights on *MTE* are different for *IV* and for the treatment parameters. Thus, not only is it true that the treatment parameters are *not* rates of return, but *IV* does not in general estimate the treatment parameters.

Figure 10a plots the marginal treatment effect (*MTE*) derived from a generalized normal Roy model using the parameterization of (17) and (18) shown at the base of Figure 10b. It displays the prototypical pattern that the returns to schooling decline for those persons who have higher costs of schooling (higher U_S), i.e., for persons less likely to attend school.[92] The same figure is implicit in the analysis of Willis and Rosen but they do not develop or exposit it. The treatment effect parameters generated from this model are presented in Table 10. It also presents *IV* and *OLS* estimates as well as the sorting gain and selection bias terms for this model.

Figure 10a also displays the weights on *MTE* used to form *ATE* (Average Treatment Effect), *TT* (Treatment on the Treated) and *TUT* (Treatment on the Untreated) for a generalized Roy model (with tuition costs).[93] *TT* overweights the *MTE* for persons with low values of U_S who, *ceteris paribus*, are more likely to attend school. *TUT* overweights the *MTE* for persons with high values of U_S who are less likely to attend school. *ATE* weights *MTE* uniformly. The decline in *MTE* reveals that the "gross return" (β) declines with U_S. Those more likely to attend school (based on lower U_S) have higher "gross returns" or higher growth rates of earnings with schooling. Not surprisingly, in light of the shape of *MTE* and the shapes of the weights, $TT > ATE > TUT$. There is a positive sorting gain ($E(U_1 - U_0|X = x, S = 1) > 0$) and a negative selection bias ($E(U_0|X = x, S = 1) - E(U_0|X = x, S = 0) < 0$). Figure 10b displays the *MTE* and the weights for *OLS* and for *IV* using $P(Z)$ as the instrument. *IV* weights

[91] The website for their paper provides software for doing so.

[92] Recall that $S = \mathbf{1}(S^* > 0) = \mathbf{1}(\mu_S(Z) > U_S)$ so that the higher U_S, the less likely is a person to attend college or have $S = 1$.

[93] The form of the Roy model we use assumes additive separability and generates U_0, U_1 and U_S from a common unobservable ε. Thus, in this example, the distribution of $U_1 - U_0$ given U_S is degenerate.

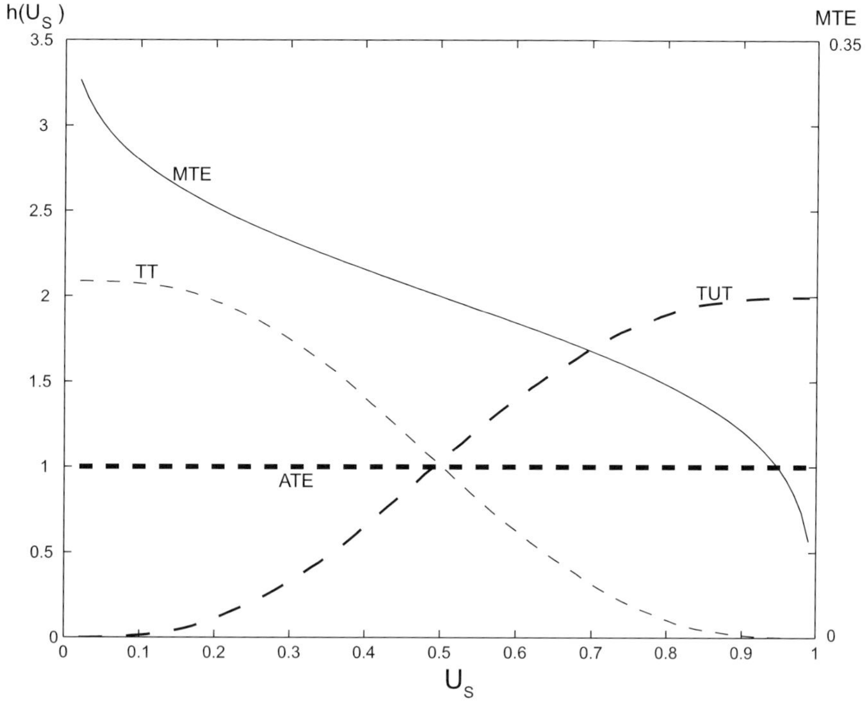

Figure 10a. Weights for the marginal treatment effect for different parameters.

the *MTE* more symmetrically and in a different fashion than *ATE*, *TUT* or *TT*. The shape of the *IV* weight is prototypical when $P(Z)$ is the instrument. However, for other instruments, including individual components of Z, the shapes of the weights are different [see Heckman, Urzua and Vytlacil (2006), for further analysis and examples]. We present examples of these weights below. *OLS* weights *MTE* very differently. The contrast between the *OLS* weight and the *IV* weight conveys the contrast between the CPS/Census literature and the modern *IV* literature. In general, neither identifies *ATE* or the other treatment effects, and the conventional treatment effects are not rates of return.

To estimate *ex post* rates of return, it is necessary to account for foregone earnings and direct costs. The treatment effect literature typically accounts for neither and reports differences in labor market payments to different schooling levels. To cast the discussion of Section 4 into the framework of this section, let $Y_{1,t}$ be the earnings of a college-educated person at age t. Let $Y_{0,t}$ be the earnings for a high school-educated person at age t. (To this point in this section we have abstracted from age-dependent growth rates of earnings.) Suppose that it takes τ periods to complete college and that direct costs are C_t per period while in college. The interest rate is r, assumed to be constant. Assume that while in school persons receive no earnings. (If they did, they could help offset costs C.) College educated persons retire at age T_1. High school educated persons

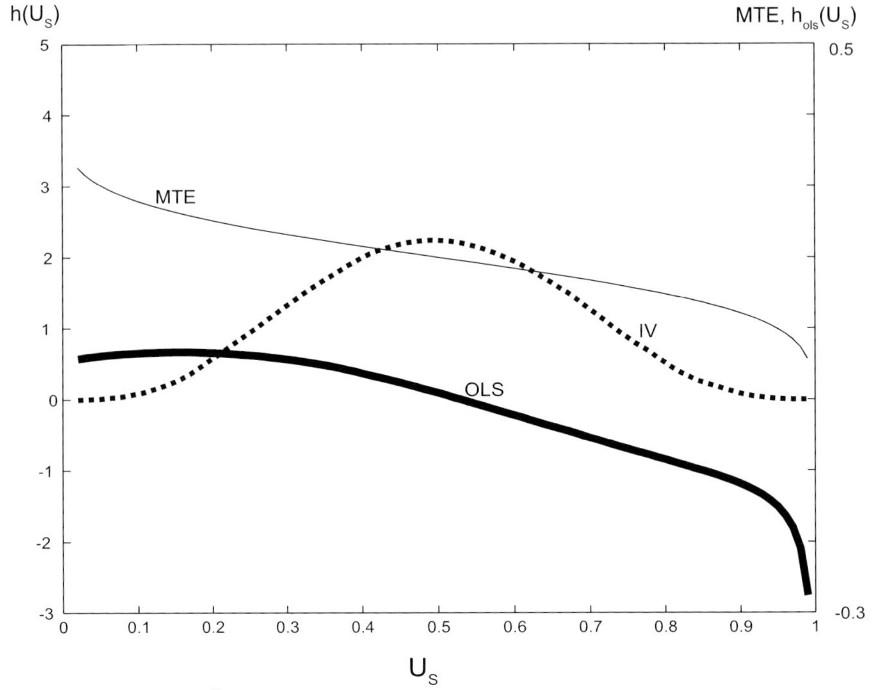

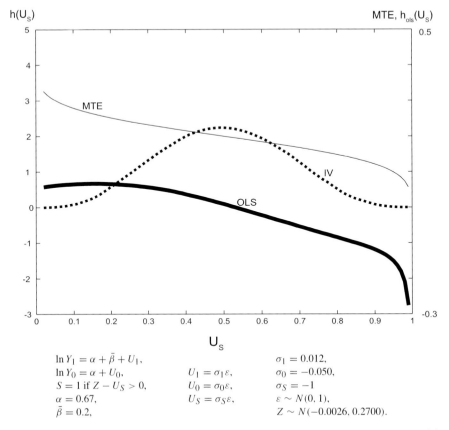

$$\ln Y_1 = \alpha + \bar{\beta} + U_1, \qquad \sigma_1 = 0.012,$$
$$\ln Y_0 = \alpha + U_0, \qquad U_1 = \sigma_1 \varepsilon, \qquad \sigma_0 = -0.050,$$
$$S = 1 \text{ if } Z - U_S > 0, \qquad U_0 = \sigma_0 \varepsilon, \qquad \sigma_S = -1$$
$$\alpha = 0.67, \qquad U_S = \sigma_S \varepsilon, \qquad \varepsilon \sim N(0, 1),$$
$$\bar{\beta} = 0.2, \qquad Z \sim N(-0.0026, 0.2700).$$

Figure 10b. Marginal treatment effect vs. linear instrumental variables and ordinary least squares weights. Roy example. Source: Heckman and Vytlacil (2005).

Table 10
Treatment parameters in the generalized Roy example

Ordinary least squares	0.1735
Treatment on the treated	0.2442
Treatment on the untreated	0.1570
Average treatment effect	0.2003
Sorting gain*	0.0440
Selection bias†	−0.0707
Linear instrumental variables‡	0.2017

$^*E[U_1 - U_0 | S = 1] = TT - ATE.$

$^\dagger E[U_0 | S = 1] - E[U_0 | S = 0] = OLS - TT.$

‡Using propensity score as the instrument.

retire at age T_0. One definition of the return to college R is

$$R = \frac{\sum_{t=\tau}^{T_1} \frac{Y_{1,t}}{(1+r)^{t-\tau}} - \sum_{t=0}^{T_0} \frac{(Y_{0,t}+C_t)}{(1+r)^t}}{\sum_{t=0}^{T_0} \frac{Y_{0,t}+C_t}{(1+r)^t}}.$$

This is a version of the Becker (1964) formula. It compares the present values of two earnings streams realized τ periods apart.

As discussed in Section 3, in the special case assumed by Mincer, log earnings are parallel in experience across schooling categories. For the case of geometric growth and defining $\overline{Y}_0 = Y_{0,0}$ and $\overline{Y}_1 = Y_{1,\tau}$, earnings may be written as:

$$Y_{0,t} = \overline{Y}_0(1+g)^t,$$
$$Y_{1,t} = \overline{Y}_1(1+g)^{t-\tau}, \quad t \geqslant \tau,$$

where g is the growth rate of earnings with age.[94] Mincer further assumes that $T_1 - T_0 = \tau$ so working lives are the same for both schooling classes. The discounted growth rate of earnings with experience, e, is

$$e = \sum_{j=0}^{T_0} \left(\frac{1+g}{1+r}\right)^j.$$

Assume that direct costs (psychic and tuition) are the same per period during the schooling years and define

$$A(\tau) = \sum_{j=0}^{\tau} \left(\frac{1}{1+r}\right)^j.$$

The return in this case is

$$R = \frac{\overline{Y}_1 e - \overline{Y}_0 e - CA(\tau)}{CA(\tau) + \overline{Y}_0 e}.$$

The growth rate of earnings with schooling is

$$\phi = \frac{\overline{Y}_1 - \overline{Y}_0}{\overline{Y}_0} \approx \ln \overline{Y}_1 - \ln \overline{Y}_0.$$

This is the "Mincer return" to schooling. An alternative expression for the return is

$$R = \frac{\phi - \frac{CA(\tau)}{\overline{Y}_0 e}}{1 + \frac{CA(\tau)}{\overline{Y}_0 e}}.$$

[94] Mincer assumes more general period-specific growth rates. The argument in the text can be modified to account for this at the cost of more notational complexity.

This shows that the Mincer return ϕ, is greater than the true return, R, whenever costs are positive. When costs are zero ($C = 0$), R equals the Mincer return, ϕ. Thus, the Mincer assumptions justify the conventional practice of equating growth rates to rates of returns, the implicit assumption in the recent literature on estimating rates of return. In general, if $1+R > (1+r)^{\tau}$, it pays to go to college; otherwise, it does not. An alternative way to state this criterion is that it pays to go to college if

$$1 + \phi > (1 + r)^{\tau}.$$

When $\tau = 1$, this simplifies to the conventional criterion that $\phi > r$.

The evidence presented in Sections 3 and 4 of this chapter argues strongly against the practice of equating growth rates with rates of return. Mincer's parallelism assumption across schooling levels (i.e., that growth rates of earnings with experience, g, are the same for all schooling levels) is not accurate for earnings profiles from more recent data. Additionally, the evidence presented below in Section 10 points to the existence of substantial psychic cost components and an adjustment for psychic cost components substantially reduces the rate of return to schooling. The current literature on estimating rates of return makes none of these adjustments and instead reports the growth rate of earnings as a "return." While the growth rate of ϕ is an ingredient of returns, it is not in general a return, as the expression for R reveals.[95]

We can use the modern literature to identify growth rates of earnings for persons at different margins of choice. Costs, discount rates and horizons need to be adjusted appropriately to get true rates of return. To our knowledge, this has not been done in the vast *IV* literature on computing rates of return.

8.3. Understanding why IV estimates exceed OLS estimates of the schooling coefficient

In the generalized Roy model, there are three sources of potential econometric problems; (a) S is correlated with U_0; (b) β is correlated with S (i.e., $U_1 - U_0$ is correlated with S); (c) β is correlated with U_0. The relative importance of the problems depends on what question the analyst seeks to answer. Source (a) arises in ability bias or measurement error models. Source (b) arises if agents partially anticipate β when making schooling decisions so that $\Pr(S = 1|X, \beta) \neq \Pr(S = 1|X)$. In this framework, β is an *ex post* "causal effect," which may not be known to agents *ex ante*. In the case where decisions about S are made in the absence of information about β, β is independent of S. Source (c) arises from the possibility that the gains to schooling (β) may be dependent on the level of potential earnings in the unschooled state (Y_0) as in the Roy model.

When $U_1 = U_0$, β is a constant for all persons (conditional on X), and we obtain the conventional *IV* model as analyzed by Griliches (1977). In this framework, because β is a constant, there is a unique effect of schooling. Indeed, β is "the" effect of schooling, and the marginal effect is the same as the average effect (conditional on X).

[95] In addition, in this two choice example, there are no option values. Accounting for them is a factor toward raising the rate of return above the measured growth rate.

In the notation of Equation (17), the usual assumption in the literature is that $COV(S, U_0) > 0$. Measured schooling S may be correlated with unmeasured U_0 because of omitted ability factors. Therefore, when β is constant across individuals, the *OLS* estimate of the "return" is an upward biased estimate of β:

$$\text{plim } \hat{\beta}_{OLS} = \beta + \frac{COV(S, U_0)}{V(S)} > \beta.$$

Following Griliches (1977) and the scholars who preceded him, many advocate using instrumental variable estimators for β to correct for this problem. If there is an instrument Z such that $COV(Z, S) \neq 0$ and $COV(Z, U_0) = 0$, then:

$$\text{plim } \hat{\beta}_{IV} = \beta + \frac{COV(Z, U_0)}{COV(Z, S)} = \beta.$$

Therefore we expect that $\hat{\beta}_{IV} < \hat{\beta}_{OLS}$.

However, as noted by Griliches (1977) and Card (1995, 1999, 2001), almost all of the empirical literature on the returns to schooling shows precisely the opposite pattern: $\hat{\beta}_{IV} > \hat{\beta}_{OLS}$. How can one rationalize this finding? One standard explanation is that schooling is measured with error. This would induce a downward bias in the schooling coefficient, which would be corrected by the use of *IV*.

This simple explanation has been questioned in two different ways. Kane, Rouse and Staiger (1999) claim that measurement error in schooling is nonclassical and therefore we might not expect the standard attenuation bias that results from nonclassical measurement error.[96] Card (1999, 2001) argues that, if measurement error is classical, the amount of measurement error in schooling that would have to exist to justify the large gaps between *OLS* and *IV* estimates is unreasonably large. He argues that, in fact, schooling is relatively well measured in the U.S., so that the measurement error explanation for the empirical regularity is likely to be of second order importance.

The explanation for the empirical regularity that Card (1999, 2001) favors is that there is heterogeneity in the returns to schooling so β is a random variable and it is correlated with schooling. For a model with two levels of schooling, this is just the generalized Roy model. In this case, it is possible that *IV* estimates of returns to schooling exceed *OLS* estimates. Implicitly, his argument has three steps: (1) *OLS* is an upward biased estimate of the average "return to schooling" (this is the standard ability bias intuition in a model in which β is the same for everyone); (2) *IV* corresponds to an estimate of the returns to schooling for individuals at the margin;[97] and therefore, (3) if the *IV* estimate of the "return" exceeds the *OLS* estimate of the "return," then individuals at the margin

[96] Nonclassical measurement error is measurement error of a true variable that is stochastically dependent on the true value of the variable. Thus the mean, the variance and other moments of the measurement error may depend on the true value.

[97] This argument is based on *LATE* [Imbens and Angrist (1994)]. Card does not provide a precise definition of the concept. Carneiro, Heckman and Vytlacil (2005) precisely define and estimate the return for the average marginal person. See also the discussion in Heckman and Vytlacil (2005).

have higher "returns" than the average individual in the economy.[98] In our notation, the probability limits of the least squares and IV estimators are

$$\text{plim}\ \hat{\beta}_{OLS} = \bar{\beta} + \frac{COV(S, U_0)}{V(S)} + \frac{COV[S, S(U_1 - U_0)]}{V(S)}, \tag{22}$$

$$\begin{aligned} \text{plim}\ \hat{\beta}_{IV} &= \bar{\beta} + \frac{COV[Z, S(U_1 - U_0)]}{COV(Z, S)} + \frac{COV(Z, U_0)}{COV(Z, S)} \\ &= \bar{\beta} + \frac{COV[Z, S(U_1 - U_0)]}{COV(Z, S)}. \end{aligned} \tag{23}$$

In general, plim $\hat{\beta}_{OLS}$ can be larger than, smaller than or equal to plim $\hat{\beta}_{IV}$. We can rewrite (22) and (23) as:

$$\begin{aligned} \text{plim}\ \hat{\beta}_{OLS} &= \bar{\beta} + E(U_0|S = 1) - E(U_0|S = 0) + E(U_1 - U_0|S = 1) \\ &= E(\beta|S = 1) + E(U_0|S = 1) - E(U_0|S = 0), \\ \text{plim}\ \hat{\beta}_{IV} &= \bar{\beta} + E(U_1 - U_0|S = 1) \\ &\quad + \frac{COV[Z, (U_1 - U_0)|S = 1]\Pr(S = 1)}{COV(Z, S)} \\ &= E(\beta|S = 1) + \frac{COV[Z, (U_1 - U_0)|S = 1]\Pr(S = 1)}{COV(Z, S)}. \end{aligned}$$

Therefore, plim $\hat{\beta}_{IV} >$ plim $\hat{\beta}_{OLS}$ if $\frac{COV[Z,(U_1-U_0)|S=1]\Pr(S=1)}{COV(Z,S)} > E(U_0|S = 1) - E(U_0|S = 0)$.[99]

The assumption implicit in Card's argument, and in the standard ability bias literature, is that $E(U_0|S = 1) - E(U_0|S = 0) > 0$. This condition is satisfied if persons who go to college are above average in high school. In such a case, current college graduates would be at the top of the high school wage distribution if they chose to become high school graduates. If this model generates the data, the only way that plim $\hat{\beta}_{IV} >$ plim $\hat{\beta}_{OLS}$ is if $\frac{COV[Z,(U_1-U_0)|S=1]\Pr(S=1)}{COV(Z,S)} > 0$.

How plausible is this condition? Recall that Z is a determinant of the cost of schooling $C(Z)$ and satisfies the standard instrumental variable assumptions. Assume that C is increasing in Z which is assumed to be scalar.[100] As a consequence of these two conditions,

$$COV(Z, S) < 0 \quad \text{and} \quad COV(Z, U_1) = COV(Z, U_0) = 0. \tag{24}$$

98 Card's model was described in Section 7. It allows for multiple levels of schooling, but assumes a common rate of return across all schooling levels or else reports an average return to schooling across schooling levels. Heckman, Urzua and Vytlacil (2006) and Heckman and Vytlacil (2005, 2007b) develop methods for identifying marginal returns to different schooling levels. For simplicity, we assume a two outcome schooling model.

99 This argument appears in Carneiro and Heckman (2002).

100 Z may be a vector, but in this example we assume it is a scalar.

In the simple two outcome model of schooling, individuals enroll in school if benefits are higher than costs as is clear from Equation (18) ($S = 1$ if $\beta - C(Z) = \bar{\beta} + (U_1 - U_0) - C(Z) > 0$). In such a model the average individual who attends school has a higher return than the marginal individual ($E(\beta|S = 1) > E(\beta|\beta = C(Z))$). Furthermore, even though $COV(Z, U_1 - U_0) = 0$, $COV(Z, U_1 - U_0|S = 1) > 0$ (if an individual has a high cost, or high Z, he or she will only attend school if he or she also has a high $U_1 - U_0$). But in that case, because $COV(Z, S) < 0$, plim $\hat{\beta}_{IV} <$ plim $\hat{\beta}_{OLS}$. Implicit in Card's analysis is the assumption that it is not possible for the average student to have a higher return than the marginal student and still find that $\hat{\beta}_{IV} > \hat{\beta}_{OLS}$. Card rationalizes $\hat{\beta}_{IV} > \hat{\beta}_{OLS}$ by assuming that the marginal student with a higher return than the average student is out of school because of some external constraint, such as a liquidity constraint so $E(\beta|S = 1) < E(\beta|\beta = C(Z))$. The less able (lower β) people are excluded from school. In Card's original model, the "returns" to schooling decrease with the amount of schooling for each individual ($k_1 < 0$ in Section 7), and those individuals whose schooling decision is more sensitive to changes in the instrument have relatively little schooling and, as a consequence, relatively high returns.

Drawing on the generalized Roy model, Carneiro and Heckman (2002) and Carneiro, Heckman and Vytlacil (2005) argue instead that the reason why $\hat{\beta}_{IV} > \hat{\beta}_{OLS}$ is not that the marginal student has a higher return than the average student ($E(\beta|S = 1) < E(\beta|\beta = C(Z))$), but instead that $E(U_0|S = 1) - E(U_0|S = 0) < 0$. They show empirically, for a nationally representative sample of U.S. white males (NLSY79), that the marginal "return" is below the average for college goers while, simultaneously, $\hat{\beta}_{IV} > \hat{\beta}_{OLS}$. In their setup, $\frac{COV[Z,(U_1-U_0)|S=1]\Pr(S=1)}{COV(Z,S)} < 0$, $E(U_0|S = 1) - E(U_0|S = 0) < 0$ and $\frac{COV[Z,(U_1-U_0)|S=1]\Pr(S=1)}{COV(Z,S)} > E(U_0|S = 1) - E(U_0|S = 0)$.[101] *OLS* estimates are downward biased for $E(\beta|S = 1)$ because $E(U_0|S = 1) - E(U_0|S = 0) < 0$. For example, if individuals with $S = 1$ become teachers and those with $S = 0$ become plumbers, then the latter are better plumbers than the average teacher would be if he became a plumber.[102] This possibility is featured in Willis and Rosen (1979), who speculate that, contrary to conventional wisdom, $COV(U_1, U_0) < 0$, although, with their model, they cannot identify this correlation from the data. Carneiro, Heckman and Vytlacil (2005) and Cunha, Heckman and Navarro (2005) identify this covariance and find evidence that supports the Willis–Rosen conjecture of a negative correlation. When analysts use *OLS*, they compare $E(Y_1|S = 1)$ with $E(Y_0|S = 0)$ (see Equation (22)), and since $E(Y_0|S = 0) > E(Y_0|S = 1)$, the *OLS* estimate is an underestimate of $E(Y_1 - Y_0|S = 1)$.

To summarize, an important lesson from the recent literature is that in a model of heterogeneous returns, intuitions about ability bias are no longer as simple as in the standard homogeneous returns model with a single measure of ability [Griliches (1977)]. In

[101] Carneiro (2002) shows that their conclusions hold for white females and across different data sets.
[102] In such a model we need to have more than one dimension of ability.

such a model, the most able people enroll in school.[103] In a more general Roy-type model, there can be multiple abilities (in this case, U_1 and U_0), which can be arbitrarily correlated (positively or negatively). The idea that individuals with "high ability" are more likely to enroll in school is no longer obvious. Recent evidence supports the claim that the most able persons in the U_0 distribution (high school skills) do not go on to college. This is true not only in models of schooling, but also in many other models in economics where returns to an activity are heterogeneous and people sort into different activities based on those returns.[104]

8.4. Estimating the MTE

We now show how the local *IV* methods of Heckman and Vytlacil (1999, 2001b, 2005, 2007b) can be used to estimate average returns to school for any population of interest. Heckman, Urzua and Vytlacil (2006) show how to estimate the *MTE* and generate all of the weights shown in Table 9b. They also provide software for doing so. Using Equation (16) the conditional expectation of $\log Y$ $(= \ln Y_0(1-S) + \ln Y_1 S)$ is

$$\begin{aligned} E(\ln Y|Z=z) &= E(\ln Y_0|Z=z) \\ &\quad + E(\ln Y_1 - \ln Y_0|Z=z, S=1)\Pr(S=1|Z=z), \end{aligned}$$

where we keep the conditioning on X implicit. From the index structure generated by decision rules (18) and (20), we may write this expectation as

$$E(\ln Y|Z=z) = E(\ln Y_0) + E\big(\beta|P(z) \geqslant U_S, P(Z)=P(z)\big)P(z).$$

Observe that the instruments enter the model through the probability of selection or the propensity score $(P(z))$. Using $P(z)$ as the instrument, and applying the Wald estimator for two different values of Z, z and z', assuming $P(z) < P(z')$, we obtain the *IV* formula:

$$\begin{aligned} &\frac{E(\ln Y|P(Z)=P(z)) - E(\ln Y|P(Z)=P(z'))}{P(z)-P(z')} \\ &\quad = \bar{\beta} + \frac{E(U_1-U_0|P(z) \geqslant U_S)P(z) - E(U_1-U_0|P(z') \geqslant U_S)P(z')}{P(z)-P(z')} \\ &\quad = E\big(\beta|P(z) < U_S \leqslant P(z')\big) \\ &\quad = \Delta^{LATE}\big(P(z), P(z')\big), \end{aligned}$$

[103] However, even in the one ability model, Griliches (1977) shows that it is possible that the most able do not enroll in school because their opportunity costs of doing so are too high.

[104] For example, returns to job training or unionism vary across individuals and individuals make choices based on them. The productivity of different inputs varies across firms and they choose different quantities of inputs according to the productivity patterns they face (this is relevant for the estimation of production functions). Different consumers have different demand elasticities for a good and their choice of quantities depends on their elasticity.

where Δ^{LATE} is the *LATE* parameter. This is the average return to schooling for individuals who have U_S between $P(z)$ and $P(z')$ $(P(z) < U_S \leqslant P(z'))$. As we make z and z' closer to each other, we identify β for a narrower group of individuals defined in terms of their U_S. The *MTE* can therefore be estimated by taking a limit of *LATE* when z and z' are arbitrarily close to each other. When $U_1 \equiv U_0$ or $(U_1 - U_0) \perp\!\!\!\perp U_S$, corresponding to the two special cases in the literature, *IV* based on $P(Z)$ estimates *ATE* $(= \bar{\beta})$ because the second term on the right-hand side (second line) of this expression vanishes. Otherwise *IV* estimates an economically difficult-to-interpret combination of *MTE* parameters with weights given in Table 9b.

Another representation of $E(\ln Y | P(Z) = P(z))$ reveals the index structure underlying this model more explicitly and writes

$$\begin{aligned}
&E\bigl(\ln Y | P(Z) = P(z)\bigr) \\
&\quad = \alpha + \bar{\beta} P(z) \\
&\qquad + \int_{-\infty}^{\infty} \int_{0}^{P(z)} (U_1 - U_0) f(U_1 - U_0 | U_S = u_S)\, \mathrm{d}u_S\, \mathrm{d}(U_1 - U_0). \qquad (25)
\end{aligned}$$

Differentiating with respect to $P(z)$, we obtain *MTE*:

$$\begin{aligned}
&\frac{\partial E(\ln Y | P(Z) = P(z))}{\partial P(z)} \\
&\quad = \bar{\beta} + \int_{-\infty}^{\infty} (U_1 - U_0) f\bigl(U_1 - U_0 | U_S = P(z)\bigr)\, \mathrm{d}(U_1 - U_0) \\
&\quad = \Delta^{MTE}\bigl(P(z)\bigr).
\end{aligned}$$

IV estimates $\bar{\beta}$ if $\Delta^{MTE}(u_S)$ does not vary with u_S. Under this condition $E(\ln Y | P(Z) = P(z))$ is a linear function of $P(z)$. Thus, under our assumptions, a test of the linearity of the conditional expectation of $\ln Y$ in $P(z)$ is a test of the validity of linear *IV* for $\bar{\beta}$. It is also a test for the validity of conditions I and II. Heckman, Urzua and Vytlacil (2006) elaborate on this point.

More generally, a test of the linearity of $E(\ln Y | P(Z) = P(z))$ in $P(z)$ is a test of whether or not the data are consistent with a correlated random coefficient model and is also a test of comparative advantage in the labor market for educated labor. If $E(\ln Y | P(z))$ is linear in $P(z)$, standard instrumental variables methods identify "the" effect of S on $\ln Y$. In contrast, if $E(\ln Y | P(z))$ is nonlinear in $P(z)$, then there is heterogeneity in the return to college attendance, individuals act at least in part on their own idiosyncratic return, and standard linear instrumental variables methods will not in general identify the average treatment effect or any other of the treatment parameters defined earlier. This test for nonlinearity in $P(Z)$ as a sign of correlated heterogeneity is simple to execute and interpret. Carneiro, Heckman and Vytlacil (2005) and Heckman, Urzua and Vytlacil (2006) implement it and find evidence in support of nonlinearity in the data they analyze.

It is straightforward to estimate the levels and derivatives of $E(\ln Y | P(Z) = P(z))$ and standard errors using the methods developed in Heckman et al. (1998). The derivative estimator of *MTE* is the local instrumental variable (*LIV*) estimator of Heckman and Vytlacil (1999, 2001b, 2005, 2007b).[105]

This framework can be extended to consider multiple treatments, which in this case can be either multiple years of schooling, or multiple types or qualities of schooling. These can be either continuous [see Florens et al. (2002)] or discrete [see Carneiro, Hansen and Heckman (2003), Heckman and Vytlacil (2005, 2007a, 2007b), Heckman, Urzua and Vytlacil (2006)].

Heckman, Urzua and Vytlacil (2006) establish the close relationship between selection models and instrumental variables models when the response of earnings to changes in education varies among persons. Essentially, *IV* estimates the derivatives of outcome equations while the control function estimates them in levels.

8.5. *Evidence from the instrumental variables literature*

Card (1999) surveys empirical estimates from the instrumental variables literature. In the case of the general model presented in this chapter, different instruments identify different weighted averages of the *MTE* and in general do not identify any interpretable economic object such as a rate of return to schooling. The intensity of the search for instruments Z uncorrelated with (U_0, U_1) and correlated with S has not been matched by an equally intense search for an interpretation of what economic question the instrumental variables estimators answer. As noted by Heckman and Vytlacil (2007a, 2007b) and Heckman, Urzua and Vytlacil (2006), since the question being addressed by the recent literature is not clearly stated, it is not obvious that *IV* is better than *OLS*. The estimates produced from many of the commonly used instruments have large standard errors in producing any particular parameter of interest except for parameters defined by instruments. On a purely statistical basis there is often little difference between *IV* and *OLS* estimates once sampling variation is accounted for. Many of the instruments used in this literature are controversial.

Parental education and number of siblings have been used as instruments by Willis and Rosen (1979) and Taber (2001). They tend to produce estimates of "effects" with small standard errors. However, they are controversial. It is necessary to assume that potential wages in both the college and high school state are independent of family background, but many studies show that these are determinants of ability [see Cunha et al. (2006)]. Unless one controls for ability, the quality of the instruments is in question. Many data sets lack direct measures of ability.

Other popular instruments are based on the geographic location of individuals at the college going age. If the decision of going to college and the location decision are correlated then these instruments are not valid. For example, individuals who are more likely to enroll in college may choose to locate in areas where colleges are abundant and inexpensive. Distance to college is used as an instrument for schooling by Card (1993),

[105] Software is available in Heckman, Urzua and Vytlacil (2006).

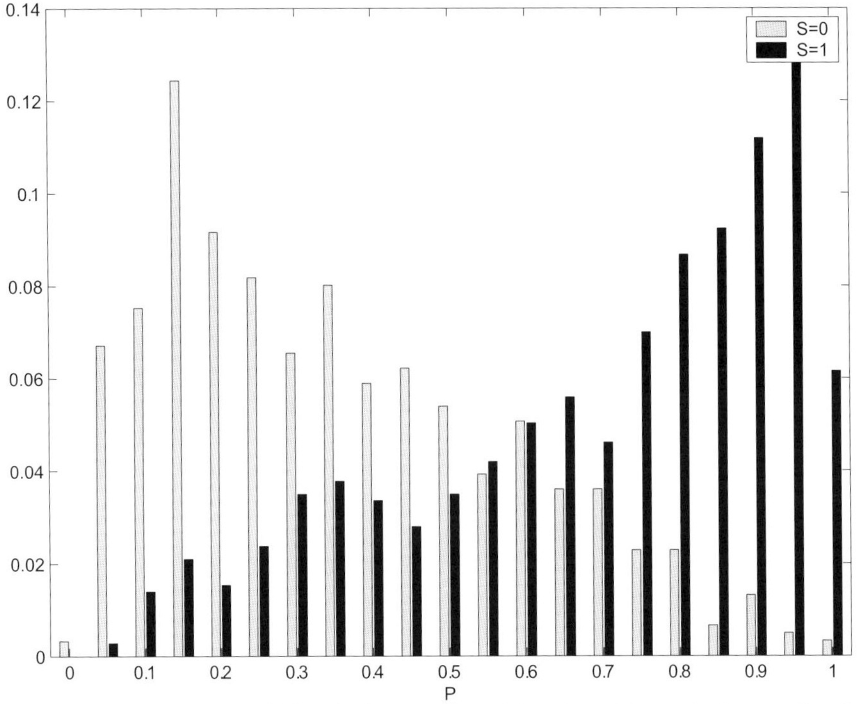

Note: P is the estimated probability of going to college. It is estimated from a logit regression of college attendance on corrected AFQT, father's education, mother's education, number of siblings, tuition, distance to college and local unemployment.

Figure 11. Density of P given $S = 0$ and $S = 1$ (estimated probability of enrolling in college). Source: Carneiro, Heckman and Vytlacil (2005).

(They trim 5% of the observations in the sample.[107]) Even after trimming, the sparseness of data in the tails results in a large amount of noise (variability) in the estimation of $E(Y|X, P(Z) = p)$ for values of p close to 0.07 or 0.98, which in turn makes problematic estimation of the parameters defined over the full support of U_S (which require estimation of $E(Y|X, P(Z) = p)$ over the full unit interval).

The lack of full support of $P(Z)$ means that *ATE*, *TT* and *TUT* are not identified nonparametrically by the method of instrumental variables. However the *MTE* can be estimated pointwise for a wide range of evaluation points without full support. This highlights what *LATE* can and cannot do in these data. It can produce a number. It cannot produce even a conventional treatment effect, much less a rate of return to schooling. The pattern of support of $P(Z)$ is similar in the Heckman, Urzua and Vytlacil (2006) study. See Figure 12 taken from their analysis.

[107] The importance of trimming in a semiparametric model similar to the one we use is illustrated in Heckman, Ichimura and Todd (1997).

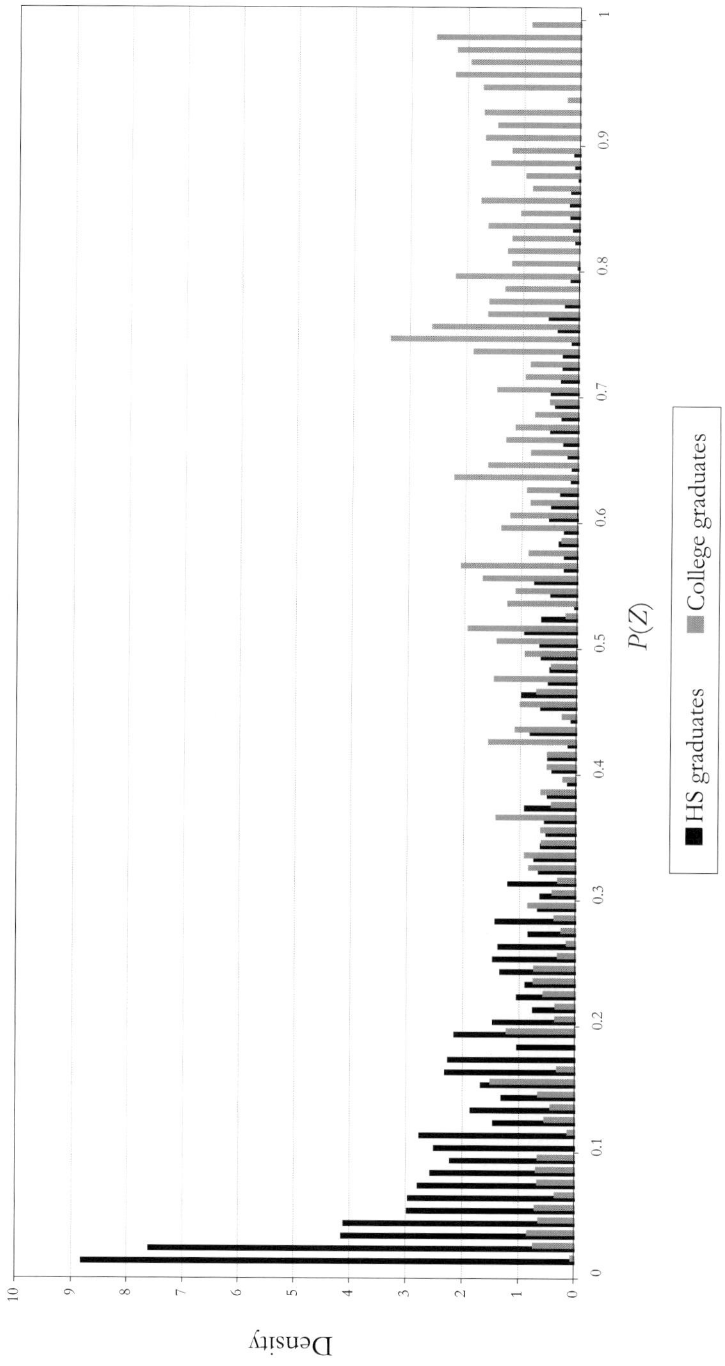

Figure 12. Frequency of the propensity score by final schooling decision. HS graduates and four year college graduates – males of the NLSY at age 30. Source: Heckman, Urzua and Vytlacil (2004).

Cognitive ability (as measured by AFQT) is an important determinant of the returns to schooling. Simple least squares regressions of log wages on schooling, ability measures, and interactions of schooling and ability (ignoring selection arising from uncontrolled unobservables) have been widely estimated in this and other data sets and generally show that cognitive ability is an important determinant of the returns to schooling.[108] Carneiro, Heckman and Vytlacil (2005) and Heckman, Urzua and Vytlacil (2006) include AFQT in their model as an observable determinant of the returns to schooling and of the decision to go to college. In the absence of such a measure of cognitive ability, selection arising from unobservables should be important. Most of the data sets that are used to estimate the returns to education (such as the Current Population Survey or the Census) lack such ability measures.

The test for selection on the individual returns to attending college checks whether $E(\ln Y|X, P)$ is a linear or a nonlinear function of P. Nonlinearity in P means that there is heterogeneity in the returns to college attendance and that individuals select into college based at least in part on their own idiosyncratic return (conditional on X). One possible way to implement this test is to approximate $K(P)$ with a polynomial in P and test whether the coefficients in the terms of the polynomial of order higher than one are jointly equal to zero. Carneiro, Heckman and Vytlacil test and reject linearity, indicating that a correlated random coefficient model describes the NLSY data.

Carneiro, Heckman and Vytlacil (2005) partition the estimated *MTE* into two components, one depending on X and the other on u_S,

$$\begin{aligned} MTE(x, u_S) &= E(\ln Y_1 - \ln Y_0 | X = x, U_S = u_S) \\ &= \mu_1(X) - \mu_0(X) + E(U_1 - U_0 | U_S = u_S). \end{aligned}$$

Figure 13 plots the component of the *MTE* that depends on U_S but not on X where the confidence interval bands are bootstrapped. The estimates are obtained using Robinson's (1988) method for estimating partially linear models. $E(U_1 - U_0|U_S = u_S)$ is declining in u_S for values of u_S below 0.7, and then it is flat and if anything it slightly rises.[109] Returns are annualized to reflect the fact that college goers on average attend 3.5 years of college. The most college worthy persons in the sense of having high gross returns are more likely to go to college (they have low U_S).[110] The magnitude of the heterogeneity in returns is substantial: returns can vary from 13% to 40% per year of college.[111]

[108] See Blackburn and Neumark (1993), Bishop (1991), Grogger and Eide (1995), Heckman and Vytlacil (2001a), Murnane, Willett and Levy (1995), Meghir and Palme (2001).

[109] Notice that the decision rule is $S = 1$ if $P(Z) - U_S \geqslant 0$ so, for a given Z, individuals with a higher U_S are less likely to go to college.

[110] U_S may be interpreted as the unobservable cost of college.

[111] The bootstrapped confidence intervals are very wide. However, the estimates of each point of the curve are highly correlated which will reduce the imprecision of the implied treatment parameters. For example, Carneiro, Heckman and Vytlacil can reject (at the 10% level) the hypothesis that $MTE(\bar{x}, U_S = 0.05) = MTE(\bar{x}, U_S = 0.5)$ (although, they cannot reject that $MTE(\bar{x}, U_S = 0.5) = MTE(\bar{x}, U_S = 0.95)$).

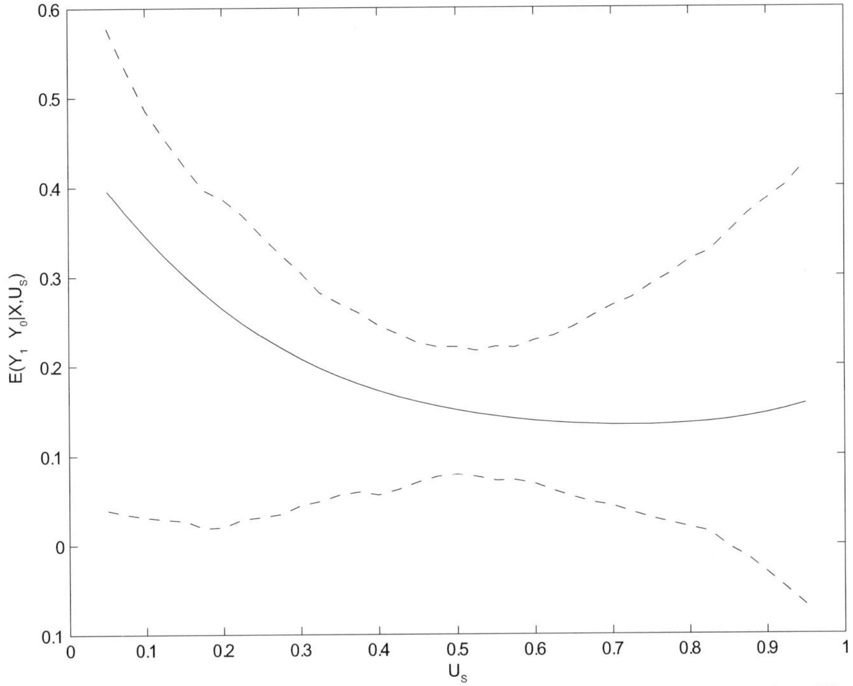

Note: To estimate the function in this figure ($E(Y_1 - Y_0|X, U_S)$) we use a two step procedure. We first estimate $\mu_0(X)$ and $\mu_1(X)$ from a regression of log wages on polynomials in X, interactions of polynomials in X and P, and a nonparametric function of P (where P is the predicted probability of attending college). We estimate a partially linear model. X includes experience, corrected AFQT and local unemployment. Then we compute the residual of this regression by subtracting $\mu_0(X) + P * [\mu_1(X) - \mu_0(X)]$ from log wages. Finally we estimate the nonlinear function in the figure by running a local quadratic regression of this residual on P and taking the coefficients on the linear term. Then we add a constant term to this function which is simply the average of $\mu_1(X) - \mu_0(X)$. $E(Y_1 - Y_0|X, U_S)$ is divided by 3.5 to account for the fact that individuals that attend college have on average 3.5 more years of schooling than those who do not. Therefore these correspond to estimates of returns to one year of college. The confidence interval bands are bootstrapped (250 replications).

Figure 13. $E(Y_1 - Y_0|X, U_S)$ estimated using locally quadratic regression (averaged over X). Source: Carneiro, Heckman and Vytlacil (2005).

The wide standard error bands are symptomatic of a phenomenon that plagues the entire *IV* literature. Estimates are not precisely determined. Figure 14 from Heckman, Urzua and Vytlacil (2004) reveals a similar pattern and a wide band of standard errors. Over broad intervals the confidence bands include zero indicating no effect of schooling on earnings. If β is independent of S, the *MTE* is flat. The evidence clearly rejects this so a correlated random coefficient model describes their data but there is a considerable loss in precision in using instrumental variables.

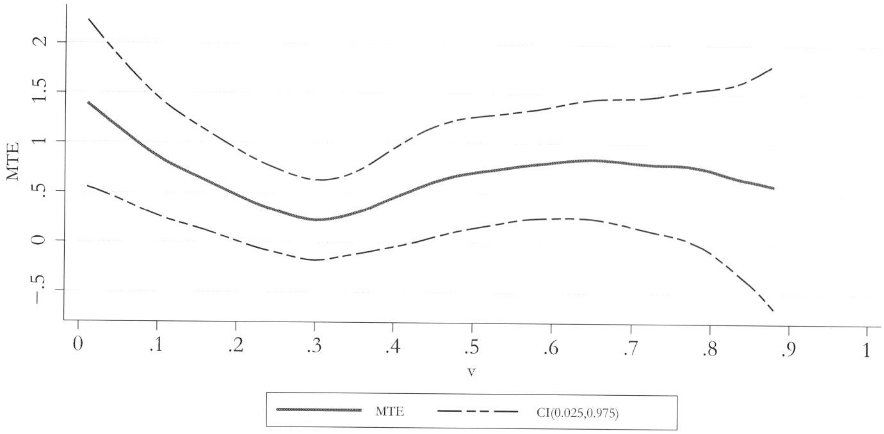

Figure 14. MTE with confidence interval. Sample of HS graduates and four year college graduates – males at age 30 – nonparametric. Source: Heckman, Urzua and Vytlacil (2004).

Table 11 presents estimates of different summary measures of returns to one year of college for two models from Carneiro, Heckman and Vytlacil (2005). In the first column they use family background as an exclusion and in the second they do not. The point estimates are similar in both models but they are more precise in the first one, and therefore we focus on those. However, this precision in estimation is obtained by using what many would argue are invalid exclusion restrictions. These parameters are obtained by using the appropriate weights for each parameter [see Carneiro, Heckman and Vytlacil (2005)].

The limited support of P near the boundary values of $P = 0$ and $P = 1$ creates a practical problem for the computation of the treatment parameters such as *ATE*, *TT*, and *TUT*, since *MTE* cannot be estimated for values of U_S outside the support of P. The sparseness of the data in the extremes does not allow accurate estimation of the *MTE* at evaluation points close to 0 or 1. The numbers presented in Table 11 are constructed after restricting the weights to integrate over the region [0.07, 0.98]. These can be interpreted as the parameters defined in the empirical (trimmed) support of $P(Z)$, which is close to the full unit interval.[112]

The sensitivity of estimates to lack of support in the tails ($P = 0$ or $P = 1$) is important for parameters, such as *ATE* or *TT*, that put substantial weight on the tails of the *MTE* distribution. Even with support over most of the interval [0, 1], such parameters

[112] Alternative ways to deal with the problem of limited support are to construct bounds for the parameters or to use a parametric extrapolation outside of the observed support. Bounds on the treatment effects are generally wide even though the support is almost full. Parametric extrapolation outside of the support is potentially sensitive to the choice of extrapolation model. Estimates based on locally adapted extrapolations show much less sensitivity than do estimates based on global approximation schemes. See Carneiro, Heckman and Vytlacil (2005) for further discussion.

Table 11
Estimates of various returns to one year of college

	Family background is exclusion $0.07 < P < 0.98$	Family background is not exclusion $0.07 < P < 0.98$
Average treatment effect	0.2124	0.1638
	(0.0648)	(0.0916)
	[0.0069; 0.2641]	[−0.0074; 0.2955]
Treatment on the treated	0.3202	0.2279
	(0.1103)	(0.1171)
	[0.0045; 0.4094]	[−0.0036; 0.3820]
Treatment on the untreated	0.1042	0.0897
	(0.0802)	(0.1285)
	[−0.0027; 0.2522]	[−0.1400; 0.3024]
Policy relevant treatment effect ($500 tuition subsidy)	0.2489	0.1905
	(0.0854)	(0.1651)
	[0.0024; 0.3520]	[−0.1037; 0.3602]
Ordinary least squares	0.0788	0.0796
	(0.0091)	(0.0114)
	[0.0654; 0.0955]	[0.0614; 0.0983]
Instrumental variables	0.1649	0.1530
	(0.0389)	(0.0758)
	[0.0888; 0.2166]	[0.0036; 0.2479]

Notes: Bootstrapped 5–95% standard errors (in parentheses) and confidence intervals (in brackets) are presented below the corresponding coefficients (250 replications).
Source: Carneiro, Heckman and Vytlacil (2005).

cannot be identified unless 0 (for both *ATE* and *TT*) and 1 (for *ATE*) are contained in the support of the distribution of $P(Z)$. Estimates of these parameters are highly sensitive to imprecise estimation or extrapolation error for $E(Y|X, P(Z) = p)$ for values of p close to 0 or 1. Even though empirical economists often seek to identify *ATE* and *TT*, usually they are not easily estimated nor are they always economically interesting parameters. As we have stressed repeatedly, they are not rates of return.

Integrating only over $P(Z)$ in the interval [0.07, 0.98], Table 11 reports estimates of the average annual return to college for a randomly selected person in the population (*ATE*) of 21.24%, which is between the annual return for the average individual who attends college (*TT*), 32.02%, and the average return for high school graduates who never attend college (*TUT*), 10.42%. Card reports *IV* estimates between 6 and 16% using different instruments but, as previously noted, different instruments weight *MTE* differently and answer different implicit questions. None of these numbers corresponds to the average annual return to college for those individuals of poor backgrounds who are induced to enroll in college by a $500 tuition subsidy (*PRTE*), which is 24.89%.[113]

[113] The policy consists of a subsidy of $500 for individuals who have higher than median ability and for whom both parents have less than a high school degree. The purpose of this simulation is to approximate a

This is the relevant return for evaluating this specific policy using a Benthamite welfare criterion. It is below *TT*, which means that the marginal entrant induced to go to college by this specific policy has an annual return well below (ten log points) that of the average college attendee.

Carneiro, Heckman and Vytlacil (2005) compare all of these estimated summary measures of returns with the *OLS* and *IV* estimates of the annual return to college, where the instrument is $\widehat{P}(Z)$, the estimated probability of attending college for individuals with characteristics Z. *OLS* estimates *ATE* if S and X are orthogonal to $U_0+S(U_1-U_0)$. Since the returns estimated by *OLS* and by *IV* both depend on X, they evaluate the *OLS* and *IV* returns at the average value of X for individuals induced to enroll in college by a \$500 tuition subsidy,[114] so that they can compare these estimates with the policy relevant treatment effect. The *OLS* estimate of the return to a year of college is 7.88% while the *IV* estimate is 16.49%.[115] Only by accident does *IV* identify policy relevant treatment effects when the *MTE* is not constant in U_S and the instrument is not the policy. Carneiro, Heckman and Vytlacil (2005) display the weights for all the treatment parameters reported in this section.

Carneiro, Heckman and Vytlacil (2005) report that $\hat{\beta}_{OLS} < \hat{\beta}_{IV}$. This finding is common in the literature [Card (2001)]. At the same time, the returns to schooling are higher for individuals more likely to enroll in college, which means that the average return for the marginal individual is below the return for the average student in college. As explained in Section 8.3 and confirmed in the empirical work of Carneiro, Heckman and Vytlacil (2005) reported here and in Cunha, Heckman and Navarro (2005), this is possible because the conventional measure of selection bias $(E(U_0|S=1) - E(U_0|S=0))$ is negative and not positive, as is implicitly assumed in Card (1999, 2001) and in most of the empirical literature. In a model of heterogeneous returns, standard intuitions about instrumental variables and ability bias break down. Carneiro, Heckman and Vytlacil (2005) confirm the conjecture of Willis and Rosen (1979). The evidence of Cunha, Heckman and Navarro (2005) shows that the single skill or efficiency units representation of the labor market which is implicit in most of the literature is invalid.

Table 12, taken from the analysis of Heckman, Urzua and Vytlacil (2004), demonstrates the sensitivity of *IV* estimates to the choice of instruments and to whether or

means tested tuition subsidy for high ability individuals. The standard error of this estimate is quite high, even though it overweights the *MTE* where it is more precisely estimated. The reason is that the flexible form we use for the selection equation, although useful for the estimation of the *MTE*, creates some imprecision in the policy simulation because not all the coefficients on the terms involving tuition are precisely estimated, at least for this policy. It is easier to simulate policies in models where tuition enters the choice equation in a simpler way, although in some cases the standard errors of the *MTE* become larger because it is important (for the standard errors) to be flexible in the way the instruments affect choices. See Carneiro, Heckman and Vytlacil (2005) for further details.

114 This is obtained by integrating X with respect to $f_X(x|PRT) = f_X(x|\mu_S(Z) - U_S < 0, \mu_S(Z') - U_S \geqslant 0)$.

115 When they compute the *IV* parameter by weighting up the *MTE* using the *IV* weights, they get an estimate of 12.12%, which is close to the *IV* estimate we obtain using the direct method.

not the estimates are conducted on samples where there is full support. As Figure 12 reveals, there are many intervals over which support is less than full, or very thin. In Table 12, for the full sample (first column) or the common support sample (second column), the *IV* estimates are all over the map. [Their estimates should be divided by 3.5 to get the annual returns to college reported in Carneiro, Heckman and Vytlacil (2005).] The final three columns show the *IV* based on an estimated *MTE* using (a) a parametric normal model (third column); (b) a semiparametric polynomial estimation method and (c) a nonparametric method based on local linear regression. The weights used to produce the *IV* estimates are given in Table 9b and are tailored to each estimation situation. There is close agreement between the two semiparametric methods and they are very different from the estimates in the third column that assume normality. The instability

Table 12
Instrumental variables estimates NLSY–HS graduates and four-year college graduates males at age 30*

Instruments	Standard IV		IV-MTE (common support)§		
	Full sample†	Common support‡	Parametric	Polynomial	Nonparametric
Number of siblings at 14	0.983 (0.512)	1.122 (0.591)	0.390 (0.121)	0.634 (0.163)	0.634 (0.160)
Family income in 1979 (thousands)	1.667 (0.432)	1.803 (0.630)	0.416 (0.121)	0.590 (0.143)	0.612 (0.147)
Local wage of HS graduates at county level at age 17	94.600 (1713.300)	41.400 (334.000)	0.407 (0.141)	0.591 (0.269)	0.618 (0.190)
Two year coll. grad's local wage at age 17	5.008 (4.077)	5.394 (4.941)	0.426 (0.135)	0.600 (0.216)	0.622 (0.188)
Four year coll. grad's local wage at age 17	2.742 (1.093)	3.149 (1.537)	0.428 (0.125)	0.614 (0.187)	0.629 (0.162)
Local unemp. rate of HS graduates at county level at age 17	0.675 (0.604)	0.612 (0.675)	0.203 (0.442)	0.523 (33.651)	0.526 (15.377)
Two year coll. grad's local unemployment rate at age 17	0.210 (0.579)	0.187 (0.727)	0.363 (0.260)	0.580 (1.824)	0.588 (1.927)
Four year coll. grad's local unemployment rate at age 17	3.465 (13.476)	4.480 (11.586)	0.405 (0.144)	0.554 (0.294)	0.588 (0.220)

(*Continued on next page*)

Table 12
(Continued)

Instruments	Standard IV		IV-MTE (common support)[§]		
	Full sample[†]	Common support[‡]	Parametric	Polynomial	Nonparametric
Distance to a two	3.369	4.603	0.416	0.606	0.621
year college	(3.223)	(6.282)	(0.139)	(0.186)	(0.165)
Distance to a four	4.810	7.440	0.415	0.629	0.634
year college	(5.180)	(12.150)	(0.120)	(0.170)	(0.161)
Two year college	−2.637	−1.870	0.417	0.798	0.677
tuition	(3.321)	(2.172)	(0.767)	(8.690)	(5.931)
Four year college	12.500	72.300	0.436	0.650	0.642
tuition	(42.780)	(1465.920)	(1.248)	(0.729)	(0.604)
Propensity score	0.496	0.505	0.420	0.572	0.604
	(0.093)	(0.103)	(0.121)	(0.138)	(0.143)

*We excluded the oversample of poor whites and the military sample.

[†]The *IV* estimates and the standard deviations (in parentheses) are computed applying the traditional formulae to the full sample. The number of observations in our sample is 982.

[‡]The *IV* estimates and the standard deviations (in parentheses) are computed applying the traditional formulae to the common support sample. This sample contains only observations for which the estimated propensity score belongs to the common support of the propensity score between the control (HS graduates) and treatment group (4 year college graduates) (912 observations).

[§]In the first column the *IV* estimates are computed by taking the weighted sum of the *MTE* estimated using the parametric approach. In the second column the *IV* estimates are computed by taking the weighted sum of the *MTE* estimated using a polynomial of degree 4 to approximate $E(Y|P)$. The *IV* estimates in the last column are computed by taking the weighted sum of the *MTE* estimated using the nonparametric approach. The propensity score ($\text{Prob}(D = 1|Z = z)$) is computed using the instruments presented in the table as well as two dummy variables as controls for the place of residence at age 14 (south and urban), and a set of dummy variables controlling for the year of birth (1958–1963). The standard deviations (in parentheses) are obtained using bootstrapping (100 draws).

Source: Heckman, Urzua and Vytlacil (2004).

manifest in the numbers reported in the first two columns is reduced by using the *MTE*. But the instability is manifest in a number of studies in the literature.

Table 13 shows estimates of the various treatment parameters based on the three versions of the *MTE*. There is a sharp contrast in the estimates produced from the parametric and nonparametric approaches. The different treatment parameters estimate different objects. The *LATE* estimators, defined for different points of evaluation $P(Z)$ (given by the arguments in parentheses) estimate very different numbers.

Figures 15a and 15b from Heckman, Urzua and Vytlacil (2004) graph the weights for the *MTE* for some of the instruments used to generate the numbers in Table 12. The weights for $P(Z)$ as an instrument are very different from the weights for four-year college tuition (Figure 15a) and especially two-year college tuition (Figure 15b).

Table 13
Treatment parameter estimates NLSY–HS graduates and four-year college graduates males at age 30*

Treatment parameter†	Parametric‡	Polynomial‡	Nonparametric§
Treatment on the treated	0.362	0.758	0.696
	(0.123)	(0.201)	(0.181)
Treatment on the untreated	0.509	0.687	0.652
	(0.149)	(0.142)	(0.167)
Average treatment effect	0.455	0.713	0.668
	(0.127)	(0.153)	(0.151)
LATE(0.62, 0.38)	0.483	0.59	0.659
	(0.138)	(0.185)	(0.192)
LATE(0.79, 0.55)	0.555	1.04	0.792
	(0.175)	(0.269)	(0.245)
LATE(0.45, 0.21)	0.412	0.157	0.383
	(0.120)	(0.184)	(0.159)

*We excluded the oversample of poor whites and the military sample.

†The treatment parameters are estimated by taking the weighted sum of the *MTE* estimated using a polynomial of degree 4 to approximate $E(Y|P)$.

‡The treatment parameters were estimated by taking the weighted sum of the *MTE* estimated using the parametric approach.

§The treatment parameters were estimated by taking the weighted sum of the *MTE* estimated using the nonparametric approach. The standard deviations (in parentheses) are computed using bootstrapping (100 draws).
Source: Heckman, Urzua and Vytlacil (2004).

This accounts for why different instruments define different parameters in terms of their weighting of a common *MTE* function. It is the *MTE* function and not an *IV* estimate that plays the role of a policy invariant parameter in the modern literature on instrumental variables.

8.6. The validity of the conventional instruments

This section examines the validity of conventional instruments in the NLSY data which is unusually rich. Many data sets on earnings and schooling do not possess measures of cognitive ability. For example, the CPS and many other data sets used to estimate the returns to schooling surveyed in Katz and Autor (1999) do not report measures of cognitive ability. In this case, ability becomes part of U_1, U_0 and U_S instead of being in X.

The assumption of independence between the instrument and U_1 and U_0 implies that the instruments have to be independent of cognitive ability. However, the instruments that are commonly used in the literature are correlated with AFQT, a widely used measure of ability. The first column of Table 14a shows the coefficient of a regression of each instrument (Z) on college attendance (S), denoted by $\beta_{S,Z}$. With the exception of the local unemployment rate, all candidate instruments are strongly correlated with

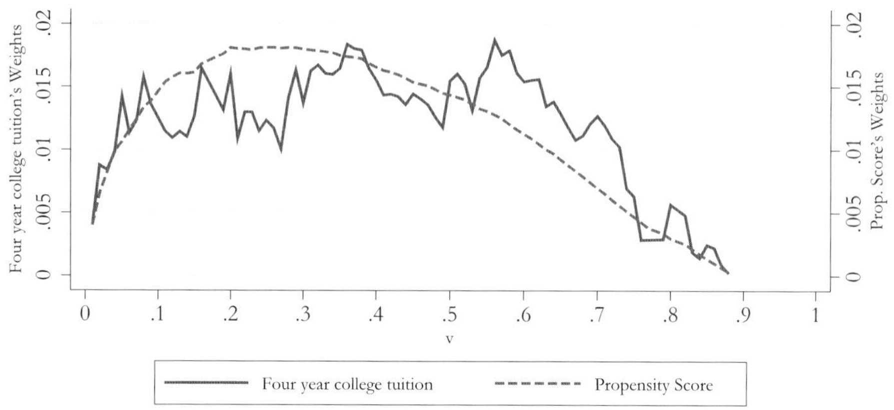

Figure 15a. IV weights for the MTE. Propensity score vs. four year college tuition as the instrument NLSY – sample of HS graduates and four year college graduates – males at age 30. Source: Heckman, Urzua and Vytlacil (2004).

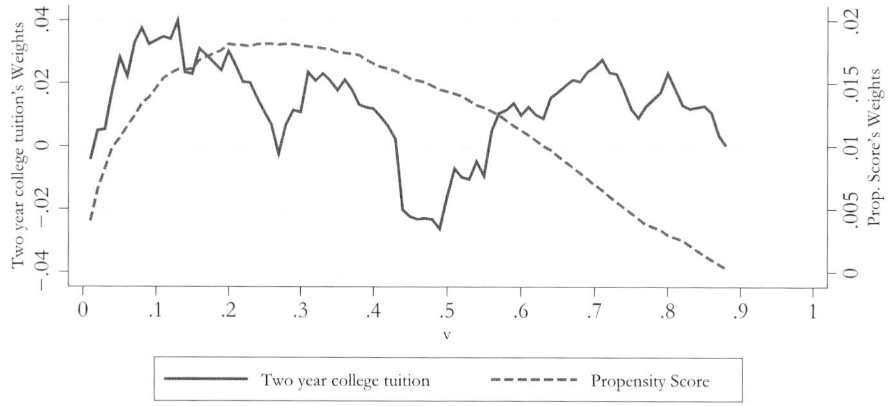

Figure 15b. IV weights for the MTE. Propensity score vs. two year college tuition as the instrument NLSY – sample of HS graduates and four year college graduates – males at age 30. Source: Heckman, Urzua and Vytlacil (2004).

schooling. The second column of this table presents the coefficient of a regression of each instrument on AFQT scores (A), denoted by $\beta_{A,Z}$. It shows that most of the candidates for instrumental variables in the literature are also correlated with cognitive ability. Therefore, in data sets where cognitive ability is not available most of these variables are not valid instruments since they violate the crucial *IV* assumption of independence. Since few data sets have measures of cognitive ability, this finding calls into question much of the *IV* literature. Notice that the local unemployment rate is not strongly correlated with AFQT. However, it is only weakly correlated with college attendance.

Table 14a
Regression of instrumental variables (Z) on schooling (S) and AFQT (A)

Instrumental variable	$\beta_{S,Z}$	$\beta_{A,Z}$	F-Stat
Number of siblings	−0.0302	−0.0468	15.04
	(0.0078)	(0.0141)	
Mother's education	0.0760	0.1286	157.56
	(0.0060)	(0.0110)	
Father's education	0.0582	0.0986	201.33
	(0.0041)	(0.0075)	
Average county tuition at 17	−0.0062	−0.0044	13.32
	(0.0017)	(0.0031)	
Distance to college at 14	−0.0038	−0.0081	8.56
	(0.0013)	(0.0023)	
State unemployment rate at 17	−0.0052	−0.0038	0.42
	(0.0081)	(0.0148)	

Source: Carneiro, Heckman and Vytlacil (2005).

The third column of Table 14a presents the F-statistic for the test of the hypothesis that the coefficient on the instrument is zero in a regression of schooling on the instrument. Staiger and Stock (1997) suggest using an F-statistic of 10 as a threshold for separating weak and strong instruments.[116] The table shows that the local unemployment variable has an F statistic well below 10 which suggests that it is a weak instrument when used by itself. Therefore either the candidate instrumental variable is correlated with ability or it is weakly correlated with schooling.

Table 14b presents coefficients of regressions of each instrument on schooling and ability, after controlling for family background variables (number of siblings and parental education). Conditioning on family background weakens the correlation between AFQT and the instruments. However the F-test for a regression of schooling on the residualized instrument is low by Staiger–Stock standards. Residualizing on family background attenuates the correlation between the instruments and ability but also between the instruments and schooling. The strength of this dependence is reported in the third column of Table 14b.

The instrument used by Carneiro, Heckman and Vytlacil (2005) is $P(Z)$. Regressing schooling on polynomials in experience, corrected AFQT, number of siblings, mother's education, father's education (the variables we include in the wage regression) and $P(Z)$, the F-statistic of the coefficient on P is 33.76. By including AFQT in the wage regression they attenuate the possibility of using invalid instruments. By using an index of instruments instead of a single instrument, it is possible to overcome the weak

[116] In a recent paper Stock and Yogo (2002) propose a different test. However they still find that the rule of thumb first proposed in Staiger and Stock (1997) works well in general.

Table 14b
Residualized regression of instrumental variables (Z) on schooling (S) and AFQT (A)

Instrumental variable	$\beta_{S,Z}$	$\beta_{A,Z}$	F-Stat
Average county tuition at 17	−0.0041	−0.0009	6.81
	(0.0015)	(0.0029)	
Distance to college at 14	−0.0008	−0.0032	0.53
	(0.0012)	(0.0022)	
State unemployment rate at 17	−0.0027	0.0005	0.13
	(0.0075)	(0.0138)	

Source: Carneiro, Heckman and Vytlacil (2005).

instrument problem. Furthermore, using an index of instruments instead of a single instrument tends to reduce support problems for any instrument. Even if one instrument has limited support, other instruments can augment the support of P. Observe that the *IV* estimates based on $P(Z)$ are more stable in Table 12 than are the estimates based on the individual components.

8.7. *Summary of the modern literature on instrumental variables*

Heckman and Vytlacil (2001a, 2005, 2007b) show how to write different conventional mean parameters and *IV* estimates as weighted averages of the marginal treatment effect (*MTE*). In a model with heterogeneous responses, different instruments define different parameters. Unless the instruments are the policies being studied, these parameters answer well-posed economic questions only by accident. It is possible to identify and estimate the *MTE* using a robust nonparametric selection model. Their method allows them to combine diverse instruments into a scalar instrument motivated by economic theory. This combined instrument expands the support of any one instrument, and allows the analyst to perform out-of-sample policy forecasts. Focusing on a policy relevant question, they construct estimators based on the *MTE* to answer it, rather than hoping that a particular instrumental variable estimator happens to answer a question of economic interest. The approach based on the *MTE* unites the selection and *IV* literatures. As noted by Heckman, Urzua and Vytlacil (2006), both methods use $P(Z)$ but one conditions on it (the selection model) while the other (the *IV* literature) does not.

The recent literature confirms in a semiparametric setting a central claim of the parametric Willis and Rosen (1979) analysis [Carneiro, Hansen and Heckman (2003), Cunha, Heckman and Navarro (2005)]. Individuals sort into schooling on the basis of both observed and unobserved gains where the observer is the economist analyzing the data. Moreover, as noted by Willis and Rosen (1979), it is not possible to rationalize labor market data with the single skill (or efficiency units) model that governs most of the standard intuitions about ability bias in schooling. In fact, these intuitions break down in a general model of heterogeneous returns, and lead to potentially wrong interpretations of the data.

Instrumental variables are not guaranteed to estimate policy relevant treatment parameters or conventional treatment parameters. Different instruments define different parameters, and in the empirical analysis of Carneiro, Heckman and Vytlacil (2005) and Heckman, Urzua and Vytlacil (2006) they produce wildly different "effects" of schooling on earnings. The current practice of reporting *IV* estimates as "returns" to schooling defines the parameter being identified by an econometric method and not by an economic question. Our examples show that the *IV* method does not produce an economically interesting or interpretable parameter, and in general does not estimate a rate of return. Different *IV* estimators weight the *MTE* differently and are not comparable in their economic content.

Even granting the validity and the strength of the instruments, the entire recent *IV* enterprise for correlated random coefficient models is premised on a fundamental asymmetry. Returns (growth rates) are allowed to be heterogeneous in a general way. Schooling may either increase or decrease rates of return. However, choices are not permitted to be heterogeneous in a general way [Heckman and Vytlacil (2005), Heckman, Urzua and Vytlacil (2006)]. The monotonicity assumptions (or index structure assumptions embodied in (18) or (20) so that schooling is determined by an index of "net utility" where the observables are separable from the nonobservables) impose the condition that all persons respond in the same way in their schooling choices for any change in Z. Thus if increasing a coordinate of Z, say Z_1, increases schooling for one person, the same increase cannot decrease schooling for anyone else. This condition rules out heterogeneity in the choice equations. These conditions are at odds with a variety of economic models for schooling such as models for dynamic discrete choice [see Heckman and Navarro (2006)]. See Belzil and Hansen (2005) for an interesting contrast between *IV* and structural estimates of returns to schooling. Their structural models and those of Heckman and Navarro do not impose monotonicity conditions on the choice data.

If the monotonicity conditions are violated, increases in Z_1 may increase participation in schooling for some and decrease it for others. In this case, instrumental variables methods do not estimate treatment effects and the local instrumental variable does not identify the marginal treatment effect. See Heckman and Vytlacil (2001c, 2005), Heckman, Urzua and Vytlacil (2006), for further discussion of this point.

9. Estimating distributions of returns to schooling

Following the representative agent tradition, economists usually summarize the distribution of the growth rate of earnings with schooling by some mean. In Section 8, we presented a variety of mean treatment effects which are defined by the conditioning variables used. Different means answer different policy questions.

The research reported in this section [based on Aakvik, Heckman and Vytlacil (2005), Heckman, Smith and Clements (1997), Carneiro, Hansen and Heckman (2001, 2003),

Cunha, Heckman and Navarro (2005, 2006), Cunha and Heckman (2006a)] moves beyond means as descriptions of policy outcomes and considers joint counterfactual distributions of outcomes (for example, $F(Y_1, Y_0)$, gains $F(Y_1 - Y_0)$ or $F(Y_1, Y_0 | S = 1)$). These are *ex post* distributions realized after schooling decisions are completed. We analyze *ex ante* distributions in the next section. From knowledge of the *ex post* joint distributions of counterfactual outcomes, it is possible to determine the proportion of people who benefit or lose from schooling, the origin and destination outcomes of those who change status because of schooling and the amount of gain (or loss) from various policy choices such as tuition subsidies by persons at different deciles of an initial prepolicy income distribution.[117] Using the joint distribution of counterfactuals, it is possible to develop a more nuanced understanding of the distributional impacts of public policies directed toward education, and to move beyond comparisons of aggregate distributions induced by different policies to consider how people in different portions of an initial distribution are affected by public policy. From knowledge of the mean treatment effects presented in Section 8, if $Y_1 - Y_0$ varies in the population, it is not possible to answer the simple question of who benefits from schooling and the proportion of people benefiting, except in the special case where everyone with the same X receives the same benefit. Our methods can be used to explain effects of schooling (and other interventions) on earnings, employment and health. In this chapter, we focus on earnings measures.

Under the assumptions of Section 8, joint distributions of counterfactuals are not identified nonparametrically [see Heckman (1990)]. We observe Y_1 or Y_0 for the same person but not both. Thus it is not possible to use cross section data to tabulate the joint distribution of (Y_0, Y_1) from the raw data. However, with additional information, it is possible.

More precisely, an agent can experience one of two possible counterfactual schooling levels with associated outcomes (Y_0, Y_1). As before, we denote X as determinants of the counterfactual outcomes (Y_0, Y_1); $S = 1$ if the agent is in state 1; $S = 0$ otherwise. The observed outcome is $Y = SY_1 + (1 - S)Y_0$. Let Z be a determinant of S that does not affect Y_1, Y_0.[118] The standard treatment effect model analyzed in Section 8 and in this section considers policies that shift Z and that affect choices of treatment but not potential outcomes (Y_0, Y_1). It ignores general equilibrium effects.[119]

The goal is to recover $F(Y_0, Y_1 | X)$ and hence $F(Y_1 - Y_0 | X)$, and related distributions such as those for gross gains $(\frac{1}{1+r} Y_1 - Y_0)$ or net gains $(\frac{Y_1}{1+r} - Y_0 - C)$ assuming one period of foregone earnings is required to move from "0" to "1".

[117] It is also possible to generate all mean, median or other quantile gains to schooling, to identify all pairwise treatment effects in a multi-outcome setting, and to determine how much of the variability in returns across persons comes from variability in the distributions of the outcome selected and how much comes from variability in opportunity distributions.

[118] Thus $(Y_1, Y_0) \perp\!\!\!\perp Z | X$ and $\Pr(S = 1 | Z, X)$ depends on Z for all X.

[119] See Heckman, Lochner and Taber (1998) for a treatment of general equilibrium policy evaluation.

The problem of recovering joint distributions from cross section data has two aspects. The first is the selection problem. From data on the distribution of earnings by schooling and characteristics X, $F(Y_1|S = 1, X)$ and $F(Y_0|S = 0, X)$, under what conditions can one recover $F(Y_1|X)$ and $F(Y_0|X)$, respectively? The second problem is how to construct the joint distribution $F(Y_0, Y_1|X)$ from the two marginal distributions of earnings for each secondary schooling level.

If the selection problem can be solved and the marginal distributions of Y_1 and Y_0 are identified, results from probability theory due to Fréchet (1951) and Hoeffding (1940) can be used to bound $F(Y_1, Y_0|S, X)$ from the marginal distributions. In practice these bounds are often very wide, and the inferences based on the bounding distributions are often not very helpful.[120]

A second approach, based on matching, postulates access to variables Q that have the property that conditional on Q, $F(Y_0|S = 0, X, Q) = F(Y_0|X, Q)$ and $F(Y_1|S = 1, X, Q) = F(Y_1|X, Q)$. Matching thus assumes that conditional on observed variables, there is no selection problem. If it is further assumed that all of the dependence between (Y_0, Y_1) given X comes through Q, then it follows that $F(Y_1, Y_0|X, Q) = F(Y_1|X, Q)F(Y_0|X, Q)$. Using these results, it is possible to create the joint distribution $F(Y_0, Y_1|X)$ because

$$F(Y_0, Y_1|X) = \int F(Y_0|X, Q)F(Y_1|X, Q)\, \mathrm{d}\mu(Q|X).$$

$\mu(Q|X)$ is the conditional distribution of Q given X. We obtain $F(Y_0|X, Q)$, $F(Y_1|X, Q)$ by matching. We know the distribution of Q given X because we observe Q and X. Thus we can construct the right-hand side of this expression. Matching makes the strong assumption that conditional on (Q, X) the marginal return to schooling is the same as the average return.[121]

One traditional approach in economics assumes that the joint distribution $F(Y_0, Y_1|X)$ is a degenerate one-dimensional distribution. It assumes that conditional on X, Y_1 and Y_0 are deterministically related,

$$Y_1 = Y_0 + \Delta, \tag{26}$$

where Δ is the difference in means between Y_1 and Y_0 for the selection corrected distribution.[122] This assumes that schooling has the same effect on everyone (with the same X) and that effect is Δ.

Heckman and Smith (1998) and Heckman, Smith and Clements (1997) relax this assumption by assuming perfect ranking in the positions of individuals $F(Y_1|X)$ and $F(Y_0|X)$ distributions. (The best in one distribution is the best in the other.) Assuming continuous and strictly increasing marginal distributions, they postulate that quantiles

[120] See Heckman and Smith (1998) and Heckman, Smith and Clements (1997).

[121] See Heckman and Vytlacil (2005, 2007b).

[122] Δ may be a function of X.

are perfectly ranked so $Y_1 = F_1^{-1}(F_0(Y_0))$ where $F_1 = F_1(y_1|X)$ and $F_0 = F_0(y_0|X)$. This assumption generates a deterministic relationship which turns out to be the tight upper bound of the Fréchet bounds.[123] An alternative assumption is that people are perfectly inversely ranked so the best in one distribution is the worst in the other: $Y_1 = F_1^{-1}(1 - F_0(Y_0))$. This is the tight Fréchet lower bound.[124]

A perfect ranking (or perfect inverse ranking) assumption generalizes the perfect-ranking, constant-shift assumptions implicit in the conventional literature. It allows analysts to apply conditional quantile methods to estimate the distributions of gains.[125] However, it imposes a strong and arbitrary dependence across distributions. When the perfect ranking assumption is relaxed and tested, it is rejected.[126]

A more general framework attacks this problem in a different way than does matching or invoking special assumptions about relationships between the ranks of persons in the Y_0 and Y_1 distribution. This line of research starts from the analysis of Heckman (1990), Heckman and Smith (1998), Aakvik, Heckman and Vytlacil (2005), Carneiro, Hansen and Heckman (2001, 2003), Cunha, Heckman and Navarro (2005, 2006) and Cunha and Heckman (2006a). In this chapter we draw on the analysis of Carneiro, Hansen and Heckman (2003).[127] They start with the marginal distributions of Y_1 and of Y_0 given X. They allow for unobservables to generate the joint dependence and do not rely on matching.

The basic idea is to restrict the dependence among the (U_0, U_1, U_S) by factor models or other restrictions. A low dimensional set of random variables generates the dependence across the unobservables. Such dimension reduction coupled with use of the

[123] An upper bound is "tight" if it is the smallest possible upper bound. A lower bound is tight if it is the largest lower bound.

[124] More generally, one can associate quantiles across distributions more freely. Heckman, Smith and Clements (1997) use Markov transition kernels that stochastically map quantiles of one distribution into quantiles of another. They define a pair of Markov kernels $M(y_1, y_0|X)$ and $\widetilde{M}(y_0, y_1|X)$ such that

$$F_1(y_1|X) = \int M(y_1, y_0|X)\, \mathrm{d}F_0(y_0|X),$$

$$F_0(y_0|X) = \int \widetilde{M}(y_0, y_1|X)\, \mathrm{d}F_1(y_1|X).$$

Allowing these kernels to be degenerate produces a variety of deterministic transformations, including the two previously presented, as special cases of a general mapping. Different $(M, \widetilde{M})$ pairs produce different joint distributions. These stochastic or deterministic transformations supply the missing information needed to construct the joint distributions.

[125] See, e.g., Heckman, Smith and Clements (1997).

[126] However, testing it requires invoking other assumptions. See Cunha, Heckman and Navarro (2005, 2006) and Cunha and Heckman (2006a).

[127] Using a version of Equation (19) separable in X and (U_0, U_1), and using Equation (20), under the assumption that $(Z, X) \perp\!\!\!\perp (U_0, U_1, U_S)$ and including the condition that (i) $\mu_S(Z)$ is a nontrivial function of Z conditional on X and that (ii) the support assumptions on $\mu_1(X)$, $\mu_0(X)$ and $\mu_S(Z)$ matches that of U_1, U_0, U_S, they establish nonparametric identification of $F(U_0, U_S)$, $F(U_1, U_S)$ up to a normalization for U_S, and full identification of $\mu_1(X)$, $\mu_0(X)$ over their supports and $\mu_S(Z)$ suitably scaled over its support.

choice data and measurements that proxy components of the (U_0, U_1, U_S), provides enough information to identify the joint distribution of (Y_1, Y_0) and of (Y_1, Y_0, S).

Assume separability between unobservables and observables and that Y_1 and Y_0 are lifetime earnings:

$$Y_1 = \mu_1(X) + U_1,$$
$$Y_0 = \mu_0(X) + U_0.$$

Denote S^* as the latent variable generating schooling choices:

$$S^* = \mu_S(Z) + U_S,$$
$$S = \mathbf{1}(S^* \geqslant 0).$$

Recall that we allow any X to be in Z. To motivate the approach, assume that (U_0, U_1, U_S) is normally distributed with mean zero and covariance matrix Σ_G ("G" for Generalized Roy). If the distributions are normal, they can be fully characterized by means and covariances. To simplify the discussion, we focus our exposition on normal models although that is not essential. We assume that (U_0, U_1, U_S) are statistically independent of (X, Z).

Under normality, standard results in the selection bias literature show that from data on Y_1 given $S = 1$, and X, and data on Y_0 for $S = 0$ and X, and data on choices of schooling given Z, one can identify $\mu_1(X)$, $\mu_0(X)$ and $\mu_S(Z)$, the latter up to scale σ_S (where $\sigma_S^2 = \mathrm{Var}(U_S)$). See Heckman (1976) or Cunha, Heckman and Navarro (2005). In addition, one can identify the joint densities of $(U_0, U_S/\sigma_S)$ and $(U_1, U_S/\sigma_S)$. Without further information, one cannot identify the joint density of $(U_0, U_1, U_S/\sigma_S)$.

Recent developments in microeconometrics show that analysts can identify these same objects without a normality assumption provided that there are variables Z that generate enough variation in $\mu_S(Z)$. The intuition for why variation identifies the model is presented in Heckman and Honoré (1990), Heckman (1990) and Cunha, Heckman and Navarro (2006). If Z has sufficient variation, there are limit sets where $P(Z) = 1$ and other sets where $P(Z) = 0$ so there is no selection problem in those limit sets.[128] Formal proofs and general conditions are given in Carneiro, Hansen and Heckman (2003). Normality plays no central role in the analysis of this section. We use it because it is familiar in the economics of education due to the application of the Generalized Roy model by Willis and Rosen (1979).[129]

To get the gist of the method underlying recent work, we adopt a factor structure model for the U_0, U_1, U_S. Other restrictions across the unobservables are possible [see

[128] We identify $F(Y_0|X)$ in the limit sets where $P(Z) = 0$ and $F(Y_1|X)$ in the limit sets where $P(Z) = 1$. Heckman and Navarro (2006) present evidence on the failure of the limit set conditions in a schooling example. When the limit sets fail to exist, identification can be secured using functional forms of the distributions of the unobservables. An alternative is to construct bounds or equivalently to perform a sensitivity analysis of the estimates to alternative values of the parameters of the model.

[129] Separability can also be relaxed using the methods of Matzkin (2003).

Urzua (2005)]. Factor models are extensively developed by Jöreskog and Goldberger (1975). Aakvik, Heckman and Vytlacil (2005) and Carneiro, Hansen and Heckman (2001, 2003) apply their analysis to generate counterfactuals. For simplicity, we assume a one factor model where θ is the factor that generates dependence across the unobservables:

$$U_0 = \alpha_0\theta + \varepsilon_0,$$
$$U_1 = \alpha_1\theta + \varepsilon_1,$$
$$U_S = \alpha_S\theta + \varepsilon_S.$$

We assume $E(U_0) = 0$, $E(U_1) = 0$, $E(U_S) = 0$. In addition, $E(\theta) = 0$, $E(\varepsilon_0) = 0$, $E(\varepsilon_1) = 0$ and $E(\varepsilon_S) = 0$. To set the scale of the unobserved factor, we can normalize one "loading" (coefficient on θ) to 1. Other normalizations are possible. We assume that θ is a scalar factor (say unmeasured ability) and the $(\varepsilon_0, \varepsilon_1, \varepsilon_S)$ are independent of θ and of each other. All the dependence across the unobservables arises from θ.

Under normality or from the general semiparametric identification analysis of Carneiro, Hansen and Heckman (2003), we can identify

$$COV\left(U_0, \frac{U_S}{\sigma_S}\right) = \frac{\alpha_0\alpha_S}{\sigma_S}\sigma_\theta^2,$$
$$COV\left(U_1, \frac{U_S}{\sigma_S}\right) = \frac{\alpha_1\alpha_S}{\sigma_S}\sigma_\theta^2.$$

From the ratio of the second covariance to the first we obtain $\frac{\alpha_1}{\alpha_0}$, assuming $\alpha_0 \neq 0$. Thus we obtain the sign of the dependence between U_0, U_1 because

$$COV(U_0, U_1) = \alpha_0\alpha_1\sigma_\theta^2.$$

From the ratio, we obtain α_1 if we normalize $\alpha_0 = 1$. Without further information, we can only identify the variance of U_S up to scale, which can be normalized to 1. (Alternatively, we could normalize the variance of ε_S to 1.) Below, we present a condition that sets the scale of U_S.

Knowledge of the sign of $\frac{\alpha_1}{\alpha_0}$ is informative on the sign of the correlation between college and high school skills, a key unanswered question in the analysis of Willis and Rosen (1979). They conjecture that $COV(U_0, U_1) < 0$. The evidence reported in Carneiro, Hansen and Heckman (2001, 2003), Cunha, Heckman and Navarro (2005, 2006) and Cunha and Heckman (2006a) supports their conjecture. Those with high levels of U_1 have lower levels of U_0.[130]

[130] Our terminology is different from that of Willis and Rosen (1979). What they call a "one factor model" is an efficiency units model where $U_1 = U_0$ (or, more generally, that U_1 and U_0 are perfectly dependent). As our analysis reveals, it is possible to have (U_1, U_0) not perfectly dependent and have a one factor representation. U_1 and U_0 would be perfectly dependent in a one factor model only when the uniquenesses are identically zero: $\varepsilon_0 = \varepsilon_1 = 0$.

With additional information, we can identify the full joint distribution. We now present some examples. Cunha, Heckman and Navarro (2005) present a more comprehensive analysis.

Example 1. Access to a single test score

Assume access to data on Y_0 given $S = 0, X, Z$; to data on Y_1 given $S = 1, X, Z$; and data on S given X, Z. Suppose that the analyst also has access to a single test score T that is a proxy for θ,

$$T = \mu_T(X) + U_T,$$

where $U_T = \alpha_T\theta + \varepsilon_T$ so

$$T = \mu_T(X) + \alpha_T\theta + \varepsilon_T,$$

where ε_T is independent of $\varepsilon_0, \varepsilon_1, \varepsilon_S$ and (X, Z). We can identify the mean $\mu_T(X)$ from observations on T and X. We pick up three additional covariance terms, conditional on X, Z:

$$COV(Y_1, T) = \alpha_1\alpha_T\sigma_\theta^2,$$
$$COV(Y_0, T) = \alpha_0\alpha_T\sigma_\theta^2,$$
$$COV(S^*, T) = \frac{\alpha_S}{\sigma_S}\alpha_T\sigma_\theta^2.$$ [131]

To simplify the notation we keep the conditioning on X and Z implicit. Suppose that we normalize the loading on the test score to one ($\alpha_T = 1$). It is no longer necessary to normalize $\alpha_0 = 1$ as in the preceding section. From the ratio of the covariance of Y_1 with S^* with the covariance of S^* with T, we obtain the left-hand side of

$$\frac{COV(Y_1, S^*)}{COV(S^*, T)} = \frac{\alpha_1\alpha_S\sigma_\theta^2}{\alpha_S\alpha_T\sigma_\theta^2} = \alpha_1,$$

because $\alpha_T = 1$ (normalization). From the preceding argument without the test score, we obtain α_0 since

$$\frac{COV(Y_1, S^*)}{COV(Y_0, S^*)} = \frac{\alpha_1\alpha_S\sigma_\theta^2}{\alpha_0\alpha_S\sigma_\theta^2} = \frac{\alpha_1}{\alpha_0}.$$

From knowledge of α_1 and α_0 and the normalization for α_T, we obtain σ_θ^2 from $COV(Y_1, T)$ or $COV(Y_0, T)$. We obtain α_S (up to scale σ_S) from $COV(S^*, T) = \alpha_S\alpha_T\sigma_\theta^2$ since we know α_T ($= 1$) and σ_θ^2. The model is overidentified. We can set

[131] Conditioning on X, Z, we can remove the dependence of Y_1, Y_0, T and S^* on these variables and effectively work with the residuals $Y_0 - \mu_0(X) = U_0$, $Y_1 - \mu_1(X) = U_1$, $T - \mu_T(X) = U_T$, $S^* - \mu_S(Z) = U_S$.

the scale of σ_S by a standard argument from the discrete choice literature. See the discussion below.

Observe that if we write out the decision rule for schooling in terms of costs, we can characterize the latent variable determining schooling choices as:

$$S^* = Y_1 - Y_0 - C,$$

where $C = \mu_C(Z) + U_C$ and $U_C = \alpha_C\theta + \varepsilon_C$, where ε_C is independent of θ and the other ε's. $E(U_C) = 0$ and U_C is independent of (X, Z). Then,

$$\begin{aligned}\alpha_S &= \alpha_1 - \alpha_0 - \alpha_C,\\ \varepsilon_S &= \varepsilon_1 - \varepsilon_0 - \varepsilon_C,\\ \operatorname{Var}(\varepsilon_S) &= \operatorname{Var}(\varepsilon_1) + \operatorname{Var}(\varepsilon_0) + \operatorname{Var}(\varepsilon_C).\end{aligned}$$

Identification of α_0, α_1 and α_S implies identification of α_C. Identification of the variance of ε_S implies identification of the variance of ε_C since the variances of ε_1 and ε_0 are known.

Observe further that the scale σ_{U_S} is identified if there are variables in X but not in Z [see Heckman (1976, 1979), Heckman and Robb (1985, 1986), Willis and Rosen (1979)].[132] From the variance of T given X, we obtain $\operatorname{Var}(\varepsilon_T)$ since we know $\operatorname{Var}(T)$ (conditional on X) and we know $\alpha_T^2\sigma_\theta^2$:

$$\operatorname{Var}(T) - \alpha_T^2\sigma_\theta^2 = \sigma_{\varepsilon_T}^2.$$

(Recall that we keep the conditioning on X implicit.) By similar reasoning, it is possible to identify $\operatorname{Var}(\varepsilon_0)$, $\operatorname{Var}(\varepsilon_1)$ and the fraction of $\operatorname{Var}(U_S)$ due to ε_S. We can thus construct the joint distribution of (Y_0, Y_1, C) since we know $\mu_C(Z)$ and all of the factor loadings.

We have assumed normality because it is convenient. Carneiro, Hansen and Heckman (2003), Cunha, Heckman and Navarro (2005, 2006) and Cunha and Heckman (2006a) show that it is possible to nonparametrically identify the distributions of θ, ε_0, ε_1, ε_S and ε_T so these results do not hinge on arbitrary distributional assumptions.

There are other ways to construct the joint distributions that do not require a test score. Access to panel data on earnings affords identification. One way, that leads into our analysis of *ex ante* vs. *ex post* returns in Section 10, is discussed next.

[132] The easiest case to understand writes

$$\mu_C(Z) = Z\gamma, \qquad \mu_1(X) = X\beta_1, \qquad \mu_0(X) = X\beta_0, \qquad \mu_S(Z, X) = X(\beta_1 - \beta_0) - Z\gamma.$$

We identify the coefficients of the index $\mu_S(Z, X)$ up to scale σ_{U_S}, but we know $\beta_1 - \beta_0$ from the earnings functions. Thus if one X is not in Z and its associated coefficient is not zero, we can identify σ_{U_S}. See, e.g., Heckman (1976).

Example 2. Two (or more) periods of panel data on earnings

Suppose that for each person we have two periods of earnings data in one counterfactual state or the other. We write

$$Y_{1t} = \mu_{1t}(X) + \alpha_{1t}\theta + \varepsilon_{1t}, \quad t = 1, 2,$$
$$Y_{0t} = \mu_{0t}(X) + \alpha_{0t}\theta + \varepsilon_{0t}, \quad t = 1, 2.$$

We observe one or the other lifecycle stream of earnings for each person, but never both streams for the same person. We assume that the interest rate is zero and that agents maximize the present value of their income. Thus in terms of the index

$$S^* = (Y_{12} + Y_{11}) - (Y_{02} + Y_{01}) - C,$$

$$S = 1 \quad (S^* \geqslant 0),$$

where C was defined previously. We assume no test score – just two periods of panel data.

Under normality, application of the standard normal selection model allows us to identify $\mu_{1t}(X)$ for $t = 1, 2$; $\mu_{0t}(X)$ for $t = 1, 2$ and $\mu_{11}(X) + \mu_{12}(X) - \mu_{01}(X) - \mu_{02}(X) - \mu_C(X)$, the latter up to a scalar σ_S, the standard deviation of

$$U_S = (\alpha_{12} + \alpha_{11} - \alpha_{02} - \alpha_{01} - \alpha_C)\theta + \varepsilon_{11} + \varepsilon_{12} - \varepsilon_{01} - \varepsilon_{02} - \varepsilon_C.$$

Following our discussion of Example 1, we can recover the scale if there are variables in $(\mu_{11}(X) + \mu_{12}(X) - (\mu_{01}(X) + \mu_{02}(X)))$ not in $\mu_C(Z)$. For simplicity we assume that this condition holds.[133]

From normality, we can recover the joint distributions of (S^*, Y_{11}, Y_{12}) and (S^*, Y_{01}, Y_{02}) but not directly the joint distribution of $(S^*, Y_{11}, Y_{12}, Y_{01}, Y_{02})$. Thus, conditioning on X and Z we can recover the joint distribution of (U_S, U_{01}, U_{02}) and (U_S, U_{11}, U_{12}) but apparently not that of $(U_S, U_{01}, U_{02}, U_{11}, U_{12})$. However, under our factor structure assumptions this joint distribution can be recovered as we next show.

From the available data, we can identify the following covariances:

$$COV(U_S, U_{12}) = (\alpha_{12} + \alpha_{11} - \alpha_{02} - \alpha_{01} - \alpha_C)\alpha_{12}\sigma_\theta^2,$$
$$COV(U_S, U_{11}) = (\alpha_{12} + \alpha_{11} - \alpha_{02} - \alpha_{01} - \alpha_C)\alpha_{11}\sigma_\theta^2,$$
$$COV(U_S, U_{01}) = (\alpha_{12} + \alpha_{11} - \alpha_{02} - \alpha_{01} - \alpha_C)\alpha_{01}\sigma_\theta^2,$$
$$COV(U_S, U_{02}) = (\alpha_{12} + \alpha_{11} - \alpha_{02} - \alpha_{01} - \alpha_C)\alpha_{02}\sigma_\theta^2,$$
$$COV(U_{11}, U_{12}) = \alpha_{11}\alpha_{12}\sigma_\theta^2,$$
$$COV(U_{01}, U_{02}) = \alpha_{01}\alpha_{02}\sigma_\theta^2.$$

133 If not, then $\mu_C(Z)$, $\sigma_{U_S}^2$ and ε_C are identified up to normalizations.

If we normalize $\alpha_{01} = 1$ (recall that one normalization is needed to set the scale of θ), we can form the ratios

$$\frac{COV(U_S, U_{12})}{COV(U_S, U_{01})} = \alpha_{12}, \qquad \frac{COV(U_S, U_{11})}{COV(U_S, U_{01})} = \alpha_{11},$$
$$\frac{COV(U_S, U_{02})}{COV(U_S, U_{01})} = \alpha_{02}.$$

From these coefficients and the remaining covariances, we identify σ_θ^2 using $COV(U_{11}, U_{12})$ and/or $COV(U_{01}, U_{02})$. Thus if the factor loadings are nonzero,

$$\frac{COV(U_{11}, U_{12})}{\alpha_{11}\alpha_{12}} = \sigma_\theta^2$$

and

$$\frac{COV(U_{01}, U_{02})}{\alpha_{01}\alpha_{02}} = \sigma_\theta^2.$$

We can recover σ_θ^2 (since we know $\alpha_{11}\alpha_{12}$ and $\alpha_{01}\alpha_{02}$) from $COV(U_{11}, U_{12})$ and $COV(U_{01}, U_{02})$. We can also recover α_C since we know $\sigma_\theta^2, \alpha_{12}+\alpha_{11}-\alpha_{02}-\alpha_{01}-\alpha_C$, and α_{11}, α_{12}, α_{01}, α_{02}. We can form (conditional on X) $COV(Y_{11}, Y_{01}) = \alpha_{11}\alpha_{01}\sigma_\theta^2$; $COV(Y_{12}, Y_{01}) = \alpha_{12}\alpha_{01}\sigma_\theta^2$; $COV(Y_{11}, Y_{02}) = \alpha_{11}\alpha_{02}\sigma_\theta^2$ and $COV(Y_{12}, Y_{02}) = \alpha_{12}\alpha_{02}\sigma_\theta^2$. Thus we can identify the joint distribution of $(Y_{01}, Y_{02}, Y_{11}, Y_{12}, C)$ since we can identify $\mu_C(Z)$ from the schooling choice equation since we know $\mu_{01}(X)$, $\mu_{02}(X)$, $\mu_{11}(X)$, $\mu_{12}(X)$ and we have assumed that there are some Z not in X so that σ_S is identified.

As in Example 1, this analysis can be generalized to a general nonnormal setting using the analysis of Carneiro, Hansen and Heckman (2003). For simplicity, we have worked with a one factor model. The analyses of Carneiro, Hansen and Heckman (2003), Cunha, Heckman and Navarro (2005, 2006), Cunha and Heckman (2006a) and Heckman and Navarro (2006) use multiple factors. We offer an example in the next section.

The key idea in constructing joint distributions of counterfactuals using the analysis of Cunha, Heckman and Navarro (2005, 2006) and Cunha and Heckman (2006a) is *not* the factor structure for unobservables although it is convenient. The motivating idea is the assumption that a low-dimensional set of random variables generates the dependence across outcomes. Other low-dimensional representations such as the ARMA model or the dynamic factor structure model [see Sargent and Sims (1977)] can also be used. Urzua (2005) develops such a model and applies it to estimating rates of returns to schooling. The factor structure model presented in this section is easy to exposit and has been used to estimate joint distributions of counterfactuals. We present some examples in the next section. That section reviews recent work that generalizes the analysis of this section to derive *ex ante* and *ex post* outcome distributions, and measure the fundamental uncertainty facing agents in the labor market. With these methods it is possible to compute the distributions of both *ex ante* and *ex post* rates of return to schooling.

10. *Ex ante* and *ex post* returns: Distinguishing heterogeneity from uncertainty

In computing *ex ante* returns to schooling, it is necessary to characterize what is in the agent's information set at the time schooling decisions are made. To do so, the recent literature exploits the key idea that if agents know something and use that information in making their schooling decisions, it will affect their schooling choices. With panel data on earnings and other measurements of the factors, which may be test scores or information on other choices, we can assess what components of those outcomes were known at the time schooling choices were made.[134]

The literature on panel data earnings dynamics [e.g., Lillard and Willis (1978), MaCurdy (1982)] is not designed to estimate what is in agent information sets. It estimates earnings equations of the following type:

$$Y_{i,t} = X_{i,t}\beta + S_i\tau + U_{i,t}, \tag{27}$$

where $Y_{i,t}$, $X_{i,t}$, S_i, $U_{i,t}$ denote (for person i at time t) the realized earnings, observable characteristics, educational attainment, and unobservable characteristics, respectively, from the point of view of the observing economist. The variables generating outcomes realized at time t may or may not have been known to the agents at the time they made their schooling decisions.

The error term $U_{i,t}$ is usually decomposed into two or more components. For example, it is common to specify that

$$U_{i,t} = \phi_i + \delta_{i,t}. \tag{28}$$

The term ϕ_i is a person-specific effect. The error term $\delta_{i,t}$ is often assumed to follow an ARMA(p, q) process [see Hause (1980), MaCurdy (1982)] such as $\delta_{i,t} = \rho\delta_{i,t-1}+m_{i,t}$, where $m_{i,t}$ is a mean zero innovation independent of $X_{i,t}$ and the other error components. The components $X_{i,t}$, ϕ_i, and $\delta_{i,t}$ all contribute to measured *ex post* variability across persons. However, the literature is silent about the difference between heterogeneity and uncertainty, the unforecastable part of earnings as of a given age. The literature on income mobility and on inequality measures all variability *ex post* as in Chiswick (1974), Mincer (1974) and Chiswick and Mincer (1972).

An alternative specification of the error process postulates a factor structure for earnings, that uses the representation introduced in Section 9:

$$U_{i,t} = \theta_i\alpha_t + \varepsilon_{i,t}, \tag{29}$$

where θ_i is a vector of skills (e.g., ability, initial human capital, motivation, and the like), α_t is a vector of skill prices, and the $\varepsilon_{i,t}$ are mutually independent mean zero shocks independent of θ_i. Hause (1980) and Heckman and Scheinkman (1987) analyze such earnings models. Any process in the form of Equation (28) can be written in

[134] An alternative approach summarized by Manski (2004) is to use survey methods to elicit expectations. We do not survey that literature in this chapter.

terms of (29). The latter specification is more directly interpretable as a pricing equation than (28).

Depending on the available market arrangements for coping with risk, the predictable components of $U_{i,t}$ will have a different effect on choices and economic welfare than the unpredictable components, if people are risk averse and cannot fully insure against uncertainty. Statistical decompositions based on (27), (28), and (29) or versions of them describe *ex post* variability but tell us nothing about which components of (27) or (29) are forecastable by agents *ex ante*. Is ϕ_i unknown to the agent? $\delta_{i,t}$? Or $\phi_i + \delta_{i,t}$? Or $m_{i,t}$? In representation (29), the entire vector θ_i, components of the θ_i, the $\varepsilon_{i,t}$, or all of these may or may not be known to the agent at the time schooling choices are made.

The methodology developed in Carneiro, Hansen and Heckman (2003), Cunha, Heckman and Navarro (2005) and Cunha and Heckman (2006a, 2006b) provides a framework within which it is possible to identify components of life cycle outcomes that are forecastable and acted on at the time decisions are taken from ones that are not. In order to choose between high school and college, agents forecast future earnings (and other returns and costs) for each schooling level. Using information about educational choices at the time the choice is made, together with the *ex post* realization of earnings and costs that are observed at later ages, it is possible to estimate and test which components of future earnings and costs are forecast by the agent. This can be done provided we know, or can estimate, the earnings of agents under both schooling choices and provided we specify the market environment under which they operate as well as their preferences over outcomes.

For market environments where separation theorems are valid, so that consumption decisions are made independently of wealth maximizing decisions, it is not necessary to know agent preferences to decompose realized earnings outcomes in this fashion. Carneiro, Hansen and Heckman (2003), Cunha, Heckman and Navarro (2005) and Cunha and Heckman (2006a, 2006b) use choice information to extract *ex ante* or forecast components of earnings and to distinguish them from realized earnings under different market environments. The difference between forecast and realized earnings allows them to identify the distributions of the components of uncertainty facing agents at the time they make their schooling decisions.

10.1. A generalized Roy model

To state these issues more precisely, consider a version of the generalized Roy (1951) economy with two sectors.[135] This builds on the second example of Section 9. Let S_i denote different schooling levels. $S_i = 0$ denotes choice of the high school sector for person i, and $S_i = 1$ denotes choice of the college sector. Each person chooses to be

[135] See Heckman (1990) and Heckman and Smith (1998) for discussions of the generalized Roy model. In this chapter we assume only two schooling levels for expositional simplicity, although our methods apply more generally.

in one or the other sector but cannot be in both. Let the two potential outcomes be represented by the pair $(Y_{0,i}, Y_{1,i})$, only one of which is observed by the analyst for any agent. Denote by C_i the direct cost of choosing sector 1, which is associated with choosing the college sector (e.g., tuition and nonpecuniary costs of attending college expressed in monetary values). We have used this framework throughout this chapter.

$Y_{1,i}$ is the *ex post* present value of earnings in the college sector, discounted over horizon T for a person choosing at a fixed age, assumed for convenience to be zero,

$$Y_{1,i} = \sum_{t=0}^{T} \frac{Y_{1,i,t}}{(1+r)^t},$$

and $Y_{0,i}$ is the *ex post* present value of earnings in the high school sector at age zero,

$$Y_{0,i} = \sum_{t=0}^{T} \frac{Y_{0,i,t}}{(1+r)^t},$$

where r is the one-period risk-free interest rate. $Y_{1,i}$ and $Y_{0,i}$ can be constructed from time series of *ex post* potential earnings streams in the two states: $(Y_{0,i,0}, \ldots, Y_{0,i,T})$ for high school and $(Y_{1,i,0}, \ldots, Y_{1,i,T})$ for college. A practical problem is that we only observe one or the other of these streams. This partial observability creates a fundamental identification problem which can be solved using the methods described in Section 9 and the references cited.

The variables $Y_{1,i}$, $Y_{0,i}$, and C_i are *ex post* realizations of returns and costs, respectively. At the time agents make their schooling choices, these may be only partially known to the agent, if at all. Let $\mathcal{I}_{i,0}$ denote the information set of agent i at the time the schooling choice is made, which is time period $t = 0$ in our notation. Under a complete markets assumption with all risks diversifiable (so that there is risk-neutral pricing) or under a perfect foresight model with unrestricted borrowing or lending but full repayment, the decision rule governing sectoral choices at decision time '0' is

$$S_i = \begin{cases} 1, & \text{if } E(Y_{1,i} - Y_{0,i} - C_i | \mathcal{I}_{i,0}) \geqslant 0, \\ 0, & \text{otherwise.}^{136} \end{cases} \tag{30}$$

Under perfect foresight, the postulated information set would include $Y_{1,i}$, $Y_{0,i}$, and C_i. Under either model of information, the decision rule is simple: one attends school if the expected gains from schooling are greater than or equal to the expected costs. Thus under either set of assumptions, a separation theorem governs choices. Agents maximize expected wealth independently of their consumption decisions over time.

The decision rule is more complicated in the absence of full risk diversifiability and depends on the curvature of utility functions, the availability of markets to spread risk, and possibilities for storage. [See Cunha and Heckman (2006a) and Navarro (2005), for a more extensive discussion.] In these more realistic economic settings, the components

[136] If there are aggregate sources of risk, full insurance would require a linear utility function.

of earnings and costs required to forecast the gain to schooling depend on higher moments than the mean. In this chapter we use a model with a simple market setting to motivate the identification analysis of a more general environment analyzed elsewhere [Carneiro, Hansen and Heckman (2003), Cunha and Heckman (2006b)].

Suppose that we seek to determine $\mathcal{I}_{i,0}$. This is a difficult task. Typically we can only partially identify $\mathcal{I}_{i,0}$ and generate a list of candidate variables that belong in the information set. We can usually only estimate the distributions of the unobservables in $\mathcal{I}_{i,0}$ (from the standpoint of the econometrician) and not individual person-specific information sets. Before describing the analysis of Cunha, Heckman and Navarro (2005), we consider how this question might be addressed in the linear-in-the-parameters Card model.

10.2. Identifying information sets in the Card model

We seek to decompose the "returns" coefficient or the gross gains from schooling in an earnings–schooling model into components that are known at the time schooling choices are made and components that are not known. For simplicity assume that, for person i, returns are the same at all levels of schooling. Write the log of discounted lifetime earnings of person i as

$$Y_i = \alpha + \rho_i S_i + U_i, \tag{31}$$

where ρ_i is the person-specific *ex post* return, S_i is years of schooling, and U_i is a mean zero unobservable.[137] We seek to decompose ρ_i into two components $\rho_i = \eta_i + \nu_i$, where η_i is a component known to the agent when he/she makes schooling decisions and ν_i is revealed after the choice is made. Schooling choices are assumed to depend on what is known to the agent at the time decisions are made, $S_i = \lambda(\eta_i, Z_i, \tau_i)$, where the Z_i are other observed determinants of schooling and τ_i represents additional factors unobserved by the analyst but known to the agent. Both of these variables are in the agent's information set at the time schooling choices are made. We seek to determine what components of *ex post* lifetime earnings Y_i enter the schooling choice equation.

If η_i is known to the agent and acted on, it enters the schooling choice equation. Otherwise it does not. Component ν_i and any measurement errors in $Y_{1,i}$ or $Y_{0,i}$ should not be determinants of schooling choices. Neither should future skill prices that are unknown at the time agents make their decisions. If agents do not use η_i in making their schooling choices, even if they know it, η_i would not enter the schooling choice equation. Determining the correlation between realized Y_i and schooling choices based on *ex ante* forecasts enables economists to identify components known to agents and acted on in making their schooling decisions. Even if we cannot identify ρ_i, η_i, or ν_i for each person, under conditions specified in this chapter we can identify their distributions.

[137] We could equally well work with levels of discounted lifetime earnings but then ρ_i is no longer a "rate of return," i.e., a growth rate in earnings, which is the conventional focus in the literature.

If we correctly specify the X and the Z that are known to the agent at the time schooling choices are made, local instrumental variable estimates of the *MTE* as described in Section 8 identify *ex ante* gross gains. Any dependence between U_S and $Y_1 - Y_0$ arises from information known to the agent at the time schooling choices are made. If the conditioning set is misspecified by using information on X and Z that accumulates after schooling choices are made and that predicts realized earnings (but not *ex ante* earnings), the estimated *MTE* identifies an *ex post* return relative to that information set. Thus, it is important to specify the conditioning set correctly to obtain the appropriate *ex ante* return. How to pick the information set?

Suppose that the model for schooling can be written in linear in parameters form, as in the Card model exposited in Section 7:

$$S_i = \lambda_0 + \lambda_1 \eta_i + \lambda_2 \nu_i + \lambda_3 Z_i + \tau_i, \tag{32}$$

where τ_i has mean zero and is assumed to be independent of Z_i. The Z_i and the τ_i proxy costs and may be correlated with U_i and ρ_i in (31). In this framework, the goal of the analysis is to determine the η_i and ν_i components. By definition, $\lambda_2 = 0$ if ν_i is not known when agents make their schooling choices.

As a simple example, consider the model of Section 7.1. We drop "i" subscripts unless they clarify notation. We observe the cost of funds, r, and assume $r \perp\!\!\!\perp (\rho, \alpha)$. This assumes that the costs of schooling are independent of the "return" ρ and the payment to raw ability, α. We established identification of $\bar{\rho}$. (If there are observed regressors X determining the mean of $\bar{\rho}$, we identify $\bar{\rho}(X)$, the conditional mean of ρ.)

Suppose that agents do not know ρ at the time they make their schooling decisions but instead know $E(\rho) = \bar{\rho}$.[138] If agents act on this expected return to schooling, decisions are given by

$$S = \frac{\bar{\rho} - r}{k}$$

and *ex post* earnings observed after schooling are

$$Y = \bar{\alpha} + \bar{\rho} S + \big\{(\alpha - \bar{\alpha}) + (\rho - \bar{\rho}) S\big\}.$$

In the notation introduced in the Card model, $\eta = \bar{\rho}$ and $\nu = \rho - \bar{\rho}$.

In this case,

$$COV(Y, S) = \bar{\rho}\,\mathrm{Var}(S)$$

because $(\rho - \bar{\rho})$ is independent of S. Note further that $(\bar{\alpha}, \bar{\rho})$ can be identified by least squares because $S \perp\!\!\!\perp [(\alpha - \bar{\alpha}), (\rho - \bar{\rho}) S]$.

If, on the other hand, agents know ρ at the time they make their schooling decisions, *OLS* breaks down for identifying $\bar{\rho}$ because ρ is correlated with S. We can identify $\bar{\rho}$ and

[138] This is a version of a rational expectations assumption for a particular information set, where the agent forecasts ρ by $\bar{\rho}$, the overall population mean. Under rational expectations, the mean *ex ante* return is the same as the mean *ex post* return, but the distributions of these returns may be very different.

the distribution of ρ using the method of instrumental variables presented in Section 7.1. Under our assumptions, r is a valid instrument for S.

In this case

$$COV(Y, S) = \bar{\rho}\text{Var}(S) + COV\big(S, (\rho - \bar{\rho})S\big).$$

Since we observe S, we can identify $\bar{\rho}$ and can construct $(\rho - \bar{\rho})$ for each S, we can form both terms on the right-hand side. Under the assumption that agents do not know ρ but forecast it by $\bar{\rho}$, ρ is independent of S so we can test for independence directly. In this case the second term on the right-hand side is zero and does not contribute to the explanation of $COV(\ln Y, S)$. Note further that a Durbin (1954)–Wu (1973)–Hausman (1978) test can be used to compare the *OLS* and *IV* estimates, which should be the same under the model that assumes that ρ is not known at the time schooling decisions are made and that agents base their choice of schooling on $E(\rho) = \bar{\rho}$. If the economist does not observe r, but instead observes determinants L satisfying the conditions in Section 7.2, then we can still conduct the Durbin–Wu–Hausman test to discriminate between the two hypotheses, but we cannot form $COV(\rho, S)$ directly.

If we add selection bias to the Card model (so $E(\alpha|S)$ depends on S), we can identify $\bar{\rho}$ by *IV* as shown in Section 7.3 but *OLS* is no longer consistent even if, in making their schooling decisions, agents forecast ρ using $\bar{\rho}$. Selection bias can occur, for example, if fellowship aid is given on the basis of raw ability. Thus the Durbin–Wu–Hausman test is not helpful in assessing what is in the agent's information set.

Even ignoring selection bias, if we misspecify the information set, in the case where r is not observed, the proposed testing approach based on the Durbin–Wu–Hausman test breaks down. Thus if we include in L variables that predict *ex post* gains $(\rho - \bar{\rho})$ and are correlated with S, we do not identify $\bar{\rho}$. The Durbin–Wu–Hausman test is not informative on the stated question. For example, if local labor market variables proxy the opportunity cost of school (the r), and also predict the evolution of *ex post* earnings $(\rho - \bar{\rho})$, they are invalid. The question of determining the appropriate information set is front and center and cannot in general be inferred using *IV* methods.

The method developed by Cunha, Heckman and Navarro (2005, 2006) and Cunha and Heckman (2006a, 2006b) exploits the covariance between S and the realized Y_t to determine which components of Y_t are known at the time schooling decisions are made. It explicitly models selection bias and allows for measurement error in earnings. It does not rely on linearity of the schooling relationship in terms of $\rho - r$. Their method recognizes the discrete nature of the schooling decision. It builds on the modern literature on constructing counterfactual schooling models discussed in Section 9.

10.3. Identifying information sets

Cunha, Heckman and Navarro (2005, 2006) henceforth CHN, exploit covariances between schooling and realized earnings that arise under different information structures to test which information structure characterizes the data. To see how the method works, simplify the model to two schooling levels. Heckman and Navarro (2006) analyze models with multiple schooling levels, but do not present empirical estimates of their model.

Suppose, contrary to what is possible, that the analyst observes $Y_{0,i}$, $Y_{1,i}$, and C_i. Such information would come from an ideal data set in which we could observe two different lifetime earnings streams for the same person in high school and in college as well as the costs they pay for attending college. From such information, we could construct $Y_{1,i} - Y_{0,i} - C_i$. If we knew the information set $\mathcal{I}_{i,0}$ of the agent that governs schooling choices, we could also construct $E(Y_{1,i} - Y_{0,i} - C_i | \mathcal{I}_{i,0})$. Under a given model of expectations, we could form the residual

$$V_{\mathcal{I}_{i,0}} = (Y_{1,i} - Y_{0,i} - C_i) - E(Y_{1,i} - Y_{0,i} - C_i | \mathcal{I}_{i,0}),$$

and from the *ex ante* college choice decision, we could determine whether S_i depends on $V_{\mathcal{I}_{i,0}}$. It should not if we have specified $\mathcal{I}_{i,0}$ correctly. In terms of the model of Equations (31) and (32), if there are no direct costs of schooling, $E(Y_{1,i} - Y_{0,i} | \mathcal{I}_{i,0}) = \eta_i$, and $V_{\mathcal{I}_{i,0}} = \nu_i$.

A test for correct specification of candidate information set $\widetilde{\mathcal{I}}_{i,0}$ is a test of whether S_i depends on $V_{\widetilde{\mathcal{I}}_{i,0}}$, where $V_{\widetilde{\mathcal{I}}_{i,0}} = (Y_{1,i} - Y_{0,i} - C_i) - E(Y_{1,i} - Y_{0,i} - C_i | \widetilde{\mathcal{I}}_{i,0})$. More precisely, the information set is valid if $S_i \perp\!\!\!\perp V_{\widetilde{\mathcal{I}}_{i,0}} | \widetilde{\mathcal{I}}_{i,0}$. In terms of the simple linear schooling model of Equations (31) and (32), this condition says that ν_i should not enter the schooling choice equation ($\lambda_2 = 0$). A test of misspecification of $\widetilde{\mathcal{I}}_{i,0}$ is a test of whether the coefficient of $V_{\widetilde{\mathcal{I}}_{i,0}}$ is statistically significantly different from zero in the schooling choice equation.

More generally, $\widetilde{\mathcal{I}}_{i,0}$ is the correct information set if $V_{\widetilde{\mathcal{I}}_{i,0}}$ does not help to predict schooling. One can search among candidate information sets $\widetilde{\mathcal{I}}_{i,0}$ to determine which ones satisfy the requirement that the generated $V_{\widetilde{\mathcal{I}}_{i,0}}$ does not predict S_i and what components of $Y_{1,i} - Y_{0,i} - C_i$ (and $Y_{1,i} - Y_{0,i}$) are predictable at the age schooling decisions are made for the specified information set.[139] There may be several information sets that satisfy this property.[140] For a properly specified $\widetilde{\mathcal{I}}_{i,0}$, $V_{\widetilde{\mathcal{I}}_{i,0}}$ should not cause (predict) schooling choices. The components of $V_{\widetilde{\mathcal{I}}_{i,0}}$ that are unpredictable are called intrinsic components of uncertainty, as defined in this chapter.

It is difficult to determine the exact content of $\mathcal{I}_{i,0}$ known to each agent. If we could, we would perfectly predict S_i given our decision rule. More realistically, we might find variables that proxy $\mathcal{I}_{i,0}$ or their distribution. Thus, in the example of Equations (31) and (32) we would seek to determine the distribution of ν_i and the allocation of the variance of ρ_i to η_i and ν_i rather than trying to estimate ρ_i, η_i, or ν_i for each person. This strategy is pursued in Cunha, Heckman and Navarro (2005, 2006) for a two-choice

[139] This procedure is a Sims (1972) version of a Wiener–Granger causality test.

[140] Thus different combinations of variables may contain the same information. The issue of the existence of a smallest information set is a technical one concerning a minimum σ-algebra that satisfies the condition on $\mathcal{I}_{i,0}$.

model of schooling, and generalized by Cunha and Heckman (2006a). To implement such a test requires overcoming the problem of missing counterfactual earnings equations. We now describe a method for doing so developed in Carneiro, Hansen and Heckman (2003) and Cunha, Heckman and Navarro (2005, 2006, 2007).

10.4. An approach based on factor structures

The essence of the idea underlying the method of testing for what is in an agent's information set at the time schooling decisions are made is communicated by adapting Example 2 presented in Section 9. Suppose that at the time they make their schooling decisions, agents do not know θ or the future $\varepsilon_{1t}, \varepsilon_{0t}, t = 1, 2$. (Recall that period 1 is the initial period in that example.) θ is realized after schooling choices are made. The agents know X, Z and ε_C. Thus $\mathcal{I}_{i,0} = \{X_i, Z_i, \varepsilon_C\}$. Suppose that θ is independent of X, Z, ε_C and $E(\theta|X, Z, \varepsilon_C) = 0$. Under rational expectations U_S is independent of all future earnings disturbances so that $COV(U_S, U_{11}) = 0$, $COV(U_S, U_{12}) = 0$, $COV(U_S, U_{01}) = 0$, $COV(U_S, U_{02}) = 0$. However realized earnings are correlated with each other through the realized θ.

Under the assumptions of Example 2, we can test for the zero covariances. If nonzero covariances are found, then θ is a component of heterogeneity. Otherwise θ contributes to *ex ante* uncertainty. By design, this example is overly simplistic. It is more likely that there are multiple sources of unobserved heterogeneity (θ is a vector) and that they may only partially know the X that are realized after schooling decisions are made (e.g., macro shocks or new trends in skill prices). A more general procedure is required to account for those possibilities which we now describe.

Consider the following linear in parameters model for a full T periods. This analysis generalizes the example just presented. Write earnings in each counterfactual state as

$$\begin{aligned} Y_{0,i,t} &= X_{i,t}\beta_{0,t} + U_{0,i,t}, \\ Y_{1,i,t} &= X_{i,t}\beta_{1,t} + U_{1,i,t}, \quad t = 0, \dots, T. \end{aligned}$$

We let costs of college be defined as

$$C_i = Z_i\gamma + U_{i,C}.$$

Assume that the life cycle of the agent ends after period T. Linearity of outcomes in terms of parameters is convenient but not essential to the method of CHN.

Suppose that there exists a vector of factors $\theta_i = (\theta_{i,1}, \theta_{i,2}, \dots, \theta_{i,L})$ such that $\theta_{i,k}$ and $\theta_{i,j}$ are mutually independent random variables for $k, j = 1, \dots, L, k \neq j$. They represent the error term in earnings at age t for agent i in the following manner:

$$\begin{aligned} U_{0,i,t} &= \theta_i\alpha_{0,t} + \varepsilon_{0,i,t}, \\ U_{1,i,t} &= \theta_i\alpha_{1,t} + \varepsilon_{1,i,t}, \end{aligned}$$

where $\alpha_{0,t}$ and $\alpha_{1,t}$ are vectors and θ_i is a vector distributed independently across persons. The $\varepsilon_{0,i,t}$ and $\varepsilon_{1,i,t}$ are mutually independent of each other and independent of the θ_i. We can also decompose the cost function C_i in a similar fashion:

$$C_i = Z_i\gamma + \theta_i\alpha_C + \varepsilon_{i,C}.$$

All of the statistical dependence across potential outcomes and costs is generated by θ, X, and Z. Thus, if we could match on θ_i (as well as X and Z), we could use matching to infer the distribution of counterfactuals and capture all of the dependence across the counterfactual states through the θ_i. Thus we could use θ as the Q in Section 9 if we could observe it. However, in general, CHN allow for the possibility that not all of the required elements of θ_i are observed.

The parameters α_C and $\alpha_{s,t}$ for $s = 0, 1$, and $t = 0, \dots, T$ are the factor loadings. $\varepsilon_{i,C}$ is independent of the θ_i and the other ε components. In this notation, the choice equation can be written as:

$$S_i^* = E\left(\sum_{t=0}^{T} \frac{(X_{i,t}\beta_{1,t} + \theta_i\alpha_{1,t} + \varepsilon_{1,i,t}) - (X_{i,t}\beta_{0,t} + \theta_i\alpha_{0,t} + \varepsilon_{0,i,t})}{(1+r)^t} - (Z_i\gamma + \theta_i\alpha_C + \varepsilon_{iC})|\mathcal{I}_{i,0}\right), \tag{33}$$

$$S_i = 1 \quad \text{if } S^* \geqslant 0; \qquad S_i = 0 \quad \text{otherwise.}$$

The sum inside the parentheses is the discounted earnings of agent i in college minus the discounted earnings of the agent in high school. The second term is the cost of college.

Constructing (33) entails making a counterfactual comparison. Even if the earnings of one schooling level are observed over the lifetime using panel data, the earnings in the counterfactual state are not. After the schooling choice is made, some components of the $X_{i,t}$, the θ_i, and the $\varepsilon_{i,t}$ may be revealed (e.g., unemployment rates, macro shocks) to both the observing economist and the agent, although different components may be revealed to each and at different times. For this reason, application of *IV* even in the linear schooling model is problematic. If the wrong information set is used, the *IV* method will not identify the true *ex ante* returns.

Examining alternative information sets, one can determine which ones produce models for outcomes that fit the data best in terms of producing a model that predicts date $t = 0$ schooling choices and at the same time passes the CHN test for misspecification of predicted earnings and costs. Some components of the error terms may be known or not known at the date schooling choices are made. The unforecastable components are intrinsic uncertainty as CHN define it. The forecastable information is called heterogeneity.[141]

To formally characterize the CHN empirical procedure, it is useful to introduce some additional notation. Let $\odot$ denote the Hadamard product ($a \odot b = (a_1b_1, \dots, a_Lb_L)$)

[141] The term 'heterogeneity' is somewhat unfortunate. Under this term, CHN include trends common across all people (e.g., macrotrends). The real distinction they are making is between components of realized earnings forecastable by agents at the time they make their schooling choices vs. components that are not forecastable.

for vectors a and b of length L. This is a componentwise multiplication of vectors to produce a vector. Let Δ_{X_t}, $t = 0, \ldots, T$, Δ_Z, Δ_θ, Δ_{ε_t}, Δ_{ε_C}, denote coefficient vectors associated with the X_t, $t = 0, \ldots, T$, the Z, the θ, the $\varepsilon_{1,t} - \varepsilon_{0,t}$, and the ε_C, respectively. These coefficients will be estimated to be nonzero in a schooling choice equation if a proposed information set is not the actual information set used by agents. For a proposed information set $\widetilde{\mathcal{I}}_{i,0}$ which may or may not be the true information set on which agents act, CHN define the proposed choice index $\widetilde{S}_i^*$ in the following way:

$$
\begin{aligned}
\widetilde{S}_i^* = {} & \sum_{t=0}^{T} \frac{E(X_{i,t} | \widetilde{\mathcal{I}}_{i,0})}{(1+r)^t} (\beta_{1,t} - \beta_{0,t}) \\
& + \sum_{t=0}^{T} \frac{[X_{i,t} - E(X_{i,t} | \widetilde{\mathcal{I}}_{i,0})]}{(1+r)^t} (\beta_{1,t} - \beta_{0,t}) \odot \Delta_{X_t} \\
& + E(\theta_i | \widetilde{\mathcal{I}}_{i,0}) \left[\sum_{t=0}^{T} \frac{(\alpha_{1,t} - \alpha_{0,t})}{(1+r)^t} - \alpha_C \right] \\
& + \left[\theta_i - E(\theta_i | \widetilde{\mathcal{I}}_{i,0})\right] \left\{ \left[\sum_{t=0}^{T} \frac{(\alpha_{1,t} - \alpha_{0,t})}{(1+r)^t} - \alpha_C \right] \odot \Delta_\theta \right\} \\
& + \sum_{t=0}^{T} \frac{E(\varepsilon_{1,i,t} - \varepsilon_{0,i,t} | \widetilde{\mathcal{I}}_{i,0})}{(1+r)^t} \\
& + \sum_{t=0}^{T} \frac{[(\varepsilon_{1,i,t} - \varepsilon_{0,i,t}) - E(\varepsilon_{1,i,t} - \varepsilon_{0,i,t} | \widetilde{\mathcal{I}}_{i,0})]}{(1+r)^t} \Delta_{\varepsilon_t} \\
& - E(Z_i | \widetilde{\mathcal{I}}_{i,0}) \gamma - \left[Z_i - E(Z_i | \widetilde{\mathcal{I}}_{i,0})\right] \gamma \odot \Delta_Z - E(\varepsilon_{iC} | \widetilde{\mathcal{I}}_{i,0}) \\
& - \left[\varepsilon_{iC} - E(\varepsilon_{iC} | \widetilde{\mathcal{I}}_{i,0})\right] \Delta_{\varepsilon_C}.
\end{aligned} \tag{34}
$$

To conduct their test, CHN fit a schooling choice model based on the proposed model (34). They estimate the parameters of the model including the Δ parameters. This decomposition for $\widetilde{S}_i^*$ assumes that agents know the β, the γ, and the α.[142] If that is not correct, the presence of additional unforecastable components due to unknown coefficients affects the interpretation of the estimates. A test of no misspecification of information set $\widetilde{\mathcal{I}}_{i,0}$ is a joint test of the hypothesis that the Δ are all zero. That is, when $\widetilde{\mathcal{I}}_{i,0} = \mathcal{I}_{i,0}$ then the proposed choice index $\widetilde{S}_i^* = S_i^*$.

In a correctly specified model, the components associated with zero Δ_j are the unforecastable elements or the elements which, even if known to the agent, are not acted on in making schooling choices. To illustrate the application of the method of CHN, we elaborate on the example based on Example 2 of Section 9, previously discussed, and

[142] Cunha, Heckman and Navarro (2005) and Cunha and Heckman (2006a, 2006b) relax this assumption.

assume for simplicity that the $X_{i,t}$, the Z_i, the $\varepsilon_{i,C}$, the $\beta_{1,t}$, $\beta_{0,t}$, the $\alpha_{1,t}$, $\alpha_{0,t}$, and α_C are known to the agent, and the $\varepsilon_{j,i,t}$ are unknown and are set at their mean zero values. We can infer which components of the θ_i are known and acted on in making schooling decisions if we postulate that some components of θ_i are known perfectly at date $t = 0$ while others are not known at all, and their forecast values have mean zero given $\mathcal{I}_{i,0}$.

If there is an element of the vector θ_i, say $\theta_{i,2}$ (factor 2), that has nonzero loadings (coefficients) in the schooling choice equation and a nonzero loading on one or more potential future earnings, then one can say that at the time the schooling choice is made, the agent knows the unobservable captured by factor 2 that affects future earnings. If $\theta_{i,2}$ does not enter the choice equation but explains future earnings, then $\theta_{i,2}$ is unknown (not predictable by the agent) at the age schooling decisions are made. An alternative interpretation is that the second component of $[\sum_{t=0}^{T} \frac{(\alpha_{1,t}-\alpha_{0,t})}{(1+r)^t} - \alpha_C]$ is zero, i.e., that even if the component is known, it is not acted on. CHN can only test for what the agent knows and acts on.

One plausible case is that for their model $\varepsilon_{i,C}$ is known (since schooling costs are incurred up front), but the future $\varepsilon_{1,i,t}$ and $\varepsilon_{0,i,t}$ are not, have mean zero, and are insurable. If there are components of the $\varepsilon_{j,i,t}$ that are predictable at age $t = 0$, they will induce additional dependence between S_i and future earnings that will pick up additional factors beyond those initially specified. The CHN procedure can be generalized to consider all components of (34). With it, the analyst can test the predictive power of each subset of the overall possible information set at the date the schooling decision is being made.[143,144]

In the context of the factor structure representation for earnings and costs, the contrast between the CHN approach to identifying components of intrinsic uncertainty and the approach followed in the literature is as follows. The traditional approach as exemplified by Keane and Wolpin (1997) assumes that the θ_i are known to the agent while the $\{\varepsilon_{0,i,t}, \varepsilon_{1,i,t}\}_{t=0}^{T}$ are not.[145] The CHN approach allows the analyst to determine which

[143] This test has been extended to a nonlinear setting, allowing for credit constraints, preferences for risk, and the like. See Cunha and Heckman (2006b) and Navarro (2005).

[144] A similar but distinct idea motivates the Flavin (1981) test of the permanent income hypothesis and her measurement of unforecastable income innovations. She picks a particular information set $\widetilde{\mathcal{I}}_{i,0}$ (permanent income constructed from an assumed ARMA(p, q) time series process for income, where she estimates the coefficients given a specified order of the AR and MA components) and tests if $V_{\widetilde{\mathcal{I}}_{i,0}}$ (our notation) predicts consumption. Her test of 'excess sensitivity' can be interpreted as a test of the correct specification of the ARMA process that she assumes generates $\widetilde{\mathcal{I}}_{i,0}$ which is unobserved (by the economist), although she does not state it that way. Blundell and Preston (1998) and Blundell, Pistaferri and Preston (2004) extend her analysis but, like her, maintain an *a priori* specification of the stochastic process generating $\mathcal{I}_{i,0}$. Blundell, Pistaferri and Preston (2004) claim to test for 'partial insurance.' In fact their procedure can be viewed as a test of their specification of the stochastic process generating the agent's information set. More closely related to our work is the analysis of Pistaferri (2001), who uses the distinction between expected starting wages (to measure expected returns) and realized wages (to measure innovations) in a consumption analysis.

[145] Keane and Wolpin assume one factor where the θ is a discrete variable and they assume all factor loadings are identical across periods. However, their specification of the uniquenesses or innovations is more general

components of θ_i and $\{\varepsilon_{0,i,t}, \varepsilon_{1,i,t}\}_{t=0}^{T}$ are known and acted on at the time schooling decisions are made.

Statistical decompositions do not tell us which components of (29) are known at the time agents make their schooling decisions. A model of expectations and schooling is needed. If some of the components of $\{\varepsilon_{0,i,t}, \varepsilon_{1,i,t}\}_{t=0}^{T}$ are known to the agent at the date schooling decisions are made and enter (34), then additional dependence between S_i and future $Y_{1,i} - Y_{0,i}$ due to the $\{\varepsilon_{0,i,t}, \varepsilon_{1,i,t}\}_{t=0}^{T}$, beyond that due to θ_i, would be estimated.

It is helpful to contrast the dependence between S_i and future $Y_{0,i,t}$, $Y_{1,i,t}$ arising from θ_i and the dependence between S_i and the $\{\varepsilon_{0,i,t}, \varepsilon_{1,i,t}\}_{t=0}^{T}$. Some of the θ_i in the *ex post* earnings equation may not appear in the choice equation. Under other information sets, some additional dependence between S_i and $\{\varepsilon_{0,i,t}, \varepsilon_{1,i,t}\}_{t=0}^{T}$ may arise. The contrast between the sources generating realized earnings outcomes and the sources generating dependence between S_i and realized earnings is the essential idea in the analysis of CHN. The method can be generalized to deal with nonlinear preferences and imperfect market environments.[146] A central issue, discussed next, is how far one can go in identifying income information processes without specifying preferences, insurance, and market environments.

10.5. More general preferences and market settings

To focus on the main ideas in the literature, we have used the simple market structures of complete contingent claims markets. What can be identified in more general environments? In the absence of perfect certainty or perfect risk sharing, preferences and

than that used in factor analysis. See our discussion of their model in Section 10.8. The analysis of Hartog and Vijverberg (2002) is another example and uses variances of *ex post* income to proxy *ex ante* variability, removing "fixed effects" (person specific θ).

[146] In a model with complete autarky with preferences Ψ, ignoring costs,

$$I_i = \sum_{t=0}^{T} E\left[\frac{\Psi(X_{i,t}\beta_{1,t} + \theta_i\alpha_{1,t} + \varepsilon_{1,i,t}) - \Psi(X_{i,t}\beta_{0,t} + \theta_i\alpha_{0,t} + \varepsilon_{0,i,t})}{(1+\rho)^t}\,\middle|\,\widetilde{\mathcal{I}}_{i,0}\right],$$

where ρ is the time rate of discount, we can make a similar decomposition but it is more complicated given the nonlinearity in Ψ. For this model we could do a Sims noncausality test where

$$\begin{aligned}V_{\widetilde{\mathcal{I}}_{i,0}} &= \sum_{t=0}^{T} \frac{\Psi(X_{i,t}\beta_{1,t} + \theta_i\alpha_{1,t} + \varepsilon_{1,i,t}) - \Psi(X_{i,t}\beta_{0,t} + \theta_i\alpha_{0,t} + \varepsilon_{0,i,t})}{(1+\rho)^t} \\ &\quad - \sum_{t=0}^{T} E\left[\frac{\Psi(X_{i,t}\beta_{1,t} + \theta_i\alpha_{1,t} + \varepsilon_{1,i,t}) - \Psi(X_{i,t}\beta_{0,t} + \theta_i\alpha_{0,t} + \varepsilon_{0,i,t})}{(1+\rho)^t}\,\middle|\,\widetilde{\mathcal{I}}_{i,0}\right].\end{aligned}$$

This requires some specification of Ψ. See Carneiro, Hansen and Heckman (2003), who assume $\Psi(Y) = \ln Y$ and that the equation for $\ln Y$ is linear in parameters. Cunha and Heckman (2006b) and Navarro (2005) generalize that framework to a model with imperfect capital markets where some lending and borrowing is possible.

market environments also determine schooling choices. The separation theorem allowing consumption and schooling decisions to be analyzed in isolation of each other that we have used thus far breaks down.

If we postulate information processes *a priori*, and assume that preferences are known up to some unknown parameters as in Flavin (1981), Blundell and Preston (1998) and Blundell, Pistaferri and Preston (2004), we can identify departures from specified market structures. Cunha and Heckman (2006b) postulate an Aiyagari (1994)–Laitner (1992) economy with one asset and parametric preferences to identify the information processes in the agent's information set. They take a parametric position on preferences and a nonparametric position on the economic environment and the information set.

An open question, not yet fully resolved in the literature, is how far one can go in nonparametrically jointly identifying preferences, market structures and information sets. [See Cunha, Heckman and Navarro (2005).] Navarro (2005) adds consumption data to the schooling choice and earnings data to secure identification of risk preference parameters (within a parametric family) and information sets, and to test among alternative models for market environments. Alternative assumptions about what analysts know produce different interpretations of the same evidence. The lack of full insurance interpretation given to the empirical results by Flavin (1981) and Blundell, Pistaferri and Preston (2004) may be a consequence of their misspecification of the agent's information set generating process. We now present some evidence on *ex ante* vs. *ex post* returns presented by Cunha and Heckman (2006b), henceforth CH.

10.6. Evidence on uncertainty and heterogeneity of returns

Few data sets contain the full life cycle of earnings along with the test scores and schooling choices needed to directly estimate the CHN model and extract components of uncertainty. It is necessary to pool data sets. CHN (2005) combine NLSY and PSID data sets. We summarize the analysis of CH in this subsection. See their paper for their exclusions and identification conditions.

Following the preceding theoretical analysis, they consider only two schooling choices: high school and college graduation.[147] For simplicity and familiarity, we focus on their results that are based on assuming that complete contingent claims markets characterize the data. We consider evidence from other market settings in Section 10.7. Because they assume that all shocks are idiosyncratic and that complete markets operate, schooling choices are made on the basis of expected present value income maximization. Carneiro, Hansen and Heckman (2003) assume the absence of any credit markets or insurance. Navarro (2005) checks whether the CHN and CH findings about components of uncertainty are robust to different assumptions about the availability of credit markets and insurance markets. He estimates an Aiyagari–Laitner economy with

[147] Heckman and Navarro (2006) present a model with multiple schooling levels.

a single asset and borrowing constraints and discusses risk aversion and the relative importance of uncertainty. We summarize the evidence from alternative assumptions about market structures below. We now summarize the model of CH (2006b).

10.6.1. Identifying joint distributions of counterfactuals and the role of costs and ability as determinants of schooling

Suppose that the error term for $Y_{s,t}$ is generated by a two factor model,

$$Y_{s,t} = X\beta_{s,t} + \theta_1\alpha_{s,t,1} + \theta_2\alpha_{s,t,2} + \varepsilon_{s,t}. \tag{35}$$

We omit the "i" subscripts to eliminate notational burden. Cunha and Heckman (2006b) report that two factors are all that is required to fit the data.

They use a test score system of K ability tests:

$$T_{jT} = X_T\omega_{jT} + \theta_1\alpha_{jT} + \varepsilon_{jT}, \quad j = 1, \dots, K. \tag{36}$$

Thus factor 1 is identified as an ability component. The cost function C is specified by:

$$C = Z\gamma + \theta_1\alpha_{C,1} + \theta_2\alpha_{C,2} + \varepsilon_C. \tag{37}$$

They assume that agents know the model coefficients and X, Z, ε_C and some, but not necessarily all, components of θ. Let the components known to the agent be $\bar{\theta}$. The decision rule for attending college is based on:

$$S^* = E\left(Y_{1,0} + \frac{Y_{1,1}}{1+r} - Y_{0,0} - \frac{Y_{0,1}}{1+r}\,\middle|\, X, \bar{\theta}\right) - E(C|Z, X, \bar{\theta}, \varepsilon_C), \tag{38}$$

$$S = \mathbf{1} \quad (S^* \geqslant 0).$$

Cunha and Heckman (2006b) report evidence that the estimated factors are highly non-normal.[148]

Table 15 presents the conditional distribution of *ex ante* potential college earnings given *ex ante* potential high school earnings, decile by decile, as reported by Cunha and Heckman (2006b). The table displays positive dependence between the relative positions of individuals in the two distributions, but it is not especially strong. In all high school deciles save the highest, almost 90% of persons are in a different college decile. Observe that this comparison is not made in terms of positions in the overall distribution of earnings. CH can determine where individuals are located in the distribution of

[148] They assume that each factor k, $k \in \{1, 2\}$, is generated by a mixture of J_k normal distributions,

$$\theta_k \sim \sum_{j=1}^{J_k} p_{k,j}\phi(f_k|\mu_{k,j}, \tau_{k,j}),$$

where the $p_{k,j}$ are the weights on the normal components.

Table 15
Ex-ante conditional distributions for the NLSY79 (College earnings conditional on high school earnings)

High school	College 1	2	3	4	5	6	7	8	9	10
1	0.1833	0.1631	0.1330	0.1066	0.0928	0.0758	0.0675	0.0630	0.0615	0.0535
2	0.1217	0.1525	0.1262	0.1139	0.1044	0.0979	0.0857	0.0796	0.0683	0.0498
3	0.1102	0.1263	0.1224	0.1198	0.1124	0.0970	0.0931	0.0907	0.0775	0.0506
4	0.0796	0.1083	0.1142	0.1168	0.1045	0.1034	0.1121	0.1006	0.0953	0.0652
5	0.0701	0.0993	0.1003	0.1027	0.1104	0.1165	0.1086	0.1112	0.1043	0.0768
6	0.0573	0.0932	0.1079	0.1023	0.1110	0.1166	0.1130	0.1102	0.1059	0.0825
7	0.0495	0.0810	0.0950	0.1021	0.1101	0.1162	0.1202	0.1174	0.1134	0.0950
8	0.0511	0.0754	0.0770	0.1006	0.1006	0.1053	0.1244	0.1212	0.1297	0.1147
9	0.0411	0.0651	0.0841	0.0914	0.1039	0.1117	0.1162	0.1216	0.1442	0.1206
10	0.0590	0.0599	0.0622	0.0645	0.0697	0.0782	0.0770	0.1028	0.1181	0.3087

$\Pr(d_i < Y_c < d_i + 1 | d_j < Y_h < d_j + 1)$ where d_i is the ith decile of the college lifetime ex-ante earnings distribution and d_j is the jth decile of the high school ex-ante lifetime earnings distribution. Individual fixes known θ at their means, so information set $= \{\theta_1 = 0, \theta_2 = 0\}$. Correlation$(Y_C, Y_H) = 0.4083$.
Source: Cunha and Heckman (2006b).

population potential high school earnings and the distribution of potential college earnings although in the data we only observe them in either one or the other state. Their evidence shows that the assumption of preservation of ranks across counterfactual distributions that is maintained in much of the recent literature [e.g., Juhn, Murphy and Pierce (1993)] is far too strong. They also report evidence of less than perfect sorting on *ex post* earnings.

Figure 16 presents the marginal density of predicted (actual) present value of earnings for college students and the counterfactual density of the present value of their earnings if they were high school students. When we compare the densities of present value of earnings in the college sector for persons who choose college against the densities of counterfactual high school earnings for college graduates, the density of the present value of earnings for college graduates in college is to the right of the counterfactual density of the present value of high school earnings for college graduates. A parallel analysis for high school graduates reveals that the density of college earnings for high school graduates is to the right of the distribution of their high school earnings so that many high school graduates would earn more by going to college.

Table 16 from CHN reports the fitted and counterfactual present value of earnings for agents who choose high school. The typical high school student would earn \$968.5 thousand over the life cycle. He would earn \$1,125.8 thousand if he had chosen to be a college graduate.[149] This implies a return of 20.5% to a college education over the whole life cycle (i.e., a monetary gain of \$157.3 thousand). In Table 17, CHN note

[149] These numbers may appear to be large but are a consequence of using a 3% discount rate.

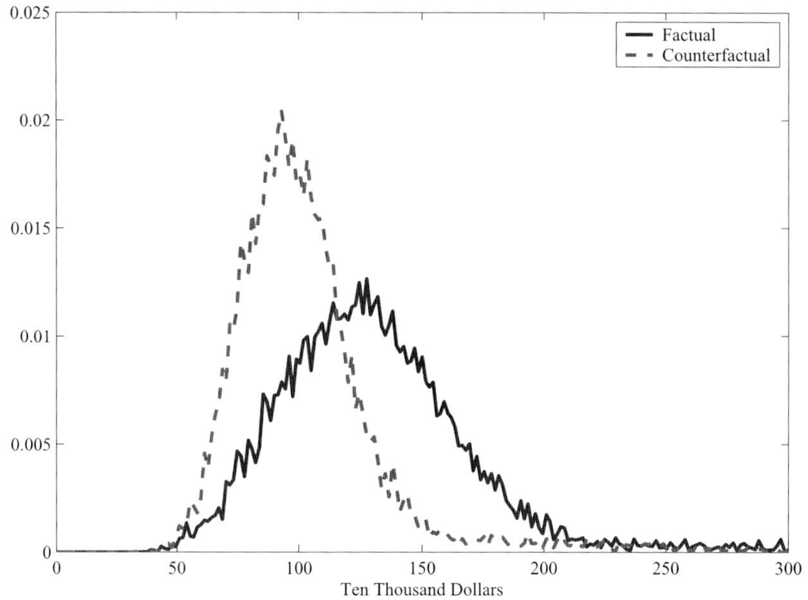

Present value of lifetime earnings from age 18 to 65 for college graduates using a discount rate of 3%. Let Y_0 denote present value of earnings in high school sector. Let Y_1 denote present value of earnings in college sector. In this graph we plot the counterfactual density function $f(y_0|S = 1)$ (the dashed line), against the factual density function $f(y_1|S = 1)$.

Figure 16. Densities of present value of earnings for college graduates. Factual and counterfactual NLSY/1979 sample. Source: Cunha and Heckman (2006b).

Table 16
Average present value of *ex post* earnings[1] for high school graduates fitted and counterfactual[2] white males from NLSY79

	High school (fitted)	College (counterfactual)	Returns[3]
Average	968.5100	1125.7870	0.2055
Standard error	7.9137	9.4583	0.0113

Source: Cunha and Heckman (2006b).

[1]Thousands of dollars. Discounted using a 3% interest rate.

[2]The counterfactual is constructed using the estimated college outcome equation applied to the population of persons selecting high school.

[3]As a fraction of the base state, i.e., $\frac{(\mathrm{PV}_{\text{earnings}}(\mathrm{Col})-\mathrm{PV}_{\text{earnings}}(\mathrm{HS}))}{\mathrm{PV}_{\text{earnings}}(\mathrm{HS})}$.

that the typical college graduate earns $1,390.3 thousand if he goes to college (above the counterfactual earnings of what a typical high school student would earn in col-

Table 17
Average present value of *ex post* earnings[1] for college graduates fitted and counterfactual[2] white males from NLSY79

	High school (counterfactual)	College (fitted)	Returns[3]
Average	1033.721	1390.321	0.374
Standard error	14.665	30.218	0.280

Source: Cunha and Heckman (2006b).

[1]Thousands of dollars. Discounted using a 3% interest rate.

[2]The counterfactual is constructed using the estimated high school outcome equation applied to the population of persons selecting college.

[3]As a fraction of the base state, i.e., $\frac{(\text{PV}_{\text{earnings}}(\text{Col})-\text{PV}_{\text{earnings}}(\text{HS}))}{\text{PV}_{\text{earnings}}(\text{HS})}$.

lege), and would make only $1,033.7 thousand over his lifetime if he chose to be a high school graduate instead. The returns to college education for the typical college graduate (which in the literature on program evaluation is referred to as the effect of Treatment on the Treated) is almost double that of the return for a high school graduate. In monetary terms a college graduate has a gain of going to college almost $175 thousand higher over his lifetime than does the typical high school graduate.

Figure 17 plots the density of *ex post* gross returns to education excluding direct costs and psychic costs for agents who are high school graduates (the solid curve), and the density of returns to education for agents who are college graduates (the dashed curve). In reporting our estimated returns, CH follow conventions in the literature and actually present growth rates in terms of present values, and not true rates of return (ignoring option values).[150] Thus these figures report the growth rates in present values $(\frac{PV(1)-PV(0)}{PV(0)})$ where "1" and "0" refer to college and high school and all present values are discounted to a common benchmark level. Tuition and psychic costs are ignored. College graduates have returns distributed somewhat to the right of high school graduates, so the difference is not only a difference for the mean individual but is actually present over the entire distribution. Agents who choose a college education are the ones who tend to gain more from it.

With their methodology, CHN can also determine returns to the marginal student. This could also be estimated by the *MTE* method discussed in Section 8. Under rational expectations, mean *ex post* and *ex ante* returns are the same although the distributions may differ. Table 18 reveals that the average individual who is just indifferent between a college education and a high school diploma earns $976.04 thousand as a high school graduate or $1,208.26 thousand as a college graduate. This implies a return of 28%. The returns to people at the margin are above those of the typical high school graduate,

[150] Recall our discussion of treatment effects in the generalized Roy model and their relationship to true rates of return in Section 8.2.

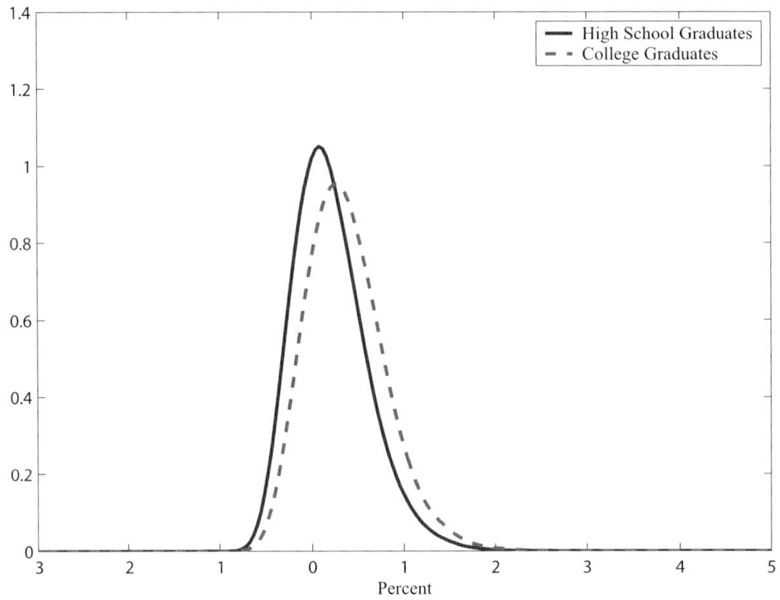

Let Y_0 denote present value of earnings in high school sector. Let Y_1 denote present value of earnings in college sector. Let $R = (Y_1 - Y_0)/Y_0$ denote the gross rate of return to college. In this graph we plot the density function of the returns to college conditional on being a high school graduate, $f(r|S = 0)$ (the solid line), against the density function of returns to college conditional on being a college graduate, $f(r|S = 1)$. We use kernel density estimation to smooth these functions.

Figure 17. Densities of returns to college. NLSY/1979 sample. Source: Cunha and Heckman (2006b).

but below those for the typical college graduate. Since persons at the margin are more likely to be affected by a policy that encourages college attendance, their returns are the ones that should be used in order to compute the marginal benefit of policies that induce people into schooling.

A major question that emerges from the analyses of CHN and CH is, why, if high school graduates have such positive returns to attending college, don't more attend? People do not pick schooling levels based only on monetary returns. Recall that their choice criterion (Equation (38)) also includes both pecuniary and nonpecuniary costs of attending college. Figure 18 shows the estimated density of the monetary value of this cost both overall and by schooling level. Fewer high school graduates perceive a benefit (negative cost) of attending college than college graduates. Table 19 explores this point in more detail by presenting the mean total cost of attending college (first row) and the mean cost that is due to ability (i.e., factor 1), given in the second row. The mean cost of attending college is negative for the average college graduate and positive for the average high school graduate. Costs are substantially smaller for college graduates. Average college graduates have higher ability. The average contribution of

Table 18

Average present value of *ex post* earnings[1] for individuals at the margin fitted and counterfactual[2] white males from NLSY79

	High school	College	Returns[3]
Average	976.04	1208.26	0.2828
Std. Err.	21.503	33.613	0.0457

Source: Cunha and Heckman (2006b).

[1]Thousands of dollars. Discounted using a 3% interest rate.

[2]The counterfactual is defined as the result of taking a person at random from the population regardless of his schooling choice.

[3]As a fraction of the base state, i.e., $\frac{(PV_{\text{earnings}}(\text{Col}) - PV_{\text{earnings}}(\text{HS}))}{PV_{\text{earnings}}(\text{HS})}$.

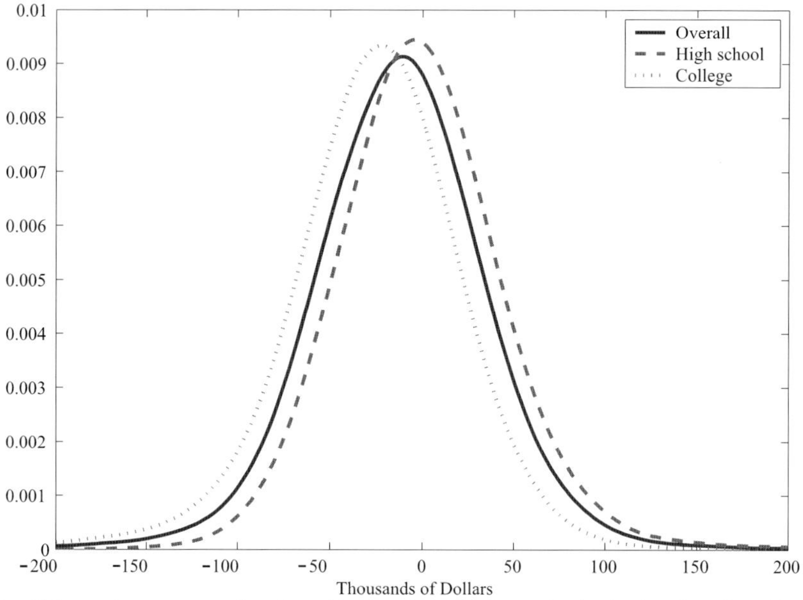

Let C denote the monetary value of psychic costs. Let $f(c)$ denote the density function of psychic costs in monetary terms. The dashed line shows the density of psychic costs for high school graduates, that is $f(c|S = 0)$. The dotted line shows the density of psychic costs for college graduates, that is, $f(c|S = 1)$. The solid line is the unconditional density of the monetary value of psychic costs, $f(c)$.

Figure 18. Densities of monetary value of psychic cost both overall and by schooling level. Source: Cunha and Heckman (2006b).

Table 19
Monetary costs of schooling levels

	High school	College	Overall
Mean monetary value of total cost of attending college	0.4393	−26.8651	−11.9223
Mean monetary value of ability cost of attending college	12.7152	−14.8924	0.0000

Values in thousands of dollars (2000).
Let C denote the psychic costs in monetary terms. Then C is given by

$$C = Z\gamma + \theta_1 \alpha_{C_1} + \theta_2 \alpha_{C_2} + \varepsilon_C.$$

The contribution of ability to the costs of attending college in monetary value is $\theta_1 \alpha_C$. Recall that, on average, the ability is different between those attending college and those attending high school.
Source: Cunha and Heckman (2006b).

ability to costs is positive for high school graduates (a true cost). It is negative for college graduates, so it is perceived as a benefit.

This is one answer to the stated puzzle. People do not only (or even mainly) make their schooling decisions by looking at their monetary returns in terms of earnings. Psychic costs play a very important role. More able people have lower psychic costs of attending college. The high estimated psychic cost is one reason why the rates of return that ignore psychic costs (and tuition) discussed in Section 4 are so high. This high psychic cost is one explanation why the college attendance rate is so low when the monetary returns are so high. One convention in the classical human capital literature – that tuition and psychic costs are negligible – is at odds with this evidence.[151] The evidence against strict income maximization is overwhelming.

However, explanations based on psychic costs are intrinsically unsatisfactory. One can rationalize any economic choice data by an appeal to psychic costs. Heckman, Stixrud and Urzua (2006) show the important role played by noncognitive skills as well as cognitive skills in explaining schooling (and other decisions). They show how, in principle, conventional risk aversion, time preference and leisure preference parameters can be related to psychometric measures of cognitive and noncognitive skills. Establishing this link will provide a better foundation for understanding what "psychic costs" actually represent.

[151] "Psychic costs" can stand in for expectational errors and attitudes towards risk. We do not distinguish among these explanations in this chapter. The estimated costs are too large to be due to tuition alone. As noted below, given that returns are far from perfectly forecast, an important role for expectational errors is impossible.

"Psychic costs" may also be a stand in for credit constraints and risk aversion. However, the evidence on psychic costs in schooling choice equations is more sturdy than this discussion might suggest. Carneiro, Hansen and Heckman (2003) obtain similar conclusions on the importance of psychic costs from a model where people are not allowed to borrow or lend and there is risk aversion. In Cunha, Heckman and Navarro (2005), on the other hand, there are no constraints on borrowing or lending, and they also show sizeable components of psychic costs.

10.6.2. *Ex ante and ex post returns: Heterogeneity versus uncertainty*

Figures 19 through 21, from Cunha and Heckman (2006b) separate the effect of heterogeneity from uncertainty in earnings. The figures plot the distribution of *ex ante* and *ex post* outcomes under different information sets. The information set of the agent is $\mathcal{I} = \{X, Z, X_T, \varepsilon_C, \Theta\}$, Θ contains some or all of the factors. In this paper and in the analyses of Cunha, Heckman and Navarro (2005, 2006, 2007) and Carneiro, Hansen and Heckman (2003), the various information sets consist of different components of θ.

First consider Figure 19. It presents results for a variety of information sets. First assume that agents do not know their factors; consequently, $\Theta = \varnothing$. This is the *ex post* or realized distribution of the variation that is observed in the data. If the agents learn about factor 1,[152] so that, $\Theta = \{\theta_1\}$, the reduction in the forecast variance is very small. Factor 1, which is associated with cognitive ability, is important for forecasting educational choices, but does not do a very good job in forecasting earnings. If the agent is given knowledge of factor 2, but not factor 1, so that $\Theta = \{\theta_2\}$, then the agent is able to substantially reduce the forecast variance of earnings in high school. Factor 2 does not greatly affect college choices, but it greatly informs the agent about his future earnings. When the agent is given knowledge of both factors 1 and 2, that is, $\Theta = \{\theta_1, \theta_2\}$, he can forecast earnings marginally better. Figure 20 reveals much the same story about the college earnings distribution. These results suggest that selection into college is not based primarily on expected economic returns to education. Cost factors play an important role.

Table 20 presents agent forecast variances of the present value of future earnings and their return. CH establish that agents know (θ_1, θ_2), the (X, Z) and the coefficient vectors of the model at the time that agents make college enrollment decisions. Agents do not know the ε's. They forecast 65% of the variance of the present value of college earnings, 56% of the variance of the present value of high school earnings and 56% of the gross lifetime gain to attending college. The unforecastable components are due to uncertainty by the agent at the time schooling decisions are made. There are substantial roles for both heterogeneity and uncertainty.

[152] As opposed to the econometrician who never gets to observe either θ_1 or θ_2.

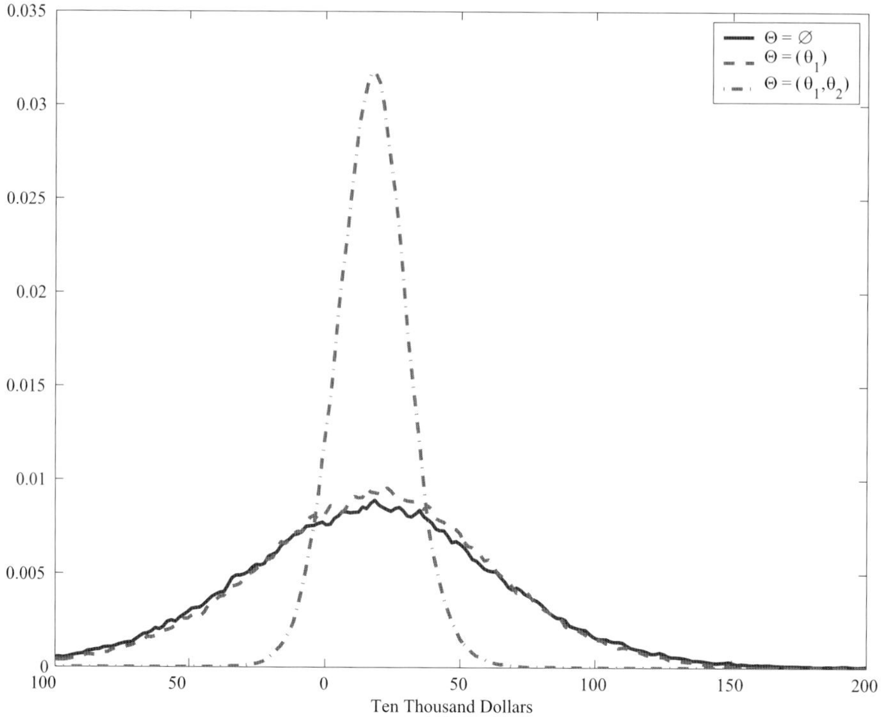

Let Θ denote the information set of the agent. Let Y_0 denote the present value of returns (discounted at a 3% interest rate). Let $f(y_0|\Theta)$ denote the density of Y_0 conditional on information set Θ. The solid line plots the density of Y_0 when $\Theta = \varnothing$. The dashed line plots the density of Y_0 when $\Theta = \{\theta_1\}$. The dotted and dashed line plots the density of Y_0 when $\Theta = \{\theta_1, \theta_2\}$. The X variables are in the information set of the agent. The factors θ, when known, are evaluated at their mean, which is zero.

Figure 19. Densities of present value of returns – NLSY/1979 under different information sets for the agent calculated for the entire population regardless of schooling choice. Source: Cunha and Heckman (2006b).

10.6.3. Ex ante versus ex post

Once the distinction between heterogeneity and uncertainty is made, it is possible to be precise about the distinction between *ex ante* and *ex post* decision making. From their analysis, CH conclude that, at the time agents pick their schooling, the ε's in their earnings equations are unknown to them. These are the components that correspond to "luck." It is clear that decision making would be different, at least for some individuals, if the agent knew these chance components when choosing schooling levels, since the decision rule would now be

$$S^* = Y_{1,0} + \frac{Y_{1,1}}{1+r} - Y_{0,0} - \frac{Y_{0,1}}{1+r} - C > 0,$$

$$S = 1 \quad \text{if } S^* > 0; \qquad S = 0 \quad \text{otherwise,}$$

return. While many of these assumptions turn out to hold in the 1960 data for the U.S. labor market that he analyzed (e.g., separability in education and experience, log-linearity of earnings in schooling, negligible tuition costs of school, and negligible taxes), this chapter shows that in recent U.S. data they no longer hold. After documenting evidence against Mincer's assumptions, Section 4 considers alternative approaches to estimating the marginal internal rate of return to schooling across different schooling levels.

We estimate general nonparametric earnings functions and generate from them marginal internal rates of return that account for taxes and tuition. The levels and time series patterns of marginal internal rates of return differ dramatically from those produced by a Mincer model. Deviations from parallelism and linearity in schooling in log earnings equations – keystones of the Mincer approach – are quantitatively important in determining internal rates of return, as are the effects of taxes and tuition. Economists cannot continue to pretend that violations of the required assumptions are innocuous when using Mincer regressions to estimate 'returns to schooling'. Although we report estimates based on U.S. data, we conjecture that similar problems with Mincer's assumptions apply to many other countries. Replication of our study on data from other countries would be highly desirable.[155]

Our analysis shows how to use nonparametric earnings profiles reported in the recent literature to estimate rates of return. The recent literature surveyed in Katz and Autor (1999) establishes that the payment to college graduates has gone up relative to that of high school graduates in the past two decades. It does not determine whether rates of return have increased. We show that using the Mincer estimate of the rate of return misrepresents trends in actual rates of return, because of misspecification of the earnings–schooling–experience relationship and because of neglecting components of the return such as tuition costs and taxes. It also leads to inaccurate estimates of earnings associated with different schooling levels.

The standard representative agent income maximizing model that serves as the foundation for many analyses of returns to schooling motivated by economic theory suggests that marginal internal rates of return should be the same across observed schooling choices and should equal the common real interest rate faced by students. Yet, our reported estimates of the return to high school and college completion for recent years are substantially larger than the real interest rates faced by consumers, even on credit card debt.

One possible explanation for this disparity is the failure of the income maximizing concept, rather than the utility maximizing concept, to represent schooling decisions. Psychic costs or distaste for schooling may explain why more than fifteen percent of new cohorts of American youth do not receive a high school degree despite its high

[155] There is a considerable volume of work on estimating returns to schooling in other countries. See, e.g., Blundell, Dearden and Sianesi (2005) for the U.K., or Adda et al. (2005) for Germany. Zamarro (2005) uses the *MTE* methods developed in Heckman and Vytlacil (1999, 2005) and Heckman, Urzua and Vytlacil (2006) to estimate returns to schooling in Spain. None of these studies make the *ex ante–ex post* distinction, and none estimate the internal rate of return to schooling or the more general return measures discussed in this chapter.

estimated financial return. Results from Carneiro, Hansen and Heckman (2003), Cunha, Heckman and Navarro (2005, 2006) and Cunha and Heckman (2006a, 2006b) discussed in Section 10 show high psychic cost components estimated under different assumptions about the economic environments facing agents. Although in theory substantial credit constraints could explain the patterns of college-going decisions, recent research finds them to be quantitatively unimportant in the U.S. economy [see the survey by Cunha et al. (2006)], and the estimates of high psychic costs are robust to alternative assumptions about credit markets.

Heckman, Stixrud and Urzua (2006) establish the importance of both cognitive and noncognitive skills in explaining schooling decisions, wages and a variety of risky behaviors. Psychic costs are related to both cognitive and noncognitive skills. They discuss, but do not definitively establish, the link between psychometric measures of cognitive and noncognitive skills and conventional measures of risk aversion, preference for leisure and time preference that would be a more satisfactory foundation for explaining "psychic costs."

Mincer and many other researchers use cross sections of earnings to estimate life-cycle earnings of the various cohorts sampled in the cross-section, the so-called synthetic cohort approach. This practice is problematic when labor markets are nonstationary as in recent years. The use of repeated cross-section or panel data that follow the experience of actual cohorts is essential for accurately measuring rates of return to schooling. However, use of repeated cross section data does not produce lower estimated returns. If anything, the return from repeated cross section data is higher, leaving the puzzle of high estimated returns to schooling in place.

If analysts seek to estimate *ex post* returns, a cohort analysis is clearly preferred to a cross-section approach. However, if analysts are interested in estimating *ex ante* returns in a changing economic environment, the choice is less clear cut. Expectations about the future need to be specified or, better, estimated or measured.[156]

We summarize an emerging literature that moves beyond estimating mean growth rates of earnings with schooling or treatment effects to estimate distributions of growth rates and rates of return. This approach is based on the principle that dependence across counterfactual distributions is generated by low-dimensional unobservables. The new methods can be implemented using panel data on earnings and schooling. Access to test scores or other proxies for the latent factors facilitates identification of the distribution of rates of return.

Application of the new methods to rich panel data allows analysts to disentangle uncertainty from measured variability. We review evidence from Cunha, Heckman and Navarro (2005, 2006) and Cunha and Heckman (2006a, 2006b), who develop and implement an approach for empirically distinguishing *ex ante* from *ex post* returns to schooling using rich panel data. They find that uncertainty about the future is empirically important for understanding schooling decisions. To the extent that individuals are

[156] Manski (2004) presents a comprehensive survey of recent research on measuring expectations.

risk averse, the evidence on uncertainty helps to explain some of the high estimated returns to schooling reported in Section 4 and in the entire literature [see Navarro (2005), Cunha and Heckman (2006b)]. At the same time, a substantial amount of observed variability in earnings is predictable at the date schooling decisions are made.

In a dynamic setting, uncertainty about future earnings and schooling outcomes creates a wedge between *ex post* average rates of return and real interest rates due to the option value of continuing on in school and updating information. For example, some individuals may attend college, knowing that the expected returns to only a few years of college are low but the expected returns from finishing college are quite high. Even if college graduation is not certain, many individuals may be willing to take the gamble of attending with the hope that they will finish successfully. Our estimates of low returns to college attendance and high returns to college completion are consistent with this story.

Our analysis of option values raises questions about the internal rate of return – a pillar of classical human capital theory – as a useful measure of returns to schooling. In a model with uncertainty and sequential decision making, there may be many discount rates that equate theoretically correct value functions across different schooling choices. The validity of internal rate of return measures depends crucially on the amount of uncertainty in future earnings associated with different education levels. The recent literature finds a substantial amount of predictability in future earnings and empirical estimates of option values that are relatively small. This mitigates concerns about using internal rates of return as a criterion for evaluating educational policy. However, work on this topic has just begun, so any conclusion about the empirical importance of option values has to be tempered with caution.

The most common criticism directed against the Mincerian approach questions the strong assumption that individuals making different schooling choices are *ex ante* identical [see, e.g., Griliches (1977), Willis (1986), Willis and Rosen (1979), Card (1995, 1999), Heckman and Vytlacil (1999, 2005), Carneiro, Hansen and Heckman (2003), Carneiro, Heckman and Vytlacil (2005)]. The recent literature that attempts to address the consequences of heterogeneity on estimated rates of return focuses on mean growth rates of earnings with schooling and not on true rates of return. Card's (1995, 1999) version of Becker's Woytinsky lecture offers a useful framework for analyzing growth rates in earnings in a heterogeneous world. Under strong assumptions that schooling choice equations are linear in growth rates and in costs of schooling, instrumental variable methods can be used to identify the average effect of schooling on earnings.

However, researchers are often interested in other treatment parameters that can be directly linked to the effects of a particular policy intervention. These parameters are not typically estimated by instrumental variable estimators. Since schooling is a discrete outcome, traditional instrumental variables methods produce parameters that are instrument-dependent and are rarely economically interpretable.

The empirical debate on the importance of accounting for the endogeneity of schooling in estimating rates of return is far from settled. Much of this literature does not estimate rates of return but instead focuses on various treatment effects. An entire recent literature has directed attention away from estimating rates of return, or other economically interpretable parameters, toward estimating the probability limits of *IV* estimators which often lack any economic interpretation. Many of the popular instruments are weak and the *IV* literature has lost sight of estimating distributions of returns.

Much of the recent literature has focused on the rising returns to college. The estimates presented in this chapter suggest a substantially greater increase in the returns to high school, raising the obvious questions: why do so many individuals continue to drop out of high school and why is the correctly measured high school dropout rate increasing? The answer may rely on high "psychic" costs of school, credit constraints, risk and uncertainty, or unobserved differences in ability between dropouts and graduates. It remains to be established whether the enormous increase in the returns to high school in recent decades estimated using the internal rates of return implicit in the recent Census-CPS literature can be explained by changes in ability differences between high school dropouts and graduates. The relatively slow growth in high school dropout rates since 1970 and the continued increase in rates of return to high school (as measured by cross-section or cohort-based estimates) since that time poses a serious challenge to simple explanations based on this premise.[157] The new literature is beginning to sort out these competing explanations. Recent developments in the literature employ new methods to take advantage of rich longitudinal microdata in order to begin distinguishing among the many possibilities.

With better tools and better data, the conventions of 1960s labor economics should no longer guide estimation of rates of return to schooling in the 21st century. The Mincer model is no longer a valid guide to estimating the returns to schooling or accounting for heterogeneity in returns. The modern *IV* literature aims to recover growth rates of earnings with schooling, allowing for heterogeneity, but has lost sight of the economic questions posed by Mincer. Recent developments in econometrics and the economics of education coupled with rich panel data make it possible to estimate economically interpretable parameters including true *ex ante* and *ex post* rates of return to schooling and their distributions in the population.

Appendix A: Derivation of the overtaking age

Based on the text,

$$\begin{aligned}\ln Y(s,x) &= \ln P_{s+x} + \ln(1-k_{s+x})\\ &\approx \ln P_s + \rho_0 \sum_{j=0}^{x-1} k_{s+j} - k_{s+x}.\end{aligned}$$

[157] Recent work by Heckman and LaFontaine (2006) suggests that in recent cohorts dropouts are relatively more educated than in earlier cohorts so the basic facts work against the hypothesis suggested in the text. For a survey of recent evidence on college–high school wage differentials, see Katz and Autor (1999).

Further using the assumption of linearly declining investment yields

$$\ln Y(s, x) \approx \ln P_s + \kappa\left(\rho_0 \sum_{j=0}^{x-1}(1 - j/T) - (1 - x/T)\right).$$

Assuming only initial earnings potential (P_s) and investment levels (κ) vary in the population, the variance of log earnings is given by

$$\begin{aligned}\operatorname{Var}\bigl(\ln Y(s, x)\bigr) &= \operatorname{Var}(\ln P_s) + \left(\rho_0 \sum_{j=0}^{x-1}(1 - j/T) - (1 - x/T)\right)^2 \operatorname{Var}(\kappa)\\ &\quad + 2\left(\rho_0 \sum_{j=0}^{x-1}(1 - j/T) - (1 - x/T)\right) COV(\ln P_s, \kappa).\end{aligned}$$

If κ and $\ln P_s$ are uncorrelated, then earnings are minimized (and equal to $\operatorname{Var}(\ln P_s)$) when

$$\rho_0 \sum_{j=0}^{x-1}(1 - j/T) = 1 - x/T, \quad \text{or}$$

$$\rho_0\left(x - \frac{x(x-1)}{2T}\right) = \rho_0(1 - x/T).$$

Clearly, $\lim_{T\to\infty} x^* = \frac{1}{\rho_0}$, so the variance minimizing age is $\frac{1}{\rho_0}$ when the work-life is long. More generally, re-arranging terms and solving for the root of this equation[158] yields the variance minimizing experience level of

$$\begin{aligned}x^* &= T + \frac{1}{2} + \frac{1}{\rho_0} - \sqrt{\left(T + \frac{1}{2} + \frac{1}{\rho_0}\right)^2 - \frac{2T}{\rho_0}}\\ &\approx \left(\rho_0 + \frac{\rho_0}{2T} + \frac{1}{T}\right)^{-1},\end{aligned}$$

where the final approximation comes from a first-order Taylor approximation of the square root term around the squared term inside. The approximation suggests that the variance minimizing age will generally be less than or equal to $\frac{1}{\rho_0}$, with the difference disappearing as T grows large.

[158] There is a second root which is greater than T (the maximum working age), so it is ignored.

Appendix B: Data description

Census data

The Census samples used in this chapter are taken from the 1940, 1950, 1960, 1970, 1980 and 1990 Public-Use Census Samples. The 1940 sample consists of the self-weighting subsample which represents 1% of the population. The 1950 sample consists of sample-line persons (for whom questions regarding earnings were asked) which represent about 0.303% of the population. The 1960 sample is a self-weighting 1% sample. The 1970 sample is taken from two Public-Use A samples: the 1% State sample (5% form) and the 1% State sample (15% form). It is a self-weighting sample of 2% of the population. The 1980 and 1990 Census samples are both 5% Public Use A samples. The 1980 sample is self-weighting but the 1990 sample is not. For 1990, we use person weights to re-weight the sample back to random proportions.

The following sample restrictions are imposed for each Census year:

***age*:** Sample includes individuals age 16–64. For Census years when a *quarter-of-birth* variable is available, we take into account the quarter of birth in calculating the age of each individual from the *year of birth* variable provided in the data set.

***race*:** Only individuals reported as being black or white are included in the analysis.

***earnings*:** The earnings measure used is annual earnings, which includes both wage and salary and business income for the Census years when business income is available. For Census years when earnings are reported in intervals, we use the midpoint of the interval as the individual's earnings.

***imputations*:** Individuals with imputed information on age, race, sex, education, weeks worked or income are excluded. For years when all the imputation flags are not provided, we omit individuals on the basis of the available imputation flags.

The following variables are constructed:

***experience*:** Potential experience is measured by Age–Years of Education–6.

***years of education*:** For the 1940–1980 Censuses, years of education are reported as the highest grade completed. For the 1990 Census, years of education are reported differently: by categories for first through fourth grade and for fifth through eighth grade, by year for ninth through 12th grade, and then by degree attained. To maintain comparability with the other Census samples, we impute the number of years of school associated with each category or degree. For those with some college but no degree or for those with an associate degree, we assign 14 years of school. For those with a bachelor's degree, we assign 16 years of school. For professional degrees we assign 17 years and for masters degrees and beyond, including doctoral degrees, we assign 18 years of school.

Current Population Survey (CPS) data

The CPS samples used in this chapter are taken from the 1964–2000 CPS March Supplements.

The following sample restrictions are used for each year:

***age*:** Sample includes individuals age 18–65.
***race*:** Sample separated into whites and all nonwhites.
***earnings*:** Annual wage and salary income (deflated using the CPI-U) is used as the earnings measure in each year.

The following variables are constructed for our analysis:

***experience*:** Potential experience is measured by Age–Years of Education–6.
***years of education*:** For 1964–1991, years of education are reported as the highest grade completed. Categories of schooling include 9–11 years, 12 years, and 16 years. From 1992–2000, years of education are reported differently. Those completing 12 years of schooling but who do not receive a high school diploma are assigned 11 years. Only those with 12 years of schooling and a diploma are assigned 12 years of schooling. For those with a bachelor's degree, we assign 16 years of school.

Tuition time series

To estimate the private cost of college, we use the time series Total Revenue from Student Fees and Tuition obtained from Snyder (1993, Table 33). Tables 24 and 33 of this publication provide, for all institutions, statistics on total educational revenue, total tuition revenue, and total enrollment. We divide total revenue for all institutions by total enrollment. Supplementing this data with data from Snyder (2000, Tables 175 and 331), we create a consistent time series of total educational revenue, total tuition revenue, and total enrollment for 1940–1995.

Tax rate time series

We obtain the average marginal tax rate time series from Barro and Sahasakul (1983) and Mulligan and Marion (2000, Table 1, column 1). The tax rates used in our progressive tax analysis are obtained from the federal schedule for a single adult with no dependents. All income is assumed to be earned income and standard deductions are assumed. To obtain after-tax income for 1960–90, we use the TAXSIM version 4.0 program available at http://www.nber.org/taxsim/taxsim-calc4/index.html. For 1940 and 1950, we use the actual federal tax schedules (Form 1040) as reported in the Statistics of Income.

Appendix C: Local linear regression

In estimating the nonparametric regressions, we use local linear regression methods. As discussed in Fan and Gijbels (1996), the local linear estimator for the conditional expectation $E[y_i|x_i = x_0]$ can be computed from the minimization problem

$$\min_{a,b} \sum_{i=1}^{n} \big(y_i - a - b_1(x_i - x_0)\big)^2 K\left(\frac{x_i - x_0}{h_n}\right),$$

where $K(\cdot)$ is a kernel function and $h_n > 0$ is a bandwidth which converges to zero as $n \to \infty$.[159] The estimator of the conditional mean $E[y_i|x_i = x_0]$ is $\hat{a}$. The local linear estimator can be expressed as a weighted average of the y_i observations, $\sum_{i=1}^{n} y_i W_i(x_0)$, where the weights are

$$W_i(x_0) = \frac{K_i \sum_{j=1}^{n} K_j^2 - K_i \sum_{k=1}^{n} K_k}{\sum_{k=1}^{n} K_k \sum_{j=1}^{n} K_j^2 - (\sum_{k=1}^{n} K_k)^2}.$$

Our local regression estimator is given by

$$\hat{m}(x_0) = \sum_{i=1}^{N} y(x_i) W_i(x_0),$$

where $y(x_i)$ represents log earnings at experience level x_i and N represents the number of observations.[160]

The asymptotic distribution of the estimator $\hat{m}(x_0)$ for $m(x_0) = E(y_i|x_i = x_0)$ is given by

$$\sqrt{nh_n}\big(\hat{m}(x_0) - m(x_0)\big) \sim N(B_n, V_n) + o_p(1),$$

where the bias and variance expressions are given by

$$B_n = h_n^2 \cdot \big(0.5m''(x_0)\big) \cdot \int_{-\infty}^{\infty} u^2 K(u)\, du,$$

$$V_n = \frac{\sigma^2(x_0)}{f(x_0)} \int_{-\infty}^{\infty} K^2(u)\, du,$$

and where $\sigma^2(x_0) = E(\{y_i - E(y_i|x_i = x_0)\}^2|x_i = x_0)$ and $f(x_0)$ is the density of x_i at x_0.[161]

159 The kernel function we use in the empirical work is the quartic kernel, given by

$$K(s) = \begin{cases} (15/16)(s^2 - 1)^2 & \text{if } |s| < 1, \\ 0 & \text{otherwise.} \end{cases}$$

The bandwidth used is equal to 5.

160 For some of the Census years, there is a problem of nonrandom sampling with sampling weights provided in the data. The sampling weights are taken into account when calculating the mean log earnings at each experience level.

161 See, e.g., Fan and Gijbels (1996), for derivation of these formulae.

Tests of parallelism

In Section 3 of this chapter, we perform nonparametric tests of whether the log-earnings–experience profiles are parallel across schooling levels. Let s_1 and s_2 denote two different schooling levels (16 years and 12 years, for example). We test whether

$$E(y_i|x_i, s = s_1) - E(y_i|x_i, s = s_2) = \text{constant across } x_i \in \{10, 20, 30, 40 \text{ years}\}.$$

We select the experience values at which the hypothesis is tested to be at least 2 bandwidths apart from the other experience levels, so that the nonparametric estimates are independent from one another. Let $\hat{m}(x_i, s_1)$ denote the estimator for $E(y_i|x_i, s = s_1)$ for experience level x_i and schooling level $s = s_1$. The test statistic for testing parallelism for two different schooling levels s_1 and s_2 and two experience levels x_i and x_k is given by

$$\begin{aligned}&\big(\hat{m}(x_i, s_1) - \hat{m}(x_i, s_2)\big) - \big(\hat{m}(x_k, s_1) - \hat{m}(x_k, s_2)\big)\\&\quad\times (\widehat{V}_1 + \widehat{V}_2 + \widehat{V}_3 + \widehat{V}_4)^{-1}\\&\quad\times \big(\hat{m}(x_i, s_1) - \hat{m}(x_i, s_2)\big) - \big(\hat{m}(x_k, s_1) - \hat{m}(x_k, s_2)\big),\end{aligned}$$

where $\widehat{V}_1$, $\widehat{V}_2$, $\widehat{V}_3$, and $\widehat{V}_4$ are estimators for $V_1 = \operatorname{Var}(\hat{m}(x_i, s_1))$, $V_2 = \operatorname{Var}(\hat{m}(x_i, s_2))$, $V_3 = \operatorname{Var}(\hat{m}(x_k, s_1))$, $V_4 = \operatorname{Var}(\hat{m}(x_k, s_2))$.

To estimate the variances, we use

$$\operatorname{Var}\big(\hat{m}(x_i, s_\ell)\big) = \sum_{i=1}^{N} \hat{\varepsilon}(x_i, s_\ell)^2 W_i^2(x_i), \qquad \ell = 1, 2,$$

where $\hat{\varepsilon}(x_i, s_\ell) = y(x_i, s_\ell) - \hat{m}(x_i, s_\ell)$, $\ell = 1, 2$, is the fitted residual from the nonparametric regression evaluated at experience level x_i.[162] In Table 1, we report test results based on the test statistic that straightforwardly generalizes the test statistic given above to four experience levels.

References

Aakvik, A., Heckman, J.J., Vytlacil, E.J. (2005). "Estimating treatment effects for discrete outcomes when responses to treatment vary: An application to Norwegian vocational rehabilitation programs". Journal of Econometrics 125 (1–2), 15–51.

Adda, J., Dustmann, C., Meghir, C., Robin, J.-M. (2005). "Career progression and formal versus on the job training". Unpublished manuscript, University College London and Université Paris I. March.

Aiyagari, S.R. (1994). "Uninsured idiosyncratic risk and aggregate saving". Quarterly Journal of Economics 109 (3), 659–684. August.

Amemiya, T. (1985). Advanced Econometrics. Harvard University Press, Cambridge, MA.

[162] Heckman et al. (1998) show that this estimator has better finite sample performance than a "plug-in" estimator based on the asymptotic variance formulae.

Angrist, J.D., Imbens, G.W. (1995). "Two-stage least squares estimation of average causal effects in models with variable treatment intensity". Journal of the American Statistical Association 90 (430), 431–442. June.

Angrist, J.D., Krueger, A.B. (1991). "Does compulsory school attendance affect schooling and earnings?". Quarterly Journal of Economics 106 (4), 979–1014. November.

Angrist, J.D., Krueger, A.B. (1999). "Empirical strategies in labor economics". In: Ashenfelter, O., Card, D. (Eds.), Handbook of Labor Economics, vol. 3A. North-Holland, New York, pp. 1277–1366.

Angrist, J.D., Krueger, A.B. (2001). "Instrumental variables and the search for identification: From supply and demand to natural experiments". Journal of Economic Perspectives 15 (4), 69–85. Fall.

Arias, O., McMahon, W.W. (2001). "Dynamic rates of return to education in the U.S.". Economics of Education Review 20 (2), 12–138. April.

Atkeson, A., Lucas, R.E. (1992). "On efficient distribution with private information". The Review of Economic Studies 59 (3), 427–453. July.

Barro, R.J., Sahasakul, C. (1983). "Measuring the average marginal tax rate from the individual income tax". Journal of Business 56 (4), 419–452. October.

Becker, G.S. (1964). Human Capital: A Theoretical and Empirical Analysis, with Special Reference to Education. National Bureau of Economic Research, New York. Distributed by Columbia University Press.

Becker, G.S. (1967). Human Capital and the Personal Distribution of Income: An Analytical Approach. Woytinsky Lecture No. 1. University of Michigan, Institute of Public Administration, Ann Arbor.

Becker, G.S., Chiswick, B.R. (1966). "Education and the distribution of earnings". The American Economic Review 56 (1/2), 358–369. March.

Behrman, J.R., Birdsall, N. (1983). "The quality of schooling: Quantity alone is misleading". American Economic Review 73 (5), 928–946. December.

Belzil, C., Hansen, J. (2002). "Unobserved ability and the return to schooling". Econometrica 70 (5), 2075–2091. September.

Belzil, C., Hansen, J. (2005). "A structural analysis of the correlated random coefficient wage regression model with an application to the OLS-IV puzzle". Discussion Paper 1585, IZA. May.

Ben-Porath, Y. (1967). "The production of human capital and the life cycle of earnings". Journal of Political Economy 75 (4), 352–365. Part 1. August.

Bils, M., Klenow, P.J. (2000). "Does schooling cause growth?". American Economic Review 90 (5), 1160–1183. December.

Bishop, J.H. (1991). "Achievement, test scores, and relative wages". In: Kosters, M.H. (Ed.), Workers and Their Wages: Changing Patterns in the United States. AEI Studies, vol. 520. AEI Press, Washington, DC, pp. 146–186.

Björklund, A., Moffitt, R. (1987). "The estimation of wage gains and welfare gains in self-selection". Review of Economics and Statistics 69 (1), 42–49. February.

Blackburn, M.L., Neumark, D. (1993). "Omitted-ability bias and the increase in the return to schooling". Journal of Labor Economics 11 (3), 521–544. July.

Blundell, R., Dearden, L., Sianesi, B. (2005). "Evaluating the effect of education on earnings: Models, methods and results from the National Child Development Survey". Journal of the Royal Statistical Society: Series A (Statistics in Society) 168 (3), 473–512. July.

Blundell, R., Pistaferri, L., Preston, I. (2004). Consumption inequality and partial insurance. Technical Report WP04/28, Institute for Fiscal Studies. October.

Blundell, R., Preston, I. (1998). "Consumption inequality and income uncertainty". Quarterly Journal of Economics 113 (2), 603–640. May.

Blundell, R., Reed, H., Stoker, T. (2003). "Interpreting aggregate wage growth: The role of labor market participation". American Economic Review 93 (4), 1114–1131. September.

Bound, J., Jaeger, D.A., Baker, R.M. (1995). "Problems with instrumental variables estimation when the correlation between the instruments and the endogenous explanatory variable is weak". Journal of the American Statistical Association 90 (430), 443–450. June.

Buchinsky, M., Leslie, P. (2000). "Educational attainment and the changing U.S. wage structure: Dynamic implications without rational expectations". Unpublished Manuscript, UCLA Department of Economics. January.

Cameron, S.V., Heckman, J.J. (1998). "Life cycle schooling and dynamic selection bias: Models and evidence for five cohorts of American males". Journal of Political Economy 106 (2), 262–333. April.

Cameron, S.V., Taber, C. (2004). "Estimation of educational borrowing constraints using returns to schooling". Journal of Political Economy 112 (1), 132–182. February.

Card, D. (1993). "Using geographic variation in college proximity to estimate the return to schooling". Technical Report 4483, National Bureau of Economic Research. October.

Card, D. (1995). "Earnings, schooling, and ability revisited". In: Polachek, S. (Ed.), Research in Labor Economics. JAI Press, Greenwich, CT, pp. 23–48.

Card, D. (1999). "The causal effects of education on earnings". In: Ashenfelter, O., Card, D. (Eds.), Handbook of Labor Economics, vol. 5. North-Holland, New York, pp. 1801–1863.

Card, D. (2001). "Estimating the returns to schooling: Progress on some persistent econometric problems". Econometrica 69 (5), 1127–1160. September.

Card, D., Krueger, A.B. (1992). "Does school quality matter? Returns to education and the characteristics of public schools in the United States". Journal of Political Economy 100 (1), 1–40. February.

Card, D., Lemieux, T. (2001). "Can falling supply explain the rising return to college for younger men? A cohort-based analysis". Quarterly Journal of Economics 116 (2), 705–746. May.

Carneiro, P. (2002). Heterogeneity in the Returns to Schooling: Implications for Policy Evaluation. Ph.D. thesis, University of Chicago.

Carneiro, P., Hansen, K., Heckman, J.J. (2001). "Removing the veil of ignorance in assessing the distributional impacts of social policies". Swedish Economic Policy Review 8 (2), 273–301. Fall.

Carneiro, P., Hansen, K., Heckman, J.J. (2003). "Estimating distributions of treatment effects with an application to the returns to schooling and measurement of the effects of uncertainty on college choice". International Economic Review 44 (2), 361–422. 2001 Lawrence R. Klein Lecture. May.

Carneiro, P., Heckman, J.J. (2002). "The evidence on credit constraints in post-secondary schooling". Economic Journal 112 (482), 705–734. October.

Carneiro, P., Heckman, J.J., Vytlacil, E.J. (2005). "Understanding what instrumental variables estimate: Estimating marginal and average returns to education". Presented at Harvard University, 2001. Submitted for publication.

Chandra, A. (2003). "Is the convergence of the racial wage gap illusory?" Working Paper 9476, National Bureau of Economic Research.

Chiswick, B.R. (1974). Income Inequality: Regional Analyses Within a Human Capital Framework. National Bureau of Economic Research, New York.

Chiswick, B.R., Mincer, J. (1972). "Time–series changes in personal income inequality in the United States from 1939, with projections to 1985". Journal of Political Economy 80 (3), S34–S66. May/June. Part II.

Comay, Y., Melnik, A., Pollatschek, M.A. (1973). "The option value of education and the optimal path for investment in human capital". International Economic Review 14 (2), 421–435. June.

Cunha, F., Heckman, J.J. (2006a). "A framework for the analysis of inequality". Journal of Macroeconomics. In press.

Cunha, F., Heckman, J.J. (2006b). "Identifying and estimating the distributions of *Ex Post* and *Ex Ante* returns to schooling: A survey of recent developments". Labour Economics. Submitted for publication.

Cunha, F., Heckman, J.J., Lochner, L.J., Masterov, D.V. (2006). "Interpreting the evidence on life cycle skill formation". In: Hanushek, E.A., Welch, F. (Eds.), Handbook of the Economics of Education. North-Holland, Amsterdam, in this issue.

Cunha, F., Heckman, J.J., Navarro, S. (2005). "Separating uncertainty from heterogeneity in life cycle earnings, The 2004 Hicks lecture". Oxford Economic Papers 57 (2), 191–261. April.

Cunha, F., Heckman, J.J., Navarro, S. (2006). "Counterfactual analysis of inequality and social mobility". In: Morgan, S.L., Grusky, D.B., Fields, G.S. (Eds.), Mobility and Inequality: Frontiers of Research in Sociology and Economics. Stanford University Press, Palo Alto. Chapter 4.

Cunha, F., Heckman, J.J., Navarro, S. (2007). "The identification and economic content of ordered choice models with stochastic cutoffs". International Economic Review. Submitted for publication.
Cunha, F., Heckman, J.J., Urzua, S. (2006). "Nonmonotonicity arises in many classes of economic choice models". Unpublished Manuscript, University of Chicago, Department of Economics.
Dixit, A.K., Pindyck, R.S. (1994). Investment Under Uncertainty. Princeton University Press, Princeton.
Dooley, M.D., Gottschalk, P. (1984). "Earnings inequality among males in the United States: Trends and the effect of labor force growth". Journal of Political Economy 92 (1), 59–89. February.
Durbin, J. (1954). "Errors in variables". Review of the International Statistical Institute 22, 23–32.
Eckstein, Z., Wolpin, K.I. (1999). "Why youths drop out of high school: The impact of preferences, opportunities, and abilities". Econometrica 67 (6), 1295–1339. November.
Ellwood, D.T., Kane, T.J. (2000). "Who is getting a college education? Family background and the growing gaps in enrollment". In: Danziger, S., Waldfogel, J. (Eds.), Securing the Future: Investing in Children from Birth to College. Russell Sage Foundation, New York, pp. 283–324.
Fan, J., Gijbels, I. (1996). Local Polynomial Modelling and its Applications. Chapman and Hall, New York.
Flavin, M.A. (1981). "The adjustment of consumption to changing expectations about future income". Journal of Political Economy 89 (5), 974–1009. October.
Florens, J.-P., Heckman, J.J., Meghir, C., Vytlacil, E.J. (2002). "Instrumental variables, local instrumental variables and control functions". Technical Report CWP15/02, CEMMAP. Under revision, Econometrica.
Fréchet, M. (1951). "Sur les tableaux de corrélation dont les marges sont données". Annales de l'Université de Lyon A (Series 3, 14) 3 (14), 53–77.
Friedman, M., Kuznets, S.S. (1945). Income from Independent Professional Practice. National Bureau of Economic Research, New York.
Glewwe, P. (2002). "Schools and skills in developing countries: Education policies and socioeconomic outcomes". Journal of Economic Literature 40 (2), 436–482. June.
Greene, W.H. (2003). Econometric Analysis, 5th ed. Prentice-Hall, Upper Saddle River, NJ.
Griliches, Z. (1977). "Estimating the returns to schooling: Some econometric problems". Econometrica 45 (1), 1–22. January.
Grogger, J., Eide, E. (1995). "Changes in college skills and the rise in the college wage premium". Journal of Human Resources 30 (2), 280–310. Spring.
Hanoch, G. (1967). "An economic analysis of earnings and schooling". Journal of Human Resources 2 (3), 310–329. Summer.
Hansen, L.P. (1982). "Large sample properties of generalized method of moments estimators". Econometrica 50 (4), 1029–1054. July.
Hartog, J., Vijverberg, W. (2002). "Do wages really compensate for risk aversion and skewness affection?" Technical Report IZA DP No. 426, IZA, Bonn, Germany. February.
Hause, J.C. (1980). "The fine structure of earnings and the on-the-job training hypothesis". Econometrica 48 (4), 1013–1029. May.
Hausman, J.A. (1978). "Specification tests in econometrics". Econometrica 46, 1251–1272. November.
Heckman, J.J. (1976). "A life-cycle model of earnings, learning, and consumption". Journal of Political Economy 84 (4), S11–S44. Part 2. August. Journal Special Issue: Essays in Labor Economics in Honor of H. Gregg Lewis.
Heckman, J.J. (1979). "Sample selection bias as a specification error". Econometrica 47 (1), 153–162. January.
Heckman, J.J. (1990). "Varieties of selection bias". American Economic Review 80 (2), 313–318. May.
Heckman, J.J. (1997). "Instrumental variables: A study of implicit behavioral assumptions used in making program evaluations". Journal of Human Resources 32 (3), 441–462. Summer. Addendum published vol. 33, no. 1 (Winter 1998).
Heckman, J.J., Honoré, B.E. (1990). "The empirical content of the Roy model". Econometrica 58 (5), 1121–1149. September.
Heckman, J.J., Ichimura, H., Smith, J., Todd, P.E. (1998). "Characterizing selection bias using experimental data". Econometrica 66 (5), 1017–1098. September.

Heckman, J.J., Ichimura, H., Todd, P.E. (1997). "Matching as an econometric evaluation estimator: Evidence from evaluating a job training programme". Review of Economic Studies 64 (4), 605–654. October.
Heckman, J.J., LaFontaine, P. (2006). "Bias corrected estimates of GED returns". Journal of Labor Economics. Submitted for publication.
Heckman, J.J., Layne-Farrar, A., Todd, P.E. (1996). "Human capital pricing equations with an application to estimating the effect of schooling quality on earnings". Review of Economics and Statistics 78 (4), 562–610. November.
Heckman, J.J., Lochner, L.J., Taber, C. (1998). "Explaining rising wage inequality: Explorations with a dynamic general equilibrium model of labor earnings with heterogeneous agents". Review of Economic Dynamics 1 (1), 1–58. January.
Heckman, J.J., Lyons, T.M., Todd, P.E. (2000). "Understanding black–white wage differentials: 1960–1990". American Economic Review 90 (2), 344–349. May.
Heckman, J.J., Navarro, S. (2006). "Dynamic discrete choice and dynamic treatment effects". Journal of Econometrics. Submitted for publication.
Heckman, J.J., Robb, R. (1985). "Alternative methods for evaluating the impact of interventions". In: Heckman, J., Singer, B. (Eds.), Longitudinal Analysis of Labor Market Data, vol. 10. Cambridge University Press, New York, pp. 156–245.
Heckman, J.J., Robb, R. (1986). "Alternative methods for solving the problem of selection bias in evaluating the impact of treatments on outcomes". In: Wainer, H. (Ed.), Drawing Inferences from Self-Selected Samples. Springer-Verlag, New York, pp. 63–107. Reprinted in 2000, Lawrence Erlbaum Associates, Mahwah, NJ.
Heckman, J.J., Scheinkman, J. (1987). "The importance of bundling in a Gorman–Lancaster model of earnings". Review of Economic Studies 54 (2), 243–355. April.
Heckman, J.J., Sedlacek, G.L. (1985). "Heterogeneity, aggregation, and market wage functions: An empirical model of self-selection in the labor market". Journal of Political Economy 93 (6), 1077–1125. December.
Heckman, J.J., Smith, J.A. (1998). "Evaluating the welfare state". In: Strom, S. (Ed.), Econometrics and Economic Theory in the Twentieth Century: The Ragnar Frisch Centennial Symposium. Cambridge University Press, New York, pp. 241–318.
Heckman, J.J., Smith, J.A., Clements, N. (1997). "Making the most out of programme evaluations and social experiments: Accounting for heterogeneity in programme impacts". Review of Economic Studies 64 (221), 487–536. October.
Heckman, J.J., Stixrud, J., Urzua, S. (2006). "The effects of cognitive and noncognitive abilities on labor market outcomes and social behavior". Journal of Labor Economics. Submitted for publication.
Heckman, J.J., Tobias, J.L., Vytlacil, E.J. (2001). "Four parameters of interest in the evaluation of social programs". Southern Economic Journal 68 (2), 210–223. October.
Heckman, J.J., Tobias, J.L., Vytlacil, E.J. (2003). "Simple estimators for treatment parameters in a latent variable framework". Review of Economics and Statistics 85 (3), 748–754. August.
Heckman, J.J., Urzua, S., Vytlacil, E.J. (2004). "Understanding instrumental variables in models with essential heterogeneity: Unpublished results". Unpublished Manuscript, University of Chicago, Department of Economics.
Heckman, J.J., Urzua, S., Vytlacil, E.J. (2006). "Understanding instrumental variables in models with essential heterogeneity". Review of Economics and Statistics. In press.
Heckman, J.J., Vytlacil, E.J. (1998). "Instrumental variables methods for the correlated random coefficient model: Estimating the average rate of return to schooling when the return is correlated with schooling". Journal of Human Resources 33 (4), 974–987. Fall.
Heckman, J.J., Vytlacil, E.J. (1999). "Local instrumental variables and latent variable models for identifying and bounding treatment effects". Proceedings of the National Academy of Sciences 96, 4730–4734. April.
Heckman, J.J., Vytlacil, E.J. (2000). "The relationship between treatment parameters within a latent variable framework". Economics Letters 66 (1), 33–39. January.
Heckman, J.J., Vytlacil, E.J. (2001a). "Identifying the role of cognitive ability in explaining the level of change in the return to schooling". Review of Economics and Statistics 83 (1), 1–12. February.

Heckman, J.J., Vytlacil, E.J. (2001b). "Local instrumental variables". In: Hsiao, C., Morimune, K., Powell, J.L. (Eds.), Nonlinear Statistical Modeling: Proceedings of the Thirteenth International Symposium in Economic Theory and Econometrics: Essays in Honor of Takeshi Amemiya. Cambridge University Press, New York, pp. 1–46.
Heckman, J.J., Vytlacil, E.J. (2001c). "Policy-relevant treatment effects". American Economic Review 91 (2), 107–111. May.
Heckman, J.J., Vytlacil, E.J. (2005). "Structural equations, treatment effects and econometric policy evaluation". Econometrica 73 (3), 669–738. May.
Heckman, J.J., Vytlacil, E.J. (2007a). "Econometric evaluation of social programs, Part I: Causal models, structural models and econometric policy evaluation". In: Heckman, J., Leamer, E. (Eds.), Handbook of Econometrics, vol. 6, Elsevier, Amsterdam. In press.
Heckman, J.J., Vytlacil, E.J. (2007b). "Econometric evaluation of social programs, Part II: Using the marginal treatment effect to organize alternative economic estimators to evaluate social programs and to forecast their effects in new environments". In: Heckman, J., Leamer, E. (Eds.), Handbook of Econometrics, vol. 6, Elsevier, Amsterdam. In press.
Hirshleifer, J. (1970). Investment, Interest, and Capital. Prentice-Hall, Englewood Cliffs, NJ.
Hoeffding, W. (1940). "Masstabinvariante Korrelationtheorie". Schriften des Mathematischen Instituts und des Instituts für Angewandte Mathematik und Universität Berlin 5, 197–233.
Hungerford, T., Solon, G. (1987). "Sheepskin effects in the returns to education". Review of Economics and Statistics 69 (1), 175–177. February.
Imbens, G.W., Angrist, J.D. (1994). "Identification and estimation of local average treatment effects". Econometrica 62 (2), 467–475. March.
Jaeger, D.A., Page, M.E. (1996). "Degrees matter: New evidence on sheepskin effects in the returns to education". Review of Economics and Statistics 78 (4), 733–740. November.
Jöreskog, K.G., Goldberger, A.S. (1975). "Estimation of a model with multiple indicators and multiple causes of a single latent variable". Journal of the American Statistical Association 70 (351), 631–639. September.
Juhn, C., Murphy, K.M., Pierce, B. (1993). "Wage inequality and the rise in returns to skill". Journal of Political Economy 101 (3), 410–442. June.
Kane, T.J., Rouse, C.E. (1995). "Labor-market returns to two- and four-year college". American Economic Review 85 (3), 600–614. June.
Kane, T.J., Rouse, C., Staiger, D. (1999). "Estimating returns to schooling when schooling is misreported". Technical Report 7235, NBER.
Katz, L.F., Autor, D.H. (1999). "Changes in the wage structure and earnings inequality". In: Ashenfelter, O., Card, D. (Eds.), Handbook of Labor Economics, vol. 3. North-Holland, New York, pp. 1463–1555. Chapter 25.
Katz, L.F., Murphy, K.M. (1992). "Changes in relative wages, 1963–1987: Supply and demand factors". Quarterly Journal of Economics 107 (1), 35–78. February.
Keane, M.P., Wolpin, K.I. (1997). "The career decisions of young men". Journal of Political Economy 105 (3), 473–522. June.
Kling, J.R. (2001). "Interpreting instrumental variables estimates of the returns to schooling". Journal of Business and Economic Statistics 19 (3), 358–364. July.
Laitner, J. (1992). "Random earnings differences, lifetime liquidity constraints, and altruistic intergenerational transfers". Journal of Economic Theory 58 (2), 135–170. December.
Lewis, H.G. (1963). Unionism and Relative Wages in the United States: An Empirical Inquiry. University of Chicago Press, Chicago.
Lewis, H.G. (1986). Union Relative Wage Effects: A Survey. University of Chicago Press, Chicago.
Lillard, L.A., Willis, R.J. (1978). "Dynamic aspects of earning mobility". Econometrica 46 (5), 985–1012. September.
Lochner, L.J., Moretti, E. (2004). "The effect of education on crime: Evidence from prison inmates, arrests, and self-reports". American Economic Review 94 (1), 155–189. March.
MaCurdy, T.E. (1982). "The use of time series processes to model the error structure of earnings in a longitudinal data analysis". Journal of Econometrics 18 (1), 83–114. January.

MaCurdy, T.E., Mroz, T. (1995). "Estimating macro effects from repeated cross-sections". Unpublished Working Paper, Stanford University.
Manski, C.F. (2004). "Measuring expectations". Econometrica 72 (5), 1329–1376. September.
Matzkin, R.L. (2003). "Nonparametric estimation of nonadditive random functions". Econometrica 71 (5), 1339–1375. September.
Meghir, C., Palme, M. (2001). "The effect of a social experiment in education". Technical Report W01/11, Institute for Fiscal Studies.
Mincer, J. (1958). "Investment in human capital and personal income distribution". Journal of Political Economy 66 (4), 281–302. August.
Mincer, J. (1974). Schooling, Experience and Earnings. Columbia University Press for National Bureau of Economic Research, New York.
Mincer, J. (1997). "Changes in wage inequality, 1970–1990". In: Polachek, S.W., Robst, J. (Eds.), Research in Labor Economics, vol. 16. JAI Press, Greenwich, CT, pp. 1–18.
Mincer, J., Polachek, S. (1974). "Family investment in human capital: Earnings of women". Journal of Political Economy 82 (2), S76–S108. Part II, March–April.
Mulligan, C.B. Marion, J.G. (2000). "Average marginal tax rates revisited: A comment". Working Paper 01.4, Harris School of Public Policy.
Murnane, R.J., Willett, J.B., Levy, F. (1995). "The growing importance of cognitive skills in wage determination". Review of Economics and Statistics 77 (2), 251–266. May.
Murphy, K.M., Welch, F. (1990). "Empirical age–earnings profiles". Journal of Labor Economics 8 (2), 202–229. April.
Murphy, K.M., Welch, F. (1992). "The structure of wages". Quarterly Journal of Economics 107 (1), 285–326. February.
Navarro, S. (2005). Understanding Schooling: Using Observed Choices to Infer Agent's Information in a Dynamic Model of Schooling Choice When Consumption Allocation Is Subject to Borrowing Constraints. Ph.D. Dissertation, University of Chicago, Chicago, IL.
Neal, D. (2004). "The measured black–white wage gap among women is too small". Journal of Political Economy 112 (1, Part 2 Supplement), S1–S28. February.
Noyes, C.R. (1945). "Director's comment". In: Friedman, M., Kuznets, S.S. (Eds.), Income from Independent Professional Practice. National Bureau of Economic Research, New York, pp. 405–410.
Pistaferri, L. (2001). "Superior information, income shocks, and the permanent income hypothesis". Review of Economics and Statistics 83 (3), 465–476. August.
Psacharopoulos, G. (1981). "Returns to education: An updated international comparison". Comparative Education 17 (3), 321–341. October.
Psacharopoulos, G., Patrinos, H.A. (2004). "Returns to investment in education: A further update". Education Economics 12 (2), 111–134. August.
Quandt, R.E. (1958). "The estimation of the parameters of a linear regression system obeying two separate regimes". Journal of the American Statistical Association 53 (284), 873–880. December.
Quandt, R.E. (1972). "A new approach to estimating switching regressions". Journal of the American Statistical Association 67 (338), 306–310. June.
Robinson, P.M. (1988). "Root-N-consistent semiparametric regression". Econometrica 56 (4), 931–954. July.
Rosen, S. (1977). "Human capital: A survey of empirical research". In: Ehrenberg, R. (Ed.), Research in Labor Economics, vol. 1. JAI Press, Greenwich, CT, pp. 3–40.
Roy, A. (1951). "Some thoughts on the distribution of earnings". Oxford Economic Papers 3 (2), 135–146. June.
Rutherford, R.S.G. (1955). "Income distributions: A new model". Econometrica 23 (3), 277–294. July.
Ruud, P.A. (2000). An Introduction to Classical Econometric Theory. Oxford University Press, New York.
Sargent, T.J., Sims, C.A. (1977). "Business cycle modeling without much a priori economic theory". In: New Methods in Business Cycle Research: Proceedings from a Conference. Federal Reserve Bank of Minneapolis, Minneapolis.

Schultz, T.P. (1975). "Long-term change in personal income distribution: Theoretical approaches, evidence, and explanations". In: Levine, D.M., Bane, M.J. (Eds.), The Inequality Controversy: Schooling and Distributive Justice. Basic Books, New York.
Sims, C.A. (1972). "Money, income, and causality". American Economic Review 62 (4), 540–552. September.
Smith, J.P., Welch, F.R. (1979). "Inequality: Race differences in the distribution of earnings". International Economic Review 20 (2), 515–526. June.
Snyder, T.D. (1993). 120 Years of American Education: A Statistical Portrait. U.S. Dept. of Education, Office of Educational Research and Improvement, National Center for Education Statistics, Washington, DC.
Snyder, T.D. (2000). Digest of Education Statistics 1999. U.S. Dept. of Education, Office of Educational Research and Improvement, National Center for Educational Statistics, Washington, DC.
Staiger, D., Stock, J.H. (1997). "Instrumental variables regression with weak instruments". Econometrica 65 (3), 557–586. May.
Stock, J.H., Yogo, M. (2002). "Testing for weak instruments in linear IV regression". Technical Working Paper 284, NBER.
Taber, C.R. (2001). "The rising college premium in the eighties: Return to college or return to unobserved ability?". Review of Economic Studies 68 (3), 665–691. July.
Urzua, S. (2005). "Schooling choice and the anticipation of labor market conditions: A dynamic choice model with heterogeneous agents and learning". Unpublished Manuscript, University of Chicago, Department of Economics.
Vytlacil, E.J. (2002). "Independence, monotonicity, and latent index models: An equivalence result". Econometrica 70 (1), 331–341. January.
Weisbrod, B.A. (1962). "Education and investment in human capital". Journal of Political Economy 70 (5), 106–123. Part 2: Investment in human beings.
Willis, R.J. (1986). "Wage determinants: A survey and reinterpretation of human capital earnings functions". In: Ashenfelter, O., Layard, R. (Eds.), Handbook of Labor Economics. North-Holland, New York, pp. 525–602.
Willis, R.J., Rosen, S. (1979). "Education and self-selection". Journal of Political Economy 87 (5), S7–S36. Part 2. October.
Wu, D. (1973). "Alternative tests of independence between stochastic regressors and disturbances". Econometrica 41, 733–750. July.
Zamarro, G. (2005). "Accounting for heterogeneous returns in sequential schooling decisions". Unpublished Manuscript, CEMFI, Madrid. May.

Chapter 8

THE SOCIAL VALUE OF EDUCATION AND HUMAN CAPITAL

FABIAN LANGE

Department of Economics, Yale University, 27 Hillhause, Rm 38, New Haven, CT 06511, USA
e-mail: fabian.lange@yale.edu

ROBERT TOPEL

Urban and Labor Economics, University of Chicago, Chicago, IL 60637, USA
e-mail: robert.topel@gsb.uchicago.edu

Contents

Handbook of the Economics of Education, Volume 1
Edited by Eric A. Hanushek and Finis Welch
© 2006 Elsevier B.V. All rights reserved
DOI: 10.1016/S1574-0692(06)01008-7

Abstract

We review and extend the empirical literature that seeks evidence of a wedge between the private and social returns to human capital, specifically education. This literature has two main strands. First, much of modern growth theory puts human capital at center-stage, building on older notions of human capital externalities as an engine of economic growth. Empirical support for these ideas, based on both the comparative growth of national outputs and on the geographic dispersion of wages within countries, is meager. There is a strong association between average earnings and average education across nations and regions in the U.S. that exceeds the private returns to education. However, problems of omitted variables and endogeneity inherent in spatial equilibrium models mean that this association can hardly be understood as evidence for social returns. There is no evidence from this literature that social returns are *smaller* than private ones, yet neither is there much to suggest that they are *larger*. We then turn to the literature on job market signaling, which implies that social returns to education are smaller than private returns. Consistent with our earlier conclusions, we find scant evidence of this. We construct a model of the speed of employer learning about workers' unobserved talents, and we estimate the model using panel data on young workers. We find that employer learning about productivity occurs fairly quickly after labor market entry, implying that the signaling effects of schooling are small.

Keywords

education externality, spacial equilibrium, migration, skill biased productivity growth

JEL classification: I-20, J-31, J-61, O-15, O-42, R23, R30

Economists (and others) have generally had little success in estimating the social effects of different investments, and, unfortunately, education is no exception.
Becker, Human Capital (1964)

1. Introduction

This chapter reviews and extends the literature on the social returns to accumulation of human capital, with particular emphasis on the social returns to education. Here and in what follows we define "social returns" to be the sum of the private and external marginal benefits of a unit of human capital. In other words, we study the problem of human capital externalities – does an individual's private decision to accumulate human capital confer external benefits or costs on others?

There are three main strands to the literature on human capital externalities, each of which touches on externalities created by the accumulation of education. First, in a formalization of ideas that go back at least as far as Marshall (1890)[1] recent theories of economic growth emphasize human capital accumulation as an engine of growth. Following Lucas (1988), who built on earlier work by Uzawa (1965) and others, growth theorists have emphasized interactions amongst agents that may cause the social returns to human capital to exceed the private ones. Persons with greater skill may raise the productivity of others with whom they interact, so accumulation of human capital may increase total factor productivity in an economy. We provide an overview of growth models that generate such externalities, and we critique the empirical literature that seeks to identify these effects from both aggregate and micro data. We then extend this literature, modeling the contribution of education to growth in total factor productivity in states and regions of the U.S. since 1940. Looking ahead, our conclusion is that empirical evidence for important human capital externalities is, at best, weak.

In contrast to the growth literature – where education is alleged to produce positive externalities – models of the signaling value of education raise the possibility that some component of schooling is a social waste. In the extreme form first formulated by Spence (1973) schooling acts as a signal of private information about individual productivities, for which employers are willing to pay, though it does not raise anyone's productivity. It is privately optimal to invest in schooling – education has a private return because it transfers wealth from less to more skilled individuals – but the social return is negative since schooling does not raise individuals' productivities and it reduces social output by using valuable resources.[2] We review and critique the existing

[1] Marshall emphasized the social benefits of valuable ideas, which are public goods and, he implies, are more likely to be produced by the highly educated. "...[F]or one new idea, such as Bessemer's chief invention, adds as much to England's productive power as the labour of a hundred thousand men. ... All that is spent ... [in educating the masses] would be well paid for if it called out one more Newton or Darwin, Shakespeare, or Beethoven." *Principles of Economics, 8th Edition* (1920).

[2] It could be that signaling improves the allocation of individuals to tasks and thus generates social returns. Butt in its most basic form we would expect that the social returns are lower than the private ones.

empirical literature on signaling, which we find provides little convincing evidence for an important role of Job Market Signaling. We extend that literature with an empirically tractable model of employer learning about individuals' talents. Applying our model to panel data from the National Longitudinal Study of Youth (NLSY) we find that learning about individual talents occurs fairly quickly. This allows us to put an empirical upper bound on the contribution of signaling to the private returns to schooling. We conclude that the impact of signaling on private returns is small – no more than about a tenth of the private return – so most of the returns to schooling reflect a positive impact of education on productivity.

A third strand of literature emphasizes possible external benefits of education that do not apply directly to the production process. They are not reflected in factor payments,[3] and so they are often less amenable to empirical research. Such external benefits might arise because education reduces criminal behavior [Lochner and Moretti (2004)], because education enables individuals to participate more efficiently in the political process [Friedman (1962), Miligan, Moretti and Oreopoulos (2003)], or because education carries direct consumption externalities. If knowledge of Shakespeare or Astronomy makes one more interesting, then investment in education raises the welfare of others through a form of network externality borne of social interactions. (Study of say, accounting, might have the opposite effect.) This raises welfare without any discernable impact on wages or productivity. With rare exceptions – crime is the only one that we can think of – these putative social benefits of education are unmeasured. So our empirical review touches them only in passing.

The remainder of the paper is organized in 2 major sections. Section 2 considers the evidence concerning external effects of education in production. Section 3 examines the empirical evidence on Job Market Signaling. Section 4 concludes.

2. Growth and production externalities of human capital

This section reviews and extends the empirical literature on production externalities of human capital, as measured (mainly) by education. For such externalities to exist, an individual's human capital must cause an unpriced increase in the productivity of others. Typically these effects are thought to occur through proximity and human interaction, though when productive interactions occur within firms they are merely complementarities that will be internalized and priced. This has led to an emphasis – both in theories and in applied work – on social interactions in cities, where ideas are sort of 'in the air.' Then the external benefits of human capital are localized, which has empirical implications for wages and land prices that are taken up in Section 2.2. But the idea of

[3] By definition externalities are not reflected in the payments to factors generating the external effects. However, they might be reflected in payments to those benefiting from the external effects. This forms the basis of most existing empirical studies of external effects of education.

productive externalities from human capital is not limited by geography, as Marshall's (1920) emphasized with his example of Pasteur's contribution to public health. Members of the "charmed circle" that produce such ideas "have probably earned for the world a hundred times or more as much as they have earned for themselves."[4] Such global externalities will not show up in geographic variation of factor prices and are thus outside of the scope of existing empirical attempts (including ours) to identify the social benefits from education.

We begin in Section 2.1 with a review of the place of human capital in modern theories of economic growth, and the state of empirical evidence derived from growth of national outputs. Section 2.2 outlines a model for evaluating the impact of human capital on local productivities, and reviews empirical work that seeks to identify externalities from geographic differences in wages and educational attainment. This research is extended in Section 2.3, where we apply the model to data on the growth of U.S. states from 1940 to 2000.

2.1. Human capital, education and economic growth

Recent interest among macroeconomists in the possibility of human capital externalities follows the revival of growth theory, which is built on the idea that human capital is central to growth. Following Lucas (1988), neoclassical models of growth treat human capital as a produced input to a standard constant returns technology, so that growth of human capital and growth of output are nearly synonymous.

To appreciate the special place of human capital in modern growth models, we begin with two key facts. First, as noted by Kaldor (1961), most countries have experienced sustained growth over very long periods of time – for example, growth in U.S. per-capita income averaged 1.75 percent per year over the 20th century. Second, the capital/output ratio is remarkably stable across countries, both rich and poor.[5] To accommodate these facts, Solow's (1956) original formulation of a growth model introduced an exogenous rate of labor-augmenting technical change to generate sustained growth in the face of diminishing returns to physical capital. To fix ideas let aggregate production be Cobb–Douglas with constant returns to capital and labor, with zero labor force growth:

$$Y_t = K_t^{\alpha}(A_t L)^{1-\alpha}. \tag{1}$$

Here A_t denotes the state of labor-augmenting technical progress, which grows at exogenous rate $\dot{a}_t = \mathrm{d}\log(A_t)/\mathrm{d}t$. Let $\dot{y}_t$ and $\dot{k}_t$ denote the growth rates of output per worker and capital per worker, so (1) implies

$$\dot{y}_t = \alpha \dot{k}_t + (1-\alpha)\dot{a}_t. \tag{2}$$

With a constant savings rate, output, capital and consumption grow at the common rate $\dot{a}$. This also means that the capital/output ratio is fixed in the steady state.

[4] Marshal (1920, p. 598).

[5] See Young (1995) or Figure 1 in Topel (1999).

Human capital entered the picture when Theodore Schultz (1963) and other development economists interpreted the Solow residual $\dot{a}$ as growth in human capital. This was formalized by Uzawa (1965) and Lucas (1988) who interpreted A_t as the average stock of human capital per worker, so $H = AL$ is the human capital stock. In Lucas' formulation aggregate human capital is an input to its own production, much as private human capital is in Ben-Porath's (1967) model of human capital investment for individuals:

$$
\begin{aligned}
Y_t &= K_t^{\alpha}(uH_t)^{1-\alpha},\\
\frac{\mathrm{d}H_t}{\mathrm{d}t} &= BH_t(1-u) - \delta H_t,
\end{aligned}
\tag{3}
$$

where $1-u$ is the proportion of time devoted to production of new human capital. Here workers embody skills that accumulate through wealth maximizing investment decisions – schooling, training and learning by doing. As above, in the steady state the economy's stocks of physical and human capital grow at a common endogenous rate, which sustains economic growth. As specified the model admits no distortions between private and social values, so growth and investment in human capital are socially efficient. There is no efficiency argument for government participation in human capital production.

Yet publicly financed education is near-universal, at least in the lower grades in many countries but all the way through college in others. An efficiency rationale for government participation in education rests on the possibility of positive externalities: do individual decisions to acquire human capital create external benefits for others?[6] For example, it is plausible that one individual's human capital is more productive when other members of society are more skilled. As we noted above, the benefits of such complementarities will be internalized when they occur within firms, but not if they are produced by social and other interactions that are external to firms. There are many ways to model these interactions [see Acemoglu (1996), Jovanovic and Rob (1989), or Glaeser (1999), for examples] which need not concern us here. The possibility of such external effects of human capital motivated Lucas (1988) to study a reduced-form extension of (3) in which output of each firm depends on the human capital of its workers and also on the average human capital of workers in the economy as a whole.

The hypothesis of human capital externalities is not easy to test – it requires evidence that the social return to a "unit" of human capital is different from the private return. If we take schooling as our prototypical measure of a human capital component, then Mincerian estimates of the private return to schooling investments abound. Further, the consensus of surveys of this literature indicates that the "true" return to schooling is not much different than what is found from an OLS regression of individual log earnings on years of completed schooling, which would put the private return to an additional year of schooling on the order of 5–8 percent, though recent returns in the U.S. are slightly higher.[7] Given this base for the private return, the question of interest here is whether

[6] See Heckman and Klenow (1998).

[7] See Card (1999) for a comprehensive survey of earlier literature.

the social return to an additional year of average schooling – the "Macro-Mincerian" return – substantially exceeds the "Micro-Mincerian" private return that is estimated from the wage and schooling outcomes of individuals. And of course the opposite is possible: the Macro-Mincer return might be smaller than the micro return – a negative externality – as in signaling models (see Section 3, below).

To put some structure on this question in an empirical model of growth let the stock of human capital be $H = hL$ where h is human capital per worker while A is the state of labor-augmenting technology. With Cobb–Douglas production output per worker in country j follows

$$\ln y_{jt} = \alpha_j \ln k_{jt} + (1 - \alpha_j) \ln h_{jt} + (1 - \alpha_j) \ln A_{jt}, \tag{4}$$

where lower case letters denote per-worker quantities. Now exploit the observation that the capital/output ratio is approximately constant, as would occur with a perfectly elastic supply of capital. Then $\ln y_{jt} - \ln k_{jt} = \tilde{\kappa}_j$ and appropriate substitution yields

$$\ln y_{jt} = \kappa_j + \ln h_{jt} + \ln A_{jt}, \tag{5}$$

where $\kappa_j = \frac{\alpha_j}{1-\alpha_j}\tilde{\kappa}_j$ is a country-specific constant. According to (5) output per worker grows in proportion to human capital h and labor-augmenting technical knowledge, A. Consistent with the form of human capital earnings functions pioneered by Mincer (1974), let the human capital of person i in country j and in period t satisfy

$$\begin{aligned}\ln h_{ijt} &= X_{ijt}\beta^P + u_{ijt} = X_{jt}\beta^P + (X_{ijt} - X_{jt})\beta^P + u_{ijt} \\ &= X_{jt}\beta^P + z_{ijt},\end{aligned} \tag{6}$$

where X is a vector of human capital determinants such as schooling and experience and X_{jt} is the mean of X in j at t. The parameters β^P measure the private returns to a unit increase in X on an *individual's* stock of human capital – the Micro-Mincer return in reference to schooling. Aggregating (6) over the labor force, log human capital per workers is

$$\ln h_{jt} = X_{jt}\beta^P + \ln \sum_i \exp(z_{ijt}) = X_{jt}\beta^P + \xi_{jt}. \tag{7}$$

Notice that ξ_{jt} depends on the distribution of human capital in the workforce. Since z_{ij} is the deviation of an individual's human capital from the economy-wide mean, and ξ is convex in z, a mean-preserving spread of the distribution of human capital increases ξ and hence $\ln h$.[8]

To complete the model we need to incorporate Lucas' (1988) notion of human capital externalities. One form of this hypothesis is that greater amounts of measurable human

[8] This raises obvious econometric issues. When we apply the model to the returns to schooling, the effect of schooling on productivity will be biased down (up) if an increase in average schooling reduces (increases) overall inequality of human capital.

capital – say schooling or experience – raise total factor productivity. So let

$$\ln A_{jt} = X_{jt}\beta^E + a_{jt}, \tag{8}$$

where β^E measures the extent of human capital externalities. Inserting (7) and (8) in (5) yields

$$\ln y_{jt} = \kappa_j + X_{jt}\beta^S + \xi_{jt} + a_{jt}, \tag{9}$$

where $\beta^S = \beta^P + \beta^E$ is the social impact of human capital measures on output per worker. Then the empirical question of (positive) human capital externalities comes down to whether $\beta^S > \beta^P$: e.g., does a unit increase in *average* years of schooling raise aggregate productivity by more than the private return?

Topel (1999) estimates various forms of (9) using an unbalanced panel of 111 countries at 5 year intervals between 1960 and 1990.[9,10] Tables 1 and 2 summarize his estimates, in which the only measure of human capital per worker is average years of schooling. Table 1 applies a fixed effects estimator to (9), so the estimates of the impact of a year of additional average schooling are generated by within-country variation in productivity and educational attainment of the workforce. In the estimates that contain year effects (column 3) – inclusion of which seems appropriate – the estimated social return is 0.10 per year of schooling. This is somewhat higher than the typical estimate of private returns, but given the quality of the data and the lack of other controls we are reluctant to interpret this as firm evidence in favor of $\beta^S > \beta^P$. On the other hand, Table 1 provides little comfort to those who would argue that social returns are smaller than private ones, as in signaling models.

The fixed effects (deviations from means) estimates in Table 1 are not an explicit model of economic growth. Take first differences in (5) and (7)

$$\Delta \ln y_{jt} = \Delta X_{jt}\beta^P + \Delta\xi_{jt} + \Delta \ln A_{jt}. \tag{10}$$

The last term in (10) is growth in total factor productivity. In Lucas' formulation of externalities the level of productivity depends on the average level of human capital per worker, so a surge in investment in human capital would lead to a one-time surge in productivity. But it is equally plausible that the *level* of human capital affects growth, as suggested by Nelson and Phelps (1965). In their model skilled workers are more likely to innovate new technologies and more capable of adopting existing technologies to local production. Further, as noted by Barro and Sala-i-Martin (1997) the opportunities to grow may be greater for economies that are inside the technological frontier, which they term "convergence." We represent these ideas as

$$\Delta \ln A_{jt} = \Delta X_{jt}\beta^E + X_{jt}\delta_X + \ln y_{jt}\delta_y + X_{jt}\ln y_{jt}\delta_{Xy} + \Delta a_{jt}, \quad \text{where } \delta_X > 0 \tag{11}$$

[9] Output and productivity data were from the Summers-Heston Mark 5.6 (1995) files, while information on educational attainment of the labor force was collected by Barro and Lee (1993).

[10] See also Barro (1991), Bils and Klenow (2000), Barro and Sala-i-Martin (1997), Benhabib and Spiegel (1994), Krueger and Lindahl (2000), Mankiw, Romer and Weil (1992), Pritchett (2001).

Table 1
The effects of education on labor productivity fixed country effects, 1960–1990 ($N = 719$)

	(1)	(2)	(3)	(4)
Avg. years of schooling	0.23		0.10	
	(0.010)		(0.016)	
Avg. years of primary schooling		0.20		0.06
		(0.019)		(0.029)
Avg. years of secondary schooling		0.28		0.14
		(0.037)		(0.024)
Country effects	Yes	Yes	Yes	Yes
Year Effects	No	No	Yes	Yes
R^2	0.46	0.46	0.58	0.59

Standard errors in parentheses. Based on Summers-Heston Mark 5.6 and Barro and Lee (1993) data.

Table 2
The effects of education on productivity and growth first-difference estimator at various growth intervals (dependent variable: Δy_{jt})

	5-year growth ($N = 608$)	10-year growth ($N = 290$)	15-year growth ($N = 186$)	20-year growth ($N = 101$)	5-year growth, fixed effects ($N = 604$)	10-year growth, fixed effects ($N = 290$)
Δ Education:	0.058	0.115	0.155	0.246	0.022	0.086
ΔX_{jt}	(0.016)	(0.022)	(0.030)	(0.043)	(0.017)	(0.030)
Years of schooling:	0.004	0.003	0.003	0.004	0.004	0.009
X_{jt}	(0.001)	(0.001)	(0.001)	(0.001)	(0.003)	(0.004)
Ln output/worker:	−0.005	−0.004	−0.005	−0.009	−0.043	−0.047
$\ln y_{jt}$	(0.002)	(0.003)	(0.003)	(0.004)	(0.007)	(0.008)
$\Delta X_{jt} \times \ln y_{jt}$	−0.36	−0.060	−0.041	−0.025	−0.020	−0.049
	(0.159)	(0.022)	(0.032)	(0.044)	(0.016)	(0.025)
R^2	0.224	0.332	0.391	0.399	0.287	0.493

Standard errors in parentheses. Based on Summers-Heston Mark 5.6 and Barro and Lee (1993) data. All models include year effects. Effects of ΔX_{jt} are evaluated at the mean level of $\ln y_{jt}$. Table A1 from Krueger and Lindahl (2000).

if the level of human capital is a boon to growth and $\delta_{Xy} < 0$ if the impact of human capital on growth is greater in less advanced countries.

Estimates based on (11) are shown in Table 2, again taken from Topel (1999), who estimates the effects of education on growth at various growth intervals. With measurement error and serial correlation in schooling there is an econometric tradeoff: short growth intervals increase sample size, but admit larger downward bias in estimated

Table 3
Correlation between Barro and Lee's (1993) and Kyriacou's (1991) measures of schooling as reported by Krueger and Lindahl (2000)

	Barro–Lee (1993)	Barro–Lee (1993)	Kyriacou (1991)	Kyriacou (1991)	Δ Barro–Lee	Δ Kyriacou
Barro–Lee (1993)	1.00					
Barro–Lee (1993)	0.97	1.00				
Kyriacou (1991)	0.91	0.92	1.00			
Kyriacou (1991)	0.81	0.86	0.88	1.00		
ΔBarro–Lee	0.23	0.46	0.36	0.51	1.00	
ΔKyriacou	−0.12	−0.03	−0.17	0.33	0.34	1.00

returns due to measurement error. Topel's estimates are consistent with this: at long growth intervals (e.g., 15 or 20 years) the estimated impact of education on productivity is much larger than at short intervals (5 years). At a 20 year growth interval the estimated impact of one year of average schooling on productivity is .246, which is vastly larger than the typical private returns to schooling estimated from micro data. And unless human capital externalities are truly grand, it also implausibly large as an estimate of the social return to schooling, β^S.

These estimates do not control for other elements of human capital than schooling, and it is reasonable to assume that growth in other forms of human capital is correlated with growth in schooling. That is, if investment in education is worthwhile, then investments in other forms of skill acquisition are also likely to be profitable. Then the impact of education on growth will be biased up for the usual omitted variables reasons. Given the quality of the data, measurement of these variables is infeasible. An alternative is to assume that unmeasured elements of human capital evolve at a constant rate within each country, which adds a fixed country effect λ_j to (11). With this assumption the estimates are unaffected by correlation between innovations to education and unmeasured factors in λ_j. A limitation is that the estimator can only be applied to fairly short growth intervals – 5 or 10 years in the available data – which increases the importance of measurement error in recorded schooling. With this limitation in mind, the last two columns of Table 2 show the results of applying this "diffs-in-diffs" methodology to growth data. At a 10-year interval the main effect of schooling on productivity is 0.086 per year, which is near the top of the range of estimates of private returns typically estimated from micro data.

Two recent studies [Krueger and Lindahl (2000), de la Fuente and Domenech (2001)] focus on the importance of measurement error in aggregate education measures for estimating Macro-Mincer returns to schooling. Table 3 reports the correlations between the two most prominent measures of education in the literature, produced by Barro and Lee (1993) and by Kyriacou (1991). They report average years of schooling for 68 countries in 1965 and 1985, based on differing methodologies. Both data-sets pick-up the large differences in education between less and more highly developed countries, reflected in the high correlations between the contemporaneous measures of education in 1965 and also in 1985. But for specifications like (11) that rely on first-differences the correlations in *growth* of education are decisive. The correlation between growth in average years of schooling between 1965 and 1985 is fairly low (.34). For shorter time-horizons the correlation is likely to be even smaller. This clearly underlines the importance of measurement error in the education data and motivates Krueger and Lindahl (2000) to instrument the Barro–Lee measure of schooling with Kyriacou's measure of the same thing. The resulting point estimate[11] of the Macro-Mincer return to schooling (0.069) implies a private return to schooling of 11.5% if we assume that human capital has a share in GDP of 60%. The standard error for this estimate is large, however, and Krueger and Lindahl are unable to reject the hypothesis of zero returns at conventional levels significance levels.

So what do we learn from macroeconomic data on growth and average educational attainment? Our reading is that the evidence is inconclusive. There is no plausible evidence that the social returns to education are *smaller* than the private returns, which one might take as evidence inconsistent with important signaling effects in the returns to schooling (see Section 3). The Macro-Mincer estimates tend to be at the upper end of the usually reported 6–9% range for private returns to education, and are often substantially higher. Yet the macroeconomic evidence for positive educational externalities is at best weak (see also Chapter 11 by Lant Pritchett in this Handbook). In part this weakness is due to the limitations of growth accounting data. Measures of educational attainment are not typically comparable across countries, educational attainment may be measured with substantial error, and other forms of human capital remain unmeasured, among other shortcomings. This has led some researchers to seek evidence of excess social returns in more traditional (for labor economists) sources of micro data in the U.S. We now turn to that approach.

2.2. Evidence from local data: States and cities

Several studies [Rauch (1993), Acemoglu and Angrist (2000), Ciccone and Peri (2006), Moretti (2003, 2004)] have sought evidence of human capital externalities from the spatial distribution of wages in the United States. These studies examine the effect of variation in aggregate measures of education at a local level on wages. The presumption is that production externalities of education increase individuals' marginal product and by extension their wages. A prototype empirical specification in these studies is

$$w_{li} = X_{li} B + S_{li} \beta^P + \bar{S}_l \beta^E + \varepsilon_{li}, \tag{12}$$

where w_{li} is the log wage of individual i in local market (e.g., state or city) l, X_{il} is a vector of controls, and S_{li} is person i's years of completed schooling. Then β^P is the Micro-Mincer return to schooling. The twist introduced by the cited studies is to include

[11] See Krueger and Lindahl (2000, Table 5, column (5)).

$\bar{S}_l$, the average years of schooling in market l, in the regression. $\bar{S}_l$ is intended to pick up the effect of human capital externalities – a more educated local labor force increases local productivity. This impact on productivity raises the price of land as firms choose where to locate, and it raises wages because mobile labor must be indifferent among locales. This literature attempts to control for unobserved factors that may be correlated with $\bar{S}_l$ in a variety of ways, mainly involving the use of instrumental variables, which we discuss below.

In what follows we outline a spatial equilibrium model of local wage determination, based on Lange and Topel (2005). This model serves two purposes. First, it guides our review of the empirical studies of educational externalities based on micro data, cited above. Each of these studies appeals to the theoretical framework formulated by Roback (1982) to justify the empirical model (12). Looking ahead, our view is that these studies give insufficient weight to endogeneity issues implied by a spatial equilibrium, so that the econometric methods they apply are unlikely to be valid. Second, the model guides our own attempts to identify the determinants of long term growth in American states, and the role of education in that process. We take up these issues in Section 2.4.

2.2.1. *A model of spatial equilibrium in labor markets*

In Roback's (1982) spatial model land is both a consumption good and a productive input. Firms' and individuals' location decisions are made conditional on rental prices of land as well as wages in different places. In equilibrium prices leave individuals and firms indifferent between locales, so that local externalities are reflected both in rental prices and wages. Production externalities increase both. The effect on land prices is usually ignored in the empirical literature,[12] citing lack of reliable and comparable data across areas.

We consider a labor and product market equilibrium defined over a large number of locales, l. Output in l is tradable across locales for a competitive price and, consistent with the growth models outline above, it is produced by capital, land (M) and human capital (H) with constant returns to scale. We assume that capital is in perfectly elastic supply, so it can be ignored in what follows. Local output Y_l is then

$$Y_l = M_l^{\alpha_M}\left(\prod_{s=1}^{S}(A_{ls}H_{ls}N_{ls})^{\delta_s}\right)^{\alpha_H}, \tag{13}$$

where $\sum_s \delta_s = 1$, N_{ls} is the number of workers of skill-type s who live and work in l, and H_{ls} is the average amount of human capital that workers of type-s in locale l bring to the task and M_l is land used in production in l. The shares of land and human capital in production are given by (α_M, α_H). The nested Cobb–Douglas specification implies that δ_s is the share of labor income accruing to type-s workers. The restriction that

[12] A notable exception is Rauch (1993).

δ_s is fixed across locales is easily relaxed (δ_{ls}), but the Cobb–Douglas assumption of constant shares is a bit more serious. With this technology an increase in the productivity of type-j labor ($\mathrm{d}A_{lj} > 0$) leaves its income share unchanged because all inter-group elasticities of substitution are unitary ($\sigma_{jk} = 1$), so employment of type-j labor is unchanged. Relaxing this adds some complexity without much corresponding benefit in terms of additional insight, so we maintain the Cobb–Douglas assumption in our exposition.

It will be convenient to represent the production side of the market in terms of its dual, the unit cost function for locale l's output. Denoting this unit (marginal) cost by C_l and normalizing the price of the tradable good to unity, product market equilibrium requires

$$C_l = \left(\frac{R_l}{\alpha_M}\right)^{\alpha_M} \left(\prod_{s=1}^{S} \left(\frac{W_{ls}}{(1-\alpha)\delta_s A_{ls}}\right)^{\delta_s}\right)^{\alpha_H} = 1. \tag{14}$$

In (14), R_l is the rental price of land at location l and W_{ls} is the rental price (wage) of one unit of skill type s in that market.

Workers of type s are mobile across locales. We assume that utility depends on consumption of local amenities, units of the tradable good and land. Let the utility of individual i of type s in locale l take the form:

$$U_{lsi} = V_{lsi} Z_{lsi}^{\theta} M_{lsi}^{1-\theta}, \tag{15}$$

where V indexes utility from local amenities, Z is consumption of the composite tradable good, and M is land. The budget constraint is

$$Z_{lsi} = H_{si} W_{ls} - R_l M_{lsi}, \tag{16}$$

where H_{si} is the type-s human capital of person i, whose observed wage is $W_{lsi} = H_{si} W_{ls}$. We can think of H_{si} as unobserved talent or the quality of the individual's human capital – for example, if s indexes labor in different schooling and experience cells, then H_{si} is human capital that is not directly measured by the index. With this definition the indirect utility of person i in location l is:

$$U(V_{lsi}, H_{si}, R_l, W_{ls}) = V_{lsi} \theta^{\theta} (1-\theta)^{1-\theta} H_{si} W_{ls} R_l^{\theta-1}. \tag{17}$$

In spatial equilibrium the marginal worker of type s must be indifferent between living and working in l and in the best alternative locale. We treat this reservation value as constant for skill type-s, so in equilibrium:

$$V_{ls} W_{ls} R_l^{\theta-1} = U_s, \tag{18}$$

where V_{ls} is the value of local amenities for the *marginal* worker of type-s. In writing this condition we have made use of the fact that the "quality" of person i's human capital, H_{si}, raises utility by the same proportion in all locations, so H does not appear in (18).

If all individuals value local amenities identically, then V_{ls} is a constant. Then the supply of type-s skills to a locale is perfectly elastic. Heterogeneous tastes for living in a locale will generate a rising supply price of skills. In this case the marginal V_{ls} will vary with local conditions – for example, a surge in demand for type-s skills will reduce V_{ls}. This point plays an important role in our subsequent discussion of empirical evidence – most instruments for education that have been proposed in the literature will also affect V_{ls} in a systematic and predictable way.

The cost and utility conditions (14) and (18) are sufficient to characterize the spatial distribution of skill prices and land rents. Adopt the notational convention that lower-case letters represent natural logarithms. Then taking logs in (14), spatial competition in production of the tradable good yields an "indifference" relation for unit cost:

$$w_l = \lambda + a_l - \frac{\alpha_M}{\alpha_H} r_l, \tag{19}$$

where $w_l = \sum_s \delta_s w_{ls}$ is the income-share weighted average of log skill prices and $\alpha_H * a_l = \alpha_H * (\sum_s \delta_s a_{ls})$ is total factor productivity (TFP) in market l. Equation (19) must be satisfied for employers to operate in market l – wages in market l can be higher the greater is TFP, the greater is worker quality, or the lower the price of land.

Taking logs in (18) yields a family of indifference relations between skill prices and land rents for workers of each type:

$$w_{ls} = \mu_s + (1-\theta) r_l - v_{ls}. \tag{20}$$

To retain workers in l, a higher price of land in l must be offset by greater wages, while more valuable local amenities reduce wages, holding constant the price of land. Now form $w_l = \sum_s \delta_s w_{ls}$ in (20) and solve for the (log) price of land:

$$r_l = \frac{\lambda - \mu + a_l + v_l}{1 - \theta + \phi}, \tag{21}$$

where $\phi = \alpha_M / \alpha_H$ is the ratio of cost shares of land relative to the share of human capital α_H and $v_l = \sum_s \delta_s v_{ls}$ is the average valuation of location l amenities by the marginal worker of each type. According to (21), the price of land in l will be higher (a) the greater is total factor productivity in l, $\alpha_H * a_l$ or (b) the greater the value of local amenities in l, v_l.

Inserting (21) into (20) yields a solution for the price of type-s skills in l:

$$\begin{aligned} w_{ls} &= \mu_s + \gamma (a_l + v_l) - v_{ls} \\ &= \mu_s + \frac{\gamma}{\alpha_H} (\alpha_H a_l + \alpha_H v_l) - v_{ls}, \end{aligned} \tag{22}$$

where we have absorbed constants into μ_s and

$$\frac{\gamma}{\alpha_H} = \frac{1-\theta}{\alpha_H (1-\theta) + \alpha_M}. \tag{23}$$

According to (22), the log price of type-s skills consists of (a) a skill-specific component μ_s that is common to all locales; (b) a locale-specific effect reflecting the impact of total factor productivity (a_l) and the average valuation of local amenities (v_l) on the price of land; and (c) a "supply" shifter ($-v_{ls}$) that reflects the marginal cost of attracting and retaining type-s labor.

The fact that $\frac{\gamma}{\alpha_H} \neq 1$ is important. In country studies, where the dependent variable of interest is per-capita income or the average product of labor, a unit increase in TFP raises log productivity by exactly one unit, by definition. But the relation between the local TFP and local wages is not one-for-one but depends on the shares of labor and land in production as well as the share of land in consumption. How big is $\frac{\gamma}{\alpha_H}$? As a reasonable calibration, let the cost share of human capital be $\alpha_H = .60$, based on national income accounts. Then physical capital and land together account for $\alpha_K + \alpha_M = .40$ of cost. If land accounts for a quarter of this, then $\alpha_M = 0.1$. If housing accounts for $1/3$ of a typical household's expenditures,[13] and land is half of that, then $\frac{\gamma}{\alpha_H} = \frac{\frac{1}{6}}{\frac{1}{6} * \frac{6}{10} + \frac{1}{10}} = \frac{5}{6}$. So an event that raises local productivity by one percent would raise wages by a $5/6$th of that amount. Put the other way around, if econometric evidence indicates that a locale-specific productivity shifter raises wages by x percent, then it must raise local TFP by $1.2x$. This will prove important in interpreting econometric evidence on the magnitude of human capital externalities.

Equations (21) and (22) characterize a spatial equilibrium of land and labor markets. We can express the observed log wage of individual i as $w_{lsi} = w_{ls} + h_{si}$. Using (22):

$$w_{lsi} = \mu_s + \gamma a_l + (\gamma - 1)v_l + h_l + u_{lsi}, \tag{24}$$

where v_l and h_l are the within-locale means of v_{ls} and h_i, respectively.

Equation (24) is in the form of (12), and it is the foundation for our interpretation of the results of studies that attempt to estimate educational externalities from cross-sectional survey data. To put this in familiar form let μ_s represent the systematic component of a standard human-capital earnings model – including controls for an individual's years of schooling, experience and the like – the parameters and form of which need not concern us here. The issue at hand is how *market-wide* measures of human capital affect total factor productivity in l. To this end, let E_l denote human capital measures (average years of schooling, for example) for location l that may generate social returns through an impact on total factor productivity. To represent this, let TFP in l be

$$a_l = E_l \pi^E + a_l^0, \tag{25}$$

where π^E represents the parameters of interest – the magnitude of human capital externalities that are revealed through differences in land prices – and a_l^0 represents unobserved components of local TFP differences. Note that a_l^0 will not, in general, be

[13] Lucas and Rossi-Hansberg (2002) calibrate the share of land in consumption and production to equal 0.1 and 0.05 respectively. These parameter values imply $\gamma \approx 0.66$, slightly higher than the value used in our discussion here.

orthogonal to E_l; for example, with skill-biased technological change areas with greater TFP may demand greater amounts of skills. Using (25), individual log wages follow the regression model:

$$
\begin{aligned}
w_{lsi} &= \mu_s + E_l \beta^E + \varepsilon_l + u_{lsi}, \\
\varepsilon_l &\equiv \gamma a_l^0 + (\gamma - 1) v_l + h_l.
\end{aligned} \tag{26}
$$

As noted above $\beta^E = \gamma \pi^E$: the effect of E_l on *wages* is strictly smaller than its effect on *productivity*.

What can one learn about human capital externalities from econometric estimates of β^E? As (26) is essentially a comparison of wages across areas, the empirical question is whether areas with greater levels of E_l also have higher average wages and, if so, why? The unfortunate fact is that equilibrium outcomes in labor markets rarely provide clean "natural experiments," and the situation here is worse than usual. An area can be "human capital intensive" because of either supply or demand factors, and in either case the conditions for a consistent estimator $\hat{\beta}^E$ of β^E are unlikely to be satisfied. To be more precise, let Z_l denote instrumental variables that can be used to impute E_l. These instruments could represent either demand (Z_l^D) or supply (Z_l^S) forces. In the case of ordinary least squares $Z_l \equiv E_l$, but whatever the estimation method consistency requires $p \lim n^{-1}(Z'\varepsilon) = 0$ where n is the number of locales in the data. Applying this condition to the individual components of ε_l, the relevant orthogonality conditions are:

$$p \lim \left(\frac{1}{n} Z_l' a_l^0 \right) = 0, \tag{27a}$$

$$p \lim \left(\frac{1}{n} Z_l' h_l \right) = 0, \tag{27b}$$

$$p \lim \left(\frac{1}{n} Z_l' v_l \right) = 0. \tag{27c}$$

The issue is whether conditions (27a)–(27c) can be plausibly satisfied by some instrument Z_l that predicts E_l.

Condition (27a) requires that instruments for local human capital be orthogonal to productivity differences across locales. It isn't hard to see how this condition would fail. For example, suppose there are two skill groups – workers with a high school education ($s = 1$) and those with a college education ($s = 2$) – and that E_l is average years of schooling of workers in l. Assume that high school graduates are equally productive everywhere ($a_{l1} = a_1$) but college graduates are more productive in some locales than in others. If the elasticity of substitution between college and high school labor exceeds 1.0, as most studies suggest,[14] then areas with greater productivity of college graduates

[14] See, e.g., Katz and Murphy (1992) who estimate an elasticity of substitution between college and high school labor of about 1.4. Hamermesh (1986) provides a useful survey of such estimates.

will have greater TFP (a_l^0) *and* a larger share of college graduates in the local labor force, so E_l is higher. Then $p\lim n^{-1} E_l' a_l^0 > 0$: differences in relative factor demands as represented by a_l^0 are correlated with differences in average schooling levels, so $\hat{\beta}_{OLS}^E$ is biased up. Stated more broadly, if local human capital measures are correlated with local demands for human capital, then estimators for human capital externalities will be biased up – instruments Z_l must be uncorrelated with differences across locales in the *demands* for skill. Obvious candidates that would satisfy *this* condition are things that affect the supply of human capital to an area, Z_l^S, though we argue next that such "supply shifters" imply biases of their own.

Condition (27b) requires that *observable* measures (instruments) of local human capital be orthogonal to *unobservable* local human capital. For example, if E_l is average years of schooling the condition will fail if areas with more educated workers also have higher levels of other dimensions of skill, such as higher quality schooling or higher average ability of workers. It is difficult to think of instruments that would get around this – an instrument Z_l that is correlated with measured human capital in an area is highly likely to be correlated with unmeasured human capital too, for *both* supply and demand reasons. For example, if E_l in an area is high for demand (productivity) reasons, it is plausible that the demand for unmeasured components of skill will also be high. Conversely, if E_l is large because of supply factors – say area-specific investments in schooling or a climate that is unusually attractive to educated labor – those supply factors are likely to produce workers with more h_l as well. In both of these cases the estimator $\hat{\beta}^E$ is biased up, and the magnitude of local externalities is exaggerated. In Section 2.3 we will show that unmeasured components of human capital are indeed important in generating a large positive (statistical) relation between aggregate wages and education.

Condition (27c) relates measured local human capital to the valuation of local amenities for marginal workers, v_l. If the supply of skills to a locale is perfectly elastic then we can think of $v_l \equiv \sum \delta_s v_{ls}$ as an area-specific constant. In the more general case of rising supply price of skills to an area, factors Z_l^D that affect the demand for skill will be negatively related to v_l (demand shifts pull in workers who put lower value on local amenities), while factors Z_l^S that affect the supply of skill will be positively related to v_l (supply shifts reduce the cost of retaining the marginal worker). In either case condition (27c) is unlikely to be satisfied – if E_l varies across locales for demand reasons then an estimator of human capital externalities is biased up, and if E_l varies for supply reasons the estimator is biased down. And, sadly, it is hard to think of an instrument that represents neither demand nor supply differences, but which affects the observed stock of human capital in an area.

In the introduction we referred to a strand of the literature that emphasizes consumption externalities in education. Such externalities will also cause condition (27c) to fail and result in biases in the estimation of production externalities of education. If education produces positive consumption externalities, then individuals will be willing to pay for living in cities with high levels of education. Firms can only maintain their unit costs and remain competitive if wages decline. In equilibrium we therefore predict a positive relation between rents and average education and a negative relation between wages and average education due to consumption externalities in education. This represents a fundamental identification problem for disentangling external effects in production and consumption – a problem that is not addresses in the existing literature, nor in our contribution.[15]

2.2.2. *Empirical studies of schooling externalities*

With this framework as a guide, we turn to existing estimates of human capital externalities. As noted above, these have the common form of (12), which we repeat here:

$$w_{li} = X_{li}B + S_{li}\beta^P + \bar{S}_l\beta^E + \varepsilon_{li}. \tag{12}$$

The issue is whether the evidence from these studies provides evidence of $\beta^E > 0$.

Rauch (1993) Rauch's (1993) study is the first attempt to identify human capital externalities in cross-sectional data. An attractive feature of his study is that he estimates effects of productivity shifters on both wages and "land" rents, as implied by a spatial model. Using data on wages and housing rents (imputed for home owners) for individuals in 237 SMSAs, taken from the 1980 U.S. Census Public Use files, he estimates models of the form:

$$\begin{aligned} w_{li} &= X_i^w\beta^w + E_l\beta^{wE} + u_l^w + e_{li}^w, \\ r_{li} &= X_i^r\beta^r + E_l\beta^{rE} + u_l^r + e_{li}^r, \end{aligned} \tag{28}$$

where the left-side variables are the log wage of individual i in location $l(w_{li})$ and log monthly housing expenditures (r_{li}). His measure of E_l is average years of schooling for individuals in SMSA l, while the Xs are standard controls – including an individual's education, experience and so on – that are incidental to our discussion.

Rauch finds that an additional year of SMSA-average education raises wages (β^{wE}) by from 2.8 (se = .016) to 5.1 percent (se = .013). An additional year of average schooling raises "rents" by about 13 percent. An additional year of SMSA-average experience has a small positive impact on wages, but raises rents by about 1.5–2.0 percent. Rauch interprets these results as being consistent with an environment in which higher average human capital raises overall productivity, which is reflected in both wages and land values.

If there are human capital externalities, then the magnitudes of Rauch's wage estimates are not implausible. Yet the econometric conditions necessary to identify such externalities are unlikely to be satisfied by his regression procedure, which fails to ask

[15] The spatial equilibrium model presented here however suggests, that education should in the presence of consumption externalities raise housing prices and lower wages. The lack of good data on land prices makes testing this hypothesis difficult. The findings of Rauch (1993) that we review next are consistent with this hypothesis.

why some SMSAs have more educated workers than others. Specifically, these estimates are likely to overstate the size of local externalities, especially if human capital differences among locales are demand-driven.

Acemoglu and Angrist (2000) Acemoglu and Angrist's (A–A) implementation of the spatial equilibrium model uses Census data from 1950 to 1990. They define a "locale" as the state a person resides in, and they estimate models of the form:

$$w_{lsti} = \mu_{st} + \delta_l + \delta_t + E_{lt}\beta^E + u_{lt} + \varepsilon_i. \tag{29}$$

Similar to Rauch (1993) they measure local human capital by average years of schooling in the state-l labor force, so β^E measures the return to average schooling over and above the return to individual schooling, which is embedded in μ_{st}. For their main results they focus on white men between the ages of 40 and 49, and Census cross sections from 1960–1980.

A–A are concerned with two main sources of bias in estimating (29). First, demand-side changes that spur growth and raise wages may also raise the demand for schooling. Then E is positively correlated with the residual in (27). Second, "labor productivity and taste for schooling may change at the same time," which they assert may also generate an upward bias. To deal with these sources of bias, they instrument E with compulsory schooling laws that were in effect in an individual's state of birth at age 14. As it turns out, roughly 2/3 of persons schooled in a state stay there, so compulsory schooling laws (CSL) – which mandate that all individuals must complete a minimum number of years of schooling – raise average completed schooling in a state. Note that CSLs will raise average schooling by impacting the lower end of the schooling distribution – more students will be required to complete the 10th grade, for example, so this component of the stock of human capital must be an important source of externalities in order for the experiment to make sense. A–A argue that this instrument is "unlikely to be correlated with state-specific shocks since they are derived from laws passed 30 years before education and wages are recorded." CSLs then generate "exogenous variation," as they put it, so that conditions (27) are satisfied. Notice also that their model contains fixed effects for state of residence, δ_l, so identification comes from within-state time series variation in (imputed) average schooling and average wages.

It is true that the component of E that is predicted by CSLs is unlikely to be correlated with current "shocks," but it is not true that this component is econometrically exogenous in the sense of conditions (27). To see this, suppose that supplies of skill types were perfectly elastic, so v_l defined above is fixed. Then differences in CSLs would not predict E_l in a spatial model: if all workers are indifferent among areas and are freely mobile, then the place where human capital was *produced* bears no relation to where it *works*. If an area produced more educated workers then, absent mobility, the returns to education would fall. With mobility, educated labor would migrate elsewhere to equate the returns across areas, and with perfectly elastic supply a "shock" to the local number of, say, high school graduates would not affect the number of high school graduates who reside in the locale in the long run. But A–A find that CSLs *do* predict average education levels 30 years down the road, which means that labor supply is not perfectly elastic. Areas with more stringent CSLs have higher values of v_l (lower costs of retaining workers). In the notation used above, CSLs are supply side instruments, Z_l^S, that reduce the cost of local human capital. So the instrumental variables estimator $\hat{\beta}_{IV}^E$ is biased down because $p\lim(n^{-1}Z_l'v_l) > 0$.[16] Bluntly put, if CSLs "work" as instruments, they must be invalid.[17]

Viewed in this light, A–A's estimator might be viewed as a lower bound on human capital externalities. This lower bound is not that informative, however, as their IV estimates of β^E are very close to zero.[18] A–A estimate $\hat{\beta}_{IV}^E = .004$ in their most complete specification, compared to an OLS estimate of .073. A–A interpret their results as indicating that virtually all of the returns to education are private. This may be too pessimistic, for two reasons. First, their findings may indicate that increases in average education that are produced by CSLs reduce the cost of retaining an educated workforce – presumably part of the purpose of such laws – which will cause a downward bias in estimated externalities. Second, as noted above, CSLs increase average schooling by raising completion rates at lower schooling levels. If these generate small or no externalities – say because high school graduates are not the source of new ideas that drive growth – then the effects will be small in any case.

Moretti (2003) Moretti's (2003) analysis of spatial wage differentials is more ambitious than earlier studies. Using data from the 1980 and 1990 Censuses, he considers a variety of conceptual experiments that typically produce evidence of higher wages in locales with greater aggregate schooling, controlling for the private returns to schooling. He interprets this as evidence in favor of positive human capital externalities. His measure of externality-producing educational attainment is the percentage of the local labor force with college degrees, where "local" means a Metropolitan Statistical Area (MSA). Concerned about the correlation of this index with local demand shocks, he uses two instrumental variables: the age structure of cities calculated from Census data

[16] There can also be an upward bias. Condition (27b) requires that instruments be orthogonal to the average quality of human capital. If areas that invest in schooling be requiring more years of schooling also improve school qualities, then this condition may fail.

[17] In a recent paper Lochner and Moretti (2004) exploit compulsory schooling laws to estimate the effect of education on crime rates. They provide evidence that compulsory schooling laws "work" in raising education of different states by reporting F-values of close to 50 for whites [see Lochner and Moretti (2004)]. While this suggests that indeed compulsory schooling laws predict schooling, closer inspection also shows that the variation predicted is small. The degrees of freedom for the F-test are 3 and approximately 3,000,000 which implies that compulsory schooling laws explain at most 1/200 of a percent of the residual variance of schooling in the sample. This in turn implies for the study by Angrist and Acemoglu that even small violations of conditions (27a)–(27c) will result in large biases. We were able to confirm the finding that the variation in schooling explained by compulsory schooling and attendance laws is small using the census data that forms the basis of the empirical results in Section 2.3.

[18] A two standard error band for their preferred estimate is [−.053,.061], which includes some substantial positive effects, but also admits a substantial range of negative social returns.

(younger cohorts are more educated) and an indicator for the presence of a land-grant college in the MSA.

Whether these instruments are plausibly orthogonal to unobserved components of productivity and labor force quality is largely a matter of faith, but in our view their ability to satisfy conditions (27) are not apparent.[19] And the magnitudes of "externalities" they produce strike us as implausibly large. For example, Moretti reports that a *one percentage point* increase in the share of college graduates in an MSA raises average wages in that locale by about 1 percent, after controlling for the private returns to schooling and other factors. To put this in familiar units, think of its implications for the Macro-Mincer return to schooling. In 1990 the average share of college graduates in MSAs was about .20 [Moretti (2003, Table1)]. For the sake of argument, assume that average years of schooling in the other 80 percent of the workforce is 12 (they are high school graduates, on average). Then it takes a change in the college share of .25 to increase average years of schooling by 1 year. Further, we know that the effect of local human capital externalities on wages is smaller than the external impact on productivity – that is, $\gamma < 1$ in our previous notation. Our back-of-the envelope calculations suggested $\gamma \approx 5/6$, so Moretti's estimates imply a Macro-Mincer impact of a year of average schooling on average productivity on the order of .30. This is close to *four times* the Micro-Mincer private return to schooling. It would be nice if this were true – then education is surely the path to economic development. But we doubt it.

2.3. *Conclusion: What have we learned from micro-data?*

Estimates of productivity externalities based on augmented Micro-Mincer earnings regressions range from zero (Acemoglu and Angrist) to not-so-implausible (Rauch) to simply huge (Moretti). Combined with Macro-Mincer estimates from the growth literature, we think its fair say that there is little evidence in favor of *negative* external returns to education. This finding alone is useful, as it casts doubt on earlier studies [e.g., Pritchett (2001), Benhabib and Spiegel (1994)] that argued for small or even zero aggregate returns to schooling. Yet the evidence for positive external returns is weak, at best, and founded on dubious identifying assumptions. The next section attempts to

[19] All three of (27a)–(27c) may fail. For example, the age structure is unlikely to be orthogonal to productivity differences across locales, especially as younger families are more geographically mobile. Then serial correlation in productivity growth will cause (27a) to fail even in differenced data. Further, areas with more young people, who tend to be more educated, may also have higher h when more able quality workers congregate due to complementarities, or when there are cohort effects in the quality of human capital and schooling, causing (27b) to fail. Moretti attempts to deal with the latter effects by controlling for individual effects within cities in NLSY data, but these estimates do not employ the instruments mentioned in the text. Finally, as in Acemoglu and Angrist (2000), the fact that these instruments predict education at all implies that supplies are not perfectly elastic across locales, so (27c) is unlikely to hold. In a more recent paper Moretti (2004) attempts to directly estimate firms productivity linking data from the Census of Manufacturing with the Census of Population. However, any of the sources of bias summarized in Equation (27c) survive since the spatial mobility of firms ensures that wage differences have to correspond to difference in productivity by firms.

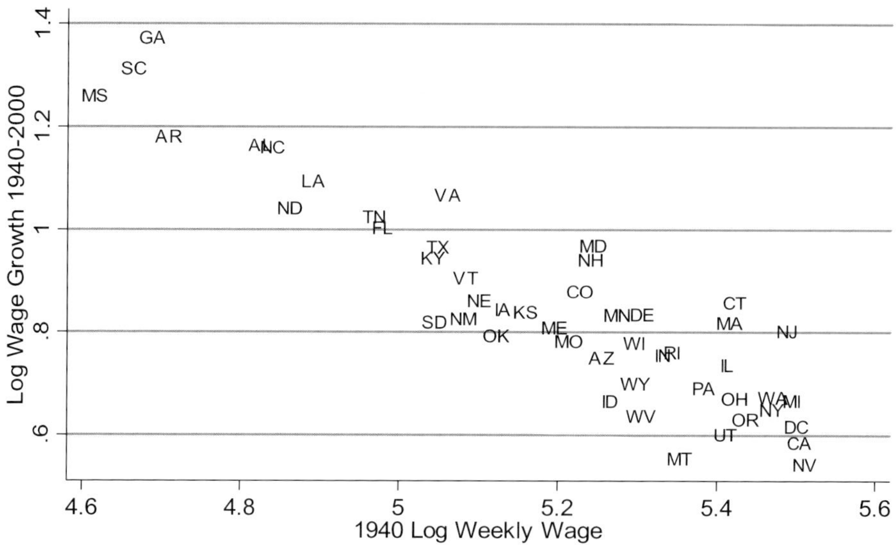

Figure 1a. Level and growth of wages. Log weekly wages, 1940–2000.

cast new light on these issues by combining the two approaches: we study the growth of wages and productivity in U.S. states between 1940 and 2000, using the spatial model of Section 3.2 as a framework.

2.4. Human capital and growth revisited: American States, 1940–2000

This section uses individual level data from the 1940–2000 U.S. Censuses to study wage and productivity growth in American states. Our framework for this exercise is the model of spatial equilibrium outlined in Section 3.2. In differenced form, this model can be viewed as a standard model of economic growth augmented by mobility decisions that connect geographically disparate markets.

A rough look at the data suggests a (perhaps too) strong relationship between growth in educational attainment and growth in wages. Figures 1a–b graph 1940–2000 growth in state averages of log wages and years of schooling of employed individuals against the initial, 1940, values of these variables. There is no doubt that low-wage (mainly Southern) states led the way in terms of growth, and that states with growing educational attainment also experienced the greatest growth of wages (Figure 1c). A simple regression of 60-year wage growth on growth in schooling yields a coefficient of 0.21 ($t = 8.4$) per year of schooling. This is a big number. Either growth in average years of schooling is correlated with other determinants of productivity or the external benefits of schooling are very large.

We use the model summarized by Equation (24) to guide our analysis. In addition to the usual earnings and schooling measures recorded in micro-data, Census files record

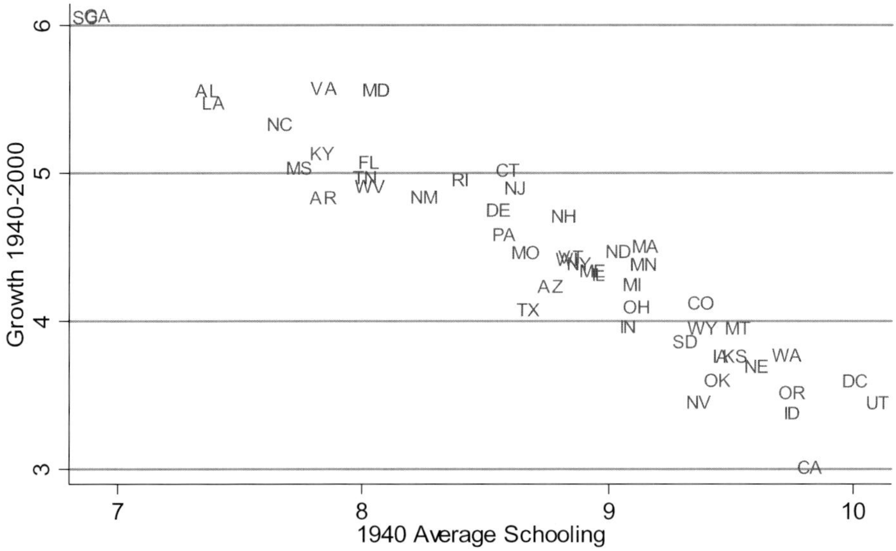

Figure 1b. Level and growth of schooling. Average years, 1940–2000.

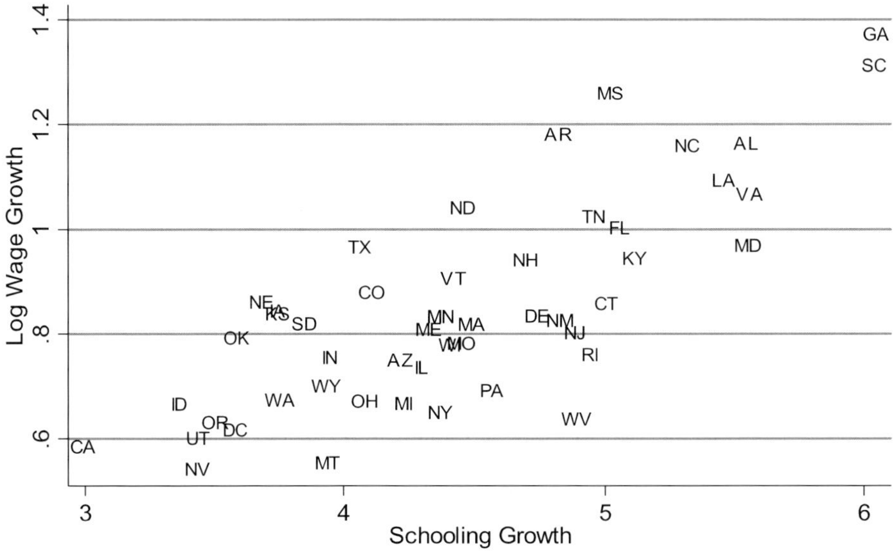

Figure 1c. Growth in wages and schooling. Log weekly wages and average years of schooling, 1940–2000.

each respondent's state of birth. To the extent that area-specific differences in schooling quality and other environmental factors experienced while young affect adult productivity, this information provides additional leverage for assessing the average "quality" of human capital in local labor markets. Specifically, augmenting (26) we express the (log) wage of individual i in market l at time t as:

$$w_{it} = X_{it}\beta_t + T_{lt} + \delta_{bc} + u_{it}, \tag{30a}$$

$$T_{lt} = E_{lt}\beta^E + \gamma a_{lt}^0 + (\gamma - 1)v_{lt} + h_{lt}. \tag{30b}$$

Model (30a) expresses wages in terms of observable human capital controls X_{it} (education and potential experience), state-specific productivity T_{lt}, and a fixed-over-time effect of an individual's birth-state (b) and birth-cohort (c), δ_{bc}. In turn, state-specific productivity is determined by human capital externalities, unobserved demand (a_{lt}^0) and supply (v_{lt}) conditions and the unobserved quality of state-l workers, h_{lt}.

We estimate (30a) by pooling the data over Census years. We adopt an unrestrictive form for the component $X_{it}\beta_t$, with a set of indicators for completed schooling and 5-year intervals of potential experience. We estimate state-specific productivity with fixed effects for each of the 48 contiguous states, plus the District of Columbia, in each year. The birthstate/cohort "quality" effects δ_{bc} are estimated from birthstate-by-cohort indicators, where we define birth cohorts by 10 year intervals; e.g., persons born in Michigan between 1920 and 1930. As experience, year and cohort effects are not separately identified, we impose the restriction

$$\sum_b \delta_{bc} = 0 \tag{31}$$

so that the δ_{bc} measure the within-cohort *relative* "quality" of persons born in state b.

We estimate (30a) on 7 cross-sections (1940–2000) of Census data. This yields estimates of local productivity differences $\widehat{T}_{lt}$ and birthstate-cohort effects $\hat{\delta}_{bc}$, along with the usual cross-sectional returns to schooling and experience $\hat{\beta}_t$. Now take means by state and year, and linearize the aggregate returns to schooling and experience. Differencing the data between Census years yields a growth model:

$$\Delta w_{lt} = A_{0t} + \Delta \text{Educ}_{lt} A_1 + \Delta \text{Exp}_{lt} A_2 + \Delta T_{lt} + \Delta\bar{\delta}_{lt} + e_{lt}. \tag{32}$$

The parameter A_1 measures the aggregate return to schooling: conditional on other factors that determine local wages, by how much does an additional year of *average* schooling in a state raise the average log wage in that state? Note that there is no necessary relation between this growth-based estimate of the impact of schooling on average log wages and the "private" return that is typically estimated from cross-sectional data. For example, the extreme form of signaling models of education implies $A_1 = 0$ – education does not raise aggregate productivity – even if education commands a positive cross-sectional return.

Estimates of model (32) for various growth intervals are shown in Table 4. The estimates in column 1 under each growth interval are analogous to the country-based

Table 4
Wage growth in U.S. States: 1940–2000[a]

	10 year growth			20 year growth[b]			30 year growth[c]			60 year growth	
	(1)	(2)	(3)	(1)	(2)	(3)	(1)	(2)	(3)	(1)	(2)
ΔEduc_{lt}	0.117	0.072	0.067	0.166	0.076	0.068	0.187	0.083	0.075	0.203	0.097
	(0.018)	(0.006)	(0.007)	(0.022)	(0.006)	(0.009)	(0.021)	(0.006)	(0.011)	(0.023)	(0.006)
ΔExp_{lt}	−0.006	0.017	0.017	0.008	0.019	0.018	0.029	0.019	0.020	0.077	0.022
	(0.005)	(0.002)	(0.002)	(0.008)	(0.002)	(0.002)	(0.011)	(0.004)	(0.004)	(0.021)	(0.005)
ΔT_{lt}		1.01	1.01		1.03	1.04		1.04	1.10		1.01
		(0.020)	(0.022)		(0.021)	(0.028)		(0.031)	(0.052)		(0.032)
$\Delta\bar{\delta}_{lt}$		1.15	1.39		1.10	1.72		1.02	1.74		0.780
		(0.141)	(0.282)		(0.134)	(0.256)		(0.135)	(0.281)		(0.163)
State effects	No	No	Yes	No	No	Yes	No	No	Yes	No	No
R^2	0.887	0.990	0.991	0.941	0.997	0.998	0.968	0.998	0.999	0.693	0.993

$\Delta w_{lt} = A_{0t} + \Delta\text{Educ}_{lt} A_1 + \Delta\text{Exp}_{lt} A_2 + \Delta T_{lt} A_3 + \Delta\bar{\delta}_{lt} A_4 + e_{lt}$.
Standard errors are estimated taking into account the generated regressor problem arising because the independent variable $\Delta\delta$ is estimated in the first step regression. See Murphy and Topel (1985).
[a]Estimated using state averages for indicated variables from U.S. Census files, 1940–2000. All models contain year effects.
[b]20-year growth intervals are 1940–60, 1960–80, and 1980–2000.
[c]30-year growth intervals are 1940–70, 1970–2000.

growth models of Table 2 above, though they are based on average log wages rather than log income per capita. columns 2 condition on estimates of ΔT_{lt} and $\Delta\bar{\delta}_{lt}$ from the cross-section model (30a). Given the setup of the model, we expect $A_3 = 1$ and $A_4 = 1$: growth in TFP or in the average quality of workers raises wages proportionally. As these regressions must pass through the means of the data, estimates of A_1 and A_2 reproduce the average cross sectional Micro-Mincer returns to schooling and experience. As in the country-based results the estimated social returns to schooling in columns 1 exceed the typical private return, and they are larger the longer is the growth interval used for estimation. For example, at 30-year intervals the Macro-Mincer return to an additional year of average schooling is .187, which is more than double the corresponding Micro-Mincer estimate.

It isn't plausible that the estimated social returns to schooling in Table 4 are merely redistributive, as implied by the pure form of signaling models. The wage bill, and hence productivity, must rise with the average educational attainment of the workforce in order to generate these results. The evidence in columns 1 shows that aggregate earnings increase in aggregate education. Comparison with columns 2 and 3 shows that aggregate earnings increase by more with education than private returns. In other words, Table 4 indicates that additional education really does raise individual and aggregate productivities, quite apart from issues of externalities. We have more to say on the plausibility of signaling as an explanation for the private returns to schooling in Section 3.

Table 5
Regression estimates of the effect of average state years of schooling on total factor productivity, U.S. States, 1940–2000

	1940	1950	1960	1970	1980	1990	2000	Pooled 1940–2000	
1. Levels	0.071	0.086	0.094	0.059	0.071	0.093	0.093	0.079[a]	0.092[a]
	(0.026)	(0.019)	(0.022)	(0.026)	(0.029)	(0.046)	(0.049)	(0.010)	(0.010)
2. Growth[a]									
10 years	−0.053	0.084	0.087	−0.030	0.161	0.015	–	0.046[b]	0.029[b]
	(0.048)	(0.021)	(0.036)	(0.042)	(0.061)	(0.030)		(0.017)	(0.021)
20 years	0.041	0.115	0.086	0.098	0.086	–	–	0.067[c]	0.050[c]
	(0.034)	(0.028)	(0.026)	(0.023)	(0.037)			(0.019)	(0.031)
30 years	0.077	0.092	0.149	0.059	–	–	–	0.067[d]	0.034[d]
	(0.032)	(0.020)	(0.022)	(0.017)				(0.018)	(0.033)
40 years	0.057	0.140	0.107	–	–	–	–	–	–
	(0.058)	(0.020)	(0.019)						
50 years	0.100	0.117	–	–	–	–	–	–	–
	(0.021)	(0.017)							
60 years	0.081	–	–	–	–	–	–	–	–
	(0.021)								
State fixed effects	no	no	no	no	no	no	no	no	yes

[a]All pooled models contain fixed year effects.

[b]Pooled estimates of 10 year growth using 1940–50, 1950–60, . . . , 1990–2000.

[c]Pooled estimates of 20 year growth using 1940–60, 1960–80, 1980–2000.

[d]Pooled estimates of 30 year growth using 1940–70, 1970–2000.

The evidence in Table 4 indicates that education is an important contributor to economic growth, with social returns that are at least the equal of private ones. But they do not address the externality issue, which is that increases in aggregate schooling raise total factor productivity. In terms of the model, the issue is whether $\beta^E > 0$ in (30b).

Table 5 shows least squares estimates of β^E based on (30b) from both levels and growth regressions. The cross-sectional estimates in row 1 are consistent with previous findings of Rauch (1993), Acemoglu and Angrist (2000) and Moretti (2003, 2004), all of whom find a positive impact of average schooling on local wages, after controlling for private returns. As $\beta^E = \gamma\pi^E$, the pooled estimate of 7.9 percent implies a huge impact of education on TFP: if we calibrate $\frac{\gamma}{1-\alpha} = 5/6$ then the external impact of an additional year of average schooling is to raise local productivity by about 10 percent. Estimates at various growth intervals also produce large effects; at 20 years the impact of an additional year of schooling on T_l is .068 and at 60 years it is .081, which also implies an external impact on TFP of about 10 percent.

As in the papers Acemoglu and Angrist (2000) and Moretti (2003, 2004) the issue is whether these effects are caused by externalities ($\beta^E > 0$) or by other omitted factors (a^0, v, and h in our notation) that are correlated with average years of schooling.

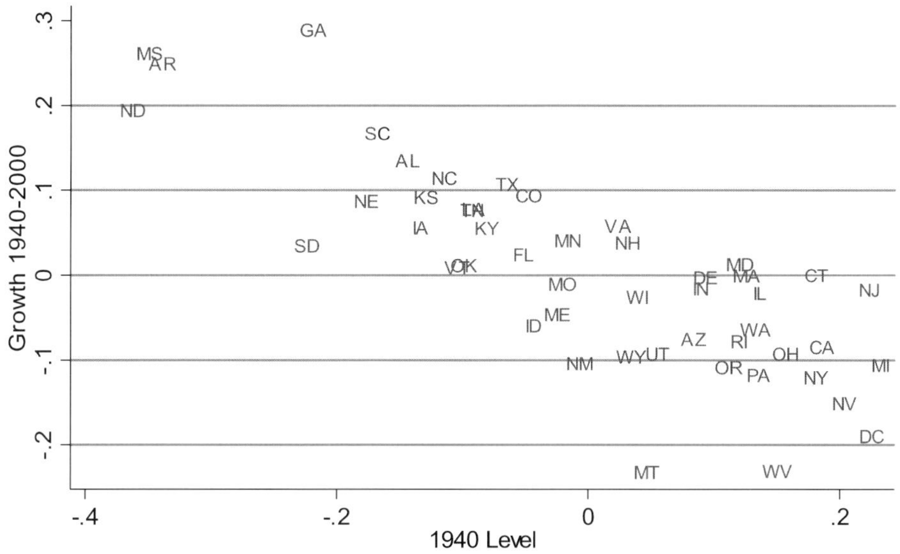

Figure 2a. Level and growth of TFP. Estimated state specific productivity, 1940–2000.

Previous authors have sought consistent estimators of β^E via instrumental variables techniques, but our view (see above) is that the validity of any instrument that successfully predicts education is dubious at best. So we take an alternative approach. Instead of seeking exogenous variation via an instrument, we seek to measure factors that are omitted from the simple regression relationship between T_l and average years of schooling. We focus on labor force quality, h_l.

Our candidate is $\bar{\delta}_l$ which is a labor force weighted average of estimated birthstate-cohort effects, δ_{bc}, for individuals who work in state l. As Equation (30a) includes state fixed effects for each Census year, estimates of δ_{bc} are formed from within-state comparisons of wages for people who were born in different states. These comparisons are uncontaminated by externalities, which (according to the theory) affect all wages in a locale by the same proportional amount. Then $\bar{\delta}_l$ is a measure of labor force quality in l, which we can take as a measure or correlate of h_l in (30b). In terms of growth, δ_{bc} is fixed over time for a given birthstate-cohort pair, so *changes* in $\bar{\delta}_l$ are generated by changes in the labor force shares of different cohorts.

Figures 2a and 2b show the relationships between long run (1940–2000) growth and 1940 levels for T_l and $\bar{\delta}_l$. As with wages and education, estimates of T_l and $\bar{\delta}_l$ converge in the sense that states with low values of T_l (quality) in 1940 experienced the greatest productivity (quality) growth.

Inspection of the figures reveals that rapid growth on both fronts occurred in Southern states, where relative wages and schooling also grew. Figure 2c shows that states with growing educational attainment also had greater growth in $\bar{\delta}_l$, and Figure 2d demonstrates a similar relationship between productivity growth and growth of $\bar{\delta}_l$.

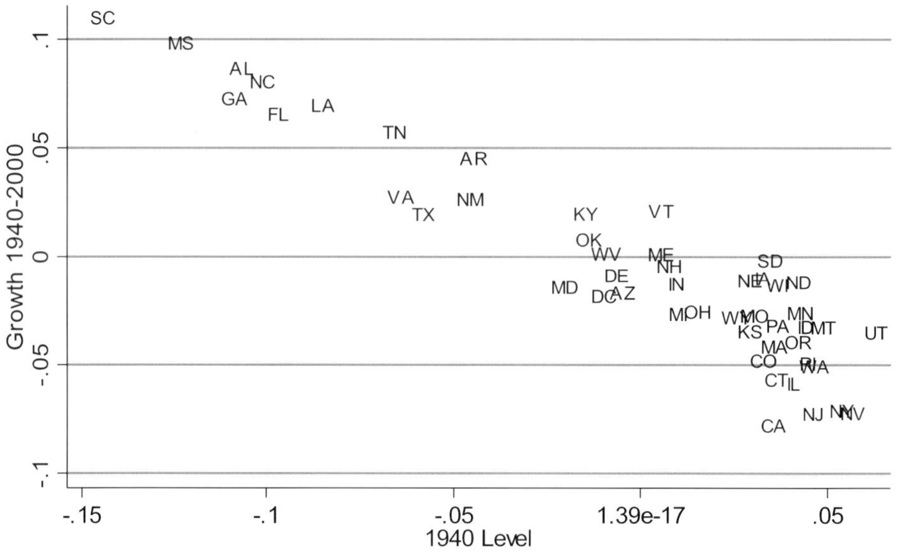

Figure 2b. Level and growth of unobserved skills. Estimated unobserved talents, 1940–2000.

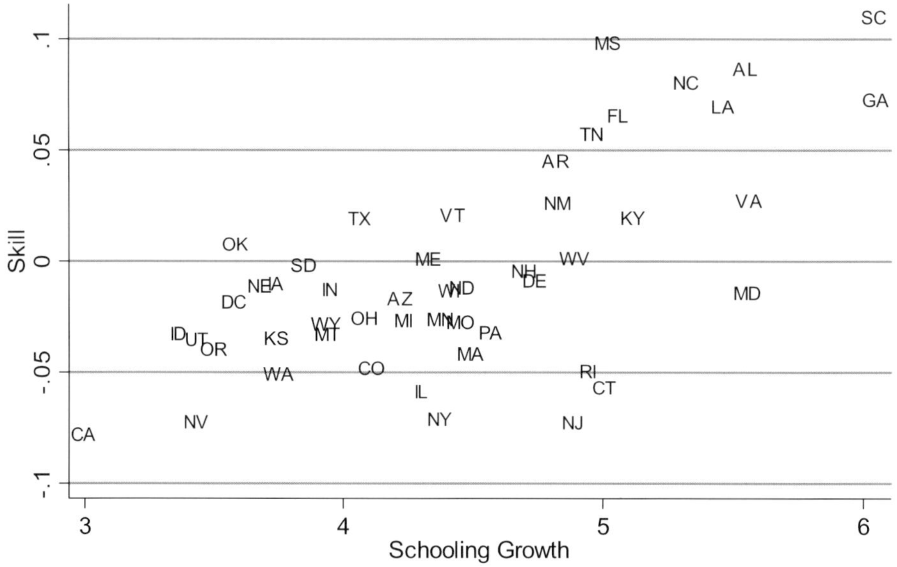

Figure 2c. Growth in skills and schooling. Growth in estimated skills and mean years of schooling, 1940–2000.

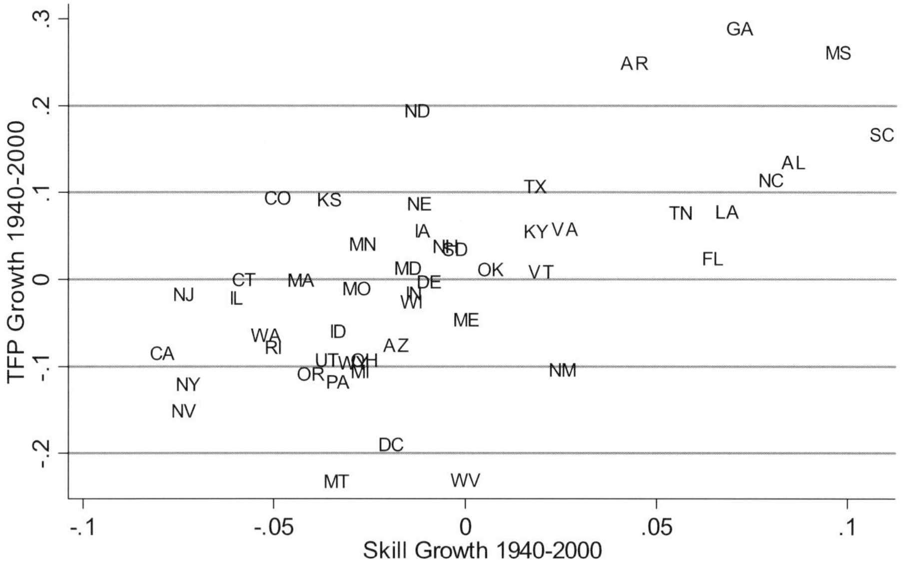

Figure 2d. Growth in skills and local TFP. Growth in estimated skills and state specific productivity, 1940–2000.

These data indicate that states with rapidly growing educational attainment, which experienced growing productivity, also experienced an upgrading in the measured *quality* of their labor forces. As we indicated above, if education and labor force quality go hand-in-hand, a simple regression of changes in productivity on changes in education may "find" externalities where none exist.

How big might the bias be? Table 6 makes some headway on this question by simply adding $\Delta\bar{\delta}_l$ to the growth models of Table 5. For each growth interval we reproduce in column 1 the corresponding growth estimate from Table 5. All of these estimates of β^E are numerically large, with the biggest effects for the longest growth intervals. For example, the 60 year estimate is .081, suggesting that an additional year of education raises T_l by 8.1 percent. Adding changes in "unobserved" labor force quality $\Delta\bar{\delta}_l$ in columns 2 reduces the impact of education in each case. For the longest (60 year) interval, the point estimate falls from .081 to .021. None of the column 2 estimates are significantly different from zero by conventional standards.

The evidence in Table 6 does not demonstrate that externalities are unimportant. For example, the 20-year growth point estimate of .04 implies an external impact on productivity of about .05, which rivals conventional estimates of the private return to schooling. But this evidence surely raises doubts about the importance of externalities, estimates of which are surely overstated by least squares. The evidence is that states with growing productivity and educational attainment also attracted or produced "better" workers, and even a simple measure of labor force quality eliminates up to three-fourths of the al-

Table 6
Education and productivity growth: U.S. States 1940–2000[a]

	10 year growth		20 year growth[b]		30 year growth[c]		60 year growth	
ΔEduc	0.046	0.026	0.068	0.040	0.067	0.036	0.081	0.023
	(0.017)	(0.018)	(0.019)	(0.021)	(0.017)	(0.020)	(0.021)	(0.024)
$\Delta\bar{\delta}_l$		1.23		1.08		1.01		1.35
		(0.44)		(0.40)		(0.34)		(0.38)
R^2	0.894	0.897	0.952	0.954	0.978	0.980	0.248	0.415

$\Delta T_{lt} = B_{0t} + \Delta \text{Educ}_{lt} B_1 + \Delta\bar{\delta}_{lt} B_2 + e_{lt}$.
Standard errors are estimated taking into account the generated regressor problem arising because the independent variable $\Delta\delta$ is estimated in the first step regression. See Murphy and Topel (1985).
[a]See notes to Table 5.
[b]20-year growth intervals are 1940–60, 1960–90, and 1980–2000.
[c]30-year growth intervals are 1940–70 and 1970–2000.

leged relation between education and TFP. In our view, the data do not provide a strong reason to believe in the importance of productive externalities from schooling.

3. Job market signaling and the social value of schooling

In the standard Human Capital model (hereafter HC) without externalities the private returns to schooling equal the social returns. The Job Market Signaling (JMS) model provides a competing explanation for the observed private returns to schooling. JMS – in contrast to HC – generates a wedge between private returns and social returns to schooling, as individual returns from signaling do not fully translate into productivity increases at the aggregate level.

In this section we review the available empirical evidence on the JMS and HC models, mindful of the need not only to test, but also to quantify the relative importance of each. As Wolpin (1977) puts it: "[T]he real issue concerns not the mere existence of one or the other effect, but the extent to which schooling performs each of these roles." We come to the conclusion that the available empirical evidence is insufficient to achieve either goal. There are few convincing tests of JMS and even less evidence that allows us to quantify the contribution of HC relative to JMS. This leads us to provide some new evidence of our own in Section 3.3.1.

In Section 2.3 we presented evidence of a large positive relation of aggregate wages and education between 1940–2000 from US Census data (Tables 4–6) and from cross-national studies [Tables 1, 2 from Topel (1999)]. Most formulations of JMS generate private returns in excess of the social returns to schooling. The fact that observed Macro-Mincer returns are as large as or larger than the Micro-Mincer returns is prima facie evidence against JMS. The empirical findings reviewed in Section 2 therefore constitute important evidence against a signaling explanation of the cross-sectional relation

Table 7
The basic structure of the job market signaling model

Individual type	Marginal product for schooling = 0 and 1	Costs of schooling level = 1
I	(1, 1)	y
II	(2, 2)	$y/2$

between wages and education. At the very least it raises the standard of empirical proof required to take JMS seriously.

The JMS model traces its roots to Spence (1973), who developed an equilibrium model of the labor market with positive individual returns to schooling absent any productivity effects of schooling. Testing JMS against HC is complicated by the fact that both rely on similar assumptions regarding individuals' and firms' objectives. This means that JMS and HC are observationally equivalent with regard to data generated within a single labor market and time-period.

JMS relies on 3 crucial assumptions:

1. Individuals have private information on their productive types.
2. Costs of schooling and productivity of individuals are negatively related.
3. Contracts cannot be written conditional on information that is initially private.

Any model with incomplete information requires a restriction on how agents form expectations. Spence's asymmetric information setup owes its prominence in the literature to the fact that both firm and individual expectations and decisions are fully rational. Agents' expectations are based on the mathematical distributions that pertain in equilibrium (macro-economists would say that agents hold rational expectations). Firms' expectations of unobserved characteristics of individuals are consistent with the stochastic relation between observed and unobserved characteristics obtained in equilibrium. Many of the difficulties[20] of testing JMS can be traced to this consistency requirement.

Spence's original formulation allows schooling to be continuous. This raises the possibility of multiple separating equilibria, each with a different set of employer beliefs about the relation between schooling and unobserved productivity. We assume instead that there are only 2 possible levels of schooling: $s = 0$ or $s = 1$ and two types of individuals (I, II). In this case there is a unique separating equilibrium. The basic structure of the model is summarized in Table 7. The two-dimensional vectors in the second columns of Tables 7 (and 8) describe the productivity associated with each schooling choice. The first entry denotes the productivity of the individual of type I or II given $s = 0$ and the second if schooling is $s = 1$. Type II is more skilled since his productivity exceeds type I irrespective of schooling choice.

[20] The discussion concerning the difficulties of testing JMS against the Human Capital Model summarized in Tables 7–9 benefited tremendously from a conversation with Robert Willis.

Table 8
A human capital model

Individual type	Marginal product for schooling = 0 and 1	Costs of schooling level = 1
I	$(1, 1 + r)$	y
II	$(2/(1 + r), 2)$	$y/2$

Table 9
Data generated by the signaling and the human capital model

Type/school	0	1
I	$(1, 1)$	$(1, 1 + r)$
II	$\left(2, \frac{2}{1+r}\right)$	$(2, 2)$

In the pure signaling model schooling does not raise the productivity of either type. Individuals' productive types are not directly observed and the costs of schooling decline with productivity. Firms eventually learn the true productivity of individuals, but it is not possible to write enforceable contracts contingent on this information. We are interested in the separating equilibrium where individuals' types are revealed by their choice of schooling – i.e. where type I workers choose $s = 0$ and type II workers choose $s = 1$. Both types are paid their productivity, which is revealed by their choice of schooling. Condition (33) ensures existence of a separating equilibrium where higher ability individuals attend school and less able individuals do not.[21]

$$1 < y < 2. \tag{33}$$

Compare this signaling model to a human capital model with a similar cost condition. Assume again that there are 2 types of individuals and 2 levels of schooling. Assume that schooling raises productivity by r percent. The productivity of a type I with no schooling is 1 and that of type II with no schooling is $2/(1 + r)$. Costs are the same as in Table 7. Table 8 lists the fundamentals of this model.

Schooling is sufficiently expensive to deter type I, but not expensive enough to also deter type II:

$$r < y < 4r/(1 + r). \tag{34}$$

Table 9 shows the outcomes for individuals of different types in the JMS and HC models. The first entry of each row in the table corresponds to the signaling model and the second to the human capital model.

[21] This discussion is extremely simplified. See Riley (2001) for a more detailed discussion of the theoretical considerations, in particular the problem of the existence and the uniqueness of equilibria that arise in more complex models.

The observed (equilibrium) data are on the diagonal. To distinguish JMS from HC using data on schooling and wages requires access to the off-diagonal cells, which are not observed in equilibrium. The decentralizing role of the price mechanism implies that equilibrium models of job market signaling and human capital are observationally equivalent. Maximizing individuals do not consider the impact of schooling on productivity, but instead consider only the relation between wages and schooling itself. Likewise firms do not inquire about the mechanisms generating productivity differences across schooling levels, but instead are interested only in the relation between individual productivities and what must be paid for them. This simple problem makes testing JMS against the Human Capital model a difficult endeavor, a fact acknowledged by Lang and Kropp (1986): "[M]any members of the profession maintain (at least privately) that these hypotheses cannot be tested against each other and that the debate must therefore by relegated to the realm of ideology."

An early paper illustrates the difficulties of testing the JMS-model against the HC-model. Layard and Psacharopoulos (1974) mistakenly argue that JMS implies that the returns to schooling decline with experience as employers learn about individuals' characteristics. This is not a prediction of the JMS model. The assumption that agents' beliefs are rational implies that any wage-schooling gradient reflects real productivity differences. These productivity differences will persist across the life-cycle unless we make additional assumptions external to the JMS-model.

Layard and Psacharopoulos (1974) also propose that JMS predicts excess returns for years of schooling that correspond to degrees, such as 16 for college graduates – diplomas carry special weight in transferring information. They did not observe diploma effects and rejected JMS on that basis. Subsequent empirical work has consistently demonstrated the existence of diploma effects in a variety of countries and time-periods [Hungerford and Solon (1987), Belman and Heywood (1991), Jaeger and Page (1996), Frazis (2002)], which some interpret as evidence against the HC model and in favor of JMS [Frazis (2002)]. We disagree. Instead we interpret diploma effects as evidence that individuals resolve uncertainty about their individual returns to schooling while still in school. Whether these returns are generated by a HC or a JMS model is immaterial. This argument was first made (informally) by Chiswick (1973) and relies on modeling the drop-out decision directly. Then diploma effects are consistent both with both the HC and JMS models.

We next consider 2 papers [Lang and Kropp (1986), Bedard (2001)] motivated by the difficulties in testing the JMS against the HC-model. These papers study differences in equilibrium outcomes across segmented labor markets that differ in the structure of their education system. They relate data on differences in regional education systems to data on the variation in the equilibrium distribution of schooling in these regions. The JMS and the HC model differ in their prediction of how a change in the cost structure of education affects the equilibrium distribution of schooling. Roughly speaking, the idea is that agents' decisions in the HC-model are affected by only their own costs of schooling. Variation in the costs of schooling faced by type-j individuals does not affect outcomes for type-k individuals. This contrasts with JMS where the returns to schooling are determined by the equilibrium distribution of ability types across schooling levels. Then the returns to schooling depend on the schooling decisions of other agents, and variation in the costs of schooling for some agents affect the schooling decisions of *all* agents. If we can identify such variation for some (but not all) schooling levels, then the HC-model predicts that only those agents directly affected will change their schooling decisions. The JMS-model instead predicts that such variation in the costs of schooling will affect the schooling decisions of all agents in the market in a predictable manner. Lang and Kropp (1986) and Bedard (2001) do provide some support for the JMS-model, though they cannot provide guidance on the magnitude of JMS and HC motives.

Finally we consider empirical approaches to testing JMS that exploit the assumption that firms ultimately learn about individuals' productive types. An early body of work [Wolpin (1977), Riley (1979), Albrecht (1981)] examines the implications of differences in the speed with which employers learn across occupations or industries. The evidence on JMS from this literature is mixed. Riley (1979) finds evidence in favor of the signaling model with employer learning, Wolpin (1977) and Albrecht (1981) are not supportive. We present new evidence from more recent data that rejects Riley's predictions.

More recently the literature on statistical discrimination and employer learning assumes that the data contain a measure of individual productivity that is hard to observe for firms [Foster and Rosenzweig (1994), Farber and Gibbons (1996), Altonji and Pierret (2001), Galindo-Rueda (2003), Lange (2006)]. This assumption generates testable predictions for the interaction between schooling and ability with experience in earning regressions. The literature on employer learning can be understood as a test of the core assumption of JMS that firms statistically discriminate on the basis of schooling. Altonji and Pierret (1997) and Lange (2006) point out that the speed with which employers learn ultimately limits the contribution of JMS to the private returns to schooling. Lange (2006) estimates this speed to be rapid and therefore argues that JMS can only explain a small fraction of the private gains from schooling, even if we maintain the assumptions of the employer learning literature.[22]

3.1. Diploma effects

The existence of diploma effects ranks among the most persistent empirical findings in labor economics. Completion of degree years is associated with an increase in wages above that observed for other years, and the distribution of completed years of schooling in the population exhibits spikes at those years. Table 10 demonstrates these 2 facts using the 1998 wave of the NLSY for white males.

The returns to high school (12th grade) and college (16th grade) graduation are 16% and 38% respectively. These 2 years also stand out in the distribution of schooling.

[22] Lange (2004) also points out that the same empirical patterns emphasized in the Employer Learning model can be generated by post-schooling investment behavior and provides evidence in favor of this explanation.

Table 10
Diploma effects in the distribution of and the returns to schooling[a]

Highest grade completed[b]	Frequency	Return to grade
⩽8	2.63%	Omit
9	2.28%	−3.89% (11.77%)
10	2.28%	+14.51% (11.78%)
11	2.28%	7.39% (11.80%)
12	42.32%	+16.18% (8.54%)
13	7.47%	+20.11% (9.59%)
14	8,85%	−0.23% (9.51%)
15	3.25%	−2.07% (11.16%)
16	16.74%	+37.51% (9.28%)
17	3.67%	−19.15% (11.06%)
18+	8.23%	+34.61% (11.62%)
Observations	1,446	1,446

Obtained from a regression of log(wage) on schooling and cubic in experience.
[a]The sample consists of white males in NLSY (year = 1999).
[b]Schooling is bottom coded at 8 years and top-coded at 18 years.

42.45% of the male population graduate from high school but do not continue further in their education. 16.74% terminate their education after 16 years. This compares with less than 9% of the population for any other year of schooling.

Diploma effects are often [Layard and Psacharopoulos (1974), Jaeger and Page (1996), Frazis (2002), Habermalz (2004), Park (1994)] presented as evidence for screening theories of schooling. We disagree. Instead we view diploma effects as evidence that individuals face uncertainty about their individual returns to schooling and that this uncertainty is revealed as individuals acquire schooling. Those least capable to profit from schooling drop out before the completion of degree years. Those graduating exhibit larger returns than those who dropped out at lower levels of schooling. This reasoning was informally developed by Chiswick (1973).[23] Since then, a number of authors

[23] Altonji (1993) analyzes the effect of uncertainty about completion of degrees on observed returns to schooling in a model incorporating choice of college major and learning about tastes and ability while in school. He as well as Heckman, Lochner and Todd (2003) show that uncertainty associated with the returns

[Altonji (1993), Heckman, Lochner and Todd (2003), Keane and Wolpin (1997)] examined different aspects of sequential schooling choice under uncertainty. We build a simple model in this spirit with the intention to show how individual's schooling decisions can generate (large) diploma effects if individuals learn about their returns while in school.

Suppose that individuals can choose 3 levels of schooling. They might decide not to enter into a degree program ($S = 0$), to enroll but drop out after 1 period ($S = 1$) or to complete the degree program, which takes 2 periods ($S = 2$). The returns to schooling depend on ability, β, which is either high (β_H) or low (β_L). At $t = 0$ an individual knows the probability p of being high ability. By attending school the agent discovers at the end of period 1 the true value of β. He then needs to decide whether or not to complete the program. Individual life-times are infinite and all individuals start with the same initial level of human capital H_0. All individuals also have the same discount rate r. The present discounted value of choosing $S = 0$ is then

$$V(S = 0, t = 1) = \frac{H_0}{r}. \tag{35}$$

An individual who attends school for 1 period and has productivity $\beta_i > 1, i = L, H$, has a present discounted value (at $S = 1$) of income given by

$$V(S = 1, \beta_i; t = 1) = \frac{\beta_i H_0}{r}, \quad i \in \{L, H\}. \tag{36}$$

If the agent attends schooling for 2 periods then

$$V(S = 2, \beta_i; t = 2) = \frac{\beta_i^2 H_0}{r}, \quad i \in \{L, H\}. \tag{37}$$

The agent's problem can be solved by backwards induction. At $t = 1$ he chooses $S = 2$ iff

$$\begin{aligned} V(S = 1, \beta_i; t = 1) = \frac{\beta_i H_0}{r} &< \frac{1}{1+r}\frac{\beta_i^2 H_0}{r} = V(S = 2, \beta_i; t = 2) \\ \Leftrightarrow 1 &< \frac{\beta_i}{1+r}. \end{aligned} \tag{38}$$

Imposing the restriction $\beta_H > \frac{1}{1+r} > \beta_L$ implies that all individuals who are of high ability complete their degree and those of low ability drop out. At $t = 0$ individuals only know their individual probability of being of high ability and therefore choose to enroll in the degree program iff

$$\frac{H_0}{r} < E\left[\mathrm{Max}\left\{\frac{\beta_H^2 H_0}{r}\left(\frac{1}{1+r}\right)^2, \frac{\beta_L H_0}{r}\left(\frac{1}{1+r}\right)\right\}\middle| p\right]$$

to schooling can generate option values for education that can substantially affect the returns to schooling. Keane and Wolpin (1997) analyze a model of sequential choices between various discrete education and work alternatives.

$$\Leftrightarrow 1 < p\left(\frac{\beta_H}{1+r}\right)^2 + (1-p)\frac{\beta_L}{1+r} \tag{39}$$

which defines an optimal cut-off point p^* below which individuals do not enroll into the degree program. Observed returns are β_L for those completing one period and β_H^2/β_L for those completing two periods. The true return to schooling for agents who complete their degree is β_H, less than the estimated return.

The observed returns for completion of the degree are higher than the returns observed during the initial year of the degree since those individuals that complete the degree earn larger returns to schooling during the entire duration of the degree program. The excess returns observed in the last year captures not just the difference in the return generated during the last year between high and low ability individuals. These observed returns also reflect the greater learning in the initial years of schooling for those individuals who continue schooling rather than drop out.

The process of learning about individual ability also generates the spikes in the distribution of completed schooling observed during degree years. Individuals with $p < p^*$ will attend only schooling $= 0$. The fraction of individuals who drop out will be relatively small. This is because these are individuals who ex ante believe they have a high return and only find out ex-post that they actually have low returns to education. If individuals make fairly good predictions about their own ability then only a small portion will choose to drop out before the completion of their degree (making mistakes is a low probability event).

This argument implies that diploma effects do not provide evidence for or against JMS. That individuals are uncertain about their own ability to learn and that this uncertainty is (at least partially) resolved while in school naturally imply the existence of diploma effects as well as of bunching at degree years. We therefore dismiss diploma effects as evidence for or against JMS. We turn to other evidence that might inform us on the existence and size of JMS.

3.2. Testing JMS using segmented labor markets

The value of signaling through schooling depends on the difference in the average productivity by schooling level. In turn average productivity by schooling level depends on individuals' costs of acquiring schooling. JMS therefore implies that if costs vary for one part of the support of schooling, then this will affect the returns of schooling throughout the entire support. As individuals adjust to the changing costs along one part of the support of schooling they affect the returns for adjacent schooling levels. Then changes in the costs of schooling cause ripple effects in the distribution of schooling at all levels, even if these cost changes only apply to part of the schooling support. If one can identify variation in costs for only a subset of the schooling distribution, then one can test JMS by evaluating the changes in the distribution of schooling across the entire support. This idea lies at the heart of the empirical approach in Lang and Kropp (1986) and Bedard (2001).

Lang and Kropp exploit variation in compulsory attendance laws (CALs) across states. Imagine an increase in the compulsory schooling age from 12 to 14 years. HC predicts[24] that this regulatory change will only affect individuals previously constrained by compulsory attendance laws. JMS predicts that the change in regulation will affect the entire schooling distribution. Children who previously left school at age 12 will now remain in school until age 14. These children are less able than those who chose to remain in school until age 14 before the change in the CAL, so the average productivity of individuals who leave school at age 14 declines. This raises the return to schooling at age 14, so some individuals who otherwise would have left will remain in school longer. The JMS implies that the fraction of individuals who remain in school longer than age 14 will increase. By extension JMS also predicts an increase in the fraction of individuals who remain in school past age 15, and so on. Lang and Kropp (1986) find this "ripple effect" in response to increases in CALs across U.S. states enacted during the 1908–1968 period.[25]

An important criticism of this work is that an increase in the compulsory schooling age plausibly reflects an overall increase in the value of education. This would cause a rightward shift of the education distribution, which is consistent with the data. A recent study by Bedard (2001) is not subject to this critique. Bedard examines how the presence of post-secondary education institutions in local labor markets affects the high school drop-out decision. The assumption is that proximity reduces the costs of attending post-secondary education. JMS predicts that lower costs of post-secondary education lead the more capable high-school graduates to continue on, which reduces the average productivity of the remaining pool of high school graduates. This reduces the signaling return to graduating from high school, so the drop-out rate will rise. This is indeed the pattern that Bedard finds, which is robust to the criticism that the presence of a post-secondary institution might indicate a greater value attached to education in the local labor market. The papers by Lang and Kropp (1986) and Bedard (2001) therefore do provide some evidence for sorting in determining schooling choices and the distribution of schooling in the population.

3.3. *Employer learning models*

JMS assumes firms are initially unsure about individuals' productive types. They therefore use schooling to infer individuals' productivity. It seems reasonable to assume that firms learn about individuals productive types as time passes and productivity is observed. This assumption forms the basis to a stimulating and active branch of the empirical literature on JMS.

[24] This relies on the assumption that there are no general equilibrium effects on the wage structure. Lang and Kropp (1986) rely on factor prize equalization to rule out such GE effects.

[25] Recent work on the impact of compulsory attendance laws on the distribution of educational attainment does not confirm this prediction [see Lochner and Moretti (2004, Table 4)].

Two approaches have been used to exploit the idea of employer learning. A number of authors use presumed differences in the ease with which firms can learn about individual productivity between different industries [Wolpin (1977), Riley (1979)] or types of applicants [Albrecht (1981)]. More recent contributions test for statistical discrimination and employer learning by assuming that the econometrician can observe a pre-market ability measure, based on test scores, that is not observed by employers. This literature [Foster and Rosenzweig (1994), Farber and Gibbons (1996), Altonji and Pierret (1997, 2001), Galindo-Ruedo (2003), Lange (2006) and others] evaluates how the estimated returns to schooling and ability evolve over time. We will examine this literature first.

We present here a recent formulation by Lange (2006), who extends the analysis of Altonji and Pierret (2001) to estimate the speed with which employers learn about individuals' abilities. The speed of employer learning is crucial for JMS since it limits the time interval during which schooling can be a useful signal of unobserved ability – the presumption is that repeated observations of productive outcomes "reveal" a person's true talents. Then wages reflect new information learned about workers' true talents as time passes. This framework then carries a testable hypothesis about learning and signaling: as labor market experience increases, pre-market signals such as schooling have declining influence on observed wages, while unobserved talents have ever increasing weight. The rate at which this shift occurs is determined by the speed of employer learning. Following Lange (2006) we demonstrate how to estimate the speed of employer learning from the set of OLS-coefficients on schooling and a pre-market ability measure, fully interacted with experience, in an earnings regression. And we show how this estimate and the first-order condition for choosing schooling can be used to bound the contribution of signaling to the returns of schooling.

The key assumption for what follows is that a source of panel data on individuals records a pre-market ability measure z_i that is not directly observed by employers.[26] Assume further that the log of individual productivity x_i depends linearly on z_i, years of completed schooling s_i, and on information that is observed by employers but that is not recorded in the data, q_i. Adding an individual effect u_i, productivity follows:

$$x_i = \alpha_0 + \alpha_1 s_i + \alpha_2 z_i + \alpha_3 q_i + u_i. \tag{40}$$

It will be convenient to write $\tilde{x} = x - (\alpha_0 + \alpha_1 s + \alpha_3 q)$ and to suppress individual subscripts from now on. $\tilde{x}$ is the component of individual productivity that is not directly observed by employers. Following the JMS framework, we suppose this component to be private information of individuals – there is asymmetric information.[27] Firms use

[26] Altonji and Pierret used the AFQT-score, father's education and siblings' wages in the NLSY. Their main analysis proceeds with the AFQT-score. Test-scores have also been used in UK and German data [Galindo-Rueda (2003), Bauer and Haisken-DeNew (2001)]. In an interesting paper Foster and Rosenzweig (1995) use earnings of rural workers observed in a period when these were paid piece rates.

[27] It may seem equally plausible that neither workers nor employers observe z_i and q_i, and that both learn about talent from repeated observations of market outcomes. Then schooling plays no signaling role because

s and q to make predictions about $\tilde{x}$. Assume that the conditional expectation of $\tilde{x}$ is linear:

$$E[\tilde{x}|s,q] = \beta_1 s + \beta_2 q. \tag{41}$$

Productivity x is then linear in s, q and an error e_1:

$$\begin{aligned} x &= E[x|s,q] + e_1 = \alpha_0 + \alpha_1 s + \alpha_3 q + E[\tilde{x}|s,q] + e_1 \\ &= \alpha_0 + (\alpha_1 + \beta_1)s + (\alpha_3 + \beta_2)q + e_1 \\ &= b_0 + b_1 s + b_2 q + e_1. \end{aligned} \tag{42}$$

We assume $e_1 \sim N(0, \sigma_1^2)$. Then the information (s, q) generates a noisy signal of log productivity that, by assumption, is available to firms. Firms also learn about worker productivity from repeated observations on productive outcomes, y_t, during each period an individual spends in the labor market. This learning is common to all firms.

$$y_t = x + \varepsilon_t, \tag{43}$$

where $\varepsilon_t \sim N(0, \sigma_\varepsilon^2)$. Firms update their expectations as new information becomes available. Denote by $y^t = [y_0, y_1, \ldots, y_{t-1}]$ the vector of measurements available for forming expectations at t and write $\bar{y}^t$ for the average of these measurements. Then[28] a firm's best guess of productivity x at experience level t is:

$$E\big[x|s, y^t\big] = \big(1 - \theta(t)\big)E[x|s,q] + \theta(t)\bar{y}^t. \tag{44}$$

The weight $\theta(t) = \frac{tK}{1+(t-1)K}$ placed on new information tends to 1 as experience grows. This weight on new information is greater the larger is $K = \frac{\sigma_1^2}{\sigma_1^2+\sigma_\varepsilon^2}$, which Lange (2006) calls the "speed of employer learning" (SEL). The SEL is greater as subsequent measures of productivity y_t become more informative relative to initial estimates based on (s, q).

Now add a competitive spot market for labor services so workers are paid their expected productivity in each period. The normal structure of the problem implies that log wages follow:

$$w\big(s, y^t\big) = \big(1 - \theta(t)\big)E[x|s,q] + \theta(t)\bar{y}^t + \frac{1}{2}\sigma^2(t), \tag{45}$$

where $\sigma^2(t)$ denotes the variance of the prediction error in x conditional on the information (s, y^t). Equation (45) describes wages as a weighted average of the estimate based on the initial information (s, q) available to employers and subsequent observations of log productivity. The econometrician does not have the same information (s, q) available as the firm, but instead observes (s, z). To estimate K we need to understand what

workers do not condition their choice of schooling on knowledge of their individual talents. We can in this case still estimate the speed of employer learning with the methodology described here.

[28] For a simple introduction to Kalman updating see Appendix 21 in Lungqvist and Sargent (2000).

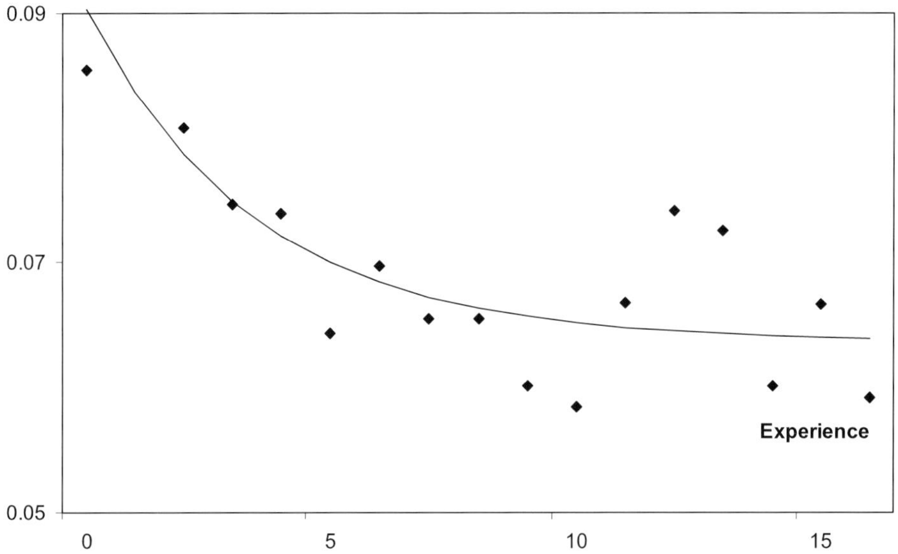

Shown are the estimated return to a standard deviation in the AFQT-score for each experience level as described in Section 3. The line represents the predicted returns over the life-cycle corresponding to Table 2, column 1.

Figure 3a. The returns to ability over the life-cycle.

(45) implies for the relation between wages and the information (s, z) available to the researcher. At $t = 0$ the linear projection of wages on (s, z) is given by the projection of $E[x|s, q]$ on (s, z). With increasing experience the coefficients on (s, z) in a wage regression converge to the coefficients obtained from the linear projection of $\bar{y}$ on (s, z). The speed of this convergence depends entirely on K, the speed of employer learning. This parameter can therefore be estimated using the pattern of convergence from the initial[29] to the final[30] cross-sectional coefficients on (s, z). To be precise: With the above structure the probability limit of the OLS coefficients for schooling and ability at each experience level will be given by

$$p\lim\left(\hat{b}^j_{OLS}\right) = \left(1 - \theta(t)\right)b^j_1 + \theta(t)b^j_T, \quad j = s, z, \tag{46}$$

where b^j_1 is the coefficient obtained from regressing wages on schooling and the productivity measure z before any learning takes place and b^j_T is the limit value of the coefficient.

We apply this framework to panel data from the National Longitudinal Study of Youth (NLSY). The NLSY records an individual's score on the Armed Forces Qualifying Test

[29] Experience $= 0$.

[30] Experience ∞.

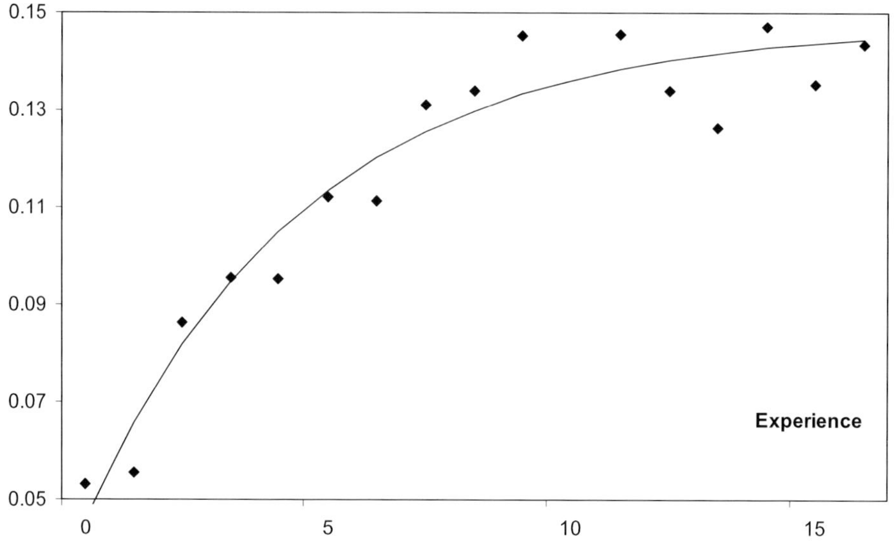

Shown are the estimated coefficients on schooling for each experience level as described in Section 3. The line shows the predicted returns to schooling over the life-cycle implied by the estimates in column 2, Table 11.

Figure 3b. The returns to schooling over the life-cycle.

(AFQT), which was administered to each member of the panel while still in school. This plays the role of z_i in the above analysis – a measure of ability that is plausibly unobserved by employers. Following these individuals after labor market entry, we regressed log wages on indicators for each year of labor market experience, and interactions of these experience dummies with both years of completed schooling and AFQT score. The scatters in Figure 3, panels A and B show the estimated returns to schooling and the AFQT at each experience level. These scatters confirm the findings that Altonji and Pierret (2001) report in a linear context. Consistent with employer learning about true productivity, returns to schooling decline with experience while returns to pre-market "ability" increase.[31] The scatter also reveals that returns to schooling and ability converge fairly quickly from their initial value to a more stable long-run level. This means that most learning occurs within the first few years of careers, so any role of education as a signal diminishes fairly quickly.

The solid lines in each panel depict the predicted returns to schooling and AFQT-score at each experience level, obtained by fitting the non-linear function (46) to the estimated returns by choice of (b_1^x, b_T^x, K). Estimated values of these parameters are

[31] Hause (1972) reports findings consistent with the findings of Altonji and Pierret (2001). Their findings refer to test scores from 4 different samples and a different time period than that analyzed by Altonji and Pierret (2001). See also Galindo-Rueda (2003) for similar findings from UK data.

Table 11
The speed of employer learning[a,b]

	Schooling	AFQT-score
The speed of learning K	0.2855***	0.2130***
	(0.1153)	(0.0799)
Initial value b_1	0.1039***	0.0066
	(0.0122)	(0.0259)
Limit value b_T	0.0568***	0.1788***
	(0.0061)	(0.0186)

[a]Parameters are estimated by non-linear least squares using the coefficient estimates on schooling and AFQT-score at different experience levels obtained from the NLSY as described in Lange (2006).
[b]Standard errors are boot-strapped with 2,000 repetitions.

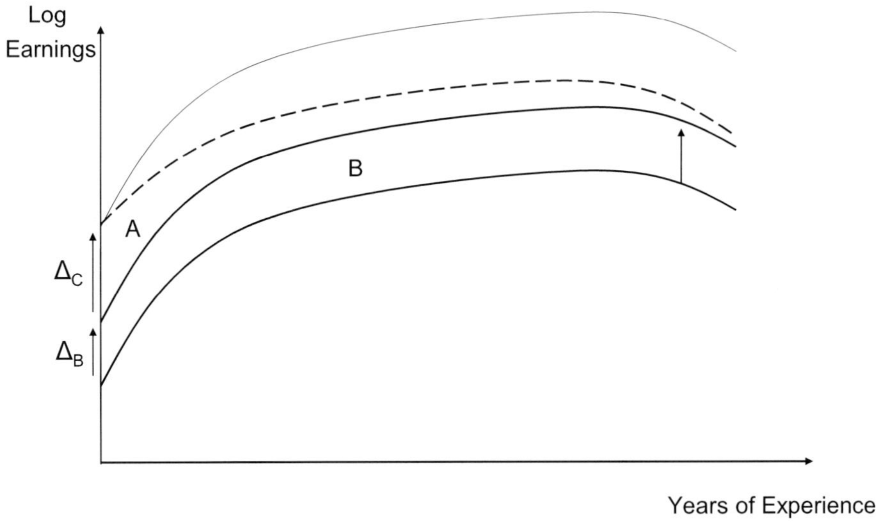

Figure 4. Decomposing the returns to schooling into a signaling and human capital component.

provided in Table 11. These estimates imply that employer learning is fast. One way to gauge the speed of learning is by asking how quickly the impact of an initial expectation error on wages will decline with experience. Using the definition $\theta(t) = \frac{tK}{1+(t-1)K}$ in the wage equation (46), a value of $K = 0.25$ means that the weight on an initial expectation error will decline by half in the first three years of labor market experience, and by three-fourths in the first 9 years. To us, this speed of employer learning seems "fast" in comparison with the 40–45 year decision horizon relevant for schooling decisions.

Table 12
The contribution of signaling to the gains from schooling with an estimated speed of learning of $K(1) = 0.25$[a]

Interest rate	Contribution of signaling	Productivity effects of schooling
3%	31.65%	2.9%
4%	25.23%	3.6%
5%	19.30%	4.6%
6%	13.52%	5.6%
7%	7.90%	6.8%
8%	2.53%	8.1%
8.70%	−1.17%	9%

[a]The table shows the contribution of signaling and of the human capital model for different discount rates. This decomposition is arrived at in the manner proposed by Lange (2006) and described in more detail in that paper (see Table 3, panel A).

How much of the private return to schooling might be due to signaling? At each level of experience the estimates above allow us to gauge the impact of signaling on the wage, so the impact on wealth is the net present value of these effects, viewed from the start of a career. Lange (2006)[32] performs these calculations, based on wealth maximizing schooling choices. The basic idea is illustrated in Figure 4, which shows how the life-time gains from an additional year of schooling decompose into a productivity component and a signaling component.[33] At labor market entry the effect of an additional year of schooling on the log wage is composed of a productivity increase α_1 and a signaling component β_1. The productivity component persists along the life-cycle, whereas the expected contribution from signaling declines as firms can be anticipated to learn about true productivity. For any *given* productivity effect we can decompose the total gains into a signaling and a productivity contribution. Yet the true productivity effect of schooling is unknown. The overall gains from schooling are monotonically increasing in the productivity contribution of schooling. There is therefore just one productivity effect of schooling that equates total gains to an estimate of the costs of schooling (not graphed). We can obtain such an estimate of schooling costs based on a discount rate, an estimate of tuition and the life-cycle patterns of earnings observed in the data. With this estimate of the costs of schooling we can identify a single productivity contribution that equates the gains to the costs of schooling. Based on this productivity contribution we decompose the gains from schooling into a signaling and a human capital contribution.

[32] A similar argument has been made previously by Altonji and Pierret (1997). Their work does not arrive at an estimate of the speed of employer learning. They demonstrate however that if the speed of learning is fast, then the contribution of JMS to the gains from schooling has to be low.

[33] The figure examines the particular case where firms do not have any additional information about individuals productivity (q is constant).

Table 12 shows the upper bounds for the contribution of signaling to the gains of schooling for various discount rates, as well as the implied productivity effects of schooling. For a wide range of plausible discount rates the contribution of signaling is fairly small. For example, suppose the appropriate discount rate for returns on human capital investments is 6 percent – roughly the post-tax rate of return on physical capital observed in the US since World War II.[34] Then the upper bound on the contribution of signaling is smaller than 15%.

Our conclusion from these estimates is that signaling is a minor contributor to the returns to schooling. This result is conditional on accepting the (strong) assumptions necessary to test for statistical discrimination using the method proposed by Farber and Gibbons (1996), Altonji and Pierret (2001), and Lange (2006). But even with these restrictions the speed of employer learning is so fast that job market signaling is unlikely to be an important determinant of individual schooling decisions.

3.3.1. Differences in the speed of employer learning across industries and occupation

The analysis above is based on the assumption that employers learn about individuals' productive types as labor market experience accumulates. An earlier literature tests the JMS-model by assuming that the speed with which employers learn varies across industries [Riley (1979)] or by other identifiable characteristics [Albrecht (1981), Wolpin (1977)]. For example, Riley's (1979) model predicts that average years of schooling should be lower in industries where employers learn more rapidly – the signaling returns to schooling conditional on unobserved ability $\tilde{x}$ are lower in those industries. This implies (i) fewer years of schooling in industries with faster employer learning and (ii) conditional on years of schooling, higher ability in industries with faster learning. Empirically, Riley's sorting model implies that, conditional on schooling, earnings should be higher in industries with lower average schooling.

Riley's prediction is contradicted by the data. Murphy and Topel (1990) estimated industry and occupational wage premiums, conditional on education, potential experience and other controls, using micro-data from the Current Population Surveys. Then they estimated "second stage" models that regressed the estimated industry and occupation premiums on education, experience and other typical controls. Their salient finding for present purposes was that the "effect" of years of schooling in the second stage was *positive*. That is, persons with more schooling also tend to work in industries and occupations that pay more for unobserved characteristics of workers – the opposite of what the signaling model would suggest. Table 13 implements this idea using more recent data for white males from the NLSY. Industry is defined using the first full-time job following completion of schooling. Again, the effect of schooling on estimated industry wage premiums is positive.

[34] See Mulligan (2002).

Table 13
The relation between industry effects and average schooling[a]

Dependent variable = industry specific effects in earnings equation[a]		
Average schooling[b]	0.0380***	0.0564***
	(0.0109)	(0.0104)
Experience	−0.0056	0.0165
	(0.0580)	(0.0529)
Experience squared	0.0014	−0.0002
	(0.0032)	(0.0029)
Fraction black		−0.1396
		(0.1327)
Fraction female		−0.3186***
		(0.0504)
R^2	0.0772	0.2473
Observations[c]	205	205

[a]The dependent variable is obtained from regressing log wages on schooling, experience, year dummies NLSY. The estimated industry effects from the first stage serve as dependent variable in second stage. Regressions are weighted by number of observations by industry in first stage.
***Denotes significance at the 1% level.
[b]Average years of schooling are average of highest grade completed by individuals working in this industry.
[c]3-digit industries.

4. Conclusions: What do we know about the social value of education?

We have reviewed and extended the literature on possible differences between the private and social values of education. In theory, such a "wedge" could be positive or negative. The possibility that social returns exceed private ones is typically ascribed to productive externalities – my productivity is raised by your human capital, in a way that markets do not take into account. The possibility that social returns are smaller than private ones typically views education as merely redistributive – able individuals use schooling to signal their ability, which may raise wages even if it has not impact on productivity.

The most striking finding from local aggregate data on education and wage growth in the US between 1940 and 2000 is that aggregate human capital measures are highly correlated with productivity, even after controlling for private returns. This finding is consistent with the evidence from cross-national data sets and so elemental that we believe that any account of income growth in the US must come to terms with it.

A number of authors have argued that education has substantial external benefits. This strand of the literature uses ordinary least squares [Rauch (1993)] or instrumental variable methods [Acemoglu and Angrist (2000), Moretti (2003, 2004)] to examine whether variation in education causes increases in aggregate wages after controlling for private returns. We believe that this type of evidence is inherently flawed, as it does not sufficiently account for endogeneity issues implied by a spatial equilibrium. We show that controlling for variation in skills by birthplace in aggregate wage regressions reduces the association between aggregate wages and schooling substantially. The fact that instrumental variable methods are incompatible with the restrictions imposed by a spatial equilibrium model also does not allow us to rule out skill-biased technological change as a cause for the association between schooling and aggregate wages.

The strong positive link between productivity and education is also problematic for adherents of the Job Market Signaling model. Job Market Signaling generates private returns to schooling without the corresponding social returns. This means that if one seriously entertains Job Market Signaling as an explanation for observed private returns to schooling, then the problem of explaining observed aggregate returns becomes even more severe. Our review of the available empirical evidence on Job Market Signaling leads us to conclude that there is little in the data that supports Job Market Signaling as an explanation for the observed returns to schooling.

Appendix

The sample consists of US males aged 18–65 from the Census. We used the standard 1940–2000 1-% micro data sample provided by the IPUMS (www.ipums.org). For 1940, 1950 and 1960 we use the general 1%-sample, for 1970 the "form 2 state" sample, for 1980 the 1% Metro (B sample), for 1990 the 1% Metro sample and for 2000 the general 1% sample. We base our analysis on employees with valid wage observations who worked 40 weeks or more. Employees can not be fully consistently defined over the sample period. In 1940 we defined employees as those for whom no substantial non-wage income is reported. From 1950 onwards employees were those without income from businesses or farms. We drop residents of Hawaii and Alaska since these states are not sampled in 1940 and 1950. Individuals with top-coded wages were excluded.

Table A.1
Descriptive statistics for Census IPUMS

	1940	1950	1960	1970	1980	1990	2000
Education	8.74	9.71	10.30	11.27	12.33	12.98	13.13
	(3.64)	(3.58)	(3.53)	(3.27)	(2.88)	(2.62)	(2.60)
Experience	22.31	22.23	23.01	21.92	18.94	18.75	19.98
	(13.08)	(13.66)	(13.51)	(13.82)	(13.35)	(12.05)	(11.69)
Age	37.05	37.93	39.31	39.19	37.27	37.73	39.10
	(11.69)	(12.31)	(12.13)	(12.68)	(12.58)	(11.64)	(11.54)
Log weekly wage	5.28	5.50	5.95	6.16	6.16	6.12	6.07
	(0.69)	(0.61)	(0.60)	(0.67)	(0.70)	(0.67)	(0.67)
N	164,307	97,688	298,153	358,355	399,746	437,905	512,599

The coding of education in the census underwent some changes in 1990. From 1940–1980 the variable *HIGRADE* coded education as the highest year of schooling or college completed. In 1990 and 2000 the variable *EDUC99* codes the highest grade of schooling completed through 11th Grade and classifies high school graduates by their degree completed. The schooling variable we used EDUCREC. The census provides this variable to make education variables comparable across census years. It classifies individuals in 9 categories of completed schooling (0 and Kindergarten, grades 1–4, 5–8, 9, 10, 11, 1–3 years of college, 4+ years of college). In the first stage regressions we use EDUCREC as a categorical variable. We calculated mean education by state by assigning to the categories provided by EDUCREC the vector of years of schooling (0, 2.5, 6.5, 9, 10, 11, 12, 14, 16).

The dependent variable in the first state is the log weekly wage (in 1990 dollars). In the first stage we define the skill categories using both the schooling variable and experience, where experience is chosen to be age minus cohort. We categorize experience into 10-year cells. Thus we have 9 education categories and 6 experience categories (18–20, 21–30, ..., 61–65) and therefore arrive at 54 skill groups. We interact the skill effects with each census year and therefore estimate in total $54 \cdot 7 = 378$ skill effects. We define the cohorts by decades and have 11 cohorts (1870–79, 1880–1889, ..., 1980–1989). We therefore have $49 \cdot 11 = 539$ birthstate · cohort categories. Finally we estimate state-effects for each census year and thus estimate a total of $49 \cdot 7 = 343$ state effects. These state effects will provide the basis of the 2nd step estimation. Table A.1 presents summary statistics for the Census Extracts used.

References

Acemoglu, D. (1996). "A microfoundation for social increasing returns in human capital accumulation". Quarterly Journal of Economics 111 (3), 779–804.

Acemoglu, D., Angrist, J. (2000). "How large are the social returns to education? Evidence from compulsory schooling laws". NBER Macroannual 9-59.

Albrecht, J.W. (1981). "A procedure for testing the signaling hypothesis". Journal of Public Economics 15, 123–132.

Altonji, J. (1993). "The demand for and return to education when education outcomes are uncertain". Journal of Labor Economics 11 (1), 48–83.

Altonji, J., Pierret, C. (1997). "Employer learning and the signaling value of education". In: Ohashi, I., Tachibanaki, T. (Eds.), Industrial Relations, Incentives and Employment. Macmillan Press Ltd., London.

Altonji, J., Pierret, C. (2001). "Employer learning and statistical discrimination". Quarterly Journal of Economics 116 (1), 313–350.

Barro, R. (1991). "Economic growth in a cross section of countries". Quarterly Journal of Economics CVI, 363–394.

Barro, R., Lee, J.-W. (1993). "International comparison of educational attainment". NBER Working Paper No. 4349.

Barro, R., Sala-i-Martin, X. (1997). "Technological diffusion, convergence, and growth". Journal of Economic Growth 2 (1), 1–26.

Bauer, T., Haisken-DeNew, J. (2001). "Employer learning and the returns to schooling". Labor Economics 8, 161–180.

Becker, G. (1964). Human Capital. Columbia University Press, New York.
Bedard, K. (2001). "Human capital versus signaling models: University access and high school dropouts". Journal of Political Economy 109 (4), 749–775.
Belman, D., Heywood, J. (1991). "Sheepskin effects in the returns to education: An examination of women and minorities". Review of Economics and Statistics 73, 720–724.
Benhabib, J., Spiegel, M. (1994). "The role of human capital in economic development, evidence from aggregate cross-country data". Journal of Monetary Economics 34 (2), 143–173.
Ben-Porath, Y. (1967). "The production of human capital and the life cycle of earnings". The Journal of Political Economy 75 (4), 352–365.
Bils, M., Klenow, P. (2000). "Does schooling cause growth". American Economic Review 90, 1160–1193.
Card, D. (1999). "The causal effect of education on earnings". In: Ashenfelter, O., Card, D. (Eds.), Handbook of Labor Economics, vol. 3. North-Holland, Amsterdam.
Chiswick, B.R. (1973). "Schooling, screening, and income". In: Solomon, L.C., Taubman, P.J. (Eds.), Does College Matter? Academic Press, New York.
Ciccone, A., Peri, G. (2006). "Identifying human capital externalities: Theory with applications". Review of Economic Studies 73, 381–412.
De la Fuente, A., Domenech, R. (2001). "Schooling data, technological diffusion and the neoclassical model". American Economic Review 91 (2), 323–327.
Farber, H., Gibbons, R. (1996). "Learning and wage dynamics". Quarterly Journal of Economics 111 (4), 1007–1047.
Foster, A., Rosenzweig, M. (1994). "Information, learning and wage rates in rural labor markets". Journal of Human Resources 28, 759–790.
Foster, A., Rosenzweig, M. (1995). "Learning by doing and learning from others: Human capital and the technical change in agriculture". Journal of Political Economy 103 (6), 1176–1209.
Frazis, H. (2002). "Human capital, signaling and the patterns of returns to education". Oxford Economic Papers – New Series 54 (2), 298–320.
Friedman, M. (1962). Capitalism and Freedom. University of Chicago Press, Chicago.
Galindo-Rueda, F. (2003). "Employer learning and schooling-related statistical discrimination in Britain". IZA Discussion Papers No. 777.
Glaeser, E. (1999). "Learning in cities". Journal of Urban Economics 46, 254–277.
Habermalz, S. (2004). "An examination of sheepskin effects over time". Working Paper.
Hamermesh, D. (1986). "The demand for labor in the long run". In: Ashenfelter, O., Layard, R. (Eds.), Handbook of Labor Economics. North-Holland.
Hause, J. (1972). "Earnings profile: Ability and schooling". Journal of Political Economy 80 (3), S108–S138.
Heckman, J., Klenow, P. (1998). "Human capital policy". In: Boskin, M. (Ed.), Policies to Promote Capital Formation.
Heckman, J., Lochner, L., Todd, P. (2003). "Fifty years of Mincer earnings regressions". NBER Working Paper 9732.
Hungerford, T., Solon, G. (1987). "Sheepskin effects in the returns to education". Review of Economic Studies 69, 176–178.
Jaeger, D., Page, M. (1996). "Degrees matter: New evidence on sheepskin effects in the returns to education". Review of Economics and Statistics 76, 733–739.
Jovanovic, B., Rob, R. (1989). "The growth and diffusion of knowledge". Review of Economic Studies 56 (4), 569–582.
Kaldor, N. (1961). "Capital accumulation and economic growth". In: Lutz, F., Hague, D.C. (Eds.), The Theory of Capital. St. Martin's Press, New York, pp. 177–222.
Katz, L., Murphy, K. (1992). "Changes in relative wages, 1963–1987: Supply and demand factors". Quarterly Journal of Economics 107 (1), 35–78.
Keane, M., Wolpin, K. (1997). "The career decisions of young men". Journal of Political Economy 105 (3), 473–522.
Krueger, A., Lindahl, M. (2000). "Education for growth: Why and for whom?" National Bureau of Economic Research 7591.

Kyriacou, G. (1991). "Level and growth effects of human capital". C.V. Starr Centre, New York University.
Lang, K., Kropp, D. (1986). "Human capital vs. sorting: The effects of compulsory attendance laws". Quarterly Journal of Economics 101, 609–624.
Lange, F. (2004). "The returns of schooling and ability during the early career: Evidence on employer learning and past-school investment". Manuscript available at http://www.econ.yale.edu/~fl88/.
Lange, F. (2006). "The speed of employer learning". Journal of Labor Economics, in press.
Lange, F., Topel, R. (2005). "Social returns to education". Manuscript available at http://www.econ.yale.edu/~fl88/.
Layard, R., Psacharopoulos, G. (1974). "The screening hypothesis and the returns to education". Journal of Political Economy 82, 985–998.
Lochner, L., Moretti, E. (2004). "The effect of education on criminal activity: Evidence from prison inmates, arrests and self-reports". American Economic Review 94 (1).
Lucas, R.E. (1988). "On the mechanics of economics development". Journal of Monetary Economics XXII, 3–42.
Lucas, R.E., Rossi-Hansberg, E. (2002). "On the internal structure of cities". Econometrica 70 (4), 1445–1476.
Lungqvist, L., Sargent, T. (2000). Recursive Macroeconomic Theory. MIT Press.
Mankiw, G., Romer, D., Weil, D. (1992). "A contribution to the empirics of economic growth". Quarterly Journal of Economics 107 (2), 407–438.
Marshall, A. (1920). Principles of Economics. Macmillan, London, 1890, 8th ed.
Miligan, K., Moretti, E., Oreopoulos, P. (2003). "Does education improve citizenship? Evidence from the U.S. the U.K." NBER Working Paper 9584.
Mincer, J. (1974). Schooling, Experience and Earnings. National Bureau of Economics Research, New York.
Moretti, E. (2003). "Estimating the social return to higher education: Evidence from longitudinal and cross-section data". Journal of Econometrics.
Moretti, E. (2004). "Workers' education, spillovers and productivity: Evidence from plant-level production functions". American Economic Review 94 (3).
Mulligan, C. (2002). "Capital, interest, and aggregate intertemporal substitution". NBER Working Paper 9373.
Murphy, K.M., Topel, R.H. (1985). "Estimation and inference in two-step econometric models". Journal of Business Economic Statistics 3 (4).
Murphy, K.M., Topel, R.H. (1990). "Efficiency wages reconsidered: Theory and evidence". In: Weiss, Y., Fishelson, G. (Eds.), Advances in the Theory and Measurement of Unemployment. Macmillan, London.
Nelson, R., Phelps, E. (1965). "Investment in humans, technological diffusion and economic growth". Cowles Foundation Discussion Paper.
Park, J.H. (1994). "Returns to schooling: A peculiar deviation from linearity". Working Paper No. 335, Industrial Relations Section, Princeton University.
Pritchett, L. (2001). "Where has all the education gone?" World Bank Economic Review.
Rauch, J. (1993). "Productivity gains from geographic concentration in cities". Journal of Urban Economics 34, 380–400.
Roback, J. (1982). "Wages, rents, and the quality of life". Journal of Political Economy 90, 1257–1278.
Riley, J. (1979). "Testing the educational screening hypothesis". Journal of Political Economy 87, S227–S252.
Riley, J. (2001). "Silver signal – twenty five years of screening and signaling". Journal of Economics Literature 39, 432–478.
Schultz, T. (1963). The Economic Value of Education. Columbia University Press, New York.
Solow, R.M. (1956). "A contribution to the theory of economic growth". Quarterly Journal of Economics 70, 65–94.
Spence, M. (1973). "Job market signaling". Quarterly Journal of Economics 87, 355–379.
Topel, R. (1999). "Labor markets and economic growth". In: Ashenfelter, O., Card, D. (Eds.), Handbook of Labor Economics. Elsevier Science, Amsterdam, pp. 2943–2984.
Uzawa, H. (1965). "Optimum technical change in an aggregative model of economic growth". International Economic Review 6, 18–31.

Wolpin, K. (1977). "Education and screening". American Economics Review 67, 949–958.
Young, A. (1995). "The tyranny of numbers: Confronting the statistical realities of the East Asian growth experience". The Quarterly Journal of Economics 110 (3), 641–680.

Chapter 9

WHY HAS BLACK–WHITE SKILL CONVERGENCE STOPPED?

DEREK NEAL

University of Chicago and NBER

Contents

Handbook of the Economics of Education, Volume 1
Edited by Eric A. Hanushek and Finis Welch
© 2006 Elsevier B.V. All rights reserved
DOI: 10.1016/S1574-0692(06)01009-9

Abstract

All data sources indicate that black–white skill gaps diminished over most of the 20th century, but black–white skill gaps as measured by test scores among youth and educational attainment among young adults have remained constant or increased in absolute value since the late 1980s. I examine the potential importance of discrimination against skilled black workers, changes in black family structures, changes in black household incomes, black–white differences in parenting norms, and education policy as factors that may contribute to the recent stability of black–white skill gaps. Absent changes in public policy or the economy that facilitate investment in black children, best case scenarios suggest that even approximate black–white skill parity is not possible before 2050, and equally plausible scenarios imply that the black–white skill gap will remain quite significant throughout the 21st century.

Keywords

basic skills, black–white differences, convergence

JEL classification: I20, J15, J20

1. Introduction

Four decades after the adoption of civil rights laws that prohibit racial discrimination by employers in hiring, pay, and promotion practices, black–white differences in standards of living remain a fact of life in the United States. These differences fuel much public debate about the government's role in regulating the labor market, the effects of alternative means of financing and governing public schools, procedures that determine admission to institutions of higher education, and other policies that affect the distribution of income and opportunity. In this chapter, I do not explore all factors that contribute to observed black–white differences in employment rates or incomes. Instead, I focus on black–white differences in skill and how these differences have changed over time.

According to all available measures, blacks are less skilled than whites. Black adults of all ages report less completed schooling than their white counterparts. Black youth and adults also score lower than their white counterparts on numerous tests that measure cognitive function and academic achievement, and this is true even among students or adults with the same level of completed schooling. In modern economies, most wealth takes the form of human capital, which consists of the knowledge, skills, and abilities that determine the productive capacities of individual workers. Long before cohorts of young persons reach adulthood, significant black–white skill gaps emerge, and these gaps are an important determinant of black–white differences in lifetime earnings. Thus, as long as one assumes that large scale redistribution from white to black Americans is not politically feasible, one must conclude that closing the black–white skill gap is a necessary although possibly not sufficient condition for economic equality between blacks and whites in the United States.

Section two of this chapter documents the evolution of black–white gaps in completed schooling and measured skill over the past four decades and highlights several patterns in the data. To begin, all data sources indicate that overall black–white skill gaps have diminished over time. A large literature documents the progress made throughout most of the previous century in closing black–white gaps in schooling attainment, and more recent data show a dramatic closing of the black–white test score gap during the 1970s and 1980s. Existing trends in 1990 suggested that successive generations of black children were making steady progress toward approximate skill parity with white children. However, during the 1990s, black–white skill gaps as measured by test scores among youth and educational attainment among young adults remained constant or increased in absolute value. Further, there is evidence that black youth in large cities actually lost significant ground relative to white students during much of the 1980s and 1990s. Data on employment rates and incarceration rates also indicate that, since 1980, the number of young black men who spend more time interacting with corrections officials than employers has grown at an alarming rate.

To date, much of the literature on the black–white skill gap explores the determinants of past improvements in relative achievement and attainment among blacks, but recent developments challenge scholars to think carefully about why the black–white skill gap remains so large and why many black youth may have actually fallen farther behind their white peers during the past fifteen years or more. In section three, I argue that low skill levels among black youth cannot be easily understood as a rational response to labor discrimination against skilled black adults. In recent decades, estimated gains from investments in education and skills have almost always been greater among blacks adults than among whites. This pattern is most striking in data on employment rates and total labor market earnings.

Having shown that black youth can expect significant returns from skill investments, I turn in section four to the determinants of investments in children and the intergenerational transmission of human capital. Standard models clearly indicate that current wealth differences between black and white parents do contribute directly to current black–white skill gaps among youth, and shocks to the wage structure in recent decades may have lowered wealth among black families. However, the effects of these shocks or other temporary negative shocks to black families and communities cannot cause black–white skill gaps to remain at current levels indefinitely. Given the stability of black–white skill gaps since 1990, I explore the possibility that more persistent barriers to skill development among black youth may exist. I deal explicitly with the ways that education policies may impede black progress, and I also examine the potential role of norms concerning academic achievement within black families and communities.

The concluding section looks forward. It is possible to form estimates of future black–white skill gaps by using existing data to calibrate rates of skill convergence between black and white youth. Results based on convergence rates that represent best case scenarios for black youth suggest that even approximate black–white skill parity is not possible before 2050, and equally plausible scenarios imply that the black–white skill gap will remain quite significant throughout the 21st century. Absent changes in public policy or shocks to the economy that facilitate investment in black children, there is little reason to be optimistic about the future pace of black–white skill convergence. I close by discussing the possibility that early childhood interventions among disadvantaged children may be an important policy tool for closing the black–white skill gap earlier rather than later in the 21st century.

2. Trends in measures of the black–white skill gap

At the dawn of the 20th century, the educational attainment of blacks lagged well behind that of whites for many reasons. In the antebellum period, the vast majority of blacks were slaves who had almost no access to formal schooling. Thus, blacks began the post-war period with low adult levels of education. Further, most blacks lived in the South, and the South lagged behind the rest of the nation in providing education. Even whites in the South attended schools that received fewer resources than schools in the rest of the country, and after reconstruction, the disenfranchisement of blacks and the resulting segregationist policies regarding the provision of public schooling guaranteed that blacks in the South only had access to schools that were worse yet than the substandard schools that their white neighbors attended. There is little evidence that blacks born during the period from the end of reconstruction through the first decade of the twentieth century made any attainment gains relative to their white counterparts, and Collins and Margo (2003) report that, among those born in the South between 1905 and 1909, the average final attainment of six years among blacks fell three years below the average white attainment. The corresponding attainment gap for the nation as a whole was almost 3.5 years.[1]

For subsequent birth cohorts, the story is different. A large existing literature documents how successive cohorts of black young adults born after the first decade of the twentieth century obtained higher and higher schooling levels relative to whites. In another chapter in this Handbook, Collins and Margo document these trends and discuss their causes. Collins and Margo focus on the period before 1960. In their seminal work on black progress during the 20th century, Smith and Welch (1989) employ data from the period 1940–1980. Here, I present results based on data from the 1960–2000 census files. The rows of Table 1 give birth years, the columns give age groups, and each diagonal row running from lower left to upper right contains results from a particular census. The top diagonal row contains data from 1960. The bottom such row presents data from the 2000 census.

Table 1 shows that, during the 1980s, the black–white attainment gap continued to narrow at a pace that one might expect given the experience of previous decades. Among men ages 26–30, the black–white education gap fell from roughly one year to about two thirds of a year between 1980 and 1990, and this change is simply an extension of the 1960–1980 trends in relative attainment. Starting in 1990 and going back to 1960, the black–white education gap among men 26–30 is always two thirds of the corresponding gap in the previous decade. The rate of convergence among women is not quite as rapid over this period, but the initial gap in 1960 was not nearly as large. Black women made steady gains in attainment relative to white women over the entire period, and by 1990 the black–white attainment gap among young adult women was just under one half of a year of schooling. The results in Table 1 combined with those in Smith (1984) and Smith and Welch (1989) indicate that each decade from 1940 through 1990 brought a decline in the measured black–white attainment gap for both men and women at all ages, and in 1990, the overall black–white gap in years of attainment among young adults ages 26–30 represented less than 5 percent of the average schooling level among whites.[2]

However, this trend toward black–white parity in attainment stops in 1990. Among men and women ages 26–30 in 2000, the black–white educational attainment gap is slightly larger than the corresponding gap in 1990. Similar results hold for men and women ages 31–35.[3] In terms of school cohorts, the black–white gap in educational

[1] Smith and Welch (1989) report an even larger black–white attainment gap for this cohort. The Smith and Welch number of 3.9 is larger because they report results for males only.

[2] The gaps in 1960–1980 are larger in Smith and Welch. The differences result because the census changed the coding of education in 1990, and in order to make results comparable over the entire 1960–2000 period, I adopted a less disaggregate coding scheme for education.

[3] These changes are small, but given the large samples sizes in the census files, they are statistically significant among women.

Table 1
Black–white differences in average education

Men

Year of birth	Age 26–30	31–35	36–40	41–45	46–50
1910–1914					−3.13
1915–1920				−3.03	
1920–1924			−2.81		−2.60
1925–1929		−2.48		−2.30	
1930–1934	−2.26		−1.95		−1.81
1935–1939		−1.71		−1.53	
1940–1944	−1.50		−1.38		−1.29
1945–1949		−1.21		−1.29	
1950–1954	−0.99		−0.97		−1.10
1955–1959		−0.76		−0.84	
1960–1964	−0.66		−0.76		
1965–1969		−0.81			
1970–1974	−0.72				

Notes: Data are from the decennial census IPUMS. Mean education for whites 26–30 years old was 11.6 in the 1960 census, 12.5 in the 1970 census, 13.3 in the 1980 census, 13.1 in the 1990 census and 13.6 in the 2000 census. The IPUMS variables used for constructing years of schooling are "higraded" for 1960, 1970 and 1980 and "educ99" for 1990 and 2000. Individuals with allocated age, sex, race or education have been dropped from the sample. Sample weights "perwt" are used for year 2000.

Women

Year of birth	Age 26–30	31–35	36–40	41–45	46–50
1910–1914					−2.53
1915–1920				−2.25	
1920–1924			−2.04		−2.00
1925–1929		−1.68		−1.54	
1930–1934	−1.46		−1.21		−1.06
1935–1939		−1.07		−0.80	
1940–1944	−1.06		−0.72		−0.73
1945–1949		−0.68		−0.65	
1950–1954	−0.64		−0.64		−0.71
1955–1959		−0.47		−0.63	
1960–1964	−0.45		−0.59		
1965–1969		−0.64			
1970–1974	−0.62				

Notes: Data are from the decennial census IPUMS 1960–2000. Mean education for whites 26–30 years old was 11.3 in the 1960 census, 12.1 in the 1970 census, 13.0 in the 1980 census, 13.3 in the 1990 census and 13.9 in the 2000 census. The IPUMS variables used for constructing years of schooling are "higraded" for 1960, 1970 and 1980 and "educ99" for 1990 and 2000. Individuals with allocated age, sex, race or education have been dropped from the sample. Sample weights "perwt" are used for year 2000.

Appendix Table 1

Average years of schooling and black–white education gaps

Men

Year	Dataset	Age 26–30 black	26–30 white	26–30 gap	31–35 black	31–35 white	31–35 gap	36–40 black	36–40 white	36–40 gap	41–45 black	41–45 white	41–45 gap	46–50 black	46–50 white	46–50 gap
1990	CPS	12.58	13.03	−0.45	12.55	13.28	−0.73	12.85	13.58	−0.73	12.41	13.60	−1.19	11.80	13.10	−1.30
	Census	12.47	13.13	−0.66	12.56	13.33	−0.77	12.66	13.64	−0.98	12.40	13.68	−1.28	11.94	13.23	−1.29
2000	CPS	13.12	13.43	−0.31	13.14	13.52	−0.38	13.10	13.39	−0.29	12.93	13.55	−0.62	13.09	13.83	−0.74
	Census	12.88	13.59	−0.71	12.83	13.64	−0.81	12.83	13.59	−0.76	12.84	13.68	−0.84	12.84	13.95	−1.11
	ACS	12.88	13.47	−0.59	13.13	13.50	−0.37	12.89	13.53	−0.64	12.99	13.57	−0.58	12.94	13.90	−0.96
2001	CPS	13.09	13.44	−0.35	13.07	13.56	−0.49	13.03	13.41	−0.38	12.85	13.55	−0.70	13.09	13.76	−0.67
	ACS	13.03	13.45	−0.42	13.12	13.58	−0.46	12.89	13.53	−0.64	12.92	13.56	−0.64	12.93	13.84	−0.91

Women

Year	Dataset	Age 26–30 black	26–30 white	26–30 gap	31–35 black	31–35 white	31–35 gap	36–40 black	36–40 white	36–40 gap	41–45 black	41–45 white	41–45 gap	46–50 black	46–50 white	46–50 gap
1990	CPS	12.65	13.18	−0.53	12.92	13.26	−0.34	12.76	13.38	−0.62	12.28	13.14	−0.86	11.95	12.74	−0.79
	Census	12.82	13.27	−0.45	12.88	13.35	−0.47	12.85	13.50	−0.65	12.63	13.28	−0.65	12.12	12.85	−0.73
2000	CPS	13.35	13.72	−0.37	13.25	13.64	−0.39	13.32	13.50	−0.18	13.23	13.57	−0.34	13.10	13.70	−0.60
	Census	13.30	13.92	−0.62	13.20	13.84	−0.64	13.17	13.75	−0.58	13.16	13.79	−0.63	13.14	13.85	−0.71
	ACS	13.30	13.80	−0.50	13.15	13.74	−0.59	13.16	13.64	−0.48	12.95	13.70	−0.75	13.04	13.80	−0.76
2001	CPS	13.31	13.77	−0.46	13.45	13.72	−0.27	13.19	13.63	−0.44	13.10	13.55	−0.45	13.24	13.78	−0.54
	ACS	13.31	13.79	−0.48	13.19	13.82	−0.63	13.14	13.68	−0.54	13.14	13.68	−0.54	13.06	13.77	−0.71

Notes: This table compares average years of schooling and black–white gaps across three datasets: CPS, Census and ACS. The calculations use sample weights for ACS, CPS and Census 2000. Individuals with allocated age, sex, race or education have been dropped from the samples. Entries for the black–white gaps using Census data may differ from Table 1 because of rounding. Table 1 calculates black–white gaps rounding to the nearest hundredth while this appendix table rounds average years of schooling and then calculates the black–white gap.

attainment may have stopped closing and even begun to widen with the cohorts of children who began their schooling during the late 1960s and early 1970s. I have examined educational attainment by individual birth cohorts over the period 1960 to 1974. Regardless of gender, the black–white attainment gaps for those born after 1965 are almost always slightly greater than the attainment gaps associated with birth cohorts from the early 60s.

Because the black–white attainment gap also increases between 1990 and 2000 within several birth cohorts who reached adulthood before 1990, i.e., as one moves along rows in the table, there is some concern that the increase in black–white attainment gaps observed among the most recent cohort of young adults may, in part, reflect a change in sampling procedures between 1990 and 2000. To provide more information about trends in black–white attainment gaps during the 1990s, I have also examined education gaps in the March Current Population Surveys and the American Community Surveys. Appendix Table 1 describes the results. These surveys are not exactly comparable to census files because the CPS does not include persons in the military or in institutional quarters, and the ACS does not include persons in institutions. The ACS did not exist in 1990, but the 1990 March CPS and 1990 Census provide similar estimates of black–white attainment gaps. Thus it is somewhat surprising that, in contrast to the census results reported in Table 1, a comparison of results from the March 2000 and March 1990 CPS files indicates that three of four black–white education gaps among men and women in the 26–30 and 31–35 age groups grew smaller in absolute value over the 1990s. At the same time, the CPS files are much smaller than the census files, and none of these changes is statistically significant.

While the CPS results provide some suggestion that young black adults continued to close the black–white attainment gap during the 1990s, the balance of the evidence indicates that the attainment gap remained constant at best during the 1990s. The case for convergence during the 1990s is strongest among men ages 31–35. Here, the ACS 2000 and 2001 results are clearly more in line with the CPS results than the census numbers. However, the 2000 ACS results for men ages 26–30 are quite consistent with the 2000 census results.[4] Further, among young adult women, black–white education gaps in the 2000 census, the 2000 ACS, and the 2001 ACS are always larger in absolute value than corresponding gaps taken from either the 2000 or 2001 March CPS files. In fact, among women ages 26–35, black–white education gaps in the 2000 census, 2000 ACS and 2001 ACS are always larger than the corresponding gaps in the 1990 census, implying that young adult black women in 2000 were no closer to educational parity with white women than were their predecessors in 1990.

[4] In 2001, the implied black–white attainment gap among men ages 26–30 is larger in the ACS than the CPS but still smaller than the gap implied by the 2000 census data. To compare census and ACS results directly, one must adjust the census numbers by removing the institutionalized population. The prison population grew substantially over the 1990s, especially among black men. Black–white education gaps among men ages 26–35 in the 2000 census are almost 0.1 smaller in absolute value when men living in institutions are not included in the sample.

In sum, Table 1 provides significant but not definitive evidence that black–white convergence in educational attainment stopped during the 1990s. One can have more confidence that convergence in relative attainment actually stopped if other measures of attainment tell a similar story. Next, I present results concerning how black–white differences in rates of graduating from high school and college have evolved over recent decades.

Although cohorts born in the late seventies or the eighties have not completed their schooling, one can compare high school graduation rates for cohorts born in the early 1960s to those of cohorts born in the early 1980s by examining data from the National Longitudinal Surveys of Youth. Table 2a gives high school graduation rates by age and birth cohort for samples taken from the National Longitudinal Surveys of Youth, NLSY79 and NLSY97. The NLSY79 provides panel data on persons born between 1957 and 1964. The NLSY97 provides panel data on persons born between 1980 and 1984. Using recent data from the NLSY97, I compute the fraction of people born in 1980 or 1981 who graduated from high school by the date of their 19th, 20th, or 21st birthdays. I calculate the corresponding graduation rates for all the NLSY79 cohorts, and in addition, I calculate the number who graduate high school by age 30.

Each cell in Table 2a contains two graduation rates. The top number is a graduation rate based on the number of persons with regular high school diplomas. The bottom number includes as graduates those persons who receive a high school equivalency credential by passing the General Educational Development (GED) test. For the moment, focus on the results concerning regular diplomas. The numbers are averages for people born in adjacent birth cohorts who share the same race and gender. There is no evidence that black men born in the early 1980s were generally more likely to graduate high school than black men born in the late 1950s and early 1960s. Among black men born in 1980–1981, 62 percent graduate from high school by their 21st birthday. This graduation rate is lower than corresponding rates for three of the four pairs of adjacent birth cohorts taken from the NLSY79. In contrast, the 82 percent graduation rate among white males born in 1980–1981 is higher than three of the four graduation rates associated with the NLSY79 cohorts of white males. The rate among white males born in 1957–1958 is 0.83, but the graduation rates for cohorts born in 1959–1964 are all below 0.80. The overall comparison of the NLSY79 and NLSY97 results indicates that, among men, there may have been no net closing of the black–white gap in high school graduation rates over roughly two decades of cohorts born between 1960 and 1980, although black–white differences in graduation rates do diminish over the cohorts born in the late 1950s and early 1960s, in large part because white graduation rates decline over this period. The time pattern of black–white gaps in graduation rates is consistent with the results in Table 1 concerning final attainment gaps. The black–white attainment gap among men reached a historic low among those born in the early 1960s and appears to remain constant or widen slightly among later cohorts.

The results for women in Table 2a are quite similar. Although high school graduation rates for those born in 1980–1981 are higher than rates for birth cohorts from the late 50s and early 60s regardless of race, the improvement in graduation rates since the early

Table 2a

High school graduation rates by age, gender and race. Actual graduation rates (top line, bold), high school diplomas and GED (bottom line)

	Year of birth	Men				Women			
		19	20	21	30	19	20	21	30
Whites	1957–1958	**0.75**	**0.81**	**0.83**	**0.84**	**0.80**	**0.83**	**0.84**	**0.85**
		0.77	0.84	0.85	0.89	0.82	0.86	0.87	0.91
	1959–1960	**0.69**	**0.78**	**0.79**	**0.79**	**0.79**	**0.81**	**0.81**	**0.83**
		0.71	0.81	0.83	0.86	0.81	0.85	0.86	0.90
	1961–1962	**0.69**	**0.74**	**0.75**	**0.75**	**0.74**	**0.79**	**0.79**	**0.79**
		0.73	0.79	0.81	0.84	0.78	0.83	0.84	0.89
	1963–1964	**0.66**	**0.72**	**0.72**	**0.74**	**0.74**	**0.78**	**0.78**	**0.78**
		0.71	0.78	0.79	0.85	0.79	0.83	0.84	0.88
	1980–1981	**0.67**	**0.78**	**0.82**		**0.76**	**0.85**	**0.88**	
		0.71	0.84	0.86		0.78	0.87	0.91	
Blacks	1957–1958	**0.51**	**0.61**	**0.65**	**0.66**	**0.64**	**0.74**	**0.75**	**0.77**
		0.55	0.66	0.71	0.74	0.67	0.78	0.80	0.86
	1959–1960	**0.48**	**0.62**	**0.67**	**0.68**	**0.62**	**0.70**	**0.70**	**0.72**
		0.50	0.67	0.72	0.79	0.66	0.74	0.76	0.82
	1961–1962	**0.50**	**0.61**	**0.61**	**0.63**	**0.69**	**0.76**	**0.76**	**0.77**
		0.56	0.68	0.71	0.80	0.71	0.79	0.80	0.85
	1963–1964	**0.53**	**0.64**	**0.67**	**0.68**	**0.66**	**0.72**	**0.73**	**0.74**
		0.59	0.72	0.76	0.83	0.68	0.77	0.78	0.84
	1980–1981	**0.43**	**0.56**	**0.62**		**0.66**	**0.76**	**0.78**	
		0.47	0.62	0.70		0.69	0.79	0.81	

Notes: Data are from NLSY 1979 and NLSY 1997. Only individuals who were observed after the age of interest are included. Individuals with coding errors for the age variable have been dropped from the sample.

Table 2b

College graduation rates by gender and race – ages 26–35

	Women			Men		
	Black	White	Ratio	Black	White	Ratio
1960	4.45	7.74	1.74	4.05	16.08	3.97
1970	5.30	12.04	2.27	5.38	20.27	3.77
1980	11.73	21.30	1.82	12.23	29.08	2.38
1990	13.41	23.50	1.75	11.48	24.50	2.13
2000	17.90	32.75	1.83	13.91	30.22	2.17

Notes: Data are from the decennial census IPUMS 1960–2000. The variable used for constructing college graduation rates is "educrec". Individuals with allocated age, sex, race or education have been dropped from the sample. Sample weights "perwt" are used for year 2000.

1960s is slightly greater among white females, and thus the black–white gap in graduation rates is slightly greater among those born in 1980–1981 than among those born in the 1961–1964 period. Table 1 indicates that the black–white gap in attainment among women declined to roughly 0.45 of one year of schooling for women born between 1955 and 1964 and then widened slightly among later cohorts.

Table 2a also provides a cautionary tale concerning the measurement of educational attainment. Data from the NLSY79 cohorts show that a notable number of those who receive a high school diploma by age 30 are GED recipients who never graduated from a particular high school. Among both black and white men in NLSY79, the rate of GED receipt was higher among later birth cohorts, and over 15 percent of all black men born between 1961 and 1964 received a GED. The corresponding figure for white men is around 10 percent. Table 2a shows that, within the NLSY79 cohort, most high school credentials received after a respondent's 21st birthday are GEDs. Because census data do not distinguish between GEDs and regular diplomas, educational attainment data from census files do not capture the true magnitude of black–white differences in actual graduation rates.[5]

Table 1 presents overall attainment gaps, and Table 2a explores differences in high school graduation rates. Another important marker of education attainment is college graduation. Table 2b presents college graduation rates among men and women ages 26–35 in each census year from 1960 through 2000. The final column in each panel presents ratios of these race-specific graduation rates (white to black). In 1960, the white graduation rate for men was almost four times greater than the corresponding rate for blacks. This ratio falls to 2.13 by 1990, but increases slightly between 1990 and 2000 to 2.17. College graduation rates for white women were quite low in 1960. Thus, the time trend in the ratio of white to black graduation rates among women before 1990 is not nearly as dramatic. Nonetheless, in the 1990s, graduation rates did not increase as rapidly among young black women as among young white women.[6]

In sum, data on attainment gaps as well as trends in high school and college graduation rates suggest that, among both men and women, the dramatic black–white convergence in attainment that began with cohorts born around 1910 came to a halt just over 50 years later. The attainment outcomes among blacks born in the late 1960s and early 1970s as well as the high school graduation rates of those born in the early 1980s may reflect only a pause in the long-term process of black–white convergence in attainment, but this pause is noteworthy because it is a clear departure from the trend toward black–white parity in attainment that dominated most of the 20th century. It is ironic that the cohorts of black youth born immediately after the passage of the Civil Rights

[5] See Cameron and Heckman (1993) for differences in outcomes between GED and regular diploma recipients.

[6] The 2000 Census and 2000 March CPS provide fairly comparable estimates of race-specific college graduation rates for young adults. The same is true in 1990. Neither data series indicates that young black adults closed the black–white gap in college graduation rates during the 1990s.

Act of 1964 did not add to previous decades of progress toward racial equality in educational attainment. However, the next section demonstrates that the cohorts born in the late 1960s and the 1970s did participate in a dramatic narrowing of the black–white test score gap.

2.1. *Achievement gaps*

Years of schooling is an indirect measure of human capital. It provides an accounting of time devoted to acquiring skills through formal schooling. However, schools differ in curricula, and some schools facilitate learning more effectively than others. Further, even within the same school, some children learn faster than others, and these differences reflect more than simple differences in individual aptitudes. Children differ greatly in the extent to which adults direct their activities outside school toward learning. Thus, for many reasons, persons who reach the same level of educational attainment may have significantly different skill sets.

In this section, I review existing data on black–white differences in test scores, and I focus on tests that measure basic math and reading skills among children and teenagers. These basic skills provide the foundation for acquiring new skills as an adult both in the work place and in institutions of higher education. Table 3 presents statistics based on the data found in the National Assessment of Education Progress – Long Term Trend study (NAEP-LTT). The NAEP-LTT is a series of nationwide assessments in reading, math, and science. The tests have been given periodically since 1971 to students who are in school and age 9, 13, or 17. These assessments maintain a consistent testing framework and are designed to measure trends in achievement over time. Here, I do not employ data from the tests for the age 17 sample. The assessments of 17 year old students provide a select sample of scores because the NAEP-LTT first samples schools and then samples enrolled students within schools. All 17 year old dropouts are therefore not eligible for testing. Because drop out rates are not the same for blacks and whites, these data are not ideal for inferences concerning black–white achievement differences among 17 year old students. In addition, compared to the age 9 and 13 assessments, response rates are significantly lower in the 17 year old samples.

Table 3 presents test score gaps for students who share a common age and birth cohort. To determine the year that a particular test was given simply sum the appropriate row and column labels. Each entry is the black–white test score gap for a particular birth cohort in a given subject at a given age. The score gaps are normalized by the population standard deviation on the particular assessment in question. The sample standard deviations on these tests vary from year to year, and although standard deviations tend to be higher in the early assessments, there is no trend in the standard deviation of scores over most of the period.[7] The NAEP-LTT reveal significant test score gaps at both ages,

[7] The score gaps from the 1973 math assessments are normalized by the standard deviations from the 1978 assessments because I cannot find a report containing the 1973 standard deviations.

Table 3
Black–white math and reading score gaps in NAEP. Entries are black–white gaps in mean scores expressed in standard deviation units

	Reading		Math	
Cohort/age	9	13	9	13
1958		−1.08		
1960				−1.18
1962	−1.04	−1.02		
1964			−0.97	
1965				−1.08
1966	−0.92			
1967		−0.91		
1969			−0.88	−1.02
1971	−0.84	−0.74		
1973			−0.84	−0.79
1975	−0.79	−0.53		
1977		−0.58	−0.74	−0.87
1979	−0.71	−0.73		−0.93
1981	−0.79	−0.77	−0.81	−0.90
1983	−0.83	−0.82	−0.82	−0.92
1985	−0.80		−0.74	
1986		−0.74		−0.98
1987	−0.74		−0.75	
1990	−0.91		−0.82	

Notes: Data are from 1999 NAEP Long-Term Trend Summary Data Tables. Entries are calculated as the score gap divided by the overall standard deviation for the corresponding test year. The standard deviations for the 1973 age 9 and age 13 math tests are not available, and therefore the standard deviations of the 1978 math tests are used instead.

for both subjects, and among all birth cohorts. Black–white test score gaps are always greater than 0.5 standard deviations and several are roughly a full standard deviation or more.

The previous section shows that the black–white gap in final educational attainment did not continue to close among cohorts born after 1965. However, black children born in the 1970s did perform better relative to white children on both math and reading tests than black children born in previous cohorts. In terms of birth cohorts, black–white test score convergence proceeds at a steady rate until the mid to late 1970s. In terms of assessment dates, the relative test scores of black children improve among both nine and thirteen years old students from the early 1970s until the late 1980s. Appendix Table 2 provides more details concerning time trends in achievement by race. From the late 1970s through the late 1980s, black children made striking gains in achievement while scores for white children remained relatively flat. The most dramatic changes occurred in the 13 year old sample. Figures 1(a) and (b) plot black–white test score gaps in the

Appendix Table 2
NAEP test scores (standard errors in parenthesis, standard deviations in brackets)

Year	Math scores				Year	Reading scores			
	9 year-olds		13 year-olds			9 year-olds		13 year-olds	
	White	Black	White	Black		White	Black	White	Black
73	225 (1.0)	190 (1.8)	274 (0.9)	228 (1.9)	71	214 (0.9)	170 (1.7)	261 (0.7)	222 (1.2)
	–	–	–	–		[39.4]	[38.3]	[32.9]	[33.5]
78	224 (0.9)	192 (1.1)	272 (0.8)	230 (1.9)	75	217 (0.7)	181 (1.2)	262 (0.7)	226 (1.2)
	[34]	[34.5]	[35.7]	[36]		[36.1]	[35.8]	[32.9]	[34.9]
82	224 (1.1)	195 (1.6)	274 (1.0)	240 (1.6)	80	221 (0.8)	189 (1.8)	264 (0.7)	233 (1.5)
	[32.8]	[33.7]	[31]	[31]		[35.2]	[37.6]	[32.7]	[32.7]
86	227 (1.1)	202 (1.6)	274 (1.3)	249 (2.3)	84	218 (0.9)	186 (1.4)	263 (0.6)	236 (1.2)
	[32.6]	[31.7]	[29.4]	[28.3]		[38.8]	[38.9]	[33.8]	[34.1]
90	235 (0.8)	208 (2.2)	276 (1.1)	249 (2.3)	88	218 (1.4)	189 (2.4)	261 (1.1)	243 (2.4)
	[31.2]	[31.5]	[29]	[28.7]		[39.3]	[39.4]	[33.9]	[32.1]
92	235 (0.8)	208 (2.0)	279 (0.9)	250 (1.9)	90	217 (1.3)	182 (2.9)	262 (0.9)	242 (2.2)
	[31]	[31.8]	[28.5]	[30.1]		[42.9]	[41.7]	[34.5]	[35.3]
94	237 (1.0)	212 (1.6)	281 (0.9)	252 (3.5)	92	218 (1.0)	185 (2.2)	266 (1.2)	238 (2.3)
	[31.4]	[30.8]	[29.8]	[31.5]		[37.5]	[39.8]	[36.6]	[39.8]
96	237 (1.0)	212 (1.4)	281 (0.9)	252 (1.3)	94	218 (1.3)	185 (2.3)	265 (1.1)	234 (2.4)
	[32.4]	[31.1]	[28.7]	[29.5]		[37.4]	[40.6]	[37.5]	[38]
99	239 (0.9)	211 (1.6)	283 (0.8)	251 (2.6)	96	220 (1.2)	191 (2.6)	266 (1.0)	234 (2.6)
	[31.8]	[33]	[30.3]	[28.8]		[36.5]	[38.6]	[36.5]	[36.4]
					99	221 (1.6)	186 (2.3)	267 (1.2)	238 (2.4)
						[35.6]	[37.9]	[36.6]	[37.6]

Notes: The table displays average NAEP scores and standard deviations for math and reading tests, ages nine and thirteen. Data are taken from the 1999 NAEP Long-Term Trend Summary Data Tables.

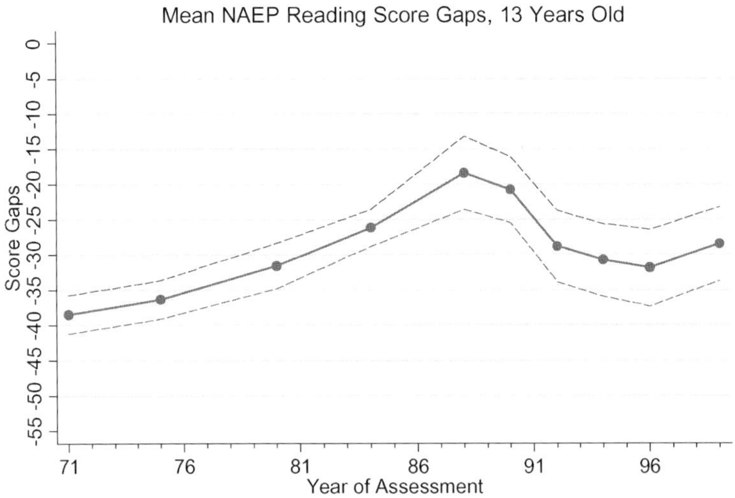

(a)

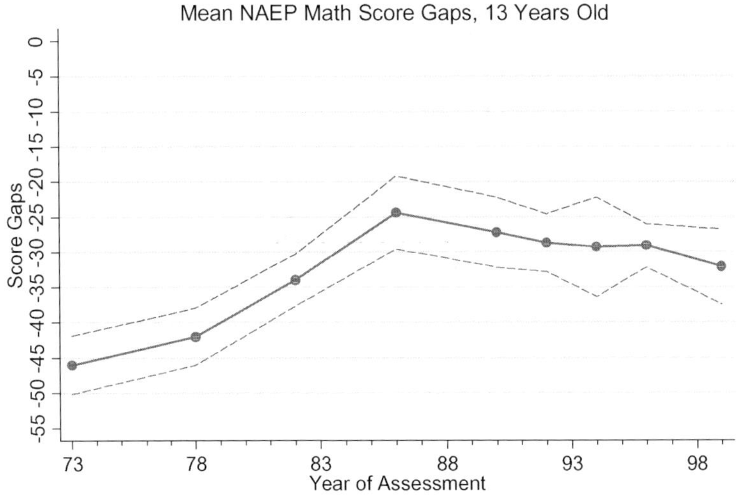

(b)

Figure 1. Data are from the 1999 NAEP Long-Term Trend. Dashed lines are 95% confidence intervals.

age 13 NAEP-LTT by assessment date. The relative gains in math and reading between the early 1970s and the late 1980s are large by any metric.

However, Table 3 and Figures 1(a) and (b) show that black–white test score gaps among 9 and 13 year old students stopped closing in the late 1980s. Since then, black test scores have shown little improvement in levels, and black–white test score gaps have either remained constant or increased modestly. Some may be tempted to draw significance from the fact that, as shown in Table 1, the 1990s are also the first decade in which census data record no further closing and possibly an increase in the black–white attainment gap among young adults. However, it is not clear exactly how the trends in Tables 1, 2b and 3 are related. Most adults between 26 and 35 in the 2000 census were born more than a decade before the cohorts of children who took NAEP-LTT tests during the late 1980s and throughout the 1990s. On the other hand, given the constraints of mandatory schooling laws, the majority of adults ages 26–35 in the 2000 census made decisions that determined their final educational attainments during the late 1980s or the 1990s. It is possible that a shock common to many black communities occurred during this period that both restrained educational attainment among young adults and harmed the development of math and reading skills among youth during the coming decade. In Section 4, I discuss changes in family income and family structure that may in part reflect changes in the wage structure that hurt less skilled workers during the 1980s. I also discuss recent work by Fryer et al. (2004) that documents how the crack epidemic ravaged urban black communities during the late 1980s and early 1990s. However, before turning to possible explanations for the time series of black–white attainment and test score gaps documented in the census files and the NAEP-LTT, I present results from other data sets concerning changes in black–white test score gaps over time.

2.2. *Evidence from other test data*

The NAEP-LTT is one of the few data sources that provides test scores for a nationally representative sample of persons sharing the same age.[8] Most data sets containing test scores provide samples of students, often high school students, who are enrolled in a particular grade at a point in time. However, the NLSY79 and NLSY97 do provide test scores for samples of students defined by birth cohort who took comparable tests almost twenty years apart. These data provide an excellent opportunity to determine whether or not the patterns observed in the NAEP-LTT data concerning black–white progress over the birth cohorts of the 1960s and 1970s hold given different tests of reading and math skills.

In 1980, the Department of Defense used the NLSY79 sample to construct a national distribution of scores for the Armed Services Vocational Aptitude Battery (ASVAB). The ASVAB contains 10 tests. Many are designed to measure aptitude for special military vocations. The Armed Forces Qualifying Test (AFQT) is a composite of four ASVAB tests that cover basic reading and math skills. The military uses AFQT scores as proxies for general aptitude in learning military jobs. Extensive evaluations of the AFQT show that it does help predict future measured performance on military jobs and

[8] The improvement of test scores among black children during the 1970s and 1980s is well documented. See Hedges and Nowell (1998) for analyses of relative gains in black achievement during this period that also include results from samples drawn based on grade of attendance.

Table 4
Black–white test score gaps

Year and age	Boys			Girls			Full sample		
	Reading	Math	Composite	Reading	Math	Composite	Reading	Math	Composite
1979									
13–14									
15–17	−1.15	−0.94	−1.11	−1.17	−0.96	−1.14	−1.16	−0.95	−1.13
1997									
13–14	−0.87	−0.90	−0.93	−0.69	−0.79	−0.78	−0.78	−0.84	−0.85
15–17	−0.87	−0.82	−0.89	−0.96	−0.92	−0.99	−0.91	−0.87	−0.94

Notes: Data are from NLSY 1979 and NLSY 1997. Test scores have been transformed into deviations from the average score among persons born in the same two-month interval and standardized so that one unit equals one standard deviation in the distribution of scores for persons of the same birth cohort and gender.

that it is not racially biased. Relationships between AFQT and post-training assessments are quite similar for black and white recruits.[9] The Defense Department gave a computer assisted version of the ASVAB to NLSY97 respondents during the fall of 1997 and early 1998. The NLSY79 follows respondents born between 1957 and 1964. The NLSY97 includes respondents born between 1980 and 1984.

Table 4 presents test scores for three different groups of birth cohorts drawn from the NLSY panels. These students took the AFQT at ages 13–17. To facilitate comparisons among the NLSY panels and the NAEP-LTT, I transformed all test score data from the NLSY panels into deviations from the average score among persons born in the same two month interval.[10] The scores are also standardized so that one unit equals one standard deviation in the distribution of scores for persons of the same birth cohort and gender.

The NAEP-LTT reports do not provide separate scores for boys and girls within racial groups. However, the NLSY data allow me to report separate black–white score gaps by gender. The results for 15–17 year old respondents allow direct comparisons over time under the assumption that the 1997–1998 and 1980 administrations of the ASVAB are comparable assessments. This comparison indicates clear improvement for black

[9] See Wigdor and Green (1991).

[10] The NAEP-LTT is a random sample of students who were a particular age at a point in time. The NLSY samples are drawn according to birth dates. Therefore, over the two calendar intervals that the AFQT was given to the NLSY panels, the shares of persons with the youngest and oldest ages in each panel were less than their corresponding shares in the population. In NLSY79, the share of 15 year olds is too small. In the NLSY97, the share of 17 year olds is to small.

The NLSY97 provides the date that each respondent took the ASVAB. Thus, in the NLS97, I standardized scores for birth date and whether or not the student took the test during the summer of 1997, the fall of 1997, or the winter of 1998. Test dates are not available in the NLSY79, but the NLSY79 exams were given over a shorter time interval.

teenagers relative to their white counterparts among boys and girls. Note that this improvement mirrors secular trends in the NAEP-LTT data for age 13 assessments.

The NAEP reading scores for those born in 1962 and the NAEP math scores for those born in 1965 are the best points of comparison for the NLSY79 scores. The estimated size of the black–white reading gap among those age 13 in 1975 was just over one standard deviation. The absolute value of the estimated black–white gap in math scores among those age 13 in 1978 was about 1.1 standard deviations. The NLSY79 sample of those tested at ages 15–17 includes persons born in 1962–1964. The black–white test score gaps in this sample are similar in magnitude to those in the 1975 and 1978 NAEP-LTT for age 13, but the relative sizes of the reading and math gaps are reversed. The AFQT scores imply that reading gaps are larger than the math gaps.

The AFQT scores from the 1997–1998 administration of the ASVAB yield black–white test score gaps in reading of −0.78 and −0.91 standard deviations among those ages 13–14 and 15–17, respectively. In math, the corresponding gaps are −0.84 and −0.87. Compared to the NLSY79 scores for those ages 15–17, these gaps represent relative improvements for black youth of 0.38 to 0.25 standard deviations in reading and 0.11 to 0.08 standard deviations in math. Because the NLSY97 respondents were born in 1980–1984, the NAEP-LTT scores that provide the best points of comparison are the age 13 scores for students born in 1981 and 1983 and tested in 1994 and 1996. Relative to the black–white score gaps in the 1975 reading assessment and the 1978 math assessment, Table 3 shows that the 1994–1996 assessments imply relative score gains for black youth of 0.2–0.25 standard deviations in reading and 0.16–0.18 standard deviations in math. Taking the differences between the NLSY79 and NLSY97 results as baselines, the implied achievement gains in the NAEP-LTT over roughly the same period are slightly larger in math and somewhat smaller in reading. Nonetheless, the shrinking of black–white gaps in scores on the math and reading sections of the AFQT between 1979 and 1997 lends credit to the hypothesis that the NAEP-LTT data reported in Table 3 capture a real and noteworthy closing of the black–white skill gap among teenagers.[11]

The narrowing of the black–white test score gap is an important development in the post-civil rights era. Because there are no reliable measures of individual achievement prior to the NAEP-LTT data, we do not know the extent to which the narrowing of black–white test score gaps among cohorts born during the 1960s and 1970s was part of a long term trend toward skill convergence, but the amount of convergence documented in Tables 3 and 4 is noteworthy. Both Neal and Johnson (1996) and Hansen, Heckman and Mullen (2004) estimate that one year of high school raises average AFQT scores by roughly 0.2 standard deviations. Thus, the final column of Table 4 indicates that,

[11] The AFQT data are consistent with the relative improvement of blacks scores in the NAEP-LTT over the 1978–1999 period, but no data from random samples based on age allow an independent check on the conclusion, often drawn from the NAEP-LTT, that the post-1978 improvements in black achievement took place before 1990. Hedges and Nowell (1998) do document noteworthy improvement during the 1980s in the relative scores of black students included in grade-based samples.

between 1980 and 1997–1998, the overall improvement in AFQT scores among those ages 15–17 represents the addition of roughly one year's worth of achievement for black students relative to white students. While this gain is impressive, it also highlights the enormous magnitude of the black–white skill gap that remains. Work by Neal and Johnson (1996) and Johnson and Neal (1998) suggests that the black–white skill gap among teenagers in the NLSY97 will likely translate into at least a 15 percent difference in lifetime earning capacity.[12]

I have followed accepted practice by discussing these gaps in terms of units created by transforming all sets of scores so that the sample average is zero and the sample standard deviation is one. Because some test score distributions are approximately normal by design, standard deviation units often serve as a cardinal metric for test score gaps, and given this metric, the NAEP-LTT data and the NLSY panels provide fairly consistent information about the magnitude of the black–white test score gap at different points in time among different birth cohorts. However, ability has no natural units.[13] In most cases, test scores provide only a ranking of individuals. Whatever the scoring system, one assumes that if person A has a higher score than person B, then A performed better on the exam than B, but statements about the distance between A's performance and B's performance usually rely on arbitrary scales that have no inherent cardinal significance.

Figures 2(a) and (b) present results for respondents in the NLSY79 and NLSY97 who were ages 15–17 when they took the ASVAB. The figures give matches between percentile rankings in white and black math score distributions by gender.[14] For example, in the 1980 administration of the test, the tenth percentile in the distribution of math scores for black males equaled the second percentile in the distribution of math scores for white males. Several aspects of these figures are noteworthy. To begin, these figures provide a useful perspective on the size of black–white differences in the distributions of scores that remain in 1997. Roughly 80 percent of black males and females scored below the corresponding median score among whites, and just over five percent of black males and females scored in the top 25% of the corresponding score distributions for whites. Further, the pattern of changes in relative rankings over time is what one would expect given the results in Table 4. Compared to blacks born in the early 1960s, those born in the early 1980s were more likely to be in at least the middle of the white distribution of scores. Among boys, the fraction of blacks who scored above the median

[12] Neal and Johnson (1996) employ wage data from the 1990–1991 wave of the NLSY79. The next section includes results from the 2000 wave of the NLSY79, and the results suggest an even stronger relationship between AFQT and future earnings capacity.

[13] If the distributions of black scores and white scores were both normal with the same variance, then knowledge of the black–white gap in mean scores expressed in standard deviation units would fully reveal the mapping between percentile ranks in the black distribution and percentile ranks in the white distribution. However, it is obvious that these conditions do not hold in many data sets. In fact, distributions of AFQT composites from the NLSY panels are not always normal and are skewed as well.

[14] I do not include reading scores because I was not able to get the required individual NAEP-LTT data as points of comparison in enough relevant years.

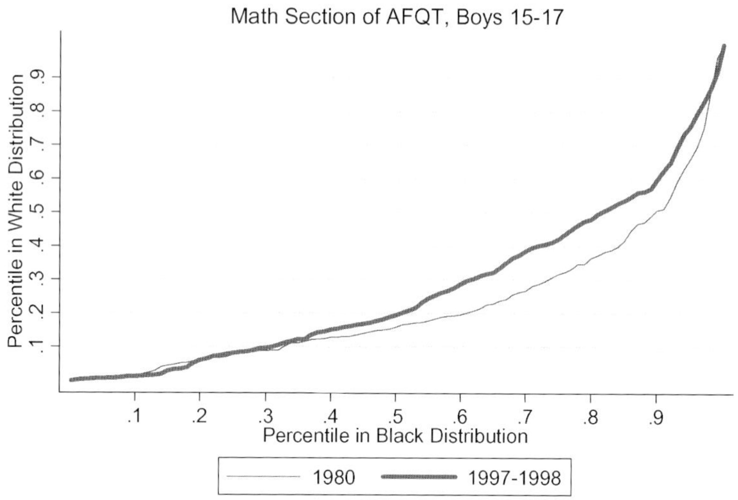

(a)

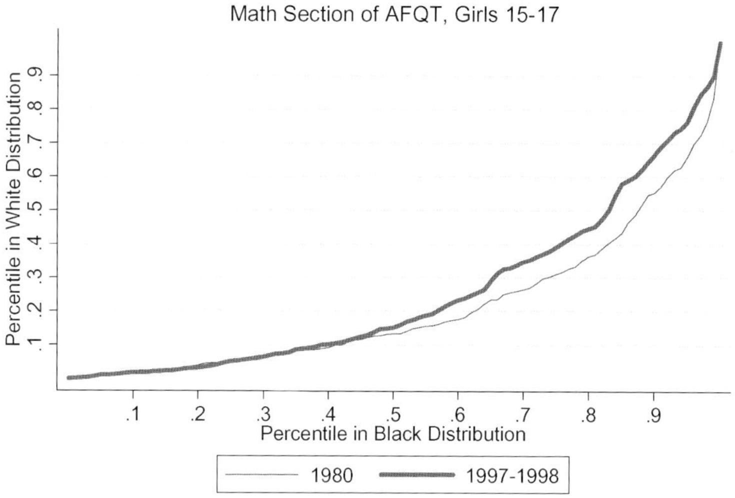

(b)

Figure 2. (a), (b) The figures use standardized AFQT scores from the 1979 and 1997 NLSY. (c), (d) The figures use math scores from the 1978, 1982 and 1992–1996 NAEP.

white score increased from roughly 10 percent to about 20 percent. Still, progress toward racial equality in scores was not the same at all percentiles in the black score distributions. While the right tails of the black score distributions moved farther into the upper half of the white score distribution, the left tails of the black score distributions remained below all but a handful of white scores.

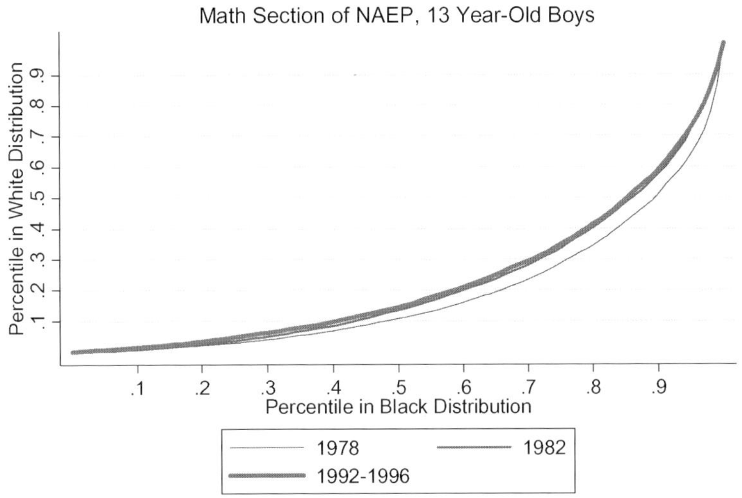

(c)

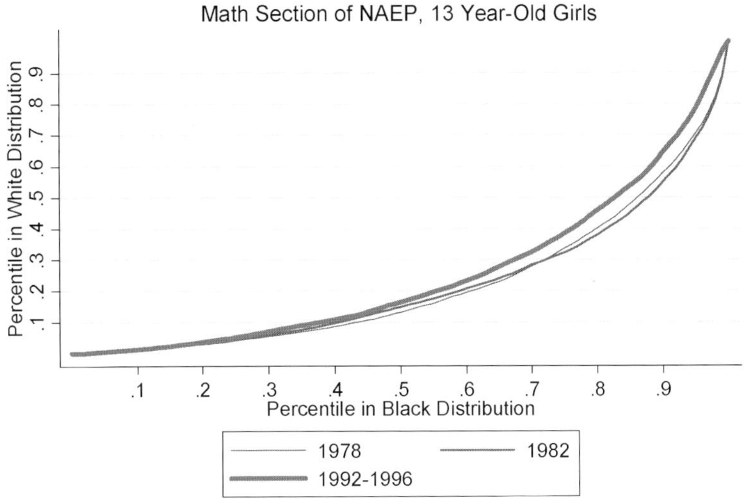

(d)

Figure 2. (*Continued.*)

Figures 2(c) and (d) present similar results based on individual data from the NAEP-LTT math assessments. The figures present relative ranks for three samples of 13 year old students. The first two samples are the 1978 and 1982 NAEP-LTT math assessments.

The third sample combines data from the 1992, 1994, and 1996 assessments.[15] Once again, the NLSY and NAEP-LTT paint similar pictures. Black teenagers improved their relative ranks over this period, but they remain far behind white teenagers in terms of math achievement. Further, blacks in the lower percentiles of test score distributions are making the least progress relative to whites. However, the timing of black relative progress differs by gender. Almost all of the improvements in relative scores for black males came between 1978 and 1982, but the significant improvements for black girls come after 1982. In addition, among boys, the overall improvement of black NAEP scores relative to white scores is not as dramatic as the relative improvement in the math components of AFQT scores observed between the two NLSY cohorts. This is somewhat surprising given that results from Tables 3 and 4, where black–white score gaps are expressed in standard deviation units, suggest that blacks made larger relative gains in math on the NAEP-LTT assessments than on the AFQT.[16]

Because the NAEP-LTT is designed to test the same math skills in every assessment year and because all scores from all years are on a common scale, one can also determine whether or not there was improvement over time within the black sample. The scale scores of those in the lower percentiles of the black score distributions did improve between the 1978 and mid 1990s assessments, but this improvement did not result in noticeable improvements in the rank of lower scoring black students in the white score distribution for two reasons. To begin, the black and white math score distributions for those age 13 in 1978 did not effectively share a common support. The lower percentile scores for blacks born in 1965 were so low that these scores could have improved without generating notable changes in the relative ranks of black and white test scores, even if the white score distribution remained completely constant over time. In addition, scores at the lower percentiles of the white distribution also improved over time.

The NLSY79 respondents took a paper and pencil version of the ASVAB. Those born in 1961 through 1964 took the test as teenagers, and the distribution of raw scores among black teenagers in this sample provides some context for just how poorly less skilled blacks from cohorts born before 1965 performed on cognitive tests. The version of the AFQT administered to NLSY79 respondents contains 105 questions. Each question is a multiple choice question with four possible answers and one correct answer. Thus, if a given respondent simply guessed randomly, he or she would have expected a raw score between 26 and 27. Further, among a group of respondents who guessed randomly, we expect over 20 percent to have answered 30 or more questions correctly. Thus, a score

15 I was not able to obtain individual NAEP data for many years. I combined results from the 1992–1996 wave because the data sets from the 1990s are much smaller than those from previous years. I present math results because I was not able to verify the quality of the 1996 data on individual reading scores by reproducing the published tables that summarize the assessment.

16 I do not present graphs for reading scores because I was not able to obtain a reliable version of the 1996 reading test results from the NAEP. For the analyses involving math scores, I was able to recreate the published tables that document percentiles in score distributions for various years and subpopulations.

of 30 constitutes far less than decisive evidence against the null hypothesis that a given respondent knew the correct answer to none of the questions and simply chose answers randomly. Still, 19 percent of black male respondents and 11 percent of black female respondents answered 27 or less questions correctly, and almost 27 percent of black males and roughly 18 percent of black females posted a raw score of 30 or less. In contrast, more than 94 percent of whites scored above 30 regardless of gender.

Given these results, it seems fair to conclude that a substantial fraction of the NLSY79 sample of black males who took the ASVAB test lacked the basic math and reading skills covered by the exam, lacked any motivation to put forth effort during the exam, or both. The results for black females are not quite as bleak, but they still indicate very low levels of performance in the left-tail of the black score distribution. The NLSY97 and the NAEP-LTT tests do not permit the type of "number correct" counts that I have done for the NLSY79, but taken as a whole, the results presented here suggest that cohorts of black youth and young adults born in the 1980s and 1990s may still contain a significant number of individuals who do not possess the basic math and reading skills that young teenagers are expected to acquire in school. Although scaled NAEP-LTT scores for black youth at the fifth and tenth percentiles of the distributions did improve between 1978 and the mid 1990s, these achievement gains were not sufficient to create notable changes in the score ranks of lower performing black youth relative to white students, and Figures 2(a) and (b) also show little, if any, improvement between 1980 and 1997 in relative AFQT score ranks for youth scoring in the lower percentiles of the black score distributions.

Finally, Figures 3(a)–(b) present the relative ranks of black youth from large cities in the nationwide distribution of white math scores. As in Figures 2(c) and (d), the data come from the NAEP-LTT math assessments, and I define large cities as central cities with a total metropolitan area population of at least two million in 1990. Note that the relative ranks of blacks in these large cities who are age 13 actually tended to fall, especially among boys, between 1978 and the mid 1990s. Compare Figures 2(c) and 3(a). The falling achievement of black boys in large cities over the 1980s and early 1990s is comparable in magnitude to the significant overall improvements made by black boys during the 1978–1982 period. By the mid 1990s, black youth in large cities performed notably worse than black youth in small towns or rural areas. This development is noteworthy because prior to 1980, rural blacks performed worse than other blacks on tests of academic achievement.

Flanagan and Grissmer (2002) provide evidence that reinforces the results in Figures 3(a)–(b). Table 5 is taken directly from their paper. In order to create samples that provide significant numbers of observations for various subgroups defined by race and geography, Flanagan and Grissmer combined data from nine different grade level NAEP assessments conducted during the 1990s. These include three 4th grade reading tests, three 8th grade math tests, two 4th grade math tests and one 8th grade reading test.

The population percentage figures refer to shares in the national sample of public school students. Among both blacks and whites, students in central cities perform be-

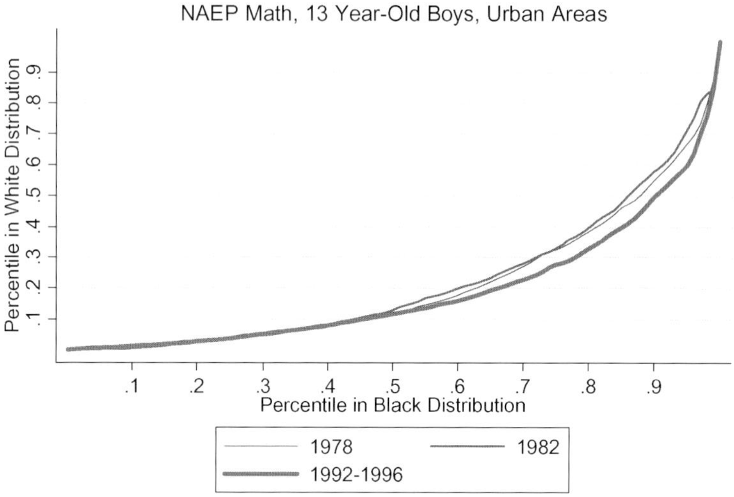

(a)

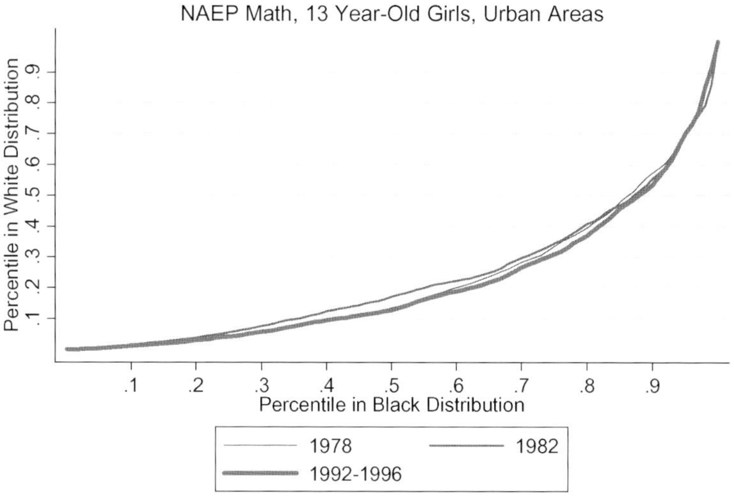

(b)

Figure 3. The figures use math scores from the 1978, 1982 and 1992–1996 NAEP for MSAs with population greater than 2 million.

low average.[17] However, less than one in four white students attend public schools in cities while over half of all black students in the Flanagan and Grissmer sample are

[17] These samples of central city students contain scores from many cities that are not included in the results for Figures 3(a)–(b) because Grissmer and Flanagan do not restrict their attention to the largest central cities.

Table 5
Average test scores and population percentages by race, region and locality

Race	Locality	Region	Student population percentage	Avg score (standard deviation)
White	Suburban	Northeast	9.4	0.47
White	Suburban	Midwest	11	0.37
White	Rural	Northeast	3.3	0.37
White	Rural	Midwest	5.1	0.31
White	Suburban	Southeast	10.1	0.23
White	Suburban	West	8.5	0.18
White	Central city	Southeast	5.1	0.17
White	Rural	West	2.9	0.16
White	Central city	West	4.6	0.15
White	Central city	Midwest	4.1	0.14
White	Central city	Northeast	2.2	0.03
White	Rural	Southeast	5.6	0
Black	Suburban	Northeast	1.4	−0.38
Black	Suburban	Midwest	0.8	−0.49
Black	Rural	Southeast	1.2	−0.65
Black	Rural	Northeast	0.2	−0.68
Black	Rural	Midwest	0.1	−0.71
Black	Suburban	Southeast	3.1	−0.76
Black	Central city	Southeast	3.7	−0.79
Black	Central city	Midwest	1.9	−0.79
Black	Central city	West	0.6	−0.81
Black	Central city	Northeast	2.2	−0.84
Black	Suburban	West	0.7	−0.93
Black	Rural	West	0.1	−0.99

Notes: This table is taken from Flanagan and Grissmer (2002), Table 4. Column 4 reports the students living in each location as a percentage of the national student population.

in central cities. Further, with the exception of a small number of black students in suburbs and rural areas in the West, blacks in central cities score lower than all other black students. For the vast majority of the 20th century, any result suggesting that black children in the rural South were better educated than black children in northern cities would have been completely incredible, but note that by the 1990s, black students in the rural southeast score more than 0.2 standard deviations higher than black students in northeastern cities.

Several existing studies of the relative performance of public versus private schools document particularly poor educational outcomes for black students who attend public schools in large cities.[18] These results as well as the results in Figures 3(a)–(b) and Table 5 stand in stark contrast to a literature that documents the experiences of blacks

[18] See Neal (1997) and Grogger and Neal (2000).

Appendix Table 3
NAEP national test scores (standard errors in parenthesis)

Year	Math scores							
	4th grade				8th grade			
	White		Black		White		Black	
90	220	(1.00)	188	(1.80)	270	(1.30)	237	(2.70)
92	227	(0.80)	193	(1.40)	277	(1.00)	237	(1.30)
96	232	(1.00)	198	(1.60)	281	(1.10)	240	(1.90)
00	234	(0.80)	203	(1.20)	284	(0.80)	244	(1.20)
03	243	(0.20)	216	(0.40)	288	(0.30)	252	(0.50)
Year	Reading scores							
	4th grade				8th grade			
	White		Black		White		Black	
92	224	(1.20)	192	(1.70)	267	(1.10)	237	(1.70)
94	224	(1.30)	185	(1.80)	267	(1.00)	236	(1.80)
98	225	(1.00)	193	(1.90)	270	(0.90)	244	(1.20)
00	224	(1.10)	190	(1.80)	–	–	–	–
02	229	(0.30)	199	(0.50)	272	(0.40)	245	(0.70)
03	229	(0.20)	198	(0.40)	272	(0.20)	244	(0.50)

Notes: The table displays average NAEP National scores and standard errors for math and reading tests, grades 4 and 8. Data are taken from the NAEP sponsored The Nation's Report Card. In 2000, reading tests for 8th graders were not administered.

during the pre-Civil Rights era. In the decades prior to the Civil Rights Act of 1964, large numbers of blacks migrated from the rural South to seek a better life for themselves and their children in cities, especially northern cities, but by the end of the 20th century, black children in cities possessed lower levels of skill than black children in the rural South.

In summary, there is considerable evidence that during the 1970s and 1980s black youth made significant achievement gains relative to white youth. The gains are present in math and reading using different data sets and different measures of progress. On the other hand, both the NAEP-LTT and AFQT data suggest that youth in the lower deciles of black test score distributions did not improve their relative ranks in distributions of test scores for whites over this period, and black youth in large cities, especially boys, likely lost ground relative to white youth.

In terms of overall trends, it is most important to note that Table 3 provides no evidence that black–white test score gaps continued to close during the 1990s. This development is puzzling in light of the sizeable gains made by black youth during the 1970s and 1980s. The AFQT data in the NLSY panels provide two snapshots that are almost two decades apart, and although these snapshots allow comparisons between two specific sets of birth cohorts, the NLSY panels provide no information about achievement trends during the 1990s. It would be useful to examine other measures of trends in black–white achievement gaps during the 1990s, but the NAEP-LTT assessments are the only nationally representative data on achievement intended to measure trends over time. The best available points of comparison may come from the national NAEP math and reading assessments for 4th and 8th graders. These assessments are not designed to be comparable over time, but the National Center for Educational Statistics (NCES) suggests that they may in some instances provide useful information about short term achievement trends in samples defined by grade attending rather than age.[19] Appendix Table 3 presents results from these assessments. During the 1990s, the NAEP national assessments suggest that black elementary and junior high school students gained no ground on their white peers in terms of overall achievement. Reading scores for black eighth graders rose relative to scores for their white peers, but the opposite was true for math scores, and black–white test score gaps among fourth graders were roughly the same at the end of the 1990s as they were at the beginning. Results from these assessments are not directly comparable to those from the NAEP-LTT assessments, and the two sets of assessments do not always paint exactly the same picture. However, neither set of assessments indicate that the overall black–white skill gap narrowed during the 1990s.

It is worth noting that the 2002 reading assessments and the 2003 math assessments show significant gains in achievement for black fourth graders both in levels and relative to whites. These results may signal the beginning of another period of test score convergence between black and white youth. However, it is important not to draw too much from these two data points. The national NAEP scores are reported on a common scale across years, but the national NAEP program does not maintain a fixed assessment framework over time. In addition, even if one is willing to use these data to measure trends from the early 1900s through 2003, there is no clear evidence of overall progress for black youth relative to white youth. The black–white gap in fourth grade math scores is significantly smaller in 2003 than in the early 1990s, but this is not true for the other three assessments. Finally, the reading assessments in 2002 and the math assessments in 2003 involved dramatic changes in the administration of the tests. In these years, the state NAEP assessments were folded into the national NAEP assessments creating a set of national assessments that involved more than 10 times as many students as in previous years. The NAEP-LTT assessments for 2003 will be released in 2005. These data should tell us much more about trends in black–white achievement after 1999.[20]

[19] See http://www.nces.ed.gov/nationsreportcard/about/national.asp. The difference between the national and LTT assessment is described as follows: "As the content and nature of the NAEP instrument evolve to match instructional practice, the ability of the assessment to measure change over time is reduced. While short-term trends can be measured in many of the NAEP subjects (e.g., mathematics, reading), the most reliable instrument of change over time are the NAEP long-term trend assessments".

[20] These assessments were released while this volume was in press. While these most recent NAEP-LTT results do suggest some closing of back–white test score gaps after 1999, the most recent gaps remain at least as large, on average, as the gaps observed between 1986 and 1990.

3. Skills and adult outcomes

The future will reveal whether the 1990s were only a pause in a secular process of skill convergence between black and white Americans, or whether the late 1980s and early 1990s marked the beginning of an important period of constant or falling relative skill levels for blacks. In either case, the results presented in the previous section raise important questions. Why have relative skill levels for black youth apparently remained constant at best for the past fifteen years or more given the large black–white skill gap that remains? Why do so many black youth apparently fail to master the basic math and reading skills covered by their schools' curricula? Can a large black–white skill gap persist for the indefinite future?

I begin my discussion of these issues by reviewing modern models of statistical discrimination. A large theoretical literature explores the idea that black youth may fail to acquire skills because they believe that employers are not likely to view them as skilled regardless of their true skill level. In these models, the response of black youth to the anticipated prejudice of employers confirms the prejudice, and the black community finds itself in an equilibrium characterized by low levels of skill investment and low gross returns to the skill investments that are made. In this section, I flesh out the logic of statistical discrimination models, and I assess whether or not these models can explain recent data on skill levels and racial wage gaps.

I illustrate the key features of statistical discrimination models by describing a particular model that has been quite influential. In Coate and Loury (1993), firms must assign workers to one of two tasks. Task one yields higher output if and only if the worker assigned to task one is a skilled worker. Workers are skilled if they make particular investments in their own human capital. These skill investments are costly to workers but not verifiable. Firms have prior beliefs, π_b and π_w, concerning the fraction of black workers and white workers respectively who invest in skills, and for each worker i, firms see only a noisy signal of worker i's productivity, θ_i, and worker i's race. Based on these two pieces of information, firms form posterior beliefs about worker i's productivity and assign the worker to the task that maximizes his expected output. Firms use a cutoff rule such that every worker with a signal greater than some standard, s, is assigned to task one. Because firms' prior beliefs may differ by race, firms may establish $s_w \neq s_b$ as race-specific standards for assignment. Individual workers face heterogeneous costs of investing in skill, but these costs are independent draws from the same distribution $G(c)$ for both black and white workers. An individual worker invests in skills if the expected return is positive given the standard he faces. An equilibrium in the model consists of pairs of beliefs and standards (π_w, s_w) and (π_b, s_b) such that worker investment behavior is an optimal response to the standards set by employers, and given these optimal responses, employer beliefs are self-confirming. The equilibrium is defined by the following condition:

$$\pi_i = G\big(B\big(s^*(\pi_i)\big)\big), \quad \text{where } s_i = s^*(\pi_i),\ i = b, w.$$

The key term is $B(s^*(\pi_i))$. This is the expected wage increase associated with investing in skill for a member of group i. Although all workers assigned to the same task earn the same wage regardless of race, $B(s_i)$ declines with the assignment standard s_i because higher cutoffs imply lower chances of assignment to task one.

There are many variations on this theme in the literature on statistical discrimination. However, throughout the literature, the structure of models implies that blacks invest less in skills than whites as a rational response to employer discrimination. In equilibrium, $\pi_b < \pi_w$, is not only a statement about beliefs but also a statement about racial differences in actual levels of investment, and here, $\pi_b < \pi_w$ holds precisely because $s_b > s_w$, which implies directly that $B(s^*(\pi_b)) < B(s^*(\pi_w))$. The irony is that there is little or no evidence from recent decades that blacks do earn lower returns from skill investments and much evidence suggesting that blacks earn equal or higher returns to investments in skill. It is plausible that, before the 1960s, statistical or other types of discrimination against highly skilled black workers may have dampened incentives for skill acquisition among black youth, but I demonstrate in the next section that apparent returns to investments in skills have been as great or greater among black adults than white adults for many decades. I begin by discussing returns to skills that are not directly observed by most firms. These results speak most clearly to the empirical content of statistical discrimination models. I then turn to race-specific relationships between education and labor market outcomes. In both cases, the evidence indicates that, in recent decades, the correlation between skill levels and labor market outcomes has been at least as strong and likely stronger among blacks than whites.

The analyses presented below are restricted to samples of adult men. A significant literature demonstrates that sample selection bias contaminates standard measures of black–white wage gaps because patterns of selection into work differ by race. Since relationships between participation rates and measured skills also differ by race, selection bias contaminates estimates of black–white gaps in standard measures of the return to skills. In analyses of men, it is possible to make some progress by assuming that men who have not worked for significant periods of time face relatively low potential wages. However, this is not a fruitful approach in analyses of women. For significant numbers of white women, the choice to work at home appears to be driven not by low potential wages but the high earnings potential of their spouse.[21]

3.1. Returns to cognitive skills

In previous work, Neal and Johnson (1996) and Johnson and Neal (1998), William Johnson and I have examined race-specific returns to skills measured by the ASVAB tests taken by respondents in the NLSY79. Using labor market data from the early 1990s, we found that the correlation between AFQT scores at ages 15–18 and subsequent log wages observed at ages 26–30 was at least as strong among black males as among

[21] See Neal (2004) for more on racial differences in selection patterns among women.

white males. We also found that the AFQT-log earnings gradient was clearly steeper among black males than among white males. Here, I repeat our previous analyses using wage and earnings data from the 2000 wave of the NLSY79.[22] The specifications I adopt here differ from those in the earlier analyses because I use data from all birth cohorts in the NLSY79 sample. In the previous work, we excluded cohorts that were old enough to have engaged in a significant period of full-time work before taking the AFQT. We adopted this approach because we were trying to assess the importance of black–white differences in pre-market skill acquisition. If employers discriminate against black workers by denying them access to jobs with significant opportunities for learning, AFQT scores posted after labor market entry could be contaminated by discrimination in the labor market.[23] However, between the early 1990s and 2000, the NLSY suffered noteworthy attrition bias, and to increase sample sizes, I performed the analyses presented in Figures 4(a)–(c) on the full NLSY sample.

Similar figures based on data from only the 1962–1964 birth cohorts are available upon request. These figures illustrate the same patterns that I highlight below. Wage and earnings profiles with respect to AFQT are as steep or steeper among blacks than the corresponding profiles among whites. However, the absolute value of AFQT-constant wage and earnings gaps is somewhat larger among respondents from these later birth cohorts.

Figures 4(a)–(c) present three sets of results on relationships between AFQT and wages for blacks and whites separately. Figure 4(a) presents results from regressions of log wages on a quadratic in AFQT. These regressions are weighted to account for non-random attrition, and the wage observation used is the hourly rate of pay associated with the job identified in the 2000 wave of the NLSY79 as the CPS job. The figure graphs these predicted wages between the 10th and 90th percentiles of the race-specific AFQT distributions. Figures 4(b) and (c) present results from median regressions. The median regressions corresponding to the lines in Figure 4(b) employ the same samples used in the mean regressions. However, the median regressions associated with Figure 4(c) include imputed wages of one dollar per hour for all men who report not working any job since their last interview. Since the previous wave of the NLSY was administered in 1998, the imputations are restricted to men who have not worked at all for at least two years.[24]

[22] The sample includes males from all birth years. It does not include respondents from the oversamples of Hispanics, economically disadvantaged whites or military personnel. However, the sample does include respondents from the oversample of black males. The white sample here differs from the white sample used in the Neal and Johnson (1996). Here, I construct a white category that matches, as closely as possible, the census definition of white. In the earlier paper, we used the non-black, non-Hispanic category that forms the basis for the NLSY sampling frame.

[23] In this scenario, the age-adjusted score for black respondents from earlier birth cohorts may measure not only cognitive function but also a separate ability to overcome discrimination.

[24] Johnson, Kitamura and Neal (2000) use panel data from earlier waves of the NLSY79 to show that workers, who report past or future wages rates but are currently in the middle of a multiple year spell of non-employment, almost always earn less than the median wage observed among workers with similar demographic characteristics.

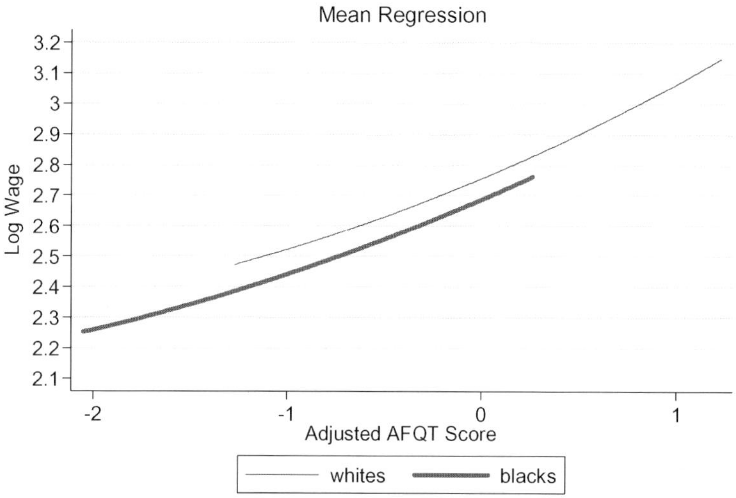

(a)

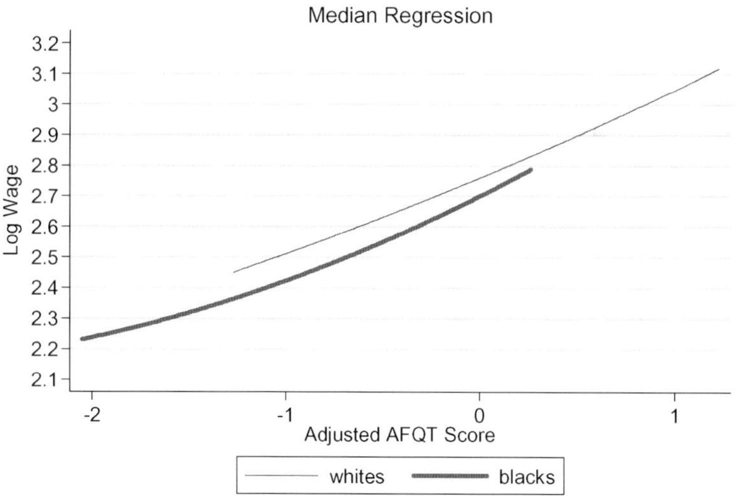

(b)

Figure 4. The figures show predicted values from a regression of log wages on a quadratic in adjusted AFQT score for black and white males separately. Data are from the 2000 wave of the NLSY79. In the median regressions (c) for individuals who did not work since their 1998 interview are imputed a wage equal to one dollar.

Several patterns in these figures are noteworthy. First, the black and white AFQT distributions do overlap but the right tail of the white score distribution and the left tail of the black score distribution represent regions with little if any overlap. A sig-

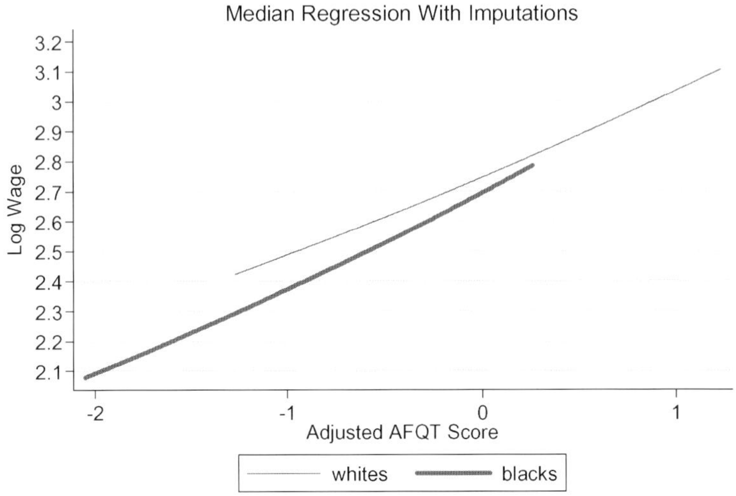

(c)

Figure 4. (*Continued.*)

nificant fraction of males in the black sample score more than 1.5 standard deviations below the mean, and these males have few white peers.[25] There is also a clear absence of black scores in the upper tail of the distribution. Thus, meaningful comparisons of race-specific returns to AFQT must focus on respondents who score from just below -1 to just above 0. Second, in all three figures, the wage-AFQT gradient is as steep or steeper among black men than white men. The difference in slopes for the mean regressions is small and not statistically significant. The racial difference in slopes for the median regressions is much more significant economically but still falls short of conventional standards of statistical significance. Third, the low levels of employment among black men with low AFQT scores drive the important differences between Figures 4(b) and (c). Within the upper half of the black skill distribution, the wage-AFQT profiles for black men in Figures 4(b) and (c) are similar, but the two profiles diverge dramatically as one moves down through the bottom half of the black skill distribution. This result foreshadows a theme that will be repeated several times in this section. In recent decades, employment levels among less skilled and less educated black men have been quite low by any historical standard for adult men. One possible explanation is that changes in the relative demands for workers of different skill levels have adversely affected less-skilled black workers in a manner that has no counterpart among white workers because there are so few white workers who struggle with basic math and reading skills.

[25] This result is not surprising given the results reported above concerning the fraction of black teens in NLSY79 who did not do better on the AFQT than one would expect from guessing.

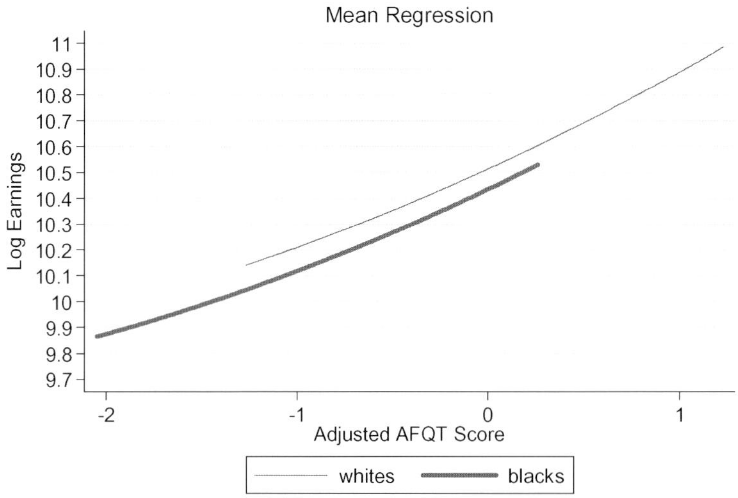

(a)

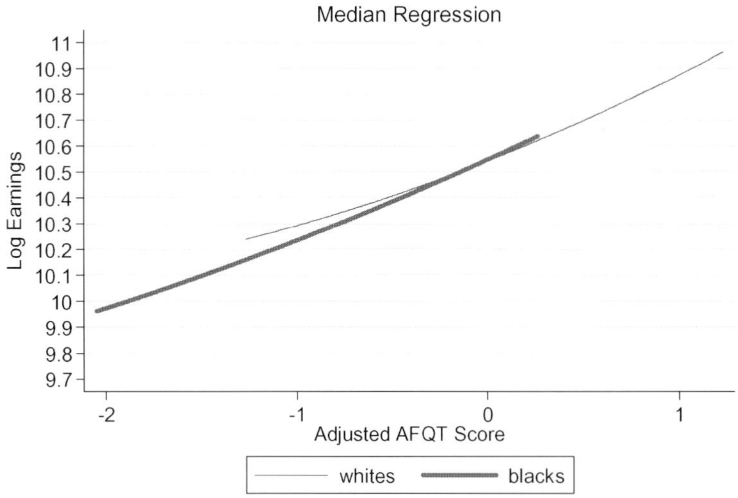

(b)

Figure 5. The figures show predicted values from a regression of log earnings on a quadratic in adjusted AFQT score for black and white males separately. Data are from the 2000 wave of the NLSY79.

Figures 5(a)–(b) present two sets of results based on earnings levels in the previous calendar year. Figure 5(a) presents results from a regression of log earnings on a quadratic in AFQT. Figure 5(b) presents results from a corresponding median regression. I do not present results that incorporate earnings imputations for workers with missing earnings.[26] The patterns are similar to those observed in Figures 4(a)–(b). However, the difference in slopes is more pronounced for the median regression. The median regression results are quite robust to the use of various cutoff rules for trimming earnings levels that imply either coding error or short spells of employment, and these results indicate that median earnings rise quite a bit faster with skill among black men.

Such results present a challenge for models that explain low black skill levels as a rational response to the presence of statistical discrimination by employers. The Coate and Loury model is a one period model, but it seems natural to interpret it in the following way. Firms acquire signals about workers' talents through interviews, observing their performance in entry level jobs, and checking their work records with other employers. Based on these signals, employers make assignment decisions. Because employers statistically discriminate against black workers, blacks who invest in skills will see a smaller increase in their probability of promotion to good jobs than whites who invest.[27] This implies that the gradient between wages and productive skills, that are not directly observed by the employer, should be greater among whites than blacks. Figures 4(a)–5(b) provide no evidence that this prediction is true, and they provide considerable suggestive evidence that this prediction is false.

Some may argue that what matters is not realized returns to investments but rather the fact that many blacks believe that the labor market will not reward them or their children for investing in human capital. The literature on statistical discrimination began with Arrow (1973) and Phelps (1972). When Arrow and Phelps first developed these ideas, existing cohorts of adult workers had lived most of their lives in labor markets where blacks may well have earned lower returns to education and skills than whites workers.[28] However, it is hard to find data that would support this belief today. Blacks who reached adulthood after the Civil Rights Act of 1964 have not earned systematically lower returns to attainment or achievement than their white peers. During the past decade or more, black adult respondents in the NLSY79 have earned relatively high

[26] There is no 1999 wave of the NLSY79. Wage data are collected with reference to the time since the last interview. Earnings data are collected with reference to the past calendar year. Thus, if someone worked in 1998 but not in 1997 or 1999, his most recent wage is likely recorded but his most recent calendar earnings are not recorded. Thus, I cannot identify earnings levels for all persons who worked since their 1998 interview.

[27] Because employers hold all blacks to a higher promotion standard whether they have invested or not, it may seem possible that discrimination of this type could raise returns from skill investment for blacks. However, this cannot occur in equilibrium because higher returns for blacks would generate higher investment levels for blacks and the original discriminatory beliefs that led to the racial difference in promotion standards would not be self-confirming.

[28] No data provide gradients of labor market outcomes with respect to cognitive test scores during the 1970s and early 1980s. However, Cutright (1973) matched social security earnings data from 1964 with AFQT scores for persons drafted in the Korean war. His results suggest that prior to the Civil Rights Act, blacks may well have earned lower gross returns to basic skills. Nonetheless, Welch (1973) notes that shortly after the passage of the Civil Rights Acts, blacks began enjoying comparable or better implied returns to investments in education than whites.

returns to skills measured by the AFQT.[29] Further, as I demonstrate below, apparent returns to formal schooling among black young adults have typically been as large or larger than the corresponding returns among whites since at least 1970.

In the balance of this section, I present details concerning the relationship between education and labor market outcomes among black and white adult men. Existing panel data sets do not provide information concerning racial differences in the relationship between cognitive skills and adult outcomes for birth cohorts other than those included in the NLSY79.[30] However, census data document the relationship between educational attainment and labor market outcomes for a broad range of cohorts. Education differs from reading and math scores in that it is an indirect measure of skill that is easily observed by employers, but the patterns documented below are similar to those in Figures 4(a)–5(b). Correlations between schooling and positive labor market outcomes among blacks are as strong or stronger than the corresponding correlations among whites, especially in recent decades.

3.2. *Education and labor market outcomes*

The Integrated Public Use Micro Samples (IPUMS) drawn from decennial census records provide individual data on education, earnings and labor force activity in the various census years. Most of the results below come from 1980 through 2000 census files, but in some cases, I also include results from 1960 and 1970. I begin by describing data on rates of employment and incarceration. Table 6 describes outcomes for groups of men who fall in the same (race $*$ education $*$ age) cell in a given census year. The diagonal rows in the table provide results from the same census file, which in this case is either 1980, 1990, or 2000. Moving across a row, one can follow a birth cohort over time. Moving down columns, one can track the evolution over birth cohorts of outcomes at specific ages. The three education groups are: (1) completed some high school but no credential (2) finished high school or obtained a GED but completed no post-secondary schooling and (3) college degree but no post-graduate degrees. These education groups provide the opportunity to measure cell means with respectable sample sizes. Each cell contains three numbers. The top number is the fraction working or enrolled in school at the time of the census. The second number is the fraction who worked in the previous calendar year. The final number is the fraction institutionalized. For men ages 26–45, correctional institutions are by far the most common form of institutional housing.

[29] Both Altonji and Pierret (2001) and Lange (2004) present evidence consistent with the view that employers learn a great deal over time about aspects of worker productivity that are correlated with AFQT scores. These findings raises concerns about all models in which the reason that blacks cannot earn a market return to skill investments is that they cannot reveal their true skill levels to employers.

[30] The National Educational Longitudinal Surveys provide panel data on high school experiences and adult labor market outcomes. However, these samples are drawn from students who are enrolled in specific grades at a point in time, and thus they provide select samples from persons born in a set of birth years. In addition, the follow-up data on earnings and employment are of relatively poor quality in the NELS surveys when compared to NLSY79 on work outcomes.

Table 6
(1) Fraction working or at school in reference week
(2) Fraction worked last calendar year
(3) Fraction institutionalized

Year of birth and education	White				Black			
	26–30	31–35	36–40	41–45	26–30	31–35	36–40	41–45
9–11 years								
1935–1939				0.86				0.77
				0.91				0.79
				0.01				0.03
1940–1944			0.86				0.75	
			0.92				0.80	
			0.01				0.03	
1945–1949		0.84		0.81		0.71		0.64
		0.91		0.85		0.75		0.68
		0.02		0.01		0.06		0.05
1950–1954	0.81		0.80		0.62		0.62	
	0.90		0.85		0.69		0.65	
	0.02		0.02		0.09		0.09	
1955–1959		0.80		0.71		0.56		0.47
		0.86		0.77		0.63		0.51
		0.03		0.03		0.14		0.13
1960–1964	0.79		0.73		0.51		0.49	
	0.86		0.78		0.58		0.53	
	0.04		0.04		0.19		0.19	
1965–1969		0.74				0.44		
		0.79				0.47		
		0.05				0.28		
1970–1974	0.73				0.43			
	0.79				0.47			
	0.05				0.26			

(Continued on next page)

Two gradients in Table 6 deserve particular attention. First, black–white differences in employment rates decline dramatically with worker education levels. Among black men ages 26–45 without a high school diploma or GED, less than half were employed at their 2000 Census interview date and less than half worked at all during the calendar year 1999. In contrast, the corresponding employment rates among less educated white men, whether measured in terms of current status or employment last year, are all more than 20 percentage points higher and in four cases are as much as 30 percentage points higher. But, the third panel shows that employment rates for college graduates do not differ greatly by race. In 2000, no black–white difference in employment rates for college educated workers is greater than eight percentage points. The racial differences in employment rates among high school graduates fall between these extremes. It is clear that the relationship between employment and education is much stronger among black

Table 6
(*Continued*)

Year of birth and education	White				Black			
	26–30	31–35	36–40	41–45	26–30	31–35	36–40	41–45
12 years								
1935–1939				0.93				0.84
				0.95				0.84
				0.00				0.01
1940–1944			0.93				0.81	
			0.95				0.85	
			0.01				0.03	
1945–1949		0.91		0.89		0.80		0.76
		0.95		0.92		0.84		0.79
		0.01		0.01		0.03		0.04
1950–1954	0.89		0.89		0.77		0.75	
	0.95		0.92		0.82		0.77	
	0.01		0.01		0.04		0.06	
1955–1959		0.89		0.85		0.73		0.65
		0.93		0.87		0.76		0.70
		0.01		0.02		0.07		0.07
1960–1964	0.89		0.85		0.74		0.67	
	0.93		0.87		0.78		0.71	
	0.02		0.02		0.08		0.09	
1965–1969		0.85				0.67		
		0.87				0.71		
		0.03				0.11		
1970–1974	0.84				0.65			
	0.87				0.68			
	0.03				0.11			

(*Continued on next page*)

workers than white workers. This was also true in 1980 and 1990, but the strength of the relationship between education and employments rates among black men has grown dramatically over time.

In Table 6, I define working last year based on the presence of information provided by the respondent that either directly indicates actual work last year or at least suggests that an allocated positive value of weeks worked last year is credible. If I were to simply calculate employment rates for the previous calendar year based on published census data, employment rates for less educated men would be notably higher among both black and white men in 2000. However, the 2000 data contain many allocated values of positive weeks worked that are not credible. For example, roughly 1 in 6 black men ages 26–45 who have nine to eleven years of schooling receive positive allocated weeks worked even though they did not provide answers to any of the questions about work or earned income sources during the previous calendar year. Further, more than half of

Table 6
(Continued)

Year of birth and education	White				Black			
	26–30	31–35	36–40	41–45	26–30	31–35	36–40	41–45
16 years								
1935–1939				0.97				0.91
				0.97				0.91
				0.00				0.01
1940–1944			0.97				0.94	
			0.97				0.93	
			0.00				0.01	
1945–1949		0.97		0.96		0.93		0.92
		0.97		0.97		0.93		0.91
		0.00		0.00		0.01		0.02
1950–1954	0.96		0.96		0.91		0.90	
	0.97		0.97		0.92		0.89	
	0.00		0.00		0.01		0.03	
1955–1959		0.97		0.95		0.93		0.90
		0.97		0.94		0.89		0.90
		0.00		0.00		0.02		0.01
1960–1964	0.97		0.96		0.95		0.89	
	0.96		0.95		0.91		0.88	
	0.00		0.00		0.01		0.02	
1965–1969		0.96				0.90		
		0.96				0.90		
		0.00				0.02		
1970–1974	0.96				0.91			
	0.95				0.89			
	0.00				0.01			

Notes: Data for this table are from the decennial census IPUMS 1960–2000. The table displays the fraction of males working or in school in the census reference week, fraction who worked last year and fraction of people institutionalized. In order to be counted as working in the previous calendar year, a respondent must have (a) an affirmative, non-allocated response to the question "Did this person work . . . (during the previous calendar year)?" or (b) positive, non-allocated weeks worked or (c) positive non-allocated earned income or (d) positive, allocated weeks worked and a non-allocated indication of working since January 1st of the census year in question. Sample weights "perwt" are used for year 2000.

these men were institutionalized at the time of the census. I have also calculated rates of working last year based only on samples of persons who answered at least one question concerning work last year or earned income in the previous year. This method yields results that are quite similar to those in Table 6.

When considering the strikingly low employment rates among less educated black men reported in Table 6, one must also remember that not all black men are counted in the census. Robinson, Adlakha and West (2002) use vital statistics data to estimate how many persons should have been counted in the 2000 census in various demographic groups defined by age, race, and gender. They report that black men are the only adult group in 2000 for which a significant undercount is present, and their estimates imply that at least 9 percent of black males ages 25–44 were not counted in the 2000 census. If less educated black men are over-represented in the undercount of black men, the true gradient between education and employment among black men could be even steeper than the relationship implied by Table 6.

The second noteworthy gradient in Table 6 involves the sizes of institutionalized populations. Among black men, the fraction institutionalized declines dramatically with education, and this is particularly true among men ages 26–35. Note that over one in four black high school dropouts in this age group were institutionalized at the time of the 2000 census. This is roughly 5 times the rate of institutionalization among white men in the same age and education cells, and at least three times greater than the corresponding rate among black men in 1980. If one assumes that rates of institutionalization correspond closely to rates of imprisonment, it is clear that incarceration rates have risen among black men of all ages and education levels since 1980, but the increase among black college graduates is trivial compared to increases among black men who have no high school credential or a high school credential with no post-secondary schooling.[31]

Next, I turn to wages and earnings and their relationships with education. Table 7 presents black–white differences in mean log wages within cells defined by education and levels of potential experience.[32] Because the census gathers information on income from the past calendar year, the data describe wage gaps in 1979, 1989, and 1999. In a recent paper, Baum-Snow and Neal (2004), Nathaniel Baum-Snow and I document serious problems with hours worked information in census data.[33] Thus, I construct predicted log hours per week for each employed individual using data from the March CPS of the corresponding year and form log wages for each individual in the census by subtracting reported log weeks worked and predicted log hours per week from reported log annual earnings. I present mean black–white gaps in log wages for workers who fall in 45 cells defined by three education groups, three census years, and five experience levels. The education groups are the same ones used in Table 6.

The results in Table 7 demonstrate that in the vast majority of cases black–white log wage gaps decline with education level among men who have similar levels of potential

[31] The results presented in Table 6 also underscore why results that follow concerning wages and earnings draw on census data and not data from the Current Population Surveys (CPS). The CPS do not sample incarcerated individuals and thus, in recent years, are not useful for constructing representative samples of less educated black men.

[32] Here, I define potential experience as the $\max\{\min(\text{age} - 18,\ \text{age} - \text{years of schooling} - 6), 0\}$. The education variable used here is a measure of school completed not school attended. Data on highest grade attended is not available in 1990 and 2000. By marking age 18 as the beginning of adult work experience, I minimize the number of high school dropouts that are falsely given credit for a year of potential work experience simply because they started school after age 6, repeated a grade, or did not graduate from the last grade they attended.

[33] We show that many persons respond to the question on usual hours worked per week as if it were a question about usual hours worked per day. The frequency of these apparent errors is correlated with race and gender and varies across census years.

Table 7
Black–white differences in average log hourly wages (predicted hours from CPS). No imputations. Standard deviations in parentheses

Year and education	Experience				
	1–5	6–10	11–15	16–20	21–25
9–11 years					
1980	−0.21	−0.24	−0.25	−0.27	−0.24
	(0.02)	(0.02)	(0.02)	(0.02)	(0.02)
1990	−0.18	−0.24	−0.22	−0.21	−0.17
	(0.02)	(0.02)	(0.02)	(0.02)	(0.02)
2000	−0.15	−0.14	−0.22	−0.23	−0.25
	(0.02)	(0.03)	(0.03)	(0.02)	(0.02)
12 years					
1980	−0.14	−0.16	−0.16	−0.18	−0.19
	(0.01)	(0.01)	(0.01)	(0.01)	(0.01)
1990	−0.12	−0.21	−0.22	−0.16	−0.19
	(0.01)	(0.01)	(0.01)	(0.01)	(0.01)
2000	−0.07	−0.14	−0.16	−0.18	−0.21
	(0.02)	(0.02)	(0.01)	(0.01)	(0.01)
16 years					
1980	−0.01	−0.06	−0.12	−0.15	−0.25
	(0.02)	(0.02)	(0.03)	(0.03)	(0.04)
1990	−0.02	−0.14	−0.17	−0.18	−0.17
	(0.02)	(0.02)	(0.02)	(0.02)	(0.03)
2000	−0.03	−0.12	−0.16	−0.27	−0.27
	(0.03)	(0.02)	(0.02)	(0.02)	(0.02)

Notes: This table displays black–white average log wage gaps. Data are from the decennial census IPUMS 1960–2000. Log hourly wages are created using the IPUMS variables "incwage" and "wkswork1" and predicted hours using CPS data. The sample includes non self-employed males with positive wage income who worked last year. Working last year is defined using the rules described in the notes to Table 6. Sample weights "perwt" are used for year 2000. Wages are trimmed at the 1st and 99th percentile. Values are expressed in 1999 USD. Current monetary values have been adjusted using the CPI-U. Potential experience is defined as $\max\{0, \min(\text{age} - 18, \text{age} - \text{years of schooling} - 6)\}$.

labor market experience, and these declines tend to be larger at lower levels of experience. The results in Table 7 permit the calculation of 45 racial differences in the log wage gain associated with a given increase in completed schooling. These include differences in the wage gains associated with finishing high school, finishing high school and going on to finish college, and completing college given a high school credential. In 43 of 45 cases, the implied gain for black men is either greater than or not statistically different than the implied gain for white men. The exceptions involve wage gains associated with obtaining a college education among workers with more than 16 years of experience. Table 8 presents black–white log earnings gaps in the same format as Table 7. Table 8 also includes data from the 1960 and 1970 census files. The results from the 1980–2000 data follow the same patterns found in Table 7, and in the earlier census years, implied log earnings gains associated with education tend also to be as large or larger for blacks. However, the pattern of racial differences in returns in 1960 is more mixed than in other years.

Table 6 demonstrates that, across a broad age range, black–white employment ratios rise with education levels. Similar patterns emerge if one calculates employment rates by race for groups defined by education and potential experience. Even among workers with decades of potential experience, employment rates among black men with no post-secondary schooling have fallen dramatically in recent decades, both in absolute terms and relative to those of comparably educated white men.[34] Economists often assume that, among men who share a common set of demographic characteristics, the mean observed wage is greater than the mean of potential wages among those who do not work. Thus, the mean wage among workers in a given group may be a poor approximation of the mean potential wage in that group when a significant percentage of persons in the group do not work. The results in Table 6 suggest that selection bias may attenuate the measured racial wage and earnings gaps in Tables 7 and 8, and this bias may be most severe among less educated workers. The entries in Tables 7 and 8 for high school dropouts in 2000 are calculated based on samples of black men who report employment rates of roughly 50 percent or less at all experience levels.

Tables 9 and 10 represent versions of Tables 7 and 8 that are corrected for selection in the following manner. For each cell defined by race, experience level, and education, I calculate the average log wage and average log earnings. I subtract 0.4 from these log averages to form imputed average log wages and earnings for men in these same cells who did not work in the previous calendar year. I then calculate the implied averages for overall log potential wages and log potential earnings in each cell and calculate black–white differences in these averages.[35] These tables suggest that selection bias does tend to dampen black–white differences in gradients between education and either wages or earnings. In the 2000 census data, the largest black–white differences in log potential

[34] The participation rates in Table 6 do not provide precise information about racial differences in selection rates for the entries in Tables 7 and 8 because Table 6 presents results for age groups rather than experience groups and because Table 6 includes self-employed persons in the sample of workers even if they have no wage and salary income.

[35] After examining wage levels of workers in the NLSY79 who were not employed for entire interview years, I have concluded that 0.4 is a conservative adjustment factor. I also performed analyses in which I calculated the average log wage and average log earnings among workers between the 40th and 60th percentiles of the wage and earnings distributions associated with each of the cells in Tables 7 and 8. I then calculated selection adjustments for these averages under the assumption that all non-workers who report multiple years of non-employment or institutional living quarters face potential wages and earnings below the 40th percentile of the relevant potential wage and earnings distributions for each cell. This approach generated even greater black–white differences in the slopes of the gradients between education and log potential wages or log potential earnings.

Table 8
Black–white differences in average log earnings. No imputations. Standard deviations in parentheses

Year and education	Experience				
	1–5	6–10	11–15	16–20	21–25
9–11 years					
1960	−0.36	−0.47	−0.49	−0.41	−0.44
	(0.02)	(0.02)	(0.02)	(0.02)	(0.02)
1970	−0.26	−0.35	−0.39	−0.37	−0.39
	(0.02)	(0.02)	(0.02)	(0.02)	(0.02)
1980	−0.40	−0.35	−0.34	−0.34	−0.30
	(0.02)	(0.02)	(0.03)	(0.03)	(0.03)
1990	−0.41	−0.41	−0.42	−0.37	−0.29
	(0.03)	(0.03)	(0.03)	(0.03)	(0.03)
2000	−0.35	−0.35	−0.35	−0.30	−0.37
	(0.03)	(0.04)	(0.04)	(0.03)	(0.03)
12 years					
1960	−0.34	−0.43	−0.49	−0.47	−0.42
	(0.02)	(0.02)	(0.02)	(0.02)	(0.02)
1970	−0.16	−0.30	−0.30	−0.34	−0.36
	(0.02)	(0.01)	(0.01)	(0.02)	(0.02)
1980	−0.32	−0.34	−0.29	−0.32	−0.31
	(0.01)	(0.01)	(0.01)	(0.02)	(0.02)
1990	−0.22	−0.36	−0.40	−0.31	−0.33
	(0.02)	(0.02)	(0.02)	(0.02)	(0.02)
2000	−0.23	−0.30	−0.27	−0.29	−0.34
	(0.02)	(0.02)	(0.02)	(0.02)	(0.02)
16 years					
1960	−0.27	−0.37	−0.47	−0.42	−0.54
	(0.06)	(0.04)	(0.04)	(0.04)	(0.08)
1970	0.00	−0.23	−0.28	−0.42	−0.48
	(0.05)	(0.04)	(0.04)	(0.05)	(0.06)
1980	−0.15	−0.19	−0.21	−0.28	−0.37
	(0.03)	(0.03)	(0.03)	(0.04)	(0.05)
1990	−0.04	−0.21	−0.29	−0.29	−0.23
	(0.03)	(0.02)	(0.02)	(0.03)	(0.03)
2000	−0.09	−0.19	−0.25	−0.32	−0.33
	(0.03)	(0.03)	(0.03)	(0.03)	(0.03)

Notes: This table displays black–white average log earnings gaps. Data are from the decennial census IPUMS 1960–2000. The IPUMS variable used is "incwage". The sample includes non self-employed males with positive wage income who worked last year. Working last year is defined using the rules described in the notes to Table 6. Earnings are trimmed at the 1st and 99th percentile. Values are expressed in 1999 USD. Current monetary values have been adjusted using the CPI-U. Potential experience is defined as $\max\{0, \min(\text{age} - 18, \text{age} - \text{years of schooling} - 6)\}$. Sample weights "perwt" are used for year 2000.

Table 9
Black–white differences in average log hourly wages (predicted hours from CPS). With imputations for non-workers. Standard deviations in parentheses

Year and education	Experience				
	1–5	6–10	11–15	16–20	21–25
9–11 years					
1980	−0.32	−0.33	−0.32	−0.32	−0.28
	(0.02)	(0.02)	(0.02)	(0.02)	(0.02)
1990	−0.30	−0.35	−0.33	−0.29	−0.24
	(0.02)	(0.02)	(0.02)	(0.02)	(0.02)
2000	−0.27	−0.26	−0.35	−0.34	−0.35
	(0.02)	(0.03)	(0.03)	(0.02)	(0.02)
12 years					
1980	−0.21	−0.22	−0.21	−0.22	−0.23
	(0.01)	(0.01)	(0.01)	(0.01)	(0.01)
1990	−0.19	−0.28	−0.28	−0.23	−0.24
	(0.01)	(0.01)	(0.01)	(0.01)	(0.01)
2000	−0.15	−0.23	−0.23	−0.24	−0.28
	(0.02)	(0.02)	(0.01)	(0.01)	(0.01)
16 years					
1980	−0.04	−0.09	−0.13	−0.17	−0.28
	(0.02)	(0.02)	(0.03)	(0.03)	(0.04)
1990	−0.05	−0.16	−0.20	−0.21	−0.19
	(0.02)	(0.02)	(0.02)	(0.02)	(0.03)
2000	−0.06	−0.15	−0.19	−0.30	−0.30
	(0.03)	(0.02)	(0.02)	(0.02)	(0.02)

Notes: This table displays black–white average log wage gaps, with imputations for non-workers. See notes to Table 7 for sample and variable definitions, and notes to Table 6 for the definition of working status. Each entry is equal to $[p_b x_b + (1 - p_b)(x_b - 0.4)] - [p_w x_w + (1 - p_w)(x_w - 0.4)]$, where x_w (x_b) is the mean log wage in the white (black) year–experience–education cell among working men, and p_w (p_b) is the fraction working in the white (black) year–experience–education cell.

wages and earnings are always found among workers who have not obtained any high school credential, and in recent decades, new cohorts of college educated blacks have fared much better relative to whites than less educated blacks.

Here, I am using the cross-section relationships between education and earnings or education and wages as indicators of the gains from education that individual young persons might expect at a given point in time. Heckman, Lochner and Todd (2004) adopt a life-cycle investment framework and calculate rates of return on investments in education by following the earnings histories of synthetic cohorts over recent census years. They find consistent evidence that blacks earn higher rates of return to education than whites.

Table 10
Black–white differences in average log earnings. With imputations for non-workers. Standard deviations in parentheses.

Year and education	Experience				
	1–5	6–10	11–15	16–20	21–25
9–11 years					
1960	−0.40	−0.49	−0.50	−0.43	−0.47
	(0.02)	(0.02)	(0.02)	(0.02)	(0.02)
1970	−0.32	−0.38	−0.42	−0.39	−0.41
	(0.02)	(0.02)	(0.02)	(0.02)	(0.02)
1980	−0.51	−0.44	−0.42	−0.39	−0.34
	(0.02)	(0.02)	(0.03)	(0.03)	(0.03)
1990	−0.53	−0.52	−0.53	−0.45	−0.36
	(0.03)	(0.03)	(0.03)	(0.03)	(0.03)
2000	−0.47	−0.48	−0.48	−0.41	−0.47
	(0.03)	(0.04)	(0.04)	(0.03)	(0.03)
12 years					
1960	−0.37	−0.45	−0.51	−0.49	−0.44
	(0.02)	(0.02)	(0.02)	(0.02)	(0.02)
1970	−0.20	−0.32	−0.32	−0.35	−0.38
	(0.02)	(0.01)	(0.01)	(0.02)	(0.02)
1980	−0.39	−0.40	−0.33	−0.36	−0.35
	(0.01)	(0.01)	(0.01)	(0.02)	(0.02)
1990	−0.29	−0.43	−0.47	−0.37	−0.38
	(0.02)	(0.02)	(0.02)	(0.02)	(0.02)
2000	−0.31	−0.39	−0.34	−0.35	−0.40
	(0.02)	(0.02)	(0.02)	(0.02)	(0.02)
16 years					
1960	−0.28	−0.38	−0.47	−0.42	−0.53
	(0.06)	(0.04)	(0.04)	(0.04)	(0.08)
1970	−0.01	−0.24	−0.28	−0.42	−0.50
	(0.05)	(0.04)	(0.04)	(0.05)	(0.06)
1980	−0.17	−0.21	−0.22	−0.31	−0.39
	(0.03)	(0.03)	(0.03)	(0.04)	(0.05)
1990	−0.07	−0.23	−0.32	−0.32	−0.25
	(0.03)	(0.02)	(0.02)	(0.03)	(0.03)
2000	−0.12	−0.22	−0.28	−0.34	−0.36
	(0.03)	(0.03)	(0.03)	(0.03)	(0.03)

Notes: This table displays black–white average log earnings gaps, with imputations for non-workers. See notes to Table 7 for sample and variable definitions and notes to Table 6 for the definition of working status. Each entry is equal to $[p_b x_b + (1 - p_b)(x_b - 0.4)] - [p_w x_w + (1 - p_w)(x_w - 0.4)]$, where x_w (x_b) is the mean log earnings in the white (black) year–experience–education cell among working men, and p_w (p_b) is the fraction working in the white (black) year–experience–education cell.

4. Investments in children

Section 2 of this chapter demonstrates that recent cohorts of black young adults have not continued to close the black–white attainment gap and that cohorts of black youth born after the late 1970s appear to have either fallen farther behind their white counterparts or simply made no progress toward closing the black–white achievement gap. The preceding section demonstrates that these measures of the black–white skill gap stopped closing during a time when the correlations between adult labor market outcomes and measured skills were at least as strong and likely stronger among black adults than among white adults. It is possible that race-specific correlations between measured skills and labor market outcomes paint a misleading picture concerning racial differences in the distributions of potential gains from skill investments, but no existing studies provide clear evidence that this is the case.[36] Regardless of the degree to which blacks still suffer from labor market discrimination, recent labor market data do not support the view that discrimination harms skilled blacks more than unskilled blacks, and there is no evidence that some recent surge in discrimination against skilled black workers could serve as a plausible explanation for the recent lack of progress toward closing black–white skill and attainment gaps among youth.[37]

Because black youth can apparently expect relatively high returns from investments in skills, the observed low and stagnant relative skill levels among black youth suggest that there exist barriers to skill acquisition in black families and communities. In this section, I discuss black–white skill convergence in terms of a simple model of the intergenerational transmission of human capital that illustrates how various factors affect investments in children and the evolution of group differences in human capital over time.

Assume that each person lives two periods, and each family has one parent and one child. Children make no decisions. Parents divide their time between market work and investment activities with their children. They divide their income between current household consumption and investment in their child's human capital. Each parent has a utility function

$$U(c, h'),$$

where c = family consumption, and h' = the human capital that her child enjoys in adulthood. In this framework, h' enters the utility function directly. Parents may care about the future well-being of their children, but parents also derive utility directly from

[36] See Card (1999), Carneiro and Heckman (2002) and Carneiro, Hansen and Heckman (2003) for work on individual heterogeneity and measured returns to schooling.

[37] The empirical work in the previous section did not address heterogeneity in returns to skill investments among blacks. While it is possible that the returns to skill and attainment implied by the results in the previous section are not available to some black children, it is important to remember that the NAEP data from the 1990s indicate that a significant fraction of black youth still perform at levels that are approximately below the support of the white skill distribution. For the parents of these black students, what information could sustain the belief that their children have little to gain from improving their reading and math skills, especially given the well documented increase in the apparent labor market returns to education and cognitive skills during the past two decades or more?

having a well educated child.[38] Each parent has one unit of time and devotes a fraction s to investments in her child and a fraction $(1-s)$ to market work. Three factors determine human capital accumulation for a child. These are purchased inputs, d, effective parental time, sh, and the child's ability, θ. Thus, each parent faces the following constraints:

$$h' = g(\theta, sh, d),$$
$$(1 - s)h = pc + td,$$

where h is the human capital of the parent, p is the price of the consumption good, t is the price of the purchased investments in children, and wages are normalized to one. A key finding in the literature on black–white skill gaps is that black children often find themselves well behind their white peers at young ages. I use this model, in large measure, to analyze parents' decisions to invest in young children, and thus I assume that a parent does not know her child's ability to learn, θ, when making these decisions. The abilities of individual children are i.i.d. draws from an ability distribution $F(\theta)$.[39] I impose the standard restriction that parents cannot borrow on behalf of their children. I also ignore bequests, but the results that I highlight remain in a slightly modified version of the model that permits financial transfers to children.

Consider the following special case of the model:

$$U(c, h') = \ln(c) + \alpha \ln(h'),$$
$$h' = \theta(sh)^{\gamma}(d)^{\delta}, \quad \gamma > 0, \quad \delta > 0, \quad (\gamma + \delta) < 1.$$

Given this specification, it is straightforward to derive the following equation describing the evolution of human capital over generations.

$$\ln h' = \ln \theta + (\gamma + \delta) \ln h + k(\alpha, \gamma, \delta) - \delta \ln t,$$

where k is a constant determined by preference and production parameters. I maintain the assumption that the distribution of θ does not vary by race. Existing psychometric studies offer many results that are inconsistent with the view that the black–white skill gap is genetic in origin.[40] Here, I also assume that blacks and whites have the same utility functions and home production functions. Thus, $k(\alpha, \gamma, \delta)$ is the same for black and white families and does not affect the black–white skill gap. Given these assumptions, three factors determine the evolution of black–white skill gaps across generations.[41]

[38] This assumption simplifies the presentation of the model. However, it is not central to the analysis. Below, I solve a specific version of the model to illustrate several basic points. It is straightforward to reformulate this version of the model as a recursive problem in which parents care only about their consumption and the indirect utility of their children.

[39] In the special case of the model that I solve below, investment decisions are not a function of $F(\theta)$, and the analysis of group differences would not change if I allowed correlations within families among realizations of θ.

[40] See Ceci (1991) and Nisbett (1995).

[41] The form of the utility function in this example is such that preference parameters do not enter this equation. Here, the income elasticity of demand for h' would equal one if parents acquired h' at a constant price. If h' is a luxury good, there will be less regression to the mean in human capital across generations.

To begin, the current black–white skill gap affects the skill gap in the next generation. All wealth in this model is held in the form of human capital, and wealth matters here because all investments in children are financed through forgone consumption. Second, the size of this wealth effect varies inversely with the degree of diminishing returns to investments in a given child. Finally, racial differences in the cost of investment goods, $\Delta \ln t$, influence future human capital gaps through their effect on the racial gap in current investments in children.

A little algebra gives the following equation for the steady-state black–white skill gap,

$$\Delta \ln h = \frac{-\delta}{1 - \gamma - \delta} \Delta \ln t,$$

where Δx denotes the mean value of x among blacks minus the corresponding mean among whites. Two steady-state scenarios present themselves. First, if blacks and whites face the same investment cost, $\Delta \ln t = 0$, the black–white skill gap will equal zero in steady state regardless of the size of the initial black–white skill gap. This outcome is not peculiar to this model. In models with perfect capital markets, full convergence may take place in one generation, but even in models with borrowing constraints, diminishing returns to child-specific investments tend to eliminate group differences in human capital as long as both groups enjoy the same opportunities to invest in children.[42] Diminishing returns is a natural assumption in this context because each child's own time and energy are fixed factors in the production of h'.

On the other hand, if blacks face higher costs than whites, $\Delta \ln t > 0$, then $\Delta \ln h < 0$ will be the steady state outcome. A large literature documents significant relative improvements in school quality for blacks during the 20th century. Further, compared to the pre-Civil Rights era, blacks enjoy much greater freedom to choose communities, schools, and colleges. The extent to which black and white families now face the same costs of investing in their children will influence the degree to which the skills of black youth converge to those of white youth in future generations.

Below, I examine three possible explanations for the halt in black–white skill convergence during the 1990s. I begin by discussing shocks that black families and communities suffered during the 1980s and 1990s. I then turn to the roles of schools and culture. These potential explanations have very different implications for black–white skill convergence in the future. One time shocks to black families or communities can only slow the process of black–white skill convergence for a limited period of time, but persistent racial differences in access to quality schooling or racial differences in social norms concerning investments in children or the organization of families can create more permanent barriers to black–white skill convergence.

[42] See Becker and Tomes (1986) and Loury (1981) for examples. Mulligan (1997) provides a useful exposition of these models and provides analyses of intergenerational correlations for consumption as well as potential income.

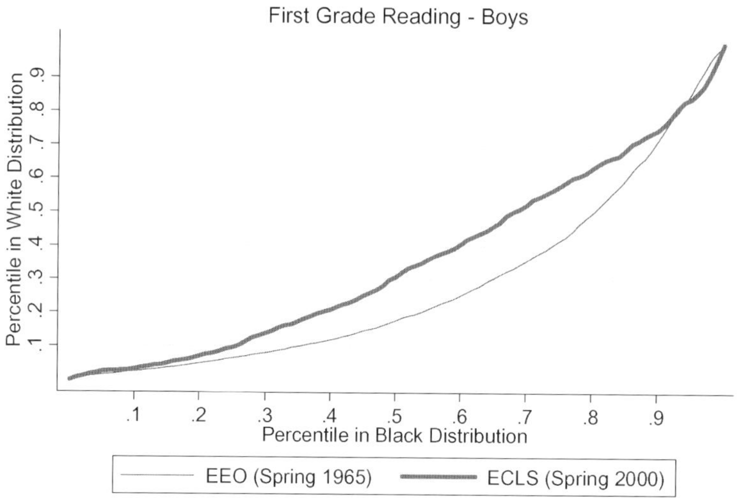

(a)

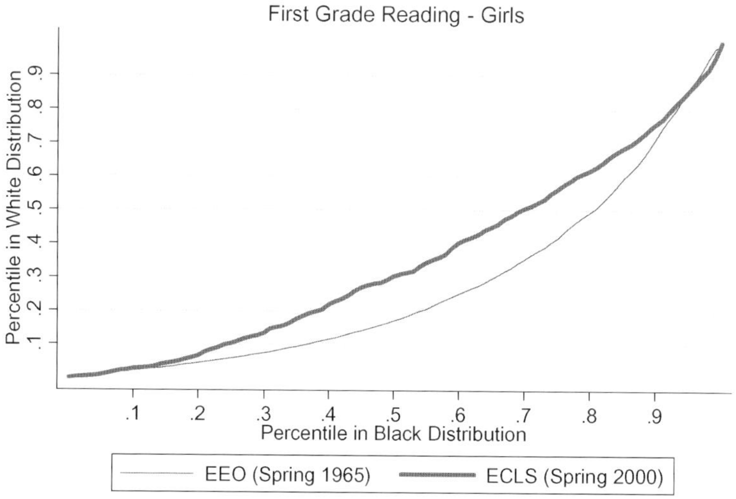

(b)

Figure 6. The figures use verbal and reading EEO and ECLS test scores.

4.1. Shocks to families and communities

The importance of family resources comes into sharper focus when one realizes that black–white achievement gaps are large even among children in their first few years of school. Figures 6(a)–(b) present results based on first grade reading scores from the

Equality of Education Opportunity Study of 1965 (EEO) and the Educational Childhood Longitudinal Study – Kindergarten Class of 1998–1999 (ECLS-K). The figures give matches between percentiles in the black and white score distributions separately by gender. While black first graders did make significant gains relative to their white counterparts over the last three and one half decades of the 20th century, roughly 70 percent of black first-graders in 2000 still performed below the median score among white first-graders of the same gender.[43]

The fact that test scores among black children lag well behind scores among white children at early ages is consistent with the idea that the black–white skill gap among young adults can be traced, in large measure, to black–white differences in the types of investments made in children at early ages. These investments are, for the most part, made by families, and Tables 11 and 12 show that, among young children, the black–white gap in family resources remains large today. Table 11 describes trends in family structure for children ages five and under. The data come from the 1960–2000 census files. The numbers in each cell give the fraction of children of a given race in a given census year who live with either one parent, two parents, or neither of their parents. In 2000, only 1/3 of black pre-school children lived with two parents, and just over one in ten lived with neither of their parents. Black family structures differed from white family structures even in 1960, and in the decades that followed, the rate of decline in two-parent households was much more dramatic in the black community. However, rising black incomes more than made up for the adverse effects of changes in family structure on black household incomes during the period from 1960 to 1980. Table 12 presents weighted averages of household incomes by race, census year, and family structure for families with children ages five and under. The weights are the number of pre-school children in each household. The table shows that between 1960 and 1980, black incomes increased dramatically regardless of family structure, and despite adverse changes in family structures, overall average black household incomes rose considerably relative to white household incomes.

Yet, beginning around 1980, many factors worked together to diminish the resources available to black children. Two-parent families became even more rare in the black community, and for the first time, never-married motherhood became quite common.[44] Further, real wages for less skilled workers fell, and the real value of transfers offered by various welfare programs declined. Thus, Table 12 shows that mean black household income fell during the 1980s and that the ratio of mean black income to mean white income remained lower in 2000 than it was in 1980. Further, within any family structure category, the incomes of black families in that structure did not keep pace

[43] Measured in standard deviation gaps, the black–white gaps for boys are 0.65 and 0.57 for the EEO and ECLS-K respectively. The corresponding gaps for girls are 0.66 and 0.53. Brooks-Gunn, Duncan and Klebanov (1996) document IQ gaps of roughly one full standard deviation in a sample of five year olds.

[44] Neal (2004b) shows that, between 1980 and 1990, the prevalence of never-married motherhood among black women with no postsecondary schooling increased quite dramatically. Never-married mothers may receive much less financial support than divorced mothers.

Table 11
Fraction of children with zero, one, and two parents

	Black			White		
	Zero	One	Two	Zero	One	Two
1960	0.08	0.24	0.68	0.01	0.06	0.93
1970	0.06	0.36	0.58	0.01	0.09	0.90
1980	0.06	0.49	0.46	0.01	0.13	0.86
1990	0.07	0.59	0.34	0.02	0.18	0.80
2000	0.11	0.56	0.33	0.03	0.19	0.79

Notes: The table displays fractions of children aged 0–5 who live in a household with zero, one or two parents. Data are from the decennial census IPUMS, 1960–2000. The IPUMS variables used for defining the number of parents are "momloc" and "poploc". Individuals with allocated sex, age or race have been dropped from the sample. Sample weights "perwt" are used for year 2000.

Table 12
Average household income of children with zero, one, and two parents

Year	Parents							
	Black				White			
	Average	Zero	One	Two	Average	Zero	One	Two
1960	18,280	15,730	13,282	20,323	34,769	24,386	21,076	35,725
1970	28,065	23,376	19,264	33,934	45,779	34,477	27,427	47,664
1980	31,017	29,674	22,150	40,670	45,480	41,464	27,671	48,136
1990	30,933	29,299	22,590	45,634	52,828	42,965	31,773	57,740
2000	35,756	35,591	25,197	53,894	64,065	46,149	37,495	71,016

Notes: The table displays average total household income for children aged 0–5. Data are from the decennial census IPUMS, 1960–2000. The IPUMS variable used for constructing total household income is "inctot". Total household income is the sum of "inctot" across individuals who live in the same household. Negative values of "inctot" have been recoded to zeros. Values are expressed in 1999 USD. Current monetary values have been adjusted using the CPI-U. The variables used for defining the number of parents are "momloc" and "poploc". Individuals with allocated sex, age or race have been dropped from the sample. Sample weights "perwt" are used for year 2000.

with the incomes of their white counterparts from 1980 to 2000. Still, it is clear that the magnitude of the overall relative decline in black family income since 1980 is related to changes in black family structure and the weak growth of household income among black single parents. Mean household incomes for black children in two-parent families did increase by one third during the 1980s and 1990s, but two-parent black families declined in numbers over this period, and mean household income for black children in single parent homes barely increased in real terms during the 1980s and grew at an anemic pace during the 1990s.

A large literature documents dramatic changes in the wage structure during the 1980s and 1990s.[45] These changes involved falling real wages for less skilled workers throughout the 1980s, and because black adults entered the 1980s with less human capital than white adults, these changes in the wage structure lowered the earnings of black adults relative to white adults, especially in the early 1980s.[46] This earnings shock lowered wealth among black adults, and may have also lowered gains from marriage in the black community, helping foster changes in family structures that further widened the effective family resource gap between black and white children. The 1980s were preschool years for most of the nine and thirteen year old respondents tested in the NAEP-LTT assessments of the late 1980s and early 1990s, and these assessments were the first NAEP assessments that showed no closing of the black–white test score gap. The timing of these episodes may be purely coincidental, but the model outlined above suggests that a negative shock to parental wealth should lower human capital accumulation among children, and several recent empirical studies, Mayer (1997) and Blau (1999), find that increases in family wealth are associated with increases in cognitive test scores among children.

Although the magnitudes of existing estimates of the effects of long-term family income on achievement are not large, the sharp declines in family income among black families during the early 1980s were likely accompanied by many episodes of job displacement and family disruption that harm development in children.[47] If negative shocks to black families in the 1980s did reduce investments in black preschoolers, these shocks likely played a role in creating the large and stagnant black–white test score gaps observed during the 1990s. Further, the rising relative incomes of black families during the late 1990s may provide a reason to expect smaller black–white test score gaps in the near future.[48]

Fryer et al. (2004) point to another shock to black families and communities that occurred in the late 1980s and early 1990s. The crack epidemic began around 1985, and it may be no coincidence that this increase in drug market activity began as real wages for unskilled workers were declining. Although the crack epidemic was generally confined to cities, crack distribution did create significant disruptions in urban black communities during the late 1980s and early 1990s. I noted above how Figures 3(a) and (b) show that between 1982 and the period 1992–1996, black youth in large cities actually lost ground in math, relative to the overall distribution of scores for whites. This is quite striking given that overall results for black youth show a narrowing of black–white test

[45] See Katz and Autor (1999).

[46] See Bound and Freeman (1992) and Juhn, Murphy and Pierce (1991). Further, CPS data on yearly averages of household income indicate that the significant declines in black family income prior to 1985 contributed greatly to the overall decline in black family incomes during the 1980s.

[47] McLanahan and Sandefur (1994) and Sandefur and Wells (1999) present much suggestive evidence that children benefit in many ways from growing up in stable homes with two parents.

[48] CPS data indicate that the rising black incomes during the late 1990s generated much of the overall increase in black family incomes during the 1990–2000 period.

score gaps during most of the 1980s and relatively constant gaps during the 1990s. I have not been able to acquire individual NAEP-LTT data for years between 1982 and 1992, and thus I cannot determine the extent to which black achievement in large cities moves with the spread of crack among large cities. However, Figures 3(a)–(b) suggest that this may be an important task for future research.

4.2. Schools

The discussion above focuses on the possibility that changes in the wage structure may have harmed black families and communities in ways that have temporarily stalled the process of black–white skill convergence.[49] However, the model of investment in children presented earlier demonstrates that, if black families face persistently higher costs of investing in their children, black–white skill convergence is not inevitable, and the experience of the past 15 years or more could mark the beginning of a long period of large and stable black–white skill gaps. In this section, I discuss schools as potential sources of fixed racial differences in the levels of investments made in children.

Governments greatly influence the cost of investing in children by selecting policies that regulate the funding and operation of public schools serving different groups in society, and there is no doubt that, during much of the 20th century, blacks were only allowed to attend schools that were funded poorly relative to schools that served predominately white populations. In contrast, black and white students today attend schools that receive comparable resources in terms of standard measures of school inputs.[50] Still, there is some evidence that blacks attend less effective schools than white students, and although this racial gap in school quality cannot be linked to racial differences in school funding levels, it may indicate that blacks pay higher implicit, if not explicit, costs to attend quality schools. Here, I review some of the evidence on the contribution of schools to the black–white achievement gap.

In a recent paper, Fryer and Levitt (2004) analyze data from a panel of students who entered kindergarten in 1998. Fryer and Levitt report that black–white gaps in reading and math are large when students begin kindergarten, and they also report that these gaps grow as children progress through kindergarten and first grade. When they control for school fixed effects, they find little evidence that black–white test score gaps grow over time among students attending the same school, and they interpret this result as suggestive evidence that blacks, on average, attend schools that are less effective than the schools that whites attend.

De los Santos, Heckman and Larenas (2004) use a different methodology to address black–white differences in school quality. Using data from the NLSY79, they estimate how AFQT scores change with years of schooling prior to the date of the test. They con-

[49] Note that even if the drop in real wages for unskilled workers is permanent, this change amounts to a one time negative shock to the relative wealth of black families. This shock would slow but not stop the process of black–white skill convergence.

[50] See Neal (2004b), Grogger (1996), and Boozer, Krueger and Wolkon (1992) for details.

trol for endogeneity in attainment at the time of the test using two methods developed in Hansen, Heckman and Mullen (2004) and conclude that, on average, AQFT scores do increase with schooling faster among white students than black students. However, their results also suggest that these racial differences in how scores change with additional schooling may only be important among children with low latent ability, which they interpret as poor pre-school preparation.

These studies suggest that either racial differences in available school quality or black–white differences in how families and children interact with schools cause the black–white skill gap to grow as children age, but several other data sets offer little evidence that the black–white achievement gap grows at all with time in school. Table 13a summarizes results from three different panel studies of achievement. Each study follows a nationally representative cohort of students who are in the same grade in the first year of the panel. The table describes how the black–white test score gap evolves as students in these cohorts progress through school. The High School and Beyond Study of 1980 (HSB80) follows 10th graders through high school. Follow-up testing took place in 1982 when most respondents were high school seniors. The National Educational Longitudinal Study of 1988 (NELS88) began with a cohort of eighth graders and included follow up testing in 1990 and 1992. In the ECLS-K, black–white test score gaps are clearly wider at the end of first grade than the beginning of kindergarten, and this widening appears to be slightly more dramatic among boys. The NELS88 data show small increases in the absolute value of test score gaps between 8th and 10th grade. However, neither the HSB80 or NELS88 data show that blacks fall farther behind whites after 10th grade. In some cases, black–white gaps in raw test scores widen as students progress through school even though the corresponding gaps measured in standard deviation units shrink over the same time interval. This reflects the fact that, with the exception of the ECLS-K data, the changes in black–white test score gaps reported here are quite small and in some cases they are significantly smaller than the increase in the overall standard deviation of scores between two grades.

Table 13b compares how the relative ranks of black students in distributions of white test scores change between assessments. I assign each black student a percentile score based on where his or her score falls in the corresponding distribution of scores for white students and then calculate the average for these percentile scores. The change in the average percentile rank of black students within the white test score distribution is an attractive index of the change in the achievement of blacks relative to whites because it is invariant to all monotonic transformations of the distributions of test scores. Using this metric, there is no clear evidence that black students lose ground relative to their white peers after 8th grade, and some suggestion of improvement between grades 10 and 12 in the relative ranks of black students in the HSB. The ECLS-K results follow the same pattern found in Table 13a, but the average changes in relative rank among young black girls are quite small.

Table 14 addresses the issue of black–white test score divergence during school ages using synthetic cohort data from the NAEP-LTT studies. I calculate the change in the black–white score gap between ages 9 and 13 for various birth cohorts by subject using

Table 13a
Changes in black–white score gaps. Gap in followup year – gap in base year

Data set	Boys				Girls			
	Reading		Math		Reading		Math	
	Score gain (se)	Stand dev. gain	Score gain (se)	Stand dev. gain	Score gain (se)	Stand dev. gain	Score gain (se)	Stand dev. gain
High School & Beyond Sophomore	−0.123	0.005	0.188	0.078	−0.302	−0.021	−0.206	0.047
1980 Cohort (10th–12th grade)	0.371		0.744		0.323		0.627	
NELS 1988–1990	−1.154	−0.013	−1.176	0.037	−0.527	0.024	−1.894	−0.047
(8th–10th grade)	0.844		1.066		0.737		0.954	
NELS 1990–1992	−0.316	−0.017	−0.750	−0.012	−0.214	−0.013	0.529	0.071
(10th–12th grade)	0.905		1.166		0.725		0.999	
ECLS 1998–1999	−4.386	−0.122	−2.417	−0.130	−3.429	−0.096	−1.876	−0.071
(Fall K–Spring 1st grade)	1.171		0.846		1.217		0.837	

This table displays the changes in the black–white score gaps (referred to as score gains) in score terms and in standard deviation terms for the HSB, NELS and ECLS data. The ECLS base period is fall kindergarten and followup period is spring first grade for 1998–1999. The HSB base period is 10th grade and the followup period is 12th grade for the 1980 cohort. The NELS data covers two time periods. In the first the base period is 8th grade and followup is 10th grade for 1988–1990. The second has a base period of 10th grade and a followup of 12th grade for 1990–1992.

Table 13b
Average percentile ranking in white test scores among black children

Year	HSB			
	Reading		Math	
	Male	Female	Male	Female
1980	0.34	0.33	0.27	0.28
1982	0.35	0.32	0.30	0.30
	NELS			
	Reading		Math	
	Male	Female	Male	Female
1988	0.31	0.31	0.26	0.28
1990	0.31	0.32	0.27	0.29
1992	0.31	0.31	0.27	0.31
	ECLS			
	Reading		Math	
	Male	Female	Male	Female
1998	0.36	0.36	0.32	0.30
1999	0.34	0.35	0.28	0.29

Notes: Each entry represents the average white percentile for black scores. The ECLS data corresponds to fall kindergarten in 1998 and to spring first grade in 1999. The HSB data are for 10th grade in 1980 and 12th in 1982. The NELS data are for 8th grade in 1988, 10th grade in 1990 and 12th grade in 1992.

published reports from the NAEP-LTT. For nine different birth cohorts from 1962 to 1983, there is not one instance of a statistically significant increase in the absolute value of the black–white test score gap in either math or reading. Further, the most notable entries in Table 14 involve instances where black students gained ground on white students, especially in reading. Other studies have found that black–white test score gaps widen as children age,[51] but the ECLS-K is the only nationally representative sample involving multiple waves of testing which provides consistent evidence that blacks fall farther behind whites as they progress through school.

Black–white achievement gaps are quite large before students enter school, and before children leave elementary school, black–white test score gaps are comparable to the gaps that will be observed later when these children are young adults. It seems unlikely that one can understand the black–white skill gap and its recent stability without a

[51] See Carneiro and Heckman (2002) and Phillips, Crouse and Ralph (1998). These studies examine the Children of the National Longitudinal Survey (CNLSY) samples and the Prospects sample. Both studies provide evidence that achievement gaps widen during elementary school years.

Table 14
Relative test score gains of black students. Ages 9–13 NAEP-LTT

Cohort	Reading		Math	
	Score gain (se)	Stand dev. gain	Score gain (se)	Stand dev. gain
1962	7.50 (2.37)	0.03	–	–
1969	–	–	−2.30 (2.36)	−0.14
1971	5.80 (2.38)	0.11	–	–
1973	–	–	4.70 (3.28)	0.04
1975	14.10 (3.12)	0.26	–	–
1977	–	–	−1.90 (3.20)	−0.13
1979	0.40 (3.80)	−0.02	–	–
1981	4.40 (4.13)	0.01	−2.50 (4.31)	−0.09
1983	1.50 (3.69)	0.01	−2.00 (2.67)	−0.10

Notes: The table displays the changes in the black–white reading and math score gap between ages 9 and 13 for various birth cohorts. The data are taken from the 1999 NAEP Long-Term Trend Assessment Summary Data Tables.

better understanding of black–white differences in experiences during early childhood. Because parents play such a large role in preparing children for school and then aiding their children's transition into school, it is worthwhile to consider the potential obstacles that black families may face as they attempt to build their children's human capital. I take up this task in the next section.

Before turning to the role of families, I must add one clarifying comment about schools and education policy. It is well known that black students now, on average, attend public schools that receive resource levels equal to or slightly greater than national averages.[52] Given this fact, and the result that black students do not fall farther behind their white peers after elementary school, some may conjecture that schools per

[52] See Boozer, Krueger and Wolkon (1992), Grogger (1996) and Neal (2004c) for recent statistics on black–white differences in public school resources.

Ferguson (2004) adds a cautionary note concerning teacher quality. He reviews several studies that report a negative correlation between the average level of academic quality among teachers and the percentage of minority students in their classrooms. The measures of teacher quality in these studies include teacher test scores and college major.

se contribute little to the black–white skill gap among today's youth, but even if this conjecture is correct, it does not imply that changes in education policy cannot help close the black–white achievement gap. A recent book edited by Chubb and Loveless (2002) reviews evidence from several experiments involving class size changes, vouchers for disadvantaged students, changes in school management and curriculum, and the introduction of test-based accountability systems. Many of the papers conclude that specific policy changes could contribute to a narrowing of the black–white achievement gap. Krueger and Whitmore (2002) argue that, even though no racial difference in class size currently exists, further across the board reductions in class size would shrink the black–white test score gap because black students benefit more than white students from class size reductions, and they argue that black students were hurt by the fact that average class sizes shrank at a slower rate during the 1990s than in previous decades. Howell and Peterson (2002) argue that vouchers targeted to economically disadvantaged students in cities should reduce the black–white skill gap because black students make up a large portion of disadvantaged urban students and because voucher experiments in cities have shown particularly impressive gains from vouchers for black students.[53]

These results and others reported in the Chubb and Loveless (2002) volume are important for stimulating informed debate about potential changes in public policy that may be particularly beneficial for black children, but I know of no change in public policy during the last 20 years that systematically took resources away from black children. Changes in education policy may be needed to restart the process of convergence, but it is difficult to identify a specific policy change that could have caused black–white convergence in achievement and attainment to suddenly halt after decades of steady progress.

4.3. The role of norms

Black–white differences in family wealth play some role in determining black–white skill gaps among children by shaping investments in children at early ages, and the extremely slow growth of black household income during the 1980s may have contributed to the lack of progress toward closing the black–white skill gap among children born at the end of the 1970s and during the 1980s. However, as I noted earlier, negative wealth shocks should only slow the process of black–white skill convergence for a period of time, and black household income per child began to grow again at a respectable rate at some point during the 1990s. If the below-trend academic performance of black-children born during the 1980s and early 1990s is attributable to the relatively weak

[53] The Krueger and Whitmore paper follows up Krueger's earlier 1999 paper that evaluates the Tennessee STAR experiment. The Howell and Peterson paper summarizes selected results from a larger study of voucher experiments in Dayton, New York City, and Washington, DC, Howell and Peterson (2002b).

Slavin and Madden (2002) contribute another interesting chapter on the use of the "Success for All" school management model in schools with significant populations of minority students.

growth of black family incomes during this period, the process of black–white skill convergence may resume in the near future.

Nonetheless, there is a more ominous potential explanation for the recent stability of the black–white skill gap. Black families may pay consistently higher costs to invest in their children and these cost differences may support persistent and significant black–white gaps in test scores and attainment. This scenario is not compelling unless one can be specific about the form that these cost differences might take, and I have already noted that black and white children now attend schools that receive comparable resources. Further, in stark contrast to the state of affairs a century ago, no legal structures today explicitly place black families at a legal disadvantage relative to whites when investing in their children. Civil Rights laws now guarantee that black families have the right to live in any neighborhood in any house they can afford and also apply to any school they choose without fear of being denied admission solely because of their race. On the other hand, race appears to matter per se in determining how persons organize their social interactions. Rates of inter-marriage are far too low to be explained by economic differences between blacks and whites. Further, neighborhoods and schools are much more segregated by race than one would expect if purely economic considerations determined patterns of sorting. Because social interactions are so segregated by race, one must ask whether or not black–white differences in norms or culture affect patterns of investment in children.

This issue is salient because some evidence suggests that black–white differences in parenting styles contribute to black–white skill gaps among children. Brooks-Gunn, Duncan and Klebanov (1996) follow a sample of low-birth weight infants through age 5. At age 5, these children took IQ tests that revealed a full standard deviation gap in IQ between black and white children. The authors found that measures of family wealth and neighborhood quality did account for roughly half of the black–white gap in IQ scores, but the analyses also included measures of maternal parenting behavior that were constructed from data gathered at ages 12 and 36 months by trained observers who made visits to each child's home. These measures of parenting behavior accounted for over half of the black–white IQ gap among children from families who enjoyed comparable wealth and neighborhood quality even in regression specifications that included additional controls for maternal education and verbal ability. It is possible that parenting behaviors serve as proxies for unmeasured dimensions of maternal human capital. Even among mothers with similar measured skills, those with greater intellectual sophistication likely make better parenting choices. Nonetheless, the fact that parenting behaviors differ greatly by race among families that are similar with respect to wealth, neighborhood quality, family structure, and measured maternal human capital raises the possibility that norms concerning child rearing differ among blacks and whites in important ways.[54]

[54] See also Brooks-Gunn et al. (1998) and Ferguson (2004). Lightfoot (1978) provides a more qualitative analysis of how black families and schools interact and discusses the role on culture in these interactions.

In the economics and sociology literature, there are at least two different lines of argument that deal with social norms and human capital accumulation among children. I begin with the literature on "acting white". A substantial literature examines the possibility that blacks may invest less in human capital than whites because they fear social sanctions from other blacks. If academic achievement is viewed as a "white" accomplishment, higher achieving blacks may be ostracized by other blacks. Austen-Smith and Fryer (2005) develop an explicit model of human capital investment in a setting where this type of social sanction is possible. In their model, residents of a particular neighborhood or social group who invest in academic achievement risk being excluded from social interactions in their neighborhood or group. Contributing to group functions is more costly for skilled people because they have a higher shadow price of time. Thus, the group expects that persons who invest in market skills are more likely to default on future obligations to the group. This social dynamic reduces aggregate investment in human capital because the expected loss of cooperation within the group acts as an extra cost of investing in market skills. Anecdotal evidence in media reports and ethnographic work often suggests that something like this pattern of social interactions hinders human capital accumulation among black youth,[55] but at this point, the existing empirical literature does not provide conclusive evidence that high-achieving black children experience different social benefits or sanctions than high-achieving white children. Further, there is no evidence that black parents suffer social sanctions when they encourage their children to excel in school.[56]

Another important argument about group norms involves attitudes towards marriage and single motherhood. The most striking demographic difference between black and white children is the greater likelihood that a black child will live in a home with one or no parents. Further, many single parent homes in the black community do not arise because of divorce or the death of a parent. Neal (2004b) demonstrates that never-married motherhood became common among black women by 1990, and never-married mothers are even less likely to receive support from the fathers of their children or the families of these fathers than women who are widowed or divorced.

Nechyba (2001) describes a model of unwed motherhood in which the fraction of women who are unwed mothers in one generation determines the stigma associated with unwed motherhood in the next generation. Nechyba argues that, because behavior today affects group norms tomorrow, changes in economic returns to marriage versus single motherhood can create changes in behavior that endogenously generate new norms that persist much longer than the original change in the economic returns to marriage. The possibility that black–white differences in marriage rates reflect not only black–white differences in the economic gains from marriage but also black–white differences in

[55] Ogbu (1990) presents the hypothesis that historical discrimination against blacks has created a belief among blacks that investment in individual skills is a "white" strategy for success and not an attractive strategy for them.

[56] Austen-Smith and Fryer survey this literature. Cook and Ludwig (1998) is one well-known study that finds no support for the claim that highly skilled black students suffer social penalties for "acting white".

norms concerning the desirability of marriage may have implications for how we understand black–white differences in youth outcomes. Weiss and Willis (1985) present a model that shows how investments in children are likely to be below efficient levels when parents do not live in the same household because parents who live together can better coordinate investments in children. When parents live apart, an agency problem arises. The non-custodial parent cannot be sure that transfers intended for expenditures on their child are spent entirely on the child. This monitoring problem acts as a tax on investments in children.

We do not fully understand the causes of existing black–white differences in family structure, but if important black–white differences in norms concerning the desirability of marriage do exist, these differences could be a source of racial differences in investment in children, even among sets of parents with similar wealth and education levels. Further, to the extent that black–white differences in norms concerning marriage affect the expected stability of existing marriages or the likelihood that single mothers will marry the father of their children in the future, black–white differences in parenting behaviors may arise even among families that currently share the same structures and enjoy the same wealth levels. In sum, black–white differences in norms concerning marriage may create differences in the mapping between parental human capital and investments in children that could support persistent black–white skill differences among adults across generations.

Here, I have discussed these potential differences in norms as black–white differences in the cost of investing in children. This seems natural when discussing the Willis and Weiss model because the moral hazard problem they discuss raises the cost of purchasing investment goods for children. However, some may prefer to think of acting white theories or other theories concerning black culture as hypotheses concerning racial differences in preferences or home production technologies. This distinction has no effect on the analysis presented here because such black–white differences in preferences or technology that retard investment in children, $\Delta k(\alpha, \gamma, \delta) < 0$, will yield a non-zero steady-state skill gap, $\Delta \ln h = \Delta k(\alpha, \gamma, \delta)$, even if one assumes that $\Delta \ln t = 0$.

5. Conclusion

It is not clear why the process of black–white skill convergence appeared to stop around 1990. In the previous section, I highlight several possible explanations, but the task of gathering definitive evidence concerning the relative merit of these competing hypotheses remains for future research. I have stressed how some potential explanations imply that the 1990s will one day be seen as an aberration, while other scenarios highlight the possibility that black–white skill gaps may be constant and large indefinitely. However, no plausible scenario implies that one should expect anything approaching black–white skill parity over the next several generations.

After some experimentation, I conclude that even the most optimistic projections imply that the black–white skill gap will be large throughout much of this century. To construct a best-case scenario, I draw on NAEP-LTT data from the late 1970s and the 1980s. Between 1978 and 1986, the black–white test score gap in math for 13 year old students shrank from 1.08 standard deviations to 0.79 standard deviations. Further, between 1980 and 1988, the reading gap for those age 13 shrank from 0.91 to 0.53. These gaps of 0.53 and 0.79 are the smallest gaps ever recorded in the NAEP-LTT for reading and math respectively, and the rates of convergence between black and white test scores during these eight year periods are more rapid than rates observed during any other periods of equal or greater length. What would happen if test scores for black and white youth converged at these rates throughout the 21st century using 1999 gaps as baselines?[57] The black–white test score gap among teenagers in 1999 was roughly 0.75 standard deviations in reading and 0.9 standard deviations in math in 1999.[58] Given the rates of convergence observed during the 1978–1988 period and the 1999 baselines, one would expect the black–white reading gap to remain above 0.1 standard deviations until roughly 2030 and above 0.05 standard deviations until after 2040. For math, one would expect the gap to remain above these thresholds until after 2055 and 2070, respectively.

These dates represent best-case scenarios.[59] It is easy to construct plausible scenarios in which black–white test score gaps remain large throughout the next century. Further, Figures 2(a)–(d) demonstrate that the relative achievement gains among black students observed during the 1980s were concentrated in the middle and upper percentiles of the black skill distribution. In terms of relative ranks in white test score distributions, black students in the lower percentiles of the black skill distribution appear to have made little progress since the late 1970s, and black students in large cities have actually lost ground.

Now is an appropriate time to consider what policy makers can do to enhance the skill levels of black youth in this generation and those to come. In a recent book, James Heckman and Alan Krueger (2003) engage in a detailed debate concerning the desirability of various human capital policies. The two disagree on much, but both agree

[57] I use NAEP-LTT data and the formula $\text{gap}(t) = \text{gap}(0)\exp(-rt)$ evaluated at $t = 8$ to pin down r. Assume that a generation equals 20 years. The rates of convergence that I recover imply that the ratio of the math test score gaps at $t + 20$ and t is 0.46. The corresponding figure for reading gaps is 0.26.

Solon (2002) surveys the literature on intergenerational earnings mobility. He concludes that the expected value of the ratio of a son's log earnings to his father's log earnings, given the father's earnings, is "about 0.4 or a bit higher". In more recent work, Haider and Solon (2004) present results suggesting that the expected value of this ratio may well be between 0.5 and 0.6.

Thus, my best case projections assume that measured cognitive achievement is even less persistent across generations than log earnings.

[58] I use these figures as approximations based on the results in Table 4 from the NLSY97 and the results for 13 years old in the 1999 wave of NAEP-LTT. The black–white test score gaps in these NAEP-LTT samples are roughly one standard deviation in math and 0.75 standard deviations in reading.

[59] Sampling error affects each of the NAEP-LTT estimates of race-specific achievement means for a given year. Since I chose convergence rates by selecting the most rapid documented period of convergence and since the end points of these periods represent record lows for the absolute value of these black–white score gaps, it is reasonable to suspect that the NAEP-LTT data overstate the actual convergence that occurred during these two periods. True rates of convergence may have never been this rapid.

that high quality pre-school programs may yield large returns for disadvantaged youth. Further, this debate and the related literature provide considerable support for the view that many of the important consequences of black–white differences in parental wealth arise during the pre-school years.

I argue above that the black–white differences in early childhood experiences contribute significantly to measured black–white skill gaps later in life. In another chapter in this Handbook, Blau and Currie (2004) review the literature on the effectiveness of early childhood intervention programs. Many early interventions have yielded positive results, but I will not review that literature again here. Rather, I focus on one particular experiment that is rather distinctive because it involved intense interventions that began while children were still infants. The Carolina Abecederian Project (CAP) began in the early 1970s in North Carolina. 98% of the children in the study were black and all were economically disadvantaged. The study randomly assigned infants to four different treatment and control groups. One group received high-quality day care services with special emphasis on skill and social development during pre-school years. Another group received these services as well as mentoring services during school years. A third group received no pre-school treatment but mentoring services while in school. The final group received no treatment. Treatments for school aged children were associated with few benefits. However, the day care services provided during pre-school years had long lasting impacts on adult employment, attainment, and test scores. Campbell et al. (2001) report that the achievement gains associated with pre-school treatment at age 15 are 0.45 standard deviations in reading and 0.37 standard deviations in math. Figures 4(a)–5(b) suggest that such large increases in basic reading and math skills may translate into significant increases in lifetime earnings.

Prudence requires that one refrain from drawing too many conclusions from a single study which involved only slightly over 100 children. The pre-school treatment services were quite expensive, and no existing studies provide a full cost–benefit analysis for the project. Nonetheless, the results of the CAP show that direct interventions at an early age can generate significant increases in basic skills even among black children who are quite disadvantaged. This is an important finding because the results presented in Section 2 show that a significant portion of black youth still possess basic reading and math skills that place them in the far left tails of the white skill distribution. Further, Figures 2(a)–(d) show that, relative to their white peers, youth in the lower percentiles of the black skill distribution have made the least progress in recent decades.

Among the mothers of children in the CAP, the average IQ is 85 and the average education level is 10.6 years of schooling.[60] Women with such low skill levels may find it difficult to provide early childhood experiences for their children that stimulate cognitive growth and prepare them for school. Although a large literature explores the effect of credit market imperfections on investments in post-secondary education,[61] the large

[60] See Campbell and Ramey (1994).

[61] See Cameron and Heckman (2001), Carneiro and Heckman (2002) and Card (1999).

and lasting benefits of the CAP treatments suggest that, for women in these circumstances, the inability to finance the type of high quality pre-school instruction provided by CAP may be the single most important credit constraint they face as parents. Further, seen in the light of the Brooks-Gunn, Duncan and Klebanov (1996) results concerning racial differences in parenting behaviors, the CAP results also suggest that the mothers in the CAP control group may have benefited greatly from mentoring, instruction and education in effective parenting practices.[62]

There is much evidence that changes in government policies concerning the funding and governance of schools contributed in important ways to the relative academic progress of blacks during the 20th century, but at the dawn of the 21st century, black–white differences in family environments are by far the most important source of black–white differences in levels of resources devoted to children. Important future work is required to more fully understand black–white differences in how parents invest in young children because the black–white skill gap among today's young children is considerably larger than existing estimates of the potential achievement gains associated various education reform proposals.[63] The first generation of black children who enter kindergarten with the same basic language and arithmetic skills as white children may well be the first generation of black adults to enter the labor market on equal footing with their white peers.

Acknowledgements

I thank Nathaniel Baum-Snow, Mario Macis, and Marie Tomarelli for research assistance. I thank Greg Duncan, Steven Durlauf, Eric French, Roland Fryer, James Heckman, Larry Hedges, Steven Levitt, Casey Mulligan, Ananth Sheshadri, Eric Hanushek, and Finis Welch for their comments. I thank the D&D Foundation for research support. I thank summer workshop participants at IRP and IZA.

References

Altonji, J.G., Pierret, C.R. (2001). "Employer learning and statistical discrimination". Quarterly Journal of Economics 116 (1), 313–350.

Arrow, K. (1973). "The theory of discrimination". In: Ashenfelter, O., Rees, A. (Eds.), Discrimination in Labor Markets. Princeton University Press.

Austen-Smith, D., Fryer Jr., R.G. (2005). "An economic analysis 'Acting White' ". Quarterly Journal of Economics. In press.

[62] However, a recent literature survey by Magnuson and Duncan (2005) concludes that interventions targeted directly at young children are more effective means of improving child outcomes than interventions that aim to improve parenting skills.

[63] There are also reasons to worry that gains from class size reductions, voucher programs and other experiments may be difficult to replicate on a large scale.

Baum-Snow N., Neal D. (2004). "Data problems and the measurement of racial and gender wage gaps over time". Mimeo, University of Chicago.
Becker, G.S., Tomes, N. (1986). "Human capital and the rise and fall of families". Journal of Labor Economics 4 (3), S1–S39.
Blau, D., Currie, J. (2004). "Pre-school, day care, and after school care: Who's minding the kids". In: Handbook of Economics of Education. Elsevier, New York.
Blau, D.M. (1999). "The effect of income on child development". Review of Economics and Statistics 81 (2), 261–276.
Boozer, M.A., Krueger, A.B., Wolkon, S. (1992). "Race and school quality since brown versus the board of education". Brookings Papers on Economic Activity: Microeconomics, 269–338.
Bound, J., Freeman, R.B. (1992). "What went wrong? The erosion of relative earnings and employment among young black men in the 1980s". Quarterly Journal of Economics 107 (1), 201–232.
Brooks-Gunn, J., Duncan, G.J., Klebanov, P. (1996). "Ethnic differences in children's intelligence test scores: Role of economics deprivation, home environment and maternal characteristics". Child Development 67 (2), 396–408.
Brooks-Gunn, J., Phillips, M., Duncan, G.J., Klebanov, P., Crane, J. (1998). "Family background, parenting practices, and the black–white test score gap". In: Jencks, C., Philips, M. (Eds.), The Black–White Test Score Gap. Brookings Institution, Washington, DC.
Cameron, S.V., Heckman, J.J. (1993). "The nonequivalence of high school equivalents". Journal of Labor Economics 11 (1), 1–47.
Cameron, S.V., Heckman, J.J. (2001). "The dynamics of educational attainment for black, Hispanic, and white males". Journal of Political Economy 109 (3), 455–499.
Campbell, F.A., Ramey, C.T. (1994). "Effects of early intervention on intellectual and academic achievement: A follow-up study of children from low-income families". Child Development 65, 684–698.
Campbell, F.A., Pungello, E.E., Miller-Johnson, S., Burchinal, M., Ramey, C.T. (2001). "The development of cognitive and academic abilities: Growth curves from an early childhood educational experiment". Developmental Psychology 37 (2), 231–242.
Card, D. (1999). "The causal effect of education on earnings". In: Handbook of Labor Economics, vol. 3A. Elsevier, New York.
Carneiro, P., Heckman, J.J. (2002). "The evidence on credit constraints in post-secondary schooling". Economic Journal 112 (482), 705–734.
Carneiro, P., Hansen, K., Heckman, J.J. (2003). "Estimating distributions of treatment effects with an application to the returns to schooling and measurement of the effects of uncertainty on college choice". International Economic Review 44 (2), 361–422.
Ceci, S. (1991). "How much does schooling influences general intelligence and its cognitive components? A reassessment of the evidence". Development Psychology 27 (5), 703–722.
Chubb, J.E., Loveless, T. (Eds.) (2002). Bridging the Achievement Gap. Brookings Institution, Washington, DC.
Coate, S., Loury, G.C. (1993). "Will affirmative-action policies eliminate negative stereotypes?" American Economic Review 83 (5), 1220–1240.
Collins W.J., Margo R.A. (2003). "Historical perspectives on racial differences in schooling in the United States", NBER Working Paper #9770.
Cook, P.J., Ludwig, J. (1998). "The burden of "Acting White": Do black adolescents disparage academic achievement?" In: Jencks, C., Philips, M. (Eds.), The Black–White Test Score Gap. Brookings Institution, Washington, DC.
Cutright P. (1973). "Achievement, mobility, and the draft: Their impact on the earnings of men", Social Security Administration.
De los Santos B., Heckman J., Larenas M. (2004). "Explaining the gap in achievement test scores for blacks, Hispanics and whites". Mimeo, University of Chicago.
Ferguson, R.F. (2004). "Why America's black–white school achievement gap persists". In: Loury, G.C., Teles, S., Modood, T. (Eds.), Ethnicity, Social Mobility and Public Policy. Cambridge University Press. In press.

Flanagan, A., Grissmer, D. (2002). "The role of federal resources in closing the achievement gap". In: Chubb, J.E., Loveless, T. (Eds.), Bridging the Achievement Gap. Brookings Institution, Washington, DC.
Fryer Jr., R.G., Heaton P., Levitt S., Murphy K. (2004). "The impact of crack cocaine". Mimeo, University of Chicago.
Fryer Jr., R.G., Levitt, S. (2004). "Understanding the black–white test score gap in the first two years of school". Review of Economics and Statistics 86 (2), 447–464.
Grogger, J., Neal, D. (2000). "Further evidence on the effects of catholic secondary schooling". Brookings–Wharton Papers on Urban Affairs 1 (1). Brookings Institution, Washington, DC.
Grogger, J. (1996). "Does school quality explain the recent black–white wage trend". Journal of Labor Economics 14 (2), 231–253.
Haider S., Solon G. (2004). "Life-cycle variation in the association between current and lifetime earnings". Mimeo, University of Michigan.
Hansen, K.T., Heckman, J.J., Mullen, K.J. (2004). "The effect of schooling and ability of achievement test scores". Journal of Econometrics 121 (1).
Heckman J.J., Lochner L., Todd P. (2004). "Fifty years of mincer earnings equations". Mimeo, University of Chicago.
Heckman, J.J., Krueger, A. (2003). Inequality in America: What Role For Human Capital Policy? MIT Press, Cambridge.
Hedges, L., Nowell, A. (1998). "Black–white test score convergence since 1965". In: Jencks, C., Philips, M. (Eds.), The Black–White Test Score Gap. Brookings Institution, Washington, DC.
Howell, W.G., Peterson, P. (2002). The Education Gap: Vouchers and Urban Schools. Brookings Institution, Washington, DC.
Howell, W.G., Peterson, P. (2002b). "Voucher programs and the effect of ethnicity on test scores". In: Chubb, J.E., Loveless, T. (Eds.), Bridging the Achievement Gap. Brookings Institution, Washington, DC.
Johnson, W., Kitamura, Y., Neal, D. (2000). "Evaluating a simple method for estimating black–white gaps in median wages". American Economic Review 90.
Johnson, W., Neal, D. (1998). "Basic skills and the black–white earnings gap". In: Jencks, C., Philips, M. (Eds.), The Black–White Test Score Gap. Brookings Institution, Washington, DC.
Juhn, C., Murphy, K., Pierce, B. (1991). "Accounting for the slowdown in black–white wage convergence". In: Workers and Their Wages: Changing Patterns in the U.S. American Enterprise Institute.
Katz, L., Autor, D. (1999). "Changes in the wage structure and earnings inequality". In: Ashenfelter, O., Card, D. (Eds.), Handbook of Labor Economics, vol. 3A. Elsevier, Amsterdam.
Krueger, A.B. (1999). "Experimental estimates of education production functions". Quarterly Journal of Economics 114 (2), 497–532.
Krueger, A.B., Whitmore, D. (2002). "Would smaller classes help close the black–white achievement gap?" In: Chubb, J.E., Loveless, T. (Eds.), Bridging the Achievement Gap. Brookings Institution, Washington, DC.
Lange F. (2004). "The returns to schooling and ability during the early career: Evidence on job market signaling, employer learning, and post school investments". Mimeo, Yale University.
Lightfoot, S.L. (1978). Worlds Apart. Basic Books, New York.
Loury, G.C. (1981). "Intergenerational transfers and the distribution of earnings". Econometrica 49 (4), 843–867.
Mayer, S. (1997). What Money Can't Buy: Family Income and Children's Life Chances. Harvard University Press.
Magnuson K., Duncan G. (2005). "Parent-vs.-child based intervention strategies for promoting children's well-being". Mimeo, Columbia University.
McLanahan, S., Sandefur, G. (1994). Growing Up With a Single Parent, What Hurts, What Helps. Harvard University Press.
Mulligan, C.B. (1997). Parental Priorities and Economic Inequality. University of Chicago Press.
Neal, D. (1997). "The effects of catholic secondary schooling on educational achievement". Journal of Labor Economics 15 (1).

Neal, D. (2004). "The measured black–white wage gap among women is too small". Journal of Political Economy 112, S1–S28.
Neal, D. (2004b). "The relationship between marriage market prospects and never-married motherhood". The Journal of Human Resources 39 (4), 938–957.
Neal, D. (2004c). "Resources and educational outcomes among black children". In: Peterson, P. (Ed.), In One Generation: The Elimination of Race Differences in Educational Achievement. Rowman & Littlefield.
Neal, D., Johnson, W. (1996). "The role of pre-market factors in black–white wage differences". Journal of Political Economy 104, 869–895.
Nechyba, T. (2001). "Social approval, values, and AFDC: A reexamination of the illegitimacy debate". Journal of Political Economy 109, 637–672.
Nisbett, R.E. (1995). "Race, IQ, and scientism". In: The Bell Curve Wars. Basic Books, New York, NY.
Ogbu, J. (1990). "Minority education in comparative perspective". Journal of Negro Education 59, 45–57.
Phillips, M., Crouse, J., Ralph, J. (1998). "Does the black–white test score gap widen after children enter school?" In: Jencks, C., Philips, M. (Eds.), The Black–White Test Score Gap. Brookings Institution, Washington, DC.
Phelps, E.S. (1972). "The statistical theory of racism and sexism". American Economic Review 62 (4), 659–661.
Robinson J.G., Adlakha A., West K. (2002). "Coverage of population in census 2000: Results from demographic analysis", U.S. Census Bureau, Washington, DC.
Sandefur, G.D., Wells, T. (1999). "Does family structure really influence educational attainment?" Social Science Research 28 (4), 331–357.
Slavin, R.E., Madden, N. (2002). " 'Success for all' and African American and Latino student achievement". In: Chubb, J.E., Loveless, T. (Eds.), Bridging the Achievement Gap. Brookings Institution, Washington, DC.
Smith, J.P., Welch, F.R. (1989). "Black economic progress after Myrdal". Journal of Economic Literature 27 (2), 519–564.
Smith, J.P. (1984). "Race and human capital". American Economic Review 74 (4), 685–698.
Solon, G. (2002). "Cross-country differences in intergenerational earnings mobility". Journal of Economic Perspectives 16 (3), 59–66.
Weiss, Y., Willis, R.J. (1985). "Children as collective goods and divorce settlements". Journal of Labor Economics 3 (3), 268–292.
Welch, F. (1973). "Black–white differences in returns to schooling". American Economic Review 63 (5), 893–907.
Wigdor, A.K., Green Jr., B.F. (Eds.) (1991). Performance Assessment For the Workplace. National Academy Press, Washington, DC.

Chapter 10

EDUCATION AND NONMARKET OUTCOMES

MICHAEL GROSSMAN

City University of New York Graduate Center and National Bureau of Economic Research

Contents

Handbook of the Economics of Education, Volume 1
Edited by Eric A. Hanushek and Finis Welch
© 2006 Elsevier B.V. All rights reserved
DOI: 10.1016/S1574-0692(06)01010-5

Abstract

This chapter explores the effects of education on nonmarket outcomes from both theoretical and empirical perspectives. Examples of outcomes considered include general consumption patterns at a moment in time, savings and the rate of growth of consumption over time, own (adult) health and inputs into the production of own health, fertility, and child quality or well-being reflected by their health and cognitive development. They are distinguished from the labor market outcomes of education in terms of higher earnings and wage rates. The focus is on identifying causal effects of education and on mechanisms via which these effects operate. The chapter pays a good deal of attention to the effects of education on health for a variety of reasons. They are the two most important sources of human capital: knowledge capital and health capital. They interact in their levels and in the ways they affect the cost and usefulness of the other. There is a large literature addressing the nature of their complementarities. While each affects the production and usefulness of the other, there are important dynamics of their interaction, seen in the age-structure of the net and gross production of the two. This sequencing also affects their optimal amounts. In the conceptual foundation section, models in which education has productive efficiency and allocative efficiency effects are considered. These frameworks are then modified to allow for the endogenous nature of schooling decisions, so that observed schooling effects can be traced in part to omitted "third variables" such as an orientation towards the future. An additional complication is that schooling may contribute to a future orientation in models with endogenous preferences. The empirical review provides a good deal of evidence for the proposition that the education effects are causal but is less conclusive with regard to the identification of specific mechanisms.

Keywords

education, nonmarket, efficiency, health, time preference

JEL classification: I10, I20

1. Introduction

Are more educated people healthier? Are they less likely to smoke cigarettes, more likely to quit smoking if they do smoke, and less likely to be obese? Are they more likely to have fewer children, healthier children, and better educated children? Do their consumption patterns differ from those of persons with less education? These are examples of the potential nonmarket outcomes of education that are considered in this chapter. I define these outcomes as those associated with the time that the consumer does not spend in the labor market, and I distinguish them from the labor market outcomes of education in terms of higher earnings and wage rates.

Until the early 1960s, treatments of the effects of education on nonmarket outcomes or behaviors were not explored by economists. The argument was that the impacts of variables other than real income or real wealth and relative prices must operate through tastes, and economists had little to say about the formation of tastes. Gary S. Becker changed all that, and this chapter is heavily influenced by his contributions [Becker (1960, 1965, 1991, 1996), Becker and Lewis (1973), Becker and Murphy (1988), Becker and Mulligan (1997)]. In his early work, Becker introduced the idea that consumers produce their fundamental objects of choice, called commodities, in the nonmarket sector using inputs of market goods and services and their own time. Education is quite likely to influence the efficiency of these production processes. Thus it may affect the absolute and relative marginal costs or shadow prices of home produced commodities and real income evaluated at shadow prices, with market prices of goods and money income held constant. In his later work, Becker stressed that the determinants and consequences of addictions, time preference, and other variables typically labeled as tastes can be approached by standard economic models of rational behavior, with important implications for the role of schooling in decisions pertaining to, for example, the rate of growth in consumption with age, savings, investment in children, and consumption of harmfully addictive substances.

In the next section of this chapter, I outline several conceptual frameworks that generate effects of education on nonmarket outcomes. Empirical evidence with regard to these effects is summarized and critiqued in the sections that follow. The focus is on identifying causal effects of education and on mechanisms via which these effects operate. Before proceeding, a few comments on the scope of the chapter are in order.

First, the knowledge that a person has acquired through schooling is embedded within himself and accompanies him wherever he goes: to the labor market where money earnings are produced, to the doctor where health is produced, to the bedroom where sexual satisfaction and perhaps children are produced, to plays and movies where entertainment is produced, and to the tennis court and the ski slope where exercise and recreation are produced. If knowledge and traits acquired through schooling influence decisions made at work, they are just as likely to influence decisions made with regard to cigarette smoking, the types of food to eat, the type of contraceptive technique to use, and the portion of income to save. While these examples suggest an infinite number of nonmarket outcomes that may be influenced by education, I keep the scope of this chapter manageable by considering a few. They include general consumption patterns at a moment in time, savings and the rate of growth of consumption over time, own (adult) health and inputs into the production of own health, fertility, and child quality or well-being reflected by their health and cognitive development.[1]

Second, I pay a good deal of attention to the effects of education on health for a variety of reasons. They are the two most important sources of human capital: knowledge capital and health capital. They interact in their levels and in the ways they affect the cost and usefulness of the other. There is a large literature addressing the nature of their complementarities. While each affects the production and usefulness of the other, there are important dynamics of their interaction, seen in the age-structure of the net and gross production of the two. This sequencing also affects their optimal amounts.

Finally, my survey of the literature is meant to be selective rather than definitive. I highlight studies, mostly from the 1970s and early 1980s, that laid the foundations for empirical investigations of the impacts of schooling on nonmarket outcomes. I also highlight very recent research that focuses on mechanisms and causality. The reader can fill in the gaps by consulting the studies that I cite.

2. Conceptual foundations

2.1. Productive efficiency

Becker's (1965) model of the allocation of time serves as the point of departure for approaches that assume that increases in knowledge capital, in general, and education or years of formal schooling completed, in particular, (from now on these two terms are used as synonyms) raise efficiency in the nonmarket sector. Becker draws a sharp distinction between fundamental objects of choice – called commodities – that enter the utility function and market goods and services. Consumers produce these commodities using inputs of market goods and services and their own time.

In seminal contributions to the literature, Michael (1972, 1973b) develops theoretical tools to study the effects of variations in nonmarket efficiency. In the context of a static or one-period model, consumers maximize a utility function given by

$$U = U(Z_1, Z_2, \dots, Z_n), \tag{1}$$

where each Z_i ($i = 1, 2, \dots, n$) is a commodity produced in the nonmarket or household sector. The set of household production functions is given by

$$Z_i = e^{\rho_i S} F_i(X_i, T_i), \tag{2}$$

where X_i is a market good or service input, T_i is an input of the own time of the consumer, S is a measure of the efficiency of the production process, and ρ_i is a positive

[1] For an earlier survey that considers additional nonmarket effects of education, see Michael (1982).

parameter. Each production function is linear homogeneous in X_i and T_i. For simplicity, I assume that each production process uses a single unique good or service purchased in the market and a single unique own time input. Conceptually, X_i and T_i could be treated as vectors rather than scalars, and joint production (an increase in X_i raises Z_i and simultaneously raises or lowers other commodities) could be introduced. These modifications are useful when the commodities can be measured empirically, but are ruled out in Michael's empirical applications. I will return to these issues below.

The efficiency variable S in equation (2) coincides with the consumer's stock of knowledge or human capital, a theoretical concept, and operationalized by the number of years of formal schooling that he or she has completed. Of course, the stock of human capital depends on such additional factors as the quality of schooling, on-the-job training, and health capital, but the focus of this chapter is on the effects of schooling. Health is treated as one of the outputs of household production and is discussed in detail both theoretically and empirically later in the chapter. While the goods and time inputs are endogenous variables, schooling is predetermined. Complications due to the endogeneity of schooling are addressed after the basic model is developed.

Since each production function is linear homogeneous in the goods and time inputs, an increase in S raises each commodity only if it raises the marginal products of the inputs on average. In fact, according to equation (2), an increase in S raises the marginal product of X_i and T_i by the same percentage (ρ_i). This is the Hicks- or factor-neutrality assumption applied to production in the nonmarket sector. As is the case with the other assumptions just made, Michael (1972, 1973b) requires it in his empirical work but not in the theoretical development of his model.

Michael makes empirical predictions about the impacts of schooling on the demand for commodities and market goods by considering variations in schooling, with money "full income" (the sum of property income and earnings when all available time is allocated to work in the market), the prices of market goods, and wage rates held constant. Because the more educated are more efficient, the marginal or average cost of each commodity is lower for them than for the less educated. Indeed, since a one unit increase in education raises the marginal products of X_i and T_i by ρ_i percent and since the Z_i production function is linear homogeneous in these two inputs, the marginal cost or average cost or "shadow price" of Z_i falls by ρ_i percent. Hence, with money full income evaluated at shadow prices held constant, real full income rises by ρ percent:

$$\rho = \sum_{i=1}^{n} k_i \rho_i, \tag{3}$$

where k_i is the share of Z_i in full income.[2] Since real income rises, an increase in education raises the demand for commodities with positive income elasticities. In addition,

[2] The marginal cost or average cost or shadow price of Z_i is

$$\pi_i = \frac{P_i}{e^{\rho_i S} \partial F_i / \partial X_i} = \frac{W}{e^{\rho_i S} \partial F_i / \partial T_i} = \frac{P_i X_i + W T_i}{e^{\rho_i S} F_i},$$

there may be substitution effects since relative commodity prices will change unless ρ_i is the same for each commodity.

Define the schooling parameter in the demand function for Z_i as $\tilde{Z}_i \equiv \partial \ln Z_i / \partial S$, and keep in mind that this parameter summarizes an effect that holds money income, the prices of market goods, and the wage rate constant. This parameter is given by

$$\tilde{Z}_i = \eta_i \rho - k_i \sigma_{ii} \rho_i - \sum_{j \neq i=1}^{n} k_j \sigma_{ij} \rho_j, \tag{4}$$

where η_i is the income elasticity of demand for Z_i, $\sigma_{ii} < 0$ is the Allen own partial elasticity of substitution in consumption of Z_i, and σ_{ij} is the Allen cross partial elasticity of substitution in consumption between Z_i and Z_j. Given that Z_i is a superior commodity, the first term on the right-hand side of equation (4) is positive. The second term reflects an own substitution effect and also is positive. The third term reflects cross price effects and is negative since σ_{ij} is positive on average unless the prices of commodities that are strong complements to Z_i fall substantially (ρ_j is large when σ_{ij} is negative and large in absolute value).

Since most of the Z commodities cannot be measured empirically, assume that all cross partial elasticities of substitution in consumption are the same ($\sigma_{ij} = \sigma > 0$). Hence,[3]

$$\tilde{Z}_i = \eta_i \rho + \sigma(\rho_i - \rho). \tag{5}$$

According to equation (5), the quantity of Z_i demanded unambiguously rises as schooling rises provided more schooling raises marginal products in the Z_i production function by the same percentage as on average or by a greater percentage than on average ($\rho_i \geqslant \rho$). The sign of $\tilde{Z}_i$ is ambiguous if the reverse holds ($\rho_i < \rho$).

where P_i is the price of X_i, W is the wage rate, and the last equality follows from linear homogeneity. The full income constraint for utility maximization is

$$W\Omega + V = \sum_{i=1}^{n} \pi_i Z_i = \sum_{i=1}^{n} (P_i X_i + W T_i),$$

where Ω is the constant amount of time available in the period (the sum of time allocated to the market and time allocated to the nonmarket), and V is property or nonearnings income. Real full income evaluated at shadow prices is $(W\Omega + V)/\Pi$, where Π is a Laspeyres geometric price level:

$$\Pi = \pi_1^{k_1} \pi_2^{k_2} \cdots \pi_n^{k_n}, \qquad k_i = \frac{\pi_i Z_i}{\sum_{i=1}^{n} \pi_i Z_i}.$$

[3] To obtain equation (5), note

$$-k_i \sigma_{ii} = \sum_{j \neq i=1}^{n} k_j \sigma_{ij},$$

since $\sigma_{ij} = \sigma$, $-k_i \sigma_{ii} = (1 - k_i)\sigma$.

From equation (5), the schooling parameter in the demand function for the market good or service input in the production function of Z_i (X_i) is[4]

$$\tilde{X}_i = (\eta_i - 1)\rho + (\sigma - 1)(\rho_i - \rho). \tag{6}$$

Equation (6) highlights that changes in the quantity of X_i consumed as schooling rises close the gap between the percentage change in the quantity of Z_i demanded $[\eta_i\rho + \sigma(\rho_i - \rho)]$ and the percentage increase in the quantity of Z_i supplied by fixed amounts of the good and time inputs (ρ_i). Three pieces of information are required to predict the sign of $\tilde{X}_i$: (1) whether η_i is greater than, smaller than, or equal to one; (2) whether σ is greater than, equal to, or smaller than one; and (3) whether ρ_i is greater than, equal to, or smaller than ρ. Information on the third item would be available only if the full set of household production functions were estimated. If one could do this, one might not want to assume that all the partial elasticities of substitution in consumption are the same. But then one would need to estimate the full set of these elasticities.

Given the problems just mentioned, Michael (1972, 1973b) assumes that all ρ_i are the same and equal to ρ. He terms this assumption "commodity neutrality". It implies that relative prices remain the same and that no substitution effects accompany increases in education. Equation (6) becomes

$$\tilde{X}_i = (\eta_i - 1)\rho \gtreqless 0 \quad \text{as } \eta_i \gtreqless 1. \tag{7}$$

In words, an increase in schooling increases the demand for goods inputs associated with commodities that have income elasticities greater than one, reduces the demand for goods inputs associated with commodities that have income elasticities less than one, and has no impact on goods inputs associated with commodities that have income elasticities equal to one. This is the empirical test of the hypothesis that education has a productive efficiency effect devised by Michael. It can be implemented with detailed cross-sectional data on outlays on goods and services for items that exhaust total consumption. For each item, estimate an Engel curve that relates expenditures on that item to income and schooling. If the resulting income elasticity of demand for the item exceeds one, the schooling coefficient should be positive, while the schooling coefficient should be negative if the income elasticity is less than one. Schooling effects should be zero for items with unitary income elasticities.[5] Put differently, with money income held constant, an increase in education should cause a reallocation of consumption expenditures towards luxuries and away from necessities. This same test could be applied to time budget surveys, although these surveys are less numerous and less detailed than consumer expenditure surveys.

[4] Since the production function is linear homogeneous and input prices are held constant,

$$\tilde{X}_i = \tilde{T}_i = \tilde{Z}_i - \rho_i + \rho - \rho.$$

Replace $\tilde{Z}_i$ with the right-hand side of equation (5) to obtain equation (6).

[5] Since all production functions are homogeneous of degree one in the goods and time inputs and since input prices are held constant, a one percent change in Z_i due to a given percentage change in money income is accompanied by a 1 percent change in X_i. Hence, the income elasticities of Z_i and X_i are the same.

2.1.1. Productive efficiency, total consumption, and hours of work

A modified version of Michael's (1972, 1973b) model can be employed to study the effect of an increase in schooling on total consumption and hours of work when schooling varies, with the wage rate and property income held constant.[6] Suppose that the utility function is

$$U = U(Z, X) = U\left(e^{\rho_Z S} T, X\right). \tag{8}$$

In this formulation, utility depends on a single good purchased in the market (X) and a commodity produced at home (Z) with a time input (T) alone. The marginal product of the time input ($e^{\rho_Z S}$) rises as schooling rises. Obviously, since there is only one use of time in the nonmarket, T corresponds to leisure and is given by the difference between total available time and time allocated to work in the market. It can be measured as long as data on working time are available.

Consider demand functions for T and X that depend on the wage rate, property income, and schooling. The schooling parameters in these demand functions ($\tilde{T}$ and $\tilde{X}$, respectively) are

$$\tilde{T} = \left\{\left[k\eta_Z + (1-k)\sigma_{ZX} - 1\right]\right\}\rho_Z, \tag{9}$$

$$\tilde{X} = \frac{k}{1-k}\left[1 - k\eta_Z - (1-k)\sigma_{ZX}\right]\rho_Z. \tag{10}$$

In these equations, k is the share of Z in full income, η_Z is the income elasticity of demand for Z or T and σ_{ZX} is the elasticity of substitution in consumption between Z or T and X. Note that $k\eta_Z + (1-k)\sigma_{ZX}$ define the absolute value of the uncompensated price elasticity of demand for Z (ε_Z). Hence, the quantity of leisure or nonmarket time is positively related to schooling and total consumption is negatively related to schooling if ε_Z is larger than one. The reverse holds if ε_Z is smaller than one. Empirically, this parameter can be retrieved from estimates of the elasticities of hours of leisure with respect to the wage rate and property income.[7]

The preceding model controls for market productivity effects of schooling because the wage rate is held constant. An alternative model is one in which a one-year increase in schooling raises market and nonmarket productivity by ρ_Z percent. In that model the schooling parameters become

$$\tilde{T} = \left[(1-s)\eta_Z - 1\right]\rho_Z, \tag{9a}$$

[6] The model developed in this subsection is based to some extent on Morris (1976). I depart from his analysis, however, because I focus on a case where schooling varies, with the wage rate held constant.

[7] Based on the definition of full income in footnote 2, the elasticity of Z or T with respect to property income is $s\eta_Z$, where s is the ratio of property income to full income and η_Z is the elasticity of Z with respect to full income. The elasticity of T or Z with respect to the wage rate is $[(1-s-k)\eta_Z - (1-k)\sigma_{ZX}]$. This elasticity holds schooling constant.

$$\tilde{X} = \left[(1-s)\left(\frac{1-k\eta_Z}{1-k}\right)\right]\rho_Z, \tag{10a}$$

where s is the share of property income in full income. According to equation (9a), hours of leisure fall as schooling rises and hours of work rise unless η_Z is greater than $1/(1-s)$. If s is relatively small, hours of work increase, remain constant, or fall as schooling rises according to whether η_Z is less than, equal to, or greater than one. This model suggests that only schooling and property income should be included in empirical estimates of demand functions for leisure and total consumption. Comparisons of the two models and the constraints they imply via goodness-of-fit tests allow one to distinguish between them.

2.1.2. *Productive efficiency and health production*

I [Grossman (1972a), (1972b), (2000)] explore the productive efficiency effect of schooling in the context of a model of the production of health and the demand for health. My model is somewhat complicated because it involves the selection of an optimal life cycle path of a durable stock of health capital and associated profiles of gross investment in that stock and inputs in the gross investment production function. My model also contains both investment and consumption motives for demanding health. As a consumption commodity, health is a direct source of utility. As an investment commodity, it determines the total amount of time in a period that can be allocated to work in the market and to the production of commodities in the nonmarket sector.

I simplify my model while retaining the aspects required to study the impacts of schooling on the demand for health and health inputs by employing a static version of my pure investment model in which health does not enter the utility function directly.[8] In the period at issue, say a year, the total amount of time that can be allocated to market and nonmarket production (h) is not fixed. Instead, it is a positive function of health (H) because increases in health lower the time lost from these activities due to illness and injury ($\partial h/\partial H \equiv G > 0$). Because the output of health has a finite upper limit of 8,760 hours or 365 days times 24 hours per day if the year is the relevant period, the marginal product of health falls as H rises ($\partial^2 h/\partial H^2 \equiv G_H < 0$). Health is produced with inputs of medical care (M) and the own time of the consumer (T):

$$H = e^{\rho_H S} F(M, T), \tag{11}$$

where F is linear homogeneous in M and T. An increase in schooling raises the marginal products of M and T by the same percentage (ρ_H).

The consumer maximizes $Wh - \pi_H H$, where W is the wage rate and π_H is the marginal or average cost of producing health. The first-order condition for optimal H is

$$WG = \pi_H. \tag{12}$$

[8] I emphasize the pure investment model because it generates powerful predictions from simple analysis.

Using this equation, one obtains formulas for the optimal percentage changes in the quantities of H and M caused by a one unit increase in schooling (S):

$$\tilde{H} = \varepsilon_H \rho_H, \tag{13}$$

$$\tilde{M} = (\varepsilon_H - 1)\rho_H, \tag{14}$$

where

$$\varepsilon_H \equiv -\frac{G}{HG_H}.$$

The effects summarized by equations (13) and (14) hold the wage rate and the price of medical care constant.[9]

The parameter ε_H is the inverse of the absolute value of the elasticity of the marginal product of health (G) with respect to H. I [Grossman (1972a, 1972b, 2000)] show that ε_H is very likely to be smaller than one because the output of health has a finite upper limit. Given that this condition holds, an increase in schooling is predicted to increase the quantity of health demanded but to lower the quantity of medical care demanded.

2.2. *Allocative efficiency*

In the productive efficiency approach, an increase in knowledge capital or schooling raises the efficiency of the production process in the nonmarket or household sector, just as an increase in technology raises the efficiency of the production process in the market sector. Some persons object to this approach. In the specific context of the production of health, Deaton (2002, p. 21) writes: "In many economic models of health, education is seen as enhancing a person's efficiency as a producer of health – a suggestive phrase, but not one that is very explicit about the mechanisms involved." In a study dealing with infant health production, Rosenzweig and Schultz (1982, p. 59) argue: "It is not clear ... how education can actually alter marginal products of inputs ... unless inputs are omitted from [the production function]. That is, it is doubtful that schooling can affect the production of ... [health] without it being associated with some alteration in an input."

The statements by Deaton and by Rosenzweig and Schultz point to an allocative efficiency effect of education. Clearly, this is a very legitimate alternative to the productive efficiency hypothesis, but one can raise the same objection to the many treatments of exogenous technological change in the literature on production by firms and industries. In fact, the set of household production functions specified by equation (2) is very similar to a specification of the production of earnings in which the more educated get more

[9] Note that $G_H \equiv \partial G/\partial H$. Note also that the marginal product of medical care in the production of healthy time is GH_M. An increase in schooling raises H_M. With M constant, however, an increase in S lowers GH_M if $\varepsilon_H < 1$.

of this output with the same amount of time allocated to the market than the less educated. Thus, it is important for the reader to keep in mind that the productive efficiency hypothesis has testable implications in comparing the two approaches.

Allocative efficiency pertains to situations in which the more educated pick a different mix of inputs to produce a certain commodity than the less educated. The mix selected by the more educated gives them more output of that commodity than the mix selected by the less educated. As the quotes by Deaton and Rosenzweig and Schultz cited above imply, education will have no impact on outputs unless it alters inputs, and education coefficients in production functions will be zero if all relevant inputs are included. Since data on outputs as well as inputs are required to test the allocative efficiency hypothesis and since health is one of few outputs of household production that can be measured, most theoretical treatments of allocative efficiency are in the context of the production of health.

Theoretical underpinnings of the allocative efficiency approach are contained in Rosenzweig and Schultz (1982, 1989), Kenkel (1991, 2000), Rosenzweig (1995), Meara (1999, 2001), Goldman and Lakdawalla (2002), Goldman and Smith (2002), Lleras-Muney and Lichtenberg (2002), Glied and Lleras-Muney (2003), and de Walque (2004, 2005). These treatments correctly recognize the multivariate nature of the health production function and include a variety of market goods inputs, such as diet, cigarette smoking, and alcohol use, in addition to medical care. Some of these inputs have negative marginal products in the production of health. For example, cigarette smoking lowers health but raises utility at least for some consumers because it simultaneously produces the commodity "smoking pleasure" that is a positive source of utility. Hence, models of allocative efficiency incorporate joint production in the nonmarket sector.[10] Some of these models replace a generic time input with time allocated to such activities as exercise and weight control.

Typically, approaches to allocative efficiency assume that the more educated have more information about the true nature of the production function. For example, the more educated may have more knowledge about the harmful effects of smoking or about what constitutes an appropriate diet. In addition, they may respond to new knowledge more rapidly. These approaches also pay attention to the role of endowed or inherited health. Clearly, a favorable endowment raises current health. At the same time, the demand for inputs with positive marginal products falls while the demand for inputs with negative marginal products may rise.

To fully test the allocative efficiency hypothesis, one needs to estimate the health production function and show that the schooling coefficient is zero once all inputs are included. Difficulties arise because the production function is a structural equation that relates an output of health to endogenous inputs. Biases that are encountered when it is estimated by ordinary least squares (OLS) are discussed in detail by Rosenzweig and Schultz (1982, 1983, 1991), Corman, Joyce and Grossman (1987), Grossman and

[10] For a detailed discussion of joint production, see Grossman (1972b, pp. 74–83).

Joyce (1990), and Joyce (1994). There are two types. Adverse selection occurs when individuals with low levels of initial health obtain larger quantities of health inputs. Here the unobserved disturbance term in the production function reflects the health endowment and is negatively correlated with the inputs. In general, OLS input coefficients are biased towards zero in this case. Favorable selection occurs when there is at least one unmeasured healthy behavior input (for example, appropriate diet or exercise or absence of stress) and when individuals who are risk averse obtain larger quantities of all health inputs, which have positive effects on health and less of the inputs with negative effects. Here the unobserved disturbance term in the production function reflects unmeasured healthy behavior inputs and is positively correlated with measured inputs. These considerations suggest that the production function should be obtained by such simultaneous equations methods as two-stage least squares. Since the productive efficiency hypothesis makes predictions about reduced form coefficients, simultaneous equations methods are not required to explore its implications unless one questions the exogeneity of schooling (see Section 2.5).

One could also test the productive efficiency model by fitting the production function by simultaneous equations methods. It predicts a positive schooling coefficient with all relevant inputs held constant. On the other hand, the allocative efficiency model predicts no direct schooling effect. These models need not be viewed as competitors. Aspects of both may be relevant, and both predict positive schooling coefficients in reduced form health equations.

Some treatments formally combine aspects of productive and allocative efficiency. Typically, these treatments implicitly or explicitly assume costs of adjustment or interactions between past health status and the marginal products of health inputs. Thus, positive effects of past health on current health and negative effects of past health on current input use (positive effects of past measures of poor health on current input use) are incorporated.[11] For example, using a model developed by Nelson and Phelps (1966), Glied and Lleras-Muney (2003) postulate a lag between the introduction of a new medical technology for treating a certain illness and its adoption by a specific individual. In turn, the lag is negatively related to the person's education. In this framework, the health production function is

$$H = F\left[M_0 \mathrm{e}^{\rho(t-u)}\right], \tag{15}$$

where M_0 is the medical technology available at time 0, $M_0\mathrm{e}^{\rho t}$ is the state-of-the-art technology at time t, $M_0\mathrm{e}^{\rho(t-u)}$ is the technology actually employed by the individual or his physician at time t, and other inputs are suppressed. The variable u measures the adoption lag and is negatively related to the person's schooling. This model predicts that the marginal product of schooling in the production function is positively related

[11] For the development of a demand for health model with costs of adjustment, see Grossman (2000, pp. 390–392).

to ρ, the rate of technological progress. Hence, the impact of schooling on disease-specific mortality, for example, should be larger in absolute value for diseases for which significant advances in treatment have occurred in the recent past.

Using a somewhat related framework, Goldman and Lakdawalla (2002) examine the properties of a model in which individuals with a given initial health problem employ medical care and their own time in a Cobb–Douglas technology to improve their health:

$$H = M^{\alpha} T^{\beta}. \tag{16}$$

In their model the output elasticity of medical care (α) is positively related to schooling for some diseases – especially those where progress in treatment has been rapid in the recent past. The output elasticity of the patient's own time input (β) also may be positively related to schooling, especially treatment regimes that require significant amounts of this input. Innovations that diminish the importance of patient monitoring – for example, one that makes it less important for a patient with type 1 diabetes to monitor blood sugar – lower β and may also reduce the positive relationship between β and schooling.[12]

2.3. Schooling effects in the quantity–quality model of fertility

Parents' schooling plays an important role in the quantity–quality model of fertility developed by Becker (1960), Becker and Lewis (1973), Willis (1973), Becker (1991) and summarized in detail by Hotz, Klerman and Willis (1997). Parents maximize a utility function that depends on the number of children (N), the quality or well-being of each child (Q, assumed to be the same for each child in a given family), and the parents' standard of living (Z). These three commodities are produced with inputs of market goods and services and the own time of the parents. The full income budget constraint is

$$R = \pi_Z Z + \pi NQ + \pi_N N + \pi_Q Q, \tag{17}$$

where π_Z is the price of Z, π is the price of one unit of NQ, π_N is the fixed cost of N, and π_Q is the fixed cost of Q.

According to Becker (1991), the cost component $\pi_N N$ reflects the time and expenditure spent on pregnancy and delivery and the costs of avoiding pregnancies. These outlays are independent of quality. The component $\pi_Q Q$ represents costs that do not depend on the number of children because of joint consumption by different children

[12] Goldman and Lakdawalla (2002) do not constraint the sum of α and β to equal one because they want to examine the effect of a change in one of these output elasticities, with the other one held constant. I have simplified their model in the discussion in the text. They emphasize that the health demand function has a multiplicative form in my model and in more complicated versions of it. Hence, any variable that raises the quantity of health demanded also will increase the marginal effect of schooling or the wage rate on health. In my view, the points that I emphasize in the text are consistent with and provide a simple explanation of their empirical evidence to be discussed in Section 4.

such as acquiring information and knowledge from the parents at the same time. On the other hand, the component πNQ reflects costs that depend on both N and Q. Hence, the marginal costs or shadow prices of N and Q are

$$P_N = \pi_N + \pi Q, \tag{18}$$

$$P_Q = \pi_Q + \pi N. \tag{19}$$

The shadow price of N rises with Q because each additional child is more costly the higher is his quality. Along the same lines the shadow price of Q rises with N because an additional unit of quality is more costly the larger is the number of children in the family who will receive it.

Suppose that more educated parents face lower costs of contraception either because they are more likely to use the most effective birth control methods or are more efficient at using a given method. Note that a reduction in the cost of contraception raises π_N. The increase in the relative price of N induces a substitution effect away from N and towards Q. The expansion in the ratio of Q to N causes a further increase in the relative price of N and an additional substitution effect in favor of Q and away from N. The presence of both a direct substitution effect (π_N increases which increase the relative price of N) and a secondary substitution effect (Q/N rises which increases the relative price of N) suggests a sizable reduction in N and a sizable increase in Q even if these two commodities are not particularly good substitutes in consumption. Exactly the same analysis follows if π_Q falls as parents' education rises because more educated parents are more efficient producers of quality. Since the parents' time is spent in encouraging the child's curiosity and in training the child in how to learn and in what satisfaction comes from learning, it is highly likely that more educated parents will be more effective or successful in encouraging these traits in their children.

Clearly the quality or well-being of children is positively related to their health and cognitive development. In turn, the latter depends on such outcomes as school achievement test scores and years of formal schooling completed. Since mothers typically allocate more time to childcare than fathers, it is natural to obtain separate estimates of the effects of mother's schooling and father's schooling on these outcomes. Especially in the case of the former, one wants to take account of increases in the wage or the value of time associated with schooling. Willis (1973) assumes that the production of child quality or well-being is more intensive in the wife's time than the production of the parents' standard of living. But child quality rises with the wage while family size falls because child well-being and parents' standard of living are complements in consumption. Becker and Lewis (1973) get the same result for a different reason. They assume that the fixed costs of number of children exceed the fixed costs of quality. They then show that an increase in the value of the wife's time lowers the price of quality relative to that of number of children, although it raises the price of quality relative to parents' standard of living. Thus, they predict a small negative or even a positive effect of an increase in the wage on child well-being. The point I wish to emphasize is that in both models wage or value of time effects are extremely unlikely to reverse efficiency effects and are very likely to reinforce these effects.

2.4. Biases, biases, biases

So far I have considered frameworks that generate causal effects of schooling on a variety of outcomes. For example, regardless of whether the mechanism is productive or allocative efficiency, an increase in an individual's own schooling is predicted to increase his or her own health. Similarly, an increase in parents' schooling is expected to increase the well-being of their children as measured by their health and cognitive development. These frameworks have been questioned, however, because schooling clearly is an endogenous variable. A variety of optimal schooling models, some of which are discussed and extended by Card (1999, 2001), raise the possibility that health, for example, may cause schooling or that omitted "third variables" may cause schooling and adult health or child well-being to vary in the same direction. I illustrate the issues involved with respect to adult health and child well-being outcomes.

Causality from better health to more schooling results if healthier students are more efficient producers of additions to the stock of knowledge (or human capital) via formal schooling. In addition, they may miss fewer days of school due to illness and therefore learn more for that reason. Furthermore, this causal path may have long lasting effects if past health is an input into current health status. Thus, even for non-students, a positive relationship between health and schooling may reflect reverse causality in the absence of controls for past health. Evidence linking poor health in early childhood to unfavorable educational outcomes is contained in Edwards and Grossman (1979), Shakotko, Edwards and Grossman (1981), Chaikind and Corman (1991), Currie (2000), Alderman et al. (2001), and Case, Fertig and Paxson (2005). Health also may cause schooling because a reduction in mortality increases the number of periods over which the returns from investments in knowledge can be collected.

The third-variable hypothesis has received a good deal of attention in the literature because it is related to the hypothesis that the positive effect of schooling on earnings, explored in detail by Mincer (1974) and in hundreds of studies since his seminal work [see Card (1999, 2001) for reviews of these studies], is biased upward by the omission of ability. Fuchs (1982) identifies time preference as the third variable. He argues that persons who are more future oriented (who have a high degree of time preference for the future or discount it at a modest rate) attend school for longer periods of time and make larger investments in their own health and in the well-being of their children. Thus, the effects of schooling on these outcomes are biased if one fails to control for time preference. Behrman and Rosenzweig (2002) present an argument that is even more closely related to ability bias in the earnings-schooling literature. In their model, parents with favorable heritable endowments obtain more schooling for themselves, are more likely to marry each other, and raise children with higher levels of well-being. In turn, these endowments reflect ability in the market to convert hours of work into earnings and childrearing talents in the nonmarket or household sector.

The time preference hypothesis is worth considering in more detail because it is related to the recent and very rich theoretical models in which preferences are endogenous discussed in Section 2.5. Suppose that human capital investments and the inputs that produce these investments do not enter the utility function directly. Then differences in time preference among individuals will not generate differences in investments in human capital unless certain other conditions are met. One condition is that the ability to finance these investments by borrowing is limited, so that they must be funded to some extent by foregoing current consumption. Even if the capital market is perfect, the returns on an investment in schooling depend on hours of work if schooling raises market productivity by a larger percentage than it raises nonmarket productivity. Individuals who are more future oriented desire relatively more leisure at older ages. Therefore, they work more at younger ages and have a higher discounted marginal benefit on a given investment than persons who are more present oriented. If health enters the utility function, persons who discount the future less heavily will have higher health levels during most stages of the life cycle. Hence, a positive relationship between schooling and health does not necessarily imply causality.

De Walque (2004, 2005) constructs a specific model with some of the above aspects in which differences in time preference have causal impacts on schooling and health. In his model the capital market is perfect and nonmarket productivity effects are not relevant since time is not an input in household production. Investments in schooling raise wage rates. Returns to these investments depend on health because healthier persons live longer and lose less time from work due to illness.[13] Health is endogenous because future health is negatively related to a good that enters the current period utility function such as cigarette smoking. Persons who discount the future heavily will consume more of this good and will have lower levels of health. This reduces the returns to investments in schooling and lowers the optimal level of schooling. Clearly, one can add a component to de Walque's model and related models in which parents who are more future oriented attend school for longer periods of time and make larger investments in the well-being of their children.

The preceding discussion suggests that the coefficient of own schooling in a regression in which own health is the dependent variable and the coefficient of parents' schooling in a regression in which child well-being is the dependent variable may be biased and inconsistent estimates of the true parameters. Several econometric procedures can be employed to correct for these biases. First, one can include past health measures in regressions that relate adult health to own schooling. Second, one can control for unmeasured third variables by examining differences in outcomes due to differences in schooling between siblings or twins. Third, one can employ the technique of instrumental variables. Here the idea is to employ variables that are correlated with schooling but not correlated with such omitted third variables as ability, other inherited genetic traits, and time preference to obtain consistent estimates of schooling effects. In the context of two-stage least squares estimation and its variants, the instruments are used to predict schooling in the first stage. Then predicted schooling replaces actual schooling in the adult health or child well-being equation.

[13] De Walque only considers the mortality aspects of health, but his model can easily be extended to the morbidity aspects.

The problem with the first procedure is that measures of past health may not be available or may be measured imprecisely. The second procedure, especially if it is based, on twins has several difficulties. Typically, it is based on small samples. In addition, differencing between twins exacerbates biases due to measurement error [Griliches (1979), Bound and Solon (1999), Neumark (1999)]. Finally, Bound and Solon (1999) stress that variations in schooling between identical twins may be systematic rather than random. Given the large literature that uses the technique of instrumental variables to investigate the causal impact of schooling on earnings [see Card (1999, 2001) for reviews], the third procedure appears to be the most promising. Of course, the difficulty here is that one must uncover instruments that plausibly are not correlated with third variables. The reader should keep these factors in mind in evaluating the studies discussed in Sections 4 and 5.

2.5. *Schooling effects in models with endogenous tastes*

Typically, economists have not emphasized the effects of variations in taste variables on the optimal consumption of goods and services at a moment in time or on changes in consumption over the life cycle because they have lacked theories about the formation of tastes. They have, however, devoted attention to the impacts of time preference and addiction or habit formation – two key components of tastes – in models that assume that tastes are exogenous. In most models of consumption over the life cycle [see Frederick, Lowenstein and O'Donoghue (2002) for a recent review], consumers maximize a lifetime utility function (L) defined as the discounted sum or present value of utility at each age:

$$L = \sum_{t=0}^{n} D^t U(C_t). \tag{20}$$

Here $U(C_t)$ is the current period utility function at time or age t, C_t is consumption at age t, and D is the discount factor. In turn, $D = 1/(1+g)$, where g is the rate of time preference for the present. Consumers who discount the future heavily (have small values of D or large values of g) will exhibit much slower rates of increase in consumption over their life cycles than consumers who discount the future at modest rates. Indeed, if g is large enough, consumption by the former group may actually fall with age.[14]

Pollak (1970) and others incorporate addiction or habit formation into the standard model of consumer behavior by assuming that past consumption of certain goods influences current period tastes or utility. Let A be a good that exhibits this property and C be a good that does not, so that A is the addictive good. Then the current period utility function is $U(C_t, A_t, A_{t-1})$. An increase in A_{t-1} lowers current period utility because there is a "necessary" component of consumption due to physiological or psychological

[14] Consumption rises with age if the market rate of interest exceeds g and falls with age if the converse holds.

factors. At the same time, an increase in past consumption is assumed to increase the marginal utility of current consumption in the case of addictive goods. This suggests that the current consumption of these goods is positively related to past consumption. It is natural to associate the reductions in current period utility caused by an increase in past consumption of addictive goods with the harmful health effects of cigarette smoking, excessive alcohol use, and the consumption of such illegal drugs as cocaine, heroin, marijuana, and opium. Moreover, experimental studies by psychologists of harmful addictions [for example, Peele (1985)] usually have identified reinforcement in the sense that greater past consumption of these goods raises their current consumption.

What do economic models that emphasize the effects of time preference and addiction add to conceptual frameworks for studying the relationship between schooling and adult health or between parents' schooling and child well-being? The answer is very little if time preference and past consumption are exogenous variables. We have already seen that exogenous variations in time preference can cause schooling and health or well-being to vary in the same direction in Section 2.4. Clearly, one wants to take account of the relationship between current consumption and past consumption or between current and future consumption in estimating demand functions for addictive goods with harmful health effects. But if past consumption is exogenous, these effects were ignored by consumers when they selected the optimal value of A_{t-1}. Similarly, the harmful future effects of current consumption are ignored when the optimal amount of A_t is selected.

The story is very different if time preference is endogenous and future effects are incorporated into current decision making. For example, proponents of the time preference hypothesis assume that a reduction in the rate of time preference for the present causes years of formal schooling to rise. On the other hand, Becker and Mulligan (1997) argue that causality may run in the opposite direction: namely, an increase in schooling may *cause* the rate of time preference for the present to fall (may *cause* the rate of time preference for the future to rise). They point out that the present value of utility in equation (20) is *higher* the smaller is the rate of time preference for the present. Hence, consumers have incentives to make investments that *lower* the rate of time preference for the present.

Becker and Mulligan then show that the marginal costs of investments that lower time preference fall and the marginal benefits rise as income or wealth rises. Marginal benefits also are greater when the length of life is greater. Hence, the equilibrium rate of time preference falls as the level of education rises because education raises income and life expectancy. Moreover, the more educated may be more efficient in making investments that lower the rate of time preference for the present – a form of productive efficiency not associated with health production. To quote Becker and Mulligan: "Schooling also determines ... [investments in time preference] partly through the study of history and other subjects, for schooling focuses students' attention on the future. Schooling can communicate images of the situations and difficulties of adult life, which are the future of childhood and adolescence. In addition, through repeated practice at problem solving, schooling helps children learn the art of scenario simulation. Thus, educated people should be more productive at reducing the remoteness of future pleasures (pp. 735–736)." This argument amounts to a third causal mechanism in addition to productive and allocative efficiency in health production via which schooling can cause health.

Becker and Mulligan's model appears to contain useful insights in considering intergenerational relationships between parents and children. For example, parents can raise their children's future health, including their adulthood health, by making them more future oriented. Note that years of formal schooling completed is a time-invariant variable beyond approximately age 30, while adult health is not time invariant. Thus, parents probably have a more important direct impact on the former than the latter. By making investments that raise their offspring's schooling, parents also induce them to make investments that lower their rate of time preference for the present and therefore raise their adult health.

There appear to be important interactions between Becker and Mulligan's theory of the endogenous determination of time preference and Becker and Murphy's (1988) theory of rational addiction. Unlike in the myopic models of addiction developed by Pollak (1970) and others, in the Becker–Murphy model, consumers are farsighted in the sense that they take account of the expected future consequences of their current decisions. That is, they realize that an increase in the consumption of a harmfully addictive good in the present period lowers future utility due to adverse health effects at the same time as it increases current utility. According to Becker and Mulligan (1997, p. 744), "Since a decline in future utility reduces the benefits from a lower discount on future utilities, greater consumption of harmful substances would lead to higher rates of time preference by discouraging investments in lowering these rates ...". This is the converse of Becker and Murphy's result that people who discount the future more heavily are more likely to become addicted because they give relatively little weight to future adverse health effects. Thus, "... harmful addictions induce even rational persons to discount the future more heavily, which in turn may lead them to become more addicted" [Becker and Mulligan (1997, p. 744)].

An extreme version of the ideas contained in the endogenous time preference and rational addiction literature suggests the following econometric specification of the relationship between health and schooling:

$$H = \alpha D, \tag{21}$$

$$D = \beta S, \tag{22}$$

$$H = \alpha\beta S. \tag{23}$$

Intercepts, disturbance terms, and other determinants of health and time preference (D) are suppressed. Since D is a positive correlate of time preference for the future, α and β are positive. This specification assumes that there is no direct effect of adult schooling on adult health, with time preference held constant. It also assumes that schooling has an important indirect effect on these outcomes that operates through time preference. Hence, the reduced-form parameter of schooling ($\alpha\beta$) is positive. Clearly, this is the relevant parameter from a policy perspective.

Estimation of the model just specified would be challenging because time preference is difficult to measure and because the disturbance terms in equations (21) and (22) are likely to be correlated. Suppose that an instrument exists that affects D but not H, so that one can test the hypothesis that the direct effect of schooling on H is zero in equation (21). Acceptance of that hypothesis *does not* imply the absence of a causal schooling effect if β is positive.

I realize that the Becker–Murphy (1988) and Becker–Mulligan (1997) models are controversial.[15] In the absence of direct and comprehensive measures of time preference, an important research strategy is to treat schooling as endogenous and employ instruments that are correlated with it but not correlated with time preference. The point I wish to emphasize is the existence of a conceptual framework in the literature in which causality runs from schooling to time preference. This framework suggests that it is not appropriate to include an exogenous measure of time preference in health outcome equations to investigate the causal nature of schooling effects unless one assumes or has evidence that there is no causality from schooling to time preference.

3. Empirical evidence: consumption patterns, total consumption, and consumption growth

3.1. Consumption patterns

Michael (1972, 1973b) uses the 1960–1961 Bureau of Labor Statistics Consumer Expenditures Survey to test the predictions of a factor- and commodity-neutral model of productive efficiency. Recall that the model predicts that the schooling effect should be positive for luxuries, negative for necessities, and zero for items with unitary income elasticities. He employs total consumption as a measure of permanent income or wealth. He finds that, of 52 items that exhaust total consumption, 29 have the predicted schooling effect. These items account for 71 percent of total consumption. When the analysis is limited to nondurables, 26 of 35 items have the predicted schooling effect. These items account for 84 percent of total nondurable consumption. The findings for nondurables are particularly important because actual consumption is much better measured for these items than for durables.

Given estimates of the income elasticities and schooling parameters in equation (7) [η_i and $(\eta_i - 1)\rho$, respectively], Michael attempts to estimate ρ, the percentage increase in nonmarket productivity caused by a one-year increase in schooling. His preferred procedure is to impose alternative values of ρ on the system of Engel curves and pick the one that minimizes the weighted (by expenditure shares) residual sum of squares. He compares this estimate to the impact of education on market productivity, measured by

[15] For critiques and alternative approaches, see, for example, Gruber and Köszegi (2001) and Frederick, Lowenstein and O'Donoghue (2002).

the percentage increase in consumption caused by a one-year increase in schooling. He finds that the ratio of the nonmarket productivity effect to the market productivity effect is approximately equal to 0.6.[16] Thus, although the market effect is larger, the nonmarket effect is substantial. This estimate is comparable in magnitude to one obtained by Gronau (1980) with data on wage rates of married women and the time that they allocate to housework.

The BLS has conducted consumer expenditure surveys like the one used by Michael on an annual basis since 1980. Given these surveys, it is very surprising that his research has not been replicated and extended. The availability of detailed price data for many items from the American Chamber of Commerce Researchers Association [ACCRA (various years)] would facilitate these efforts. The ACCRA surveys cover between 250 and 300 cities on a quarterly basis since 1968. In addition to specific prices, the surveys contain cost-of-living indexes for each city. These data could be used to adjust expenditures for price variation and to include real prices as explanatory variables. It might also be possible to take account of the impacts of variations in the price of time due to schooling by adding the city-specific real wage rate to the set of independent variables.[17] In addition, the new BLS American Time Use Survey offers the possibility of doing with the time input in household production the same analysis previously done on the goods input. The time use survey, if used in combination with the consumer expenditure surveys, may be a vehicle for breaking out of the constraining data limitations faced by Michael and other researchers who have attempted to test the productive efficiency hypothesis.

3.2. Total consumption

In Section 2.1.1, I considered the impact of an increase in schooling on total consumption and hours of work when schooling varies, with the wage rate and property income held constant. The prediction is that consumption and hours of work will rise if the uncompensated price elasticity of demand for nonmarket time is less than one in absolute value. I also considered an alternative model in which the market and nonmarket productivity effects of schooling are the same. In that model hours of work rise if the income elasticity of demand for leisure is less than one. These specific hypotheses have never been tested. One reason is that the impact of schooling on consumption at a moment in time or in the cross section may reflect forces associated with its rate of growth

[16] Michael employs the logarithm of schooling rather than schooling as a regressor. Hence he obtains an estimate of ρ/S. Obviously, this does not affect the comparison of the relative magnitudes of market and nonmarket productivity effects.

[17] An increase in the wage rate generates a substitution in production towards goods inputs and a substitution in consumption towards goods-intensive commodities (commodities in which the share of the time input in total cost is smaller than on average) and towards the inputs used to produce these commodities. The substitution in consumption effect lowers the demand for goods used to produce time-intensive commodities. Hence, with real income and schooling held constant, the impact of a change in the wage on the demand for a particular market good or service is ambiguous.

over time or with age. Thus, the more educated may consume less from a given income because they desire a more rapid growth in consumption with age (see Section 3.3 for evidence in favor of this proposition). Another reason is that schooling, the wage rate, and property income may be highly correlated, although a number of studies of the determinants of health reviewed in Section 4 employ all three variables as regressors.

Morris (1976) estimates consumption functions derived from a variant of the static model presented in Section 2.1.1, but he assumes that the wage rate is strictly proportional to schooling, which is highly questionable. Moreover, his development requires one to include full income and the ratio of the wage rate to nonmarket productivity as regressors. A much more flexible specification is one in which the wage rate, schooling, and property income are the regressors. In my view little should be made of his rejection of the hypothesis that education has a nonmarket productivity effect.

If the productive efficiency model is to be tested with aggregate consumption data in future research, supply curves of hours of work or demand functions for nonmarket time should be obtained at the same time. It also seems necessary to develop a strategy to control for the life cycle components of these behaviors. One approach might be to focus on cross-sectional variations at the age or ages at which consumption and hours of work peak and to allow the peak ages to depend on schooling.[18]

3.3. *Consumption growth*

The lifetime utility function given by equation (20) implies that the rate of growth of consumption with age is approximately equal to $\sigma(r - g)$, where σ is the intertemporal elasticity of substitution in consumption, r is the market rate of interest and g is the rate of time preference for the present. If σ and r do not vary among individuals, consumption growth is governed by time preference. Persons who discount the future heavily (have large values of g) exhibit much slower growth than those who are more future oriented (have small values of g).[19]

Carroll and Summers (1991) and Lawrence (1991) present evidence that consumption grows more rapidly over the life cycle for persons with more years of formal schooling. Using the 1960–1961 BLS Consumer Expenditures Survey, Carroll and Summers (1991) find that consumption grows by 25 percent for college graduates between the ages of 27 and 32 but only by 10 percent for high school graduates who did not attend college. Between the ages of 27 and 47, the growth rates for the two schooling groups are 70 percent and 35 percent, respectively.[20] Lawrence (1991) uses annual data from

[18] Ghez and Becker (1975) show that the age at which consumption peaks may differ from the age at which hours of work peak.

[19] I assume in the text that r exceeds g. If the converse holds for people with large values of g, consumption falls over their life cycles.

[20] The above summary is based on Becker and Mulligan's (1997) analysis of data presented but not discussed in detail by Carroll and Summers (1991).

the Panel Survey of Income Dynamics for the years 1974 through 1982 to estimate regressions in which the rate of growth in consumption depends on income, age, race, the real after-tax interest rate, and a dichotomous indicator for households in which the head had a college education. Her results suggest that families with a college-educated head have a time preference rate that is about two percentage points lower than families whose head did not have a college education.

In discussing these results, especially those of Carroll and Summers, Becker and Mulligan (1997) point out that they have often been explained by liquidity constraints. Proponents of this hypothesis note that earnings grow rapidly at young ages and for the highly educated. These groups would like to borrow against their future earnings but cannot do so. Hence, their consumption is limited by their earnings. Becker and Mulligan proceed to argue that the liquidity constraint hypothesis does not explain why savings might be observed for young college graduates.

I acknowledge that the empirical evidence just discussed does not prove that schooling causes time preference. Clearly, it is consistent with the alternative hypothesis that time preference causes schooling. The point I wish to emphasize is that this evidence also does not prove that time preference causes schooling. Absent definitive tests that establish causality in one direction only, empirical evidence that time preference measures greatly reduce the effects of schooling on adult health or child well-being should be interpreted with caution. Such results do not necessarily imply absence of causality from schooling to these outcomes.

Another point worth noting is that Becker and Mulligan (1997) summarize evidence of positive relationships between parents' income and the rate of growth of consumption of their children when they become adults. They indicate that these results could be traced to exogenous inherited traits that determine time preference. But they also indicate that these genetic correlations would have to be quite large – larger than those that have been estimated in the literature – to account for the sizable relationship between the outcomes at issue. Thus a scenario in which higher income parents make larger investments in the future orientation of their children is equally likely if not more likely.

4. Empirical evidence: health

Most of the empirical evidence discussed in this paper pertains to schooling and health outcomes. As pointed out in Section 1, this is a natural focus because the evidence pertains to complementary relationships between the two most important components of the stock of human capital. The very large literature in this area has been reviewed recently by Grossman and Kaestner (1997) and by Grossman (2000). My aim in this section is to give the reader a "flavor" for this literature rather than repeating all the material in the two papers just cited. I highlight research that laid the foundations for current studies and the results of these and ongoing studies. I consider adult health in Section 4.1 and child health (defined to include the health of infants, children, and adolescents) in Section 4.2. Within each topic, I begin with studies that employ the productive efficiency framework or that relate health to schooling and variables that are not endogenous inputs into the production of health. I then turn to research on allocative efficiency and to approaches that address the time preference and other third variables hypotheses, some of which do so by treating schooling as endogenous.

At the outset, I note that Grossman and Kaestner (1997) and Grossman (2000) conclude from their extensive reviews of the literature that years of formal schooling completed is the most important correlate of good health. This finding emerges whether health levels are measured by mortality rates, morbidity rates, self-evaluation of health status, or physiological indicators of health, and whether the units of observation are individuals or groups. The studies reviewed also suggest that schooling is a more important correlate of health than occupation or income, the two other components of socioeconomic status. This is particularly true when one controls for reverse causality from poor health to low income. Of course, schooling is a causal determinant of occupation and income, so that the gross effect of schooling on health may reflect in part its impact on socioeconomic status. The studies reviewed, however, indicate that a significant portion of the gross schooling effect cannot be traced to the relationship between schooling and income or occupation. The main message of my review is that research completed since the Grossman–Kaestner and Grossman papers were published has not altered their basic conclusions.

4.1. Adult health

4.1.1. Productive efficiency and related frameworks

I [Grossman (1972b)] report positive effects of schooling on self-rated health[21] and negative effects of schooling on work-loss days due to illness and injury and on restricted activity days due to illness and injury in a nationally representative 1963 United States survey conducted by the Center for Health Administration Studies and the National Opinion Research Center of the University of Chicago. These findings control for the weekly wage rate, property income, age, and several other variables. In the demand function for medical care (measured by personal medical expenditures on doctors, dentists, hospital care, prescribed and nonprescribed drugs, nonmedical practitioners, and medical appliances), the schooling coefficient is positive but not statistically significant. This finding is not consistent with the version of my pure investment model in which the inverse of the elasticity of the marginal product of health with respect to health is less than one in absolute value (see Section 2.1.2). But note that I was forced to use a very aggregate measure of medical care and had no information on health insurance. Since more generous health insurance coverage increases the quantity of care demanded and

[21] Many of the studies discussed in Sections 4.1 and 4.2 employ self-rated health or parental rating of child health as an outcome. Thus, it is important to emphasize that these measures have been shown to be strongly predictive of mortality and other objective health outcomes. See Idler and Kasl (1995) for an extensive review of this literature.

since coverage and schooling are positively related, my estimated schooling effect is biased away from zero.

Wagstaff (1986) and Erbsland, Ried and Ulrich (1995) provide more definitive evidence in favor of the productive efficiency hypothesis. Wagstaff (1986) uses the 1976 Danish Welfare Survey to estimate a multiple indicator version of my demand for health model. He performs a principal components analysis of nineteen measures of non-chronic health problems to obtain four health indicators that reflect physical mobility, mental health, respiratory health, and presence of pain. He then uses these four variables as indicators of the unobserved stock of health. His estimation technique is the so-called MIMIC (multiple indicators–multiple causes) model developed by Jöreskog (1973) and Goldberger (1974) and employs the maximum likelihood procedure contained in Jöreskog and Sörbom (1981). His contribution is unique because it accounts for the multidimensional nature of good health both at the conceptual level and at the empirical level.

Wagstaff reports a positive and significant effect of schooling on his measure of good health and a negative and significant effect of schooling on the number of physician visits in the past eight months. The latter result differs from mine. One factor that may account for the discrepancy is that Wagstaff has a much better measure of medical care utilization than I had. Another factor is that Wagstaff is able to control for variations in the price of a physician visit. Since money cost of medical care is heavily subsidized in Denmark, this price is given by the time required by survey respondents to travel to their physicians.

Erbsland, Ried and Ulrich (1995) provide another example of the application of the MIMIC procedure to the estimation of a demand for health model. Their database is the 1986 West German Socio-economic Panel. The degree of handicap, self-rated health, the duration of sick time, and the number of chronic conditions, all as reported by the individual, serve as four indicators of the unobserved stock of health. In the reduced form demand function for health, schooling has a positive and significant coefficient. In the reduced form demand function for visits to general practitioners, the schooling effect is negative and significant.

Gilleskie and Harrison (1998) perform a direct test of the productive efficiency hypothesis by estimating a self-rated health production function with four endogenous inputs: the number of preventive doctor visits in the past year, the number of curative doctor visits in the past year, and dichotomous indicators that identify persons who smoke cigarettes and who exercise regularly. They employ the 1987 National Medical Expenditure Survey and control for the past stock of health by including the number of chronic conditions and the body mass index (weight in kilograms divided by height in meters squared) as regressors. They use Mroz's (1999) discrete factor estimator to account for the endogeneity of the inputs.

Gilleskie and Harrison report positive and significant schooling coefficients for both males and females. This is direct evidence in support of a productive efficiency effect of schooling. Some caution is required in interpreting their results because the proxies for past health may be endogenous but are treated as exogenous. Moreover, they achieve identification in part with attitudinal variables (for example, whether a person says that he or she is more than an average risk taker) that may be caused by schooling and correlated with unmeasured health inputs.

The remaining studies to be discussed in this subsection contain equations that are best interpreted as reduced form health outcome equations. A number of them contain direct controls for potential third variables such as past health, physical and mental ability, and parents' schooling. They do not attempt to distinguish between the productive and allocative efficiency hypotheses.

I [Grossman (1975)] conclude that schooling has a significant positive impact on the current self-rated health of middle-aged white males in the NBER-Thorndike sample.[22] The estimated schooling effect in my study controls for health in high school, parents' schooling, scores on physical and mental tests taken by the men when they were in their early twenties, current hourly wage rates, property income, and job satisfaction. My finding is particularly notable because all the men graduated from high school. Hence it suggests that the favorable impact of schooling on health persists even at high levels of schooling.

My analysis of the mortality experience of the Thorndike sample between 1955 and 1969 confirms the important role of schooling in health outcomes. This analysis is restricted to men who reported positive full-time salaries in 1955. In the fitted logit functions, schooling has a positive and statistically significant effect on the probability of survival. Indeed, schooling is the only variable whose logit coefficient differs from zero in a statistical sense. The schooling effect is independent of the level of median salary in 1955 and suggests that, in the vicinity of the mean death rate, a one-year increase in schooling lowers the probability of death by 0.4 percentage points. These results must be interpreted with some caution because the men in the Thorndike sample were only in their thirties in 1955, and relatively few variables were available for that year.

The importance of schooling as a determinant of self-rated health status of persons in the preretirement years is reinforced in studies by Hartog and Oosterbeek (1998) for the Netherlands and Gerdtham and Johannesson (1999) for Sweden. Hartog and Oosterbeek study the health in 1993 of men and women who were sixth grade pupils in 1953 in the Dutch province of Noord-Brabant. The schooling coefficients in their study control for IQ in 1953 and parents' schooling among other variables. Gerdtham and Johannesson fit a model of the demand for health to the 1991 Swedish level of Living Survey. The schooling coefficient in their study actually may be underestimated because they include a measure of obesity in their equation. Schooling has a well-established negative impact on this outcome [for example, Chou, Grossman and Saffer (2004)].

[22] In 1955, Robert L. Thorndike and Elizabeth Hagan collected information on earnings, schooling, and occupation for a sample of 9,700 men drawn from a population of 75,000 white males who volunteered for, and were accepted as, candidates for Aviation Cadet status in the Army Air Force in the last half of 1943. Candidates were given 17 specific tests that measured 5 basic types of ability: general intelligence, numerical ability, visual perception, psychomotor control, and mechanical ability. In 1969 and again in 1971, the National Bureau of Economic Research mailed questionnaires to the members of the Thorndike–Hagan 1955 sample.

Estimates of dynamic demand for health models in panel data by Van Doorslaer (1987), Wagstaff (1993), Bolin, Jacobson and Lindgren (2002), and Case, Fertig and Paxson (2005) also confirm the importance of schooling as a determinant of health. These studies take account of reverse causality from health at early stages in the life cycle to the amount of formal schooling completed. They also relax the assumption that there are no costs of adjustment, so that lagged health becomes a relevant determinant of current health. Van Doorslaer (1987) employs the 1984 Netherlands Health Interview Survey. While this is a cross-sectional survey, respondents were asked to evaluate their health in 1979 as well as in 1984. Both measures are ten-point scales, where the lowest category is very poor health and the highest category is very good health. Van Doorslaer's main finding is that schooling has a positive and significant coefficient in the regression explaining health in 1984, with health in 1979 held constant.

Wagstaff (1993) uses the Danish Health Study, which followed respondents over a period of 12 months beginning in October 1982. As in his 1986 study, a MIMIC model is estimated. Three health measures are used as indicators of the unobserved stock of health capital in 1982 (past stock) and 1983 (current stock). These are a dichotomous indicator of the presence of a health limitation, physician-assessed health of the respondent as reported by the respondent, and self-assessed health. Both of the assessment variables have five-point scales. Wagstaff reports positive schooling effects for adults under the age of 41 and for adults greater than or equal to that age, although only the former effect is statistically significant.

Bolin, Jacobson and Lindgren (2002) fit the exact version of the dynamic demand for health model that I developed [Grossman (2000, pp. 390–392)]. I show that a model with rising marginal cost of gross investment in health results in a second-order difference equation in which current health (health at age t) is positively related to past health (health at age $t-1$) and future health (health at age $t+1$). Bolin et al. use the 1980/81, 1988/89, and 1996/97 waves of The Swedish Survey of Living Conditions to estimate this model. Current self-rated health is taken from the second wave, and past and future self-rated health are taken from the first and third waves, respectively. Based on order-probit specifications, schooling raises the probability of being in the highest health category and reduces the probabilities of being in the lowest and intermediate categories. Since these results hold past and future health constant and since past and future health are found to raise current health, long-run schooling effects are even larger.[23]

Case, Fertig and Paxson (2005) employ a unique data set: the 1958 British National Child Development Study. All children born in England, Scotland, and Wales in the week of March 3, 1958, have been followed in this study from birth through age 42. Parents were interviewed at the time of the birth, and health and socioeconomic data

[23] Long-run effects are obtained by setting past current and future health equal to each other. Bolin, Jacobson and Lindgren (2002) cannot compute these effects because they treat past and future health as continuous variables in an ordered probit specification of current health. Some caution should be exercised in interpreting their findings because past and future health are endogenous variables in the dynamic model formulated by Grossman (2000), while Bolin, Jacobson and Lindgren (2002) treat these variables as exogenous.

have been collected on panel members at ages 7, 11, 16, 23, 33, and 42. Case, Fertig and Paxson (2005) relate self-rated health of males at age 42 to corresponding measures at ages 23 and 33, birthweight, the number of physician-assessed chronic health conditions at ages 7 and 16, own schooling, earnings at age 42, and family income age 16. The schooling coefficient is positive and significant even in models that include self-rated health at ages 23 and 33. Clearly, these two outcomes may depend on schooling.

The importance of schooling as a determinant of the self-rated health of older males and of the mortality experience of males of all ages is underscored in studies by Rosen and Taubman (1982), Taubman and Rosen (1982), and Sickles and Taubman (1986). The first study is based on the 1973 Exact Match Sample, which was obtained by matching persons in the March 1973 Current Population Survey with their Social Security and Internal Revenue Service records and then tracing their mortality experience through 1977. Rosen and Taubman estimate separate mortality regressions for white males aged 25 through 64 in 1973 and for white males aged 65 and over in that year. For both groups mortality is negatively related to education, with marital status, earnings in 1973, and health status in that year held constant. Rosen and Taubman conclude: "... the effect of education does not flow solely or primarily through income effects, does not reflect a combination of differential marriage patterns and the health benefits of having a wife, and ... those who are disabled or not working because of ill health are not found disproportionately in any one education group (p. 269)."

Taubman and Rosen (1982) use the 1969, 1971, and 1973 Retirement History Survey to study the self-rated health and survival experience of white males who were between the ages of 58 and 63 in the initial year of this panel survey. The dependent variable compares health with that of others the same age and has four categories: better, same, worse, or dead. With health in 1969, income, and marital status held constant, health levels in 1971 and 1973 and changes over time are strongly related to years of formal schooling completed. There also is evidence that own schooling is a more important predictor of health than wife's schooling for married men.

Sickles and Taubman (1986) add the 1975 and 1977 waves to the panel data employed by Taubman and Rosen and include black males as well as white males in their analysis. They fit a model with two endogenous variables: health status and retirement status. The model is recursive (health status determines retirement status) and allows for correlated errors between the two equations and heterogeneity, which is treated as a random effect. Since the health equation is an ordered polytomous probit and the retirement equation is a binary probit, full information maximum likelihood estimation methods are employed. As in the Taubman–Rosen study, higher schooling levels are associated with better health. Taken together, the two studies suggest that the schooling effect is not sensitive to very different model specifications and estimation strategies.

Hurd and Kapteyn (2003) buttress findings reported by Rosen and Taubman and by Sickles and Taubman with regard to the effect of schooling on self-rated health in the Health and Retirement Survey – households with one member between the ages of 51 and 61 in 1992. They employ baseline data and follow-ups conducted in 1994, 1996, 1998, and 2000. Controlling for baseline health, current income, and wealth, they show that more educated persons are more likely to report maintaining their health in the highest category.

Deaton and Paxson (2001) confirm the importance of schooling in mortality outcomes of both men and women in two data sets. One consists of all-cause mortality for the United States for the years 1975–1995 merged by birth cohort and sex to the 1976–1996 Current Population Survey (cohort file). The second is the National Longitudinal Mortality Study (NLMS) – a survey of individuals originally sampled in the CPS around 1980 and in the 1980 Census of Population into which death certificates have been retrospectively merged.

In both data sets negative schooling effects on mortality are observed for persons under the age of 60 as well as for persons over that age. These estimates control for family income. In the NLMS, the income effect becomes weaker as the length of time between 1980 and the year of death increases, while the schooling effect increases in absolute value for males. Deaton and Paxson argue that this is because moving forward in time reduces reverse causality from poor health to low income.

In the cohort file, the schooling coefficients are negative and significant while the income coefficients are either insignificant or positive and significant when both variables are included. Deaton and Paxson caution that the income and schooling measures are highly correlated, making it difficult to sort out the separate impacts of each variable. They mention but dismiss an argument by Fuchs (1974) and others that income can actually have harmful effects on health with schooling held constant because higher income people may consume larger quantities of items that are harmful to their health. Their dismissal is based on inconclusive evidence in the studies cited by Fuchs. They do not, however, refer to my study (Grossman 1972b) that reports a negative effect of family income on several health measures with schooling and the wage rate held constant. In any case their evidence is consistent with the mortality studies conducted in the 1980s.[24]

4.1.2. Allocative efficiency

Leigh (1983) employs data from the University of Michigan's Quality of Employment Surveys of 1973 and 1977 and considers persons 16 years of age and older who worked for pay for 20 or more hours per week in these two national surveys. He shows that most of the statistically significant positive effect of schooling on self-rated health can be explained by decisions with regard to cigarette smoking, exercise, and the choice of less hazardous occupations by the more educated. This finding provides support for the allocative efficiency hypothesis. But it also supports the alternative hypotheses that schooling causes health because of its impacts on tastes, primarily its impact on time preference. Of course, the finding also is consistent with a third hypothesis that both schooling and the determinants of health are caused by time preference.

[24] For summaries and critiques of several studies that do not find negative effects of schooling on mortality, see Grossman and Kaestner (1997).

Kenkel (1991) explores the allocative efficiency hypothesis by examining the extent to which schooling helps people choose healthier life styles by improving their knowledge of the relationships between health behaviors and health outcomes. He uses direct measures of health knowledge to test this explanation. He does this by estimating the separate effects of schooling and health knowledge on cigarette smoking (the number of cigarettes smoked per day), excessive alcohol use (the number of days in the past year on which the respondent consumed five or more drinks of an alcoholic beverage), and exercise (the number of minutes of exercise in the past two weeks) using data from the Health Promotion/Disease Prevention Supplement to the 1985 National Health Interview Survey. Cigarette knowledge is measured by the number of correct responses to whether smoking causes each of seven illnesses. Drinking knowledge is measured by the number of correct responses to whether heavy drinking causes each of three illnesses. Exercise knowledge is given by correct responses for the amount of exercise required to strengthen the heart and lungs and the required change in heart rate and breathing.

With age, family income, race, marital status, employment status, and veteran status (for males only), held constant, an increase in schooling leads to a reduction in smoking and excessive alcohol use and to an increase in exercise. Moreover, knowledge of the health consequences of smoking decreases smoking, and similar relationships hold for excessive alcohol consumption and exercise. The results also show that part of the relationship between schooling and health behaviors is due to health knowledge, but the schooling coefficients are significant with health knowledge held constant. Moreover the reductions in schooling coefficients due to the inclusion of health knowledge are relatively small; they range between 5 and 20 percent. The results are not altered when health knowledge is treated as an endogenous variable. Kenkel interprets this result as indicating that unobservables, such as individual rates of time preference, are important determinants of health behavior and schooling but acknowledges that other interpretations are possible.

Situations in which new information becomes available or in which new medical technologies are introduced provide the best setting to explore and test the allocative efficiency hypothesis. As pointed out in Section 2.2, most treatments of allocative efficiency assume that the more educated respond more rapidly to these new developments. Sander (1995a, 1995b) and de Walque (2004) present national data showing that cigarette smoking initiation and participation rates fell more rapidly and quit rates rose more rapidly as the level of education rose between the middle 1960s and the 1970s. These data suggest that those with more schooling were more responsive to new information about the harmful effects of smoking in the 1950s and early 1960s, which culminated in the issuance of the first Surgeon General's Report on Smoking and Health in 1964. These trends persisted, however, in the 1980s and 1990s. Since information concerning the health risks of smoking was widespread by the early 1980s, the more recent data are not consistent with the allocative efficiency hypothesis.

The spread of the HIV/AIDS epidemic since the early 1980s provides another setting to examine the allocative efficiency hypothesis. Glied and Lleras-Muney (2003) point out that by the late 1980s new AIDS cases among gay men (a group with high education) were significantly below predicted rates, while new cases among intravenous drug users (a group with lower levels of education) were at or above projected rates. This suggests that there had been little behavioral change in the latter group. Goldman and Smith (2002) report that more educated HIV patients are more likely to adhere to therapy, reflected by highly active antiretroviral treatments (HAART), which became available in the mid 1990s. Their data source is the HIV Cost and Services Utilization Study, conducted in three waves between 1996 and 1998, and their findings control for initial health status and insurance status. In turn, adherence to therapy leads to improvements in self-rated health between the three waves of the survey. Schooling has no impact on improvements in health with adherence to therapy held constant. Hence, adherence to therapy by the more educated appears to be an important mechanism via which schooling can improve health among persons with a relatively new disease when a new treatment regime is introduced.

Goldman and Lakdawalla (2002) reinforce the results just discussed by considering self-reported CD4 T-lymphocyte cell counts as an outcome in the same survey used by Goldman and Smith (2002). A depletion in these cells correlates strongly with the worsening of HIV disease and raises the probability of developing AIDS. They find negative and significant schooling effects on this outcome in the second and third waves of the survey, but not in the baseline wave, with insurance status, self-reported baseline health, and the number of years since the individual had been diagnosed with HIV held constant.

De Walque (2005) reinforces Goldman and Smith's results in a very different setting. He finds that, after more than a decade of prevention campaigns about the dangers of the HIV/AIDS epidemic in Uganda, there has been a significant change in the HIV/education gradient. In 1990 no relationship existed, but by 2000 education lowers the risk of being HIV positive among young individuals. He also reports a positive relationship between schooling and condom use during the recent period, which may partially explain his findings. Not enough time in the AIDS epidemic has elapsed to examine whether a permanent relationship between the prevalence and severity of the disease and schooling has emerged. The weakening of this relationship would provide further support for the allocative efficiency hypothesis, while its persistence would provide support for productive efficiency effects or for the role of third variables.

Lleras-Muney and Lichtenberg (2002) and Glied and Lleras-Muney (2003) present evidence of important interactions between education and new medical technologies in a variety of cases. Using the 1997 U.S. Medical Expenditure Panel Survey, Lleras-Muney and Lichtenberg (2002) find that the more educated are more likely to use drugs recently approved by the Federal Drug Administration. Their findings only pertain to individuals who repeatedly purchase drugs for a given condition, indicating that the more educated are better able to learn from experience.

Glied and Lleras-Muney (2003) focus on mortality from 55 diseases that account for mortality from all diseases and on cancer mortality from 81 different cancer sites. The former analysis employs the 1986–1990 Health Interview Surveys matched to the

Mortality Cause of Death files for 1986–1995 and examines disease-specific mortality within five years. The latter employs the Surveillance Epidemiology and End Results Cancer Incidence Public Use Database, which contains information on every person diagnosed with cancer from 1973 through 1998 in six states and three cities in different states. The outcome is mortality within five years of diagnosis. In the disease-specific mortality analysis, technological progress is measured by the annual percentage change in the age-adjusted mortality rate for the period 1969–1999 for each of the 55 diseases. In the cancer analysis, it is based on the percentage change in the five-year survival rate conditional on diagnosis using diagnosis data for each of the 81 sites for the years 1973–1975 and 1991–1993. Alternatively, progress in treating cancer is given by the number of drugs that existed in 1999 and the number of drugs approved between 1973 and 1999 by site.[25] Their principal result is that negative effects of schooling on mortality are largest for diseases and cancer sites in which progress has been the most rapid.

Goldman and Lakdawalla (2002) point out that not all new medical innovations require better self-management skills on the part of patients. They give as an example the introduction of new antihypertensive drugs, called beta-blockers, in the late 1960s and early 1970s. These new drugs serve as a substitute at least to some extent for the former treatment of diet, exercise, weight control, and the occasional use of diuretics. In terms of their model outlined in Section 2.2, the positive relationship between the output elasticity of the patient's own time and schooling falls when beta-blockers are introduced. Consistent with this prediction, they find that the negative effect of schooling on the presence of hypertensive cardiovascular disease as diagnosed by a physician in the Framingham Heart Study is reduced in absolute value in the post-beta-blocker period.

Goldman and Smith (2002) give an example in which the persistence of long-run schooling effects is not necessarily evidence against allocative efficiency. They study treatment regimes pursued by diabetics in the Health and Retirement Survey – households with one member between the ages of 51 and 61 in 1992. Using four waves of data and information on alternative treatment regimes (swallowed medication only, insulin shots only, medication and insulin shots an external pump, or nothing), Goldman and Smith classified treatment patterns as good or bad and report that the more educated are less likely to adhere to poor treatment regimes.[26] In turn, a poor regime is associated with a deterioration in self-rated health between the first and fourth regimes. Finally, the negative effect of schooling on a poor treatment regime is eliminated when the Wechsler Adult Intelligence Score, a measure of higher-level reasoning, is included as a regressor. This suggests that the schooling effect measures cognitive ability.

[25] Glied and Lleras-Muney (2003) cannot employ survival conditional on diagnosis in the NHIS data because there is no information on diagnosis. They argue that a drug measure is not accurate in the case of disease-specific mortality since drugs are used for conditions that can lead to death from multiple causes.

[26] For example, the same regime in each wave was considered good as was a progression from medication to insulin. Bad regimes included taking medication or insulin in one wave but not in a subsequent one or switching from one treatment to another and then back to the initial treatment.

4.1.3. Time preference, other omitted factors, and instrumental variables

Fuchs (1982) measures time preference in a telephone survey by asking respondents questions in which they choose between a sum of money now and a larger sum in the future. He includes an index of time preference in a multiple regression in which health status is the dependent variable and schooling is one of the independent variables. Fuchs is not able to demonstrate that the schooling effect is due to time preference. The latter variable has a negative regression coefficient, but it is not statistically significant. When time preference and schooling are entered simultaneously, the latter dominates the former. These results must be regarded as preliminary because they are based on one small sample of adults on Long Island and on exploratory measures of time preference.

Farrell and Fuchs (1982) explore the time preference hypothesis in the context of cigarette smoking using interviews conducted in 1979 by the Stanford Heart Disease Prevention Program in four small agricultural cities in California. They examine the smoking behavior of white non-Hispanics who were not students at the time of the survey, had completed 12 to 18 years of schooling, and were at least 24 years old. The presence of retrospective information on cigarette smoking at ages 17 and 24 allows them to relate smoking at these two ages to years of formal schooling completed by 1979 for cohorts who reached age 17 before and after the widespread diffusion of information concerning the harmful effects of cigarette smoking on health.

Farrell and Fuchs find that the negative relationship between schooling and smoking, which rises in absolute value for cohorts born after 1953, does not increase between the ages of 17 and 24. Since the individuals were all in the same school grade at age 17, the additional schooling obtained between that age and age 24 cannot be the cause of differential smoking behavior at age 24, according to the authors. Based on these results, Farrell and Fuchs reject the hypothesis that schooling is a causal factor in smoking behavior in favor of the view that a third variable causes both. Since the strong negative relationship between schooling and smoking developed only after the spread of information concerning the harmful effects of smoking, they argue that the same mechanism may generate the schooling-health relationship.

A different interpretation of the Farrell and Fuchs finding emerges if one assumes that consumers are farsighted. The current consumption of cigarettes leads to more illness and less time for work in the future. The cost of this lost time is higher for persons with higher wage rates who have made larger investments in human capital. Thus, the costs of smoking in high school are greater for persons who plan to make larger investments in human capital.

Leigh (1985) presents evidence that supports Fuchs's (1982) finding that the positive relationship between schooling and health cannot be explained by time preference. Using the Panel Study of Income Dynamics, a nationally representative panel survey conducted by the University of Michigan's Survey Research Center annually since 1968, Leigh measures health inversely with a dichotomous variable that identifies persons who became disabled (developed conditions that limited the amount or kind of work they could do) in 1971 or 1972. The independent variables in logit equations that explain the probability of becoming disabled pertain to the year prior to the onset of the disability. Schooling has a negative and statistically significant logit coefficient. When a risk preference index, which is highly correlated with a time preference index [Leigh (1986)], is introduced into the equation, the schooling coefficient declines by only 10 percent and remains statistically significant (personal communication with Leigh).

Ross and Mirowsky (1999) find that the impacts of schooling on self-rated health and on a continuous positive correlate of physical functioning are significantly reduced when a measure of sense of control is included as a regressor in the 1995 Aging, Status, and the Sense of Control Survey. This is a nationally representative U.S. sample of persons aged 18 and over, with an oversampling of the elderly. Sense of control pertains to the belief that one can and does master, control, and shape his own life. Studies by psychologists summarized by Ross and Mirowsky (1999) and by Hammond (2003) indicated that sense of control is positively related to self-efficacy and to a future orientation.

Ross and Mirowsky note that lack of personal control makes efforts to change health by quitting smoking, exercising, or limiting alcohol consumption appear to be useless. They argue: "Human capital acquired in school increases a person's real and perceived control of life. Education develops the habits and skills of communication .... Because education develops one's ability to gather and interpret information and to solve problems on many levels, it increases one's control over events and outcomes in life" (p. 446). Although Ross and Mirowsky are sociologists, their argument is very similar to the one proposed by Becker and Mulligan (1997) regarding why education makes a person more future oriented. The point I wish to make is that Ross and Mirowsky treat sense of control as a mechanism via which schooling can affect health rather than as a third variable that must be held constant is assessing whether more schooling causes better health.

A counterpoint to the point made by Ross and Mirowsky is contained in a study by Coleman and DeLeire (2003). Using the National Education Longitudinal Study, they show that sense of control measured in the eighth grade is a positive predictor of high school completion and college attendance. This suggests that sense of control may be an exogenous influence on schooling rather than a mechanism via which schooling affects health. They also report, however, that increases in personal control between the eighth and twelfth grades are positively related to increases in cognitive test scores between those two grades. This finding implies that sense of control has an endogenous component.

Ippolito (2003) takes a somewhat different approach to controlling for time preference in his study of the determinants of health in the Health and Retirement Survey used by Goldman and Smith (2002). He employs three measures of health from the 1992 baseline data: dichotomous indicators that identify respondents in poor health and respondents who have difficulty walking stairs and the number of reported ailments. He also employs death within six years of the 1992 survey from the National Death Index as a fourth health outcome. With income and several other variables held constant, schooling has a negative and significant impact on each outcome. The schooling coefficients are greatly reduced and in the case of ailments and mortality become insignificant when proxies for time preference are included as regressors. These proxies include the amount of formal schooling obtained by the oldest child in the household, whether there is an Individual Retirement Account (IRA) in the household, whether the respondent has a pension in the present job or had one in the past job, and willingness to sacrifice some lifetime consumption in favor of leaving a bequest to children or grandchildren (a five-point scale, with five indicating that the respondent definitely plans to leave a bequest).

Ippolito indicates that his results are subject to several interpretations. One is that they provide evidence in favor of the time preference hypothesis. An alternative interpretation is that the time preference variables are determined by schooling and are mechanisms via which an individual's own schooling affects his or her own health. That interpretation is the one implied by the Becker–Mulligan model and the one stressed by Ross and Mirowsky (1999). An interpretation of the findings with respect to pensions and IRAs not mentioned by Ippolito is that they reflect reverse causality from longevity to savings. Hurd (1987, 1989) points out that individuals (or couples) with a longer life expectancy have more reason to save.

Definitive estimates of the partial effects of schooling and time preference on health would treat both as endogenous in a system of equations that allows for causality between schooling and time preference in both directions. Given difficulties in measuring time preference and in identifying this system, no attempts have been made to estimate it. There is, however, an extremely promising line of research that treats schooling as endogenous and estimates the causal effect of schooling on health by the method of instrumental variables. This line of research does not attempt to distinguish between the direct effect of schooling on health and the indirect effect that operates through time preference. The latter variable is treated as the disturbance term in the health equation and is assumed to be correlated with schooling. The idea is to find instruments that are correlated with schooling but not correlated with time preference. These variables serve as instruments for schooling in estimation of health equations by two-stage least squares and its variants.[27]

[27] Let H be health, S be schooling, and D be the time discount factor (a positive correlate of future orientation). Consider the following model

$$H = \alpha_1 S + \alpha_2 D + u,$$

$$D = \beta_1 S + v,$$

$$S = \gamma_1 D + \gamma_2 X + w.$$

Here u, v, and w are disturbance terms, and X is an observed determinant of schooling that is not correlated with these disturbance terms. Substitute the second equation into the first:

$$H = (\alpha_1 + \beta_1 \alpha_2) S + \alpha_2 v + u.$$

The earliest studies to apply the instrumental variables (IV) methodology to the relationship between health and schooling are by Berger and Leigh (1989), Sander (1995a, 1995b), and Leigh and Dhir (1997). Berger and Leigh apply the methodology to two data sets: the first National Health and Nutrition Examination Survey (NHANES I) and the National Longitudinal Survey of Young Men (NLS). In NHANES I, health is measured by blood pressure, and separate equations are obtained for persons aged 20 through 40 and over age 40 in the period 1971 through 1975. The schooling equation is identified by ancestry and by average real per capita income and average real per capita expenditures on education in the state in which an individual resided from the year of birth to age 6. These variables enter the schooling equation but are excluded from the health equation. In the NLS, health is measured by a dichotomous variable that identifies men who in 1976 reported that health limited or prevented them from working and alternatively by a dichotomous variable that identifies the presence of a functional health limitation. The men in the sample were between the ages of 24 and 34 in 1976, had left school by that year, and reported no health limitations in 1966 (the first year of the survey). The schooling equation is identified by IQ, Knowledge of Work test scores, and parents' schooling.

Results from the NLS show that the schooling coefficient rises in absolute value when predicted schooling replaces actual schooling, and when health is measured by work limitation. When health is measured by functional limitation, the two-stage least squares schooling coefficient is approximately equal to the ordinary least squares coefficient, although the latter is estimated with more precision. For persons aged 20 through 40 in NHANES I, schooling has a larger impact on blood pressure in absolute value in the two-stage regressions. For persons over age 40, however, the predicted value of schooling has a positive and insignificant regression coefficient. Except for the last finding, these results are inconsistent with the time preference hypothesis and consistent with the hypothesis that schooling causes health.

In another application of the same methodology, Leigh and Dhir (1997) focus on the relationship between schooling and health among persons ages 65 and over in the 1986 wave of the Panel Survey of Income Dynamics (PSID). Health is measured by a disability index comprised of answers to six activities of daily living and by a measure of exercise frequency. Instruments for schooling include parents' schooling, parents' income, and state of residence in childhood. The schooling variable is associated with better health and more exercise whether it is treated as exogenous or endogenous.

Sander (1995a, 1995b) applies the methodology to the relationship between schooling and cigarette smoking studied by Farrell and Fuchs (1982). His data consist of the

Solve the second and third equations for S to obtain the reduced form schooling equation

$$S = \left(\frac{\gamma_2}{1-\gamma_1\beta_1}\right)X + \left(\frac{\gamma_1}{1-\gamma_1\beta_1}\right)v + \left(\frac{1}{1-\gamma_1\beta_1}\right)w.$$

The next to last equation cannot be estimated by ordinary least squares because S is correlated with v. Since X is not correlated with v and has no impact on H with S held constant, it serves as an instrument for S in an estimation of the health equation by two-stage least squares.

1986–1991 waves of the National Opinion Research Center's General Social Survey. In the first paper the outcome is the probability of quitting smoking, while in the second the outcome is the probability of smoking. Separate probit equations are obtained for men and women ages 25 and older. Instruments for schooling include father's schooling, mother's schooling, rural residence at age 16, region of residence at age 16, and number of siblings.

In general schooling has a negative effect on smoking participation and a positive effect on the probability of quitting smoking. These results are not sensitive to the use of predicted as opposed to actual schooling in the probit regressions. Moreover, the application of the Wu–Hausman endogeneity test [Wu (1973), Hausman (1978)] in the quit equation suggests that schooling is exogenous in this equation. Thus, Sander's results, like Berger and Leigh's and Leigh and Dhir's results, are inconsistent with the time preference hypothesis.

The aforementioned conclusion rests on the assumption that the instruments used to predict schooling in the first stage are uncorrelated with time preference. The validity of this assumption is most plausible in the case of measures such as real per capita income and real per capita outlays on education in the state in which an individual resided from birth to age 6 (used by Berger and Leigh in NHANES I), state of residence in childhood (used by Leigh and Dhir in the PSID), rural residence at age 16, and region of residence at that age (used by Sander). The validity of the assumption is less plausible in the case of measures such as parents' schooling (used by Sander and by Berger and Leigh in the NLS and by Leigh and Dhir in the PSID) and parents' income (used by Leigh and Dhir in the PSID).

Very recent work by Lleras-Muney (2005), Adams (2002), Arendt (2005), Spasojevic (2003), Arkes (2004), and de Walque (2004) address the schooling-health controversy by using compulsory education laws, unemployment rates during a person's teenage years, or the risk of draft induction during the Vietnam war era to obtain consistent estimates of the effect of schooling on health or on cigarette smoking – a key determinant of many adverse health outcomes. These variables, some of which result from quasi-natural experiments, are assumed to be correlated with schooling but uncorrelated with time preference. Hence, they serve as instruments for schooling in the estimation of health equations by two-stage least squares and its variants.

Lleras-Muney (2005) employs compulsory education laws in effect from 1915 to 1939 to obtain consistent estimates of the effect of education on mortality in synthetic cohorts of successive U.S. Censuses of Population for 1960, 1970, and 1980. This instrument is highly unlikely to be correlated with unobserved determinants of health, especially because she controls for state of birth and other state characteristics at age 14. Her ordinary least squares estimates suggest that an additional year of schooling lowers the probability of dying in the next ten years by 1.3 percentage points. Her IV estimate is much larger: 3.6 percentage points.

Adams (2002) uses the same instrument as Lleras-Muney in the first wave of the Health and Retirement survey, conducted in 1992. He restricts his analysis to individuals between the ages of 51 and 61 and measures health by functional ability and self-rated health. He finds positive and significant effects of education on these positive correlates of good health and larger IV coefficients than the corresponding OLS coefficients.

Arendt (2005) capitalizes on compulsory school reform in Denmark in 1958 and 1975 to study the impact of schooling on self-rated health in the 1990 and 1995 waves of the Danish National Work Environment Cohort Study. Respondents were between the ages of 18 and 59 in 1990. His results are similar to those of Adams.

Spasojevic (2003) focuses on a unique social experiment, the 1950 Swedish comprehensive school reform. Between 1949 and 1962, the school system created by the 1950 act was implemented randomly and in stages by municipalities in Sweden. Because of that, persons born between 1945 and 1955 went through two different school systems, one of which implied at least one additional year of compulsory schooling. This serves as the instrument for schooling in estimates of health equations for males born between 1945 and 1955 in the 1981 and 1991 waves of the Swedish Level of Living Survey. Health is measured by an index constructed from information on the presence of fifty different health conditions (illnesses and ailments). Results suggest that the negative IV effects of schooling on the index of poor health are at least as large in absolute value as the corresponding OLS effects.

Arkes (2004) focuses on white males aged 47 to 56 in the 1990 Census of Population. His instrument for schooling is the state unemployment rate during a person's teenage years. With state per capita income held constant, he argues that a higher unemployment rate should lead to greater educational attainment because it reduces the opportunity cost of attending school. From two-stage least squares probit models, he finds that an additional year of formal schooling lowers the probability of having a work-limiting condition by 2.6 percentage points and reduces the probability of requiring personal care by 0.7 percentage points. Both estimates exceed those that emerge from probit models that treat schooling as exogenous.

De Walque (2004) examines the effect of schooling on the probability that males born between 1937 and 1956 are current cigarette smokers in the 1983, 1985, 1987, 1988, 1990, 1991, 1992, 1994, and 1995 U.S. National Health Interview Survey. These men were of draft age during the Vietnam war era, and some of them enrolled in college to avoid the draft. Thus de Walque uses the risk of induction, defined as the average yearly number of inductions in Vietnam during the years in which a particular birth cohort was aged 19–22 divided by the size of the cohort, as an instrument for college education. In some specification, the induction risk is multiplied by the risk of being killed in Vietnam (the ratio of the number of soldiers killed in action in a year and the number of troops engaged in Vietnam in that year) to obtain the risk of being inducted and killed in action. The IV estimates of the effect of education on the probability of smoking are negative and significant. In some cases, they are at least as large in absolute value as the corresponding OLS coefficients.

The results of the six very recent studies just reviewed suggest causality from more schooling to better health. The finding that the IV estimates exceed the OLS estimates may arise because the instruments are based on policy interventions that affect the educational choices of persons with low levels of education [Card (2001)]. If different individuals face different health returns to education, IV estimates reflect the marginal rate of return of the group affected by the policies [Angrist, Imbens and Rubin (1996)]. Card (2001) points out: "For policy evaluation purposes ... the average marginal return to schooling in the population may be less relevant than the average return for the group that will be impacted by a proposed reform. In such cases, the best available evidence may be IV estimates of the return to schooling based on similar earlier reforms" (p. 1157).

A second explanation of the larger IV than OLS estimates is that the schooling variable contains random measurement error, which leads to a downward bias in the OLS estimates. As long as the instruments for schooling are not correlated with this error, the IV procedure eliminates this bias [Card (1999, 2001)]. A third explanation is that there may be spillover effects in the sense that the health outcome of an individual depends on the average schooling of individuals in his area as well as on his own schooling or that of his parents [Acemoglu (1996), Acemoglu and Angrist (2000)]. Currie and Moretti (2003) show that IV estimates of this combined effect based on area-level instruments are consistent, while OLS estimates understate it.

In summary, the six very recent studies that I have discussed in detail underscore the utility of employing IV techniques with area-level instruments to obtain consistent estimates of the effects of schooling on health and other measures of well-being. This methodology controls for time preference and other unmeasured variables that potentially are correlated with health and schooling.

4.2. Child health

4.2.1. Productive efficiency and related mechanisms

Evidence that parents' schooling causes children's health is contained in research by my colleagues and me on the determinants of child and adolescent health [Edwards and Grossman (1981, 1982, 1983), Shakotko, Edwards and Grossman (1981)]. We study child and adolescent health in the context of the nature–nurture controversy. Our research uses data primarily on whites from Cycle II of the U.S. Health Examination Survey (children aged 6 through 11 years in the period 1963 through 1965), Cycle III of the Health Examination Survey (adolescents aged 12 through 17 years in the period 1966 through 1970), and the panel of individuals (one third of the full Cycle III sample) who were examined in both cycles.

We find that the home environment in general and mother's schooling in particular play an extremely important role in the determination of child and adolescent health. It is not surprising to find that children's home environment has a positive impact on their health with no other variables held constant. Moreover, it is difficult to sort out the effect of nature from that of nurture because it is difficult to measure a child's genetic endowment and because genetic differences may induce environmental changes. Nevertheless, we have accumulated a number of suggestive pieces of evidence on the true importance of the home environment. With birthweight, mother's age at birth, congenital abnormalities, other proxies for genetic endowment, and family income held constant, parents' schooling has positive and statistically significant effects on many measures of health in childhood and adolescence. For example, children and teenagers of more educated mothers have better oral health, are less likely to be obese, and less likely to have anemia than children of less educated mothers. Father's schooling plays a much less important role in the determination of oral health, obesity, and anemia than mother's schooling. The latter findings are important because equal effects would be expected if the schooling variables were simply proxies for unmeasured genetic endowments. On the other hand, if the effect of schooling is primarily environmental, one would expect the impact of mother's schooling to be larger because she was the family member most involved with children's health care in the late 1960s and early 1970s.

Several additional pieces of evidence underscore the robustness of the above finding. When oral health is examined in a longitudinal context, mother's schooling dominates father's schooling in the determination of the periodontal index in adolescence, with the periodontal index in childhood held constant. Similar comments apply to the effect of mother's schooling on school absence due to illness in adolescence (with school absence due to illness in childhood held constant) and to the effect of mother's schooling on obesity in adolescence (with obesity in childhood held constant).

Edwards and Grossman (1979) document a variety of positive associations between good health and cognitive development, measured by IQ and school achievement, in Cycle II of the Health Examination Survey. As part of the longitudinal study just described, Shakotko, Edwards and Grossman (1981) investigate the direction of causation implied by these associations. They apply the notion of causality introduced by Granger (1969) by estimating two multivariate equations. One relates adolescent health to childhood health, childhood cognitive development, and family background measures. The second relates adolescent cognitive development to childhood cognitive development, childhood health, and family background. They find feedback both from good health to cognitive development and from cognitive development to good health, but the latter of these relationships is stronger. Since an individual's cognitive development is an important determinant of the number of years of formal schooling that he or she ultimately receives, this finding may be viewed as the early forerunner of the positive impact of schooling on good health for adults that we discussed above.

The study by Shakotko, Edwards and Grossman (1981) is unique in several respects. First, it exploits time-varying measures of health and school achievement in panel data to investigate the causal priorness of these measures. We assume that the processes governing these outcomes are Markov and can be estimated by a simple first-order autoregressive model. We show that, if the genetic impact on these outcomes is restricted to the determination of initial conditions, then the estimates of the time paths will be free of genetic bias and will reflect the true environmental effects of family background, childhood health, and childhood cognitive development variables. Second, indicators of education generally are fixed over time in panel studies of adult health, but these indicators are not fixed in our panel. Finally, most of the studies summarized in this paper measure education by years of formal schooling completed and ignore the quality of schooling. The school achievement variable that we employ reflects in part school quality.

Research by Wilcox-Gök (1983) calls into question some of the findings in the studies just described. She studies the determinants of child health in a sample of natural and adopted sibling pairs. The children in her sample were between the ages of 5 and 14 in 1978 and were all members of the Medical Care Group of Washington University (a prepaid, comprehensive medical care plan) in St. Louis, Missouri. Health is measured by the number of days a child had missed from usual activities due to illness or injury in a five month period as reported by parents. The results for natural siblings reveal that the proportion of the variation in health explained by unmeasured sources of common family background is much greater than the proportion explained by measured variables. Moreover, the correlation between natural siblings' health is significantly higher than for sibling pairs in which one child was adopted (was not the natural child of at least one parent). These results point to the importance of genetic endowment.

Clearly, Wilcox-Gök's findings are not generalizable to the population of the United States. Not only are they specific to the residents of one city, but the families in the sample had a higher mean income and a larger number of children (the prepaid group practice offered special family membership rates) than the typical U.S. family. In addition, one parental reported health indicator is employed in contrast to the variety of measures, many of which come from physical examinations, used by Shakotko, Edwards and Grossman (1981).

Corman and Grossman (1985) document the importance of mother's schooling as a determinant of neonatal mortality rates (deaths of infants within the first 27 days of life per thousand live births) in the United States. They use large counties of the United States (counties with a population of at least 50,000 persons in 1970) as the units of observation and a three-year average of the neonatal mortality rate centered on 1977 as the dependent variable. Separate regressions are obtained for whites and blacks. To examine the relative contributions of schooling, poverty, and public program measures to the recent U.S. neonatal mortality experience, Corman and Grossman apply the estimated regression coefficients to trends in the exogenous variables between 1964 and 1977, a period during which the neonatal mortality rate declined rapidly.

In the period at issue the white neonatal mortality rate fell by 7.5 deaths per thousand live births, from 16.2 to 8.7. The black neonatal mortality rate fell by 11.5 deaths per thousand live births, from 27.6 to 16.1. The statistical analysis "explains" approximately 28 percent of the white decline on average and 33 percent of the black decline on average. The increase in white female schooling makes the largest contribution to the decline in white neonatal mortality. The reduction due to schooling amounts to approximately 0.5 deaths per thousand live births. The increase in black female schooling ranks second to the increase in abortion availability as a contributing factor to the reduction in black neonatal mortality. The estimated abortion effect amounts to a decline of about 1 death per thousand live births, while the schooling trend produces a decline of about 0.7 death per thousand live births.

While Corman and Grossman (1985) fit reduced form infant health outcome equations, Grossman and Joyce (1990) obtain a direct estimate of productive efficiency by fitting birthweight production functions for blacks in New York City in 1984. They do not employ two-stage least squares estimation. Instead, they control for a variety of unobservables governing pregnancy resolutions and birthweight by pooling data on births and abortions. They then estimate a three-equation model. The first equation is a probit for the probability of giving birth, given that a woman is pregnant. With this as the criterion equation, they test for self-selection (correlations between unobserved variables and observed outcomes) in the birthweight production function and in the prenatal care demand function using Heckman's (1979) methodology.[28] They report that black women who completed at least one year of college gave birth to infants who weighed 69 grams more than the infants of women who completed at least 8 but no more than 11 years of schooling. This amounts to a 2 percent increase relative to a mean of 3,132 grams for the latter group.

Recent studies by Case, Lubotsky and Paxson (2002) and by Currie and Stabile (2003) confirm the importance of parents' schooling on child health outcomes at a variety of different ages. Case and her colleagues employ data from the 1988 U.S. National Health Interview Survey. They find positive effects of mother's and father's schooling on parental rating of child health, with family income held constant. The favorable effect of family income on this outcome is larger for older children, but this pattern is not observed for the schooling effects. The authors conclude: "It appears that income (and what it buys a child) has a different effect on a child's health from the skills that accompany parental education" (p. 1314). Currie and Stabile (2003) report cross-sectional results that mirror those of Case and her colleagues in the Canadian National Longitudinal Survey of Children and Youth – children ages 0–11 in 1994, with follow-ups in 1996 and 1998. Moreover, mother's schooling has a positive effect on her rating of the child's health in 1998, with health status in 1994 (measured by the presence of a chronic condition in 1994, the presence of asthma in 1994, or by hospitalization in 1994) held constant.

A number of the studies summarized in this subsection bear on the somewhat controversial but highly influential work by Baker (1995) and the less controversial studies by Da Stavola et al. (2000) because they report effects of parents' schooling on children's current health status, with past health status held constant. Baker (1995) suggests that in-utero growth and adolescent growth affect heart disease at age 75. Da Stavola et al. (2000) report that estrogen in-utero affects birth size, and large female babies with elevated estrogen have a much higher incidence of pre-menopausal breast cancer. In their study with the 1958 British National Child Development Survey described in Section 4.1.1, Case, Fertig and Paxson (2005) find that men who experienced poor health in

[28] Based on Wu–Hausman tests [Wu (1973), Hausman (1978), Grossman and Joyce (1990)] accept the consistency of birthweight production functions obtained by ordinary least squares once these functions are corrected for self-selection.

utero and at ages 7, 16, 23, and 33 have lower health at age 42, with parents' schooling and socioeconomic status held constant. But self-rated health at age 42 is positively related to parents' schooling, unless own schooling is included in the regression analysis.

The reader is cautioned about the difference between my emphasis on findings and that of Case, Fertig and Paxson (2005). I stress the significant effects of parent's schooling and own schooling on current health, with past health held constant. They stress the significant effects of past health on current health, with the schooling variables held constant. In general, their results and those in other studies summarized in this subsection suggest a long term association between parents' attributes and children's attributes including health. Schooling is part of this relationship, but uncoupling the causal links associated with genetic and behavioral factors is very difficult. Clearly, breaking into this complicated bundle is a challenge for future research.

4.2.2. Allocative efficiency

Thomas, Strauss and Henriques (1991) and Glewwe (1999) explore the allocative efficiency hypothesis in the context of the determinants of child health in developing countries. Both studies consider the anthropometric outcome of height standardized for age and gender, which is closely related to nutritional intakes in these countries. Low values signal stunting due to nutritional deficiencies. In a study based on approximately 1,300 children age 5 or less in the 1986 Brazilian Demographic and Health Survey, Thomas, Strauss and Henriques (1991) find that practically all of the positive effect of mother's schooling on child height is due to information as measured by whether the woman reads newspapers, watches television, and listens to the radio. These three variables are treated as endogenous. The instruments are the existence of a local newspaper in the mother's municipio (similar to a county in the U.S.) of residence, dichotomous indicators of the number of television channels in the municipio of residence, and mother's age.

Glewwe (1999) employs a sample of approximately 1,500 children ages 5 or younger in Morocco in 1990–1991 obtained as part of the World Bank's Living Standards Measurement Study. This sample contains a direct measure of the mother's general health knowledge obtained as the number of correct responses to five questions. Unlike Thomas, Strauss and Henriques (1991), he is able to control directly for the child's health endowment by employing mother's and father's height as regressors. He finds that all of the favorable impact of mother's schooling on child height operates through health knowledge. He treats knowledge as endogenous and instruments it with the number of married sisters of the mother and her husband, education of the mother's parents, number of radios and televisions in the household, and the availability of local newspapers.

Clearly, Thomas, Strauss and Henriques (1991) and Glewwe (1999) find much more support for the allocative efficiency hypothesis than Kenkel (1991), whose study was described in Section 4.1.2. This may be traced to the more general and "less noisy" information variables that they employ. Of course, their studies pertain to developing countries. Thomas et al. do, however, conduct separate analyses for children who reside in rural and urban areas. Despite the larger values of schooling and information in the urban areas, they report the same results for both areas. One caution is that issues can be raised with regard to the validity of the instruments used in the two studies. Thomas et al. do not perform overidentification tests. Glewwe does perform these tests and accepts the hypothesis that the variables employed as instruments do not belong in the health outcome equation. Yet one can still question the validity of using the education of the mother's parents as an instrument if time preference is an important omitted variable.

In another application to child health and allocative efficiency in developing countries, Jalan and Ravallion (2003) consider interactions between access to piped water and mother's schooling in determining the prevalence and duration of diarrhea in rural India. They point out that this disease causes approximately four million children under the age of five in developing countries to die each year and that unsafe water is the major cause. They use a sample of 33,000 rural households in 16 states of India conducted in 1993–1994. Approximately 25 percent of the households had access to piped water. Based on propensity score matching methods, they find that the incidence and duration of diarrhea among children is significantly lower on average for families with piped water. They also report, however, no effects if the mother is poorly educated and effects that rise in absolute value as the mother's education rises. These patterns continue to be observed when household income per capita is held constant.

Meara (1999, 2001) explores the allocative efficiency hypothesis in the context of birth outcomes in the U.S. National Maternal and Infant Health Survey, conducted in 1988. Her outcome is the probability of a low-birthweight (less than 2,500 grams) birth. Low birthweight is the most important proximate cause of infant death. She obtains separate production functions of this outcome for white and black mothers.[29] She finds that the negative and significant effects of mother's schooling on the probability of a low-birthweight birth are greatly reduced in absolute value when five health inputs are held constant. For blacks, schooling is not significant in models with the inputs. The inputs are dichotomous indicators for smoking cigarettes during pregnancy, drinking more than five drinks of alcohol during pregnancy, using cocaine during pregnancy, beginning prenatal medical care during the first trimester, and taking vitamins during pregnancy. The smoking indicator has the most important impact by far on the schooling coefficients.

Taken at face value, the results just described provide support for the allocative efficiency hypothesis, although the inputs are treated as exogenous. As pointed out in Section 2.2, health production functions that ignore the endogeneity of inputs are subject to biases due to adverse and favorable selection. Meara puts these considerations aside and proceeds to show that knowledge of the harmful effects of smoking cannot explain why more educated women of childbearing age are less likely to smoke.

[29] Technically Meara estimates a mixture of a production function and a demand function because she includes income, health insurance, distance to the prenatal care provider, and other demand determinants in the birthweight equations.

This analysis employs the 1985 and 1990 Health Promotion and Disease Prevention Supplements to the U.S. National Health Interview Survey. These results are similar to Kenkel's (1991) study, except that he includes men and women of all ages. Based on this evidence, Meara rejects the allocative efficiency hypothesis in favor of one emphasizing the role of third variables.

To buttress the importance of omitted factors, Meara (1999) examines the probabilities that adolescent girls between the ages of 14 and 20 smoked cigarettes regularly and used an illegal drug besides marijuana in the 1994–1995 Longitudinal Adolescent Health Survey. She finds that the negative effects of mother's schooling on these two probabilities are greatly reduced in absolute value when proxies for discount rates, self-control, and measures of symptoms of depression are included in the probit functions that she estimates. Like Kenkel (1991), Meara is careful to conclude that her results are subject to more than one interpretation. She does tend to emphasize the third variable hypothesis stressed by Fuchs (1982), although she points out that more educated mothers could influence health and human capital investment decisions made by their daughters in a causal sense.

I would add that her results are not inconsistent with the Becker–Mulligan (1997) story in which more educated parents make investments in their children to make them more future oriented. These investments and the amount of formal schooling acquired by the prospective mother determine her rate of time preference for the present. Hence, a finding that differences in knowledge about the harmful effects of smoking cannot explain why more educated pregnant women are less likely to smoke is not inconsistent with a causal effect of education on smoking. The mechanism here is that education causes time preference which in turn causes smoking.

4.2.3. Time preference, other omitted factors, and instrumental variables

Currie and Moretti (2003) examine the relationship between maternal education and birthweight among U.S. white women with data from individual birth certificates from the Vital Statistics Natality files for 1970 to 2000. They use information on college openings between 1940 and 1990 to construct an availability measure of college in a woman's 17th year as an instrument for schooling. They find that the positive effect of maternal schooling on birthweight increases when it is estimated by instrumental variables. They also find that the negative IV coefficient of maternal schooling in an equation for the probability of smoking during pregnancy exceeds the corresponding OLS coefficient in absolute value. Since prenatal smoking is the most important modifiable risk factor for poor pregnancy outcomes in the United States [U.S. Department of Health and Human Services (1990)], they identify a very plausible mechanism via which more schooling causes better birth outcomes. Finally, parity falls and the probability of being married rises as maternal education rises. The OLS coefficients are somewhat larger than the IV coefficients, although both sets are significant. These results suggest other mechanisms via which more schooling leads to better infant health outcomes.

Breierova and Duflo (2004) capitalize on a primary school construction program in Indonesia between 1973 and 1978. In that period 61,000 primary schools were constructed. Program intensity, measured by the number of new schools constructed per primary-school age child in 1971, varied considerably across the country's 281 districts. In a study of the effects of schooling on earnings, Duflo (2001) shows that average educational attainment rose more rapidly in districts where program intensity was greater. She also argues that the program had a bigger effect for children who entered school later in the 1970s and no effect for children who entered school before 1974. Therefore, she uses the interaction between year of birth and program intensity as an instrument for schooling for male wage earners in the 1995 intercensal survey of Indonesia who were between the ages of 2 and 24 in 1974. This instrument turns out to be an excellent predictor of schooling.

Breierova and Duflo (2004) use the instrument just described to estimate the effects of mother's and father's education on child mortality in the same survey employed by Duflo. They employ fertility and infant mortality histories of approximately 120,000 women between the ages of 23 and 50 in 1995. They find that mother's and father's schooling have about the same negative effects on infant mortality. Some, but not all, of the IV coefficients exceed the corresponding OLS coefficients. The authors treat their results as very preliminary.

5. Empirical evidence: other outcomes

Numerous studies report that more educated parents have fewer children in developed and developing countries [for example, De Tray (1973), Michael (1973a), Willis (1973), Becker (1991), Schultz (1993), Hotz, Klerman and Willis (1997), Lam and Duryea (1999)]. Indeed, Schultz (1993) terms this relationship "one of the most important discoveries in research on nonmarket returns to women's education" (p. 74). A majority of the studies indicate larger effects for mother's schooling than for father's schooling. This finding is consistent with a division of labor within the household in which the mother is the family member most involved with child care.

Theoretical bases for the negative impacts of mother's schooling on fertility were discussed in Section 2.3. I leave the reader to evaluate the detailed empirical evidence and the suggested mechanisms in the studies just mentioned and in the ones that they cite. I do, however, want to call attention to two potential mechanisms that are directly related to allocative and productive efficiency. One is the effect of education on contraceptive efficiency. Michael (1973a) studies the relationship between wife's schooling and the contraceptive technique employed by women in specific birth intervals in the 1965 National Fertility Survey. He employs published data on the monthly birth probability of each technique (a measure of contraceptive failure) and uses this as the dependent variable in a regression in which schooling, actual or desired level of fertility, age, birth interval, race, and religion (Catholic/non-Catholic) are the independent variables. The control for intended family size eliminates the differential incentive to contracept by level of schooling, which is related to different levels of desired fertility. He finds that more educated women have significantly lower risks of conception. Since these results hold constant desired fertility, they cannot be attributed to the impacts of income and the value of time. Instead, since the data pertain to a period of rapid diffusion of new and effective methods of birth control – the oral contraceptive (pill) and IUD – Michael's results suggests an interaction between schooling and the adoption of new technology. Similar interactions in the health area were found in a number of the adult health studies discussed in Section 4.1.2.

Using more recent data for the 1970s and a more complicated econometric framework in which fertility is endogenous, Rosenzweig and Schultz (1989) extend Michael's (1973a) results by showing that more educated couples have a wider knowledge of contraceptive methods in cases in which such knowledge is not widely disseminated. To be specific, the more educated had more information about such ineffective methods as withdrawal and the rhythm calendar method. This does not carry over to methods that are immune to misuse such as the condom, diaphragm, foam, IUD, and the pill. They also find that the use-effectiveness of ineffective methods increases in absolute value with wife's schooling. This result comes from the longitudinal sample of women from the 1970 National Fertility survey who were reinterviewed in 1975. The dependent variable, which measures fertility, is the number of conceptions between 1970 and 1975, divided by the number of months of exposure to the risk of conception. The fertility control variables as well as the monthly frequency of intercourse are treated as endogenous.

Finally, Rosenzweig and Schultz explore interactions between an estimate of fecundity and schooling in determining the proportion of unplanned births and between that outcome and schooling in determining the effectiveness of the method of contraception selected. An increase in fecundity has a smaller impact on unplanned pregnancies for more educated women, and an increase in previous unplanned pregnancies has a larger impact on the selection of more effective methods of contraception for women with higher levels of education. The magnitude of the latter effect is dramatic. Contraceptive use effectiveness rises by almost 93 percent for more educated women in response to an unplanned pregnancy, with birth intentions held constant.

The second mechanism that I wish to call attention to is the increased schooling levels of children of more educated parents. This relationship is analogous to the one between parents' schooling and the health of their children discussed in Section 4.2. As I indicated in Section 2.5, higher levels of child quality, measured in part by the number of years of formal schooling they acquire, are likely to be accompanied by lower optimal levels of numbers of children.[30]

[30] Refer to equations (18) and (19). Suppose that π_Q, the fixed cost of child quality, is negatively correlated with mother's schooling. Then an increase in mother's schooling causes a direct substitution effect in favor of Q and away from N since the relative price of Q falls. There also is a secondary substitution effect because an increase in Q/N lowers the relative price of Q. If one holds fixed costs constant, assumes that the fixed cost of numbers exceeds that of quality, and assumes that an increase in schooling lowers π, the price of one unit of NQ, the same result follows. That is because a reduction in π lowers the relative price of Q.

Many studies summarized by Haveman and Wolfe (1995) find that the children of more educated parents obtain more schooling. Consistent with the fertility literature, the effect of mother's schooling typically exceeds that of father's schooling. Behrman and Rosenzweig (2002) examine the extent to which these results are due to omitted third variables by examining differences in years of formal schooling completed by the offspring of 424 female and 244 male identical (monozygotic) twins in the Minnesota Twin Registry. While mother's schooling has a positive and significant effect on children's schooling in the cross section, the within-twin estimate either is insignificant or negative and marginally significant. On the other hand, the coefficient of father's schooling is positive and significant in both cases. Behrman and Rosenzweig argue that the cross-sectional mother's schooling coefficient reflects the combined effect of nature (children of more educated mother's have a more favorable genetic endowment) and nurture or the home environment (more educated mothers make larger investments in the human capital of their children). Only the latter component is present in the within-twin estimates. They also argue that their findings may be attributed to the increased amount of time that educated women spend in the labor market and consequently the reduced amount of time that they spend with their children.

While the study by Behrman and Rosenzweig is novel and provocative, several considerations suggest that their findings should not be viewed as definitive. First, it is based on a small sample. Second, differencing between twins exacerbates biases due to measurement error in schooling [Griliches (1979), Bound and Solon (1999), Neumark (1999)], although Behrman and Rosenzweig do attempt to adjust for these biases. Third, since more educated women have fewer children, their increased time in the labor market does not necessarily mean that they spend less time with their offspring than less educated women. Finally, Bound and Solon (1999) stress that variation in schooling between identical twins may be systematic rather than random.

Sacerdote (2000, 2002) presents evidence on the relative importance of nature and nurture in child schooling outcomes that conflicts with that reported by Behrman and Rosenzweig. He does this by considering parental schooling effects in samples of adopted children and comparing them to parental schooling effects in samples of children raised by their biological parents. In the latter case both nature and nurture are at work, while in the former case only nurture is at work. If the nature and nurture components are additive, the ratio of the adopted parent's schooling coefficient to the biological parent's schooling coefficient shows the percentage contribution of nurture to the intergenerational transfer of educational attainment. Using completed schooling of children of women in NLSY79 as the outcome, he finds that the ratio just defined is approximately 64 percent in the case of mother's schooling and approximately 57 percent in the case of father's schooling. Moreover, the adopted mother's education effect is 40 percent larger than the adopted father's education effect.[31] One caution in

[31] Sacerdote does not include schooling of each parent in the same regression. Hence the mother's schooling effect and its estimated environmental component, for example, do not control for father's schooling.

interpreting these results is that schooling levels of biological parents are not available for adopted children. This biases the adopted parent schooling effect unless schooling levels of biological and adopted parents are uncorrelated.

In my discussion of the empirical literature dealing with adult and child health, I highlighted studies that employ instrumental variables for schooling to establish its causal impact on these outcomes. Lochner and Moretti (2004) and Dee (2004) employ IV procedures to very different outcomes: crime in the former study and voter participation, support for free speech, and civic knowledge (reflected by the frequency of newspaper readership) in the latter study. Lochner and Moretti (2004) treat incarceration from the Census of Population and arrests from the FBI Uniform Crime Reports. Changes in state compulsory schooling laws serve as instruments for schooling. This is the same instrument that was employed by Lleras-Muney (2005) in her study of adult mortality discussed in Section 4.1.3. The negative and significant effects of schooling on the crime outcomes are at least as large in absolute value when they are obtained by IV as when they are obtained by OLS.

Dee (2004) studies voter participation in High School and Beyond (HSB), a longitudinal study of high school sophomores in 1980 conducted by the U.S. Department of Labor, with follow-ups in 1984 and 1992. He adds support for free speech and frequency of newspaper readership to the voting outcome by pooling 1972–2000 cross sections of the General Social Surveys (GSS). The availability of junior and community colleges is the instrument for schooling in HSS, while the compulsory schooling laws employed by Lochner and Moretti (2004) are the instruments in GSS. Dee's findings mirror those of Lochner and Moretti: the positive and significant OLS schooling effects on the outcomes he considers become larger when they are estimated by IV.

6. Conclusions

This paper has been written with a particular point of view: namely, theory and existing empirical evidence support the proposition that education causes a variety of nonmarket outcomes. In reaching this conclusion, I do not deny the importance of future research on the mechanisms via which schooling affects these outcomes and on the causal nature of the outcomes at issue. In my view one of the most important empirical developments in the past two decades has been the application of instrumental variables techniques to the relationship between schooling and earnings. There are many fewer examples of the application of this technique to the relationship between schooling and nonmarket outcomes. Such research deserves high priority on an agenda for future research, especially as developing countries increase the amount of compulsory schooling and invest more resources in the educational sector.

New research on mechanisms also is important, both in understanding the sources of the schooling effects and in formulating public policy. These efforts should keep in mind, however, that potential mechanisms are unlikely to be exogenous. They also should keep in mind that a finding that schooling has no impact on the outcome at issue when mechanisms are held constant does not mean that schooling has no causal impact on the outcome. All too often researchers have followed a strategy of controlling for a few mechanisms (sometimes without taking account of their endogeneity), finding that schooling still is a significant determinant of the outcome, and concluding that the observed effect must be due to a hard-to-measure variable such as time preference.

To the extent that the beneficial effects of schooling on nonmarket outcomes summarized in this paper are causal, the rate of return to investments in schooling are underestimated if the benefits of these investments are simply measured in terms of the higher wage rates or annual earnings enjoyed by the more educated. I have already called attention to Michael's (1972, 1973b) estimate that education raises nonmarket productivity by three-fifths as much as it raises market productivity. De Walque (2005) combines his estimates of the reduced risk of being HIV positive among young residents of Uganda with secondary education compared to those with primary education with mortality rates from HIV/AIDS to obtain a rate of return to secondary education that includes the value of additional longevity. He finds that the rate of return rises from 10.2 percent when additional longevity is ignored to a range between 11.5 and 13.7 percent.

Clearly, the estimates made by Michael and de Walque are suggestive and preliminary because they do not encompass all the nonmarket benefits of education. Future research should investigate this issue in more detail and should address the difficult task of how to put a dollar value on some of these benefits. Of course, even if the total rate of return (the rate inclusive of nonmarket benefits) is significantly larger than the market rate of return, it does not follow that the amount of government intervention with the education decisions of its citizens should increase. Government intervention is justified only to correct for externalities and capital market imperfections. Moreover, some of the nonmarket effects of education may take the form of external costs. For example, the more educated have fewer children, yet Lee and Miller (1990) report that the net positive externality to childbearing in the United States was approximately \$100,000 in 1985 dollars. The main contributors to this figure were public goods, intergenerational transfers supporting health, education, and pension programs, and the sharing of government debt. Grossman and Kaestner (1997) consider the rationale for government policies that use schooling as a tool to correct for health externalities, and I will not repeat that discussion here. I do think that it is appropriate to conclude by considering the value of identifying time preference as a mechanism via which schooling affects health in the context of the formulation of public policy.

Becker and Mulligan (1997) suggest a more definitive and concrete way to measure time preference and incorporate it into estimates of health demand functions than those that have been attempted to date. They point out that the natural logarithm of the ratio of consumption between consecutive time periods (N) is approximately equal to $\sigma(r - g)$, where σ is the intertemporal elasticity of substitution in consumption, r is the market rate of interest, and g is the rate of time preference for the present. If σ and r do not vary among individuals, variations in N capture variations in time preference. With panel data, N can be included as a regressor in the health demand function. Since Becker and Mulligan stress the endogeneity of time preference and its dependence on schooling, simultaneous equations techniques appear to be required. Identification of this model will not be easy, but success in this area has the potential to greatly inform public policy.

To illustrate the last point, suppose that most of the effect of schooling on health operates through time preference. Then school-based programs to promote health knowledge in areas characterized by low levels of income and education may have much smaller payoffs than programs that encourage the investments in time preference made by the more educated. Indeed, in an ever-changing world in which new information constantly becomes available, general interventions that encourage future-oriented behavior may have much larger rates of return in the long run than specific interventions designed, for example, to discourage cigarette smoking, alcohol abuse, or the use of illegal drugs.

It is well known that cigarette smoking and excessive alcohol abuse begin early in life [for example, Grossman et al. (1993)]. Moreover, bandwagon or peer effects are much more important in the case of youth smoking or alcohol consumption than in the case of adult smoking or alcohol consumption. The two-way causality between addiction and time preference and the importance of peer pressure explain why parents who care about the welfare of their children have large incentives to make investments that make their children more future oriented. These forces may also account for the relatively large impact of schooling on health with health knowledge held constant reported by Kenkel (1991).

Some parents may ignore or be unaware of the benefits of investments in time preference. Given society's concern with the welfare of its children, subsidies to school-based programs that make children more future oriented may be warranted. But much more research dealing with the determinants of time preference and its relationship with schooling and health is required before these programs can be formulated and implemented in a cost-effective manner.

Acknowledgements

I am deeply indebted to Robert T. Michael for his thorough reading of an earlier version of this paper and for his penetrating comments on that version. I also am indebted to Victor R. Fuchs and the participants at a conference on the economics of education held at the George Bush School of Public Policy of Texas A&M University, March 20–22, 2003, for helpful comments and suggestions. I wish to thank Inas Rashad and Jennifer Tennant for research assistance. This paper has not undergone the review accorded official National Bureau of Economic Research publications; in particular it has not been submitted for approval by the Board of Directors. Any opinions expressed are mine and not those of the NBER.

References

Acemoglu, D. (1996). "A microfoundation for social increasing returns in human capital accumulation". Quarterly Journal of Economics 111, 779–804.

Acemoglu, D., Angrist, J. (2000). "How large are human-capital externalities? Evidence from compulsory schooling laws". In: Bernanke, B.S., Rogoff, K. (Eds.), NBER Macroeconomics Annual, vol. 15. MIT Press, Cambridge, MA, pp. 9–59.

Adams, S.J. (2002). "Educational attainment and health: evidence from a sample of older adults". Education Economics 10, 97–109.

Alderman, H., Behrman, J.R., Lavy, V., Menon, R. (2001). "Child health and school enrollment: a longitudinal analysis". Journal of Human Resources 36, 185–205.

American Chamber of Commerce Researchers Association (various years). ACCRA Cost of Living Index. ACCRA, Arlington, VA.

Angrist, J.D., Imbens, G.W., Rubin, D.B. (1996). "Identification of causal effects using instrumental variables". Journal of the American Statistical Association 91, 444–472.

Arendt, J.N. (2005). "Does education cause better health? A panel data analysis using school reform for identification". Economics of Education Review 24, 149–160.

Arkes, J. (2004). "Does schooling improve health?" Working Paper. RAND Corporation, Santa Monica, CA.

Barker, D.J.P. (1995). "Fetal origins of coronary heart disease". British Medical Journal 311, 171–174.

Becker, G.S. (1960). "An economic analysis of fertility". In: Demographic and Economic Change in Developed Countries. Princeton University Press for the National Bureau of Economic Research, Princeton, NJ, pp. 209–231.

Becker, G.S. (1965). "A theory of the allocation of time". Economic Journal 75, 493–517.

Becker, G.S. (1991). A Treatise on the Family, second edition. Harvard University Press, Cambridge, MA.

Becker, G.S. (1996). Accounting for Tastes. Harvard University Press, Cambridge, MA.

Becker, G.S., Lewis, H.G. (1973). "On the interaction between the quantity and quality of children". Journal of Political Economy 81, S279–S288.

Becker, G.S., Mulligan, C.B. (1997). "The endogenous determination of time preference". Quarterly Journal of Economics 112, 729–758.

Becker, G.S., Murphy, K.M. (1988). "A theory of rational addiction". Journal of Political Economy 96, 675–700.

Behrman, J.R., Rosenzweig, M.R. (2002). "Does increasing women's schooling raise the schooling of the next generation?" American Economic Review 92, 323–334.

Berger, M.C., Leigh, J.P. (1989). "Schooling, self-selection, and health". Journal of Human Resources 24, 433–455.

Bolin, K., Jacobson, L., Lindgren, B. (2002). "The demand for health and health investments in Sweden". In: Lindgren, B. (Ed.), Individual Decisions for Health. Routledge, London, pp. 93–112.

Bound, J., Solon, G. (1999). "Double trouble: on the value of twins-based estimation of the return to schooling". Economics of Education Review 18, 169–182.

Breierova, L., Duflo, E. (2004). "The impact of education on fertility and child mortality: do fathers really matter less than mothers?" Working Paper no. 10513. National Bureau of Economic Research, Cambridge, MA.

Card, D. (1999). "The causal effect of education on earnings". In: Ashenfelter, O., Card, D. (Eds.), Handbook of Labor Economics, vol. 3. Elsevier, Amsterdam, pp. 1801–1863.

Card, D. (2001). "Estimating the return to schooling: progress on some persistent econometric problems". Econometrica 69, 127–1160.

Carroll, C.D., Summers, L.H. (1991). "Consumption growth parallels income growth". In: Bernheim, B.D., Shoven, J.B. (Eds.), National Saving and Economic Performance. University of Chicago Press, Chicago, pp. 305–343.

Case, A., Fertig, A., Paxson, C. (2005). "The lasting impact of childhood health and circumstances". Journal of Health Economics 24, 365–389.

Case, A., Lubotsky, D., Paxson, C. (2002). "Economic status and health in childhood: the origins of the gradient". American Economic Review 92, 1308–1334.
Chaikind, S., Corman, H. (1991). "The impact of low birthweight on special education costs". Journal of Health Economics 10, 291–311.
Chou, S.-Y., Grossman, M., Saffer, H. (2004). "An economic analysis of adult obesity: results from the behavioral risk factor surveillance system". Journal of Health Economics 23, 565–587.
Coleman, M., DeLeire, T. (2003). "An economic model of locus of control and the human capital investment decision". Journal of Human Resources 38, 701–721.
Corman, H., Grossman, M. (1985). "Determinants of neonatal mortality rates in the United States: a reduced form model". Journal of Health Economics 4, 213–236.
Corman, H., Joyce, T.J., Grossman, M. (1987). "Birth outcome production functions in the United States". Journal of Human Resources 22, 339–360.
Currie, J. (2000). "Child health". In: Culyer, A.J., Newhouse, J.P. (Eds.), Handbook of Health Economics, vol. 1B. Elsevier, Amsterdam, pp. 1053–1090.
Currie, J., Moretti, E. (2003). "Mother's education and the intergenerational transmission of human capital: evidence from college openings". Quarterly Journal of Economics 118, 1495–1532.
Currie, J., Stabile, M. (2003). "Socioeconomic status and health: why is the relationship stronger for older children?". American Economic Review 93, 1813–1823.
Deaton, A. (2002). "Policy implications of the gradient of health and wealth". Health Affairs 21, 13–30.
Deaton, A., Paxson, C. (2001). "Mortality, education, income, and inequality among American cohorts". In: Wise, D.A. (Ed.), Themes in the Economics of Aging. University of Chicago Press, Chicago, IL, pp. 129–165.
Dee, T.S. (2004). "Are there civic returns to education?". Journal of Public Economics 88, 1697–1720.
De Stavola, B.L., Hardy, R., Huh, D., dos Santos Silva, I., Wadsworth, M., Swerdlow, A.J. (2000). "Birthweight, childhood growth, and risk of breast cancer in a British cohort". British Journal of Cancer 83, 964–968.
De Tray, D.N. (1973). "Child quality and the demand for children". Journal of Political Economy 81, S70–S95.
De Walque, D. (2004). "Education, information, and smoking decisions: Evidence from smoking histories, 1940–2000". Working Paper no. 3362. World Bank, Washington, DC.
De Walque, D. (2005). "How does the impact of an HIV/AIDS information campaign vary with educational attainment? Evidence from rural Uganda". Working Paper no. 3289. World Bank, Washington, DC.
Duflo, E. (2001). "Schooling and labor market consequences of school construction in Indonesia: evidence from an unusual policy experiment". American Economic Review 91, 795–813.
Edwards, L.N., Grossman, M. (1979). "The Relationship between children's health and intellectual development". In: Mushkin, S.J., Dunlop, D.D. (Eds.), Health: What Is It Worth. Pergamon Press, Elmsford, NY, pp. 273–314.
Edwards, L.N., Grossman, M. (1981). "Children's health and the family". In: Scheffler, R.M. (Ed.), Advances in Health In Health Economics and Health Services Research, vol. II. JAI Press, Greenwich, CT, pp. 35–84.
Edwards, L.N., Grossman, M. (1982). "Income and race differences in children's health in the mid-1960s". Medical Care 20, 915–930.
Edwards, L.N., Grossman, M. (1983). "Adolescent health, family background, and preventive medical care". In: Salkever, D.S., Sirageldin, I., Sorkin, A. (Eds.), Research in Human Capital and Development, vol. III. JAI Press, Greenwich, CT, pp. 77–109.
Erbsland, M., Ried, W., Ulrich, V. (1995). "Health, health care, and the environment. Econometric evidence from German micro data". Health Economics 4, 169–182.
Farrell, P., Fuchs, V.R. (1982). "Schooling and health: the cigarette connection". Journal of Health Economics 1, 217–230.
Frederick, S., Lowenstein, G., O'Donoghue, T. (2002). "Time discounting and time preference: a critical review". Journal of Economic Literature 40, 351–401.

Fuchs, V.R. (1974). "Who Shall Live? Health Economics, and Social Choice". Basic Books, New York.
Fuchs, V.R. (1982). "Time preference and health: an exploratory study". In: Fuchs, V.R. (Ed.), Economic Aspects of Health. University of Chicago Press, Chicago, IL, pp. 93–120.
Gerdtham, U.G., Johannesson, M. (1999). "New estimates of the demand for health: results based on a categorical health measure and Swedish micro data". Social Science & Medicine 49, 1325–1332.
Ghez, G.R., Becker, G.S. (1975). "The Allocation of Time and Goods Over the Life Cycle". Columbia University Press for the National Bureau of Economic Research, New York.
Gilleskie, D.B., Harrison, A.L. (1998). "The effect of endogenous health inputs on the relationship between health and education". Economics of Education Review 17, 279–297.
Glewwe, P. (1999). "Why does mother's schooling raise child health in developing countries?". Journal of Human Resources 34, 124–159.
Glied, S., Lleras-Muney, A. (2003). "Health inequality, education and medical innovation". Working Paper no. 9738. National Bureau of Economic Research, Cambridge, MA.
Goldberger, A.S. (1974). "Unobservable variables in econometrics". In: Zarembreka, P. (Ed.), Frontiers in Econometrics. Academic Press, New York, pp. 193–213.
Goldman, D., Lakdawalla, D. (2002). "Health disparities and medical technology". Working Paper. RAND Corporation, Santa Monica, CA.
Goldman, D.P., Smith, J.P. (2002). "Can patient self-management help explain the SES health gradient?". Proceedings of the National Academy of Sciences of the United States 99, 10929–10934.
Granger, C.W.J. (1969). "Investigating causal relations by econometric models and cross-spectral methods". Econometrica 37, 424–438.
Griliches, Z. (1979). "Sibling models and data in economics: beginnings of a survey". Journal of Political Economy 87, S37–S64.
Gronau, R. (1980). "Home production – a forgotten industry". Review of Economics and Statistics 62, 408–416.
Grossman, M. (1972a). "On the concept of health capital and the demand for health". Journal of Political Economy 80, 223–255.
Grossman, M. (1972b). "The Demand for Health: A Theoretical and Empirical Investigation". Columbia University Press for the National Bureau of Economic Research, New York.
Grossman, M. (1975). "The correlation between health and schooling". In: Terleckyj, N.E. (Ed.), Household Production and Consumption. Columbia University Press for the National Bureau of Economic Research, New York, pp. 147–211.
Grossman, M. (2000). "The human capital model". In: Culyer, A.J., Newhouse, J.P. (Eds.), Handbook of Health Economics, vol. 1A. Elsevier, Amsterdam, pp. 347–408.
Grossman, M., Joyce, T.J. (1990). "Unobservables, pregnancy resolutions, and birth weight production functions in New York City". Journal of Political Economy 98, 983–1007.
Grossman, M., Kaestner, R. (1997). "Effects of education on health". In: Behrman, J.R., Stacey, N. (Eds.), The Social Benefits of Education. University of Michigan Press, Ann Arbor, MI, pp. 69–123.
Grossman, M., Sindelar, J.L., Mullahy, J., Anderson, R. (1993). "Policy watch: alcohol and cigarette taxes". Journal of Economic Perspectives 7, 211–222.
Gruber, J., Köszegi, B. (2001). "Is addiction 'rational'? Theory and evidence". Quarterly Journal of Economics 116, 1261–1303.
Hammond, C. (2003). "How education makes us healthy". London Review of Education 1, 61–78.
Hartog, J., Oosterbeek, H. (1998). "Health, wealth and happiness: why pursue a higher education?". Economics of Education Review 17, 245–256.
Hausman, J.A. (1978). "Specification tests in econometrics". Econometrica 46, 1251–1271.
Haveman, R.H., Wolfe, B.L. (1995). "The determinants of children's attainments: a review of methods and findings". Journal of Economic Literature 33, 1829–1878.
Heckman, J.J. (1979). "Sample selection bias as a specification error". Econometrica 47, 153–161.
Hotz, V.J., Klerman, J.A., Willis, R.J. (1997). "The economics of fertility in developed countries". In: Rosenzweig, M.R., Stark, O. (Eds.), Handbook of Population and Family Economics, vol. 1A. Elsevier, Amsterdam, pp. 275–347.

Hurd, M. (1987). "Saving of the elderly and desired bequests". American Economic Review 77, 289–312.
Hurd, M. (1989). "Mortality risks and bequests". Econometrica 57, 779–813.
Hurd, M., Kapteyn, A. (2003). "Health, wealth, and the role of institutions". Journal of Human Resources 38, 387–415.
Idler, E.L., Kasl, S.V. (1995). "Self ratings of health: do they also predict change in functional ability?". Journal of Gerontology: Social Sciences 508, S344–S353.
Ippolito, R. (2003), "Health, education, and investment behavior in the family". Working Paper. George Mason University School of Law, Fairfax, VA.
Jalan, J., Ravallion, M. (2003). "Does piped water reduce diarrhea for children in rural India?". Journal of Econometrics 112, 153–173.
Jöreskog, K.G. (1973). "A general method for estimating a linear structural equations system". In: Goldberger, A.S., Duncan, O.D. (Eds.), Structural Equations Models in the Social Sciences. Seminar Press, New York, pp. 85–112.
Jöreskog, K.G., Sörbom, D. (1981). LISREL: Analysis of Linear Structural Relationships by the Method of Maximum Likelihood. International Educational Services, Chicago.
Joyce, T. (1994). "Self selection, prenatal care, and birthweight among blacks, whites, and Hispanics in New York City". Journal of Human Resources 29, 762–794.
Kenkel, D.S. (1991). "Health behavior, health knowledge, and schooling". Journal of Political Economy 99, 287–305.
Kenkel, D.S. (2000). "Prevention". In: Culyer, A.J., Newhouse, J.P. (Eds.), Handbook of Health Economics, vol. 1B. Elsevier, Amsterdam, pp. 1675–1720.
Lam, D., Duryea, S. (1999). "Effects of schooling on fertility, labor supply, and investments in children, with evidence from Brazil". Journal of Human Resources 34, 161–192.
Lawrence, E.C. (1991). "Poverty and the rate of time preference: evidence from panel data". Journal of Political Economy 99, 54–77.
Lee, R., Miller, T. (1990). "Population policy and externalities to childbearing". Annals of the American Academy of Political and Social Sciences 510, 17–43.
Leigh, J.P. (1983). "Direct and indirect effects of education on health". Social Science and Medicine 17, 227–234.
Leigh, J.P. (1985). "An empirical analysis of self-reported, work-limiting disability". Medical Care 23, 310–319.
Leigh, J.P. (1986). "Accounting for tastes: correlates of risk and time preferences". Journal of Post Keynesian Economics 9, 17–31.
Leigh, J.P., Dhir, R. (1997). "Schooling and frailty among seniors". Economics of Education Review 16, 45–57.
Lleras-Muney, A. (2005). "The relationship between education and adult mortality in the United States". Review of Economic Studies 72, 189–221.
Lleras-Muney, A., Lichtenberg, F.R. (2002). "The effect of education on medical technology adoption: are the more educated more likely to use new drugs?" Working Paper no. 9185. National Bureau of Economic Research, Cambridge, MA.
Lochner, L., Moretti, E. (2004). "The effect of education on crime: evidence from prison inmates, arrests, and self-reports". American Economic Review 94, 155–189.
Meara, E. (1999). "Why is health related to socioeconomic status?" Ph.D. Dissertation. Harvard University Cambridge, MA.
Meara, E. (2001). "Why is health related to socioeconomic status? The case of pregnancy and low birth weight". Working Paper no. 8231. National Bureau of Economic Research Cambridge, MA.
Michael, R.T. (1972). "The Effect of Education on Efficiency in Consumption". Columbia University Press for the National Bureau of Economic Research, New York.
Michael, R.T. (1973a). "Education and the derived demand for children". Journal of Political Economy 81, S128–S164.
Michael, R.T. (1973b). "Education in nonmarket production". Journal of Political Economy 81, 306–327.

Michael, R.T. (1982). "Measuring non-monetary benefits of education: a survey". In: McMahon, W.W., Geske, T.G. (Eds.), Financing Education: Overcoming Inefficiency and Inequity. University of Illinois Press, Urbana, IL, pp. 119–149.
Mincer, J. (1974). "Schooling, Experience, and Earnings". Columbia University Press for the National Bureau of Economic Research, New York.
Morris, J. (1976). "Some simple tests of the direct effect of education on preferences and on nonmarket productivity". Review of Economics and Statistics 58, 112–117.
Mroz, T. (1999). "Discrete factor approximation in simultaneous equations models: estimating the impact of a dummy endogenous variable on a continuous outcome". Journal of Econometrics 92, 233–274.
Nelson, R.R., Phelps, E.S. (1966). "Investments in humans, technological diffusion, and economic growth". American Economic Review 56, 69–75.
Neumark, D. (1999). "Biases in twin estimates of the return to schooling". Economics of Education Review 18, 143–148.
Peele, S. (1985). "The Meaning of Addiction: Compulsive Experience and Its Interpretation". Lexington Books, Lexington, MA.
Pollak, R.A. (1970). "Habit formation and dynamic demand functions". Journal of Political Economy 78, 745–763.
Rosen, S., Taubman, P. (1982). "Some socioeconomic determinants of mortality". In: van der Gaag, J., Neenan, W.B., Tsukahara, T. Jr (Eds.), Economics of Health Care. Praeger Publishers, New York, pp. 255–271.
Rosenzweig, M.R. (1995). "Why are there returns to schooling?". American Economic Review 85, 153–158.
Rosenzweig, M.R., Schultz, T.P. (1982). "The behavior of mothers as inputs to child health: the determinants of birth weight, gestation, and rate of fetal growth". In: Fuchs, V.R. (Ed.), Economic Aspects of Health. University of Chicago Press for the National Bureau of Economic Research, Chicago, IL, pp. 53–92.
Rosenzweig, M.R., Schultz, T.P. (1983). "Estimating a household production function: heterogeneity, the demand for health inputs, and their effects on birth weight". Journal of Political Economy 91, 723–746.
Rosenzweig, M.R., Schultz, T.P. (1989). "Schooling, information and nonmarket productivity: contraceptive use and its effectiveness". International Economic Review 30, 457–477.
Rosenzweig, M.R., Schultz, T.P. (1991). "Who receives medical care? Income, implicit prices, and the distribution of medical services among pregnant women in the United States". Journal of Human Resources 26, 473–508.
Ross, C.E., Mirowsky, J. (1999). "Refining the association between education and health: the effects of quantity, credential, and selectivity". Demography 36, 445–460.
Sacerdote, B. (2000). "The nature and nurture of economic outcomes". Working Paper no. 7949. National Bureau of Economic Research Cambridge, MA.
Sacerdote, B. (2002). "The nature and nurture of economic outcomes". American Economic Review 92, 344–348.
Sander, W. (1995a). "Schooling and quitting smoking". Review of Economics and Statistics 77, 191–199.
Sander, W. (1995b). "Schooling and smoking". Economics of Education Review 14, 23–33.
Schultz, T.P. (1993). "Returns to women's education". In: King, E.M., Hill, M.A. (Eds.), Women's Education in Developing Countries: Barriers, Benefits, and Policies. Johns Hopkins University Press, Baltimore, MD, pp. 51–99.
Shakotko, R.A., Edwards, L.N., Grossman, M. (1981). "An exploration of the dynamic relationship between health and cognitive development in adolescence". In: van der Gaag, J., Perlman, M. (Eds.), Contributions to Economic Analysis: Health, Economics, and Health Economics. North-Holland Publishing Company, Amsterdam, pp. 305–325.
Sickles, R.C., Taubman, P. (1986). "An analysis of the health and retirement status of the elderly". Econometrica 54, 1339–1356.
Spasojevic, J. (2003). "Effects of education on adult health in Sweden: results from a natural experiment". Ph.D. Dissertation. City University of New York Graduate Center, New York.

Taubman, P., Rosen, S. (1982). "Healthiness, education, and marital status". In: Fuchs, V.R. (Ed.), Economic Aspects of Health. University of Chicago Press for the National Bureau of Economic Research, Chicago, pp. 121–140.
Thomas, D., Strauss, J., Henriques, M.-H. (1991). "How does mother's education affect child height?". Journal of Human Resources 26, 83–211.
U.S. Department of Health and Human Services (1990). The Health Benefits of Smoking Cessation: A Report of the Surgeon General. Public Health Service, U.S. Department of Health and Human Services, Rockville, MD.
Van Doorslaer, E.K.A. (1987). Health Knowledge and the Demand for Medical Care. Assen, Maastricht, The Netherlands.
Wagstaff, A. (1986). "The demand for health: some new empirical evidence". Journal of Health Economics 5, 195–233.
Wagstaff, A. (1993). "The demand for health: an empirical reformulation of the Grossman model". Health Economics 2, 189–198.
Wilcox-Gök, V.L. (1983). "The determination of child health: an application of sibling and adoption data". The Review of Economics and Statistics 65, 266–273.
Willis, R.J. (1973). "A new approach to the economic theory of fertility behavior". Journal of Political Economy 81, S14–S64.
Wu, D.-M. (1973). "Alternative tests of independence between stochastic regressors and disturbances". Econometrica 41, 733–750.

Chapter 11

DOES LEARNING TO ADD UP ADD UP? THE RETURNS TO SCHOOLING IN AGGREGATE DATA

LANT PRITCHETT

Kennedy School of Government, Harvard University and World Bank

Contents

Handbook of the Economics of Education, Volume 1
Edited by Eric A. Hanushek and Finis Welch
© 2006 Elsevier B.V. All rights reserved
DOI: 10.1016/S1574-0692(06)01011-7

Abstract

The theoretical, conceptual, and practical difficulties with the use of cross-national data on schooling are so severe using aggregate data for any purpose for which individual level data would do should be avoided. There are, however, three questions for which the use of cross-national data on schooling could potentially help answer interesting questions for which individual data is insufficient. First, do differences in the evolution and dynamics of schooling help explain the big facts about the evolution and dynamics of output growth? Largely, no. Second, the existence and magnitude of output externalities to schooling is an important question with possible normative policy implications, and evidence for externalities requires at least some level of spatial aggregation. Does the cross-national data provide support for output externalities? Largely, no. Third, cross-national (or more broadly spatially aggregated) data allows the exploration of the impact on returns to schooling (or in the gap between private and social returns) of differences in economic environments. This last question seems a promising line for future research.

Keywords

growth, education, spillovers, Mincer

JEL classification: O11, O40, J24, I20

To be a successful pirate one needs to know a great deal about naval warfare, the trade routes of commercial shipping, the armament, rigging, and crew size of potential victims, and the market for booty.

To be a successful chemical manufacturer in early twentieth century United States required knowledge of chemistry, potential uses of chemicals in different intermediate and final products, markets, and problems of large scale organization.

If the basic institutional framework makes income redistribution (piracy) the preferred economic opportunity, we can expect a very different development of knowledge and skills than a productivity increasing (a twentieth century chemical manufacturer) economic opportunity would entail. The incentives that are built into the institutional framework play the decisive role in shaping the kinds of skills and knowledge that pay off.

Douglass North, 1990

1. Introduction: Why mess with aggregate data?

The use of cross-national data to make inferences about the economic impact of schooling involves at least three fundamental and, I would argue, intractable problems: creating a valid aggregate of "schooling capital"[1] within each country from data on years of schooling and achievement; specification of an adequate model of the determinants of the dynamics of equilibrium aggregate output; and a specification of the dynamics of adjustment of output; across countries. These difficulties raise a legitimate question: "why?" Before launching an intellectual voyage across territory fraught with dangers the traveler should have some clear idea of why the destination might be worth the trip. Using aggregate data when household data would suffice, particularly when the underlying behavioral models are about decisions of firms or households, is almost certainly not good practice. Yet there are three questions for which the use of use of aggregate data is necessary.

First, what are the determinants of the level and dynamics of aggregate output? No matter what the microeconomic data say about wage returns to schooling to know

[1] I take "human capital" to refer to all purposively acquired skills that augment utility – from formal schooling to on the job training to shooting free throws to learning a second language to formal schooling to acquiring job experience to learning to fence. "Education" is the broad process of socialization and training intended to create a socially functional adult (all societies have always had "universal education"). Schooling is just one *component* of human capital and just one *mode* of education (that which is carried out in an institution called a "school" or, at the higher levels, institute, college, university). Since all of the literature I review exclusively uses measures of *schooling* I will attempt to call spade a spade and refer to schooling capital (not human or even educational capital) but for variety's sake will sometimes use the term "formal education" and sometimes use "human capital" when reviewing the literature.

whether schooling helps explain differences in levels and growth of output across regions (countries, provinces, states) one needs to aggregate. Section 1 details the basic facts about the evolution of aggregate schooling to illustrate, in a heuristic way, that schooling cannot possibly explain most of the most pressing questions about economic growth – particularly for the developing countries.

Second, are there output externalities of schooling? To generate evidence relevant for normative policy recommendations about output externalities requires at least some spatial aggregation. If the conjecture is that X's schooling raises the output of Y, one needs to link X and Y. Section 2 compares the "macro-Mincer" estimates of the returns to schooling – the impact of aggregate schooling on aggregate output or wage bill with the aggregation of the "micro-Mincer" returns. Large positive output externalities imply the output impact of an increase the aggregate schooling should exceed the aggregation of the individual impacts. The empirical evidence to date produces little support for output externalities. This is in part because many studies using cross-national data find low (or negative) estimates of the impact of aggregate schooling on output, but also in part because of low power, as confidence intervals of estimates of returns from aggregate data often include zero output impact, large negative estimates, the micro-Mincer returns (zero externalities), and estimates consistent with large externalities. In this review I show how a general parametric form for mapping years of schooling into schooling capital "encompasses" the existing literature and identifies the source of the widely varying results reported.

Third, does the private return to schooling, or the gap between private and social returns, to education vary across economic environments? For instance, one class of theories about returns to education is that the deep source of returns to education is the ability to adapt to disequilibria (of whatever source, technological innovation, economic shocks, etc.) [Welch (1970), Schultz (1975)]. Another class of theories are the *gap* between private and social returns to education might depend on institutional arrangements [Gelb, Knight and Sabot (1991)]. To test these types of theories one needs variation in the economic environment, particularly variation in which labor mobility across environments is restricted to reduce selection effects. Section 3 addresses the question of using variations across countries in the economic environment to examine questions of differential returns to schooling and differential gaps between private and social returns.

This review is already overly ambitious even though I am leaving out three critical areas. First, I am not examining all possible externalities to schooling – there may, for instance, be impacts of schooling in reducing crime levels [Garces, Thomas and Currie (2000)] or reducing social or economic inequality, or in improving health status – or facilitating democracy but I am only looking at the impact of schooling on (measured) economic output. Second, while some evidence from spatial aggregation within a national economy (states, provinces) will be mentioned, my focus is overwhelmingly on the cross-national data, in part because that is the largest branch of the literature, in part because that is the literature with which I am the most familiar, and in part because I am interested in growth in the developing economies. Third, I am relentlessly empirical and do not examine the many purely theoretical papers that propose various causal mechanisms whereby schooling might affect output or its growth.

2. Does schooling help explain puzzles in economic growth?

The advantage of a handbook chapter over a journal article or even a literature review is that some discussion of the basics is acceptable. There are two motivations for presenting some basic facts about the evolution and dynamics of output and schooling across countries. First, since one reason for cross-national aggregation is to understand the dynamics of output, reviewing the obvious facts about levels and growth rates of output helps to understand the empirical phenomena to be understood and what role schooling, or accumulation of schooling, might play. Second, the interpretation of the cross-national econometric results in the second and third sections is enhanced by an some understanding of the facts of growth rates, with particular emphasis on developing countries. In any cross-national sample the "developing" countries predominate.

There are five important stylized facts about output and growth:

- The growth rates of the leading countries (OECD) have been quite stable for over 100 years.
- There has been divergence in the average per worker output between the leading countries and the lagging countries in both absolute and relative terms.
- There has been a massive and pervasive *deceleration* of growth, especially in the developing countries, since the late 1970s.
- Medium to long-term growth rates have been enormously volatile over time with little persistence of growth rates across periods, particularly in developing countries.
- Not all growth in output per worker can be easily accounted for by increases in physical capital per worker and hence "productivity" growth is an important part of the growth process.

Basic examination of the evolution of schooling reveals that it will be difficult to explain much of the behavior of growth rates with schooling as:

- Schooling has expanded massively in the OECD.
- There has been marked convergence in the levels of education across countries.
- Schooling is nearly universally much higher, and growing as fast, as before the growth deceleration.
- Schooling per worker is not volatile and is very persistent.
- In most developing countries adding in a reasonable growth accounting contribution of schooling makes estimated rate of productivity growth very low or negative.

2.1. The "Jones critique" is general

Table 1 shows that the mean and median of the ratio of growth of output per worker 1980–1994 to 100 years ago in OECD countries is typically very near one. There is

Table 1
Output per capita growth rates in OECD countries show very little historical acceleration while levels of education have expanded enormously

Country (sorted by growth acceleration)	I	II	Ratio II/I	II	III	Ratio III/II (1997/1900)	Adult illiteracy, 1900
	Growth per capita output, ppa			Secondary Enrollment/ Population aged 15–19, 1900	Net Secondary Enrollment, 1997		
	1880–1890	1980–1994					
Australia	−0.85	1.64	–		96		
Netherlands	0.41	1.66	4.1	2.67	100	37.5	
Italy	0.76	1.94	2.5	2.93	95	32.4	48.2
Norway	1.12	2.08	1.9	9.33	98	10.5	
Belgium	0.99	1.82	1.8	4.86	100	20.6	19.6
Japan	1.79	3.22	1.8	2.87	100	34.8	
UK	1.24	2.07	1.7		92		
Austria	1.54	1.86	1.2	**4.01**	**97**	**24.2**	
Germany	**1.83**	**1.97**	**1.1**		95		
Denmark	1.92	1.97	1.0	2.97	95	32.0	
France	1.49	1.52	1.0	2.67	99	37.1	16.5
USA	1.68	1.61	1.0	7.10	96	13.5	10.7
Switzerland	1.63	1.18	0.7	22.11	84	3.8	
Finland	1.83	1.30	0.7	5.76	95	16.5	61.2
New Zealand	1.22	0.83	0.7	**3.63**	**93**	**25.6**	
Sweden	1.77	1.05	0.6	3.64	100	27.4	
Canada	2.29	1.17	0.5		95		17.1
Average	1.5	1.7	1.2	5.7	95.9	16.7	

Sources: Growth rates (based on Maddison, 1995), Enrollment (Mitchell, various editions for 1900, WDI for 1990), UNESCO (illiteracy).

no suggestion of a generalized acceleration of growth. In contrast *every* measure of schooling from the lowest (primary) to the highest (university, PhDs, research scientists) has expanded many fold – both in absolute numbers and as a proportion of the labor force. While estimates of changes in the secondary enrollment rate have their difficulties (e.g., changing and non-comparable definitions, historical estimates of age composition of the population) the crude estimates here suggest that in the median OECD country secondary enrollments increased 24 fold from 1900 to 1997. France, for example, has roughly identical growth rates in the 1880s and 1980s and secondary school enrollment rates were roughly 37 times higher.

Twinning these facts follows Jones' (1995) powerful critique of the first generation endogenous growth models, showing that in the USA R&D spending has expanded massively over the long-historical span while the growth rate, both of output per worker and of measures of technical progress, has remained remarkably constant. Many of the first generation endogenous growth models [Romer (1986), Lucas (1988)] placed a great deal of emphasis on the role of knowledge and/or human capital (or scientists or

R&D spending) in expanding the expansion of output through the creation of new ideas which were non excludable.[2] This suggested the possibility that higher *levels* of R&D (or of schooling) could *permanently* raise the *growth rate* of output per capita. But the first generation of models did have the empirically unattractive feature of plainly counterfactual predictions (like a secular acceleration of economic growth as stocks of educated labor expanded): no plausible model can propose a substantial, steady state, linear relationship between the *level* of schooling (or schooling capital or R&D) and *growth rates* of either "world" technical progress or the growth of any given country.[3]

2.2. Divergence in output per worker, convergence in schooling per worker

Schooling (and more broadly education and more broadly still human capital) has been at the center of development thinking for a long, long, time.[4] Gunnar Myrdal's (1968) classic the *Asian Drama* took the importance of education as the settled (if new) conventional wisdom – *in the 1950s*. W. Arthur Lewis (1955) classic on economic growth discussed the accumulation of knowledge and had a quite sophisticated discussion of educational policies – *before* his chapter on physical capital.[5] This academic consensus on the importance of formal schooling for development has been accompanied by action. However measured, whether total enrollments, enrollment rates, or years completed, the last 40 years have witnessed an enormous expansion in schooling at all levels in nearly every country in the world (Table 2).

[2] Kuznets (1966) discussed all of the essential consequences for economic growth of knowledge as a non-rival good. This is not to slight Romer's (1986, 1990) early endogenous growth models, which provided a way of formally modeling effects which had only been discussed.

[3] This critique does not leave the growth modeling literature in a very happy state as the same fundamental issues with the "old" models remain: there clearly is profit motivated innovative and inventive activity (the microeconomics of which can be modeled); more schooled rather than less schooled workers do appear to be better at basic science, invention, and even at innovation; knowledge does seem to have characteristics of a non-rival good. There is a second generation of models that are trying to preserve the flavor of an endogenous growth model while eliminating the counter-factual predictions (e.g., Young). How successful these are as models of growth I am not sure, but since they have been changed precisely to not predict a level of schooling-growth link they are less interesting from the point of view of schooling and growth.

[4] The story that the contribution of the "new" growth theories was to emphasize a previously neglected role for formal education in the process of growth – or that human capital had been overlooked in favor of an exclusive emphasis on physical capital – is pure myth. This mythic view emerges from a distorting lens on intellectual history with two confusions. First, it confuses what happens to be formally, mathematically modeled with the views of economists (there are plenty of important issues that do not receive attention because it is perceived they are either settled and obvious or intractable with current methods). Second, it confuses views of academic economists with the views of the economics profession at large or particularly with economists as policy makers.

[5] The caricature view that Lewis thought that the process of development was exclusively about raising the saving rate comes from the famous quote "the central problem in the theory of economic growth is to understand the process by which a community is converted from being a 5 percent to a 12 percent saver" a quote from the middle of chapter 5 on page 226. Lewis himself warned in the introduction "each sentence, or paragraph, takes for granted what is written elsewhere, and, if torn from its context, may cease to be true."

Table 2
A massive and (nearly) universal expansion in schooling attainment (enrollments, literacy and years completed)

	Gross secondary school enrollment (%)			Illiteracy rate, adults 15+			Years of schooling (average)		
	1970	1995	%Ch	1970	1995	%Ch	1960	1995	
East Asia & Pacific	24.3	62.9	159%	44.0	17.3	−61%	4.7	7.5	60%
Europe & Central Asia	...	83.1		7.4	3.8	−48%	6.2	8.9	42%
Latin America & Caribbean	28.0	55.4	98%	26.2	13.3	−49%	3.5	5.9	70%
Middle East & North Africa	23.5	62.0	164%	70.2	40.7	−42%	2.2	5.9	172%
Sub-Saharan Africa	6.3	25.9	310%	72.0	44.3	−38%	1.6	3.4	118%
South Asia	23.0	43.4	89%	68.1	49.1	−28%	1.4	3.5	145%
United States	*83.7*	*97.4*	*16%*	...	...		*8.5*	*11.9*	*40%*

Source: World Development Indicators (enrollments, illiteracy) and Barro–Lee dataset (years of schooling).

This massive and universal expansion in schooling contrasts with second big fact about the evolution of output – which is that across nations there has been historical and continued divergence in output per capita. Hence the cross-national dispersion of schooling per worker and the dispersion of output per head have moved strongly in opposite directions. The unweighted standard deviation of (natural) log real GDP per capita in the latest Summers–Heston/Penn World Tables data has *increased* by 22 percent (from 0.93 in 1960 to 1.13 in 1995).[6] The nearly universal expansion in schooling has reduced the unweighted standard deviation of (natural) log years of schooling of the 15 and older population by 40 percent (from 0.94 to 0.56). Even larger differences emerge from comparing the 90th/10th percentile ratio – the 90/10 ratio of output per worker has increased by 85 percent while the ratio of schooling per worker has decreased by 68 percent. Comparisons of specific countries (Ghana, Mexico, and India) to the USA show that even in India, which has converged in output levels, the reduction in relative schooling levels has been even more rapid.

As is explored below, these basic facts about years of schooling are not the end of the story, as there are ways of defining the mapping from schooling to schooling capital that might lead differences in schooling to contribute to absolute divergence – for example, if higher schooling of teachers leads to more schooling capital acquired per year of schooling. Or, there are models in which the same differences in schooling could lead to

[6] Of course, if one is interested in the distribution of welfare *per person* the growth rates of India and China are the key and since both have done relatively well in the 1980s and 1990s the world distribution of income/consumption expenditures has improved [Sala-i-Martin (2002)]. But there are very good reasons for treating the country as the unit of observation in growth processes (since many policies are set at this level) and understanding the numbers of countries with various growth experiences and the central tendency of those growth experiences is an important, independent, question from the evolution of world distribution of personal welfare.

Table 3
Divergence in levels of (natural log) output per worker and convergence in (natural log) schooling years per worker, 1960–1995

	Output per worker			Schooling per worker			Percentage change in ratio of output per worker to schooling per worker
	1960	1995	% Change	1960	1995	% Change	
Standard deviation (ln)	0.9	1.1	21.5%	0.9	0.6	−40.4%	104.0%
90/10 ratio	12.0	22.2	85.0%	11.7	3.7	−68.4%	485.0%
	Ratio of USA value to:						
Ghana	14.3	21.3	48.9%	8.8	3.2	−63.9%	312.8%
Mexico	2.3	2.7	18.4%	3.1	1.7	−44.4%	113.2%
India	15.2	11.1	−26.7%	5.1	2.6	−47.9%	40.7%

Source: Output per worker, PWT 6.0, Schooling Barro–Lee.

larger output gaps – for example, if knowledge acquisition is some increasing function of *relative* education and the gradient of that function increases. But the basic fact is that the raw cross-national dispersion of (in) output per capita has gone up substantially and of (ln) schooling down substantially.

2.3. Massive slowdown

The third big fact about growth rates is that there has been a nearly universal and massive slowdown in economic growth. Except for India and China and some parts of East Asia (Korea, Singapore, Taiwan) growth rates in the 1980s and 1990s were much lower than in 1960s and 1970s [Ben David and Papell (1997), Pritchett (2001), Rodrik (1999)]. In the non-OECD countries the (unweighted) average growth of output per worker slowed from 2.6 ppa in the 1960s to 2.2 ppa in the 1970s to only 0.7 in the 1980s recovering only to 1.4 ppa in the 1990s (Table 4). [By using only a sample with growth rates in all periods these calculations are likely to understate the fall in cross-national average growth rates for two reasons. First, most of the "transition" countries and all of the former Soviet Union countries are excluded because they lack comparable data over time. Second, countries with spectacularly bad economic performance tend to lack data as either lack of resources of political chaos cause the production of economic statistics to cease (e.g., Afghanistan, Somalia)].

The general growth deceleration combined with the nearly universal and persistent growth schooling implies that output growth and the level of schooling were often moving strongly in opposite directions. In Venezuela (Figure 1) output per worker has been falling since the 1960s while schooling per worker rose consistently. In the Philippines (Figure 2) growth slowed in the 1980s and 1990s to near zero, while schooling continued to climb. According to these data in Brazil (Figure 3), schooling and growth move

Table 4
Growth rates of output per worker have decelerated sharply in 1980s and 1990s relative to 1960s and 1970s while level and change in level of schooling have increased

Region	N	Variable	1960s	1970s	1980s	1990s	Change 1990s vs. 1960s
Sub-Saharan Africa	20	Growth Y/W	1.5%	0.7%	−0.1%	−0.5%	−2.0%
		S/W	1.6	2.0	2.5	3.2	1.5
		Annual change S/W	0.065	0.107	0.138	0.079	0.014
Latin America and Caribbean	22	Growth Y/W	2.5%	2.3%	−0.6%	1.6%	−0.9%
		Level S/W	3.6	4.2	5.0	5.7	2.1
		Annual change S/W	0.118	0.162	0.133	0.133	0.015
Middle East, North Africa	8	Growth Y/W	4.0%	3.2%	0.6%	2.3%	−1.7%
		Level S/W	2.5	3.3	4.6	5.7	3.2
		Annual change S/W	0.153	0.261	0.223	0.176	0.023
East Asia, Pacific	13	Growth Y/W	4.4%	4.1%	3.1%	2.7%	−1.7%
		Level S/W	4.9	5.5	6.7	7.4	2.5
		Annual change S/W	0.11	0.249	0.143	0.141	0.031
South Asia	5	Growth Y/W	1.8%	1.1%	3.1%	2.8%	1.0%
		Level S/W	1.4	1.9	2.7	3.6	2.2
		Annual change S/W	0.099	0.167	0.174	0.109	0.010
Non-OECD	66	Growth Y/W	2.6%	2.2%	0.7%	1.4%	−1.2%
		Level S/W	2.7	3.3	4.1	5.0	2.2
		Annual change S/W	0.107	0.172	0.163	0.123	0.016
Western Europe	15	Growth Y/W	3.9%	2.5%	2.5%	2.3%	−1.6%
		Level S/W	6.3	7.0	7.8	8.7	2.3
		Annual change S/W	0.13	0.157	0.179	0.129	−0.001
All	87	Growth Y/W	2.9%	2.2%	1.1%	1.6%	−1.3%
		Level S/W	3.6	4.2	5.0	5.8	2.2
		Annual change S/W	0.107	0.173	0.151	0.123	0.016

in almost exactly opposite directions: during the very rapid growth of the late 1960s and 1970s (the "Brazilian miracle") education was stagnating, while schooling growth picks up after 1975 while growth slows to nearly zero.

Schooling doesn't appear to contribute to the explanation of the slow-down in growth. Moreover, if schooling does have a large positive impact whatever else it is that does explain the growth slow-down (e.g., deteriorating terms of trade, policy shifts, delayed stabilization [Rodrik (1999)], worsening international climate [Easterly (2001)] has to work harder to explain the deceleration.[7]

[7] Another massive slow-down (or reversal) is the experience of Eastern Europe, which, again, schooling does not explain. Most Eastern European countries had substantially higher quantities of schooling (and, by some measures, quality) than countries in "Southern" Europe and yet has (a) substantially lower GDP per capita which (b) fell tremendously on liberalization.

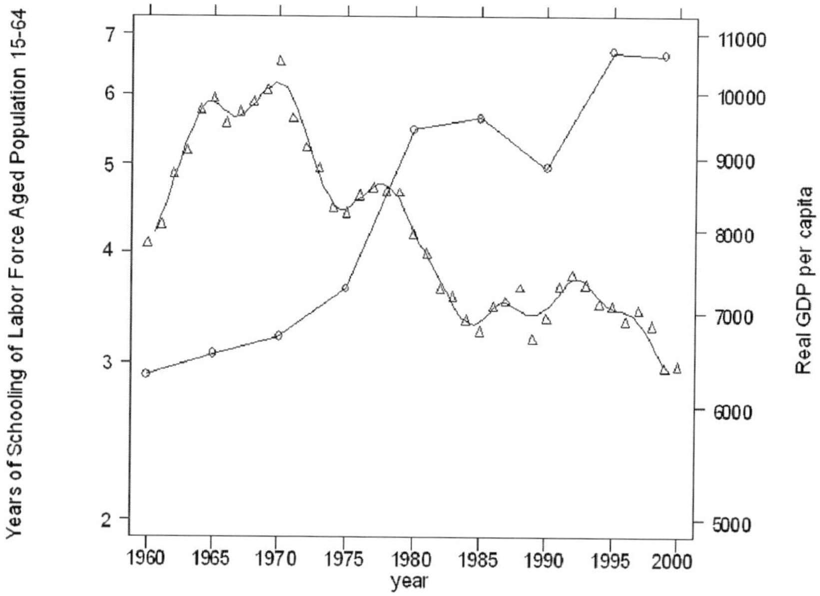

Figure 1. Schooling and GDP per person in Venezuela.

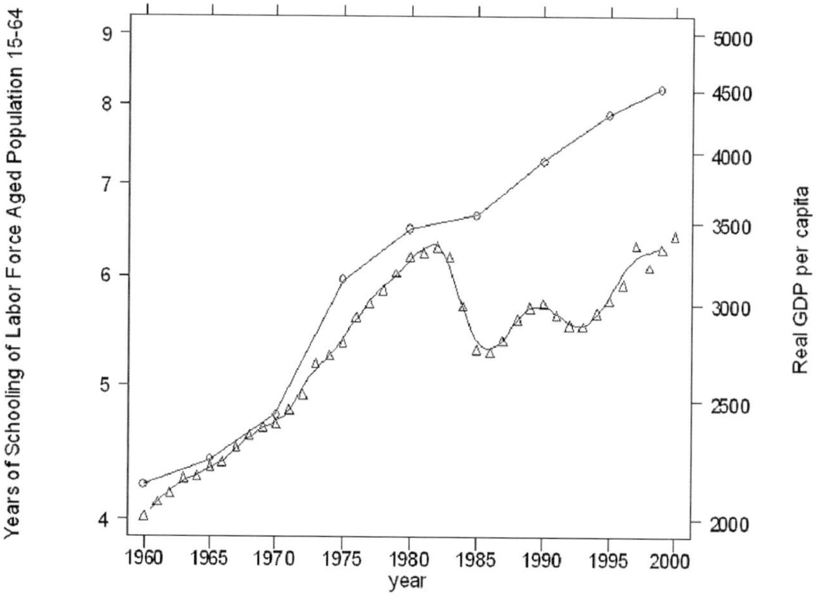

Figure 2. Schooling and GDP per person in Philippines.

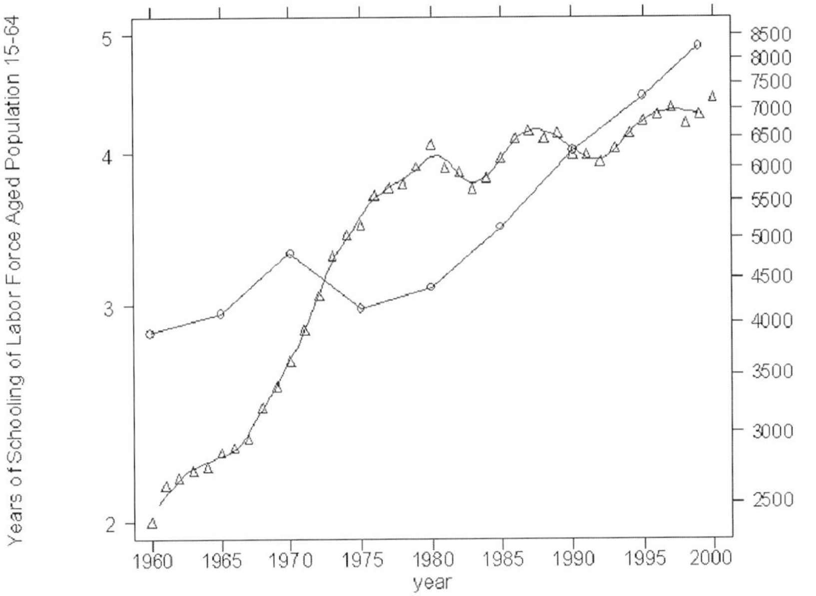

Figure 3. Schooling and GDP per person in Brazil.

2.4. *Volatility of growth*

The evolution of output in most developing countries does not fit the OECD pattern of modestly sized, business cycle frequency, fluctuations about a stable trend. Rather, developing country growth rates exhibit enormous instability over medium-run (from 5 to 10 year) and even "long" (from 15 to 20 year) horizons. Country growth rates decelerate (as shown above for Venezuela, Philippines, Brazil), accelerate as in Indonesia in 1967 (Figure 4), or simply have very large output fluctuations associated with macroeconomic crisis(es) as in Argentina (Figure 5).[8]

A stable trend explains very little of total time series variance of output in developing countries. In contrast to the OECD where the trend explains 95 percent of the variance in log output per worker over a 30 year horizon, in developing countries a stable trend explains much less of output dynamics – in 40 percent of developing countries a trend explains less than half of the time series variance [Pritchett (2001)]. Large changes in growth rates over time within countries imply there is very little persistence in growth rates – the cross-national correlation of growth rates across periods is very

[8] I think it is a misnomer to call these "business cycles" as the phrase implies both a regularity and a source of causation (it is not clear whether a "business" cycle means a cycle in business or a cycle caused by the natural processes of business) that are not present in most developing countries.

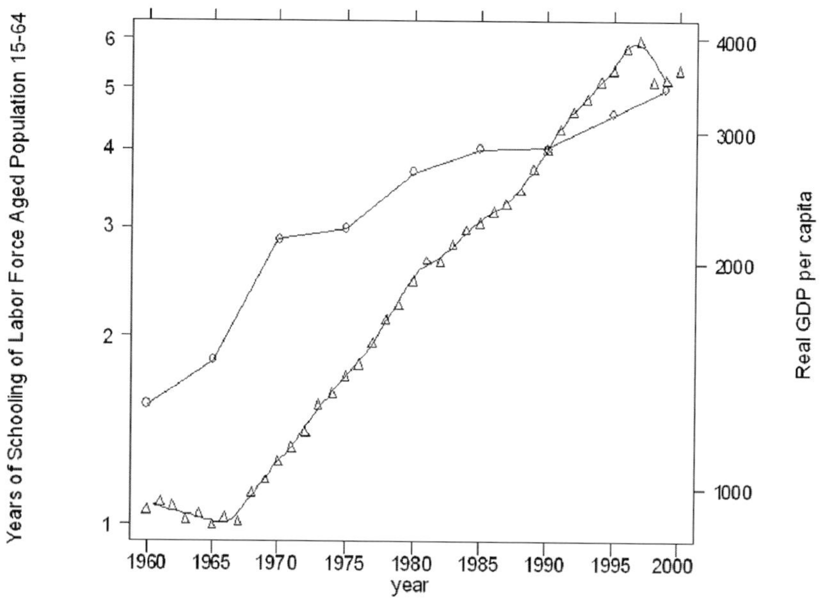

Figure 4. Schooling and GDP per person in Indonesia.

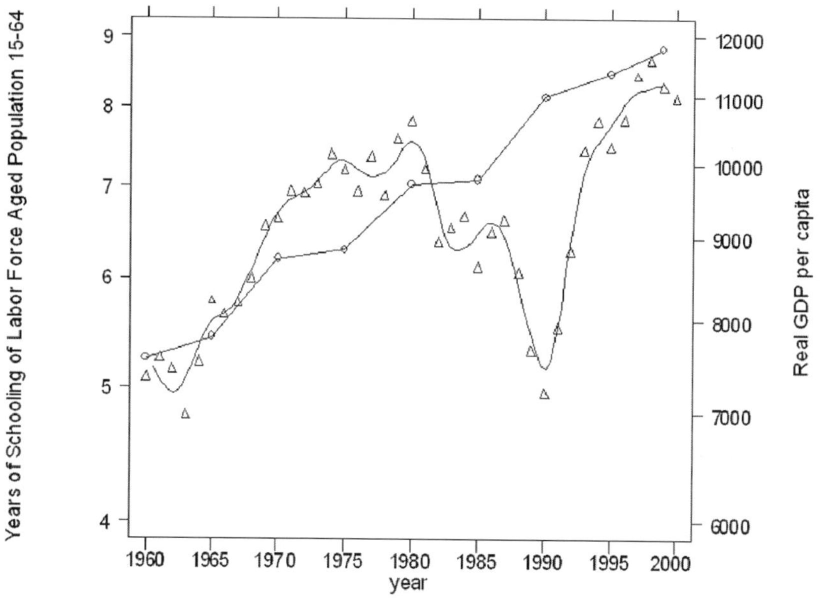

Figure 5. Schooling and GDP per person in Argentina.

low, the correlation is typically less than 0.2 over 10–15 year horizons [Easterly et al. (1993)].

In contrast the schooling of the labor force evolves very smoothly with very little time series volatility. To some extent this is a mechanical consequence of the fact that formal schooling is nearly always irreversible – people do not lose years of schooling – and hence schooling of the labor force declines only rarely (through massive emigration of the more educated). Moreover, since once in the labor force individuals rarely return to formal schooling expansion of average schooling of the labor force is driven by marginal entrants with higher schooling than existing participants and retirees. Even with rapid population growth and enormous changes in enrollment rates there are bounds to how fast average schooling can increase.[9]

Using regressions as a data summarizing device I follow up on a nice idea by Temple (2001) – which is discussed more fully below – and allow complete flexibility in the specification of the relationship between schooling and output growth. That is, I ask, how much of the variation in growth rates over 30, 10 and 5 year horizons can be explained by schooling even when I allow the data complete freedom to set the functional form? In a regression on output per worker growth over a given horizon ($t - n$ to t) I include some standard covariates. The growth of K/W[10], initial output per worker, initial infant mortality and period dummies. After experimentation across a variety of ways of entering schooling I report the transformations on S/W that maximize the incremental R2 of schooling:[11] (S/W_t, S/W_{t-n}, $(1/(S/W)_t)$, $(1/(S/W)_{t-n})$, $(S/W)_t^2$, $(S/W)_{t-n}^2$).

Not surprisingly, the ability of schooling per worker to explain cross-national differences in growth performance over medium to short horizons is very small. At 10 year horizons at most 3 percent of the variance, at five year horizons at most 1 percent of the total variance in growth rates is associated with S/W or its changes. The empirical fact is that S/W does not have sufficiently large fluctuations at the relevant frequencies to be strongly associated with changes in growth rates at medium to short term horizons. I urge the reader not to over-interpret what I (or the data) am saying as I know the incremental R2 is not a valid tool for model selection or resolving questions of causal precedence (either among the rhs variables to between the "dependent" and "independent" variables). In fact, perhaps K/W has much higher explanatory power because it is "more" endogenous.

[9] Suppose there were a labor force population growing at 2 percent per annum (so that entering cohorts are larger than previous) and suppose all current labor force entrants had zero schooling and that shifted instantaneously so that all cohorts entering had six years of schooling. The change in average labor force schooling in each five year period would be less than one year.

[10] More descriptively these are not "capital" but CUDIE (cumulated, depreciated, investment effort) which I have argued elsewhere is not even conceptually a good proxy for available "physical capital" [Pritchett (2000)].

[11] This is explicit and unashamed data mining as I am not attempting to "test" a coefficient (much less a "model"). I am exploring the data to see what is the maximum explanatory power the schooling per worker terms can achieve. I tried: percentage changes, absolute changes, levels, combinations of levels and changes with interaction terms, powers of current and lagged schooling up to a cubic.

Table 5
The maximum explanatory power of schooling per worker for growth of output per worker using a completely flexible functional form declines with the period of the growth rates

		R-squared		
		30 year	10 year	5 year
Growth of CUDIE per worker (K/W)		0.461	0.424	0.287
Growth K/W, lagged output, initial infant mortality rate, period dummies		0.647	0.530	0.390
Initial S/W, final S/W, squares of initial and final S/W, initial and final $1/(S/W)$	R2	0.714	0.563	0.400
	Incremental	0.067	0.033	0.01
All except K/W	R2	0.515	0.329	0.200
	Incremental of K/W growth	0.199	0.232	0.200
Number of observations		88	260	522
Number of countries		88	92	92

Source: Author's calculations.

2.5. Schooling and labor productivity growth

The simple accounting dictates that the larger the increase in labor productivity (output per worker) that is attributed to rising schooling per worker the lower the "residual" productivity. The combination of low output per worker growth with substantial K/W growth implies that attributing even a modestly sized impact of schooling makes the "residual" in labor productivity growth *negative* in more than half of developing countries and less than the "residual" productivity growth of the OECD countries in 80 percent of non-OECD countries.

Although I illustrate this point empirically using the very limiting assumptions of one particular specification, this general point will emerge from a variety of methods to decompose growth because of the simple combination of facts: in many developing countries output per worker grew slowly, K/W grew faster, and S/W faster still.

Output growth

≡ {Growth attributed by a theoretical relationship between changes in the quantity and quality of factors of production utilized in producing output}

plus

{A residual, which includes technical progress, measurement error in output and factors, economies of scale, misspecification of the impact of factors, etc.}

Table 6
Deducting a contribution of schooling to labor productivity implies low growth of the residual, especially in developing countries

	Output per worker growth	Per annum growth of the residual				
		Standard (augmented) Solow		Labor augmenting		
		Two factor (capital share = 0.4 (0.3 for industrial))	Three factor (1/3,1/3)	Years of schooling	Wage weighted	
					1960–1992	1980–1992[a]
China	4.0	2.3	1.2	2.2	1.8	3.3
East Asia (less China)	4.1	1.3	0.3	1.6	0.8	1.4
South Asia	2.3	1.0	0.1	0.9	0.7	1.6
SSA	0.5	−0.5	−1.7	−0.9	−0.7	−1.35
ME	1.8	1.8	−1.6	−0.6	−0.4	−0.9
LA	1.4	1.4	−0.1	0.0	0.1	−1.6
Industrial (OECD)	2.4	1.4	1.0	1.3	1.0	0.8

Source: Bosworth, Collins and Chen (1996, Tables 4 and 6).
[a]Unweighted average of reported growth rates for 1980–1986 and 1986–1992.

Attributing any significant component of growth to schooling therefore only *deepens* this puzzle as it drives the already low (or negative) growth residuals in developing countries even lower (or more negative).

Bosworth, Collins and Chen (1996) calculate TFP in two ways.[12] Their "three factor" model is the standard augmented Solow approach using the level of schooling as a proxy for human capital. As can be seen, this produces very low levels of TFP in most regions (*negative* on average in Africa, Middle East and Latin America) and very low in South Asia (0.1 percent) and lower than in the OECD on average even in East Asia (less China).[13] A negative one percent growth in TFP over this 32 year horizon implies that a worker would produce nearly 30 percent less output with the same capital and schooling. Even using their method with minimizes the growth attributed to schooling

[12] I have objected elsewhere [Pritchett (2000)] to the standard approach to TFP as it relies on cumulated, depreciated, investment effort (CUDIE) as a reasonable proxy for capital, which is likely to be wildly false in the government investment dominated, distorted, and volatile environments in most developing countries. Nevertheless, it is not a terrible way to illustrate the basic problem.

[13] Bosworth, Collins and Chen (1996), not liking these low numbers for TFP, experimented with other ways of measuring human capital that gave lower rates of increase and hence could produce larger residuals (TFP). Even with their "preferred" measure of using "wage weighted" labor force (which reduces the percentage rate of growth from 2–5 ppa to 0.5 to 0.8 ppa), I argue their procedure for computing "wage weighted" labor force mechanically constrains the growth of human capital to these low numbers.

Table 7
Adding a contribution of schooling to growth only deepens the mystery of accounting for slow growth and for the small growth residual, especially in non-OECD countries

Category of growth residual	Growth rate (ppa) of output per worker	Growth rate (ppa) of "factors of production"		Growth of output per worker less:	
		CUDIE ("K") per worker	Schooling per worker	Growth of K/W ($\alpha_K = 0.4$)	Growth of K/W, S/W ($\alpha_K = 0.4$, $\alpha_S = 0.3$)
OECD	2.51	3.33	1.04	1.17	0.86
Non-OECD	1.77	2.75	2.7	0.66	−0.01
	Numbers of non-OECD countries with low growth rates				
Less than zero	15 of 91			30 of 88	36 of 70
Less than OECD average	63 of 91			57 of 88	54 of 70

Sources: Author's calculations.

(labor augmenting, wage weighted) their measure of TFP growth 1980–1992 is negative *on average* in Latin America, SSA, and the Middle East.

Negative growth accounting residuals are difficult to escape from the combination of three facts: (1) developing country growth rates have been low (both absolutely and relative to the OECD), on average 1.77 ppa, (2) growth of *measured* K/W has typically been quite rapid, even in many low growth countries, on average 2.75 ppa, and (3) the growth of schooling has been nearly universally quite rapid, on average 2.7 ppa. Table 7 shows that 30 of the 88 non-OECD countries have a negative growth residual after just subtracting off a component attributed to K/W growth. Subtracting the percentage growth in schooling per worker times 0.3 gives negative residual growth in more than half of non-OECD countries and less than the OECD rate (in this instance, 0.86 ppa) for 77 percent of non-OECD countries.

There is no intrinsic problem or puzzle with a positive growth residual as casual observation and firm and farm level studies suggest the existence of technical progress. New knowledge does emerge and produces new products, new techniques, and new organization of production that allow greater output from the same inputs. In the early literature on growth in the USA the point was that, even after accounting for the growth of capital and labor force the residual that was attributed to "technical progress" or "TFP" seemed embarrassingly large, particularly given that within the model this component of growth was unexplainable. Introducing human capital helped reduce the residual and hence contributed to reducing the "puzzle" of largely unexplained growth.

In contrast, in developing countries the standard growth accounting produces unexpectedly *low* growth residuals even without schooling. That is, given that there has obviously been technical progress one would expect growth residuals to be positive. Moreover, since the developing countries lag the leaders in productivity many expected the residual productivity growth of "adapters" to be faster than "inventors".

This does not imply schooling does not have a large positive impact on output – it may – but the larger the growth impact attributed to increases in schooling the smaller (or most often) the more negative is the growth residual which would imply that, in spite of technical progress, a country would get less and less output from given factors, which does demand some explanation.[14]

2.6. Summary on growth and education

The results of this section are cautiously expressed as five "it is hard to" homilies. First, it is hard to explain a stable thing (historical growth rates) with a trending thing (schooling levels). Second, it is hard to explain a diverging thing (output levels) with a converging thing (schooling levels).[15] Third, it is hard to explain a falling thing (the collapse in growth rates, especially in developing countries) with a rising thing (schooling levels) or even a constant thing (absolute growth in schooling). Fourth, it is hard to explain a volatile thing (growth rates) with a stable thing (schooling levels and growth of schooling). Fifth, it is harder to attribute big output effects to schooling when they create puzzles (negative growth of the residual) than when they solve puzzles (reduce a large positive effect).

3. Does macro-Mincer exceed micro-Mincer?

Just as no economist would use market returns on bonds or equities or real estate to make inferences about *government policy* about which investments to make, no economist can infer anything about (no status) about schooling policy from regressions of private wage income/earnings on schooling.[16] The private returns to schooling are, by and large, not so spectacularly large they constitute *prima facie* evidence of a market failure or under investment in schooling – as they are typically no higher than estimates of returns to other investments.[17] In the standard normative framework the magnitude

[14] This isn't to say there are not plausible explanations. Elsewhere I have argued that physical capital stock accumulation could be dramatically overstated, sufficient to account for most of the negative growth residual, but if one pursues the 'mis-measured physical capital' explanation the magnitude of the mistake has to be larger the larger the growth attributed to capital [Pritchett (2000)].

[15] Though not impossible, as with sufficiently non-linear dynamics pretty much anything can happen. For instance, "threshold" models of poverty traps can generate divergence and then convergence even as "fundamentals" improve.

[16] Unfortunately, in policy and advocacy circles this has been a common practice: Tables of private and "social" returns assembled by Psacharopalous (e.g., 1994) have been used to justify public investment in schooling. But these are estimates of "social" returns return merely deduct some estimate of the publicly borne costs of schooling from the private returns and hence show social returns uniformly lower than private returns. My conjecture is that this confusion arose because the World Bank Articles of Agreement mandate that all investments are "productive" and there was a debate about whether schooling was "investment" or "consumption." The estimates of "social" returns were geared to demonstrating that schooling was a *productive* investment, but should have never been used to rationalize an *optimal* public subsidy.

[17] Although obviously the entire pattern of returns including covariances with other assets would need to be considered.

of the optimal public sector intervention hinges on the magnitude of the deviation of the private from the social (possibly equity adjusted) marginal costs and marginal benefits. Hence, there is some interest in the question: "If schooling of all individuals in the labor force increases by one year does that increase wages by more (or possibly less) than would have been expected from the aggregation of the individual wage impacts?" This section is in some ways the converse of the previous: while the previous section asked "Does aggregate schooling help explain facts about aggregate growth?" this section asks "Does the relationship between aggregate output and aggregate schooling in cross-national data provide compelling, or even suggestive, evidence of substantial output externalities?"

Imposing sufficient structure to interpret the results as a "rate of return" to schooling raises a host of essentially insuperable problems and requires an active suspension of disbelief. The problems with aggregation of physical capital stocks are well known from the earlier growth literature, where Fisher (1969) showed there are no plausible conditions under which the physical capital stocks of profit maximizing firms facing Cobb–Douglas production functions aggregate into an aggregate capital stock of an aggregate Cobb–Douglas production function. Aggregate physical capital stocks are as empirically successful in explaining output because they just are, not because they are theoretically well grounded. The functional forms below should be thought of as the *analogues* of, not derived from, their microeconomic counterparts.

3.1. How big of an output externality should we be looking for?

With those caveats as preface, what do the data say about output (or growth) externalities to schooling? But first, is the use of aggregate data to estimate externalities searching for a needle in a haystack? How big is the output externality to schooling that we *expect* to find? One way into that question is to ask: "*If* the common policy of (near) complete subsidization of all instructional costs of schooling *were* to be justified exclusively on the basis of an output externality to schooling, how big would that externality need to be?"[18]

To calculate this I assume the standard Mincer framework that wages are a function of experience, its square, and years of schooling,[19] a 45 year working life, 15 percent tax rate, and a discount rate of 11.5 percent. Why a discount rate 11.5 percent? – because that is the discount rate at which a 15 year old would choose to complete ninth grade at a Mincer wage increment of 9.9 percent if the only cost to the individual were

[18] This calculation is a hypothetical, in two senses. One, is that there might be many other externalities to schooling (crime reduction, promoting democracy, health spillovers) that justify public sector subsidization of schooling. Second, and much more important, the correct positive model of government support for schooling almost certainly does not depend on the normative model [Lott Jr. (1999), Pritchett (2002, 2003)].

[19] This draws on Heckman and Klenow (1997) and Heckman (1999) who do a similar calculation for college costs in the United States, with the result that the externality would need to be about 3 percentage points to justify the instructional cost subsidy at a typical public university.

Table 8
What rate excess social over private rate of return to schooling would rationalize full subsidization of instructional costs?

	I	II	III
Teacher years of schooling	15	15	17
Teacher experience	20	20	20
Primary class size	30	40	25
(secondary assumed half as large)			
Age 6, $S = 0$	4.5	3.4	6.5
Age 10, $S = 5$	2.2	1.7	3.2
Age 15, $S = 8$	2.3	1.7	3.3

The calculations assume the only private cost is wage foregone, a working life of 45 years, 15 percent tax rate, and 11.5 percent discount rate. At these assumptions a 9.9 percent wage increment is sufficient to induce a 15 year old to complete a ninth year of schooling at zero instructional cost.

the opportunity cost of the foregone wage. Now to calculate instructional costs of primary school we assume a teacher wage based on 15 years of schooling (12 plus three years teacher training) at the Mincer return of 9.9 percent and 20 years experience (with a 2.5 percent experience premium and a quadratic term such that experience premia peaks at 25 years). We explore a range of class sizes to get per student cost and assume that teacher wages are only 60 percent of total instructional costs (as construction and maintenance costs of the buildings, plus administrative costs, plus all instructional materials need to be included). I assume secondary school instructional costs are 50 percent higher than primary. This gives an estimate of instructional costs that has the main virtue of consistency, with a *patina* of plausibility.[20]

In this simple framework to justify full subsidization of instructional costs, the macro-Mincer should exceed the micro-Mincer, by about 3.5 to 6.5 percentage points at the primary level (because opportunity costs are low, instruction costs are a higher fraction of total costs) and 1.7–3.3 percent at the secondary level (Table 8). If range of micro-Mincer estimates are between 6 and 12 percent this means that the aggregate impact should be between 50 and 25 percent higher than the aggregate of the individual impacts.

3.2. Measuring years of schooling and Mincer increments

There are three elements of an estimate of the level or growth rate of "schooling capital": (a) estimates of the years of schooling (and their distribution across levels), (b) estimates

[20] Some of the ratios are taken from a review of costs that establishes "benchmarks" for costs in low-income developing countries in terms of class sizes, etc. [Bruns, Mingat and Rakotomalala (2003)]. The numbers produced are also not wildly at odds with actual estimates of cost per student in primary and secondary school.

of the returns to those years, (c) a mapping from the data on years of schooling into an estimate of aggregate "schooling capital." This Section 3.2 reviews the three elements of schooling capital while the next Section 3.3 reviews the empirical results using various specifications of the production function (or aggregate output function) which maps schooling capital to output, horizons, and estimation techniques.

3.2.1. *Years of schooling*

The first component of an estimate of aggregate of schooling capital is an estimate of the years of schooling of the labor force. Two principal methods are used in constructing estimates of the years of schooling. The perpetual inventory method uses the history of enrollment rates and mortality rates and an estimate of the initial stock to estimate cumulative years of schooling [Nehru, Swanson and Dubey (1995)] (NSD). These estimates have been extended to male/female disaggregation by Dubey and King (1994). There are two drawbacks to the perpetual inventory method. First, since this estimates schooling *acquired* in a country, not the schooling actually *present* with moderate amounts of emigration, the estimates will overstate or understate the schooling of the labor force depending on whether there has been net in or outmigration and the composition of the foreign born relative to native born population – which can go either way.[21] Second, since schooling is long lasting, measurement errors in historical data – including changes in definitions of levels of schooling – will have relatively persistent impacts.

The second method, used by Barro and Lee (1993, and in various vintages), is to use census or labor force survey based estimates of the highest levels of schooling completed (e.g., none, some primary, primary, secondary) of the labor force aged population to estimate the years of schooling. Since the survey based estimates are sporadic and coverage is incomplete they use data on enrollment rates to fill in the empty cells in the panel create a complete set of estimates with years of schooling at five year intervals. Barro and Lee have produced updated estimates with disaggregation by sex and alternative definitions of the labor force aged population (15–64 versus 24–64).

In the end, the BL and NSD estimates are quite highly correlated in levels at any point in time (around 0.9)[22] but – as Kruger and Lindahl (2001) and others have pointed out

[21] This is the likely explanation of extraordinarily high estimates of schooling in countries like Jamaica [Pritchett (2001)] and Ireland [De la Fuente and Domenech (2000)]. As Young (1998) details, in Hong Kong there was educated in-migration so that schooling capital growth was much more *rapid* than enrollment rates would suggest.

[22] An anecdote reveals why this high cross-national correlation is not an impressive indicator of data quality. When I was working on this data (in the early 1990s) I asked the person in the office next to me, Peter Lanjouw, a development economist with no particular expertise in education, to estimate the average years of schooling for each of the countries in the BL and NSD data, using only the knowledge of the minimum, maximum and mean of the data across countries. He did so in about 15 minutes and his quick guesses had a cross-national correlation of about 0.9 with both the BL and NSD estimates.

Table 9
The (rank) correlations of two alternative measures of years of schooling of the population aged 15–64: perpetual inventory (King–Dubey) and Stocks with imputation (Barro–Lee) decline with the horizon uniformly with the length of the period

	Rank correlation	Number observations/ Number of countries
Level in 1960	0.89	69
Level in 1985	0.93	72
Natural log change 1960–1985	0.69	69
Absolute change 1960–1985	0.53	69
Absolute change decades (1960s, 1970s)	0.35	147/74
Absolute change five year periods	0.27	372/76

Source: Calculations with Dubey–King and Barro–Lee data.

– the noise to total signal ratio rises the shorter the time horizon. This is born out comparing the two data sets – the correlation falls from 0.89 (1960) or 0.93 (1985) in levels to 0.68 for 25 year changes to only 0.27 for five year changes (Table 9). Comparison of the Barro–Lee estimates with estimates of years of schooling from the Demographic and Health Surveys (DHS) – a set of nationally representative, household surveys that use essentially the same questionnaire in a number of countries – produce exactly the same pattern – high correlations in levels, low correlations in changes.[23]

The principal problem with the BL method is the comparability over time of match between the educational categories in the survey data. As De la Fuente and Domenech (2000) have documented for the OECD countries the BL estimates contain sharp breaks (implausibly large increases and decreases) that almost certainly were reporting problems in the classification of various types of schooling. For instance, in the annualized growth rates in the BL data 15.9 percent of the episodes report *negative* growth rates – that is, falling attainment. De la Fuente and Domenech (2000) propose a method of smoothing the data and produce alternative estimates of the years of schooling for the OECD which produce much larger estimates of the impact of schooling – consistent with substantially larger measurement error in the BL data.[24] But, as I will show below,

[23] There are 25 countries that have B–L data and which have more than one DHS. For these countries the (rank) correlation of the levels across countries is above 0.9 while comparing the changes in average education have a correlation of only 0.18 over the available horizons which are, determined by the timing of the DHS surveys, of between 5 and 10 years.

[24] In De la Fuente and Domenech (2000, Table 6) regression of levels on levels with period and country dummies in OECD countries along the coefficient on "schooling capital" rises from 0.088 with NSD to 0.12 with BL with 0.279 with their estimates. This suggests an extraordinarily large degree of measurement error. What is even more puzzling is that with a specification in first differences with a catch up effect with country dummies and period dummies (Table 9) the coefficient on schooling capital for NSD is −0.148, for BL is −0.057 and for DD 0.271. Since pure measurement error typically produces attenuation bias something a little more complicated needs to be going on to switch from negative to positive.

except at short (five year or less) horizons, where the issue is intractable, pure measurement error of the years of schooling of the labor force is not the most serious problem as nearly all of the latest studies use empirical techniques which account for measurement error – and still find widely disparate results.

Beyond the issue of pure measurement error, there are several points about the data on years of schooling. First, both data sets estimate the education of the labor force aged population – not the labor force – as there is no attempt to correct for labor force participation rates which do differ widely across countries and across countries by gender. Second, while the estimates can be disaggregated by *level* of schooling (primary vs. secondary vs. tertiary) they cannot be disaggregated by type (e.g., public vs. private, vocational vs. general secondary, field of study). Third, there is no attempt to correct for school quality: a year of schooling is a year of schooling, a problem we return to below, several times.

3.2.2. Estimated wage increments

Some summary of the micro-Mincer coefficients on years of schooling in a wage/earnings regression is needed, for two reasons. First, if the purpose is to compare micro and macro there needs to be some sense of the central tendency of the micro. Second, the wage increment to schooling, r, is a necessary component of estimating schooling capital from schooling. Other chapters of this Handbook address the many conceptual and econometric problems with using a single such point estimate as a representation of the causal effect of the increase in any year of schooling by the marginal worker. This chapter holds all of these problems to one side and say "If we *suppose* the typical micro-Mincer coefficient represents a causal impact on labor productivity of a (roughly) uniform amount – is that grossly inconsistent with the cross-national data?"

Nearly all the available studies rely primarily on the collection of estimates of wage regressions updated most recently in Psacharopoulos and Patrinos (2002).[25] The central tendency of the coefficient on schooling in a log wage/earnings regression is between 7 percent (the average for the OECD countries) and 10 percent (the average for the non-OECD countries) (Table 10). The median in the whole sample is 8.5 percent and the standard deviation is 3.4 percentage points.

Figure 6 shows a simple bivariate scatter plot of the estimates and of the BL average years of schooling in the country and year[26] of the data (e.g., regressions on data from 1981 from Indonesia (IDN81) produce an estimate of 17 percent and just over four years of schooling while the estimate in 1995 for the USA (USA95) is 10 percent and

[25] Previous vintages were published in 1973, 1985, and 1994, see Psacharopoulos and Patrinos (2002) references.

[26] Using simple linear interpolation between the five year estimates of BL to match the user exactly.

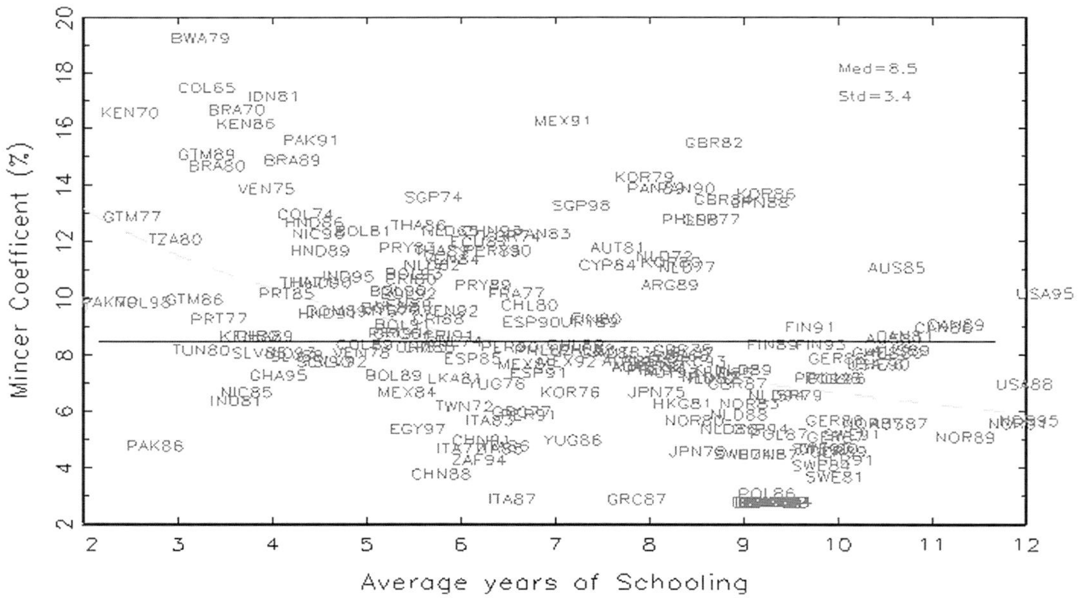

Figure 6. Estimates of the Mincer coefficient and years of schooling (observations identified with country code and year of study).

Table 10
Summary statistics of estimated coefficient on schooling in Mincer regressions

Region		1980s	1990s
OECD	Mean	7.3	6.9
	Min	2.6	4.1
	Max	13.2	10.0
	N	17	12
Non-OECD	Mean	10.9	9.4
	Min	3.6	4.1
	Max	28.8	15.4
	N	32	21

Source: Psacharapolous and Patrinos (2002), Tables A2 and A4.

12 years of schooling). Reported Mincer coefficients tend to be lower in countries with higher levels of schooling.[27]

While, at least in the development literature and practice, it has become the conventional wisdom that returns are higher for primary than secondary schooling there are two reasons why adjusting for this issue is not particularly central. First, there is a difference between the estimated wage increment or Mincer coefficient and the estimated rate of return to schooling, which takes into account costs, including direct costs and opportunity costs. For growth accounting purposes it is plausible that the conceptually right approach is the current wage increment, not the current estimate of the return, which is an *ex ante* concept. If one is asking "how much higher is output today because schooling of the labor force is higher by one year" the opportunity cost for current or past students is not directly relevant. Second, the average *wage increments* in Psacharopoulos (1994) data are nearly equal for primary and secondary schooling. The higher rates of *returns* for primary schooling emerge because his method assumes (with no particular evidence) *zero* opportunity cost for all years of primary schooling but assumes the opportunity cost of secondary schooling includes a primary schooling premia inclusive wage foregone [Bennell (1996)].

3.2.3. *Specification of schooling capital from years of schooling and returns*

With estimates of S and of r one can estimate the schooling capital of the labor force. Bils and Klenow work with the most general formulation. In their work output is a function of $H(t)$ which are units of effective labor and the current stock

[27] The regression of estimates of returns on the Barro–Lee average years of schooling of the population aged 15–64 for a sample that included multiple observations for countries gives a coefficient on schooling of -0.66 with a standard error of 0.093, $\bar{R}^2 = 0.205$, $N = 192$.

of $H(t)$ is the result of integrating the quality adjusted labor force over all ages a, $H(t) = \int_a^T h(a,t)L(a,t)\,da$.

Where the quality adjustment for a person of age a with schooling s (and hence experience of $a - s$), is given by:

$$h(a,t) = h(a+n)^{\varphi} e^{f(s)+g(a-s)}. \tag{1}$$

The first term allows the quality of those aged a to depend on the quality of previous cohorts (those aged n years older than a) as "parents/teachers" human capital contributes to accumulation of schooling capital. They also posit a general function, $f(s)$, to map from schooling to quality and they allow for experience effects.

If $f(s) = rs$ and $g(a-s) = \gamma_1(a-s) + \gamma_2(a-s)^2$ and $\varphi = 0$ then this is the exact aggregate equivalent of the standard Mincer wage equation assuming returns are constant across countries. If one also ignores the age terms then schooling capital per worker is:

$$\text{SK} = e^{rs} \tag{2}$$

and $f'(s) = r$. This is the functional form that has been used (explicitly or implicitly) in much of the growth regression and growth accounting [Hall and Jones (1999), Wössmann (2002)].

In their own empirical work Bils and Klenow (2000) allow for a more general function form for $f(s)$ which allows the returns to schooling to decline with additional schooling: $f(s) = \frac{\theta}{1-\psi} s^{1-\psi}$ and hence $f'(s) = \theta/s^{\psi}$ with θ chosen so that the mean of θ/s^{ψ} is equal to the mean Mincerian return across countries. Their regression based estimate of ψ is 0.58 (consistent with Figure 6 and the regression in footnote 23 above as ψ is the negative of the regression coefficient) while $\psi = 0$ implies the simple functional form above.

As it turns out, understanding the apparently widely varying empirical results hinges critically on this choice of specification, so it is worth developing the intuition. There is almost no correlation between the *absolute* change in the years of schooling and the initial level of schooling in 1960 (Figure 7). But this implies that the *percentage change* in schooling was enormously higher for countries that began with a low than with a high level of schooling in 1960 – so while schooling expanded only 2 years in Brazil 1960 to 1999 (from 2.8 to 4.8) and 3.5 years in the USA (from 8.5 to 12.0) this was a 71 percent increase in Brazil versus a 41 percent increase in the USA. Initial enrollment rates were strongly *negatively* correlated with the subsequent percentage growth of schooling.[28]

[28] Since the *change* in the stock is related to the *difference* in schooling of labor force entrants versus those existing the labor force it is obvious that, if enrollments rates have changed differentially across countries in the recent past then past enrollment rates will not be well correlated with changes in stocks. In the data, for instance, the initial secondary enrollment rate is *negatively* correlated with the subsequent (percentage) growth of schooling. Comparing Korea and Great Britain provides a simple illustration. Korea's secondary enrollment rate in 1960 was 27 percent while Great Britain's was 66 percent. But the level of schooling of

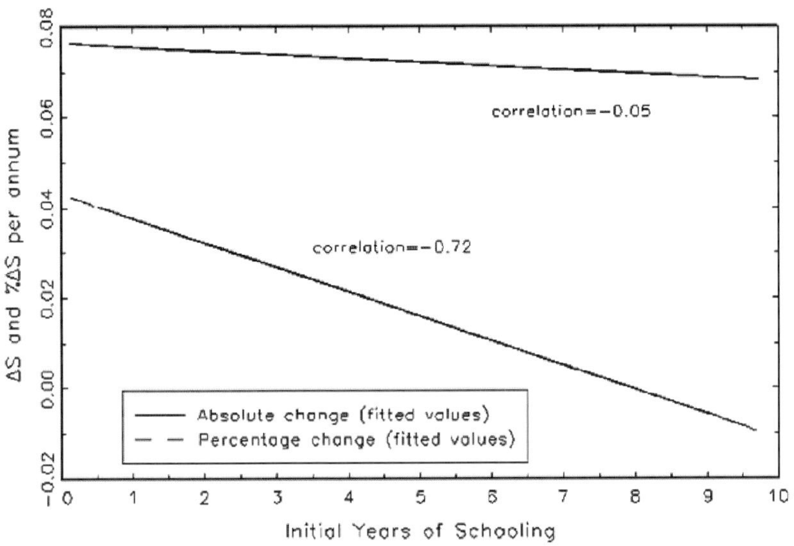

Figure 7. The absolute change in S has a weak correlation with initial S while the percentage change has a negative correlation.

In the BK formula the effect of assuming a more sharply declining return w.r.t. schooling is to raise the contribution of a year of schooling to the growth in schooling capital the lower the initial level of schooling. Over the ranges of values for ψ that BK use the correlation with the level of schooling implied by initial enrollments switches from strongly negative at $\psi = 0.58$ to positive at $\psi = 0$. Figure 8 shows the fitted values of the regression of SK on initial S for three values of ψ.

Changes in assumptions about the contribution of past cohorts have two effects: one is to raise the *average* growth in schooling capital and the second is, since this means that countries with higher past enrollments have higher contributions of a year of current schooling to schooling capital, moving from zero to higher values of φ changes the correlation of schooling capital growth with initial schooling (enrollments) from negative to positive for a given φ (in Figure 9 $\psi = 0.28$).

Estimates of the per annum growth of schooling capital per worker using data on schooling and various values of the parameters do not just switch the sign of the cross-national correlation of SK/W growth with initial schooling or enrollments but they are

Great Britain's labor force in 1960 was 7.7 years while the level of Korea's was 3.2 years. Subsequently, Great Britain's enrollment rate increased to 83 percent by 1975 and then remained relatively constant, while Korea's enrollment rate also increased from 27 to 87 percent by 1983. Given these differences in initial stocks and the large changes in enrollment rates, Korea's average years of schooling expanded massively from 3.2 to 7.8 by 1985 while Great Britain's expanded only modestly from 7.7 to 8.6, even though Great Britain enrollment rate was higher than Korea's for most of the period.

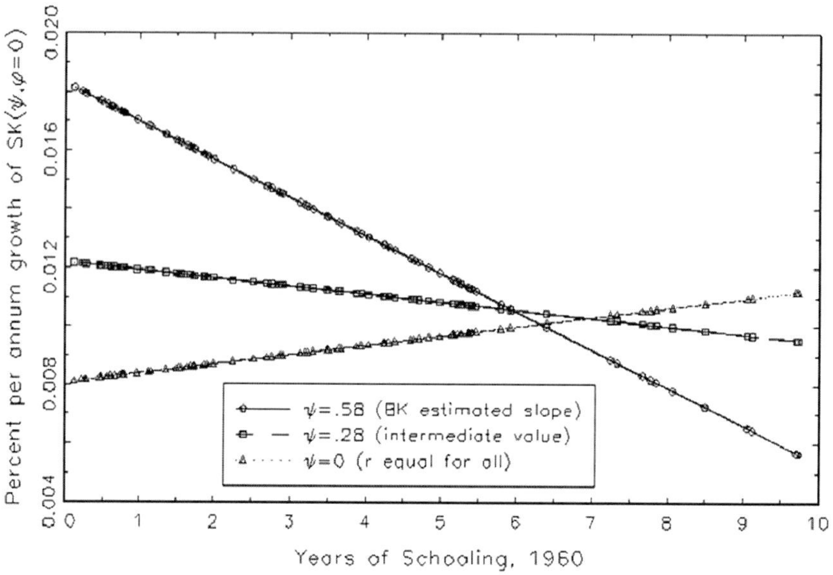

Figure 8. OLS predicted values of $g_{SK}(\psi, \varphi)$ using lagged S for various level of ψ. (Relationship of returns and level of S.)

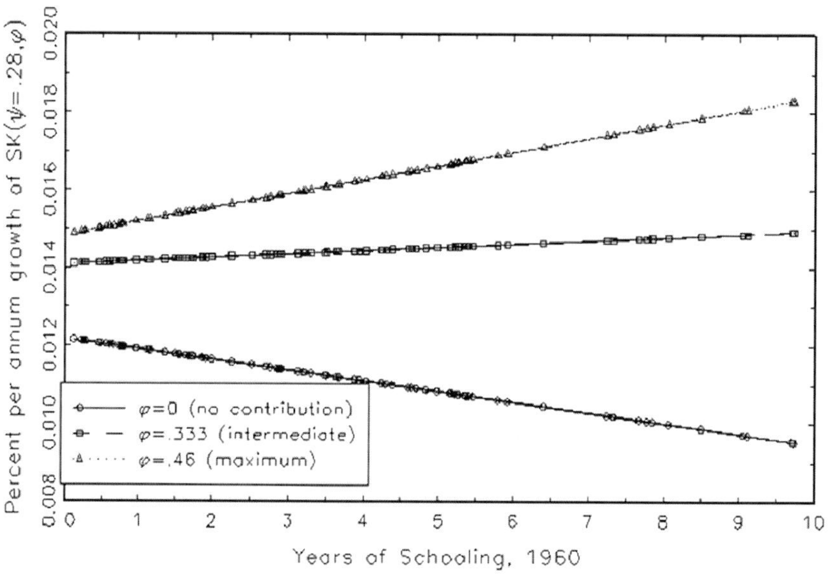

Figure 9. Higher φ (past education contributes more to current SK) raises growth of SK and the correlation of SK with S.

Table 11
(Rank) correlations of various measures of the growth of schooling capital with initial enrollments and changes in schooling and percentage changes in schooling

Bils and Klenow (2000) versions of the growth of schooling capital	Changes in schooling of the labor force			Growth of schooling capital per worker		
	Initial enrollments (schooling)	Absolute change	Percentage change	$(\psi = 0.58, \varphi = 0)$	$(\psi = 0.28, \varphi = 1/3)$	$(\psi = 0, \varphi = 0)$
$(\psi = 0.58, \phi = 0)$	−0.66	0.12	0.66	1	0.423	0.198
$(\psi = 0.28, \phi = 1/3)$	0.33	0.46	0.08	0.423	1	0.947
$(\psi = 0, \phi = 0)$	0.53	0.43	−0.09	0.198	0.947	1

Source: Author's calculations with B–K data.

not positively correlated amongst *themselves* or with other measures of the growth of schooling (Table 11). So $g_{SK}(\psi = -0.58, \varphi = 0)$ is strongly *positively* correlated with the percentage change in schooling ($\rho = 0.66$) and has a weak correlation with the absolute change in years of schooling ($\rho = 0.12$) while $g_{SK}(\psi = 0, \varphi = 0)$ is (weakly) *negatively* correlated with the percentage change ($\rho = -0.09$) and strongly *positively* correlated with the absolute change ($\rho = 0.43$). And $g_{SK}(\psi = -0.58, \varphi = 0)$ is only very weakly correlated with $g_{SK}(\psi = 0, \varphi = 0)$ ($\rho = 0.2$) and is negatively correlated with measures with $\varphi > 0$ and $\psi = 0$. Even if two researchers use the exact same data on schooling of the labor force aged population, and use the exact same data set on returns but just make different assumptions about the functional form of the mapping from schooling to schooling capital they will produce entirely different estimates of the associations of other variables with schooling capital (Table 10). Measures of the growth schooling capital are not robust to assumptions about the values of parameters within a general functional form. Obviously, I return to this issue below.

Wössmann (2002) has an excellent summary of the measurement issues as they apply to growth accounting exercises and explores the consequences of using different combinations or specifications in constructing schooling capital. While it might seem attractive to use the ith country's own estimates of wage increments r in constructing schooling capital there are (at least) two reasons to be dubious. First, in the cross-national collection of studies comparability is often quite limited and the studies vary widely in quality. Second, the estimates are often based on samples of formal sector wage earners only which are, in poorer countries, often a tiny fraction of the labor force and it is at least conceivable that markets are segmented and that returns outside the formal wage sector are much lower. Reported estimates often vary widely across countries in ways it is difficult to believe reflect principally true differences in returns. Wössmann's estimates using the country specific estimates of returns attribute much *less* of output variation to schooling capital because for the countries with high estimated returns it attributes enormously large increases in output to schooling capital (Table 12).

Table 12
Results of the covariance attribution to various factors, using different schooling capital and methods

Method of constructing schooling capital	Fraction to schooling capital	$(k/y)^{\alpha/(1-\alpha)}$	A	
Hall and Jones (replicated)	0.21	0.19	0.60	All
Accounting for differential returns across levels	0.33	0.19	0.48	All
Country specific estimates	0.18	0.19	0.63	All
Adjusted for schooling quality	0.45	0.19	0.36	All

Source: Wössmann (2002), Table 2.2a.

In contrast, using the same return to a year of schooling across countries but correcting for school quality leads to much larger attribution to schooling. He also allows the returns to vary across level of schooling, and finds that using a piece wise linear specification of $\phi(s)$ that allows r to vary between primary and secondary schooling provides a higher share of output attributed to schooling.

The aggregation by age assumes perfect substitutability between workers of different ages but similar education and attributes the average return to new labor market entrants. There are many ways in which this assumption could go badly wrong [Kremer and Thomson (1998)], but to my knowledge no one has worked out the implications for estimates of aggregate schooling capital.

3.3. *Are macro-Mincer and micro-Mincer consistent*

As the determinants of economic growth has always been a pressing issue – especially for development economists – there is a long history of estimates of the impact of schooling on output. But only fairly recently has the question been posed to ask whether the cross-national evidence suggests that output increase associated by an increase in the years of schooling of the labor force is equal, larger, or smaller than what would have been expected from the microeconomic estimates of the returns to schooling.[29] To answer this question the definition of schooling capital and specification of the regression equation have to be consistent with a microeconomic interpretation. There have been

[29] Many of these studies did not find statistically significant results – or the results were mixed across regions. Lau, Jamison and Louat (1991) estimate the effects of education by level of schooling (primary versus secondary) and allow different coefficients in five regions. They find that primary education has an estimated *negative* effect in Africa and Middle East North Africa, insignificant effects in South Asia and Latin America, and positive and significant effects only in East Asia. Jovanovich, Lach and Lavy (1992) use annual data on a different set of physical capital stocks and NSD's education data and find negative coefficients on education in a non-OECD sample. Behrman (1987) and Dasgupta and Weale (1992) find that changes in adult literacy are not significantly correlated with changes in output.

Table 13
Regression of the level of industrial sector wages on economy-wide capital stocks and average schooling of the labor force

Regression	$\ln(K/W)$	Average schooling	N	$\bar{R}^2$
All years	0.57 (0.081)	0.035 (0.033)	165	0.504
All years, year dummies	0.60 (0.075)	0.009 (0.031)	165	0.588
Just 1985–1990	0.61 (0.15)	0.046 (0.066)	43	0.595
Just 1990–1994	0.63 (0.172)	0.084 (0.074)	41	0.610

Source: Data on wages from Rama and Arcetona (2002), physical capital/CUDIE per worker from Easterly and Levine (2001). Standard errors are in parenthesis.

two approaches – a specification in which the coefficient on schooling has (roughly) the interpretation as the macro-Mincer coefficient and another is the "augmented Solow" specification in which the coefficient on an estimate of *schooling capital* has (roughly) the interpretation as the schooling capital share in output.

3.3.1. *Macro-Mincer*

Nearly all of the literature relies exclusively on GDP data, but the simplest possible approach would be to regress average wages on average years of schooling. Rama and Arcetona (2002) have assembled a collection of estimates of wages of industrial workers – measured as labor costs per worker per year and hence includes all renumeration and contributions to social security. The data has limited coverage and the usual problems of comparability but it serves as a useful introduction as it has actual data on wages as opposed to inferring wages from output data. Table 13 reports the regressions of the aggregate analogue of the micro-Mincer regression: natural log wages on an estimate of capital per worker and the Barro–Lee data on years of schooling.[30]

$$\ln\left(w_{i,t}^{\text{industry}}\right) = \alpha + \gamma \ln(K/W_{i,t}) + r S_{i,t}. \tag{3}$$

These simple regressions raise all the issues that will recur with the regressions using GDP and growth rates – the impact of capital is large and precisely estimated while the coefficient on schooling is small and imprecisely estimated.

The simplest possible approach using GDP data is to just assume factor payments exhaust total product so that: $Y = rK + wL$. If in addition one assumes the aggregate

[30] Since the wage data is given for some point in a five year period (e.g., from 1990 to 1994) we use the schooling at the beginning of that period.

wage of a labor force with S years of schooling is[31]

$$w(S) = w(0)e^{rS}. \tag{4}$$

Then the expected impact on output of an increase of one year of schooling in the labor force is

$$\frac{dY/Y}{dS} = (\text{wage share}) \times r. \tag{5}$$

Alternatively, imagine the specification of the relation between aggregate output and schooling is

$$\frac{Y}{L} = A\left(\frac{K}{L}\right)^{\alpha} e^{\phi(S)}. \tag{6}$$

Then

$$\frac{\partial \ln(Y/L)}{\partial S} = \phi'(S), \tag{7}$$

and if the equation is linear, $\phi(S) = rS$, a regression of growth rates of output per worker on the absolute change in schooling should recover an estimate of r and, if it is assumed that all of the output effect is via wages, then the division of r divided by labor share in output recovers a macro-Mincer estimate of the impact of schooling on wages.

Krueger and Lindahl's (K–L) (2001) OLS estimate of this functional form – growth in output per person on the change in schooling per labor force aged population and other covariates – produces an estimated macro-Mincer return of 2.2 percent (Table 14). In that paper they place a great deal of emphasis on measurement error and their instrumental variables estimates do imply a macro-Mincer estimate of 11.6 percent, which is slightly higher than the average of the micro-Mincer estimates. However what is striking about their IV estimate are the enormous standard errors – even a one standard error bound of the macro-Mincer estimate runs from *negative* 16 to *positive* 40 percent – both equally implausible. Hence while this article is sometimes interpreted as demonstrating that the source of low macro-Mincer estimates is measurement error – it does not produce any estimates from a plausible specification that are statistically different from zero.

K–L also illustrate the important role of controlling for the growth of physical capital in estimating the impact of schooling capital across countries. Since in nearly any production function higher capital per worker raises the marginal product of labor and labor is not fully mobile across countries it seems difficult to believe a cross-national wage determination equation should not control in some way for the different physical capital stocks across countries.[32] But in growth regressions the data want to put a

[31] While this looks exactly like the Mincer specification this ignores issues of aggregation as the log of the average wage is not the average of log wages.

[32] The simple fact that the wages of workers who migrate from low wage to high wage countries increase enormously – even though none of their human capital has changed – suggest that capital stocks play some substantial role.

Table 14
Krueger–Lindahl estimates of schooling returns

Growth variable	Annualized change in log GDP per capita, 1965–1985			
Coefficient on ΔS (std. err.)	0.013 (0.052)	0.069 (0.167)	0.083 (0.043)	0.182 (0.051)
Implied rate of return (r) (coefficient divided by labor share = 0.6)	2.2%	11.6%		
One standard error bound	((−6.5), 10.8%)	((−16.3), 39.3%)		
Coefficient on $\Delta K/W$	0.608	0.597	0.35* (constrained)	0 (excluded)
Number of countries	66 0.56	66 0.55	92 0.12[a]	97 0.281
Other included covariates	Growth K/W, initial log K/W, initial schooling		Initial schooling, initial K/W	Initial schooling, initial Y
Estimation technique (instruments)	OLS	IV (Kyricacou estimates as instrument)	OLS (constrained)	

Source: Table 5 of Krueger and Lindahl (2001), columns 4, 5, 6.
[a]The R2 from the equivalent sample size regression (column 3 of Table 5) is 0.58.

very high weight on the growth of K/W – often much higher than the capital share observed in the national accounts – which is plausibly the result of the endogeneity of capital accumulation. Since K/W and human capital growth are correlated it is obvious that lowering the K/W coefficient will raise the human capital coefficient. Krueger and Lindahl (2001) demonstrate this (fully or partially) omitted variable bias in two ways – by constraining the K/W coefficient to 0.35 and by excluding it altogether – both of which naturally raise the estimate of schooling substantially. Notice the data strongly resent this imposed constraint as the regression R2 falls from 0.56 to 0.12.

Bloom, Canning and Sevilla (2002) use a similar specification of the production function but improve on K–L in a number of ways. First, they start from a functional form for aggregate output, which includes experience:

$$Y = AK^{\alpha}L^{\beta}\mathrm{e}^{\phi S+\gamma_1(\text{experience})+\gamma_2(\text{experience})^2}. \tag{8}$$

Second, they deal with one of the problems of aggregation (assumed away above) show that only if one ignores all distributional effects can ϕ/β be interpreted as the return to education. Third, they use instruments for the growth of all inputs – including physical capital – however, in order to have instruments they must use ten-year periods, which as we have seen above will limit the ability to estimate schooling impacts precisely. Interestingly if one allows for long-run TFP to vary (column II of Table 15) the estimates

Table 15
Allowing for different steady state TFP levels reduces the estimated return to schooling

	Annual growth in GDP, ten year periods (1970–1980, 1980–1990)	
Growth in inputs:	Long-run TFP fixed	Long-run TFP varies with included variables (tropics and governance)
Capital (CUDIE)	0.424 (0.094)	0.479 (0.068)
Labor	0.633 (0.121)	0.589 (0.088)
Experience	0.208 (0.176)	−0.074 (0.034)
Technological catch-up	0.191 (0.041)	0.194 (0.042)
Percent of land in tropics		−0.329 (0.204)
Governance		0.104 (0.047)
Schooling	0.081 (0.048)	−0.026 (0.045)
Implied rate of return (r) (Schooling coefficient/labor coefficient)	12.8%	−4.4%
One standard deviation range	(6.5, 19.1%)	((−12.3), 3.5%)
p-level of Chi-Square test that the estimate of aggregate returns to schooling equals 9.1% (paper's average of the Mincer)	0.559	0.087
Number of countries/observations	104 countries 175 observations	104 countries 147 observations
Estimation technique (instruments)	Non-linear 2SLS (lagged levels as instruments)	

Source: Bloom, Canning and Sevilla (2002), Table 1, column 2 and Table 2, column 2.

of the returns to schooling are negative and the hypothesis the returns are equal to the micro returns can be rejected at the 10% level ($p = 0.087$).

Most researchers have avoided level on level regressions of output directly on physical and schooling capital, in part because one would expect the problems of reverse causation – high income leading to higher demand for schooling – becomes more severe the longer to the period. Heckman and Klenow (1997) examine specifically the question of whether the cross-national data provide support for externalities to schooling. In their cross-national results for 1960 and 1985 which do not control for physical capital but which do control for experience and life expectancy (they argue as a proxy for technological levels, but could be picking up many other features) they find Mincerian estimates of 10.6 percent in 1985 and 7.0 percent in 1960. When they control for

Table 16
Estimates of using levels on levels and first difference data with country and year fixed effects

Dependent variable	Other included variables	Fixed effects	Coefficient on schooling (std. err.)	Rate of return (one std. err.)
$\ln(y)$	–	Country: yes Year: no	0.226 (0.0099)	13.6% (12.6–14.6%)
$\ln(y)$	–	Country: yes Year: yes	0.102 (0.016)	6.1% (4.5–7.8%)
$(\ln(y) - 0.35\ln(k))/0.65$	–	Country: yes Year: yes	0.085 (0.02)	5.1% (3.1–7.1%)
$\ln(y)$	Life exp., age	Country: yes Year: yes	0.062 (0.025)	3.7% (1.1–6.3%)
$\ln(y)_t - \ln(y)_0$ (20 years)	$S_0, \ln(y)_0$	Country: No Year: yes	0.252 (0.041)	15.1% (11.0–19.3%)
$\ln(y)_t - \ln(y)_0$ (15 years)	$S_0, \ln(y)_0$	Country: No Year: Yes	0.148 (0.029)	8.9% (6.0–11.8%)
$\ln(y)_t - \ln(y)_0$ (10 years)	$S_0, \ln(y)_0$	Country: No Year: Yes	0.085 (0.020)	5.1% (3.1–7.1%)
$\ln(y)_t - \ln(y)_0$ (10 years)	$S_0, \ln(y)_0$	Country: Yes Year: Yes	0.058 (0.027)	3.5% (0.8–6.2%)
$\ln(y)_t - \ln(y)_0$ (5 years)	$S_0, \ln(y)_0$	Country: No Year: Yes	0.041 (0.014)	2.5% (1.1–3.8%)
$\ln(y)_t - \ln(y)_0$ (5 years)	$S_0, \ln(y)_0$	Country: Yes Year: Yes	0.013 (0.015)	0.8% (−0.7–2.3%)

Source: Topel (1999), Table 2 (cols. 1, 3, 5), Table 3 (col. 4), Table 4 (cols. 2, 5, 8, 11), Table 5 (cols. 1, 3).

physical capital they "find lower macro-Mincer coefficients on schooling.... But the reductions are modest – only a few percentage points" (p. 16). Therefore the inclusion of physical capital in explaining levels of output – not an unreasonable procedure – puts "macro-Mincer" coefficients at or below the cross-national average of the micro-Mincer estimates of 8 to 10 percent. They interpret their results as "providing no decisive support for or against externalities" (p. 16).

Topel (1999) runs a variety of macro-Mincer type regressions of output per worker on the schooling of the labor force (without any regression based controls for physical capital). Taken as a whole his results are broadly consistent with returns in the range of the micro-Mincer results (though on average are lower than 10 percent except in two cases). His results also illustrate several elements of the literature. First, the estimated return to schooling is lower if differences in physical capital are taken into account (row 3, 6.1% versus row 2, 5.1%) – even if the physical capital coefficient is imposed not estimated (Table 16). Second, shorter horizons of first differences (growth rates) give progressively smaller estimates of returns (15% (20 years) to 9% (15 years) to 5.1% (10 years) to 2.5% (5 years)) – as is consistent with either increased measurement error or differing output and schooling dynamics. Third, controlling for other dimensions of

Table 17
Long-period regressions allowing for flexible functional form and robust estimation from Temple (2001)

	Growth of output per worker		
Change in log capital per worker	0.462 (5.97)	0.483 (6.25)	0.585 (14.0)
$S_{1987}-S_{1960}$	0.062 (1.76)		
$\ln(S_{1987})-\ln(S_{1960})$		0.170	0.181 (1.83)
$1/S_{1987}-1/S_{1960}$		0.035	0.066 (1.40)
N	91	91	84
R2	0.71	0.71	0.85
Implied rates of return to wages – the increment to output per worker – $d\phi(S)/dS$ then divided by the wage share – by level of education			
2.7[a]	10.3%	9.56%	9.66%
4.3	10.3%	6.22%	6.42%
6.8	10.3%	4.02%	4.20%
Estimation technique	OLS	Least trimmed squares	RWLS[b]

Source: Temple (2001), Table 2, columns 9, 12, and 13. All regressions include regional dummies.
[a]These values are the 25th, 50th, and 75th percentiles of the years of schooling the Barro–Lee data for 1980.
[b]The RWLS estimates exclude Hong Kong, Haiti, Indonesia, Jordan, Mozambique, Zaire (now DRC), and Zimbabwe.

"human capital" – such as life expectancy – can reduce estimated schooling returns. Fourth, as seen below (in Table 19) using 5 to 10 year horizons *and* allowing country fixed effects causes the standard errors to widen.

Temple (2001) examines two important issues with the estimates like the above: the sensitivity of the estimates of aggregate returns to assumptions about functional form in the specification of schooling to schooling capital and the robustness of the estimates to outliers. He starts with a general production function of the form:

$$\frac{Y}{L} = A\left(\frac{K}{L}\right)^{\alpha} e^{\phi(S)}, \tag{9}$$

and allows a flexible specification $\phi(S) = \lambda_0+\lambda_1 \ln(S)+\lambda_2(1/S)$ that allows the impact to vary across years of schooling (Table 17). While his standard estimates are (reassuringly) quite close to the estimates above, with least trimmed squares (which reduces the weight on outliers) and RWLS (which deletes influential observations) Temple finds "the impact of schooling is close to micro estimates only a very low levels of average schooling (0–3 years) and is below 5% for higher levels" (p. 913).[33]

3.3.2. Augmented Solow and effective labor production function

Following the influential paper of Mankiw, Romer and Weil (1992) there have been a number of growth regressions that estimate an augmented Solow regression. While this paper is influential and has many attractive features, its use of "initial secondary enrollment stocks" as a proxy for human capital is most unfortunate as this has been widely replicated in spite of the fact that it is not a good proxy for either flows or stocks and limiting attention to secondary schooling has no particular empirical[34] or theoretical[35] justification. But the approach remains a standard in the growth literature, so if the aggregate output assumed to be:

$$Y = AK^{\alpha_k} H^{\alpha_h} L^{\alpha_l}, \tag{10}$$

then increment to output is equal to the share of returns to schooling in output:

$$\frac{dy/Y}{dH/H} = \alpha_h. \tag{11}$$

There are two simple ways to estimate this share – one which estimates the "human capital" share of the wage bill while the other estimates the "schooling capital" share directly. As MRW point out, if one assumes the minimum wage represents the "zero human capital" wage then the inverse of ratio of the average wage at average schooling of S to the minimum wage represents an estimate of the "human capital" share of the wage bill. Using a recent database on the ratio of industrial wages to the government mandated minimum wage (which admittedly may be higher or lower than a completely market driven minimum wage) in around sixty countries in the period 1990–1994 sug-

[33] He also explores a CES like specification and finds that while the points estimates suggest that educated (secondary school) labor is 1.52 (implying educated labor is 2.52 time more productive than uneducated labor) the 95 percent confidence interval extends from −0.45 to 3.49.

[34] The Mincer evidence suggests that primary and secondary schooling have very similar wage increments, especially in developing country settings. As Hall and Jones (1999) have pointed out, Mankiw, Romer and Weil (1992) use of secondary enrollments alone to proxy stocks implies human capital varies by a factor of 1200 in their sample. Since GDP per person (at PPP) varies by a factor of 65 (USA at P$34870 versus Tanzania at P$540) and average years of schooling vary by a factor of 14 (USA at 12 years versus Guinea-Bissau at 0.84) that schooling capital would vary by two orders of magnitude more than schooling and an order of magnitude more that output seems implausible (at best).

[35] In fact, nearly all arguments about an externality to schooling focus on either primary schooling – which, it is argued, creates network externalities by creating mass literacy – or on tertiary schooling which, it is argued, augments technical progress through invention and innovation.

Table 18

Estimates of human capital share of wage bill using the ration of minimum to average wage

Country	Average wages in industry (US $)	Minimum wage (US $)	Estimate of human capital share of wage bill $1 - w_{\min}/w_{\text{average}}$
OECD	23,608	9,871	0.57
Non-OECD	4,319	1,195	0.66
All	10,320	3,894	0.63

Based on data base on wages and minimum wages of Rama and Arcetona (2002).

gests a share of schooling capital in the wage bill of about 2/3, surprisingly similar in OECD[36] and non-OECD countries (Table 18).[37]

Alternatively, the share of the wage bill due to educational attainment by assuming a wage premium for each attainment category and applying Equation (12)

$$\text{Schooling capital share of wage bill} = \frac{\sum_{A=0}^{K}(w_A - w_0)\gamma_A}{wL}, \tag{12}$$

where, for each of the seven educational attainment categories, $w_i = w(0)e^{r_A S(A)}$, r_A is the return in that category, $S(A)$ is the assumed years of schooling and the γ_A are the shares of the labor force in each educational attainment category. These estimates suggest that, on average across all countries the schooling capital share of the wage bill is between one third and one half. Moreover, the schooling capital share under these assumptions rises with the level of schooling – but to some degree that is an artifact as the wage increment is assumed constant across levels of schooling.

The combination of the estimates of the human or schooling capital share of the wage bill and the wage share of output allow us to estimate the expected share of schooling capital in output. This is at most 46 percent (wage bill = 0.7, schooling capital share = 0.66) or at a minimum 0.20 (wage bill = 0.6, schooling share = 1/3) assumption of a schooling capital share in output of roughly 1/3 is a plausible value.

A number of papers, following Mankiw, Romer and Weil (1992) have used panel data to allow for country specific level and growth of "A" in the augmented Solow production function. In these models the estimates of the physical and schooling capital shares are

[36] Since these are reports of the government mandated minimum wages, a binding minimum wage above the market clearing level would make the share of human capital smaller as the implicit tax/subsidy across wage categories would compress wage differentials.

[37] Although the range is much narrower in the OECD – between 0.74 (USA) and 0.39 (Ireland) while in the non-OECD it varies from 20% to 87%.

Table 19
Estimates of the schooling capital share of output derived from educational attainment and estimates of the return to schooling, by region

	Wage premia by educational attainment under assumption set		Share of work force by educational attainment, 1985 (percent except where noted)				
	A	B	Developing countries	Sub-Saharan Africa	Latin American and Caribbean	South Asia	OECD
No schooling	1.00	1.00	49.7	48.1	22.4	69.0	3.3
Some primary	1.40	1.56	21.3	33.2	43.4	8.9	19.4
Primary complete	1.97	2.44	10.1	8.5	13.2	4.8	18.3
Some secondary	2.77	3.42	8.7	7.7	8.4	8.8	20.7
Secondary	3.90	4.81	5.9	1.6	5.5	5.3	20.1
Some tertiary	5.47	6.06	1.4	0.2	2.5	0.9	7.7
Tertiary	7.69	7.63	3.0	0.8	4.6	2.3	10.5
Average years of schooling			3.56	2.67	4.47	2.81	8.88
Calculated percentage share of wage bill due to schooling capital across regions under each assumption (percent)							
Assumption set A (wage increment is constant at 10 percent)			36	26	43	30	62
Assumption set B (wage increments are: primary 16 percent, secondary 12 percent, tertiary 8 percent)			49	38	56	42	73

Source: Pritchett (2001), Table 1. Based on educational attainment by region from Barro and Lee (1993).

a non-linear function of the parameters of the growth regression as the growth rates are transitional dynamics to a steady state. Short period panel regression results all find either a negative coefficient or a human capital estimate very much smaller than the expected schooling capital share (Table 20). Islam (1995), who uses OLS with fixed effects, and Casselli, Esquivel and Lefort (CEL) (1996), who use GMM, both report negative estimates and are able to statistically reject that the schooling capital coefficient is as large as any plausible human capital share (as they are nearly able to reject zero from below).[38] Bond, Hoeffler and Temple (2001) show that the *large* negative results

[38] Bond, Hoeffler and Temple (2001) show that essentially the difference between their results and Casselli, Esquivel and Lefort (1996) is the use of system GMM (which uses lagged levels as instruments as well as first differences as instruments for levels) versus the "first difference GMM" used by Casselli, Esquivel and Lefort (1996).

Table 20
Augmented Solow estimates using panel data

Study	Islam (1995)	Casselli, Esquivel and Lefort (1996)	Bond, Hoeffler and Temple (2001)	Dowrick and Rogers (2001)
Growth variable	Growth GDP per person (SH)	Growth GDP per capita	Same data as CEL	GDP per worker
Implied estimate of SK share in output	−0.199 (0.11)	−0.259 (0.124)	−0.018	0.01
Schooling source	Barro and Lee (1993)	Secondary enrollment rate	Same as CEL	Barro–Lee
Sk definition	ln(years)	ln(enrollment rate)	ln(enrollment rate)	Growth of secondary years
Period(s)	1960–1985, five year	1960–1985	1960–1985	1970–1990
Number of countries/observations	Non-oil, 79 countries			51 countries, 201 observations
Estimation technique (instruments)	LSDV	GMM (first difference)	System GMM	GMM

of appear to be due to estimation technique as the difference between first difference GMM and system GMM are large – but they also find a negative estimate of schooling. Dowrick and Rogers (2001) use different data and periods and find a non-negative, but very small term for schooling. The failure of the high frequency transitional dynamics to precisely estimate the output impact schooling is not surprising given the basic facts about the differing short to medium run volatilities in output growth versus schooling growth outlined in Section 2.[39]

While the cross sectional data has the problem it cannot allow for country fixed effects it does do not have the problem of the widely different short to medium run dynamics of output versus schooling. One of the earliest cross sectional regression estimates were Benhabib and Spiegel (1994) and Spiegel (1994) report growth regressions in which the coefficient on the growth of schooling years was small and insignificant while the lagged level of schooling was significant. A clearer application of the augmented Solow approach is Knowles and Owen (1997) who specify a reduced form equation that allow

[39] This is *not* a simple issue of the attenuation bias due to measurement error: the problem that over frequencies of five years or less the growth of schooling of the labor force and the growth of output per person (worker) do not covary strongly. Note that while using fixed effects will exacerbate measurement error problems for the standard reasons and Krueger and Lindahl (2001) have shown the measurement problems with short period panels these estimates cannot be explained as the result of *pure* measurement error issue as the GMM estimates should be consistent even in the presence of pure measurement error.

Table 21
Long-period cross sectional growth composition regressions estimating the schooling capital share

Study	Knowles and Owen (1997)[a]	Pritchett (2001)			
Estimated schooling capital share (one std. err.)	0.132 (−0.02, 0.284)	−0.104 (−0.15, −0.05)	−0.091 (−0.15, −0.03)	−0.12 (−0.20, −0.03)	−0.088 (−0.24, 0.06)
Estimated physical capital share (one std. err.)	0.498 (0.408, 0.588)	0.501 (0.47, 0.53)	0.458 (0.41, 0.50)	0.460 (0.51, 0.41)	0.527 (0.57, 0.48)
N	77	79	70	70	77
Schooling data		NSD	Barro–Lee		
Estimation technique (instruments)	OLS	OLS	OLS	IV (NSD)	IV (Neighbor)

[a]This equation also includes life expectancy as a proxy for "health capital" which has an estimated share of 0.411.

them to embed nearly all of the popular functional forms – both an augmented Solow (as in Equation (10)) or an "effective labor" approach which allow them to test the restrictions embedded in the usual specifications.[40] Their results suggest that neither the augmented Solow approach nor the "effective labor" specifications are rejected nor are they superior to each other – but the educational capital terms are not significant in any specification.[41]

In Pritchett (2001) I pay particular attention to measurement error. I used two different data sources for each of variables: growth rates of GDP per worker were from either the World Bank or PWT, K/W was constructed from WB or PWT investment rates and schooling data was either from NSD or BL (1994 version). Using each of these two data sets I estimated the simplest possible model of a standard augmented Solow growth decomposition by regressing the growth of output per worker on the growth of CUDIE per worker and growth of schooling capital per worker and the OLS results for both CUDIE and schooling are surprisingly similar: −0.10 with NSD and −0.09 with BL. Given the two (partially) independent

[40] While nearly all of the literature uses a Cobb–Douglas functional form, Duffy and Papageorgiou (2000) test those restrictions by estimating a more flexible functional form with "human capital adjusted labor supply" as an input into a CES specification by adjusting labor as: $\mathrm{HL} = S^{\phi} L$. They report that they "tried estimating ϕ in our non-linear production function, but the estimates were either implausibly negative or the iteration failed to converge" (p. 95). They report they also tried the alternative specification $\mathrm{HL} = \mathrm{e}^{\Phi(S)} L$ with $\Phi(S)$ piecewise linear and using the standard rates of return evidence with no "qualitative change" in the results (p. 117).

[41] The Non-Linear OLS or IV estimates of the effective-labor growth model produce negative point estimates for the schooling term in the whole sample (Table 1 and Table 3).

measures of schooling I use the NSD schooling data as an instrument for the BL data (and vice versa) and the IV results are, as expected *more* negative. In addition I use the growth in schooling capital of a country's neighbor as an instrument for its own growth[42] and also find a negative estimate. Unlike in Krueger and Lindahl (2001) where using instruments blows up the standard error, even with the increased imprecision of instruments the estimates can reject most plausible growth accounting schooling capital shares – the upper limit of the two standard error confidence interval of the IV estimates (using NSD data as an instrument for BL data) is only 0.05.[43]

3.3.3. Parametrically encompassing the literature

The estimates of the growth rate of schooling capital constructed by Bils and Klenow (2000) can be used in a pure growth accounting regression to examine how the different assumptions in the construction of the estimates of schooling capital affect the estimates of the share of output the regressions attribute to schooling capital.[44] Based on the discussion above and using a bit of intuition it is reasonably easy to guess how the regressions will turn out. The formulations that attribute large changes in schooling capital to countries with low initial schooling (large (absolute value) ψ, low φ) will behave more like the specifications that use "percentage change"-like measures. For instance, an increase in a year of schooling would increase schooling capital by 10 percent at all levels of s if $f(s) = rs$ and $r = 0.10$ but if $\psi = 0.58$ then an additional year increases schooling capital by 32 percent if $s = 2$ but by less than ten percent when $s = 8$ – a three-fold difference.[45] Conversely, combinations of parameters that make contributions of an additional year of schooling high in high initial human capital (small (absolute value) ψ, high φ) will give much higher estimates. Using what is in some ways the most plausible estimate of schooling capital – the regression based estimate of the returns-schooling relationship ($\psi = -0.58$) and $\varphi = 0$[46] produces estimates of

[42] This is a generic technique for generating instruments to address measurement error in cross-national data. A neighbor's (e.g., Malawi and Tanzania, Nepal and India, Paraguay and Bolivia) growth of schooling is likely to be correlated as they share some common underlying economic or social determinants or directly influence each other through imitation. But, if measurement error is based on country sources (e.g., changing definitions, incompatible classifications) there is little reason to believe the measurement error is correlated across countries.

[43] I also illustrate that the problem is not "low power" by calculating TFP growth using an imputation of the output effect of schooling capital based on any plausible share and then regressing TFP growth on the growth of schooling capital the coefficient is large, negative, and statistically significant – which is just an arithmetic rearrangement of the hypothesis test that the growth decomposition regression coefficient is equal to its national accounting share.

[44] I am doing this even though Klenow did not do so as he was uncertain what such a regressions represented theoretically – especially if schooling contributes to output both directly and through changes in A.

[45] This is following Bils and Klenow (2000) who set $\theta = 0.32$ so as to equal the average r over the sample.

[46] There are three arguments for a very low contribution of past cohorts to current schooling capital. First, as Wössmann (2002) points out, it is not at all clear why, once one had accounted for the market based

the schooling capital share which are negative (and highly imprecise). Using $\psi = 0$ produces estimates of the schooling capital share that are far too large (=1.25) – and have troubling implications for growth accounting residuals with estimated shares as well. Similarly, if one varies over values of φ, even moderately large values of φ produce estimates which are "too large" and produce sharply negative estimates of the growth accounting residual. The only plausible estimates are those with intermediate values of the two parameters (although keep in mind the "intermediate" value of $\psi = -0.28$ is soundly rejected by the data) which produce a human capital share of growth of output per worker of 0.44 – but with a standard error of 0.44 as well.

These results go back to the basic logic of the cross-national data – since per worker growth rates were low (especially in many initially quite poor and low schooling countries) and growth in schooling was universal and rapid, the larger the growth of output net of physical capital ($= g_{SK} + g_A$) one attributes to schooling capital growth the lower one has to believe that growth would have been in the absence of schooling (g_A). To believe output impact of the growth of schooling capital as large as the regressions with $g_{SK}(\psi = -0.28, \varphi = 0.46)$ suggest one has to believe that output g_A is very low – in fact output would have *fallen* one percent per year. While this is conceivable – the logic of a positive growth residual of about one percent a year due to the obvious technical change that surrounds us (e.g., computers, telecommunications, power generation, biotechnology, etc.) does not seem implausible.

Figure 10(a), (b), (c), (d) shows the partial scatter plots that produce the regression results in Table 22 to show how the mappings from the change in average years of schooling into a specification of schooling capital parametrically encompasses the previous literature in the sense that with combinations of assumed values of the two parameters in a general specification of schooling capital from schooling one can reproduce nearly any finding in the literature.

3.4. Reduced form regressions

As an alternative to the production function specifications, which relate output to its underlying inputs, reduced form regressions estimate the pattern of partial correlations between growth and a variety of underlying factors – geographical, policy, political, institutional, historical, etc.[47] In reduced form regressions the lagged level of some type

return to schooling via r, an independent role for past education is appropriate as if this contributed to greater skills from a year of schooling this should be reflected in the r. Second, if φ represents school learning this is inconsistent with the actual evaluation of achievement tests in the OECD, which have been on average stagnant over the last 30 years – a period in which average attainment has increased considerably. Moreover, the highest student achievement levels are in countries with low. Third, if φ is very large it is difficult to square with the long-run growth evidence in Table 1 above as schooling capital has grown by several orders of magnitude.

[47] This is a factual characterization of this endeavor as what the statistical procedures applied do in fact accomplish is the estimation of partial correlations (or more generally, of functions, such as moments, of the

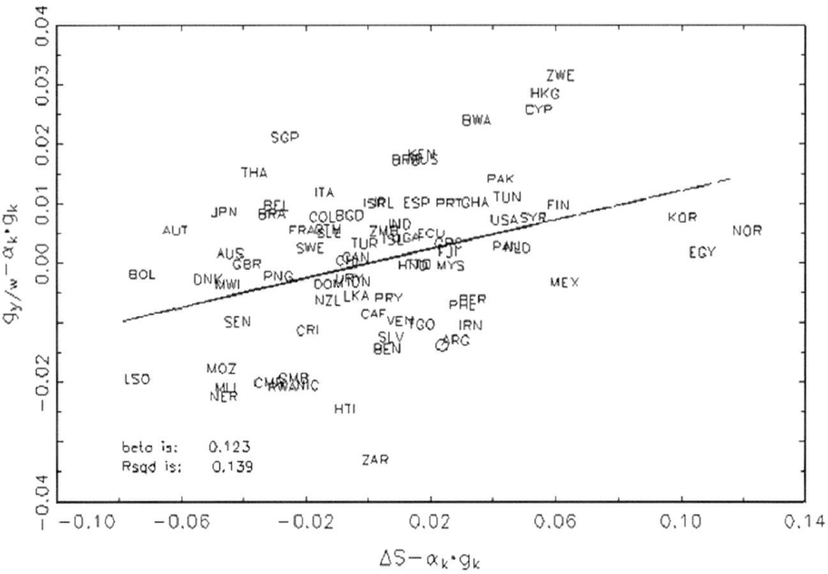

(a)

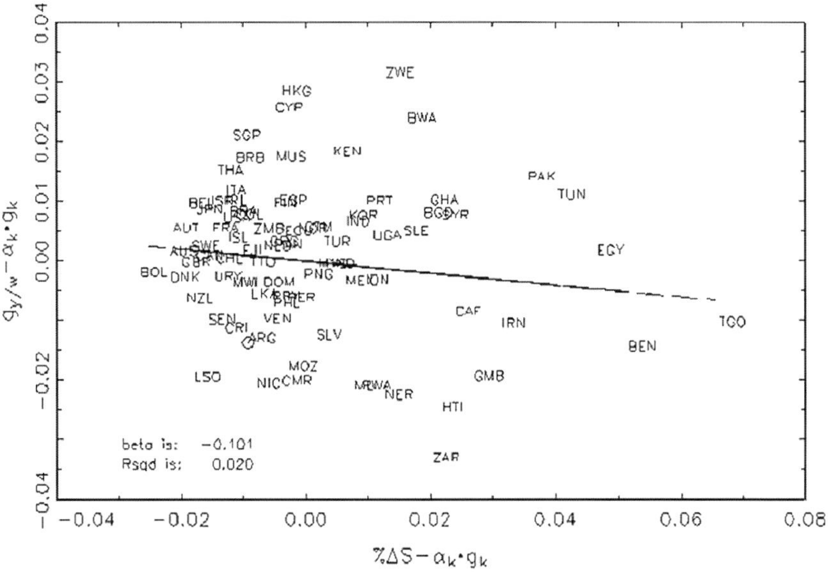

(b)

Figure 10. (a) Partial scatter plot, growth of output per worker on absolute change in schooling per year. (b) Partial scatter plot, growth in output per worker and percentage change in schooling per year. (c) Partial scatter plot, growth in output per worker and growth in SK($\psi = 0.58$, $\varphi = 0$). (d) Partial scatter plot, growth in output per worker and growth in SK($\psi = 0$, $\varphi = 0$).

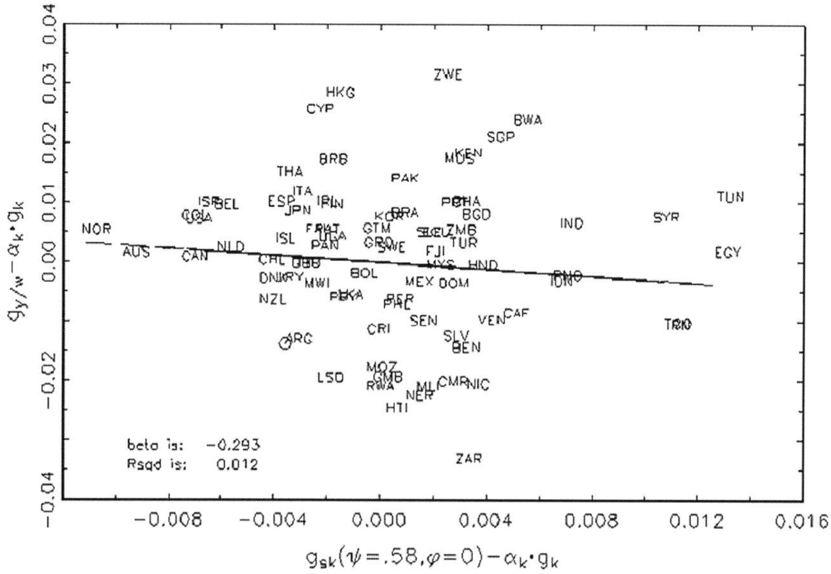

(c)

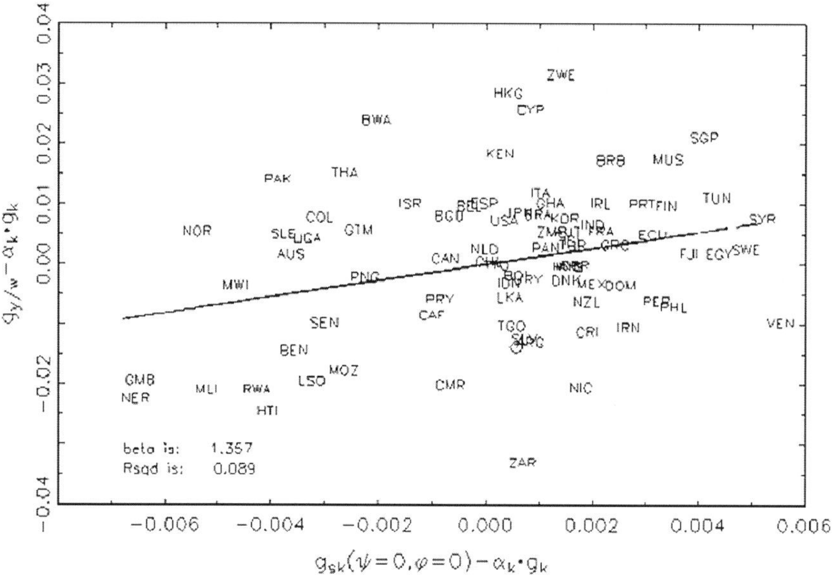

(d)

Figure 10. (*Continued.*)

Table 22

Regressions of growth of output per worker growth on K/W growth and growth of schooling capital per worker of Bils and Klenow (2000) with various parameters (and with simple percentage change and absolute change per year)

Variable	Growth K/W (ppa)	Growth SK/W (ppa)	$\bar{R}^2$	Average: $g_y - \hat{\alpha}_k g_k - \hat{\alpha}_{sh} g_{SK}$
Variation over ψ (slope of return-schooling relationship)				
$g_{SK}(\psi = -0.58, \varphi = 0)$	0.496	−0.097	0.445	0.64%
	(0.061)	(0.340)		
$g_{SK}(\psi = -0.28, \varphi = 0)$	0.490	0.442	0.452	0.03%
	(0.061)	(0.446)		
$g_{SK}(\psi = 0, \varphi = 0)$	0.452	1.25	0.479	−0.52%
	(0.062)	(0.55)		
Variation over φ (contribution of past to current schooling capital)				
$g_{SK}(\psi = -0.28, \varphi = 0)$	0.490	0.442	0.452	0.03%
	(0.061)	(0.446)		
$g_{SK}(\psi = -0.28, \varphi = 1/3)$	0.465	0.886	0.474	−0.68%
	(0.061)	(0.422)		
$g_{SK}(\psi = -0.28, \varphi = 0.46)$	0.449	1.05	0.488	−1.1%
	(0.061)	(0.411)		
Percentage change	0.494	−0.048	0.447	−0.63%
	(0.061)	(0.093)		
Absolute change	0.455	0.117	0.517	−0.24%
	(0.058	(0.034)		

Source: Author's calculations.

of schooling variable – either levels or enrollments is frequently statistically significant. Some variable of this type is, at times, a statistically significant correlate of growth (notably Barro and Sala-i-Martin in various versions of their empirical work, say 1995). Some have interpreted the presence of the *level* of schooling in a *growth* regression as support for the "new growth" or output externality effects of schooling, but this interpretation is untenable for three reasons.

First, as above in section I, since levels of schooling are trending and per capita output growth is stable there cannot be an empirically large steady state relationship between the *growth* of output per worker and the level (or lagged level) of schooling. In the language of integration and co-integration the only way for there to be a relationship between a stationary variable and a non-stationary variable is if the specification includes two non-stationary variables which are co-integrated themselves such that the

data). Any interpretation that these results represent causal or structural relationships is model dependent and is an interpretation of the results of the statistical procedures, not a result.

difference is stationary. If output and schooling levels are co-integrated (which they could be for any number of causal reasons – e.g. schooling is a consumption good) then a regression of growth on the lagged level of output and schooling identifies a *level* effect of schooling. As Topel (1999) concludes "it is impossible to interpret Barro Sala-i-Martin's estimates as the effect of human capital on economic growth."

Second, the rationale for a reduced form that includes schooling has never been made clear – if the role of schooling in the growth regression is as a proxy for schooling capital, then why not add a proxy for physical capital to the regression as well? Otherwise, the specification becomes strikingly unclear: why is there a mix of production function inputs (schooling) and other underlying determinants in the same equation – but not physical capital/CUDIE? Why treat schooling and physical capital asymmetrically?

Third, Bils and Klenow (2000) address whether, even supposing the partial correlation of growth with lagged schooling levels is robust and even supposing the specification could be meaningfully interpreted, whether the growth regression results reflect a causal impact of schooling on output. They find that if ψ is set to its regression value and $\phi = 0$ that the level of years of attainment implied by enrollment rates in 1960 and the growth of schooling capital from 1960 to 1990 are strongly *negatively* correlated. This means, strikingly, that *none* of the impact of initial enrollments on growth is mediated by an impact of enrollments on raising schooling capital. The only way around this problem is to either lower (in absolute value) ψ which makes the correlation with initial schooling less negative (as Figure 8 above) or raise the estimate of ϕ which also makes the correlation less negative (as in Figure 9 above). However these parameters have empirical implications – as ϕ is raised the estimate of g_h is raised which means that (for a given α_k and g_k) the estimate of g_A must be lower. Given the discussion of growth accounting above (Section 2.4) very substantial values of ϕ cause the average estimate of g_A to be zero so that *all* of (non-capital) growth is attributed to human capital, which seems implausible. So, if one maintains the regression estimate of the relationship of the return/schooling relationship then even the value of ϕ which drives average g_A to zero still implies a negative correlation of initial enrollments with growth of schooling capital. This again makes it very difficult to interpret the lagged level of enrollments as representing a direct causal effect of schooling on output.

3.5. Summary of cross-national estimates of returns to schooling

In the fantasy movie *Willow* a village of "small people" meet to discuss a serious problem. The wise magician declares that to make a decision they must consult the bones. Dramatically taking the magic bones from the bag around his neck, he casts the bones in front of the crowd. Peering carefully at the bones the magician says "The bones say ... the bones tell me nothing!" What do the cross-national data on output and schooling say about the question of whether there is *excess* of social over private return to schooling? At times the data really is insufficiently informative to decide amongst interesting alternatives and a range of beliefs can be supported depending on how one structures the question and filters the answer. As detailed above in reviewing the existing literature there are four dimensions of empirical technique and specification that affect the estimates: (a) mapping from years of schooling (and their distribution) into an aggregate "schooling capital," (b) mapping from schooling capital into output (the "production function", (c) the way in which physical capital is allowed to affect output and (d) how one addresses the joint question of measurement error/length of horizon of the data.

There is no compelling, and very little even suggestive, evidence of substantial (on the order of 3 to 5 percentage points) output externalities of schooling in the typical economic environments observed in the cross-national samples during this particular period. While occasionally some variant throws up a large macro-Mincer coefficient these tend to either have very large standard errors or not be robust to reasonable variations in technique or both.

If one wants to produce the result that the output effects of schooling from cross-national data are *consistent with* the micro wage increments then one should: (a) assume a combination of schooling capital and production function functional forms such that the *percentage* change in output per worker is regressed on something like the *absolute* change in schooling per worker (or levels on levels) – so that the contribution of a year of schooling to schooling capital is roughly as large in high and low schooling environments, *and* (b) constrain the coefficient on the proxy for capital to be near is national accounting value[48] *and* (c) use exclusively long-period growth or levels. This combination can produce macro-Mincer estimates that are consistent with wage increments of 10 percent [Krueger and Lindahl (2001), Topel (1999)]. The drawback of this approach is two-fold. First, the data very clearly suggest that returns are declining in the level of schooling – as Bils and Klenow (2000) point out the assumption that the slope of the returns/schooling relationship is zero is four standard errors from their cross sectional relationship.[49] Second, the larger the contribution of growth attributed to schooling the smaller one has to believe that "the residual" contribution to was – and even modestly large contributions of schooling require negative growth of the residual.

If, on the other hand one either:

(a) specifies the combination of schooling capital and production function such that either something like percentage changes in schooling [Benhabib and Spiegel (1994), Knowles and Owen (1997), Pritchett (2001)], *or*

(b) greater weight is given to years of schooling acquired when schooling years are low about of the magnitude suggested by returns/schooling regressions (*a la* Bils and Klenow) as in Table 21, *or*

(c) if one allows a flexible functional form for schooling [Temple (2001), Duffy and Papageorgiou (2000)], *or*

[48] While it is reasonably consistent to constrain the coefficient on K/W to make the schooling returns look equal to micro-Mincer, it does seem odd to constrain by assumption the evidence for human capital externalities the results of regressions which exclude or arbitrarily constrain the coefficient on physical capital – as there are plausible arguments that at least some types of physical capital investments convey externalities [de Long and Summers (1991)].

[49] In the simple bivariate regression based on Figure 6 the coefficient is 0.66 with a standard error of 0.099 so zero is *six* standard errors from the point estimate.

(d) one uses periods of ten years or less and panel data to allow for country specific levels or growth of TFP – even with econometric tools to address measurement error [Bloom, Canning and Sevilla (2002)], all of the panel augmented Solow regressions in Table 19, Topel (1999), *or*

(e) one allows the coefficient on physical capital (in practice, CUDIE) to be unconstrained,

then (1) the resulting estimates of the return to education from the cross-national data are rather smaller (running from negative to 6 percent) than if one takes the micro wage increments at face value *and* (2) these estimates frequently have enormous imprecision so that a wide range of estimates are not rejected by the data.

In particular, while there is no particular evidence *for* an output externality of substantial magnitude there is no compelling evidence *against* externalities of a policy relevant magnitude either. Output externalities on the order of 3 percent excess of social over private returns – are a needle in the haystack relative to the available statistical power and the existing data and method simply are not powerful enough to distinguish among a variety of plausible alternatives – particularly with respect to the specification of functional forms, which turn out to be crucial.[50]

Four methodological points to conclude this section (the last of which motivates the final section).

First, what is quite striking about the fact that estimates from aggregate data are many times rather "too low" than "too high" is that there are a number of reasons why the cross-national regressions might exhibit substantial *upward* bias (since most of the estimates already control for the attenuation bias of pure measurement error). The micro wage/earnings-schooling literature has spilled oceans of ink[51] in the search to eliminate the upward bias created by the fact that individuals choose more schooling when its return is high (either because of high quality schooling Behrman and Birdsall (1983)[52] or individual ability (see the twins studies – [Ashenfelter and Krueger (1994), Ashenfelter and Rouse (1998), Behrman, Rosenzweig and Taubman (1994), Behrman and Rosenzweig (1999)]) or market conditions. Rosenzweig (1998) uses panel data from regions of India to create cross-village regressions of wages on schooling that mimics a typical cross-national regression specification. But, while he finds a macro (village) Mincer coefficient of 0.098, when he uses instruments to control for the endogeneity of education to technology shocks, which are positively associated with education returns across villages, the estimated coefficient falls to 0.029.

While the simple "growth accounting" regressions have many "omitted variables" – in the sense that there are other variables that explain growth in a reduced form –

[50] A point recognized by most who have attempted these regressions: "Determining rates of return to inputs from macro-data with any precision is likely to be difficult" [Bloom, Canning and Sevilla (2002, p. 21)], "The principal message of this paper is that the aggregate evidence on education and growth, for large samples of countries, continues to be clouded with uncertainty" [Temple (2001, p. 916)].

[51] Here's hoping they mostly used recycled.

[52] They show for Brazil, that not controlling for school quality leads to *overestimating* the returns to years of schooling by a factor of two.

in the simple bivariate case this omitted variable bias would cause the OLS estimate to *overstate* schooling if the omitted variable had the same correlation with growth as with schooling capital.[53] So, suppose if "corruption" or "rule of law" or "institutional quality" was excluded from the growth regression this would likely cause the estimate of schooling capital to be biased *up*.[54]

Second, while it is relatively easy to dismiss cross-national research for its many flaws it is not entirely clear what other evidence one could use to form judgments about the magnitude of the *excess* of social over private return in a *typical* country, which from the normative policy view is a key quantity. While there is some mixed evidence at aggregate level from the United States [Acemoglu and Angrist (1999)] there is no reason to believe this would generalize to Nepal, Malawi, or Paraguay. There is also some micro-level evidence about specific spillovers (e.g., especially farm practices) but there is no way to know how that translates into economy wide estimates or generalizes over time (see Section 4 below).[55] There is a coherent view of the methodological skeptic that all unproven effects should be assumed to be of zero magnitude. But taking a particular position about the output externalities of schooling – say, to take a common position, that they are of sufficient magnitude to justify normatively public provision of tuition free schooling *and* reject any evidence from cross-national regressions because of their methodological shortcomings is *not* a coherent view. To form beliefs without perfect evidence and then take the stance that only perfect evidence could alter those beliefs is not methodological purism – it is just plain stubbornness.

Third, the "normative" set up in Section 2.2 about the magnitude of output externality was a purely academic exercise and I want to return to three points about the relationship of normative to positive. First, one cannot use a "normative as positive" circle as

[53] The simple formula of omitted variable bias with only two variables, say, schooling capital, SK, and the omitted variable, OV, is that $\hat{\beta}^{\mathrm{SK}}_{\mathrm{OLS}} = \beta^{\mathrm{SK}} + \beta^{\mathrm{OV}}\delta_{\mathrm{SK,OV}}$, where δ is the coefficient of SK and the omitted variable.

[54] With other variables, such as physical capital, in the regression it is complex as the bias in any one variable depends on the covariances both with the omitted variable and with the included variables. So if tildes represent the estimates of after projections from h and OV into k then the bias to OLS depends on the correlation of h and OV not with "raw" growth but with the residual of growth projected into physical capital growth, $\hat{\beta}^{\mathrm{HK}}_{\mathrm{OLS}} = \beta^{\mathrm{HK}} + \tilde{\beta}^{\mathrm{OV}}\tilde{\pi}_{\mathrm{HK,OV}}$. While this suggests that an upward bias is not inevitable, no one has made an argument that the omitted variable problem would produce a downward bias.

[55] Suppose the body of the cross-national evidence suggested zero output externality and that somehow there were a perfect, rigorous, controlled experiment to estimate the externality to schooling in country Z or in section S of country Z at time T and that this perfect evidence suggested a large (*pi* percentage points) externality. What should be the view about the output externality of schooling in country W? One view would be that since the *best* evidence should get *all* of the weight and hence "the best evidence is that the output externality in W is *pi*." This view is unsound. Without a compelling model and *evidence* that suggests that the output externality to schooling in W and Z is exactly the same (which is dubious) or is constant across policy/institutional environments evidence from Z is just as unreliable in making inferences about W as the cross-national evidence – probably more so. The slogan "one good study trumps a hundred lousy ones" is in this case just nonsense as this is only true if the good and lousy studies were attempting to make inferences about exactly the same quantity – and even one perfect study about spillovers to in country Z in sector S in time T does not trump anything except other studies about spillovers in country Z in sector S in time T.

evidence of output externalities. The argument "(a) there is a coherent model in which *if* the excess return was 3 percentage points government then would provide tuition free schooling, and (b) governments do provide tuition free schooling, therefore (c) there must be output externalities even if the data cannot find them (or 'policy makers believe there are output externalities')" is a pure logical fallacy.[56] Second, the weakness of the evidence for output externalities makes "normative as positive" an extremely dubious positive model. There is an important *positive* question "why do governments finance (and produce) schooling?" One possible answer to this question is "governments do so *because* a welfare maximizing planner would do so *because* of the existing market failures and/or equity objectives." As I have argued elsewhere this "normative as positive" is an extraordinarily bad positive model as it explains *nothing* about the actual educational policies[57] nor why (nearly) *all* governments produce nearly *all* types of schooling [Pritchett (2003)].[58] I have proposed an alternative positive model of schooling [Pritchett (2003)] that explains (nearly) everything about educational policies of governments with no reference at all to output externalities.

Fourth, the changes in estimated impact of schooling as the weight on the change in schooling at low levels and the large standard errors mean something. One possibility is that the assumptions that schooling has a constant (or varying only by level of schooling) impact on schooling capital and schooling capital has a constant (or varying only by level of schooling) impact on output in all country environments are broadly correct but that the data have insufficient power to identify this impact. The other thing imprecise estimates might mean is that what is being estimated – the incremental impact of a year of schooling on aggregate output – itself varies enormously across countries.

Figure 11 shows that the cross-national variance of the growth rate of schooling capital is enormously smaller than the variance of the growth of output. While some countries have growth rates of output per worker above 4 percent and many have growth rates less than zero the data on growth rate of schooling capital is rather narrowly centered, 25th percentile of 1.1 and 75th percentile of 1.6. Below an initial output per worker of P$10,000 the standard deviation of growth of Y/W is 1.93 percent while

[56] This has exactly the structure: If A then B, B, therefore A.

[57] Temple (2001), after a excellent examination of the empirical evidence comes to a similar view: that the evidence probably isn't that important anyway: "It is perhaps also becoming clear that the questions currently driving this research are not necessarily the most important in the field. ... it is not clear the what extent decisions about education spending will ever be informed by empirical evidence. A perhaps more interesting task for future research is to explore the fine detail of the institutional and incentive structure that best allocates a fixed amount of educational expenditures" (p. 917).

[58] In reviewing the evidence Poterba (1996) says [roughly, there is no evidence about the policy relevant magnitudes'] – but viewed in another light, if in *1996* there is no evidence to base educational policies, but educational policies have in fact been made for more than 100 years, this is pretty compelling evidence that in the correct positive model of educational policy making *no one really cares* about those specific pieces of evidence that would be relevant *if* normative were positive – as point well made in Zeckhauser's (1996) response to Poterba.

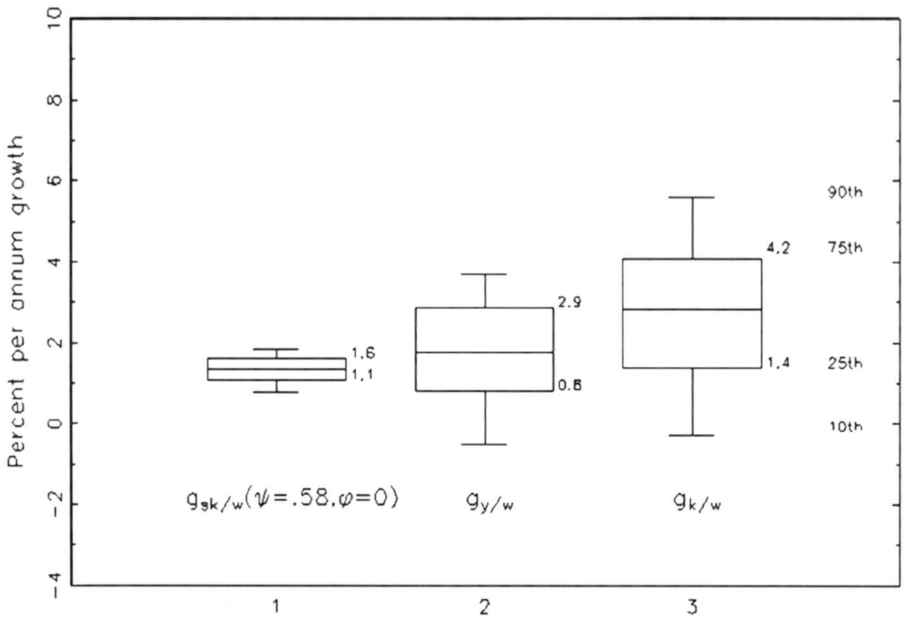

Figure 11. Variability of growth of SK per worker is much lower than of output or capital.

the standard deviation of schooling capital growth is 0.41 percent.[59] In contrast, the variation in K/W growth is even wider than in output per worker. This narrow range of growth in schooling capital obviously makes the identification of a single "impact" effect of schooling unlikely.

4. Directions forward on estimating cross-national returns to schooling

> *Rent seeking in our [African] economies is not a more or less important phenomenon, as would be the case in most economies. It is the centerpiece of our economies. It is what defines and characterizes our economic life.*
>
> *H.E. Prime Minister Meles Zenawi of Ethiopia, September 5, 2000*

The final line of research to be reviewed examines cross-national data, not to make inferences about a "parameter" that is assumed constant across countries

[59] Of course if the returns/schooling relationship is assumed to be less steep the standard deviation of schooling capital growth is even smaller. If $\psi = 0$ the standard deviation is only 0.31 percent.

but the opposite – to use the variation across countries to identify the ways in which the micro or aggregate returns to schooling *vary* across countries. The problem with studying the impact of variations in economic conditions or policies using household data sets that collect information from lots of workers in one location/country is (a) there may be little usable variation in the variables of interest – because all households face the same economic policies – and (b) if labor is mobile then if workers move to maximize utility the spatial distribution of workers by level education is endogenous. In contrast, using cross-national data generates variation in economic conditions, policies, institutions, structures of schooling, labor markets, etc and barriers to labor mobility across countries are large (as witnessed by the enormous gaps in wages across countries for workers with similar attributes).

The impact of increasing schooling on aggregate output can vary across countries either because (a) the *private* return to schooling is different country j because of factors X other than schooling:

$$r_j^{\text{private}}(X^j, S^{ji}) \neq r^{\text{private}}(\bar{X}, S^j), \tag{13}$$

or (b) because the gap between the social (by which I mean the contribution to aggregate output) and private rates is different in country j (for reasons other than level of schooling):

$$r_j^{\text{social}}(Z^j, S^j) - r_j^{\text{private}}(Z^j, S^{ji}) \neq r^{\text{social}}(\bar{Z}, S^j) - r^{\text{private}}(\bar{Z}, S^j). \tag{14}$$

I am only going to skim very lightly over this literature, I will treat first those that operate mainly by augmenting the private return and then those that operate on the gap between social and private.

Private returns

In a private (and unregulated) labor market with mobility the country wide wage premia to schooling are determined by the demand for skilled labor of employers (including self-employers) and the supply of labor skilled by schooling. The question is then, "what are the factors which drive higher returns to schooling in country j for a given level of schooling?" Many possibilities have been explored.

First, the "adaptation to disequilibria" view explains returns to schooling as the results of the ability to adopt and apply new technologies [Nelson and Phelps (1966)]. A great deal of economics of schooling, learning, and innovation has taken place in the context of the farm (e.g., the classic empirical study of Welch (1970)). Methodologically the farm is ideal as there are individual decisions that affect output, individual farmers are, for the most part, truly economic competitive and there are reasonable measures of inputs and outputs.[60] The rightly recent classic study in this regard is Foster and Rosenzweig (1996) who use data from regions of India and the regional differences in the

[60] Moreover, Schultz illustrates quite well the contrasting views of the value of education. He both argued that in "traditional" agriculture peasant farmers would be technically and economically efficient – which would

adaptability to the package of innovations of the Green Revolution to show differences in returns to schooling across regions of India.[61] In areas that had high technological change the return to schooling (measured by farmer profits) was substantially higher than in regions with low technical change. In fact, the returns in regions with low technical change were quite near zero – consistent with the low returns in stagnant agricultural environments found elsewhere.[62]

Second, either structural change or technical progress that is skill enhancing leads to greater demands for educated labor. If a country had an expansion in the supply of the labor force with schooling without a corresponding increase in the demand then the returns to schooling would drop – perhaps quite rapidly. Hence, even if two countries had equivalent measured returns to schooling at the beginning of a period, the growth impact returns would vary by how much the return itself varied over time. Certainly, the degree to which the labor market demands of economies were transformed varied enormously over the period of these regressions. Table 23 shows that in many countries in Sub-Saharan Africa the expansion of schooled labor exceeded the growth in wage employment by an order of magnitude. Since these are also environments in which farming has not been particularly technologically progressive one suspects that private returns to schooling in farming are also quite low.

Gap between private and "social" returns

In a fully market economy with no labor market distortions (and no ability to create distortions to generate "rents") then it is difficult to believe that the gap between private and social returns to schooling could be large. After all, if employers are willing to pay more for a worker with more schooling it seems most plausible that this is because a more schooled worker has a higher marginal product for the employer. The only competing hypothesis is that some type of signaling accounts for the wage premia – but while it is easy to believe that signaling plays some role it is very difficult to believe the magnitude and pervasiveness of signaling would be large enough to generate large macro-micro gaps. But it is not the case that most labor markets are undistorted, nor is it the case that in most countries the opportunities for rent seeking have been few. For

seem to imply that, under the conditions of "traditional" agriculture there would be to "return" to education. At the same time, Schultz (1975) is equally famous for emphasizing an important role for human capital in the process of development. This suggests that returns to education for farmers should vary according to the pace of technical change, both in agriculture and in the rest of the economy. Early reviews of the microeconomic literature on education and farmer productivity found that there were only modest returns in technologically stagnant settings.

61 There are a number of other papers examining both the issue of how returns vary as new techniques are introduced and how adoption dynamics create spillovers from educated farmers to less educated farmers within countries [Appleton and Balihuta (1996), Foster and Rosenzweig (1996), Besley and Case (1994)].

62 Jamison and Louat in their review of the literature find that, on average farmers with a primary education had productivity 8 percent higher than farmers with no schooling but that the pattern of results was suggestive of higher returns in more dynamic areas. While 8 percent is not zero, this far below the typically Mincer of 8 per year of schooling.

Table 23
Growth of enrollments and of wage employment in selected sub-Saharan African countries

Country	Change in enrollments ('000)	Change in wage employment ('000)	Ratio, expansion of enrollment to wage employment	Wage employment as percentage of total labor force
Enrollment growth positive, wage employment falling				
Zambia	446	−4.3	–	13.1
Cote d'Ivoire	323	−7.7	–	9
Enrollment growth exceeds wage employment growth by an order of magnitude				
Sierra Leone	257	8.9	29	4.9
Uganda	225	13.2	17	4.7
Ghana	1312	80	16	3.8
Burkina Faso	351	35.4	10	3.8
Lesotho	142	14.9	10	5.4
Enrollment growth higher by factor of 4				
Senegal	180	45.4	4.0	5.5
Kenya	1709	436	3.9	14.1
Malawi	546	143	3.8	13.7
Rough equality of enrollment and wage sector growth				
Botswana	157	122	1.3	50.4
Zimbabwe	135	111.1	1.2	36.6

Note: Growth rates of enrollments and wage sector growth are calculated beginning from the date of the study estimating Mincerian return study and ending in 1990 (or the most recent data). Source: Bennell (1996), Table 5.

instance, in a centrally planned economy in which workers were assigned both to education and to jobs after education one could imagine that observed wage returns could be meaningless as a reflection of marginal products and the gap between impact of schooling on aggregate output and the observed private wage returns could be positive or negative.

In many developing countries, the public sector has accounted for a large share of the expansion of wage employment in the 1960s and 1970s (Table 24). This is not to equate government, or the magnitude or growth of government employment, with the magnitude of rent seeking. Nor am I saying that the expansion of education in government is necessarily unproductive. On the contrary, the most successful of developing countries have had strong and active governments and highly educated civil servants hired through a very competitive process [World Bank (1993)].[63] The question is not *whether*

[63] Wade (1990) asserts that college graduates are as likely to enter government service in Korea and Taiwan as in African economies.

Table 24
Share of wage employment growth accounted for by public sector growth in selected developing countries

Country	Period	Average growth of wage employment (percent per annum)			Public sector (percentage of total increase)
		Public	Private	Total	
Public sector employment growth positive, private wage employment growth zero or less					
Ghana	1960–1978	3.4	−5.9	−0.6	
Zambia	1966–1980	7.2	−6.2	0.9	418
Tanzania	1962–1976	6.1	−3.8	1.6	190
Peru	1970–1984	6.1	−0.6	1.1	140
Egypt	1966–1976	2.5	−0.5	2.2	103
Brazil	1973–1983	1.4	0	0.3	100
Public sector employment growth more than half of total wage employment growth					
Sri Lanka	1971–1983	8	0.9	3.9	87
India	1960–1980	4.2	2.1	3.2	71
Kenya	1963–1981	6.4	2	3.7	67
Public sector growth faster, but less than half of total wage employment growth					
Panama	1963–1982	7.5	1.8	2.7	45
Costa Rica	1973–1983	7.6	2.8	3.5	34
Thailand	1963–1983	6.3	5.5	5.7	33
Venezuela	1967–1982	5.1	3.4	3.7	27
Unweighted mean		5.5	0.3	2.4	

Source: Derived from Gelb, Knight and Sabot (1991), Table 1.

the educated labor flows into the government, but *why* the government hires educated workers (actual need versus employment guarantee) and *what* they do once they are in the government (productive versus unproductive or rent-seeking activities).

Murphy, Shleifer and Vishny (1991) present a simple model of the allocation of talent in which, if returns to ability are the greatest in rent seeking, then economic growth is inhibited by drawing the most talented people away from productive sectors into rent seeking. Anecdotal evidence that rent seeking attracts educated labor abounds. There is the possibly apocryphal, but nevertheless instructive, story of Nigeria which had a public sector employment guarantee for all university graduates. In a year when the exchange rate was heavily overvalued (and hence, there was a large premium on evading import controls), 60 percent of university graduates in all fields designated the customs service as their preference for government employment.

Explicit or implicit government guarantees of employment for the educated have been common and have led to large distortions in the labor market. In Egypt, government employment guarantees led to notoriously overstaffed enterprises and bureaucracies. In 1998, the government and public enterprises employed 70 percent of all university graduates and 63 percent of those with education at the intermediate level and above [Assaad (1997)]. Gersovitz and Paxson (1995) calculate that in 1986–1988 in Cote d'Ivoire, 50 percent of all workers between 25 and 55 that had completed even *one grade* of post-primary education worked in the public sector. Gelb, Knight and Sabot (1991) build a dynamic general equilibrium model in which government responds to political pressures from potentially unemployed educated job seekers and becomes the employer of last resort for educated labor force entrants. They show that when both employment pressures are strong and the government is highly responsive to those pressures, the employment of surplus educated labor in the public sector can reduce growth of output per worker by as much as 2 percent a year (from a base case growth of 2.5 percent).

Finally, let me turn in this context of differential returns to the important paper by Hanushek and Kimko (2000). In this paper they show that once one accounts for the quality of schooling by using internationally comparable test scores that (a) the impact of the quantity of schooling years is statistically insignificant and (b) the measure of labor force quality is statistically significant and very large. In fact, too large, as the author's point out "the estimated impact of quality on growth, indicating that a one standard deviation in mathematics and science skills translates into more than one percentage point in average annual real growth, also looks implausibly large ... the growth equation results are much larger than the corresponding results for individual earnings.... The estimated growth effect of one standard deviation of quality is larger than would be obtained from over nine years in average schooling" (p. 23). One way to reconcile these results with the findings above is if the ability of governments to run schools that produce high test score results is strongly correlated with other measures of a country's "institutional quality". In that case, the enormous estimate effect of the quality of schooling is because it picks up a number of variables that are strongly correlated with higher private returns, higher excess of social over private returns and, with growth itself.

5. Conclusion

The empirical conclusions have been summarized in the respective sections so I would like to devote the conclusion to making clear my views about the implications of the empirical findings.

First, none of the arguments in this paper suggest that governments should invest less in basic schooling, for many reasons. For one thing, most, if not all, societies believe that (at least) basic education is a merit good, a fundamental human right, so that its provision is not, and need not be, justified on economic grounds at all – a position with which I strongly agree. To deny a child an education because of a small expected economic growth impact would be a moral travesty. In addition, schooling has a large number of direct beneficial effects beyond raising economic output, such as lower child mortality. The implication, therefore, of an empirically poor aggregate payoff from past increases in schooling due to a perverse policy or institutional environment that lowered private returns or the gap between social and private returns is not "don't educate", but rather "reform now so that investments (past and present) in schooling will pay off".

Second, and related, in conversations with some colleagues and friends I have sensed a reluctance to evaluate the evidence for output externalities *because* they believe (as I do) that expanding educational opportunities is key to improving human welfare and they believe (as I do not) that evidence in favor of output externalities helps expand educational opportunities. This is because in their (usually implicit) positive model of government support for education the larger the (beliefs about) output externalities the larger the support for education. But since I do not believe that beliefs about output externalities have played any significant role in creating or expanding support for education I am perfectly comfortable that my assessment that there is no evidence for output externalities in the cross-national data does not work at cross purposes with my normative beliefs that expanding high quality schooling through public sector support is key to expansions in human welfare. In fact, there is a plausible argument that excessive emphasis on government provision of schooling because of *externalities* has been an *obstacle* to creating the right institutional environments for high quality schooling by placing excessive emphasis on the interests of the state over and above the interests of parents and students themselves.

Acknowledgements

I would like to thank for comments and discussions, without implication, William Easterly, Deon Filmer, Ricardo Hausmann, Rick Hanushek, Dani Rodrik, Mark Rosenzweig, Jonathan Temple and Ludger Wössmann. I would like to especially thank Mark Bils for providing raw data.

References

Acemoglu, D., Angrist, J. (1999). "How large are the social returns to education? Evidence from compulsory schooling laws". Working Paper 7444. National Bureau of Economic Research.

Appleton, S., Balihuta, A. (1996). "Education and agricultural productivity: Evidence from Uganda". Working Paper Series 96/05. Center for the Study of African Economies, p. 15.

Ashenfelter, O., Krueger, A. (1994). "Estimates of the economic return to schooling from a new sample of twins". American Economic Review 84 (5), 1157–1174.

Ashenfelter, O., Rouse, C. (1998). "Income, schooling, and ability: Evidence from a new sample of identical twins". Quarterly Journal of Economics 113 (1), 253–284.

Assad, R. (1997). "The effects of public sector hiring and compensation policies on the Egyptian labor market". World Bank Economic Review 11 (1), 85–118.

Barro, R., Lee, J. (1993). "International comparisons of the educational attainment". Journal of Monetary Economics 32 (3), 363–394.

Barro, R., Sala-i-Martin, X. (1995). Economic Growth. McGraw-Hill, New York.

Behrman, J. (1987). "Schooling in developing countries: Which countries are the over and underachievers and what is the schooling impact?" Economics of Education Review 6 (2), 111–127.

Behrman, J., Birdsall, N. (1983). "The quality of schooling: Quantity alone is misleading". World Bank Reprint Series (International) 311, 928–946.

Behrman, J., Rosenzweig, M.R., Taubman, P. (1994). "Endowments and the allocation of schooling in the family and marriage market: The twins experiment". Journal of Political Economy 102 (6), 1131–1174.

Behrman, J., Rosenzweig, M.R. (1999). "The returns to schooling: New evidence from twins data". Economics of Education Review 18, 159–167.

Ben David, D., Papell, D. (1997). "Slowdowns and meltdowns: Post-war growth evidence from 74 countries". Working Paper 6266. National Bureau of Economic Research.

Benhabib, J., Spiegel, M. (1994). "Role of human capital in economic development: Evidence from aggregate cross-country data". Journal of Monetary Economics 34, 143–173.

Bennell, P. (1996). "Rates of return to education: Does the conventional pattern prevail in sub-Saharan Africa?" World Development 24, 183–199.

Besley, T., Case, A. (1994). "Diffusion as a learning process: Evidence from HYV cotton". Woodrow Wilson School Development Studies Papers 174. Princeton.

Bils, M., Klenow, P. (2000). "Does schooling cause growth or the other way around?" American Economic Reviev 90 (3), 1160–1183.

Bloom, D.E., Canning, D., Sevilla, J. (2002). "The effect of health on economic growth: Theory and evidence". NBER Working Paper 8587.

Bond, S., Hoeffler, A., Temple, J. (2001). "GMM estimation of empirical growth models", Economics Papers 2001-W21. Economics Group, Nuffield College, University of Oxford.

Bosworth, B., Collins, S.M., Chen, Y. (1996). "Accounting for differences in economic growth". In: Conference on Structural Adjustment Policies in the 1990s. Experience and Prospects. Tokyo.

Bruns, B., Mingat, A., Rakotomalala, R. (2003). A Change for Every Child: Achieving Universal Primary Education by 2015. World Bank, Washington, DC.

Caselli, F., Esquivel, G., Lefort, F. (1996). "Reopening the convergence debate: A new look at cross-country growth empirics". Journal of Economic Growth 1 (3), 363–390.

Dasgupta, P., Weale, M. (1992). "On measuring the quality of life". World Development 20 (1), 119–131.

De la Fuente, A., Domenech, R. (2000). "Human capital in growth regressions: How much difference does data quality make?" Working Paper 262. Economics Department.

De Long, B., Summers, L. (1991). "Equipment investment and economic growth". Quarterly Journal of Economics 106 (2), 445–502.

Dowrick, S., Rogers, M. (2001). "Classical and technological convergence: Beyond the Solow–Swan growth model". Unpublished manuscript.

Dubey, A., King, E. (1994). "A new cross-country education stock series differentiated by age and sex". Mimeo. The World Bank.

Duffy, J., Papageorgiou, C. (2000). "A cross-country empirical investigation of the aggregate production function specification". Journal of Economic Growth 5 (1), 87–120.

Easterly, W. (2001). "The lost decades: Developing countries stagnation in spite of policy reform: 1980–1998". Journal of Economic Growth 6 (2), 135–157.

Easterly, W., Levine, R. (2001). "It's not factor accumulation: Stylized facts and growth models". World Bank Economic Review 15 (2), 177–219.

Easterly, W., Kremer, M., Pritchett, L., Summers, L. (1993). "Good policy or good luck? Country growth performance and temporary shocks". Journal of Monetary Economics 32 (3), 459–483.

Fisher, F. (1969). "The existence of aggregate production functions". Econometrica 37 (4), 553–577.

Foster, A.D., Rosenzweig, M.R. (1996). "Technical change and human capital returns and investments: Evidence from the green revolution". American Economic Review 86 (4), 931–953.

Garces, E., Thomas, D., Currie, J. (2000). "Longer term effects of head start". Working Paper 8054. National Bureau of Economic Research.

Gelb, A., Knight, J.K., Sabot, R. (1991). "Public sector employment, rent seeking, and economic growth". Economic Journal 101, 1186–1199.

Gersovitz, M., Paxson, C. (1995). "The revenues and expenditures of African governments: Modalities and consequences". Mimeo, World Bank.

Hall, R.E., Jones, C.I. (1999). "Why do some countries produce so much more output per worker than others?" The Quarterly Journal of Economics 114 (1), 83–116.
Hanushek, E., Kimko, D. (2000). Schooling, Labor Force Quality, and the Growth of Nations. American Economic Review.
Heckman, J.J., Klenow, P.J. (1997). "Human capital policy". In: Boskin, M. (Ed.), Capital Formation. Hoover Economic Growth Conference, Hoover Institution.
Heckman, J.J. (1999). "Policies to foster human capital". Working Paper 7288. National Bureau of Economic Research.
Islam, N. (1995). "Growth empirics: A panel data approach". The Quarterly Journal of Economics 110 (4), 1127–1170.
Jones, C. (1995). "R&D-based models of economic growth". Journal of Political Economy (August).
Jovanovich, B., Lach, S., Lavy, V. (1992). Growth and Human Capital's Role as an Investment in Cost Reduction. New York University, New York. Processed.
Knowles, S., Owen, P.D. (1997). "Education and health in an effective-labor empirical growth model". The Economic Record 73 (223), 314–328.
Kremer, M., Thomson, J. (1998). "Why isn't convergence instantaneous? Young workers, old workers, and gradual adjustment". Journal of Economic Growth 3 (1), 5–28.
Kruger, A., Lindahl, M. (2001). "Education for growth: Why and for whom?" Journal of Economic Literature 39 (4), 1101–1136.
Kuznets, S. (1966). Modern Economic Growth: Rate, Structure, Spread. Yale University Press, New Haven.
Lau, L., Jamison, D., Louat, L. (1991). Impact of Education by Region. World Bank, Washington, DC. Processed.
Lewis, W.A. (1955). The Theory of Economic Growth. R.D. Irwin, Homewood, IL.
Lott Jr., J.R. (1999). "Public schooling, indoctrination, and totalitarianism". Journal of Political Economy 107 (S6), S127–S129.
Lucas Jr., R.E. (1988). "On the mechanics of economic development". Journal of Monetary Economics 22 (1), 3–42.
Maddison, A. (1995). Monitoring the World Economy: 1820–1992. OECD, Paris.
Mankiw, G., Romer, D., Weil, D. (1992). "A contribution to the empirics of economic growth". Quarterly Journal of Economics 107, 407–437.
Murphy, K., Shliefer, A., Vishny, R. (1991). "The allocation of talent: Implications for growth". Quarterly Journal of Economics 106 (2), 503–530.
Myrdal, G. (1968). Asian Drama: An Inquiry Into the Poverty of Nations. Twentieth Century Fund, New York.
Nehru, V., Swanson, E., Dubey, A. (1995). "A new database on human capital stock". Policy Research Paper 1124. World Bank.
Nelson, R., Phelps, E. (1966). "Investment in humans, technological diffusion, and economic growth". American Economic Review Papers and Proceedings 56, 69–75.
Poterba, J.M. (1996). "Government intervention in the markets for health care and education: How and why?". In: Fuchs, V.R. (Ed.), Individual and Social Responsibility. University of Chicago Press, pp. 277–304.
Psacharopoulos, G. (1994). "Returns to investment in education: A global update". World Development 22 (9), 1325–1343.
Psacharopoulos, G., Patrinos, H.A. (2002). "Returns to investment in education: A further update". Policy Research Working Paper 2881. World Bank.
Pritchett, L. (2000). "The tyranny of concepts: CUDIE is not capital". Journal of Economic Growth 5 (4), 361–384.
Pritchett, L. (2001). "Where has all the education gone?". The World Bank Economic Review 15 (3), 367–391.
Pritchett, L. (2002). "Ought ain't is: Midnight thoughts on education". Mimeo, Harvard University (www.lpritchett.org).
Pritchett, L. (2003). "When will they ever learn? Why all governments produce schooling". Working Paper 031. Bureau for Research in Economic Analysis of Development.

Rama, M., Arcetona, R. (2002). A Database of Indicators of Labor Market Indicators Across Countries. World Bank, Washington, DC.
Rodrik, D. (1999). "Where did all the growth go? External shocks, social conflict and growth collapses". Journal of Economic Growth 4 (4), 385–412.
Romer, P.M. (1986). "Increasing returns and long-run growth". Journal of Political Economy 94 (5), 1002–1037.
Romer, P.M. (1990). "Endogenous technological change". Journal of Political Economy 98 (5), S71–S102, part II.
Rosenzweig, M. (1998). "Schooling, economic growth and aggregate data". In: Srinivasan, T.N., Saxonhouse, G. (Eds.), Development, Duality and the International Regime: Essays in Honor of Gustav Ranis. University of Michigan Press, Ann Arbor, MI, pp. 107–129.
Sala-i-Martin, X. (2002) "The disturbing 'rise' of global income inequality". Working Paper 8904, National Bureau of Economic Research.
Schultz, T.W. (1975). "The value of the ability to deal with disequilibria". Journal of Economic Literature 13 (3), 827–846.
Spiegel, M. (1994). Determinants of Long-Run Productivity Growth: A Selective Survey with Some New Empirical Results. Department of Economics, University of Rochester, Rochester, New York. Processed.
Temple, J.R.W. (2001). "Generalizations that aren't? Evidence on education and growth". European Economic Review 45 (4–6), 905–918.
Topel, R. (1999). "Labor markets and economic growth". In: Ashenfelter, O., Card, D. (Eds.), Handbook of Labor Economics. Elsevier Science, Amsterdam, pp. 2943–2984.
Wade, R. (1990). Governing the Market. Princeton University Press, Princeton.
Welch, F. (1970). "Education in production". Journal of Political Economy 78 (1), 35–59.
World Bank (1993). The East Asian Miracle. Oxford University Press, New York.
Wössmann, L. (2002). Schooling and the Quality of Human Capital. Springer, Berlin.
Young, A. (1998). "Growth without scale effects". Journal of Political Economy 106 (1), 41–63.
Zeckhauser, R. (1996). "Comment on: Government intervention in the markets for education and health care: How and why?" In: Fuchs, V.R. (Ed.), Individual and Social Responsibility: Child Care, Education, Medical Care, and Long-Term Care in America. National Bureau of Economic Research Conference Report Series. University of Chicago Press, Chicago and London, pp. 304–306.

Chapter 12

INTERPRETING THE EVIDENCE ON LIFE CYCLE SKILL FORMATION

FLAVIO CUNHA

University of Chicago

JAMES J. HECKMAN

University of Chicago, University College London and The American Bar Foundation

LANCE LOCHNER

University of Western Ontario

DIMITRIY V. MASTEROV

University of Michigan

Contents

Handbook of the Economics of Education, Volume 1
Edited by Eric A. Hanushek and Finis Welch
© 2006 Elsevier B.V. All rights reserved
DOI: 10.1016/S1574-0692(06)01012-9

Abstract

This paper presents economic models of child development that capture the essence of recent findings from the empirical literature on skill formation. The goal of this essay is to provide a theoretical framework for interpreting the evidence from a vast empirical literature, for guiding the next generation of empirical studies, and for formulating policy. Central to our analysis is the concept that childhood has more than one stage. We formalize the concepts of self-productivity and complementarity of human capital investments and use them to explain the evidence on skill formation. Together, they explain why skill begets skill through a multiplier process. Skill formation is a life cycle process. It starts in the womb and goes on throughout life. Families play a role in this process that is far more important than the role of schools. There are multiple skills and multiple abilities that are important for adult success. Abilities are both inherited and created, and the traditional debate about nature versus nurture is scientifically obsolete. Human capital investment exhibits both self-productivity and complementarity. Skill attainment at one stage of the life cycle raises skill attainment at later stages of the life cycle (self-productivity). Early investment facilitates the productivity of later investment (complementarity). Early investments are not productive if they are not followed up by later investments (another aspect of complementarity). This complementarity explains why there is no equity-efficiency trade-off for early investment. The returns to investing early in the life cycle are high. Remediation of inadequate early investments is difficult and very costly as a consequence of both self-productivity and complementarity.

Keywords

skill formation, education, government policy, educational finance

JEL classification: J31, I21, I22, I28

1. Introduction

The most valuable of all capital is that invested in human beings; and of that capital the most precious part is the result of the care and influence of the mother.
Marshall (1890, paragraph VI.IV.11)

The study of human skill formation is no longer handicapped by the taboo that once made it impermissible to discuss differences among people. It is well documented that individuals are very diverse in a variety of abilities, that these abilities account for a substantial amount of the interpersonal variation in socioeconomic outcomes, and that this diversity is already apparent at an early age. The family plays a powerful role in shaping these abilities, contributing both genetic endowments and pre- and post-natal environments, which interact to determine the abilities, behavior and talents of children. Some families do this task poorly, with detrimental consequences for their children. From a variety of intervention studies, we know that it is possible to partially compensate for exposure to adverse environments if high-quality interventions are made sufficiently early in children's lives. The remediation efforts that appear to be most effective are those that supplement family resources for young children from disadvantaged environments. Since the family is the fundamental source of inequality in American society, programs that target children from disadvantaged families can have substantial economic and social returns.

This chapter presents formal models of skill formation that distill the essence of recent empirical findings from the literature on child development. The goal is to provide a theoretical framework for interpreting the evidence from a large empirical literature, for guiding the next generation of empirical studies, and for formulating policy.

Recent empirical research has substantially improved our understanding of how skills and abilities are formed over the life cycle. The early human capital literature [Becker (1964)] viewed human capital as a rival explanation for human ability in explaining earnings. It emphasized that acquired human capital could explain many features of earnings distributions and earnings dynamics that models of innate and invariant cognitive ability could not. This point of view still underlies many recent economic models of family influence [e.g., Aiyagari, Greenwood and Sechadri (2002), Becker and Tomes (1979, 1986)]. Related work [Ben-Porath (1967), Griliches (1977)] emphasized that invariant innate ability was an input into the production of human capital, although its effect on human capital accumulation was ambiguous. More innate ability could lead to less schooling if all schooling does is to teach what an able person could learn without formal instruction. On the other hand, more innate ability might make learning easier and promote schooling. The signaling literature [Spence (1973), Stiglitz (1975)] focused on the latter interpretation in developing models of education where higher levels of schooling signal higher innate ability. In its extreme form, this literature suggested that there was no learning content in schooling.

The entire literature assumed that ability is an innate, scalar, age-invariant measure of cognitive skill. This early point of view still prevails in most quarters of economics.

Except for work by Marxist economists [see, e.g., Bowles and Gintis (1976), Edwards (1976)], noncognitive traits like motivation, persistence, time preference, and self control were neglected in empirical research and treated as "soft skills," peripheral to educational and labor market outcomes.

In contrast to the wisdom of Marshall (1890), as encapsulated in the quotation that begins this chapter, the recent economic literature on family influence on child outcomes focuses on family income constraints and heritability as the principal sources of parental influence on child development. Becker and Tomes (1979, 1986) initiated a large literature that emphasized the importance of credit constraints and family income on the schooling and earnings of children. Important developments of this work by Benabou (2000, 2002), Aiyagari, Greenwood and Seshadri (2002), Caucutt and Kumar (2003), Hanushek, Leung and Yilmaz (2004), and Seshadri and Yuki (2004), emphasize the role of credit constraints and altruism in forming the skills of children. In this work, ability is treated as determined by genetic factors. The life cycle of the child at home is collapsed into a single period so that there is no distinction between early and late investments in children. Becker and Tomes (1986) show that there is no trade-off between equity and efficiency in making government transfers directed toward credit-constrained families because the return to human capital investment in children from such families is high due to the presence of credit constraints. We show that their insight holds true for early period investments in a multi-period model of child investment, but not for investments in later periods. We also generalize their discussion of credit constraints to a multiperiod setting following work by Caucutt and Lochner (2004), Cunha (2004), and Cunha and Heckman (2004, 2006).

Recent research, summarized in Heckman (2000) and Carneiro and Heckman (2003), presents a richer picture of schooling, life cycle skill formation and earnings determination. It recognizes the importance of both cognitive and noncognitive abilities in explaining schooling and socioeconomic success. These abilities are produced by the family and by personal actions. The role of the mother is especially important, as anticipated in the quote by Marshall that begins this chapter. Both genes and environments are involved in producing these abilities. Environments affect genetic expression mechanisms [see, e.g., Turkheimer et al. (2003)]. This interaction has important theoretical and empirical implications for skill policies. It suggests an important role for environment-enriching policies in fostering human skills.

In the light of a substantial body of recent research, the traditional sharp distinction between acquired skills and genetically determined cognitive ability maintained in the human capital literature is no longer tenable. Abilities are multiple in nature. They are both cognitive and noncognitive. Measured cognitive ability is susceptible to environmental influences, including *in utero* experiences. So is measured noncognitive ability. There are genetic components to both.[1] We have come to understand that achievement tests used to monitor performance in school and to determine acceptance

[1] See Robinson, Grozinger and Whitfield (2005) for a summary of recent research on primates and other animals. See Knudson et al. (2006).

into the military are not the same as IQ tests. Achievement test scores are determined by IQ, noncognitive inputs and by environmental factors. Even IQ can be affected by environmental interventions at least up to age 10 or so.[2] It is hard to change IQ after this age. In the popular literature, achievement tests and IQ tests are often confused.[3] Achievement test scores are affected by IQ, schooling inputs, and noncognitive skills, and are malleable over a much greater range of ages than is IQ. Noncognitive abilities such as motivation, self-discipline, and time preference – associated with the development of the prefrontal cortex – are also affected by environmental influences. They are more malleable at later ages than IQ. Achievement test outcomes can be influenced until very late ages and are affected by both cognitive and noncognitive skills. Noncognitive abilities and cognitive abilities affect schooling attainment and performance, and a wide array of behaviors [Heckman, Stixrud and Urzua (2006)]. Abilities have an acquired character although they differ in their malleability at different ages.

We characterize the human skill formation process in the following fashion. Skills and abilities are used interchangeably throughout this chapter because both are affected by environments, investment and genes. Agents possess a vector of abilities at each age. These abilities – or skills – are multiple in nature and range from pure cognitive abilities (e.g., IQ) to noncognitive abilities (patience, self control, temperament, time preference). Achievement test scores are affected by cognitive, noncognitive and environmental inputs. These abilities are used with different weights in different tasks in the labor market and in social life more generally.

The human skill or ability formation process is governed by a multistage technology. Each stage corresponds to a period in the life cycle of a child. Inputs or investments at each stage produce outputs at that stage. Unlike the Ben-Porath (1967) model, in our models qualitatively different inputs can be used at different stages and the technologies may be different at different stages.[4] The outputs at each stage are the levels of each skill achieved at that stage. Some stages of the technology may be more productive in producing some skills than other stages, and some inputs may be more productive at some stages than at other stages. Those stages that are more productive in producing certain skills are called "sensitive periods" for those skills. If one stage alone is effective in producing a skill (or ability) it is called a "critical period" for that skill.

An important feature of this technology is that the skills produced at one stage augment the skills attained at later stages. This is termed *self-productivity*. It embodies the

[2] Until age 4 or 5, measures of IQ do not predict adult IQ very well. Using parental IQ actually yields a better prediction of the child's score at age 15 than any test given before age 5. After age 10, however, IQ becomes stable within the constraints of psychometric measurement error. See Jensen (1980) for a discussion.

[3] See, e.g., Herrnstein and Murray (1994).

[4] Heckman, Lochner, and Taber (1998) generalize and estimate the Ben-Porath model by allowing the technology producing schooling human capital to be different from the technology producing post-school investment. Su (2004) and Cardak and Givon (2004) develop multistage models of secondary and postsecondary schooling choices focusing on determinants of progression through school. However, their emphasis is on later stages of the life cycle, not the early years.

idea that skills acquired in one period persist into future periods. It also embodies the idea that skills are self-reinforcing. For example, self-control and emotional security may reinforce intellectual curiosity and promote more vigorous learning of cognitive skills. A second key feature of skill formation is *complementarity*. Skills produced at one stage raise the productivity of investment at subsequent stages. In a multistage technology, complementarity also implies that levels of skill investments at different ages bolster each other. They are synergistic. Complementarity also implies that early investment has to be followed up by later investment in order for the early investment to be productive. Together, complementarity and self-productivity produce multiplier effects which explain how skills beget skills and abilities beget abilities.

Complementarity, self-productivity of human capital and multiplier effects imply an equity-efficiency trade-off for late child investments but not for early investments. These features of the technology of skill formation have consequences for the design and evaluation of public policies toward families. In particular, the returns to late childhood investment and remediation for young adolescents from disadvantaged backgrounds are low, while the returns to early investment in children from disadvantaged environments are high.

Our analysis demonstrates the quantitative insignificance of credit constraints in the college-going years in explaining child college enrollment. Controlling for cognitive ability, under meritocratic policies currently in place in American society, family income during the child's college-going years plays only a minor role in determining child college participation, although much public policy is predicated on precisely the opposite point of view. Abilities (and skills) are formed over time, and the early periods in a child's life cycle are crucial for development. Augmenting family income only in the time period when a child goes to college will not make up for suboptimal investment in the 18 years before. *Permanent* family income plays an important role in explaining educational choices, insofar as it is a proxy for the high level of investment in abilities and skills that wealthier families provide, but it is not synonymous with family income in the adolescent years, nor with tuition and fees.

Carneiro and Heckman (2002, 2003) present evidence for the United States that only a small fraction (at most 8%) of the families of American adolescents are credit constrained in making their college decisions. The quantitatively important constraints facing disadvantaged children are the ones determining their early environments – parental background, and the like. The empirically important market failure in the life cycle of child skill formation is the inability of children to buy their parents or the lifetime resources that parents provide, and not the inability of families to secure loans for a child's education when the child is an adolescent. Our analysis has major implications for the way policies should be designed in order to help low income and disadvantaged populations. Evidence from disadvantaged populations demonstrates that enriched early interventions can raise measured ability and other skills.

Ours is an unusual survey. The standard approach to survey writing in empirical economics is to compile lists of facts and "treatment effects" from various empirical studies. Instead, in this chapter, we develop a comprehensive model of the skill formation process that is grounded in the best available empirical evidence. We distill general theoretical principles that can guide skill formation policy. We present economic models that focus on basic principles. Any study of skill formation policy grounded in economic and scientific fundamentals improves on a purely empirical approach to policy evaluation that relies on evaluations of the programs and policies in place or those previously experienced. Although economic policy analysis should be grounded in data, it is important to recognize that those policies that can be evaluated empirically are only a small subset of the policies that might be tried.[5] If we base speculation about economic policies on economic fundamentals, rather than solely on estimated "treatment effects" that are only weakly related to those fundamentals, we are in a better position to think beyond what has been tried to propose more innovative answers to skill formation questions. We investigate the study of skill formation policy by placing it in the context of economic models of life cycle learning and skill accumulation rather than focusing exclusively on which policies have "worked" in the past. The current literature on childhood skill formation abounds in facts and figures, but lacks a clear interpretive framework that is faithful to the evidence. If a picture (graph) is worth a thousand words, then a model is worth a thousand pictures (graphs). Our models summarize the existing evidence succinctly and point the way to future developments.

Any model that is faithful to the evidence summarized in this paper must recognize that (a) parental influences are key factors governing child development; (b) early child investments must be distinguished from late child investments and that an equity-efficiency trade-off exists for late investments, but not for early investments; (c) abilities are created, not solely inherited, and are multiple in variety; and (d) the traditional ability-skills dichotomy is obsolete. These insights change the way we interpret evidence and design policy. Point (a) is emphasized in many papers. Point (b) is ignored by models that consider only one period of childhood investment. Points (c) and (d) have received scant attention in the formal literature on child investment.

The central concept in this paper is the production function for skills. Since both skills and abilities can be acquired, we do not distinguish between these two concepts. Both skills and abilities are affected by genes, environments and personal actions.[6] We use a skill production technology to interpret the evidence on the life cycle evolution of skills and abilities, developing the technology and its implications more formally in Section 3.

Here, we provide an intuitive summary of the main theoretical ideas that organize the evidence presented in this paper. Assume, for the sake of simplicity, that there are two stages in the life cycle of the child prior to attaining adulthood. Adulthood is a third and

[5] See Heckman and Vytlacil (2005, 2007a, 2007b) for comprehensive discussions of econometric policy evaluation.

[6] One possible distinction between abilities and skills is that the latter are acquired by personal actions while the former are acquired by external influences. This distinction is not sharp since personal actions may affect the operation of the environment on the individuals, and personal actions (self help programs) may alter abilities.

final stage. Denote investment in a child during period t as I_t, and the skill produced from that investment as S_t for $t = 1, 2$. Both I_t and S_t may be vectors (e.g., cognitive and noncognitive skills), and they may be of different dimensions. The S_t are different levels of the same skills or abilities at different stages. Thus S_t could contain a variety of abilities and skills, ranging from pure IQ to noncognitive skills like motivation. It could also include cognitive skills as measured in achievement tests that are affected by IQ, motivation and self-control. I_t is a vector of investments at stage t. These may be stage-specific investments (e.g., phonics lessons) or general investments that are not stage-specific. Some stages may be uniquely suited to the formation of some skills. These are the critical or sensitive periods.

Let S_0 be the vector of initial skills of the child, say at birth. These skill levels may be influenced by *in utero* experiences and genetics.[7] We define the technology of skill formation at stage t in a recursive fashion:

$$S_t = f_t(I_t, S_{t-1}), \tag{1}$$

where $f_t(\cdot)$ is increasing in (I_t, S_{t-1}) and is concave in I_t. For simplicity, we assume differentiability, except in special cases. Each stage of the life cycle may have a different production technology using different inputs.[8]

Different adult tasks $j = 1, \ldots, J$ require skills that can be combined in different ways to produce task-specific output at period t in adult life, $T_{j,t}$. The tasks correspond to the outputs in the J different occupations (e.g., lawyer, ditch digger, full time mother, athlete):

$$T_{j,t} = T_{j,t}(S_t) \quad \text{for } j = 1, 2, \ldots, J. \tag{2}$$

In some tasks, components of S_t can substitute for each other. In other tasks, those same components may be strongly complementary. For example, to be a good mother requires many skills. To be a good ditch digger requires fewer skills.

Appendix A presents a more general discussion of our specification of the technology of skill formation and compares it to the conventional Ben-Porath (1967) model which is a very special case of our framework. Throughout much of this paper, we focus on technology (1), and for simplicity we assume that there is one task in the economy. However, task function (2) reminds us that remediation for early disadvantage may take two forms: (a) through later investments or (b) through subsidy and technical change in the tasks that disadvantaged children can perform in adulthood.[9]

Given the technology of skill formation (1), the concept of universal *self-productivity* is captured by the assumption that $\frac{\partial S_2}{\partial S_1} = \frac{\partial f_2}{\partial S_1} > 0$.[10] More generally, some components

[7] As emphasized in the studies in Keating and Hertzman (1999) these endowments are influenced by parental genes and environment.

[8] This technology and its properties are developed more formally in Appendix A.

[9] For example, remediation through technological change might involve automatic change machines for cashiers who are innumerate.

[10] A better terminology would be "recursive productivity," where the output from one stage is the input in the next stage because S_1 and S_2 can be vectors.

of S_1 may be productive for S_2 while others may not or may even have a negative effect. This formulation is sufficiently general to allow cross effects of knowledge of one skill (or ability) on another skill (or ability).[11] The concept of universal *direct complementarity* of investments in stage 2 technology is that

$$\frac{\partial^2 f_2(I_2, S_1)}{\partial I_2 \partial S_1'} > 0.$$

For the vector case, this says that higher levels of the stocks of all skills increase the productivity of period 2 investment. More generally, $\frac{\partial^2 f_2(I_2, S_1)}{\partial I_2 \partial S_1'} \gtrless 0$, since some inputs may not be complementary with stocks of past skills or abilities. Even more generally, some skills may have a negative effect on the productivity of some investments.[12]

In addition to the notions of direct complementarity and self-productivity in skill production, there is the notion of complementarity or substitution of period t skills in each task, as determined by the task function (2). The story of the tortoise and the hare tells us that it is sometimes possible to compensate with effort for what one lacks in pure athletic skill. In the general case with J different task functions corresponding to different adult jobs or occupations, tasks will have different degrees of substitution among the skills, and some components of skills are irrelevant for certain tasks, so it is possible in some tasks to compensate for skill deficits while for other tasks it may not be. A failure to acquire one skill can be offset by choosing to do tasks that do not require it or else by compensating for investments in other skills.

The structure of complementarity or substitutability in investments over time as governed by equation (1) is crucial in determining whether or not there is an equity-efficiency trade-off for late investments.[13] To see this, consider two children, A and B, with $S_0^A = S_0^B$ but who differ, for whatever reason, in their level of period 1 investment, I_1. We assume that there is only one investment good. Suppose that A comes from

[11] In capital theory, the "Crusonia vine" of Knight (1944) is a pure version of a self productive process. His vine grows at a fixed rate of g per year, independently of any inputs once the seed is sown. In our notation, for a scalar S_t this would be $S_t = (1+g)S_{t-1}$, so that $S_t = (1+g)^t S_0$ and $\partial f_t / \partial I_t \equiv 0$ for $t > 0$. Our notation is more general because we allow for multiple inputs that may interact synergistically.

[12] In capital theory, Hayek's (1941) stages of production of capital entail investments at each stage that are stage-specific. His theory encompasses both self-productivity and direct complementarity.

[13] Complementarity has multiple definitions in economics and these definitions are not equivalent [Samuelson (1974)]. The two polar cases, perfect substitutes and perfect complements, have been a part of the economist's toolkit at least since Fisher (1982). A production function for output, $g(x, y)$, defined in terms of inputs (x, y) is said to exhibit *perfect substitution* among the inputs if the output $g(x, y)$ is

$$g(x, y) = g\big(ax + (1-a)y\big), \quad 0 < a < 1.$$

Thus x and y substitute perfectly in the sense that one unit of y produces exactly the same output as $(1-a)/a$ units of x for all levels of x and y. If x is an early input and y is a late input, technically one can always remediate for a low x input by a compensation in terms of y. If $a = 1$, this is *not* possible. The closer a is to 1, the greater the required remediation in y. As we note in this chapter, it may not be economically feasible or efficient to remediate.

a deprived environment whereas B does not so $\bar{I}_1^A < \bar{I}_1^B$.[14] Given period 1 investments, what is the appropriate investment allocation for period 2? If there is one skill, and the goal is to maximize the sum of adult skills in society, the problem is

$$\max\left(S_2^A + S_2^B\right) \quad \text{given } I_1^A = \bar{I}_1^A,\ I_1^B = \bar{I}_1^B.^{15}$$

This is the "social planner's" problem.

Perfect complementarity characterizes $g(x, y)$ if

$$g(x, y) = g\big(\min(x, y)\big).$$

This is an "O ring" technology where output is limited by the weakest link (the lowest level of input). Thus if x is an early input, a low level of x cannot be remediated by any investment in y. Another implication of this technology is that if x is big, a low level of y undoes the early investment.

A second definition of complementarity and substitution, sometimes called direct substitution or complementarity, for a twice differentiable $g(x, y)$ is that (x, y) are direct complements if

$$\partial^2 g(x, y)/\partial x \partial y > 0,$$

while (x, y) are direct substitutes if

$$\partial^2 g(x, y)/\partial x \partial y < 0.$$

Inputs (x, y) are independent if

$$\partial^2 g(x, y)/\partial x \partial y = 0.$$

What is confusing is that the two definitions do not always agree. Suppose that $g(x, y) = ax + (1 - a)y$. Then (x, y) are perfect substitutes under the first definition, but they are independent inputs under the second definition. Note further that if (x, y) are perfect complements under the first definition, g is not everywhere differentiable. However, if g is strictly concave and differentiable, (x, y) are perfect substitutes under either definition. To make matters worse if $g(x, y)$ is homogeneous of degree one and $\partial^2 g(x, y)/\partial x^2 < 0$, then it is a consequence of Euler's Theorem that

$$\partial^2 g(x, y)/\partial x \partial y > 0,$$

so that inputs are direct complements.

The CES technology for two inputs,

$$g(x, y) = \left[ax^\sigma + (1 - a)y^\sigma\right]^{1/\sigma},$$

nests the two polar cases subsumed in the first definition ($\sigma = 1$ perfect substitutes; $\sigma = -\infty$ for perfect complements). The parameter σ is a measure of substitution or complementarity. However for $0 < a < 1$ and $-\infty < \sigma < 1$,

$$\partial^2 g(x, y)/\partial x \partial y > 0,$$

so that (x, y) are direct complements for all values of the substitution/complementarity parameter σ. In the general case with more than 2 inputs, direct complementarity is not imposed as a consequence of assumptions about substitution or complementarity in the CES case. In the example, we use the two polar cases because they are intuitive.

[14] Plausibly $S_0^A < S_0^B$, but we abstract from this.

[15] This criterion is the same as maximizing human capital if adult skill is the same as adult human capital.

Assume that the resources available for investment are M.[16] We assume that the social planner is free to impose taxes and lump sum transfers. For large enough M (i.e., assuming that investment is feasible), this problem yields the interior solution

$$\frac{\partial f_2(I_2^A, S_1(\bar{I}_1^A))}{\partial I_2^A} = \frac{\partial f_2(I_2^B, S_1(\bar{I}_1^B))}{\partial I_2^B}.$$

The marginal return to second period investment should be equated across persons.[17]

Consider the role of complementarity and substitutability by first studying the polar case in which inputs are perfect substitutes in the intuitive [Fisher (1982)] sense of the term. If I_2 and S_1 are perfect substitutes, the second period technology can be written as $S_2 = f_2(\gamma S_1 + (1-\gamma)I_2)$ for $0 \leqslant \gamma \leqslant 1$. The parameter γ determines the relative productivity of investment in the different periods. For interior solutions, the problem of maximizing social output yields the first order condition:

$$f_2'\big(\gamma \bar{S}_1^A + (1-\gamma)I_2^A\big) = f_2'\big(\gamma \bar{S}_1^B + (1-\gamma)I_2^B\big),$$

which implies that adult skill levels are equated. Specifically, second period investments are fully equalizing:

$$I_2^A = I_2^B + \frac{\gamma}{1-\gamma}\big(\bar{S}_1^B - \bar{S}_1^A\big),$$

so there is full compensation for adverse early environments.

If S_1 and I_2 are strong complements in the intuitive sense of that term, we obtain a very different result. Consider the polar opposite case of perfect complementarity (i.e., the so-called "Leontief case") with

$$S_2 = f_2\big(\min\{S_1, I_2\}\big).$$

It takes a unit of S_1 and a unit of I_2 together to produce S_2. In the Leontief case, efficiency dictates that lower first period investments in A relative to B be followed by lower second period investments in A relative to B ($\bar{I}_1^A < \bar{I}_1^B$ implies $I_2^A < I_2^B$). Efficiency in this case dictates a policy that perpetuates the initial inequality of inputs due to disadvantaged environments. Attempts to remediate early deficits are not possible due to the structure of the technology of skill formation. There is an efficiency-equity trade-off for period 2 investments, but not for period 1 investments. With this production technology, the skill level attained in period 2 is restricted by the skill level attained earlier. Period 1 is a bottleneck period. Efficient period 2 investment can be no larger than period 1 investment. This example is a bit artificial because we have postulated only a single skill. More generally, there may be some skills (abilities) that are essential for making investment in the second period productive.

[16] This may include social and private resources.

[17] Low M may imply zero investment for one or both persons unless Inada conditions (which guarantee infinite marginal product at zero levels of input) are imposed on the production function.

Complementarity has a dual face. Investments in the young are essential and cannot easily be substituted for by later investments. At the same time, later investments are needed to make the early investments pay off. On efficiency grounds, the Leontief example shows that early disadvantages will be perpetuated and compensatory investments at later ages may be inefficient if complementarity is sufficiently strong.

On the other hand, a technology with perfect substitutes and equal productivity of investments at all ages implies that the timing of investment is irrelevant for producing a given level of human capital. Indeed, with discounting and common unit investment costs across periods, common productivity in both periods (i.e., $\gamma = 1/2$), and $S_1 = I_1$, later investments are preferred to early investments because it is cheaper to defer costs. Second period compensation for adverse environments will be efficient. Delaying all investments to the second period is optimal. However, if γ is close to 1 it may be very costly to remediate deficient first period investments. When $\gamma = 1$, it is impossible.

We develop some implications of complementarity and age-specific productivity in this paper for the general vector case in Appendix A. We organize the evidence we present in this chapter around the concepts of self-productivity and complementarity. We introduce the notion of a skill multiplier in Section 3.1. The available empirical evidence on human skill formation is consistent with both self-productivity and complementarity. These features of the technology of human skill formation explain why early interventions targeted towards disadvantaged young children are more effective than interventions given to older disadvantaged children, and why later investments yield higher returns for the more able.

The plan of this chapter is as follows. Section 2 presents the evidence. Section 3 presents simple formal models that summarize the evidence by using economic theory, applying the concepts of complementarity, self-productivity, and the derived investment multiplier. Section 4 concludes the paper.

2. A summary of the empirical evidence on life cycle skill formation

2.1. *Human capital accumulation*

Skill formation is a dynamic process. The skills and abilities acquired in one stage of the life cycle affect the productivity of learning in the next stage. Human capital, as we define it in this chapter, consists of different types of skills and abilities. It is now well established that cognitive ability is an important determinant of schooling and labor market outcomes [see Heckman (1995)]. At the same time, noncognitive abilities, although harder to measure, play an important role as well [see the evidence in Heckman, Stixrud and Urzua (2006). As emphasized in recent studies of child development [e.g., Shonkoff and Phillips (2000)], different abilities are formed and shaped at different stages of the life cycle. Empirical evidence from human and animal species tells us that when the opportunities for formation of these abilities are missed, remediation can be costly, and full remediation prohibitively costly [Cameron (2004), Knudsen (2004), Knudsen et al. (2006)]. These findings highlight the need for economists to take a comprehensive view of skill formation over the life cycle.

The dynamic feature of human capital accumulation has implications for how investments in human skills should be distributed over the life cycle. Figure 1A summarizes the major finding of an entire literature. It plots the rate of return to human capital at different stages of the life cycle for a person of given abilities. The horizontal axis represents age, which is a surrogate for the agent's stage in the life cycle of skill formation. The vertical axis represents the rate of return to investment assuming the same amount of investment is made at each age. This is an out-of-equilibrium productivity curve. *Ceteris paribus*, the rate of return to a dollar of investment made while a person is young is higher than the rate of return to the same dollar invested at a later age. Optimal investment profiles equate the marginal rate of return to investment with the opportunity cost of funds in all periods and for all persons, assuming that these investments are feasible. For an externally specified constant opportunity cost of funds r (represented by the horizontal line with intercept r in Figure 1A), an optimal investment strategy is to invest relatively less when a person is old and more at younger ages (see Figure 1B). For persons with higher "innate" ability (higher S_0 in the production technology of Section 1), both curves shift to the right.

Cognitive ability is only one aspect of S_0. It is necessary for success in life, but for many aspects of performance in social life, it is not sufficient. Noncognitive abilities also matter for success both in the labor market and in schooling. Even when early childhood

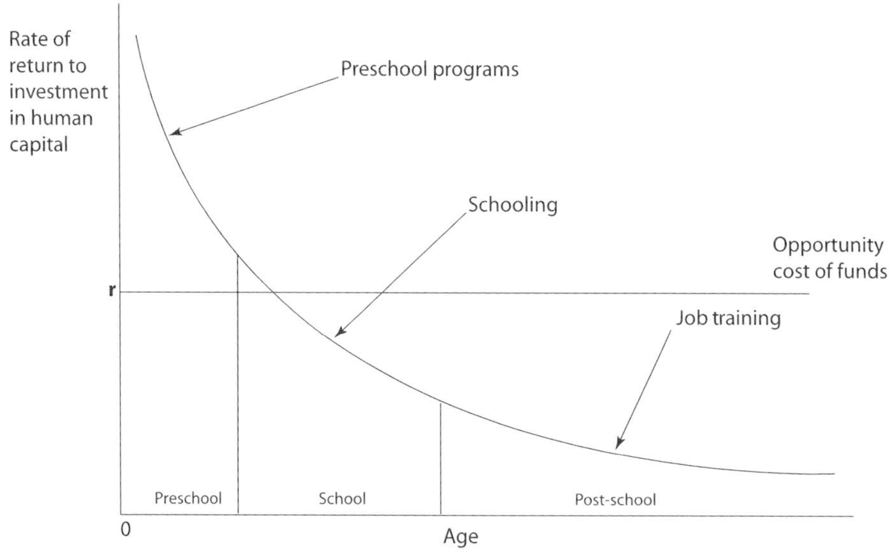

Figure 1A. Rates of return to human capital investment initially setting investment to be equal across all ages.

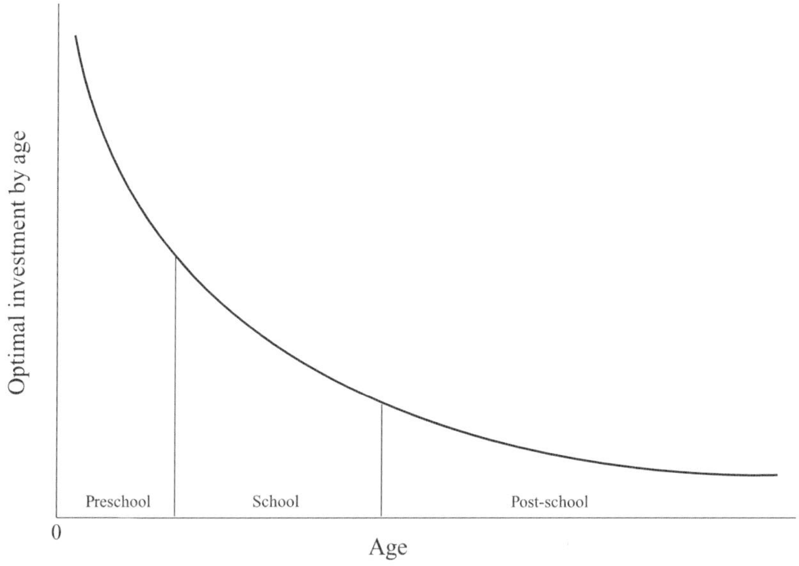

Figure 1B. Optimal investment levels.

interventions do not boost IQ, they improve noncognitive skills, with substantial effects on schooling, labor market outcomes, and behavioral outcomes such as teenage pregnancy and participation in criminal activities. They raise achievement test scores, which can be influenced by schooling (and other inputs), even when they do not boost IQ. In light of this evidence, the neglect of noncognitive ability in evaluating human capital interventions, and in formalizing the skill formation process, is unwarranted. We summarize the evidence on the importance of noncognitive skills in Section 2.3. For now, it will suffice to say that both types of skills or abilities are affected by families and schools, but they differ in their malleability over the life cycle. Differences in levels of cognitive and noncognitive skills by family income and family background emerge early and persist. If anything, schooling widens these early differences, but the main gaps in these skills that are found in adulthood emerge before schooling begins.

2.2. Early test score differentials

Important differences in the ability of children across family types appear at early ages and persist. Figure 2A plots average percentile ranks[18] on the Peabody Individual

[18] In constructing the graph in Figure 2A, we computed each individual's position in the distribution of test scores at each age. Then we divided individuals into different quartiles of permanent family income and computed the average percentile rank at each age. Because the scale of test scores is arbitrary, an analysis of test scores can only determine how the factors being studied shift people in the overall distribution of ability.

Achievement Test in Math (PIAT Math) by age for different quartiles of family income. This test is a measure of age-appropriate math knowledge. There are large gaps by the time children enter school. The gaps in ranks across income quartiles remain relatively stable as children develop. Such gaps also appear in other test scores, although for some test scores they widen slightly.[19] Just as income gradients in schooling participation rates are evident, racial differences in early test scores also emerge. Figure 2B presents evidence on the emergence of racial gaps in ranks on the PIAT Math Test.

Ability affects schooling participation and affects wages as we document below. It is shaped early in life. The available evidence indicates that IQ is relatively more malleable early in the life cycle than in later years [see Shonkoff and Phillips (2000), and Carneiro and Heckman (2003)]. Having access to more and higher-quality resources that contribute to improving cognitive ability early in life affects skill acquisition later in life. IQ is not the same as what is measured by achievement tests. Achievement tests are affected by schooling and other environmental influences into adolescence even if IQ is not [see Hansen, Heckman and Mullen (2004), Heckman, Stixrud and Urzua (2006)].

Figures 3A and 3B present the gaps in PIAT Math from the previous two figures after controlling for some main features of the child's family background. The gaps across racial and income groups are significantly reduced when we control for maternal education and cognitive ability,[20] and for family structure. Measured long-term family factors

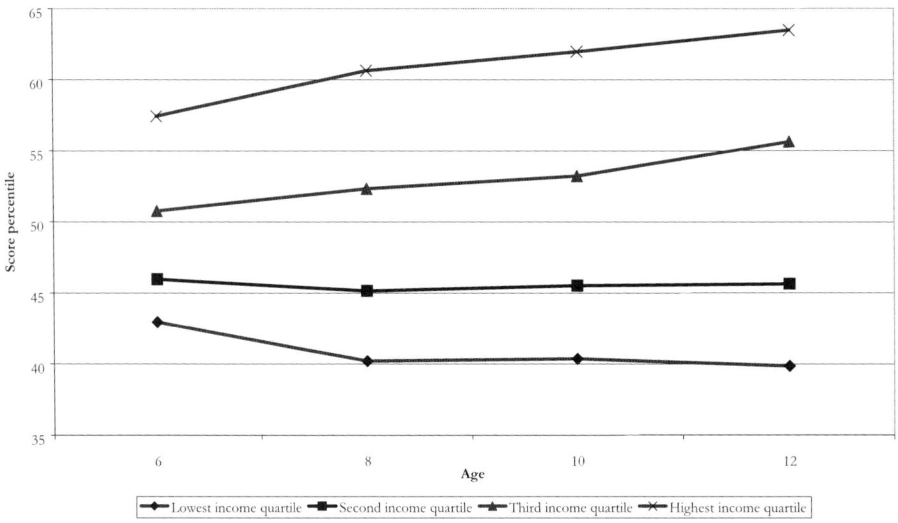

Figure 2A. Children of NLSY79. Average percentile rank on PIAT Math score, by income quartile.*
* Income quartiles are computed from average family income between the ages of 6 and 10.

[19] For evidence on other tests, see Carneiro, Heckman and Masterov (2005).

[20] Cognitive ability is measured using the Armed Forces Qualifications Test, corrected for the effect of schooling using the methodology of Hansen, Heckman and Mullen (2004).

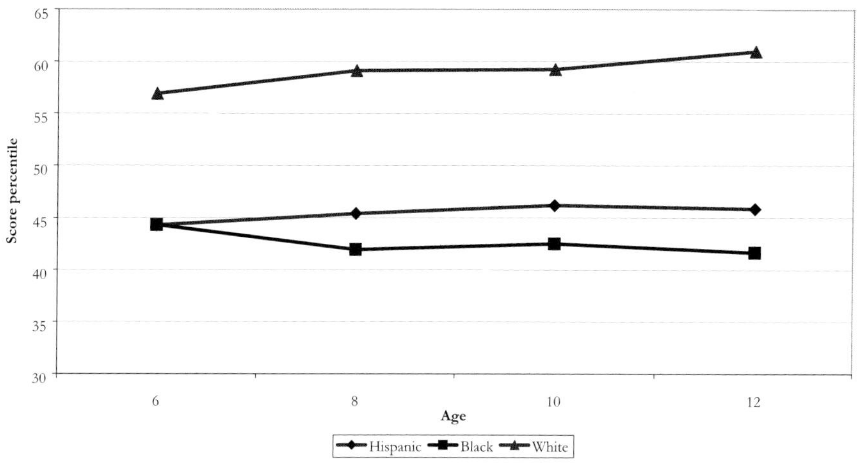

Figure 2B. Average percentile rank on PIAT Math score, by race.

play a powerful role in a correlational sense. The gaps at age 12 do not disappear entirely, however, when we compare the highest and lowest income quartiles or whites with blacks. The evidence from early intervention programs with randomized assignment that we discuss in Section 2.6 shows that these correlational results have a causal basis. When disadvantaged children are given enriched early environments, the gaps in academic achievement test scores between advantaged and disadvantaged children can be partially remedied.

The emergence of early test score gradients is not limited to cognitive measures. At early ages, differences in children's behavior across income and racial groups are also evident, as Figures 4A and 4B illustrate. These figures present differences in ranks on an index of Anti-Social Behavior across different income and racial groups. The Anti-Social Behavior index is based on exhibiting age-specific behaviors like cheating and telling lies, bullying and cruelty to others, not feeling sorry for misbehaving, breaking things deliberately, disobedience at school, and trouble getting along with teachers. High values of the index correspond to a higher prevalence of behavioral problems. As we discuss further in Section 2.3, understanding the gaps in these behavioral skills across different income and racial groups and how to eliminate them is important for understanding the determinants of economic success. Figures 5A and 5B present Anti-Social Behavior index adjusted for mother's ability, mother's score on the Armed Forces Qualification Test (AFQT), and broken home.[21] Adjusting for early family background

[21] We first regress the Anti-Social score on mother's education, mother's AFQT, and broken home at the same age at which the score is measured. We then rank individuals on the residuals of this regression and construct percentiles. We then include family income in the regression as well as the other variables mentioned above before taking the residuals and constructing the ranks.

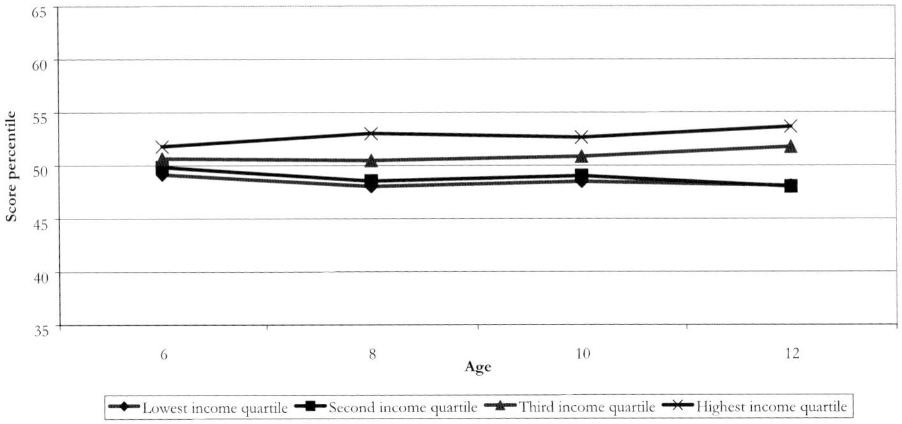

Figure 3A. Children of NLSY79. Adjusted average PIAT Math score percentiles by income quartile.*
* Adjusted by maternal education, maternal AFQT (corrected for the effect of schooling) and broken home at each age.

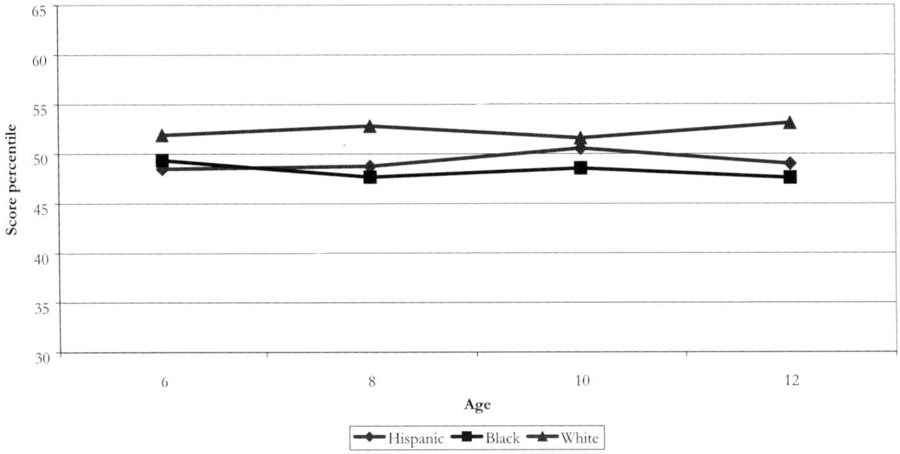

Figure 3B. Adjusted average PIAT Math score percentile by race.*
* Adjusted by maternal education, maternal AFQT (corrected for the effect of schooling) and broken home at each age.

factors substantially reduces gaps in ranks in noncognitive skills across income and racial groups. Comparing adjusted cognitive and noncognitive test scores reveals the importance of long-term factors in reducing the gaps in behavioral scores across these groups. Although noncognitive ability gaps across income and racial groups cannot be fully eliminated by a regression adjustment, controlling for mother's ability and education, family income, and family structure significantly reduces the gaps in noncognitive

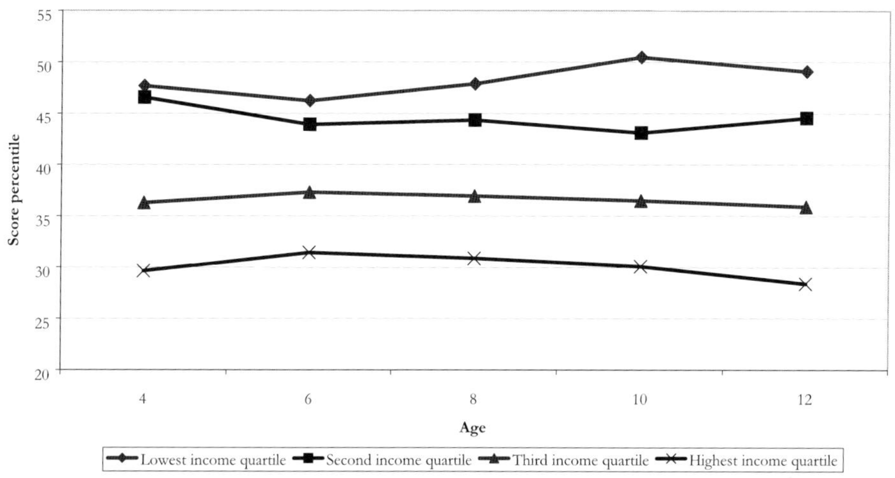

Figure 4A. Children of NLSY79. Average percentile rank on anti-social behavior score, by income quartile.

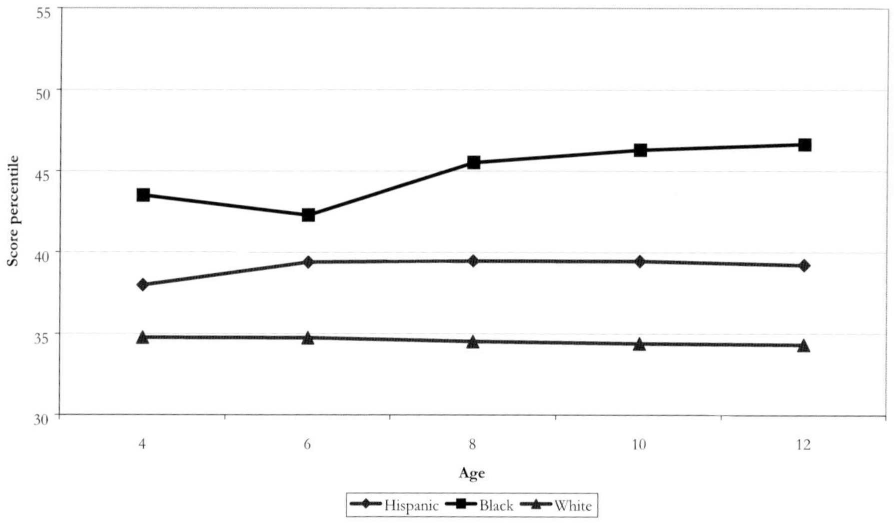

Figure 4B. Average percentile rank on anti-social behavior score, by race.

abilities across these groups at both early and later ages. The experimental evidence discussed in Section 2.6 confirms that these findings on noncognitive skills have a causal basis. Indeed, the evidence across a variety of studies suggests that early childhood interventions affect motivation and other noncognitive skills.

This evidence suggests that strong families (those with enriched parental environments) promote cognitive, social, and behavioral skills. Weak families do not. This

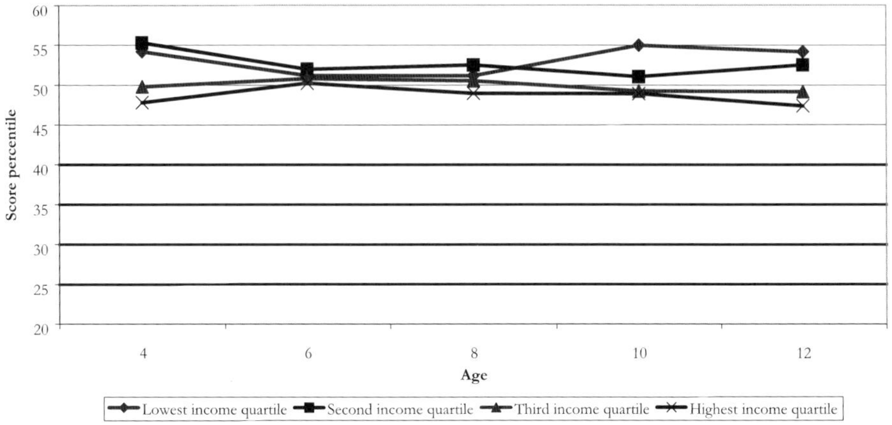

Figure 5A. Children of NLSY79. Adjusted average anti-social behavior score percentile by income quartile.*
* Adjusted by maternal education, maternal AFQT (corrected for the effect of schooling) and broken home at each age.

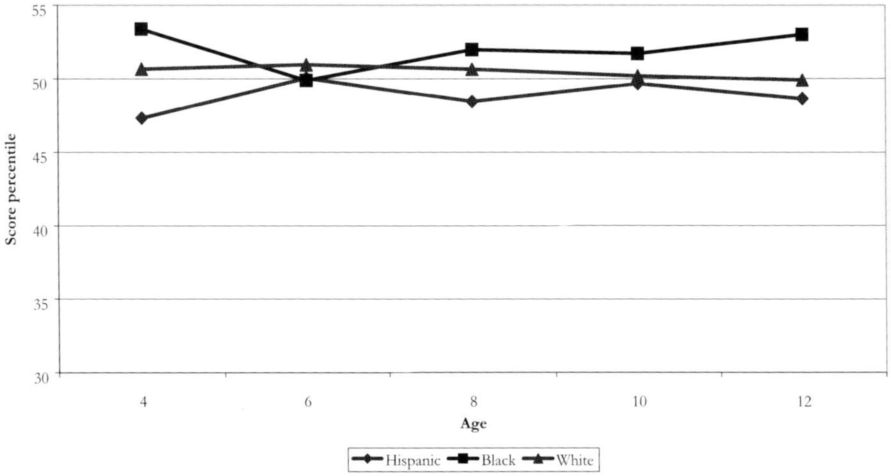

Figure 5B. Adjusted average anti-social behavior score percentile by race.*
* Adjusted by maternal education, maternal AFQT (corrected for the effect of schooling) and broken home at each age.

evidence is consistent with a large body of evidence in sociology and economics [see, e.g., Duncan and Brooks-Gunn (1997b)]. The relevant policy issue is to determine what interventions in dysfunctional families, if any, are successful. The evidence presented in Section 2.6 addresses this question.

2.3. *The evidence on the importance of noncognitive skills*

Much of the neglect of noncognitive skills in analyses of earnings, schooling, and other life outcomes is due to the lack of any reliable means of measuring them. Many different personality traits are lumped into the category of noncognitive skills. Psychologists have developed batteries of tests to measure these skills [Sternberg (1985)]. Companies use these tests to screen workers, but they are not yet widely used to ascertain college readiness or to evaluate the effectiveness of schools or reforms of schools. The literature on cognitive tests ascertains that one dominant factor (g) summarizes cognitive tests and their effects on outcomes. No single factor has emerged as dominant in the literature on noncognitive skills and it is unlikely that one will ever be found, given the diversity of traits subsumed under the category of noncognitive skills. Heckman, Stixrud and Urzua (2006), test and reject the g theory of noncognitive skills.

Studies by Bowles and Gintis (1976), Edwards (1976), and Klein, Spady and Weiss (1991) demonstrate that job stability and dependability are the traits most valued by employers as ascertained by supervisor ratings and questions of employers, although they present no direct evidence of the effects of these traits on wages and educational attainment. Perseverance, dependability and consistency are the most important predictors of grades in school [Bowles and Gintis (1976)].

Self-reported measures of persistence, self-esteem, optimism, future orientedness, and the like are now collected in major data sets, and some recent papers discuss estimates of the effects of these measures on earnings and schooling outcomes [see Bowles and Gintis (1976), Duncan, Claessens and Engel (2004)]. These studies shed new light on the importance of noncognitive skills for success in social life. Yet these studies are not without controversy. For example, *ex post* assessments of self-esteem may be as much the consequence as the cause of the measures being investigated.

Heckman and Rubinstein (2001) avoid the problems inherent in these *ex post* assessments by using evidence from the GED testing program in the United States to demonstrate the quantitative importance of noncognitive skills in determining earnings and educational attainment. The GED program is a second-chance program that administers a battery of cognitive tests to self-selected high school dropouts to determine whether or not their level of academic attainment is equivalent to that of high school graduates.

The GED examination is successful in psychometrically equating GED test takers with ordinary high school graduates who do not go on to college. Recipients are as smart as ordinary high school graduates who do not go on to college, where cognitive ability is measured by an average of cognitive components of the AFQT or by the first principal component (g) derived from the components. According to these same measures, GED recipients are smarter than other high school dropouts who do not obtain a GED [see Heckman and Rubinstein (2001)]. In the raw data, GED recipients earn more than ordinary high school dropouts, have higher hourly wages, and finish more years of high school before they drop out. This is entirely consistent with the literature that emphasizes the importance of cognitive skills in determining labor market outcomes.

When measured ability is controlled for, however, GED recipients earn the same as or less than other dropouts. Heckman and Rubinstein (2001) note that noncognitive skills play an important role in this gap. GEDs have higher cognitive skills than dropouts but exhibit the same problems of self control and self discipline exhibited by dropouts, and on some behaviors are worse than other dropouts.

Heckman, Stixrud and Urzua (2006) and Urzua (2006) present evidence that both cognitive and noncognitive skills affect schooling and the returns to schooling.[22] They analyze the changes in the probabilities of various outcomes that arise from changing cognitive or noncognitive abilities. Figures 6A and 6B, taken from their 2006 study, shows that both higher levels of cognitive and noncognitive skills are associated with lower rates of attrition from high school. For many outcome measures, increasing noncognitive ability over the same decile range as cognitive ability has a greater effect on outcomes than increasing cognitive ability over the same decile range. These effects are not always uniform across genders.[23]

Increasing noncognitive ability to the highest level reduces the probability of being a high school dropout to virtually zero for females with average cognitive ability (see Figure 6B).[24] This effect is especially pronounced at the bottom of the distribution (going up from the bottom fifth). The effect is less strong for males. Both cognitive and noncognitive skills are strong predictors of who graduates from a four year college but the effects of noncognitive skills are stronger for females (see Figures 6C and 6D). Increases in both types of ability have the same effect on reducing the likelihood of spending time in jail by age 30 for males (see Figure 6E).[25] Figures 6F and 6G show strong effects of both cognitive and noncognitive skills on smoking. Here there is a larger effect for males of increasing noncognitive ability. Figure 6H shows the strong effect of both cognitive and noncognitive skills on non-marital

[22] Cognitive and noncognitive abilities are estimated using a two-factor model and the NLSY79 data. The cognitive skill is identified by using a subset of five Armed Forces Vocational Aptitude Battery (ASVAB) tests (word knowledge, paragraph comprehension, numerical operations, coding speed and mathematics knowledge). The noncognitive factor is identified using the Rosenberg Self-Esteem and Rotter Locus of Control scales. The Rosenberg scale contains ten statements of self-approval and disapproval with which respondents are asked to strongly agree, agree, disagree or strongly disagree. A high score indicates a high self-approval rating. The Rotter scale is based on four questions about the extent to which respondents believe themselves to have control over the various domains of their lives. A higher score indicates more control over one's life. All tests were administered in 1979–1981, when the respondents were 14–24 years old. The estimation of the model is carried out using an MCMC routine. Heckman, Stixrud and Urzua use only the young sample to analyze the data (the scores are measured at least 3–4 years before the outcomes). They also show results from other data sets where the separation between the age of the test and the outcome is more substantial, and they find very similar results. They apply the method developed in Hansen, Heckman and Mullen (2004) to account for spurious feedback between outcomes and test scores.

[23] Heckman, Stixrud and Urzua (2006) show how this nonuniformity in the effects of cognitive and noncognitive skills on outcomes across genders can explain the differential effectiveness of early intervention programs across genders.

[24] Heckman, Stixrud and Urzua (2006) show the same patterns apply to college attendance.

[25] Incarceration is not an important phenomenon for females.

pregnancy. For this outcome both cognitive and noncognitive ability are important.[26] Higher levels of noncognitive skills promote success on achievement tests even when they do not affect IQ. This effect operates because noncognitive skills affect schooling and schooling raises measured achievement [Hansen, Heckman and Mullen (2004), Heckman, Larenas and Urzua (2004)]. Responses to changes in cognitive and noncognitive skills are not always uniform across genders.

Current systems of evaluating educational reforms are based predominantly on changes in scores on cognitive tests. These tests capture only one of the many skills required for a successful life [see Heckman (1999)]. A more comprehensive evaluation of educational systems would account for their effects on producing the noncognitive traits that are also valued in the market. There is substantial evidence that mentoring and motivational programs oriented toward disadvantaged teenagers are effective. We review this evidence in Section 2.6.

Much of the effectiveness of early childhood interventions comes from boosting noncognitive skills and from fostering motivation.[27] While IQ is fairly well set after the first decade of life, motivation and self-discipline are more malleable at later ages [Heckman (2000)]. More motivated children are more likely to stay in school and have higher achievement tests. Our analysis suggests that social policy should be more active in attempting to alter noncognitive traits, including values, especially for children from disadvantaged environments who receive poor discipline and little encouragement at home. This more active social policy approach would include mentoring programs and stricter enforcement of discipline in the schools. Although such programs are controversial, they are likely to be effective and to produce substantial saving to society from reduced pathological behavior (see Section 2.6).

We now turn to some evidence from animal and human populations that bolsters our case that early factors matter and socioemotional skills, shaped at an early age, also matter.

2.4. *Critical periods, sensitive periods, and socioemotional bases of skill formation and remediation*

Early experience exerts a profound influence on socioemotional outcomes directly, but it also interacts with genetic endowments, with consequences that are at least as important for development.[28] Experimental studies using animals have produced several suggestive findings that enhance our understanding of the evidence on human behavior.

[26] Heckman, Stixrud and Urzua (2006) show the same pattern for other reproductive outcomes, such as marital childbearing.

[27] See Karoly et al. (1998), Currie and Blau (2006), and Heckman (2000) for comprehensive reviews of the literature.

[28] A twins study by Turkheimer et al. (2003) found that in poor families, 60% of the variance in IQ is accounted for by the shared environments, and the contribution of genes is close to zero, whereas in wealthy families a nearly opposite result is found.

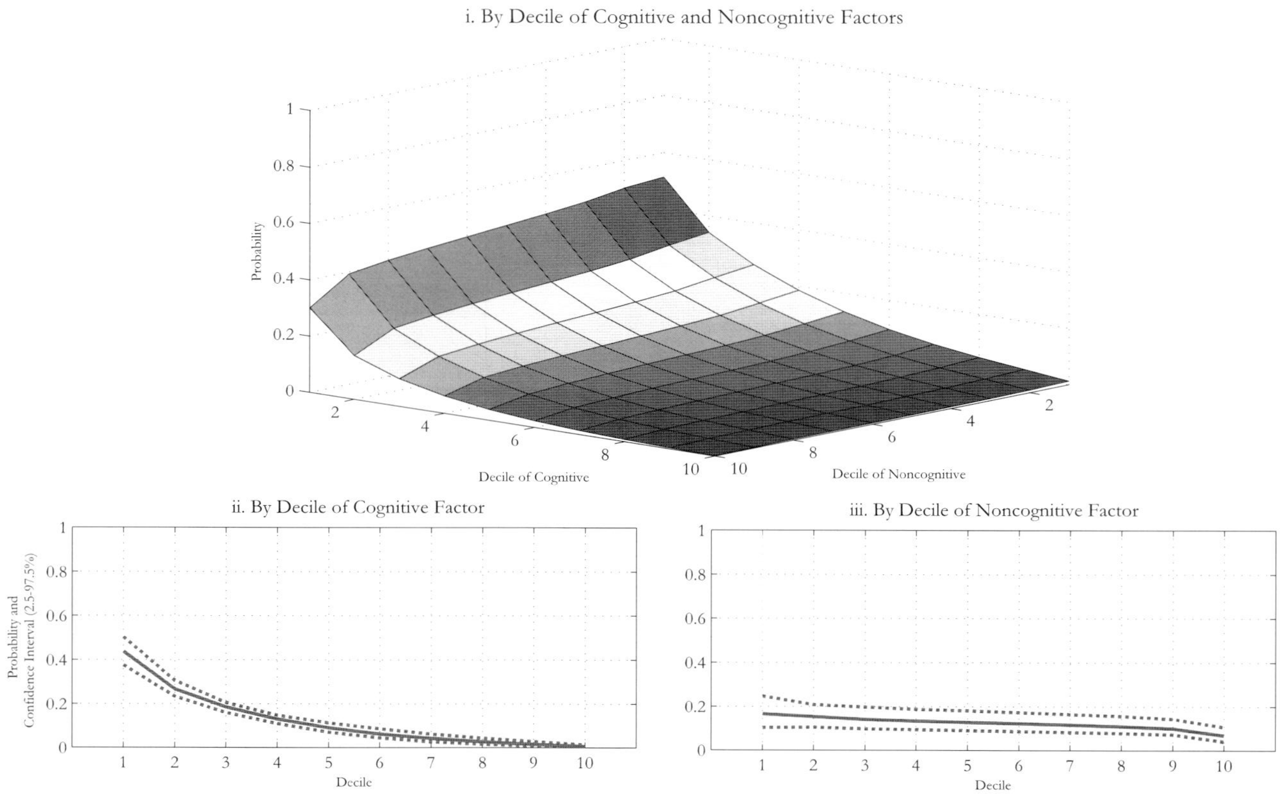

Figure 6A. Probability of being a high school dropout by age 30 – males.

Notes: The data are simulated from the estimates of the model and our NLSY79 sample. We use the standard convention that higher deciles are associated with higher values of the variable. The confidence intervals are computed using bootstrapping (200 draws). Source: Heckman, Stixrud and Urzua (2006).

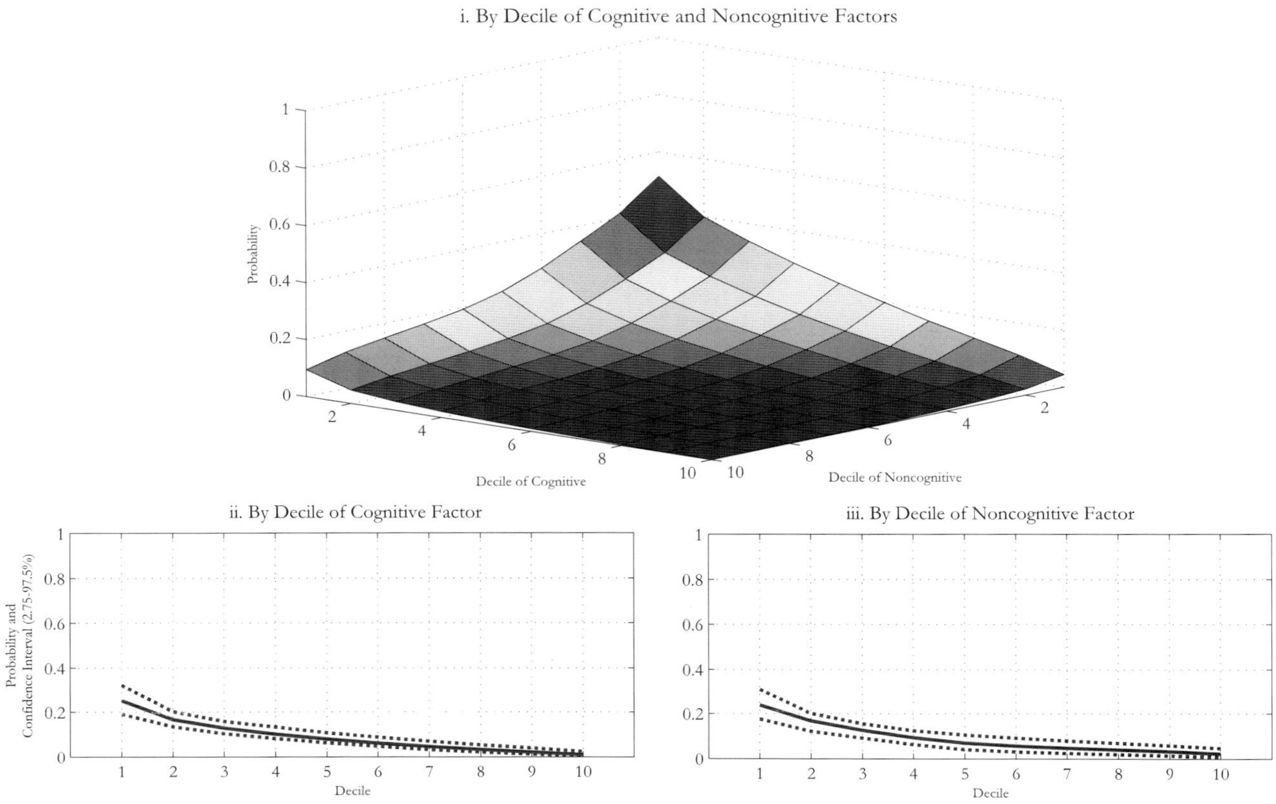

Figure 6B. Probability of being a high school dropout by age 30 – females.

Notes: The data are simulated from the estimates of the model and our NLSY79 sample. We use the standard convention that higher deciles are associated with higher values of the variable. The confidence intervals are computed using bootstrapping (200 draws). Source: Heckman, Stixrud and Urzua (2006).

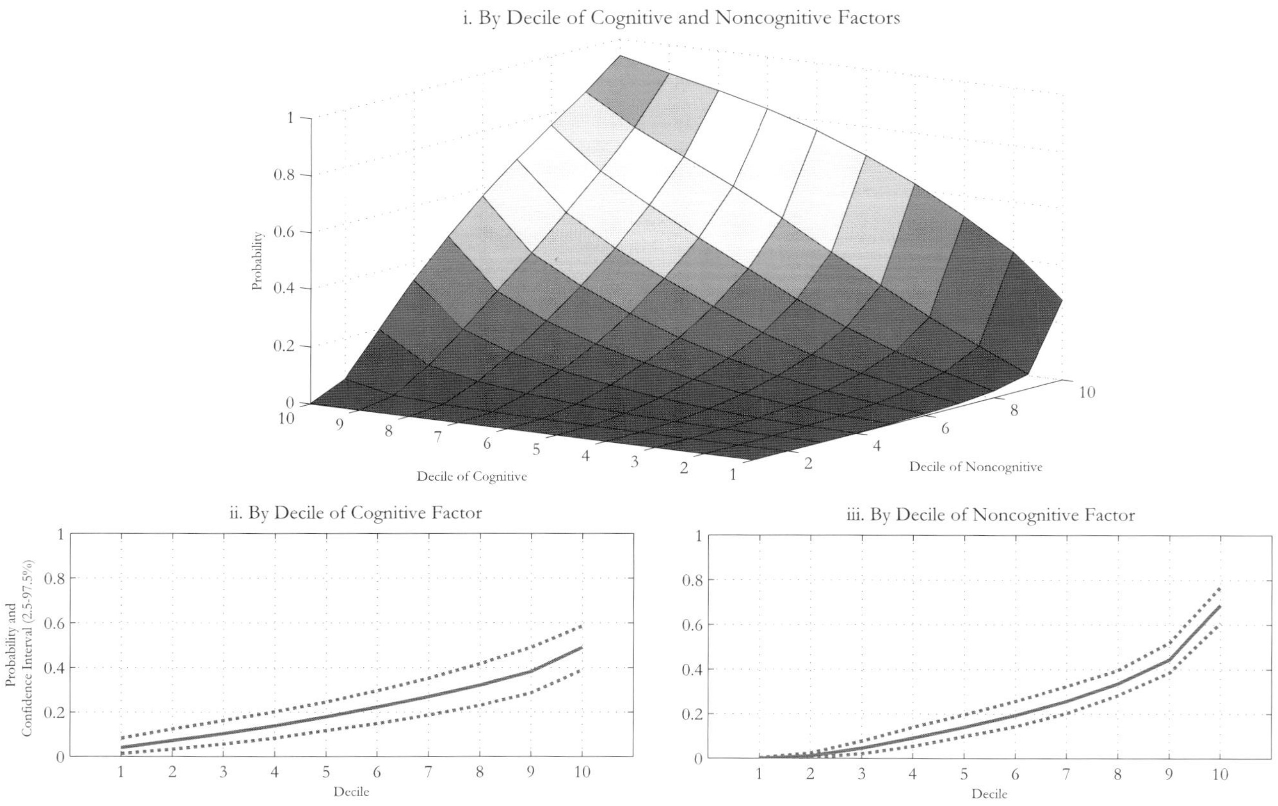

Figure 6C. Probability of being a 4-yr college graduate by age 30 – males.

Notes: The data are simulated from the estimates of the model and our NLSY79 sample. We use the standard convention that higher deciles are associated with higher values of the variable. The confidence intervals are computed using bootstrapping (200 draws). Source: Heckman, Stixrud and Urzua (2006).

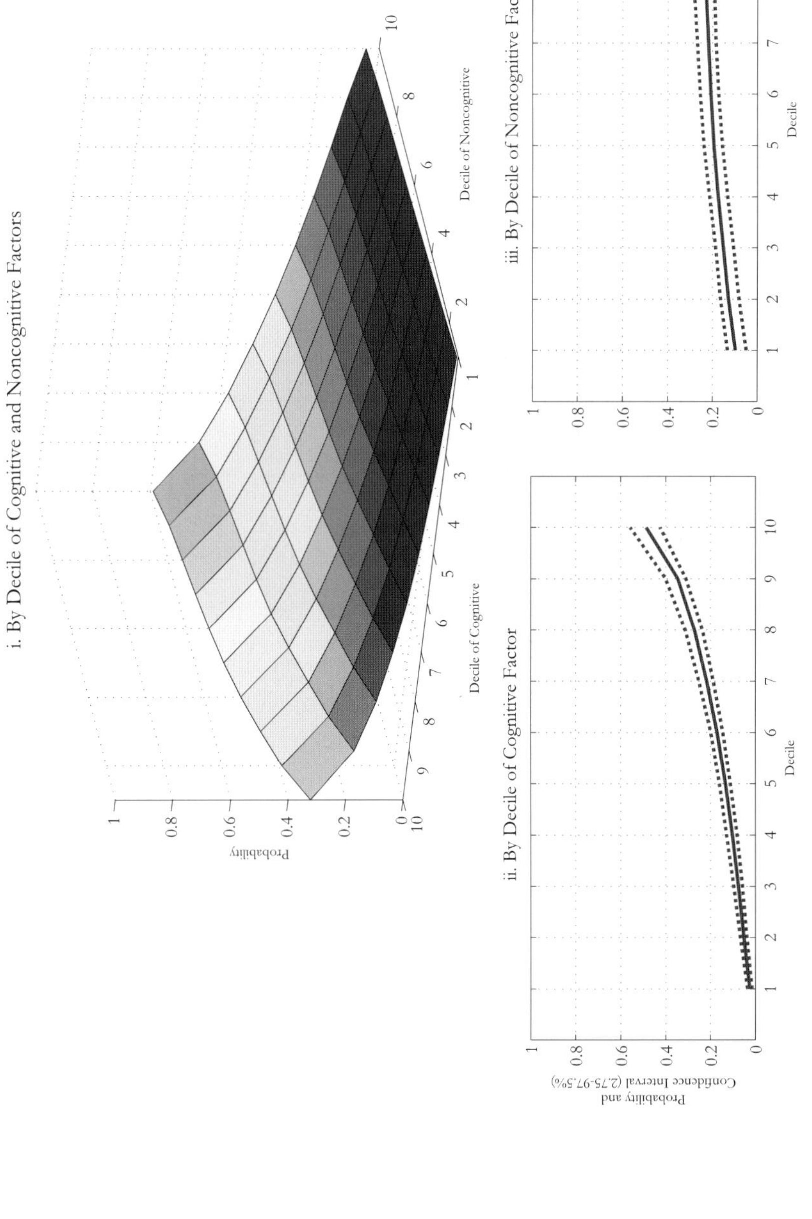

Figure 6D. Probability of being a 4-yr college graduate by age 30 – females.

Notes: The data are simulated from the estimates of the model and our NLSY79 sample. We use the standard convention that higher deciles are associated with higher values of the variable. The confidence intervals are computed using bootstrapping (200 draws). Source: Heckman, Stixrud and Urzua (2006).

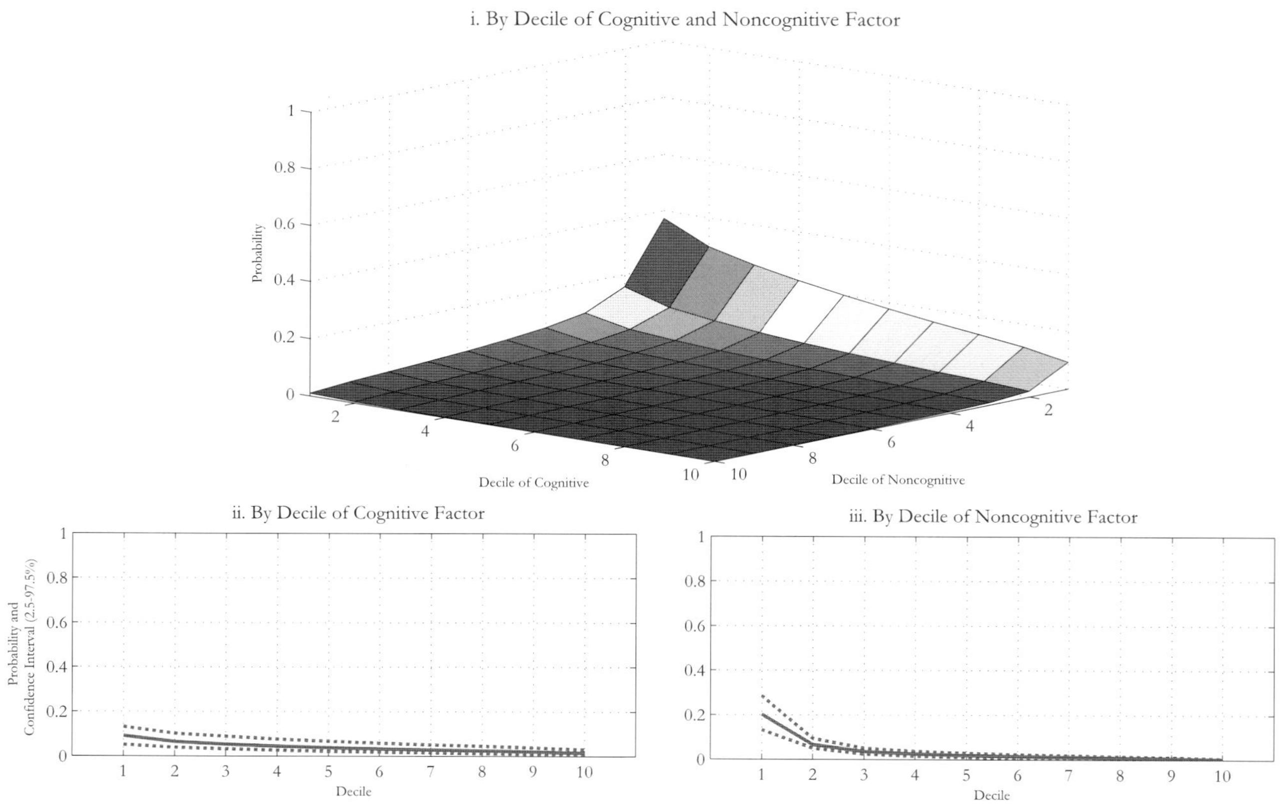

Figure 6E. Probability of incarceration by age 30 – males.

Notes: The data are simulated from the estimates of the model and our NLSY79 sample. We use the standard convention that higher deciles are associated with higher values of the variable. The confidence intervals are computed using bootstrapping (200 draws). Source: Heckman, Stixrud and Urzua (2006).

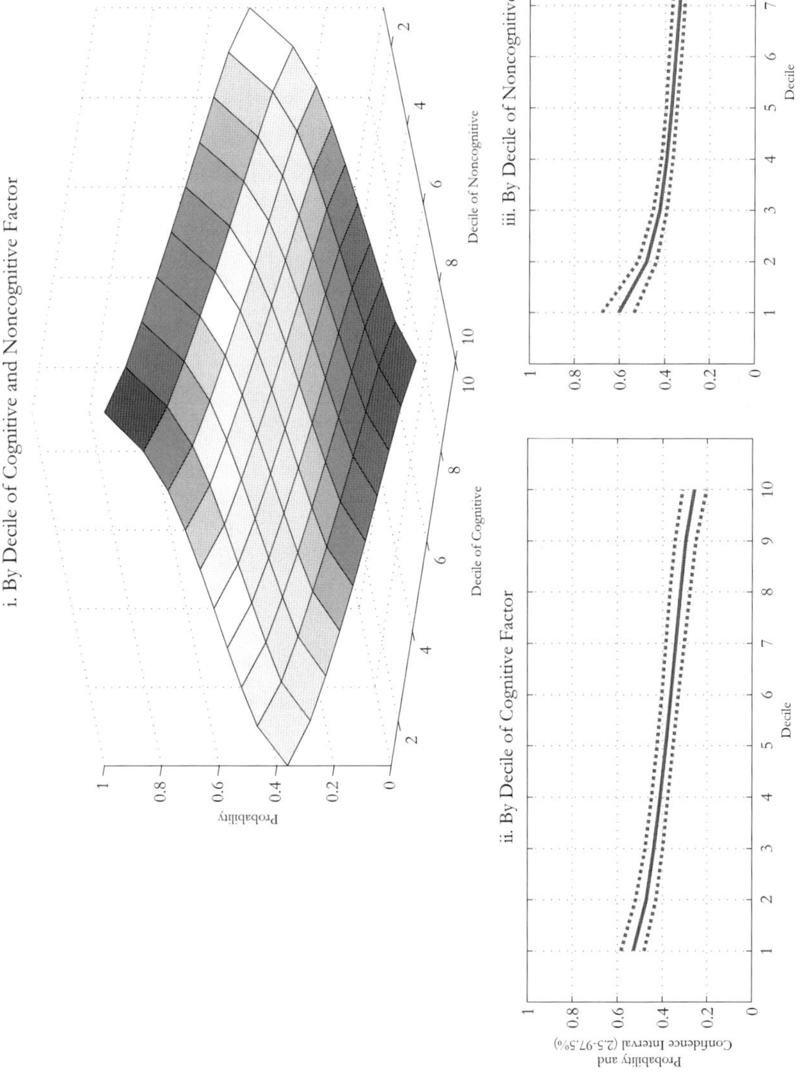

Figure 6F. Probability of daily smoking by age 18 – males.

Notes: The data are simulated from the estimates of the model and our NLSY79 sample. We use the standard convention that higher deciles are associated with higher values of the variable. The confidence intervals are computed using bootstrapping (200 draws). Source: Heckman, Stixrud and Urzua (2006).

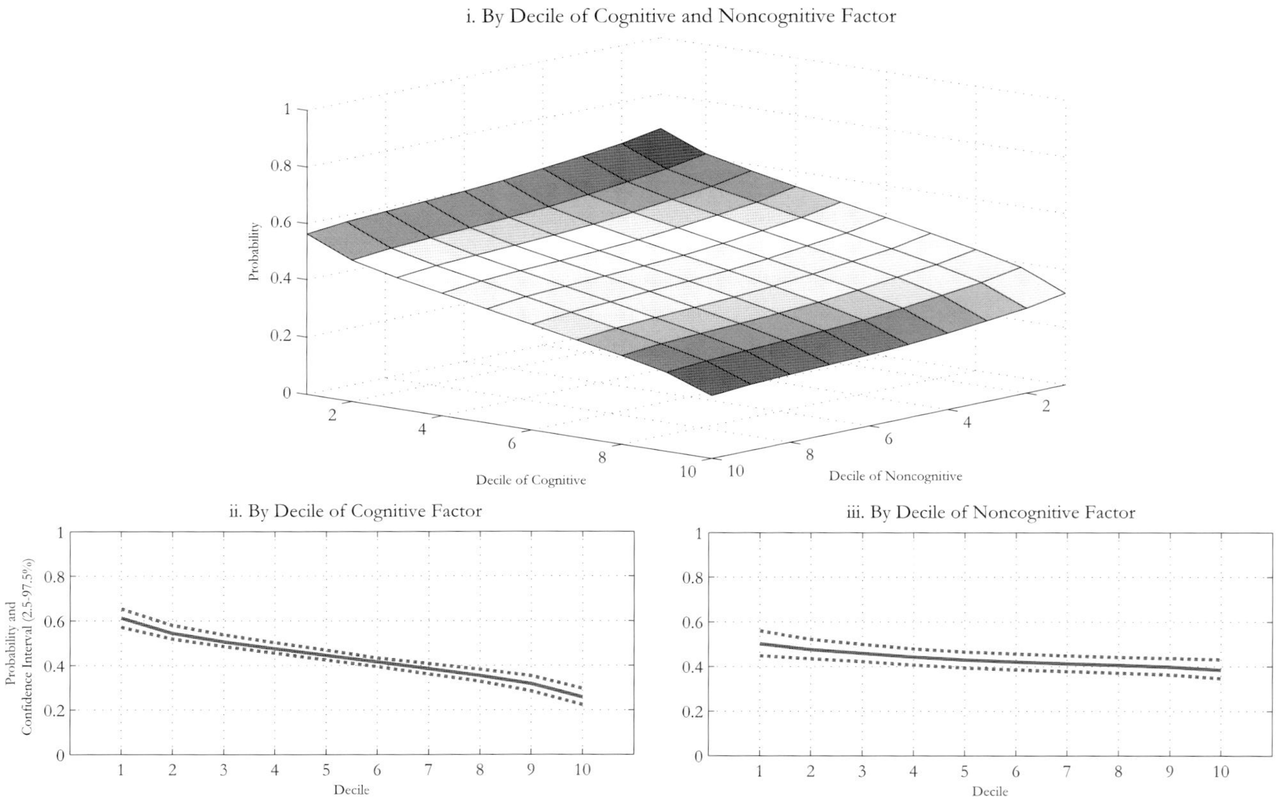

Figure 6G. Probability of daily smoking by age 18 – females.

Notes: The data are simulated from the estimates of the model and our NLSY79 sample. We use the standard convention that higher deciles are associated with higher values of the variable. The confidence intervals are computed using bootstrapping (200 draws). Source: Heckman, Stixrud and Urzua (2006).

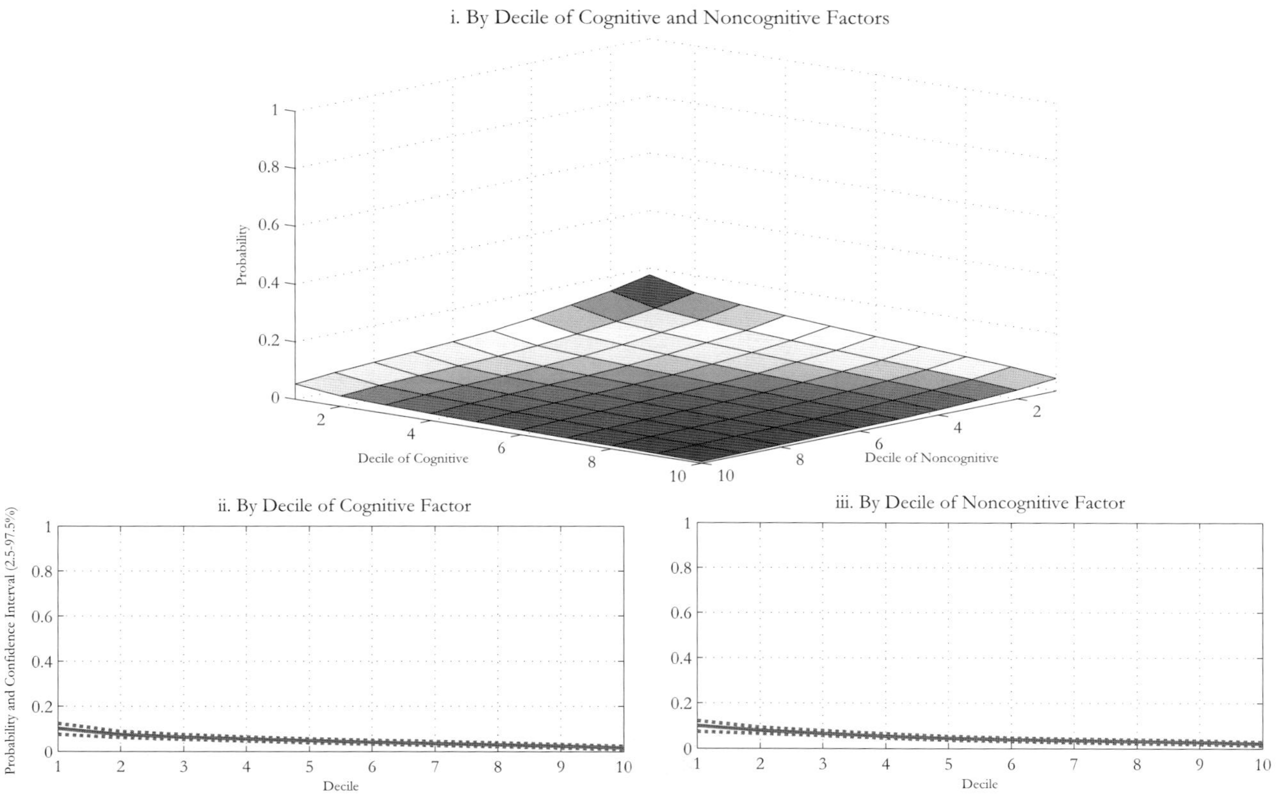

Figure 6H. Probability of being single with child at age 18 – females.

Notes: The data are simulated from the estimates of the model and our NLSY79 sample. We use the standard convention that higher deciles are associated with higher values of the variable. The confidence intervals are computed using bootstrapping (200 draws). Source: Heckman, Stixrud and Urzua (2006).

Suomi (1999) provides a summary of his research on the malleability of temperament. He and his colleagues selectively bred rhesus monkeys to be highly fearful. They then reassigned some of these infants to nurturing mothers, while pairing some infants of normal mothers with fearful adoptive mothers. Their results suggest that normal infants take on their foster mother's fearful characteristics. Infants born to fearful mothers assigned to nurturing mothers become even more socially precocious than their normal counterparts. They engage in autonomous exploration of their environment earlier and more frequently, and they do not display disproportionate responses to minor alarming stimuli. When they are moved into larger social groups, they are able to recruit allies and attain higher positions in the monkey hierarchy. Regardless of their genetic background, young females acquired the nurturing style of their adoptive mother with their own offspring rather than the style predicted by their genetic profile or own biological mother's behavior. These results suggest that positive early experiences can dramatically modify genetic tendencies, as expressed in behavior. Knudson et al. (2006) review the evidence from animal and human studies.

Knudsen (2004) shows that early experience can modify the biochemistry and architecture of neural circuits. When such experiences operate within a *limited* time frame in the life cycle, that period is termed "sensitive." During a sensitive period, certain patterns of connectivity among neurons become stable as a result of environmental influence. This stability is environmentally adaptive.[29] These pathways can be altered after the sensitive period, but their plasticity is limited by the structure created during the sensitive period, i.e., it is less efficient to invest in later periods. When experience in a given period is crucial for normal development, that period is called "critical." We formally define sensitive and critical periods in Section 3. Intuitively, if late investment is a good substitute for early investment, the early years are not critical. If it is not a good substitute, then the early period is critical.

Critical periods have been extensively documented in the development of binocular vision in the cortex of mammals, auditory space processing in the midbrain of barn owls, filial imprinting in the forebrain of ducks and chickens, and song learning in the forebrain of songbirds [see Knudsen (2004)]. For our purposes, the most relevant example is language acquisition and the fact that children tend to perform better in acquiring language skills than do adults, despite being more limited in most cognitive domains. Age of exposure to a language is negatively related to ultimate proficiency achieved in that language [see Newport (2002), for a summary of the evidence]. The decline in proficiency begins as early as 4 and 6, and continues until a plateau is reached in adulthood. This pattern is evident for many aspects of language proficiency, such as control over sounds as well as grammatical structure, and has been shown for both first

[29] Knudsen (2004) argues that experience provides information about the individual and his environment that cannot be predicted accurately and, therefore, cannot be encoded genetically. This may explain why the early experience of deprivation may result in maladaptive development and corresponding behavior. In some sense, the adaptation may only be adaptive locally, rather than globally.

and second languages.[30] However, not all aspects of language acquisition are equally sensitive. Newport (2002) cites evidence that the acquisition of vocabulary and semantic processing can be accomplished relatively easily even in adulthood, while the more formal dimensions of language (such as syntax, phonology, and morphology) are less easily acquired. These differences are apparent even on a neurological level. In short, both critical and sensitive periods are features of language learning.

Other types of social behavior are characterized by sensitive and critical periods. Independent research by Cameron (2004) suggests that development of normal social behavior in infant rhesus monkeys can be disrupted by removing the mother from the social group. When mothers and infants are separated when the infants are one week old, their subsequent adult behavior is profoundly antisocial, anxious, and aggressive. When the disruption takes place at a later age, the effects are qualitatively different and their severity declines with age at separation. The impact on the youngest monkeys can be offset by pairing them with an experienced mother, but the degree of catch-up decreases with the age at which the "foster" placement takes place. Remediation is possible, though its timing is crucial.

The monkeys who are emotionally secure explore more and learn more. This evidence shows how noncognitive skills feed into the formation of cognitive skills. It helps to explain how the Perry Preschool Program, discussed in Section 2.6, which did not raise IQ but raised noncognitive skills, affected achievement test outcomes. We formalize the notion of critical and sensitive periods in Section 3 and in Appendix A to this paper. Closely related is the concept of a "bottleneck" period. If skills at one stage of the life cycle are not formed at a sufficiently high level, it is difficult to proceed to excellence at the next stage. The Leontief technology discussed in Section 3.1 crystallizes this point.

It is important to understand how families invest in their children and why many youth do not pursue a higher education despite the purportedly high returns. As we discuss next, children from disadvantaged families often reach college-going ages without adequate preparation or skills to make college attendance worthwhile. We turn to a discussion of the importance of credit constraints and other long-term family factors on adolescent schooling decisions.

2.5. Interpreting the role of family income: The evidence on credit constraints

There is a strong relationship between family income and college attendance. Figure 7 displays aggregate time series of college participation rates for eighteen- to twenty-four-year-old American males classified by their parental income measured in the child's late adolescent years. There are substantial differences in college participation rates across family income classes in each year. The cross sectional pattern of schooling attendance by family income levels that is evident in this figure is found in many other

[30] The age-of-exposure effect appears even in the grammatical skills of deaf adults who learn sign language. See Pinker (1994) and Newport (2002) for more on this topic.

countries [see the essays in Blossfeld and Shavit (1993)]. In the late 1970s or early 1980s, college participation rates began to increase in response to increasing economic rates of return to schooling, but only for youth from the top family income groups. With a lag, children from other groups also responded, but the gaps in rates did not close. This differential educational response by income class threatens to perpetuate or widen income inequality across generations and among racial and ethnic groups. See Figure 8 for the time-series evidence on college attendance rates by race.

There are two different, but not necessarily mutually exclusive, interpretations of this evidence. The common and more influential one is the most obvious one. Credit constraints facing families in a child's adolescent years affect the resources required to finance a college education. A second interpretation emphasizes the long-run factors associated with higher family income. It notes that family income is strongly correlated over a child's life cycle. Families with high income in a child's adolescent years are more likely to have high income before that period. Higher levels of family resources in a child's formative years are associated with higher quality education and better environments that foster cognitive and noncognitive skills.

Both interpretations of the evidence are consistent with a form of credit constraint. The first, more common interpretation, is clearly compatible with this point of view. But the second interpretation is consistent with another type of credit constraint: the inability of a child to buy the parental environments and genes (or their substitutes) that form the

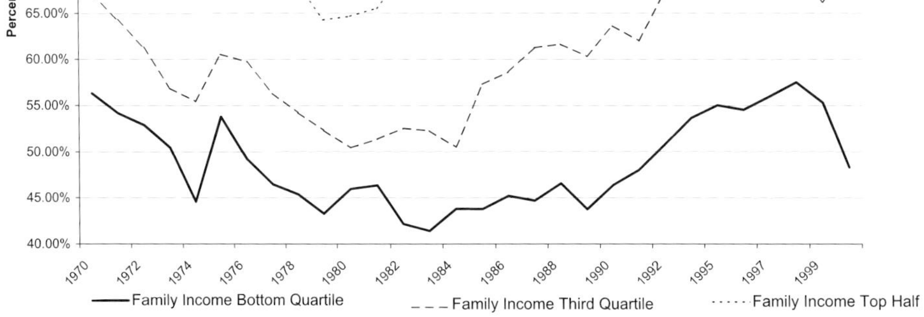

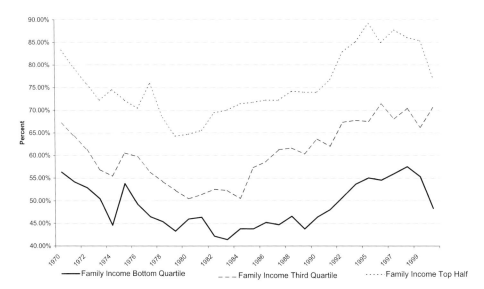

Figure 7. College participation, 18 to 24 yrs, HS graduates and GED holders. Dependent* White Males. Source: These number were computed from the CPS P-20 School Reports and the October CPS.
* Dependent is living at parental home or supported by parental family while at college.

cognitive and noncognitive abilities required for success in school. Some parents may never earn enough to provide the best developmental environments for their children.

Carneiro and Heckman (2002, 2003) argue on quantitative grounds that the inability of a child to acquire the family resources provided to children by wealthy families is the most important factor underlying Figure 7. After controlling for the ability formed by the early teenage years, they show that parental income in the adolescent years plays only a minor role in explaining college enrollment decisions. The evidence from the U.S. presented in their research suggests that at most 8 percent of American adolescents are affected by short-term liquidity constraints that inhibit their participation in post-secondary schooling. Most of the family income gap in enrollment is due to long-term factors that produce the abilities needed to benefit from participation in college.

The evidence reviewed here suggests that the first-order explanation for gaps in enrollment in college by family income is long-run family factors that are crystallized in ability. Short-run income constraints affecting families during the child's college-going years play a role in creating these gaps, albeit a quantitatively minor one. There is scope for intervention to alleviate these short-term constraints and the returns to carefully targeted interventions are potentially high. One should not expect to reduce the enrollment gaps evident in Figure 7 substantially by eliminating such constraints.

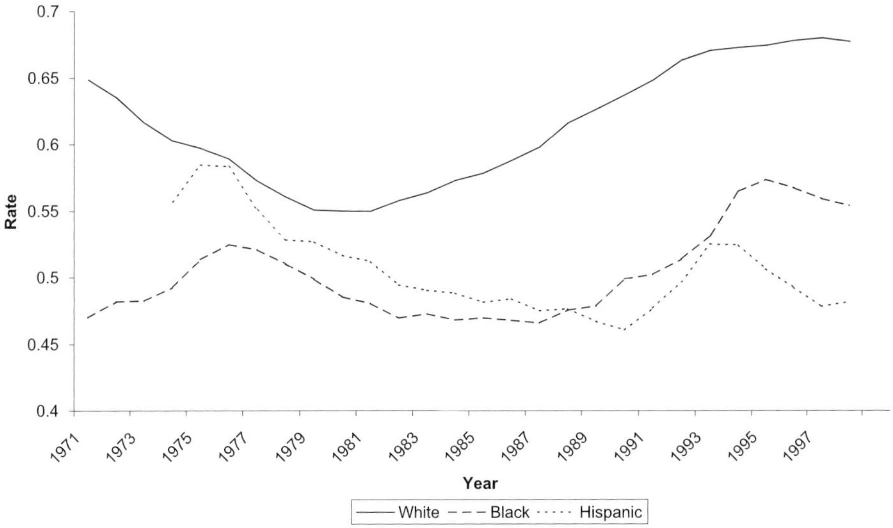

Figure 8. College participation by race. Dependent* high school graduates and GED holders. Males, ages 18–24.

Note: Three-year moving averages are shown. Source: These number were computed from the CPS P-20 School Reports and the October CPS.

* Dependent is living at parental home or supported by parental family while at college.

2.5.1. *Family income and enrollment in college*

The argument that short-term family credit constraints are the most plausible explanation for the relationship depicted in Figure 7 starts by noting that human capital is different from physical capital. There is no asset market for human capital. People cannot sell rights to their future labor earnings to potential lenders to secure financing for their human capital investments in the way that indentured servants once financed the cost of travel to the New World with their labor. Even if they could, there would be substantial problems in enforcing performance of contracts on future earnings given that persons control their own labor supply and the effort and quality of their work. The lack of collateral on the part of borrowers and the inability to monitor effort by lenders are widely cited reasons for current large-scale government interventions to finance education.

If people had to rely on their own resources to finance all of their schooling costs the level of educational attainment in society would be much lower. To the extent that subsidies do not cover the full costs of college tuition, persons are forced to raise funds to pay tuition through private loans, through work while in college, or through foregone consumption [see Keane and Wolpin (2001)]. Such constraints may affect the choice of college quality, the content of the educational experience, the decision of when to enter college, the length of time it takes to complete schooling, and even graduation from college. Children from families with higher incomes have access to resources that are not available to children from low-income families; although children from higher-income families still depend on the good will of their parents to gain access to these resources. Limited access to credit markets means that the costs of funds are higher for the children of the poor, and this limits their enrollment in college.[31] Proponents of this view argue the reductions in real income among parents in the bottom half of the family income distribution, coupled with a growth in real tuition costs, has prevented low income whites and minorities from taking advantage of the rising education premium.

An alternative interpretation of the same evidence is that long-run family and environmental factors play a decisive role in shaping the ability and expectations of children. Families with higher levels of resources produce higher-quality children who are better able to perform in school and take advantage of the new market for skills.

Children whose parents have higher incomes have access to better-quality primary and secondary schools. Children's tastes for education and their expectations about their life chances are shaped by those of their parents. Educated parents are better able to develop scholastic aptitude in their children by assisting and directing their studies. We

[31] Evidence on educational responses to tuition subsidies is sometimes mistakenly interpreted as evidence on credit constraints. The purchase of education is governed by the same principles that govern the purchase of other goods: the lower the price, the more likely are people to buy the good. Dynarski (2000) presents recent evidence about the strength of tuition effects on college participation that is consistent with a long line of research. In addition, there is, undoubtedly, a consumption component to education. Families with higher incomes may buy more of the good for their children and may buy higher quality education as well. This will contribute to the relationship displayed in Figure 7.

have reviewed the evidence that ability gaps open up early and are strongly related to family characteristics. The influences of family factors present from birth through adolescence accumulate to produce ability and college readiness. By the time individuals finish high school and their scholastic ability is largely determined, the scope of tuition policy for promoting college attendance is greatly diminished.

The interpretation that stresses the role of family and the childhood environment in producing college readiness does not necessarily rule out short-term borrowing constraints as a partial explanation for the patterns revealed in Figure 7. However, if the finances of poor but motivated families hinder them from providing high quality elementary and secondary schooling for their children, and produce a low level of college readiness, government policy aimed at reducing the short-term borrowing constraints for the college expenses of those children during their college-going years is unlikely to be effective in substantially closing the gaps evident in Figure 7. In these circumstances, policies that improve the early environments that shape ability will be more effective in the long run.

The following experiment captures the essence of the distinction we are making. Suppose two poor families participate in lotteries that are adjusted to have the same expected present value (at age zero of the child) but have different award dates. Markets are assumed to be imperfect in the sense that families cannot borrow against the future awards. Compare a family that wins the lottery in the child's adolescent years with a family that wins in the child's early formative years. The former child would lack all of the benefits of investment during the early childhood years that the child from the family that wins early would receive. The child from the late-winning family would be likely to have lower levels of cognitive and noncognitive abilities than the child from the early-winning family. To the extent that investments are complementary and self-productive, the children of the early winner will be much more likely to attend college. Although none of the data we possess are as clean as the data generated by this hypothetical experiment, taken as a whole, they point in this direction.

2.5.2. Racial and family income gaps: Long-term family factors vs. short-term credit constraints

A simple approach to testing the relative importance of long-run factors versus short-run credit constraints in accounting for the evidence in Figure 7 is to condition on long-run factors and examine if there is any additional role for short-run credit constraints.

Cameron and Heckman (1998, 1999, 2001) compare the estimated effects of family background and family income on college attendance, controlling for scholastic ability (as measured by the Armed Forces Qualifying Test, or AFQT). Measured scholastic ability is influenced by long-term family and environmental factors, which are in turn produced by long-term family factors. To the extent that the influence of family income on college attendance is diminished by the inclusion of scholastic ability in an analysis of college attendance, one would conclude that long-run family factors crystallized in AFQT scores are the driving force behind schooling attainment, and not short-term credit constraints. Fitting a life cycle model of schooling to a subsample of the National Longitudinal Survey of Youth (NLSY79) data with AFQT measured before high school graduation, Cameron and Heckman examine what portion of the gap between minority youth and whites in school attendance at various levels is due to family income, to tuition costs, and to family background.[32] They find that when they do not control for ability measured at an early age, about half (five points) of the eleven-point gap between black and white college attendance rates is due to family income; more than half (four points) of the seven-point difference between Hispanics and whites is due to family income. When scholastic ability is accounted for, only one half of one point of the eleven-point black-white gap is explained by family income. The gap between Hispanics and whites actually widens when family income is included in the empirical model. Adjusting for ability at the age people enter college more than accounts for minority-majority college attendance gaps. Cameron and Heckman obtain comparable results when they adjust for parental education and family structure.[33] The effects of tuition on college entry are greatly weakened when measures of ability are included. This analysis suggests that it is long-run factors that determine college attendance, not short-term borrowing constraints, that explain the evidence in Figure 7.

It is sometimes claimed that enrollment responses to tuition should be larger for constrained (low-income) persons [see Kane (1994), and the survey in Ellwood and Kane (2000)], although there is no theoretical basis for this.[34] Cameron and Heckman (1999) address this issue empirically. Even without adjusting for AFQT, they find no pattern in the estimated tuition response by family income level. When conditioning on ability, tuition effects become smaller for everyone (in absolute value) and the influence of family income becomes negligible. In a separate study of the HOPE Scholarship program in Georgia [Dynarski (2000)], the tuition elasticity for youth from middle- and high-income families is as high as other estimates found in the literature for lower income youth.

Based on NLSY79 data, Figures 9 and 10 illustrate the relative importance of family income and academic ability in determining a number of college-related outcomes.[35] Classifying white males by ability (as measured by AFQT scores) results in a clear ordering that shows that more able people are more likely to go to college than those who are less able. Within test score terciles, we further display college enrollment rates by family income measured in the child's adolescent years. Inspecting the graphs on the left (panels A, C, and E), we observe a clear ordering by family income within ability

[32] See Bureau of Labor Statistics (2001) for a description of the NLSY data.

[33] Cameron and Heckman condition on an early measure of ability not contaminated by the feedback from schooling to test scores. Such feedback is documented in Hansen, Heckman and Mullen (2004).

[34] Mulligan (1997) shows in the context of a Becker–Tomes model that tuition elasticities for human capital accumulation are greater (in absolute value) for unconstrained people. His proof easily generalizes to more general preferences. Carneiro and Heckman (2002) use a discrete choice schooling framework to demonstrate that constrained persons may respond less than unconstrained persons.

[35] See Carneiro and Heckman (2002) for details.

groups – persons from families with higher income are more likely to enroll in college. However, this does not necessarily mean that short-run credit constraints are operative in the college-going years. Family income in the adolescent years is strongly correlated with family income throughout the life cycle, and long-run family resources are likely to produce many skills that are not fully captured by a single test score. When we control for early family background factors (parental education, family structure, and place of residence), the relationship between family income and school enrollment is greatly weakened for all college outcomes as the graphs in the right-hand side (panels B, D, and E) reveal. Adjusted gaps are much smaller than the unadjusted ones.

Most of the analysis in the literature focuses on college enrollment and much less on other dimensions of college attendance, such as completion, quality of school, and delay of entry into college.[36] When we perform a parallel analysis for completion of four-year college, we find no evidence of constraints for white males and, in fact, over-adjust the gaps in college enrollment. Figures 9(C) and (D) present the raw and adjusted gaps respectively, for completion of four-year college. Figures 9(E) and (F) show the raw and adjusted gaps for delay of entry into college. There is no evidence of short-run credit constraints in these measures. Carneiro and Heckman (2003) present evidence of short-run credit constraints among the least able poor in completing two years of college, but not for the brightest poor.

Using the difference in each outcome between the highest income category and the lower income categories as a rough measure of the fraction of persons constrained, Carneiro and Heckman (2002, 2003) find that there is weak evidence among certain subgroups for short-term credit constraints in years of entry delay and for choice of two-year versus four-year colleges, a measure of school quality. Depending on the measure of college participation selected, the estimated percentage of white males constrained ranges from 0 to 8 percent. Comparable results hold for other demographic groups.

The strongest evidence for short-term credit constraints is for Hispanic males. This is not surprising since those in the country illegally are not eligible for the same schooling aid as legal residents. The weakest evidence for credit constraints is for black males. On many measures, the effective constraint for this group is zero [see Carneiro and Heckman (2002, 2003)].

Many of the variables used to control for long-term family factors also predict family income in the adolescent years. Does the preceding analysis simply project family income in adolescent years onto other long term family factors? Carneiro and Heckman (2002) claim it does not. Independent variation in family income remains even after controlling for other family factors. When they reverse the roles of family income and family background – e.g., examining how differences in family background affect college enrollment rates after conditioning on family income levels – a strong long-run family background effect remains. As Figure 9 shows, adjusting for family income in

[36] Work while attending school is studied in Keane and Wolpin (2001). Delay in entry is studied in Kane (1996).

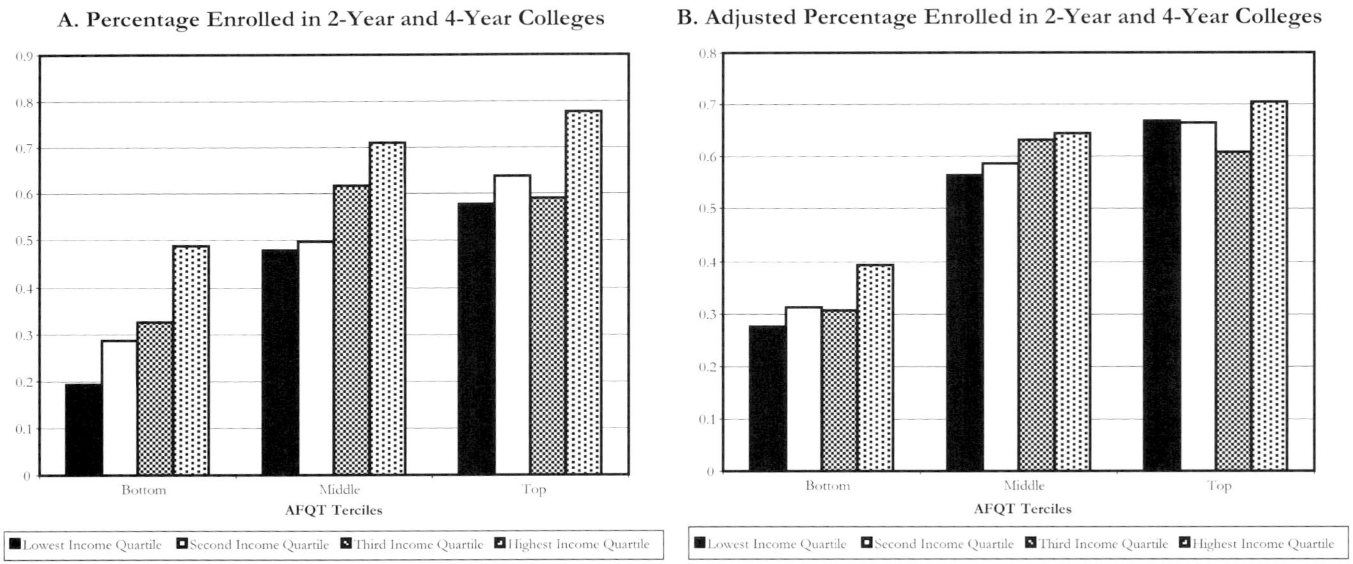

Figure 9. Enrollment, completion and no delay rates by family income quartiles and age-adjusted AFQT terciles white males, NLSY79.

Note: To draw these graphs we performed the following steps. (1) Within each AFQT tercile, we regress percentage enrolled, completion rate, and percentage with no delay on family background: $y = \alpha + F\gamma + Q_1\beta_1 + Q_2\beta_2 + Q_3\beta_3$, where y is percentage enrolled, completion rate, or percentage with no delay, F is a vector of family background variables (southern origin, broken home, urban origin, mother's education and father's education), Q_1 is a dummy for being in the first quartile of the distribution of family income at 17, Q_2 is for being in the second quartile and Q_3 is for being in the third quartile. (2) Then, within each AFQT tercile, the height of the first bar is given by $\alpha + \bar{F}\gamma + \beta_1$, the second is given by $\alpha + \bar{F}\gamma + \beta_2$, the third by $\alpha + \bar{F}\gamma + \beta_3$ and the fourth by $\alpha + \bar{F}\gamma$ (where $\bar{F}$ is a vector of the mean values for the variables in F). The coefficients for the regression are given in the Appendix Table B-3 of Carneiro and Heckman (2003).

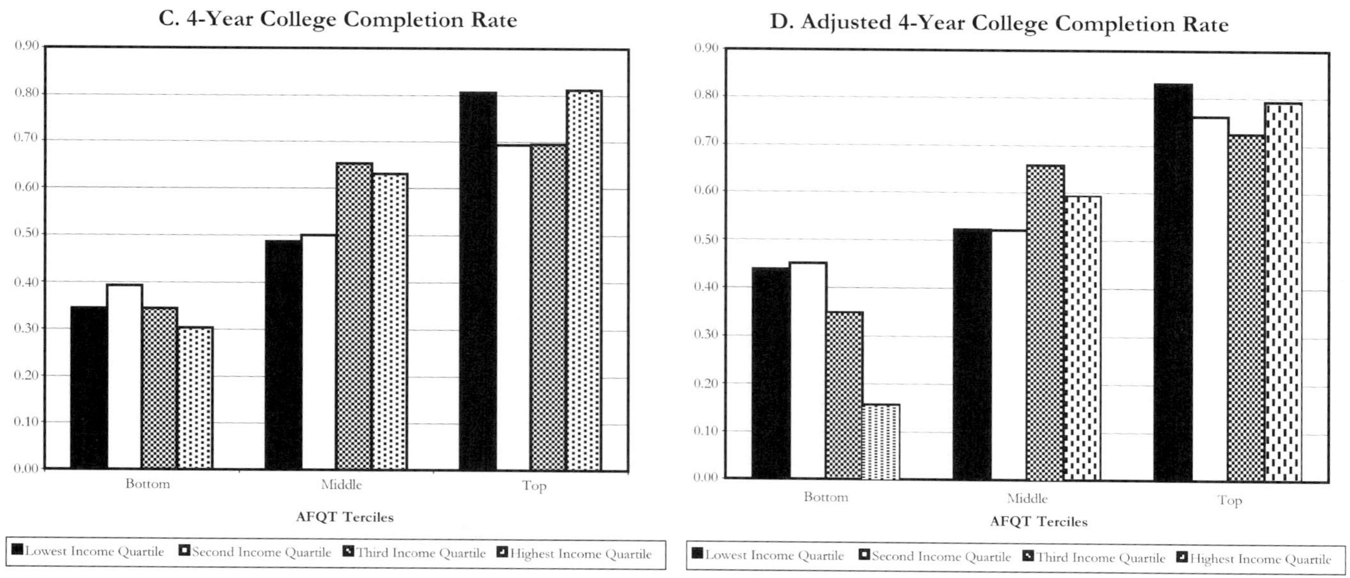

Figure 9. (*Continued.*)

Note: To draw these graphs we performed the following steps. (1) Within each AFQT tercile, we regress percentage enrolled, completion rate, and percentage with no delay on family background: $y = \alpha + F\gamma + Q_1\beta_1 + Q_2\beta_2 + Q_3\beta_3$, where y is percentage enrolled, completion rate, or percentage with no delay, F is a vector of family background variables (southern origin, broken home, urban origin, mother's education and father's education), Q_1 is a dummy for being in the first quartile of the distribution of family income at 17, Q_2 is for being in the second quartile and Q_3 is for being in the third quartile. (2) Then, within each AFQT tercile, the height of the first bar is given by $\alpha + \bar{F}\gamma + \beta_1$, the second is given by $\alpha + \bar{F}\gamma + \beta_2$, the third by $\alpha + \bar{F}\gamma + \beta_3$ and the fourth by $\alpha + \bar{F}\gamma$ (where $\bar{F}$ is a vector of the mean values for the variables in F). The coefficients for the regression are given in the Appendix Table B-3 of Carneiro and Heckman (2003).

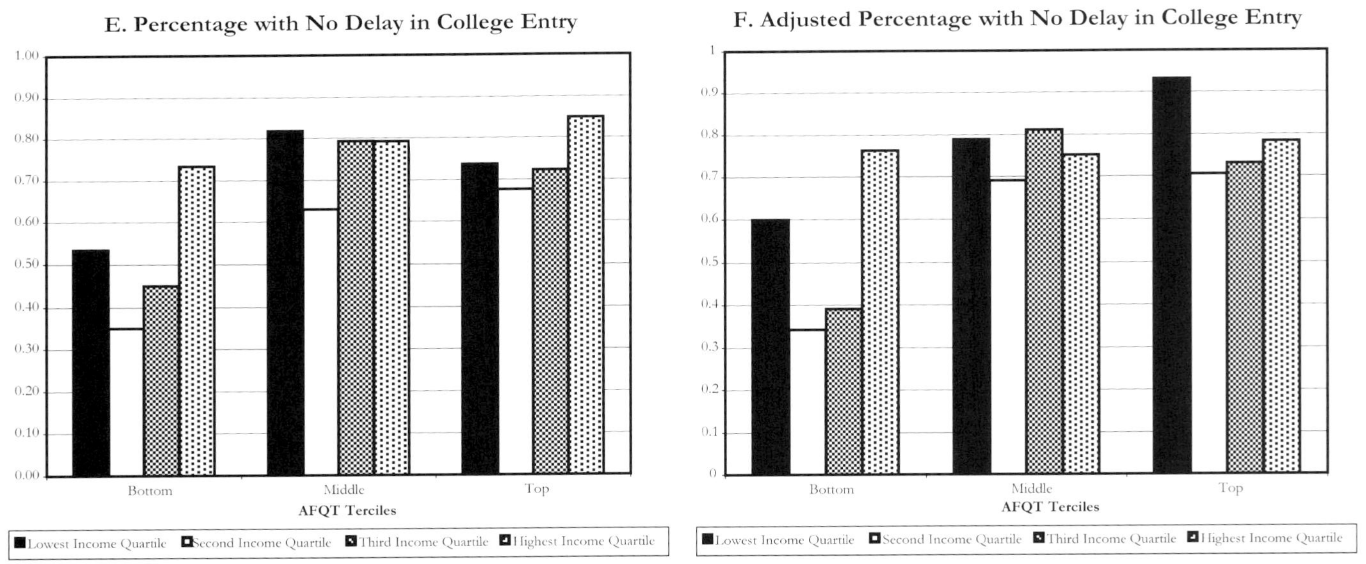

Figure 9. (*Continued.*)

Note: To draw these graphs we performed the following steps. (1) Within each AFQT tercile, we regress percentage enrolled, completion rate, and percentage with no delay on family background: $y = \alpha + F\gamma + Q_1\beta_1 + Q_2\beta_2 + Q_3\beta_3$, where y is percentage enrolled, completion rate, or percentage with no delay, F is a vector of family background variables (southern origin, broken home, urban origin, mother's education and father's education), Q_1 is a dummy for being in the first quartile of the distribution of family income at 17, Q_2 is for being in the second quartile and Q_3 is for being in the third quartile. (2) Then, within each AFQT tercile, the height of the first bar is given by $\alpha + \bar{F}\gamma + \beta_1$, the second is given by $\alpha + \bar{F}\gamma + \beta_2$, the third by $\alpha + \bar{F}\gamma + \beta_3$ and the fourth by $\alpha + \bar{F}\gamma$ (where $\bar{F}$ is a vector of the mean values for the variables in F). The coefficients for the regression are given in the Appendix Table B-3 of Carneiro and Heckman (2003).

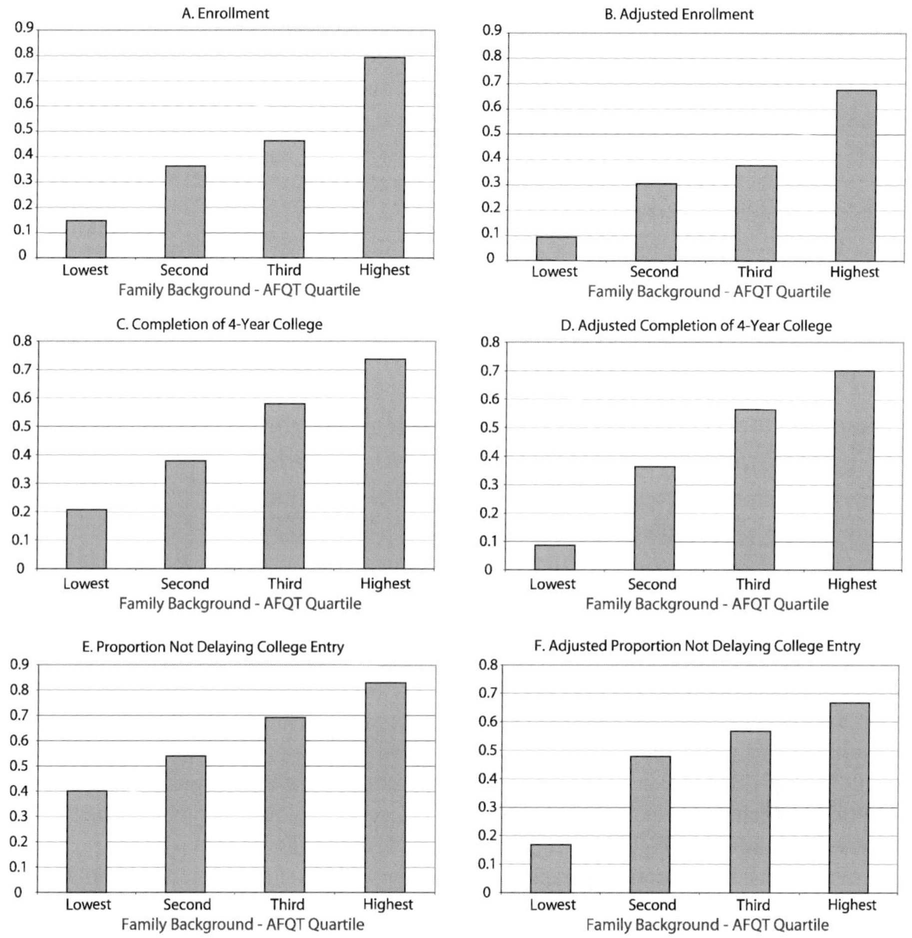

Figure 10. Enrollment, completion and delay by family background-AFQT Quartiles. NLSY79 white males. We correct for the effect of schooling at the test date on AFQT. The family background-AFQT index is based on a linear combination of south, broken home, urban, mother's education, father's education and AFQT. For the residual plots, we condition on family income at age 17. See Table B-4 in the appendix to Carneiro and Heckman (2003) for the coefficients of the linear combination of the variables forming this index.

adolescent years does not substantially affect differences in college decisions by family background.

Tables 1A and 1B report further evidence on the unimportance of short-run credit constraints on college attendance. Using data from the Children of the NLSY79 (CNLSY79) survey, they present estimates of child enrollment in college on family per capita permanent income and on family per capita income flows received at various stages of the life cycle (transitory income). Permanent income is formed as an average

Table 1A
Regression of college enrollment on various measures of family income and PIAT math at age 12

	(1) College enrollment	(2) College enrollment	(3) College enrollment	(4) College enrollment
Permanent family income at ages 0–18 (in 10K)	0.0839*	0.0747*	0.0902*	0.0779*
	(0.0121)	(0.0184)	(0.0185)	(0.0284)
PIAT math at age 12	0.0077*	0.0076*	0.0076*	0.0075*
	(0.0017)	(0.0018)	(0.0018)	(0.0018)
Permanent family income at ages 0–5 (in 10K)	–	0.0158	–	0.0149
	–	(0.0238)	–	(0.0261)
Permanent family income at ages 16–18 (in 10K)	–	–	−0.0069	−0.0023
	–	–	(0.0177)	(0.0194)
Constant	0.1447*	0.1404*	0.1410*	0.1380*
	(0.0264)	(0.0272)	(0.0268)	(0.0273)
Observations	863	863	861	861
R-squared	0.1	0.1	0.11	0.11

Standard errors in parentheses. Permanent family income is discounted to age 0 using a 5% rate.
*Significant at 1%.

discounted income flow to the family over the life of the child at home (ages 0 to 18).[37] Two features are clear from these tables: (a) permanent income matters a lot for college enrollment and (b) given permanent income, transitory income flows matter little. This result is robust whether or not one controls for ability at age 12: compare Table 1A with Table 1B which does not control for ability at age 12. We discuss other studies on the importance of the timing of family income in Section 2.5.3.

Policies that improve the educational financing of *identified* constrained subgroups in the college-going years will increase their human capital and may well be justified on objective cost–benefit criteria. The potential economic loss from delay in entering college can be substantial. If V is the economic value of attending school, and schooling is delayed one year, then the costs of delaying schooling by one year and not earning any income, are $\frac{rV}{1+r}$, where r is the rate of return. For $r = 0.10$, which is not out of line with estimates in the literature, this delay is 9 percent of the lifetime value of schooling (roughly $20,000 in 2004 dollars). For the identified constrained subgroups, the benefits to reducing delay and promoting earlier college completion, higher college quality and graduation are likely to be substantial even when earnings net of disutility costs of work in the year of delay are taken into account.

Stinebrickner and Stinebrickner (2004) examine the role of credit constraints in determining college attrition at a small liberal arts college in Kentucky. Since the probability

[37] We obtain the same empirical patterns reported in the text whether or not we use per capita income measures.

Table 1B
Regression of college enrollment on various measures of family income

	(1) College enrollment	(2) College enrollment	(3) College enrollment	(4) College enrollment
Permanent family income at ages 0–18 (in 10K)	0.0942*	0.0829*	0.1031*	0.0887*
	(0.0108)	(0.0170)	(0.0169)	(0.0270)
Permanent family income at ages 0–5 (in 10K)	–	0.0259	–	0.0233
	–	(0.0220)	–	(0.0246)
Permanent family income at ages 16–18 (in 10K)	–	–	−0.0108	−0.0048
	–	–	(0.0170)	(0.0188)
Constant	0.1367*	0.1179*	0.1329*	0.1158
	(0.0243)	(0.0251)	(0.0246)	(0.0252)
Observations	1015	987	1013	985
R-squared	0.07	0.08	0.07	0.08

Standard errors in parentheses. Permanent family income is discounted to age 0 using a 5% rate.
*Significant at 1%.

of dropping out of college differs substantially by family income in their sample, it is natural to ask whether this may be the result of borrowing constraints. They utilize a unique set of questions asked of all survey respondents to infer the role played by borrowing constraints in determining college attrition and the relationship between family income and attrition. The survey asks whether students would like to borrow more money for school if they could and, if so, how much they would like to borrow. They find that only 20% of the sample would like to borrow more for school, and the median amount those individuals would like to borrow is only $500. Based on these findings, they estimate that the inability to borrow plays little role in attrition decisions.

A few other studies have attempted to model borrowing constraints and schooling decisions more explicitly. Cameron and Taber (2004) examine the empirical importance of borrowing constraints in a model that incorporates the insight that borrowing constraints will influence both schooling choices and returns to schooling. Using a variety of methods, they find no evidence that borrowing constraints in the adolescent years play a role in explaining the years of schooling attained by recent cohorts of American youth. Keane and Wolpin (2001) estimate a more formally explicit sequential dynamic model and reach the same conclusion. Students are estimated to be constrained in the short-run, but alleviate the constraints they face by working while in college. Relaxing the budget constraint barely affects schooling decisions but affects work while in school. Neither study looks at delay or quality effects, which have been found to be quantitatively important.

In designing policies to alleviate short-term constraints, it is important to specifically target the interventions toward the constrained in ways that previous programs have not.

Broad-based policies generate deadweight. For example, Dynarski (2003) and Cameron and Heckman (1999) estimate that 93 percent of President Clinton's Hope Scholarship funds, which were directed toward middle-class families, were given to children who would have attended school even without the program. Stanley (2003) studies the impact of the GI Bill on the college-going decisions of Korean War veterans and finds that most college subsidies under the bill were used by veterans from families in the top half of the socioeconomic distribution. In an analysis of Georgia's HOPE Scholarship program, Dynarski (2000) finds that most of the funds went to middle- and high-income students. These studies all suggest that previous government attempts to finance college have primarily benefited the most well-off with little impact on those most likely to be constrained. This conclusion is further supported by simulations from the model of dynamic schooling choices in Keane and Wolpin (2001).

While targeting those identified as constrained may be good policy, it is important not to lose sight of the main factors accounting for differences in schooling attainment. Family background factors crystallized in ability are the first-order factors explaining college attendance and completion gaps. Differences in ability by family income groups appear at early ages and persist. They affect schooling decisions and wages. A major conclusion of the studies reviewed in this section is that the abilities decisive in producing differentials in college attendance are shaped early in life.

Lochner and Monge (2004) argue that the current structure of the student lending system in the U.S. minimizes the effect of liquidity problems on college attendance decisions, even though it may severely distort consumption patterns. This is because the student loan system directly links borrowing limits to schooling expenditures, a feature neglected in most studies of credit constraints and schooling. That is, students who spend more on college can borrow more as long as their total borrowing remains below an upper limit set by government lending programs. While Stafford loan limits for dependent students are limited to a cumulative amount of $23,000, students from poorer families can borrow up to an additional $40,000 from the Perkins loan program in addition to any direct transfers from the Pell Grant program. Finally, parents can borrow up to the student's determined need from the PLUS loan program.[38] Thus, the effective constraint on family borrowing for many college students is simply the amount needed for tuition, fees, books, and room and board at the institution of choice. In this sense, college costs can be fully covered by student loans.[39] While students cannot borrow

[38] PLUS take-up rates are low relative to the roughly 50% take-up rates of other student loans. It is difficult to know whether this reflects a reluctance of parents to take on debt when students would choose to do so themselves if they could or whether it reflects the fact that other lending and grants satisfy the needs of most students. Parents are not eligible for PLUS loans if they have a bad credit rating (they are eligible with no credit rating or a good one), but students with ineligible parents are able to borrow considerably more (at the levels set for independent students) from the Stafford loan program than other dependent students.

[39] While loans cannot be taken out to cover foregone earnings, room and board does not, strictly speaking, represent a cost of college. To the extent that these roughly offset each other for individuals who work a few hours a week during the school year and full-time during the summer, the full costs of college, including direct and indirect costs, can be borrowed.

above and beyond the costs of college to buy fancy cars or expensive apartments (even if their future prospects are bright and they would like to consume more while in college), the constraints embodied in the federal student loan system tend not to distort schooling decisions.[40] The analysis of Lochner and Monge (2004) is consistent with the analysis and evidence in Keane and Wolpin (2001).[41]

2.5.3. Borrowing constraints as determinants of family investment in children

While many recent studies have analyzed the importance of borrowing constraints among college-age students, very little attention has been given to the role played by borrowing constraints in determining family investments in younger children. Two conceptually distinct types of constraints may limit family investments in their younger children. First, parents may be unable to borrow against their children's future income even if they can borrow against their own future income. This suggests that bright children born to poor parents may not receive the efficient amount of investment because their parents may never earn enough to pay for those investments. The timing of income receipts for the parents is assumed to be irrelevant in this case. Only the discounted present value of their income matters. A second, more severe, constraint on parents may limit them from borrowing fully against their own future income. This is the constraint most commonly associated with the notion of borrowing constraints, and it implies that the timing of a parent's income matters for child investment decisions. Parents who earn a smaller share of their lifetime income when their children are young are likely to invest less in their young children. Two families with the same lifetime income may make different early investment decisions. These early investment decisions may affect later decisions about college attendance.

While it seems likely that the first form of constraint is relevant for most families, the empirical importance of the second is a matter of some controversy. The obvious test for the second borrowing constraint examines whether the timing of family income matters for child achievement and schooling outcomes. Only a few studies speak to

[40] Furthermore, the option for students to default on their student loans after leaving school may actually encourage some of the least able to attend low quality colleges that offer little net return. While this may sound farfetched, cohort default rates reached 20% in the early 1990s. Many institutions had default rates above 50%.

[41] The take-up rate on Pell Grants and Perkins Loans targeted toward students from low-income families is low [Orfield (1992)]. Many more people are eligible for support than those who claim it. Binding borrowing constraints are not a plausible explanation for the lack of utilization of these potential resources. Kane (1999) suggests that nonmonetary costs of applying for financial aid may be high, especially for low-income people, because the application process is complex. He argues that decreasing these costs may be a more promising avenue for relaxing financing constraints for low-income people than expanding existing programs. He provides no evidence, however, in support of this conjecture. An alternative explanation consistent with our evidence is that many eligible persons perceive that even with a substantial tuition subsidy, the returns to college education for them are too low to pay for the foregone earnings required to attend school. Risk aversion due to the uncertainty of income flows may also reduce the returns relative to the benefits.

this issue. Duncan and Brooks-Gunn (1997b) use PSID data to estimate the effects of family income earned at different stages of a child's life (ages 0–5, 6–10 and 11–15) on final schooling outcomes. Both standard cross-sectional OLS and sibling fixed effects models reveal that early income (ages 0–5) has a significantly larger impact on years of completed schooling and high school graduation rates than does income at later ages. Levy and Duncan (2000) report similar results using the PSID and siblings fixed effects models. Carneiro and Heckman (2003) argue that these findings do not necessarily imply that timing matters, since one should discount income in all stages back to the same base year. Otherwise, the income earned when a child is young is worth more than when the child is older, simply because the latter needs to be discounted. When they control for the discounted present value of lifetime income over the child's ages 0–18, they do not find any significant additional effect of early income on college enrollment decisions using data from the Children of the NLSY79 (recall our discussion of Tables 1A and 1B). They conclude that the timing of parental income within the life cycle of the child is unimportant.

Caucutt and Lochner (2004) use the Children of NLSY79 to conduct three tests for determining whether the timing of (discounted) family income affects adolescent math and reading achievement levels. Their estimates suggest that (i) income earned at earlier ages has a slightly larger (and statistically significant) impact on adolescent test scores than does income earned at later ages, (ii) future income has less of an effect on current outcomes than does past income and (iii) the slope of a family's income profile is negatively related to test scores, even after controlling for the discounted present value of family income taken over a twenty-year period. While most of their findings are consistent with the presence of constraints on parental borrowing against their own income, none of them suggest that the timing of parental income within the life cycle of the child plays a large role in determining child outcomes. Consistent with Carneiro and Heckman (2003), their results suggest a strong effect of permanent lifetime income on child development outcomes.

Overall, the evidence on whether the timing of income matters on children's outcomes is mixed. While some of the evidence suggests that timing does matter, some does not. Even those studies that suggest a role for timing do not find large effects. Because it is necessary to observe individuals over a long time period in order to examine the role of income timing, most studies are based on a fairly small number of individuals and are forced to make strong assumptions about the dynamic process by which income may affect achievement and schooling outcomes. Additional studies of this issue are certainly warranted to explore the robustness of the findings to alternative specifications.

2.5.4. High rate of return to schooling compared to the return on physical capital

Least squares estimates of the rate of return to schooling, based on the Mincer earnings function, are often above 10 percent and sometimes are as high as 17 to 20 percent. Estimates based on instrumental variables are even higher. [See, for example, the evidence surveyed by Card (1999, 2001), and the discussion of the quality of the instruments used in this literature presented in Carneiro and Heckman (2002)]. It is sometimes claimed that the returns to schooling are very high relative to the returns to physical capital, and therefore people are credit-constrained or that some other market failure is present.

The cross-sectional Mincer rate of return to schooling does not, in general, estimate the marginal internal rate of return to schooling, and the internal rate of return is not well-defined in sequential dynamic programming models.[42] Willis (1986) and Heckman, Lochner and Todd (2006) state the conditions under which the Mincer rate of return will equal the marginal internal rate of return to schooling. The latter paper shows that these assumptions are at odds with U.S. earnings data. Even if these conditions are satisfied, implicit comparisons are usually made against a risk-free interest rate. However, this is not the relevant comparison for evaluating schooling decisions. Carneiro, Hansen and Heckman (2001, 2003), Cunha, Heckman and Navarro (2005), and Navarro (2005) estimate that agents face considerable uncertainty in their returns to schooling. The illiquidity and irreversibility of human capital investments drive the premium on human capital far above the safe interest rate [see Judd (2000)]. Consequently, comparisons of Mincer returns and returns to capital are intrinsically uninformative about the existence of credit constraints or the need for intervention in human capital markets. See Carneiro and Heckman (2002), Cunha, Heckman and Navarro (2005), and Navarro (2005) for further discussion of this point.

2.5.5. *Are rates of return to investment higher for persons from low-income families?*

If low-income families are credit-constrained, under conditions specified in Carneiro and Heckman (2002), at the margin, the returns to schooling for children from constrained families should be higher, since they are investing less than the efficient amount.[43] We develop this analysis formally in Section 3. Carneiro and Heckman (2002) establish that if choices are made at the margin of schooling quality, the estimated Mincer return may be lower for constrained persons, unless adjustments for schooling quality are made in the estimated returns. The empirical literature on this topic, which does not adjust for quality, finds that returns to secondary schooling and post-secondary schooling are higher for high-ability people than for low-ability people. [See, for example, Cawley et al. (2000), Meghir and Palme (1999), Tabler (2001), or the evidence presented in Section 2.5.6.] Family income and child ability are positively correlated, so one would expect higher returns to schooling for children of high-income families for this reason alone. Altonji and Dunn (1996) find in their preferred empirical specification that the returns to schooling are higher for children from more-educated

[42] See Heckman, Lochner and Todd (2006) and Heckman, Lochner and Taber (1998) for examples in which cross-sectional rates of return are uninformative about the return to schooling that any person experiences.

[43] Carneiro and Heckman (2002) show that for this prediction to be valid, it is necessary to assume that all families face the same technology of schooling (relating inputs to outputs) and that there be no comparative advantage in the labor market. Cameron and Taber (2004) derive a different set of conditions.

families than for children of less-educated families. This effect operates in part through higher schooling participation rates and hence higher earnings. There is no evidence that rates of return to secondary and postsecondary schooling are higher for children from low-income families than for children from high-income families. Indeed all of the evidence points to returns in the later stages of child schooling being higher for high ability children from more advantaged environments. This is consistent with complementarity and self-productivity as discussed in Section 1. We elaborate on this point in Section 3.

Interventions at very early ages, however, have *higher* returns for the most disadvantaged. This empirical pattern holds across many studies. For example, this holds true for a nurse home visitation program in Elmira, NY [Olds (2002)], where there was no statistically significant effect of the program on child socioeconomic outcomes for the sample as a whole, but modest effects were found for the disadvantaged subsample of unmarried, young, and poor white mothers and their children. The nurse home visitation program in Memphis replicated this pattern of results, though the overall effects of treatment were much weaker.[44] The IHDP[45] study of low-birth weight babies by Brooks-Gunn et al. (1992) finds that the increase in IQ is higher among children of poorly educated mothers.[46] Non-experimental studies of preschool by Magnuson et al. (2004); Magnuson, Ruhm and Waldfogel (2004) and the Gormley et al. (2004) study of Oklahoma universal pre-K program find the effect of preschool on achievement test scores to be higher among the disadvantaged children.

By the late adolescent years, the pattern is reversed and returns are lower for low ability and disadvantaged children. An equity-efficiency trade-off becomes evident. This is clear in the higher returns to the most able in job training and in the military AFQT studies, both of which we summarize below. This reversal in the pattern of returns to investment in disadvantaged persons is a consequence of the technology of skill formation that we formalize in Section 3 of this paper. Distinguishing returns from early investment from returns to late investment reveals the value of self-productivity and complementarity as useful conceptual tools for organizing the evidence on child development.

[44] We discuss the evidence on other visitation programs in Section 2.6.1.4.

[45] The Infant Health and Development Program was a randomized study of low-birthweight infants conducted at 8 sites around the country. The treatment group received home visits by program staff, child attendance at a child development center, and parent group meetings. Both treatment and control children received medical, developmental, and social assessments, with referral for pediatric care and other services. All services were provided at no cost to the families. The intervention lasted until children were 36 months of age, adjusted for prematurity.

[46] However, any cognitive effect of IHDP are almost entirely attenuated by age 8 [see McCarton et al. (1997)].

Table 2
Average marginal effect on participation in company training (the probability of participating in training)

	Average marginal effect					
	White males		Black males		Hispanic males	
	(1)	(2)	(1)	(2)	(1)	(2)
Age-adjusted AFQT	0.0149	–	0.0182	–	0.0066	–
	(0.0024)	–	(0.0033)	–	(0.0037)	–
Family income in 1979	−0.0021	−0.0005	−0.0047	−0.0019	0.0011	0.0015
(in $10,000)	(0.0012)	(0.0011)	(0.0024)	(0.0023)	(0.0024)	(0.0023)
Grade completed	0.0382	–	0.0060	–	0.0036	–
	(0.001)	–	(0.0014)	–	(0.0014)	–
Father's education	−0.0014	0.0007	0.0003	0.0010	0.0002	0.0008
	(0.0006)	(0.0005)	(0.0008)	(0.0008)	(0.0007)	(0.0007)
	White females		Black females		Hispanic females	
	(1)	(2)	(1)	(2)	(1)	(2)
Age-adjusted AFQT	0.0076	–	0.0169	–	0.0159	–
	(0.0025)	–	(0.0038)	–	(0.0045)	–
Family income in 1979	−0.0007	0.0001	−0.0006	0.0014	−0.0065	−0.0043
(in $10,000)	(0.0011)	(0.0011)	(0.0024)	(0.0023)	(0.0031)	(0.0029)
Grade completed	0.0027	–	0.0014	–	0.0013	–
	(0.0010)	–	(0.0016)	–	(0.0016)	–
Father's education	0.0001	0.0009	0.0015	0.0021	−0.00001	0.0007
	(0.0006)	(0.0006)	(0.0008)	(0.0008)	(0.0009)	(0.0008)

The panel data set was constructed using NLSY79 data from 1979–1994. Data on training in 1987 is combined with 1988 in the original dataset. Company training consists of formal training run by employer, and military training excluding basic training. Standard errors are reported in parentheses. Specification (1) includes a constant, age, father's education, mother's education, number of siblings, southern residence at age 14 dummy, urban residence at age 14 dummy, and year dummies. Specification (2) drops age-adjusted AFQT and grade completed. Average marginal effect is estimated using average derivatives from a probit regression.

2.5.6. *The role of ability in returns to schooling and in choice of post-school investment*

Ability is not only a primary determinant of schooling decisions and hence earnings, but it also affects the return per unit of schooling as well as participation in job training. Table 2 gives our evidence on the effect of ability on participation in post-school job training programs. For different demographic groups it shows the effect of measured ability (AFQT) on participation in company training programs. More able people are substantially more likely to participate in company training. Far from remediating credit constraints, as they are sometimes conjectured to do, private-sector post-school investment programs reveal that those who start with higher initial conditions make more investments throughout their lifetimes.

Table 3
Return to one year of college for individuals at different percentiles of the math test score distribution. White males from High School and Beyond

	5%	25%	50%	75%	95%
Average return in the population	0.1121	0.1374	0.1606	0.1831	0.2101
	(0.0400)	(0.0328)	(0.0357)	(0.0458)	(0.0622)
Return for those who attend college	0.1640	0.1893	0.2125	0.2350	0.2621
	(0.0503)	(0.0582)	(0.0676)	(0.0801)	(0.0962)
Return for those who do not attend college	0.0702	0.0954	0.1187	0.1411	0.1682
	(0.0536)	(0.0385)	(0.0298)	(0.0305)	(0.0425)
Return for those at the margin	0.1203	0.1456	0.1689	0.1913	0.2184
	(0.0364)	(0.0300)	(0.0345)	(0.0453)	(0.0631)

Wages are measured in 1991 by dividing annual earnings by hours worked per week multiplied by 52. The math test score is an average of two 10th grade math test scores. There are no dropouts in the sample and the schooling variable is binary (high school–college). The gross returns to college are divided by 3.5 (average difference in years of schooling between high school graduates that go to college and high school graduates that do not in a sample of white males in the NLSY79). To construct the numbers in the table we proceed in two steps. First we compute the marginal treatment effect using the method of local instrumental variables as in Carneiro, Hansen and Heckman (2001). The parameters in the table are different weighted averages of the marginal treatment effect. Therefore, in the second step we compute the appropriate weight for each parameter and use it to construct a weighted average of the marginal treatment effect (see also Carneiro (2002)). Individuals at the margin are indifferent between attending college or not.

We have already discussed the evidence that the wage returns to schooling are higher for children from the most advantaged environments. This evidence is consistent with complementarity and self-productivity. Ability also affects the economic return to schooling. Carneiro and Heckman (2003) study the economic returns to college for people of different ability (see Table 3). Those at the bottom 5% of the ability distribution get half of the return to college of those at the top 5% of the ability distribution. Ability also affects wages independently of its effect on schooling, as shown in Carneiro, Heckman and Masterov (2005). This is further evidence on complementarity and self-productivity.

A strong connection between ability and job performance has been established in a series of studies conducted for the military. The armed services rely heavily on aptitude testing to screen recruits. Aptitude is defined in terms of performance on the Armed Forces Qualification Test (AFQT), which is a subset of the Armed Forces Vocational Aptitude Battery (ASVAB). Category I corresponds to the highest ability level, while V is the lowest, representing scores below the 10th percentile.[47] Armor and Roll (1994)

[47] Recruits whose scores fall in category V are ineligible for enlistment. Category I corresponds to AFQT scores in the 93–99th percentiles, II to 65–92th, IIIA to 50–64th, IIIB to 31–49th, IV to 10–30, and V to 1–9th.

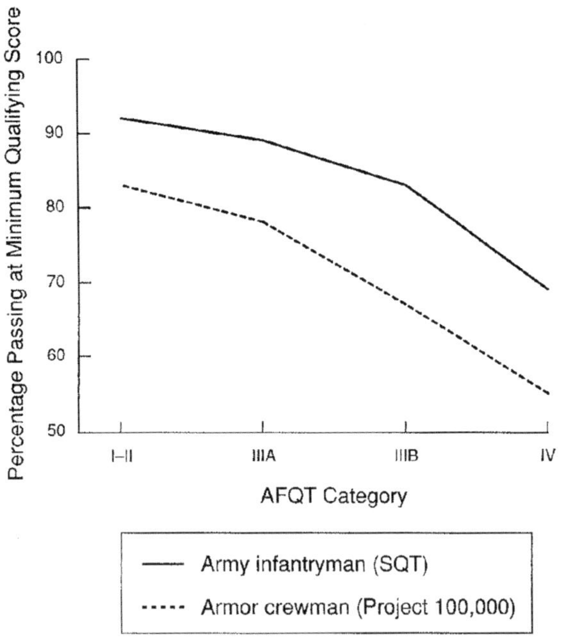

Figure 11A. Military job performance and AFQT. Source: Armor and Roll (1994).

establish that the test is predictive of true productivity and that initial deficits in productivity are not remedied by work experience. Figure 11A shows the relationship between the percentage passing at a minimum qualifying score on two job-performance tests and AFQT for the two largest combat specialties. The two tests are the Skill Qualification Test (SQT) for infantrymen and the Project 100,000 Test for armor crewmen.[48] The strong positive relationship between AFQT and the measures on job performance tests is unambiguous. Moreover, job experience does not appear to mediate these performance gaps substantially. Remediation through experience, which is sometimes claimed to be effective [Bruer (1999)], is actually ineffective in closing skill gaps. Early disadvantages are not easily remedied by compensatory investments or work experience at later ages.

Figure 11B shows the link between time on the job and the average score on the hands-on performance test developed by the Job Performance Measurement/Enlistment Standards Project (JPM) for first-term soldiers from all branches of the military. While the performance of soldiers at all ability levels improves with experience, the difference

[48] The Project 100,000 measure was a field test using real equipment of some task in which performance of each subtask was scored by an officer as correct or incorrect. The passing rate is set at 50% correct. The SQT includes a hands-on performance test, a job knowledge test, and a certification component (e.g., firing range qualifications). A score of 60% correct is considered a minimum level of job proficiency. This accounts for the gap between the two lines in the figure.

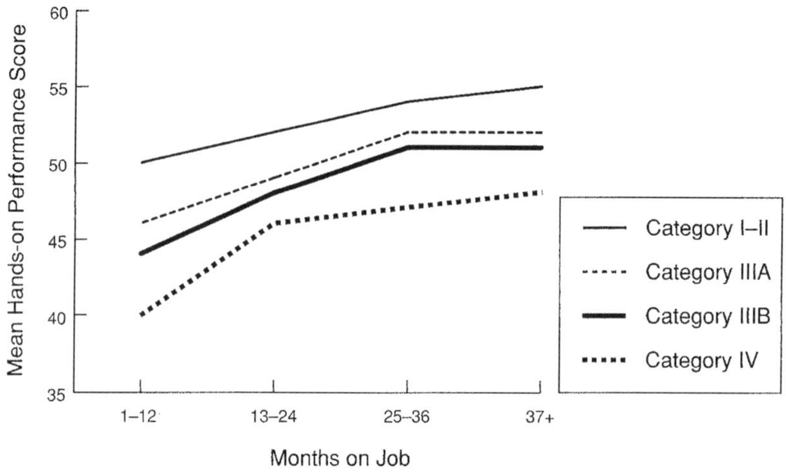

Figure 11B. Military job performance on JPM, AFQT and experience. Source: Armor and Roll (1994).

between categories I–II and IV remains constant at approximately one-half of a standard deviation. To put it differently, the average category IV soldier with three years of experience performs at the level of a category IIIA soldier with one year of service.

Ability formed in the early years is also important in explaining crime, teenage pregnancy and a variety of social pathologies. Figure 12A shows that women with low cognitive ability are more likely to bear children when they are young. Figure 12B shows that men of low cognitive ability are more likely to spend time in jail by the time they are 30. Figures 12C and 12D show that maternal ability is positively associated with how much cognitive and emotional stimulation children receive. Maternal ability is an important ingredient in eliminating test score gaps of children as demonstrated in Section 2.2. Not only do less able women bear children at earlier ages, but they propagate themselves across generations by investing less in their children.

We next turn to an analysis of the evidence on the effectiveness of specific policies in supplementing the environments of disadvantaged children.

2.6. *What is known about specific policies to foster ability and skill?*

2.6.1. *Early interventions*

Karoly et al. (1998), Currie (2001) and Currie and Blau (2006) present comprehensive surveys of numerous preschool intervention programs targeted toward disadvantaged populations and their measured effects. The programs they analyze vary, both in terms of age of enrollment and age of exit. The effects are generally consistent, although in some

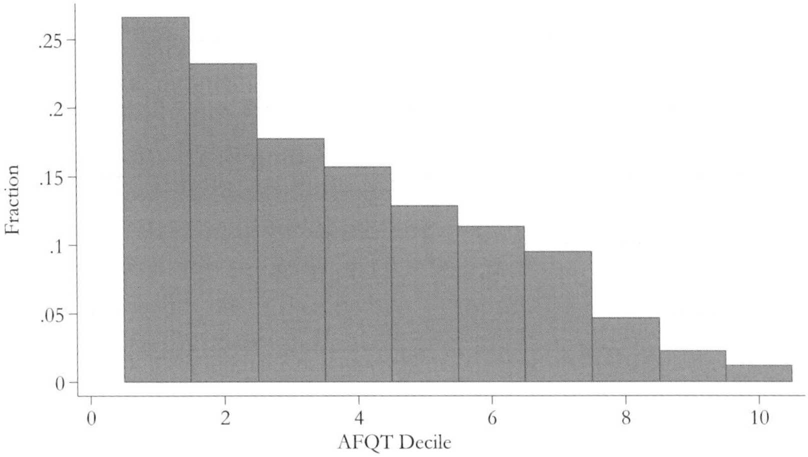

Figure 12A. Fraction of women who gave birth by 18th birthday. Data from NLSY79.
Note: Uses the AFQT calculation procedure as defined by the Department of Defense in 1989. Data used 1979–2000.

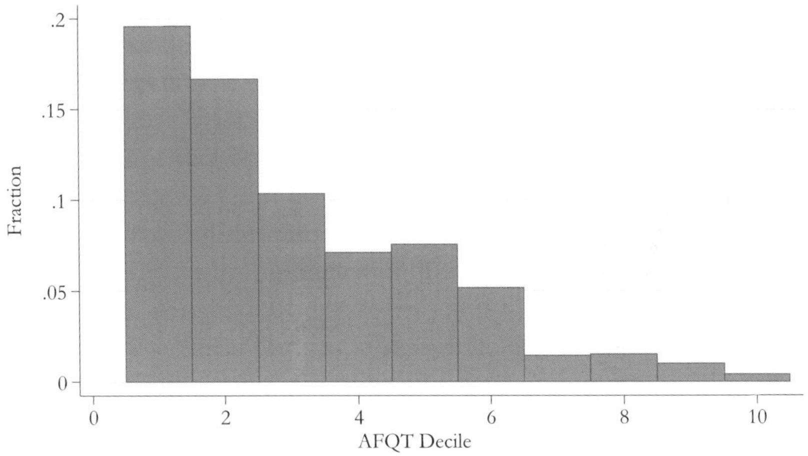

Figure 12B. Fraction of male respondents in jail at age 30 or below. Data from NLSY79.
Note: Uses the AFQT calculation procedure as defined by the Department of Defense in 1989. Data used 1979–2000.

cases they are quite small.[49] Generally, performance of children in school is improved in terms of less grade repetition, more graduation and higher test scores. Unfortunately,

[49] For example, Currie and Thomas (2000) show that test score gains of participants in the Head Start program tend to fade completely for blacks but not for whites. Their paper suggests that one reason may be that

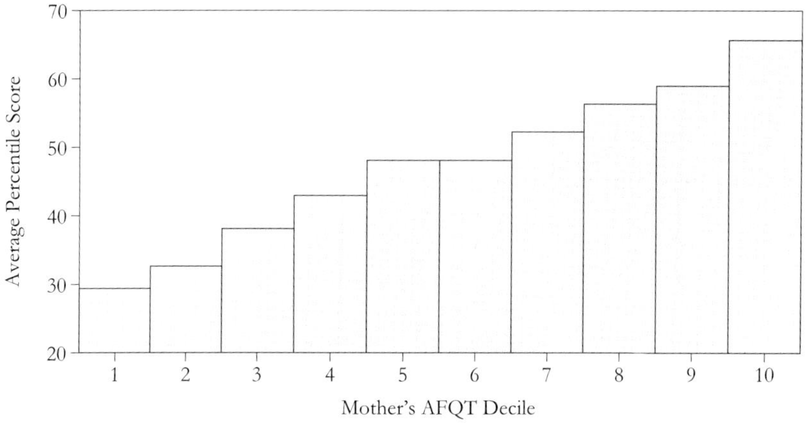

Figure 12C. Average cognitive stimulation score by mother's AFQT decile. Data from CNLSY79. Note: Overall stimulation is a measure of the quality of the child's home environment. It comprises emotional and cognitive stimulation subscores. It is based on measures of resources, such as books, and on interactions with parents. The score is measured in percentiles.

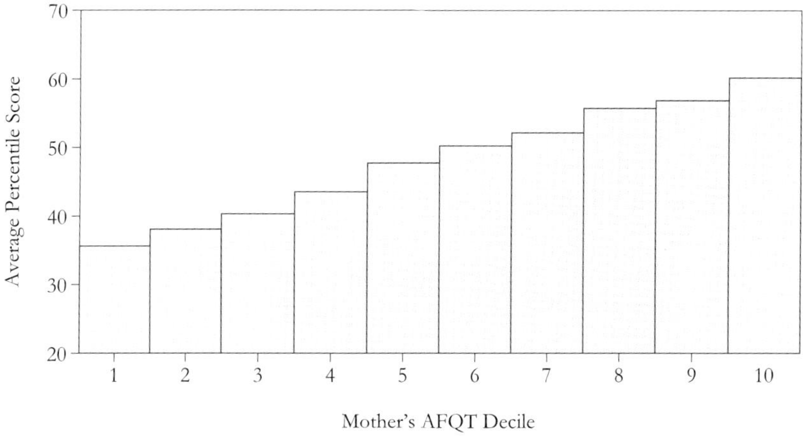

Figure 12D. Average emotional stimulation score by mother's AFQT decile. Data from CNLSY79. Note: Overall stimulation is a measure of the quality of the child's home environment. It comprises emotional and cognitive stimulation subscores. It is based on measures of resources, such as books, and on interactions with parents. The score is measured in percentiles.

blacks attend worse schools than whites, and therefore blacks are not able to maintain initial test score gains. However, Heckman, Larenas and Urzua (2004) dispute this finding. They show that schooling quality differences which are substantial across ethnic groups have only a slight effect on the levels or rates of growth in many of the evaluations of these programs do not follow children into late adolescence or adulthood. Interventions at younger ages seem to produce larger effects.[50]

Three programs have long-term follow-ups, and we focus on them here. They all targeted high-risk children from disadvantaged families. The first is the High/Scope Perry Preschool, a half-day program on a small scale in the Ypsilanti, MI public schools. Children were typically enrolled at age 4 and stayed in the program for two years. It was an experiment with a sample size of 123 and follow-up to age 40. The Abecedarian program, the second one we consider, was a full-day, year-round educational child care program in Chapel Hill, NC. Children entered around the age of 4 months and continued until age 5. Half of all children were then enrolled in a school-age program until age 8. It was evaluated by randomization and has 111 participants, and students are followed to age 21.

The final program we consider is the Chicago Child–Parent Centers (CPC), a half-day program during the school year and full-time for six weeks during the summer, conducted on a large scale in the Chicago public schools. It was evaluated by a non-experimental method (matching) and has a sample of about 1,500 children. All three programs had some sort of parental involvement component.

The programs differ by duration and child age at entry. Abecedarian started with young children in the first months of life. Perry and the CPC program start with older children, 3–5 years old. The programs differ in intensity. For some programs the comparison group received some supplementary resources relative to ordinary children, and for others they did not. Moreover, some comparison group members attended alternative preschool and kindergarten programs.

2.6.1.1. Perry preschool experiment. The Perry preschool experiment was an intensive preschool program that was administered to 65 randomly selected black children who were enrolled in the program over 5 different waves between 1962 and 1967. All the children came from Ypsilanti, MI. A control group of roughly the same size provides researchers with an appropriate benchmark to evaluate the effects of the preschool program.

The experimental group assignment was performed in the following way. Candidate families were identified from a census of the families of the students attending the Perry school at the date of operation of the program, neighborhood group referrals and door to door canvassing. Poor children who scored between 75 and 85 on the standard Stanford-Binet IQ test were randomly divided into two undesignated groups.[51] The children were

test scores. Garces, Thomas and Currie (2002) find comparable results. The Mathematica evaluation of Early Head Start by Love et al. (2002) shows very modest effects as well. However, Head Start is a considerably less intensive program than many of the other programs considered in this section, which may explain why it has limited consequences for the developmental trajectories of disadvantaged children.

[50] Morris, Duncan and Clark-Kauffman (2005) find that the biggest impact of a parental wage-subsidy intervention on children's achievement is for preschool children.

[51] Poverty status was determined by a formula that considered rooms per person in the child's household, parental schooling and occupational level. The IQ range was labeled as "borderline educable mentally re-

then transferred across groups to equalize the socioeconomic status, cognitive ability (as measured by the IQ test) and gender composition of the samples. Finally, a coin was tossed to determine which group received the treatment and which did not. Initially the treatment and control groups included 64 children each, but the actual treatment and control groups contained 58 and 65 children, respectively.[52]

Children entered the Perry School in five waves, starting with wave zero (of four-year-olds) and wave one (of three-year-olds) in 1962, then waves two, three and four (of three-year-olds) entered in each subsequent year through 1965. The average age at entry was 42.3 months. With the exception of wave zero, treatment children spent two years attending the program. In the final year of the program, 11 three-year-olds who were not included in the data attended the program with the 12 4-year-olds who were. About half of the children were living with two parents. The average mother was 29 years old and completed 9.4 years of school.

The treatment consisted of a daily $2\frac{1}{2}$ hour classroom session on weekday mornings and a weekly ninety minute home visit by the teacher on weekday afternoons to involve the mother in the child's educational process. The length of each preschool year was 30 weeks, beginning in mid-October and ending in May. Ten female teachers filled the four teaching positions over the course of the study, resulting in an average child-teacher ratio of 5.7 for the duration of the program.[53] All teachers were certified to teach in elementary, early childhood or special education.[54] If it were administered today, the Perry preschool program would cost approximately $9,785 per participant per year in 2004 dollars.

tarded" by the state of Michigan at the time of the experiment. Only children without an organic mental handicap were included in the study.

52 Some aspect of the assignment was clearly nonrandom and this has led some to call the Perry results into question. First, younger children were assigned to the same group as their older siblings. Two treatment children were transferred to the control group because their mothers were not able to participate in any classes or home visits because they were employed far from home. Four treatment children left the program before completing the second year of preschool when their families relocated, and one control child died. Thus, the final sample consisted of 123 children. The 123 children in the sample came from 100 families. In the control group, 41 families contributed 1 child each, and 12 families contributed 2 children each. In the treatment group, 39 families contributed 1 child apiece, 6 families contributed 2 children apiece, 1 family contributed 3 and another 4 children. Assigning younger siblings to the same group effectively made the family, rather than the individual, the unit of analysis. Still, it is difficult to argue that assigning siblings at random would have been a better strategy. So-called spillovers to the control siblings from home visits would have been one possible source of bias since mothers cannot be expected to treat siblings in accordance with their experimental status. Another potential source of bias is spillover from one sibling to another. In any case, differences in background characteristics between the two experimental groups are virtually nonexistent, with the exception of much higher rates of maternal employment at program entry in the treatment group.

53 This number is low relative to other early education experiments. For instance, the student–teacher ratio for the Chicago Child–Parent Center and Expansion Program ranged from 8 to 12 [see Fuerst and Fuerst (1993)].

54 Schweinhart, Barnes and Weikart (1993) argue that the certification of the teachers is an important component in the success of the Perry preschool.

2.6.1.2. Abecedarian project. The Abecedarian Project recruited 111 children born between 1972 and 1977 whose 109 families scored high on the High Risk Index.[55] It enrolled families and intervened in the lives of children beginning a few months after birth. Enrollment was based on the characteristics of the families more than on the characteristics of the children, as in the Perry program. Virtually all of the children were Black, and their parents had low levels of education, income, cognitive ability and high levels of pathological behavior. The children were screened for mental retardation. 76% of the children lived in a single parent or multigenerational household. The average mother in this group was less than 20 years old, completed 10 years of schooling and had an IQ of 85. There were 4 cohorts of about 28 students each. By the time they were 6 weeks old, the children were assigned randomly to either a preschool intervention or a control group. The mean age of entry was 4.4 months. At age 5, just as they were about to enter kindergarten, all of the children were reassigned to either a school age intervention through age 8 or to a control group. This yielded 4 groups: children who experienced no intervention at all, those who experienced an intervention when they were young, those who experienced it when they were older, and finally those who enjoyed a high-quality intervention throughout their whole childhood. The children were followed up until age 21.

The Abecedarian intervention was more intensive than the Perry one. The preschool program was a year-round, full-day intervention. The initial infant-to-teacher ratio was 3:1, though it grew to a child-to-teacher ratio of 6:1 as the kids progressed through the program. Infants in the control group received an iron-fortified formula for 15 months and diapers as needed to create an incentive for participation. Many of the control children were enrolled in preschool and/or kindergarten.

During the first 3 primary school years, a home-school teacher would meet with the parents and help them in providing supplemental educational activities at home. The teacher provided an individually-tailored curriculum for each child. This home-school teacher also served as a liaison between the ordinary teachers and the family, and she would interact with the parents and the teachers about every two weeks. She would also help the family deal with other issues that might improve their ability to care for the child, such as finding employment, navigating the bureaucracy of social services agencies, and transporting children to appointments. Data were collected regularly up to age 21.

2.6.1.3. Chicago Child–Parent Center program. The Chicago Child–Parent Center was not evaluated by the method of random assignment but by the method of matching treated children to comparable nontreated children on the basis of age, eligibility

[55] The factors used to form the index consist of weighted measures of maternal and paternal education levels, family income, absence of the father from the home, poor social or family support for the mother, indication that older siblings have academic problems, the use of welfare, unskilled employment, low parental IQ, and family members who sought counseling or support from various community agencies. Parental income and education were considered most important in calculating the index.

for intervention, and family socioeconomic status. It was started in 1967 in 11 public schools serving impoverished neighborhoods of Chicago. Using federal funds, the center provided half-day preschool program for 3- and 4-year-olds during the 9 months that they were in school. The program provided an array of services, including health and social services, and free meals. Parental participation was encouraged. Parents were helped to complete school and participated in home visits and field trips. In 1978, state funding became available, and the program was extended through third grade and included a full-day kindergarten experience. Eventually, 24 centers provided preschool and after-school activities, up to second or third grade. This is the period during which the sample analyzed by Reynolds, Ou and Topitzes (2004) was enrolled in the program. The preschool program ran 3 hours per day during the week for the 9 months that school was in session, and usually included a 6-week summer program. During the kindergarten years, more services were provided at the affiliated school. Teacher-child ratios were 17:2 for the preschool component and 25:2 for the kindergarten. Participation during the primary years was open to any child in the school. Program participants experienced reduced class sizes of 25 pupils rather than the standard of 35 or more in the Chicago public schools. Teachers' aides, extra instructional materials, and enrichment activities were also available. Some children continued to participate in CPC through age 9, for a maximum total of 6 years. 93% of the children were black and 7% were Hispanic.

2.6.1.4. The effects of early interventions. These and other studies of interventions for children from low-income families find that participants experienced increased achievement test scores, decreased grade retention, decreased time in special education, decreased crime and delinquency and increased high school graduation. The gains vary with quality and age at which the program is started, and there are important differences by the sex of the child.

Programs differ in the measures they use to evaluate the outcomes and in their intensity and quality. As a result, it is hard to compare the programs using a standard basket of benefits. The CPC program, which is less intensive, produced substantial effects on high school graduation rates, reductions in special (remedial) education, grade repetition and juvenile arrest (see Figure 13).

The Perry Preschool Program is the flagship experimental intervention study. Children are followed through age 40. The initial boost in IQ faded by the time the children were in second grade (see Figure 14A), but the program had substantial effects on educational achievement. Achievement test scores for the treatment group were consistently and statistically significantly higher through age 14. Participants had higher grades and were more likely to graduate from high school. Substantially less time was spent in special education, and higher high school graduation rates were achieved by participants (Figure 14B). Participants were more likely to be employed[56] and to earn more (Figure 14C) and they were less dependent on welfare. There was substantially less crime

[56] The difference in employment rates was only statistically significant at age 19.

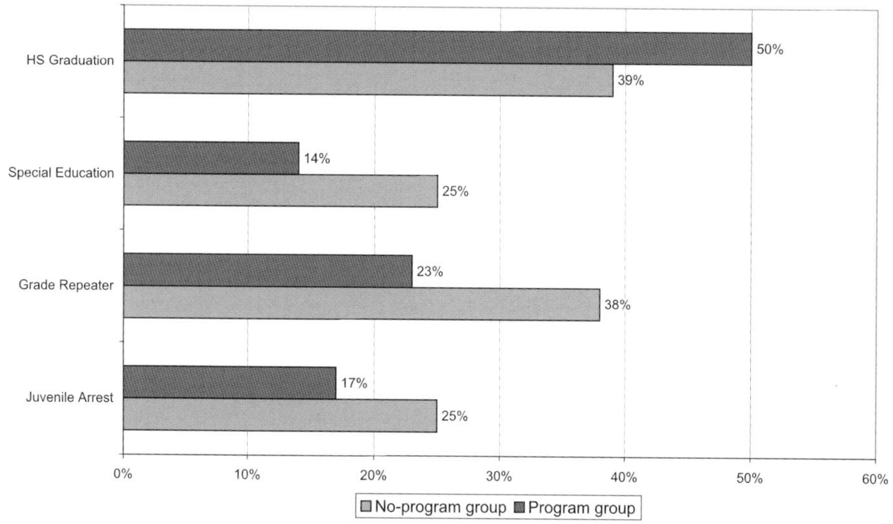

Figure 13. Academic and social benefits at school exit for CPC participants. Source: Barnett (2004).

among participants (Figure 14D) – both in terms of incidence and severity, a recurrent finding of early intervention programs. However, there was no statistically significant difference in grade retention by age 27 between the two groups, although teenage pregnancy was lower, and marriage rates were higher by age 27 for program participants. Results at age 27 are generally more favorable for girls. This reverses when outcomes at age 40 are studied [see Heckman (2005), and Heckman, Savelyev and Yavitz (2006)].

The Abecedarian program boosted IQ, but its effect is concentrated primarily among girls. Figure 15A shows the overall IQ gap between treatments and controls. It is persistent over time.[57] The Abecedarian program intervenes in the very early years, and it is known that IQ is malleable when children are very young (see, e.g., the discussion in Armor, 2003). This message is reinforced by the fact that the IQ boost was not found among children who only experienced the later intervention. Comparable effects are found for reading scores (Figure 15B) and math achievement scores (Figure 15C). The test score effects persist through age 21, which is the last age analyzed in the reports available to us.

There were substantial academic benefits as recorded in Figure 15D. Treatment group members participated less in remedial special education at age 15 and repeated fewer grades at all ages. High school graduation and four-year college participation rates were high. Participants were less likely to smoke and had better jobs (see Figure 15E).

[57] The decline in IQ over time for both groups may be a consequence of the "Flynn Effect" (see Flynn (1987)). Scores are normed against national averages, but over cohorts IQ is increasing.

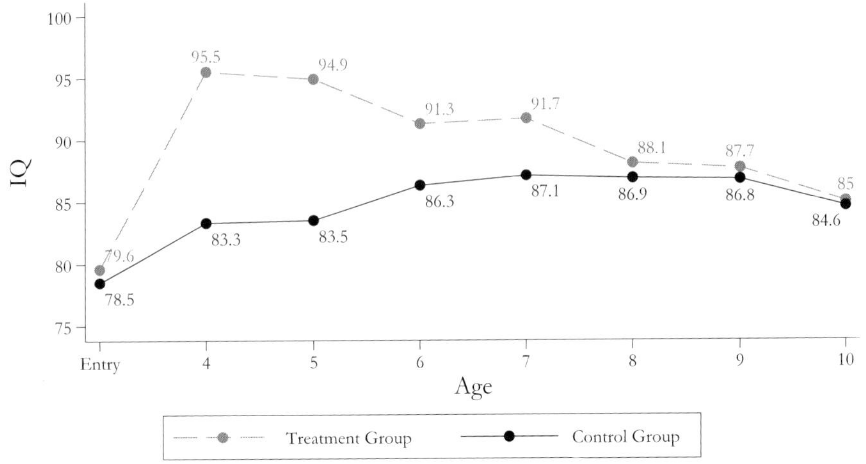

Figure 14A. Perry Preschool Program: IQ, by age and treatment group. Source: Perry Preschool Program. IQ measured on the Stanford–Binet Intelligence Scale (Terman and Merrill, 1960). Test was administered at program entry and each of the ages indicated.

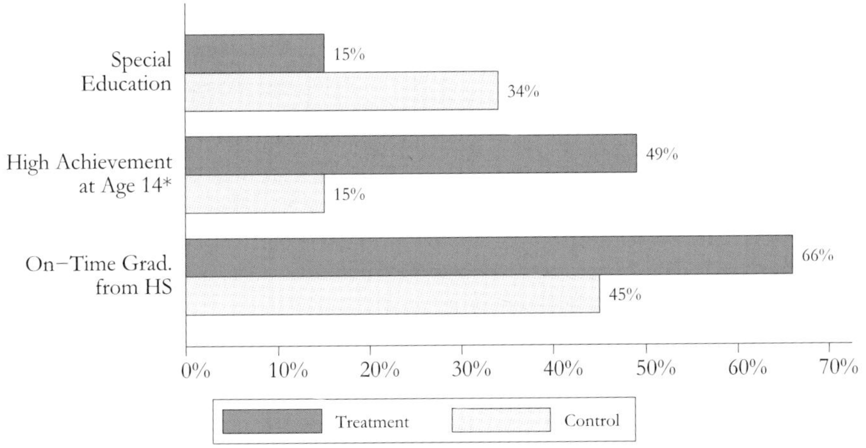

Figure 14B. Perry Preschool Program: Educational effects, by treatment group. Source: Barnett (2004). *High achievement defined as performance at or above the lowest 10th percentile on the California Achievement Test [Tiegs and Clark (1970)].

Table 4 presents estimated costs and benefits of the Perry and Chicago programs with benefits discounted at a 3% rate. All figures are in 2004 dollars. The benefits vary among programs.[58] Perry produced some gain to parents in terms of reduced child care costs,

[58] There is a cost benefit study of the Abecedarian program [Barnett and Masse (2002)], but it is highly speculative, so that we did not include it here.

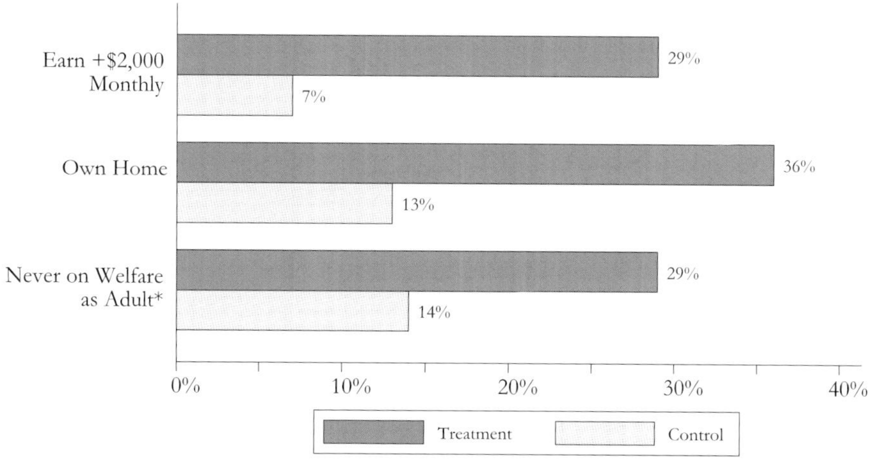

Figure 14C. Perry Preschool Program: Economic effects at age 27, by treatment group. Source: Barnett (2004).
*Updated through age 40 using recent Perry Preschool Program data, derived from self-report and all available state records.

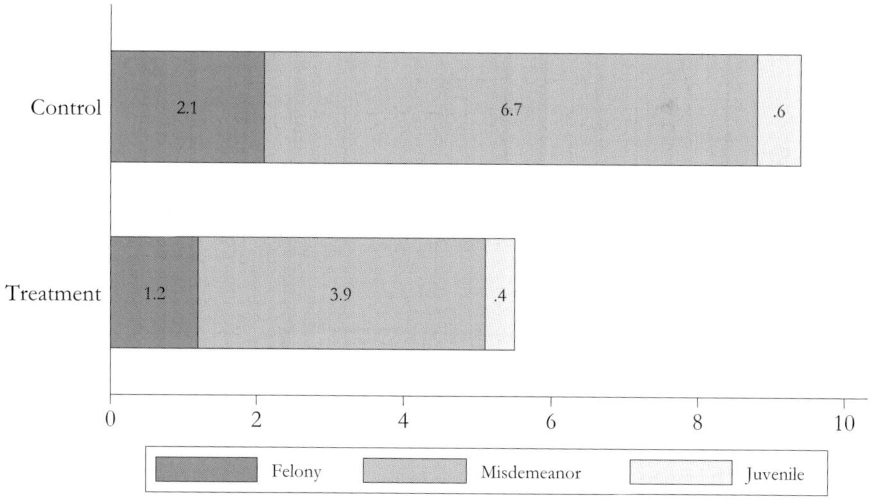

Figure 14D. Perry Preschool Program: Arrests per person before age 40, by treatment group. Source: Barnett (2004). Juvenile arrests are defined as arrests prior to age 19.

and earnings gains for participants were substantial. The K-12 benefit arises from the increment in student quality and a reduction in special education costs. This benefit is substantial across all programs. The college/adult category represents the extra tuition paid by students who go to college. Crime represents the reduction in direct costs (incar-

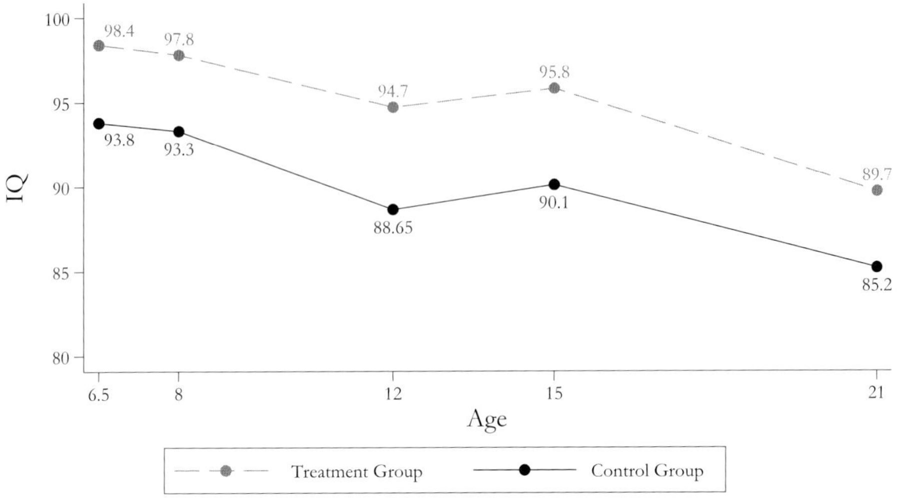

Figure 15A. Abecedarian Program: IQ, by age and treatment group. Source: Barnett (2004).

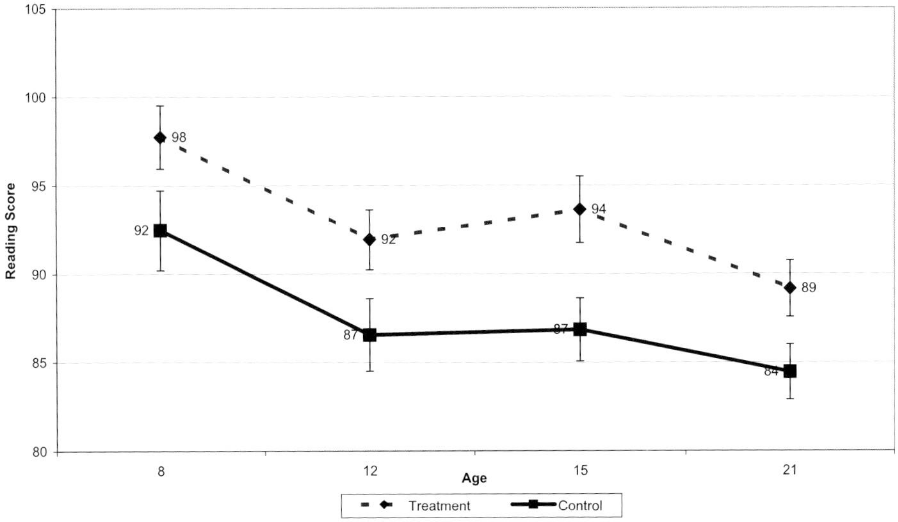

Figure 15B. Abecedarian reading achievement over time. Source: Barnett (2004).

ceration and criminal justice system) as well as damage done to victims. This excludes transfers. Welfare effects are modest. Future Generation (FG) Earnings represents the improvement in the earnings of the descendents of the program participants.

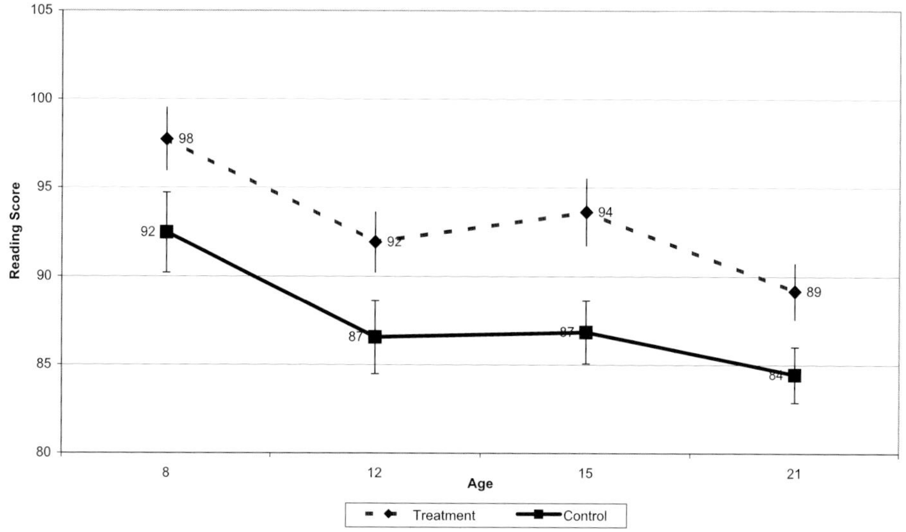

Figure 15C. Abecedarian math achievement over time. Source: Barnett (2004).

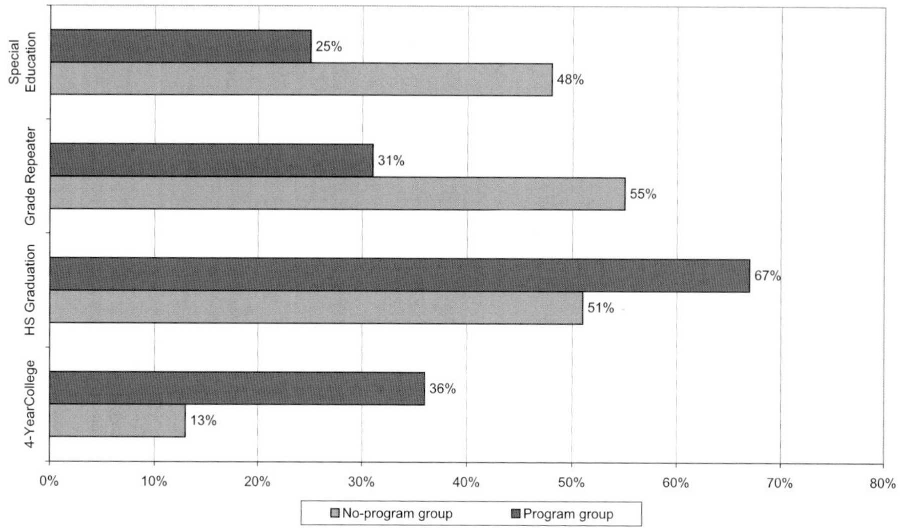

Figure 15D. Abecedarian academic outcomes. Source: Barnett (2004).

Smoking and health benefits were not measured in the Perry and Chicago data. For Abecedarian, there were substantial effects, including major differences in smoking rates. CPC documents a decline in child abuse and the costs of treating abused children.

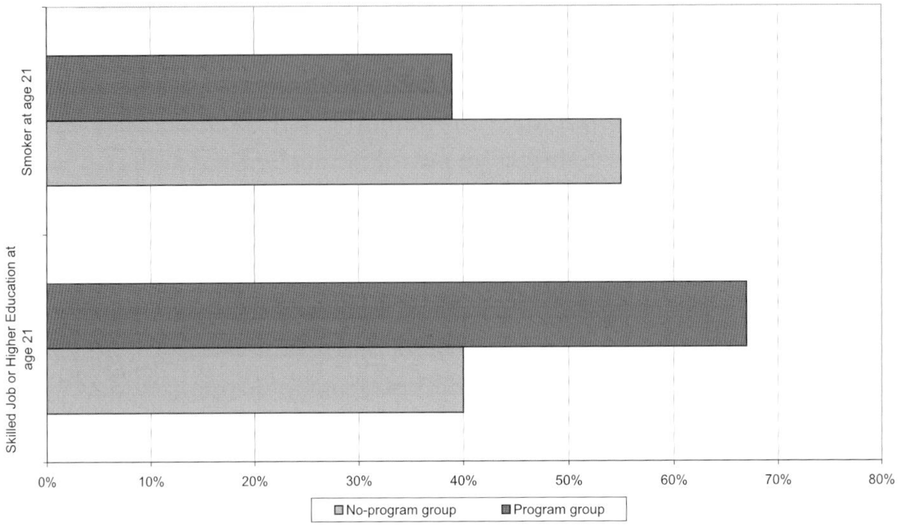

Figure 15E. Other benefits of Abecedarian. Source: Barnett (2004).

Table 4
Economic benefits and costs per treated child

	Perry	Chicago CPC
Child care	986	1,916
Earnings	40,537	32,099
K-12	9,184	5,634
College/adult	−782	−644
Crime	94,065	15,329
Welfare	355	546
FG earnings	6,181	4,894
Abuse/neglect	0	344
Total benefits	150,525	60,117
Total costs	16,514	7,738
Net present value	134,011	52,380
Benefits-to-costs ratio	9.11	7.77

All values discounted at 3% and are in \$2004. Numbers differ slightly from earlier estimates because FG Earnings for Perry and Chicago were estimated using the ratio of Future Generations Earnings Effect (FG) to Earnings Effect (about 15%) that was found in Abecedarian. Source: Barnett (2004).

The costs of Perry were substantial but per year were about the average cost of expenditure on public school students. CPC per year costs about \$6,796 for the preschool and \$3,428 for the school-age component (in 2004 dollars). The benefit cost ratios are substantial: 9 to 1 for Perry; 8 to 1 for Chicago CPC. By projecting from the age 27 results, Rolnick and Grunewald (2003) estimate that the annual rate of return for Perry is 4% for participants and 12% for society at large. Belfield, Nores, Barnett (2004) use the data on Perry participants through age 40 to estimate that the rate of return for the participants and the general public as a whole is 18.4%. The rate varies by sex of the participants: the rate of return for males alone is 21.9%, while the rate for females is only 12.6%.[59]

Some of the home visitation programs for low-income young mothers have been shown to have modest effects on maternal and offspring behavior and health.[60] Olds (2002) summarizes the results from two randomized trials in Elmira, NY and Memphis, TN, which served predominantly rural white and urban black populations, respectively. The treatment in both trials involved a series of pre- and postnatal home visits of poor, unmarried, and young women by specially-trained nurses.[61] The visits typically lasted 75–90 minutes, and nurses spent more time with women they deemed to have higher needs. The target areas for this intervention were health related behavior during and after pregnancy, childcare skills, and personal development (family planning, education, job search assistance).

The Elmira treatment group made better use of community services and exhibited reduced prenatal-period smoking, with 75% fewer premature deliveries among smokers. At ages 3–4, children whose mothers smoked 10 or more cigarettes during pregnancy had a mean IQ of 4.5 points lower than women who smoked 0–9 cigarettes. Among the 14- to 16-year-old treatment women, the newborn children were almost 400 grams heavier relative to the children of the control women. The beneficial effects of the program were especially apparent for the most disadvantaged women (i.e., young, poor, and unmarried).[62] After the birth of the child, the disadvantaged mothers who were visited showed better parenting skills and higher quality of the home environment. They also had 80% fewer verified cases of child abuse and neglect. Children of visited mothers had 32% fewer visits to the emergency room, and this effect persisted after the end of the program, though the differences in abuse and neglect faded.[63] The disadvantaged

[59] Excluding the benefits of the program for the participants, the rate for the general public alone is 16.9%. Belfield, Nores, Barnett (2004) do not calculate a rate of return for participants only because they do not bear any significant costs of the program. The rate for the general public on investing in males and females separately is 21.0% and 7.6%, respectively. The greater return for men comes from the effect of the intervention on crime, a predominantly male activity.

[60] Gomby et al. (1999) and Brooks-Gunn, Berlin and Fuligni (2000) show much more modest effects of home visitation programs, though these implementations are considerably less intensive.

[61] Only women who were pregnant with their first child were eligible. The mean frequency of nurse visits in the prenatal and postnatal (age 0–2) stages were 9 and 23 for Elmira, and 7 and 27 for Memphis. The treatment group was divided into two subgroups, where the first received only prenatal visits. The control group was also divided. See Olds (2002) for more details on the intervention.

[62] This result is found in many studies. Brooks-Gunn et al. (1992), Magnuson et al. (2004), Magnuson, Ruhm and Waldfogel (2004), and Gormley et al. (2004) find higher effects for the disadvantaged population.

[63] This may have been due to improved reporting of abuse by the nurses.

subsample of the treatment group had fewer subsequent pregnancies, longer periods between births, and greater employment rates. These effects were also evident by the time the child was 15. The children of the disadvantaged women reported fewer instances of running away, less criminal activity, promiscuous sexual behavior and smoking. Both parents and children reported less use of drugs and alcohol. Importantly, there were no differences in other behavioral problems. A cost–benefit analysis of the Elmira trial by Karoly et al. (1998) suggests that the program was very successful for low-income, unmarried women. Extrapolating from the results at age 15, the benefits of the program were 4 times its costs. The program paid for itself before the child's fourth birthday, with the primary savings coming from reduced welfare and criminal justice expenditures, as well as increases in tax revenue. However, the program provided no net savings for the sample as a whole, suggesting that targeting, rather than universal provision, is appropriate.

The effects for the Memphis trial were considerably weaker, even for the disadvantaged subsample. There were no effects on birth outcomes and parenting skills. Many fewer women smoked in this sample, so any reductions were very small. The same may be the case for child abuse and neglect. Children of visited women had fewer health-care visits, especially among the disadvantaged subsample. In the first 2 years of life, more visited mothers attempted breast feeding. At age 4, there were no differences in mental development or reported behavior problems. Visited mothers reported fewer subsequent pregnancies. There were no differences in employment and some evidence of reduced AFDC and Food Stamp use. The children are still too young to perform a reliable cost–benefit analysis on their outcomes.

Much more research is needed on Perry, CPC, and a wide variety of other early childhood programs (shown in Tables 5 and 6). These samples and measurements need to be placed in a common analytical framework to better understand the differences in samples, treatments, and effects. For example, are the persistent Abecedarian effects on IQ due to the intensity or the age (4 months) at which the intervention is administered? How important are home visitation efforts? Joint analysis of the multiplicity of generally favorable treatment outcomes using methods appropriate for the small samples that are available, needs to be applied to supplement analyses of one-at-a-time outcome measure studies. A much more careful analysis of the effects of scaling up the model programs to the target population, and its effects on costs, has to be undertaken before these estimates can be considered definitive.

2.6.1.5. Extreme deprivation and remediation. Institutional rearing of children, insofar as it tends to be exceptionally poor, provides scientists with a unique natural experiment that can be used to ascertain the effects of severe environmental deprivation. Evidence on children from such environments allows us to answer questions about the developmental consequences of negative early experience and how amenable exposed children are to interventions such as foster care. It may also enable us to learn if there are critical or sensitive periods for development, which would have important implications for the relationship between the timing of an intervention and the extent

Table 5
Effects of early intervention programs

Program/study	Costs*	Program description	Test scores	Schooling	Pre-delinquency crime
Abecedarian project** [Ramey et al. (1988)]	N/A	Full-time year round classes for children from infancy through preschool	High scores at ages 1–4	34% less grade retention by 2nd grade; better reading and math proficiency	
Early training** [Gray et al. (1982)]	N/A	Part-time classes for children in summer; weekly home visits during school year	Higher scores at ages 5–10	16% less grade retention; 21% higher HS grad. rates	
Harlem study [Palmer (1983)]	N/A	Individual teacher-child sessions twice-weekly for young males	Higher scores at ages 3–5	21% less grade retention	
Houston PCDC** [Johnson (1988)]	N/A	Home visits for parents for 2 yrs; child nursery care 4 days/wk in year 2 (Mexican Americans)	Higher scores at age 3		Rated less aggressive and hostile by mothers (ages 8–11)
Milwaukee project** [Garber (1988)]	N/A	Full-time year-round classes for children through 1st grade; job training for mothers	Higher scores at ages 2–10	27% less grade retention	
Mother–child home program [Levenstein, O'Hara and Madden (1983)]	N/A	Home visits with mothers and children twice weekly	Higher scores at ages 3–4	6% less grade retention	
Perry preschool program** [Schweinhart, Barnes and Weikart (1993)]	$13,400	Weekly home visits with parents; intensive, high quality preschool services for 1–2 years	Higher scores in all studied years (ages 5–27)	21% less grade retention or special services; 21% higher HS grad. rates	2.3 vs. 4.6 lifetime arrests by age 27 7% vs. 35% arrested 5 or more times

(Continued on next page)

Table 5
(*Continued*)

Program/study	Costs*	Program description	Test scores	Schooling	Pre-delinquency crime
Rome head start [Monroe and McDonald (1981)]	$5,400	Part-time classes for children; parent involvement		12% less grade retention; 17% higher HS grad. rates	
Syracuse university family development [Lally et al. (1988)]	$38,100	Wekly home visits for family; day care year round	Higher scores at ages 3–4		6% vs. 22% had probation files; offenses were less severe
Yale experiment	$23,300	Family support; home visits and day care as needed for 30 months	Better language development at 30 months	better-school attendance and adjustment; fewer special adjustment; school services (age $12\frac{1}{2}$)	Rated less aggressive and pre-delinquent by teachers and parents (age $12\frac{1}{2}$)

All comparisons are for program participants vs. non-participants. Source: Heckman et al. (1997).
*Costs valued in 1990 dollars.
**Studies used a random assignment experimental design to determine program impacts. Data from Donohue and Siegelman (1998), Schweinhart, Barnes and Weikart (1993), and Seitz (1990) for the impacts reported here.

of its success. Some good evidence on this issue comes from the longitudinal studies of initially institutionalized Romanian infants and toddlers who were later placed into foster care abroad. In this section, we will outline the historical context for these studies, some of their results, and the implications that these data have for our model of human development.

The Ceauşescu regime in Romania, which was in power from 1966 to 1989, attempted to enlarge the country's workforce by increasing the birth rate.[64] Virtually all types of abortion were criminalized, and divorce was made much more difficult. Contraceptives were neither manufactured domestically nor imported. Progressive income taxes on childless adults over 25 were imposed. Monthly cash subsidies were awarded to families with children, and the average allowance per child rose as family size increased. Various labor laws eased working conditions for pregnant and nursing mothers by eliminating overtime and night work entirely, and by reducing physically demanding work. Over three months of paid maternity leave were available, as were additional breaks or reductions in work hours of up to two hours per day. Early retirement was available for

[64] Moskoff (1980) enumerates the regime's pronatalist policies.

Table 6
Outcomes of early intervention programs

	Program (years of operation)	Outcome	Followed up to age	Age when treatment effect last statistically significant	Control group	Change in treated group
Cognitive measures						
	Early Training Project (1962–1965)	IQ	16–20	6	82.8	+12.2
	Perry Preschool Project (1962–1967)	IQ	27	7	87.1	+4.0
	Houston PCDC (1970–1980)	IQ	8–11	2	90.8	+8.0
	Syracuse FDRP (1969–1970)	IQ	15	3	90.6	+19.7
	Carolina Abecedarian (1972–1985)	IQ	21	12	88.4	+5.3
	Project CARE (1978–1984)	IQ	4.5	3	92.6	+11.6
	IHDP (1985–1988)	IQ (HLBW sample)	8	8	92.1	+4.4
Educational outcomes						
	Early Training Project	Special education	16–20	18	29%	−26%
	Perry Preschool Project	Special education	27	19	28%	−12%
		High school graduation		27	45%	+21%
	Chicago CPC (1967–present)	Special education	20	18	25%	−10%
		Grade retention		15	38%	−15%
		High school graduation		20	39%	+11%
	Carolina Abecedarian	College enrollment	21	21	14%	+22%

(*Continued on next page*)

Table 6
(*Continued*)

	Program (years of operation)	Outcome	Followed up to age	Age when treatment effect last statistically significant	Control group	Change in treated group
Economic outcomes						
	Perry Preschool Project	Arrest rate	27	27	69%	−12%
		Employment rate		27	32%	+18%
		Monthly earnings		27	$766	+$453
		Welfare use		27	32%	−17%
	Chicago CPC (preschool vs. no preschool)	Juvenile arrests	20	18	25%	−8%
	Syracuse FDRP	Probation referral	15	15	22%	−16%
	Elmira PEIP (1978–1982)	Arrests (HR sample)	15	15	0.53	−0.029

HLBW = heavier, low birth weight sample; HR = high risk. Cognitive measures include Stanford-Binet and Weshler Intelligence Scales, California Achievement Tests, and other IQ and achievement tests measuring cognitive ability. All results significant at 0.05 level or higher. Source: Karoly (2001). For a discussion of the specific treatments offered under each program see Heckman (2000) and Karoly (2001).

women as a function of the number of children they raised to age 10. Increasing economic hardship coupled with Ceauşescu's goal of paying off all international debt by imposing rationing, obliged many women to work outside the home. Since childcare for the young (or any other alternative) was scarce, many children were simply abandoned.

Institutionalization of children was not stigmatized, and was even encouraged officially. When the Ceauşescu regime fell in 1989, there were roughly 170,000 children in 700 overcrowded state institutions [see Rosapepe (2001)]. While no rigorous statistics on the conditions in these homes are available, foreign visitors described the situation as appalling [see Rosapepe (2001), Rutter (1998)]. Children remained in their cots all day, with no toys or other types of stimulation. Caregiving and personalized affection were all but nonexistent. Many young children were fed only gruel from bottles that were propped up, and some continued to have difficulty even chewing solid food some years later. Orphanages were frequently located in remote areas of the country; some children were transferred far away from where they were born and were "lost" in the system. By the late 1980s, many institutions had no hot water, no constant heat during winter, no diapers or even detergent. Medical supplies, including antibiotics and syringe needles, were extremely scarce. Children were often tied down or locked in rooms to keep them under control and some were abused. While the prevalence and incidence of these problems are unknown, most children exhibited a range of emotional, behavioral and medical problems when they were adopted abroad.

Several studies have been conducted to evaluate the effects of interventions at various ages on these children. The largest study of this sort was completed in the UK by Michael Rutter, his colleagues and the English and Romanian Adoptees Study Team. The most recent results are summarized in O'Connor et al. (2000). This group studied 165 children who were adopted from Romania into UK families between 1990 and 1992 and compared them at ages 4 and 6 to 52 adopted children from within the UK who were all placed before age 6 months.[65] Selected results are shown in Table 7. Rutter (1998) shows that at the time of adoption, the orphans showed substantial developmental retardation, malnutrition, and a range of health problems. Relative to ordinary English children, half of the Romanian orphans were below the third percentile on weight, and over a third were below the third percentile on height. The overall mean score on the Denver developmental quotient was 63, indicating mild retardation.[66] Interestingly, there were no significant differences in weight or Denver scale by age of adoption. By age 4, only 2% of the orphans were below the third percentile on weight, and only 1% was below that threshold on height. The extent of catch-up to British adoptees on the

[65] Only 87% of the Romanian children were adopted from institutions. The others came from a family setting, but there were no differences in origin by age at the time of adoption. It is true, however, that the non-institutionalized children exhibited fewer problems.

[66] The Denver Developmental Scales were used to conduct this assessment. Parents were asked to recall specific behavior (e.g., standing while holding on to something, lifting the head, making meaningful "da-da" sounds) at the time of adoption. The majority of parents used baby books that recorded these developmental milestones, which made recollection much better. See Rutter (1998) for more details on the analysis.

Table 7
Anthropomorphic, developmental, and cognitive outcomes of Romanian and within-UK adoptees over time

	Within-UK adoptees	Romanian orphans		
Age of adoption (months):	6	Before 6	At 6–24	At 24–42
Weight at adoption	–	−2.1	−2.3	–
	–	(1.7)	(1.7)	–
Height at adoption	–	−1.8	−2.2	–
	–	(1.6)	(2.4)	–
Denver Developmental	–	76.5	48.1	–
Scale at adoption	–	(48.1)	(25.4)	–
Weight at age 4	0.45	−0.02	0.04	–
	(0.79)	(0.92)	(0.94)	–
Height at age 4	0.25	−0.29	−0.36	–
	(0.91)	(0.89)	(1.02)	–
Denver Developmental	117.7	115.7	96.7	–
Scale at age 4	(24.3)	(23.4)	(21.3)	–
McCarthy GCI at age 4	109.4	105.9	91.7	–
	(14.8)	(17.9)	(18.0)	–
Weight at age 6	0.30	0.02	−0.25	−0.85
	(0.90)	(0.97)	(0.96)	(0.98)
Percentage with	2	0	5	18
Denver Developmental	(1)	(0)	(2)	(7)
Scale at age 6 below 70				
McCarthy GCI at age 6	117	114	99	90
	(17.8)	(18.3)	(19.2)	(23.8)

Standard deviations are reported below in parentheses. All anthropometric measurements are standardized using the UK age-specific distributions. The Denver Developmental Scale is are based on specific behaviors (e.g., standing while holding on to something, lifting the head, making meaningful "da-da" sounds). Due to ceiling effects, the Denver scale is not meaningful at age 6, so O'Connor et al. (2000) use the percentage with impairment (defined as a score below 70) as the test criterion. The GCI is the total score on the McCarthy Scales of Children's Abilities. It summarizes verbal, quantitative, perceptual, and memory performance. See Rutter et al. (1998) and O'Connor et al. (2000) for more details on the analysis.

Denver developmental quotient was greater for the orphans who entered foster care before they were 6 months of age.[67] At age 6, the same result was obtained.[68] The same

[67] The mean Denver scale for within-UK adoptees was 117.7 ($SD = 24.3$), 115.7 ($SD = 23.4$) for Romanians adopted before 6 months, and 96.7 ($SD = 21.3$) for those adopted when they were between 6 and 24 months of age. See Rutter (1998).

[68] O'Connor et al. (2000) add a third group of Romanian children who were adopted between the ages of 24 to 42 months. This group exhibits the worst performance on the Denver scale. Due to ceiling effects, the Denver scale is not meaningful at age 6, so O'Connor et al. (2000) use the presence of impairment (defined as a score below 70) as a test criterion. For within-UK adoptees, only 2% ($SD = 1$) qualify as impaired. The corresponding percentages for the Romanians adopted before 6, 6–24 and 24–42 months are 0 ($SD = 0$), 5 ($SD = 2$), and 18 ($SD = 7$). See O'Connor et al. (2000).

pattern appears to hold for cognitive development at ages 4 and 6, as measured using the McCarthy General Cognitive Index.[69]

Romanian orphans who were adopted into UK families from an environment of severe early deprivation exhibited remarkable improvement. This recovery was characterized by a negative linear dose-response relationship with the duration (or perhaps severity) of the exposure to poor pre and postnatal environments. The children who caught up to ordinary UK adoptees were the ones who were adopted before 6 months of age. This shows the importance of early vs. late intervention that we have documented throughout this chapter. This evidence is also consistent with the notion that early environments are a sensitive, rather than a critical period of development for many child outcomes. Had the interventions occurred later in the life of the children, it is likely that they would have been less effective.

2.6.2. *Intervention in the adolescent years*

How effective are interventions in the adolescent years? Is it possible to remedy the consequences of neglect in the early years? These questions are relevant because cognitive abilities are fairly well determined and stable by age 10 in the sense that IQ at later ages is highly correlated with IQ at ages 8–10. Just as early intervention programs have a high payoff primarily from the social skills and motivation they impart to the child and the improved home environment they produce, so do interventions that operate during the adolescent years.

Tables 8 and 9 summarize evidence on the effects of adolescent interventions on education, earnings, and crime rates. There are few estimates of rates of return for these programs. School-based and training-based programs are compared in the tables. We briefly discuss what is known about school-based interventions during the adolescent years. A few recent studies of mentoring programs like Big Brothers/Big Sisters (BB/BS) and Philadelphia Futures Sponsor-A-Scholar (SAS) have shown that these programs have broad positive social and academic impacts on participating school-aged children and adolescents. The BB/BS program pairs unrelated adult volunteers with youth from single-parent households for the purpose of providing youth with an adult friend. This activity promotes private youth development and surrogate parenthood. No specific attempts were made to ameliorate particular deficiencies or to reach specific educational goals. A broad, supportive role is envisioned for the mentor.

In a random-assignment study, Tierney, Grossman and Resch (1995) found that eighteen months after being matched with a mentor, Little Brothers and Sisters (ages 10 to 16 at the time of the match) were less likely to have initiated drug or alcohol use, to hit someone, to skip class or a day of school, or to lie to their parents; they had higher average grades and were more likely to feel competent in their school work and report a better relationship with their parents.

[69] The GCI is the total score on the McCarthy Scales of Children's Abilities. It summarizes verbal, quantitative, perceptual, and memory performance.

Table 8
Estimated benefits of mentoring programs (Treatment group reductions compared to control group)

Program	Outcome measure	Change	Program costs per participant
Big Brother/Big Sister			$500–1500*
	Initiating drug use	−45.8%	
	Initiation alcohol use	−27.4%	
	# of times hit someone	−31.7%	
	# of times stole something	−19.2%	
	Grade point average	3.0%	
	Skipped class	−36.7%	
	Skipped day of school	−52.2%	
	Trust in parent	2.7%	
	Lying to parent	−36.6%	
	Peer emotional support	2.3%	
Sponsor-A-Scholar			$1485
	10th grade GPA (100 point scale)	2.9	
	llth grade GPA (100 point scale)	2.5	
	% attending college (1 year after HS)	32.8%	
	% attending college (2 years after HS)	28.1%	
Quantum opportunity program			
	Graduated HS or GED	+26%	
	Enrolled in 4-year college	+15%	
	Enrolled in 2-year college	+24%	
	Currently employed full time	+13%	
	Self receiving welfare	−22%	
	% ever arrested	−4%	

Sources: Benefits from Heckman (1999) and Taggart (1995), costs from Johnson (1996) and Herrera et al. (2000).
*Costs, in 1996 dollars, for school-based programs are as low as $500 and more expensive community based mentoring programs cost as high as $1500; HS = high school.

The primary goal of Sponsor-A-Scholar (SAS) was to help students from Philadelphia public high schools make it to college. The program provides long-term mentoring (throughout high school and for one year beyond), substantial academic support, help with college application and financial-aid procedures, and financial support for college-related expenses. Individually matched mentors served as surrogate parents, provided a successful role model, monitored student progress, and provided encouragement and support. SAS provided students with $6,000 in financial assistance throughout college for those choosing to enroll in an accredited two- or four-year postsecondary institution. The program also provided a coordinator for groups of about thirty students to ensure a successful relationship is built between mentors and students. Using a matched sample of non-SAS students in Philadelphia high schools, Johnson (1996) estimates statisti-

Table 9
Effects of selected adolescent social programs on schooling, earnings, and crime

Program/Study	Costs*	Program Description	Schooling	Earnings*	Crime*
Job Corps [Long et al. (1981)]	$11,000	7 mo. of educ. and vocational training for 16–21 yr. olds (mostly male)	no effect	disc. pres. value of increased earnings of $10,000	Estimated Reduction in crime valued at approx.
STEP [Walker and Viella-Velez (1992)]	N/A	2 summers of employment, academic/ remediation and life skills for 14 and 15 year olds	short-run gains in test scores; no effect on school completion rates		
Quantum opportunities program** [Taggart (1995)]	$10,600	counseling; educ., comm., and devp. services; financial incentives for part. (4 yrs. beginning in 9th grade)	34% higher HS grad./GED rates (2 yrs. post- program)		4% vs. 16% convicted; 0.28 vs. 0.56 avg. number of arrests (2 yrs. post-program)

Notes: All comparisons are for program participants vs. nonparticipants.
Source: Heckman et al. (1997).
*All dollar figures are in 1990 values.
**Studies used a random assignment experimental design to determine program impacts.

cally significant increases in grade point averages for tenth and eleventh grades, as well as a 22 percent (16 percent) increase in college attendance one year (two years) after graduation from high school. Because the primary goal of SAS is to increase college enrollment, Johnson did not collect other social and psychological measures.

Much like SAS, the Quantum Opportunity Program (QOP) offered disadvantaged minority students counseling and financial incentives (one dollar up front and one dollar put in a college fund) for every hour spent in activities aimed at improving social and market skills. Students who were randomly chosen to participate in the program were provided with a mentor at the beginning of ninth grade. All participants were kept in the program for four years regardless of whether they stayed in school. Over four years, the average participant logged 1,286 hours of educational activities like studying with tutors or visiting museums. Two years after program completion, about a third more participating students graduated from high school (or obtained a GED) than similar nonparticipants. Since many participants were enrolled in postsecondary schooling at the time of the follow-up study, it is difficult to determine the program's effect on earnings. Arrest rates for program participants, however, were one-half those for non-participants. These benefits did not come without substantial expenditures, however, as the average four-year cost per participant was $10,600. Still, a cost–benefit analysis estimated positive net social returns to QOP. [See Taggart (1995) for a more detailed description of the program and an evaluation of its impacts]. Tables 8 and 9 present evidence from a randomized-trial evaluation of the QOP program. Again, the evidence shows that QOP and programs like it can dramatically improve social skills and the adaptation of adolescents to society. However, these programs do not produce miracles. The recent evaluation of QOP by Maxfield, Schirm and Rodriguez-Planas (2003) found that the program did not improve grades or achievement test scores and the effect on risky behaviors was ambiguous. It was also more effective for teens from the middle of the eligible grade distribution than for enrollees at the top or bottom of the distribution. There was considerable variability in effect by program site.

Two other studies provide additional evidence that creative programs designed to keep adolescents in school can be effective. These are discussed more extensively in Heckman (2000) and Heckman and Lochner (2000), and we briefly summarize these discussions here. Ohio's Learning, Earning, and Parenting (LEAP) program and the Teenage Parent Demonstration (TPD) provided financial incentives for teenage parents on welfare to stay in school or take GED classes (or, alternatively, imposed financial penalties for nonenrollment). LEAP showed increases in high school graduation or GED rates among randomly assigned participants who were still enrolled in school when they entered the program. TPD showed mixed results on educational attainment depending on the program site. Young women who had already dropped out of school at the time of enrollment in the program (and, to a lesser extent, those who were still attending school when they entered the program) may have substituted GED training for high school graduation as an easier way to meet program requirements, raising concerns about an unintended, potentially negative effect. Both of these programs show positive post-program effects on earnings and employment for students who were still in school when they entered the program. The estimated effects were often negative, however, for participants who had already dropped out of school before entering the program. Both studies thus show more positive impacts for individuals still enrolled in school than for dropouts. It is still unknown whether the effects of the programs are more positive for those still in school because, on average, they are of higher ability than those who have already dropped out, or because there is some advantage to intervening before adolescents leave school.

The available schooling literature demonstrates that providing disadvantaged students with financial incentives to stay in school and participate in learning activities can increase schooling and improve employment outcomes. It should be noted that although programs providing such incentives have proven to influence employment and earnings positively (and, in the case of QOP, to reduce crime), they do not perform miracles. The impacts they achieve are modest, but positive.

The Summer Training and Employment Program (STEP) provided remedial academic education and summer jobs to disadvantaged youth ages 14 and 15. Each summer, participants enrolled in 110 hours of classes and 90 hours of part-time work. Although program participants achieved modest short-term gains in reading and math skills, those gains did not last. Two to three years after program completion, program participation was found to have no effects on high school graduation rates, grades, or employment (see Table 9). The program has been criticized for not attempting to follow up on its summer program with a school year curriculum. Maryland's Tomorrow program did just that: it combined an intensive summer program with a school year follow-up, offering participants summer jobs and academic instruction, career guidance, and counseling through adult mentors, peer support, or tutoring. Although the program did not reduce final attrition rates, it did seem to delay attrition (dropout rates were lower for program participants during the ninth grade but not by the end of the twelfth grade). The program also increased the pass rate for twelfth grade students taking the Maryland Functional Tests, a series of tests of basic skills [see Heckman and Lochner (2000)].

There is also some non-experimental evidence that Catholic secondary schooling is associated with increased college participation among urban students, especially minorities [see Grogger and Neal (2000)]. This increase does not appear to be accompanied by large gains in math scores, at least for the groups whose attainment is most affected. This is consistent with our hypothesis that adolescent interventions alter noncognitive skills but have weaker effects on cognitive skills. Altonji, Elder and Taber (2005) find a similar pattern that attendance at Catholic schools raises high school graduation rates and, more tentatively, promotes college attendance but has no effect on test scores.

The evidence on programs aimed at increasing the skills and earnings of disadvantaged youth suggests that sustained interventions targeted at adolescents still enrolled in school can positively affect learning and subsequent employment and earnings. The studies discussed in this section also suggest that interventions for dropouts are much less successful. One plausible interpretation, consistent with other evidence reported in this chapter, is that those who choose to drop out have less motivation and lower ability, making programs less effective for them regardless of when the intervention takes place. It is important to note, however, that the interventions conducted by such programs only alleviate and do not fully reverse early damage caused by low quality family environments.

2.6.3. The effectiveness of late adolescent and young adult remediation programs

The evidence from public job training and second chance programs like the GED suggests that remediation targeted towards children from disadvantaged environments is costly and at current expenditure levels is ineffective [see Carneiro and Heckman (2003)]. Heckman, LaLonde and Smith (1999) survey evaluations of public job training programs in the United States. Returns are low (and sometimes negative) and even when they are positive they do not lift most persons treated out of poverty. Similar evidence is reported for remediation efforts in public schools. As discussed above, the return to GED certification is very low. While the return to private sector on-the-job training is high, access to such training is difficult for the less able and the disadvantaged (recall Table 2). Adolescent remediation programs are effective for a targeted few who use them as second chance opportunities. They are not effective for the rest.

Some look to public schooling as a way to remedy early ability deficits and to alleviate disadvantage in endowments. Hansen, Heckman and Mullen (2004) and Heckman, Larenas and Urzua (2004) address this issue. They use a variety of methods to control for the endogeneity of schooling. All methods show that schooling, while it raises measured ability, does not eliminate gaps between children from different racial and economic strata, and if anything widens them. This evidence parallels the evidence on military experience and productivity discussed in Section 2.5.6. Experience raises performance but does not close gaps.

Figures 16A and 16B, taken from Heckman, Larenas and Urzua (2004), show how schooling raises achievement test scores at different levels of ability. These authors use the methodology of Hansen, Heckman and Mullen (2004) to isolate causal effects of schooling on AFQT test scores, holding pure cognitive ability constant. The level of latent ability is determined by a version of factor analysis. Graphs are given by decile of ability from the lowest to the highest. Their analysis is based on longitudinal data to

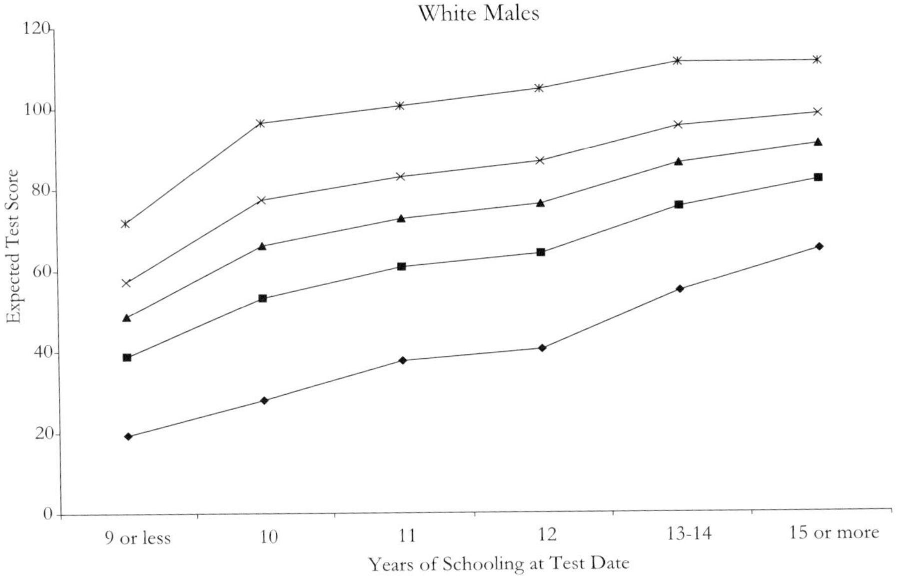

Figure 16A. Expected value of AFQT score conditional on latent ability (plots are by decile of latent ability). Notes: The structural model includes the following covariates: urban status, broken home and southern residence at age 14, number of siblings and family income in 1979, mother's and father's education, and age of the child at December 1980.

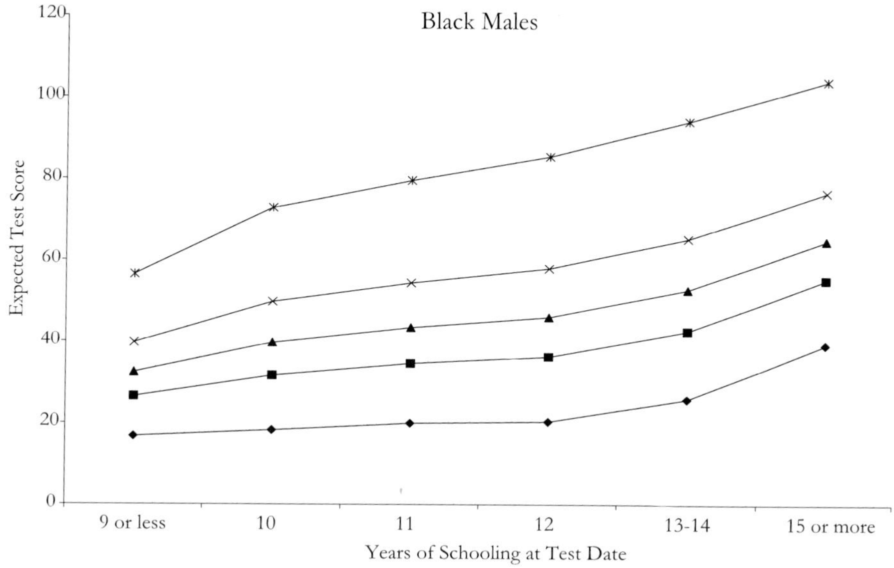

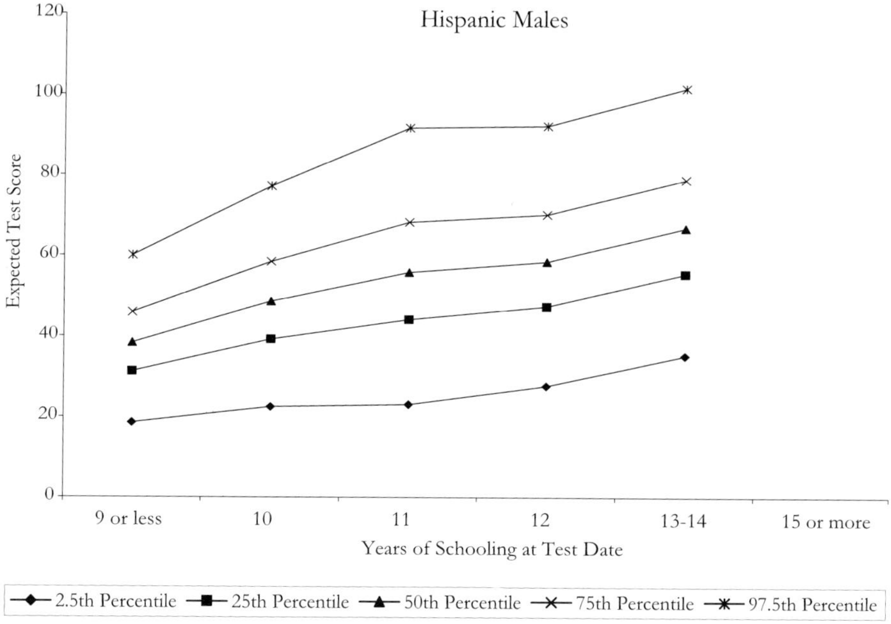

Figure 16A. (*Continued.*)

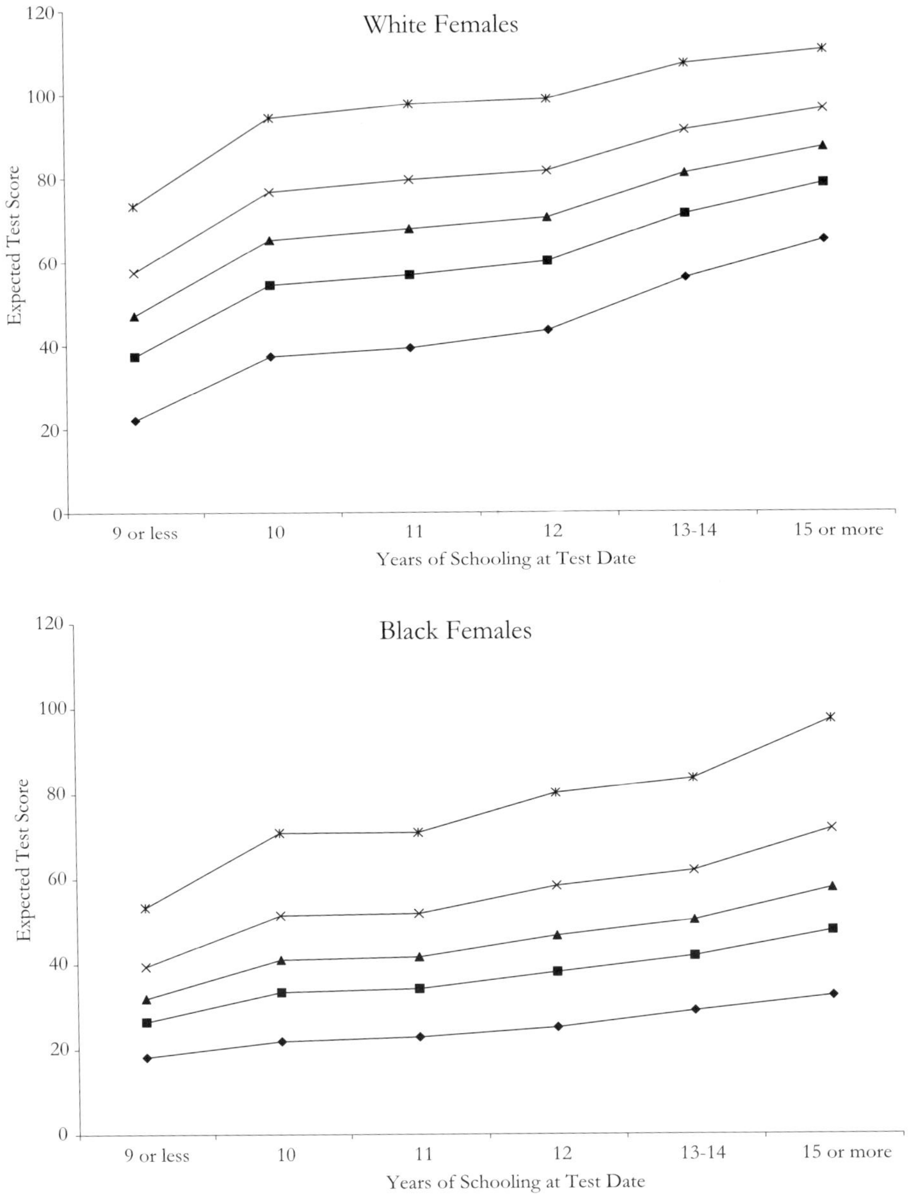

Figure 16B. Expected value of AFQT score conditional on factor.

Note: The structural model includes the following covariates: urban status, broken home and south residence at age 14, number of sibling, family income in 1979, mother's and father's education, and age of the child at December 1980.

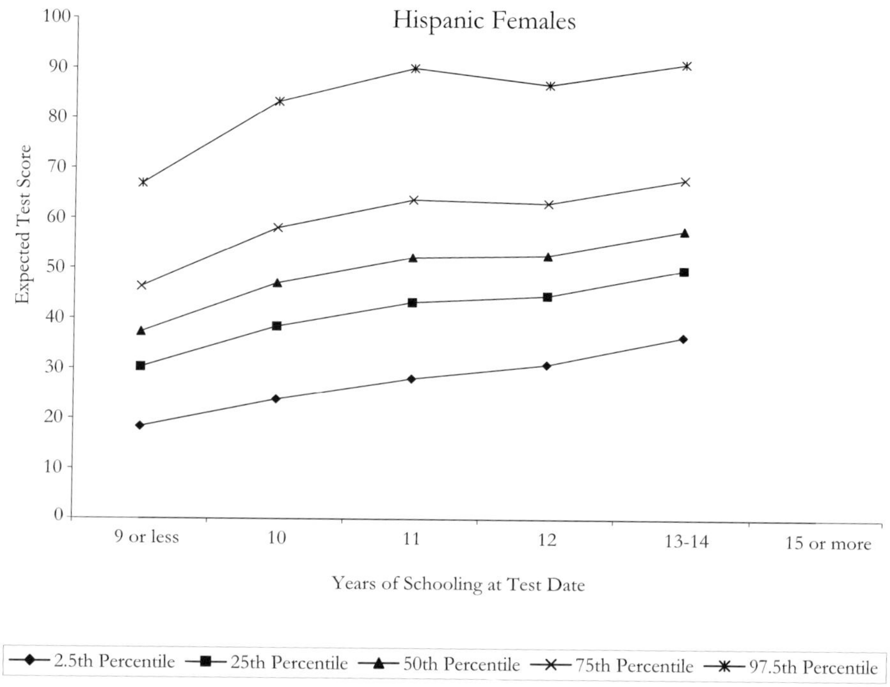

Figure 16B. (*Continued.*)

measure the effects of different levels of schooling attained at the date the test is taken on achievement for people who all eventually get the same schooling. For all major demographic groups, initial (ninth grade) test score gaps are maintained regardless of schooling level. Schooling raises test scores, but it does not equalize them. These results persist even after controlling for measures of schooling quality. One cannot count on schooling to eliminate early test score deficits. On the other hand, one cannot blame schools for widening initial test score gaps.

The evidence reviewed in Section 2 points to the empirical importance of self-productivity and complementarity. Skill begets skill. Later remediation of early skill deficits can be costly. This evidence supports the qualitative conclusions of Figures 1A and 1B that returns to investment are higher for the young and the disadvantaged. We next present a more formal model of the technology of skill formation that is a starting point for the theoretical unification of a scattered literature on treatment effects that presents "effects" for different programs in different environments directed towards different clientele.

3. Using the technology of skill formation to explain the evidence

3.1. A model of skill formation

We use simple economic models to organize the evidence presented in Section 2 as summarized in Figures 1A and 1B. We define the concepts of recursive productivity or "self-productivity" and complementarity and show how the skill multiplier (as defined in this section) and the notion of complementarity help to organize the empirical evidence surveyed in Section 2. These concepts are essential for understanding why early interventions are more effective than later interventions and why there is no trade-off between equity and efficiency in the early years of childhood but why there is such a trade-off in the later years.

In the models presented in this section, parents make decisions about their children. We ignore how the parents get to be who they are and the decisions of the children about their own children. We develop a more generationally consistent model in Section 3.2, after developing the basic framework of the technology of skill formation.

Suppose that there are two periods in a child's life, "1" and "2", before the child becomes an adult. Adulthood is a distinct third period. The child works for a fixed number of periods after the two periods of childhood. Models based on the analysis of Becker and Tomes (1979) assume only one period of childhood. We assume that there are two kinds of skills: S^C and S^N. For example, S^C can be thought of as cognitive skill and S^N as noncognitive skill. Our treatment of ability is in contrast to the view of the traditional literature on human capital formation that views IQ as innate ability. In our analysis, IQ is just another skill. What differentiates IQ from other cognitive and noncognitive skills is that IQ is subject to accumulation during critical periods. That is, parental and social interventions can increase the IQ of the child, but they can do so successfully only for a limited time. Recall our evidence that an enriched early intervention like the Abecedarian program raised IQ but Head Start and Perry Preschool – directed towards later ages – did not. Compare Figure 15A for the Abecedarian program with Figure 14A for the later-intervention Perry program.[70]

Let I_t^k denote parental investments in child skill k at period $t, k = C, N$ and $t = 1, 2$. Let h be the level of human capital as the child starts adulthood. It depends on both components of (S_2^C, S_2^N). The parents fully control the investment of the child. A richer model incorporates, among other features, investment decisions of the child as influenced by the parent through preference formation processes [see Cunha and Heckman (2004, 2006)].

We first describe how skills evolve over time. Assume that each agent is born with initial conditions $S_0 = (S_0^C, S_0^N)$. At each stage t let $S_t = (S_t^C, S_t^N)$ denote the vector

[70] One has to be careful in making this comparison because the Abecedarian program was much more intensive. One cannot separate out the effect that Abecedarian started at 4 months age (as opposed to Perry's 3–4 years) from the greater resource intensity of the Abecedarian program.

of skill or ability stocks. The technology of production of skill k at period t is:

$$S_t^k = f_t^k\left(S_{t-1}, I_t^k\right) \tag{3}$$

for $k = C, N$ and $t = 1, 2$. We assume that f_t^k is twice continuously differentiable, increasing and concave in I_t^k.[71] In this model, stocks of both skills and abilities produce next period skills and the productivity of investments. Cognitive skills can promote the formation of noncognitive skills and vice versa.

We define adult human capital h as a combination of different period 2 skills:

$$h = g\left(S_2^C, S_2^N\right). \tag{4}$$

The function g is assumed to be continuously differentiable and increasing in (S_2^C, S_2^N). This model assumes that there is no comparative advantage in the labor market or in life itself.[72]

Period 1 is a *critical period* for S_2^C if

$$\frac{\partial S_2^C}{\partial I_2^C} = \frac{\partial f_2^C(S_1, I_2^C)}{\partial I_2^C} \equiv 0 \quad \text{for all } S_1, I_2^C,$$

but

$$\frac{\partial S_1^C}{\partial I_1^C} = \frac{\partial f_1^C(S_0, I_1^C)}{\partial I_1^C} > 0 \quad \text{for some } S_0, I_1^C.$$

This says that investments in C are productive in period 1 but not in period 2. In the analysis of Section 2, the early periods (before age 8) are critical periods for IQ but not for achievement tests or for noncognitive skills.

Period 1 is a *sensitive period* for S_2^C if

$$\left.\frac{\partial S_2^C}{\partial I_2^C}\right|_{S_1=s, I_2^C=i} < \left.\frac{\partial S_1^C}{\partial I_1^C}\right|_{S_0=s, I_1^C=i}.$$

Thus, 1 is a sensitive period if, at the same level of inputs, investment is more productive in stage 1 than in stage 2. The evidence in Section 2 suggests that early investments in both cognitive and noncognitive abilities and skills are more productive than later investments.

As defined in the introduction, and clarified in the Appendix A, direct complementarity of skill l acquired in period 1 on the output of investment k in producing skill k in

[71] Twice continuous differentiability is a convenience.

[72] Thus we rule out one potentially important avenue of compensation that agents can specialize in tasks that do not require the skills in which they are deficient. In Appendix A and in Section 1, we briefly consider a more general task function that captures the notion that different tasks require different combinations of skills and abilities.

period 2 is defined by

$$\frac{\partial^2 S_2^k}{\partial I_2^k \partial S_1^l} > 0, \quad k = C, N.$$

Early stocks of abilities and skills promote later skill acquisition by making it more productive. Students with greater early cognitive and noncognitive abilities are more efficient in later learning of both cognitive and noncognitive skills. Thus the enriched early environments of the Abecedarian, Perry and CPC programs promote greater efficiency in learning in high schools and reduce problem behaviors. See the evidence in Figures 13–15 on reduction in remedial education and problem behavior for the treatment group in these programs.

This technoloy also is sufficiently rich to describe learning in rodents and rhesus monkeys as documented by Meaney (2001) and Cameron (2004). It also captures the critical and sensitive periods in animals documented by Knudsen et al. (2006). Emotionally nurturing early environments create preconditions for later cognitive learning. More emotionally secure young animals explore their environments more actively and learn more quickly. This is an instance of complementarity.

To fix ideas, consider the following specialization of our model. Ignore the effect of initial conditions and assume that first period skills are just due to first period investment:

$$S_1^C = f_1^C(S_0, I_1^C) = I_1^C$$

and

$$S_1^N = f_1^C(S_0, I_1^C) = I_1^N,$$

where I_1^C and I_1^N are scalars. For the second period technologies, we assume a CES structure:

$$\begin{aligned} S_2^C &= f_2^C(S_1, I_2^C) \\ &= \{\gamma_1 (S_1^C)^\alpha + \gamma_2 (S_1^N)^\alpha + (1 - \gamma_1 - \gamma_2)(I_2^C)^\alpha\}^{1/\alpha}, \\ &\text{where } 1 \geqslant \gamma_1 \geqslant 0,\ 1 \geqslant \gamma_2 \geqslant 0,\ 1 \geqslant 1 - \gamma_1 - \gamma_2 \geqslant 0, \end{aligned} \tag{5}$$

and

$$\begin{aligned} S_2^N &= f_2^N(S_1, I_2^N) \\ &= \{\eta_1 (S_1^C)^\sigma + \eta_2 (S_1^N)^\sigma + (1 - \eta_1 - \eta_2)(I_2^N)^\sigma\}^{1/\sigma}, \\ &\text{where } 1 \geqslant \eta_1 \geqslant 0,\ 1 \geqslant \eta_2 \geqslant 0,\ 1 \geqslant 1 - \eta_1 - \eta_2 \geqslant 0, \end{aligned} \tag{6}$$

where $\frac{1}{1-\alpha}$ is the elasticity of substitution in the inputs producing S_2^C and $\frac{1}{1-\sigma}$ is the elasticity of substitution of inputs in producing S_2^N where $\alpha \in (-\infty, 1]$ and $\sigma \in (-\infty, 1]$. Notice that I_2^N and I_2^C are direct complements with (S_1^C, S_1^N) irrespective of the substitution parameters α and σ, except in limiting cases.

The CES technology is well known and has convenient properties. It imposes direct complementarity even though inputs may be more or less substitutable depending on α or σ.[73] We distinguish between direct complementarity and CES-substitution/complementarity in this section. Focusing on the technology for producing S_2^C, when $\alpha = 1$, the inputs are perfect substitutes in the intuitive use of that term (the elasticity of substitution is infinite). The inputs S_1^C, S_1^N and I_2^C can be ordered by their relative productivity in producing S_2^C. The higher γ_1 and γ_2, the higher the productivity of S_1^C and S_1^N respectively. When $\alpha = -\infty$, the elasticity of substitution is zero. All inputs are required in the same proportion to produce a given level of output so there are no possibilities for technical substitution, and

$$S_2^C = \min\left\{S_1^C, S_1^N, I_2^C\right\}.$$

In this technology, early investments are a *bottleneck* for later investment. Compensation for adverse early environments through late investments is impossible. These polar cases generalize the cases developed in Section 1.

The evidence from numerous studies previously cited shows that IQ is no longer malleable after ages 8–10. Taken at face value, this implies that if S^C is IQ, for all values of I_2^C, $S_2^C = S_1^C$. Period 1 is a critical period for IQ but not necessarily for other skills and abilities. More generally, period 1 is a critical period if

$$\frac{\partial S_t^C}{\partial I_t^C} = 0 \quad \text{for } t > 1.$$

For parameterization (5), this is obtained by imposing $\gamma_1 + \gamma_2 = 1$.

The evidence on adolescent interventions surveyed in Section 2 shows substantial positive results for such interventions on noncognitive skills (S_2^N) and at most modest gains for cognitive skills. Technologies (5) and (6) can rationalize this pattern. Since the populations targeted by adolescent intervention studies tend to come from families with poor backgrounds, we would expect I_1^C and I_1^N to be below average. Thus, S_1^C and S_1^N will be below average. Interventions make I_2^C and I_2^N relatively large for the treatment group in comparison to the control group in the adolescent intervention experiments. At stage 2, S_2^C (cognitive ability) is essentially the same in the control and treatment groups, while S_2^N (noncognitive ability) is higher for the treated group. Large values of $(\gamma_1 + \gamma_2)$ (associated with a small coefficient on I_2^C) or small values of $(\eta_1 + \eta_2)$ (so the coefficient on I_2^N is large) and high values of α and σ can produce this pattern. Another case that rationalizes the evidence is when $\alpha \to -\infty$ and $\sigma = 1$. Under these conditions:

$$S_2^C = \min\left\{S_1^C, S_1^N, I_2^C\right\}, \tag{7}$$

[73] See footnote 13 in Section 1.

while

$$S_2^N = \eta_1 S_1^C + \eta_2 S_1^N + (1 - \eta_1 - \eta_2) I_2^N. \tag{8}$$

The attainable period 2 stock of cognitive skill (S_2^C) is limited by the minimum value of S_1^C, S_1^N, I_2^C. In this case, any level of investment in period 2 such that $I_2^C > \min\{S_1^C, S_1^N\}$ is ineffective in incrementing the stock of cognitive skills. Period 1 is a bottleneck period. Unless sufficient skill investments are made in S_C in period 1, it is not possible to raise skill S_C in period 2. This phenomenon does not appear in the production of the noncognitive skill, provided that $(1 - \eta_1 - \eta_2) > 0$. More generally, the higher σ and the larger $(1 - \eta_1 - \eta_2)$, the more productive is investment I_2^N in producing S_2^N.

To complete the CES example, assume that adult human capital h is a CES function of the two skills accumulated at stage two:

$$h = \{\tau (S_2^C)^\phi + (1 - \tau)(S_2^N)^\phi\}^{\rho/\phi}, \tag{9}$$

where $\rho \in (0, 1)$, $\tau \in [0, 1]$, and $\phi \in (-\infty, 1]$. In this parameterization, $\frac{1}{1-\phi}$ is the elasticity of substitution across different skills in the production of adult human capital. Equation (9) reminds us that the market, or life in general, requires use of multiple skills. Being smart isn't the sole determinant of success. In general, different tasks require both skills in different proportions. One way to remedy early skill deficits is to make compensatory investments. Another way is to motivate people from disadvantaged environments to pursue tasks that do not require the skill that deprived early environments do not produce. A richer theory would account for this choice of tasks and its implications for remediation.[74] For the sake of simplifying our argument, we work with equation (9) that captures the notion that skills can trade off against each other in producing effective people. Highly motivated, but not very bright, people may be just as effective as bright but unmotivated people. That is one of the lessons from the GED program. [See Heckman and LaFontaine (2007), Heckman and Rubinstein (2001), Heckman, Stixrud and Urzua (2006)].

The analysis is simplified by assuming that investments are general in nature: $I_1^C = I_1^N = I_1, I_2^C = I_2^N = I_2$.[75] Cunha and Heckman (2004, 2006) develop the more general case of skill-specific investments which requires more notational complexity.

With common investment goods, we can solve out for S_1^C and S_1^N in terms of I_1 to simplify (5) and (6) to reach

$$S_2^C = \{(\gamma_1 + \gamma_2)(I_1)^\alpha + (1 - \gamma_1 - \gamma_2)(I_2)^\alpha\}^{1/\alpha} \tag{10}$$

[74] We sketch such a model in Appendix A.

[75] Thus when a parent buys a book in the first period of childhood, this book may be an investment in all kinds of skills. It is an investment in cognitive skills, as it helps the child get exposure to language and new words. It can also be an investment in noncognitive skills, if the book may contain a message on the importance of being persistent and patient.

and

$$S_2^N = \{(\eta_1 + \eta_2)(I_1)^\sigma + (1 - \eta_1 - \eta_2)(I_2)^\sigma\}^{1/\sigma}. \tag{11}$$

If we then substitute these expressions into the production function for adult human capital (9), we obtain

$$h = \{\tau[\tilde{\gamma}(I_1)^\alpha + (1 - \tilde{\gamma})(I_2)^\alpha]^{\phi/\alpha} + (1 - \tau)[\tilde{\eta}(I_1)^\sigma + (1 - \tilde{\eta})(I_2)^\sigma]^{\phi/\sigma}\}^{\rho/\phi}, \tag{12}$$

where $\tilde{\gamma} = \gamma_1 + \gamma_2$, $\tilde{\eta} = \eta_1 + \eta_2$. Equation (12) expresses adult human capital as a function of the entire sequence of childhood investments in human capital. Current investments in human capital are combined with the existing stocks of skills in order to produce the stock of next period skills.

A conveniently simple formulation of the problem arises if we assume that $\alpha = \sigma = \phi$ so that CES substitution among inputs in producing outputs and CES substitution among skill in producing human capital are the same. This produces the convenient and familiar-looking CES expression for adult human capital stocks:

$$h = \{\gamma I_1^\phi + (1 - \gamma) I_2^\phi\}^{\rho/\phi}, \tag{13}$$

where $\gamma = \tau\tilde{\gamma} + (1 - \tau)\tilde{\eta}$ and $\phi = \alpha = \sigma$. The parameter γ is *a skill multiplier*. It arises because I_1 affects the accumulation of S_1^C and S_1^N. These stocks of skills in turn affect the productivity of I_2 in forming S_2^C and S_2^N. Thus γ captures the net effect of I_1 on h through both self-productivity and direct complementarity.[76] $\frac{1}{1-\phi}$ is a measure of how easy it is to substitute between I_1 and I_2 where the substitution arises from both the task performance (human capital) function in equation (9) and the technology of skill formation. Within the CES technology, ϕ is a measure of the ease of substitution of inputs. In this analytically convenient case, the parameter ϕ plays a dual role. First, it informs us how easily one can substitute across different skills in order to produce one unit of adult human capital h. Second, it also represents the degree of complementarity

[76] To repeat an observation made in Section 1, direct complementarity between I_1 and I_2 arises if

$$\frac{\partial^2 h}{\partial I_1 \partial I_2} > 0.$$

As long as $\rho > \phi$, I_1 and I_2 are direct complements, because

$$\text{sign}\left(\frac{\partial^2 h}{\partial I_1 \partial I_2}\right) = \text{sign}(\rho - \phi).$$

This definition of complementarity is to be distinguished from the notion based on the elasticity of substitution between I_1 and I_2, which is $\frac{1}{1-\phi}$. When $\phi < 0$, I_1 and I_2 are sometimes called complements. When $\phi > 0$, I_1 and I_2 are sometimes called substitutes. When $\rho = 1$, I_1 and I_2 are always direct complements, but if $1 > \phi > 0$, they are CES substitutes.

(or substitutability) between early and late investments in producing skills. In this second role, the parameter ϕ dictates how easy it is to compensate for low levels of stage 1 skills in producing late skills.

In principle, compensation can come through two channels: (i) through skill investment or (ii) through choice of market activities, substituting deficits in one skill by the relative abundance in the other through choice of tasks. We do not develop the second channel of compensation in this chapter, deferring it to later work.

When ϕ is small, low levels of early investment I_1 are not easily remediated by later investment I_2 in producing human capital. The other face of CES complementarity is that when ϕ is small, high early investments should be followed with high late investments. In the extreme case when $\phi \to -\infty$, (13) converges to $h = (\min\{I_1, I_2\})^{\rho}$. We analyzed this case in Section 1. The Leontief case contrasts sharply with the case of perfect CES substitutes, which arises when $\phi = 1$: $h = [\gamma I_1 + (1-\gamma)I_2]^{\rho}$. When we impose the further restriction that $\gamma = 1/2$, we generate the model that is implicitly assumed in the existing literature on human capital investments that collapses childhood into a single period. In this special case, only the total amount of human capital investments, regardless of how it is distributed across childhood periods, determines adult human capital. In the case of perfect CES substitutes, it is possible in a physical productivity sense to compensate for early investment deficits by later investments, although it may not be economically efficient to do so.

When $\rho = 1$, we can rewrite (13) as

$$h = I_1\{\gamma + (1-\gamma)\omega^{\phi}\}^{1/\phi},$$

where $\omega = I_2/I_1$. Fixing I_1 (early investment), an increase in ω is the same as an increase in I_2. The marginal productivity of late investment is

$$\frac{\partial h}{\partial \omega} = (1-\gamma)I_1\{\gamma + (1-\gamma)\omega^{\phi}\}^{\frac{1-\phi}{\phi}}\omega^{\phi-1}.$$

For $\omega > 1$ and $\gamma < 1$, marginal productivity is increasing in ϕ and $(1-\gamma)$. Thus, provided that late investments are greater than earlier investments, the more substitutable I_2 is with I_1 (the higher ϕ) and the lower the skill multiplier γ, the more productive are late investments. Figure 17A graphs the isoquants for $\frac{\partial h}{\partial \omega}$ when $\omega = 2$. It shows that a high ϕ trades off with a high γ. As $(\phi, 1-\gamma)$ increases along a ray, $\frac{\partial h}{\partial \omega}$ increases. For a fixed skill multiplier γ, the higher ϕ, the higher the marginal productivity of second period investment.

If, however, $\omega < 1$, as in Figure 17B, then $\frac{\partial h}{\partial \omega}$ could be decreasing as $(\phi, 1-\gamma)$ increases along a ray and the trade-off between ϕ and $(1-\gamma)$ along a $(\frac{\partial h}{\partial \omega}, \omega)$ isoquant is reversed. If I_1 is large relative to I_2 (i.e., $\omega < 1$), for a fixed γ the marginal product of I_2 is decreasing in ϕ. More CES complementarity implies greater productivity (see Figure 17B).[77] The empirically relevant case for the analysis of investment in disadvantaged children is $\omega > 1$, as shown in Figure 17A, so greater CES-substitutability and

[77] One can show that at sufficiently low values of ϕ, the marginal productivity is no longer increasing in ϕ.

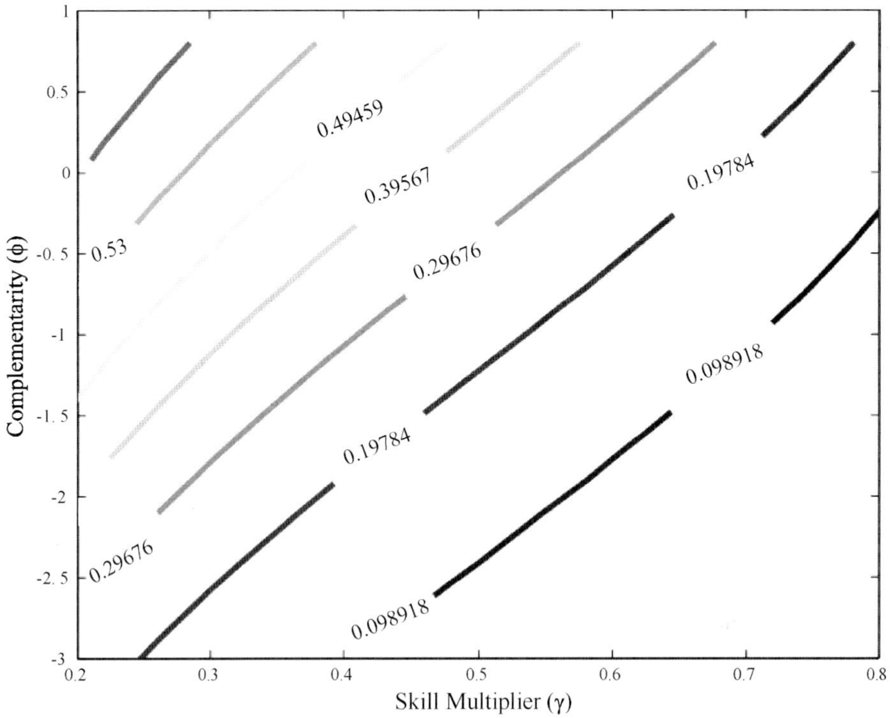

Figure 17A. The indifference curves of the marginal productivity of the ratio of late to early investments as a function of ϕ and γ when $I_2/I_1 = 2$.
Define $\omega = I_2/I_1$, the ratio of late to early investments in human capital. From the homogeneity of degree one we can rewrite the technology as:

$$h = I_1\left[\gamma + (1-\gamma)\omega^{\phi}\right]^{1/\phi}.$$

The marginal product of the ratio of late to early investment, ω, holding early investment constant, is

$$\frac{\partial h}{\partial \omega} = (1-\gamma)I_1\left[\gamma + (1-\gamma)\omega^{\phi}\right]^{\frac{1-\phi}{\phi}}\omega^{\phi-1}.$$

This figure displays the indifference curves of $\frac{\partial h}{\partial \omega}$ when $\omega = 2$. Each indifference curve shows the corresponding level of $\frac{\partial h}{\partial \omega}$. Note that for a given value of γ the value of the function tends to increase as we increase ϕ. The function also increases as we decrease γ.

a smaller skill multiplier produce a higher marginal productivity of remedial second period investment.

It is important to distinguish the case when it is technologically efficient to compensate for adverse early environments from the case when it is economically efficient to do so. If γ is near 1, it may be very costly to remediate shortfalls in early investments even though it is technically possible to do so. We return to this point below.

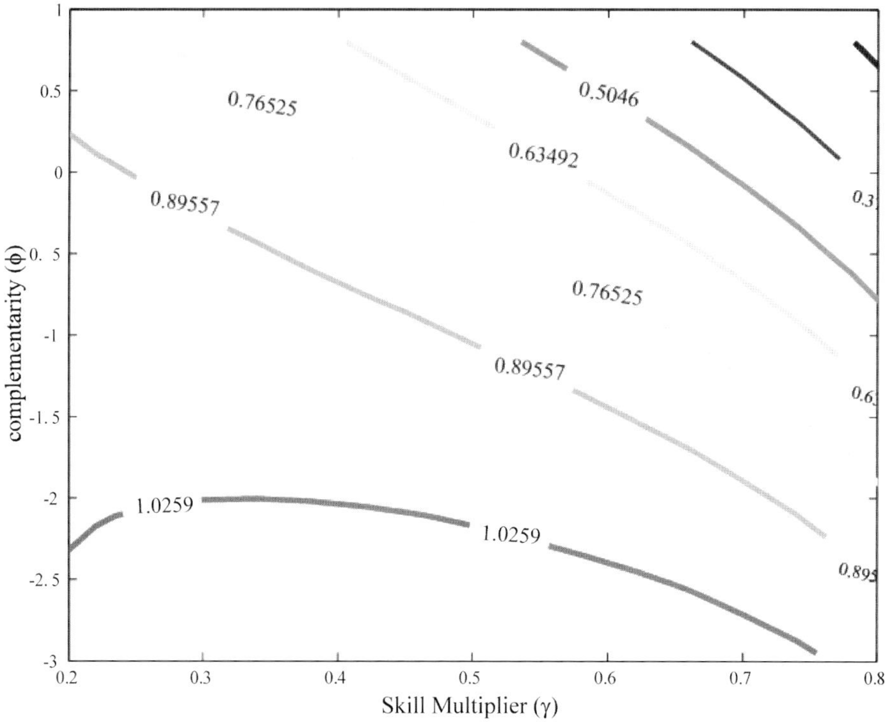

Figure 17B. The indifference curves of the marginal productivity of the ratio of late to early investments as a function of ϕ and γ when $I_2/I_1 = 1/2$.
Consider the CES specification for the technology of human capital formation:

$$h = \left[\gamma I_1^{\phi} + (1-\gamma) I_2^{\phi}\right]^{1/\phi}.$$

Define $\omega = I_2/I_1$, the ratio of late to early investments in human capital. From the homogeneity of degree one we can rewrite the technology as:

$$h = I_1\left[\gamma + (1-\gamma)\omega^{\phi}\right]^{1/\phi}.$$

The marginal product of the ratio of late to early investment, ω, holding early investment constant, is

$$\frac{\partial h}{\partial \omega} = (1-\gamma) I_1\left[\gamma + (1-\gamma)\omega^{\phi}\right]^{\frac{1-\phi}{\phi}} \omega^{\phi-1}.$$

This figure displays the indifference curves of $\frac{\partial h}{\partial \omega}$ when $\omega = 0.5$. Each indifference curve shows the corresponding level of $\frac{\partial h}{\partial \omega}$. Note that for a given value of γ the value of the function tends to decrease as we increase ϕ. However, the function may not be monotonic with respect to γ.

In analyzing the optimal timing of investment, it is convenient to work with the technology embodied in (13). We now show how the ratio of early to late investments varies as a function of ϕ, γ, and ρ. Consider the following model in which parents maximize the present value of net wealth of their children.[78] In order to do that, parents decide how much to invest in period "1," I_1, how much to invest in period "2," I_2, and how much to transfer in risk-free assets, b, given total parental resources M. Period "1" could include *in utero* investments. Parents cannot extract resources from children, so $b \geqslant 0$. From period "3" to period T, the age of retirement from the workforce, persons are assumed to work full time. Let r denote the time-invariant interest rate, set exogenously and assumed to be constant for all periods, and let q denote the present value of future earnings per efficiency unit of adult human capital $\{w_t\}_{t=3}^{T}$:

$$q = \sum_{t=3}^{T} \left(\frac{1}{1+r}\right)^{t-3} w_t.$$[79]

Lifetime earnings of children when they start working at period "3" are given by $qg(I_1, I_2)$, where g is the function determining the adult stock of human capital. Discounted to period 1, the present value of lifetime earnings is $\frac{q}{(1+r)^2} g(I_1, I_2)$. The problem of the parents is to maximize the present value of the child's net wealth:

$$\max_{I_1, I_2, b} \left\{ \frac{1}{(1+r)^2} \left[qg(I_1, I_2) + b \right] \right\},$$

subject to the standard budget constraint

$$I_1 + \frac{1}{1+r} I_2 + \frac{1}{(1+r)^2} b = M, \tag{14}$$

and the constraint that parents cannot leave negative bequests to their children

$$b \geqslant 0, \tag{15}$$

where $g(I_1, I_2)$ is as defined in equation (13) and is concave in I_1 and I_2.

When $\phi = 1$, early and late investments are perfect CES substitutes. The optimal investment strategy for this technology in this simple environment is straightforward. The price of early investment is \$1. The price of the late investment is $\$\frac{1}{(1+r)}$. Thus the parents can purchase $(1 + r)$ units of I_2 for every unit of I_1. The amount of human capital produced from one unit of I_1 is γ, while $\$(1 + r)$ of I_2 produces $(1 + r)(1 - \gamma)$ units of human capital. Therefore, the parent invests early if $\gamma > (1 - \gamma)(1 + r)$ and late otherwise. Two forces act in opposite directions. High productivity of initial investment (the skill multiplier) drives the agent toward making early investments. Intertemporal prices (the interest rate) drive the agent to invest late. It is optimal to invest early if $\gamma > \frac{1+r}{2+r}$.

[78] This setup is overly simplistic but allows us to focus on the important points. See Caucutt and Lochner (2004), Cunha (2004) and Cunha and Heckman (2004, 2006) for more general models.

[79] We abstract from endogenously determined on-the-job training, learning-by-doing, and assume that agents supply labor inelastically.

As $\phi \to -\infty$, the CES production function converges to the Leontief case and the optimal investment strategy is to set $I_1 = I_2$. CES complementarity dominates and the profile of investments is such that $\frac{I_1}{I_2}$ converges to one. In this extreme case, CES complementarity has a dual face. Investments in the young are essential. At the same time, later investments are needed to harvest early investments. On efficiency grounds, early disadvantages should be perpetuated, and compensatory investments at later ages are economically inefficient.

For $-\infty < \phi < 1$, the first-order conditions are necessary and sufficient given concavity of the technology in terms of I_1 and I_2. Let μ, λ denote the Lagrange multipliers associated with restrictions (14) and (15), respectively. The first-order conditions for I_1, I_2, and b are

$$\frac{q}{(1+r)^2}\rho\gamma\{\gamma I_1^{\phi} + (1-\gamma)I_2^{\phi}\}^{\frac{\rho-\phi}{\phi}} I_1^{\phi-1} = \mu, \tag{16}$$

$$\frac{q}{(1+r)}\rho(1-\gamma)\{\gamma I_1^{\phi} + (1-\gamma)I_2^{\phi}\}^{\frac{\rho-\phi}{\phi}} I_2^{\phi-1} = \mu, \tag{17}$$

$$\mu - 1 = \lambda(1+r)^2. \tag{18}$$

Notice that if restriction (15) is not binding, then $\lambda = 0$, $\mu = 1$ and optimal early and late investments are only functions of (q, r). In this case, all unconstrained families that make bequests will invest the same in their children. The only difference is in the transfers of assets to their children. If $M_A > M_B$ then $b_A > b_B$.

For an interior solution, if we take the ratio of (16) to (17) and rearrange terms we obtain

$$\frac{I_1}{I_2} = \left[\frac{\gamma}{(1-\gamma)(1+r)}\right]^{\frac{1}{1-\phi}}. \tag{19}$$

Figure 18 plots the ratio of early to late investments as a function of the skill multiplier γ, under different values of the complementarity parameter ϕ. When $\phi \to -\infty$, we obtain the Leontief technology and there is high CES-complementarity between early and late investments. In this case, the ratio is not sensitive to variations in γ. CES-complementarity dominates, and the optimal investment profile distributes investments equally across different periods. When $\phi = 0$, the function g is given by the Cobb–Douglas function:

$$h = (I_1)^{\rho\gamma}(I_2)^{\rho(1-\gamma)}.$$

In this case, from equation (19), I_1/I_2 is close to zero for low values of γ, but explodes to infinity as γ approaches one.

Another way to express these conclusions is to work in terms of growth rates of investment, which yields the expression

$$\ln\left(\frac{I_1}{I_2}\right) = \frac{1}{1-\phi}\left[\ln\left(\frac{\gamma}{1-\gamma}\right) - \ln(1-r)\right]. \tag{20}$$

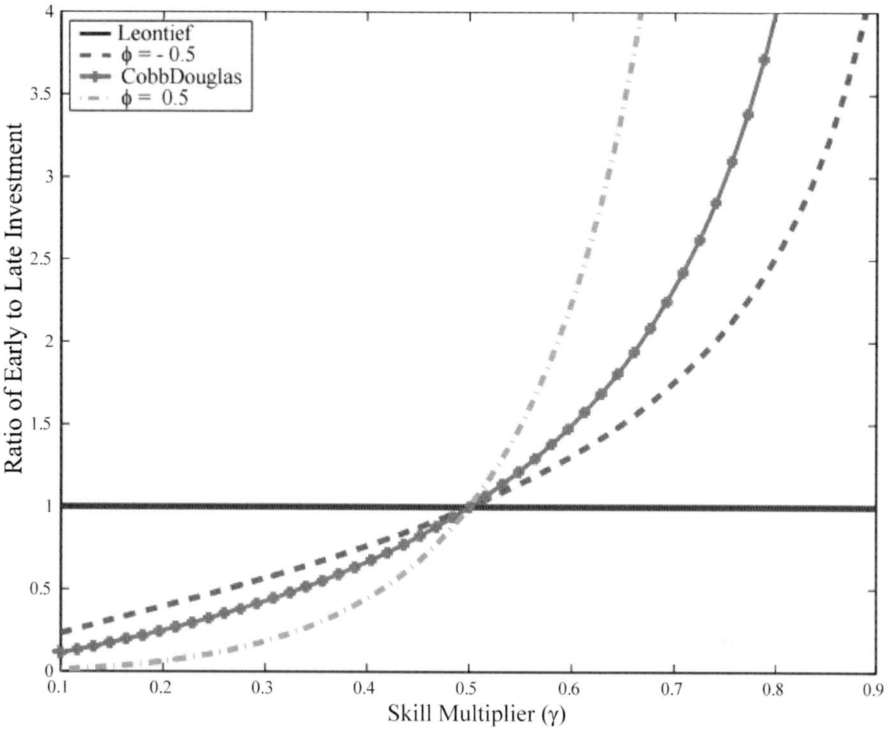

Figure 18. The ratio of early to late investment in human capital as a function of the skill multiplier for different values of complementarity.

This figure shows the optimal ratio of early to late investments, I_1/I_2, as a function of the skill multiplier parameter γ, for different values of the complementarity parameter ϕ, assuming that the interest rate r is zero. The optimal ratio I_1/I_2 is the solution of the parental problem of maximizing the present value of the child's wealth through investments in human capital, h, and transfers of risk-free bonds, b. In order to do that, parents have to decide how to allocate a total of M dollars into early and late investments in human capital, I_1 and I_2, respectively, and risk-free bonds. Let q denote the present value as of period "3" of the future prices of one efficiency unit of human capital: $q = \sum_{t=3}^{T} \frac{w_t}{(1+r)^{t-3}}$. The parents solve

$$\max \left(\frac{1}{1+r}\right)^2 [gh + b]$$

subject to the budget constraint

$$I_1 + \frac{I_2}{(1+r)} + \frac{b}{(1+r)^2} = M$$

and the technology of skill formation:

$$h = \left[\gamma I_1^{\phi} + (1-\gamma) I_2^{\phi}\right]^{\rho/\phi}$$

for $0 < \rho < 1$, $0 \leqslant \gamma \leqslant 1$, and $\phi \leqslant 1$. From the first-order conditions it follows that $\frac{I_1}{I_2} = [\frac{\gamma}{(1-\gamma)(1+r)}]^{\frac{1}{1-\phi}}$. This ratio is plotted in this figure when $\phi \to -\infty$ (Leontief), $\phi = -0.5$, $\phi = 0$ (Cobb–Douglas) and $\phi = 0.5$ and for values of the skill multiplier γ between 0.1 and 0.9.

This expression does not depend on ρ. In the special case $\gamma = \frac{1+r}{2+r}$, investment will be the same in both periods regardless of the value assumed by ϕ. More generally, the ratio of early to late investments varies with the complementarity between early and late investments, ϕ, with the skill multiplier for human capital, γ, and with the interest rate. *Ceteris paribus*, the higher the skill multiplier, γ, the higher the ratio of early to late investments. Intuitively, if early investments have a substantial impact in determining future stocks of human capital, optimality implies that early investments should also be high. The higher the interest rate, the lower the ratio of early to late investments. This result reflects the opportunity costs of investing today relative to investing tomorrow. The higher the interest rate today, the cheaper it is to postpone investments. *Ceteris paribus*, if $(\frac{\gamma}{1-\gamma}) > (1+r)$ and $(\frac{I_1}{I_2}) > 1$, the higher ϕ, the higher $(\frac{I_1}{I_2})$. If $(\frac{\gamma}{1-\gamma}) < (1+r)$, the higher ϕ, the lower $(\frac{I_1}{I_2})$.

The lessons we take from this simple analysis are summarized in Table 10. When CES complementarity is high, the skill multiplier γ plays a limited role in shaping the ratio of early to late investments. High early investments should be followed by high late investments. As the degree of CES complementarity decreases, the role of the skill multiplier increases, and the higher the multiplier, the more investments should be concentrated in the early ages.

This simple model also has implications for the timing of interventions. If $M_A > M_B$ and family A is unconstrained while family B is constrained, then for family B, $\lambda_B > 0$, $\mu_B = [1 + \lambda_B(1+r)^2]$. Consequently, in equilibrium, the marginal return to one dollar invested in the poor child from family B is above the marginal return to the same dollar invested in the rich child from family A, so family B underinvests compared to the less constrained family A.

Table 10
The ratio of optimal early and late investments I_1/I_2 under different assumptions about the skill formation technology

	Low self-productivity: $\gamma < \frac{1+r}{2+r}$	High self-productivity: $\gamma > \frac{1+r}{2+r}$
High degree of complementarity: $\phi < 0$	$\frac{I_1}{I_2} \to 1$ as $\phi \to -\infty$	$\frac{I_1}{I_2} \to 1$ as $\phi \to -\infty$
Low degree of complementarity: $0 \leqslant \phi \leqslant 1$	$\frac{I_1}{I_2} \to 0$ as $\phi \to 1$	$\frac{I_1}{I_2} \to \infty$ as $\phi \to 1$

This table summarizes the behavior of the ratio of optimal early to late investments according to four cases: I_1 and I_2 have high complementarity, but self-productivity is low; I_1 and I_2 have both high complementarity and self-productivity; I_1 and I_2 have low complementarity and self-productivity; and I_1 and I_2 have low complementarity, but high self-productivity. When I_1 and I_2 exhibit high complementary, complementarity dominates and is a force towards equal distribution of investments between early and late periods. Consequently, self-productivity plays a limited role in determining the ratio I_1/I_2 (row 1). On the other hand, when I_1 and I_2 exhibit a low degree of complementarity, self-productivity tends to concentrate investments in the *late* period if self-productivity is low, but in the *early* period if it is high (row 2).

There is no trade-off between equity and efficiency in *early* childhood investments. Government policies to promote early accumulation of human capital should be targeted to the children of poor families. However, the optimal second period intervention for a child from a disadvantaged environment depends critically on the nature of human capital aggregation and function (13), the technology of skill production. If I_1 and I_2 are perfect CES complements, then a low level of I_1 cannot be compensated at any level of investment by a high I_2.

On the other hand, suppose that $\phi = 1$, so the reduced form technology can be written with inputs as perfect CES substitutes:

$$h = \left[\gamma I_1 + (1-\gamma) I_2\right]^{\rho}, \quad 0 \leqslant \gamma \leqslant 1. \tag{21}$$

Then a second-period intervention can, in principle, eliminate initial skill deficits (low values of I_1). At a sufficiently high level of second-period investment, it is technically possible to offset low first period investments. However, it may not be cost effective to do so. For example, if $\rho = 1$ and $q(1-\gamma) < 1 + r$, then the gains from future earnings do not justify the costs of investment. It would be more efficient to give the child a bond that earns interest rather than to invest in human capital in order to put the child at a certain level of income. Carneiro and Heckman (2003) show that classroom size reductions at current levels of funding in the U.S. are an example of such a policy.

We previously discussed the concepts of critical and sensitive periods in terms of the technical possibilities of remediation. These were defined in terms of the technology of skill formation. Here, we consider the net effects operating through investment and market substitution. The higher ϕ, the greater are the possibilities for alleviating early disadvantage. When $\phi = 1$, as in this example, it is always technically possible to remediate early disadvantage. But it may not be economically efficient to do so. From an economic point of view, critical and sensitive periods should be defined in terms of the costs and returns of remediation, and not solely in terms of technical possibilities.

Cunha and Heckman (2004, 2006) estimate a log linear (Cobb–Douglas) version of technology (3) and establish the importance of sensitive periods for parental investments in cognitive and noncognitive skills. The sensitive periods for cognitive skills occur earlier in the life cycle of the child than do the sensitive periods for noncognitive skills. Cunha, Heckman and Schennach (2006) develop and apply a methodology for estimating the key substitution parameters. We next embed the technology developed in this section into a market setting where choices and credit constraints can be clearly articulated.

3.2. The technology of skill formation in overlapping generations economies

In this section we embed the technology (13) developed in the preceding section into simple dynamic economies. These simple economies serve as baselines for the discussion of two conceptually distinct market failures: credit constraints in a deterministic economy, and an economy with incomplete markets with uncertainty in the labor mar-

Table 11
The generational structure

Generation born at period	Periods $t = 0$	$t = 1$	$t = 2$	$t = 3$	$t = 4$
−3	Old adult				
−2	Young adult	Old adult			
−1	Adolescent	Young adult	Old adult		
0	Child	Adolescent	Young adult	Old adult	
1		Child	Adolescent	Young adult	Old adult
2			Child	Adolescent	Young adult
3				Child	Adolescent
4					Child

ket, as analyzed in Cunha (2004), Cunha and Heckman (2004, 2006) and subsequent work by Caucutt and Lochner (2004).

3.2.1. *Generational structure and the human capital production function*

The environment we consider is an overlapping generations economy with an infinite number of periods, each one denoted $t \in \{0, 1, 2, \ldots\}$. Each agent lives for four periods. In the first period of his life, the agent is a young child. In the second period of his life the agent is an adolescent. In the third period of his life, the agent is a young adult and has a child of his own. In the fourth period of his life the agent is an old adult. At the end of the old adult period, the agent dies and is replaced by the generation of his grandchild. Note that in every period there are agents of every possible demographic type (child, adolescent, young adult and old adult). Life goes on in the future in similar fashion. Table 11 describes the demographics of the economy.

3.2.2. *Formalizing the problem of the agent*

First, we describe the way agents go through life. Children and adolescents do not work. They only receive investments in human capital which may include components of their consumption. When they become young adults they conceive one child. In this setup, neither children nor adolescents have volition and make no economic decisions at this stage of their life cycles. As long as parents' and children's objectives are aligned, this assumption is not crucial, but a more general model would allow for child volition and parental actions to promote preference alignment through incentives [Akabayashi (1996), Weinberg (2001)].

The young parent starts the third period of his life with a stock of human capital (or efficiency units) h, an inheritance in the form of physical assets b, and gives birth to one child. We assume that labor supply is perfectly inelastic, so that the labor income of the parents is given by wh, where w is the wage rate of one efficiency unit. Because the focus is on steady states, we assume that $w_t = w$ for all $t = 0, 1, 2, \ldots$. Given h and b, the young parent chooses consumption when he is young and old, (c_y, c_o); early and late investments, (I_1, I_2), in the human capital of his child; and how much to bequeath in physical capital to his child, b'. "s" is the savings of the young parent. Let β be the discount factor and r the interest rate. The agent's problem is to maximize the value of lifetime utility defined as

$$V(h, b) = \max \left\{ u(c_y) + \beta u(c_o) + \beta^2 V(h', b') \right\},$$

subject to

$$c_y + I_1 + \frac{s}{1+r} = wh + b, \tag{22}$$

$$c_o + I_2 + \frac{b'}{1+r} = wh + s, \tag{23}$$

and technology (13).

Cunha and Heckman (2004) close the model by introducing a firm that operates under a constant returns to scale technology and uses both human and physical capital to produce a good that can be used for consumption, human capital investment, or physical capital investment. In this chapter, we focus our attention on the behavior of investments in the child's human capital in an economy in which the equilibrium allocation is first best.

In this simple economy, the equation describing the ratio of the marginal productivity of investments is the same as equation (19) obtained in the simple static model:

$$\frac{I_1}{I_2} = \left(\frac{\gamma}{(1-\gamma)(1+r)} \right)^{\frac{1}{1-\phi}}.$$

Thus, the main conclusions of the simple, static model developed in Section 3.1 are valid in a more fully specified economic environment.

3.3. The technology of skill formation in a model with credit constraints

We now study how the technology of skill formation affects investment in human capital when we introduce market imperfections into the economy just described. Caucutt and Lochner (2004) use a general technology to analyze how the interaction between the technology of skill formation and credit constraints during different periods affects the life cycle profile of the sequence of investments in human capital. They assume that parents make monetary transfers to children every period. These transfers cannot be negative, because parents cannot extract resources from children. Here, for the sake of simplicity, we focus on the implications for the profile of investments when there exists a limit $d \geqslant 0$ on how much parents can borrow when children are young:

$$s \geqslant -d,$$

$$b' \geqslant 0.$$

Allocations over time will depend on whether or not borrowing constraints bind. Taking the first-order condition for savings s it follows that

$$u'(c_y) = \beta(1+r)u'(c_o) + \beta^{-1}\lambda,$$

where $\lambda \geqslant 0$ represents the Lagrange multiplier on the debt constraint. If $\beta(1+r) = 1$ and the technology is described by (13), it is straightforward to show that relative investments are generated by the following equation:

$$\log\left(\frac{I_1}{I_2}\right) = \frac{1}{1-\phi}\log\left(\frac{\gamma}{1-\gamma}\right) - \frac{1}{1-\phi}\log(1+r) + \frac{1}{1-\phi}\log\frac{u'(c_o)}{u'(c_y)}.$$

Note that in comparison to first order condition (20), we acquire a new term, given by the ratio of the marginal utility of consumption, which reflects the severity of credit constraints. Investment in early childhood will be reduced with age among constrained families compared with unconstrained families.

The effects of early constraints on later investment decisions will depend on the CES-complementarity or substitutability of investment across ages. When investments are very CES-substitutable, families will tend to respond to early constraints by re-allocating investments to later periods. In this case, investments during constrained periods should decline, while investments at later ages should increase to partially offset any reductions in human capital. On the other hand, when investments are very CES-complementary over time, any reduction in early investments makes later investments less productive. If investments are strongly complementary, investment may decline at all ages in response to constraints that only bind for a few.

3.4. *The technology of skill formation in a model with market incompleteness*

We now consider a stochastic version of this model with incomplete markets, following the analyses of Cunha (2004) and Cunha and Heckman (2004, 2006).[80] We focus here on the assumption that parental earnings are subject to temporary idiosyncratic shocks ε (when parents are young) and η (when parents are old). The ε and η are statistically independent. The support of ε is given by the interval $[\varepsilon_{\min}, \varepsilon_{\max}]$, with $\varepsilon_{\min} > 0$. The distribution of ε is given by F_ε. Similarly, we have that the support of η is given by the interval $[\eta_{\min}, \eta_{\max}]$, with $\eta_{\min} > 0$. The distribution of η is given by F_η. The market failure in their analysis is that there are no markets that allow agents to insure against realizations of ε or η. Furthermore, parents cannot leave debts to their children. Their setup extends the framework developed in the income fluctuation literature analyzed by Schechtman (1976), Bewley (1986), Clarida (1987), Laitner (1979, 1992), Huggett (1993), and Aiyagari (1994) to account for child investment decisions.

[80] Recent work by Caucutt and Lochner (2004) also considers a stochastic version of this model.

In a simplified version of Cunha (2004) and Cunha and Heckman (2004, 2006), the problem of the parent is to maximize the utility of the parents using the recursive representation for first period preferences:

$$V_1(h, b, \varepsilon) = \max_{c_y, I_1, s} \{u(c_y) + \beta E[V_2(h, s, I_1, \eta) \mid \varepsilon]\},$$

where c_y is the consumption of the parents while their children are young, subject to

$$c_y + I_1 + \frac{s}{1+r} = wh\varepsilon + b, \tag{24}$$

where s is saving and

$$s \geqslant -wh\eta_{\min}. \tag{25}$$

The second period parental utility problem in recursive form is

$$V_2(h, s, I_1, \eta) = \max_{c_0, I_2, b'} \{u(c_o) + \beta E[V_2(h', b', \varepsilon') \mid \eta]\}$$

where c_o is the consumption of the parents in the second period of their child's life cycle, subject to the constraints

$$c_o + I_2 + \frac{b'}{1+r} = wh\eta + s, \tag{26}$$

$$b' \geqslant 0, \tag{27}$$

and technology (13).

Restriction (25) is what Aiyagari (1994) calls the natural borrowing limit. It arises as a combination of the restrictions that parents cannot leave negative debts to their children and that consumption cannot be negative. Note that the natural borrowing limit varies with parental human capital h. The higher the parental human capital, the more parents can borrow to finance consumption and early investments. The first-order condition for bequest b' may bind or not. Assuming it does not bind, the first order condition is given by

$$-\lambda_2 \frac{1}{1+r} + \beta \frac{\partial E[V_2(h', b', \varepsilon') \mid \eta]}{\partial b'} = 0 \quad \text{if } b' > 0.$$

The fact that parents cannot extract resources from their descendents has consequences for the profile of investments in the human capital of the child. The inability of the parents to leave debts for their children in order to finance human capital investments makes both early and late investments a function of parental lifetime resources. Parents who are very poor tend to invest much less, both early and late, than parents who are better off. Consequently, gaps in skill formation arise even in the early ages of child development, a fact consistent with the evidence presented in Section 2 and in an entire literature (see, e.g. the essays in Duncan and Brooks-Gunn, 1997a).

Figure 19 is reproduced from Cunha and Heckman (2004), who study educational policies in a Laitner (1992) economy. It is based on their provisional estimates for the

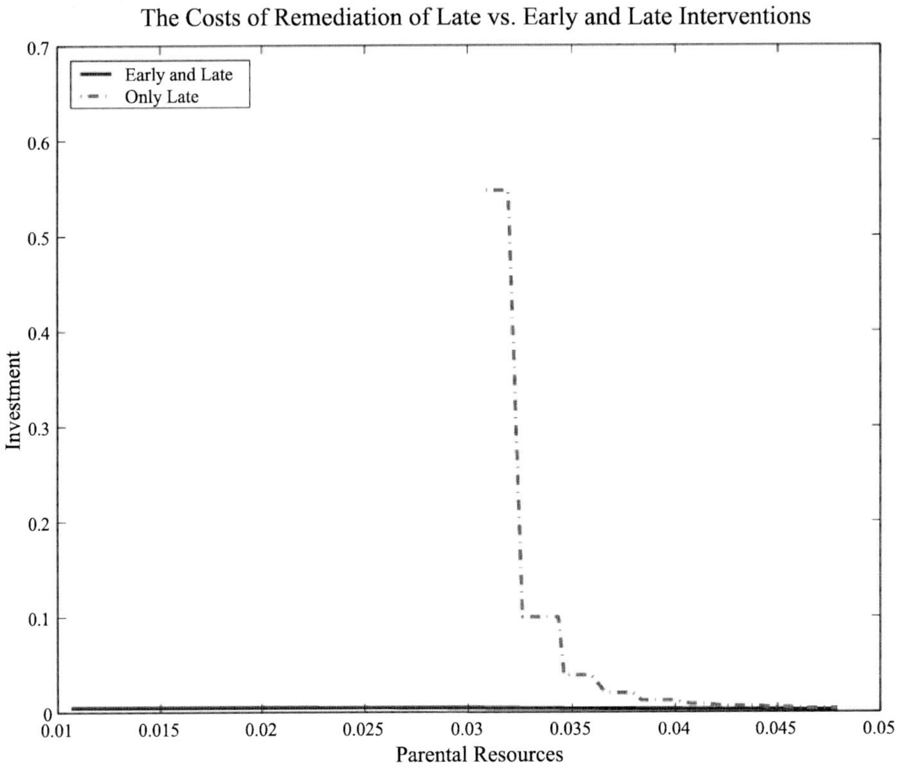

Figure 19. The costs of remediation of late vs. early and late interventions.
This figure is from Cunha and Heckman (2004), and is based on estimates reported above: $\rho = 0.7012, \gamma = 0.8649$, and $\phi = -0.4108$. It shows the costs of remediation when the government makes up for parental deficits in investments due to binding lifetime credit constraints. Formally, the young parents solve $V_1(h, b, \varepsilon) = \max\{u(c_y) + \beta E[V_2(h, s, I_1, \eta) \mid \varepsilon]\}$, subject to the young budget constraint $c_y + I_1 + \frac{s}{1+r} = wh\varepsilon + b$, and the natural borrowing limit $s \geqslant wh\eta_{\min}$. When old, the parents solve $V_2(h, s, I_1, \eta) = \max\{u(c_0) + \beta E[V_2(h', b', \varepsilon') \mid \eta]\}$, subject to the budget constraint when old, $c_0 + I_2 + \frac{b'}{1+r} = wh\eta + s$; the constraint that prevents parents from extracting resources from their children, $b' \geqslant 0$; and the technology of skill formation. This figure plots the remediation costs for parents that receive no bequest in risk-free bonds, so that $b = 0$. The goal is to calculate the short-run costs of implementing a policy that attains the counterfactual human capital stock of the child if parents had access to full insurance against realizations of idiosyncratic shocks. There are two ways the government can pursue this policy. In the first case, the government provides educational goods and services in both early and late investment periods. In the second case, the government intervenes only during the late investment period. The message from this figure is clear: when the government intervenes only in the late period, remediation costs are much higher than when the government acts in both periods for all levels of parental income. Furthermore, for parents with very low income, there is no amount of government-provided educational goods and services that can attain the objective of the policy. In this figure, it is assumed that the government policy is unexpected when parents allocate resources to investments. See Cunha (2004) for long-run effects of government remediation policies.

technology of skill formation.[81] It shows the costs of remediation when the government makes up for parental deficits in investments due to binding lifetime credit constraints, so that $b = 0$ (that is, the parents receive no bequests from the grandparents).[82] The graph plots the short-run costs, by a measure of parental resources, of a policy that attains the counterfactual human capital stock of the child that would arise if households had access to complete markets in an Arrow-Debreu sense.[83] There are two ways the government can pursue this policy. In the first case, the government provides educational goods and services in both early and late investment periods. In the second case, the government intervenes only during the late investment period (e.g., a tuition policy).

The lesson from their analysis is that when the government intervenes only in the late period but not the early period and attempts to achieve a first best solution at all levels of parental income, remediation costs are much higher than when the government intervenes in both periods. Furthermore, for parents with very low income, so that early investments are very low, there is no amount of government-provided educational goods and services that can attain the objectives of the policy due to the high level of CES-complementarity and self-productivity.[84]

In long-run equilibrium, the possibility of substitution among investments at different stages of the life cycle raises challenges for designing an optimal economic policy. If in the first period agents know that late investments are subsidized, such subsidies may either encourage or discourage early investments. It will discourage early investment if I_1 and I_2 are close substitutes. It will encourage early investment if I_1 and I_2 are strong complements. Empirically, the latter appears to be the relevant case. Cunha (2004) shows that for the parameter values of Cunha and Heckman (2004), a tuition subsidy causes parents to increase the amount of early investments in human capital of the child. The case for tuition subsidies lies more in their effect on early childhood investment than in their effect on alleviating credit constraints operating on the family during the child's adolescent years.

4. Summary and conclusions

This paper reviews the evidence on the life cycle of human skill formation and interprets it using basic economic models. The new economics of the life cycle recognizes that childhood is a multistage process where early investments feed into later investments. Skill begets skill; learning begets learning. The early influential work of Becker and

[81] In recent work Cunha, Heckman and Schennach (2006) develop more refined estimates of the technology of skill formation.

[82] The estimates of the parameters of (13) reported in Cunha and Heckman (2004) are $\rho = 0.7012$, $\gamma = 0.8649$, and $\phi = -0.4108$.

[83] By complete markets in this case we mean that parents can buy insurance against the realizations of temporary shocks in earnings ε and η.

[84] Note, however, that this is not the pure Leontief case.

Tomes (1979, 1986) collapsed childhood into a single period and implicitly assumed that all investments at all ages of the child are perfect substitutes. This misses important features of the skill development process.

The evidence reported here is broadly consistent with the self-productivity of human capital investment and the complementarity of investments at different ages. Both factors combine to produce the phenomenon that skill begets skill. Complementarity implies that early investments need to be followed by later investments if the early investments are to pay off.

We formalize the concept of critical and sensitive periods and introduce the concept of the skill multiplier which captures the combined effects of complementarity and self-productivity on the child development process. Complementarity and the skill multiplier produce no trade-off between equity and efficiency at early ages of human development but a substantial trade-off at later ages. Once skills are crystallized, complementarity implies that the returns are highest for investment in the most able. At the youngest ages, it is possible to form ability and create the complementarity that characterizes late adolescent and early adult human capital investment processes. Thus early interventions targeted toward the disadvantaged can be highly effective. Later investments are not.

The main findings of the literature can be summarized succinctly. First, abilities matter. A large number of empirical studies document that cognitive ability affects both the likelihood of acquiring advanced training and higher education, and the economic returns to those activities. Both cognitive and noncognitive abilities matter in determining participation in crime, teenage pregnancy, drug use and participation in other deviant activities. The evidence that abilities matter tells us nothing whatsoever about whether they are genetically determined.

Second, ability is multidimensional. IQ has to be distinguished from what is measured by achievement tests, although it partly determines success on achievement tests. Noncognitive skills (perseverance, motivation, self-control and the like) have direct effects on wages (given schooling), schooling, teenage pregnancy, smoking, crime and achievement tests. Both cognitive and noncognitive skills affect socioeconomic success. Both are strongly influenced by family environments. The old dichotomy between an invariant, genetically determined ability and acquired skills is a false one that still continues to influence the literature in economics. Abilities and skills are both acquired. They are influenced both by genes and the environment.

Third, ability gaps in both cognitive and noncognitive skills across individuals and across socioeconomic groups open up at early ages. They are strongly correlated with family background factors, like parental education and maternal ability, which, when controlled for in a statistical sense, largely eliminate these gaps. Inputs of schooling quality and resources have relatively small effects on early ability deficits. Parenting practices have strong effects on emotional development and motivation. This correlational evidence is supported by the experimental evidence from the Perry Preschool Program and the Abecedarian program.

Fourth, the importance of family credit constraints in the child's adolescent years in explaining college attendance (and other) differentials across socioeconomic groups is greatly exaggerated in the recent literature. While there is an identifiable group of families constrained in this fashion, it is not numerically large. Interventions targeted toward this group can be effective but will not substantially eliminate gaps in college attendance. The real binding constraint is the inability of children to buy favorable family environments at early ages.

Fifth, it is possible to partially compensate for adverse family environments. Evidence from randomized trials conducted on intervention programs targeted at disadvantaged children who are followed into adulthood, suggests that it is possible to eliminate some of the gaps due to early disadvantage. Enriched and sustained interventions at the youngest ages raise IQ. The Abecedarian program provided an enriched intervention for disadvantaged children starting at age 4 months. The children who received the intervention score consistently higher than the children who do not, even long after the treatment is discontinued. Later interventions like the Perry Preschool program show no lasting effect on IQ. However, effects on motivation and, hence, achievement test scores are found. Children are less likely to commit crime and have out of wedlock births and are more likely to participate in regular schooling. Early interventions have a substantial effect on adult performance and have a high economic return.

Sixth, different types of abilities appear to be manipulable at different ages. Thus, while factors affecting IQ deficits need to be addressed at very early ages for interventions to be effective, there is evidence that later interventions in the adolescent years can affect noncognitive skills as well as the knowledge measured by achievement tests. Achievement is determined by both cognitive and noncognitive factors. This evidence is rooted in the neuroscience that establishes the malleability of the prefrontal cortex into the early 20s. This is the region of the brain that governs emotion and self-regulation.

Seventh, the later the remediation, the less effective it is. Classroom remediation programs designed to combat early cognitive deficits have a poor track record. Public job training programs and adult literacy and educational programs, like the GED, that attempt to remediate years of educational and emotional neglect among disadvantaged individuals have a low economic return, and for young males, the return is negative. This evidence is consistent with strong complementarity of investment over the life cycle of the child.

Eighth, the economic returns to initial investments at early ages are high. The economic return to investment at older ages is lower. The technology of skill formation which we analyze in this essay suggests a strong skill multiplier effect of investment. Investment at an early age produces a high return through self-productivity and direct complementarity. Early investment in cognitive and noncognitive skills lowers the cost of later investment by making learning at later ages more efficient. The skill multiplier highlights the value of early investment. It also demonstrates that there is no trade-off between equity (targeting programs at disadvantaged families) and efficiency (getting the highest economic returns), provided that the investments are made at early ages. There is such a trade-off at later ages.

Ninth, CES-complementarity of early with late investments implies that early investments must be followed up by later investments in order to be effective. Nothing in the new economics of human skill formation suggests that we should starve later educational and skill enhancement efforts. The main finding from the recent literature is that we should prioritize, and shift our priorities, in a marginal fashion by redirecting a given total sum of expenditure on skill investment to earlier ages relative to how it is currently allocated toward disadvantaged populations that do not provide enriched environments for their children.

Acknowledgements

This research was supported by NICHD R01-34598-03 and by a grant from the Pew Charitable Trusts through the Committee for Economic Development. Cunha acknowledges support by the Claudio Haddad Dissertation Fund at the University of Chicago. Lochner acknowledges support from Social Sciences and Humanities Research Council of Canada grant 410-2004-1026. An early version of this paper was presented at a conference at the Minneapolis Federal Reserve, October 2003; at the meetings of the Society of Economic Dynamics in Florence, July 2004; at a seminar at Washington University, St. Louis in April 2004; at the Conference on Wages, Education and Risk at the Centre for Applied Microeconometrics of the Copenhagen University, sponsored by Martin Browning in August 2004; in a special Institute for Research on Poverty Lecture on Poverty in America, November 2004; at a presentation at the Chicago Labor Seminar, April 1, 2005, at the Federal Reserve Bank of Chicago; and at the Roy Geary Institute Inaugural Lecture, Dublin, April 22, 2005. We thank Pedro Carneiro, John Kennan, John Laitner and Robert Pollak for comments on the first draft. We thank Greg Duncan for helpful comments on the second draft. We thank Jeff Campbell, Jeff Grogger and Chris Taber for comments on this draft. Finola Kennedy of University College Dublin directed us to the apt quote from Marshall that begins this chapter.

Appendix A

A.1. The general technology of skill formation

Let S_t be a $L \times 1$ vector of skills or abilities at stage t. Included are pure cognitive abilities (e.g., IQ) as well as noncognitive abilities (time preference, self control, patience, judgment). The notation is sufficiently flexible to include acquired skills like general education or a specific skill. Agents start out life with vector S_0 of skills (abilities). The S_0 are produced by genes and *in utero* environments which are known to affect child outcomes (see the essays in Keating and Hertzman, 1999).

Let I_t be a $K \times 1$ vector of investments at stage t. These include all inputs invested in the child including parental and social inputs. The technology of skill formation can be written as

$$S_t = f_t(S_{t-1}, I_t),$$

where f_t is a stage-t function mapping skill (ability) levels and investment at stage t into skill (ability) levels at the end of the period. For simplicity we assume that f_t is twice continuously differentiable in its arguments. Its domain of definition is the same for all inputs. The inputs may be different at different stages of the life cycle, so the inputs in I_t may be different from the inputs at period τ different from t.

Universal self-productivity at stage t is defined as

$$\frac{\partial S_t}{\partial S_{t-1}} = \frac{\partial f_t}{\partial S_{t-1}} > 0.$$

In the general case this is a $L \times L$ matrix. More generally, some components of this matrix may be zero at all stages while other components may always be positive. In principle, some skills could have negative effects in some periods. At some stages, some components may be zero while at other stages they may be positive.

Universal direct complementarity at stage t is defined by the $L \times K$ matrix:

$$\frac{\partial^2 S_t}{\partial S_{t-1} \partial I_t'} > 0.$$

Higher levels of S_t raise the productivity of I_t. Alternatively, higher levels of I_t raise the productivity of S_t. Again, in the general case, some components at some or all stages may have zero effects, and some may have negative effects. They can switch signs across stages.

This notation is sufficiently general to allow for the possibility that some components of skill are produced only at certain critical periods. Period t is critical for skill (ability) j if

$$\frac{\partial S_{t,j}}{\partial I_t} \neq 0, \quad \text{for some levels of } S_{t-1} = s_{t-1},\ I_t = i_t,$$

but

$$\frac{\partial S_{t+k,j}}{\partial I_{t+k}} = 0, \quad k > 0,\ \text{for all levels of } S_{t-1} = s_t,\ I_t = i_t.$$

Sensitive periods might be defined as those periods where, at the same level of input S_{t-1}, I_t, the $\frac{\partial S_t}{\partial I_t}$ are high. More formally, letting $S_{t-1} = s$, $I_t = i$, t is a sensitive period for skill (or ability) j if

$$\left.\frac{\partial S_{t+k,j}}{\partial I_{t+k}}\right|_{S_{t+k-1}=s, I_{t+k}=i} < \left.\frac{\partial S_{t,j}}{\partial I_t}\right|_{S_{t-1}=s, I_t=i}, \quad \text{for all } k \neq 0.$$

Clearly there may be multiple sensitive periods, and there may be sensitivity with respect to one input that is not true of other inputs.

An alternative definition of critical and sensitive periods works with a version of the technology that solves out $S_{t,j}$ as a function of lagged investments and initial conditions $S_0 = s_0$:

$$S_{t,j} = M_{t,j}(I_t, I_{t-1}, \ldots, I_1, S_0), \quad S_0 = s_0,\ j = 1, \ldots, J.$$

Stage t^* is a *critical period* for $S_{t,j}$ if investments are productive at t^* but not at any other stage $k \neq t^*$. Formally,

$$\frac{\partial S_{t,j}}{\partial I_k} = \frac{\partial M_{t,j}(I_t, I_{t-1}, \ldots, I_1, S_0)}{\partial I_k} \equiv 0, \quad k \neq t^*, \ j = 1, \ldots, J,$$

for all $S_0, I_1, \ldots, I_t$, but

$$\frac{\partial S_{t,j}}{\partial I_{t^*}} = \frac{\partial M_{t,j}(I_t, I_{t-1}, \ldots, I_1, S_0)}{\partial I_{t^*}} > 0, \quad j = 1, \ldots, J,$$

for some $S_0, I_1, \ldots, I_t$.

Stage t^* is a *sensitive period* for $S_{t,j}$ if at the same level of inputs, investment is more productive at stage t^* than at stage t. Formally, t^* is a sensitive period for $S_{t,j}$ if for $k \neq t^*$,

$$\left.\frac{\partial S_{t,j}}{\partial I_k}\right|_{S_0=s_0, I_k=i_k, k=1,\ldots,t, k\neq t^*} \leqslant \left.\frac{\partial S_{t,j}}{\partial I_{t^*}}\right|_{S_0=s_0, I_k=i_k, k=1,\ldots,t}.$$

The inequality is strict for at least one period $k = 1, \ldots, t$, $k \neq t^*$.

This definition of critical periods agrees with the previous one. Our second definition of sensitive periods may not agree with the previous one, which is defined only in terms of the effect of investment on the next period's output. The second definition fixes the period at which output is measured and examines the marginal productivity of inputs in producing the output. It allows for feedback effects of the investment in j on output beyond j through self-productivity in a way that the first definition does not.

At each stage t, agents can perform certain tasks. The level of performance in task l at stage t is $T_{l,t} = T_{l,t}(S_t)$. For some tasks, and some stages, components of S_t may be substitutes or complements. Thus we distinguish complementarity or substitution in skills (abilities) in stage t in task performance from complementarity or substitution in skill production. Agents deficient in some skills may specialize in some tasks. This is an alternative form of remediation compared to remediation through skill investment.

A.2. Relationship with the Ben-Porath (1967) model

The conventional formulation of the technology of skill formation is due to Ben-Porath. Let h_t be a scalar human capital. This corresponds to a model with one skill (general human capital) and one task. In his setup, $T_t(S_t) = h_t(S_t)$. Ben-Porath makes the additional (implicit) assumption that $h_t(S_t) = h(S_t)$. His model postulates that human capital at time $t+1$ depends on human capital at t, invariant ability (denoted θ), and investment at t, I_t. I_t may be a vector. The same type of investments are made at each stage. Skill is measured in the same units over time. His specification of the investment technology is

$$h_{t+1} = f(I_t, h_t, \theta),$$

where f is concave in I_t. The technology is specialized further to allow for depreciation of scalar human capital at rate σ. Thus we obtain

$$h_{t+1} = g(I_t, h_t, \theta) + (1 - \sigma)h_t.$$

When $\sigma = 0$, there is no depreciation. "h_t" is carried over (not fully depreciated) as long as $\sigma < 1$.

Self-productivity in his model arises when $\frac{\partial h_{t+1}}{\partial h_t} = \frac{\partial g(\theta, h_t, I_t)}{\partial h_t} + (1 - \sigma) > 0$. This comes from two sources: a carry over effect, $(1 - \sigma) > 0$, arising from the human capital that is not depreciated, and the effect of h_t on gross investment $(\frac{\partial g(\theta, h_t, I_t)}{\partial h_t} > 0)$. If $g(I_t, h_t, \theta) = \phi_1(h_t, \theta) + \phi_2(I_t, \theta)$, there is no essential distinction between $(1-\sigma)h_t$ and $g(I_t, h_t, \theta)$ as sources of self-productivity if we allow σ to depend on $\theta(\sigma(\theta))$.

Complementarity of all inputs is

$$\frac{\partial^2 g(I_t, h_t, \theta)}{\partial h_t \partial I_t'} > 0.$$

In a more general case, some components of this vector may be negative or zero. In the case of universal complementarity, the stock of h_t raises the marginal productivity of I_t. Direct complementarity and self-productivity, singly and together, show why skill begets skill. Our model generalizes the Ben-Porath model by (a) allowing for different skill formation technologies at different stages; (b) allowing qualitatively different investments at different stages; (c) allowing for both skill and ability formation and (d) considering the case of vector skills and abilities.

References

Aiyagari, S.R. (1994). "Uninsured idiosyncratic risk and aggregate saving". Quarterly Journal of Economics 109 (3), 659–684.

Aiyagari, S.R., Greenwood, J., Seshadri, A. (2002). "Efficient investment in children". Journal of Economic Theory 102 (2), 290–321.

Akabayashi, H. (1996). On the Role of Incentives in the Formation of Human Capital in the Family. Ph.D. Thesis, University of Chicago.

Altonji, J.G., Dunn, T.A. (1996). "The effects of family characteristics on the return to education". Review of Economics and Statistics 78 (4), 692–704.

Altonji, J.G., Elder, T.E., Taber, C.R. (2005). "Selection on observed and unobserved variables: Assessing the effectiveness of catholic schools". Journal of Political Economy 113 (1), 151–184.

Armor, D.J. (2003). Maximizing Intelligence. Transaction Publishers, New Brunswick, NJ.

Armor, D.J., Roll Jr., C.R. (1994). "Military manpower quality: Past, present, future". In: Green Jr., B.F., Mavor, A.S. (Eds.), Modeling Cost and Performance for Military Enlistment: Report of a Workshop. National Academy Press, Washington, DC, pp. 13–34.

Barnett, W.S. (2004). "Benefit–cost analysis of preschool education". PowerPoint presentation. November. Available at: http://nieer.org/resources/files/BarnettBenefits.ppt.

Barnett, W.S., Masse, L.N. (2002). "A benefit–cost analysis of the Abecedarian early childhood intervention". Technical report. National Institute for Early Education Research (NIEER), New Brunswick, NJ.

Becker, G.S. (1964). Human Capital: A Theoretical and Empirical Analysis, with Special Reference to Education. National Bureau of Economic Research, New York. Distributed by Columbia University Press.

Becker, G.S., Tomes, N. (1979). "An equilibrium theory of the distribution of income and intergenerational mobility". Journal of Political Economy 87 (6), 1153–1189.
Becker, G.S., Tomes, N. (1986). "Human capital and the rise and fall of families". Journal of Labor Economics 4 (3, Part 2), S1–S39.
Belfield, C.R., Nores, M., Barnett, W.S. (2004). "The high/scope Perry pre-school program: Cost–benefit analysis using data from the age-40 follow-up". Technical report. National Institute for Early Education Research (NIEER), New Brunswick, NJ.
Ben-Porath, Y. (1967). "The production of human capital and the life cycle of earnings". Journal of Political Economy 75 (4, Part 1), 352–365.
Benabou, R. (2000). "Unequal societies: Income distribution and the social contract". American Economic Review 90 (1), 96–129.
Benabou, R. (2002). "Tax and education policy in a heterogeneous agent economy: What levels of redistribution maximize growth and efficiency?" Econometrica 70 (2), 481–517.
Bewley, T.F. (1986). "Stationary monetary equilibrium with a continuum of independently fluctuating consumers". In: Hildenbrand, W., Mas-Collel, A. (Eds.), Contributions to Mathematical Economics in Honor of Gerard Debreu. North-Holland, Amsterdam.
Blossfeld, H.-P., Shavit, Y. (1993). Persistent Inequality: Changing Educational Attainment in Thirteen Countries. Westview Press, Boulder, CO.
Bowles, S., Gintis, H. (1976). Schooling in Capitalist America: Educational Reform the Contradictions of Economic Life. Basic Books, New York.
Brooks-Gunn, J., Berlin, L.J., Fuligni, A.S. (2000). "Early childhood intervention programs: What about the family?". In: Meisels, S., Shonkoff, J. (Eds.), The Handbook of Early Childhood Interventions. Cambridge University Press, New York, pp. 549–588.
Brooks-Gunn, J., Gross, R., Kraemer, H., Spiker, D., Shapiro, S. (1992). "Enhancing the cognitive outcomes of low birth weight, premature infants: For whom is the intervention most effective?" Pediatrics 89 (6, Part 2), 1209–1215.
Bruer, J.T. (1999). The Myth of the First Three Years: A New Understanding of Early Brain Development and Lifelong Learning. Free Press, New York.
Bureau of Labor Statistics (2001). NLS Handbook 2001: The National Longitudinal Surveys. U.S. Department of Labor, Washington, DC.
Cameron, J. (2004). "Evidence for an early sensitive period for the development of brain systems underlying social affiliative behavior". Unpublished manuscript. Oregon National Primate Research Center.
Cameron, S.V., Heckman, J.J. (1998). "Life cycle schooling and dynamic selection bias: Models and evidence for five cohorts of American males". Journal of Political Economy 106 (2), 262–333.
Cameron, S.V., Heckman, J.J. (1999). "Can tuition policy combat rising wage inequality?" In: Kosters, M. (Ed.), Financing College Tuition: Government Policies and Educational Priorities. AEI Press, Washington, DC, Chapter 5, p. 125.
Cameron, S.V., Heckman, J.J. (2001). "The dynamics of educational attainment for black, Hispanic, and white males". Journal of Political Economy 109 (3), 455–499.
Cameron, S.V., Taber, C. (2004). "Estimation of educational borrowing constraints using returns to schooling". Journal of Political Economy 112 (1), 132–182.
Card, D. (1999). "The causal effect of education on earnings". In: Ashenfelter, O., Card, D. (Eds.), Handbook of Labor Economics, vol. 5. North-Holland, New York, pp. 1801–1863.
Card, D. (2001). "Estimating the return to schooling: Progress on some persistent econometric problems". Econometrica 69 (5), 1127–1160.
Cardak, B.A., Givon, D. (2004). "Why the poor don't go to university: Attainment constraints and two-staged education." Presented at the Fifth APET International Conference on Public Economics, Peking University, Beijing, China, 25–29 August, 2004.
Carneiro, P. (2002). "Heterogeneity in the returns to schooling: Implications for policy evaluation." Ph.D. thesis, University of Chicago.
Carneiro, P., Hansen, K., Heckman, J.J. (2001). "Removing the veil of ignorance in assessing the distributional impacts of social policies". Swedish Economic Policy Review 8 (2), 273–301.

Carneiro, P., Hansen, K., Heckman, J.J. (2003). "Estimating distributions of treatment effects with an application to the returns to schooling and measurement of the effects of uncertainty on college choice". International Economic Review 44 (2), 361–422. 2001 Lawrence R. Klein Lecture.
Carneiro, P., Heckman, J.J. (2002). "The evidence on credit constraints in post-secondary schooling". Economic Journal 112 (482), 705–734.
Carneiro, P., Heckman, J.J. (2003). "Human capital policy". In: Heckman, J.J., Krueger, A.B., Friedman, B.M. (Eds.), Inequality in America: What Role for Human Capital Policies? MIT Press, Cambridge, MA.
Carneiro, P., Heckman, J.J., Masterov, D.V. (2005). "Labor market discrimination and racial differences in pre-market factors". Journal of Law and Economics 48 (1), 1–39.
Caucutt, E., Kumar, K. (2003). "Higher education subsidies and heterogeneity: A dynamic analysis". Journal of Economic Dynamics and Control 27 (8), 1459–1502.
Caucutt, E., Lochner, L.J. (2004). "Early and late human capital investments, credit constraints, and the family". Unpublished manuscript. University of Western Ontario, Department of Economics.
Cawley, J., Heckman, J.J., Lochner, L.J., Vytlacil, E.J. (2000). "Understanding the role of cognitive ability in accounting for the recent rise in the return to education". In: Arrow, K., Bowles, S. (Eds.), Meritocracy and Economic Inequality. Princeton University Press, Princeton, NJ.
Clarida, R.H. (1987). "Consumption, liquidity constraints and asset accumulation in the presence of random income fluctuations". International Economic Review 28 (2), 339–351.
Cunha, F. (2004). Skill formation in a laitner economy. Ph.D. Thesis. University of Chicago.
Cunha, F., Heckman, J.J. (2004). "The technology of skill formation". Unpublished manuscript, University of Chicago, presented at AEA Meetings, January 2003, San Diego, CA, and Federal Reserve Bank of Minneapolis, October 2004 and Society for Economic Dynamics Meetings in Florence, Italy, 2004. Revised May 2005 for presentation at the Society for Economic Dynamics and Control.
Cunha, F., Heckman, J.J. (2006). "Formulating identifying and estimating the technology of cognitive and noncognitive skill formation". Unpublished manuscript. University of Chicago, Department of Economics.
Cunha, F., Heckman, J.J., Navarro, S. (2005). "Separating uncertainty from heterogeneity in life cycle earnings, the 2004 Hicks lecture". Oxford Economic Papers 57 (2), 191–261.
Cunha, F., Heckman, J.J., Schennach, S.M. (2006). "Estimating the technology of cognitive and noncognitive skill formation". Unpublished manuscript, University of Chicago, Department of Economics. Presented at the Yale Conference on Macro and Labor Economics, May 5–7, 2006.
Currie, J. (2001). "Early childhood education programs". Journal of Economic Perspectives 15 (2), 213–238.
Currie, J., Blau, D. (2006). "Who's minding the kids? Preschool day care, and after school care, and after school case". In: Welch, F., Hanushek, E. (Eds.), Handbook of the Economics of Education. Elsevier, Amsterdam. In Volume 2 of this Handbook.
Currie, J., Thomas, D. (2000). "School quality and the longer-term effects of head start". Journal of Human Resources 35 (4), 755–774.
Donohue, J.J., Siegelman, P. (1998). "Allocating resources among prisons and social programs in the battle against crime". Journal of Legal Studies 27 (1), 1–43. January.
Duncan, G., Claessens, A., Engel, M. (2004). "The contributions of hard skills and socio-emotional behavior to school readiness". Unpublished manuscript. Northwestern University.
Duncan, G.J., Brooks-Gunn, J. (1997a). Consequences of Growing Up Poor. Russell Sage Foundation, New York.
Duncan, G.J., Brooks-Gunn, J. (1997b). "Income effects across the life span: Integration and interpretation". In: Duncan, G., Brooks-Gunn, J. (Eds.), Consequences of Growing Up Poor. Russell Sage Foundation, New York, pp. 596–610.
Dynarski, S.M. (2000). "Hope for whom? Financial aid for the middle class and its impact on college attendance". National Tax Journal 53 (3, Part 2), 629–661.
Dynarski, S.M. (2003). "Does aid matter? Measuring the effect of student aid on college attendance and completion". American Economic Review 93 (1), 279–288.
Edwards, R.C. (1976). "Individual traits and organizational incentives: What makes a "good" worker?" Journal of Human Resources 11 (1), 51–68.

Ellwood, D.T., Kane, T.J. (2000). "Who is getting a college education? Family background and the growing gaps in enrollment". In: Danziger, S., Waldfogel, J. (Eds.), Securing the Future: Investing in Children from Birth to College. Russell Sage Foundation, New York, pp. 283–324.

Fisher, I. (1982). "Mathematical investigations in the theory of value and prices". Transactions of the Connecticut Academy of Arts and Sciences 9, 1–124.

Flynn, J.R. (1987). "Massive IQ gains in 14 nations: What IQ tests really measure". Psychological Bulletin 101, 171–191.

Fuerst, J., Fuerst, D. (1993). "Chicago experience with an early childhood program: The special case of the child parent center program". Urban Education 28 (1), 69–96.

Garber, H.L. (1988). The Milwaukee Project: Preventing Mental Retardation in Children at Risk. American Association on Mental Retardation, Washington, DC.

Garces, E., Thomas, D., Currie, J. (2002). "Longer-term effects of head start". American Economic Review 92 (4), 999–1012.

Gomby, D.S., Larson, C.S., Lewit, E.M., Behrman, R.E. (1999). "Home visiting: Recent program evaluations – analysis and recommendations". The Future of Children 9 (1), 4–26.

Gormley, W., Gayer, T., Phillips, D., Dawson, B. (2004). "The effect of universal pre-K on cognitive development". Unpublished manuscript. Georgetown University.

Gray, S.W., Ramsey, B.K., Klaus, R.A. (1982). From 3 to 20: The Early Training Project. University Park Press, Baltimore, MD.

Griliches, Z. (1977). "Estimating the returns to schooling: Some econometric problems". Econometrica 45 (1), 1–22.

Grogger, J., Neal, D. (2000). "Further evidence of the effects of catholic secondary schooling". Brookings-Wharton Papers on Urban Affairs, 151–193.

Hansen, K.T., Heckman, J.J., Mullen, K.J. (2004). "The effect of schooling and ability on achievement test scores". Journal of Econometrics 121 (1–2), 39–98.

Hanushek, E., Leung, C.K.Y., Yilmaz, K. (2004). "Borrowing constraints, college aid, and intergenerational mobility". Technical Report 10711, NBER.

Hayek, F.A.V (1941). The Pure Theory of Capital. University of Chicago Press, Chicago.

Heckman, J.J. (1995). "Lessons from the bell curve". Journal of Political Economy 103 (5), 1091.

Heckman, J.J. (1999). "Doing it right: Job training and education". The Public Interest 135, 86–107.

Heckman, J.J. (2000). "Policies to foster human capital". Research in Economics 54 (1), 3–56. With discussion.

Heckman, J.J. (2005). "Invited comments". In: Schweinhart, L.J., Montie, J., Xiang, Z., Barnett, W.S., Belfield, C.R., Nores, M. (Eds.), Lifetime Effects: The High/Scope Perry Preschool Study Through Age 40. Monographs of the High/Scope Educational Research Foundation, vol. 14. High/Scope, Ypsilanti, MI, pp. 229–233.

Heckman, J.J., LaFontaine, P. (2007). America's Dropout Problem: The GED and the Importance of Social and Emotional Skills. University of Chicago Press, Chicago. In press.

Heckman, J.J., LaLonde, R.J., Smith, J.A. (1999). "The economics and econometrics of active labor market programs". In: Ashenfelter, O., Card, D. (Eds.), Handbook of Labor Economics, vol. 3A. North-Holland, New York. Chapter 31, pp. 1865–2097.

Heckman, J.J., Larenas, M.I., Urzua, S. (2004). "Accounting for the effect of schooling and abilities in the analysis of racial and ethnic disparities in achievement test scores". Unpublished manuscript. University of Chicago, Department of Economics.

Heckman, J.J., Lochner, L.J. (2000). "Rethinking myths about education and training: Understanding the sources of skill formation in a modern economy". In: Danziger, S., Waldfogel, J. (Eds.), Securing the Future: Investing in Children from Birth to College. Russell Sage Foundation, New York.

Heckman, J.J., Lochner, L.J., Smith, J., Taber, C. (1997). "The effects of government policy on human capital investment and wage inequality". Chicago Policy Review 1 (2), 1–40.

Heckman, J.J., Lochner, L.J., Taber, C. (1998). "Explaining rising wage inequality: explorations with a dynamic general equilibrium model of labor earnings with heterogeneous agents". Review of Economic Dynamics 1 (1), 1–58.

Heckman, J.J., Lochner, L.J., Todd, P.E. (2006). "Earnings equations and rates of return: The Mincer equation and beyond". In: Hanushek, E.A., Welch, F. (Eds.), Handbook of the Economics of Education. Elsevier, Amsterdam. In this Handbook.

Heckman, J.J., Rubinstein, Y. (2001). "The importance of noncognitive skills: Lessons from the GED testing program". American Economic Review 91 (2), 145–149.

Heckman, J.J., Savelyev, P., Yavitz, A. (2006). "The Perry preschool project: A reanalysis". Unpublished manuscript, University of Chicago, Department of Economics.

Heckman, J.J., Stixrud, J., Urzua, S. (2006). "The effects of cognitive and noncognitive abilities on labor market outcomes and social behavior". Journal of Labor Economics 24 (3), 411–482.

Heckman, J.J., Vytlacil, E.J. (2005). "Structural equations, treatment effects and econometric policy evaluation". Econometrica 73 (3), 669–738.

Heckman, J.J., Vytlacil, E.J. (2007a). "Econometric evaluation of social programs, part I: Causal models, structural models and econometric policy evaluation". In: Heckman, J., Leamer, E. (Eds.), Handbook of Econometrics, vol. 6. Elsevier, Amsterdam. In press.

Heckman, J.J., Vytlacil, E.J. (2007b). "Econometric evaluation of social programs, part II: Using the marginal treatment effect to organize alternative economic estimators to evaluate social programs and to forecast their effects in new environments". In: Heckman, J., Leamer, E. (Eds.), Handbook of Econometrics, vol. 6. Elsevier, Amsterdam. In press.

Herrera, C., Sipe, C.L., McClanahan, W.S. (2000). Mentoring School-Age Children: Relationship Development in Community-Based and School-Based Programs. Public/Private Ventures, Philadelphia, PA.

Herrnstein, R.J., Murray, C.A. (1994). The Bell Curve: Intelligence and Class Structure in American Life. Free Press, New York.

Huggett, M. (1993). "The risk-free rate in heterogeneous-agent incomplete-insurance economies". Journal of Economic Dynamics and Control 17 (5–6), 953–969.

Jensen, A.R. (1980). Bias in Mental Testing. Free Press, New York.

Johnson, A.W. (1996). An Evaluation of the Long-Term Impacts of the Sponsor-A-Scholar Program on Student Performance. Mathematica Policy Research, Princeton, NJ.

Johnson, D.L. (1988). "Primary prevention of behavior problems in young children: The Houston parent-child development center". In: Cowen, E., Price, R., Ramos-McKay, J., Lorion, R. (Eds.), 14 Ounces of Prevention: A Casebook for Practitioners. American Psychological Association, Washington, DC, pp. 44–52. Chapter 4.

Judd, K.L. (2000). "Is education as good as gold? A portfolio analysis of human capital investment." Unpublished working paper. Hoover Institution, Stanford University.

Kane, T.J. (1994). "College entry by blacks since 1970: The role of college costs, family background, and the returns to education". Journal of Political Economy 102 (5), 878–911.

Kane, T.J. (1996). "College cost, borrowing constraints and the timing of college entry". Eastern Economic Journal 22 (2), 181–194.

Kane, T.J. (1999). The Price of Admission: Rethinking How Americans Pay for College. Brookings Institution, Washington, DC.

Karoly, L.A. (2001). "Investing in the future: Reducing poverty through human capital investments". In: Danziger, S., Haveman, R. (Eds.), Understanding Poverty. Russell Sage Foundation, New York, pp. 314–356.

Karoly, L.A., Greenwood, P.W., Everingham, S.S., Hoube, J., Kilburn, M.R., Rydell, C.P., Sanders, M., Chiesa, J. (1998). Investing in Our Children: What We Know and Don't Know About the Costs and Benefits of Early Childhood Interventions. RAND, Santa Monica, CA.

Keane, M.P., Wolpin, K.I. (2001). "The effect of parental transfers and borrowing constraints on educational attainment". International Economic Review 42 (4), 1051–1103.

Keating, D.P., Hertzman, C. (1999). Developmental Health and the Wealth of Nations: Social, Biological, and Educational Dynamics. Guilford Press, New York.

Klein, R., Spady, R., Weiss, A. (1991). "Factors affecting the output and quit propensities of production workers". Review of Economic Studies 58 (5), 929–953.

Knight, F.H. (1944). "Diminishing returns from investment". Journal of Political Economy 52 (1), 26–47.
Knudsen, E.I. (2004). "Sensitive periods in the development of the brain and behavior". Journal of Cognitive Neuroscience 16 (1), 1412–1425.
Knudsen, E.I., Heckman, J.J., Cameron, J., Shonkoff, J.P. (2006). "Economic, neurobiological, and behavioral perspectives on building America's future workforce". Proceedings of the National Academy of Sciences 103 (27), 10155–10162.
Laitner, J. (1979). "Household bequest behaviour and the national distribution of wealth". Review of Economic Studies 46 (3), 467–483.
Laitner, J. (1992). "Random earnings differences, lifetime liquidity constraints, and altruistic intergenerational transfers". Journal of Economic Theory 58 (2), 135–170.
Lally, J.R., Manggione, P.L., Honig, A.S. (1988). "Syracuse university family development research program: Long-range impact of an early intervention with low-income children and their families". In: Powell, D.R. (Ed.), Parent Education as Early Childhood Intervention: Emerging Directions in Theory, Research, and Practice. Ablex Publishing Company, Norwood, NJ, pp. 79–104.
Levenstein, P., O'Hara, J., Madden, J. (1983). "The mother–child program of the verbal interaction project." In: Consortium for Longitudinal Studies (Ed.), As the Twig is Bent: Lasting Effects of Preschool Programs. Erlbaum, Hillsdale, NJ.
Levy, D., Duncan, G.J. (2000). "Using sibling samples to assess the effect of childhood family income on completed schooling." Working paper, JCPR.
Lochner, L.J., Monge, A. (2004). "Education default incentives with government student loan programs". Unpublished manuscript. University of Western Ontario, Department of Economics.
Long, D.A., Mallar, C.D., Thornton, C.V. (1981). "Evaluating the benefits and costs of the job corps". Journal of Policy Analysis and Management 1 (1), 55–76.
Love J.M., Eliason-Kisker, E., Ross C.M., Schochet, P.Z., Brooks-Gunn, J. Paulsell, D., Boller, K. Constantine, J., Vogel, C. Sidle Fuligni, A., Brady-Smith, C. (2002). "Making a difference in the lives of infants and toddlers and their families: The impacts of early head start". Technical Report PR02-30a, Mathematica Policy Research Report.
Magnuson, K.A., Meyers, M., Ruhm, C.J., Waldfogel, J. (2004). "Inequality in preschool education and school readiness". American Educational Research Journal 41 (1), 115–157.
Magnuson, K.A., Ruhm, C.J., Waldfogel, J. (2004). "Does prekindergarten improve school preparation and performance?" Technical Report 10452, NBER.
Marshall, A. (1890). Principles of Economics. Macmillan, New York.
Maxfield, M., Schirm, A., Rodriguez-Planas, N. (2003). "The quantum opportunity program demonstration: Implementation and short-term impacts". Technical Report, MPR reference No. 8279-093, Mathematica Policy Research, Washington, DC.
McCarton, C.M., Brooks-Gunn, J., Wallace, I.F., Bauer, C., Bennett, F.C., Bernbaum, J.C., Broyles, R.S., Casey, P.H., McCormick, M.C., Scott, D.T., Tyson, J., Tonascia, J., Meinert, C.L. (1997). "Age 8 years of early intervention for low-birth-weight premature infants: The infant health and development program". Journal of the American Medical Association 277 (2), 126–132.
Meaney, M.J. (2001). "Maternal care, gene expression, and the transmission of individual differences in stress reactivity across generations". Annual Review of Neuroscience 24 (1), 1161–1192.
Meghir, C., Palme, M. (1999). "Assessing the effect of schooling on earnings using a social experiment." Technical Report W99/10, IFS.
Monroe, E., McDonald, M.S. (1981). "Follow up study of the 1966 Head Start program, Rome city schools, Rome, Georgia." Unpublished manuscript, Georgia Public Schools.
Morris, P., Duncan, G.J., Clark-Kauffman, E. (2005). "Child well-being in an era of welfare reform: The sensitivity of transitions in development to policy change". Developmental Psychology 41 (6), 919–932.
Moskoff, W. (1980). "Pronatalist policies in Romania". Economic Development and Cultural Change 28 (3), 597–614.
Mulligan, C.B. (1997). Parental Priorities and Economic Inequality. University of Chicago Press, Chicago, IL.

Navarro, S. (2005). "Understanding schooling: Using observed choices to infer agent's information in a dynamic model of schooling choice when consumption allocation is subject to borrowing constraints". Ph.D. dissertation, University of Chicago, Chicago, IL.

Newport, E.L. (2002). "Critical periods in language development". In: Nadel, L. (Ed.), Encyclopedia of Cognitive Science. Macmillan/Nature Publishing Group, London, pp. 737–740.

O'Connor, T.G., Rutter, M., Beckett, C., Keaveney, L., Kreppner, J.M., The English and Romanian Adoptees Study Team (2000). "The effects of global severe privation on cognitive competence: Extension and longitudinal follow-up". Child Development 71 (2), 376–390.

Olds, D.L. (2002). "Prenatal and infancy home visiting by nurses: From randomized trials to community replication". Prevention Science 3 (2), 153–172.

Orfield, G. (1992). "Money, equity, and college access". Harvard Educational Review 62 (3), 337–372.

Palmer, F. (1983). "The Harlem study: Effects by type of training, age of training and social class." In: Consortium for Longitudinal Studies (Ed.), As the Twig is Bent: Lasting Effects of Preschool Programs. Lawrence Erlbaum, Hillsdale, NJ.

Pinker, S. (1994). The Language Instinct: How the Mind Creates Language. W. Morrow, New York.

Ramey, C.T., Bryant, D.M., Wasik, B.H., Sparling, J.J., Campbell, F.A. (1988). "Early intervention for high-risk children: The Carolina early intervention program". In: Price, R.H. (Ed.), 14 Ounces of Prevention: A Casebook for Practitioners. American Psychological Association, Washington, DC.

Reynolds, A.J., Ou, S.-R., Topitzes, J.W. (2004). "Paths of effects of early childhood interventions on educational attainment and deliquency: A confirmatory analysis of the Chicago parent–child centers". Child Development 75 (5), 1299–1328.

Robinson, G.E., Grozinger, C.M., Whitfield, C.W. (2005). "Sociogenomics: Social life in molecular terms". Nature Review Genetics 6 (4), 257–270.

Rolnick, A., Grunewald, R. (2003). "Early childhood development: Economic development with a high public return." Technical Report. Federal Reserve Bank of Minneapolis, Minneapolis, MN.

Rosapepe, J.C. (2001). "Half way home: Romania's abandoned children ten years after the revolution". Report of the US Ambassador to Romania, accessed on 12/05/2004.

Rutter, M.A., The English and Romanian Adoptees Study Team (1998). "Developmental catch-up, and deficit, following adoption after severe global early privation". Journal of Child Psychology and Psychiatry 39 (4), 465–476.

Samuelson, P.A. (1974). "Complementarity: An essay on the 40th anniversary of the Hicks–Allen revolution in demand theory". Journal of Economic Literature 12 (4), 1255–1289.

Schechtman, J. (1976). "An income fluctuation problem". Journal of Economic Theory 12 (2), 218–241.

Schweinhart, L.J., Barnes, H.V., Weikart, D. (1993). Significant Benefits: The High-Scope Perry Preschool Study Through Age 27. High/Scope Press, Ypsilanti, MI.

Seitz, V. (1990). "Intervention programs for impoverished children: A comparison of educational and family support models". In: Vasta, R. (Ed.), Annals of Child Development: A Research Annual, vol. 7. Jessica Kingsley, London, pp. 73–103.

Seshadri, A., Yuki, K. (2004). "Equity and efficiency effects of redistributive policies". Journal of Monetary Economics 51 (7), 1415–1447.

Shonkoff, J.P., Phillips, D. (2000). From Neurons to Neighborhoods: The Science of Early Child Development. National Academy Press, Washington, DC.

Spence, A.M. (1973). "Job market signaling". Quarterly Journal of Economics 87 (3), 355–374.

Stanley, M. (2003). "College education and the midcentury GI bills". Quarterly Journal of Economics 118 (2), 671–708.

Sternberg, R.J. (1985). Beyond IQ: A Triarchic Theory of Human Intelligence. Cambridge University Press, New York.

Stiglitz, J.E. (1975). "The theory of 'screening', education, and the distribution of income". American Economic Review 65 (3), 283–300.

Stinebrickner, R., Stinebrickner, T.R. (2004). "Time-use and college outcomes". Journal of Econometrics 121 (1–2), 243–269.

Su, X. (2004). "The allocation of public funds in a hierarchical educational system". Journal of Economic Dynamics and Control 28 (12), 2485–2510.

Suomi, S.J. (1999). "Developmental trajectories, early experiences, and community consequences: Lessons from studies with rhesus monkeys". In: Keating, D.P., Hertzman, C. (Eds.), Developmental Health and the Wealth of Nations: Social, Biological, and Educational Dynamics. Guilford Press, New York, pp. 185–200.

Taber, C.R. (2001). "The rising college premium in the eighties: Return to college or return to unobserved ability?" Review of Economic Studies 68 (3), 665–691.

Taggart, R. (1995). Quantum Opportunity Program. Opportunities Industrialization Centers of America, Philadelphia, PA.

Terman, L.M., Merrill, M.A. (1960). Stanford-Binet Intelligence Scale: Manual for the Third Revision Form L-M. Houghton Mifflin, Boston.

Tiegs, E.W., Clark, W.W. (1970). Examiner's Manual and Test Coordinator's Handbook: California Achievement Tests. McGraw-Hill.

Tierney, J.P., Grossman, J.B., Resch, N.L. (1995). Making a Difference: An Impact Study of Big Brothers/Big Sisters. Public/Private Ventures, Philadelphia, PA.

Turkheimer, E., Haley, A., Waldron, M., D'Onofrio, B., Gottesman, I.I. (2003). "Socioeconomic status modifies heritability of IQ in young children". Psychological Science 14 (6), 623–628.

Urzua, S. (2006). "The effects of cognitive and noncognitive skills on racial and ethnic wage gaps." Unpublished manuscript. University of Chicago, Department of Economics.

Walker, G.C., Vilella-Velez, F. (1992). Anatomy of a Demonstration: The Summer Training and Education Program (STEP) from Pilot Through Replication and Postprogram Impacts. Public/Private Ventures, Philadelphia, PA.

Weinberg, B.A. (2001). "An incentive model of the effect of parental income on children". Journal of Political Economy 109 (2), 266–280.

Willis, R.J. (1986). "Wage determinants: A survey and reinterpretation of human capital earnings functions". In: Ashenfelter, O., Layard, R. (Eds.), Handbook of Labor Economics. North-Holland, New York, pp. 525–602.

AUTHOR INDEX

n indicates citation in a footnote.

SUBJECT INDEX